MW00650024

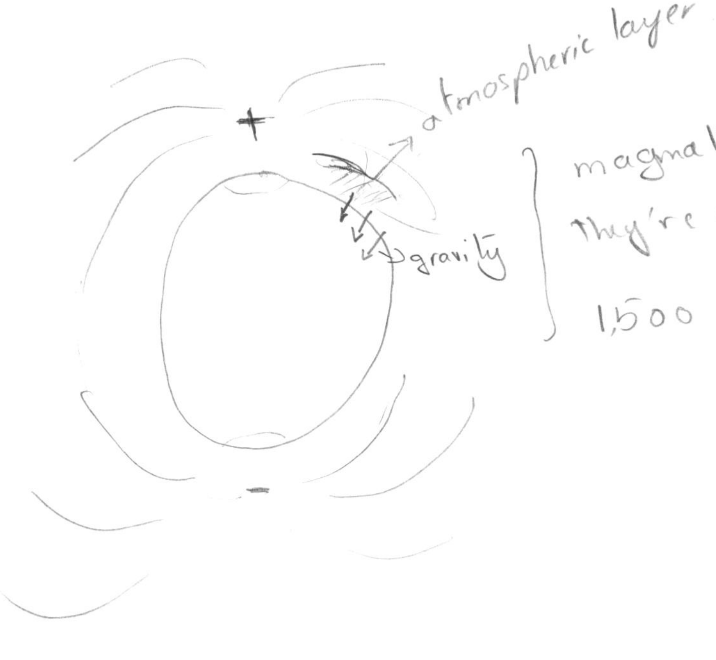

magnatic field
they're creating.
1,500 Earth rotation

e-exam

math → 22 of 40 | 55 %

English → 35 of 70 | 70 %

Arabic → 24.3 of 30 | 81 %

HOLT SCIENCE & TECHNOLOGY

Integrated Science

level BLUE

HOLT, RINEHART AND WINSTON
A Harcourt Education Company
Orlando • Austin • New York • San Diego • London

Acknowledgments

Contributing Authors

Katy Z. Allen
Science Writer
Wayland, Massachusetts

Linda Ruth Berg, Ph.D.
Adjunct Professor of Natural Sciences
St. Petersburg College
St. Petersburg, Florida

Andrew Champagne
Former Physics Teacher
Ashland, Massachusetts

Leila Dumas, MA
Former Physics Teacher
Lago Vista, Texas

Jennie Dusheck, MA
Science Writer
Santa Cruz, California

Robert H. Fronk, Ph.D.
Chair of Science and Mathematics Education
Florida Institute of Technology
West Melbourne, Florida

Mary Kay Hemenway, Ph.D.
Research Associate and Senior Lecturer
Department of Astronomy
The University of Texas at Austin
Austin, Texas

Kathleen Kaska
Life and Earth Science Teacher
Oak Harbor Middle School
Oak Harbor, Washington

Karen J. Meech, Ph.D.
Associate Astronomer
Institute for Astronomy
University of Hawaii
Honolulu, Hawaii

Lee Summerlin, Ph.D.
Professor of Chemistry (retired)
University of Alabama
Birmingham, Alabama

Mark F. Taylor, Ph.D.
Associate Professor of Biology
Biology Department
Baylor University
Waco, Texas

Safety Reviewer

Jack Gerlovich, Ph.D.
Associate Professor
School of Education
Drake University
Des Moines, Iowa

Inclusion Specialist

Karen Clay
Inclusion Consultant
Boston, Massachusetts

Ellen McPeek Glisan
Special Needs Consultant
San Antonio, Texas

Academic Reviewers

Glenn Adelson, Ph.D.
Instructor
Department of Organismic and Evolutionary Biology
Harvard University
Cambridge, Massachusetts

Katy Z. Allen
Science Writer
Wayland, Massachusetts

Linda Ruth Berg, Ph.D.
Adjunct Professor of Natural Sciences
St. Petersburg College
St. Petersburg, Florida

Kenneth H. Brink, Ph.D.
Senior Scientist and Physical Oceanography Director
Coastal Ocean Institute and Rinehart Coastal Research Center
Woods Hole Oceanographic Institution
Woods Hole, Massachusetts

John Brockhaus, Ph.D.
Director of Geospatial Science Information Program
Department of Geography and Environmental Engineering
United States Military Academy
West Point, New York

Acknowledgments
continued on page 807

ISBN-13: 978-0-03-095869-4
ISBN-10: 0-03-095869-5

7 8 9 10 11 0868 15 14 13 12 11
4500280197

Contents in Brief

Contents

yasmin
Rashad
wz here and she ♡'s you.

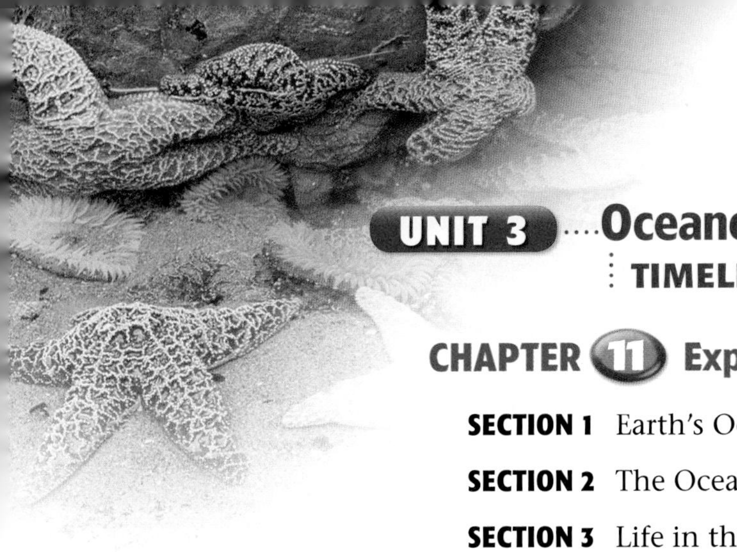

UNIT 3 Oceanography

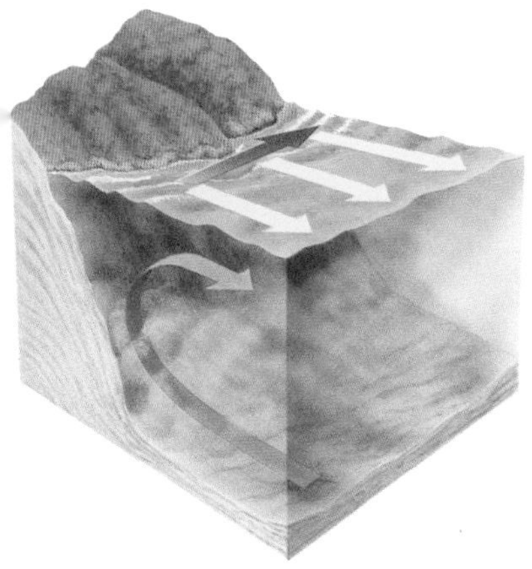

I ♥ U
- Y.R

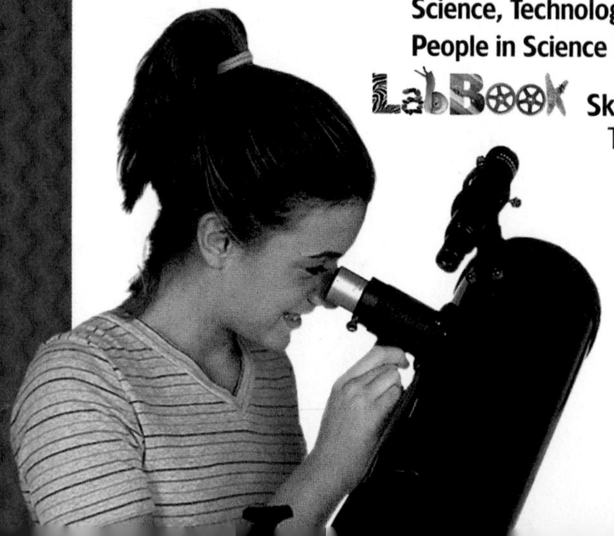

Yasmine Khair

yasmine khair. ♡ you ♥ -bs and aktar -Y.R. ♥

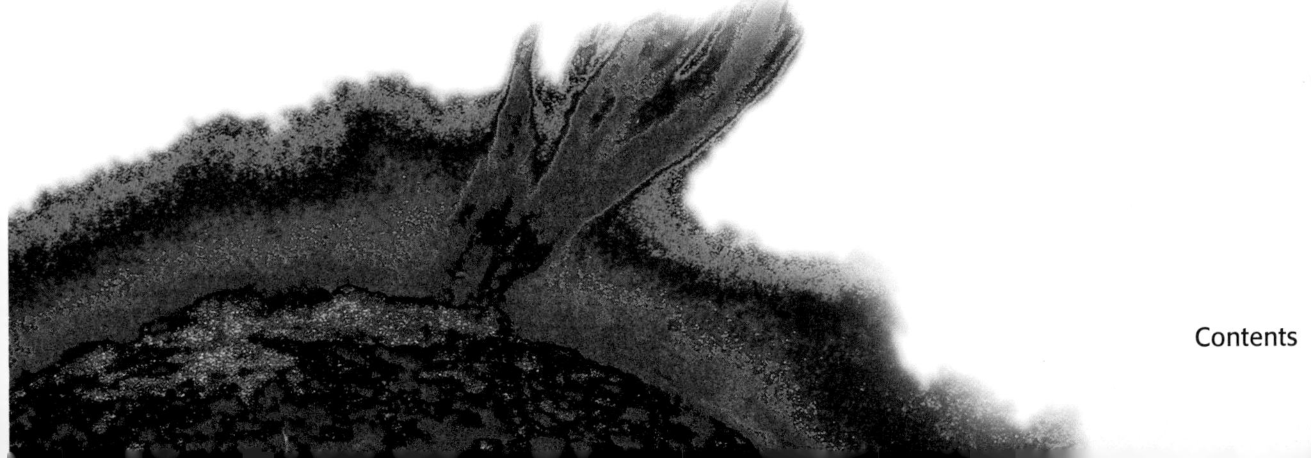

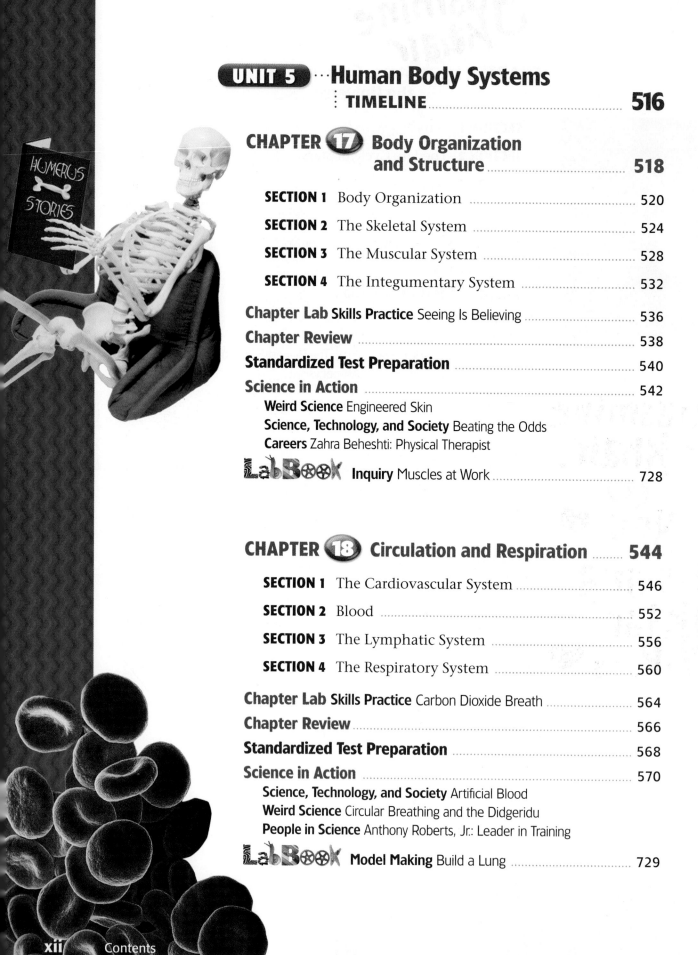

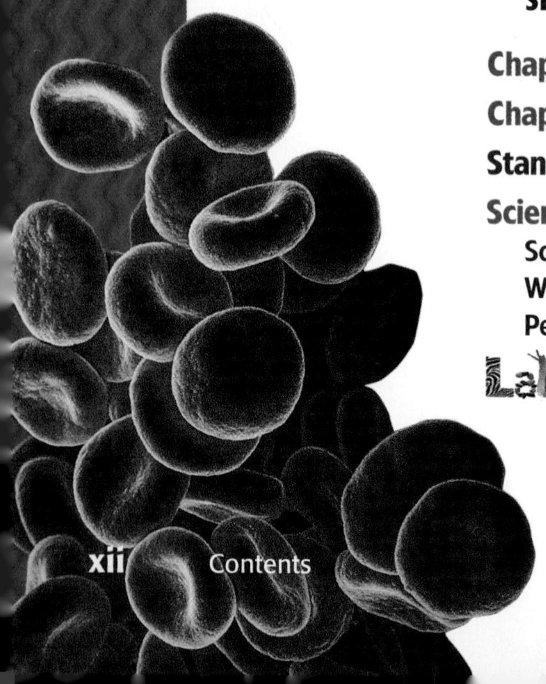

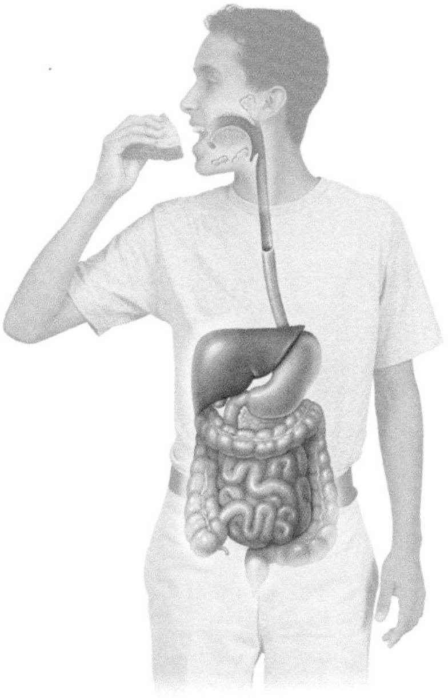

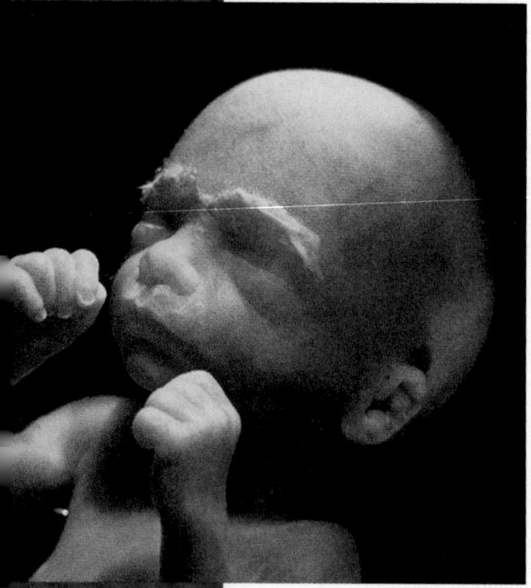

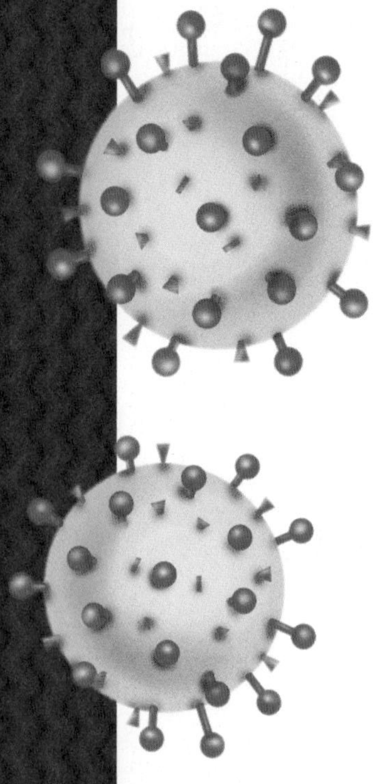

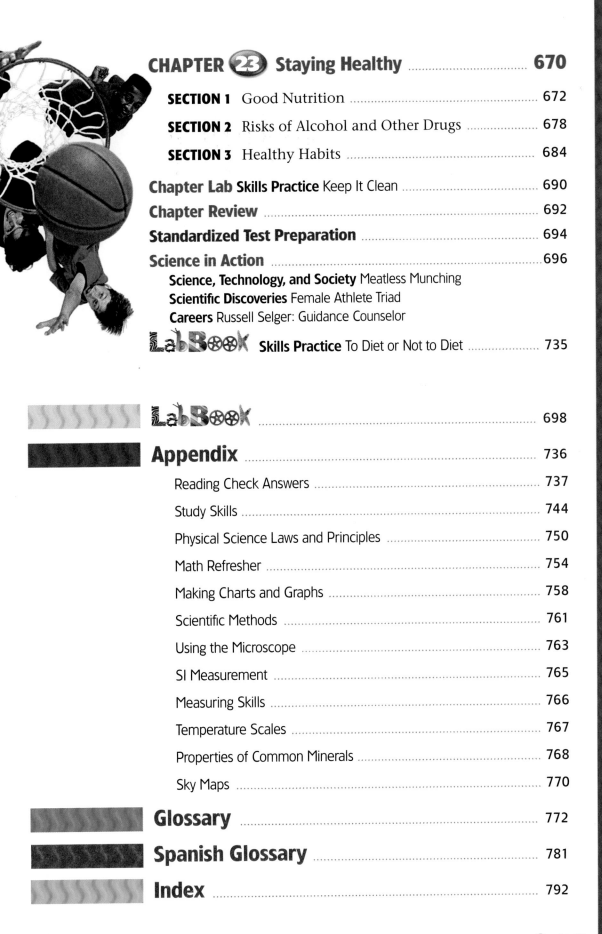

Chapter Labs

Make science a "hands-on" experience.

Each chapter ends with a chapter lab designed to help you experience science firsthand. But please don't forget to be safe. Read the **Safety First!** section before starting any of the labs.

LabBook Labs

The more labs, the better!

Take a minute to browse the variety of exciting labs in this textbook. Additional chapter labs appear in a special **LabBook** in the back of the textbook. **Quick Labs** appear within each chapter and are designed to require only a small amount of time and limited equipment. Don't forget to read the **Safety First!** section before starting any of the labs.

Quick Labs

Pre-Reading Activities

FOLDNOTES

Graphic Organizer

Start your engines with an activity!

Get motivated to learn by doing the two activities at the beginning of each chapter. The **Pre-Reading Activity** helps you organize information as you read the chapter. The **Start-Up Activity** helps you gain scientific understanding of the topic through hands-on experience.

Start-Up Activities

Reading Strategies

Remembering what you read doesn't have to be hard!

A **Reading Strategy** at the beginning of every section provides tips to help you remember and/or organize the information covered in the section.

Internet Activities

Get caught in the Web!

Go to **go.hrw.com** for **Internet Activities** related to each chapter. To find the Internet Activity for a particular chapter, just type in the keyword listed on this page.

School to Home

Science brings you closer together!

Bring science into your home by doing **School-to-Home Activities** with a family member or another adult in your household.

Math Practice

Science and math go hand in hand.

Each **Math Practice** activity contains a word problem related to the topic at hand. **Math Focus** activities provide step-by-step instructions and practice questions designed to help you apply math directly to science.

Math Focus

Connection to...

One subject leads to another.

You may not realize it at first, but different subjects are related to each other in many ways. Each **Connection** explores a topic from the viewpoint of another discipline. In this way, all of the subjects you learn about in school merge to improve your understanding of the world around you.

Science In Action

Science moves beyond the classroom!

Read **Science in Action** articles to learn more about science in the real world. These articles will give you an idea of how interesting, strange, helpful, and action-packed science is. At the end of each chapter, you will find three short articles. And if your thirst is still not quenched, go to **go.hrw.com** for in-depth coverage.

Science Fiction

Science, Technology, and Society

Scientific Debate

Weird Science

Scientific Discoveries

Careers

People in Science

How to Use Your Textbook

Your Roadmap for Success with Holt Science and Technology

What You Will Learn

At the beginning of every section you will find the section's objectives and vocabulary terms. The objectives tell you what you'll need to know after you finish reading the section.

Vocabulary terms are listed for each section. Learn the definitions of these terms because you will most likely be tested on them. Each term is highlighted in the text and is defined at point of use and in the margin. You can also use the glossary to locate definitions quickly.

STUDY TIP Reread the objectives and the definitions to the terms when studying for a test to be sure you know the material.

Get Organized

A Reading Strategy at the beginning of every section provides tips to help you organize and remember the information covered in the section. Keep a science notebook so that you are ready to take notes when your teacher reviews the material in class. Keep your assignments in this notebook so that you can review them when studying for the chapter test.

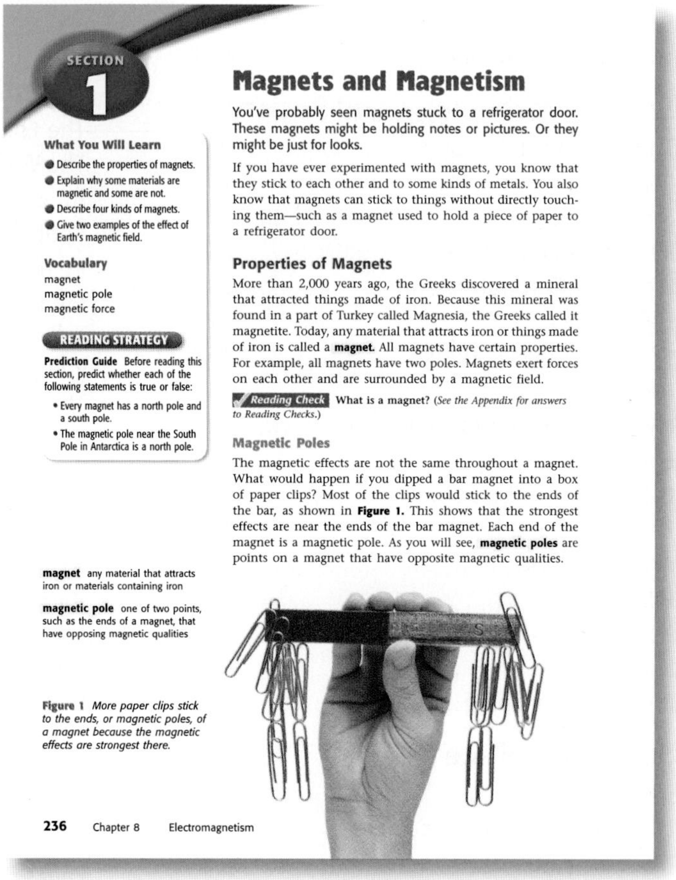

SECTION 1

What You Will Learn

- Describe the properties of magnets.
- Explain why some materials are magnetic and some are not.
- Describe four kinds of magnets.
- Give two examples of the effect of Earth's magnetic field.

Vocabulary

magnet
magnetic pole
magnetic force

READING STRATEGY

Prediction Guide Before reading this section, predict whether each of the following statements is true or false:

- Every magnet has a north pole and a south pole.
- The magnetic pole near the South Pole in Antarctica is a north pole.

Magnets and Magnetism

You've probably seen magnets stuck to a refrigerator door. These magnets might be holding notes or pictures. Or they might be just for looks.

If you have ever experimented with magnets, you know that they stick to each other and to some kinds of metals. You also know that magnets can stick to things without directly touching them—such as a magnet used to hold a piece of paper to a refrigerator door.

Properties of Magnets

More than 2,000 years ago, the Greeks discovered a mineral that attracted things made of iron. Because this mineral was found in a part of Turkey called Magnesia, the Greeks called it magnetite. Today, any material that attracts iron or things made of iron is called a **magnet.** All magnets have certain properties. For example, all magnets have two poles. Magnets exert forces on each other and are surrounded by a magnetic field.

Reading Check What is a magnet? *(See the Appendix for answers to Reading Checks.)*

Magnetic Poles

The magnetic effects are not the same throughout a magnet. What would happen if you dipped a bar magnet into a box of paper clips? Most of the clips would stick to the ends of the bar, as shown in **Figure 1.** This shows that the strongest effects are near the ends of the bar magnet. Each end of the magnet is a magnetic pole. As you will see, **magnetic poles** are points on a magnet that have opposite magnetic qualities.

magnet any material that attracts iron or materials containing iron

magnetic pole one of two points, such as the ends of a magnet, that have opposing magnetic qualities

Figure 1 *More paper clips stick to the ends, or magnetic poles, of a magnet because the magnetic effects are strongest there.*

236 Chapter 8 Electromagnetism

Be Resourceful—Use the Web

SciLinks boxes in your textbook take you to resources that you can use for science projects, reports, and research papers. Go to **scilinks.org** and type in the **SciLinks code** to find information on a topic.

Visit go.hrw.com
Check out the **Current Science®** magazine articles and other materials that go with your textbook at **go.hrw.com.** Click on the textbook icon and the table of contents to see all of the resources for each chapter.

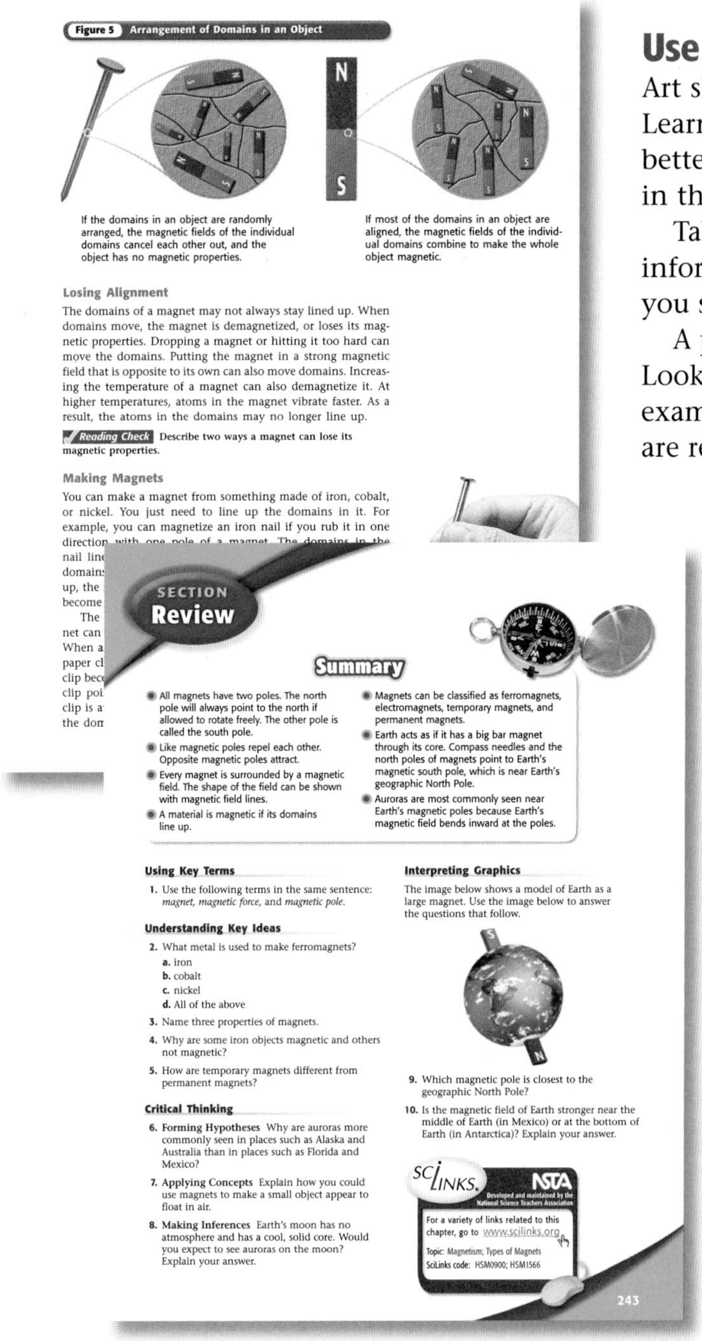
Figure 5 Arrangement of Domains in an Object

If the domains in an object are randomly arranged, the magnetic fields of the individual domains cancel each other out, and the object has no magnetic properties.

If most of the domains in an object are aligned, the magnetic fields of the individual domains combine to make the whole object magnetic.

Losing Alignment

The domains of a magnet may not always stay lined up. When domains move, the magnet is demagnetized, or loses its magnetic properties. Dropping a magnet or hitting it too hard can move the domains. Putting the magnet in a strong magnetic field that is opposite to its own can also move domains. Increasing the temperature of a magnet can also demagnetize it. At higher temperatures, atoms in the magnet vibrate faster. As a result, the atoms in the domains may no longer line up.

Reading Check Describe two ways a magnet can lose its magnetic properties.

Making Magnets

You can make a magnet from something made of iron, cobalt, or nickel. You just need to line up the domains in it. For example, you can magnetize an iron nail if you rub it in one direction ...

SECTION Review

Summary

- All magnets have two poles. The north pole will always point to the north if allowed to rotate freely. The other pole is called the south pole.
- Like magnetic poles repel each other. Opposite magnetic poles attract.
- Every magnet is surrounded by a magnetic field. The shape of the field can be shown with magnetic field lines.
- A material is magnetic if its domains line up.
- Magnets can be classified as ferromagnets, electromagnets, temporary magnets, and permanent magnets.
- Earth acts as if it has a big bar magnet through its core. Compass needles and the north poles of magnets point to Earth's magnetic south pole, which is near Earth's geographic North Pole.
- Auroras are most commonly seen near Earth's magnetic poles because Earth's magnetic field bends inward at the poles.

Using Key Terms

1. Use the following terms in the same sentence: *magnet, magnetic force,* and *magnetic pole.*

Understanding Key Ideas

2. What metal is used to make ferromagnets?
   a. iron
   b. cobalt
   c. nickel
   d. All of the above
3. Name three properties of magnets.
4. Why are some iron objects magnetic and others not magnetic?
5. How are temporary magnets different from permanent magnets?

Critical Thinking

6. **Forming Hypotheses** Why are auroras more commonly seen in places such as Alaska and Australia than in places such as Florida and Mexico?
7. **Applying Concepts** Explain how you could use magnets to make a small object appear to float in air.
8. **Making Inferences** Earth's moon has no atmosphere and has a cool, solid core. Would you expect to see auroras on the moon? Explain your answer.

Interpreting Graphics

The image below shows a model of Earth as a large magnet. Use the image below to answer the questions that follow.

9. Which magnetic pole is closest to the geographic North Pole?
10. Is the magnetic field of Earth stronger near the middle of Earth (in Mexico) or at the bottom of Earth (in Antarctica)? Explain your answer.

SciLinks NSTA Developed and maintained by the National Science Teachers Association
For a variety of links related to this chapter, go to www.scilinks.org
Topic: Magnetism; Types of Magnets
SciLinks code: HSM0900; HSM1566

243

Use the Illustrations and Photos

Art shows complex ideas and processes. Learn to analyze the art so that you better understand the material you read in the text.

Tables and graphs display important information in an organized way to help you see relationships.

A picture is worth a thousand words. Look at the photographs to see relevant examples of science concepts that you are reading about.

Answer the Section Reviews

Section Reviews test your knowledge of the main points of the section. Critical Thinking items challenge you to think about the material in greater depth and to find connections that you infer from the text.

STUDY TIP When you can't answer a question, reread the section. The answer is usually there.

Do Your Homework

Your teacher may assign worksheets to help you understand and remember the material in the chapter.

STUDY TIP Don't try to answer the questions without reading the text and reviewing your class notes. A little preparation up front will make your homework assignments a lot easier. Answering the items in the Chapter Review will help prepare you for the chapter test.

Holt Online Learning

Visit Holt Online Learning

If your teacher gives you a special password to log onto the **Holt Online Learning** site, you'll find your complete textbook on the Web. In addition, you'll find some great learning tools and practice quizzes. You'll be able to see how well you know the material from your textbook.

SAFETY FIRST!

Exploring, inventing, and investigating are essential to the study of science. However, these activities can also be dangerous. To make sure that your experiments and explorations are safe, you must be aware of a variety of safety guidelines. You have probably heard of the saying, "It is better to be safe than sorry." This is particularly true in a science classroom where experiments and explorations are being performed. Being uninformed and careless can result in serious injuries. Don't take chances with your own safety or with anyone else's.

The following pages describe important guidelines for staying safe in the science classroom. Your teacher may also have safety guidelines and tips that are specific to your classroom and laboratory. Take the time to be safe.

Safety Rules!

Start Out Right

Always get your teacher's permission before attempting any laboratory exploration. Read the procedures carefully, and pay particular attention to safety information and caution statements. If you are unsure about what a safety symbol means, look it up or ask your teacher. You cannot be too careful when it comes to safety. If an accident does occur, inform your teacher immediately regardless of how minor you think the accident is.

If you are instructed to note the odor of a substance, wave the fumes toward your nose with your hand. Never put your nose close to the source.

Safety Symbols

All of the experiments and investigations in this book and their related worksheets include important safety symbols to alert you to particular safety concerns. Become familiar with these symbols so that when you see them, you will know what they mean and what to do. It is important that you read this entire safety section to learn about specific dangers in the laboratory.

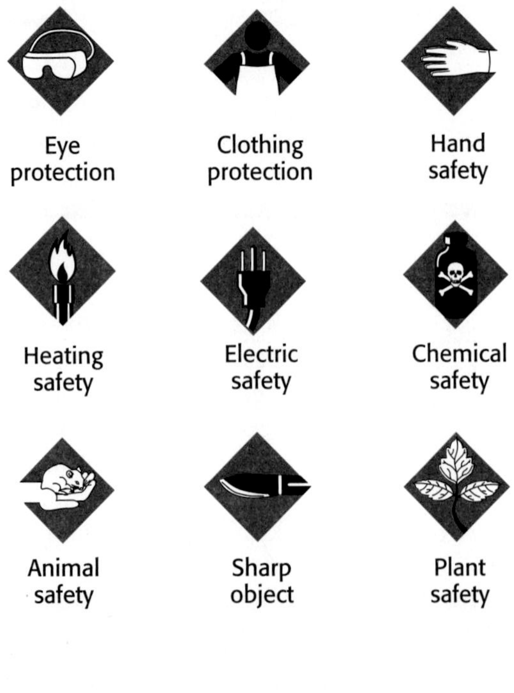

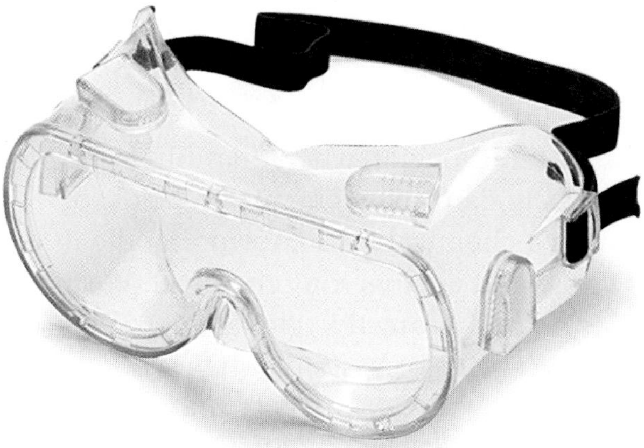

Eye Safety

Wear safety goggles when working around chemicals, acids, bases, or any type of flame or heating device. Wear safety goggles any time there is even the slightest chance that harm could come to your eyes. If any substance gets into your eyes, notify your teacher immediately and flush your eyes with running water for at least 15 minutes. Treat any unknown chemical as if it were a dangerous chemical. Never look directly into the sun. Doing so could cause permanent blindness.

Avoid wearing contact lenses in a laboratory situation. Even if you are wearing safety goggles, chemicals can get between the contact lenses and your eyes. If your doctor requires that you wear contact lenses instead of glasses, wear eye-cup safety goggles in the lab.

Safety Equipment

Know the locations of the nearest fire alarms and any other safety equipment, such as fire blankets and eyewash fountains, as identified by your teacher, and know the procedures for using the equipment.

Neatness

Keep your work area free of all unnecessary books and papers. Tie back long hair, and secure loose sleeves or other loose articles of clothing, such as ties and bows. Remove dangling jewelry. Don't wear open-toed shoes or sandals in the laboratory. Never eat, drink, or apply cosmetics in a laboratory setting. Food, drink, and cosmetics can easily become contaminated with dangerous materials.

Certain hair products (such as aerosol hair spray) are flammable and should not be worn while working near an open flame. Avoid wearing hair spray or hair gel on lab days.

Sharp/Pointed Objects

Use knives and other sharp instruments with extreme care. Never cut objects while holding them in your hands. Place objects on a suitable work surface for cutting.

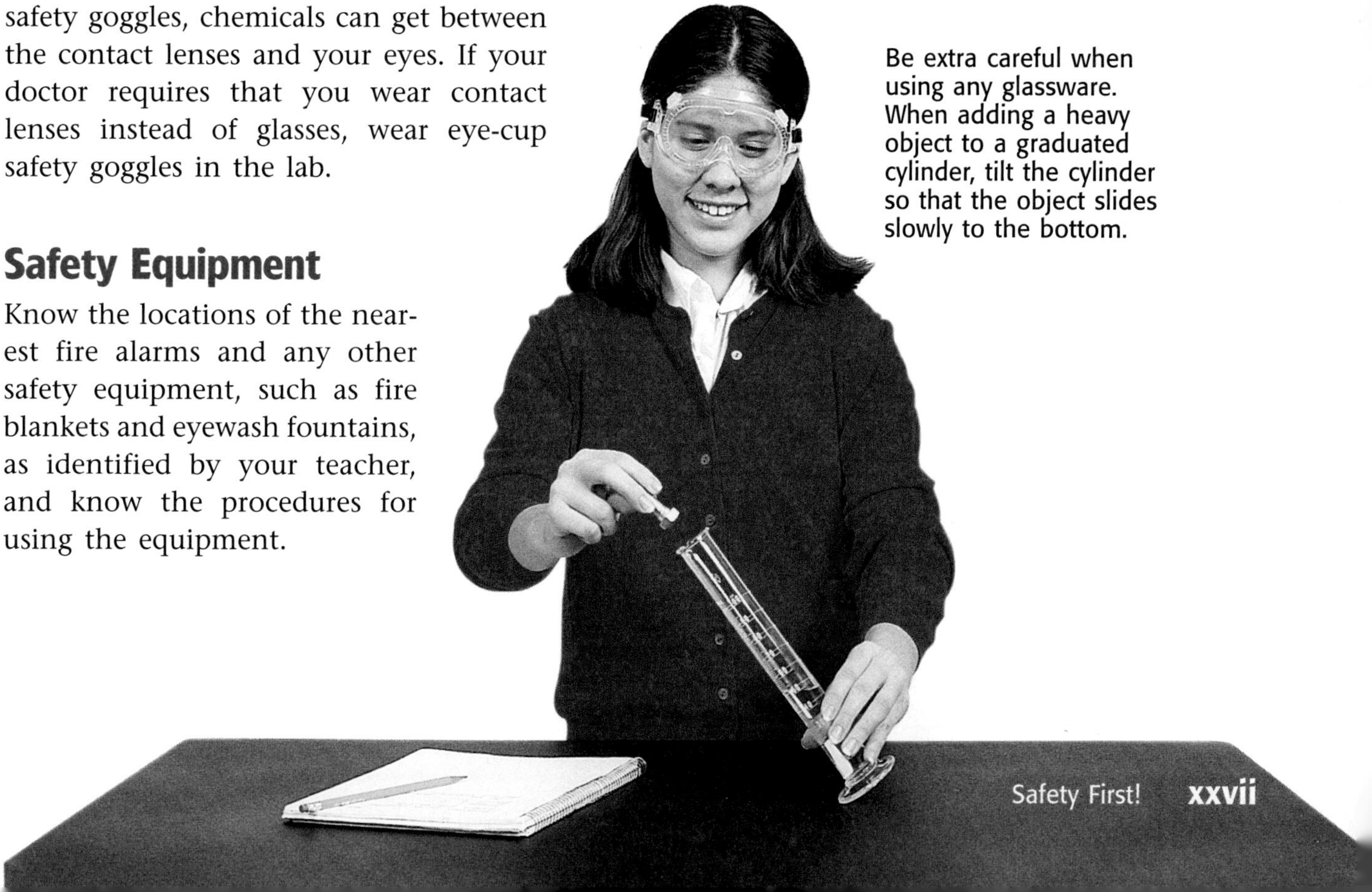

Be extra careful when using any glassware. When adding a heavy object to a graduated cylinder, tilt the cylinder so that the object slides slowly to the bottom.

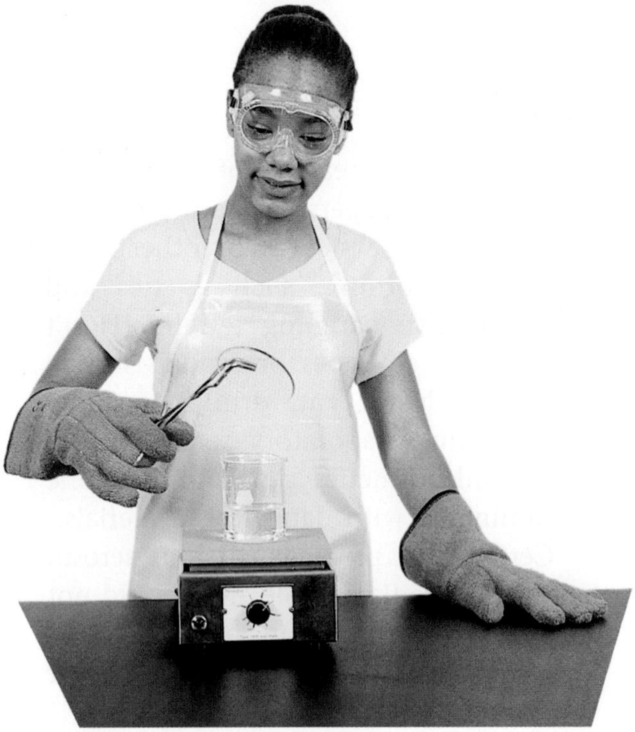

Heat

Wear safety goggles when using a heating device or a flame. Whenever possible, use an electric hot plate as a heat source instead of using an open flame. When heating materials in a test tube, always angle the test tube away from yourself and others. To avoid burns, wear heat-resistant gloves whenever instructed to do so.

Electricity

Be careful with electrical cords. When using a microscope with a lamp, do not place the cord where it could trip someone. Do not let cords hang over a table edge in a way that could cause equipment to fall if the cord is accidentally pulled. Do not use equipment with damaged cords. Be sure that your hands are dry and that the electrical equipment is in the "off" position before plugging it in. Turn off and unplug electrical equipment when you are finished.

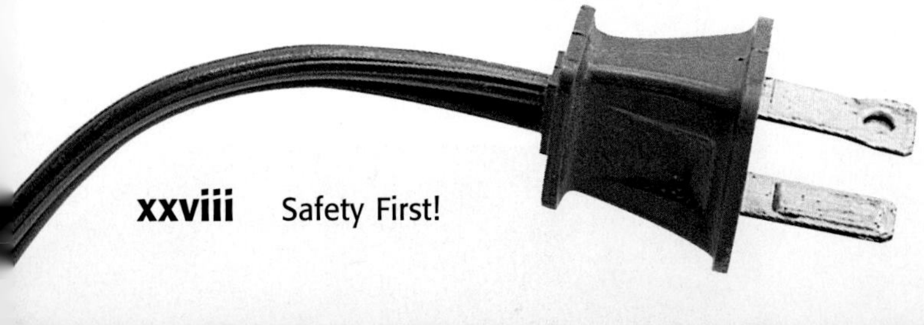

Chemicals

Wear safety goggles when handling any potentially dangerous chemicals, acids, or bases. If a chemical is unknown, handle it as you would a dangerous chemical. Wear an apron and protective gloves when you work with acids or bases or whenever you are told to do so. If a spill gets on your skin or clothing, rinse it off immediately with water for at least 5 minutes while calling to your teacher.

Never mix chemicals unless your teacher tells you to do so. Never taste, touch, or smell chemicals unless you are specifically directed to do so. Before working with a flammable liquid or gas, check for the presence of any source of flame, spark, or heat.

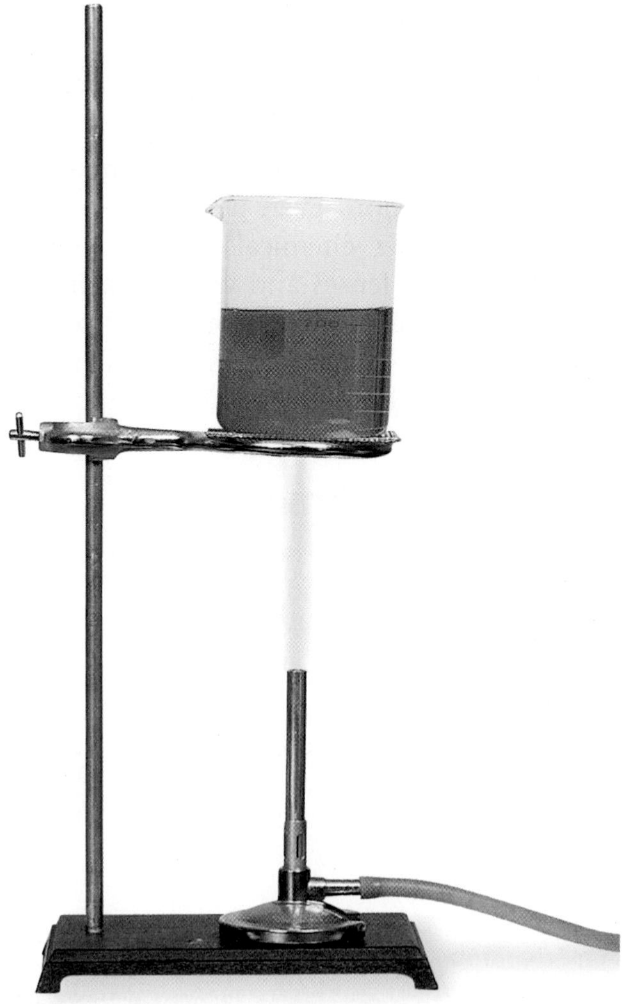

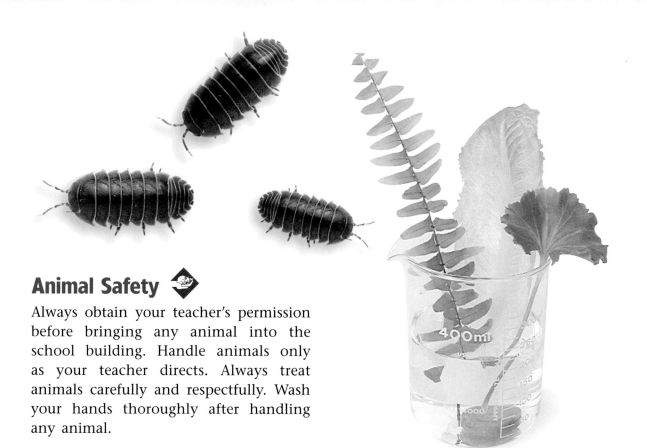

Animal Safety

Always obtain your teacher's permission before bringing any animal into the school building. Handle animals only as your teacher directs. Always treat animals carefully and respectfully. Wash your hands thoroughly after handling any animal.

Plant Safety

Do not eat any part of a plant or plant seed used in the laboratory. Wash your hands thoroughly after handling any part of a plant. When in nature, do not pick any wild plants unless your teacher instructs you to do so.

Glassware

Examine all glassware before use. Be sure that glassware is clean and free of chips and cracks. Report damaged glassware to your teacher. Glass containers used for heating should be made of heat-resistant glass.

1

Science in Our World

The Big Idea Scientific progress is made by asking meaningful questions and conducting careful investigations.

SECTION

About the Photo

Flippers work great to help penguins move through the water. But could flippers help ships, too? Two scientists have been trying to find out. By using scientific methods, they are asking questions such as, "Would flippers use less energy than propellers do?" As a result of these investigations, ships may have flippers like those of penguins someday!

PRE-READING ACTIVITY

Graphic Organizer

Spider Map Before you read the chapter, create the graphic organizer entitled "Spider Map" described in the **Study Skills** section of the Appendix. Label the circle "Scientific Models." Create a leg for each type of scientific model. As you read the chapter, fill in the map with details about each type of scientific model.

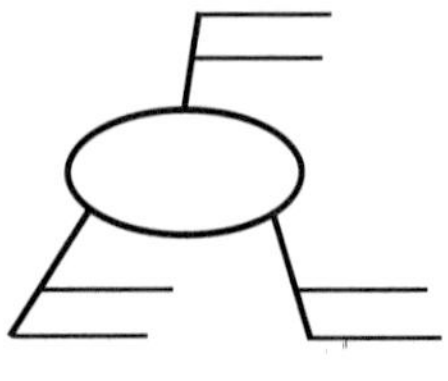

START-UP ACTIVITY

Figure It Out

In this activity, you will make observations and use them to solve a puzzle, just as scientists do.

Procedure

1. Get the **five shapes** shown here from your teacher.

2. Observe the drawing at right. Predict how the five shapes could be arranged to make the fish.

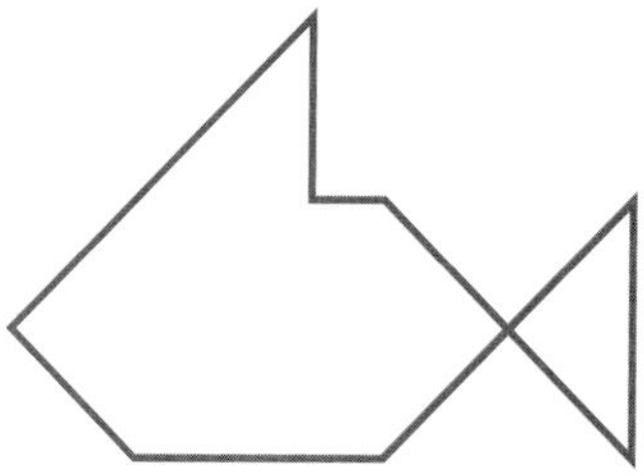

3. Test your idea. You may have to try several times. (Hint: Shapes can be turned over.)

Analysis

1. Did you solve the puzzle just by making observations? What observations helped the most?
2. How did testing your ideas help?

SECTION 1

Science and Scientists

You're eating breakfast. You look down and notice your reflection in your spoon is upside down! You wonder, Why is my reflection upside down even though I'm holding the spoon right side up?

What You Will Learn

- Describe three methods of investigation.
- Identify benefits of science in the world around you.
- Describe jobs that use science.

Vocabulary

science

READING STRATEGY

Reading Organizer As you read this section, create an outline of the section. Use the headings from the section in your outline.

Congratulations! You just completed the first steps of being a scientist. How did you do it? You observed the world around you. Then you asked questions about your observations. And that's part of what science is all about.

Science Starts with a Question

The process of gathering knowledge about the natural world is called **science**. Asking a question is often the first step in the process of gathering knowledge. The world around you is full of amazing things that can lead you to ask questions, such as those in **Figure 1.**

science the knowledge obtained by observing natural events and conditions in order to discover facts and formulate laws or principles that can be verified or tested

In Your Own Neighborhood

Take a look around your school and around your neighborhood. Most of the time, you take things that you use or see every day for granted. However, one day you might look at something in a new way. That's when a question hits you! The student in **Figure 1** didn't have to look very far to realize that she had some questions to ask.

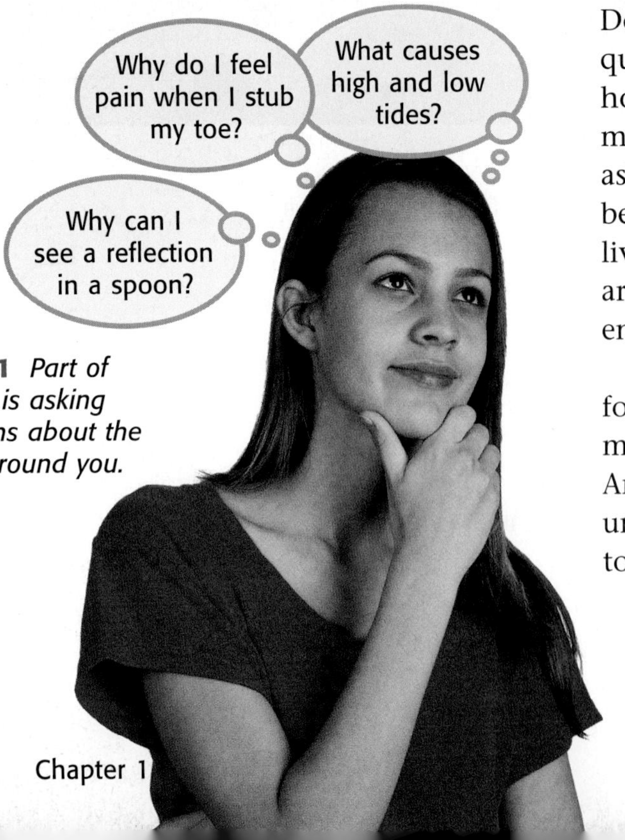

Why do I feel pain when I stub my toe?
What causes high and low tides?
Why can I see a reflection in a spoon?

Figure 1 *Part of science is asking questions about the world around you.*

The World and Beyond

Do you think you might get tired asking questions about things in your neighborhood? Then just remember that the world is made up of many different places. You could ask questions about deserts, forests, or sandy beaches. Many different plants and animals live in each of these places. And then there are the rocks, soil, and flowing water in the environment.

But Earth is not the final place to look for questions. You can look outward to the moon, sun, and planets in our solar system. And beyond that, you have the rest of the universe! There seem to be enough questions to keep scientists busy for a long time.

Investigation: The Search for Answers

Once you ask a question, it's time to find an answer. There are several different methods that you can use to start your investigation.

Figure 2 *A library is a good place to begin your search for answers.*

Research

You can find answers to some of your questions by doing research, as shown in **Figure 2.** You can ask someone who knows a lot about the subject of your question, or you can look up information in textbooks, encyclopedias, and magazines. You can also search on the Internet for information. You can find information by reading about an experiment that someone did. But be sure to think about where the information you find comes from. You want to use information only from reliable sources.

Observation

You can find answers to questions by making careful observations. For example, if you want to know if cloud type and weather are associated, you could make daily observations. By daily recording the types of clouds that you see and the day's weather, you may find associations between the two.

Experimentation

You can answer some of your questions by doing an experiment, as shown in **Figure 3.** Your research might help you plan your experiment. And, you'll need to make careful observations. What do you do if your experiment needs materials or conditions that are hard to get? For example, what do you do if you want to see how a rat runs through a maze in space? Don't give up! Do more research, and try to find the results from someone else's experiment!

Reading Check **What do you do if materials for your experiment are hard to find?** (*See the Appendix for answers to Reading Checks*)

Figure 3 *This student is doing an experiment to find out how her reflection changes in different mirrors.*

Why Ask Why?

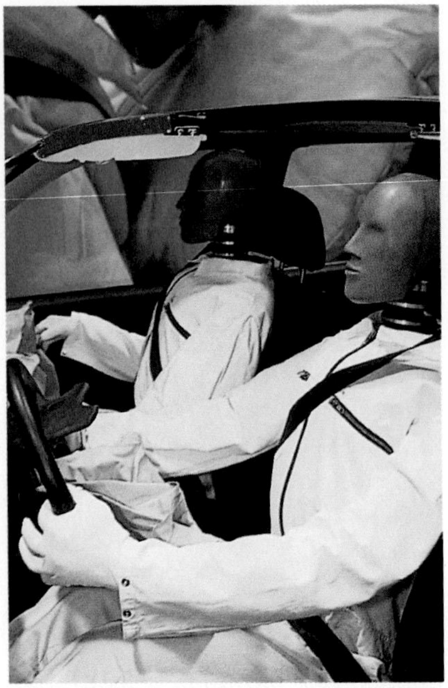

Figure 4 *The results of this test are used to improve air bags.*

Although people cannot use science to answer every question, they do find some interesting answers. But do any of the answers really matter? Absolutely! As you study science, you will see how it affects you and everything around you.

Saving Lives

Using science, people have come up with several answers to the question "How can people be protected during an automobile accident?" One answer is to require people to wear seat belts. Other answers include designing and building cars that are made of stronger materials and that have air bags. **Figure 4** shows how air bags are tested under scientific conditions. In this way, science helps make cars safer.

Saving Resources

Science has also helped answer the question, How can resources be made to last longer? Recycling is one answer. Science has helped people invent ways to recycle a variety of materials. For example, when a car becomes worn out or is wrecked, its steel can be recycled and used to make new products. And recycling steel saves more than just the steel, as shown in **Figure 5.** Using science, people develop more-efficient methods and better equipment for recycling steel, aluminum, paper, glass, and even some plastics. In this way, science helps make resources last longer.

Figure 5 **Resources Saved Through Recycling**

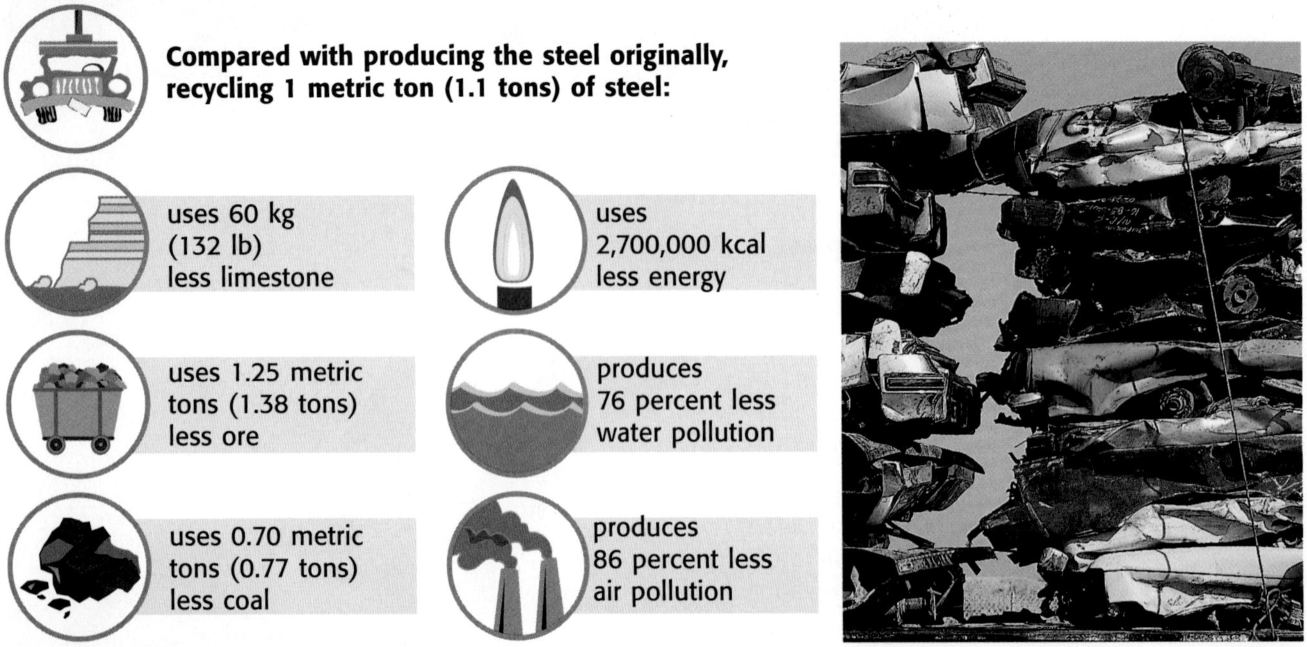

Compared with producing the steel originally, recycling 1 metric ton (1.1 tons) of steel:
uses 60 kg (132 lb) less limestone
uses 1.25 metric tons (1.38 tons) less ore
uses 0.70 metric tons (0.77 tons) less coal
uses 2,700,000 kcal less energy
produces 76 percent less water pollution
produces 86 percent less air pollution

Saving the Environment

Science has helped answer the question, How can the ozone layer be protected? Substances called chlorofluorocarbons (KLAWR oh FLUR uh KAHR buhnz) (CFCs), which can be found in aerosols, have had a role in damaging the ozone layer. But using science, people have made other substances that can take the place of CFCs. These substances do not harm the ozone layer.

Why does the loss of this layer matter? The ozone that makes up this layer protects everything on the planet from a harmful type of light called ultraviolet (UV) light. Without the protection of the ozone layer, higher levels of UV light will reach the ground. Higher rates of skin cancer could result. By finding ways to reduce the use of these chemicals, we can help protect the environment and make the world a healthier place.

SCHOOL to HOME

Challenging Topics

Although science can be used to explain or answer many questions about the world around us, there are some topics that cannot be examined usefully in a scientific way. With a parent, discuss two or three possible topics that may not be explained by science.

ACTIVITY

Scientists Are All Around You

Believe it or not, scientists work in many different places. If you think about it, any person who asks questions and looks for answers could be called a scientist! Keep reading to learn about just a few jobs that use science.

Meteorologist

A *meteorologist* (MEET ee uhr AHL uh jist) is a person who studies the atmosphere. One of the most common careers that meteorologists have is that of weather forecaster. But some meteorologists specialize in—and even chase—tornadoes! These meteorologists predict where a tornado is likely to form. Then, they drive very near the site to gather data, as shown in **Figure 6.** These data help meteorologists and other scientists understand tornadoes better. A better understanding of tornadoes enables scientists to more accurately predict the behavior of these violent storms. The ability to make more-accurate predictions allows scientists to give earlier warnings of storms, which helps reduce injuries and deaths caused by storms.

Reading Check What is a meteorologist?

Figure 6 *These meteorologists are risking their lives to gather data about tornadoes.*

Figure 7 *This geochemist takes rock samples from the field. Then she studies them in her laboratory.*

Geochemist

Look at **Figure 7.** A *geochemist* (JEE oh KEM ist) is a person who specializes in the chemistry of rocks, minerals, and soil. Geochemists determine the economic value of these materials. They also try to find out what the environment was like when these materials formed and what has happened to the materials since they first formed.

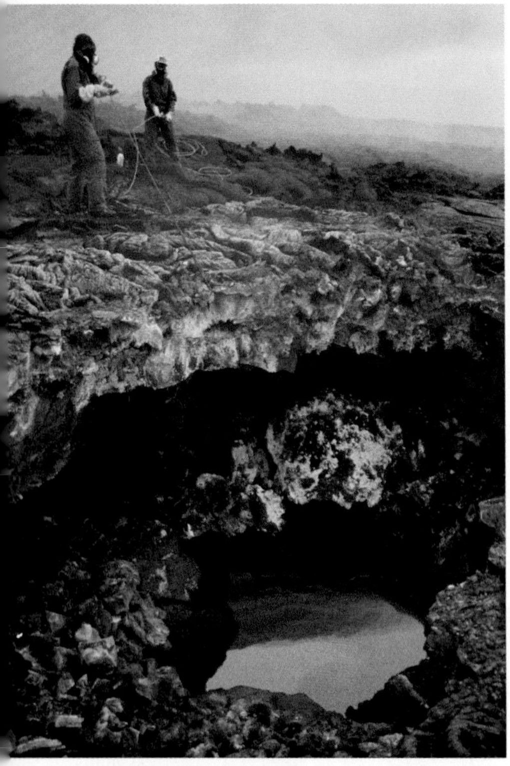

Figure 8 *Volcanologists study volcanoes. Many volcanologists study volcanic patterns in order to predict when a volcano will erupt.*

Ecologist

To understand the behavior of living things, you also need to know about the surroundings. An *ecologist* (ee KAHL uh jist) is a person who studies a community of organisms and their nonliving environment. Ecologists work in many fields, such as wildlife management, agriculture, forestry, and conservation.

Volcanologist

Imagine that your workplace was at the edge of 1,000°C pool of lava, as seen in **Figure 8**. That's where you might work if you were a volcanologist! A *volcanologist* (VAHL kuh NAHL uh jist) is a scientist who studies volcanoes. Volcanologists must know the structure and the chemistry of Earth and its rocks. They must also understand how volcanic materials interact with air and water. This knowledge helps volcanologists learn how and why volcanoes erupt. If volcanologists can predict when a volcano will erupt, they can help save lives.

Science Illustrator

You may be surprised to learn that there is a career that uses both art and science skills. *Science illustrators* draw scientific diagrams, such as the one in **Figure 9.**

Science illustrators often have a background in art and variety of sciences. However, some science illustrators focus on one area of science. For example, some science illustrators draw only medical diagrams. These diagrams are used in medical textbooks, or in brochures that patients receive from their doctors.

Reading Check What is a science illustrator?

Figure 9 *A science illustrator drew this diagram so students can learn about the digestive system in birds.*

SECTION Review

Summary

- Science is the process of gathering knowledge about the natural world.
- Science begins by asking a question.
- Three methods of investigation are research, observation, and experimentation.
- Science affects people's daily lives. Science can help save lives, save resources, and improve the environment.
- There are several types of scientists and many jobs that use science.

Using Key Terms

1. In your own words, write a definition for the term *science.*

Understanding Key Ideas

2. Which of the following items describes what volcanologists must know in order to help them predict the eruption of a volcano?

a. the structure of Earth
b. the chemistry of Earth's rocks
c. the interaction between volcanic material and air
d. All of the above.

3. Describe three jobs that use science.

4. What are three methods of investigation?

5. Describe how science can help people save resources such as coal.

Math Skills

6. A slow flow of lava is traveling at a rate of 3 m per day. How far will the lava have traveled at the end of 30 days?

Critical Thinking

7. Applying Concepts Your friend wants to know the average amount of salt added to her favorite fast-food French fries. What would you recommend that she do to find out the amount of salt?

8. Making Inferences The slogan for a package delivery service is "For the fastest shipping from port to port, call Holt Speedy Transport!" What inferences about the service can you make from this slogan? Describe how science could help you figure out whether this service really ships packages faster than other services do.

SCILINKS. NSTA Developed and maintained by the National Science Teachers Association

For a variety of links related to this chapter, go to www.scilinks.org

Topic: Scientific Inquiry; Careers in Science

SciLinks code: HSM1357; HSM0225

SECTION 2

Scientific Methods

What You Will Learn

- Identify the steps used in scientific methods.
- Formulate testable hypotheses.
- Explain how scientific methods are used to answer questions and solve problems.

Vocabulary

scientific methods
observation
technology
hypothesis
data

READING STRATEGY

Mnemonics As you read this section, create a mnemonic device to help you remember scientific methods.

Imagine that you are trying to improve ships. Would you study the history of shipbuilding? Would you investigate different types of fuel? Would you observe creatures that move easily through the water, such as dolphins and penguins?

Two scientists from the Massachusetts Institute of Technology (MIT) thought that studying penguins was a great way to improve ships! In the next few pages, you'll learn about James Czarnowski (zahr NOW SKEE) and Michael Triantafyllou (tree AHN ti FEE loo). These two scientists from MIT used scientific methods to develop *Proteus* (PROH tee uhs), the penguin boat.

What Are Scientific Methods?

The ways in which scientists answer questions and solve problems are called **scientific methods**. As scientists look for answers, they often use the same steps. But there is more than one way to use the steps. Look at **Figure 1.** Scientists may use all of the steps or just some of the steps during an investigation. They may even repeat some of the steps or do them in a different order. It all depends on what works best to answer their question.

Figure 1 Scientific Methods

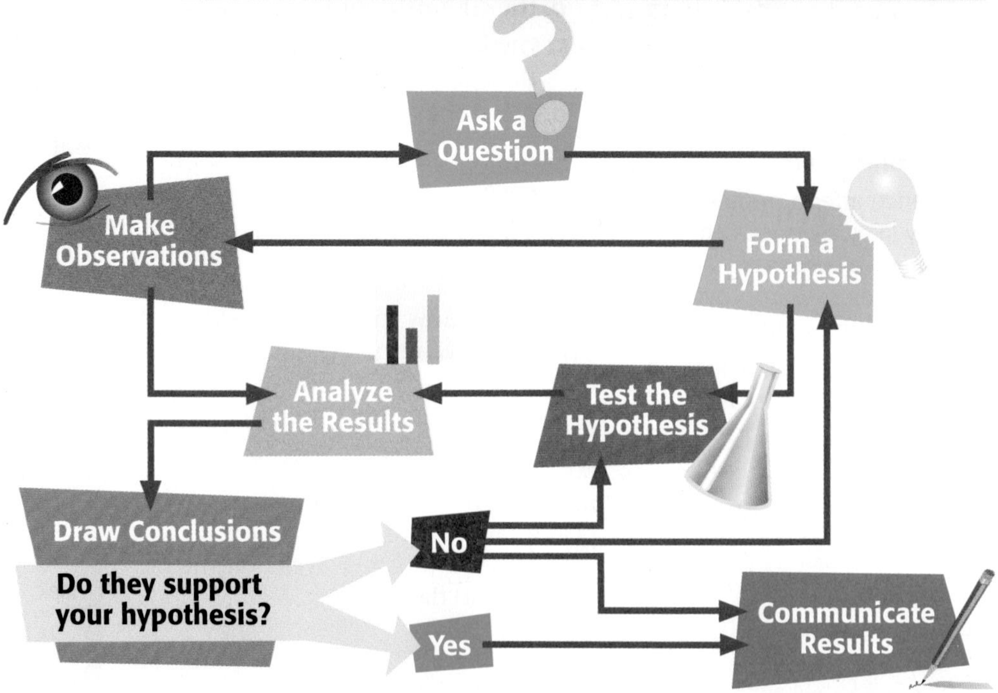

Figure 2 *James Czarnowski (left) and Michael Triantafyllou (right) made observations about how boats work in order to develop Proteus.*

Ask a Question

Asking a question helps focus the purpose of an investigation. Scientists often ask a question after making observations. An **observation** is any use of the senses to gather information. Noting that the sky is blue or that a cotton ball feels soft is an observation. Measurements are observations that are made with tools such as metersticks and stopwatches.

Observations should be accurately recorded so that scientists can use the information in future investigations. In an investigation, if information is not gathered from a large enough number of samples, the study's results may be misleading.

A Real-World Question

Czarnowski and Triantafyllou, shown in **Figure 2,** are engineers (EN juh NIRZ), scientists who put scientific knowledge to practical human use. Engineers create **technology** or use science to make tools for practical purposes. Czarnowski and Triantafyllou observed boat propulsion (proh PUHL shuhn) systems, which are what make boats move. Then, they studied ways to improve these systems. Most boats move by using propellers. These engineers studied the efficiency (e FISH uhn see) of boat propulsion systems. *Efficiency* compares energy output (the energy used to move the boat) with energy input (the energy supplied by the engine). The engineers learned from their observations that boat propellers are not very efficient.

Reading Check **What is technology?** (*See the Appendix for answers to Reading Checks.*)

scientific methods a series of steps followed to solve problems, including collecting data, formulating a hypothesis, testing the hypothesis, and stating conclusions

observation the process of obtaining information by using the senses

technology the application of science for practical purposes; the use of tools, machines, materials, and processes to meet human needs

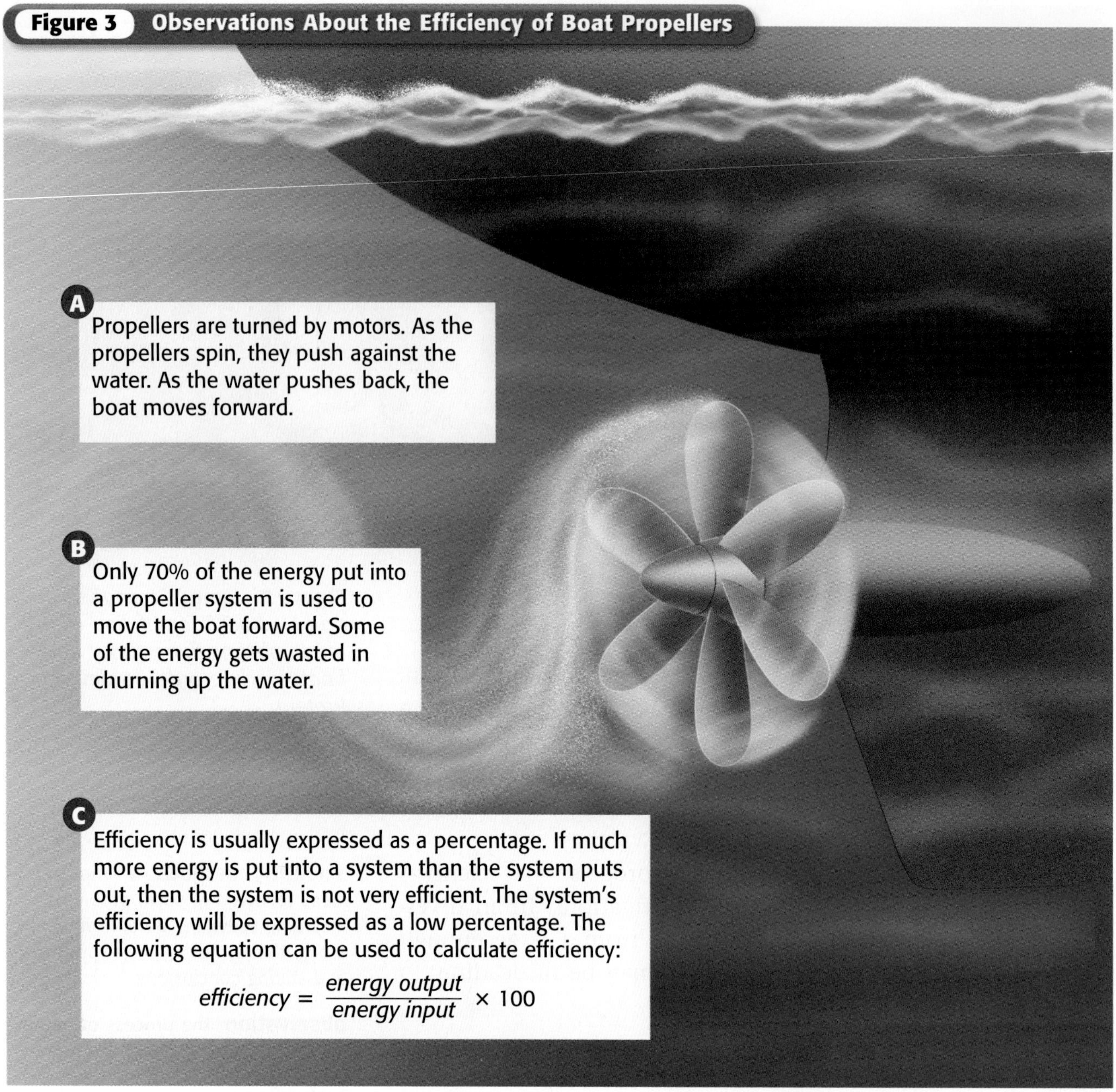

A
Propellers are turned by motors. As the propellers spin, they push against the water. As the water pushes back, the boat moves forward.
B
Only 70% of the energy put into a propeller system is used to move the boat forward. Some of the energy gets wasted in churning up the water.
C
Efficiency is usually expressed as a percentage. If much more energy is put into a system than the system puts out, then the system is not very efficient. The system's efficiency will be expressed as a low percentage. The following equation can be used to calculate efficiency:
$$efficiency = \frac{energy\ output}{energy\ input} \times 100$$

Figure 3 Observations About the Efficiency of Boat Propellers

The Importance of Boat Efficiency

Look at **Figure 3.** Czarnowski and Triantafyllou found that only 70% of the energy put into a propeller system is used to move the boat forward. Why is boat efficiency important? Making only a small fraction of the United States' boats and ships just 10% more efficient would save millions of liters of fuel per year. Saving fuel means saving money. It also means using less of Earth's supply of fossil fuels. Based on their observations and all of this information, Czarnowski and Triantafyllou were ready to ask the following question: How can boat propulsion systems be made more efficient?

Figure 4 *Penguins use their flippers to "fly" underwater. As they pull their flippers toward their body, they push against the water, which propels them forward.*

Form a Hypothesis

Once you've asked your question and made observations, you are ready to form a *hypothesis*. A **hypothesis** is a possible explanation or answer to a question. You can use what you already know and what you have observed in order to form a hypothesis. A good hypothesis is testable. This means that information can be gathered or an experiment can be designed to test it. A hypothesis that is not testable is not necessarily wrong. But there is no way to support the hypothesis or to show that it is wrong.

hypothesis an explanation that is based on prior scientific research or observations and that can be tested

Nature Provides a Possible Answer

Czarnowski observed how quickly and easily penguins at the New England Aquarium moved through the water. **Figure 4** shows how penguins propel themselves. Czarnowski also observed that penguins have a rigid body, similar to a boat. These observations led to a hypothesis: A propulsion system that mimics the way a penguin swims will be more efficient than a propulsion system that uses propellers.

Make Predictions

Before scientists test a hypothesis, they often make predictions that state what they think will happen during the actual test of the hypothesis. Scientists usually state predictions in an if-then format. The engineers at MIT might have made the following prediction: *If* two flippers are attached to a boat, *then* the boat will be more efficient than a boat powered by propellers.

Reading Check What is a prediction?

CONNECTION TO Biology

Not Tested on Humans? Did you know that scientists use people as subjects for certain investigations? Of course, these humans first have to agree to participate! Research and describe the types of investigations that use people. Why is it important to inform each person about the risks and benefits of an investigation?

Quick Lab

That's Swingin'!

1. Make a pendulum. Tie a **piece of string** to a **ring stand.** Hang a **small weight** from the string.
2. Form a testable hypothesis about one factor (such as the mass of the weight) that may affect the rate at which the pendulum swings.
3. Predict the results as you change this factor (the variable).
4. Test your hypothesis. Record the number of swings made in 10 seconds for each trial.
5. Was your hypothesis supported? Analyze your results.

Math Practice

Number of Observations

Making several observations during an experiment is important because if you based your conclusions on a small number of observations, you may reach the wrong conclusion. Imagine you flipped a coin 3 times, and each time the coin landed heads-up. You might make the generalization, "Every time I flip a quarter, it will land heads-up." But this generalization is dangerous, because if the coin lands tails up even once, your generalization is incorrect. Now, flip a coin 30 times. Can you make a more accurate generalization now? Why?

Test the Hypothesis

After you form a hypothesis, you must test it. You must find out whether it is a reasonable answer to your question. Testing helps you find out if your hypothesis is pointing you in the right direction or if it is way off the mark. Often, a scientist will test a prediction that is based on the hypothesis.

Keep It Under Control

One way to test a hypothesis is to do a controlled experiment. A *controlled experiment* compares the results from a control group with the results from one or more experimental groups. The control group and the experimental groups are the same except for one factor. This factor is called a *variable*. The experiment will then show the effect of the variable. If your experiment has more than one variable, determining which variable is responsible for the experiment's results will be difficult or impossible.

Sometimes, such as in a study of the stars, doing a controlled experiment is not possible. In such cases, you can make more observations or do research. Or you may have to build technology that you want to test as a model or model system. That's just what Czarnowski and Triantafyllou did. They built *Proteus*, the penguin boat, shown in **Figure 5.** *Proteus* is 3.4 m long and 50 cm wide, too narrow for even a single passenger.

Figure 5 **Proteus**

Proteus has two flipperlike paddles, called *foils*. Both foils move out and then in, much as a penguin uses its flippers underwater.

Proteus
A Two car batteries supply energy to the motors that drive Proteus's flapping foils.
B A desktop computer programs the number of times the foils flap per second.
C As the foils flap, they push water backward. The water pushes against the foils, to propel the boat forward.

Figure 6 Graphs of the Test Results

This line graph shows that *Proteus* was most efficient when its foils were flapping about 1.7 times per second.

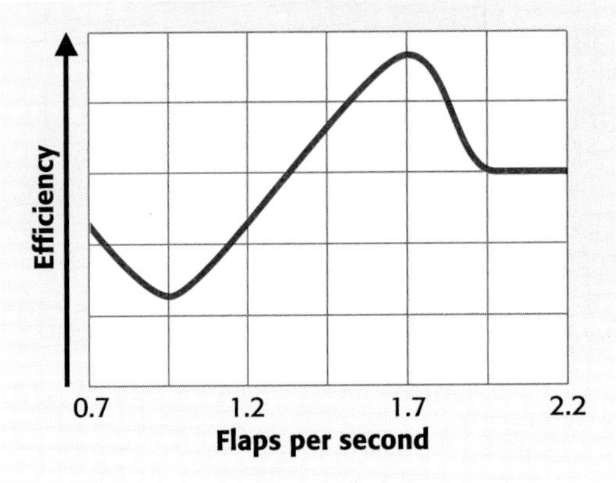

This bar graph shows that *Proteus* is 17 percent more efficient than a propeller-driven boat.

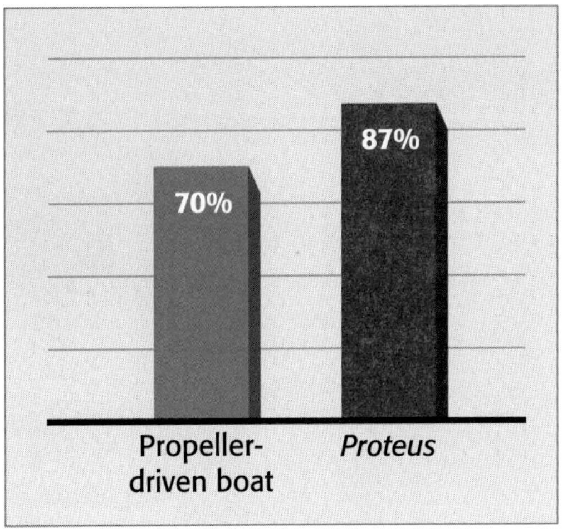

Testing *Proteus*

The engineers took *Proteus* into open water when they were ready to collect data. **Data** are pieces of information acquired through experimentation. The number of data samples in an experiment is important. The sample number must be large enough for scientists to be sure that the experiment's results are due to the variable and not to normal variation between samples. The engineers did several tests. Only the flapping rate varied between tests. Data such as the flapping rate, the energy used by the motor, and the boat's speed were recorded for each test. Input energy was determined by how much energy was used. Output energy was determined from *Proteus*'s speed.

data any pieces of information acquired through observation or experimentation

Analyze the Results

Once you have your data, you must analyze them. You must find out whether the results of your test support the hypothesis. You can analyze your results by doing calculations, or by organizing data into tables and graphs.

Reading Check What must you do after you have your data?

Analyzing *Proteus*

Czarnowski and Triantafyllou used the data for input energy and output energy to calculate *Proteus*'s efficiency for different flapping rates. These data are graphed in **Figure 6.** The scientists compared *Proteus*'s highest level of efficiency with the average efficiency of a propeller-driven boat. Look at the bar graph in **Figure 6.** Do the data support the original hypothesis?

Figure 7 *Could a penguin propulsion system be used on large ships, such as oil tankers? The research continues!*

Draw Conclusions

At the end of an investigation, you must draw a conclusion. You could conclude that your results support your hypothesis. Or you could conclude that your results do *not* support your hypothesis. Or you might even conclude that you need more information. Your conclusion can help guide what you do next. You could ask new questions or gather more information. You could change the procedure or check your calculations for errors. Or you could do another investigation.

The *Proteus* Conclusion

After analyzing their data, Czarnowski and Triantafyllou did many more trials. Each time they found that the penguin propulsion system was more efficient than a propeller propulsion system. So they concluded that their hypothesis was supported. But this conclusion led to more questions, as you can see in **Figure 7.**

Communicate Results

One of the most important steps in any investigation is to communicate your results accurately and honestly. Accurate reporting ensures the credibility of a scientist. You can communicate your results in a report or on a Web site. People who read your report can reproduce your experiment and verify your data.

Communicating About *Proteus*

Czarnowski and Triantafyllou published their results in academic papers. They also displayed their project and its results on the Internet. In addition, science magazines and newspapers have reported their work. These reports allow you to conduct some research of your own about *Proteus*.

CONNECTION TO Social Studies

Biased Samples Sometimes, the samples of data collected during an investigation may be biased. Information shows bias when it is not objective. For example, in the presidential election of 1936, a polling publication determined that Franklin Roosevelt's opponent, Alf Landon, would win the election by a landslide. The pollsters did not realize that their sample had a greater percentage of supporters of Alf Landon than were in the general population. Their information was biased. When President Roosevelt won the election, the pollsters were very surprised. Research the dangers of biased samples and make a poster about what you have learned.

ACTIVITY

SECTION Review

Summary

- Scientific methods are the ways in which scientists answer questions and solve problems.
- Asking a question helps you focus the purpose of an investigation.
- A hypothesis is a possible answer to a question. A good hypothesis is testable.
- Testing a hypothesis helps you find out if the hypothesis is a reasonable answer to your question.
- Analyzing the data collected during an investigation will help you find out whether the results of your test support your hypothesis.
- Conclusions that you draw from your results will show you if your test supported your hypothesis.
- Communicating your results will allow other scientists to use your investigation for research or conduct an investigation of their own.

Using Key Terms

In each of the following sentences, replace the incorrect term with the correct term from the word bank.

scientific methods	observations
hypotheses	data

1. Hypotheses are any use of the senses to gather information.
2. Data are possible explanations or answers to a question.

Understanding Key Ideas

3. The statement, "If I don't study for this test, then I will not get a good grade," is an example of a(n)
   a. law.
   b. theory.
   c. observation.
   d. prediction.
4. How do scientists and engineers use scientific methods?
5. Name the steps that can be used in scientific methods.

Critical Thinking

6. **Analyzing Methods** Explain how a small amount of data cannot prove that a prediction is always correct but can prove that a prediction is NOT always correct.
7. **Applying Concepts** You want to test different shapes of kites to see which shape produces the strongest lift. What are some factors that need to be the same for each trial so that the only variable is the shape of the kite?

Interpreting Graphics

Use the graph below to answer the question that follows.

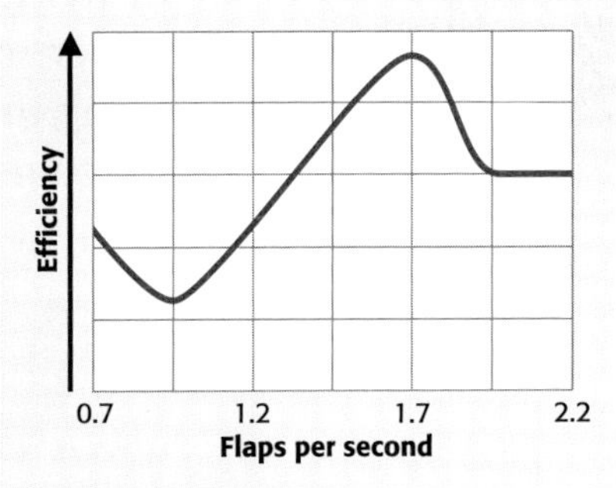

8. What is the flapping rate at the point of lowest efficiency?

SCiLINKS® NSTA
Developed and maintained by the National Science Teachers Association

For a variety of links related to this chapter, go to www.scilinks.org

Topic: Scientific Methods
SciLinks code: HSM1359

SECTION 3

Scientific Models

How much like a penguin was Proteus? Well, Proteus didn't have feathers and wasn't a living thing. But its "flippers" were designed to create the same kind of motion as a penguin's flippers.

The MIT engineers built *Proteus* to mimic the way a penguin swims. They wanted to get a greater understanding about boat propulsion. In other words, they made a *model*.

What You Will Learn

- Describe how models are used to represent the natural world.
- Identify three types of scientific models.
- Describe theories and laws.

Vocabulary
model
theory
law

READING STRATEGY

Prediction Guide Before reading this section, write the title of each heading in this section. Next, under each heading, write what you think you will learn.

Types of Scientific Models

A representation of an object or system is called a **model**. Models often use familiar objects or ideas that stand for other things. That's how a model can be a tool for understanding the natural world. A model uses something familiar to help you understand something that is not familiar. Models can be used to explain the past and the present. They can even be used to predict future events. However, keep in mind that models have limitations. Three major kinds of scientific models are physical, mathematical, and conceptual models.

model a pattern, plan, representation, or description designed to show the structure or workings of an object, system, or concept

Physical Models

Model airplanes, dolls, and even many drawings are all physical models. Some physical models, such as the model flower in **Figure 1,** look like the thing they model. However, a limitation of the model flower is that it does not grow like a real flower. Other physical models, such as *Proteus*, act somewhat like the thing they model. *Proteus* was a model of how penguins swim. Of course, *Proteus* doesn't eat fish like penguins do!

Figure 1 *The model flower makes learning the different parts of a flower much easier. But the model does not smell as sweet!*

Mathematical Models

Every day, people try to predict the weather. One way that they predict the weather is to use mathematical models. **Figure 2** shows a mathematical model that is expressed as a weather map. A mathematical model is made up of mathematical equations and data. Some mathematical models are simple. These models allow you to calculate things such as forces and acceleration. Others are so complex that only computers can handle them. Some of these very complex models have many variables. Using the most correct data does not make the prediction correct. A change in a variable that was not thought of could cause the model to fail.

Figure 2 *Weather maps that you see on the evening news are mathematical models.*

Conceptual Models

The third kind of model is a conceptual model. Some conceptual models are systems of ideas. Others are based on making comparisons with familiar things to help illustrate or explain an idea. The big bang theory, illustrated in **Figure 3**, is a conceptual model. This model says that the universe was once a small, hot, and dense volume of matter. Although the big bang theory is widely accepted by astronomers, some data do not quite fit the model. For example, scientists have calculated the ages of some old, nearby stars. If the calculations are right, then some of these stars are older than the universe itself.

Reading Check **What is a conceptual model?** (*See Appendix for answers to Reading Checks.*)

SCHOOL to HOME

Models and Scale

Models are often built to scale. This means that the size of the parts of the model are proportional to the parts of the real object. Make a scale drawing of a room in your home, including some of the objects in the room. Then, exchange drawings with a classmate. Can you determine the actual size of the room and its objects from your classmate's drawing?

ACTIVITY

Figure 3 *The big bang theory says that 12 billion to 15 billion years ago, an event called the big bang sent matter in all directions to eventually form the galaxies and planets.*

Figure 4 *Looking at a model of a cell can show you what is inside an actual cell.*

Models Are Just the Right Size

Models are often used to represent things that are very small or very large. Particles of matter are too small to see. The Earth or the solar system is too large to see completely. In these cases, a model can help you picture the thing in your mind. How can you learn about the parts of a cell? That's not an easy thing to do because you can't see inside a cell with just your eyes. But you can look at a model, such as the one being used by the student in **Figure 4.**

Models Build Scientific Knowledge

Models are often used to help illustrate and explain scientific theories. In science, a **theory** is a unifying explanation for a broad range of hypotheses and observations that have been supported by testing. A theory not only can explain an observation you've made but also can predict what might happen in the future.

theory an explanation for some phenomenon that is based on observation, experimentation, and reasoning

law a summary of many experimental results and observations; a law tells how things work.

Scientists use models to help guide their search for new information. This information can help support a theory or show it to be wrong. Keep in mind that models can be changed or replaced. These changes happen because new observations that cause scientists to change their theories are made. You can compare an old model with a current one in **Figure 5.**

Reading Check What is a theory?

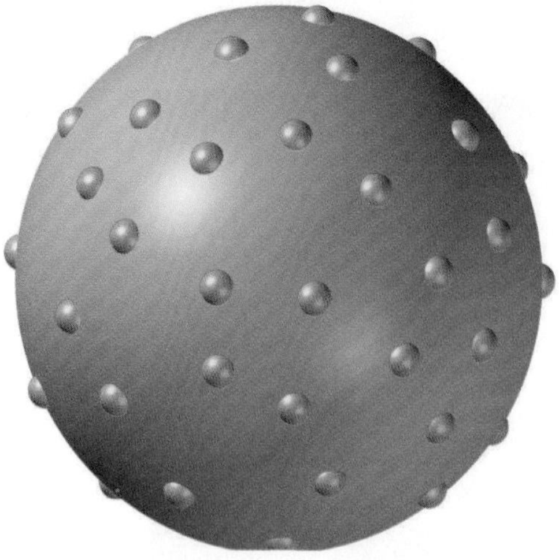

1897 atomic model

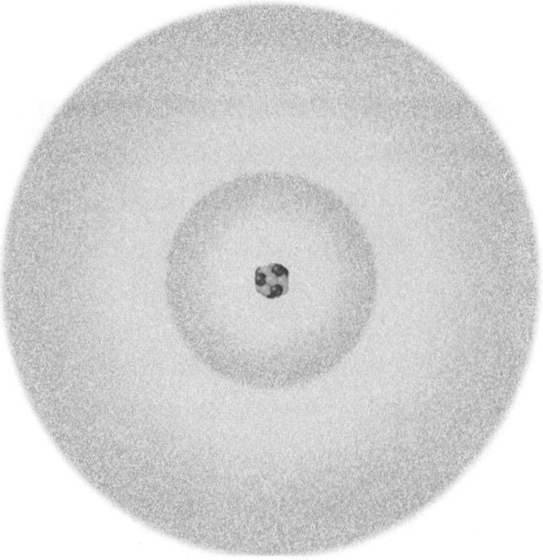

Current atomic model

Figure 5 *These models show the way scientists' idea of the atom has changed over time as new information was gathered.*

Scientific Laws

What happens when a theory and its models correctly predict the results of many different experiments? A scientific law could be formed. In science, a **law** is a summary of many experimental results and observations. A law tells you how things work. Laws are not the same as theories. Laws tell you only what happens, not why it happens.

A law tells you to expect the same thing to happen every time. Look at **Figure 6.** A chemical change took place when the flask was turned over. A light-blue solid and a dark-blue solution formed. Notice that the mass did not change. This is a demonstration of the *law of conservation of mass.* This law says that during a chemical change, the total mass of the materials formed is the same as the total mass of the starting materials. The law describes every single chemical change! However, the law doesn't explain why this happens. It says only that you can be sure that it will happen.

Figure 6 *The total mass before the change is always the same as the total mass after the change.*

SECTION Review

Summary

- A model uses familiar things to describe unfamiliar things.
- Physical, mathematical, and conceptual models are commonly used in science.
- A scientific theory is an explanation for many hypotheses and observations.
- A scientific law summarizes experimental results and observations. It describes what happens, but not why.

Using Key Terms

1. In your own words, write a definition for the term *model.*

Understanding Key Ideas

2. Which kind of model would you use to represent a human heart?
   - **a.** a mathematical model
   - **b.** a physical model
   - **c.** a conceptual model
   - **d.** a natural model
3. Explain the difference between a theory and a law.

Critical Thinking

4. **Analyzing Methods** Both a globe and a flat world map can model features of Earth. Give an example of when you would use each of these models.
5. **Applying Concepts** Identify two limitations of physical models.

Math Skills

6. For a science fair, you want to make a model of the moon orbiting Earth by using a ball. The diameter of the ball that will represent Earth will be about 62 cm. You want your model to be to scale. If the moon is about 4 times smaller than Earth, what should the diameter of the ball that represents the moon be?

SCILINKS® NSTA
Developed and maintained by the National Science Teachers Association

For a variety of links related to this chapter, go to www.scilinks.org

Topic: Using Models
SciLinks code: HSM1588

SECTION 4

Tools, Measurement, and Safety

What You Will Learn

- Identify tools used to collect and analyze data.
- Explain the importance of the International System of Units.
- Identify the appropriate units to use for particular measurements.
- Identify safety symbols.

Vocabulary

meter
area
mass
volume
density
temperature

READING STRATEGY

Discussion Read this section silently. Write down questions that you have about this section. Discuss your questions in a small group.

Would you use a spoon to dig a hole to plant a tree? You wouldn't if you had a shovel!

To dig a hole, you need the correct tools. Scientists use many different tools to help them in their experiments. A *tool* is anything that helps you do a task.

Tools for Measuring

You might remember that one way to collect data is to take measurements. To get the best measurements, you need the proper tools. Stopwatches, metersticks, and balances are some of the tools you can use to make measurements. Thermometers, spring scales, and graduated cylinders are also helpful tools. Some of the uses of these tools are shown in **Figure 1.**

Reading Check **What kinds of tools are used to make measurements?** (*See the Appendix for answers to Reading Checks.*)

Tools for Analyzing

After you collect data, you need to analyze them. Perhaps you need to find the average of your data. Calculators are handy tools to help you do calculations quickly. Or you might show your data in a graph or a figure. You may use a pencil and graph paper or even a computer to graph your data.

Figure 1 **Measurement Tools**

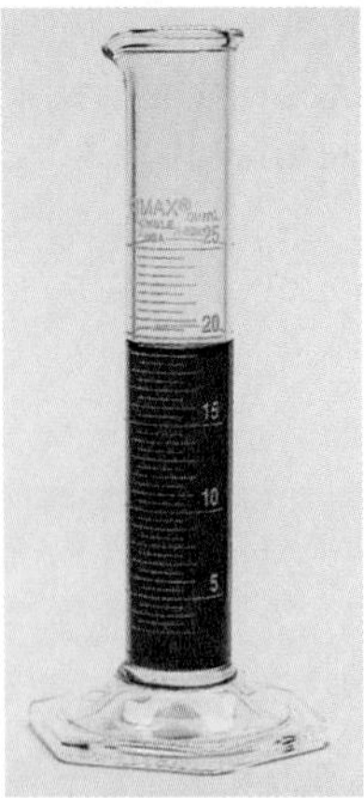

You can use a **graduated cylinder** to measure volume.

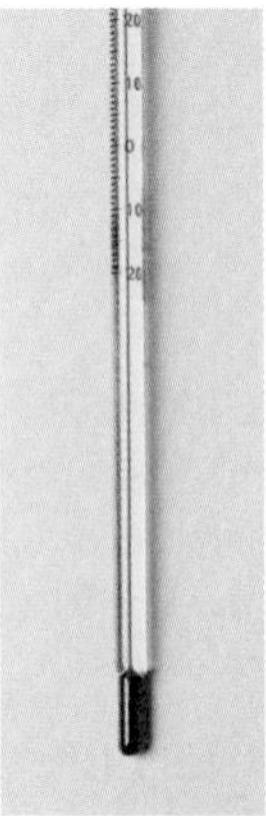

You can use a **thermometer** to measure temperature.

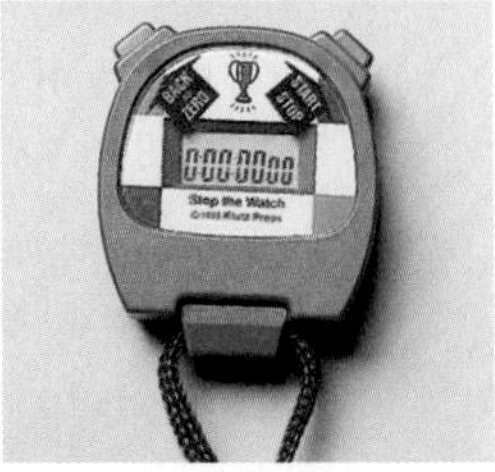

You can use a **stopwatch** to measure time.

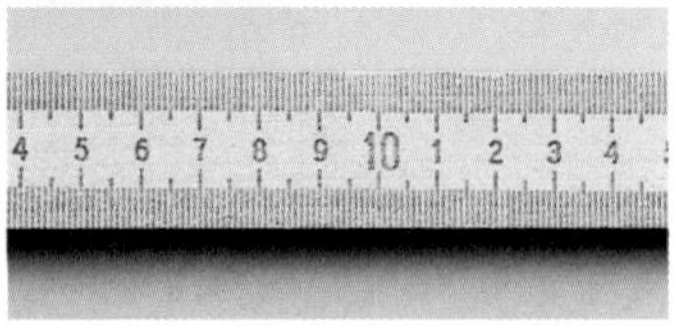

You can use a **meterstick** to measure length.

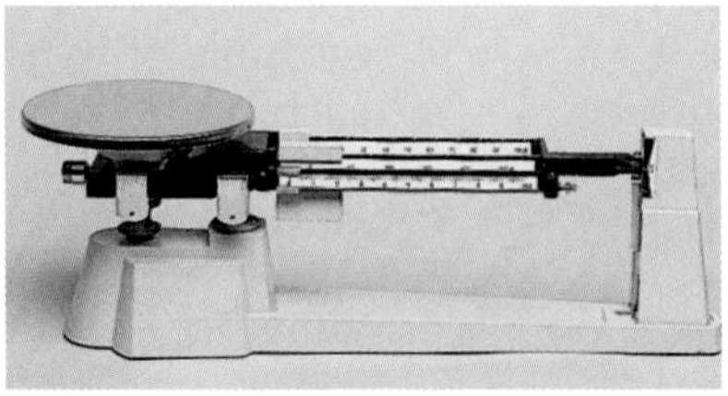

You can use a **balance** to measure mass.

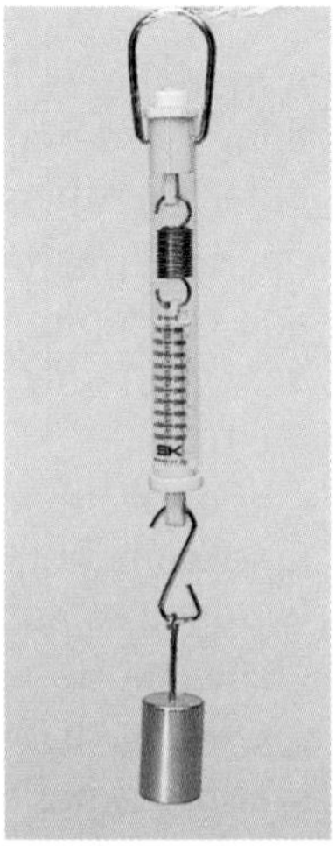

You can use a **spring scale** to measure force.

Measurement

Hundreds of years ago, different countries used different systems of measurement. In England, the standard for an inch used to be three grains of barley placed end to end. Other modern standardized units were originally based on parts of the body, such as the foot. Such systems were not very reliable. Their units were based on objects that had different sizes.

The International System of Units

In time, people saw that they needed a simple and reliable measurement system. In the late 1700s, the French Academy of Sciences set out to make that system. Over the next 200 years, the metric system was formed. This system is now called the International System of Units (SI).

Today, most scientists and almost all countries use the International System of Units. One advantage of using SI measurements is that they help all scientists share and compare their observations and results. Another advantage of SI is that all units are based on the number 10. This makes changing from one unit to another easier. **Table 1** shows SI units for length, volume, mass, and temperature.

MATH PRACTICE

Units of Measure

Pick an object to use as a unit of measure. You can pick a pencil, your hand, or anything else. Find out how many units wide your desk is, and compare your measurement with those of your classmates. What were some of the units used? Now, choose two of the units that were used in your class, and make a conversion factor. For example, 1.5 pencils equal 1 board eraser.

***Table 1* Common SI Units and Conversions**

Length 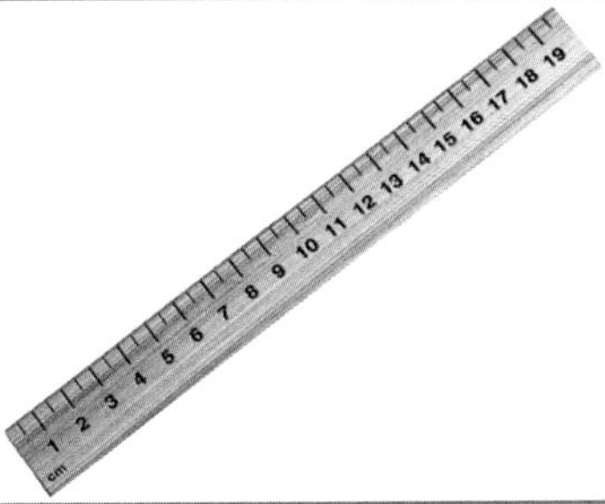	**meter (m)** kilometer (km) decimeter (dm) centimeter (cm) millimeter (mm) micrometer (µm) nanometer (nm)	1 km = 1,000 m 1 dm = 0.1 m 1 cm = 0.01 m 1 mm = 0.001 m 1 µm = 0.000001 m 1 nm = 0.000000001 m
Volume 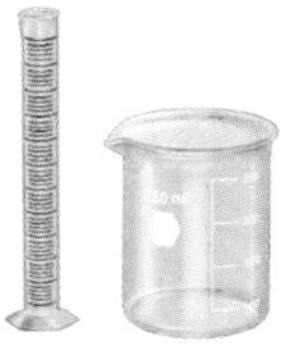	**cubic meter (m^3)** cubic centimeter (cm^3) liter (L) milliliter (mL)	1 cm^3 = 0.000001 m^3 1 L = 1 dm^3 = 0.001 m^3 1 mL = 0.001 L = 1 cm^3
Mass 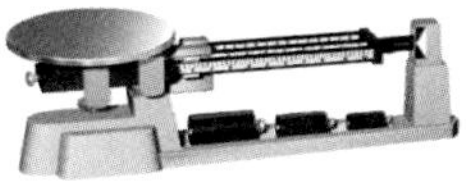	**kilogram (kg)** gram (g) milligram (mg)	1 g = 0.001 kg 1 mg = 0.000001 kg
Temperature 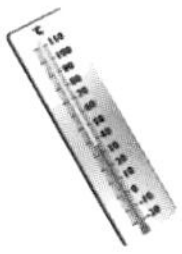	**Kelvin (K)** **Celsius (°C)**	0°C = 273 K 100°C = 373 K

Figure 2 *This scientist is measuring the thickness of an ice sheet.*

Length

meter the basic unit of length in the SI (symbol, m)

area a measure of the size of a surface or a region

mass a measure of the amount of matter in an object; a fundamental property of an object that is not affected by the forces that act on the object, such as the gravitational force

How thick is the ice sheet in **Figure 2**? To describe this length, a scientist would probably use meters (m). A **meter** is the basic SI unit of length. Other SI units of length are larger or smaller than the meter by multiples of 10. For example, if you divide 1 m into 1,000 parts, each part equals 1 mm. This means that 1 mm is one-thousandth of a meter. To describe the length of a grain of salt, scientists use micrometers (µm) or nanometers (nm).

Area

How much wallpaper would you need to cover the walls of your classroom? To answer this question, you must find the area of the walls. **Area** is a measure of how much surface an object has. Area is based on two measurements. To calculate the area of a square or a rectangle, first measure the length and width. Then, use the following equation:

$$area = length \times width$$

The units for area are square units, such as square kilometers (km^2), square meters (m^2), and square centimeters (cm^2).

Mass

How many cars can a bridge support? The answer depends on the strength of the bridge and the mass of the cars. **Mass** is the amount of matter that something is made of. The kilogram (kg) is the basic SI unit for mass. The kilogram is used to describe the mass of a car. The gram is used to describe the mass of small objects. One thousand grams equals 1 kg. A medium-sized apple has a mass of about 100 g. Masses of very large objects are given in metric tons. A metric ton equals 1,000 kg.

Volume

Look at **Figure 3.** Think about moving some bones to a museum. How big would your box need to be? To answer that question, you need to understand volume. **Volume** is the amount of space that something occupies or, as in the case of the box, the amount of space that something contains.

The volume of a liquid is often given in liters (L). Liters are based on the meter. A cubic meter (1 m^3) is equal to 1,000 L. So 1,000 L will fit into a box measuring 1 m on each side. A milliliter (mL) will fit into a box measuring 1 cm on each side. So 1 mL = 1 cm^3. Graduated cylinders are used to measure the volume of liquids.

The volume of a large, solid object is given in cubic meters (m^3). The volumes of smaller objects can be given in cubic centimeters (cm^3) or cubic millimeters (mm^3). To calculate the volume of a box-shaped object, multiply the object's length by its width and then by its height. To find the volume of an irregularly shaped object, measure the volume of liquid that the object displaces. **Figure 4** shows how this method works.

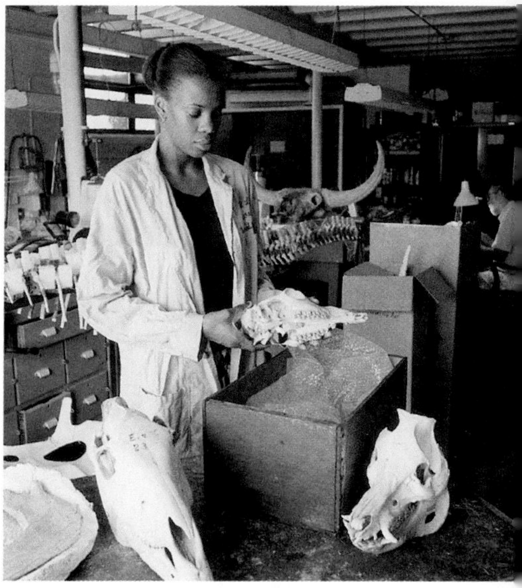

Figure 3 *The box has a volume, so it can hold only a limited number of bones.*

Density

If you measure the mass and the volume of an object, you have the information that you need in order to find the density of the object. **Density** is the amount of matter in a given volume. You cannot measure the density directly. But you can calculate density using the following equation:

$$density = \frac{mass}{volume}$$

Because mass is expressed in grams and volume is expressed in milliliters or cubic centimeters, density can be expressed in grams per milliliter or grams per cubic centimeter.

volume a measure of the size of a body or region in three-dimensional space

density the ratio of the mass of a substance to the volume of the substance; often expressed as grams per cubic centimeter for solids and liquids and as grams per liter for gases

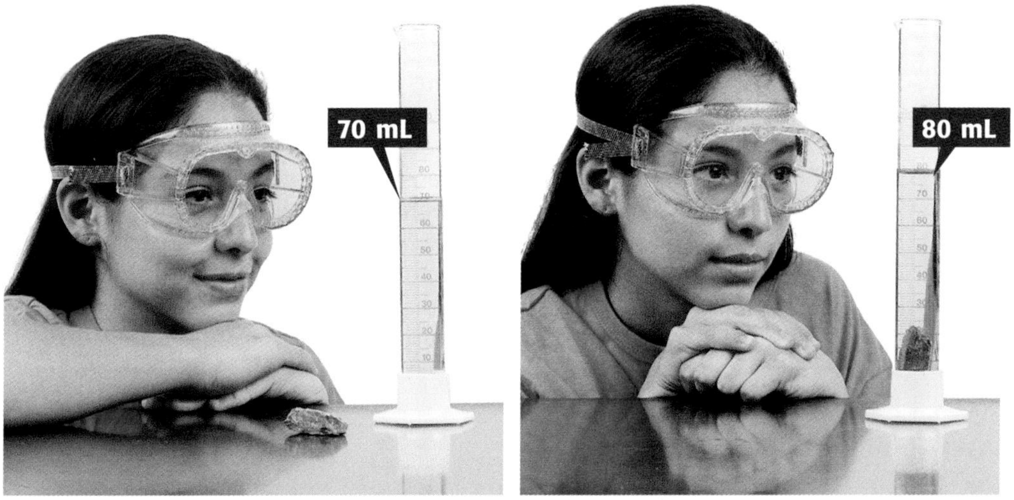

Figure 4 *Adding the rock changes the water level from 70 mL to 80 mL. So, the rock displaces 10 mL of water. Because 1 mL = 1 cm^3, the volume of the rock is 10 cm^3.*

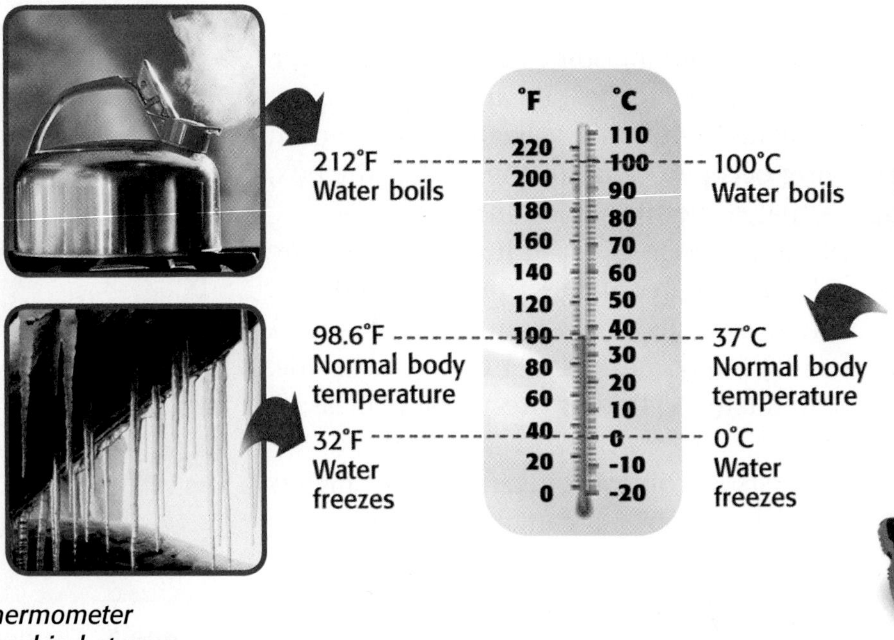

Figure 5 *This thermometer shows the relationship between degrees Fahrenheit and degrees Celsius.*

Temperature

Temperature a measure of how hot (or cold) something is; specifically, a measure of the average kinetic energy of the particles in an object

How hot does it need to be to kill bacteria? How cold does it have to be before mercury freezes? To answer these questions, a scientist would measure the temperature at which bacteria die, or the temperature of the air at which mercury freezes. **Temperature** is a measure of how hot (or cold) something is. You are probably used to describing temperature with degrees Fahrenheit (°F). Scientists often use degrees Celsius (°C). However, kelvins (K), the SI base unit for temperature, is also used. The thermometer in **Figure 5** shows how the Fahrenheit scale compares with the Celsius scale. Degrees Celsius is the unit you will see most often in this book.

Reading Check What is the SI base unit for temperature?

CONNECTION TO Social Studies

Thermal Pollution Factories are often built along the banks of rivers. The factories use the river water to cool the engines of their machinery. Then, the hot water is poured back into the river. Energy, in the form of heat, is transferred from this water to the river water. The increase in temperature results in the death of many living things. Research how thermal pollution causes fish to die. Also, find out what many factories are doing to prevent thermal pollution. Make a brochure that explains what thermal pollution is and what is being done to prevent it.

Safety Rules!

Science is exciting and fun, but it can also be dangerous. Always follow your teacher's instructions. Don't take shortcuts, even when you think that there is no danger. Read lab procedures carefully and thoroughly. Pay special attention to safety information and caution statements. **Figure 6** shows the safety symbols used in this book. Learn these symbols and their meanings by reading the safety information at the start of the book. **Knowing the safety information is important!** If you are still not sure about what a safety symbol means, ask your teacher.

Figure 6 Safety Symbols

SECTION Review

Summary

- Tools are used to make observations, take measurements, and analyze data.
- The International System of Units (SI) is the standard system of measurement.
- Length, volume, mass, and temperature are quantities of measurement.
- Density is the amount of matter in a given volume.
- Safety symbols are for your protection.

Using Key Terms

The statements below are false. For each statement, replace the underlined term to make a true statement.

1. The length multiplied by the width of an object is the <u>density</u> of the object.
2. The measure of the amount of matter in an object is the <u>area</u>.

Understanding Key Ideas

3. Which SI unit would you use to express the height of your desk?
   a. kilogram
   b. gram
   c. meter
   d. inch
4. Explain the relationship between mass and density.
5. What is normal body temperature in degrees Fahrenheit and degrees Celsius?
6. What tools would you select to find the force needed to move a 1 kg object 1 m in 30 seconds?
7. Explain the importance of having a standard method of measurement such as the SI system.

Math Skills

8. A certain bacterial cell has a diameter of 0.50 µm. The tip of a pin is about 1,100 µm in diameter. How many of these bacterial cells would fit on the tip of the pin?
9. What is the density of lead if a cube measuring 2 cm per side has a mass of 90.8 g?

Critical Thinking

10. **Analyzing Ideas** What safety icons would you see on a lab that asks you to pour acid into a beaker?
11. **Applying Concepts** To find the area of a rectangle, multiply the length by the width. Why is area called a *derived quantity*?

SciLinks® NSTA
Developed and maintained by the National Science Teachers Association

For a variety of links related to this chapter, go to www.scilinks.org

Topic: SI Units
SciLinks code: HSM1390

Skills Practice Lab

Measuring Liquid Volume

OBJECTIVES

Measure accurately different volumes of liquids with a graduated cylinder.

Transfer exact amounts of liquids from a graduated cylinder to a test tube.

MATERIALS

- beakers, filled with colored liquid (3)
- funnel, small
- graduated cylinder, 10 mL
- marker
- tape, masking
- test-tube rack
- test tubes, large (6)

SAFETY

In this lab, you will use a graduated cylinder to measure and transfer precise amounts of liquids. Remember that, to accurately measure liquids in a graduated cylinder, you should first place the graduated cylinder flat on the lab table. Then, at eye level, read the volume of the liquid at the bottom of the meniscus, which is the curved surface of the liquid.

Procedure

1. Using the masking tape and marker, label the test tubes A, B, C, D, E, and F. Place them in the test-tube rack.
2. Make a data table as shown on the next page.
3. Using the graduated cylinder and the funnel, pour 14 mL of the red liquid into test tube A. (To do this, first measure out 10 mL of the liquid in the graduated cylinder, and pour it into the test tube. Then, measure an additional 4 mL of liquid in the graduated cylinder, and add this liquid to the test tube.)
4. Rinse the graduated cylinder and funnel with water each time you measure a different liquid.
5. Measure 13 mL of the yellow liquid, and pour it into test tube C.
6. Measure 13 mL of the blue liquid, and pour it into test tube E. Record the initial color and the volume of the liquid in each test tube.

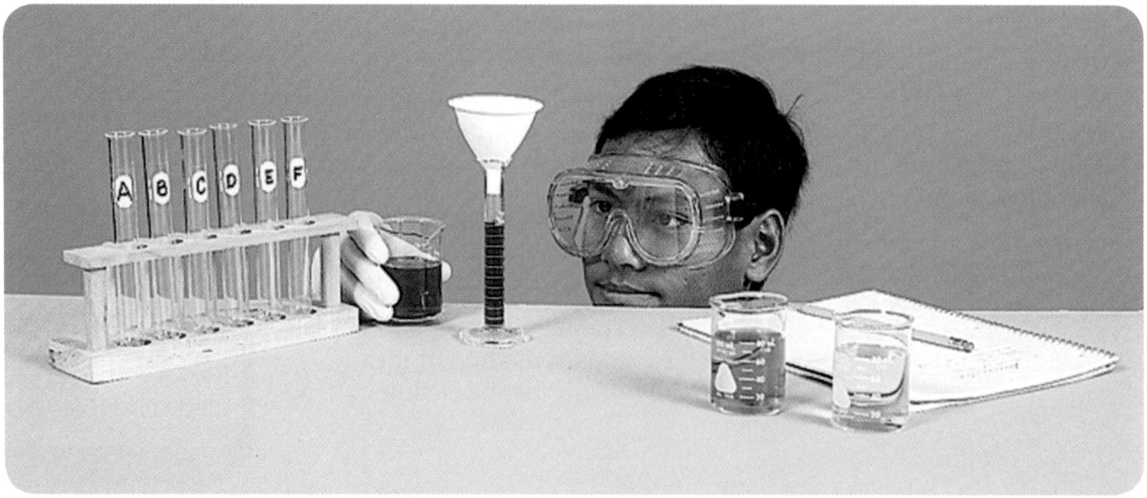

Data Table				
Test tube	**Initial color**	**Initial volume**	**Final color**	**Final volume**
A				
B				
C				
D				
E				
F				

7. Transfer 4 mL of liquid from test tube C into test tube D. Transfer 7 mL of liquid from test tube E into test tube D.
8. Measure 4 mL of blue liquid from the beaker, and pour it into test tube F. Measure 7 mL of red liquid from the beaker, and pour it into test tube F.
9. Transfer 8 mL of liquid from test tube A into test tube B. Transfer 3 mL of liquid from test tube C into test tube B.

Analyze the Results

1. **Analyzing Data** Record your final color observations in your data table.
2. **Examining Data** What is the final volume of all of the liquids? Use the graduated cylinder to measure the volume of liquid in each test tube. Record the volumes in your data table.
3. **Organizing Data** Record your final color observations and final volumes in a table of class data prepared by your teacher.

Draw Conclusions

4. **Interpreting Information** Did all of your classmates report the same colors? Form a hypothesis that could explain why the colors were the same or different after the liquids were combined.
5. **Evaluating Methods** Why should you not fill the graduated cylinder to the top?

Chapter Review

USING KEY TERMS

1. In your own words, write a definition for each of the following terms: *meter, temperature,* and *density*.

For each pair of terms, explain how the meanings of the terms differ.

2. *science* and *scientific methods*

3. *observation* and *hypothesis*

4. *theory* and *law*

5. *model* and *theory*

6. *volume* and *mass*

UNDERSTANDING KEY IDEAS

Multiple Choice

7. Which of the following are methods of investigation?
   - **a.** research
   - **b.** observation
   - **c.** experimentation
   - **d.** All of the above

8. The statement "Sheila has a stain on her shirt" is an example of a(n)
   - **a.** law.
   - **b.** hypothesis.
   - **c.** observation.
   - **d.** prediction.

9. A hypothesis
   - **a.** may or may not be testable.
   - **b.** is supported by evidence.
   - **c.** is a possible answer to a question.
   - **d.** All of the above

10. A variable
    - **a.** is found in an uncontrolled experiment.
    - **b.** is the factor that changes in an experiment.
    - **c.** cannot change.
    - **d.** is rarely included in experiments.

11. Organizing data into a graph is an example of
    - **a.** collecting data.
    - **b.** forming a hypothesis.
    - **c.** asking a question.
    - **d.** analyzing data.

12. How many milliliters are in 3.5 kL?
    - **a.** 0.0035
    - **b.** 3,500
    - **c.** 35,000
    - **d.** 3,500,000

13. A map of Seattle is an example of a
    - **a.** physical model.
    - **b.** mathematical model.
    - **c.** conceptual model.
    - **d.** All of the above

14. Ten meters is equal to
    - **a.** 100 cm.
    - **b.** 1,000 cm.
    - **c.** 100,000 mm.
    - **d.** 1,000 μm.

Short Answer

15. Describe three kinds of models used in science. Give an example and explain one limitation of each model.

16 Name two SI units that can be used to describe the volume of an object and two SI units that can be used to describe the mass of an object.

17 What are the steps used in scientific methods?

18 If a hypothesis is not testable, is the hypothesis wrong? Explain.

Math Skills

19 The cereal box on the right has a mass of 340 g. Its dimensions are 27 cm × 19 cm × 6 cm. What is the volume of the box? What is its density?

CRITICAL THINKING

20 **Concept Mapping** Use the following terms to create a concept map: *science, scientific methods, hypothesis, problems, questions, experiments,* and *observations.*

21 **Applying Concepts** A tailor is someone who makes or alters items of clothing. Why might a standard system of measurement be helpful to a tailor?

22 **Analyzing Ideas** Imagine that you are conducting an experiment. You are testing the effects of the height of a ramp on the speed at which a toy car goes down the ramp. What is the variable in this experiment? What factors must be controlled?

23 **Evaluating Assumptions** Suppose a classmate says, "I don't need to study science because I'm not going to be a scientist, and scientists are the only people who use science." How would you respond? In your answer, give examples of careers that use science.

24 **Making Inferences** You build a model boat that you predict will float. However, your tests show that the boat sinks. What conclusion would you draw? Suggest some logical next steps.

INTERPRETING GRAPHICS

Use the picture below to answer the questions that follow.

25 How similar is this model to a real object?

26 What are some of the limitations of this model?

27 How might this model be useful?

Multiple Choice

Use the picture below to answer question 1.

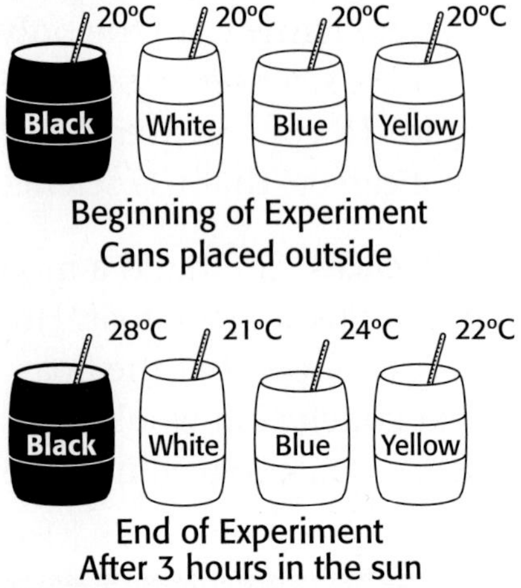

1. **A student set up the experiment shown above to determine what color absorbs the most energy from sunlight. Which of the following would make this a better-designed experiment?**

   A. Use larger thermometers.

   B. Use same-sized containers for each color.

   C. Use glass containers instead of metal containers.

   D. Place the containers in the shade instead of in direct sunlight.

2. **A nanometer is 0.000000001 m. Which answer expresses this number in scientific notation?**

   A. 10×10^{-10}

   B. 10×10^{10}

   C. 1×10^{-9}

   D. 1×10^{9}

3. **After swimming in the ocean, Jorge sits in the sun to dry off. After a while, he notices that he has small white crystals on his skin. Analyze the explanations below as to their strengths and weaknesses based on this evidence. Which is the most reasonable explanation of what happened?**

   A. The water evaporated and attracted dust to Jorge's skin.

   B. The white crystals are dead skin cells that are being shed.

   C. Jorge has developed a rare skin disorder.

   D. Salt that is dissolved in the water remained on Jorge's skin after the water evaporated.

4. **Sarah observed that there are 4 people in her class that are left-handed. If there are 36 students in her class, which answer gives the ratio of left-handed students to right-handed students as a fraction?**

   A. $\frac{1}{9}$

   B. $\frac{8}{9}$

   C. $\frac{1}{8}$

   D. $\frac{8}{1}$

5. **Which factor would have the LEAST effect on the results of an experiment designed to determine which brand of bar soap most effectively kills bacteria?**

   A. the color of the soaps

   B. the volume of soap used

   C. the surface on which the soap is used

   D. the ingredients found in the soaps

Use the picture below to answer question 6.

6. The image above shows a quarter next to a ruler marked in centimeters. What is the approximate diameter of the quarter in millimeters?

A. 2.4 mm

B. 4.4 mm

C. 24 mm

D. 44 mm

7. An environmental scientist suspects that acid precipitation is beginning to affect certain lakes in Minnesota. What is the best way to test this hypothesis?

A. Do library research on the harmful effects of acid precipitation in lakes.

B. Experiment with acid precipitation on water plants native to Minnesota.

C. Count the number of water-plant species found in a Minnesota lake.

D. Collect lake water samples and test the pH of each sample.

8. Lucia is measuring how fast bacteria grow in a Petri dish by measuring the area the bacteria cover. On day 1 the bacteria cover 0.25 cm^2. On day 2 they cover 0.50 cm^2. On day 3 they cover 1.00 cm^2. If you extrapolate from this information, what is the best prediction for the area covered on day 4?

A. 1.25 cm^2

B. 1.50 cm^2

C. 1.75 cm^2

D. 2.00 cm^2

9. Katie wants to learn about the effect that different amounts of sunlight have on plants. Which of the following is the only variable that she should change?

A. the type of plant

B. the amount of light

C. the volume of water

D. the amount of nutrients

Open Response

10. Mammoth Cave in Kentucky is one of the largest cave systems on Earth. Laishan works as a park ranger in Mammoth Cave National Park. Describe three ways that Laishan can use science in her job.

11. Describe three different kinds of scientific models and explain which type of model would be most useful for studying the structure of an atom.

Science in Action

Science Fiction

"Inspiration" by Ben Bova

What if you were able to leap back and forth through time? Novelist H. G. Wells imagined such a possibility in his 1895 novelette *The Time Machine*. Most physicists said that time travel was against all the laws of physics. But what if Albert Einstein, then 16 and not a very good student, had met Wells and had an inspiration? Ben Bova's story "Inspiration" describes such a possibility. Young Einstein meets Wells and the great physicist of the time, Lord Kelvin. But was the meeting just a lucky coincidence or something else entirely? Escape to the *Holt Anthology of Science Fiction,* and read "Inspiration."

Social Studies ACTIVITY

Research the life of Albert Einstein from high school through college. Make a poster that describes some of his experiences during this time. Include information about how he matured as a student.

Weird Science

A Palace of Ice

An ice palace is just a fancy kind of igloo, but it takes a lot of ice and snow to make an ice palace. One ice palace was made from 27,215.5 metric tons of snow and 9,071.85 metric tons of ice! Making an ice palace takes time, patience, and temperatures below freezing. Sometimes, blocks of ice are cut with chain saws from a frozen river or lake and then transported in huge trucks. On location, the huge ice cubes are stacked on each other. Slush is used as mortar between the "bricks." The slush freezes and cements the blocks of ice together. Then, sculptors with chain saws, picks, and axes fashion elegant details in the ice.

Math ACTIVITY

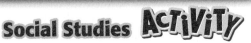

One block of ice used to make the ice palace in the story above has a mass of 181.44 kg. How many blocks of ice were needed to make the ice palace if 9071.85 metric tons of ice was used?

Julie Williams-Byrd

Electronics Engineer Julie Williams-Byrd uses her knowledge of physics to develop better lasers. She started working with lasers when she was a graduate student at Hampton University in Virginia. Today, Williams-Byrd works as an electronics engineer in the Laser Systems Branch (LSB) of NASA. She designs and builds lasers that are used to study wind and ozone in the atmosphere. Williams-Byrd uses scientific models to predict the nature of different aspects of laser design. For example, laser models are used to predict output energy, wavelength, and efficiency of the laser system.

Her most challenging project has been building a laser transmitter that will be used to measure winds in the atmosphere. This system, called *Lidar,* is very much like radar except that it uses light waves instead of sound waves to bounce off objects. Although Williams-Byrd works with high-tech lasers, she points out that lasers are a part of daily life for many people. For example, lasers are used in scanners at many retail stores. Ophthalmologists use lasers to correct vision problems. Some metal workers use them to cut metal. And lasers are even used to create spectacular light shows!

Language Arts ACTIVITY

WRITING SKILL Research lasers and how they can be used in everyday life. Then, write a one-page essay on how lasers have made life easier for people.

go.hrw.com

To learn more about these Science in Action topics, visit **go.hrw.com** and type in the keyword **HP5WPSF.**

Current Science

Check out Current Science® articles related to this chapter by visiting go.hrw.com. Just type in the keyword HP5CS01.

UNIT 1

TIMELINE

Matter, Sound, and Light

When you hear the word *waves,* you probably think of waves in the ocean. But waves that you encounter every day have a much bigger effect on your life than do water waves! In this unit, you will learn about different types of waves, how waves behave and interact, and how sound energy and light energy travel in waves. This timeline shows some events and discoveries that have occurred throughout history as scientists have sought to learn more about the energy of waves.

Around 1600

Italian astronomer and physicist Galileo Galilei attempts to calculate the speed of light by using lanterns and shutters. He writes that the speed is "extraordinarily rapid."

1903

The popularity of an early movie called *The Great Train Robbery* leads to the establishment of permanent movie theaters.

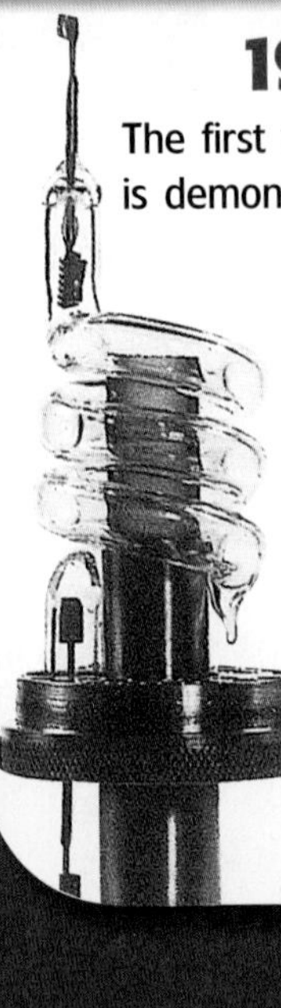

1960

The first working laser is demonstrated.

1971

Hungarian physicist Dennis Gabor wins the Nobel Prize in physics for his invention of holography, the method used to make holograms.

1704

Sir Isaac Newton publishes his book *Optiks*, which contains his theories about light and color.

1711

English trumpeter John Shore invents the tuning fork, an instrument that produces a single-frequency note.

1801

British scientist Thomas Young is the first to provide experimental data showing that light behaves as a wave.

1905

Physicist Albert Einstein suggests that light sometimes behaves as a particle.

1929

American astronomer Edwin Hubble uses the Doppler effect of light to determine that the universe is expanding.

1947

Anne Frank's *The Diary of a Young Girl* is published. The book is an edited version of the diary kept by a Jewish teenager while in hiding during World War II.

1983

A "mouse" is first used on personal computers.

1997

British pilot Andy Green drives a jet-powered car at 341 m/s, when he becomes the first person to travel faster than the speed of sound on land.

2002

Scientists develop a thermoacoustic refrigerator. The device is cooled using high amplitude sound instead of chemical refrigerants.

2

Introduction to Matter

The Big Idea

Matter has properties that are observable and measurable.

SECTION

About the Photo

Matter is all around you. Everything you can hold in your hand is made of matter. In fact, everything in this picture is made of matter. Even the air that fills the hot air balloon is made of matter. But what is matter? In this chapter, you will learn that matter is anything that has mass and volume.

PRE-READING ACTIVITY

FOLDNOTES

Booklet Before you read the chapter, create the FoldNote entitled "Booklet" described in the **Study Skills** section of the Appendix. Label each page of the booklet with a main idea from the chapter. As you read the chapter, write what you learn about each main idea on the appropriate page of the booklet.

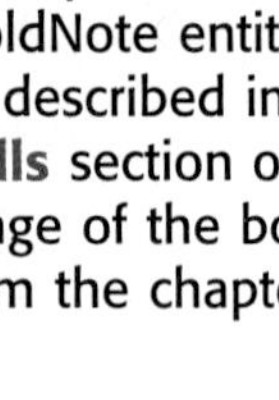

START-UP ACTIVITY

What's the Matter?

In this activity, you will test your ability to identify a substance based on its properties and its ability to change.

Procedure

1. Your teacher will give your group a **sealed box.** Do not open the box.
2. When instructed to do so, have one member of your group open the box and follow the directions written on the lid.
3. Only one person should see what the substance is and how it changes. The rest of the group will need to determine what the substance is from the observer's verbal clues.
4. Record important clues that might help you identify the substance.

Analysis

1. Spend three minutes comparing notes with the other members of your group.
2. Make a single list of all of the properties of this substance.
3. With your group, develop a hypothesis about the identity of the substance.
4. Look at the substance. Did you correctly identify the substance? What other observations were needed to correctly identify the substance? Record your answers.

SECTION 1

What Is Matter?

What You Will Learn

- Define *matter*.
- Describe the two common properties of all matter.
- Compare mass and weight.
- Describe density as the relationship between mass and volume.
- Identify ways in which substances differ.

Vocabulary

matter
mass
volume
weight
density

READING STRATEGY

Prediction Guide Before reading this section, write the title of each heading in this section. Next, under each heading, write what you think you will learn.

Look around you. What do you see? Do you see a window, a tree, a book, or your classmates? What do these things have in common? Everything that you see has at least one thing in common. Even the objects that you can't see have the same thing in common.

Every object that you can think of, including you, is made of matter. **Matter** is anything that has mass and takes up space.

Common Properties of All Matter

The food you eat, the liquid you drink, and the air you breathe are examples of matter. These things seem so different. For example, you can't see the air you breathe because it is not visible. But all matter shares two properties. First, all matter has mass. **Mass** is a measure of the amount of matter in an object. Second, all matter has volume. **Volume** is a measure of the amount of space that an object takes up.

Both mass and volume are measurable and observable properties. **Figure 1** shows how the mass and volume of a balloon change when the balloon is filled with matter in the form of air. Mass and volume can also be used to distinguish one substance from another.

Reading Check **What are two properties of all matter?** *(See the Appendix for answers to Reading Checks.)*

Figure 1 *When the balloon is filled with air, the mass and volume of the balloon change because air takes up space and consists of matter.*

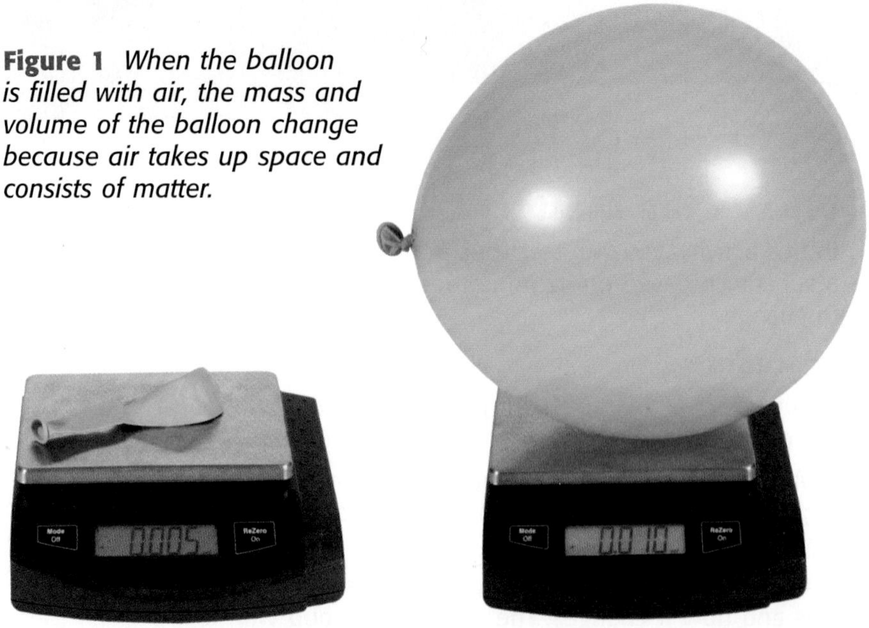

Figure 2 *The amount of matter making up this astronaut is the same on Earth and in space, but his weight is different.*

Mass

Looking at an object is not a reliable way to measure how much matter is in the object. Sometimes, very large objects can be made of a small amount of matter. For example, even large sponges have little mass. This is true because sponges are made of matter that is not packed very closely together. Also, it is possible for small objects, such as lead fishing sinkers, to be made up of a great deal of matter. Scientists often measure an object's mass by using a balance. A balance compares an object's mass to known standards of mass. The mass of an object remains the same regardless of where the object is located in the universe.

matter anything that has mass and takes up space

mass a measure of the amount of matter in an object

volume a measure of the size of a body or region in three-dimensional space

Mass, Not Weight

You probably do not know your mass. On the other hand, you have been weighed many times over the course of your life. Are mass and weight two ways to measure how heavy something is? No, mass and weight measure two different things.

Weight is a measure of the gravitational force on an object. An object feels heavy because of the force of gravity. Because the force of gravity changes based on an object's location, the object's weight also changes based on the object's location. For example, the weight of the astronaut in **Figure 2** changed when the astronaut left Earth and went into space. If this astronaut landed on the moon, he would weigh less than he did on Earth. This is true because the gravitational force of the moon is smaller than the gravitational force on Earth. But the astronaut has the same mass on Earth as he does in space.

weight a measure of the gravitational force exerted on an object; its value can change with the location of the object in the universe

Reading Check How are weight and mass different?

Figure 3 *These students are using three different methods to measure the volumes of three different objects.*

Volume

The way in which you measure volume depends on the kind of matter you are measuring. The volume of a regularly shaped solid, such as a cube or rectangular block, can be measured by using a ruler. The student on the left in **Figure 3** is finding the volume of a regularly shaped solid. She is measuring the length, width, and height of the object. By multiplying these measurements, she will find the volume of the block.

$$length \times width \times height = volume$$

MATH PRACTICE

Calculating Volume

A regularly shaped block of cheese is measured. Its height is 12 cm. Its width is 10 cm, and its length is 8 cm. What is the volume of this cheese? To answer the question, use the following equation:

$$volume = length \times width \times height$$

Volume of Liquids

Can you imagine using a ruler to measure the volume of a liquid? Instead of using a ruler, you measure the volume of a liquid by using a graduated cylinder. A graduated cylinder is a measuring device that is specifically designed for measuring liquids. When poured into a graduated cylinder, a liquid often forms a *meniscus,* or curve, at its surface. When you use a graduated cylinder, the liquid's volume is read by finding the mark that is closest to the bottom of the meniscus. The middle student in **Figure 3** is measuring the volume of a liquid.

Volume of Irregularly Shaped Solids

Think about all of the solid objects that have odd shapes. How do you find the volume of a rock, a coin, or a marble? A graduated cylinder comes in handy in these situations, too. Look at **Figure 3.** The student on the right is measuring the volume of a marble. He has placed the marble in a graduated cylinder that contains a known volume of water. The marble's volume is equal to the amount that the volume of the water increased when the marble was placed in the graduated cylinder.

Density: Relating Mass and Volume

You have learned that mass and volume are important properties that all matter possesses. Another property of all matter is density. **Density** is a measure of the amount of matter in a given amount of space. You can calculate density by dividing the mass of an object by the volume of the object.

Two different objects that have the same volume may have different masses. For example, the ducks in **Figure 4** have roughly the same volume. But, the duckling has more mass than the rubber duck has. Because the duckling has more matter packed into about the same amount of space, the duckling has a greater density than the rubber duck has. Density is an important way in which substances can differ. Scientists often use density calculations to determine the kind of substance with which they are dealing. The reason is that the density of most substances differs from the density of other substances.

Reading Check **Describe how you can tell the difference between two substances if they have the same volume.**

Figure 4 *These ducks have similar volumes, but their densities are very different.*

density the ratio of the mass of a substance to the volume of the substance

SECTION Review

Summary

- Matter is anything that has mass and volume.
- Mass is the amount of matter in an object.
- Volume is the space that matter occupies.
- Weight is a measure of the gravitational pull on an object. Mass does not depend on gravity.
- Density measures how closely particles in an object are packed. Density is the ratio of mass to volume.
- Mass, volume, and density can be used to distinguish between various kinds of matter.

Using Key Terms

1. Write an original definition for *matter, weight,* and *volume.*

Understanding Key Ideas

2. Which of the following is matter?
   - **a.** dust
   - **b.** the moon
   - **c.** strand of hair
   - **d.** All of the above
3. Mass is measured in
   - **a.** liters.
   - **b.** centimeters.
   - **c.** newtons.
   - **d.** kilograms.
4. Why can mass be used to distinguish between equal volumes of two substances?
5. List the three ways in which volume can be measured.

Math Skills

6. Density is calculated by dividing an object's mass by the object's volume. What is the density of a 5 g piece of metal that has a volume of 2 cm^3?

Critical Thinking

7. **Applying Ideas** What happens to an astronaut's weight and mass when the astronaut leaves Earth and travels to the moon?

SECTION 2

Particles of Matter

An orange appears to be a solid object. But when you eat an orange, you're able to see that it is composed of many smaller parts. Did you know that a single drop of orange juice can be broken down into smaller particles?

What You Will Learn

- Explain that all matter is composed of atoms.
- Describe the general structure of the atom.
- Identify subatomic particles by charge and mass.
- Calculate the charge of an atom.
- Predict what happens when atoms lose, gain, or share electrons.

Vocabulary

atom
element
proton
neutron
electron
nucleus
ion

READING STRATEGY

Reading Organizer As you read this section, make a concept map by using the terms above.

All matter—regardless of what it is or where it comes from—is made of very small particles called atoms. An **atom** is the smallest unit of an element that maintains the properties of that element. **Figure 1** shows that citric acid, one of the substances in orange juice, is made of several kinds of atoms.

Atoms Forming Matter

All matter is made of a unique combination of one or more atoms. Just as combinations of different letters of the alphabet make different words, combinations of different atoms yield substances that have different properties. There are roughly 100 kinds of atoms that occur naturally on Earth. Each kind of atom makes up a substance called an element. An **element** is a pure substance that cannot be broken into simpler substances.

All atoms in an element are alike. However, the properties of atoms of one element differ from the properties of atoms of any other element. The properties of an atom are determined by the particles that compose the atom. For example, every atom of the element gold is composed of 78 positively charged particles. Atoms from no other element have exactly the same properties as atoms of gold.

atom the smallest unit of an element that maintains the properties of that element

element a substance that cannot be separated or broken down into simpler substances by chemical means

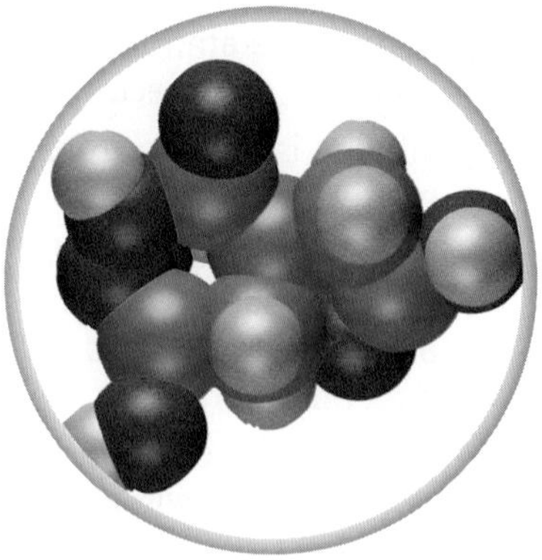

Figure 1 *Every substance that you can think of is composed of atoms. Citric acid is just one kind of substance in orange juice. Citric acid is made of three kinds of atoms.*

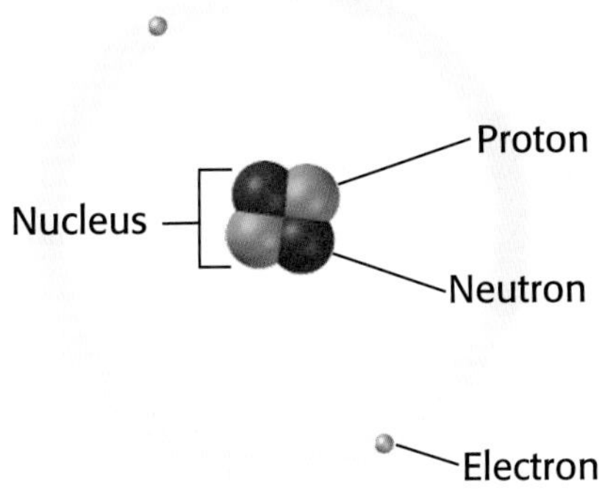

Figure 2 *A helium atom is composed of two protons, two neutrons, and two electrons. Each subatomic particle has a special place in the atom.*

Structure of the Atom

Atoms are so small that even the most powerful microscope cannot look inside them. What we know about atoms has been determined through experimentation over several centuries. While there is still much to learn, we know that all atoms have some features in common. For example, all atoms are made of the same three particles. These particles are called *subatomic particles* because they are smaller than atoms. The subatomic particles that make up atoms are protons, neutrons, and electrons. The particles each play a special role in determining the properties and behavior of the atoms that they compose.

Reading Check **What particles make up an atom?** (*See the Appendix for answers to Reading Checks.*)

SCHOOL to HOME

Edible Atoms

With an adult family member, make several cookies. Use food dye to prepare three colors of icing. Make models of the atoms in the figures in this section. Be sure to make a key that explains which color represents each subatomic particle. After you have read the entire section, find the charge of each atom.

ACTIVITY

Protons and Neutrons

Protons and neutrons make up the nucleus of an atom, as shown in **Figure 2.** A **proton** is a subatomic particle of an atom and has a positive charge. Protons are important for several reasons. Scientists use the number of protons in an atom to identify what kind of atom they are working with. For example, all atoms that have one proton are hydrogen atoms. The number of protons in an atom is called the *atomic number.* Protons are massive, at least by subatomic standards. The mass of a proton is 1 atomic mass unit (amu). A **neutron** is a subatomic particle with no charge. Like protons, neutrons form the nucleus and have a mass of 1 amu.

proton a subatomic particle that has a positive charge and that is found in the nucleus of an atom

neutron a subatomic particle that has no charge and that is found in the nucleus of an atom

electron a subatomic particle that has a negative charge

Electrons

Electrons are found in the area surrounding the nucleus. An **electron** is a subatomic particle with a negative charge. Because opposite charges attract, electrons are attracted to protons in the nucleus. When two atoms come in contact with one another, the electrons of each atom interact first. The mass of an electron is so much smaller than the mass of a proton or neutron that an electron is said to have a mass of 0 amu. For this reason, electrons are not considered when calculating the mass of an atom.

Figure 3 The Nucleus

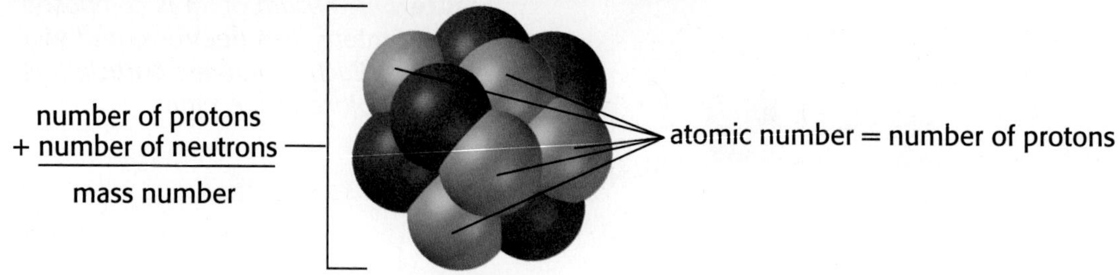

The Nucleus

nucleus in physical science, an atom's central region, which is made up of protons and neutrons

The **nucleus** is the dense center of an atom and is made up of neutrons and protons. Even though most of an atom's mass is located in the nucleus, the nucleus is very small. The nucleus is so small that if an atom were the size of your classroom, the atom's nucleus would be the size of a small dust particle! So, most of the atom is empty space. Because protons are part of the nucleus, the nucleus has a positive charge. And because opposite charges attract, electrons are attracted to the nucleus. Atoms of different elements have different numbers of protons in their nuclei. Also, atoms of different elements are different in size. So, the attraction of electrons to the nucleus of each atom is different. Both the number of protons and the strength of the attractions of electrons to the nucleus influence the properties of the atom.

Reading Check **Why is the charge of the nucleus important?**

Atoms and Isotopes

Because neutrons have no charge, it is possible for atoms of a single element to have different numbers of neutrons. *Isotopes* are atoms that have the same number of protons but different numbers of neutrons. A single element can have many isotopes. Isotopes of an element have different masses because each isotope contains a different number of neutrons. As **Figure 3** shows, the mass number of an atom is calculated by adding the number of protons and the number of neutrons. Isotopes of an element appear identical in most physical and chemical properties. However, each isotope of an element has some unique properties.

For example, carbon has several isotopes. Carbon-12 is an isotope of carbon that has six neutrons in its nucleus. Carbon-14 is an isotope of carbon that has eight neutrons in its nucleus. Both of these isotopes react with oxygen to form identical compounds. However, carbon-14 is a radioactive isotope and will undergo radioactive decay over time.

MATH FOCUS

Mass Number An atom of chlorine has 17 protons, 18 neutrons, and 17 electrons. What is the mass number of this atom?

Step 1: Identify the number of protons and the number of neutrons in the atom. Electrons are not counted because they have very little mass.

protons = 17; neutrons = 18

Step 2: Add these numbers to find the mass number of the atom.

$$17 + 18 = 35$$

Now It's Your Turn

1. What is the mass number of an iodine atom that has 53 protons, 53 electrons, and 74 neutrons?

Atoms: Neutral Particles

Atoms have no overall charge because the number of protons is always equal to the number of electrons in an atom. **Figure 4** calculates the overall charge for atoms of two elements. The atom on the left is lithium. It has three protons and three electrons. Finding the overall charge of the atom is as simple as adding the total charge of the protons to the total charge of the electrons. For lithium, the sum of 3+ and 3– is 0. Because neutrons have no charge, they do not change the overall charge of the atom. In the same way, you can find the charge of the oxygen atom on the right in **Figure 4.** Oxygen has eight positive protons and eight negative electrons. When you add the charges of the protons and electrons, you find that the oxygen atom has an overall charge of 0. The atom is neutral.

Figure 4 Calculating an Atom's Charge

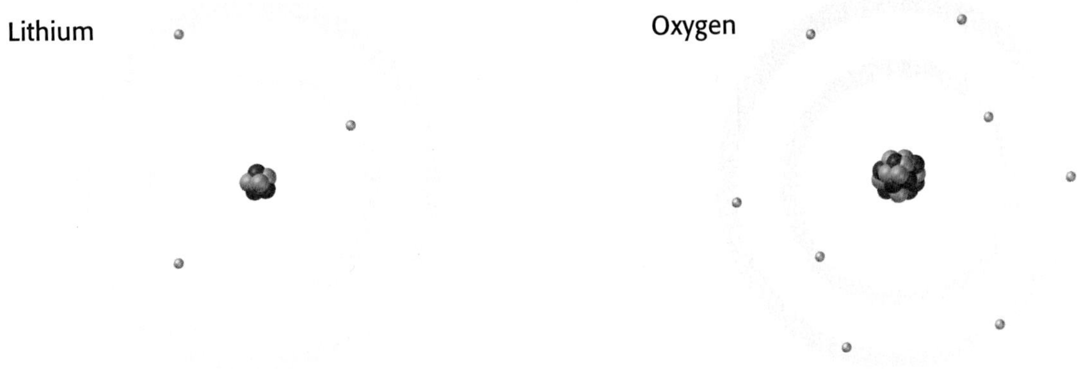

charge of	=
3 protons	3+
3 neutrons	0
3 electrons	3–
overall	0

charge of	=
8 protons	8+
8 neutrons	0
8 electrons	8–
overall	0

Figure 5 The Formation of a Positive Ion

A lithium atom will lose an electron in certain circumstances. As a result, a positive lithium ion forms.

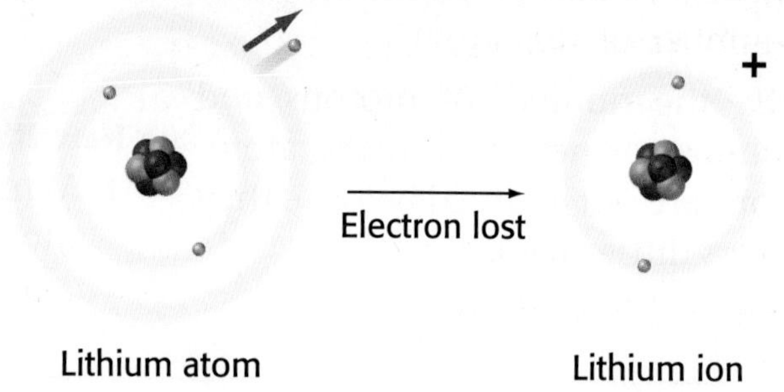

Atoms Losing, Gaining, or Sharing Electrons

ion a charged particle that forms when an atom or group of atoms gains or loses one or more electrons

Atoms are always neutral. However, sometimes atoms can lose or gain electrons to become more stable. Because electrons are charged particles, when the number of electrons in an atom changes, the overall charge of the atom changes, too. An **ion** forms when an atom gains or loses one or more electrons. **Figure 5** shows that a positive ion forms when an electron is lost. **Figure 6** shows that a negative ion forms when an electron is gained. Notice the *-ide* ending that is used for the name of the negative ion that forms.

Ionic Bonds

The same force that causes protons and electrons to be attracted to one another causes positive ions to be attracted to negative ions. Ions that have opposite charges are attracted to each other. The attraction between oppositely charged ions is called an *ionic bond.* A substance that has ionic bonds, such as table salt, is composed of ions in a specific ratio based on the charges of the ions. For example, lithium ions, which have a charge of 1+, form a compound with fluoride ions, which have a charge of 1–. The ions in this compound have a 1:1 ratio.

Figure 6 The Formation of a Negative Ion

A fluorine atom will gain an electron in certain circumstances. As a result, a negative fluoride ion forms.

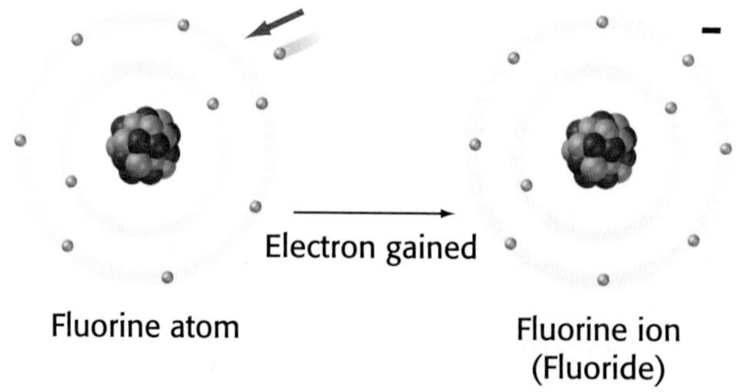

Covalent Bonds

Ions are not the only particles that combine to form substances. Many atoms are able to combine to form more complex substances. When atoms share electrons, a bond that holds the atoms together forms. This type of bond is called a *covalent bond*. Covalent bonds can form between similar atoms. Sometimes, covalent bonds can form between two atoms of the same element. Covalent bonds are in particles called *molecules*. For example, hydrogen and oxygen atoms share electrons and form water molecules, such as the molecule in **Figure 7.**

Reading Check How do atoms form substances?

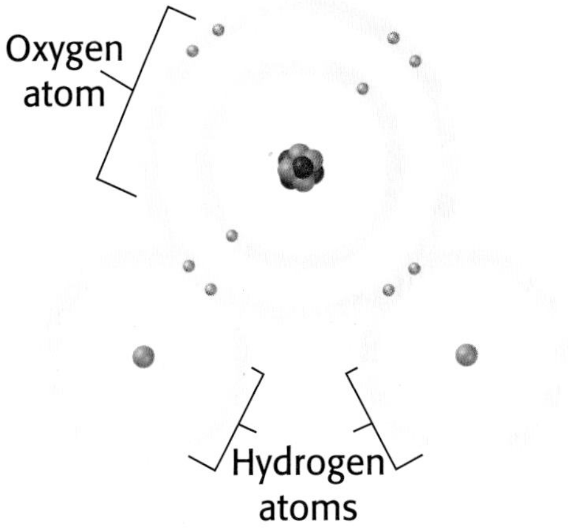

Figure 7 *Two hydrogen atoms and one oxygen atom are held together by covalent bonds to form water.*

SECTION Review

Summary

- All matter is composed of atoms.
- Atoms are made of protons, neutrons, and electrons. The nucleus of an atom contains protons and neutrons.
- The atomic number of an atom is the number of protons in the atom.
- The mass number of an atom is the sum of the number of protons and the number of neutrons.
- All atoms are neutral because they have equal numbers of protons and electrons.
- One force that holds atoms together is the attraction between the oppositely charged protons and electrons.
- Atoms gain or lose electrons to become ions.

Understanding Key Ideas

1. How are protons and neutrons alike? How are they different?
2. A carbon atom has six protons and six neutrons. Determine its atomic number.
3. How does an atom become a positive ion? How does an atom become a negative ion?
4. What is the charge of an ion that has 12 protons and 10 electrons? Write the ion's symbol.
5. An element whose mass number is 9 has four protons. The element also has
   a. nine neutrons.
   b. five neutrons.
   c. four neutrons.
   d. no neutrons.
6. The smallest piece of an element that maintains the properties of that element is a(n)
   a. particle.
   b. piece.
   c. atom.
   d. fragment.

Math Skills

7. How many electrons does an atom of lithium need to lose to form an ion with a +1 charge?
8. How many electrons does an atom of oxygen need to gain to form an ion with a –2 charge?

Critical Thinking

9. **Identifying Relationships** Explain why ionic compounds are neutral even though they are made up of charged particles.
10. **Identifying Relationships** How would an atom be different if its nucleus had a negative charge?
11. **Applying Concepts** Explain why almost the entire mass of an atom is in the nucleus.

SECTION 3

Three States of Matter

What You Will Learn

- Describe three states of matter.
- Explain the differences between the states of matter.
- Describe the conversion of matter from one state to another.
- Compare several changes of state.

Vocabulary

states of matter
solid
liquid
gas
change of state

READING STRATEGY

Paired Summarizing Read this section silently. In pairs, take turns summarizing the material. Stop to discuss ideas that seem confusing.

You have just walked home on one of the hottest days of the year. The air conditioner is on full blast. And there is a pitcher of lemonade on the kitchen table.

You pour yourself a glass of lemonade and add ice cubes to your glass. You take the lemonade out to the front porch to drink. After you have been on the porch for a short time, you notice drops of water forming on the outside of your glass. The scene described above has examples of the three most familiar states of matter: solid, liquid, and gas.

States of Matter

The **states of matter** are the physical forms in which a substance can exist. For example, water exists in three states of matter: solid (ice), liquid (water), and gas (steam). The state of matter is determined by the motion and position of the atoms or molecules in a substance. **Figure 1** shows matter in different states. Atoms or molecules in a solid have a fixed position. Atoms or molecules in a liquid or a gas do not have a fixed position and thus are free to move around. Atoms or molecules in a solid move more slowly than the atoms or molecules in a liquid or gas of the same substance. In fact, atoms or molecules in a solid are able only to vibrate and rotate in place.

Reading Check **Describe the three states of matter.** *(See the Appendix for answers to Reading Checks.)*

Figure 1 **Models of a Solid, a Liquid, and a Gas**

Particles of a solid do not move fast enough to overcome the strong attraction between them. So, they are close together and vibrate and rotate in place.

Particles of a liquid move fast enough to overcome some of the attraction between them. The particles are close together but can slide past one another.

Particles of a gas move fast enough to overcome almost all of the attraction between them. The particles are far apart and move independently of one another.

Solids

Imagine dropping a marble into a bottle. Would anything happen to the shape or size of the marble? If you put the marble in a larger bottle, would its shape or size change?

Definite Shape and Volume

Even in a bottle, a marble keeps its original shape and volume. Because the marble is a solid, its shape and volume stay the same no matter how big the bottle into which you drop the marble is. A **solid** is the state of matter that has a fixed shape and volume.

The particles of a substance in a solid are very close together. The attraction between them is stronger than the attraction between the particles of the same substance in a liquid or gas. The particles in a solid move, but they do not move fast enough to overcome the attraction between them. Each particle is locked in place by the particles around it. Therefore, each particle in a solid vibrates and rotates in place.

Two Kinds of Solids

There are two kinds of solids—*crystalline* (KRIS tuhl in) and *amorphous* (uh MAWR fuhs). Crystalline solids have a very orderly, three-dimensional arrangement of particles. The particles of crystalline solids are in a repeating pattern of rows. Iron, diamond, and ice are examples of crystalline solids.

Amorphous solids are made of particles that do not have a special arrangement. So, each particle is in one place, but the particles are not arranged in a pattern. Examples of amorphous solids are glass, rubber, and wax. **Figure 2** shows a photo of quartz (a crystalline solid) and glass (an amorphous solid).

Reading Check How are the particles in a crystalline solid arranged?

CONNECTION TO Physics

Is Glass a Liquid? At one time, there was a theory that glass was a liquid. This theory came about because of the observation that ancient windowpanes were often thicker at the bottom than at the top. People thought that glass flowed to the bottom of the pane and so must be a liquid. Research this theory. Present your research to your class in an oral presentation.

ACTIVITY

states of matter the physical forms of matter, which include solid, liquid, and gas

solid the state of matter in which the volume and shape of a substance are fixed

Figure 2 Crystalline and Amorphous Solids

The particles of crystalline solids, such as this quartz crystal, have an orderly, three-dimensional pattern.

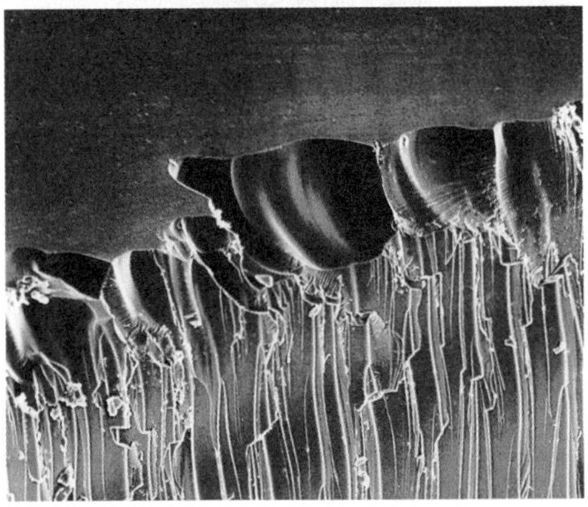

Glass, an amorphous solid, is made of particles that are not arranged in any particular pattern.

Figure 3 *Although their shapes are different, the beaker and the graduated cylinder each contain 350 mL of juice.*

Liquids

How does orange juice change if you pour the juice from a can into a glass? Is the volume of juice different? Does the shape of the juice change?

A Change in Shape but Not in Volume

The only thing that changes when you pour the juice into the glass is the shape of the juice. The shape changes because juice is a liquid. A **liquid** is the state of matter that has a definite volume but that takes the shape of its container. The particles in a liquid move fast enough to overcome some of the attractions between them. The particles slide past each other until the liquid takes the shape of its container.

Although liquids change shape, they do not easily change volume. A can of juice contains a certain volume of liquid. That volume stays the same whether you pour the juice into a large container or a small one. **Figure 3** shows the same volume of liquid in two different containers.

liquid the state of matter that has a definite volume but not a definite shape

gas a form of matter that does not have a definite volume or shape

change of state the change of a substance from one physical state to another

Unique Characteristics of Liquids

A special property of liquids is surface tension. *Surface tension* is a force that acts on the particles at the surface of a liquid. Surface tension causes some liquids to form spherical drops, such as the beads of water shown in **Figure 4.** Different liquids have different surface tensions. For example, gasoline has a very low surface tension and forms flat drops. Water forms spherical drops because it has a high surface tension.

Another important property of liquids is viscosity. *Viscosity* is a liquid's resistance to flow. Usually, the stronger the attractions between the molecules of a liquid, the more viscous the liquid is. For example, honey flows more slowly than water does. So, honey has a higher viscosity than water does.

Figure 4 *Water forms spherical drops as a result of surface tension.*

Reading Check What is viscosity?

Gases

Would you believe that one small tank of helium can fill almost 700 balloons? How is this possible? After all, the volume of a tank is equal to the volume of only about 5 filled balloons. The answer has to do with helium's state of matter.

A Change in Both Shape and Volume

The helium in a balloon is a gas. A **gas** is the state of matter that has no fixed shape or volume. The particles of a gas move quickly. So, they can break away from one another completely. The particles of a gas are less attracted to each other than particles of the same substance in the solid or liquid state are.

The amount of empty space between gas particles can change. Look at **Figure 5.** The particles of helium in the balloons are farther apart than the particles of helium in the tank. The particles spread out as helium fills the balloon. So, the amount of empty space between the gas particles increases.

Reading Check **How does the motion and position of the atoms or molecules in a gas differ from the motion and position of the atoms or molecules in a liquid?**

Figure 5 *Many balloons can be filled from one tank of helium because the particles of helium gas in the balloons are far apart.*

Changes of State

A **change of state** occurs when a substance changes from one physical state to another. This change happens when the attraction between the particles of a substance is overcome. The motion of the particles in a substance affects the attraction between the particles. For the motion and position of atoms and molecules in a substance to change, the amount of energy that the atoms and molecules have has to change.

Melting and Freezing

Melting and freezing describe the changes of state that occur between solids and liquids. *Melting* is the change of state in which a solid becomes a liquid when energy is added to the substance. The amount of energy required to melt a solid depends on the attraction between the atoms or molecules in the substance. Some substances, such as water, melt below room temperature. Other substances, such as table salt, melt at much higher temperatures.

Freezing is the change of state in which a liquid becomes a solid when energy is removed. For example, you make ice by placing liquid water in a freezer, which draws energy away from the water. Because water freezes at 0°C, you may associate freezing with cold temperatures. But some substances freeze at fairly high temperatures. For example, lead changes into a solid at 379°C.

Quick Lab

Boiling Water Is Cool

1. Remove the cap from a **syringe.**
2. Place the tip of the syringe in the **warm water** that is provided by your teacher. Pull the plunger out until you have 10 mL of water in the syringe.
3. Tighten the cap on the syringe.
4. Hold the syringe, and slowly pull the plunger out.
5. Observe any changes that you see in the water. Record your observations.
6. Why doesn't the water in the syringe burn you?

Evaporation, Boiling, and Condensation

Three changes of state may occur between a liquid and a gas. *Evaporation* (ee VAP uh RAY shuhn) happens when a substance changes from a liquid to a gas. Evaporation can occur at the surface of a liquid that is below its boiling point. *Boiling* occurs when a substance changes from a liquid to a gas throughout the entire substance. Boiling happens in a liquid at its boiling point. As energy is added to the liquid, particles throughout the liquid move faster until they evaporate and become a gas.

Condensation is the reverse of evaporation and boiling. As the middle image of **Figure 6** shows, *condensation* happens when a substance changes from a gas to a liquid. Gas condenses when it comes in contact with a cooler surface. The gas, whose particles are far apart, loses energy and changes into a liquid, whose particles are closer together.

Reading Check **Give an example of condensation.**

Figure 6 **Three Common Changes of State**

Solid ice melts as its thermal energy increases. This change of state will result in a liquid.

Water vapor in the air condenses as its thermal energy transfers to the cool glass.

Water evaporates as its thermal energy increases. This change of state results in a gas.

Sublimation: Solid to Gas

The fog effect in **Figure 7** is made with dry ice. Dry ice is carbon dioxide in a solid state. It is called *dry ice* because instead of melting into a liquid, it goes through sublimation. *Sublimation* is the change of state in which a solid changes directly into a gas. Dry ice is much colder than ice made from water.

For a solid to change directly into a gas, the particles of the substance must change from being very tightly packed to being spread far apart. So, the attractions between the particles must be overcome completely. The substance must gain energy for the particles to overcome their attractions. You might have experienced sublimation in your freezer. Ice that is left for a long time seems to disappear as a result of sublimation.

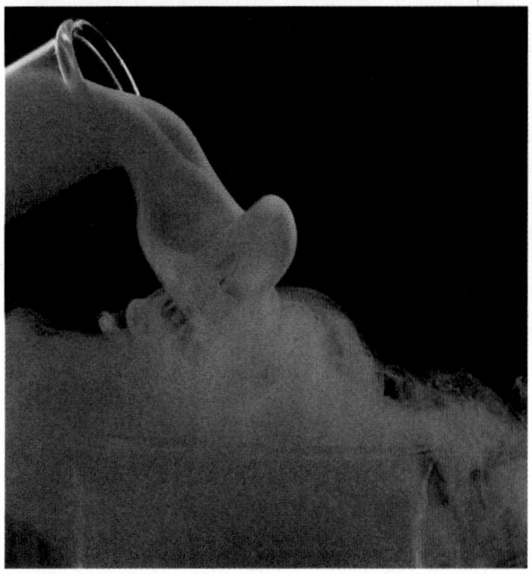

Figure 7 *The dry ice in the beaker changes directly from a solid to a gas as water is poured onto the ice.*

SECTION Review

Summary

- The three most familiar states of matter are solid, liquid, and gas.
- The physical state of matter is determined by the arrangement and movement of the particles of matter.
- A solid has a definite shape and volume.
- A liquid has a definite volume, but not a definite shape.
- A gas does not have a definite shape or volume.
- A change of state happens when a substance changes from one physical form to another.

Understanding Key Ideas

1. How does melting differ from freezing? Give an example to support your answer.
2. How do condensation and evaporation differ? Give an example to support your answer.
3. What is one property that all particles of matter in a substance share?
   a. They never move in solids.
   b. They move only in gases.
   c. They move constantly.
   d. None of the above
4. Use shape and volume to describe solids, liquids, and gases.
5. Describe how the motion and arrangement of particles in a substance change as the substance freezes.

Math Skills

6. The volume of a substance in the gaseous state is 1,000 times the volume of the same substance in the liquid state. What is the volume of this substance in its gaseous state if its volume is 18 ml as a liquid?

Critical Thinking

7. **Identifying Relationships** The volume of a gas can change, but the volume of a solid cannot change. Explain why this statement is true.
8. **Applying Concepts** Drops of moisture appear on the outside of a cold soda can. Explain why.
9. **Making Comparisons** How does the movement of the atoms or molecules in a substance determine the state of matter of that substance?
10. **Predicting Consequences** Dry ice sublimates. Would sublimating dry ice make a puddle on the floor?

SCILINKS. NSTA
Developed and maintained by the National Science Teachers Association

For a variety of links related to this chapter, go to www.scilinks.org

Topic: Solids, Liquids, and Gases
SciLinks code: HSM1420

SECTION 4

Matter and Its Properties

Think about all of the cars that you've seen today. They all have some features in common. But in many ways, they are very different. How are they the same? How do they differ?

Just as cars have certain features that distinguish them from other cars, different kinds of matter have distinguishing features, or properties.

What You Will Learn

- Identify various ways in which substances differ.
- Identify six examples of physical and chemical properties.
- Identify appropriate uses of materials based on properties.

Vocabulary

physical property
chemical property

READING STRATEGY

Reading Organizer As you read this section, create a mnemonic device to help you remember physical and chemical properties.

Chemical and Physical Properties

Would you make a truck out of paper? Of course not! Paper is not strong enough. The burning of gasoline that powers most trucks would cause the paper truck to catch on fire! The substances used to make a truck must be strong and unreactive. The steel and plastic used to make the truck in **Figure 1** have the right properties for their purposes.

All matter has physical and chemical properties that distinguish it from other kinds of matter. **Physical properties** are characteristics of a substance that can be observed without changing the substance. **Chemical properties** are properties of matter that describe a substance's ability to change into a new substance. Chemical properties describe how and under what circumstances a particular substance will change into a new substance. Generally, chemical properties describe how a substance is able to interact with other substances.

Reading Check **Distinguish between physical and chemical properties.** (*See the Appendix for answers to Reading Checks.*)

physical property a characteristic of a substance that does not involve a chemical change, such as density, color, or hardness

chemical property a property of matter that describes a substance's ability to participate in chemical reactions

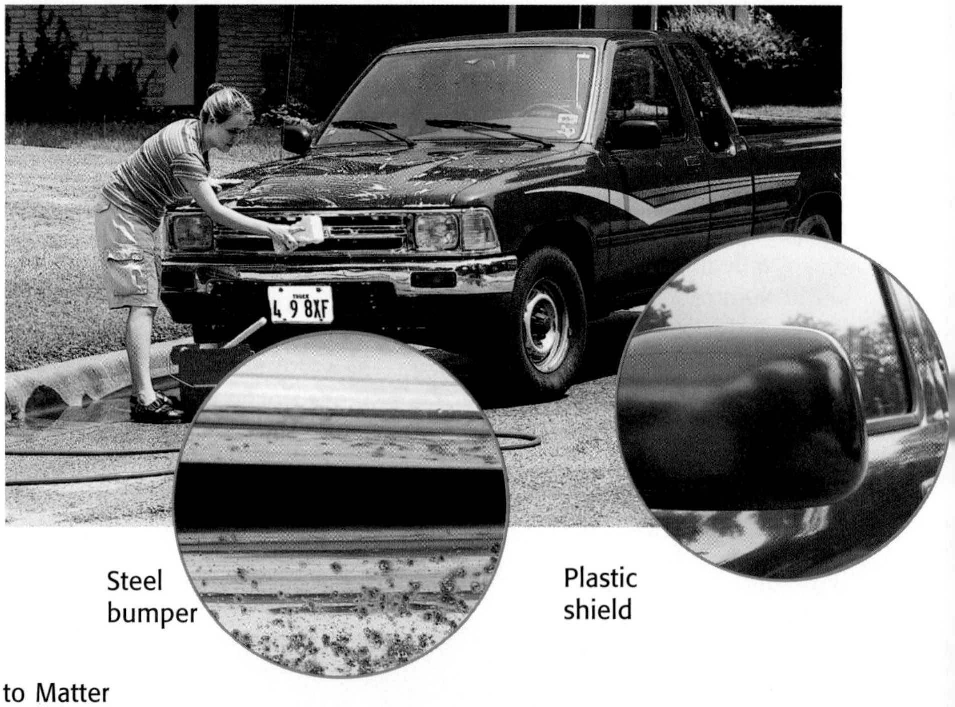

Figure 1 *Because of their physical and chemical properties, steel and plastic are useful materials for constructing a truck.*

Figure 2 *Steel nails are attracted to this magnet because of the physical property of magnetism.*

Physical Properties

The metal magnet in **Figure 2** has many of the physical properties that the steel used in trucks does. Both the material in the magnet and steel are solid, dense substances. Both substances can be shaped and bent. On the other hand, each object has unique physical properties. Each has a different shape and size. And the object in **Figure 2** is magnetic. You can observe physical properties, such as magnetism, without changing the substance.

Measuring and Observing Physical Properties

Your senses are helpful in identifying the properties of substances. For example, even your sense of smell can identify a physical property—odor. There are many other ways to detect and measure physical properties. Tools, such as rulers and graduated cylinders, extend our ability to measure and record the physical properties of a substance. No matter how you measure and observe properties,the identity of a substance does not change when a physical property is observed.

Common Physical Properties

Length, height, width, mass, shape, and state are familiar physical properties. Yet there are many other physical properties. The most useful physical properties are characteristic properties. *Characteristic properties* are properties that do not change when the amount of the substance changes. Characteristic properties are most useful in identifying an unknown substance because even the smallest sample will have the same characteristic properties that the whole has.

There are many examples of characteristic properties. *Thermal conductivity* is the rate at which a substance transfers heat. *Solubility* is the ability of a substance to dissolve in another substance. *Ductility* is the ability of a substance to be pulled into a wire. *Malleability* is the ability of a substance to be rolled or pounded into sheets.

SCHOOL to HOME

Properties and Function

WRITING SKILL With an adult family member, choose two objects or substances in your house that are used to do something. For example, one substance that you could choose is dish soap, which cleans dishes. Make a poster that describes the properties that make the objects or substances well suited to their jobs. Share your findings with your class.

ACTIVITY

MATH FOCUS

Calculating Density What is the density of a liquid that has a mass of 25 g and a volume of 50 mL?

Step 1: Write the equation for density.

$$D = m \div V$$

Step 2: Replace m and V with the measurements given in the problem, and solve.

$$D = 25 \text{ g} \div 50 \text{ mL} = 0.5 \text{ g/mL}$$

Now It's Your Turn

1. Find the density of a marble that has a mass of 52 g and a volume of 25 cm^3. If water has a density of 1.0 g/mL, will the marble float or sink?
2. Find the density of a book that has a mass of 502 g and a volume of 250 mL.
3. Platinum has a density of 21.5 g/cm^3. What is the mass of 10 cm^3 of platinum?

Density

Density is another characteristic property. You calculate density by dividing the mass of a substance by the volume of the substance. A substance's density is the same no matter how much of the substance is being measured. Density is very useful in determining whether a substance will float or sink in water. If a substance is less dense than water, the substance will float. If a substance is denser than water, the substance will sink.

Chemical Properties

Chemical properties, such as those in **Figure 3,** describe how a substance changes into new substances. To observe chemical properties, you must observe a substance when it might change into new substances. For example, substances in your saliva have chemical properties that allow these substances to react with and change food you eat as soon as you start chewing. You can experience this chemical property in action if you chew a saltine cracker for 60 seconds or more. The salty cracker will start to taste sweet as the chemical reaction occurs.

Figure 3 Examples of Chemical Properties

Reactivity Baking soda reacts with vinegar.

Decay Compounds in the food react with oxygen.

Reactivity Aluminum and iron(III) oxide react violently.

Observing Chemical Properties

Because chemical properties must be observed while a substance might change into new substances, they are not as easy to observe with your senses as physical properties are. But as the reactions in **Figure 3** show, there are many signs that indicate that new substances might be forming. For example, if you were exploring the chemical properties of an unknown solid, you might start by testing a small amount of this substance with water. You might observe the formation of bubbles, a change in color, or an increase in temperature. If one or more of these changes occur, you might be observing a chemical property. However, even if no change happens, you are still observing a chemical property of the substance—the substance does not react with water!

Reactivity

Reactivity is an example of a chemical property. *Reactivity* is the ability of two or more substances to combine and form one or more new substances. When baking soda and vinegar are combined, as **Figure 3** shows, a chemical reaction occurs and new substances form. A chemical property of baking soda is that baking soda reacts with vinegar and forms carbon dioxide.

Flammability

A chemical property that you may be familiar with is flammability. *Flammability* is the ability of a substance to burn. Flammable materials, such as wood, burn in the presence of oxygen. The wood reacts with oxygen in the air to produce water, carbon dioxide, and ash. These new substances have different chemical and physical properties than the wood had.

Reading Check **What are two chemical properties that can be used to tell one substance from another?**

Quick Lab

Signs, Signs, Everywhere!

1. Copy the data table your teacher has placed on the chalkboard.
2. Take a sample of your **unknown powder.**
3. Perform the tests listed on the far left column of the table.
4. Record your results carefully.
5. Compare your data to the information that your teacher has provided about known substances.
6. Was your unknown substance salt, baking soda, or powdered sugar? How do you know?

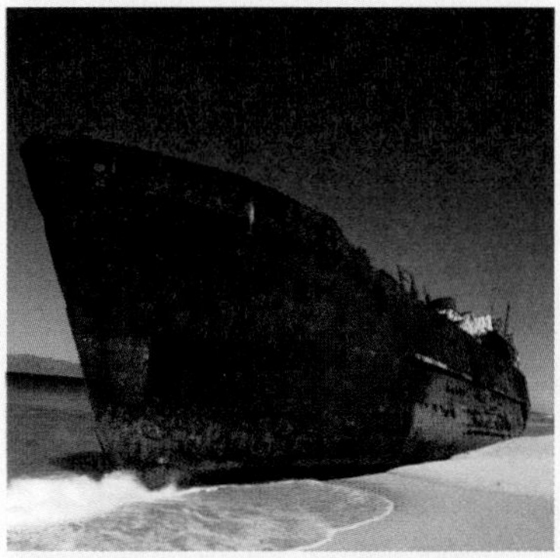

Rusting Iron reacts with oxygen and water.

Reactivity Sodium sulfide and cadmium nitrate react.

Digestion Chemicals in your body break down food.

Comparing Physical and Chemical Properties

Physical and chemical properties both describe matter. Observing physical properties does not change the identity of the substance. For example, when you observe the malleability of an object by pounding on the object with a hammer, you are changing the shape of the object. The composition of the substance does not change. It is important to remember that when you observe a substance's chemical properties, the substance can be changed. As a result of observing chemical properties, new substances whose structure differs from the structure of the original substance or substances can form.

Using Properties to Identify Substances

A scientist uses both physical and chemical properties to identify matter. The student in **Figure 4** has an unknown white powder. She uses the powder's physical properties to create a list of substances that the powder could be. Her list might include sugar, salt, baking soda, and powdered sugar, all of which are white powders. She can now test the powder to see if it has the chemical properties of any of the substances on her list. She begins testing the powder's chemical properties by mixing the powder with vinegar because she knows that only one of the four substances on her list reacts with vinegar. When the powder reacts with vinegar to form bubbles of carbon dioxide, she is able to confirm that the powder has the physical and chemical properties of baking soda. Both chemical and physical properties were used to identify the substance.

Reading Check **How are physical and chemical properties used to find the identity of a substance?**

Figure 4 *In this experiment, a student is using both physical properties and chemical properties to determine the identity of a substance.*

Using Properties to Help Determine Use

You use physical and chemical properties every day. Physical properties are useful when you are deciding what clothes to wear. For example, the physical properties of wool make wool ideal for cold, wet weather. You use chemical properties when you decide how to remove a stain from your clothes. Suppose that you want to build a bridge. You would want to use a metal that could be shaped into beams but that was strong enough to support a lot of weight. You might select iron because it has these physical properties. But iron rusts when it comes in contact with moisture. Because you know these chemical properties, you might decide to paint the bridge to protect it from rusting.

INTERNET ACTIVITY

For another activity related to this chapter, go to **go.hrw.com,** and type in the keyword **HP5MATW.**

SECTION Review

Summary

- Matter has physical and chemical properties.
- Physical properties can be determined without changing the composition of matter.
- Density is the mass of a substance per unit volume.
- Chemical properties can be determined only by trying to change the composition of matter.
- Properties can be used to identify matter.

Understanding Key Ideas

1. Flammability of a substance is
   a. a physical property.
   b. a chemical property.
   c. not a property.
   d. Both (a) and (b)
2. For each statement, identify whether the statement describes a physical property or a chemical property.
   a. A substance bubbles when placed in water.
   b. A substance has a boiling point of 100°C.
   c. A substance is bright green.
   d. A substance dissolves in water.
   e. A substance is very hard.
3. Explain how to tell the difference between a physical property and a chemical property.

Math Skills

4. Calculate the density of a liquid that has a mass of 20 g and a volume of 56 mL.
5. Gold has a density of 19.3 g/cm^3. What is the volume of a 100 g sample of gold?
6. Silver has a density of 10.5 g/cm^3. What is the mass of a sample of silver with a volume of 100 cm^3?

Critical Thinking

7. **Applying Concepts** Why is the melting point of a substance not a chemical property?
8. **Analyzing Processes** What physical properties would you use to find the right materials to build a birdhouse?
9. **Identifying Relationships** How can you determine that a coin is not pure silver if you know the mass and volume of the coin?
10. **Analyzing Ideas** Identify two physical and two chemical properties of a bag of microwave popcorn before and after popping.

SCILINKS. NSTA Developed and maintained by the National Science Teachers Association

For a variety of links related to this chapter, go to www.scilinks.org

Topic: Describing Matter
SciLinks code: HSM0391

SECTION 5

Matter and Change

What You Will Learn

- Describe two ways that matter can change.
- Explain what happens during a physical change.
- Explain what happens during a chemical change.
- Compare physical and chemical changes.

Vocabulary

physical change
chemical change

READING STRATEGY

Reading Organizer As you read this section, make a table comparing physical changes with chemical changes.

You're helping your parent prepare dinner. You chop vegetables and put them on the grill. As the vegetables cook, you notice the difference in how they smell and the way they slowly brown. When they are finished, you eat!

The vegetables undergo the physical change of being cut into smaller pieces. And the vegetables undergo the chemical changes of cooking and digestion. Those vegetables, like all of the food in **Figure 1,** are going through dramatic changes!

Kinds of Change

Matter is constantly changing. If you think carefully about your day, you may have seen ice melting, water boiling, and food being eaten. Most changes that matter undergoes can be classified as either physical changes or chemical changes.

A **physical change** occurs when matter changes from one physical form to another. The chemical properties of matter do not change during a physical change. The melting of ice and the boiling of water are physical changes. In both cases, the properties of water remain the same.

A **chemical change** is a change that occurs when one or more substances change into entirely new substances. The properties of the new substances differ from the properties of the original substances. Many of the changes that food undergoes as it is eaten and digested are examples of chemical changes.

Reading Check **How does a physical change differ from a chemical change?** (*See the Appendix for answers to Reading Checks.*)

Figure 1 *Preparing food involves physical changes, such as cutting vegetables and meat, and chemical changes, such as cooking.*

Figure 2 *This piece of glass art has been formed through a series of physical changes.*

Physical Changes

Many things happen during a physical change. The appearance, shape, size, or other physical properties of a substance may be altered during a physical change. However, the chemical properties of a substance are never altered during a physical change. No new substances are formed during a physical change.

Figure 2 shows an example of a physical change. Artists are creating a piece of glass by physically altering a few substances. Silica, in the form of sand, is one of these substances. Sand exists as many small particles that are not held together. After being heated to very high temperatures, the sand forms molten glass. Even though the appearance of the beginning substance has changed dramatically, no new substance has been formed. If examined chemically, the glass that was formed would have the same chemical properties that the original silica did.

physical change a change of matter from one form to another without a change in chemical properties

chemical change a change that occurs when one or more substances change into entirely new substances with different properties

Signs of a Physical Change

Physical changes take many forms. Some physical changes, such as rolling metal into a sheet, are easy to see. The metal has changed shape but keeps many of the same characteristics that first allowed you to identify it. Other physical changes are more difficult to see. For example, dissolving salt in water is a physical change. It would be difficult to see that a physical change has occurred if you compared a glass of water with a glass of salt water. But several physical properties of the salt water differ from the properties of pure water. Salt water is denser than pure water. Salt water also has a higher boiling point than pure water does. But the identity of the water has not changed, so these changes are merely signs of a physical change.

CONNECTION TO Geology

Igneous Rock Igneous rock forms when magma cools and hardens. This process can happen below the surface of Earth or at Earth's surface. When magma cools at Earth's surface, the magma is called *lava*. Research where active lava flows occur on Earth, and describe how the lava is changing physically.

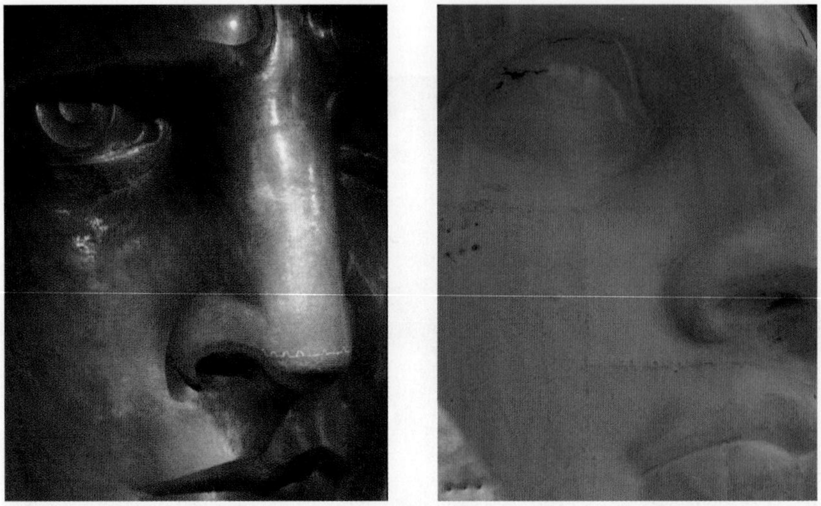

Figure 3 *The copper used to form the Statue of Liberty has changed chemically as it has been exposed to water and air.*

Chemical Changes

Chemical changes, sometimes called *chemical reactions,* take many forms. Some chemical reactions are explosive and release heat and light. Some chemical reactions, such as the one shown in **Figure 3,** are visible but do not release energy explosively. Other chemical reactions, such as the chemical reaction that occurs between aluminum and oxygen, are not easily noticed. The substance that forms during the reaction between aluminum and oxygen looks like pure aluminum.

What Happens During a Chemical Change?

Even though chemical reactions appear different, all chemical reactions have one thing in common. They all result in the formation of one or more new substances. All matter is made of atoms. During a chemical change, the atoms of a substance are rearranged to form new substances. For example, when a chemical reaction between oxygen gas and hydrogen gas occurs, atoms in both substances are rearranged to form water. Because the atoms have been rearranged, the substance formed during the chemical reaction has new chemical properties.

Reading Check **What event happens during a chemical change but does not happen during a physical change?**

Physical and Chemical Changes Together

Often, a combination of chemical and physical changes are used to complete a task. For example, the welder in **Figure 4** has physically changed the steel by cutting it. Then, the welder uses a welding tool to cause a chemical reaction that bonds the two pieces of metal. When you cook, you also use a combination of physical and chemical changes. When you bake cookies, you physically change the ingredients by mixing them together. Then, you change the mixture chemically as a result of the high temperature in the oven.

Figure 4 *A welder uses both physical and chemical changes to form metal.*

When the welder cuts the steel, a physical change happens.

A chemical change occurs during welding.

SECTION Review

Summary

- Physical changes do not alter the chemical properties of matter.
- Chemical changes alter the chemical properties of matter.
- Chemical changes always result in new substances.
- Chemical changes result in the rearrangement of atoms in a substance.
- Physical and chemical changes are used together in art and industry.

Using Key Terms

1. Write an original definition for *physical change* and *chemical change*.

Understanding Key Ideas

2. A change occurs, but the chemical properties of the substance are not altered. What kind of change has occurred?
   a. a chemical change
   b. a physical change
   c. a chemical reaction
   d. an ionic change
3. The Statue of Liberty was originally a copper color. After being exposed to the air, the statue turned a greenish color. What kind of change occurred?

Math Skills

4. The temperature of an acid solution is 25°C. A strip of magnesium is added. The temperature rises 2°C each minute for the first 3 minutes. What is the final temperature?

Critical Thinking

5. **Applying Concepts** How could you prove that grinding a bar of iron into a powder is not a chemical change?
6. **Analyzing Ideas** The boiling point of water changes when salt is dissolved in water. Explain if a chemical change occurs.

SCILINKS® NSTA
Developed and maintained by the National Science Teachers Association

For a variety of links related to this chapter, go to www.scilinks.org

Topic: Physical Changes; Chemical Changes
SciLinks code: HSM1142; HSM0266

Skills Practice Lab

Volumania!

You have learned how to measure the volume of a solid object that has square or rectangular sides. But there are many objects in the world that have irregular shapes. In this lab activity, you'll learn some ways to find the volume of objects that have irregular shapes.

OBJECTIVES

Determine the volume of irregularly shaped objects.

Compare the volumes of similar objects.

MATERIALS

Part A

- graduated cylinder
- various small objects supplied by your teacher
- water

Part B

- bottle, plastic (or similar container), 2 L, bottom half
- funnel
- graduated cylinder
- pan, aluminum pie
- paper towels
- water

SAFETY

Part A: Finding the Volume of Small Objects

Procedure

1. Fill a graduated cylinder half full with water. Read and record the volume of the water. Be sure to look at the surface of the water at eye level and to read the volume at the bottom of the meniscus, as shown below.

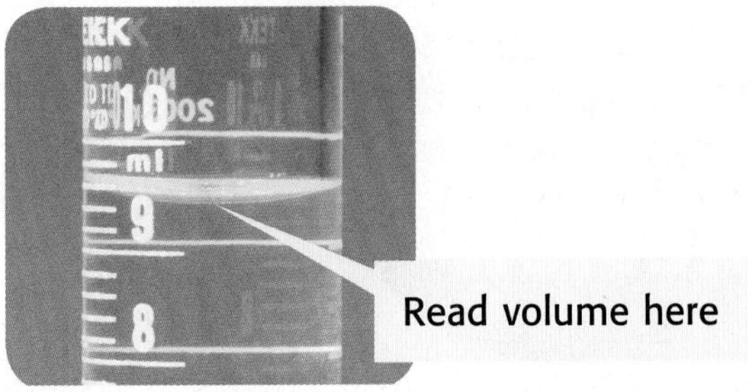

2. Carefully slide one of the objects into the tilted graduated cylinder, as shown below.
3. Read the new volume, and record it.
4. Subtract the original volume from the new volume. The resulting amount is equal to the volume of the solid object.
5. Use the same method to find the volume of the other objects. Record your results.

Analyze the Results

1. What changes do you have to make to the volumes that you determine in order to express the volumes correctly?
2. Do the heaviest objects have the largest volumes? Why or why not?

Part B: Finding the Volume of Your Hand

Procedure

1. Completely fill the container with water. Put the container in the center of the pie pan. Be sure not to spill any of the water into the pie pan.
2. Make a fist, and put your hand into the container up to your wrist.
3. Remove your hand, and let the excess water drip into the container, not the pie pan. Dry your hand with a paper towel.
4. Use the funnel to pour the overflow water into the graduated cylinder. Measure the volume. This measurement is the volume of your hand. Record the volume. (Remember to use the correct unit of volume for a solid object.)
5. Repeat this procedure with your other hand.

Analyze the Results

1. Did your hands have the same volume? If not, were you surprised? What might be the reason that a person's hands have different volumes?
2. Would placing your open hand instead of your fist into the container change the results? Explain your reasoning.
3. Compare the volume of your right hand with the volume of every classmates' right hand. Create a class graph that shows the volume of each student's right hand. What is the average volume for your class?

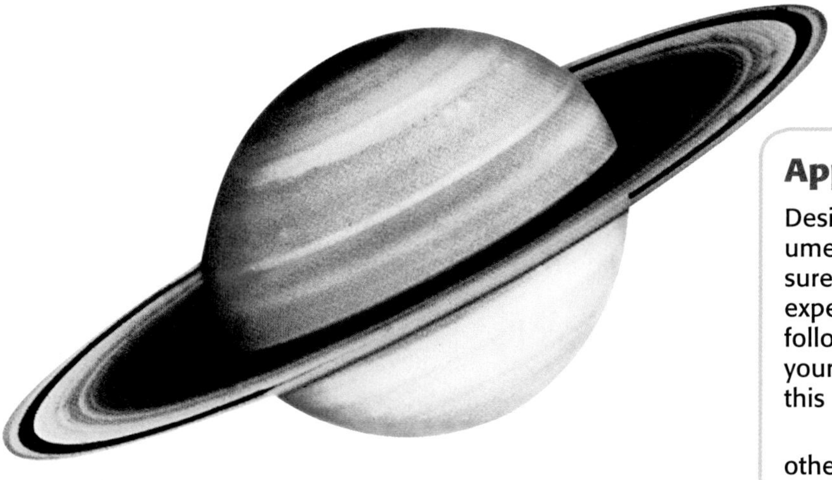

Applying Your Data

Design an experiment to determine the volume of a person's body. In your plans, be sure to include the materials needed for the experiment and the procedures that must be followed. Include a sketch that shows how your materials and methods would be used in this experiment.

Using an encyclopedia, the Internet, or other reference materials, find out how the volumes of very large samples of matter—such as an entire planet—are determined.

Chapter Review

USING KEY TERMS

1 Use each of the following terms in a separate sentence: *matter, element, states of matter*, and *physical property*.

For each pair of terms, explain how the meanings of the terms differ.

2 *volume* and *mass*

3 *atom* and *ion*

4 *liquid* and *gas*

UNDERSTANDING KEY IDEAS

Multiple Choice

5 Maria and Gretchen have entered a science fair. They are exploring ways that sugar undergoes change. Which of the following actions changes sugar's identity?

a. dissolving sugar in water
b. mixing salt and sugar
c. forming small sugar cubes
d. burning sugar

6 Atoms are the smallest particles of matter to have distinct properties. They are composed of three subatomic particles: electrons, neutrons, and protons. Which particles make up the nucleus?

a. protons and electrons
b. protons and neutrons
c. only protons
d. neutrons and electrons

7 Two substances are placed side by side on a lab table. Substance A is a flammable, clear liquid. Substance B is a nonflammable, clear liquid. Which of the following is true?

a. Substances A and B are identical.
b. Substance A would be useful in starting a campfire.
c. Substance B is safe to drink.
d. Substance A takes the shape and volume of its container.

8 Which of the following is a characteristic property?

a. density
b. mass
c. volume
d. height

Short Answer

9 Jonathan has been asked to develop a model that illustrates how mass and weight differ. Propose an argument that he can use to demonstrate this difference.

10 What happens to a liquid when it evaporates?

11 Describe the difference between melting and freezing.

12 What is the difference between a physical change and a chemical change?

Math Skills

13 What is the density of a liquid that has a mass of 206 g and a volume of 321 mL?

14 Calculate the mass number of an atom that has 92 protons and 108 neutrons.

15 What is the charge of an atom that has 15 protons, 16 neutrons, and 15 electrons?

CRITICAL THINKING

16 **Concept Mapping** Use the following terms to create a concept map: *matter, volume, mass, density, physical property, chemical property, solid, liquid,* and *gas.*

17 **Identifying Relationships** The three most common physical states of matter are solid, liquid, and gas. Devise a way to distinguish between each state by using the movement and spacing of a substance's particles.

18 **Applying Concepts** Shari dissolves a cup of sugar in a liter of water. Explain why this change is not a chemical change.

19 **Analyzing Processes** Explain how physical and chemical properties are used to distinguish between different substances. Use at least one example.

20 **Analyzing Ideas** Describe the importance of the following statement: "All matter is composed of atoms." How do you think the study of matter changed as this statement gained support?

INTERPRETING GRAPHICS

Use the photographs below to answer the questions that follow.

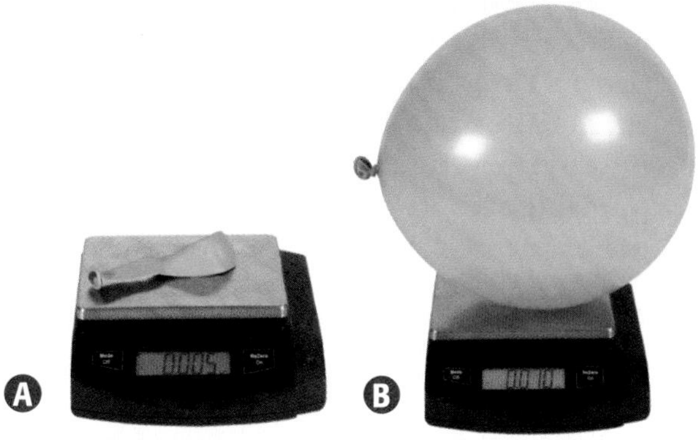

21 List three physical properties of the balloon.

22 What kind of change in the balloon occurred from picture A to picture B? Describe the change.

23 What two properties of this balloon changed from picture A to picture B?

24 What caused the balloon to change from picture A to picture B?

25 How do picture A and picture B prove that air is made up of matter?

Standardized Test Preparation

Multiple Choice

1. **Ethan knows that atoms are the smallest particles of matter and that there are only about 100 different kinds of atoms. Atoms vary in their chemical properties. Also, atoms combine to form all of the substances found on Earth. What subatomic particle participates in chemical bonds with other atoms?**

   A. electron

   B. ion

   C. neutron

   D. proton

2. **In her physical science class, Aileen is learning about three different states of matter. Aileen's teacher has explained that each of these states results from the speed at which the particles move, as well as the attraction between particles. Which of the following would have the fastest moving particles?**

   A. paper

   B. milk shake

   C. soda water

   D. steam

3. **Which physical property could be used to classify oxygen, helium, propane, and hydrogen as in the same group?**

   A. flammability

   B. state of matter

   C. reactivity

   D. malleability

Use the table below to answer questions 4–5.

Densities of Common Substances*

Substance	Density (g/cm^3)	Substance	Density (g/cm^3)
Helium (gas)	0.0001663	Copper (solid)	8.96
Oxygen (gas)	0.001331	Silver (solid)	10.50
Water (liquid)	1.00	Lead (solid)	11.35
Iron pyrite (solid)	5.02	Mercury (liquid)	13.55
Zinc (solid)	7.13	Gold (solid)	19.32

* at 20°C and normal atmospheric pressure

4. **Shawna created the chart above, which compares the densities of common substances. Using the chart, what could Shawna conclude about mercury?**

   A. It is the densest substance listed.

   B. Its density is less than the density of water.

   C. It is solid at 20°C and normal atmospheric pressure.

   D. It is the densest liquid listed in the chart.

5. **A certain substance has a mass of 68.1 g and a volume of 6 cm^3. Based on the chart above, what is the substance?**

   A. lead

   B. gold

   C. copper

   D. silver

6. **A certain substance is liquid at room temperature, has no color, and dissolves table salt. What is the substance?**

   A. oxygen

   B. gold

   C. mercury

   D. water

7. **Which of the following could describe oxygen at room temperature?**

   A. Its fast-moving particles form a definite shape.

   B. It has a volume that remains constant over time.

   C. Its particles have overcome their attraction to each other.

   D. Its particles may become crystalline as they collide.

8. **Iron oxide, or rust, forms from iron and the oxygen in the air. Which property makes iron susceptible to the formation of rust?**

   A. solubility

   B. reactivity

   C. malleability

   D. flammability

9. **An element is shiny and conducts electric current well. It is malleable and ductile. Which of the following could this element be?**

   A. silver

   B. carbon

   C. silicon

   D. chlorine

Use the figure below to answer question 10.

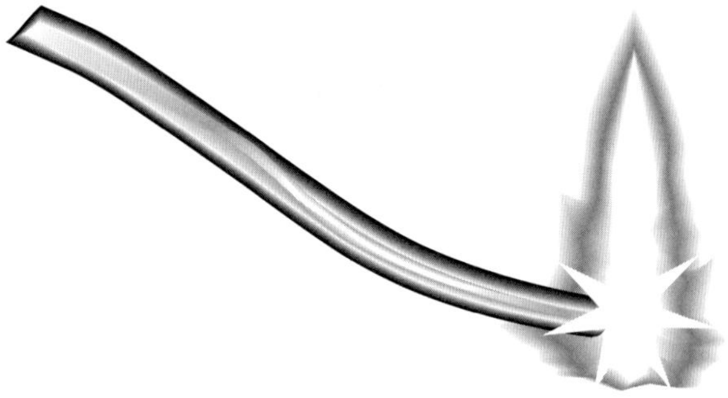

10. **The figure shows magnesium burning in the presence of oxygen during a laboratory investigation. What can be concluded from the figure?**

   A. A chemical change is taking place.

   B. The identity of the oxygen is not changing.

   C. A physical change is taking place.

   D. The identity of the magnesium is not changing.

Open Response

11. **Caitlin's teacher gives her a cube of a shiny element. How could Caitlin use lab materials to identify the element?**

12. **Guillermo claims that any pure substance is also an element. Give two reasons why he is wrong.**

Standardized Test Preparation

Science in Action

Scientific Debate

Paper or Plastic?

What do you choose at the grocery store: paper or plastic bags? Plastic bags are waterproof and take up less space. You can use them to line waste cans and to pack lunches. Some places will recycle plastic bags. But making 1 ton of plastic bags uses 11 barrels of oil, which can't be replaced, and produces polluting chemicals. On the other hand, making 1 ton of paper bags destroys 13 to 17 trees, which take years to replace. Paper bags, too, can be reused for lining waste cans and wrapping packages. Recycling paper pollutes less than recycling plastic does. What is the answer? Maybe we should reuse both!

Language Arts ACTIVITY

WRITING SKILL There are advantages and disadvantages of each kind of bag. Write a one-page essay defending your position on this subject. Support your opinion with facts.

Scientific Discoveries

The Fourth State of Matter

If you heat water, it will eventually turn into a gas. But what would happen if you kept on heating the gas? Scientists only had to look to the sun for the answer. The sun, like other stars, is made of the fourth state of matter—plasma. Plasma is a superheated gas. Once a gas's temperature rises above 10,000°C to 20,000°C, its particles start to break apart and it becomes plasma. Unlike gas, plasma can create, and be affected by, electrical and magnetic fields. More than 99% of the known universe is made of plasma! Even Earth has some naturally occurring plasma. Plasma can be found in auroras, flames, and lightning.

Social Studies ACTIVITY

Research plasma. Find out how plasma is used in today's technology, such as plasma TVs. How will this new technology affect you and society in general? Describe your findings in a poster.

Careers

Aundra Nix

Metallurgist Aundra Nix is a chief metallurgist for a copper mine in Sahuarita, Arizona, where she supervises laboratories and other engineers. "To be able to look at rock in the ground and follow it through a process of drilling, blasting, hauling, crushing, grinding, and finally mineral separation—where you can hold a mineral that is one-third copper in your hand—is exciting."

Although she is a supervisor, Nix enjoys the flexible nature of her job. "My work environment includes office and computer work, plant work, and outdoor work. In this field you can 'get your hands into it,' which I always prefer," says Nix. "I did not want a career where it may be years before you see the results of your work." Aundra Nix enjoyed math and science, "so engineering seemed to be a natural area to study," she says. Nix's advice to students planning their own career is to learn all that they can in science and technology, because that is the future.

Math ACTIVITY

A large copper-mining company employed about 2,300 people at three locations in New Mexico. Because of an increase in demand for copper, 570 of these employees were hired over a period of a year. Of the 570 new employees, 115 employees were hired within a three-week period. What percentage of the total work force do the newly hired employees represent? What percentage of the new employees were hired during the three-week hiring period?

go.hrw.com

To learn more about these Science in Action topics, visit go.hrw.com and type in the keyword HT6FMF6F.

Current Science

Check out Current Science® articles related to this chapter by visiting go.hrw.com. Just type in the keyword HP5CS04.

3

The Energy of Waves

The Big Idea

Waves transfer energy, have describable properties, and interact in predictable ways.

SECTION

About the Photo

A surfer takes advantage of a wave's energy to catch an exciting ride. The ocean wave that this surfer is riding is just one type of wave. You are probably familiar with water waves. But did you know that light, sound, and even earthquakes are waves? From music to television, waves play an important role in your life every day.

PRE-READING ACTIVITY

FOLDNOTES

Three-Panel Flip Chart

Before you read the chapter, create the FoldNote entitled "Three-Panel Flip Chart" described in the **Study Skills** section of the Appendix. Label the flaps of the three-panel flip chart with "The nature of waves," "Properties of waves," and "Wave interactions." As you read the chapter, write information you learn about each category under the appropriate flap.

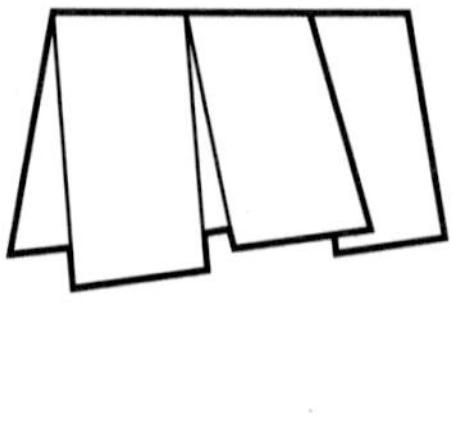

START-UP ACTIVITY

Energetic Waves

In this activity, you will observe the movement of a wave. Then, you will determine the source of the wave's energy.

Procedure

1. Tie one end of a **piece of rope** to the back of a **chair.**
2. Hold the other end in one hand, and stand away from the chair so that the rope is almost straight but is not pulled tight.
3. Move the rope up and down quickly to create a wave. Repeat this step several times. Record your observations.

Analysis

1. In which direction does the wave move?
2. How does the movement of the rope compare with the movement of the wave?
3. Where does the energy of the wave come from?

28 October 2013

SECTION 1

The Nature of Waves

What You Will Learn

- Describe how waves transfer energy without transferring matter.
- Distinguish between waves that require a medium and waves that do not.
- Explain the difference between transverse and longitudinal waves.

Vocabulary

wave
medium
transverse wave
longitudinal wave

READING STRATEGY

Discussion Read this section silently. Write down questions that you have about this section. Discuss your questions in a small group.

Imagine that your family has just returned home from a day at the beach. You had fun playing in the ocean under a hot sun. You put some cold pizza in the microwave for dinner, and you turn on the radio. Just then, the phone rings. It's your friend calling to ask about homework.

In the events described above, how many different waves were present? Believe it or not, there were at least five! Can you name them? Here's a hint: A **wave** is any disturbance that transmits energy through matter or empty space. Okay, here are the answers: (1) water waves in the ocean; (2) light waves from the sun; (3) microwaves inside the microwave oven; (4) radio waves transmitted to the radio; (5) and sound waves from the radio, (6) telephone, and (7) voices. Don't worry if you didn't get very many. You will be able to name them all after you read this section.

Examples →

Reading Check **What do all waves have in common?** (*See the Appendix for answers to Reading Checks.*)

Wave Energy

Energy can be carried away from its source by a wave. You can observe an example of a wave if you drop a rock in a pond. Waves from the rock's splash carry energy away from the splash. However, the material through which the wave travels does not move with the energy. Look at **Figure 1.** Can you move a leaf on a pond if you are standing on the shore? You can make the leaf bob up and down by making waves that carry enough energy through the water. But you would not make the leaf move in the same direction as the wave.

wave a periodic disturbance in a solid, liquid, or gas as energy is transmitted through a medium

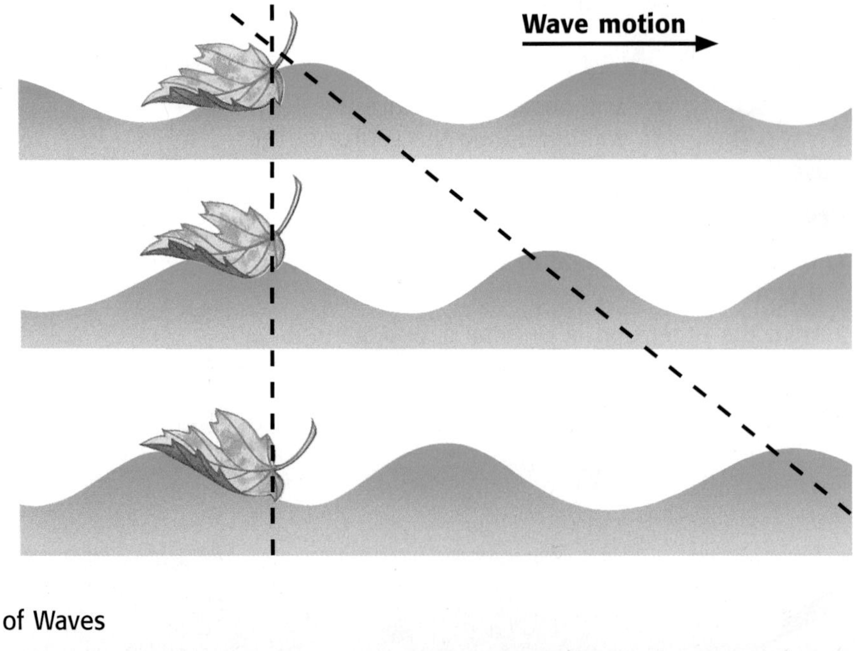

Figure 1 *Waves on a pond move toward the shore, but the water and the leaf floating on the surface only bob up and down.*

Waves and Work

As a wave travels, it does work on everything in its path. The waves in a pond do work on the water to make it move up and down. The waves also do work on anything floating on the water's surface. For example, boats and ducks bob up and down with waves. The fact that these objects move tells you that the waves are transferring energy.

Energy Transfer Through a Medium

Most waves transfer energy by the vibration of particles in a medium. A **medium** is a substance through which a wave can travel. A medium can be a solid, a liquid, or a gas. The plural of *medium* is *media*.

When a particle vibrates (moves back and forth, as in **Figure 2**), it can pass its energy to a particle next to it. The second particle will vibrate like the first particle does. In this way, energy is transmitted through a medium.

Sound waves need a medium. Sound energy travels by the vibration of particles in liquids, solids, and gases. If there are no particles to vibrate, no sound is possible. If you put an alarm clock inside a jar and remove all the air from the jar to create a vacuum, you will not be able to hear the alarm.

Other waves that need a medium include ocean waves, which move through water, and waves that are carried on guitar and cello strings when they vibrate. Waves that need a medium are called *mechanical waves*. **Figure 3** shows the effect of a mechanical wave in Earth's crust: an earthquake.

Figure 2 *A vibration is one complete back-and-forth motion of an object.*

medium a physical environment in which phenomena occur

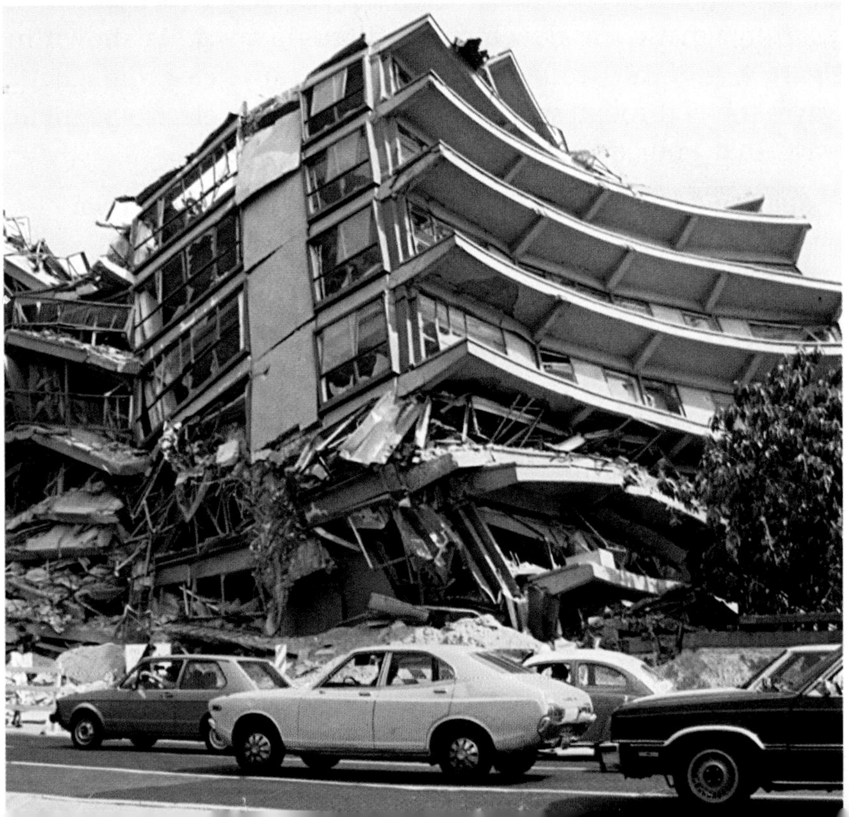

Figure 3 *Earthquakes cause seismic waves to travel through Earth's crust. The energy they carry can be very destructive to anything on the ground.*

Figure 4 *Light waves are electromagnetic waves, which do not need a medium. Light waves from the Crab nebula, shown here, travel through the vacuum of space billions of miles to Earth, where they can be detected with a telescope.*

Energy Transfer Without a Medium

Some waves can transfer energy without going through a medium. Visible light is one example. Other examples include microwaves made by microwave ovens, TV and radio signals, and X rays used by dentists and doctors. These waves are *electromagnetic waves*.

Although electromagnetic waves do not need a medium, they can go through matter, such as air, water, and glass. The energy that reaches Earth from the sun comes through electromagnetic waves, which go through space. As shown in **Figure 4,** you can see light from stars because electromagnetic waves travel through space to Earth. Light is an electromagnetic wave that your eyes can see.

Reading Check **How do electromagnetic waves differ from mechanical waves?**

CONNECTION TO Astronomy

Light Speed Light waves from stars and galaxies travel great distances that are best expressed in light-years. A light-year is the distance a ray of light can travel in one year. Some of the light waves from these stars have traveled billions of light-years before reaching Earth. Do the following calculation in your **science journal:** If light travels at a speed of 300,000,000 m/s, what distance is a light-minute? (Hint: There are 60 s in a minute.)

ACTIVITY

Types of Waves

All waves transfer energy by repeated vibrations. However, waves can differ in many ways. Waves can be classified based on the direction in which the particles of the medium vibrate compared with the direction in which the waves move. The two main types of waves are *transverse waves* and *longitudinal* (LAHN juh TOOD'n uhl) *waves.* Sometimes, a transverse wave and a longitudinal wave can combine to form another kind of wave called a *surface wave.*

INTERNET ACTIVITY

For another activity related to this chapter, go to **go.hrw.com** and type in the keyword **HP5WAVW.**

Transverse Waves

Waves in which the particles vibrate in an up-and-down motion are called **transverse waves.** *Transverse* means "moving across." The particles in this kind of wave move across, or perpendicularly to, the direction that the wave is going. To be *perpendicular* means to be "at right angles."

transverse wave a wave in which the particles of the medium move perpendicularly to the direction the wave is traveling

A wave moving on a rope is an example of a transverse wave. In **Figure 5,** you can see that the points along the rope vibrate perpendicularly to the direction the wave is going. The highest point of a transverse wave is called a *crest,* and the lowest point between each crest is called a *trough* (TRAWF). Although electromagnetic waves do not travel by vibrating particles in a medium, all electromagnetic waves are considered transverse waves. The reason is that the waves are made of vibrations that are perpendicular to the direction of motion.

Figure 5 Motion of a Transverse Wave

A wave on a rope is a transverse wave because the particles of the medium vibrate perpendicularly to the direction the wave moves.

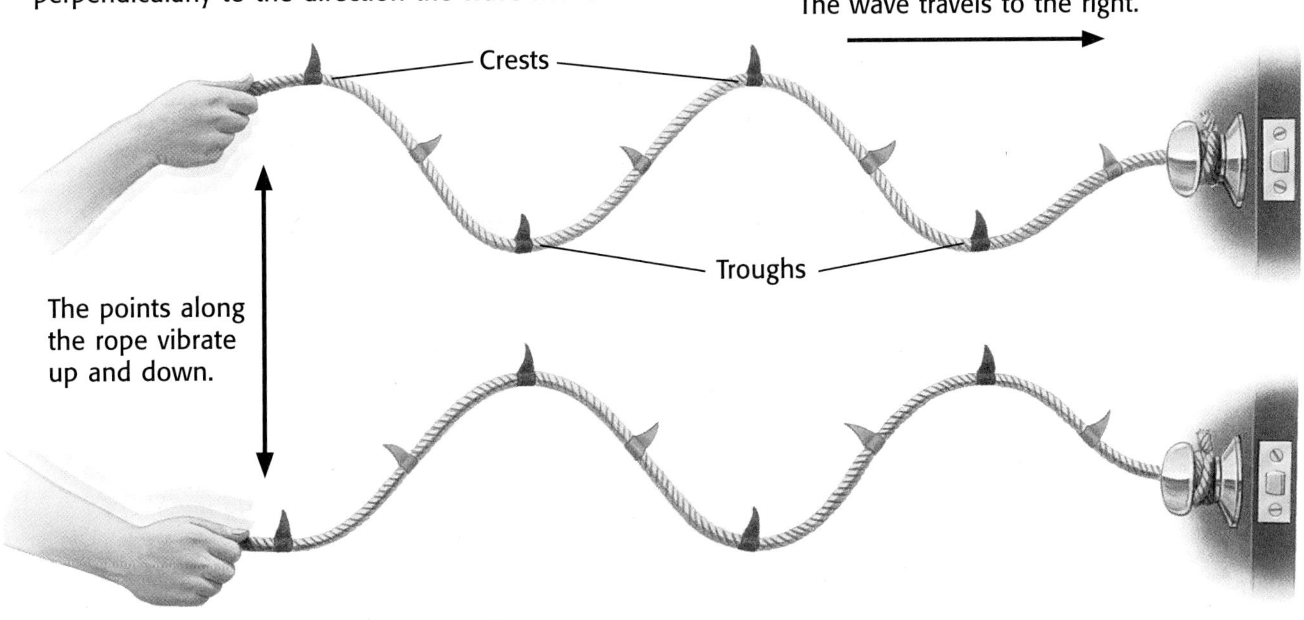
The wave travels to the right.
Crests
Troughs
The points along the rope vibrate up and down.

Figure 6 **Comparing Longitudinal and Transverse Waves**

Examples

Pushing a spring back and forth creates a longitudinal wave, much the same way that shaking a rope up and down creates a transverse wave.

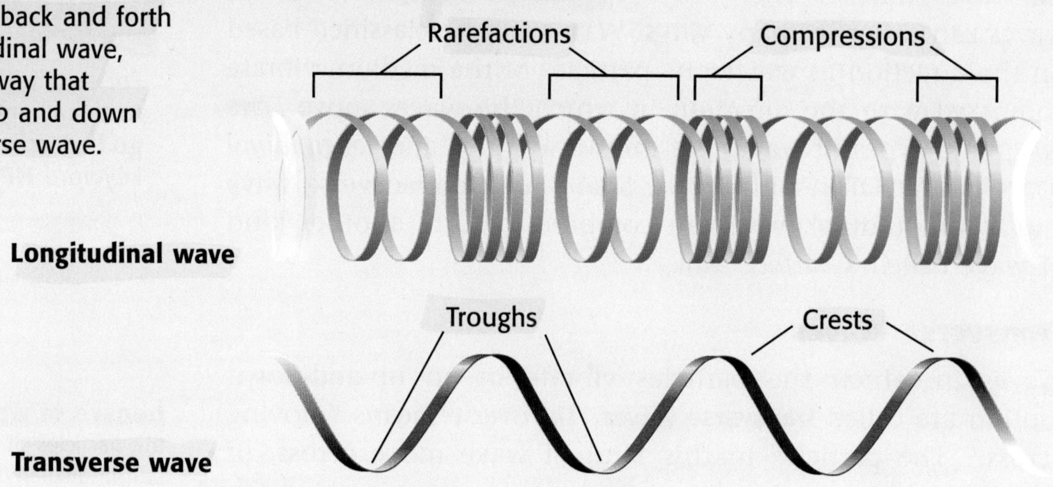

Longitudinal Waves

longitudinal wave a wave in which the particles of the medium vibrate parallel to the direction of wave motion

In a **longitudinal wave,** the particles of the medium vibrate back and forth along the path that the wave moves. You can make a longitudinal wave on a spring. When you push on the end of the spring, the coils of the spring crowd together. A part of a longitudinal wave where the particles are crowded together is called a *compression.* When you pull back on the end of the spring, the coils are pulled apart. A part where the particles are spread apart is a *rarefaction* (RER uh FAK shuhn). Compressions and rarefactions are like the crests and troughs of a transverse wave, as shown in **Figure 6.**

Sound Waves

A sound wave is an example of a longitudinal wave. Sound waves travel by compressions and rarefactions of air particles. **Figure 7** shows how a vibrating drum forms compressions and rarefactions in the air around it.

Reading Check What kind of wave is a sound wave?

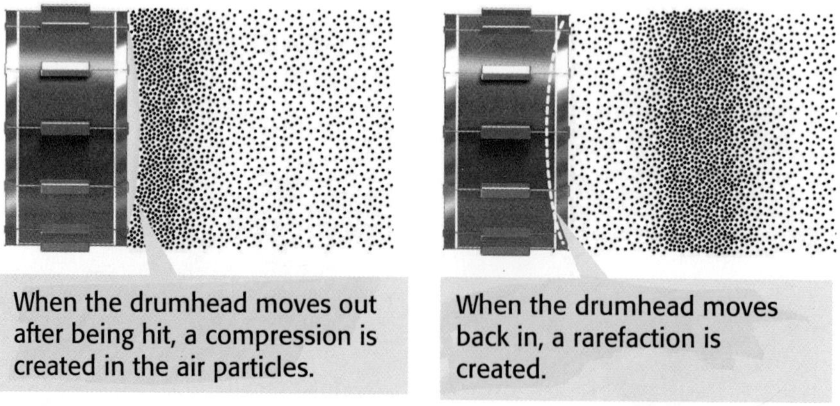

When the drumhead moves out after being hit, a compression is created in the air particles.

When the drumhead moves back in, a rarefaction is created.

Figure 7 *Sound energy is carried away from a drum by a longitudinal wave through the air.*

Combinations of Waves

When waves form at or near the boundary between two media, a transverse wave and a longitudinal wave can combine to form a *surface wave*. An example is shown in **Figure 8.** Surface waves look like transverse waves, but the particles of the medium in a surface wave move in circles rather than up and down. The particles move forward at the crest of each wave and move backward at the trough.

Figure 8 *Ocean waves are surface waves. A floating bottle shows the circular motion of particles in a surface wave.*

SECTION Review

Summary

- A wave is a disturbance that transmits energy.
- The particles of a medium do not travel with the wave.
- Mechanical waves require a medium, but electromagnetic waves do not.
- Particles in a transverse wave vibrate perpendicularly to the direction the wave travels.
- Particles in a longitudinal wave vibrate parallel to the direction that the wave travels.

Using Key Terms

Complete each of the following sentences by choosing the correct term from the word bank.

~~transverse wave~~	~~wave~~
~~longitudinal wave~~	medium

1. In a ___, the particles vibrate parallel to the direction that the wave travels. Longitudinal wave
2. Mechanical waves require a ___ through which to travel. Medium
3. Any ___ transmits energy through vibrations. wave
4. In a ___, the particles vibrate perpendicularly to the direction that the wave travels. transverse wave

Understanding Key Ideas

5. Waves transfer
   a. matter. c. particles.
   (b.) energy. d. water.
6. Name a kind of wave that does not require a medium. Visible light waves.

Critical Thinking

7. **Applying Concepts** Sometimes, people at a sports event do "the wave." Is this a real example of a wave? Why or why not?
   No, because no energy is transmitted.
8. **Making Inferences** Why can supernova explosions in space be seen but not heard on Earth?
   Because light waves don't require a medium while sound waves require a medium.

Interpreting Graphics

9. Look at the figure below. Which part of the wave is the crest? Which part of the wave is the trough?

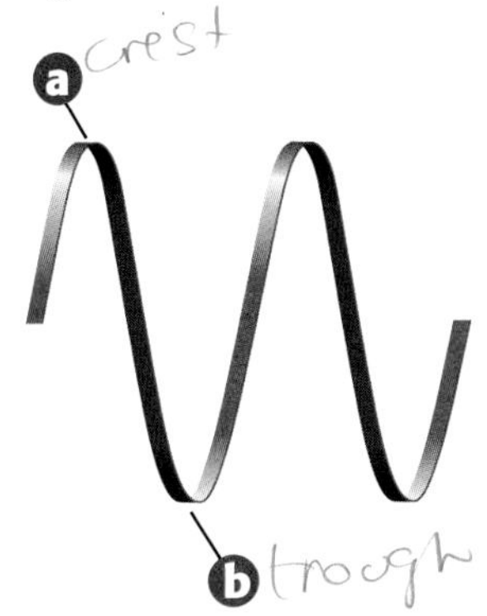

SECTION 2

Properties of Waves

What You Will Learn

- Identify and describe four wave properties.
- Explain how frequency and wavelength are related to the speed of a wave.

Vocabulary

amplitude
frequency
wavelength
wave speed

READING STRATEGY

Mnemonics As you read this section, create a mnemonic device to help you remember the wave equation.

You are in a swimming pool, floating on your air mattress, enjoying a gentle breeze. Your friend does a "cannonball" from the high dive nearby. Suddenly, your mattress is rocking wildly on the waves generated by the huge splash.

The breeze generates waves in the water as well, but they are very different from the waves created by your diving friend. The waves made by the breeze are shallow and close together, while the waves from your friend's splash are tall and widely spaced. Properties of waves, such as the height of the waves and the distance between crests, are useful for comparing and describing waves.

Amplitude

If you tie one end of a rope to the back of a chair, you can create waves by moving the free end up and down. If you shake the rope a little, you will make a shallow wave. If you shake the rope hard, you will make a tall wave.

The **amplitude** of a wave is related to its height. A wave's amplitude is the maximum distance that the particles of a medium vibrate from their rest position. The rest position is the point where the particles of a medium stay when there are no disturbances. The larger the amplitude is, the taller the wave is. **Figure 1** shows how the amplitude of a transverse wave may be measured.

amplitude the maximum distance that the particles of a wave's medium vibrate from their rest position

Larger Amplitude—More Energy

When using a rope to make waves, you have to work harder to create a wave with a large amplitude than to create one with a small amplitude. The reason is that it takes more energy to move the rope farther from its rest position. Therefore, a wave with a large amplitude carries more energy than a wave with a small amplitude does.

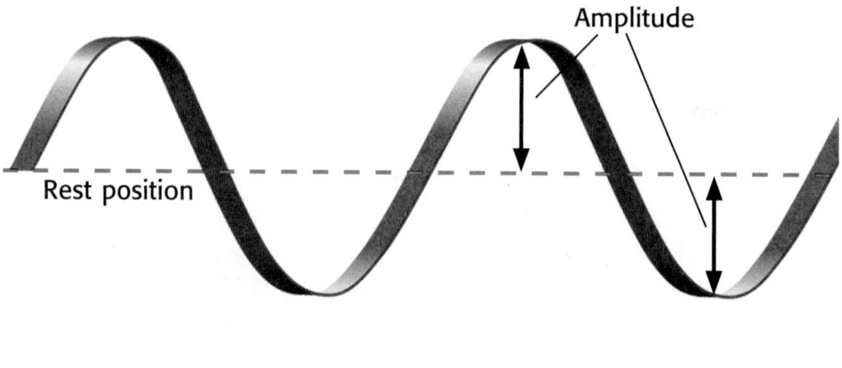

Figure 1 *The amplitude of a transverse wave is measured from the rest position to the crest or to the trough of the wave.*

Wavelength

Another property of waves is wavelength. A **wavelength** is the distance between any two crests or compressions next to each other in a wave. The distance between two troughs or rarefactions next to each other is also a wavelength. In fact, the wavelength can be measured from any point on a wave to the next corresponding point on the wave. Wavelength is measured the same way in both a longitudinal wave and a transverse wave, as shown in **Figure 2.**

wavelength the distance from any point on a wave to an identical point on the next wave

Shorter Wavelength—More Energy

If you are making waves on either a spring or a rope, the rate at which you shake it will determine whether the wavelength is short or long. If you shake it rapidly back and forth, the wavelength will be shorter. If you are shaking it rapidly, you are putting more energy into it than if you were shaking it more slowly. So, a wave with a shorter wavelength carries more energy than a wave with a longer wavelength does.

Reading Check **How does shaking a rope at different rates affect the wavelength of the wave that moves through the rope?** *(See the Appendix for answers to Reading Checks.)*

Quick Lab

Springy Waves

1. Hold a coiled **spring toy** on the floor between you and a classmate so that the spring is straight. This is the rest position.
2. Move one end of the spring back and forth at a constant rate. Note the wavelength of the wave you create.
3. Increase the amplitude of the waves. What did you have to do? How did the change in amplitude affect the wavelength?
4. Now, shake the spring back and forth about twice as fast as you did before. What happens to the wavelength? Record your observations.

Figure 2 **Measuring Wavelengths**

Wavelength can be measured from any two corresponding points that are adjacent on a wave.

Longitudinal wave

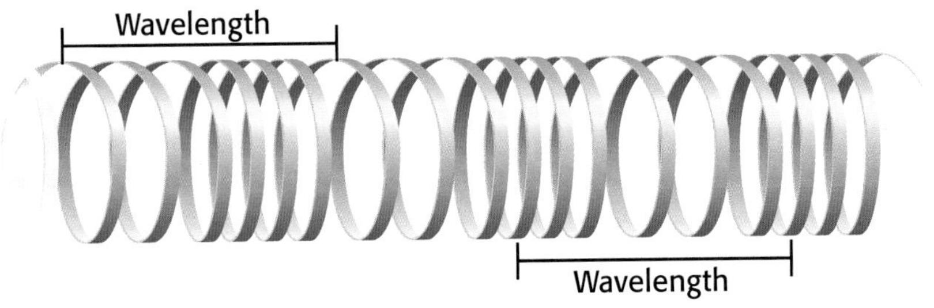

Transverse wave

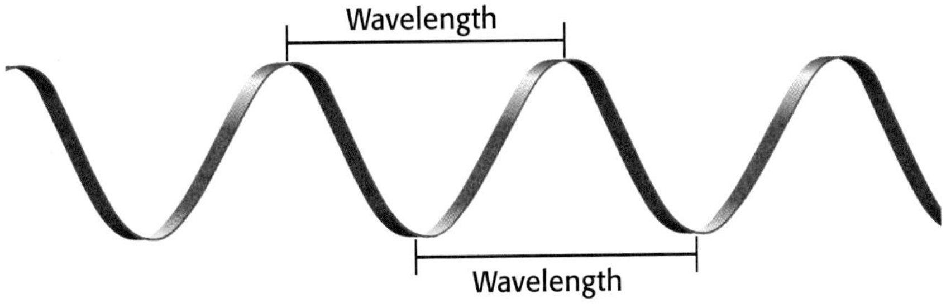

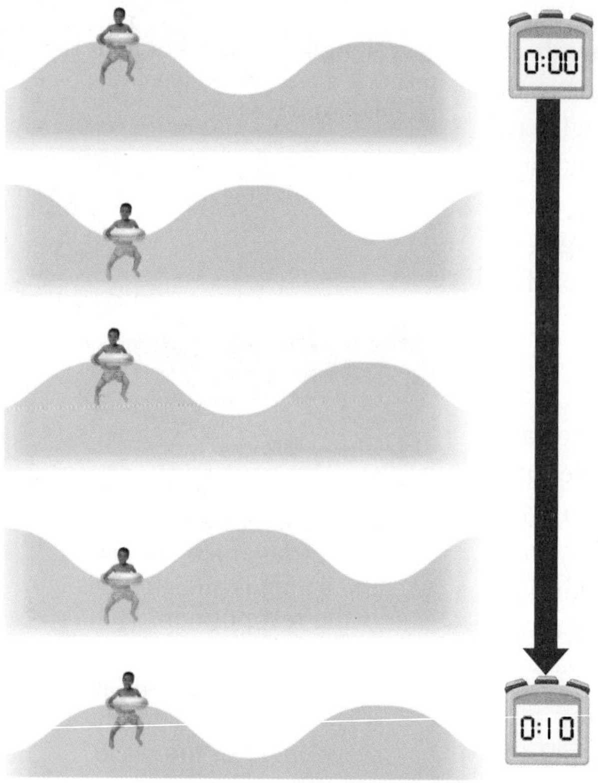

Figure 3 *Frequency can be measured by counting how many waves pass by in a certain amount of time. Here, two waves went by in 10 s, so the frequency is 2/10 s = 0.2 Hz.*

Frequency

Think about making rope waves again. The number of waves that you can make in 1 s depends on how quickly you move the rope. If you move the rope slowly, you make only a small number of waves each second. If you move it quickly, you make a large number of waves. The number of waves produced in a given amount of time is the **frequency** of the wave. Frequency is usually expressed in *hertz* (Hz). For waves, one hertz equals one wave per second (1 Hz = 1/s). **Figure 3** shows a wave with a frequency of 0.2 Hz.

Reading Check **If you make three rope waves per second, what is the frequency of the wave?** 3 Hz

Higher Frequency—More Energy

To make high-frequency waves in a rope, you must shake the rope quickly back and forth. To shake a rope quickly takes more energy than to shake it slowly. Therefore, if the amplitudes are equal, high-frequency waves carry more energy than low-frequency waves.

Wave Speed

Wave speed is the speed at which a wave travels. Wave speed (v) can be calculated using wavelength (λ, the Greek letter *lambda*) and frequency (f), by using the *wave equation*, which is shown below:

$$v = \lambda \times f$$

MATH FOCUS

Wave Calculations Determine the wave speed of a wave that has a wavelength of 5 m and a frequency of 4 Hz.

Step 1: Write the equation for wave speed.

$$v = \lambda \times f$$

Step 2: Replace the λ and f with the values given in the problem, and solve.

$$v = 5 \text{ m} \times 4 \text{ Hz} = 20 \text{ m/s}$$

The equation for wave speed can also be rearranged to determine wavelength or frequency, as shown at top right.

$$\lambda = \frac{v}{f} \text{ (Rearranged by dividing by } f\text{.)}$$

$$f = \frac{v}{\lambda} \text{ (Rearranged by dividing by } \lambda\text{.)}$$

Now It's Your Turn

1. What is the frequency of a wave if the wave has a speed of 12 cm/s and a wavelength of 3 cm?
2. A wave has a frequency of 5 Hz and a wave speed of 18 m/s. What is its wavelength?

Frequency and Wavelength Relationship

Three of the basic properties of a wave are related to one another in the wave equation—wave speed, frequency, and wavelength. If you know any two of these properties of a wave, you can use the wave equation to find the third.

One of the things the wave equation tells you is the relationship between frequency and wavelength. If a wave is traveling a certain speed and you double its frequency, its wavelength will be cut in half. Or if you were to cut its frequency in half, the wavelength would be double what it was before. So, you can say that frequency and wavelength are *inversely* related. Think of a sound wave, traveling underwater at 1,440 m/s, given off by the sonar of a submarine like the one shown in **Figure 4.** If the sound wave has a frequency of 360 Hz, it will have a wavelength of 4.0 m. If the sound wave has twice that frequency, the wavelength will be 2.0 m, half as big.

The wave speed of a wave in a certain medium is the same no matter what the wavelength is. So, the wavelength and frequency of a wave depend on the wave speed, not the other way around.

Figure 4 *Submarines use sonar, sound waves in water, to locate underwater objects.*

frequency the number of waves produced in a given amount of time

wave speed the speed at which a wave travels through a medium

SECTION Review

Summary

- Amplitude is the maximum distance the particles of a medium vibrate from their rest position.
- Wavelength is the distance between two adjacent corresponding parts of a wave.
- Frequency is the number of waves that pass a given point in a given amount of time.
- Wave speed can be calculated by multiplying the wave's wavelength by the frequency.

Using Key Terms

1. In your own words, write a definition for each of the following terms: *amplitude, frequency,* and *wavelength.*

Understanding Key Ideas

2. Which of the following results in more energy in a wave?
   - **a.** a smaller wavelength
   - **b.** a lower frequency
   - **c.** a shallower amplitude
   - **d.** a lower speed
3. Draw a transverse wave, and label how the amplitude and wavelength are measured.

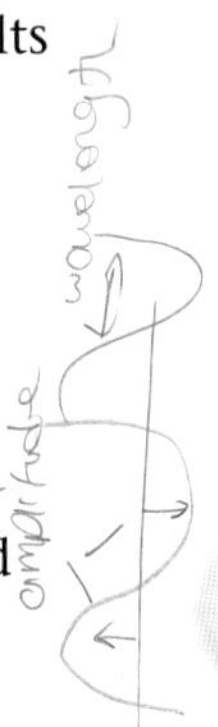

Math Skills

4. What is the speed (v) of a wave that has a wavelength (λ) of 2 m and a frequency (f) of 6 Hz?

   V = λ x f
   = 2 x 6
   = 12 m/s

Critical Thinking

5. **Making Inferences** A wave has a low speed but a high frequency. What can you infer about its wavelength? The wavelength is short.
6. **Analyzing Processes** Two friends blow two whistles at the same time. The first whistle makes a sound whose frequency is twice that of the sound made by the other whistle. Which sound will reach you first? The less frequent whistle will reach you faster

SCILINKS. NSTA Developed and maintained by the National Science Teachers Association

For a variety of links related to this chapter, go to www.scilinks.org

Topic: Properties of Waves
SciLinks code: HSM1236

SECTION 3

Wave Interactions

What You Will Learn

- Describe reflection, refraction, diffraction, and interference.
- Compare destructive interference with constructive interference.
- Describe resonance, and give examples.

Vocabulary

reflection	interference
refraction	standing wave
diffraction	resonance

READING STRATEGY

Reading Organizer As you read this section, make a concept map by using the terms above.

If you've ever seen a planet in the night sky, you may have had a hard time telling it apart from a star. Both planets and stars shine brightly, but the light waves that you see are from very different sources.

All stars, including the sun, produce light. But planets do not produce light. So, why do planets shine so brightly? The planets and the moon shine because light from the sun *reflects* off them. Without reflection, you would not be able to see the planets. Reflection is one of the wave interactions that you will learn about in this section.

Reflection

Reflection happens when a wave bounces back after hitting a barrier. All waves—including water, sound, and light waves—can be reflected. The reflection of water waves is shown in **Figure 1.** Light waves reflecting off an object allow you to see that object. For example, light waves from the sun are reflected when they strike the surface of the moon. These reflected waves allow us to enjoy moonlit nights. A reflected sound wave is called an *echo*.

Waves are not always reflected when they hit a barrier. If all light waves were reflected when they hit your eyeglasses, you would not be able to see anything! A wave is *transmitted* through a substance when it passes through the substance.

reflection the bouncing back of a ray of light, sound, or heat when the ray hits a surface that it does not go through

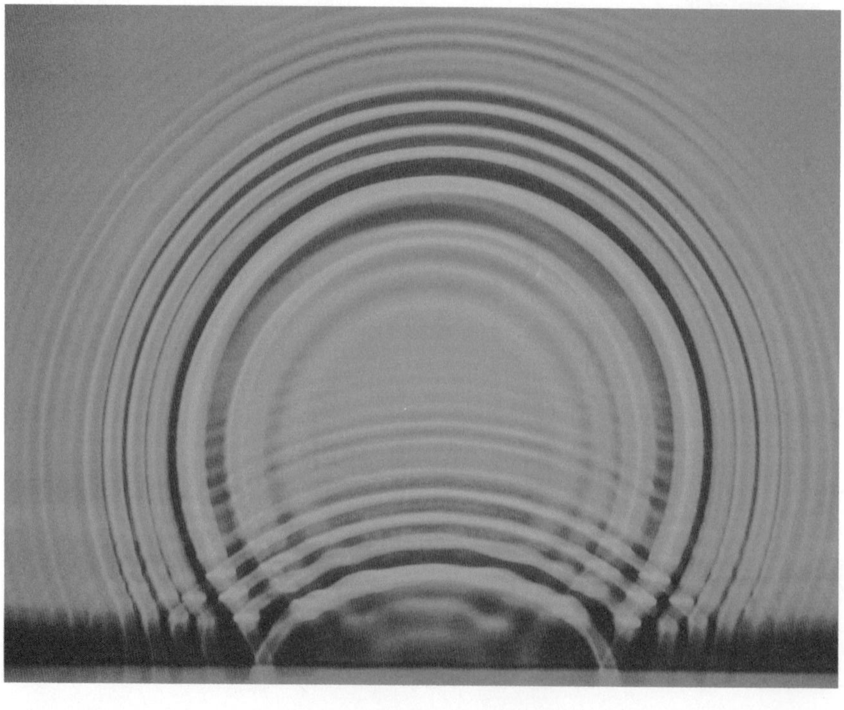

Figure 1 *These water waves are reflecting off the side of the container.*

Figure 2 *A light wave passing at an angle into a new medium—such as water—is refracted because the speed of the wave changes.*

Refraction

Try this simple activity: Place a pencil in a half-filled glass of water. Now, look at the pencil from the side. The pencil appears to be broken into two pieces! But as you can see when you take the pencil out of the water, it is still in one piece.

What you saw in this experiment was the result of the *refraction* of light waves. **Refraction** is the bending of a wave as the wave passes from one medium to another at an angle. Refraction of a flashlight beam as the beam passes from air to water is shown in **Figure 2.**

refraction the bending of a wave as the wave passes between two substances in which the speed of the wave differs

When a wave moves from one medium to another, the wave's speed changes. When a wave enters a new medium, the wave changes wavelength as well as speed. As a result, the wave bends and travels in a new direction.

Reading Check **What happens to a wave when it moves from one medium to another at an angle?** (*See the Appendix for answers to Reading Checks.*)

Refraction of Different Colors

When light waves from the sun pass through a droplet of water in a cloud or through a prism, the light is refracted. But the different colors in sunlight are refracted by different amounts, so the light is *dispersed,* or spread out, into its separate colors. When sunlight is refracted this way through water droplets, you can see a rainbow. Why does that happen?

Although all light waves travel at the same speed through empty space, when light passes through a medium such as water or glass, the speed of the light wave depends on the wavelength of the light wave. Because the different colors of light have different wavelengths, their speeds are different, and they are refracted by different amounts. As a result, the colors are spread out, so you can see them individually.

CONNECTION TO Language Arts

WRITING SKILL **The Colors of the Rainbow** People have always been fascinated by the beautiful array of colors that results when sunlight strikes water droplets in the air to form a rainbow. The knowledge science gives us about how they form makes them no less breathtaking.

In the library, find a poem that you like about rainbows. In your **science journal,** copy the poem, and write a paragraph in which you discuss how your knowledge of refraction affects your opinion about the poem.

Figure 3 Diffraction Through an Opening

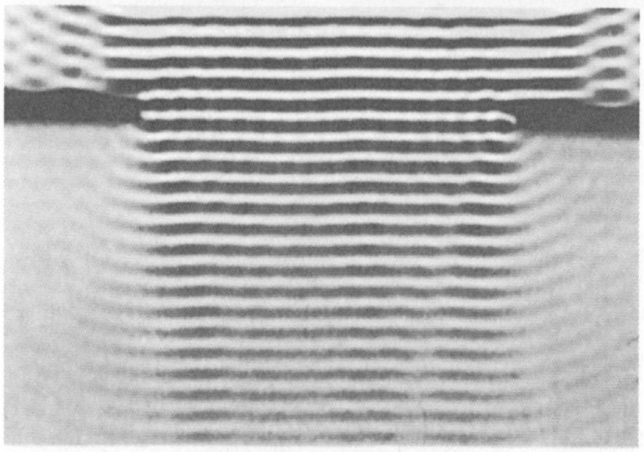

If the barrier or opening is larger than the wave-length of the wave, there is only a small amount of diffraction.

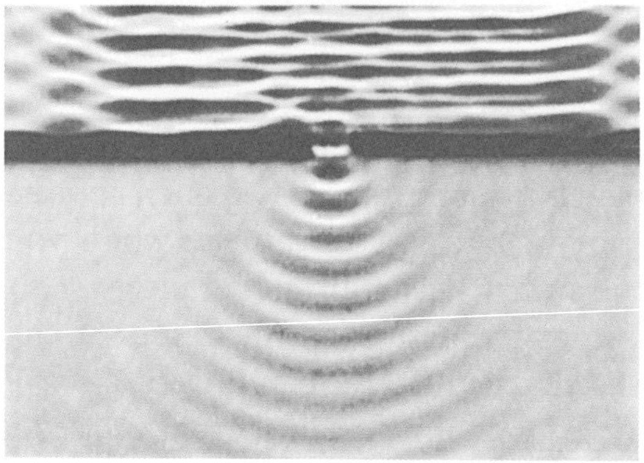

If the barrier or opening is the same size or smaller than the wavelength of an approaching wave, the amount of diffraction is large.

SCHOOL to HOME

What if Light Diffracted?

With an adult, take a walk around your neighborhood. Light waves diffract around corners of buildings much less than sound waves do. Imagine what would happen if light waves diffracted around corners much more than sound waves did. Write a paragraph in your **science journal** describing how this would change what you see and hear as you walk around your neighborhood.

ACTIVITY

Diffraction

Suppose you are walking down a city street and you hear music. The sound seems to be coming from around the corner, but you cannot see where the music is coming from because a building on the corner blocks your view. Why do sound waves travel around a corner better than light waves do?

Most of the time, waves travel in straight lines. For example, a beam of light from a flashlight is fairly straight. But in some circumstances, waves curve or bend when they reach the edge of an object. The bending of waves around a barrier or through an opening is known as **diffraction.**

If You Can Hear It, Why Can't You See It?

The amount of diffraction of a wave depends on its wavelength and the size of the barrier or opening the wave encounters, as shown in **Figure 3.** You can hear music around the corner of a building because sound waves have long wavelengths and are able to diffract around corners. However, you cannot see who is playing the music because the wavelengths of light waves are much shorter than sound waves, so light is not diffracted very much.

diffraction a change in the direction of a wave when the wave finds an obstacle or an edge, such as an opening

Interference

You know that all matter has volume. Therefore, objects cannot be in the same space at the same time. But waves are energy, not matter. So, more than one wave can be in the same place at the same time. In fact, two waves can meet, share the same space, and pass through each other! When two or more waves share the same space, they overlap. The result of two or more waves overlapping is called **interference. Figure 4** shows what happens when waves occupy the same space and interfere with each other.

interference the combination of two or more waves that results in a single wave

Constructive Interference

Constructive interference happens when the crests of one wave overlap the crests of another wave or waves. The troughs of the waves also overlap. When waves combine in this way, the energy carried by the waves is also able to combine. The result is a new wave that has higher crests and deeper troughs than the original waves had. In other words, the resulting wave has a larger amplitude than the original waves had.

Reading Check How does constructive interference happen?

Figure 4 **Constructive and Destructive Interference**

Constructive Interference When waves combine by constructive interference, the combined wave has a larger amplitude.

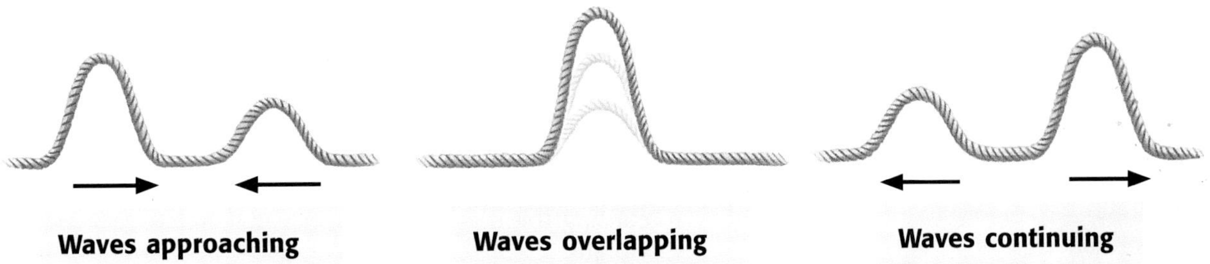

Destructive Interference When two waves with the same amplitude combine by destructive interference, they cancel each other out.

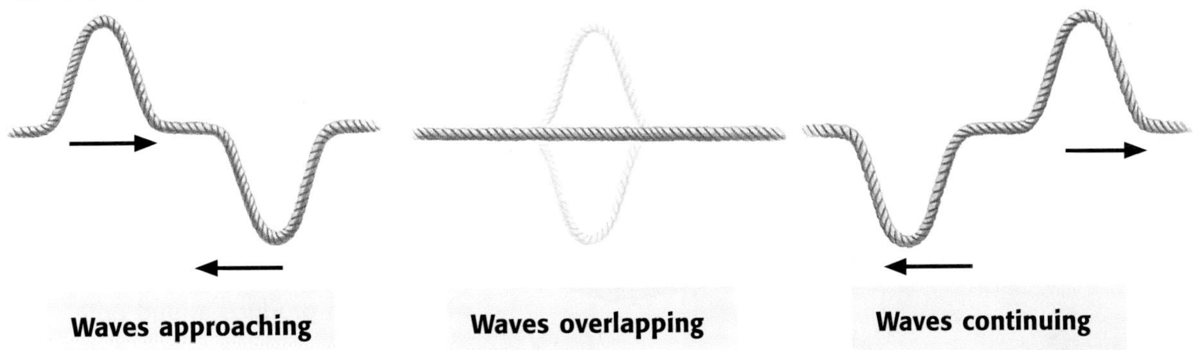

Destructive Interference

Destructive interference happens when the crests of one wave and the troughs of another wave overlap. The new wave has a smaller amplitude than the original waves had. When the waves involved in destructive interference have the same amplitude and meet each other at just the right time, the result is no wave at all.

Standing Waves

If you tie one end of a rope to the back of a chair and move the other end up and down, the waves you make go down the rope and are reflected back. If you move the rope at certain frequencies, the rope appears to vibrate in loops, as shown in **Figure 5.** The loops come from the interference between the wave you made and the reflected wave. The resulting wave is called a **standing wave.** In a standing wave, certain parts of the wave are always at the rest position because of total destructive interference between all the waves. Other parts have a large amplitude because of constructive interference.

A standing wave only *looks* as if it is standing still. Waves are actually going in both directions. Standing waves can be formed with transverse waves, such as when a musician plucks a guitar string, as well as with longitudinal waves.

Reading Check How can interference and reflection cause standing waves?

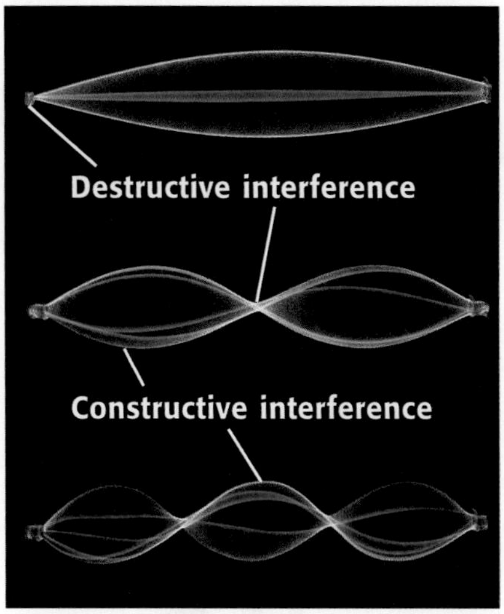

Figure 5 *When you move a rope at certain frequencies, you can create different standing waves.*

Figure 6 *A marimba produces notes through the resonance of air columns.*

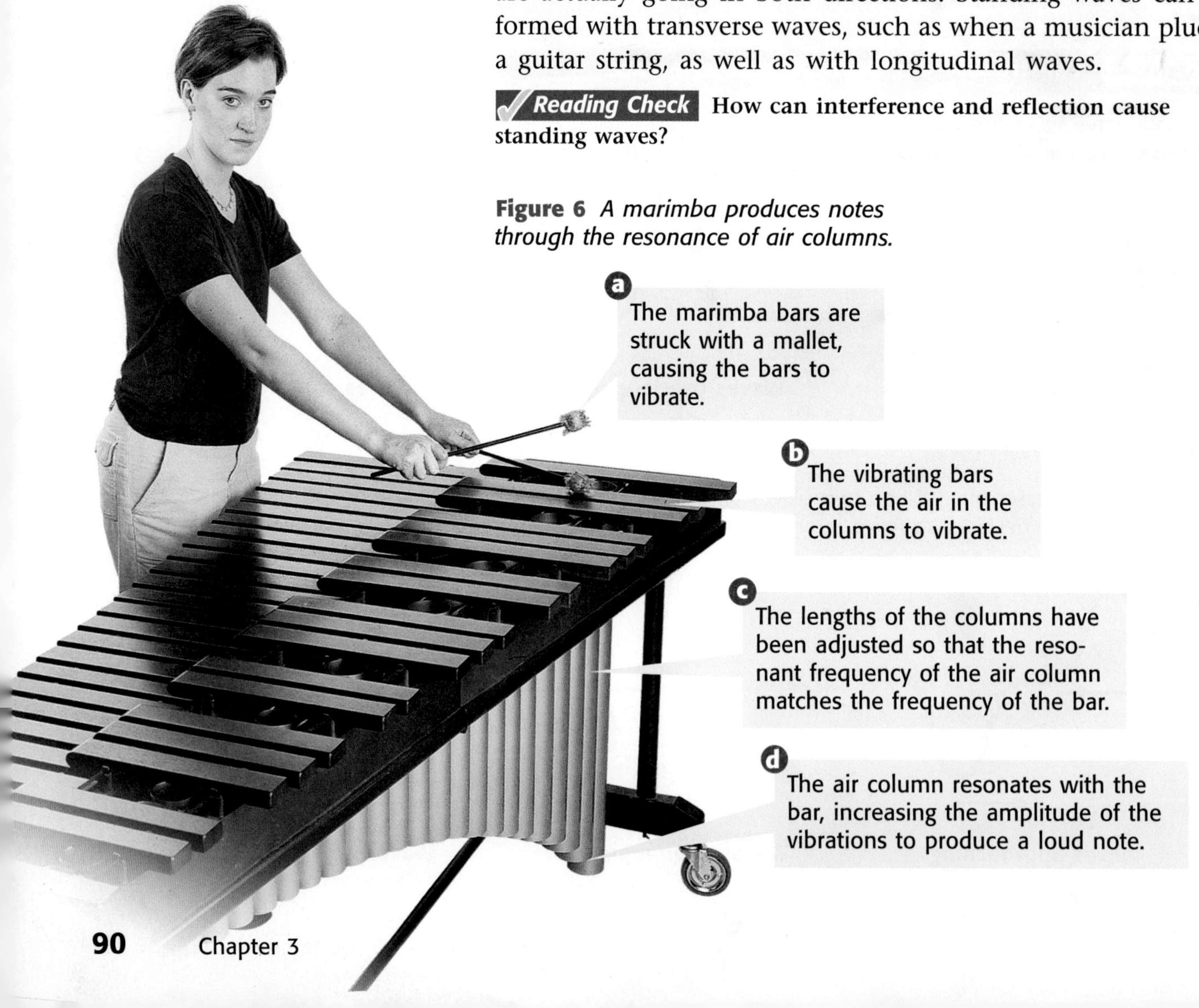

a
The marimba bars are struck with a mallet, causing the bars to vibrate.
b
The vibrating bars cause the air in the columns to vibrate.
c
The lengths of the columns have been adjusted so that the resonant frequency of the air column matches the frequency of the bar.
d
The air column resonates with the bar, increasing the amplitude of the vibrations to produce a loud note.

Resonance

The frequencies at which standing waves are made are called *resonant frequencies*. When an object vibrating at or near the resonant frequency of a second object causes the second object to vibrate, **resonance** occurs. A resonating object absorbs energy from the vibrating object and vibrates, too. An example of resonance is shown in **Figure 6** on the previous page.

You may be familiar with another example of resonance at home—in your shower. When you sing in the shower, certain frequencies create standing waves in the air that fills the shower stall. The air resonates in much the same way that the air column in a marimba does. The amplitude of the sound waves becomes greater. So your voice sounds much louder.

standing wave a pattern of vibration that simulates a wave that is standing still

resonance a phenomenon that occurs when two objects naturally vibrate at the same frequency; the sound produced by one object causes the other object to vibrate

SECTION Review

Summary

- Waves reflect after hitting a barrier.
- Refraction is the bending of a wave when it passes through different media.
- Waves bend around barriers or through openings during diffraction.
- The result of two or more waves overlapping is called interference.
- Amplitude increases during constructive interference and decreases during destructive interference.
- Resonance occurs when a vibrating object causes another object to vibrate at one of its resonant frequencies.

Using Key Terms

Complete each of the following sentences by choosing the correct term from the word bank.

a refraction c reflection
b diffraction d interference

1. _a_ happens when a wave passes from one medium to another at an angle.
2. The bending of a wave around a barrier is called _b_.
3. We can see the moon because of the _c_ of sunlight off it.

Understanding Key Ideas

4. The combining of waves as they overlap is known as
   a. interference.
   b. diffraction.
   c. refraction.
   d. resonance.
5. Name two wave interactions that can occur when a wave encounters a barrier.
6. Explain why you can hear two people talking even after they walk around a corner. diffraction
7. Explain what happens when two waves encounter one another in destructive interference.

Critical Thinking

8. **Making Inferences** Sometimes, when music is played loudly, you can feel your body shake. Explain what is happening in terms of resonance.
9. **Applying Concepts** How could two waves on a rope interfere so that the rope did not move at all?

Interpreting Graphics

10. In the image below, what sort of wave interaction is happening?

constructive

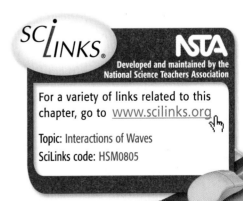

SCILINKS. NSTA Developed and maintained by the National Science Teachers Association

For a variety of links related to this chapter, go to www.scilinks.org

Topic: Interactions of Waves
SciLinks code: HSM0805

Using Scientific Methods

Skills Practice Lab

OBJECTIVES

Form hypotheses about the energy and speed of waves.

Test your hypotheses by performing an experiment.

MATERIALS

- beaker, small
- newspaper
- pan, shallow, approximately 20 cm × 30 cm
- pencils (2)
- stopwatch
- water

SAFETY

Wave Energy and Speed

If you threw a rock into a pond, waves would carry energy away from the point of origin. But if you threw a large rock into a pond, would the waves carry more energy away from the point of origin than waves caused by a small rock? And would a large rock make waves that move faster than waves made by a small rock? In this lab, you'll answer these questions.

Ask a Question

1. In this lab, you will answer the following questions: Do waves made by a large disturbance carry more energy than waves made by a small disturbance? Do waves created by a large disturbance travel faster than waves created by a small disturbance?

Form a Hypothesis

2. Write a few sentences that answer the questions above.

Test the Hypothesis

3. Place the pan on a few sheets of newspaper. Using the small beaker, fill the pan with water.
4. Make sure that the water is still. Tap the surface of the water with the eraser end of one pencil. This tap represents the small disturbance. Record your observations about the size of the waves that are made and the path they take.

5. Repeat step 4. This time, use the stopwatch to record the amount of time it takes for one of the waves to reach the side of the pan. Record your data.

6. Using two pencils at once, repeat steps 4 and 5. These taps represent the large disturbance. (Try to use the same amount of force to tap the water that you used with just one pencil.) Observe and record your results.

Analyze the Results

1. **Describing Events** Compare the appearance of the waves created by one pencil with that of the waves created by two pencils. Were there any differences in amplitude (wave height)?

2. **Describing Events** Compare the amount of time required for the waves to reach the side of the pan. Did the waves travel faster when two pencils were used?

Draw Conclusions

3. **Drawing Conclusions** Do waves made by a large disturbance carry more energy than waves made by a small one? Explain your answer, using your results to support your answer. (Hint: Remember the relationship between amplitude and energy.)

4. **Drawing Conclusions** Do waves made by a large disturbance travel faster than waves made by a small one? Explain your answer.

Applying Your Data

A tsunami is a giant ocean wave that can reach a height of 30 m. Tsunamis that reach land can cause injury and enormous property damage. Using what you learned in this lab about wave energy and speed, explain why tsunamis are so dangerous. How do you think scientists can predict when tsunamis will reach land?

Chapter Review

USING KEY TERMS

For each pair of terms, explain how the meanings of the terms differ.

1. *longitudinal wave* and *transverse wave*
2. *wavelength* and *amplitude*
3. *reflection* and *refraction*

UNDERSTANDING KEY IDEAS

Multiple Choice

4. As the wavelength increases, the frequency
   - **a.** decreases.
   - **b.** increases.
   - **c.** remains the same.
   - **d.** increases and then decreases.

5. Waves transfer
   - **a.** matter.
   - **b.** energy.
   - **c.** particles.
   - **d.** water.

6. Refraction occurs when a wave enters a new medium at an angle because
   - **a.** the frequency changes.
   - **b.** the amplitude changes.
   - **c.** the wave speed changes.
   - **d.** None of the above

7. The wave property that is related to the height of a wave is the
   - **a.** wavelength.
   - **b.** amplitude.
   - **c.** frequency.
   - **d.** wave speed.

8. During constructive interference,
   - **a.** the amplitude increases.
   - **b.** the frequency decreases.
   - **c.** the wave speed increases.
   - **d.** All of the above

9. Waves that don't require a medium are
   - **a.** longitudinal waves.
   - **b.** electromagnetic waves.
   - **c.** surface waves.
   - **d.** mechanical waves.

Short Answer

10. Draw a transverse wave and a longitudinal wave. Label a crest, a trough, a compression, a rarefaction, and wavelengths. Also, label the amplitude on the transverse wave.

11. What is the relationship between frequency, wave speed, and wavelength?

Math Skills

12. A fisherman in a row boat notices that one wave crest passes his fishing line every 5 s. He estimates the distance between the crests to be 1.5 m and estimates that the crests of the waves are 0.5 m above the troughs. Using this data, determine the amplitude and speed of the waves.

CRITICAL THINKING

13 **Concept Mapping** Use the following terms to create a concept map: *wave, refraction, transverse wave, longitudinal wave, wavelength, wave speed,* and *diffraction.*

14 **Analyzing Ideas** You have lost the paddles for the canoe you rented, and the canoe has drifted to the center of a pond. You need to get it back to the shore, but you do not want to get wet by swimming in the pond. Your friend suggests that you drop rocks behind the canoe to create waves that will push the canoe toward the shore. Will this solution work? Why or why not?

15 **Applying Concepts** Some opera singers can use their powerful voices to break crystal glasses. To do this, they sing one note very loudly and hold it for a long time. While the opera singer holds the note, the walls of the glass move back and forth until the glass shatters. Explain in terms of resonance how the glass shatters.

16 **Analyzing Processes** After setting up stereo speakers in your school's music room, you notice that in certain areas of the room, the sound from the speakers is very loud. In other areas, the sound is very soft. Using the concept of interference, explain why the sound levels in the music room vary.

17 **Predicting Consequences** A certain sound wave travels through water with a certain wavelength, frequency, and wave speed. A second sound wave with twice the frequency of the first wave then travels through the same water. What is the second wave's wavelength and wave speed compared to those of the first wave?

INTERPRETING GRAPHICS

18 Look at the waves below. Rank the waves from highest energy to lowest energy, and explain your reasoning.

a.

b.
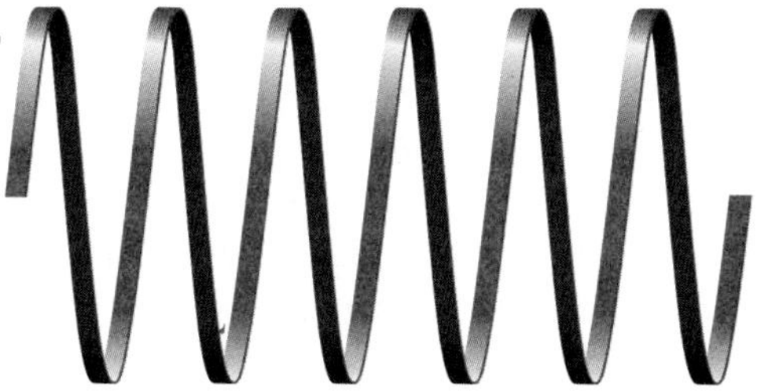

c.

Standardized Test Preparation

Multiple Choice

1. Some ocean waves are measured as traveling 45 kilometers (km) in one hour. In two minutes, 15 of these waves pass an observer on an island. What is the wavelength of these waves, in meters? (wavelength = wave speed ÷ wave frequency)

A. 1.67 m

B. 50 m

C. 100 m

D. 360 m

2. For a laboratory experiment, Antonia wanted to measure the amplitude of a transverse wave she had created using a rope. Which of the following distances should be measured?

A. the distance from one crest to the next

B. the distance from the highest to the lowest points on the wave

C. the distance from one trough to the next

D. the distance from the rest position of the wave to its highest point

3. Scott is removing laundry from a slack clothesline. He generates a wave in the clothesline that causes a shirt in the middle to bob up and down. Scott wants to move the shirt to the end of the clothesline using the wave. Why can't he do this?

A. He has generated a longitudinal wave.

B. Waves carry energy, not matter.

C. He has generated a circular wave.

D. Waves cannot be used to do work.

4. Jeff and Lyle were fishing in the ocean. Jeff bet Lyle that the ocean waves moving quickly by the floating boat would not carry away a piece of bread that Jeff threw into the water. Which of the following is a valid explanation for this claim?

A. Ocean waves are surface waves, which move the particles of their medium in circles.

B. Ocean waves are longitudinal waves, which move the particles of their medium back and forth.

C. Ocean waves are combination waves, which can move particles along the ocean surface.

D. Ocean waves are transverse waves, which move the particles of their medium up and down.

5. The amount of energy a wave carries depends partly on the wave's amplitude and wavelength. Which of the following waves would carry the most energy?

A. 

B. 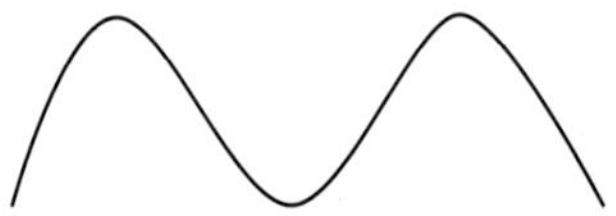

C. 

D. 

6. **All the instruments in a band are playing at the same volume. Which instrument produces sound waves that carry the most energy?**

   A. tuba

   B. trumpet

   C. drum

   D. flute

7. **Which of the following things would work well in space?**

   A. sonar

   B. flashlight

   C. drum set

   D. radio receiver

8. **Joey performed a laboratory experiment about wave movement. He and a partner each held the end of a rope and generated a wave crest at the same time. The two crests overlapped in the middle of the rope. Which of the following is a valid observation?**

   A. When the waves met, the amplitude of the new waves was smaller than the amplitude of the original waves.

   B. When the waves met, the amplitude of the new waves was the same as the amplitude of the original waves.

   C. When the waves met, the amplitude of the new waves was larger than the amplitude of the original waves.

   D. When the waves met, they cancelled each other out and the rope became straight in the middle.

Use the table below to answer question 9.

Sound Waves in Water	
Time (s)	Distance traveled (km)
1	1.5
2	3.0
3	4.5
4	?

9. **How far would the sound travel in 4 seconds?**

   A. 5.0 km

   B. 5.5 km

   C. 6.0 km

   D. 6.5 km

10. **Which of the following concerns diffraction?**

    A. Light waves bend as they pass around the edge of a wooden block.

    B. Light waves bend as they move from air to water.

    C. Light waves can disperse into different colors when passed through a prism.

    D. Light waves bounce off objects.

Open Response

11. **Why are string instruments, such as violins and cellos, hollow with a hole below the strings?**

12. **Why does a rainbow of colors appear after white light passes through a glass prism?**

Science in Action

Science, Technology, and Society

The Ultimate Telescope

The largest telescopes in the world don't depend on visible light, lenses, or mirrors. Instead, they collect radio waves from the far reaches of outer space. One radio telescope, called the Very Large Array (VLA), is located in a remote desert in New Mexico.

Just as you can detect light waves from stars with your eyes, radio waves emitted from objects in space can be detected with radio telescopes. The Very Large Array consists of 27 radio telescopes like the ones in the photo above.

Math ACTIVITY

Radio waves travel about 300,000,000 m/s. The M100 galaxy is about 5.68×10^{23} m away from Earth. How long, in years, does it take radio waves from M100 to be detected by the VLA?

Scientific Discoveries

The Wave Nature of Light

Have you ever wondered what light really is? Many early scientists did. One of them, the great 17th-century scientist Isaac Newton, did some experiments and decided that light consisted of particles. But when experimenting with lenses, Newton observed some things that he could not explain.

Around 1800, the scientist Thomas Young did more experiments on light and found that it diffracted when it passed through slits. Young concluded that light could be thought of as waves. Although scientists were slow to accept this idea, they now know that light is both particle-like and wavelike.

Language Arts ACTIVITY

WRITING SKILL Thomas Young said, "The nature of light is a subject of no material importance to the concerns of life or to the practice of the arts, but it is in many other respects extremely interesting." Write a brief essay in which you answer the following questions: What do you think Young meant? Do you agree with him? How would you respond to his statement?

Careers

Estela Zavala

Ultrasonographer Estela Zavala is a registered diagnostic medical ultrasonographer who works at Austin Radiological Association in Austin, Texas. Most people have seen a picture of a sonogram showing an unborn baby inside its mother's womb. Ultrasound technologists make these images with an ultrasound machine, which sends harmless, high-frequency sound waves into the body. Zavala uses ultrasound to form images of organs in the body. Zavala says about her education, "After graduating from high school, I went to an X-ray school to be licensed as an X-ray technologist. First, I went to an intensive one-month training program. After that, I worked for a licensed radiologist for about a year. Finally, I attended a year-long ultrasound program at a local community college before becoming fully licensed." What Zavala likes best about her job is being able to help people by finding out what is wrong with them without surgery. Before ultrasound, surgery was the only way to find out about the health of someone's organs.

Social Studies ACTIVITY

WRITING SKILL Research the different ways in which ultrasound technology is used in medical practice today. Write a few paragraphs about what you learn.

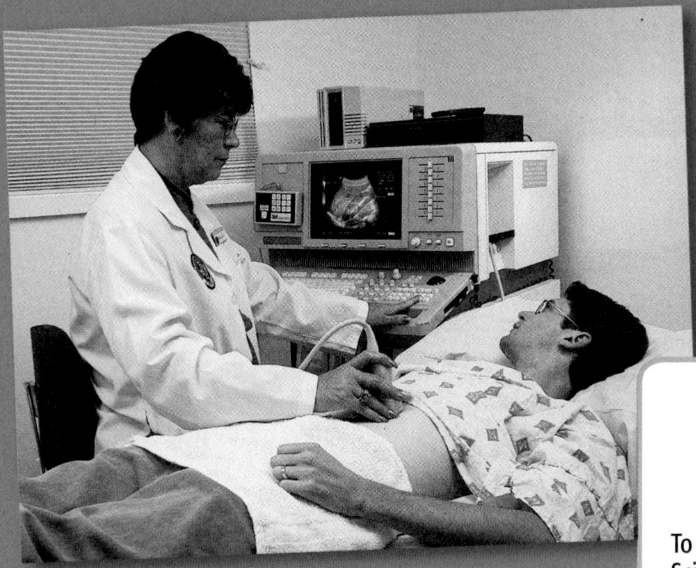

To learn more about these Science in Action topics, visit go.hrw.com and type in the keyword **HP5WAVF.**

Current Science

Check out Current Science® articles related to this chapter by visiting go.hrw.com. Just type in the keyword HP5CS20.

4

The Nature of Sound

The Big Idea

The properties and interactions of sound waves affect what one hears.

SECTION

About the Photo

Look at these dolphins swimming swiftly and silently through their watery world. Wait a minute—swiftly? Yes. Silently? No way! Dolphins use sound—clicks, squeaks, and other noises—to communicate. Dolphins also use sound to locate their food by echolocation and to find their way through murky water.

PRE-READING ACTIVITY

Graphic Organizer

Concept Map Before you read the chapter, create the graphic organizer entitled "Concept Map" described in the **Study Skills** section of the Appendix. As you read the chapter, fill in the concept map with details about each type of sound interaction.

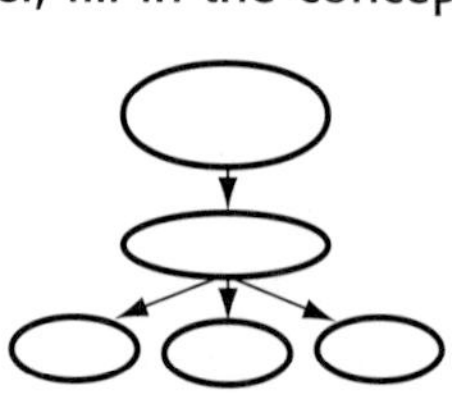

START-UP ACTIVITY

A Homemade Guitar

In this chapter, you will learn about sound. You can start by making your own guitar. It won't sound as good as a real guitar, but it will help you explore the nature of sound.

Procedure

1. Stretch a **rubber band** lengthwise around an empty **shoe box.** Place the box hollow side up. Pluck the rubber band gently. Describe what you hear.
2. Stretch **another rubber band of a different thickness** around the box. Pluck both rubber bands. Describe the differences in the sounds.
3. Put a **pencil** across the center of the box and under the rubber bands, and pluck again. Compare this sound with the sound you heard before the pencil was used.
4. Move the pencil closer to one end of the shoe box. Pluck on both sides of the pencil. Describe the differences in the sounds you hear.

Analysis

1. How did the thicknesses of the rubber bands affect the sound?
2. In steps 3 and 4, you changed the length of the vibrating part of the rubber bands. What is the relationship between the vibrating length of the rubber band and the sound that you hear?

SECTION 1

What Is Sound?

You are in a restaurant, and without warning, you hear a loud crash. A waiter dropped a tray of dishes. What a mess! But why did dropping the dishes make such a loud sound?

In this section, you'll find out what causes sound and what characteristics all sounds have in common. You'll also learn how your ears detect sound and how you can protect your hearing.

What You Will Learn

- Describe how vibrations cause sound.
- Explain how sound is transmitted through a medium.
- Explain how the human ear works, and identify its parts.
- Identify ways to protect your hearing.

Vocabulary

sound wave
medium

READING STRATEGY

Prediction Guide Before reading this section, predict whether each of the following statements is true or false:

- Sound waves are made by vibrations.
- Sound waves push air particles along until they reach your ear.

Sound and Vibrations

As different as they are, all sounds have some things in common. One characteristic of sound is that it is created by vibrations. A *vibration* is the complete back-and-forth motion of an object. **Figure 1** shows one way sound is made by vibrations.

Figure 1 **Sounds from a Stereo Speaker**

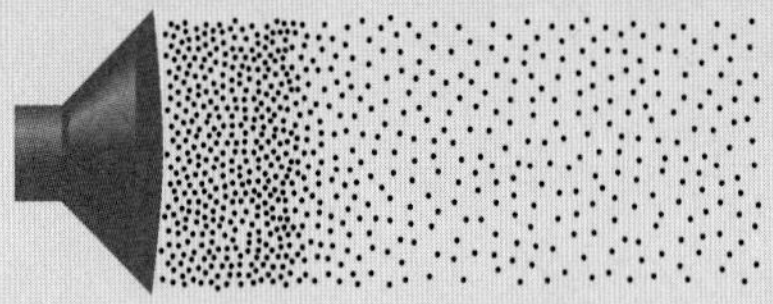

a Electrical signals make the speaker vibrate. As the speaker cone moves forward, it pushes the air particles in front of it closer together, creating a region of higher density and pressure called a *compression.*

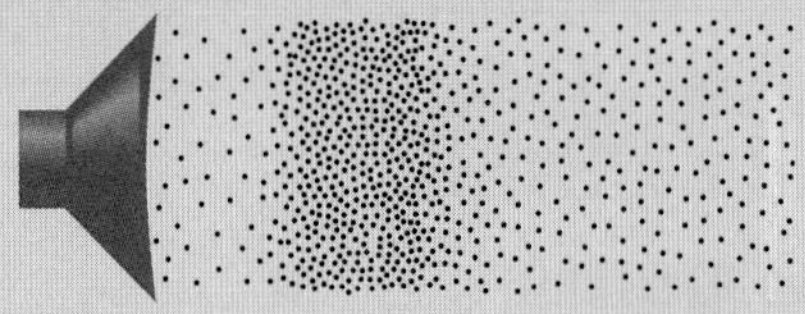

b As the speaker cone moves backward, air particles close to the cone become less crowded, creating a region of lower density and pressure called a *rarefaction.*

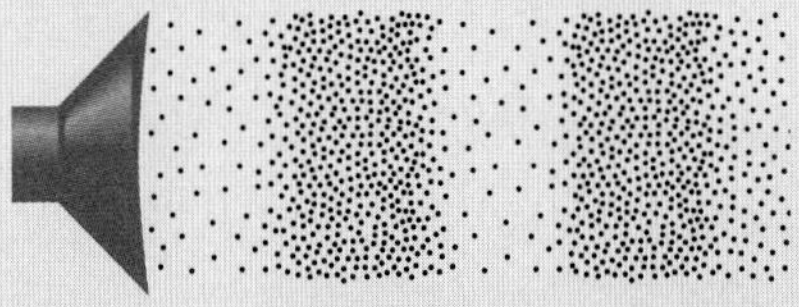

c For each vibration, a compression and a rarefaction are formed. As the compressions and rarefactions travel away from the speaker, sound is transmitted through the air.

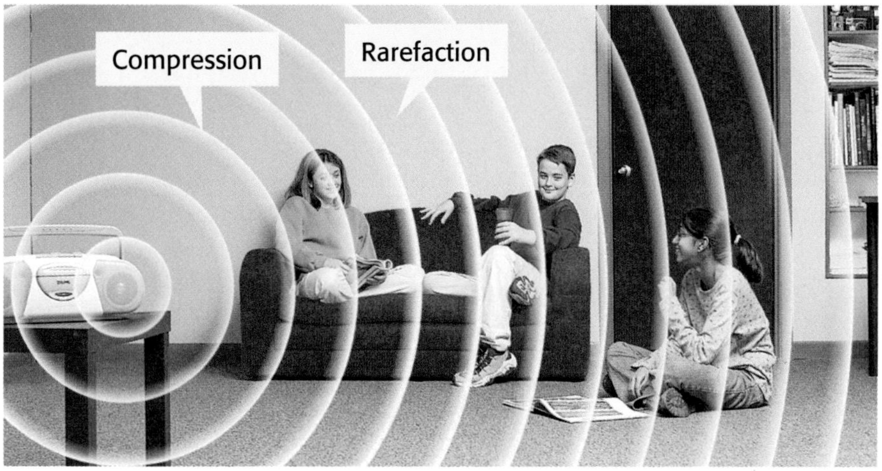

Figure 2 *You can't actually see sound waves, but they can be represented by spheres that spread out in all directions.*

Sound Waves

Longitudinal (LAHN juh TOOD'n uhl) waves are made of compressions and rarefactions. A **sound wave** is a longitudinal wave caused by vibrations and carried through a substance. The particles of the substance, such as air particles, vibrate back and forth along the path that the sound wave travels. Sound is transmitted through the vibrations and collisions of the particles. Because the particles vibrate back and forth along the paths that sound travels, sound travels as longitudinal waves.

sound wave a longitudinal wave that is caused by vibrations and that travels through a material medium

Sound waves travel in all directions away from their source, as shown in **Figure 2.** However, air or other matter does not travel with the sound waves. The particles of air only vibrate back and forth. If air did travel with sound, wind gusts from music speakers would blow you over at a school dance!

Reading Check **What do sound waves consist of?** (*See the Appendix for answers to Reading Checks.*)

Quick Lab

Good Vibrations

1. Gently strike a **tuning fork** on a **rubber eraser.** Watch the prongs, and listen for a sound. Describe what you see and what you hear.
2. Lightly touch the fork with your fingers. What do you feel?
3. Grasp the prongs of the fork firmly with your hand. What happens to the sound?
4. Strike the tuning fork on the eraser again, and dip the prongs in a **cup of water.** Describe what happens to the water.
5. Record your observations.

Figure 3 Tubing is connected to a pump that is removing air from the jar. As the air is removed, the ringing alarm clock sounds quieter and quieter.

Sound and Media

Another characteristic of sound is that all sound waves require a medium (plural, *media*). A **medium** is a substance through which a wave can travel. Most of the sounds that you hear travel through air at least part of the time. But sound waves can also travel through other materials, such as water, glass, and metal.

medium a physical environment in which phenomena occur

In a vacuum, however, there are no particles to vibrate. So, no sound can be made in a vacuum. This fact helps to explain the effect described in **Figure 3.** Sound must travel through air or some other medium to reach your ears and be detected.

Reading Check What does sound need in order to travel?

How You Detect Sound

Imagine that you are watching a suspenseful movie. Just before a door is opened, the background music becomes louder. You know that there is something scary behind that door! Now, imagine watching the same scene without the sound. You would have more difficulty figuring out what's going on if there were no sound.

Figure 4 shows how your ears change sound waves into electrical signals that allow you to hear. First, the outer ear collects sound waves. The vibrations then go to your middle ear. Very small organs increase the size of the vibrations here. These vibrations are then picked up by organs in your inner ear. Your inner ear changes vibrations into electrical signals that your brain interprets as sound.

CONNECTION TO Biology

Vocal Sounds The vibrations that produce your voice are made inside your throat. When you speak, laugh, or sing, your lungs force air up your windpipe, causing your vocal cords to vibrate.

Do some research, and find out what role different parts of your throat and mouth play in making vocal sounds. Make a poster in which you show the different parts, and explain the role they play in shaping sound waves.

ACTIVITY

Figure 4 How the Human Ear Works

a The **outer ear** acts as a funnel for sound waves. The *pinna* collects sound waves and directs them into the *ear canal.*

b In the **middle ear,** three bones—the *hammer, anvil,* and *stirrup*—act as levers to increase the size of the vibrations.

c In the **inner ear,** vibrations created by sound are changed into electrical signals for the brain to interpret.

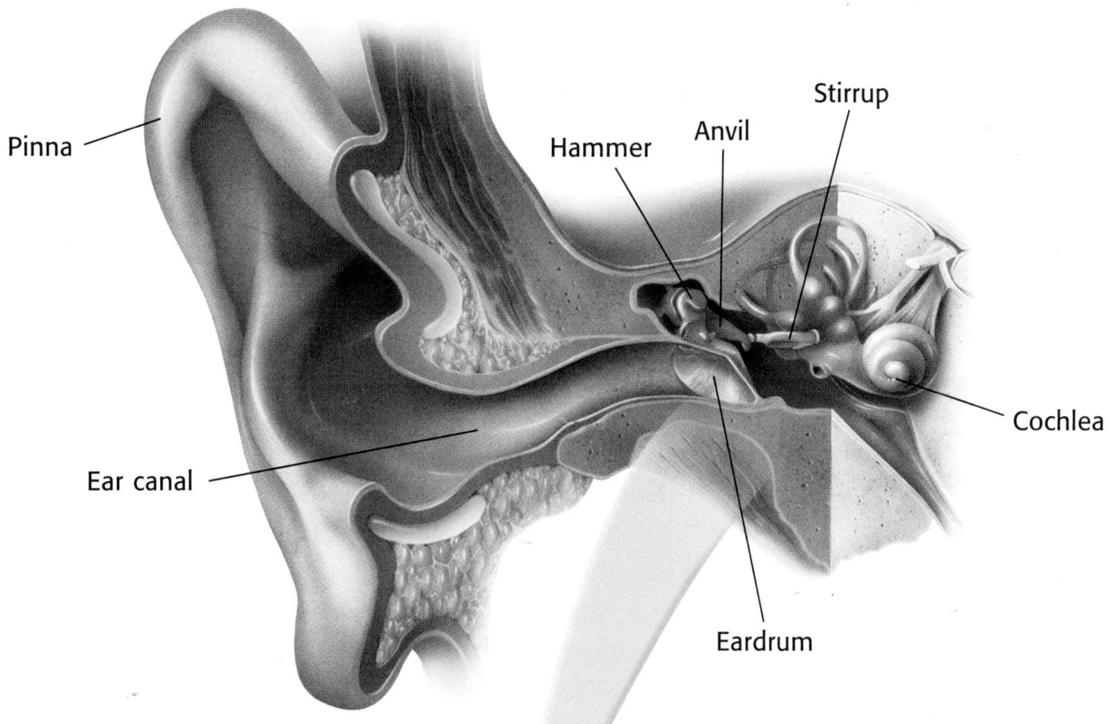

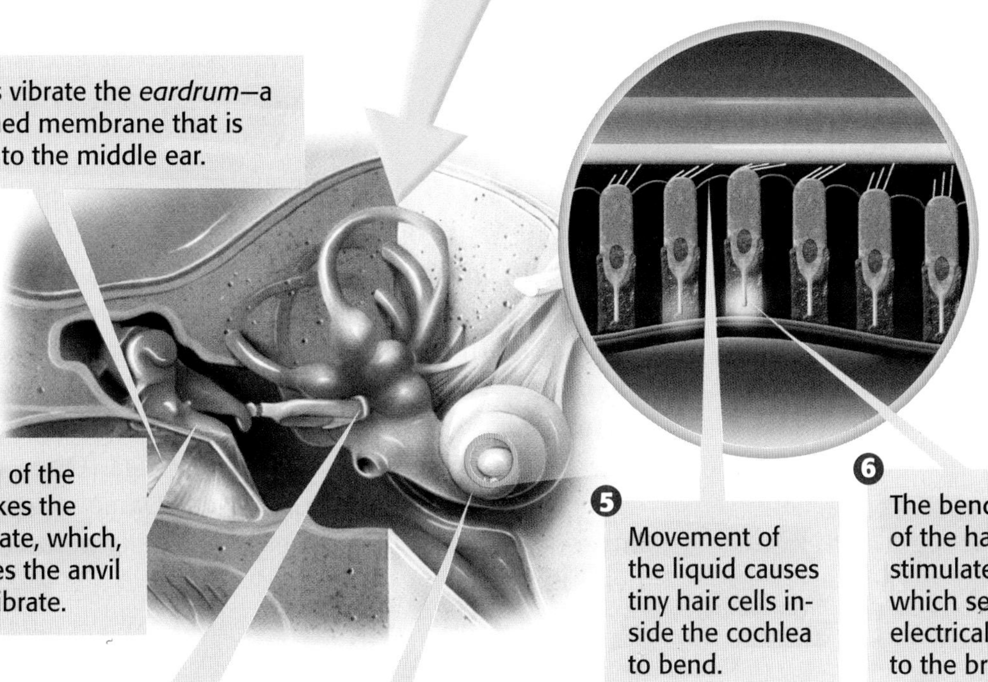

1 Sound waves vibrate the *eardrum*—a lightly stretched membrane that is the entrance to the middle ear.

2 The vibration of the eardrum makes the hammer vibrate, which, in turn, makes the anvil and stirrup vibrate.

3 The stirrup vibrates the *oval window*—the entrance to the inner ear.

4 The vibrations of the oval window create waves in the liquid inside the *cochlea.*

5 Movement of the liquid causes tiny hair cells inside the cochlea to bend.

6 The bending of the hair cells stimulates nerves, which send electrical signals to the brain.

1/12/13

Figure 5 *Sound is made whether or not anyone is around to hear it.*

INTERNET ACTIVITY

For another activity related to this chapter, go to **go.hrw.com** and type in the keyword **HP5SNDW.**

Making Sound Versus Hearing Sound

Have you heard this riddle? If a tree falls in the forest and no one is around to hear it, does the tree make a sound? Think about the situation pictured in **Figure 5.** When a tree falls and hits the ground, the tree and the ground vibrate. These vibrations make compressions and rarefactions in the surrounding air. So, there would be a sound!

Making sound is separate from detecting sound. The fact that no one heard the tree fall doesn't mean that there wasn't a sound. A sound was made—it just wasn't heard.

Hearing Loss and Deafness

The many parts of the ear must work together for you to hear sounds. If any part of the ear is damaged or does not work properly, hearing loss or deafness may result.

One of the most common types of hearing loss is called *tinnitus* (ti NIET us), which results from long-term exposure to loud sounds. Loud sounds can cause damage to the hair cells and nerve endings in the cochlea. Once these hairs are damaged, they do not grow back. Damage to the cochlea or any other part of the inner ear usually results in permanent hearing loss.

People who have tinnitus often say they have a ringing in their ears. They also have trouble understanding other people and hearing the difference between words that sound alike. Tinnitus can affect people of any age. Fortunately, tinnitus can be prevented.

Reading Check **What causes tinnitus?**

Protecting Your Hearing

Short exposures to sounds that are loud enough to be painful can cause hearing loss. Your hearing can also be damaged by loud sounds that are not quite painful, if you are exposed to them for long periods of time. There are some simple things you can do to protect your hearing. Loud sounds can be blocked out by earplugs. You can listen at a lower volume when you are using headphones, as in **Figure 6.** You can also move away from loud sounds. If you are near a speaker playing loud music, just move away from it. When you double the distance between yourself and a loud sound, the sound's intensity to your ears will be one-fourth of what it was before.

Figure 6 *Turning your radio down can help prevent hearing loss, especially when you use headphones.*

SECTION Review

Summary

- All sounds are generated by vibrations.
- Sounds travel as longitudinal waves consisting of compressions and rarefactions.
- Sound waves travel in all directions away from their source.
- Sound waves require a medium through which to travel. Sound cannot travel in a vacuum.
- Your ears convert sound into electrical impulses that are sent to your brain.
- Exposure to loud sounds can cause hearing damage.
- Using earplugs and lowering the volume of sounds can prevent hearing damage.

Using Key Terms

1. Use the following terms in the same sentence: *sound wave* and *medium.*

Understanding Key Ideas

2. Sound travels as
   a. transverse waves.
   b. longitudinal waves.
   c. shock waves.
   d. airwaves.
3. Which part of the ear increases the size of the vibrations of sound waves entering the ear?
   a. outer ear
   b. ear canal
   c. middle ear
   d. inner ear
4. Name two ways of protecting your hearing.

Critical Thinking

5. **Analyzing Processes** Explain why a person at a rock concert will not feel gusts of wind coming out of the speakers.
6. **Analyzing Ideas** If a meteorite crashed on the moon, would you be able to hear it on Earth? Why, or why not?
7. **Identifying Relationships** Recall the breaking dishes mentioned at the beginning of this section. Why was the sound that they made so loud?

Interpreting Graphics

Use the diagram of a wave below to answer the questions that follow.

8. What kind of wave is this?
9. Draw a sketch of the diagram on a separate sheet of paper, and label the compressions and rarefactions.
10. How do vibrations make these kinds of waves?

SCILINKS. NSTA Developed and maintained by the National Science Teachers Association

For a variety of links related to this chapter, go to www.scilinks.org

Topic: The Ear; What Is Sound?
SciLinks code: HSM0440; HSM1663

SECTION 2

Properties of Sound

What You Will Learn

- Compare the speed of sound in different media.
- Explain how frequency and pitch are related.
- Describe the Doppler effect, and give examples of it.
- Explain how amplitude and loudness are related.
- Describe how amplitude and frequency can be "seen" on an oscilloscope.

Vocabulary

pitch
Doppler effect
loudness
decibel

READING STRATEGY

Reading Organizer As you read this section, create an outline of the section. Use the headings from the section in your outline.

Imagine that you are swimming in a neighborhood pool. You can hear the high, loud laughter of small children and the soft splashing of the waves at the edge of the pool.

Why are some sounds loud, soft, high, or low? The differences between sounds depend on the properties of the sound waves. In this section, you will learn about properties of sound.

The Speed of Sound

Suppose you are standing at one end of a pool and two people from the opposite end of the pool yell at the same time. You would hear their voices at the same time. The reason is that the speed of sound depends only on the medium in which the sound is traveling. So, you would hear them at the same time—even if one person yelled louder!

How the Speed of Sound Can Change

Table 1 shows how the speed of sound varies in different media. Sound travels quickly through air, but it travels even faster in liquids and even faster in solids.

Temperature also affects the speed of sound. In general, the cooler the medium is, the slower the speed of sound. Particles of cool materials move more slowly and transmit energy more slowly than particles do in warmer materials. In 1947, pilot Chuck Yeager became the first person to travel faster than the speed of sound. Yeager flew the airplane shown in **Figure 1** at 293 m/s (about 480 mi/h) at 12,000 m above sea level. At that altitude, the temperature of the air is so low that the speed of sound is only 290 m/s.

Table 1 Speed of Sound in Different Media

Medium	Speed (m/s)
Air (0°C)	331
Air (20°C)	343
Air (100°C)	366
Water (20°C)	1,482
Steel (20°C)	5,200

Figure 1 *The* X-1 *airplane was the first vehicle to move faster than the speed of sound.*

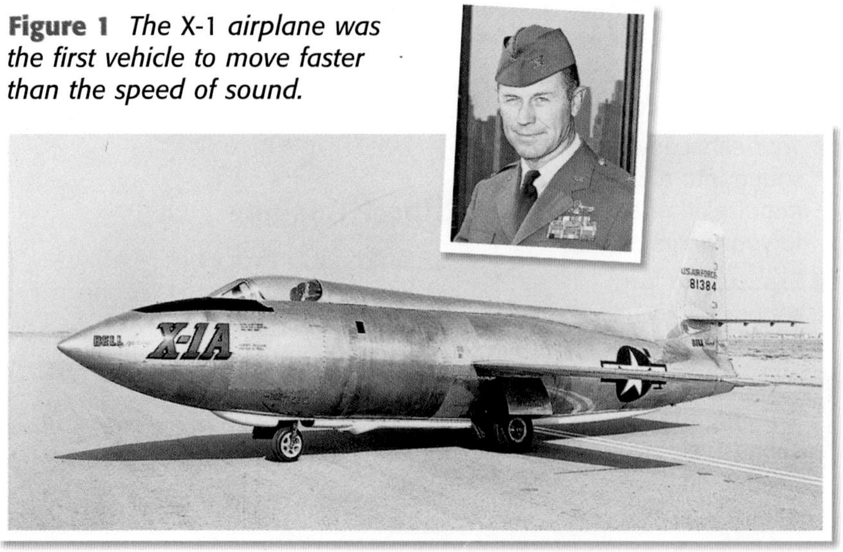

Figure 2 **Frequency and Pitch**

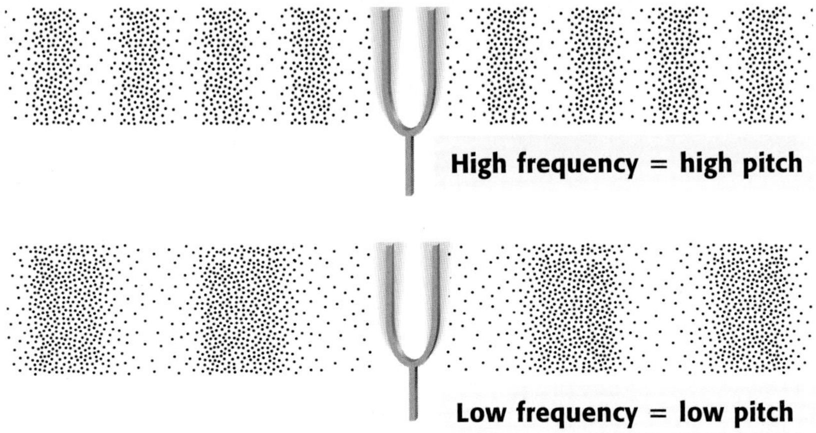

Pitch and Frequency

How low or high a sound seems to be is the **pitch** of that sound. The *frequency* of a wave is the number of crests or troughs that are made in a given time. The pitch of a sound is related to the frequency of the sound wave, as shown in **Figure 2.** Frequency is expressed in hertz (Hz), where 1 Hz = 1 wave per second. For example, the lowest note on a piano is about 40 Hz. The screech of a bat is 10,000 Hz or higher.

pitch a measure of how high or low a sound is perceived to be, depending on the frequency of the sound wave

Reading Check **What is frequency?** (*See the Appendix for answers to Reading Checks.*)

Frequency and Hearing

If you see someone blow a dog whistle, the whistle seems silent to you. The reason is that the frequency of the sound wave is out of the range of human hearing. But the dog hears the whistle and comes running! **Table 2** compares the range of frequencies that humans and animals can hear. Sounds that have a frequency too high for people to hear are called *ultrasonic.*

MATH PRACTICE

The Speed of Sound

The speed of sound depends on the medium through which sound is traveling and the medium's temperature. Sound travels at 343 m/s through air at a temperature of 20°C. How far will sound travel in 20°C air in 5 s?

The speed of sound in steel at 20°C is 5,200 m/s. How far can sound travel in 5 s through steel at 20°C?

Table 2 **Frequencies Heard by Different Animals**

Animal	Frequency range (Hz)
Bat	2,000 to 110,000
Porpoise	75 to 150,000
Cat	45 to 64,000
Beluga whale	1,000 to 123,000
Elephant	16 to 12,000
Human	20 to 20,000
Dog	67 to 45,000

Figure 3 The Doppler Effect

a A car with its horn honking moves toward the sound waves going in the same direction. A person in front of the car hears sound waves that are closer together.

b The car moves away from the sound waves going in the opposite direction. A person behind the car hears sound waves that are farther apart and have a lower frequency.

The Doppler Effect

Doppler effect an observed change in the frequency of a wave when the source or observer is moving

Have you ever been passed by a car with its horn honking? If so, you probably noticed the sudden change in pitch—sort of an *EEEEEOOooowwn* sound—as the car went past you. The pitch you heard was higher as the car moved toward you than it was after the car passed. This higher pitch was a result of the Doppler effect. For sound waves, the **Doppler effect** is the apparent change in the frequency of a sound caused by the motion of either the listener or the source of the sound. **Figure 3** shows how the Doppler effect works.

In a moving sound source, such as a car with its horn honking, sound waves that are moving forward are going the same direction the car is moving. As a result, the compressions and rarefactions of the sound wave will be closer together than they would be if the sound source was not moving. To a person in front of the car, the frequency and pitch of the sound seem high. After the car passes, it is moving in the opposite direction that the sound waves are moving. To a person behind the car, the frequency and pitch of the sound seem low. The driver always hears the same pitch because the driver is moving with the car.

Loudness and Amplitude

If you gently tap a drum, you will hear a soft rumbling. But if you strike the drum with a large force, you will hear a much louder sound! By changing the force you use to strike the drum, you change the loudness of the sound that is created. **Loudness** is a measure of how well a sound can be heard.

Energy and Vibration

Look at **Figure 4.** The harder you strike a drum, the louder the boom. As you strike the drum harder, you transfer more energy to the drum. The drum moves with a larger vibration and transfers more energy to the air around it. This increase in energy causes air particles to vibrate farther from their rest positions.

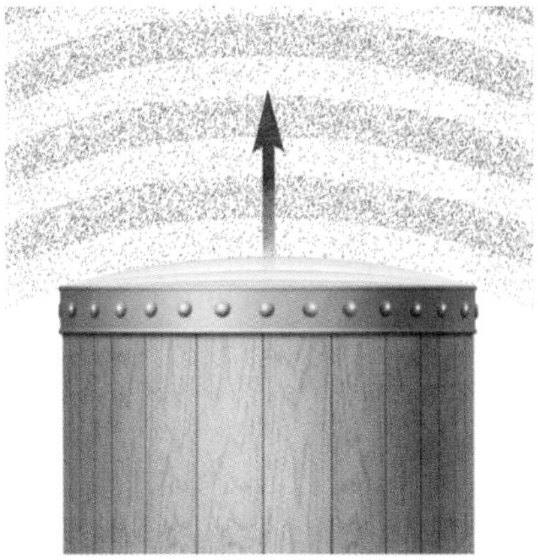

Figure 4 *When a drum is struck hard, it vibrates with a lot of energy, making a loud sound.*

Increasing Amplitude

When you strike a drum harder, you are increasing the amplitude of the sound waves being made. The *amplitude* of a wave is the largest distance the particles in a wave vibrate from their rest positions. The larger the amplitude, the louder the sound. And the smaller the amplitude, the softer the sound. One way to increase the loudness of a sound is to use an amplifier, shown in **Figure 5.** An amplifier receives sound signals in the form of electric current. The amplifier then increases the energy and makes the sound louder.

loudness the extent to which a sound can be heard

✓ Reading Check **What is the relationship between the amplitude of a sound and its energy of vibration?**

Figure 5 *An amplifier increases the amplitude of the sound generated by an electric guitar.*

Quick Lab

Sounding Board

1. With one hand, hold a **ruler** on your **desk** so that one end of it hangs over the edge.
2. With your other hand, pull the free end of the ruler up a few centimeters, and let go.
3. Try pulling the ruler up different distances. How does the distance affect the sounds you hear? What property of the sound wave are you changing?
4. Change the length of the part that hangs over the edge. What property of the sound wave is affected? Record your answers and observations.

SCHOOL to HOME

WRITING SKILL **Decibel Levels**

With an adult, listen for the normal sounds that happen around your house. In your **science journal,** write down some sounds and what you think their decibel levels might be. Then, move closer to the source of each sound, and write what you think the new decibel level of each is.

ACTIVITY

Table 3 **Decibel Levels of Common Sounds**

Decibel level	Sound
0	the softest sounds you can hear
20	whisper
25	purring cat
60	normal conversation
80	lawn mower, vacuum cleaner, truck traffic
100	chain saw, snowmobile
115	sandblaster, loud rock concert, automobile horn
120	threshold of pain
140	jet engine 30 m away
200	rocket engine 50 m away

Measuring Loudness

decibel the most common unit used to measure loudness (symbol, dB)

The most common unit used to express loudness is the **decibel** (dB). The softest sounds an average human can hear are at a level of 0 dB. Sounds that are at 120 dB or higher can be painful. **Table 3** shows some common sounds and their decibel levels.

"Seeing" Amplitude and Frequency

Sound waves are invisible. However, technology can provide a way to "see" sound waves. A device called an *oscilloscope* (uh SIL uh SKOHP) can graph representations of sound waves, as shown in **Figure 6.** Notice that the graphs look like transverse waves instead of longitudinal waves.

Reading Check **What does an oscilloscope do?** It can graph representations of sound waves.

Figure 6 **"Seeing" Sounds**

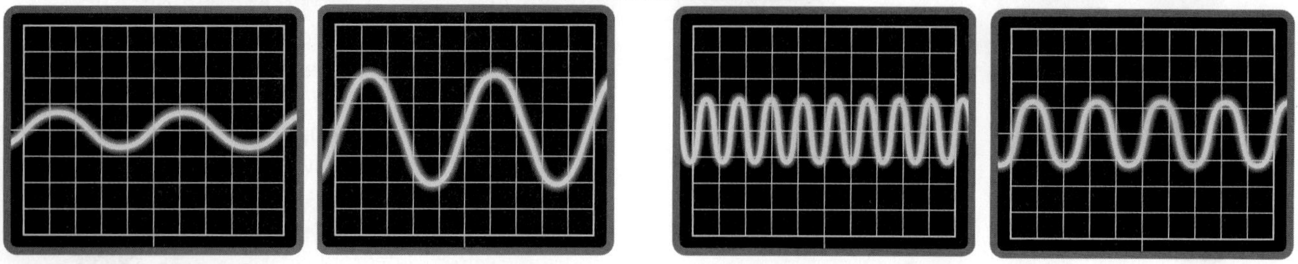

The graph on the right has a **larger amplitude** than the graph on the left. So, the sound represented on the right is **louder** than the one represented on the left.

The graph on the right has a **lower frequency** than the one on the left. So, the sound represented on the right has a **lower pitch** than the one represented on the left.

From Sound to Electrical Signal

An oscilloscope is shown in **Figure 7.** A microphone is attached to the oscilloscope and changes a sound wave into an electrical signal. The electrical signal is graphed on the screen in the form of a wave. The graph shows the sound as if it were a transverse wave. So, the sound's amplitude and frequency are easier to see. The highest points (crests) of these waves represent compressions, and the lowest points (troughs) represent rarefactions. By looking at the displays on the oscilloscope, you can quickly see the differences in amplitude and frequency of different sound waves.

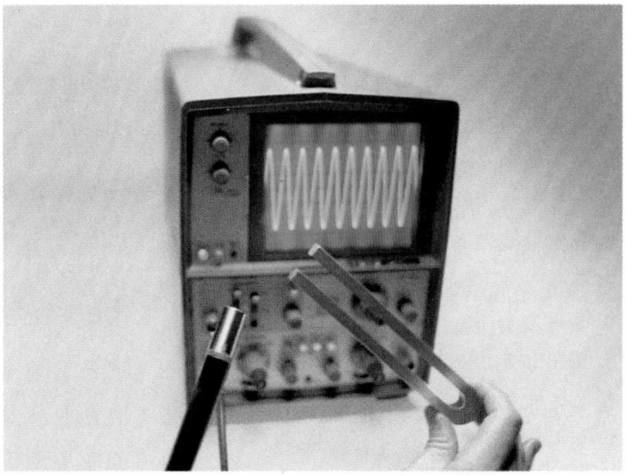

Figure 7 *An oscilloscope can be used to represent sounds.*

SECTION Review

Summary

- The speed of sound depends on the medium and the temperature.
- The pitch of a sound becomes higher as the frequency of the sound wave becomes higher. Frequency is expressed in units of Hertz (Hz), which is equivalent to waves per second.
- The Doppler effect is the apparent change in frequency of a sound caused by the motion of either the listener or the source of the sound.
- Loudness increases with the amplitude of the sound. Loudness is expressed in decibels.
- The amplitude and frequency of a sound can be measured electronically by an oscilloscope.

Using Key Terms

1. In your own words, write a definition for the term *pitch.*

2. Use the following terms in the same sentence: *loudness* and *decibel.*

Understanding Key Ideas

3. At the same temperature, in which medium does sound travel fastest?

a. air
b. liquid
c. solid
d. It travels at the same speed through all media.

4. In general, how does the temperature of a medium affect the speed of sound through that medium?

5. What property of waves affects the pitch of a sound?

6. How does an oscilloscope allow sound waves to be "seen"?

Math Skills

7. You see a distant flash of lightning, and then you hear a thunderclap 2 s later. The sound of the thunder moves at 343 m/s. How far away was the lightning?

8. In water that is near 0°C, a submarine sends out a sonar signal (a sound wave). The signal travels 1500 m/s and reaches an underwater mountain in 4 s. How far away is the mountain?

Critical Thinking

9. **Analyzing Processes** Will a listener notice the Doppler effect if both the listener and the source of the sound are traveling toward each other? Explain your answer.

10. **Predicting Consequences** A drum is struck gently, then is struck harder. What will be the difference in the amplitude of the sounds made? What will be the difference in the frequency of the sounds made?

SECTION 3

Interactions of Sound Waves

What You Will Learn

- Explain how echoes are made, and describe their use in locating objects.
- List examples of constructive and destructive interference of sound waves.
- Explain what resonance is.

Vocabulary

echo
echolocation
interference
sonic boom
standing wave
resonance

READING STRATEGY

Paired Summarizing Read this section silently. In pairs, take turns summarizing the material. Stop to discuss ideas that seem confusing.

echo a reflected sound wave

Have you ever heard of a sea canary? It's not a bird! It's a whale! Beluga whales are sometimes called sea canaries because of the many different sounds they make.

Dolphins, beluga whales, and many other animals that live in the sea use sound to communicate. Beluga whales also rely on reflected sound waves to find fish, crabs, and shrimp to eat. In this section, you will learn about reflection and other interactions of sound waves. You will also learn how bats, dolphins, and whales use sound to find food.

Reflection of Sound Waves

Reflection is the bouncing back of a wave after it strikes a barrier. You're probably already familiar with a reflected sound wave, otherwise known as an **echo.** The strength of a reflected sound wave depends on the reflecting surface. Sound waves reflect best off smooth, hard surfaces. Look at **Figure 1.** A shout in an empty gymnasium can produce an echo, but a shout in an auditorium usually does not.

The difference is that the walls of an auditorium are usually designed so that they absorb sound. If sound waves hit a flat, hard surface, they will reflect back. Reflection of sound waves doesn't matter much in a gymnasium. But you don't want to hear echoes while listening to a musical performance!

Figure 1 **Sound Reflection and Absorption**

Sound waves easily reflect off the smooth, hard walls of a gymnasium. For this reason, you hear an echo.

In well-designed auditoriums, echoes are reduced by soft materials that absorb sound waves and by irregular shapes that scatter sound waves.

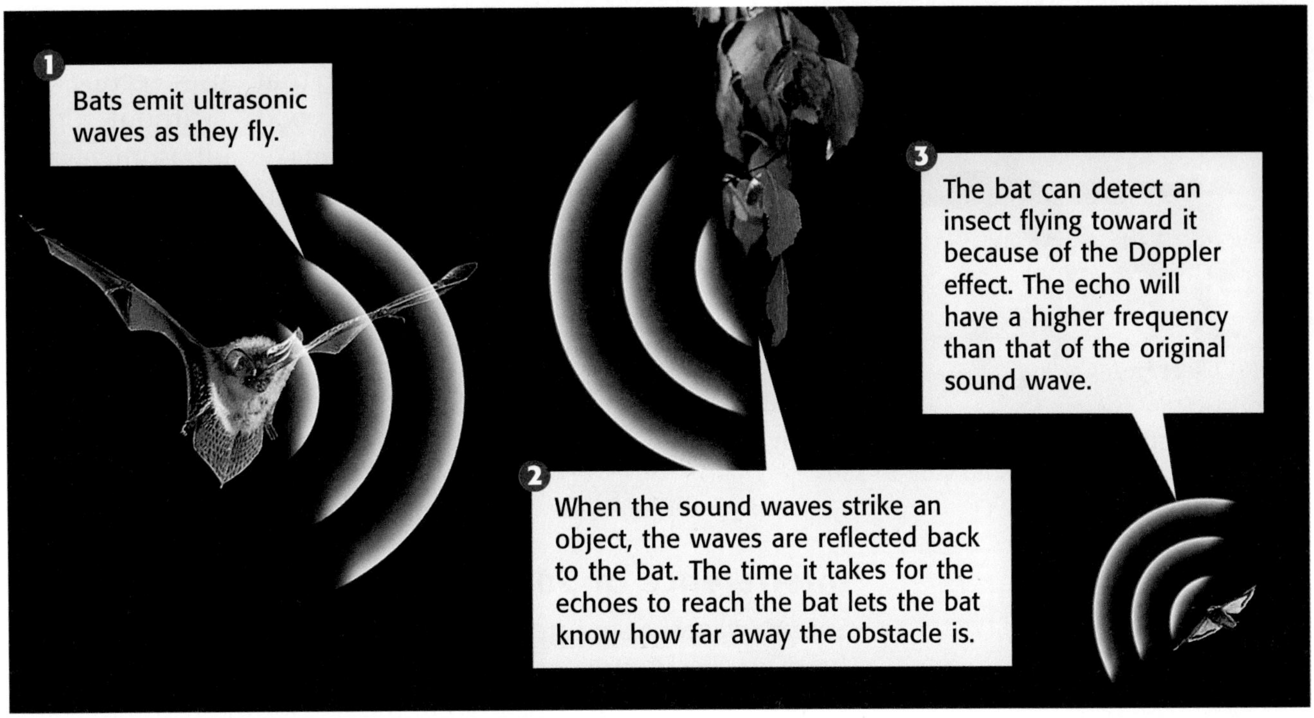

Figure 2 *Bats use echolocation to navigate around barriers and to find insects to eat.*

Echolocation

Beluga whales use echoes to find food. The use of reflected sound waves to find objects is called **echolocation.** Other animals—such as dolphins, bats, and some kinds of birds—also use echolocation to hunt food and to find objects in their paths. **Figure 2** shows how echolocation works. Animals that use echolocation can tell how far away something is based on how long it takes sound waves to echo back to their ears. Some animals, such as bats, also make use of the Doppler effect to tell if another moving object, such as an insect, is moving toward it or away from it.

echolocation the process of using reflected sound waves to find objects; used by animals such as bats

Reading Check **How is echolocation useful to some animals?** (*See the Appendix for answers to Reading Checks.*)

Echolocation Technology

People use echoes to locate objects underwater by using sonar (which stands for **so**und **n**avigation **a**nd **r**anging). *Sonar* is a type of electronic echolocation. **Figure 3** shows how sonar works. Ultrasonic waves are used because their short wavelengths give more details about the objects they reflect off. Sonar can also help navigators on ships avoid icebergs and can help oceanographers map the ocean floor.

Figure 3 *A fish finder sends ultrasonic waves down into the water. The time it takes for the echo to return helps determine the location of the fish.*

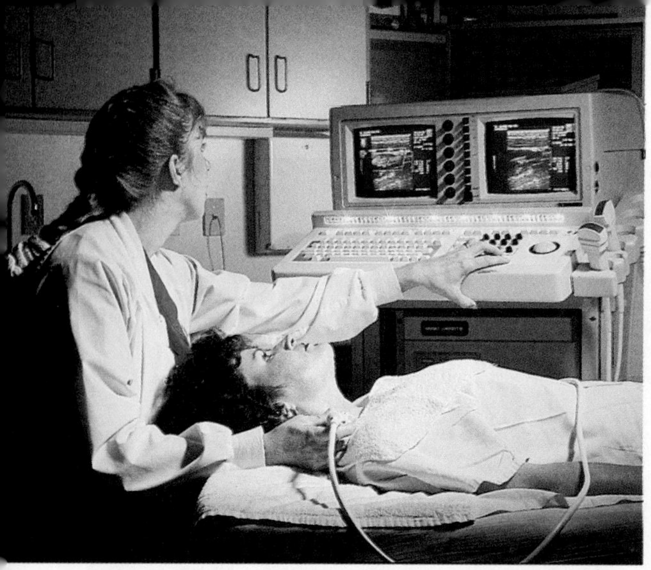

Figure 4 *Images created by ultrasonography are fuzzy, but they are a safe way to see inside a patient's body.*

Ultrasonography

Ultrasonography (UHL truh soh NAHG ruh fee) is a medical procedure that uses echoes to "see" inside a patient's body without doing surgery. A special device makes ultrasonic waves with a frequency that can be from 1 million to 10 million hertz, which reflect off the patient's internal organs. These echoes are then changed into images that can be seen on a television screen, as shown in **Figure 4.** Ultrasonography is used to examine kidneys, gallbladders, and other organs. It is also used to check the development of an unborn baby in a mother's body. Ultrasonic waves are less harmful to human tissue than X rays are.

Interference of Sound Waves

interference the combination of two or more waves that results in a single wave

sonic boom the explosive sound heard when a shock wave from an object traveling faster than the speed of sound reaches a person's ears

Sound waves also interact through interference. **Interference** happens when two or more waves overlap. **Figure 5** shows how two sound waves can combine by both constructive and destructive interference.

Orchestras and bands make use of constructive interference when several instruments of the same kind play the same notes. Interference of the sound waves causes the combined amplitude to increase, resulting in a louder sound. But destructive interference may keep some members of the audience from hearing the concert well. In certain places in an auditorium, sound waves reflecting off the walls interfere destructively with the sound waves from the stage.

Reading Check **What are the two kinds of sound wave interference?**

Figure 5 **Constructive and Destructive Interference**

Sound waves from two speakers producing sound of the same frequency combine by both constructive and destructive interference.

Constructive Interference
As the compressions of one wave overlap the compressions of another wave, the sound will be louder because the amplitude is increased.

Destructive Interference
As the compressions of one wave overlap the rarefactions of another wave, the sound will be softer because the amplitude is decreased.

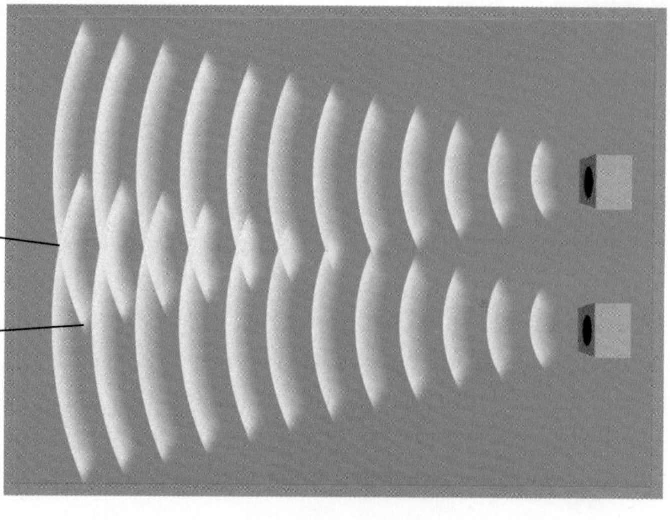

Interference and the Sound Barrier

As the source of a sound—such as a jet plane—gets close to the speed of sound, the sound waves in front of the jet plane get closer and closer together. The result is constructive interference. **Figure 6** shows what happens as a jet plane reaches the speed of sound.

For the jet in **Figure 6** to go faster than the speed of sound, the jet must overcome the pressure of the compressed sound waves. **Figure 7** shows what happens as soon as the jet reaches supersonic speeds—speeds faster than the speed of sound. At these speeds, the sound waves trail off behind the jet. At their outer edges, the sound waves combine by constructive interference to form a *shock wave*.

A **sonic boom** is the explosive sound heard when a shock wave reaches your ears. Sonic booms can be so loud that they can hurt your ears and break windows. They can even make the ground shake as it does during an earthquake.

Figure 6 *When a jet plane reaches the speed of sound, the sound waves in front of the jet combine by constructive interference. The result is a high-density compression that is called the* sound barrier.

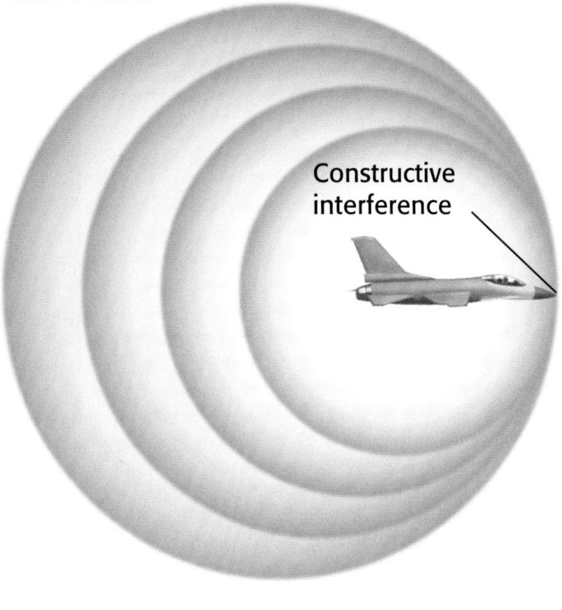

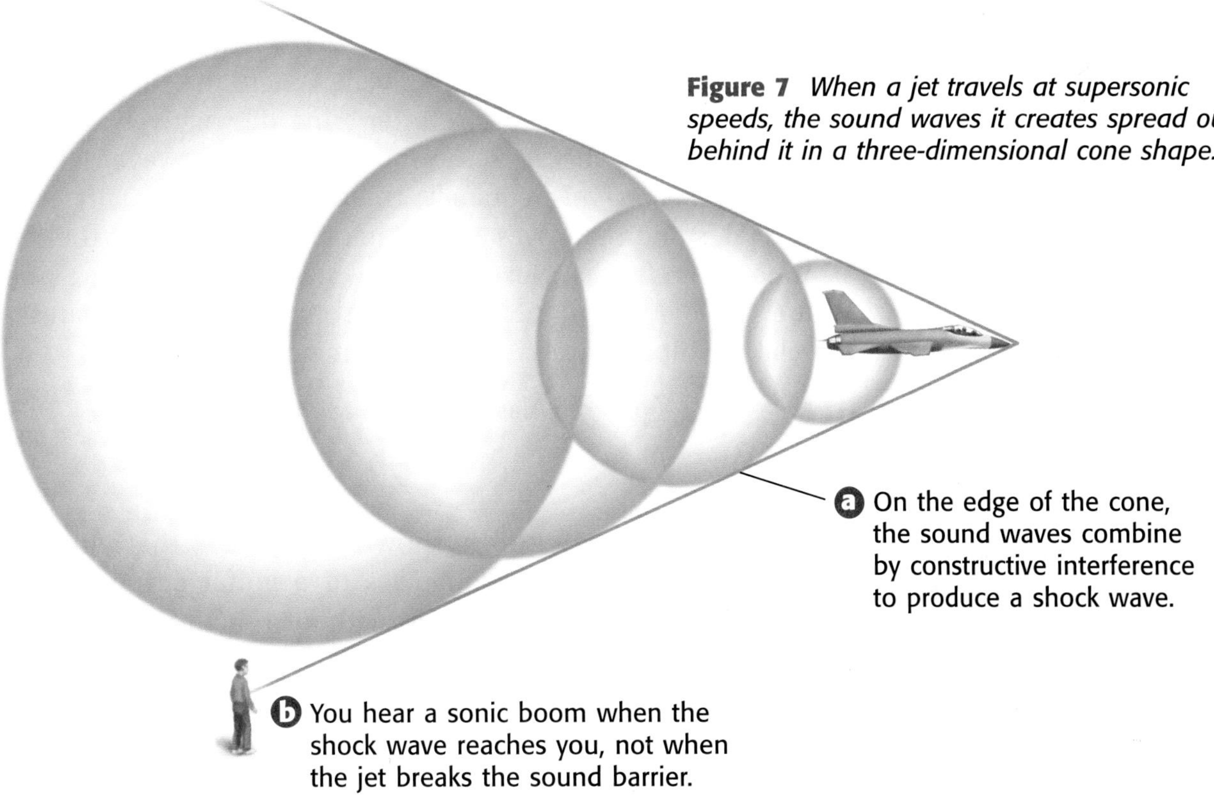

a On the edge of the cone, the sound waves combine by constructive interference to produce a shock wave.
b You hear a sonic boom when the shock wave reaches you, not when the jet breaks the sound barrier.

Figure 7 *When a jet travels at supersonic speeds, the sound waves it creates spread out behind it in a three-dimensional cone shape.*

Figure 8 Resonant Frequencies of a Plucked String

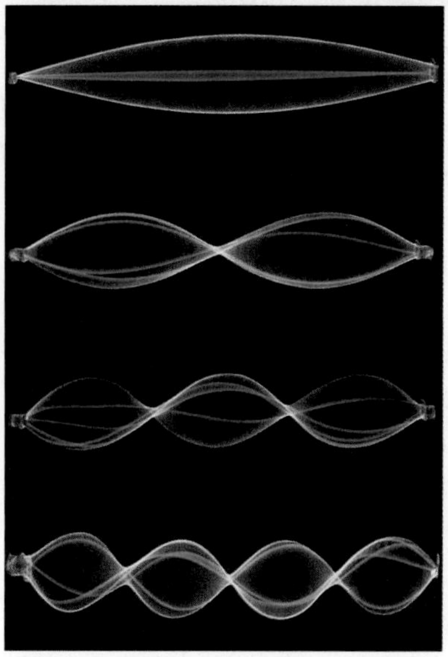

The lowest resonant frequency is called the *fundamental.*

Higher resonant frequencies are called *overtones.* The first overtone is twice the frequency of the fundamental.

The second overtone is 3 times the fundamental.

The third overtone is 4 times the fundamental.

standing wave a pattern of vibration that simulates a wave that is standing still

resonance a phenomenon that occurs when two objects naturally vibrate at the same frequency; the sound produced by one object causes the other object to vibrate

Interference and Standing Waves

When you play a guitar, you can make some pleasing sounds, and you might even play a tune. But have you ever watched a guitar string after you've plucked it? You may have noticed that the string vibrates as a standing wave. A **standing wave** is a pattern of vibration that looks like a wave that is standing still. Waves and reflected waves of the same frequency are going through the string. Where you see maximum amplitude, waves are interfering constructively. Where the string seems to be standing still, waves are interfering destructively.

Although you can see only one standing wave, which is at the *fundamental* frequency, the guitar string actually creates several standing waves of different frequencies at the same time. The frequencies at which standing waves are made are called *resonant frequencies.* Resonant frequencies and the relationships between them are shown in **Figure 8.**

Reading Check What is a standing wave?

Resonance

If you have a tuning fork, shown in **Figure 9,** that vibrates at one of the resonant frequencies of a guitar string, you can make the string make a sound without touching it. Strike the tuning fork, and hold it close to the string. The string will start to vibrate and produce a sound.

Using the vibrations of the tuning fork to make the string vibrate is an example of resonance. **Resonance** happens when an object vibrating at or near a resonant frequency of a second object causes the second object to vibrate.

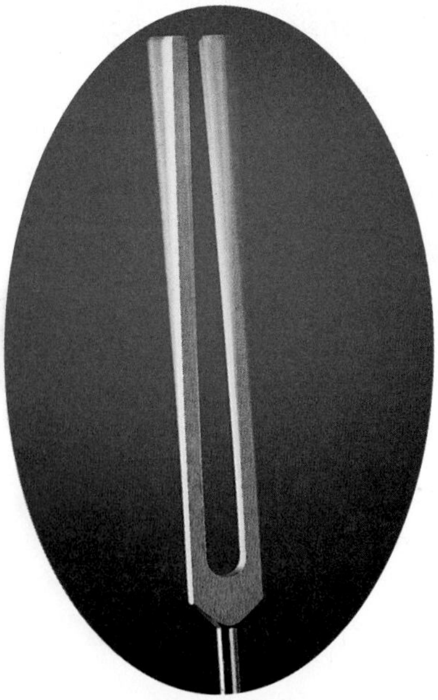

Figure 9 *When struck, a tuning fork can make another object vibrate if they both have the same resonant frequency.*

Resonance in Musical Instruments

Musical instruments use resonance to make sound. In wind instruments, vibrations are caused by blowing air into the mouthpiece. The vibrations make a sound, which is amplified when it forms a standing wave inside the instrument.

String instruments also resonate when they are played. An acoustic guitar, such as the one shown in **Figure 10,** has a hollow body. When the strings vibrate, sound waves enter the body of the guitar. Standing waves form inside the body of the guitar, and the sound is amplified.

Figure 10 *The body of a guitar resonates when the guitar is strummed.*

SECTION Review

Summary

- Echoes are reflected sound waves.
- Some animals can use echolocation to find food or to navigate around objects.
- People use echolocation technology in many underwater applications.
- Ultrasonography uses sound reflection for medical applications.
- Sound barriers and shock waves are created by interference.
- Standing waves form at an object's resonant frequencies.
- Resonance happens when a vibrating object causes a second object to vibrate at one of its resonant frequencies.

Using Key Terms

1. Use the following terms in the same sentence: *echo* and *echolocation.*

Complete each of the following sentences by choosing the correct term from the word bank.

interference	standing wave
sonic boom	resonance

2. When you pluck a string on a musical instrument, a(n) _____ forms.
3. When a vibrating object causes a nearby object to vibrate, _____ results.

Understanding Key Ideas

4. What causes an echo?
   a. reflection
   b. resonance
   c. constructive interference
   d. destructive interference
5. Describe a place in which you would expect to hear echoes.
6. How do bats use echoes to find insects to eat?
7. Give one example each of constructive and destructive interference of sound waves.

Math Skills

8. Sound travels through air at 343 m/s at 20°C. A bat emits an ultrasonic squeak and hears the echo 0.05 s later. How far away was the object that reflected it? (Hint: Remember that the sound must travel *to* the object and *back to* the bat.)

Critical Thinking

9. **Applying Concepts** Your friend is playing a song on a piano. Whenever your friend hits a certain key, the lamp on top of the piano rattles. Explain why the lamp rattles.
10. **Making Comparisons** Compare sonar and ultrasonography in locating objects.

SECTION 4

Sound Quality

What You Will Learn

- Explain why different instruments have different sound qualities.
- Describe how each family of musical instruments produces sound.
- Explain how noise is different from music.

Vocabulary

sound quality
noise

READING STRATEGY

Reading Organizer As you read this section, make a table comparing the way different instruments produce sound.

Have you ever been told that the music you really like is just a lot of noise? If you have, you know that people can disagree about the difference between noise and music.

You might think of noise as sounds you don't like and music as sounds that are pleasant to hear. But the difference between music and noise does not depend on whether you like the sound. The difference has to do with sound quality.

What Is Sound Quality?

Imagine that the same note is played on a piano and on a violin. Could you tell the instruments apart without looking? The notes played have the same frequency. But you could probably tell them apart because the instruments make different sounds. The notes sound different because a single note on an instrument actually comes from several different pitches: the fundamental and several overtones. The result of the combination of these pitches is shown in **Figure 1.** The result of several pitches mixing together through interference is **sound quality.** Each instrument has a unique sound quality. **Figure 1** also shows how the sound quality differs when two instruments play the same note.

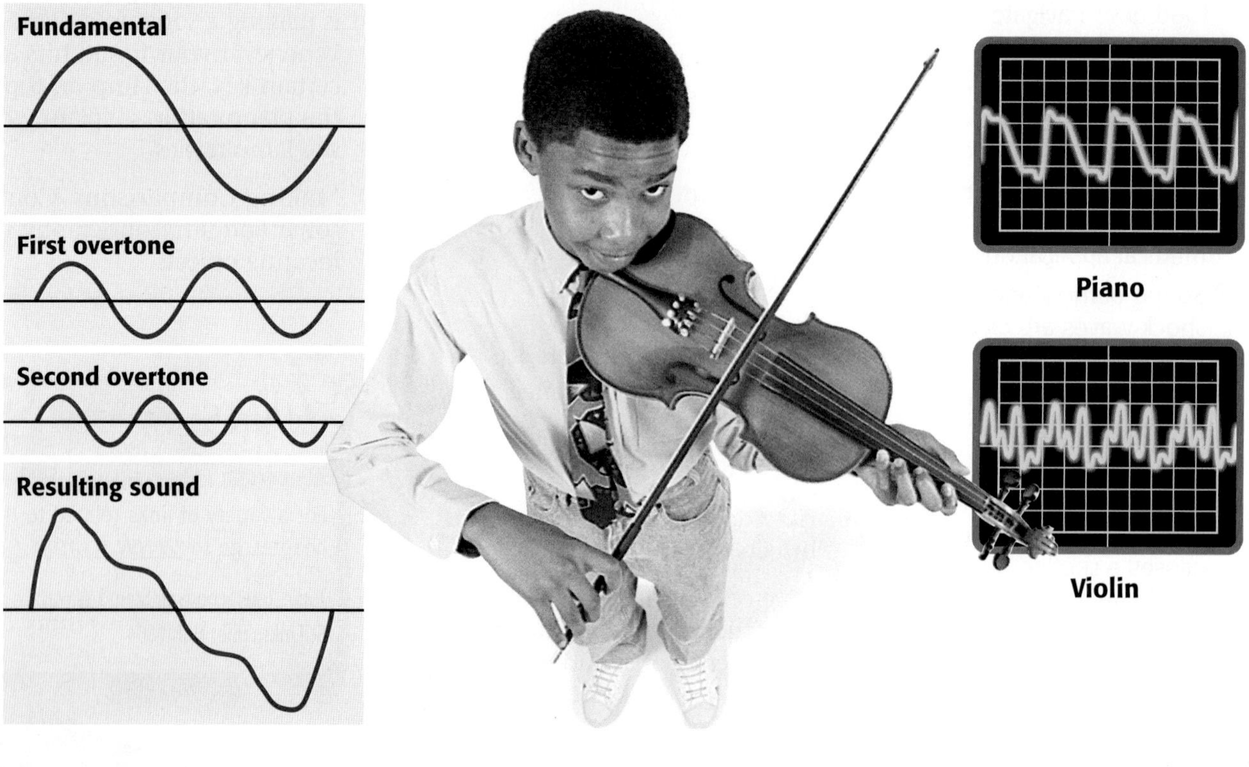

Figure 1 *Each instrument has a unique sound quality that results from the particular blend of overtones that it has.*

Sound Quality of Instruments

The difference in sound quality among different instruments comes from their structural differences. All instruments produce sound by vibrating. But instruments vary in the part that vibrates and in the way that the vibrations are made. There are three main families of instruments: string instruments, wind instruments, and percussion instruments.

sound quality the result of the blending of several pitches through interference

Reading Check **How do musical instruments differ in how they produce sound?** (*See the Appendix for answers to Reading Checks.*)

String Instruments

Violins, guitars, and banjos are examples of string instruments. They make sound when their strings vibrate after being plucked or bowed. **Figure 2** shows how two different string instruments produce sounds.

Figure 2 **String Instruments**

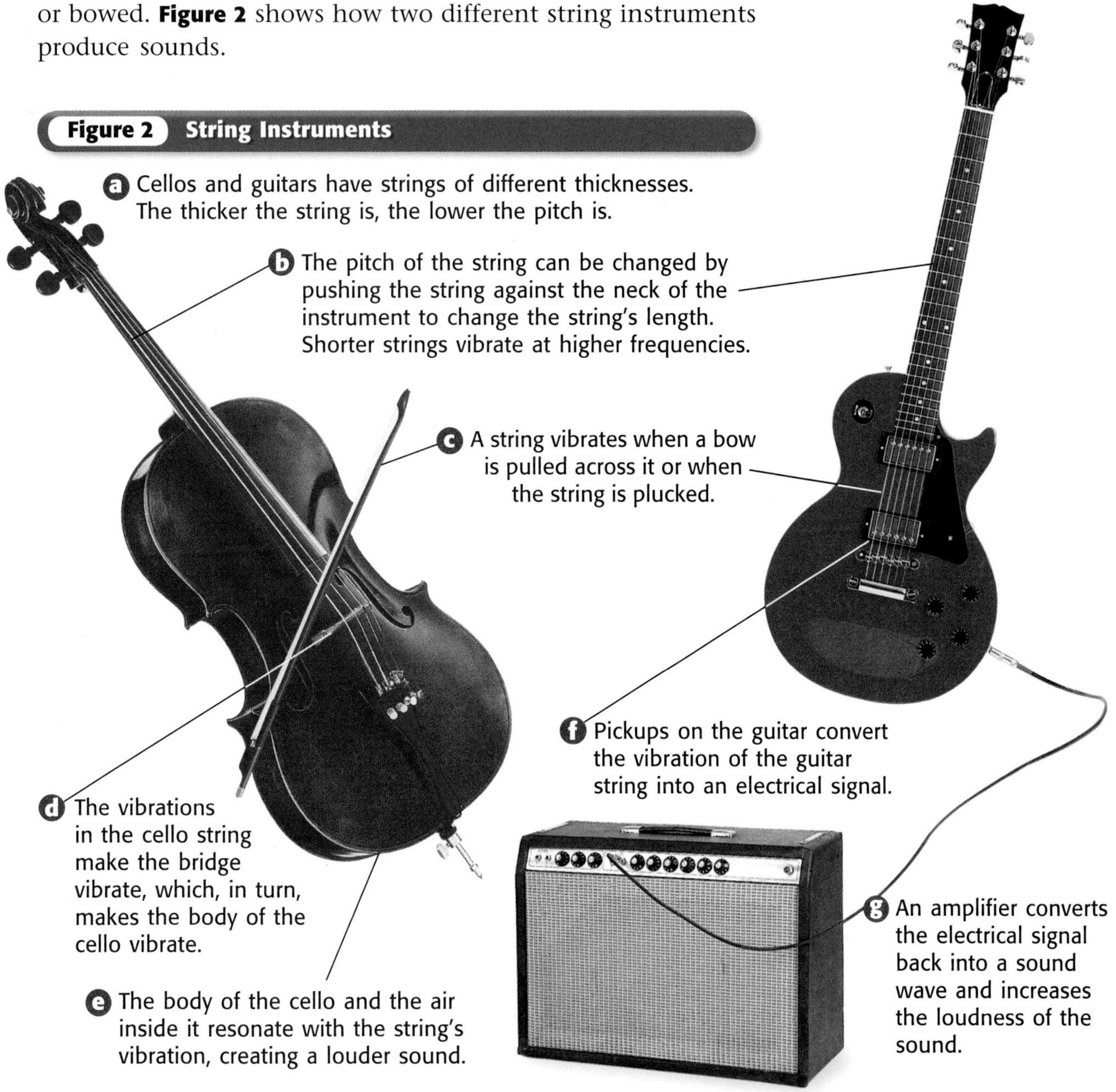

a Cellos and guitars have strings of different thicknesses. The thicker the string is, the lower the pitch is.
b The pitch of the string can be changed by pushing the string against the neck of the instrument to change the string's length. Shorter strings vibrate at higher frequencies.
c A string vibrates when a bow is pulled across it or when the string is plucked.
d The vibrations in the cello string make the bridge vibrate, which, in turn, makes the body of the cello vibrate.
e The body of the cello and the air inside it resonate with the string's vibration, creating a louder sound.
f Pickups on the guitar convert the vibration of the guitar string into an electrical signal.
g An amplifier converts the electrical signal back into a sound wave and increases the loudness of the sound.

Figure 3 **Wind Instruments**

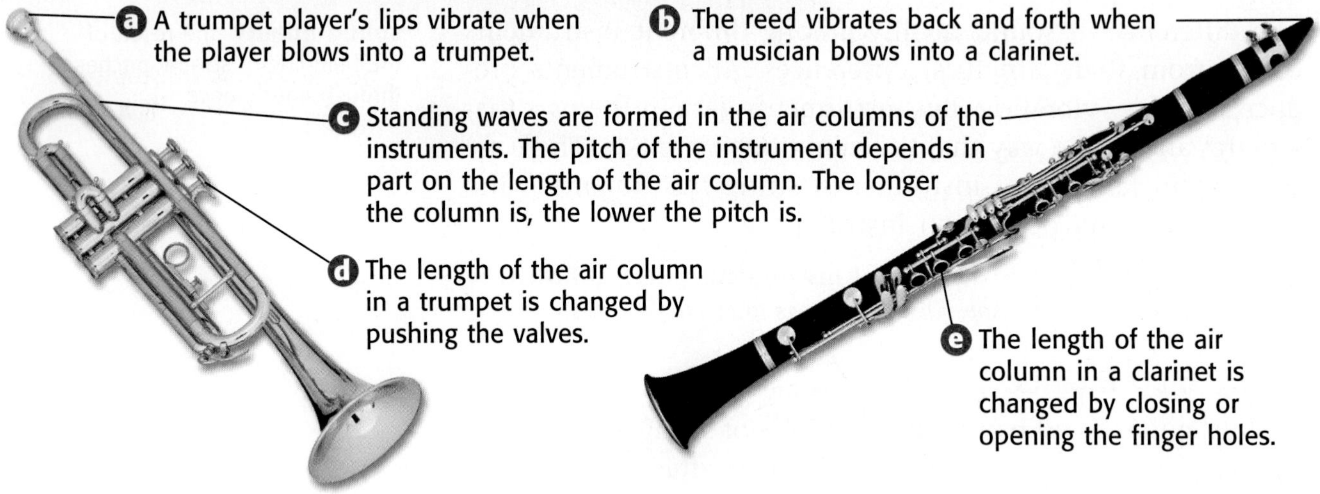

a A trumpet player's lips vibrate when the player blows into a trumpet.
b The reed vibrates back and forth when a musician blows into a clarinet.

Wind Instruments

A wind instrument produces sound when a vibration is created at one end of its air column. The vibration causes standing waves inside the air column. Pitch is changed by changing the length of the air column. Wind instruments are sometimes divided into two groups—woodwinds and brass. Examples of woodwinds are saxophones, oboes, and recorders. French horns, trombones, and tubas are brass instruments. A brass instrument and a woodwind instrument are shown in **Figure 3.**

Percussion Instruments

Drums, bells, and cymbals are percussion instruments. They make sound when struck. Instruments of different sizes are used to get different pitches. Usually, the larger the instrument is, the lower the pitch is. The drums and cymbals in a trap set, shown in **Figure 4,** are percussion instruments.

Figure 4 **Percussion Instruments**

The skins of the drums vibrate when struck with drumsticks.
Cymbals vibrate when struck together or when struck with drumsticks.
Each drum in the set is a different size. The larger the drum is, the lower the pitch is.

Music or Noise?

Most of the sounds we hear are noises. The sound of a truck roaring down the highway, the slam of a door, and the jingle of keys falling to the floor are all noises. **Noise** can be described as any sound, especially a nonmusical sound, that is a random mix of frequencies (or pitches). **Figure 5** shows on an oscilloscope the difference between a musical sound and noise.

noise a sound that consists of a random mix of frequencies

✓ Reading Check **What is the difference between music and noise?**

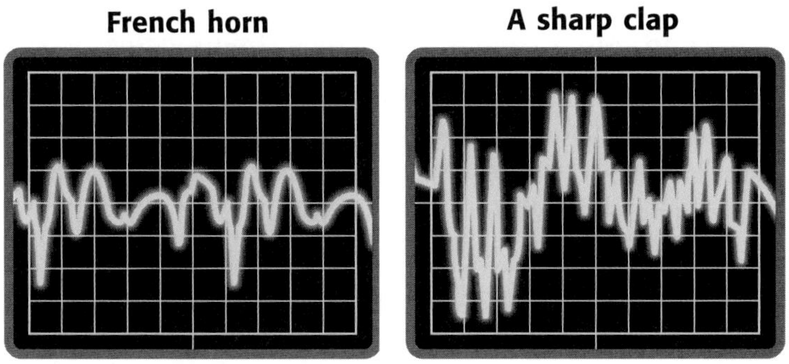

Figure 5 *A note from a French horn produces a sound wave with a repeating pattern, but noise from a clap produces complex sound waves with no regular pattern.*

SECTION Review

Summary

- Different instruments have different sound qualities.
- Sound quality results from the blending through interference of the fundamental and several overtones.
- The three families of instruments are string, wind, and percussion instruments.
- Noise is a sound consisting of a random mix of frequencies.

Using Key Terms

1. Use each of the following terms in a separate sentence: *sound quality* and *noise.*

Understanding Key Ideas

2. What interaction of sound waves determines sound quality?
   a. reflection
   b. diffraction
   c. pitch
   d. interference
3. Why do different instruments have different sound qualities?

Critical Thinking

4. **Making Comparisons** What do string instruments and wind instruments have in common in how they produce sound?
5. **Identifying Bias** Someone says that the music you are listening to is "just noise." Does the person mean that the music is a random mix of frequencies? Explain your answer.

Interpreting Graphics

6. Look at the oscilloscope screen below. Do you think the sound represented by the wave on the screen is noise or music? Explain your answer.

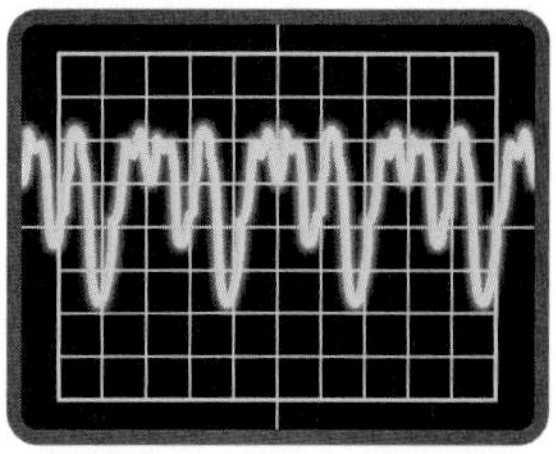

SCILINKS. NSTA Developed and maintained by the National Science Teachers Association

For a variety of links related to this chapter, go to www.scilinks.org

Topic: Sound Quality
SciLinks code: HSM1427

Using Scientific Methods

Skills Practice Lab

Easy Listening

Pitch describes how low or high a sound is. A sound's pitch is related to its frequency—the number of waves per second. Frequency is measured in hertz (Hz), where 1 Hz equals 1 wave per second. Most humans can hear frequencies in the range from 20 Hz to 20,000 Hz. But not everyone detects all pitches equally well at all distances. In this activity, you will collect data to see how well you and your classmates hear different frequencies at different distances.

OBJECTIVES

Measure your classmates' ability to detect different pitches at different distances.

Graph the average class data.

Form a conclusion about how easily pitches of different frequencies are heard at different distances.

MATERIALS

- eraser, hard rubber
- meterstick
- paper, graph
- tuning forks, different frequencies (4)

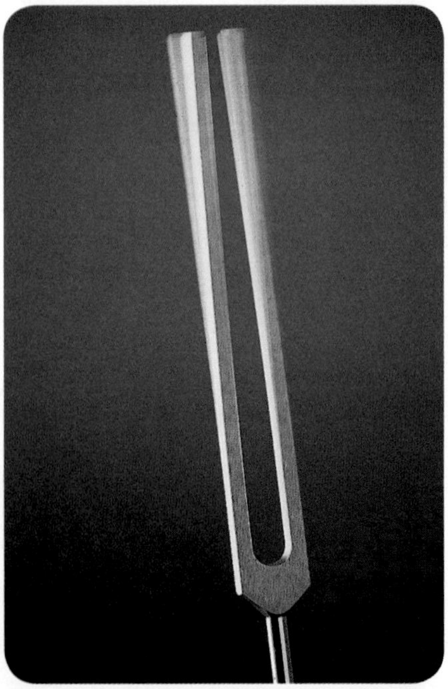

Ask a Question

1. Do most of the students in your classroom hear low-, mid-, or high-frequency sounds best?

Form a Hypothesis

2. Write a hypothesis that answers the question above. Explain your reasoning.

Test the Hypothesis

3. Choose one member of your group to be the sound maker. The others will be the listeners.

4. Copy the data table below onto another sheet of paper. Be sure to include a column for every listener in your group.

Data Collection Table

	Distance (m)			
Frequency	Listener 1	Listener 2	Listener 3	Average
1 (____Hz)				
2 (____Hz)				
3 (____Hz)				
4 (____Hz)				

DO NOT WRITE IN BOOK

5. The sound maker will choose one of the tuning forks, and record the frequency of the tuning fork in the data table.

6. The listeners should stand 1 m from the sound maker with their backs turned.

7. The sound maker will create a sound by striking the tip of the tuning fork gently with the eraser.
8. Listeners who hear the sound should take one step away from the sound maker. The listeners who do not hear the sound should stay where they are.
9. Repeat steps 7 and 8 until none of the listeners can hear the sound or the listeners reach the edge of the room.
10. Using the meterstick, the sound maker should measure the distance from his or her position to each of the listeners. All group members should record this data.
11. Repeat steps 5 through 10 with a tuning fork of a different frequency.
12. Continue until all four tuning forks have been tested.

Analyze the Results

1. **Organizing Data** Calculate the average distance for each frequency. Share your group's data with the rest of the class to make a data table for the whole class.
2. **Analyzing Data** Calculate the average distance for each frequency for the class.
3. **Constructing Graphs** Make a graph of the class results, plotting average distance (*y*-axis) versus frequency (*x*-axis).

Draw Conclusions

4. **Drawing Conclusions** Was everyone in the class able to hear all of frequencies equally? (Hint: Was the average distance for each frequency the same?)
5. **Evaluating Data** If the answer to question 4 is no, which frequency had the longest average distance? Which frequency had the shortest final distance?
6. **Analyzing Graphs** Based on your graph, do your results support your hypothesis? Explain your answer.
7. **Evaluating Methods** Do you think your class sample is large enough to confirm your hypothesis for all people of all ages? Explain your answer.

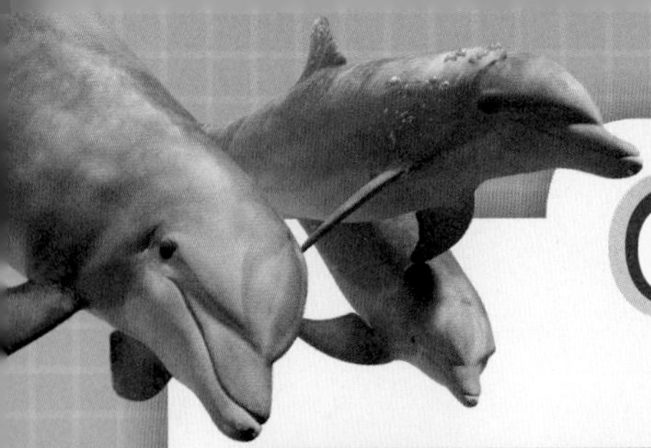

Chapter Review

USING KEY TERMS

Complete each of the following sentences by choosing the correct term from the word bank.

loudness	echoes
pitch	noise
sound quality	

1. The _____ of a sound wave depends on its amplitude.

2. Reflected sound waves are called _____.

3. Two different instruments playing the same note sound different because of _____.

UNDERSTANDING KEY IDEAS

Multiple Choice

4. If a fire engine is traveling toward you, the Doppler effect will cause the siren to sound
   - **a.** higher.
   - **b.** lower.
   - **c.** louder.
   - **d.** softer.

5. Sound travels fastest through
   - **a.** a vacuum.
   - **b.** sea water.
   - **c.** air.
   - **d.** glass.

6. If two sound waves interfere constructively, you will hear
   - **a.** a high-pitched sound.
   - **b.** a softer sound.
   - **c.** a louder sound.
   - **d.** no change in sound.

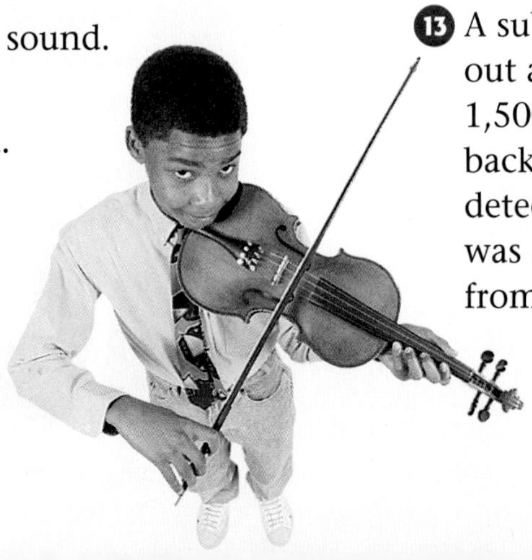

7. You will hear a sonic boom when
   - **a.** an object breaks the sound barrier.
   - **b.** an object travels at supersonic speeds.
   - **c.** a shock wave reaches your ears.
   - **d.** the speed of sound is 290 m/s.

8. Resonance can happen when an object vibrates at another object's
   - **a.** resonant frequency.
   - **b.** fundamental frequency.
   - **c.** second overtone frequency.
   - **d.** All of the above

9. A technological device that can be used to see sound waves is a(n)
   - **a.** sonar.
   - **b.** oscilloscope.
   - **c.** ultrasound.
   - **d.** amplifier.

Short Answer

10. Describe how the Doppler effect helps a beluga whale determine whether a fish is moving away from it or toward it.

11. How do vibrations cause sound waves?

12. Briefly describe what happens in the different parts of the ear.

Math Skills

13. A submarine that is not moving sends out a sonar sound wave traveling 1,500 m/s, which reflects off a boat back to the submarine. The sonar crew detects the reflected wave 6 s after it was sent out. How far away is the boat from the submarine?

CRITICAL THINKING

14 **Concept Mapping** Use the following terms to create a concept map: *sound waves, pitch, loudness, decibels, frequency, amplitude, oscilloscope, hertz,* and *interference.*

15 **Analyzing Processes** An *anechoic chamber* is a room where there is almost no reflection of sound waves. Anechoic chambers are often used to test sound equipment, such as stereos. The walls of such chambers are usually covered with foam triangles. Explain why this design eliminates echoes in the room.

16 **Applying Concepts** Would the pilot of an airplane breaking the sound barrier hear a sonic boom? Explain why or why not.

17 **Forming Hypotheses** After working in a factory for a month, a man you know complains about a ringing in his ears. What might be wrong with him? What do you think may have caused his problem? What can you suggest to him to prevent further hearing loss?

INTERPRETING GRAPHICS

Use the oscilloscope screens below to answer the questions that follow:

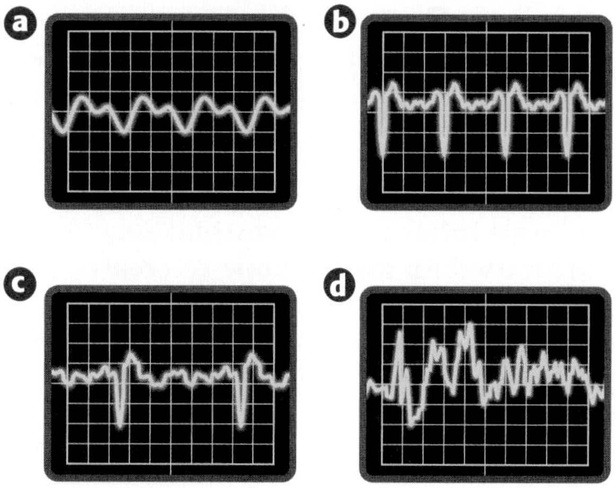

18 Which sound is noise?

19 Which represents the softest sound?

20 Which represents the sound with the lowest pitch?

21 Which two sounds were produced by the same instrument?

Standardized Test Preparation

Multiple Choice

Use the diagram below to answer questions 1–3.

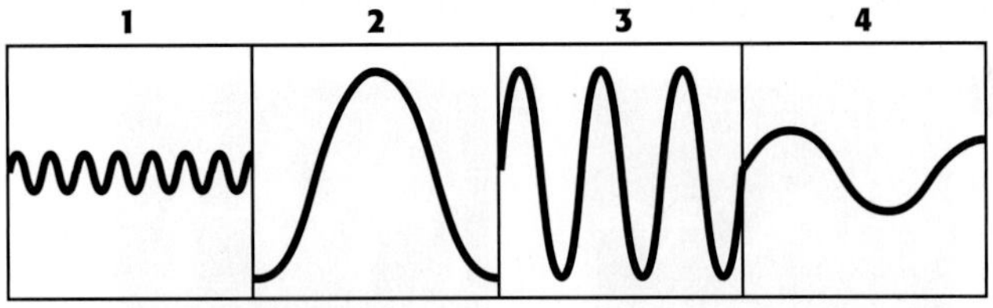

1. **During a laboratory investigation, Aaron used an oscilloscope to create graphs of sounds he produced using a whistle. Which of the graphs shows the softest sound (lowest volume)?**

   A. graph 1

   B. graph 2

   C. graph 3

   D. graph 4

2. **Which of the graphs shows a sound that would be most likely to resemble the sound made by a female opera singer hitting a high note?**

   A. graph 1

   B. graph 2

   C. graph 3

   D. graph 4

3. **Which of the graphs shows both a high volume and a high pitch?**

   A. graph 1

   B. graph 2

   C. graph 3

   D. graph 4

4. **If you were conducting an experiment to determine the speed of sound, which factor should you consider in order to formulate a testable hypothesis?**

   A. the source of the sound

   B. the temperature of the medium

   C. the loudness of the sound

   D. the amplitude of the sound wave

5. **Cletus wants to make ear protectors for people who work around loud jet engines. Which of the following materials should he experiment with for best results?**

   A. a material that amplifies sound

   B. a material that absorbs sound

   C. a material that transmits sound

   D. a material that produces sound

6. **Which of the following is a true statement about what happens when a guitar is played?**

   A. The vibrations are transmitted through a vacuum.

   B. Sound moves away from the guitar in a single direction.

   C. Sound moves as a longitudinal wave away from the guitar.

   D. Particles of air are carried farther and farther away from the guitar with each sound wave.

Use the table below to answer question 7.

Speed of Sound in Air	
Temperature (°C)	Speed (m/s)
0	331
20	343
25	346
100	366

7. In an experiment, Malik is determining the speed of sound in air at different temperatures. According to the data above, which of the following statements is true?

A. Temperature does not affect the speed of sound in air.

B. As temperature increases, the speed of sound in air decreases.

C. As temperature increases, the speed of sound in air increases.

D. As temperature decreases, the speed of sound in air increases.

8. Which statement best describes what happens in the inner ear?

A. Sound vibrations are turned into electrical signals.

B. Sound waves enter the ear and are channeled through the ear canal.

C. Sound waves are amplified by the hammer, anvil, and stirrup.

D. Electrical signals are interpreted.

9. Where can sound not travel?

A. through air

B. through water

C. through glass

D. through empty space

10. During a laboratory experiment about the nature of sound, Jesse walked into a large, dark room and yelled "Hello!" She heard a strong echo of the word almost immediately. Which of the following is a valid conclusion Jesse could draw from her observations?

A. The room has smooth, hard walls and few things in it.

B. The room is full of pillows and other soft objects.

C. The room has no walls.

D. The room is very cold.

Open Response

11. LaToya generated a longitudinal wave in a coiled spring in a toy in order to model a sound wave. Describe a limitation of LaToya's model.

12. Miguel used an oscilloscope to produce graphs of two different sounds in a laboratory investigation. One has a higher amplitude than the other, and it has repeating patterns. The other has more compressions but no repeating patterns. How can you know which graph shows music and which shows noise?

Science in Action

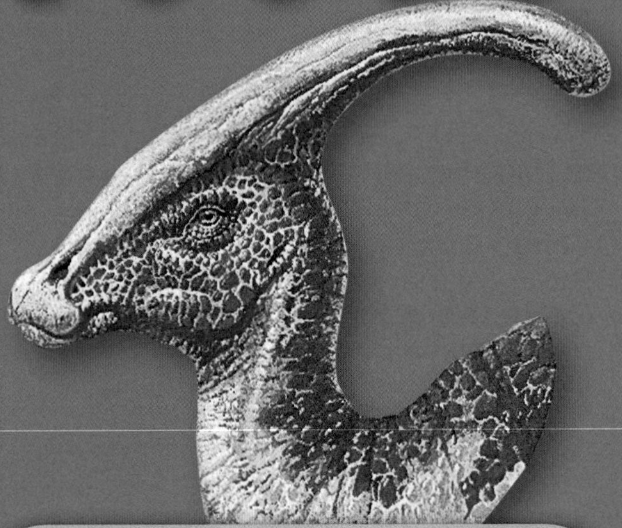

Scientific Discoveries

Jurassic Bark

Imagine you suddenly hear a loud honking sound, such as a trombone or a tuba. "Must be band tryouts," you think. You turn to find the noise and find yourself face to face with a 10 m long, 2,800 kg dinosaur with a huge tubular crest on its snout. Do you run? No—your musical friend, *Parasaurolophus,* is a vegetarian. In 1995, an almost-complete fossil skull of an adult *Parasaurolophus* was found in New Mexico. Scientists studied the noise-making qualities of *Parasaurolophus*'s crest and found that it contained many internal tubes and chambers.

Math Activity

Imagine that a standing wave with a frequency of 80 Hz is made inside the crest of a *Parasaurolophus*. What would be the frequency of the first overtone of this standing wave? the second? the third?

Science Fiction

"Ear" by Jane Yolen

Jily and her friends, Sanya and Feeny, live in a time not too far in the future. It is a time when everyone's hearing is damaged. People communicate using sign language—unless they put on their Ear. Then, the whole world is filled with sounds.

Jily and her friends visit a club called The Low Down. It is too quiet for Jily's tastes, and she wants to leave. But Sanya is dancing by herself, even though there is no music. When Jily finds Feeny, they notice some Earless kids their own age. Earless people never go to clubs, and Jily finds their presence offensive. But Feeny is intrigued.

Everyone is given an Ear at the age of 12 but has to give it up at the age of 30. Why would these kids want to go out without their Ears before the age of 30? Jily thinks the idea is ridiculous and doesn't stick around to find out the answer to such a question. But it is an answer that will change her life by the end of the next day.

Language Arts Activity

WRITING SKILL Read "Ear," by Jane Yolen, in the *Holt Anthology of Science Fiction.* Write a one-page report that discusses how the story made you think about the importance of hearing in your everyday life.

Adam Dudley

Sound Engineer Adam Dudley uses the science of sound waves every day at his job. He is the audio supervisor for the Performing Arts Center of the University of Texas at Austin. Dudley oversees sound design and technical support for campus performance spaces, including an auditorium that seats over 3,000 people.

To stage a successful concert, Dudley takes many factors into account. The size and shape of the room help determine how many speakers to use and where to place them. It is a challenge to make sure people seated in the back row can hear well enough and also to make sure that the people up front aren't going deaf from the high volume.

Adam Dudley loves his job—he enjoys working with people and technology and prefers not to wear a coat and tie. Although he is invisible to the audience, his work backstage is as crucial as the musicians and actors on stage to the success of the events.

Social Studies ACTIVITY

Research the ways in which concert halls were designed before the use of electric amplification. Make a model or diorama, and present it to the class, explaining the acoustical factors involved in the design.

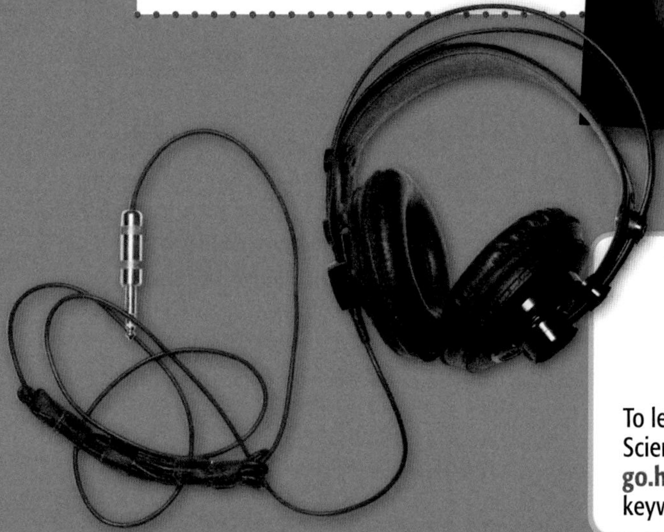

go.hrw.com

To learn more about these Science in Action topics, visit go.hrw.com and type in the keyword HP5SNDF.

Current Science

Check out Current Science® articles related to this chapter by visiting go.hrw.com. Just type in the keyword HP5CS21.

5

The Nature of Light

The Big Idea

Light is an electromagnetic wave. Electromagnetic waves interact in predictable ways.

SECTION

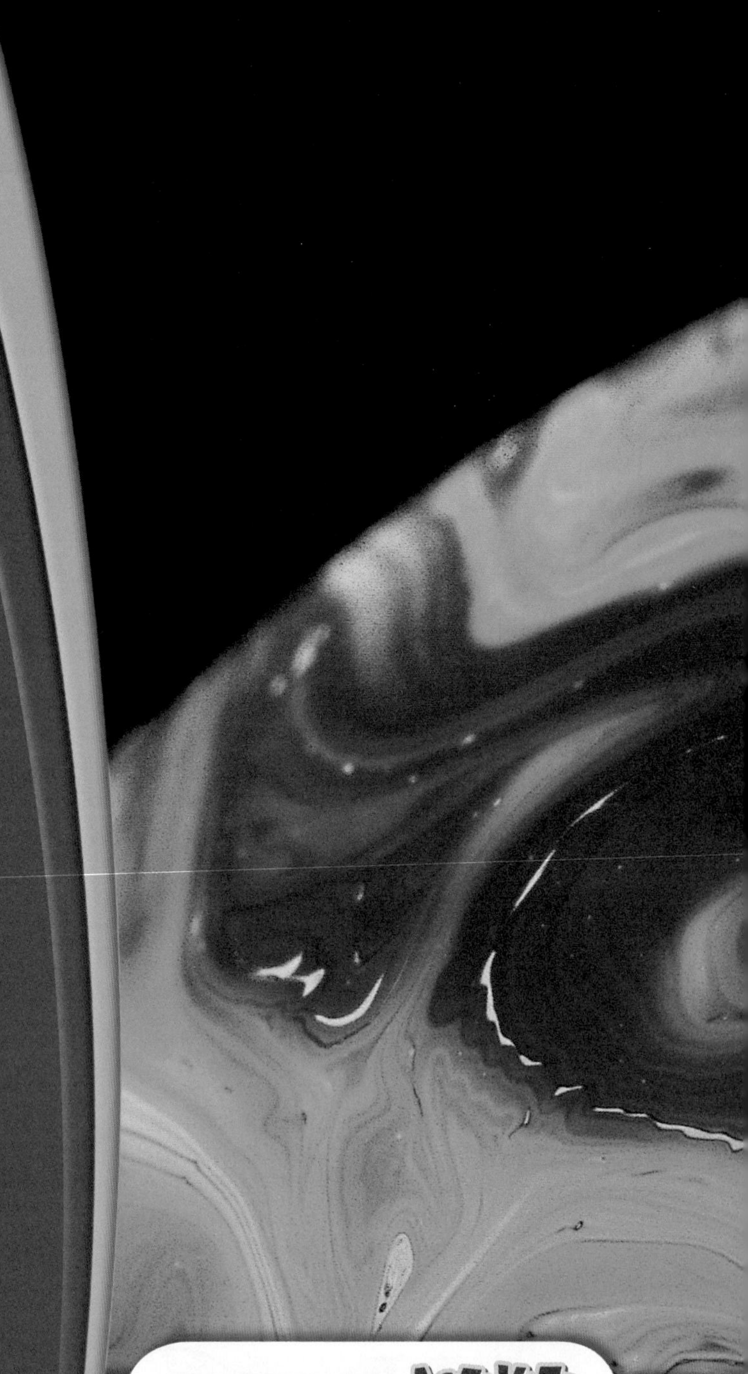

About the Photo

What kind of alien life lives on this planet? Actually, this isn't a planet at all. It's an ordinary soap bubble! The brightly colored swirls on this bubble are reflections of light. Light waves combine through interference so that you see different colors on this soap bubble.

PRE-READING ACTIVITY

FOLDNOTES **Booklet** Before you read the chapter, create the FoldNote entitled "Booklet" described in the **Study Skills** section of the Appendix. Label each page of the booklet with a main idea from the chapter. As you read the chapter, write what you learn about each main idea on the appropriate page of the booklet.

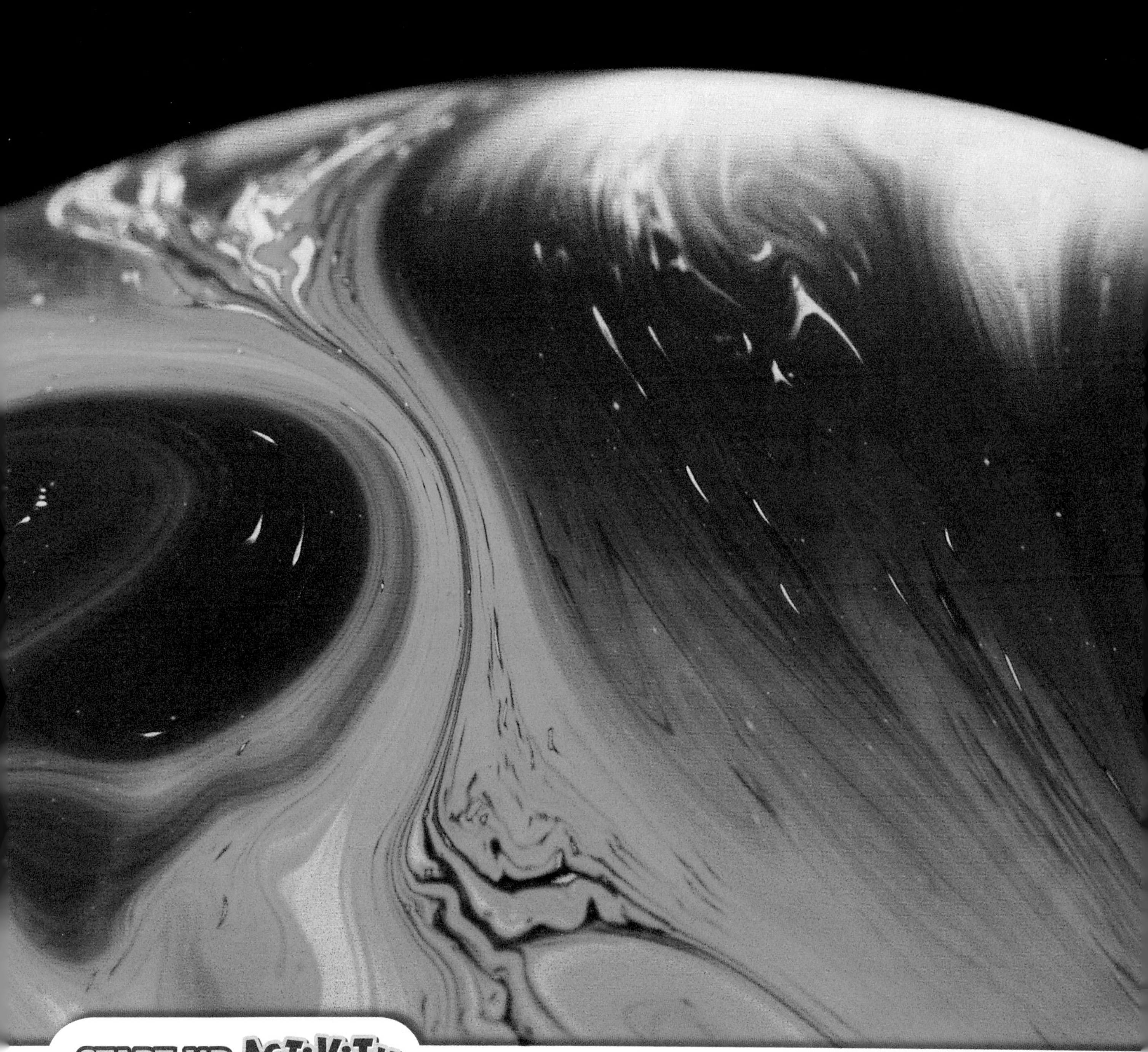

START-UP ACTIVITY

Colors of Light

Is white light really white? In this activity, you will use a spectroscope to answer that question.

Procedure

1. Your teacher will give you a **spectroscope** or instructions for making one.
2. Turn on an **incandescent light bulb.** Look at the light bulb through your spectroscope. Write a description of what you see.
3. Repeat step 2, looking at a **fluorescent light.** Again, describe what you see.

Analysis

1. Compare what you saw with the incandescent light bulb with what you saw with the fluorescent light bulb.
2. Both kinds of bulbs produce white light. What did you learn about white light by using the spectroscope?
3. Light from a flame is yellowish but is similar to white light. What do you think you would see if you used a spectroscope to look at light from a flame?

SECTION 1

What Is Light?

What You Will Learn

- Describe light as an electromagnetic wave.
- Calculate distances traveled by light by using the speed of light.
- Explain why light from the sun is important.

Vocabulary

electromagnetic wave
radiation

READING STRATEGY

Brainstorming The key idea of this section is light. Brainstorm words and phrases related to light.

You can see light. It's everywhere! Light comes from the sun and from other sources, such as light bulbs. But what exactly is light?

Scientists are still studying light to learn more about it. A lot has already been discovered about light, as you will soon find out. Read on, and be enlightened!

Light: An Electromagnetic Wave

Light is a type of energy that travels as a wave. But light is different from other kinds of waves. Other kinds of waves, like sound waves and water waves, must travel through matter. Light does not require matter through which to travel. Light is an electromagnetic wave (EM wave). An **electromagnetic wave** is a wave that can travel through empty space or matter and consists of changing electric and magnetic fields.

Fields exist around certain objects and can exert a force on another object without touching that object. For example, Earth is a source of a gravitational field. This field pulls you and all things toward Earth. But keep in mind that this field, like all fields, is not made of matter.

Figure 1 shows a diagram of an electromagnetic wave. Notice that the electric and magnetic fields are at right angles—or are *perpendicular*—to each other. These fields are also perpendicular to the direction of the wave motion.

electromagnetic wave a wave that consists of electric and magnetic fields that vibrate at right angles to each other

Figure 1 *Electromagnetic waves are made of vibrating electric and magnetic fields.*

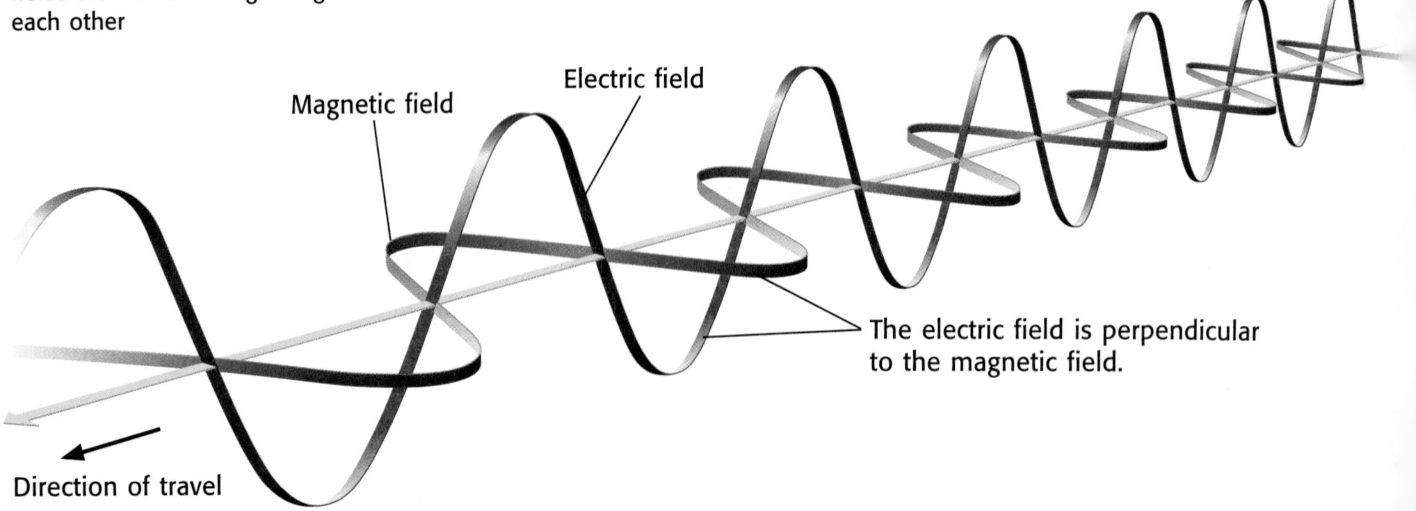

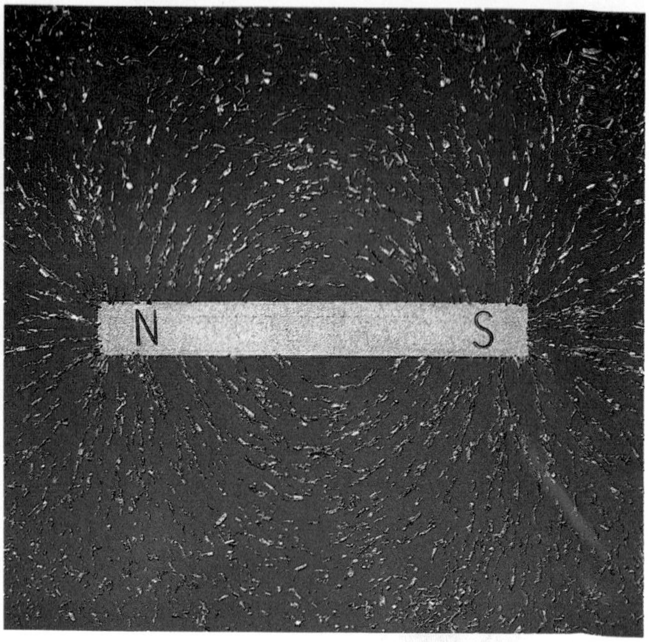

Figure 2 *The hair on the girl's head stands up because of an electric field and the iron filings form arcs around the magnet because of a magnetic field.*

Electric and Magnetic Fields

Electromagnetic waves are changing electric and magnetic fields. But what are electric and magnetic fields? An *electric field* surrounds every charged object. The electric field around a charged object pulls oppositely charged objects toward it and repels like-charged objects. You can see the effect of electric fields whenever you see objects stuck together by static electricity. **Figure 2** shows another effect of an electric field.

A *magnetic field* surrounds every magnet. Because of magnetic fields, paper clips and iron filings are pulled toward magnets. You can feel the effect of magnetic fields when you hold two magnets close together. The iron filings around the magnet in **Figure 2** form arcs in the presence of the magnet's magnetic field.

✓ *Reading Check* **Where can electric fields be found?** (*See the Appendix for answers to Reading Checks.*)

CONNECTION TO Social Studies

WRITING SKILL The Particle Model of Light

Thinking of light as being an electromagnetic wave can explain many properties of light. But some properties of light can be explained only by using a particle model of light. In the particle model of light, light is thought of as a stream of particles called *photons*. Research the history of the particle model of light. Write a one-page paper on what you learn.

How EM Waves Are Produced

An EM wave can be produced by the vibration of an electrically charged particle. When the particle vibrates, or moves back and forth, the electric field around it also vibrates. When the electric field starts vibrating, a vibrating magnetic field is created. The vibration of an electric field and a magnetic field together produces an EM wave that carries energy released by the original vibration of the particle. The transfer of energy as electromagnetic waves is called **radiation.**

radiation transfer of energy as electromagnetic waves

Figure 3 *Thunder and lightning are produced at the same time. But you usually see lightning before you hear thunder, because light travels much faster than sound.*

The Speed of Light

Scientists have yet to discover anything that travels faster than light. In the near vacuum of space, the speed of light is about 300,000,000 m/s, or 300,000 km/s. Light travels slightly slower in air, glass, and other types of matter. (Keep in mind that even though electromagnetic waves do not need to travel through matter, they can travel through many substances.)

Believe it or not, light can travel about 880,000 times faster than sound! This fact explains the phenomenon described in **Figure 3.** If you could run at the speed of light, you could travel around Earth 7.5 times in 1 s.

Reading Check **How does the speed of light compare with the speed of sound?**

MATH FOCUS

How Fast Is Light? The distance from Earth to the moon is 384,000 km. Calculate the time it takes for light to travel that distance.

Step 1: Write the equation for speed.

$$speed = \frac{distance}{time}$$

Step 2: Rearrange the equation by multiplying by time and dividing by speed.

$$time = \frac{distance}{speed}$$

Step 3: Replace *distance* and *speed* with the values given in the problem, and solve.

$$time = \frac{384{,}000 \text{ km}}{300{,}000 \text{ km/s}}$$

$$time = 1.28 \text{ s}$$

Now It's Your Turn

1. The distance from the sun to Venus is 108,000,000 km. Calculate the time it takes for light to travel that distance.

Light from the Sun

Even though light travels quickly, it takes about 8.3 min for light to travel from the sun to Earth. It takes this much time because Earth is 150,000,000 km away from the sun.

The EM waves from the sun are the major source of energy on Earth. For example, plants use photosynthesis to store energy from the sun. And animals use and store energy by eating plants or by eating other animals that eat plants. Even fossil fuels, such as coal and oil, store energy from the sun. Fossil fuels are formed from the remains of plants and animals that lived millions of years ago.

Although Earth receives a large amount of energy from the sun, only a very small part of the total energy given off by the sun reaches Earth. Look at **Figure 4.** The sun gives off energy as EM waves in all directions. Most of this energy travels away in space.

Figure 4 *Only a small amount of the sun's energy reaches the planets in the solar system.*

SECTION Review

Summary

- Light is an electromagnetic (EM) wave. An EM wave is a wave that consists of changing electric and magnetic fields. EM waves require no matter through which to travel.
- EM waves can be produced by the vibration of charged particles.
- The speed of light in a vacuum is about 300,000,000 m/s.
- EM waves from the sun are the major source of energy for Earth.

Using Key Terms

1. Use the following terms in the same sentence: *electromagnetic wave* and *radiation.*

Understanding Key Ideas

2. Electromagnetic waves are different from other types of waves because they can travel through
   a. air. **c.** space.
   b. glass. **d.** steel.
3. Describe light in terms of electromagnetic waves.
4. Why is light from the sun important?
5. How can electromagnetic waves be produced?

Math Skills

6. The distance from the sun to Jupiter is 778,000,000 km. How long does it take for light from the sun to reach Jupiter?

Critical Thinking

7. **Making Inferences** Why is it important that EM waves can travel through empty space?
8. **Making Comparisons** How does the amount of energy produced by the sun compare with the amount of energy that reaches Earth from the sun?
9. **Applying Concepts** Explain why the energy produced by burning wood in a campfire is energy from the sun.

SECTION 2

The Electromagnetic Spectrum

What You Will Learn

- Identify how electromagnetic waves differ from each other.
- Describe some uses for radio waves and microwaves.
- List examples of how infrared waves and visible light are important in your life.
- Explain how ultraviolet light, X rays, and gamma rays can be both helpful and harmful.

Vocabulary

electromagnetic spectrum

READING STRATEGY

Mnemonics As you read this section, create a mnemonic device to help you remember the kinds of EM waves.

When you look around, you can see things that reflect light to your eyes. But a bee might see the same things differently. Bees can see a kind of light—called **ultraviolet light**—that you can't see!

It might seem odd to call something you can't see *light*. The light you are most familiar with is called *visible light*. Ultraviolet light is similar to visible light. Both are kinds of electromagnetic (EM) waves. In this section, you will learn about many kinds of EM waves, including X rays, radio waves, and microwaves.

Characteristics of EM Waves

All EM waves travel at the same speed in a vacuum—300,000 km/s. How is this possible? The speed of a wave is found by multiplying its wavelength by its frequency. So, EM waves having different wavelengths can travel at the same speed as long as their frequencies are also different. The entire range of EM waves is called the **electromagnetic spectrum.** The electromagnetic spectrum is shown in **Figure 1.** The electromagnetic spectrum is divided into regions according to the length of the waves. There is no sharp division between one kind of wave and the next. Some kinds even have overlapping ranges.

Reading Check How is the speed of a wave determined? (*See the Appendix for answers to Reading Checks.*)

Figure 1 **The Electromagnetic Spectrum**

The electromagnetic spectrum is arranged from long to short wavelength or from low to high frequency.

Radio waves

All radio and television stations broadcast radio waves.

Microwaves

Despite their name, microwaves are not the shortest EM waves.

Infrared

Infrared means "below red."

Radio Waves

Radio waves cover a wide range of waves in the EM spectrum. Radio waves have some of the longest wavelengths and the lowest frequencies of all EM waves. In fact, radio waves are any EM waves that have wavelengths longer than 30 cm. Radio waves are used for broadcasting radio signals.

Broadcasting Radio Signals

Figure 2 shows how radio signals are broadcast. Radio stations encode sound information into radio waves by varying either the waves' amplitude or their frequency. Changing amplitude or frequency is called *modulation* (MAHJ uh LAY shuhn). You probably know that there are AM radio stations and FM radio stations. The abbreviation *AM* stands for "amplitude modulation," and the abbreviation *FM* stands for "frequency modulation."

1 A radio station converts sound into an electric current. The current produces radio waves that are sent out in all directions by the antenna.
2 A radio receives radio waves and then converts them into an electric current, which is then converted to sound.

Figure 2 *Radio waves cannot be heard, but they can carry energy that can be converted into sound.*

Comparing AM and FM Radio Waves

AM radio waves are different from FM radio waves. For example, AM radio waves have longer wavelengths than FM radio waves do. And AM radio waves can bounce off the atmosphere and thus can travel farther than FM radio waves. But FM radio waves are less affected by electrical noise than AM radio waves are. So, music broadcast from FM stations sounds better than music broadcast from AM stations.

electromagnetic spectrum all of the frequencies or wavelengths of electromagnetic radiation

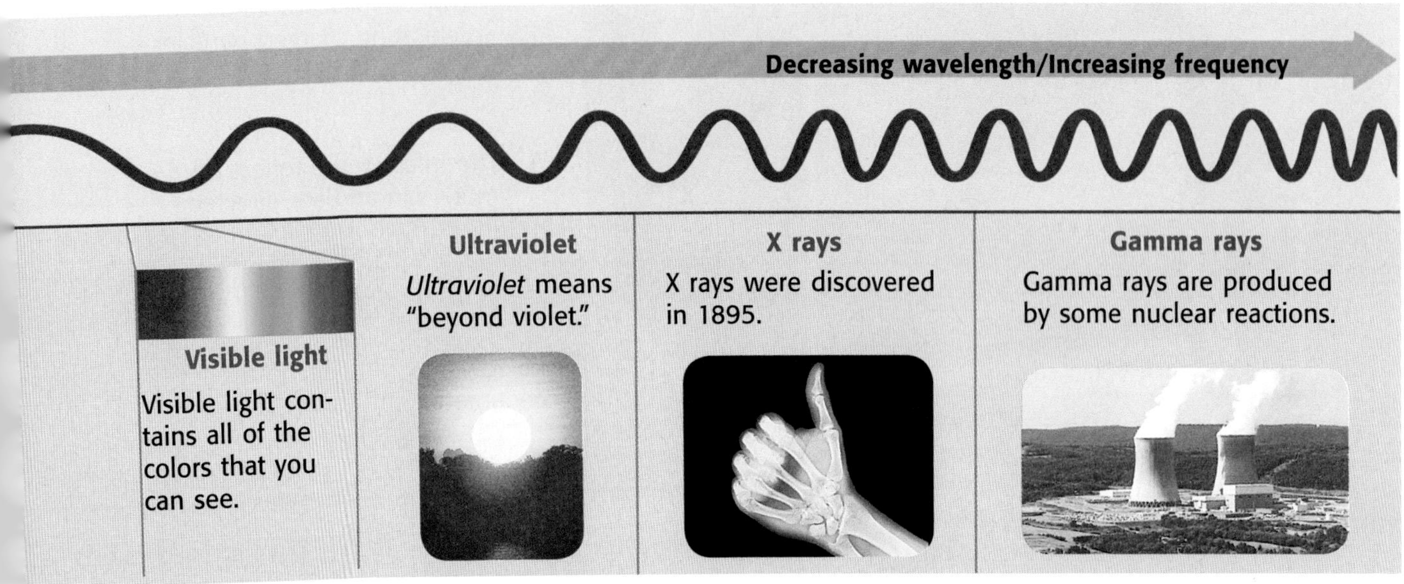

Decreasing wavelength/Increasing frequency

Ultraviolet means "beyond violet."

Gamma rays are produced by some nuclear reactions.

Radio Waves and Television

Television signals are also carried by radio waves. Most television stations broadcast radio waves that have shorter wavelengths and higher frequencies than those broadcast by radio stations. Like radio signals, television signals are broadcast using amplitude modulation and frequency modulation. Television stations use frequency-modulated waves to carry sound and amplitude-modulated waves to carry pictures.

Some waves carrying television signals are transmitted to artificial satellites orbiting Earth. The waves are amplified and sent to ground antennas. They then travel through cables to televisions in homes. Cable television works by this process.

Reading Check **Which EM waves can carry television signals?**

Microwaves

Microwaves have shorter wavelengths and higher frequencies than radio waves do. Microwaves have wavelengths between 1 mm and 30 cm. You are probably familiar with microwaves—they are created in a microwave oven, such as the one shown in **Figure 3.**

Microwaves and Communication

Like radio waves, microwaves are used to send information over long distances. For example, cellular phones send and receive signals using microwaves. And signals sent between Earth and artificial satellites in space are also carried by microwaves.

Figure 3 **How a Microwave Oven Works**

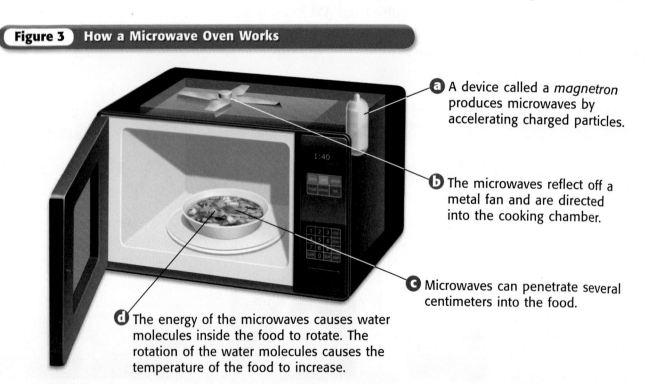

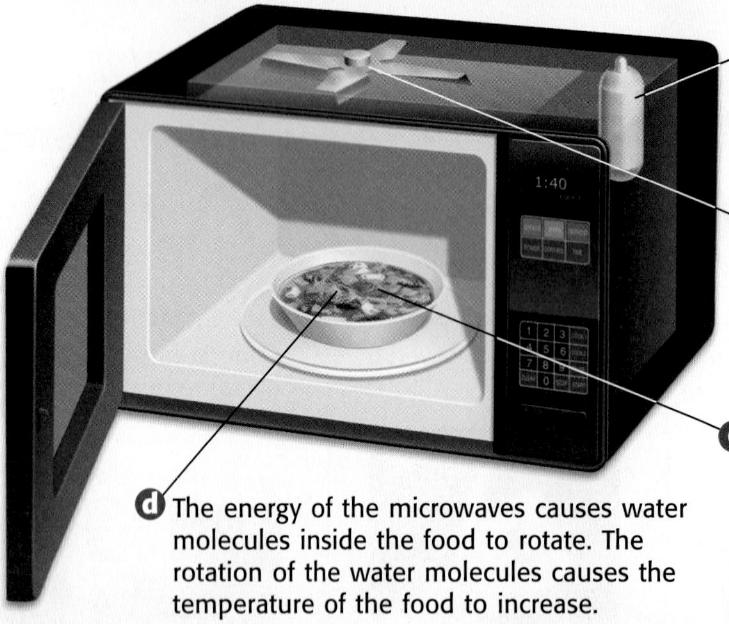

a A device called a *magnetron* produces microwaves by accelerating charged particles.

b The microwaves reflect off a metal fan and are directed into the cooking chamber.

c Microwaves can penetrate several centimeters into the food.

d The energy of the microwaves causes water molecules inside the food to rotate. The rotation of the water molecules causes the temperature of the food to increase.

Figure 4 *Police officers use radar to detect cars going faster than the speed limit.*

Radar

Microwaves are also used in radar. *Radar* (**ra**dio **d**etection **a**nd **r**anging) is used to detect the speed and location of objects. The police officer in **Figure 4** is using radar to check the speed of a car. The radar gun sends out microwaves that reflect off the car and return to the gun. The reflected waves are used to calculate the speed of the car. Radar is also used to watch the movement of airplanes and to help ships navigate at night.

Infrared Waves

Infrared waves have shorter wavelengths and higher frequencies than microwaves do. The wavelengths of infrared waves vary between 700 nanometers and 1 mm. A nanometer (nm) is equal to 0.000000001 m.

On a sunny day, you may be warmed by infrared waves from the sun. Your skin absorbs infrared waves striking your body. The energy of the waves causes the particles in your skin to vibrate more, and you feel an increase in temperature. The sun is not the only source of infrared waves. Almost all things give off infrared waves, including buildings, trees, and you! The amount of infrared waves an object gives off depends on the object's temperature. Warmer objects give off more infrared waves than cooler objects do.

You can't see infrared waves, but some devices can detect infrared waves. For example, infrared binoculars change infrared waves into light you can see. Such binoculars can be used to watch animals at night. **Figure 5** shows a photo taken with film that is sensitive to infrared waves.

Figure 5 *In this photograph, brighter colors indicate higher temperatures.*

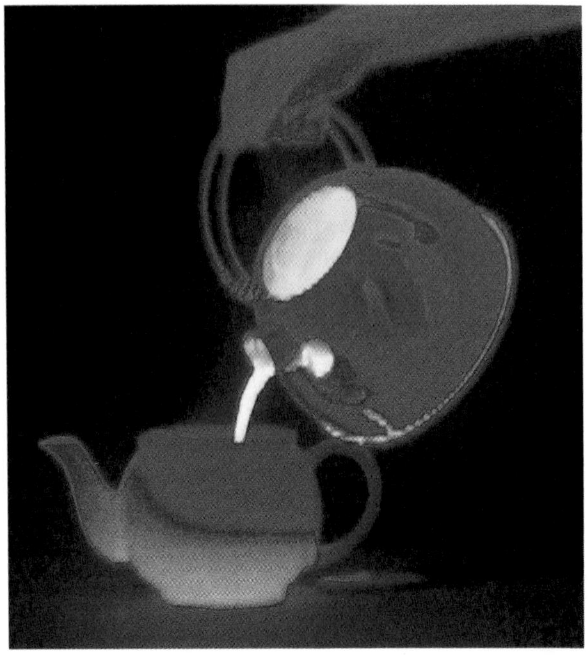

Figure 6 *Water droplets can separate white light into visible light of different wavelengths. As a result, you see all the colors of visible light in a rainbow.*

Visible Light

Visible light is the very narrow range of wavelengths and frequencies in the electromagnetic spectrum that humans can see. Visible light waves have shorter wavelengths and higher frequencies than infrared waves do. Visible light waves have wavelengths between 400 nm and 700 nm.

Visible Light from the Sun

Some of the energy that reaches Earth from the sun is visible light. The visible light from the sun is white light. *White light* is visible light of all wavelengths combined. Light from lamps in your home as well as from the fluorescent bulbs in your school is also white light.

Reading Check **What is white light?**

Colors of Light

Humans see the different wavelengths of visible light as different colors, as shown in **Figure 6.** The longest wavelengths are seen as red light. The shortest wavelengths are seen as violet light.

The range of colors is called the *visible spectrum.* You can see the visible spectrum in **Figure 7.** When you list the colors, you might use the imaginary name *ROY G. BiV* to help you remember their order. The capital letters in Roy's name represent the first letter of each color of visible light: **r**ed, **o**range, **y**ellow, **g**reen, **b**lue, and **v**iolet. What about the *i* in Roy's last name? You can think of *i* as standing for the color indigo. Indigo is a dark blue color.

SCHOOL to HOME

Making a Rainbow

On a sunny day, ask an adult to use a hose or a spray bottle to make a mist of water outside. Move around until you see a rainbow in the water mist. Draw a diagram showing the positions of the water mist, the sun, the rainbow, and yourself.

ACTIVITY

Figure 7 *The visible spectrum contains all colors of light.*

Ultraviolet Light

Ultraviolet light (UV light) is another type of electromagnetic wave produced by the sun. Ultraviolet waves have shorter wavelengths and higher frequencies than visible light does. The wavelengths of ultraviolet light waves vary between 60 nm and 400 nm. Ultraviolet light affects your body in both bad and good ways.

Reading Check **How do ultraviolet light waves compare with visible light waves?**

Bad Effects

On the bad side, too much ultraviolet light can cause sunburn, as you can see in **Figure 8.** Too much ultraviolet light can also cause skin cancer, wrinkles, and damage to the eyes. Luckily, much of the ultraviolet light from the sun does not reach Earth's surface. But you should still protect yourself against the ultraviolet light that does reach you. To do so, you should use sunscreen with a high SPF (sun protection factor). You should also wear sunglasses that block out UV light to protect your eyes. Hats, long-sleeved shirts, and long pants can protect you, too. You need this protection even on overcast days because UV light can travel through clouds.

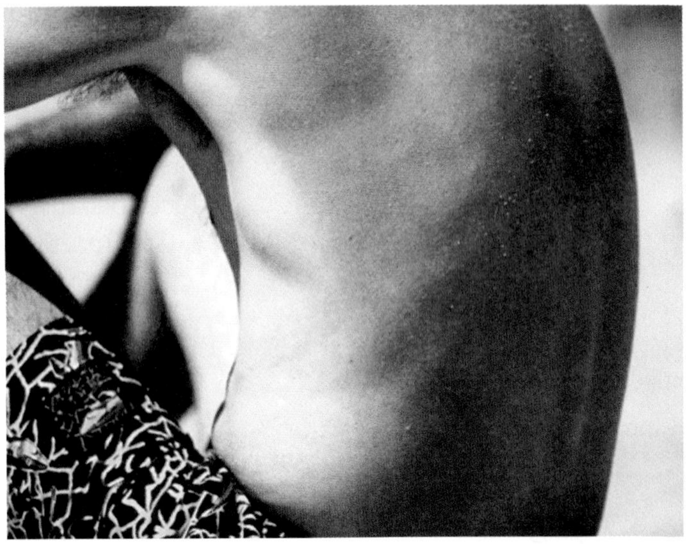

Figure 8 *Too much exposure to ultraviolet light can lead to a painful sunburn. Using sunscreen will help protect your skin.*

Good Effects

On the good side, ultraviolet waves produced by ultraviolet lamps are used to kill bacteria on food and surgical tools. In addition, small amounts of ultraviolet light are beneficial to your body. When exposed to ultraviolet light, skin cells produce vitamin D. This vitamin allows the intestines to absorb calcium. Without calcium, your teeth and bones would be very weak.

X Rays and Gamma Rays

X rays and gamma rays have some of the shortest wavelengths and highest frequencies of all EM waves.

X Rays

X rays have wavelengths between 0.001 nm and 60 nm. They can pass through many materials. This characteristic makes X rays useful in the medical field, as shown in **Figure 9.** But too much exposure to X rays can also damage or kill living cells. A patient getting an X ray may wear special aprons to protect parts of the body that do not need X-ray exposure. These aprons are lined with lead because X rays cannot pass through lead.

X-ray machines are also used as security devices in airports and other public buildings. The machines allow security officers to see inside bags and other containers without opening the containers.

Reading Check How are patients protected from X rays?

Gamma Rays

Gamma rays are EM waves that have wavelengths shorter than 0.1 nm. They can penetrate most materials very easily. Gamma rays are used to treat some forms of cancer. Doctors focus the rays on tumors inside the body to kill the cancer cells. This treatment often has good effects, but it can have bad side effects because some healthy cells may also be killed.

Gamma rays are also used to kill harmful bacteria in foods, such as meat and fresh fruits. The gamma rays do not harm the treated food and do not stay in the food. So, food that has been treated with gamma rays is safe for you to eat.

CONNECTION TO Astronomy

Gamma Ray Spectrometer In 2001, NASA put an artificial satellite called the *2001 Mars Odyssey* in orbit around Mars. The *Odyssey* is carrying a gamma ray spectrometer. A *spectrometer* is a device used to detect certain kinds of EM waves. The gamma ray spectrometer on the *Odyssey* was used to look for water and several chemical elements on Mars. Scientists hope to use this information to learn about the geology of Mars. Research the characteristics of Mars and Earth. In your **science journal,** make a chart comparing Mars and Earth.

ACTIVITY

Figure 9 How a Bone Is X Rayed

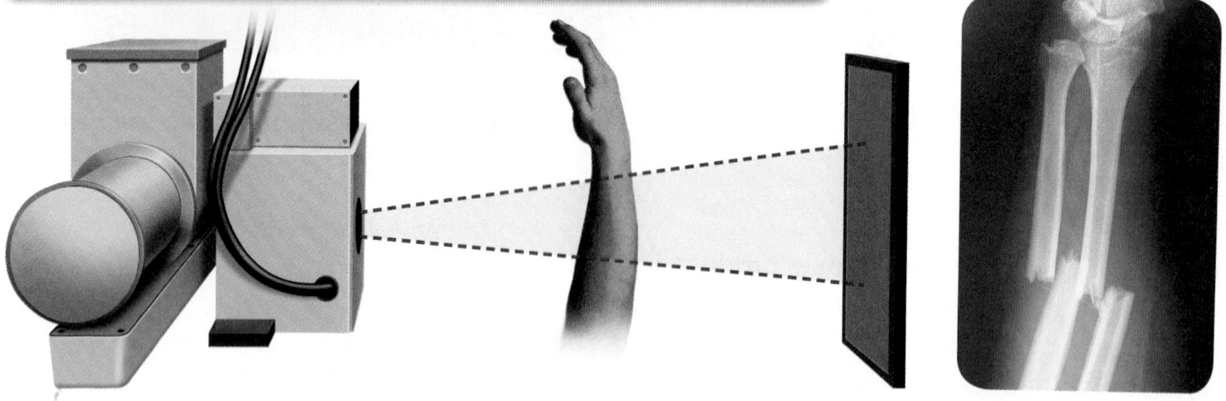

1. X rays travel easily through skin and muscle but are absorbed by bones.
2. The X rays that are not absorbed strike the film.
3. Bright areas appear on the film where X rays are absorbed by the bones.

SECTION Review

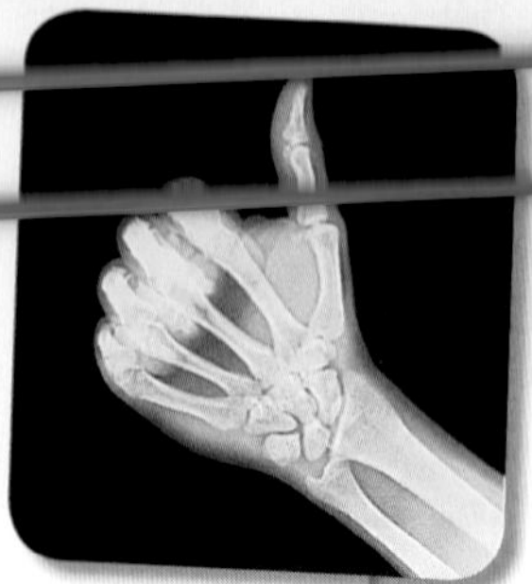

Summary

- All electromagnetic (EM) waves travel at the speed of light. EM waves differ only by wavelength and frequency.
- The entire range of EM waves is called the *electromagnetic spectrum*.
- Radio waves are used for communication.
- Microwaves are used in cooking and in radar.
- The absorption of infrared waves is felt as an increase in temperature.
- Visible light is the narrow range of wavelengths that humans can see. Different wavelengths are seen as different colors.
- Ultraviolet light is useful for killing bacteria and for producing vitamin D in the body. Overexposure to ultraviolet light can cause health problems.
- X rays and gamma rays are EM waves that are often used in medicine. Overexposure to these kinds of rays can damage or kill living cells.

Using Key Terms

1. In your own words, write a definition for the term *electromagnetic spectrum*.

Understanding Key Ideas

2. Which of the following electromagnetic waves are produced by the sun?
   a. infrared waves
   b. visible light
   c. ultraviolet light
   d. All of the above
3. How do the different kinds of EM waves differ from each other?
4. Describe two ways of transmitting information using radio waves.
5. Explain why ultraviolet light, X rays, and gamma rays can be both helpful and harmful.
6. What are two common uses for microwaves?
7. What is white light? What are two sources of white light?
8. What is the visible spectrum?

Critical Thinking

9. **Applying Concepts** Describe how three different kinds of electromagnetic waves have been useful to you today.
10. **Making Comparisons** Compare the wavelengths of infrared waves, ultraviolet light, and visible light.

Interpreting Graphics

The waves in the diagram below represent two different kinds of EM waves. Use the diagram below to answer the questions that follow.

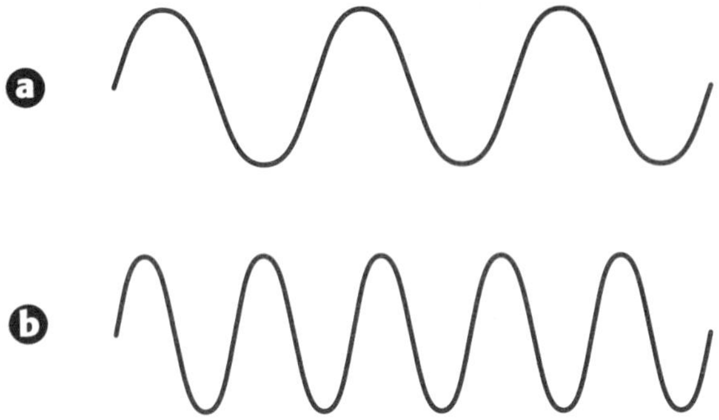

11. Which wave has the longest wavelength?
12. Suppose that one of the waves represents a microwave and one of the waves represents a radio wave. Which wave represents the microwave?

SECTION 3

Interactions of Light Waves

What You Will Learn

- Describe how reflection allows you to see things.
- Describe absorption and scattering.
- Explain how refraction can create optical illusions and separate white light into colors.
- Explain the relationship between diffraction and wavelength.
- Compare constructive and destructive interference of light.

Vocabulary

reflection	refraction
absorption	diffraction
scattering	interference

READING STRATEGY

Reading Organizer As you read this section, make a concept map by using the terms above.

Have you ever seen a cat's eyes glow in the dark when light shines on them? Cats have a special layer of cells in the back of their eyes that reflects light.

This layer helps the cat see better by giving the eyes another chance to detect the light. Reflection is one interaction of electromagnetic waves. Because we can see visible light, it is easier to explain all wave interactions by using visible light.

Reflection

Reflection happens when light waves bounce off an object. Light reflects off objects all around you. When you look in a mirror, you are seeing light that has been reflected twice—first from you and then from the mirror. If light is reflecting off everything around you, why can't you see your image on a wall? To answer this question, you must learn the law of reflection.

The Law of Reflection

Light reflects off surfaces the same way that a ball bounces off the ground. If you throw the ball straight down against a smooth surface, it will bounce straight up. If you bounce it at an angle, it will bounce away at an angle. The *law of reflection* states that the angle of incidence is equal to the angle of reflection. *Incidence* is the arrival of a beam of light at a surface. **Figure 1** shows this law.

Reading Check What is the law of reflection? (*See the Appendix for answers to Reading Checks.*)

Figure 1 The Law of Reflection

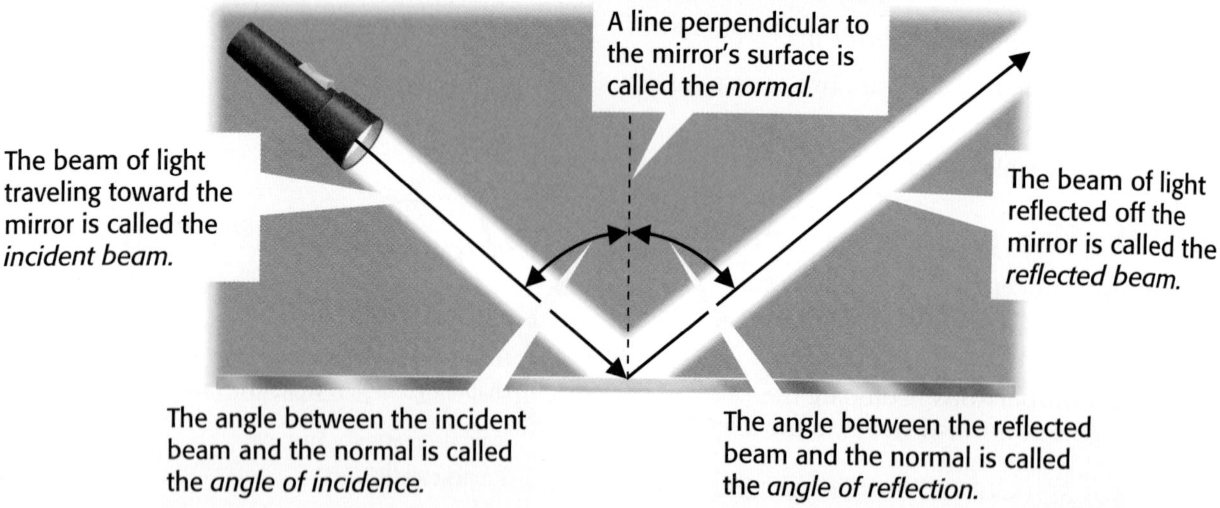

A line perpendicular to the mirror's surface is called the *normal.*
The beam of light traveling toward the mirror is called the *incident beam.*
The beam of light reflected off the mirror is called the *reflected beam.*
The angle between the incident beam and the normal is called the *angle of incidence.*
The angle between the reflected beam and the normal is called the *angle of reflection.*

Figure 2 **Regular Reflection vs. Diffuse Reflection**

Regular reflection occurs when light beams are reflected at the same angle. When your eye detects the reflected beams, you can see a reflection on the surface.

Diffuse reflection occurs when light beams reflect at many different angles. You can't see a reflection because not all of the reflected light is directed toward your eyes.

Types of Reflection

So, why can you see your image in a mirror but not in a wall? The answer has to do with the differences between the two surfaces. A mirror's surface is very smooth. Thus, light beams reflect off all points of the mirror at the same angle. This kind of reflection is called *regular reflection.* A wall's surface is slightly rough. Light beams will hit the wall's surface and reflect at many different angles. This kind of reflection is called *diffuse reflection.* **Figure 2** shows the difference between the two kinds of reflection.

reflection the bouncing back of a ray of light, sound, or heat when the ray hits a surface that it does not go through

Light Source or Reflection?

If you look at a TV set in a bright room, you see the cabinet around the TV and the image on the screen. But if you look at the same TV in the dark, you see only the image on the screen. The difference is that the screen is a light source, but the cabinet around the TV is not.

You can see a light source even in the dark because its light passes directly into your eyes. The tail of the firefly in **Figure 3** is a light source. Flames, light bulbs, and the sun are also light sources. Objects that produce visible light are called *luminous* (LOO muh nuhs).

Most things around you are not light sources. But you can still see them because light from light sources reflects off the objects and then travels to your eyes. A visible object that is not a light source is *illuminated.*

Reading Check List four different light sources.

Figure 3 *You can see the tail of this firefly because it is luminous. But you see its body because it is illuminated.*

CONNECTION TO Astronomy

Moonlight? Sometimes, the moon shines so brightly that you might think there is a lot of "moonlight." But did you know that moonlight is actually sunlight? The moon does not give off light. You can see the moon because it is illuminated by light from the sun. You see different phases of the moon because light from the sun shines only on the part of the moon that faces the sun. Make a poster that shows the different phases of the moon.

ACTIVITY

Absorption and Scattering

absorption in optics, the transfer of light energy to particles of matter

scattering an interaction of light with matter that causes light to change its energy, direction of motion, or both

Have you noticed that when you use a flashlight, the light shining on things closer to you appears brighter than the light shining on things farther away? The light is less bright the farther it travels from the flashlight. The light is weaker partly because the beam spreads out and partly because of absorption and scattering.

Absorption of Light

The transfer of energy carried by light waves to particles of matter is called **absorption.** When a beam of light shines through the air, particles in the air absorb some of the energy from the light. As a result, the beam of light becomes dim. The farther the light travels from its source, the more it is absorbed by particles, and the dimmer it becomes.

Figure 4 *A beam of light becomes dimmer partly because of scattering.*

Scattering of Light

Scattering is an interaction of light with matter that causes light to change direction. Light scatters in all directions after colliding with particles of matter. Light from the ship shown in **Figure 4** is scattered out of the beam by air particles. This scattered light allows you to see things that are outside the beam. But, because light is scattered out of the beam, the beam becomes dimmer.

Scattering makes the sky blue. Light with shorter wavelengths is scattered more than light with longer wavelengths. Sunlight is made up of many different colors of light, but blue light (which has a very short wavelength) is scattered more than any other color. So, when you look at the sky, you see a background of blue light.

Reading Check **Why can you see things outside a beam of light?**

Quick Lab

Scattering Milk

1. Fill a **2 L clear plastic bottle** with **water.**
2. Turn the lights off, and shine a **flashlight** through the water. Look at the water from all sides of the bottle. Write a description of what you see.
3. Add **3 drops of milk** to the water, and shake the bottle to mix it up.
4. Repeat step 2. Describe any color changes. If you don't see any, add more milk until you do.
5. How is the water-and-milk mixture like air particles in the atmosphere? Explain your answer.

Refraction

Imagine that you and a friend are at a lake. Your friend wades into the water. You look at her, and her feet appear to have separated from her legs! What has happened? You know her feet did not fall off, so how can you explain what you see? The answer has to do with refraction.

Refraction and Material

Refraction is the bending of a wave as it passes at an angle from one substance, or material, to another. **Figure 5** shows a beam of light refracting twice. Refraction of light waves occurs because the speed of light varies depending on the material through which the waves are traveling. In a vacuum, light travels at 300,000 km/s, but it travels more slowly through matter. When a wave enters a new material at an angle, the part of the wave that enters first begins traveling at a different speed from that of the rest of the wave.

refraction the bending of a wave as the wave passes between two substances in which the speed of the wave differs

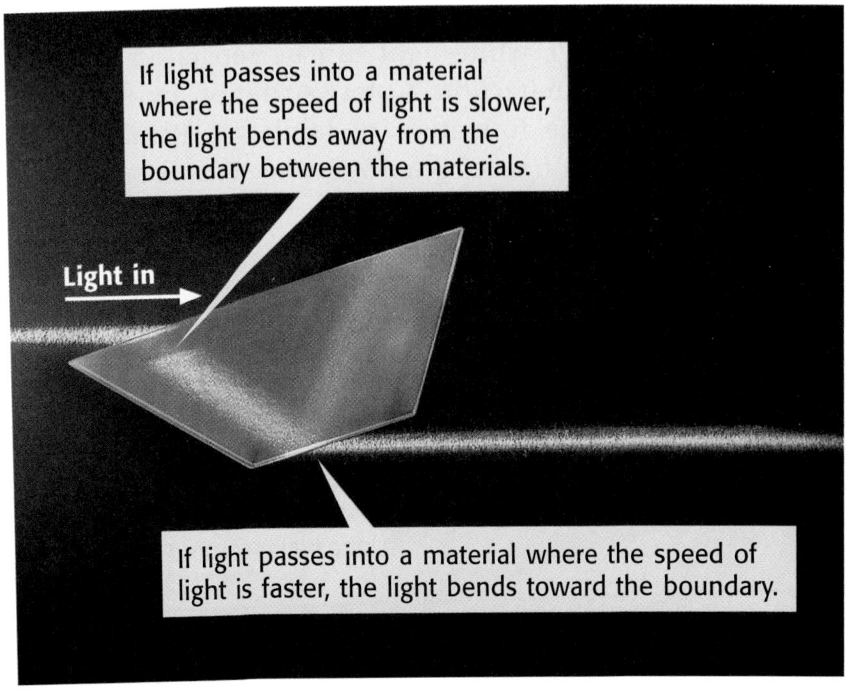

If light passes into a material where the speed of light is slower, the light bends away from the boundary between the materials.
Light in
If light passes into a material where the speed of light is faster, the light bends toward the boundary.

Figure 5 *Light travels more slowly through glass than it does through air. So, light refracts as it passes at an angle from air to glass or from glass to air. Notice that the light is also reflected inside the prism.*

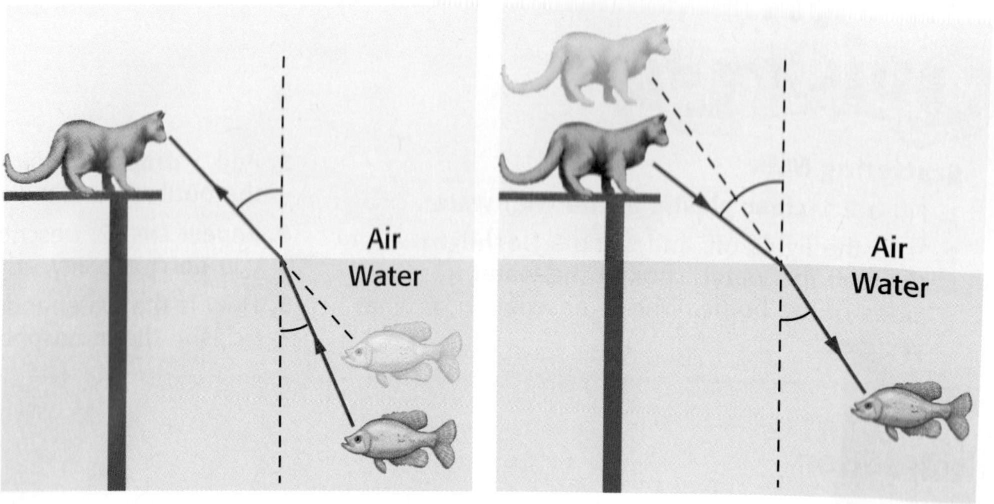

Figure 6 *Because of refraction, the cat and the fish see optical illusions. To the cat, the fish appears closer than it really is. To the fish, the cat appears farther away than it actually is.*

Refraction and Optical Illusions

Usually, when you look at an object, the light reflecting off the object travels in a straight line from the object to your eye. Your brain always interprets light as traveling in straight lines. But when you look at an object that is underwater, the light reflecting off the object does not travel in a straight line. Instead, it refracts. **Figure 6** shows how refraction creates an optical illusion. This kind of illusion causes a person's feet to appear separated from the legs when the person is wading.

Refraction and Color Separation

White light is composed of all the wavelengths of visible light. The different wavelengths of visible light are seen by humans as different colors. When white light is refracted, the amount that the light bends depends on its wavelength. Waves with short wavelengths bend more than waves with long wavelengths. As shown in **Figure 7,** white light can be separated into different colors during refraction. Color separation by refraction is responsible for the formation of rainbows. Rainbows are created when sunlight is refracted by water droplets.

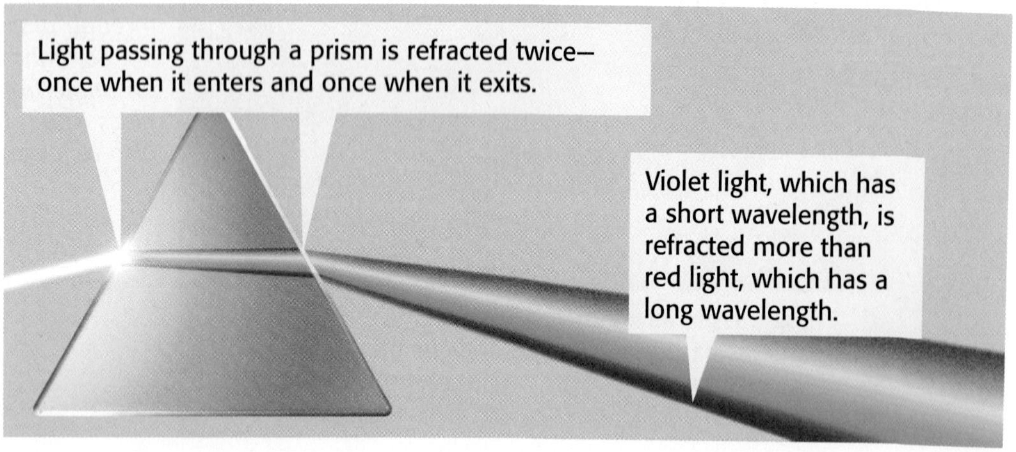

Light passing through a prism is refracted twice—
once when it enters and once when it exits.
Violet light, which has a short wavelength, is refracted more than red light, which has a long wavelength.

Figure 7 *A prism is a piece of glass that separates white light into the colors of visible light by refraction.*

Quick Lab

Refraction Rainbow

1. **Tape** a **piece of construction paper** over the end of a **flashlight.** Use **scissors** to cut a slit in the paper.
2. Turn on the flashlight, and lay it on a table. Place a **prism** on end in the beam of light.
3. Slowly rotate the prism until you can see a rainbow on the surface of the table. Draw a diagram of the light beam, the prism, and the rainbow.

Diffraction

Refraction isn't the only way light waves are bent. **Diffraction** is the bending of waves around barriers or through openings. The amount a wave diffracts depends on its wavelength and the size of the barrier or the opening. The greatest amount of diffraction occurs when the barrier or opening is the same size or smaller than the wavelength.

diffraction a change in the direction of a wave when the wave finds an obstacle or an edge, such as an opening

Reading Check **The amount a wave diffracts depends on what two things?**

Diffraction and Wavelength

The wavelength of visible light is very small—about 100 times thinner than a human hair! So, a light wave cannot bend very much by diffraction unless it passes through a narrow opening, around sharp edges, or around a small barrier, as shown in **Figure 8.**

Light waves cannot diffract very much around large obstacles, such as buildings. Thus, you can't see around corners. But light waves always diffract a small amount. You can observe light waves diffracting if you examine the edges of a shadow. Diffraction causes the edges of shadows to be blurry.

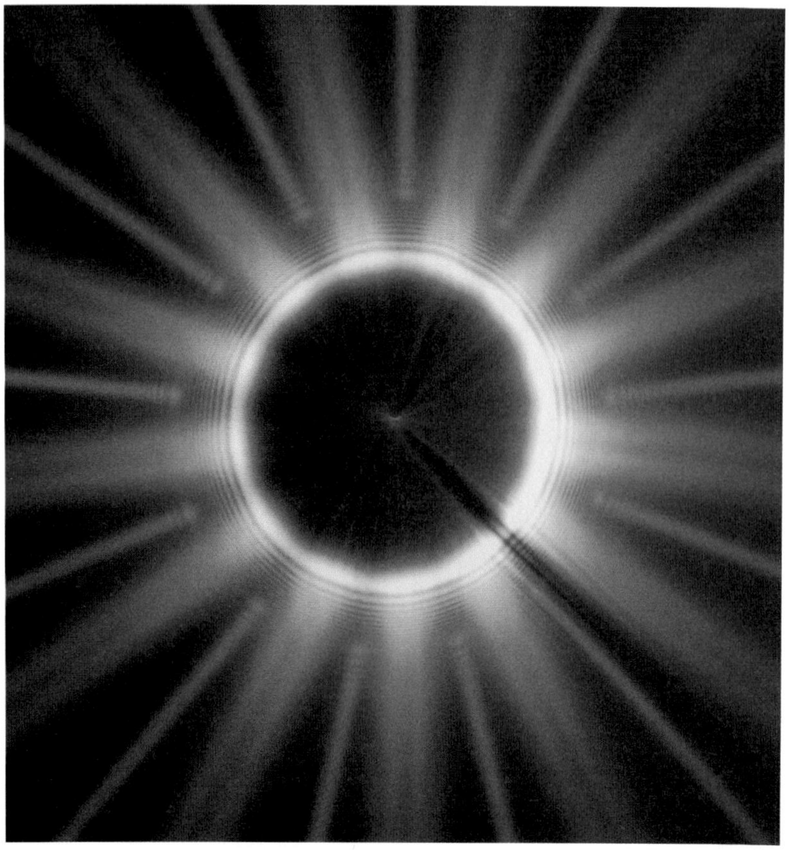

Figure 8 *This diffraction pattern is made by light of a single wavelength shining around the edges of a very tiny disk.*

interference the combination of two or more waves that results in a single wave

Interference

Interference is a wave interaction that happens when two or more waves overlap. Overlapping waves can combine by constructive or destructive interference.

Constructive Interference

When waves combine by *constructive interference,* the resulting wave has a greater amplitude, or height, than the individual waves had. Constructive interference of light waves can be seen when light of one wavelength shines through two small slits onto a screen. The light on the screen will appear as a series of alternating bright and dark bands, as shown in **Figure 9.** The bright bands result from light waves combining through constructive interference.

Reading Check What is constructive interference?

Destructive Interference

When waves combine by *destructive interference,* the resulting wave has a smaller amplitude than the individual waves had. So, when light waves interfere destructively, the result will be dimmer light. Destructive interference forms the dark bands seen in **Figure 9.**

You do not see constructive or destructive interference of white light. To understand why, remember that white light is composed of waves with many different wavelengths. The waves rarely line up to combine in total destructive interference.

INTERNET ACTIVITY

For another activity related to this chapter, go to **go.hrw.com** and type in the keyword **HP5LGTW.**

Figure 9 Constructive and Destructive Interference

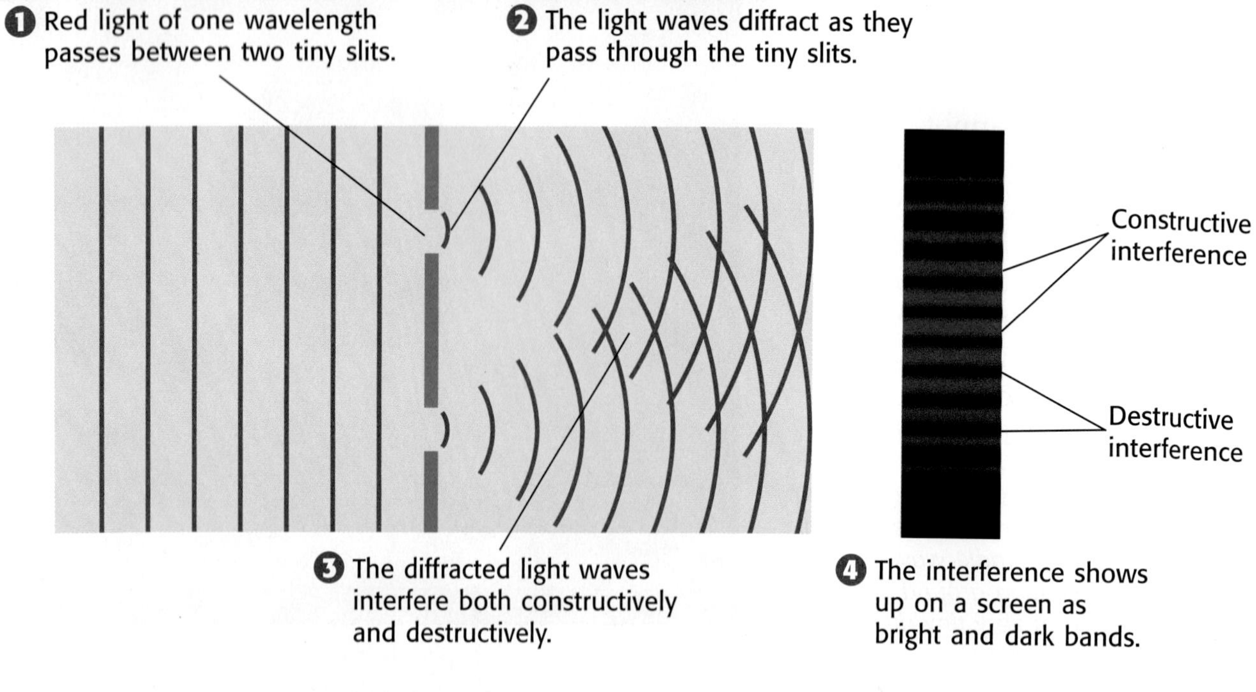

1 Red light of one wavelength passes between two tiny slits.
2 The light waves diffract as they pass through the tiny slits.
Constructive interference
Destructive interference
3 The diffracted light waves interfere both constructively and destructively.
4 The interference shows up on a screen as bright and dark bands.

SECTION
Review

Summary

- The law of reflection states that the angle of incidence is equal to the angle of reflection.
- Things that are luminous can be seen because they produce their own light. Things that are illuminated can be seen because light reflects off them.
- Absorption is the transfer of light energy to particles of matter. Scattering is an interaction of light with matter that causes light to change direction.
- Refraction of light waves can create optical illusions and can separate white light into separate colors.
- How much light waves diffract depends on the light's wavelength. Light waves diffract more when traveling through a narrow opening.
- Interference can be constructive or destructive. Interference of light waves can cause bright and dark bands.

Using Key Terms

For each pair of terms, explain how the meanings of the terms differ.

1. *refraction* and *diffraction*
2. *absorption* and *scattering*

Understanding Key Ideas

3. Which light interaction explains why you can see things that do not produce their own light?
   - **a.** absorption
   - **b.** reflection
   - **c.** refraction
   - **d.** scattering
4. Describe how absorption and scattering can affect a beam of light.
5. Why do objects that are underwater look closer than they actually are?
6. How does a prism separate white light into different colors?
7. What is the relationship between diffraction and the wavelength of light?

Critical Thinking

8. **Applying Concepts** Explain why you can see your reflection on a spoon but not on a piece of cloth.
9. **Making Inferences** The planet Mars does not produce light. Explain why you can see Mars shining like a star at night.
10. **Making Comparisons** Compare constructive interference and destructive interference.

Interpreting Graphics

Use the image below to answer the questions that follow.

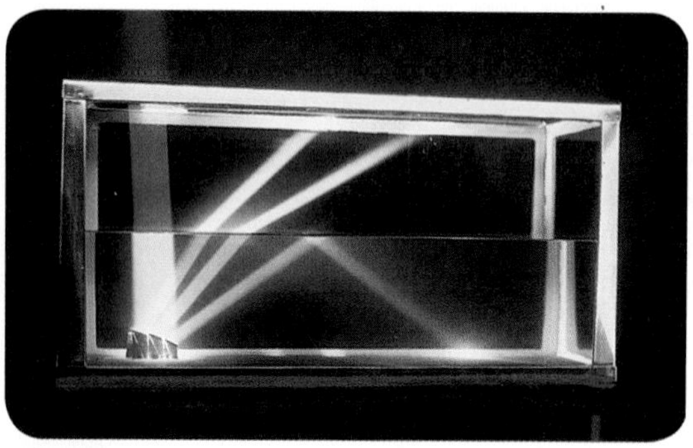

11. Why doesn't the large beam of light bend like the two beams in the middle of the tank?
12. Which light interaction explains what is happening to the bottom light beam?

SECTION 4

Light and Color

Why are strawberries red and bananas yellow? How can a soda bottle be green, yet you can still see through it?

What You Will Learn

- Name and describe the three ways light interacts with matter.
- Explain how the color of an object is determined.
- Explain why mixing colors of light is called *color addition*.
- Describe why mixing colors of pigments is called *color subtraction*.

Vocabulary

transmission
transparent
translucent
opaque
pigment

READING STRATEGY

Discussion Read this section silently. Write down questions that you have about this section. Discuss your questions in a small group.

If white light is made of all the colors of light, how do things get their color from white light? Why aren't all things white in white light? Good questions! To answer these questions, you need to know how light interacts with matter.

Light and Matter

When light strikes any form of matter, it can interact with the matter in three different ways—the light can be reflected, absorbed, or transmitted.

Reflection happens when light bounces off an object. Reflected light allows you to see things. Absorption is the transfer of light energy to matter. Absorbed light can make things feel warmer. **Transmission** is the passing of light through matter. You see the transmission of light all the time. All of the light that reaches your eyes is transmitted through air. Light can interact with matter in several ways at the same time. Look at **Figure 1.** Light is transmitted, reflected, and absorbed when it strikes the glass in a window.

transmission the passing of light or other form of energy through matter

Figure 1 Transmission, Reflection, and Absorption

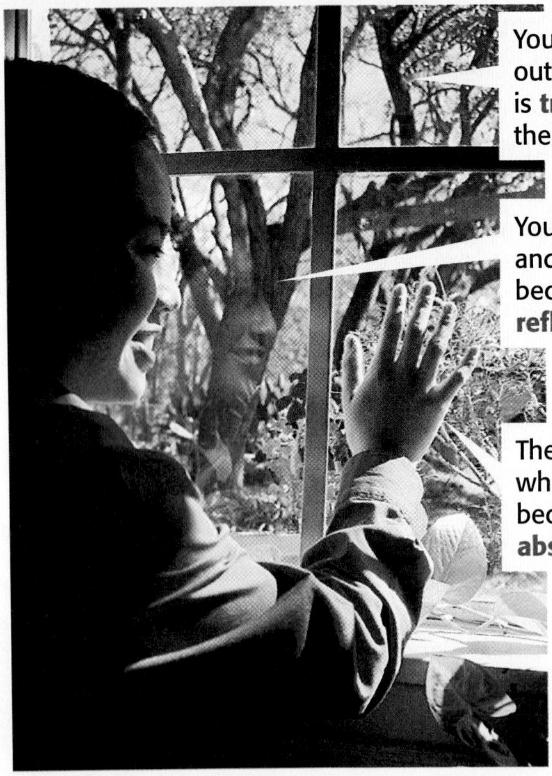

You can see objects outside because light is **transmitted** through the glass.
You can see the glass and your reflection in it because light is **reflected** off the glass.
The glass feels warm when you touch it because some light is **absorbed** by the glass.

Figure 2 **Transparent, Translucent, and Opaque**

Transparent plastic makes it easy to see what you are having for lunch.

Translucent wax paper makes it a little harder to see exactly what's for lunch.

Opaque aluminum foil makes it impossible to see your lunch without unwrapping it.

Types of Matter

Matter through which visible light is easily transmitted is said to be **transparent.** Air, glass, and water are examples of transparent matter. You can see objects clearly when you view them through transparent matter.

Sometimes, windows in bathrooms are made of frosted glass. If you look through one of these windows, you will see only blurry shapes. You can't see clearly through a frosted window because it is translucent (trans LOO suhnt). **Translucent** matter transmits light but also scatters the light as it passes through the matter. Wax paper is an example of translucent matter.

Matter that does not transmit any light is said to be **opaque** (oh PAYK). You cannot see through opaque objects. Metal, wood, and this book are examples of opaque objects. You can compare transparent, translucent, and opaque matter in **Figure 2.**

transparent describes matter that allows light to pass through with little interference

translucent describes matter that transmits light but that does not transmit an image

opaque describes an object that is not transparent or translucent

Reading Check **List two examples of translucent objects.** (*See the Appendix for answers to Reading Checks.*)

Colors of Objects

How is an object's color determined? Humans see different wavelengths of light as different colors. For example, humans see long wavelengths as red and short wavelengths as violet. And, some colors, like pink and brown, are seen when certain combinations of wavelengths are present.

The color that an object appears to be is determined by the wavelengths of light that reach your eyes. Light reaches your eyes after being reflected off an object or after being transmitted through an object. When your eyes receive the light, they send signals to your brain. Your brain interprets the signals as colors.

Figure 3 Opaque Objects and Color

When white light shines on a strawberry, only red light is reflected. Other colors of light are absorbed. Therefore, the strawberry looks red to you.

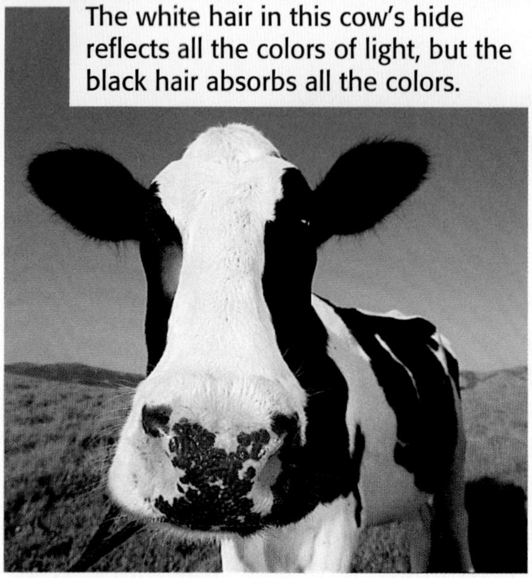

The white hair in this cow's hide reflects all the colors of light, but the black hair absorbs all the colors.

Colors of Opaque Objects

When white light strikes a colored opaque object, some colors of light are absorbed, and some are reflected. Only the light that is reflected reaches your eyes and is detected. So, the colors of light that are reflected by an opaque object determine the color you see. For example, if a sweater reflects blue light and absorbs all other colors, you will see that the sweater is blue. Another example is shown on the left in **Figure 3.**

What colors of light are reflected by the cow shown on the right in **Figure 3**? Remember that white light includes all colors of light. So, white objects—such as the white hair in the cow's hide—appear white because all the colors of light are reflected. On the other hand, black is the absence of color. When light strikes a black object, all the colors are absorbed.

Reading Check **What happens when white light strikes a colored opaque object?**

Colors of Transparent and Translucent Objects

The color of transparent and translucent objects is determined differently than the color of opaque objects. Ordinary window glass is colorless in white light because it transmits all the colors that strike it. But some transparent objects are colored. When you look through colored transparent or translucent objects, you see the color of light that was transmitted through the material. The other colors were absorbed, as shown in **Figure 4.**

Figure 4 *This bottle is green because the plastic transmits green light.*

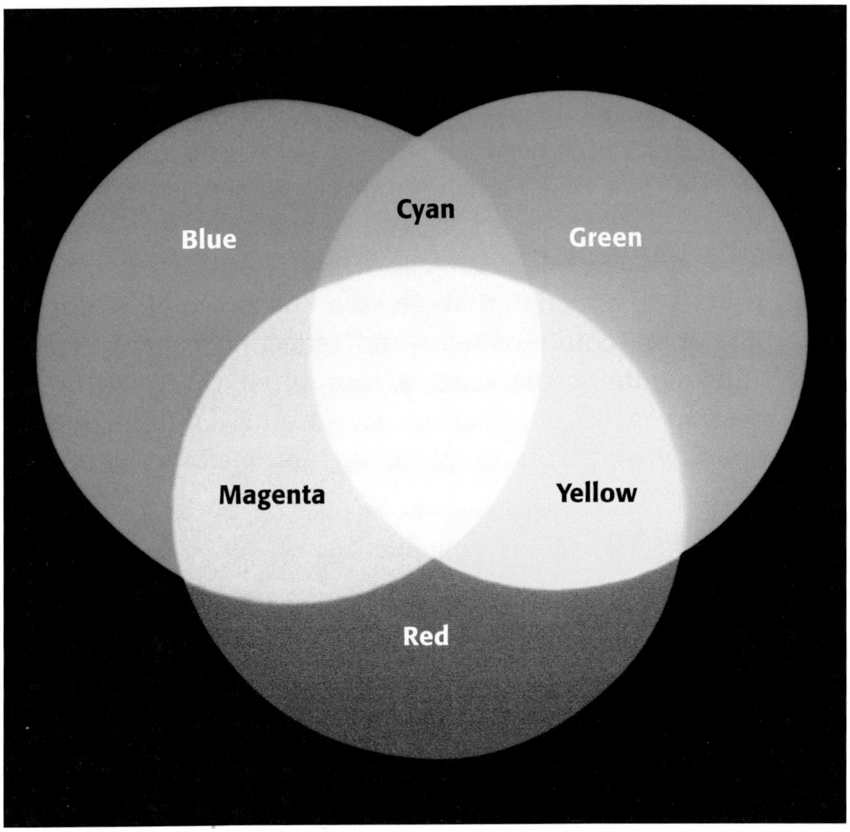

Figure 5 *Primary colors of light—written in white—combine to produce white light. Secondary colors of light—written in black—are the result of two primary colors added together.*

Mixing Colors of Light

In order to get white light, you must combine all colors of light, right? This method is one way of doing it. But you can also get light that appears white by adding just three colors of light together—red, blue, and green. The combination of these three colors is shown in **Figure 5.** In fact, these three colors can be combined in different ratios to produce many colors. Red, blue, and green are called the *primary colors of light.*

Color Addition

When colors of light combine, you see different colors. Combining colors of light is called *color addition.* When two primary colors of light are added together, you see a *secondary color of light.* The secondary colors of light are cyan (blue plus green), magenta (blue plus red), and yellow (red plus green). **Figure 5** shows how secondary colors of light are formed.

Light and Color Television

The colors on a color television are produced by color addition of the primary colors of light. A television screen is made up of groups of tiny red, green, and blue dots. Each dot will glow when the dot is hit by an electron beam. The colors given off by the glowing dots add together to produce all the different colors you see on the screen.

SCHOOL to HOME

Television Colors

Turn on a color television. Ask an adult to carefully sprinkle a few tiny drops of water onto the television screen. Look closely at the drops of water, and discuss what you see. In your **science journal,** write a description of what you saw.

ACTIVITY

Mixing Colors of Pigment

If you have ever tried mixing paints in art class, you know that you can't make white paint by mixing red, blue, and green paint. The difference between mixing paint and mixing light is due to the fact that paint contains pigments.

Pigments and Color

pigment a substance that gives another substance or a mixture its color

A **pigment** is a material that gives a substance its color by absorbing some colors of light and reflecting others. Almost everything contains pigments. Chlorophyll (KLAWR uh FIL) and melanin (MEL uh nin) are two examples of pigments. Chlorophyll gives plants a green color, and melanin gives your skin its color.

Reading Check **What is a pigment?**

Color Subtraction

Each pigment absorbs at least one color of light. Look at **Figure 6.** When you mix pigments together, more colors of light are absorbed or taken away. So, mixing pigments is called *color subtraction.*

The *primary pigments* are yellow, cyan, and magenta. They can be combined to produce any other color. In fact, every color in this book was produced by using just the primary pigments and black ink. The black ink was used to provide contrast to the images. **Figure 7** shows how the four pigments combine to produce many different colors.

Quick Lab

Rose-Colored Glasses?

1. Obtain **four plastic filters**—red, blue, yellow, and green.
2. Look through one filter at an object across the room. Describe the object's color.
3. Repeat step 2 with each of the filters.
4. Repeat step 2 with two or three filters together.
5. Why do you think the colors change when you use more than one filter?
6. Write your observations and answers.

Figure 6 *Primary pigments—written in black—combine to produce black. Secondary pigments—written in white—are the result of the subtraction of two primary pigments.*

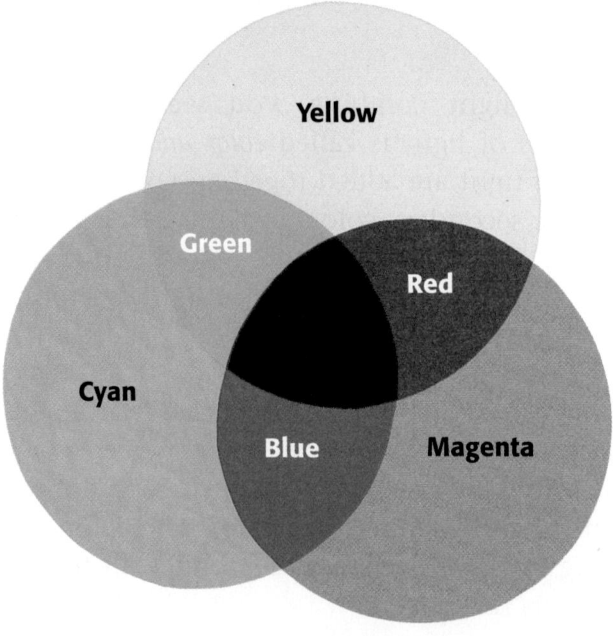

Figure 7 Color Subtraction and Color Printing

The picture of the balloon on the left was made by overlapping yellow ink, cyan ink, magenta ink, and black ink.

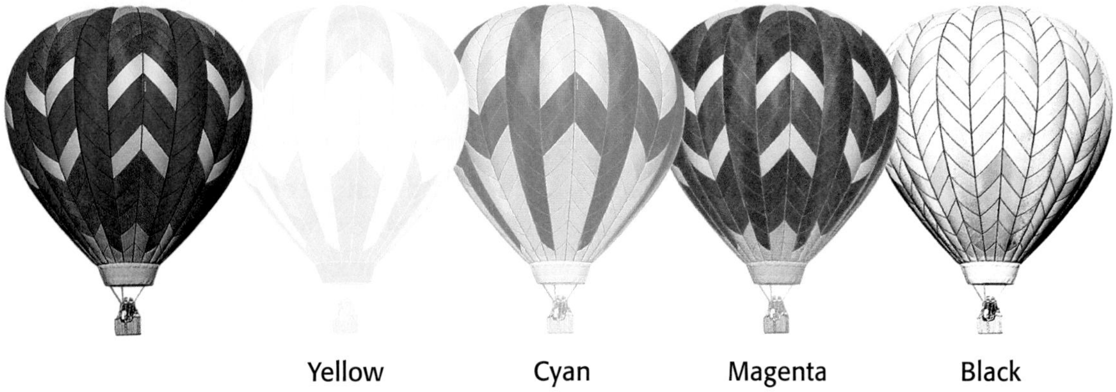

SECTION Review

Summary

- Objects are transparent, translucent, or opaque, depending on their ability to transmit light.
- Colors of opaque objects are determined by the color of light that they reflect.
- Colors of translucent and transparent objects are determined by the color of light they transmit.
- White light is a mixture of all colors of light.
- Light combines by color addition. The primary colors of light are red, blue, and green.
- Pigments give objects color. Pigments combine by color subtraction. The primary pigments are magenta, cyan, and yellow.

Using Key Terms

1. Use the following terms in the same sentence: *transmission* and *transparent*.
2. In your own words, write a definition for each of the following terms: *translucent* and *opaque*.

Understanding Key Ideas

3. You can see through a car window because the window is
   a. opaque. **c.** transparent.
   b. translucent. **d.** transmitted.
4. Name and describe three different ways light interacts with matter.
5. How is the color of an opaque object determined?
6. Describe how the color of a transparent object is determined.
7. What are the primary colors of light, and why are they called *primary colors*?
8. What four colors of ink were used to print this book?

Critical Thinking

9. **Applying Concepts** What happens to the different colors of light when white light shines on an opaque violet object?
10. **Analyzing Ideas** Explain why mixing colors of light is called *color addition* but mixing pigments is called *color subtraction*.

Interpreting Graphics

11. Look at the image below. The red rose was photographed in red light. Explain why the leaves appear black and the petals appear red.

SCILINKS. NSTA Developed and maintained by the National Science Teachers Association

For a variety of links related to this chapter, go to www.scilinks.org

Topic: Colors
SciLinks code: HSM0314

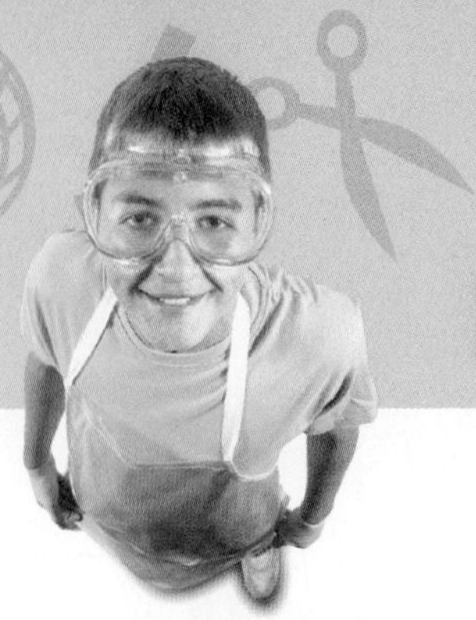

Skills Practice Lab

Mixing Colors

Mix two colors, such as red and green, and you create a new color. Is the new color brighter or darker? Color and brightness depend on the light that reaches your eye. And what reaches your eye depends on whether you are adding colors (mixing colors of light) or subtracting colors (mixing colors of pigments). In this activity, you will do both types of color formation and see the results firsthand!

OBJECTIVES

Use flashlights to mix colors of light by color addition.

Use paints to mix colors of pigments by color subtraction.

MATERIALS

Part A

- colored filters, red, green, and blue (1 of each)
- flashlights (3)
- paper, white
- tape, masking

Part B

- cups, small plastic or paper (2)
- paintbrush
- paper, white
- ruler, metric
- tape, masking
- water
- watercolor paints

SAFETY

Part A: Color Addition

Procedure

1. Tape a colored filter over each flashlight lens.
2. In a darkened room, shine the red light on a sheet of white paper. Then, shine the green light next to the red light. You should have two circles of light, one red and one green, next to each other.
3. Move the flashlights so that the circles overlap by half their diameter. What color is formed where the circles overlap? Is the mixed area brighter or darker than the single-color areas? Record your observations.

4. Repeat steps 2 and 3 with the red and blue lights.
5. Now, shine all three lights at the same point on the paper. Record your observations.

Analyze the Results

1. **Describing Events** In general, when you mixed two colors, was the result brighter or darker than the original colors?
2. **Explaining Events** In step 5, you mixed all three colors. Was the resulting color brighter or darker than when you mixed two colors? Explain your observations in terms of color addition.

Draw Conclusions

3. **Making Predictions** What do you think would happen if you mixed together all the colors of light? Explain your answer.

Part B: Color Subtraction

Procedure

1. Place a piece of masking tape on each cup. Label one cup "Clean" and the other cup "Dirty." Fill each cup about half full with water.
2. Wet the paintbrush thoroughly in the "Clean" cup. Using the watercolor paints, paint a red circle on the white paper. The circle should be approximately 4 cm in diameter.
3. Clean the brush by rinsing it first in the "Dirty" cup and then in the "Clean" cup.
4. Paint a blue circle next to the red circle. Then, paint half the red circle with the blue paint.
5. Examine the three areas: red, blue, and mixed. What color is the mixed area? Does it appear brighter or darker than the red and blue areas? Record your observations.
6. Clean the brush by repeating Step 3. Paint a green circle 4 cm in diameter, and then paint half the blue circle with green paint.

7. Examine the green, blue, and mixed areas. Record your observations.
8. Now add green paint to the mixed red-blue area so that you have an area that is a mixture of red, green, and blue paint. Clean the brush again.
9. Finally, record your observations of this new mixed area.

Analyze the Results

1. **Identifying Patterns** In general, when you mixed two colors, was the result brighter or darker than the original colors?
2. **Analyzing Results** In step 8, you mixed all three colors. Was the result brighter or darker than the result from mixing two colors? Explain what you saw in terms of color subtraction.

Draw Conclusions

3. **Drawing Conclusions** Based on your results, what do you think would happen if you mixed all the colors of paint? Explain your answer.

Chapter Review

USING KEY TERMS

Complete each of the following sentences by choosing the correct term from the word bank.

interference	radiation
scattering	opaque
translucent	transmission
electromagnetic wave	electromagnetic spectrum

1 _____ is the transfer of energy by electromagnetic waves.

2 This book is a(n) _____ object.

3 _____ is a wave interaction that occurs when two or more waves overlap and combine.

4 Light is a kind of _____ and can therefore travel through matter and space.

5 During _____, light travels through an object.

UNDERSTANDING KEY IDEAS

Multiple Choice

6 Electromagnetic waves transmit
- **a.** charges.
- **b.** fields.
- **c.** matter.
- **d.** energy.

7 Objects that transmit light easily are
- **a.** opaque.
- **b.** translucent.
- **c.** transparent.
- **d.** colored.

8 You can see yourself in a mirror because of
- **a.** absorption.
- **b.** scattering.
- **c.** regular reflection.
- **d.** diffuse reflection.

9 Shadows have blurry edges because of
- **a.** diffraction.
- **b.** scattering.
- **c.** diffuse reflection.
- **d.** refraction.

10 What color of light is produced when red light is added to green light?
- **a.** cyan
- **b.** blue
- **c.** yellow
- **d.** white

11 Prisms produce the colors of the rainbow through
- **a.** reflection.
- **b.** refraction.
- **c.** diffraction.
- **d.** interference.

12 Which kind of electromagnetic wave travels fastest in a vacuum?
- **a.** radio wave
- **b.** visible light
- **c.** gamma ray
- **d.** They all travel at the same speed.

13 Electromagnetic waves are made of
- **a.** vibrating particles.
- **b.** vibrating charged particles.
- **c.** vibrating electric and magnetic fields.
- **d.** All of the above

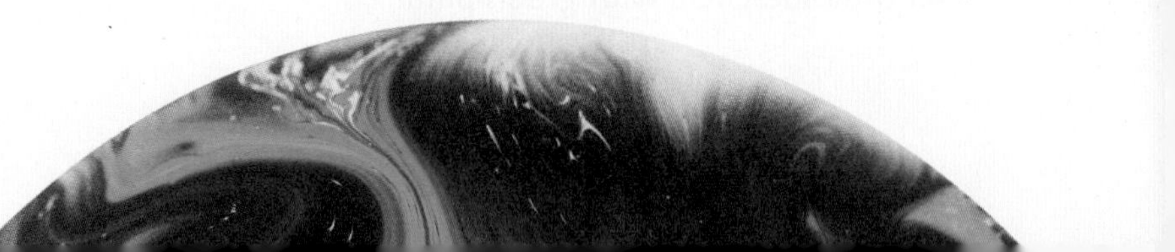

Short Answer

14 How are gamma rays used?

15 What are two uses for radio waves?

16 Why is it difficult to see through glass that has frost on it?

Math Skills

17 Calculate the time it takes for light from the sun to reach Mercury. Mercury is 54,900,000 km away from the sun.

CRITICAL THINKING

18 **Concept Mapping** Use the following terms to create a concept map: *light, matter, reflection, absorption,* and *transmission.*

19 **Applying Concepts** A tern is a type of bird that dives underwater to catch fish. When a young tern begins learning to catch fish, the bird is rarely successful. The tern has to learn that when a fish appears to be in a certain place underwater, the fish is actually in a slightly different place. Why does the tern see the fish in the wrong place?

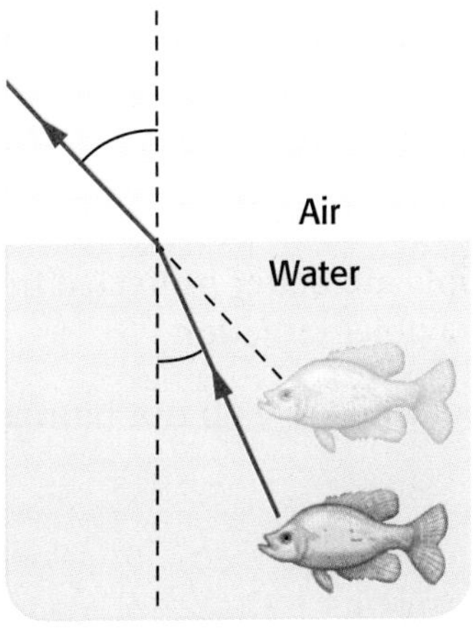

20 **Evaluating Conclusions** Imagine that you are teaching your younger brother about light. You tell him that white light is light of all the colors of the rainbow combined. But your brother says that you are wrong because mixing different colors of paint produces black and not white. Explain why your brother's conclusion is wrong.

21 **Making Inferences** If you look around a parking lot during the summer, you might see sunshades set up in the windshields of cars. How do sunshades help keep the insides of cars cool?

INTERPRETING GRAPHICS

22 Each of the pictures below shows the effects of a wave interaction of light. Identify the interaction involved.

a.

b.

c.

Standardized Test Preparation

Multiple Choice

Use the diagram below to answer questions 1–2.

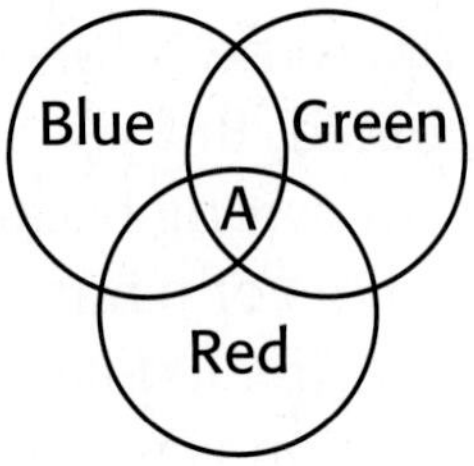

1. **While performing an experiment on the colors of light, Pablo mixed three colors of light to form the image above. What color would Pablo see at point A?**

   A. yellow

   B. magenta

   C. white

   D. black

2. **What color would Pablo find at point A if filters were used instead of colors of light?**

   A. white

   B. black

   C. green

   D. red

3. **Which of Pablo's conclusions accurately describes the difference between mixing colors of light and mixing colors of ink?**

   A. Mixing colors of light involves color addition, while mixing inks involves color subtraction.

   B. Mixing inks involves color addition, while mixing colors of light involves color subtraction.

   C. Different colors of light always combine to form black light, while different colors of ink always combine to form the ink for the color white.

   D. Inks cannot be mixed, while colors of light can.

4. **Which statement is true?**

   A. Gamma rays travel faster than X rays and microwaves.

   B. X rays travel faster than gamma rays and microwaves.

   C. Microwaves travel faster than gamma rays and X rays.

   D. All electromagnetic waves travel at the same speed.

5. **Which is the best account of the impact on society of research on sunscreen protection?**

   A. Less ultraviolet light reaches Earth.

   B. More people have developed skin cancer.

   C. People are better protected from ultraviolet radiation.

   D. Modern people do not burn as easily.

Use the diagram below to answer question 6.

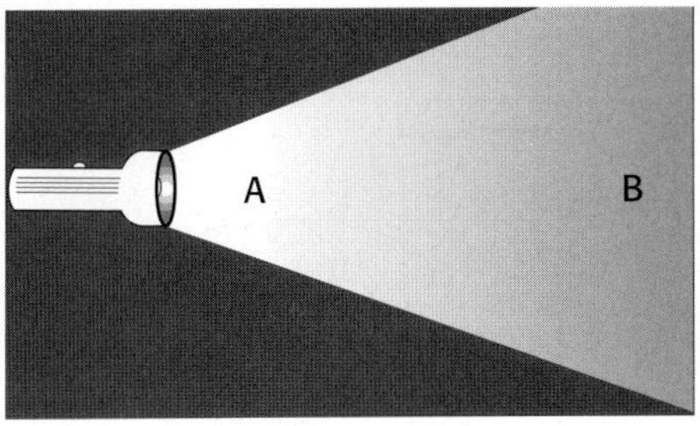

6. The light from the flashlight is brighter at point A than at point B because

A. light can travel only in a vacuum.

B. light does not travel very fast in air.

C. light energy is spread over a larger area.

D. destructive interference makes the light appear dimmer.

7. Which of the following produces a mirror image?

A. diffuse reflection

B. regular reflection

C. scattering

D. absorption

8. What precautions must be taken when a technician uses X rays to make images of patients' broken bones?

A. The patients should wear earplugs to protect their ears.

B. The patients' bodies should be protected with a lead-lined cover.

C. The patients should wear helmets.

D. The technician should wear safety goggles to protect his or her eyes.

9. A translucent material is one that

A. transmits some light.

B. transmits all light.

C. absorbs all light.

D. reflects all light.

10. A rainbow is created when visible electromagnetic waves travel through raindrops and are

A. diffracted.

B. transmitted.

C. blocked.

D. refracted.

Open Response

11. Sound is being sent from the radio station to a radio as you listen to a song. Describe the path that the electronic current takes to get from the station to the radio. Discuss two conversions of energy that occur during the process.

12. How do X rays form an image of a broken bone?

Science in Action

Weird Science

Fireflies Light the Way

Just as beams of light from lighthouses warn boats of approaching danger, the light of an unlikely source—fireflies—is being used by scientists to warn food inspectors of bacterial contamination.

Fireflies use an enzyme called *luciferase* to make light. Scientists have taken the gene from fireflies that tells cells how to make luciferase. They put this gene into a virus that preys on bacteria. The virus is not harmful to humans and can be mixed into meat. When the virus infects bacteria in the meat, the virus transfers the gene into the genes of the bacteria. The bacteria then produce luciferase and glow! So, if a food inspector sees glowing meat, the inspector knows that the meat is contaminated with bacteria.

Social Studies ACTIVITY

WRITING SKILL Many cultures have myths to explain certain natural phenomena. Read some of these myths. Then, write your own myth titled "How Fireflies Got Their Fire."

Science, Technology, and Society

It's a Heat Wave

In 1946, Percy Spencer visited a laboratory belonging to Raytheon—the company he worked for. When he stood near a device called a *magnetron,* he noticed that a candy bar in his pocket melted. Spencer hypothesized that the microwaves produced by the magnetron caused the candy bar to warm up and melt. To test his hypothesis, Spencer put a bag of popcorn kernels next to the magnetron. The microwaves heated the kernels, causing them to pop! Spencer's simple experiment showed that microwaves could heat foods quickly. Spencer's discovery eventually led to the development of the microwave oven—an appliance found in many kitchens today.

Math ACTIVITY

Popcorn pops when the inside of the kernel reaches a temperature of about 175°C. Convert this temperature to degrees Fahrenheit.

People in Science

Albert Einstein

A Light Pioneer When Albert Einstein was 15 years old, he asked himself, "What would the world look like if I were speeding along on a motorcycle at the speed of light?" For many years afterward, he would think about this question and about the very nature of light, time, space, and matter. He even questioned the ideas of Isaac Newton, which had been widely accepted for 200 years. Einstein was bold. And he was able to see the universe in a totally new way.

In 1905, Einstein published a paper on the nature of light. He knew from the earlier experiments of others that light was a wavelike phenomenon. But he theorized that light could also travel as particles. Scientists did not readily accept Einstein's particle theory of light. Even 10 years later, the American physicist Robert Millikan, who proved that the particle theory of light was true, was reluctant to believe his own experimental results. Einstein's theory helped pave the way for television, computers, and other important technologies. The theory also earned Einstein a Nobel Prize in physics in 1921.

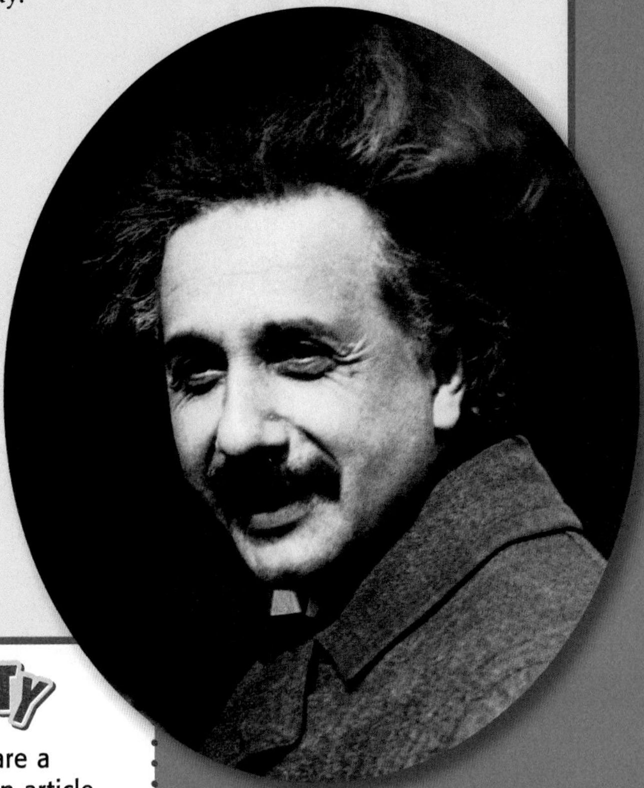

Language Arts ACTIVITY

WRITING SKILL Imagine that it is 1921. You are a newspaper reporter writing an article about Albert Einstein and his Nobel Prize. Write a one-page article about Albert Einstein, his theory, and the award he won.

go.hrw.com

To learn more about these Science in Action topics, visit **go.hrw.com** and type in the keyword **HP5LGTF.**

Current Science

Check out Current Science® articles related to this chapter by visiting go.hrw.com. Just type in the keyword HP5CS22.

6

Light and Our World

The Big Idea Mirrors and lenses change the path of light waves and affect the images that you see.

SECTION

About the Photo

This photo of Earth was taken by a satellite in space. All of the dots of light in this photo are lights in cities around the world. In areas with many dots, people live in cities that are close together. Light is very important in your everyday life. Not only does light help you see at night but light waves can also be used to send information over long distances. In fact, the satellite that took this picture sent the picture to Earth by using light waves!

PRE-READING ACTIVITY

FOLDNOTES **Tri-Fold** Before you read the chapter, create the FoldNote entitled "Tri-Fold" described in the **Study Skills** section of the Appendix. Write what you know about light in the column labeled "Know." Then, write what you want to know in the column labeled "Want." As you read the chapter, write what you learn about light in the column labeled "Learn."

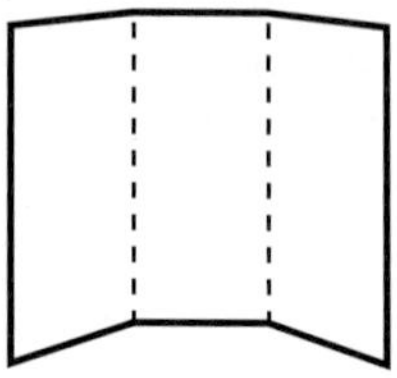

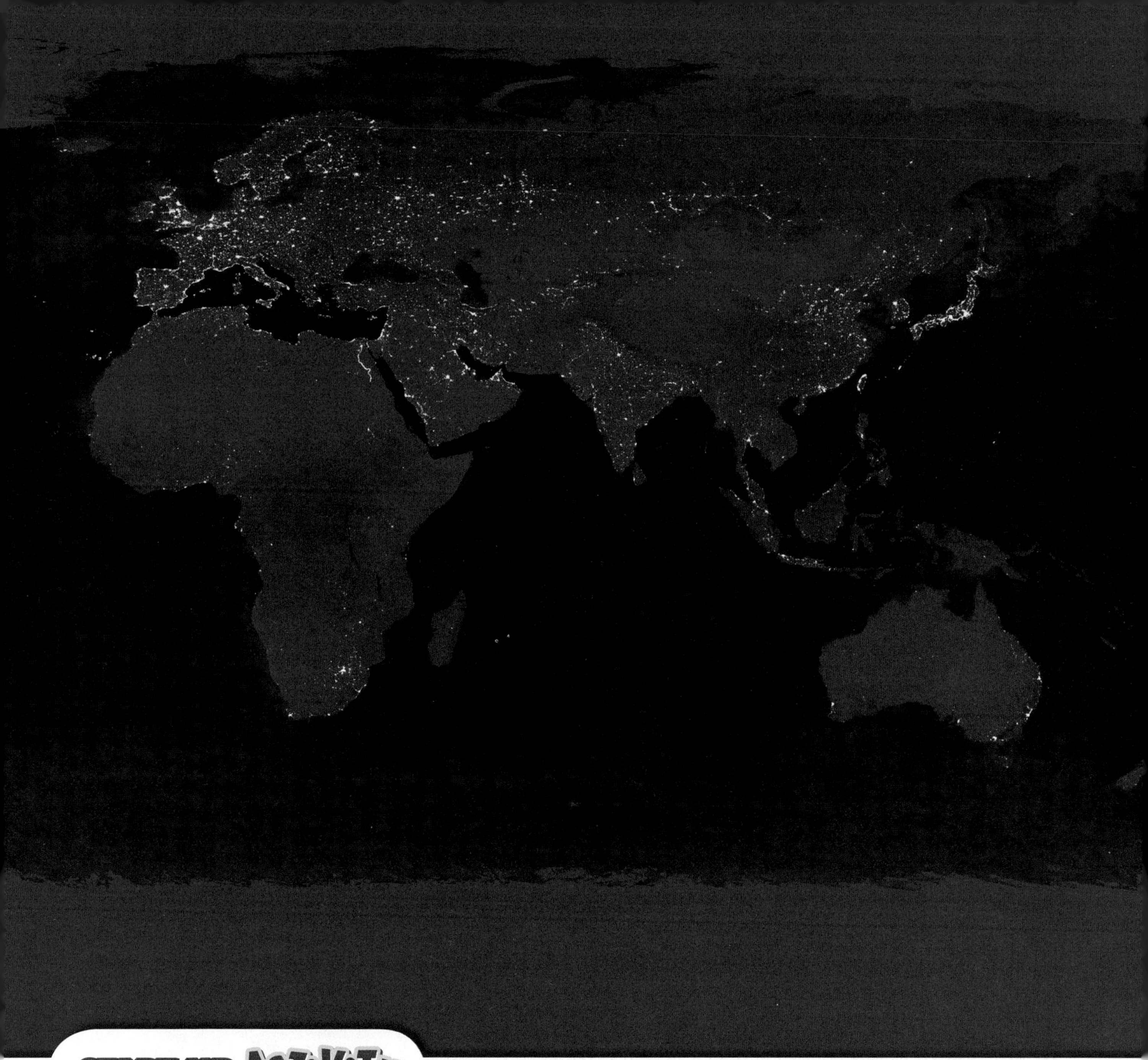

START-UP ACTIVITY

Mirror, Mirror

In this activity, you will study images formed by flat, or plane, mirrors.

Procedure

1. Tape a sheet of **graph paper** on your desk. Stand a **flat mirror** in the middle of the paper. Hold the mirror in place with pieces of **modeling clay.**
2. Place a **pen** four squares in front of the mirror. How many squares behind the mirror is the image of the pen? Move the pen farther away from the mirror. How did the image change?
3. Replace the mirror with **colored glass.** Look at the image of the pen in the glass. Compare the image in the glass with the one in the mirror.
4. Draw a square on the graph paper in front of the glass. Then, look through the glass, and trace the image of the square on the paper behind the glass. Using a **metric ruler,** measure and compare the two squares.

Analysis

1. How does the distance from an object to a plane mirror compare with the apparent distance from the mirror to the object's image behind the mirror?
2. Images formed in the colored glass are similar to images formed in a plane mirror. In general, how does the size of an object compare with that of its image in a plane mirror?

SECTION 1

Mirrors and Lenses

What You Will Learn

- Use ray diagrams to show how light is reflected or refracted.
- Compare plane mirrors, concave mirrors, and convex mirrors.
- Use ray diagrams to show how mirrors form images.
- Describe the images formed by concave and convex lenses.

Vocabulary

plane mirror
concave mirror
convex mirror
lens
convex lens
concave lens

READING STRATEGY

Reading Organizer As you read this section, make a concept map by using the terms above.

When walking by an ambulance, you notice that the letters on the front of the ambulance look strange. Some letters are backward, and they don't seem to spell a word!

Look at **Figure 1.** The letters spell the word *ambulance* when viewed in a mirror. Images in mirrors are reversed left to right. The word *ambulance* is spelled backward so that people driving cars can read it when they see an ambulance in their rearview mirrors. To understand how images are formed in mirrors, you must first learn how to use rays to trace the path of light waves.

Rays and the Path of Light Waves

Light waves are electromagnetic waves. Light waves travel from their source in all directions. If you could trace the path of one light wave as it travels away from a light source, you would find that the path is a straight line. Because light waves travel in straight lines, you can use an arrow called a *ray* to show the path and the direction of a light wave.

Rays and Reflected and Refracted Light

Rays help to show the path of a light wave after it bounces or bends. Light waves that bounce off an object are reflected. Light waves that bend when passing from one medium to another are refracted. So, rays in ray diagrams show changes in the direction light travels after being reflected by mirrors or refracted by lenses.

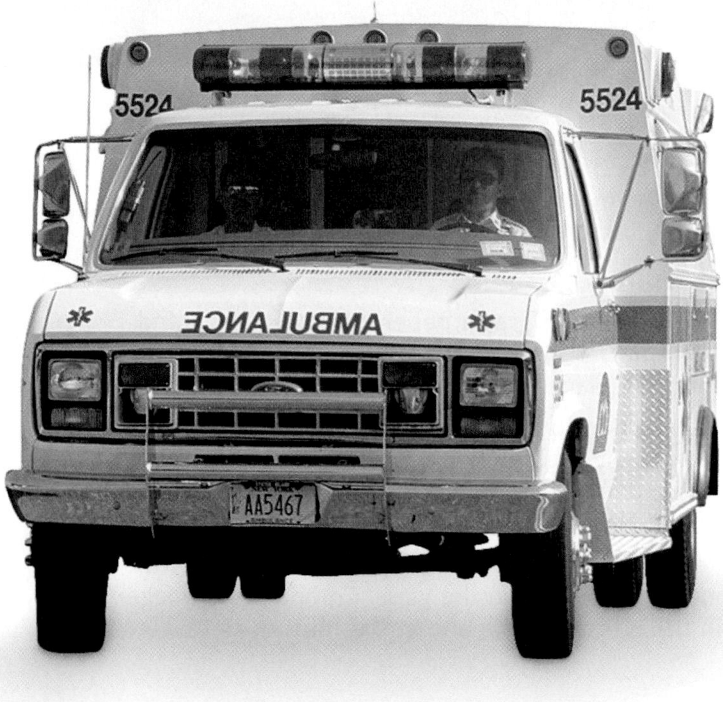

Figure 1 *If you hold this photo up to the mirror in your bathroom, you will see the word* AMBULANCE.

Figure 2 Correcting Nearsightedness and Farsightedness

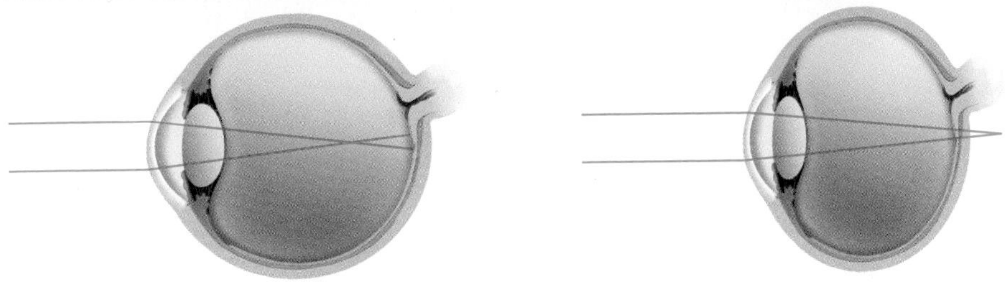

Nearsightedness happens when the eye is too long, which causes the lens to focus light in front of the retina.

Farsightedness happens when the eye is too short, which causes the lens to focus light behind the retina.

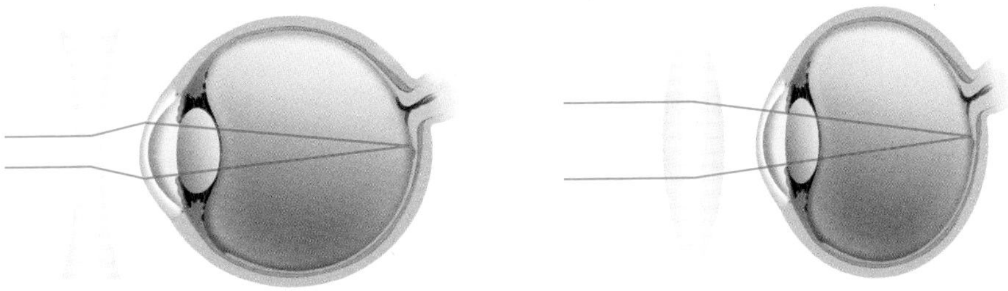

A **concave lens** placed in front of a nearsighted eye refracts the light outward. The lens in the eye can then focus the light on the retina.

A **convex lens** placed in front of a farsighted eye focuses the light. The lens in the eye can then focus the light on the retina.

Common Vision Problems

People who have normal vision can clearly see objects that are close and objects that are far away. They can also tell the difference between all colors of visible light. But because the eye is complex, it's no surprise that many people have defects in their eyes that affect their vision.

Nearsightedness and Farsightedness

The lens of a properly working eye focuses light on the retina. So, the images formed are always clear. Two common vision problems happen when light is not focused on the retina, as shown in **Figure 2. Nearsightedness** happens when a person's eye is too long. A nearsighted person can see something clearly only if it is nearby. Objects that are far away look blurry. **Farsightedness** happens when a person's eye is too short. A farsighted person can see faraway objects clearly. But things that are nearby look blurry. **Figure 2** also shows how these vision problems can be corrected with glasses.

nearsightedness a condition in which the lens of the eye focuses distant objects in front of rather than on the retina

farsightedness a condition in which the lens of the eye focuses distant objects behind rather than on the retina

Reading Check What causes nearsightedness and farsightedness? *(See the Appendix for answers to Reading Checks.)*

Figure 3 *The photo on the left is what a person who has normal vision sees. The photo on the right is a simulation of what a person who has red-green color deficiency might see.*

Color Deficiency

About 5% to 8% of men and 0.5% of women in the world have *color deficiency,* or colorblindness. The majority of people who have color deficiency can't tell the difference between shades of red and green or can't tell red from green. **Figure 3** compares what a person with normal vision sees with what a person who has red-green color deficiency sees. Color deficiency cannot be corrected.

Color deficiency happens when the cones in the retina do not work properly. The three kinds of cones are named for the colors they detect most—red, green, or blue. But each kind can detect many colors of light. A person who has normal vision can see all colors of visible light. But in some people, the cones respond to the wrong colors. Those people see certain colors, such as red and green, as a different color, such as yellow.

Reading Check **What are the three kinds of cones?**

CONNECTION TO Biology

Color Deficiency and Genes The ability to see color is a sex-linked genetic trait. Certain genes control which colors of light the cones detect. If these genes are defective in a person, that person will have color deficiency. A person needs one set of normal genes to have normal color vision. Genes that control the red cones and the green cones are on the X chromosome. Women have two X chromosomes, but men have only one. So, men are more likely than women to lack a set of these genes and to have red-green color deficiency. Research two other sex-linked traits, and make a graph comparing the percentage of men and women who have the traits.

ACTIVITY

Surgical Eye Correction

Using surgery to correct nearsightedness or farsightedness is possible. Surgical eye correction works by reshaping the patient's cornea. Remember that the cornea refracts light. So, reshaping the cornea changes how light is focused on the retina.

To prepare for eye surgery, an eye doctor uses a machine to measure the patient's corneas. A laser is then used to reshape each cornea so that the patient gains perfect or nearly perfect vision. **Figure 4** shows a patient undergoing eye surgery.

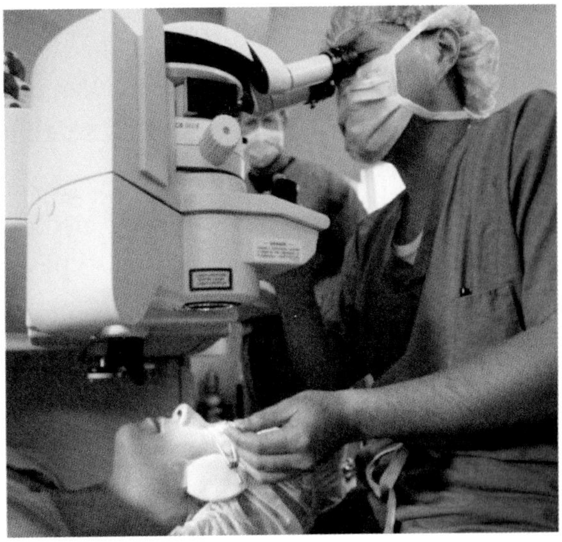

Figure 4 *An eye surgeon uses a very precise laser to reshape this patient's cornea.*

Risks of Surgical Eye Correction

Although vision-correction surgery can be helpful, it has some risks. Some patients report glares or double vision. Others have trouble seeing at night. Other patients lose vision permanently. People under 20 years old shouldn't have vision-correction surgery because their vision is still changing.

SECTION Review

Summary

- The human eye has several parts, including the cornea, the pupil, the iris, the lens, and the retina.
- Nearsightedness and farsightedness happen when light is not focused on the retina. Both problems can be corrected with glasses or eye surgery.
- Color deficiency is a condition in which cones in the retina respond to the wrong colors.
- Eye surgery can correct some vision problems.

Using Key Terms

1. Use each of the following terms in a separate sentence: *nearsightedness* and *farsightedness*.

Understanding Key Ideas

2. A person who is nearsighted will have the most trouble reading
   - **a.** a computer screen in front of him or her.
   - **b.** a book in his or her hands.
   - **c.** a street sign across the street.
   - **d.** the title of a pamphlet on a nearby table.
3. List the parts of the eye, and describe what each part does.
4. What are three common vision problems?
5. How are nearsightedness and farsightedness corrected?
6. Describe surgical eye correction.
7. What do the rods and cones in the eye do?

Math Skills

8. About 0.5% of women have a color deficiency. How many women out of 200 have a color deficiency?

Critical Thinking

9. **Forming Hypotheses** Why do you think color deficiency cannot be corrected?
10. **Expressing Opinions** Would you have surgical eye correction? Explain your reasons.

SCILINKS® NSTA Developed and maintained by the National Science Teachers Association

For a variety of links related to this chapter, go to www.scilinks.org

Topic: The Eye
SciLinks code: HSM0560

SECTION 3

Light and Technology

What do cameras, telescopes, lasers, cellular telephones, and satellite televisions have in common?

They are all types of technology that use light or other electromagnetic waves. Read on to learn how these and other types of light technology are useful in your everyday life.

What You Will Learn

- Describe three optical instruments.
- Explain what laser light is, and identify uses for lasers.
- Describe how optical fibers work.
- Explain polarized light.
- Explain how radio waves and microwaves are used in four types of communication technology.

Vocabulary

laser
hologram

READING STRATEGY

Prediction Guide Before reading this section, write the title of each heading in this section. Next, under each heading, write what you think you will learn.

Optical Instruments

Optical instruments are devices that use mirrors and lenses to help people make observations. Some optical instruments help you see things that are very far away. Others help you see things that are very small. Some optical instruments record images. The optical instrument that you are probably most familiar with is the camera.

Cameras

Cameras are used to record images. **Figure 1** shows the parts of a 35 mm camera. A digital camera has a lens, a shutter, and an aperture (AP uhr chuhr) like a 35 mm camera has. But instead of using film, a digital camera uses light sensors to record images. The sensors send an electrical signal to a computer in the camera. This signal contains data about the image that is stored in the computer, on a memory stick, card, or disk.

Figure 1 How a Camera Works

The **shutter** opens and closes behind the lens to control how much light enters the camera. The longer the shutter is open, the more light enters the camera.
The **film** is coated with chemicals that react when they are exposed to light. The result is an image stored on the film.
The **lens** of a camera is a convex lens that focuses light on the film. Moving the lens focuses light from objects at different distances.
The **aperture** is an opening that lets light into the camera. The larger the aperture is, the more light enters the camera.

Figure 2 How Refracting and Reflecting Telescopes Work

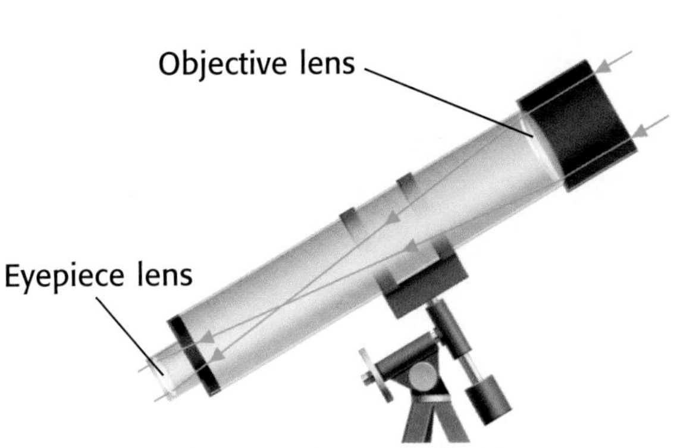

A **refracting telescope** has two convex lenses. Light enters through the objective lens and forms a real image. This real image is then magnified by the eyepiece lens. You see this magnified image when you look through the eyepiece lens.

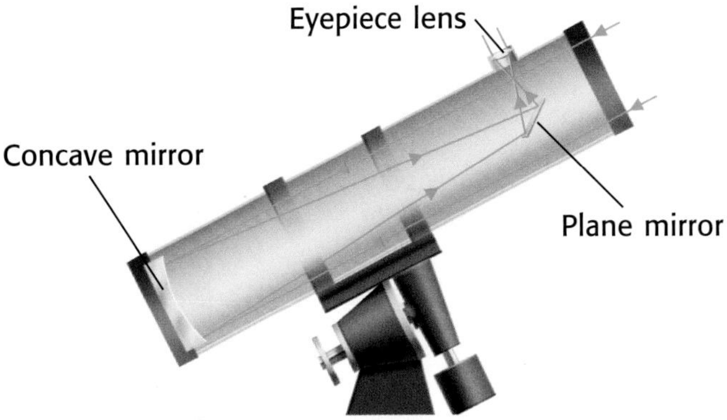

A **reflecting telescope** has a concave mirror that collects and focuses light to form a real image. The light strikes a plane mirror that directs the light to the convex eyepiece lens, which magnifies the real image.

Telescopes

Telescopes are used to see detailed images of large, distant objects. Astronomers use telescopes to study things in space, such as the moon, planets, and stars. Telescopes are classified as either refracting or reflecting. *Refracting telescopes* use lenses to collect light. *Reflecting telescopes* use mirrors to collect light. **Figure 2** shows how these two kinds of telescopes work.

Light Microscopes

Simple light microscopes are similar to refracting telescopes. These microscopes have two convex lenses. An objective lens is close to the object being studied. An eyepiece lens is the lens you look through. Microscopes are used to see magnified images of tiny, nearby objects.

Lasers and Laser Light

A **laser** is a device that produces intense light of only one color and wavelength. Laser light is different from nonlaser light in many ways. One important difference is that laser light is *coherent.* When light is coherent, light waves move together as they travel away from their source. The crests and troughs of coherent light waves are aligned. So, the individual waves behave as one wave.

Reading Check What does it mean for light to be coherent? (*See the Appendix for answers to Reading Checks.*)

MATH PRACTICE

Microscope Magnification

Some microscopes use more than one lens to magnify objects. The power of each lens indicates the amount of magnification the lens gives. For example, a 10× lens magnifies objects 10 times. To find the amount of magnification given by two or more lenses used together, multiply the powers of the lenses. What is the magnification given by a 5× lens used with a 20× lens?

laser a device that produces intense light of only one wavelength and color

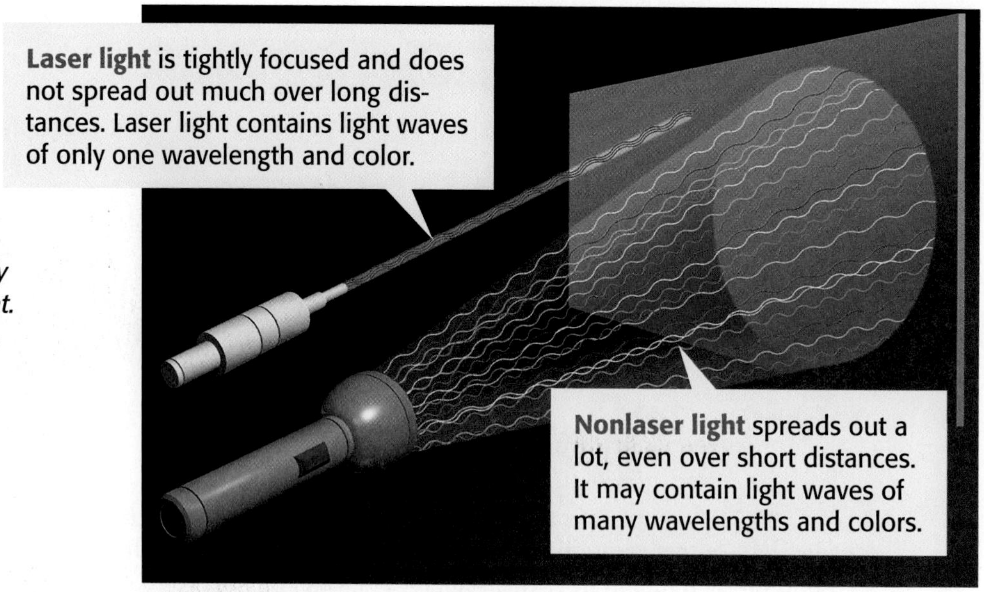

Nonlaser light spreads out a lot, even over short distances. It may contain light waves of many wavelengths and colors.

Figure 3 *Laser light is very different from nonlaser light.*

How Lasers Produce Light

Figure 3 compares laser and nonlaser light. The word *laser* stands for **l**ight **a**mplification by **s**timulated **e**mission of **r**adiation. *Amplification* is the increase in the brightness of the light. *Radiation* is energy transferred as electromagnetic waves.

What is stimulated emission? In an atom, an electron can move from one energy level to another. A photon (a particle of light) is released when an electron moves from a higher energy level to a lower energy level. The release of photons is called *emission*. *Stimulated emission* occurs when a photon strikes an atom that is in an excited state and makes the atom emit another photon. The newly emitted photon is identical to the first photon. The two photons travel away from the atom together. **Figure 4** shows how laser light is produced.

Figure 4 How a Helium-Neon Laser Works

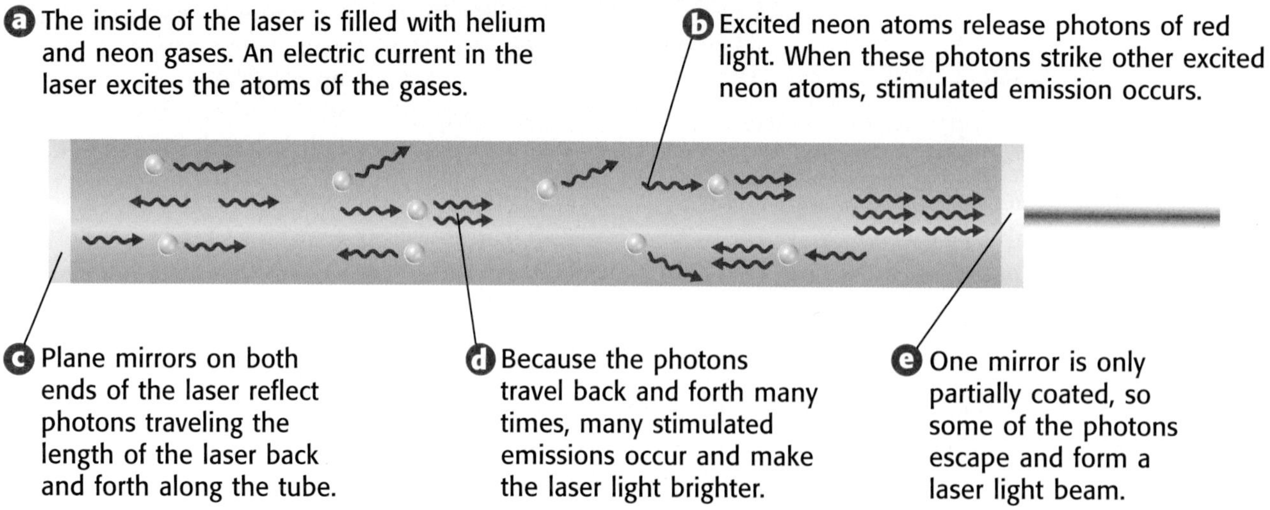

a The inside of the laser is filled with helium and neon gases. An electric current in the laser excites the atoms of the gases.
b Excited neon atoms release photons of red light. When these photons strike other excited neon atoms, stimulated emission occurs.
c Plane mirrors on both ends of the laser reflect photons traveling the length of the laser back and forth along the tube.
d Because the photons travel back and forth many times, many stimulated emissions occur and make the laser light brighter.
e One mirror is only partially coated, so some of the photons escape and form a laser light beam.

Uses for Lasers

Lasers are used to make holograms, such as the one shown in **Figure 5.** A **hologram** is a piece of film that produces a three-dimensional image of an object. Holograms are similar to photographs because both are images recorded on film. However, unlike photographs, the images you see in holograms are not on the surface of the film. The images appear in front of or behind the film. If you move the hologram, you will see the image from different angles.

Lasers are also used for other tasks. For example, lasers are used to cut materials such as metal and cloth. Doctors sometimes use lasers for surgery. And CD players have lasers. Light from the laser in a CD player reflects off patterns on a CD's surface. The reflected light is converted to a sound wave.

Reading Check How are holograms like photographs?

hologram a piece of film that produces a three-dimensional image of an object; made by using laser light

Figure 5 *Some holograms make three-dimensional images that look so real that you might want to reach out and touch them!*

Optical Fibers

Imagine a glass thread that transmits more than 1,000 telephone conversations at the same time with flashes of light. This thread, called an *optical fiber,* is a thin, glass wire that transmits light over long distances. Some optical fibers are shown in **Figure 6.** Transmitting information through telephone cables is the most common use of optical fibers. Optical fibers are also used to network computers. And they allow doctors to see inside patients' bodies without performing major surgery.

Light in a Pipe

Optical fibers are like pipes that carry light. Light stays inside an optical fiber because of total internal reflection. *Total internal reflection* is the complete reflection of light along the inside surface of the material through which it travels. **Figure 6** shows total internal reflection in an optical fiber.

Figure 6 **How Optical Fibers Work**

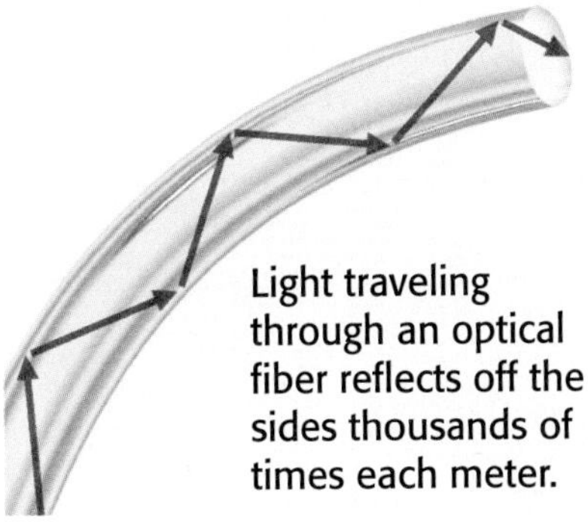

Light traveling through an optical fiber reflects off the sides thousands of times each meter.

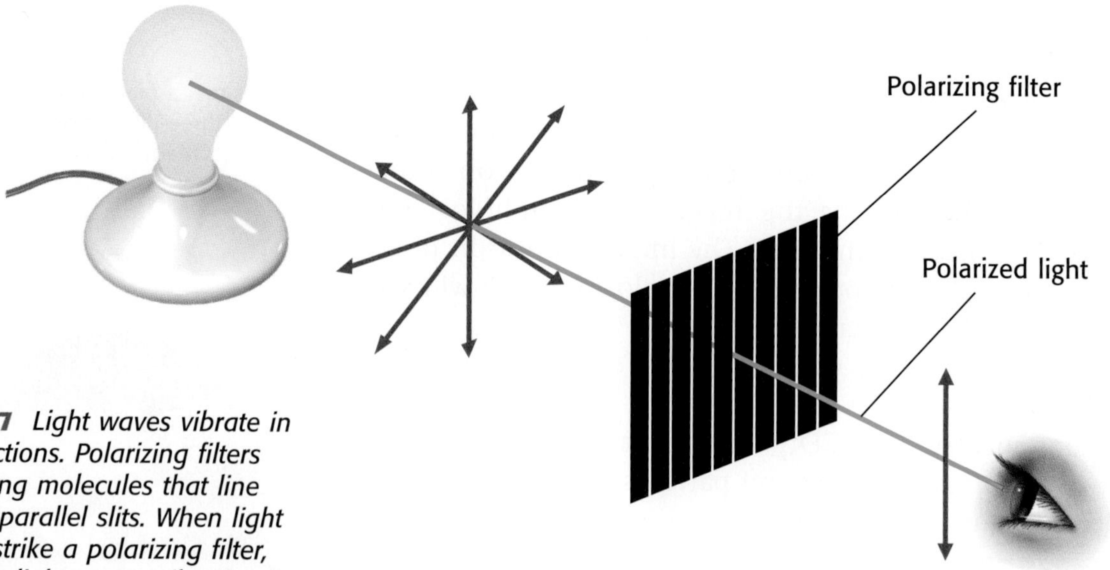

Figure 7 *Light waves vibrate in all directions. Polarizing filters have long molecules that line up like parallel slits. When light waves strike a polarizing filter, only the light waves vibrating in the same direction as the slits pass through.*

Polarized Light

The next time you shop for sunglasses, look for some that have lenses that polarize light. Such sunglasses are good for reducing glare. *Polarized light* consists of light waves that vibrate in only one plane. **Figure 7** illustrates how light is polarized.

When light reflects off a horizontal surface, such as a car hood or a body of water, the light is polarized horizontally. You see this polarized light as glare. Polarizing sunglasses reduce glare from horizontal surfaces because the lenses have vertically polarized filters. These filters allow only vertically vibrating light waves to pass through them. Polarizing filters are also used by photographers to reduce glare in their photographs, as shown in **Figure 8.**

Figure 8 *These two photos were taken by the same camera and from the same angle. There is less reflected light in the photo at right because a polarizing filter was placed over the lens of the camera.*

Quick Lab

Blackout!

1. Hold a **lens from a pair of polarizing sunglasses** up to your eye, and look through the lens. Record your observations.
2. Put a **second polarizing lens** over the first lens. Make sure both lenses are right side up. Look through both lenses, and describe your observations.
3. Rotate one lens slowly as you look through both lenses, and describe what happens.
4. Why can't you see through the lenses when they are aligned a certain way?

Communication Technology

You may think that talking on the telephone has nothing to do with light. But if you are talking on a cordless telephone or a cellular telephone, you are using a form of light technology! Light is an electromagnetic wave. There are many different kinds of electromagnetic waves. Radio waves and microwaves are kinds of electromagnetic waves. And cordless telephones and cellular telephones use radio waves and microwaves to send signals.

Figure 9 *You can make and receive calls with a cellular telephone almost everywhere you go.*

Cordless Telephones

Cordless telephones are a combination of a regular telephone and a radio. There are two parts to a cordless telephone—the base and the handset. The base is connected to a telephone jack in the wall of a building. The base receives calls through the phone line. The base then changes the signal to a radio wave and sends the signal to the handset. The handset changes the radio signal to sound for you to hear. The handset also changes your voice to a radio wave that is sent back to the base.

✓ Reading Check **What kind of electromagnetic wave does a cordless telephone use?**

Cellular Telephones

The telephone in **Figure 9** is a cellular telephone. Cellular telephones are similar to the handset part of a cordless telephone because they send and receive signals. But a cellular telephone receives signals from tower antennas located across the country instead of from a base. And instead of using radio waves, cellular telephones use microwaves to send information.

Satellite Television

Another technology that uses electromagnetic waves to transmit data is satellite television. Satellite television companies broadcast microwave signals from human-made satellites in space. Broadcasting from space allows more people to receive the signals than broadcasting from an antenna on Earth. Small satellite dishes on the roofs of houses or outside apartments collect the signals. The signals are then sent to the customer's television set. People who have satellite television usually have better TV reception than people who receive broadcasts from antennas on Earth.

CONNECTION TO Social Studies

Navigation GPS is a complex navigation system. Before GPS was developed, travelers and explorers used other techniques, such as compasses and stars, to find their way. Research an older form of navigation, and make a poster that summarizes what you learn.

ACTIVITY

The Global Positioning System

The Global Positioning System (GPS) is a network of 27 satellites that orbit Earth. These satellites continuously send microwave signals. The signals can be picked up by a GPS receiver on Earth and used to measure positions on the Earth's surface. **Figure 10** explains how GPS works. GPS was originally used by the United States military. But now, anyone in the world who has a GPS receiver can use the system. People use GPS to avoid getting lost and to have fun. Some cars have GPS road maps that can tell the car's driver how to get to a certain place. Hikers and campers use GPS receivers to find their way in the wilderness. And some people use GPS receivers for treasure-hunt games.

Reading Check **What are two uses for GPS?**

Figure 10 The Global Positioning System

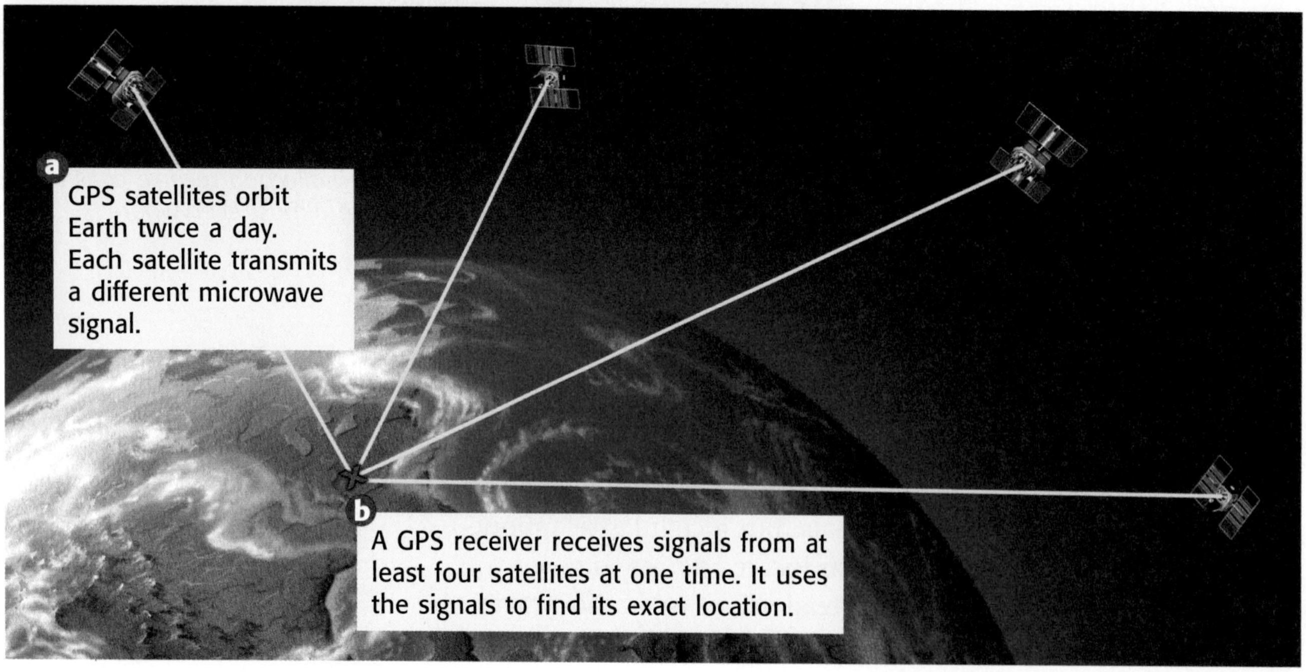

a
GPS satellites orbit Earth twice a day. Each satellite transmits a different microwave signal.
b
A GPS receiver receives signals from at least four satellites at one time. It uses the signals to find its exact location.

SECTION Review

Summary

- Optical instruments, such as cameras, telescopes, and microscopes, are devices that help people make observations.
- Lasers are devices that produce intense, coherent light of only one wavelength and color. Lasers produce light by a process called *stimulated emission*.
- Optical fibers transmit light over long distances.
- Polarized light contains light waves that vibrate in only one direction.
- Cordless telephones are a combination of a telephone and a radio. Information is transmitted in the form of radio waves between the handset and the base.
- Cellular phones transmit information in the form of microwaves to and from antennas.
- Satellite television is broadcast by microwaves from satellites in space.
- GPS is a navigation system that uses microwave signals sent by a network of satellites in space.

Using Key Terms

1. Use each of the following terms in a separate sentence: *laser* and *hologram*.

Understanding Key Ideas

2. Which of the following statements about laser light is NOT true?
   a. Laser light is coherent.
   b. Laser light contains light of only one wavelength.
   c. Laser light is produced by stimulated emission.
   d. Laser light spreads out over short distances.
3. List three optical instruments, and describe what they do.
4. What are four uses for lasers?
5. Describe how optical fibers work.
6. What is polarized light?
7. Describe two ways that satellites in space are useful in everyday life.

Critical Thinking

8. **Making Comparisons** Compare how a cordless telephone works with how a cellular telephone works.
9. **Making Inferences** Why do you think optical fibers can transmit information over long distances without losing much of the signal?

Interpreting Graphics

Use the graph below to answer the questions that follow.

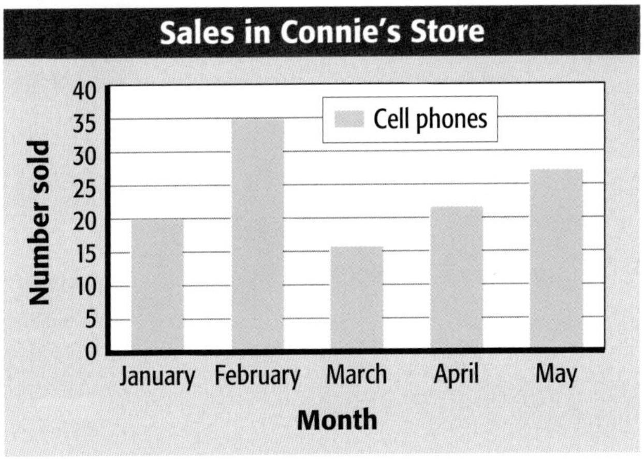

10. In which two months did Connie's store sell the most cellular telephones?
11. How many cellular telephones were sold in January?

SCILINKS. NSTA
Developed and maintained by the National Science Teachers Association

For a variety of links related to this chapter, go to www.scilinks.org

Topic: Lasers
SciLinks code: HSM0853

Using Scientific Methods

Skills Practice Lab

Images from Convex Lenses

A convex lens is thicker in the center than at the edges. Light rays passing through a convex lens come together at a focal point. Under certain conditions, a convex lens will create a real image of an object. This image will have certain characteristics, depending on the distance between the object and the lens. In this experiment, you will determine the characteristics of real images created by a convex lens—the kind of lens used as a magnifying lens.

OBJECTIVES

Use a convex lens to form images.

Determine the characteristics of real images formed by convex lenses.

MATERIALS

- candle
- card, index, 4 × 6 in. or larger
- clay, modeling
- convex lens
- jar lid
- matches
- meterstick

SAFETY

Ask a Question

1. What are the characteristics of real images created by a convex lens? For example, are the images upright or inverted (upside down)? Are the images larger or smaller than the object?

Form a Hypothesis

2. Write a hypothesis that is a possible answer to the questions above. Explain your reasoning.

Test the Hypothesis

3. Copy the table below.

Data Collection

Image	Orientation (upright/ inverted)	Size (larger/ smaller)	Image distance (cm)	Object distance (cm)
1				
2				
3				

DO NOT WRITE IN BOOK

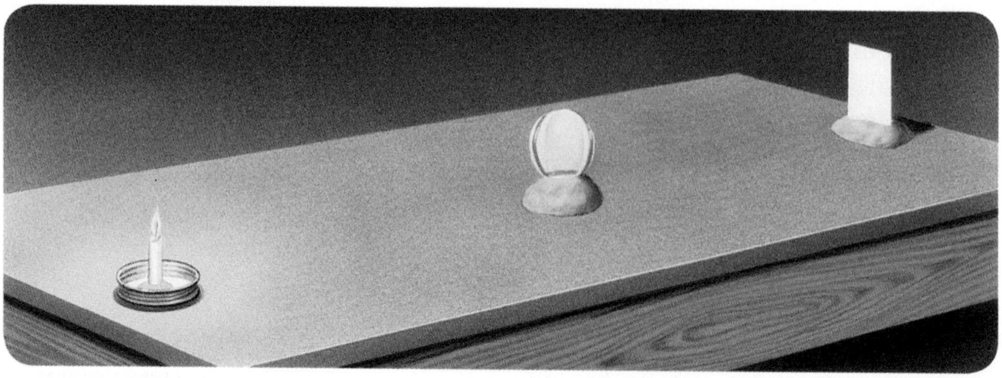

4. Use modeling clay to make a base for the lens. Place the lens and base in the middle of the table.
5. Stand the index card upright in some modeling clay on one side of the lens.
6. Place the candle in the jar lid, and anchor it with some modeling clay. Place the candle on the table so that the lens is halfway between the candle and the card. Light the candle. **Caution:** Use extreme care around an open flame.
7. In a darkened room, slowly move the card and the candle away from the lens while keeping the lens exactly halfway between the card and the candle. Continue until you see a clear image of the candle flame on the card. This is image 1.
8. Measure and record the distance between the lens and the card (image distance) and between the lens and the candle (object distance).
9. Is the image upright or inverted? Is it larger or smaller than the candle? Record this information in the table.
10. Move the lens toward the candle. The new object distance should be less than half the object distance measured in step 8. Move the card back and forth until you find a sharp image (image 2) of the candle on the card.
11. Repeat steps 8 and 9 for image 2.
12. Leave the card and candle in place and move the lens toward the card to get the third image (image 3).
13. Repeat steps 8 and 9 for image 3.

Analyze the Results

1. **Recognizing Patterns** Describe the trend between image distance and image size.
2. **Examining Data** What are the similarities between the real images that are formed by a convex lens?

Draw Conclusions

3. **Making Predictions** The lens of your eye is a convex lens. Use the information you collected to describe the image projected on the back of your eye when you look at an object.

Applying Your Data

Convex lenses are used in film projectors. Explain why your favorite movie stars are truly "larger than life" on the screen in terms of image distance and object distance.

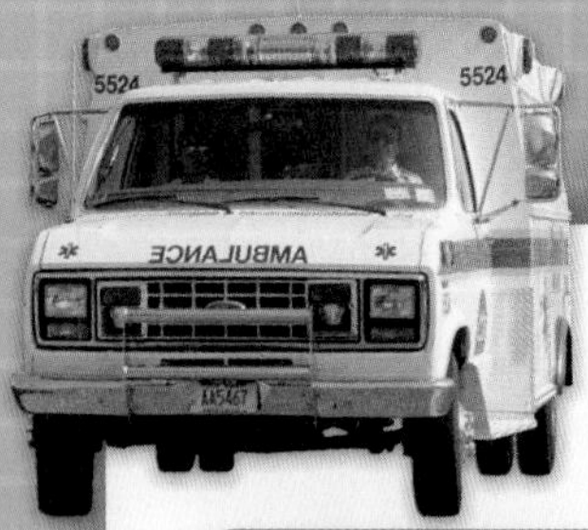

Chapter Review

USING KEY TERMS

In each of the following sentences, replace the incorrect term with the correct term from the word bank.

nearsightedness	hologram
concave mirror	laser
plane mirror	convex lens
convex mirror	farsightedness

1. A convex mirror is a mirror shaped like the inside of a spoon.

2. Eye surgeons use a hologram to reshape the cornea of an eye.

3. A person who has nearsightedness has trouble reading a book.

4. A concave lens refracts light and focuses it inward to a focal point.

5. If you move a lens around, you can see its three-dimensional image from different angles.

UNDERSTANDING KEY IDEAS

Multiple Choice

6. Which of the following parts of the eye refracts light?
   - **a.** pupil
   - **b.** iris
   - **c.** lens
   - **d.** retina

7. A vision problem that happens when light is focused in front of the retina is
   - **a.** farsightedness.
   - **b.** nearsightedness.
   - **c.** color deficiency.
   - **d.** None of the above

8. What kind of mirror provides images of large areas and is used for security?
   - **a.** a plane mirror
   - **b.** a concave mirror
   - **c.** a convex mirror
   - **d.** All of the above

9. A simple refracting telescope has
   - **a.** a convex lens and a concave lens.
   - **b.** a concave mirror and a convex lens.
   - **c.** two convex lenses.
   - **d.** two concave lenses.

10. Light waves in a laser beam interact and act as one wave. This light is called
    - **a.** coherent light.
    - **b.** emitted light.
    - **c.** polarized light.
    - **d.** reflected light.

11. When you look at yourself in a plane mirror, you see a
    - **a.** real image behind the mirror.
    - **b.** real image on the surface of the mirror.
    - **c.** virtual image that appears to be behind the mirror.
    - **d.** virtual image that appears to be in front of the mirror.

Short Answer

12 What kind of eyeglass lens should be prescribed for a person who cannot focus on nearby objects? Explain.

13 How is a hologram different from a photograph?

14 Why might a scientist who is working at the North Pole need polarizing sunglasses?

Math Skills

15 Ms. Welch's class conducted a poll about vision problems. Of the 150 students asked, 21 reported that they are nearsighted. Six of the nearsighted students wear contact lenses to correct their vision, and the rest wear glasses.

a. What percentage of the students asked is nearsighted?

b. What percentage of the students asked wears glasses?

CRITICAL THINKING

16 **Concept Mapping** Use the following terms to create a concept map: *lens, telescope, camera, real image, virtual image,* and *optical instrument.*

17 **Analyzing Ideas** Stoplights are usually mounted so that the red light is on the top and the green light is on the bottom. Why is it important for a person who has red-green color deficiency to know this arrangement?

18 **Applying Concepts** How could you find out if a device that produces red light is a laser or if it is just a red flashlight?

19 **Making Inferences** Imagine that you have a GPS receiver. When you use your receiver in the park and are surrounded by tall trees, the receiver easily finds your location. But when you use your receiver downtown and are surrounded by tall buildings, the receiver cannot determine your location. Why do you think there is a difference in reception? Describe a situation in which poor GPS reception around tall buildings could cause problems.

INTERPRETING GRAPHICS

20 Look at the ray diagrams below. For each diagram, identify the type of mirror that is being used and the kind of image that is being formed.

a

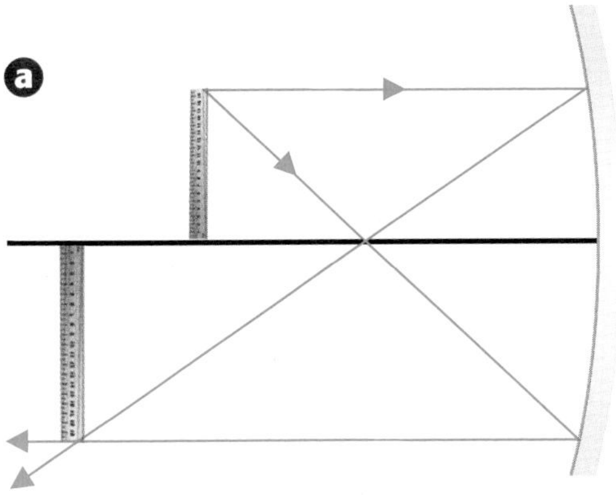

b

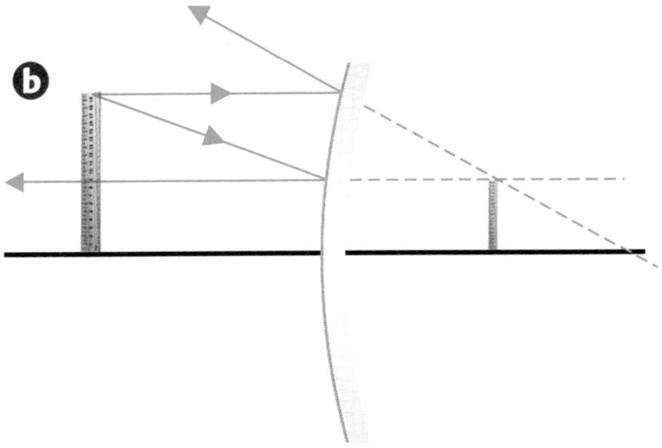

Standardized Test Preparation

Multiple Choice

1. A slide projector makes a small image larger as it projects the image onto a screen. How does a slide projector magnify an image?

A. The projector uses a convex lens.

B. The projector uses a convex mirror.

C. The projector uses a concave lens.

D. The projector uses a concave mirror.

2. Jordan is nearsighted. Which of the following describes how Jordan's eyeglasses help to correct her vision, so that she can focus on objects that are far away?

A. The concave lenses in Jordan's eyeglasses refract the light outward. The convex lenses in her eyes focus the refracted light onto her retinas.

B. The convex lenses in Jordan's eyeglasses focus the light inward. The convex lenses in her eyes focus the refracted light onto her retinas.

C. The concave lenses in Jordan's eyeglasses refract the light outward. The concave lenses in her eyes focus the refracted light onto her retinas.

D. The convex lenses in Jordan's eyeglasses focus the light inward. The concave lenses in her eyes focus the refracted light onto her retinas.

3. When Greg stands on a spot in front of a funhouse mirror, his image disappears. What conclusion can Greg draw about the mirror and his position in front of it?

A. Greg is located more than 1 focal length away from a concave mirror.

B. Greg is located less than 1 focal length away from a convex mirror.

C. Greg is located at the focal point of a concave mirror.

D. Greg is located directly between a concave and a convex mirror.

Use the figure below to answer questions 4–5.

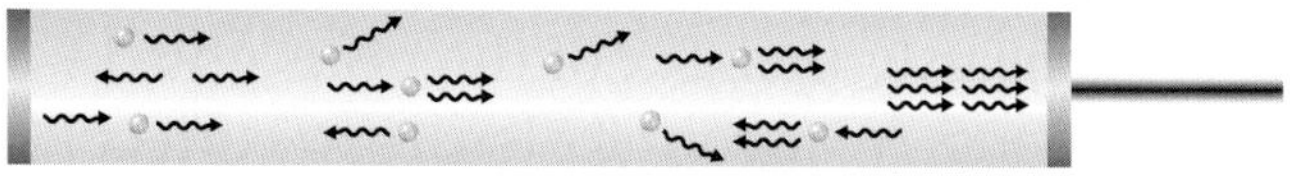

4. Katie drew the above diagram of a helium-neon laser during a lab experiment. What is the purpose of the mirrors inside a laser?

A. They focus the light into a strong beam.

B. They cause photons to bump into atoms.

C. They remove all but one wavelength of light.

D. They heat the atoms into an excited state.

5. What would happen if Katie passed the red light from the laser above through a glass prism?

A. The resulting light would be red.

B. The resulting light would be white.

C. The resulting light would be a rainbow.

D. The light would not pass through.

Use the table below to answer questions 6–7.

Image	Description of Reflection
A	Dog is life-size and right-side-up
B	Dog is smaller than life-size and upside-down
C	Dog is smaller than life-size and right-side-up
D	Dog is larger than life-size and right-side-up

6. The table above describes the reflection of a dog seen in four different mirrors. Which image was seen in a concave mirror with the dog standing less than 1 focal length away?

A. image A

B. image B

C. image C

D. image D

7. Which image described in the table above is a real image?

A. image A

B. image B

C. image C

D. image D

8. Which of the following uses electromagnetic waves that have the longest wavelength?

A. cellular telephone

B. satellite television

C. global positioning system

D. cordless telephone

9. Flying foxes have about 1 cone for every 250 rods in their eyes. What could you infer about flying foxes from this information?

A. Flying foxes are active day and night.

B. Flying foxes are visually attracted to flowers.

C. Flying foxes are nocturnal animals.

D. Flying foxes are good hunters.

10. A vertically polarized filter is placed over a camera lens. What does the photographer see?

A. horizontally vibrating light waves

B. diagonally vibrating light waves

C. vertically vibrating light waves

D. light waves vibrating in all directions

Open Response

11. Carrie creates a simple camera with a concave lens. What happens when she takes pictures with the camera?

12. List four components of a laser. Explain how the components work together to create a laser beam.

Science in Action

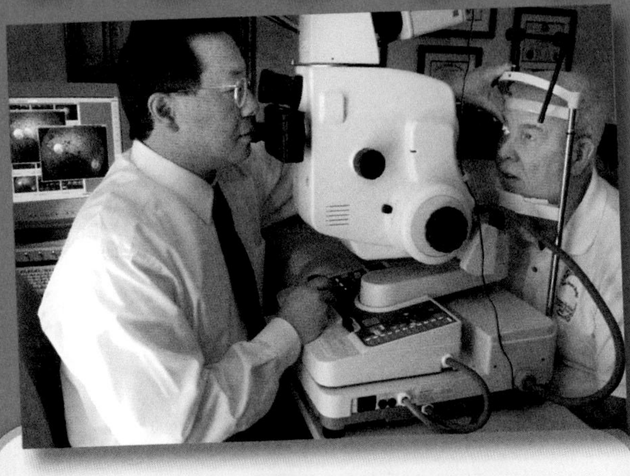

Science, Technology, and Society

Bionic Eyes

Imagine bionic eyes that allow a person who is blind to see. Researchers working on artificial vision think that the technology will be available soon. Many companies are working on different ways to restore sight to people who are blind. Some companies are developing artificial corneas, while other companies are building artificial retinas. One item that has already been tested on people is a pair of glasses that provides limited vision. The glasses have a camera that sends a signal to an electrode implanted in the person's brain. The images are black and white and are not detailed, but the person who is wearing the glasses can see obstacles in his or her path.

Language Arts Activity

WRITING SKILL Write a one-page story about a teen who has his or her eyesight restored by a bionic eye. What would the teen want to see first? What would the teen do that he or she couldn't do before?

Scientific Debate

Do Cellular Telephones Cause Cancer?

As cellular telephones became popular, people began to wonder if the phones were dangerous. Some cell-phone users claimed that the microwave energy from their cell phones caused them to develop brain cancer. So far, most research shows that the microwave energy emitted by cell phones is too low and too weak to damage human tissue. However, some studies have shown negative effects. There is some evidence that the low-power microwave energy used by cell phones may damage DNA and may cause cells to shrink. Because so many people use cellular phones, research continues around the world.

Math Activity

The American Cancer Society estimates that 0.006% of people in the United States will be diagnosed with brain cancer each year. If a city has a population of 50,000 people, how many people in that city will be diagnosed with brain cancer in one year?

People in Science

Sandra Faber

Astronomer What do you do when you send a telescope into space and then find out that it is broken? You call Dr. Sandra Faber, a professor of astronomy at the University of California, Santa Cruz (UCSC). In April 1990, after the *Hubble Space Telescope* went into orbit, scientists found that the images the telescope collected were not turning out as expected. Dr. Faber's team at UCSC was in charge of a device on *Hubble* called the *Wide Field Planetary Camera*. Dr. Faber and her team decided to test the telescope to determine what was wrong.

To perform the test, they centered *Hubble* onto a bright star and took several photos. From those photos, Dr. Faber's team created a model of what was wrong. After reporting the error to NASA and presenting the model they had developed, Dr. Faber and a group of experts began to correct the problem. The group's efforts were a success and put *Hubble* back into operation so that astronomers could continue researching stars and other objects in space.

Social Studies ACTIVITY

Research the history of the telescope. Make a timeline with the dates of major events in telescope history. For example, you could include the first use of a telescope to see the rings of Saturn in your timeline.

go.hrw.com

To learn more about these Science in Action topics, visit go.hrw.com and type in the keyword **HP5LOWF.**

Current Science

Check out Current Science® articles related to this chapter by visiting go.hrw.com. Just type in the keyword HP5CS23.

UNIT 2

TIMELINE

Electricity

Can you imagine a world without computers, motors, or even light bulbs? Your life would be very different indeed without electricity and the devices that depend on it. In this unit, you will learn how electricity results from tiny charged particles, how electricity and magnetism interact, and how electronic technology has revolutionized the world in a relatively short amount of time. This timeline includes some of the events leading to our current understanding of electricity, electromagnetism, and electronic technology.

1751

Benjamin Franklin flies a kite to which a key is attached in a thunderstorm to demonstrate that lightning is a form of electricity.

1903

Dutch physician Willem Einthoven develops the first electrocardiograph machine to record the tiny electric currents that pass through the body's tissues.

1947

The transistor is invented.

1958

The invention of the integrated circuit, which uses millions of transistors, revolutionizes electronic technology.

1773

American colonists hold the "Boston Tea Party" and dump 342 chests of British tea into Boston Harbor.

1831

British scientist Michael Faraday and American physicist Joseph Henry separately demonstrate the principle of electromagnetic induction in which magnetism is used to generate electricity.

1876

The telephone is officially invented by Alexander Graham Bell, who beats Elisha Gray to the patent office by only a few hours.

1911

Superconductivity is discovered. Superconductivity is the ability some metals and alloys have to carry electric current without resistance under certain conditions.

1945

Grace Murray Hopper, a pioneer in computers and computer languages, coins the phrase "debugging the computer" after removing from the wiring of her computer a moth that caused the computer to fail.

1984

The first portable CD player is introduced.

1997

Garry Kasparov, reigning world chess champion, loses a historic match to a computer named Deep Blue.

2003

One of the largest electricity blackouts in North American history started in the afternoon on August 14, 2003. The blackout left several large cities, including New York City; Detroit, Michigan; and Toronto, Canada, in the dark. Several days passed before electrical energy was fully restored to the millions of people affected in eight U.S. states and Canada.

7

Introduction to Electricity

The Big Idea

Electrical energy is the energy of electric charges.

SECTION

About the Photo

This incredible light display is not an indoor lightning storm, but it's close! When scientists at the Sandia National Laboratory fire this fusion device, a huge number of electrons move across the room and make giant sparks.

PRE-READING ACTIVITY

FOLDNOTES **Layered Book** Before you read the chapter, create the FoldNote entitled "Layered Book" described in the **Study Skills** section of the Appendix. Label the tabs of the layered book with "Charge," "Current," "Voltage," and "Resistance." As you read the chapter, write information you learn about each category under the appropriate tab.

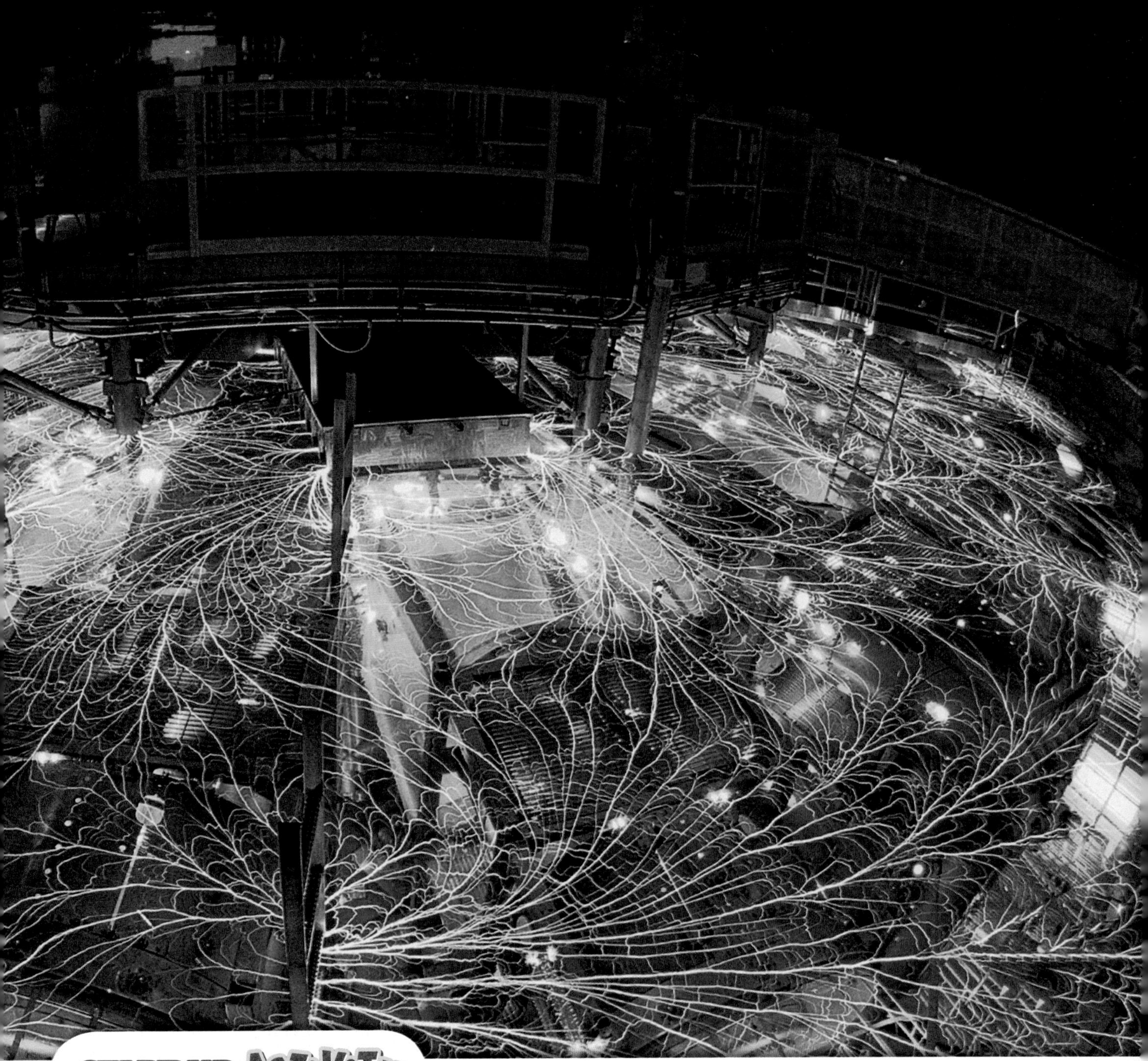

START-UP ACTIVITY

Stick Together

In this activity, you will see how a pair of electrically charged objects interact.

Procedure

1. Take **two strips of cellophane tape.** Each strip should be 20 cm long. Fold over a small part of the end of each strip to form a tab.
2. Hold each piece of tape by its tab. Bring the two pieces of tape close together, but do not let them touch. Record your observations.
3. Tape one of the strips to your lab table. Tape the second strip on top of the first strip.
4. Pull the strips of tape off the table together.
5. Quickly pull the strips apart. Bring the two pieces of tape close together, but do not let them touch. Record your observations.

Analysis

1. Compare how the pieces of tape behaved when you first brought them together with how they behaved after you pulled the pieces apart.
2. As you pulled the pieces of tape apart, electrons from one piece of tape moved onto the other piece of tape. Describe the charge on each piece of tape after you pulled the two pieces apart.
3. From your observations, draw a conclusion about how objects having the charges that you described behave toward one another.

SECTION 1

Electric Charge and Static Electricity

What You Will Learn

- Describe how charged objects interact by using the law of electric charges.
- Describe three ways in which an object can become charged.
- Compare conductors with insulators.
- Give two examples of static electricity and electric discharge.

Vocabulary

law of electric charges
electric force
electric field
electrical conductor
electrical insulator
static electricity
electric discharge

READING STRATEGY

Reading Organizer As you read this section, create an outline of the section. Use the headings from the section in your outline.

Have you ever reached out to open a door and received a shock from the doorknob? Why did that happen?

On dry days, you might get a shock when you open a door, put on a sweater, or touch another person. These shocks come from static electricity. To understand static electricity, you need to learn about atoms and charge.

Electric Charge

All matter is made up of very small particles called *atoms*. Atoms are made of even smaller particles called protons, neutrons, and electrons, which are shown in **Figure 1.** How do these particles differ? For one thing, protons and electrons are charged particles, and neutrons are not.

Reading Check **What are the two types of charged particles in atoms?** (*See the Appendix for answers to Reading Checks.*)

Protons and electrons are charged while neutrons are not

Charges Exert Forces

Charge is a physical property. An object can have a positive charge, a negative charge, or no charge. Charge is best understood by learning how charged objects interact. Charged objects exert a force—a push or a pull—on other charged objects. The **law of electric charges** states that like charges repel, or push away, and opposite charges attract. **Figure 2** illustrates this law.

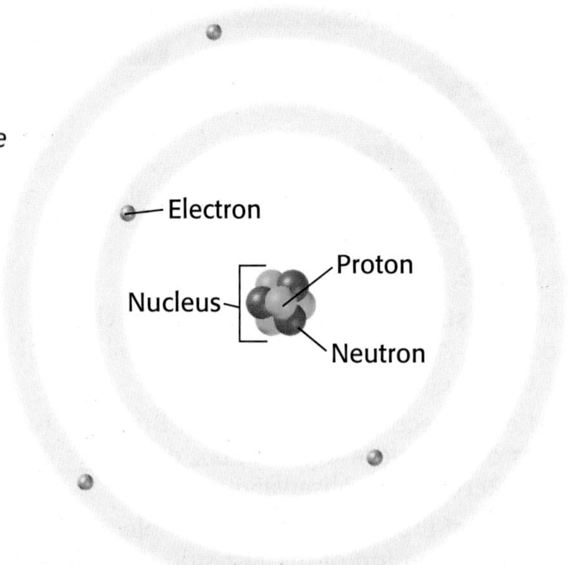

Figure 1 *Protons and neutrons make up the center of the atom, the nucleus. Electrons are found outside the nucleus.*

Figure 2 **The Law of Electric Charges**

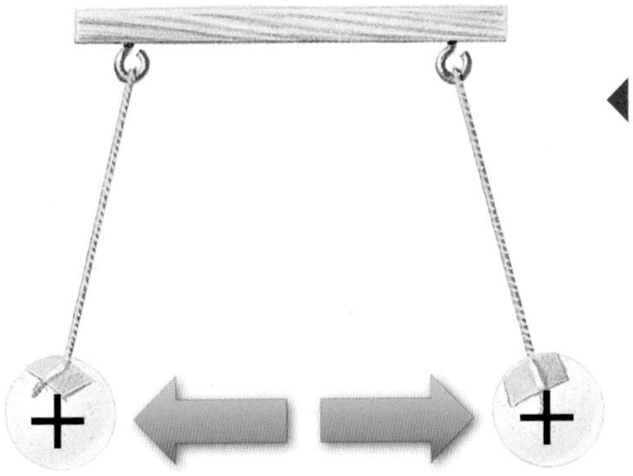

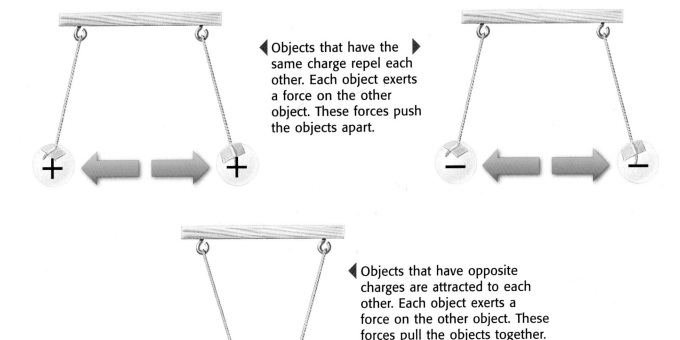

Objects that have the same charge repel each other. Each object exerts a force on the other object. These forces push the objects apart.

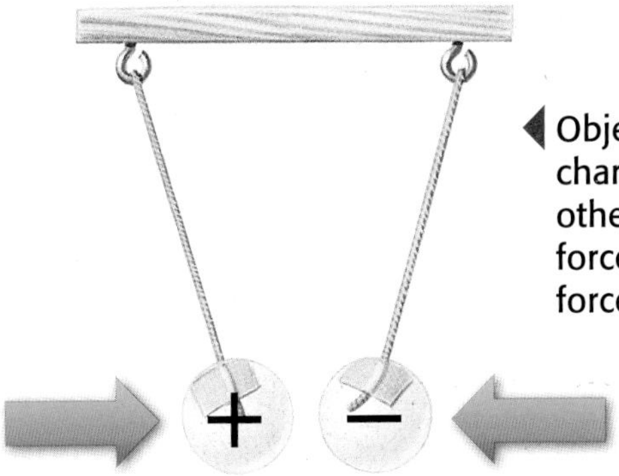

Objects that have opposite charges are attracted to each other. Each object exerts a force on the other object. These forces pull the objects together.

The Force Between Protons and Electrons

Protons are positively charged. Electrons are negatively charged. Because protons and electrons have opposite charges, they are attracted to each other. Without this attraction, electrons could not be held in atoms.

The Electric Force and the Electric Field

The force between charged objects is an **electric force.** The size of the electric force depends on two things. The first thing is the amount of charge on each object. The greater the charge is, the greater the electric force is. The other thing that determines the size of the electric force is the distance between the charges. The closer together the charges are, the greater the electric force is.

Charged things are affected by electric force because charged things have an electric field around them. An **electric field** is the region around a charged object in which an electric force is exerted on another charged object. A charged object in the electric field of another charged object is attracted or repelled by the electric force acting on it.

law of electric charges the law that states that like charges repel and opposite charges attract

electric force the force of attraction or repulsion on a charged particle that is due to an electric field

electric field the space around a charged object in which another charged object experiences an electric force

Charge It!

Atoms have equal numbers of protons and electrons. Because an atom's positive and negative charges cancel each other out, atoms do not have a charge. So, how can anything made of atoms be charged? An object becomes positively charged when it loses electrons. An object becomes negatively charged when it gains electrons. Objects can become charged by friction, conduction, and induction, as shown in **Figure 3.**

Reading Check What are three ways of charging an object?

CONNECTION TO Environmental Science

WRITING SKILL **Painting Cars** Research how charge and electric force are used by car makers to paint cars. Then, in your **science journal,** write a one-page report describing the process and explaining how the use of charge to paint cars helps protect the environment.

Friction

Charging by *friction* happens when electrons are "wiped" from one object onto another. If you use a cloth to rub a plastic ruler, electrons move from the cloth to the ruler. The ruler gains electrons and becomes negatively charged. At the same time, the cloth loses electrons and becomes positively charged.

Conduction

Charging by *conduction* happens when electrons move from one object to another by direct contact. Suppose you touch an uncharged piece of metal with a positively charged glass rod. Electrons from the metal will move to the glass rod. The metal loses electrons and becomes positively charged.

Figure 3 **Three Ways to Charge an Object**

Friction | **Conduction** | **Induction**

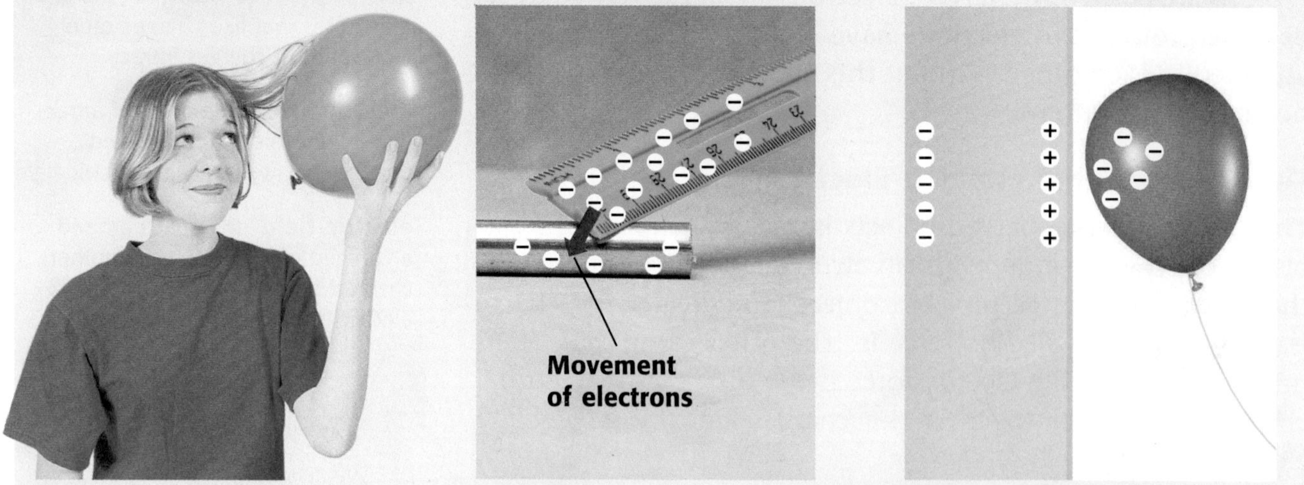

Friction: The friction of rubbing a balloon on your hair causes electrons to move from your hair to the balloon. Your hair and the balloon become oppositely charged and attract each other.

Conduction: When a negatively charged plastic ruler touches an uncharged metal rod, the electrons in the ruler travel to the rod. The rod becomes negatively charged by conduction.

Induction: A negatively charged balloon makes a small section of a metal beam have a positive charge through induction. Electrons in the metal are repelled by and move away from the balloon.

Induction

Charging by *induction* happens when charges in an uncharged metal object are rearranged without direct contact with a charged object. Suppose you hold a metal object near a positively charged object. The electrons in the metal are attracted to and move toward the positively charged object. This movement causes (or induces) an area of negative charge on the surface of the metal.

Conservation of Charge

When you charge something by any method, no charges are created or destroyed. The numbers of electrons and protons stay the same. Electrons simply move from one atom to another, which makes areas that have different charges. Because charges are not created or destroyed, charge is said to be conserved.

Detecting Charge

You can use a device called an *electroscope* to see if something is charged. An electroscope is a glass flask that has a metal rod in its rubber stopper. Two metal leaves are attached to the bottom of the rod. When the electroscope is not charged, the leaves hang straight down. When the electroscope is charged, the leaves repel each other, or spread apart.

Figure 4 shows a negatively charged ruler touching the rod of an electroscope. Electrons move from the ruler to the electroscope. The leaves become negatively charged and repel each other. If something that is positively charged touches the neutral rod, electrons move off the electroscope. Then, the leaves become positively charged and repel each other. An electroscope can show that an object is charged. However, it cannot show whether the charge is positive or negative.

Figure 4 *When an electroscope is charged, the metal leaves have the same charge and repel each other.*

✓ *Reading Check* **What can you do with an electroscope?** You can determine if the material is the charged but can't determine the kind of charge ; if it's positive or negative.

Quick Lab

Detecting Charge

1. Use **scissors** to cut **two strips of aluminum foil** that are 1 cm × 4 cm each.
2. Bend a **paper clip** to make a hook. (The clip will look like an upside-down question mark.)
3. Push the end of the hook through the middle of an **index card,** and tape the hook so that it hangs straight down from the card.
4. Lay the two foil strips on top of one another, and hang them on the hook by gently pushing the hook through them.
5. Lay the card over the top of a **glass jar.**
6. Bring **various charged objects** near the top of the paper-clip hook, and observe what happens. Explain your observations.

Figure 5 *These jumper cables are made of metal, which carries electric charges, and plastic, which keeps the charges away from your hands.*

Moving Charges

Look at **Figure 5.** Have you ever noticed that electrical cords are often made from metal and plastic? Different materials are used because electric charges move through some materials more easily than they move through others. Most materials are either conductors or insulators based on how easily charges move in them.

Conductors

An **electrical conductor** is a material in which charges can move easily. Most metals are good conductors because some of their electrons are free to move. Conductors are used to make wires. For example, a lamp cord has metal wire and metal prongs. Copper, aluminum, and mercury are good conductors.

Insulators

An **electrical insulator** is a material in which charges cannot move easily. Insulators do not conduct charges very well because their electrons cannot flow freely. The electrons are tightly held in the atoms of the insulator. The insulating material in a lamp cord stops charges from leaving the wire and protects you from electric shock. Plastic, rubber, glass, wood, and air are good insulators.

electrical conductor a material in which charges can move freely

electrical insulator a material in which charges cannot move freely

static electricity electric charge at rest; generally produced by friction or induction

Static Electricity

After you take your clothes out of the dryer, they sometimes are stuck together. They stick together because of static electricity. **Static electricity** is the electric charge at rest on an object.

When something is *static,* it is not moving. The charges of static electricity do not move away from the object that they are in. So, the object keeps its charge. Your clothes are charged by friction as they rub against each other inside a dryer. As the clothes tumble, negative charges are lost by some clothes and build up on other clothes. When the dryer stops, the transfer of charges also stops. And because clothing is an insulator, the built-up electric charges stay on each piece of clothing. The result of this buildup of charges is static cling.

Electric Discharge

Charges that build up as static electricity on an object eventually leave the object. The loss of static electricity as charges move off an object is called **electric discharge.** Sometimes, electric discharge happens slowly. For example, clothes stuck together by static electricity will eventually separate on their own. Over time, their electric charges move to water molecules in the air.

electric discharge the release of electricity stored in a source

Sometimes, electric discharge happens quickly. It may happen with a flash of light, a shock, or a crackling noise. For example, when you wear rubber-soled shoes and walk on carpet, negative charges build up on your body. When you reach out for a metal doorknob, the negative charges on your body can jump to the doorknob. The electric discharge happens quickly, and you feel a small shock.

One of the most dramatic examples of electric discharge is lightning. How does lightning form through a buildup of static electricity? **Figure 6** shows the answer.

Reading Check What is electric discharge? is the release of electricity stored in a source.

Figure 6 **How Lightning Forms**

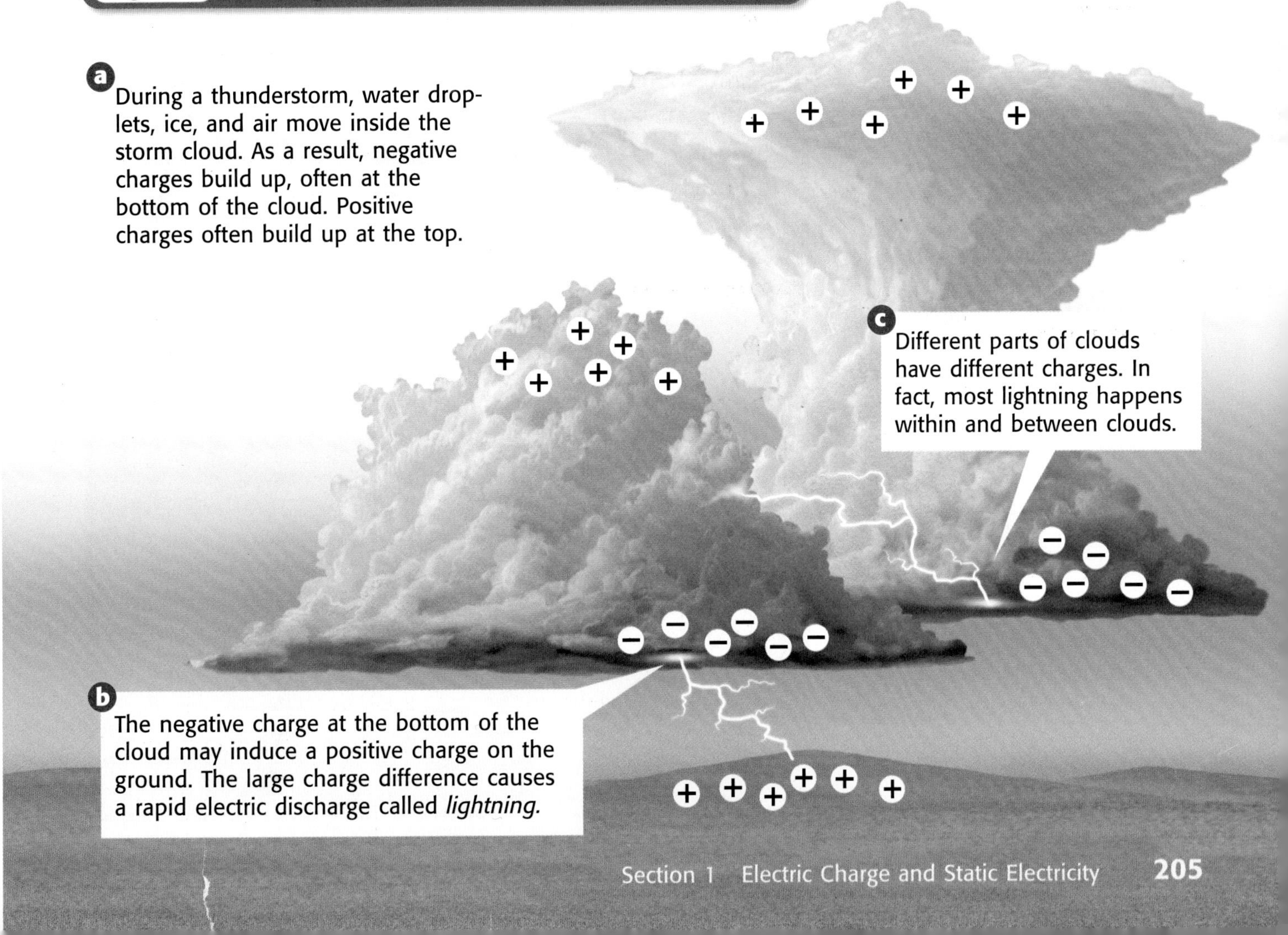

a During a thunderstorm, water droplets, ice, and air move inside the storm cloud. As a result, negative charges build up, often at the bottom of the cloud. Positive charges often build up at the top.
b The negative charge at the bottom of the cloud may induce a positive charge on the ground. The large charge difference causes a rapid electric discharge called *lightning.*
c Different parts of clouds have different charges. In fact, most lightning happens within and between clouds.

Lightning Dangers

Lightning usually strikes the highest point in a charged area because that point provides the shortest path for the charges to reach the ground. Anything that sticks up or out in an area can provide a path for lightning. Trees and people in open areas are at risk of being struck by lightning. For this reason, it is particularly dangerous to be at the beach or on a golf course during a lightning storm. Even standing under a tree during a storm is dangerous. The charges from lightning striking a tree can jump to your body.

Reading Check **Why is it dangerous to be outside in an open area during a storm?** Because when you're in open area, you are the tallest objet, so lighthing can strike you easily because you are the shortest path for lighting.

CONNECTION TO Social Studies

Benjamin Franklin In addition to being a statesman, Benjamin Franklin was a scientist. Research Franklin's discovery that lightning is a form of electricity. Make a poster describing the procedures that he used, the terms that he coined, and the inventions related to electricity that he designed.

ACTIVITY

Lightning Rods

A lightning rod is a pointed rod connected to the ground by a wire. Lightning rods are often mounted so that they are the tallest point on a building, as shown in **Figure 7.** Objects, such as a lightning rod, that are joined to Earth by a conductor, such as a wire, are *grounded*. Any object that is grounded provides a path for electric charges to move to Earth. Because Earth is so large, it can give up or absorb charges without being damaged. When lightning strikes a lightning rod, the electric charges are carried safely to Earth through the rod's wire. By directing the charge to Earth, the rods prevent lightning from damaging buildings.

Figure 7 *Lightning strikes the lightning rod rather than the building, because the lightning rod is the tallest point on the building.*

SECTION Review

Summary

- The law of electric charges states that like charges repel and opposite charges attract.
- The size of the electric force between two objects depends on the size of the charges exerting the force and the distance between the objects.
- Charged objects exert a force on each other and can cause each other to move.
- Objects become charged when they gain or lose electrons.
- Objects may become charged by friction, conduction, or induction.
- Charges are not created or destroyed and are said to be conserved.
- Charges move easily in conductors but do not move easily in insulators.
- Static electricity is the buildup of electric charges on an object. It is lost through electric discharge.

Using Key Terms

For each pair of terms, explain how the meanings of the terms differ.

1. *static electricity* and *electric discharge*
2. *electric force* and *electric field*
3. *electrical conductor* and *electrical insulator*

Understanding Key Ideas

4. Which of the following is an insulator?
   a. copper
   b. rubber
   c. aluminum
   d. iron
5. Compare the three methods of charging.
6. What does the law of electric charges say about two objects that are positively charged?
7. Give two examples of static electricity.
8. List two examples of electric discharge.

Critical Thinking

9. **Analyzing Processes** Imagine that you touch the top of an electroscope with an object. The metal leaves spread apart. Can you determine whether the charge is positive or negative? Explain your answer.
10. **Applying Concepts** Why is it important to touch a charged object to the metal rod of an electroscope and not to the rubber stopper?

Interpreting Graphics

The photograph below shows two charged balloons. Use the photograph below to answer the questions that follow.

11. Do the balloons have the same charge or opposite charges? Explain your answer.
12. How would the photograph look if each balloon were given the charge opposite to the charge it has now? Explain your answer.

SCILINKS. NSTA Developed and maintained by the National Science Teachers Association

For a variety of links related to this chapter, go to www.scilinks.org

Topic: Static Electricity
SciLinks code: HSM1451

SECTION 2

Electric Current and Electrical Energy

What You Will Learn

- Describe electric current.
- Describe voltage and its relationship to electric current.
- Describe resistance and its relationship to electric current.
- Explain how a cell generates electrical energy.
- Describe how thermocouples and photocells generate electrical energy.

Vocabulary

electric current
voltage
resistance
cell
thermocouple
photocell

READING STRATEGY

Reading Organizer As you read this section, make a table comparing electric current, voltage, and resistance.

You might not realize that when you watch TV, use a computer, or even turn on a light bulb, you depend on moving charges for the electrical energy that you need.

Electrical energy is the energy of electric charges. In most of the things that use electrical energy, the electric charges flow through wires. As you read on, you will learn more about how this flow of charges—called *electric current*—is made and how it is controlled in the things that you use every day.

Electric Current

An **electric current** is the rate at which charges pass a given point. The higher the current is, the greater the number of charges that pass the point each second. Electric current is expressed in units called *amperes* (AM PIRZ), which is often shortened to *amps*. The symbol for *ampere* is A. And in equations, the symbol for current is the letter *I*.

Reading Check **What is the unit of measurement for electric current?** (*See the Appendix for answers to Reading Checks.*) Amperes, amps, A

Making Charges Move

When you flip the switch on a flashlight, the light comes on instantly. But do charges in the battery instantly reach the bulb? No, they don't. When you flip the switch, an electric field is set up in the wire at the speed of light. And the electric field causes the free electrons in the wire to move. The energy of each electron is transferred instantly to the next electron, as shown in **Figure 1**.

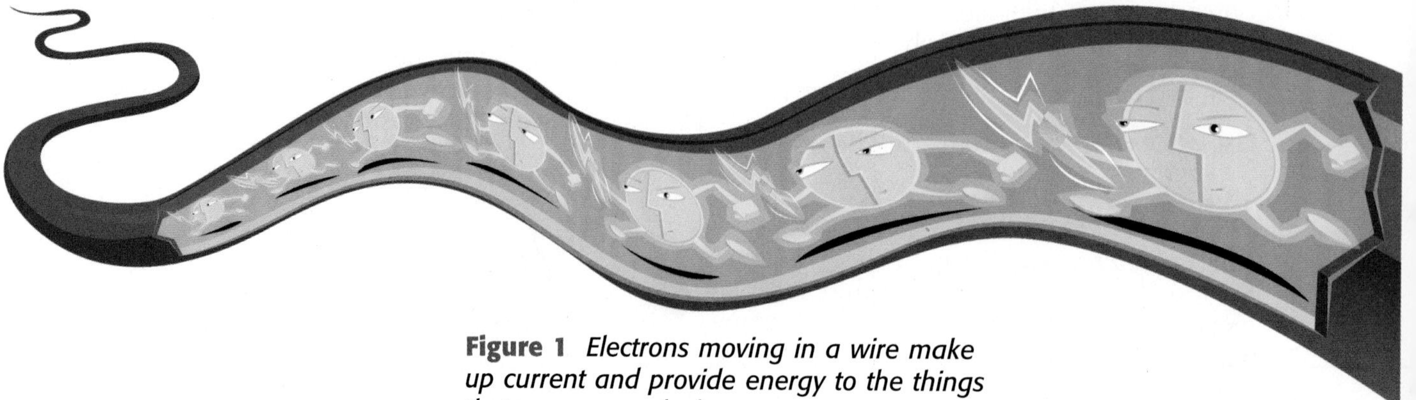

Figure 1 *Electrons moving in a wire make up current and provide energy to the things that you use each day.*

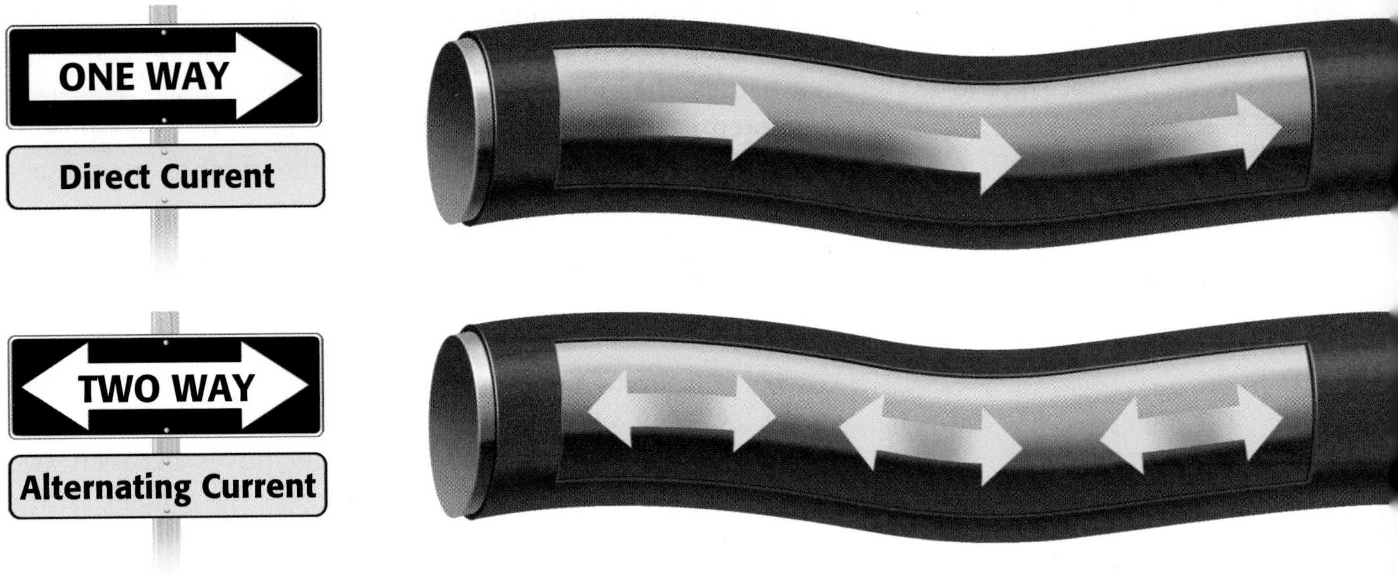

Figure 2 *Charges move in one direction in DC, but charges continually change direction in AC.*

Commanding Electrons to Move

This electric field is created so quickly that all electrons start moving through the wire at the same instant. Think of the electric field as a command to the electrons to charge ahead. The light comes on instantly because all of the electrons obey this command at the same time. So, the current that lights the bulb is established very quickly even though each electron moves quite slowly. In fact, a single electron may take more than an hour to travel 1 m through a wire.

electric current the rate at which charges pass through a given point; measured in amperes

AC and DC

There are two kinds of electric current—direct current (DC) and alternating current (AC). Look at **Figure 2.** In direct current, the charges always flow in the same direction. In alternating current, the charges continually shift from flowing in one direction to flowing in the reverse direction.

The electric current from the batteries used in a camera is DC. The electric current from outlets in your home is AC. In the United States, the alternating current changes directions 120 times each second, or has 60 cycles each second.

Both kinds of current can give you electrical energy. For example, if you connect a flashlight bulb to a battery, the light bulb will light. And you can light a household light bulb by putting it in a lamp and turning the lamp on.

Reading Check What are two kinds of electric current? AC and DC

Voltage

If you are on a bike at the top of a hill, you know that you can roll down to the bottom. You can roll down the hill because of the difference in height between the two points. The "hill" that causes charges in a circuit to move is voltage. **Voltage** is the potential difference between two points in a circuit. It is expressed in volts (V). In equations, the symbol for voltage is the letter *V*.

voltage the potential difference between two points; measured in volts

Reading Check **What is the unit of measurement for voltage?**

Voltage and Energy

Voltage is a measure of how much work is needed to move a charge between two points. You can think of voltage as the amount of energy released as a charge moves between two points in the path of a current. The higher the voltage is, the more energy is released per charge.

Voltage and Electric Current

As long as there is a voltage between two points on a wire, charges will flow in the wire. The size of the current depends on the voltage. The greater the voltage is, the greater the current is. A greater current means that more charges move in the wire each second. A large current is needed to start a car. So, the battery in a car has a fairly high voltage of 12 V. **Figure 3** shows batteries that have a number of different voltages. If you have a device that uses direct current, one of these batteries might help.

Figure 3 *Batteries are made with various voltages for use in many different devices.*

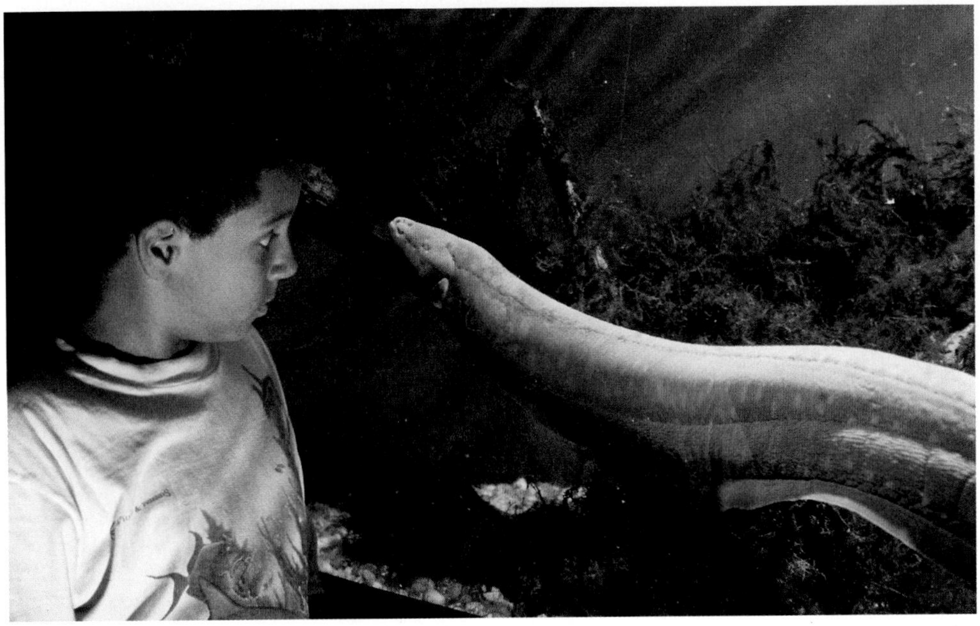

Figure 4 *An electric eel can create a voltage of more than 600 V!*

Varying Nature of Voltage

Things that run on batteries usually need a low voltage. For example, a portable radio might need only 3 V. Compare the voltage of such a radio with the voltage created by the eel in **Figure 4.** Most devices in your home use alternating current from an outlet. In the United States, electrical outlets usually supply AC at 120 V. So, most electrical devices, such as televisions, toasters, and alarm clocks, are made to run on 120 V.

CONNECTION TO Biology

Help for a Heart Pacemaker cells in the heart produce low electric currents at regular intervals to make the heart beat. During a heart attack, pacemaker cells do not work together, and the heart beats irregularly. Research how doctors sometimes "jump start" the heart during a heart attack. Make a poster to share your findings.

ACTIVITY

Resistance

Resistance is another factor that determines the amount of current in a wire. **Resistance** is the opposition to the flow of electric charge. Resistance is expressed in ohms (Ω, the Greek letter *omega*). In equations, the symbol for resistance is the letter *R*.

You can think of resistance as "electrical friction." The higher the resistance of a material is, the lower the current in the material is. So, if the voltage doesn't change, as resistance goes up, current goes down. An object's resistance depends on the object's material, thickness, length, and temperature.

resistance in physical science, the opposition presented to the current by a material or device

Resistance and Material

Good conductors, such as copper, have low resistance. Poor conductors, such as iron, have higher resistance. The resistance of insulators is so high that electric charges cannot flow in them. Materials with low resistance, such as copper, are used to make wires. But materials with high resistance are also helpful. For example, the high resistance of the filament in a light bulb causes the light bulb to heat up and give off light.

Pipe = wire
water = electric charges

Figure 5 **A Model of Resistance**

A thick pipe has less resistance than a thin pipe does because there are more spaces between pieces of gravel in a thick pipe for water to flow through.

A short pipe has less resistance than a long pipe does because the water in a short pipe does not have to work its way around as many pieces of gravel.

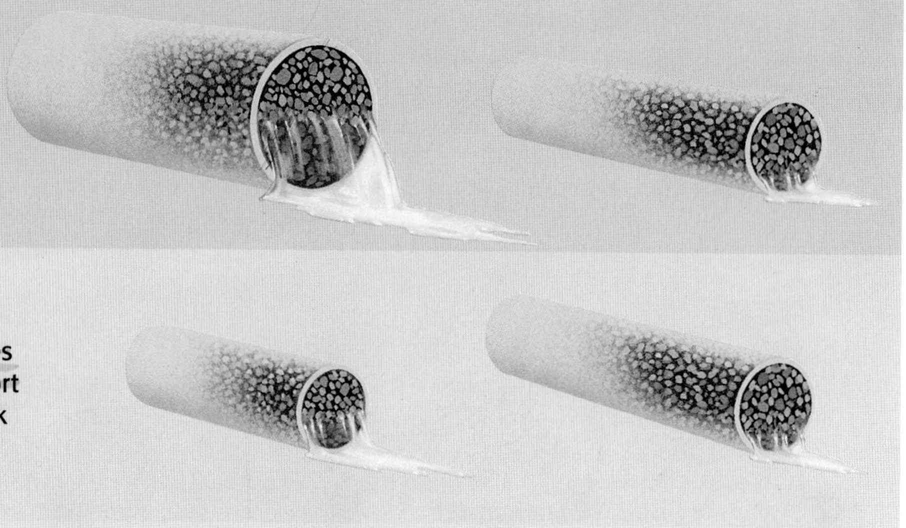

Resistance, Thickness, and Length

To understand how the thickness and length of a wire affect the wire's resistance, look at the model in **Figure 5.** The pipe filled with gravel represents a wire. The water flowing through the pipe represents electric charges.

Resistance and Temperature

Super conductors repel magnets.

Resistance also depends on temperature. In general, the resistance of metals increases as temperature rises. The atoms vibrate faster at higher temperatures and get in the way of the flowing electric charges. If you cool certain materials to a very low temperature, resistance will drop to 0 Ω. Materials in this state are called *superconductors*. A small superconductor is shown in **Figure 6.** Very little energy is wasted when electric charges move in a superconductor. However, a large amount of energy is needed to cool them. Scientists are studying how superconductors can be used to store and transmit energy.

Figure 6 *One interesting property of superconductors is that they repel magnets. The superconductor in this photo is repelling the magnet so strongly that the magnet is floating.*

Figure 7 How a Cell Works

a A chemical reaction with the electrolyte leaves extra electrons on one electrode. This electrode is made of zinc.

b A different chemical reaction causes electrons to be pulled off the other electrode. In this cell, this electrode is made of copper.

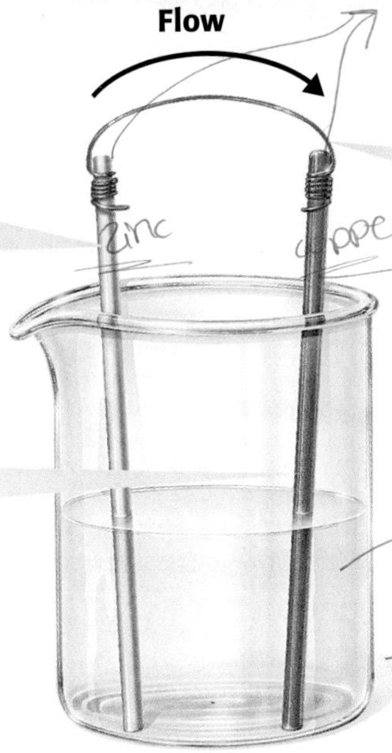

c If the electrodes are connected by a wire, electrons flow through the wire and ions move in the electrolyte. The moving charges make an electric current.

Generating Electrical Energy

You know that energy cannot be created or destroyed. It can only be changed into other kinds of energy. Many things change different kinds of energy into electrical energy. For example, generators convert mechanical energy into electrical energy. **Cells** change chemical or radiant energy into electrical energy. Batteries are made of one or more cells.

cell in electricity, a device that produces an electric current by converting chemical or radiant energy into electrical energy

Parts of a Cell

A cell, such as the one in **Figure 7**, contains a mixture of chemicals called an *electrolyte* (ee LEK troh LIET). Electrolytes allow charges to flow. Every cell also has a pair of electrodes made from conducting materials. An *electrode* (ee LEK TROHD) is the part of a cell through which charges enter or exit. Chemical changes between the electrolyte and the electrodes convert chemical energy into electrical energy.

Kinds of Cells

Two kinds of cells are wet cells and dry cells. Wet cells, such as the one in **Figure 7**, have liquid electrolytes. A car battery is made of several wet cells that use sulfuric acid as the electrolyte. You can make your own wet cell by poking strips of zinc and copper into a lemon. When the metal strips are connected, enough electrical energy is generated to run a small clock, as shown in **Figure 8**. Dry cells work in a similar way. But the electrolytes in dry cells are solid or pastelike. The cells used in small radios and flashlights are types of dry cells.

Figure 8 *This cell uses the juice of a lemon as an electrolyte and uses strips of zinc and copper as electrodes.*

Reading Check What are two kinds of cells?

thermocouple a device that converts thermal energy into electrical energy

photocell a device that converts light energy into electrical energy

Thermocouples

Thermal energy can be converted into electrical energy by a **thermocouple.** A simple thermocouple, shown in **Figure 9,** is made by joining wires of two different metals into a loop. The temperature difference within the loop causes charges to flow through the loop. The greater the temperature difference is, the greater the current is. Thermocouples usually do not generate much energy. But they are useful for monitoring the temperatures of car engines, furnaces, and ovens.

Photocells

If you look at a solar-powered calculator, you will see a dark strip called a *solar panel*. This panel is made of several photocells. A **photocell** converts light energy into electrical energy. How do photocells work? Most photocells contain silicon atoms. As long as light shines on the photocell, electrons gain enough energy to move between atoms. The electrons are then able to move through a wire to provide electrical energy to power a device, such as a calculator.

In larger panels, photocells can provide energy to buildings and cars. Large panels of photocells are even used on satellites. By changing light energy from the sun into electrical energy, the photocells provide energy to the many devices on the satellite to keep the devices working.

For another activity related to this chapter, go to **go.hrw.com** and type in the keyword **HP5ELEW.**

Reading Check **What device converts light energy into electrical energy?**

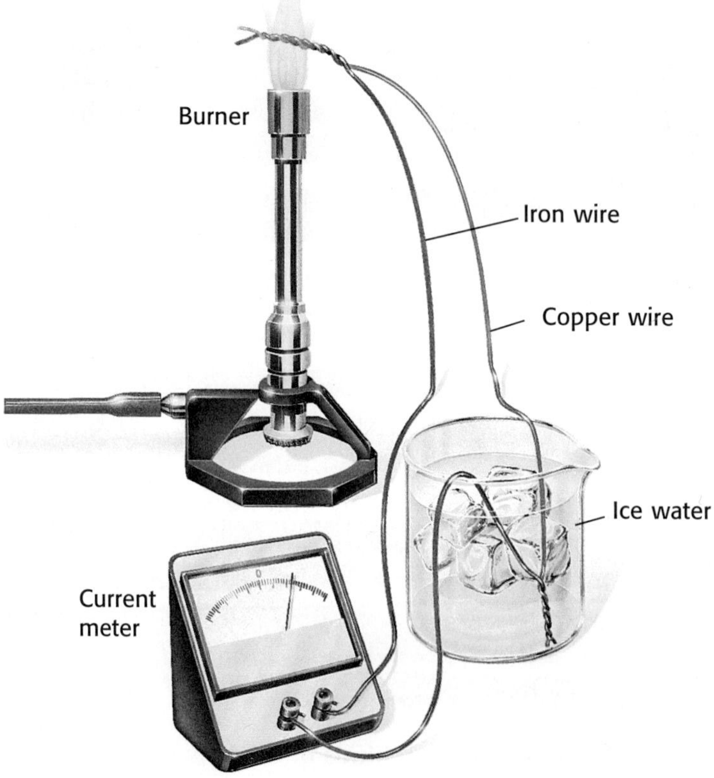

Figure 9 *In a simple thermocouple, one section of the loop is heated and one section is cooled.*

(45 mins)

SECTION Review

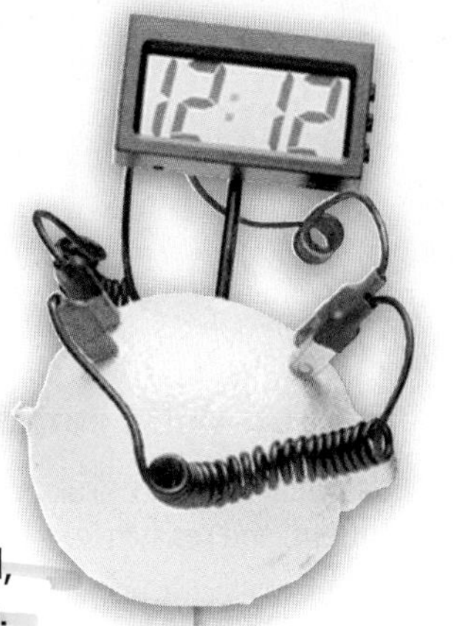

Summary

- Electric current is the rate at which charges pass a given point.
- An electric current can be made when there is a potential difference between two points.
- As voltage, or potential difference increases, current increases.
- An object's resistance varies depending on the object's material, thickness, length, and temperature. As resistance increases, current decreases.
- Cells and batteries convert chemical energy or radiant energy into electrical energy.
- Thermocouples and photocells are devices used to generate electrical energy.

Using Key Terms

Complete each of the following sentences by choosing the correct term from the word bank.

voltage	electric current
resistance	cell

1. The rate at which charges pass a point is a(n) electric current
2. The opposition to the flow of charge is resistance
3. Another term for *potential difference* is voltage
4. A device that changes chemical energy into electrical energy is a(n) cell

Understanding Key Ideas

5. Which of the following factors affects the resistance of an object?
   a. thickness of the object
   b. length of the object
   c. temperature of the object
   d. All of the above
6. Name the parts of a cell, and explain how they work together to produce an electric current.
7. Compare alternating current with direct current.
8. How do the currents produced by a 1.5 V flash-light cell and a 12 V car battery compare if the resistance is the same?
9. How does increasing the resistance affect the current?

Critical Thinking

10. **Making Comparisons** A friend is having trouble studying the types of cells in this section. Explain to your friend how the terms *photocell* and *thermocouple* hold clues that can help him or her remember the type of energy taken in by each device.
11. **Making Inferences** Why do you think some calculators that contain photocells also contain batteries?
12. **Applying Concepts** Which wire would have the lowest resistance: a long, thin iron wire at a high temperature or a short, thick copper wire at a low temperature?
    a short, thick copper wire at a low temp.

Interpreting Graphics

13. The wires shown below are made of copper and have the same temperature. Which wire should have the lower resistance? Explain your answer.

A B

Because its shorter so charges will need less energy to pass through.

SCILINKS. NSTA Developed and maintained by the National Science Teachers Association

For a variety of links related to this chapter, go to www.scilinks.org

Topic: Electric Current
SciLinks code: HSM0472

SECTION 3

Electrical Calculations

A German school teacher named Georg Ohm wondered how electric current, voltage, and resistance are related.

What You Will Learn

- Use Ohm's law to calculate voltage, current, and resistance.
- Calculate electric power.
- Determine the electrical energy used by a device.

Vocabulary

electric power

READING STRATEGY

Paired Summarizing Read this section silently. In pairs, take turns summarizing the material. Stop to discuss ideas that seem confusing.

Connecting Current, Voltage, and Resistance

Ohm (1789–1854) studied the resistances of materials. He measured the current that resulted from different voltages applied to a piece of metal wire. The graph on the left in **Figure 1** is similar to the graph of his results.

Ohm's Law

Ohm found that the ratio of voltage (V) to current (I) is a constant for each material. This ratio is the resistance (R) of the material. When the voltage is expressed in volts (V) and the current is in amperes (A), the resistance is in ohms (Ω). The equation below is often called *Ohm's law* because of Ohm's work.

$$R = \frac{V}{I}, \text{ or } V = I \times R$$

As the resistance goes up, the current goes down. And as the resistance decreases, the current increases. The second graph in **Figure 1** shows this relationship. Notice that if you multiply the current and the resistance for any point, you get 16 V.

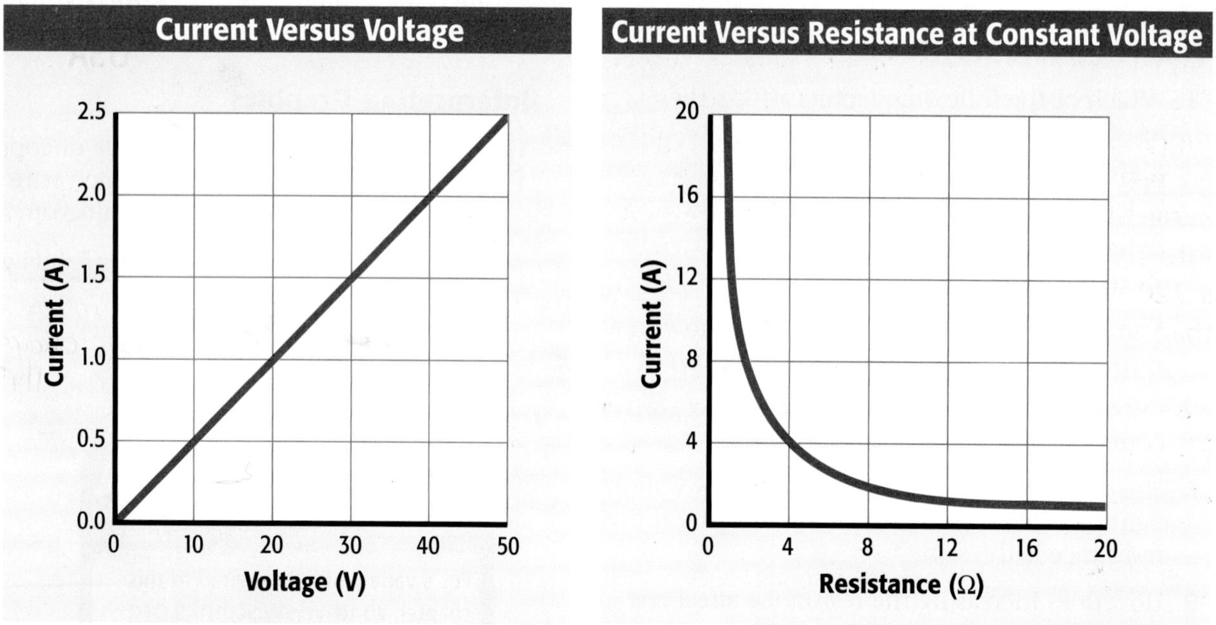

Figure 1 *The relationship between current and voltage is different from the relationship between current and resistance.*

MATH FOCUS

Using Ohm's Law What is the voltage if the current is 2 A and the resistance is 12 Ω?

Step 1: Write the equation for voltage.

$$V = I \times R$$

Step 2: Replace the current and resistance with the measurements given in the problem, and solve.

$$V = 2\text{ A} \times 12\ \Omega$$

$$V = 24\text{ V}$$

Now It's Your Turn

1. Find the voltage if the current is 0.2 A and the resistance is 2 Ω.
2. The resistance of an object is 4 Ω. If the current in the object is 9 A, what voltage must be used?
3. An object has a resistance of 20 Ω. Calculate the voltage needed to produce a current of 0.5 A.

Electric Power

The rate at which electrical energy is changed into other forms of energy is **electric power.** The unit for power is the watt (W), and the symbol for power is the letter *P*. Electric power is expressed in watts when the voltage is in volts and the current is in amperes. Electric power is calculated by using the following equation:

electric power the rate at which electrical energy is converted into other forms of energy

$$\textit{power} = \textit{voltage} \times \textit{current}, \text{ or } P = V \times I$$

Watt: The Unit of Power

If you have ever changed a light bulb, you probably know about watts. Light bulbs, such as the ones in **Figure 2,** have labels such as "60 W," "75 W," or "120 W." As electrical energy is supplied to a light bulb, the light bulb glows. As power increases, the bulb burns brighter because more electrical energy is converted into light energy. The higher power rating of a 120 W bulb tells you that it burns brighter than a 60 W bulb.

Another common unit of power is the kilowatt (kW). One kilowatt is equal to 1,000 W. Kilowatts are used to express high values of power, such as the power needed to heat a house.

Reading Check **What are two common units for electric power?** (*See the Appendix for answers to Reading Checks.*) -Watts (W) -Kilowatt (kW)

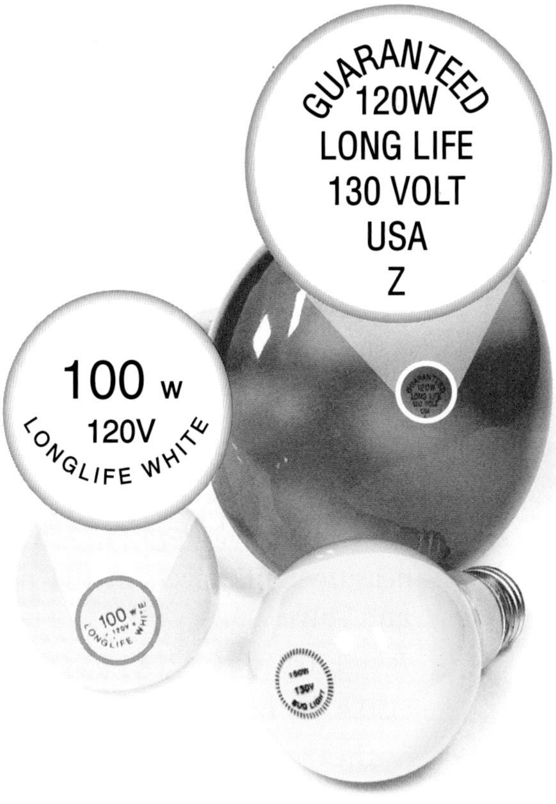

Figure 2 *These light bulbs have different wattages, so they use different amounts of electric power.*

Figure 3 *These photographs were taken 10 days apart. According to the dials on the meter, 101 kWh of energy were used.*

Measuring Electrical Energy

Electric power companies sell electrical energy to homes and businesses. Such companies determine how much a home or business has to pay based on power and time. For example, the amount of electrical energy used in a home depends on the power of the electrical devices in the house and the length of time that those devices are on. The equation for electrical energy is as follows:

$$\textit{electrical energy} = \textit{power} \times \textit{time}, \text{ or } E = P \times t$$

Measuring Household Energy Use

Different amounts of electrical energy are used each day in a home. Electric companies usually calculate electrical energy by multiplying the power in kilowatts by the time in hours. The unit of electrical energy is usually kilowatt-hours (kWh). If 2,000 W (2 kW) of power are used for 3 h, then 6 kWh of energy were used.

Electric power companies use meters, such as the one in **Figure 3,** to determine how many kilowatt-hours of energy are used by a household. These meters are often outside of buildings so that someone from the power company can read them.

Reading Check **What unit of measurement is usually used to express electrical energy?** Kilowatt hours

Math Focus

Power and Energy A small television set draws a current of 0.42 A at 120 V. What is the power rating for the television? How much energy is used if the television is on for 3 h?

Step 1: Write the equation for power.

$$P = V \times I$$

Step 2: Replace the voltage and current with the measurements given in the problem, and solve.

$$P = 120 \text{ V} \times 0.42 \text{ A}$$

$$P = 50.4 \text{ W, or } 0.0504 \text{ kW}$$

Step 3: Write the equation for electrical energy.

$$E = P \times t$$

Step 4: Replace the power and time with the measurements given in the problem, and solve.

$$E = 0.0504 \text{ kW} \times 3 \text{ h}$$

$$E = 0.1512 \text{ kWh}$$

Now It's Your Turn

1. A computer monitor draws 1.2 A at a voltage of 120 V. What is the power rating of the monitor?
2. A light bulb draws a 0.5 A current at a voltage of 120 V. What is the power rating of the light bulb?
3. How much electrical energy does a 100 W light bulb use if it is left on for 24 h?

How to Save Energy

Every appliance uses energy. But a fan, such as the one in **Figure 4,** could actually help you save energy. If you use a fan, you can run an air conditioner less. Replacing items that have high power ratings with items that have lower ratings is another way to save energy. Turning off lights when they are not in use will also help.

Figure 4 *Using a fan to stay cool and using a small toaster instead of a larger toaster oven are ways to save energy.*

SCHOOL to HOME

Saving Energy

WRITING SKILL With a parent, identify the power rating for each light in your home and estimate how long each light is on during a day. In your **science journal,** determine how much electrical energy each light uses per day. Then, describe two ways to save energy with the lights.

ACTIVITY

(15 min)

SECTION Review

Summary

- Ohm's law describes the relationship between current, resistance, and voltage.
- Electric power is the rate at which electrical energy is changed into other forms of energy.
- Electrical energy is electric power multiplied by time. It is usually expressed in kilowatt-hours.

Using Key Terms

1. In your own words, write a definition for the term *electric power.*

   The rate at which electrical energy is converted into other kinds of energy.

Understanding Key Ideas

2. Which of the following is Ohm's law?
   - **a.** $E = P \times t$
   - **b.** $I = V \times R$
   - **c.** $P = V \times I$
   - **d.** $V = I \times R$ (circled)

3. Circuit A has twice the resistance of circuit B. The voltage is the same in each circuit. Which circuit has the higher current?

   circuit B because it has less resistance

Math Skills

4. Use Ohm's law to find the voltage needed to make a current of 3 A in a resistance of 9 Ω. 27 (V)

5. How much electrical energy does a 40 W light bulb use if it is left on for 12 h? 480 watts

Critical Thinking

6. **Applying Concepts** Explain why increasing the voltage applied to a wire can have the same effect on the current in the wire that decreasing the resistance of the wire does.

7. **Identifying Relationships** Using the equations in this section, develop an equation to find electrical energy from time, current, and resistance.

For a variety of links related to this chapter, go to www.scilinks.org

Topic: Electrical Energy
SciLinks code: HSM0475

SECTION 4

Electric Circuits

Think about a roller coaster. You start out nice and easy. Then, you roar around the track. A couple of exciting minutes later, you are right back where you started!

A roller-coaster car follows a fixed pathway. The ride's starting point and ending point are the same place. This kind of closed pathway is called a *circuit.*

What You Will Learn

- Name the three essential parts of a circuit.
- Compare series circuits with parallel circuits.
- Explain how fuses and circuit breakers protect your home against short circuits and circuit overloads.

Vocabulary

series circuit
parallel circuit

READING STRATEGY

Brainstorming The key idea of this section is electric circuits. Brainstorm words and phrases related to electric circuits.

Parts of an Electric Circuit

Just like a roller coaster, an electric circuit always forms a loop—it begins and ends in the same place. Because a circuit forms a loop, a circuit is a closed path. So, an *electric circuit* is a complete, closed path through which electric charges flow.

All circuits need three basic parts: an energy source, wires, and a load. Loads, such as a light bulb or a radio, are connected to the energy source by wires. Loads change electrical energy into other forms of energy. These other forms might include thermal energy, light energy, or mechanical energy. As loads change electrical energy into other forms, they offer some resistance to electric currents. **Figure 1** shows examples of the parts of a circuit.

Reading Check **What are the three parts of an electric circuit?** *(See the Appendix for answers to Reading Checks.)*

Figure 1 **Necessary Parts of a Circuit**

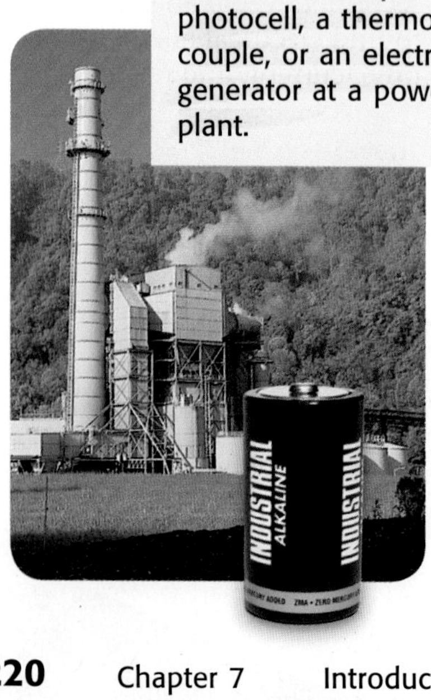

The **energy source** can be a battery, a photocell, a thermocouple, or an electric generator at a power plant.

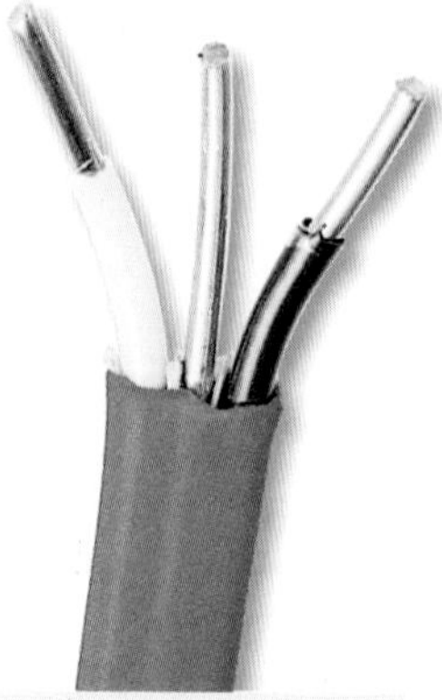

Wires connect the other parts of a circuit. Wires are made of conducting materials that have low resistance, such as copper.

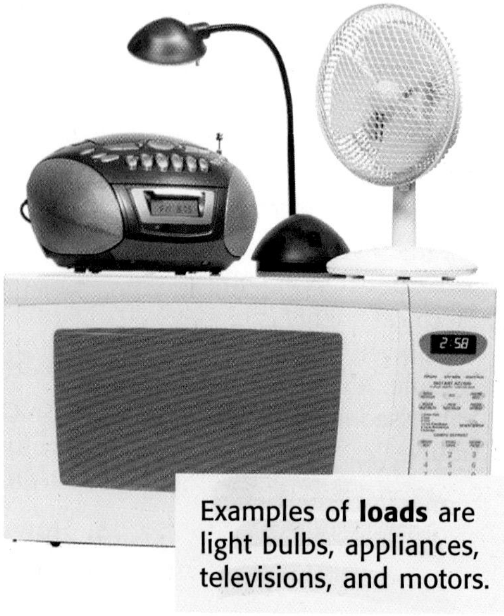

Examples of **loads** are light bulbs, appliances, televisions, and motors.

Figure 2 **Using a Switch**

When the **switch is closed,** the two pieces of conducting material touch, which allows the electric charges to flow through the circuit.

When the **switch is open,** the gap between the two pieces of conducting material prevents the electric charges from traveling through the circuit.

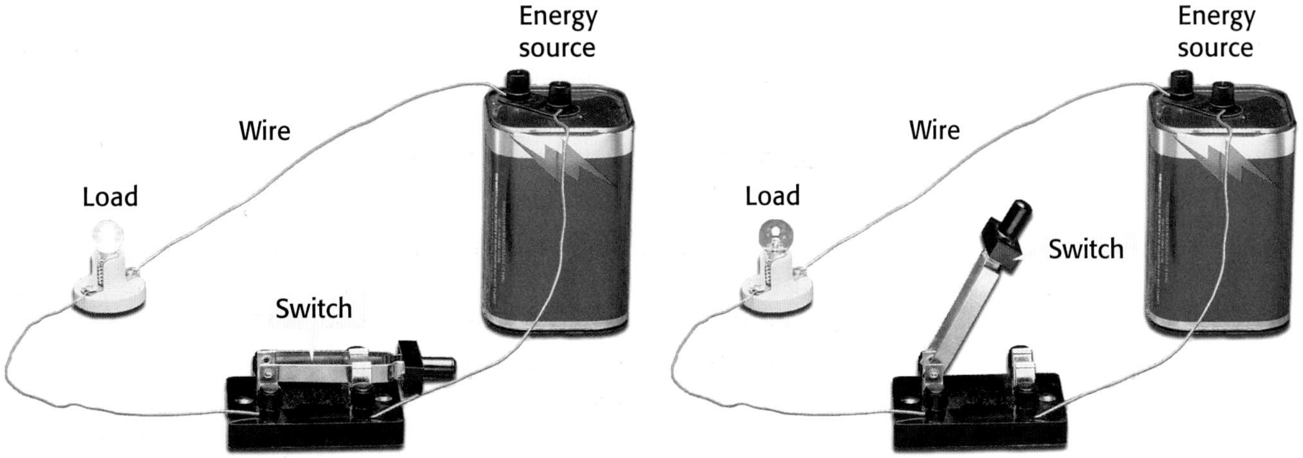

A Switch To Control a Circuit

Sometimes, a circuit also contains a switch, such as the one shown in **Figure 2.** A switch is used to open and close a circuit. Usually, a switch is made of two pieces of conducting material, one of which can be moved. For charges to flow through a circuit, the switch must be closed, or "turned on." If a switch is open, or "off," the loop of the circuit is broken. Charges cannot flow through a broken circuit. Light switches, power buttons on radios, and even the keys on calculators and computers open and close circuits.

Types of Circuits

Look around the room. Count the number of objects that use electrical energy. You might have found things, such as lights, a clock, and maybe a computer. All of the things you counted are loads in a large circuit. The circuit may connect more than one room in the building. In fact, most circuits have more than one load.

The loads in a circuit can be connected in different ways. As a result, circuits are often divided into two types. A circuit can be a series circuit or a parallel circuit. One of the main differences in these circuits is the way in which the loads are connected to one another. As you read about each type of circuit, look closely at how the loads are connected.

Reading Check **What are two types of electric circuits?** Parallel and series circuits.

CONNECTION TO Biology

WRITING SKILL **Nervous Impulses** Believe it or not, your body is controlled and monitored by electrical impulses. Research the electrical impulses that travel between your brain and the muscles and organs in your body. Then, in your **science journal,** write a one-page comparison of your nervous system and an electric circuit.

series circuit a circuit in which the parts are joined one after another such that the current in each part is the same

Series Circuits

A **series circuit** is a circuit in which all parts are connected in a single loop. There is only one path for charges to follow, so the charges moving through a series circuit must flow through each part of the circuit.

All of the loads in a series circuit share the same current. The four identical light bulbs in **Figure 3** are joined in series. Because the current in each bulb is the same, the lights glow with the same brightness. But if you add more light bulbs, the resistance of the whole circuit would go up and the current would drop. Therefore, all of the bulbs would be dimmer.

Reading Check **How are loads connected in a series circuit?**

All of the loads in a series circuit share the same current.

Uses for Series Circuits

A series circuit has only one pathway for moving charges. If there is any break in the circuit, the charges will stop flowing. For example, if one light bulb in a series circuit burns out, there is a break in the circuit. None of the light bulbs in the circuit would light. Using series circuits would not be a very convenient way to wire your home. Imagine if your refrigerator and a lamp were in a series circuit together. Your refrigerator would run only when the lamp was on. And when the bulb burns out, the refrigerator would stop working!

But series circuits are useful in some ways. For example, series circuits are useful in wiring burglar alarms. If any part of the circuit in a burglar alarm fails, there will be no current in the system. The lack of current signals that a problem exists, and the alarm will sound.

Quick Lab

A Series of Circuits

1. Connect a **6 V battery** and **two flashlight bulbs** in a series circuit. Draw a picture of your circuit.
2. Add **another flashlight bulb** in series with the other two bulbs. How does the brightness of the light bulbs change?
3. Replace one of the light bulbs with a **burned-out light bulb.** What happens to the other lights in the circuit? Why?

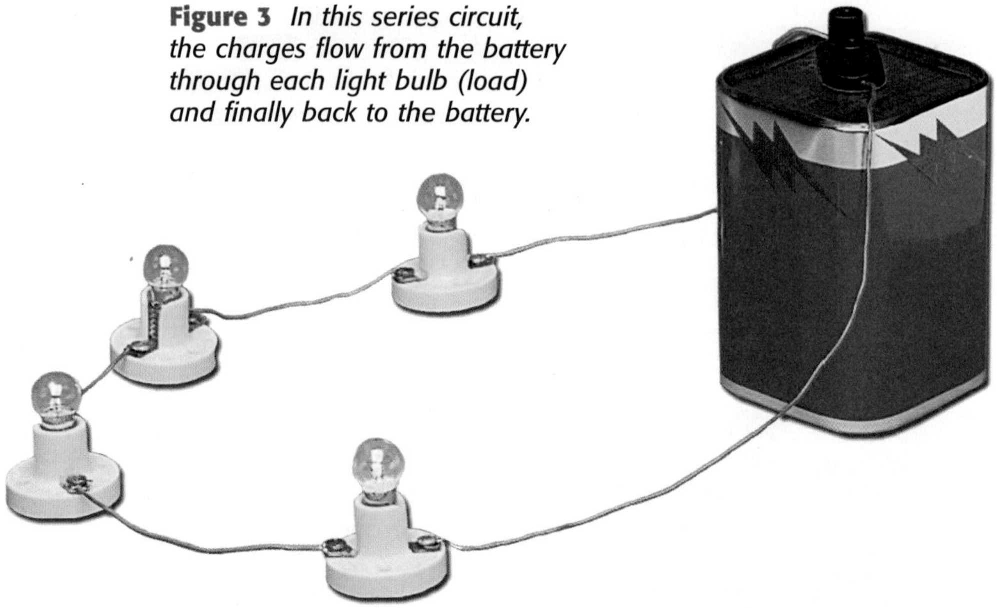

Figure 3 *In this series circuit, the charges flow from the battery through each light bulb (load) and finally back to the battery.*

Parallel Circuits

Think about what would happen if all of the lights in your home were connected in series. If you needed to turn on a light in your room, all other lights in the house would have to be turned on, too! Instead of being wired in series, circuits in buildings are wired in parallel. A **parallel circuit** is a circuit in which loads are connected side by side. Charges in a parallel circuit have more than one path on which they can travel.

Unlike the loads in a series circuit, the loads in a parallel circuit do not have the same current. Instead, each load in a parallel circuit uses the same voltage. For example, each bulb in **Figure 4** uses the full voltage of the battery. As a result, each light bulb glows at full brightness no matter how many bulbs are connected in parallel. You can connect loads that need different currents to the same parallel circuit. For example, you can connect a hair dryer, which needs a high current to run, to the same circuit as a lamp, which needs less current.

Reading Check How are loads connected in a parallel circuit?
loads in a parallel circuit are connected side by side

Uses for Parallel Circuits

In a parallel circuit, each branch of the circuit can work by itself. If one load is broken or missing, charges will still run through the other branches. So, the loads on those branches will keep working. In your home, each electrical outlet is usually on its own branch and has its own switch. Imagine if each time a light bulb went out your television or stereo stopped working. With parallel circuits, you can use one light or appliance at a time, even if another load fails.

parallel circuit a circuit in which the parts are joined in branches such that the potential difference across each part is the same

Quick Lab

A Parallel Lab

1. Connect a **6 V battery** and **two flashlight bulbs** in a parallel circuit. Draw a picture of your circuit.
2. Add **another flashlight bulb** in parallel with the other two bulbs. How does the brightness of the light bulbs change?
3. Replace one of the light bulbs with a **burned-out light bulb.** What happens to the other lights in the circuit? Why?

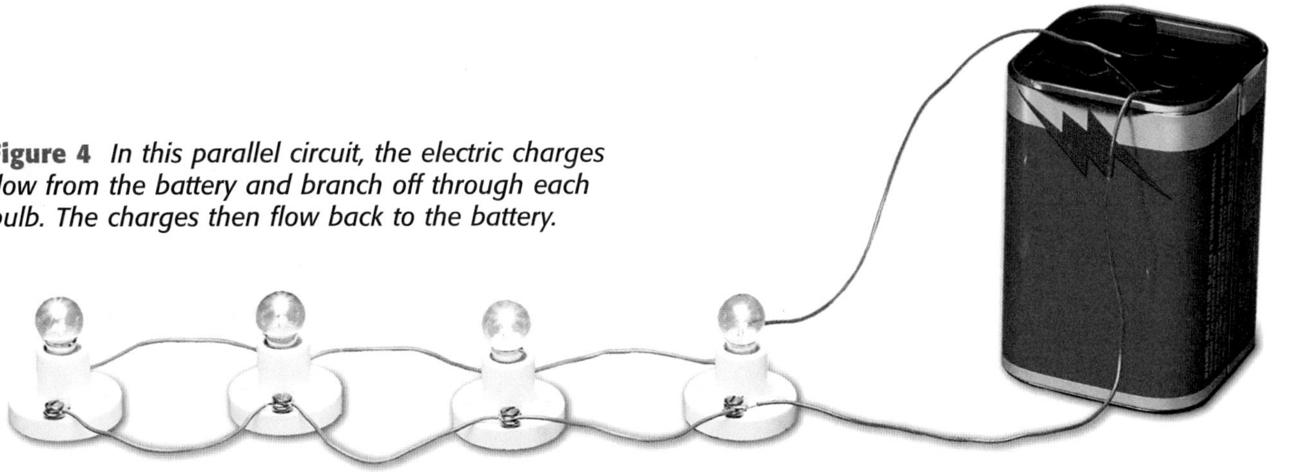

Figure 4 *In this parallel circuit, the electric charges flow from the battery and branch off through each bulb. The charges then flow back to the battery.*

Household Circuit Safety

In every home, several circuits connect all of the lights, appliances, and outlets. The circuits branch out from a breaker box or a fuse box that acts as the "electrical headquarters" for the building. Each branch receives a standard voltage, which is 120 V in the United States.

Circuit Failure

Broken wires or water can cause a short circuit. In a short circuit, charges do not go through one or more loads in the circuit. The resistance decreases, so the current increases. The wires can heat up, and the circuit could fail. The wires might even get hot enough to start a fire. Circuits also may fail if they are overloaded. When too many loads are in a circuit, the current increases, and a fire might start. Safety features, such as fuses and circuit breakers, help prevent electrical fires.

Figure 5 *The blown fuse on the left must be replaced with a new fuse, such as the one on the right.*

Fuses

A fuse has a thin strip of metal. The charges in the circuit flow through this strip. If the current is too high, the metal strip melts, as shown in **Figure 5.** As a result, the circuit is broken, and charges stop flowing.

Circuit Breakers

A circuit breaker is a switch that automatically opens if the current is too high. A strip of metal in the breaker warms up, bends, and opens the switch, which opens the circuit. Charges stop flowing. Open circuit breakers can be closed by flipping a switch after the problem has been fixed.

A ground fault circuit interrupter (GFCI), shown in **Figure 6,** acts as a small circuit breaker. If the current in one side of an outlet differs even slightly from the current in the other side, the GFCI opens the circuit and the charges stop flowing. To close the circuit, you must push the reset button.

Reading Check **What are two safety devices used in circuits?**

GFCI and a fuse

Figure 6 *GFCIs are often found on outlets in bathrooms and kitchens to protect you from electric shock.*

Electrical Safety Tips

You use electrical devices every day. So, remembering that using electrical energy can be hazardous is important. Warning signs, such as the one in **Figure 7,** can help you avoid electrical dangers. To stay safe while you use electrical energy, follow these tips:

- Make sure the insulation on cords is not worn.
- Do not overload circuits by plugging in too many electrical devices.
- Do not use electrical devices while your hands are wet or while you are standing in water.
- Never put objects other than a plug into an electrical outlet.

Figure 7 *Obeying signs that warn of high voltage can keep you safe from electrical dangers.*

SECTION Review

Summary

- Circuits consist of an energy source, a load, wires, and, in some cases, a switch.
- All parts of a series circuit are connected in a single loop. The loads in a parallel circuit are on separate branches.
- Circuits fail through a short circuit or an overload. Fuses or circuit breakers protect against circuit failure.
- It is important to follow safety tips when using electrical energy.

Using Key Terms

1. In your own words, write a definition for each of the following terms: *series circuit* and *parallel circuit.*

Understanding Key Ideas

2. Which part of a circuit changes electrical energy into another form of energy?
   - **a.** energy source
   - **b.** wire
   - **c.** switch
   - **d.** load
3. Name and describe the three essential parts of a circuit.
4. How do fuses and circuit breakers protect your home against electrical fires?

Critical Thinking

5. **Forming Hypotheses** Suppose that you turn on the heater in your room and all of the lights in your room go out. Propose a reason why the lights went out.
6. **Applying Concepts** Will a fuse work successfully if it is connected in parallel with the device it is supposed to protect? Explain your answer.

Interpreting Graphics

7. Look at the circuits below. Identify each circuit as a parallel circuit or a series circuit.

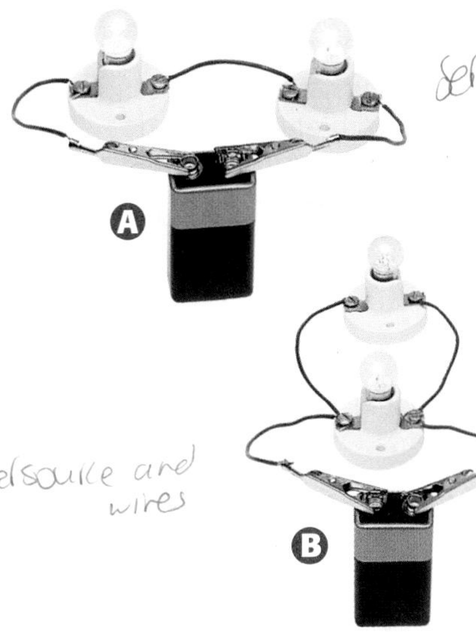

Skills Practice Lab

OBJECTIVES

Build a series circuit and a parallel circuit.

Use Ohm's law to calculate the resistance of a circuit from voltage and current.

MATERIALS

- ammeter
- energy source—dry cell(s)
- light-bulb holders (3)
- light bulbs (3)
- switch
- voltmeter
- wire, insulated, 15 cm lengths with both ends stripped

SAFETY

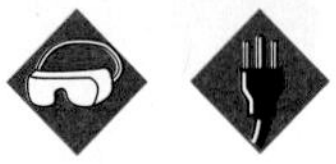

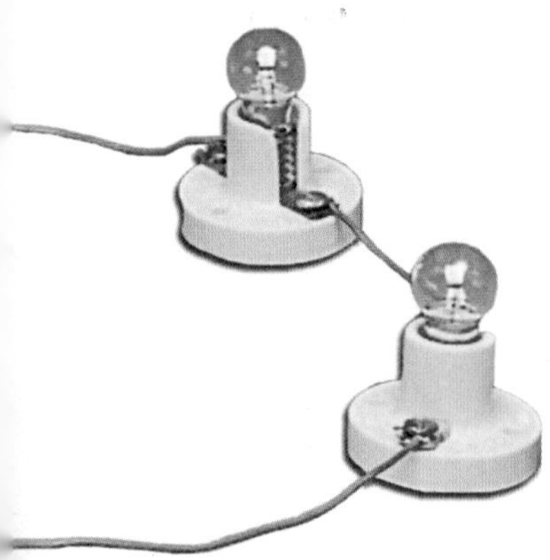

Circuitry 101

There are two basic types of electric circuits. A series circuit connects all of the parts in a single loop, and a parallel circuit connects each part on a separate branch. A switch wired in series with the energy source can control the whole circuit. If you want each part of the circuit to work on its own, the loads must be wired in parallel. In this lab, you will use an ammeter to measure current and a voltmeter to measure voltage. For each circuit, you will use Ohm's law (resistance equals voltage divided by current) to determine the overall resistance.

Procedure

1. Build a series circuit with an energy source, a switch, and three light bulbs. Draw a diagram of your circuit. **Caution:** Always leave the switch open when building or changing the circuit. Close the switch only when you are testing or taking a reading.
2. Test your circuit. Do all three bulbs light up? Are all bulbs the same brightness? What happens if you carefully unscrew one light bulb? Does it make any difference which bulb you unscrew? Record your observations.
3. Connect the ammeter between the power source and the switch. Close the switch, and record the current on your diagram. Be sure to show where you measured the current.
4. Reconnect the circuit so that the ammeter is between the first and second bulbs. Record the current, as you did in step 3.
5. Move the ammeter so that it is between the second and third bulbs, and record the current again.
6. Remove the ammeter from the circuit. Connect the voltmeter to the two ends of the power source. Record the voltage on your diagram.
7. Use the voltmeter to measure the voltage across each bulb. Record each reading.
8. Take apart your series circuit. Reassemble the same items so that the bulbs are wired in parallel. (Note: The switch must remain in series with the power source to be able to control the whole circuit.) Draw a diagram of your circuit.

9. Test your circuit, and record your observations, as you did in step 2.
10. Connect the ammeter between the power source and the switch. Record the current.
11. Reconnect the circuit so that the ammeter is right next to one of the three bulbs. Record the current.
12. Repeat step 11 for the two remaining bulbs.
13. Remove the ammeter from your circuit. Connect the voltmeter to the two ends of the power source. Record the voltage.
14. Measure and record the voltage across each light bulb.

Analyze the Results

1. **Recognizing Patterns** Was the current the same at all places in the series circuit? Was it the same everywhere in the parallel circuit?
2. **Analyzing Data** For each circuit, compare the voltage across each light bulb with the voltage at the power source.
3. **Identifying Patterns** What is the relationship between the voltage at the power source and the voltages at the light bulbs in a series circuit?
4. **Analyzing Data** Use Ohm's law and the readings for current (I) and voltage (V) at the power source for both circuits to calculate the total resistance (R) in both the series and parallel circuits.

Draw Conclusions

5. **Drawing Conclusions** Was the total resistance for both circuits the same? Explain your answer.
6. **Interpreting Information** Why did the bulbs differ in brightness?
7. **Making Predictions** Based on your results, what do you think might happen if too many electrical appliances are plugged into the same series circuit? What might happen if too many electrical appliances are plugged into the same parallel circuit?

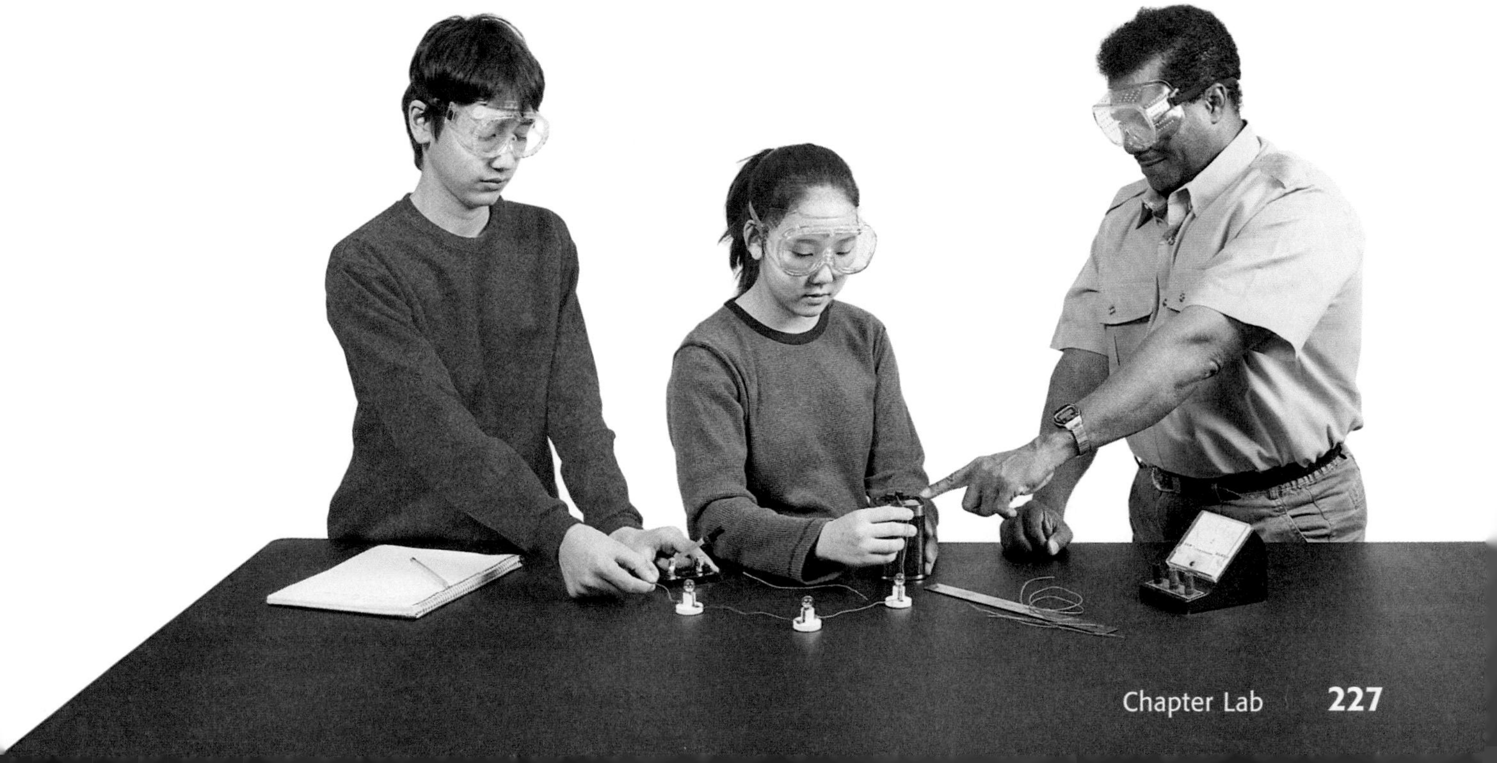

Chapter Review

USING KEY TERMS

The statements below are false. For each statement, replace the underlined term to make a true statement.

1. Charges flow easily in an electrical insulator. electrical conductor
2. Lightning is a form of static electricity. electric discharge
3. A thermocouple converts chemical energy into electrical energy. cell
4. Voltage is the opposition to the current by a material. Resistance
5. Electric force is the rate at which electrical energy is converted into other forms of energy. Electric power
6. Each load in a parallel circuit has the same current. series circuit

UNDERSTANDING KEY IDEAS

Multiple Choice

7. Two objects repel each other. What charges might the objects have?
   - **a.** positive and positive
   - **b.** positive and negative
   - **c.** negative and negative
   - **d.** Both (a) and (c)

8. Which device converts chemical energy into electrical energy?
   - **a.** lightning rod
   - **b.** cell
   - **c.** light bulb
   - **d.** switch

9. Which of the following wires has the lowest resistance?
   - **a.** a short, thick copper wire at 25°C
   - **b.** a long, thick copper wire at 35°C
   - **c.** a long, thin copper wire at 35°C
   - **d.** a short, thick iron wire at 25°C

10. An object becomes charged when the atoms in the object gain or lose
    - **a.** protons.
    - **b.** neutrons.
    - **c.** electrons.
    - **d.** All of the above

11. Which of the following devices does NOT protect you from electrical fires?
    - **a.** electric meter
    - **b.** circuit breaker
    - **c.** fuse
    - **d.** ground fault circuit interrupter

12. For a cell to produce a current, the electrodes of the cell must
    - **a.** have a potential difference.
    - **b.** be in a liquid.
    - **c.** be exposed to light.
    - **d.** be at two different temperatures.

13. The outlets in your home provide
    - **a.** direct current.
    - **b.** alternating current.
    - **c.** electric discharge.
    - **d.** static electricity.

Short Answer

14. Describe how a switch controls a circuit.

15. Name the two factors that affect the strength of electric force, and explain how they affect electric force.

16. Describe how direct current differs from alternating current.

Math Skills

17. What voltage is needed to produce a 6 A current in an object that has a resistance of 3 Ω? $V = I \times R$

18. Find the current produced when a voltage of 60 V is applied to a resistance of 15 Ω. $I = \frac{V}{R}$

19. What is the resistance of an object if a voltage of 40 V produces a current of 5 A? $R = \frac{V}{I}$

20. A light bulb is rated at 150 W. How much current is in the bulb if 120 V is applied to the bulb? $I = \frac{P}{V}$

21. How much electrical energy does a 60 W light bulb use if it is used for 1,000 hours? $E = P \times T$

CRITICAL THINKING

22. **Concept Mapping** Use the following terms to create a concept map: *electric current, battery, charges, photocell, thermocouple, circuit, parallel circuit,* and *series circuit.*

23. **Making Inferences** Suppose your science classroom was rewired over the weekend. On Monday, you notice that the lights in the room must be on for the fish-tank bubbler to work. And if you want to use the computer, you must turn on the overhead projector. Describe what mistake the electrician made when working on the circuits in your classroom.

24. **Applying Concepts** You can make a cell by using an apple, a strip of copper, and a strip of silver. Explain how you would construct the cell, and identify the parts of the cell. What type of cell did you make? Explain your answer.

25. **Applying Concepts** Your friend shows you a magic trick. First, she rubs a plastic pipe on a piece of wool. Then, she holds the pipe close to an empty soda can that is lying on its side. When the pipe is close to the can, the can rolls toward the pipe. Explain how this trick works.

INTERPRETING GRAPHICS

26. Classify the objects in the photograph below as electrical conductors or electrical insulators.

Standardized Test Preparation

Multiple Choice

Use the picture below to answer question 1.

1. The figure above shows a negatively charged plastic comb picking up pieces of uncharged tissue paper. Determine the best explanation for why this might happen.

A. Electrons are transferred from the comb to the tissue paper due to friction.

B. The comb induces a positive charge on the surface of the tissue paper.

C. Electrons move from the comb to the tissue paper by direct contact.

D. The tissue paper becomes negatively charged by conduction.

2. How is electrical energy similar to heat energy?

A. Electricity and heat are the result of moving electrons.

B. Electricity and heat can be converted into other forms of energy.

C. Electricity and heat can travel through just space.

D. Electricity and heat cannot be converted into other forms of energy.

3. How should Pedro wire four bulbs in a circuit so that all the bulbs shine as brightly as possible?

A. wire all four bulbs in series

B. wire two bulbs in parallel and the other two bulbs in series

C. wire three bulbs in parallel and the other bulb in series

D. wire all four bulbs in parallel

4. Using batteries in a portable stereo at the lake involves which energy conversions?

A. kinetic energy into electrical energy into sound energy

B. chemical energy into electrical energy into sound energy

C. electrical energy into sound energy into kinetic energy

D. sound energy into chemical energy into electrical energy

5. When Andre plugs his stereo into the same outlet as the television and lamp, all three won't work. What is the most likely hypothesis for what happened?

A. The circuit was overloaded and the circuit breaker opened.

B. The circuit was overloaded and the circuit breaker closed.

C. The stereo and lamp had incompatible electrical systems.

D. The stereo's electrical cord was faulty.

Use the diagram below to answer question 6.

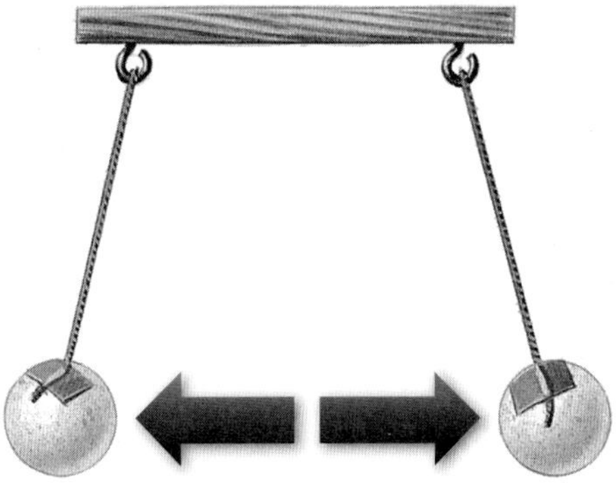

6. Kylie charged two plastic foam balls and hung them from strings. The image above shows how the foam balls behaved. What can you conclude about the foam balls?

A. The foam balls are positively charged.

B. The foam balls are negatively charged.

C. The foam balls have the same charge.

D. The foam balls have opposite charges.

7. Which of the following devices converts thermal energy into electrical energy?

A. thermocouple

B. photocell

C. dry cell

D. battery

8. Which of the following is the correct equation for Ohm's law?

A. $P = V \times I$

B. $E = P \times t$

C. $R = V \times I$

D. $V = I \times R$

9. Suki can have all five appliances in her kitchen on at the same time or she can have each appliance on one at a time. How are the appliances in Suki's kitchen wired?

A. in a voltage circuit

B. in a direct current circuit

C. in a parallel circuit

D. in a series circuit

10. Which of the following wires will have the least amount of resistance?

A. a short, thick copper wire

B. a short, thick iron wire

C. a long, thin copper wire

D. a long, thick iron wire

Open Response

11. Angelica designed an experiment using a light bulb powered by a "black box." Since light bulbs are powered by electrical energy, describe three energy conversions which could be occurring in the black box to power the light bulb. You may start with any energy source.

12. Sayid is making a pamphlet on how to conserve electrical energy in the home. Describe three ways to conserve electrical energy that Sayid could include in his pamphlet.

- Electrical energy
- light energy
- Thermo energy
- Chemical energy
- Sound energy

Science in Action

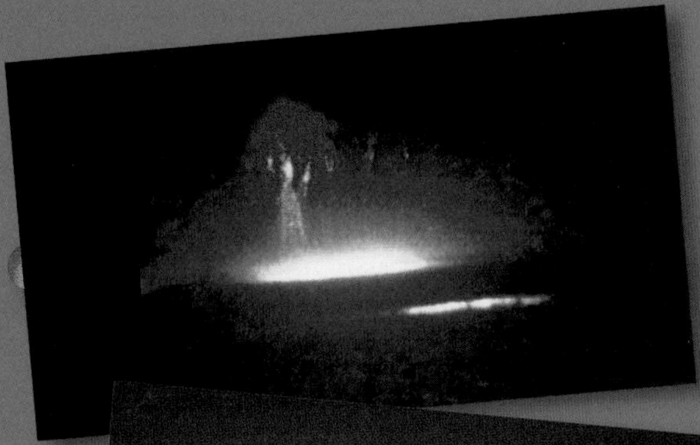

Weird Science

Electric Eels

Electric eels are freshwater fish from Central and South America. They can produce powerful jolts of electrical energy. Electric discharges from eels are strong enough to stun or kill smaller fish and frogs in the water. The eels then swallow their motionless prey whole. Early travelers to the Amazon River basin wrote that in shallow pools, the eels' discharges could knock horses and humans over. Within the body of an eel, which is 2.5 m long, are a series of electroplates, or modified muscle tissues that generate low voltages. An eel has 5,000 to 6,000 connected electroplates. In lab experiments, the bursts of voltage from a fully grown eel have been measured to be about 600 V.

Math ACTIVITY

The battery in a car provides 12 V. How many times more voltage can a fully grown eel provide than can a car battery? If the voltage provided by the eel were used in a circuit that had a resistance of 200 Ω, what would the current in the circuit be?

Scientific Discoveries

Sprites and Elves

Imagine that you are in a plane on a moonless night. You notice a thunderstorm 80 km away and see lightning move between the clouds and the Earth. Then, suddenly, a ghostly red glow stretches many kilometers above the clouds! You did not expect that!

In 1989, scientists captured the first image of this strange, red, glowing lightning. Since then, photographs from space shuttles, airplanes, telescopes, and observers on the ground have shown several types of electrical glows. Two were named sprites and elves because, like the mythical creatures, they disappear just as the eye begins to see them. Sprites and elves last only a few thousandths of a second.

Language Arts ACTIVITY

WRITING SKILL Imagine that you are a hunter living in about 5000 BCE. On a hunt, you see a sprite as described above. Write a two-page short story explaining what you saw, what your reaction was, and why you think the sprite happened.

Careers

Pete Perez

Electrician Sometimes, you forget just how much of daily life is dependent on electricity—until the electricity goes out! Then, you call an electrician, such as Pete Perez. Perez has been installing electrical systems and solving electricity problems in commercial and residential settings since 1971. "I'm in this work because of the challenge. Everywhere you go it's something new."

An electrician performs a wide variety of jobs that may include repairs, routine maintenance, or disaster prevention. One day, he or she might install wiring in a new house. The next day, he or she might replace wiring in an older house. Jobs can be as simple as replacing a fuse or as complicated as restoring an industrial machine. Also, electricians may work under many different conditions, including in a dark basement or at the top of an electrical tower. Perez's advice to aspiring young electricians is, "Open up your mind." You never know what kind of job is waiting for you around the corner, because every day brings stranger and more interesting challenges.

Social Studies ACTIVITY

Imagine that you are helping run a job fair at your school. Research the requirements for becoming an electrician. Make a brochure that tells what an electrician does and what training is needed. Describe how much the training and basic equipment to get started will cost. Include the starting salary and information about any testing or certification that is needed.

To learn more about these Science in Action topics, visit **go.hrw.com** and type in the keyword **HP5ELEF.**

Current Science

Check out Current Science® articles related to this chapter by visiting go.hrw.com. Just type in the keyword HP5CS17.

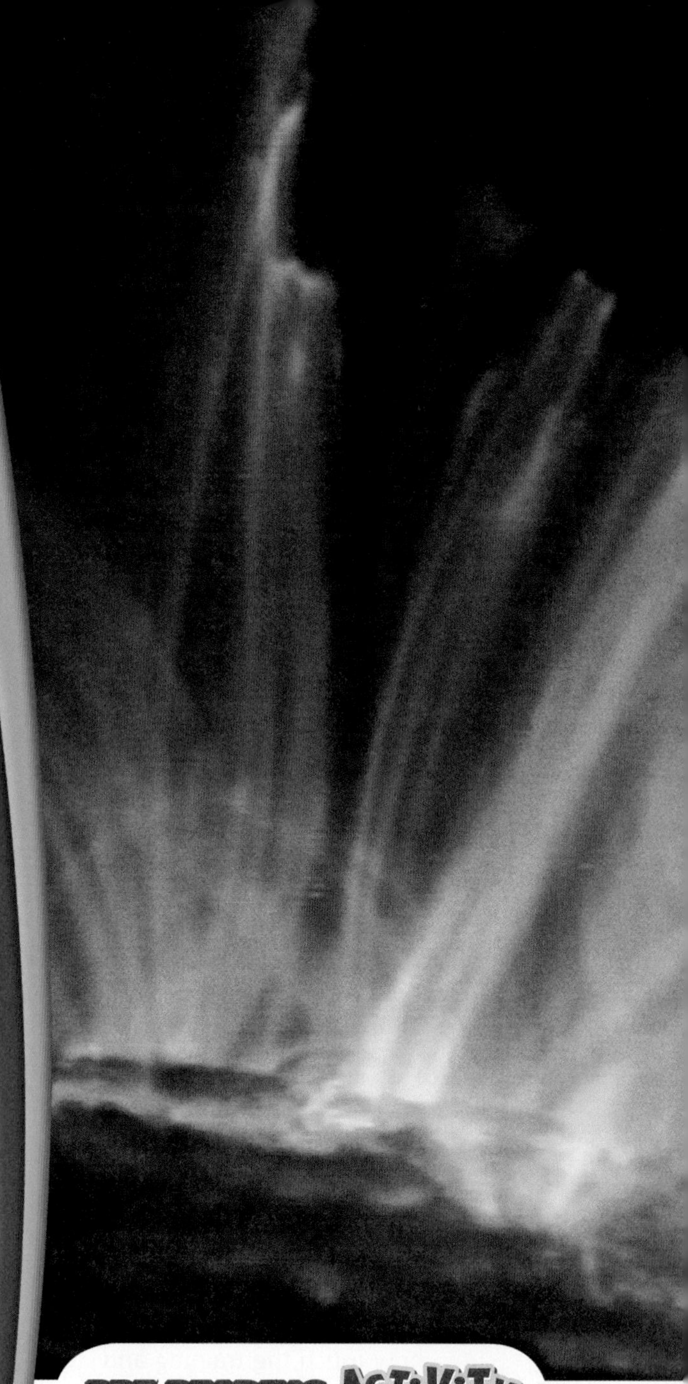

8

Electromagnetism

The Big Idea

Forces of attraction and repulsion result from magnetic and electric fields.

SECTION

About the Photo

Superhot particles at millions of degrees Celsius shoot out of the sun. But they do not escape. They loop back and crash into the sun's surface at more than 100 km/s (223,000 mi/h). The image of Earth has been added to show how large these loops can be. What directs the particles? The particles follow along the path of the magnetic field lines of the sun. You depend on magnetic fields in electric motors and generators. And you can use them to show off a good report card on the refrigerator.

PRE-READING ACTIVITY

Graphic Organizer

Comparison Table Before you read the chapter, create the graphic organizer entitled "Comparison Table" described in the **Study Skills** section of the Appendix. Label the columns with "Motor" and "Generator." Label the rows with "Energy in" and "Energy out." As you read the chapter, fill in the table with details about the energy conversion that happens in each device.

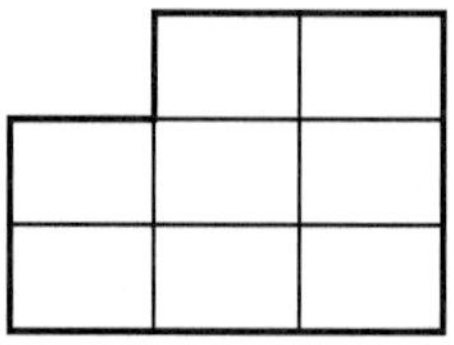

START-UP ACTIVITY

Magnetic Attraction

In this activity, you will investigate ways you can use a magnet to lift steel.

Procedure

1. Put **5 steel paper clips** on your desk. Touch the clips with an **unmagnetized iron nail.** Record the number of clips that stick to it.
2. Touch the clips with the end of a **strong bar magnet.** Record the number of clips that stick to the magnet.
3. While holding the magnet against the head of the nail, touch the tip of the nail to the paper clips. Count the number of paper clips that stick to the nail.
4. Remove the magnet from the end of the nail. Record the number of paper clips you counted in step 3 and your observations when you removed the magnet.
5. Drag one end of the bar magnet 50 times down the nail. Drag the magnet in only one direction.
6. Set the magnet aside. Touch the nail to the clips. Record the number of clips that stick to it.

Analysis

1. What caused the difference between the number of paper clips that you picked up in step 1 and in step 3?
2. What effect did the magnet have on the nail in step 5?

SECTION 1

Magnets and Magnetism

You've probably seen magnets stuck to a refrigerator door. These magnets might be holding notes or pictures. Or they might be just for looks.

What You Will Learn

- Describe the properties of magnets.
- Explain why some materials are magnetic and some are not.
- Describe four kinds of magnets.
- Give two examples of the effect of Earth's magnetic field.

Vocabulary

magnet
magnetic pole
magnetic force

READING STRATEGY

Prediction Guide Before reading this section, predict whether each of the following statements is true or false:

- Every magnet has a north pole and a south pole.
- The magnetic pole near the South Pole in Antarctica is a north pole.

If you have ever experimented with magnets, you know that they stick to each other and to some kinds of metals. You also know that magnets can stick to things without directly touching them—such as a magnet used to hold a piece of paper to a refrigerator door.

Properties of Magnets

More than 2,000 years ago, the Greeks discovered a mineral that attracted things made of iron. Because this mineral was found in a part of Turkey called Magnesia, the Greeks called it magnetite. Today, any material that attracts iron or things made of iron is called a **magnet.** All magnets have certain properties. For example, all magnets have two poles. Magnets exert forces on each other and are surrounded by a magnetic field.

Reading Check **What is a magnet?** *(See the Appendix for answers to Reading Checks.)*

magnet any material that attracts iron or materials containing iron

magnetic pole one of two points, such as the ends of a magnet, that have opposing magnetic qualities

Magnetic Poles

The magnetic effects are not the same throughout a magnet. What would happen if you dipped a bar magnet into a box of paper clips? Most of the clips would stick to the ends of the bar, as shown in **Figure 1.** This shows that the strongest effects are near the ends of the bar magnet. Each end of the magnet is a magnetic pole. As you will see, **magnetic poles** are points on a magnet that have opposite magnetic qualities.

Figure 1 *More paper clips stick to the ends, or magnetic poles, of a magnet because the magnetic effects are strongest there.*

North and South

Suppose you hang a magnet by a string so that the magnet can spin. You will see that one end of the magnet always ends up pointing to the north, as shown in **Figure 2.** The pole of a magnet that points to the north is called the magnet's *north pole*. The opposite end of the magnet points to the south. It is called the magnet's *south pole*. Magnetic poles are always in pairs. You will never find a magnet that has only a north pole or only a south pole.

Figure 2 *The needle in a compass is a magnet that is free to rotate.*

Magnetic Forces

When you bring two magnets close together, the magnets each exert a **magnetic force** on the other. These magnetic forces result from spinning electric charges in the magnets. The force can either push the magnets apart or pull them together. The magnetic force is a universal force. It is always present when magnetic poles come near one another.

magnetic force the force of attraction or repulsion generated by moving or spinning electric charges

Think of the last time you worked with magnets. If you held two magnets in a certain way, they pulled together. When you turned one of the magnets around, they pushed apart. Why? The magnetic force between magnets depends on how the poles of the magnets line up. Like poles repel, and opposite poles attract, as shown in **Figure 3.**

Reading Check **If two magnets push each other away, what can you conclude about their poles?**

Figure 3 **Magnetic Force Between Magnets**

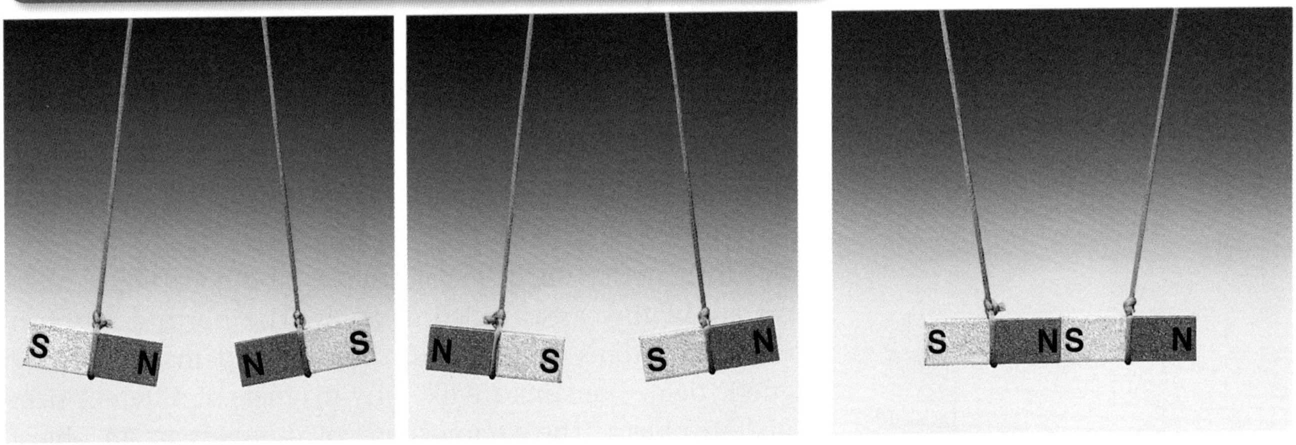

▲ If you hold the north poles of two magnets close together, the magnetic force will push the magnets apart. The same is true if you hold the south poles close together.

▲ If you hold the north pole of one magnet close to the south pole of another magnet, the magnetic force will pull the magnets together.

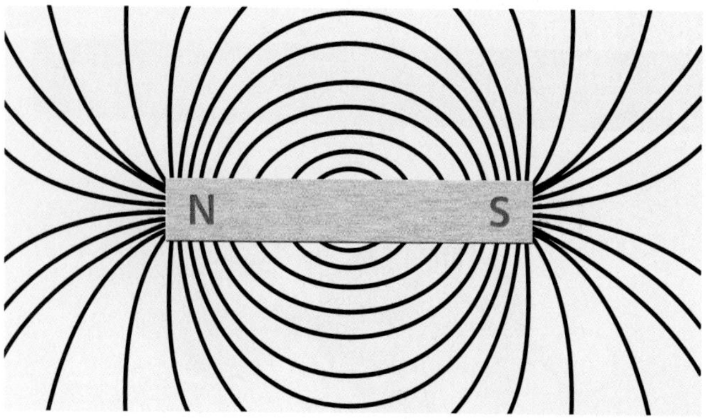

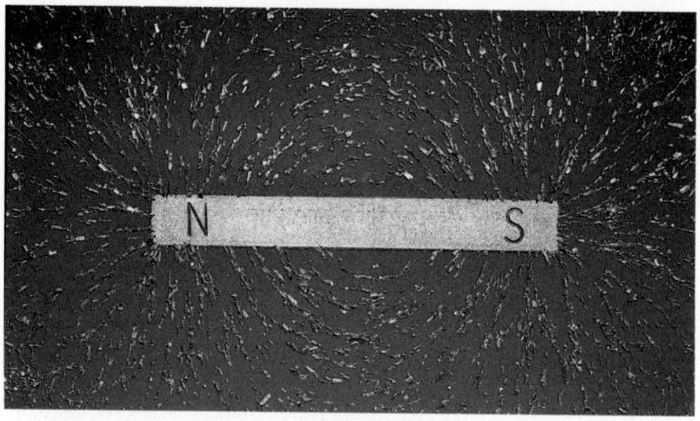

Figure 4 *Magnetic field lines show the shape of a magnetic field around a magnet. You can model magnetic field lines by sprinkling iron filings around a magnet.*

Magnetic Fields

A *magnetic field* exists in the region around a magnet in which magnetic forces can act. The shape of a magnetic field can be shown with lines drawn from the north pole of a magnet to the south pole, as shown in **Figure 4.** These lines map out the magnetic field and are called *magnetic field lines*. The closer together the field lines are, the stronger the magnetic field is. The lines around a magnet are closest together at the poles, where the magnetic force on an object is strongest.

CONNECTION TO Biology

WRITING SKILL **Animal Compasses**

Scientists think that birds and other animals may use Earth's magnetic field to help them navigate. Write a one-page paper in your **science journal** that tells which animals might find their way using Earth's magnetic field. Include evidence scientists have found that supports the idea.

The Cause of Magnetism

Some materials are magnetic. Some are not. For example, a magnet can pick up paper clips and iron nails. But it cannot pick up paper, plastic, pennies, or aluminum foil. What causes the difference? Whether a material is magnetic depends on the material's atoms.

Atoms and Domains

All matter is made of atoms. Electrons are negatively charged particles of atoms. As an electron moves around, it makes, or induces, a magnetic field. The atom will then have a north and a south pole. In most materials, such as copper and aluminum, the magnetic fields of the individual atoms cancel each other out. Therefore, these materials are not magnetic.

But in materials such as iron, nickel, and cobalt, groups of atoms are in tiny areas called *domains*. The north and south poles of the atoms in a domain line up and make a strong magnetic field. Domains are like tiny magnets of different sizes within an object. The arrangement of domains in an object determines whether the object is magnetic. **Figure 5** shows how the arrangement of domains works.

Reading Check Why are copper and aluminum not magnetic?

Figure 5 Arrangement of Domains in an Object

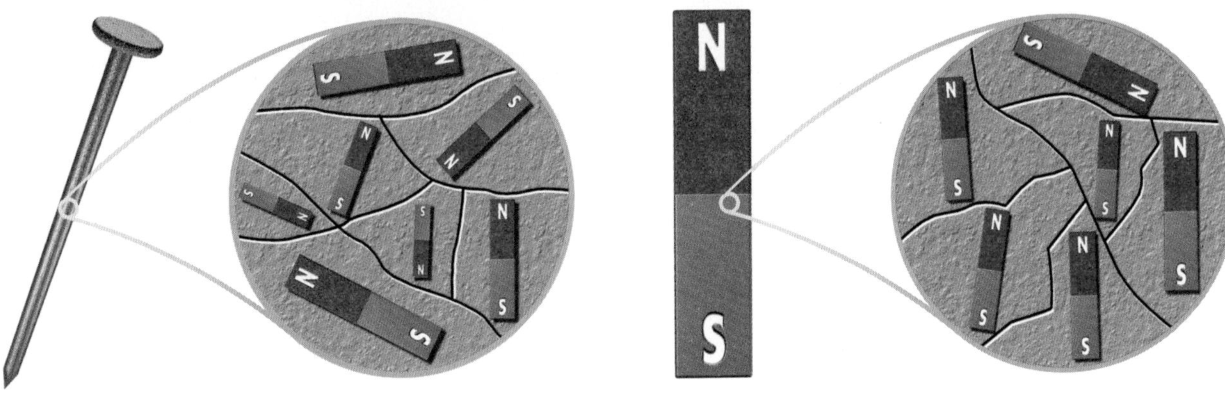

If the domains in an object are randomly arranged, the magnetic fields of the individual domains cancel each other out, and the object has no magnetic properties.

If most of the domains in an object are aligned, the magnetic fields of the individual domains combine to make the whole object magnetic.

Losing Alignment

The domains of a magnet may not always stay lined up. When domains move, the magnet is demagnetized, or loses its magnetic properties. Dropping a magnet or hitting it too hard can move the domains. Putting the magnet in a strong magnetic field that is opposite to its own can also move domains. Increasing the temperature of a magnet can also demagnetize it. At higher temperatures, atoms in the magnet vibrate faster. As a result, the atoms in the domains may no longer line up.

Reading Check **Describe two ways a magnet can lose its magnetic properties.**

Making Magnets

You can make a magnet from something made of iron, cobalt, or nickel. You just need to line up the domains in it. For example, you can magnetize an iron nail if you rub it in one direction with one pole of a magnet. The domains in the nail line up with the magnetic field of the magnet. So, the domains in the nail become aligned. As more domains line up, the magnetic field of the nail grows stronger. The nail will become a magnet, as shown in **Figure 6.**

The process of making a magnet also explains how a magnet can pick up an unmagnetized object, such as a paper clip. When a magnet is close to a paper clip, some domains in the paper clip line up with the field of the magnet. So, the paper clip becomes a temporary magnet. The north pole of the paper clip points toward the south pole of the magnet. The paper clip is attracted to the magnet. When the magnet is removed, the domains of the paper clip become scrambled again.

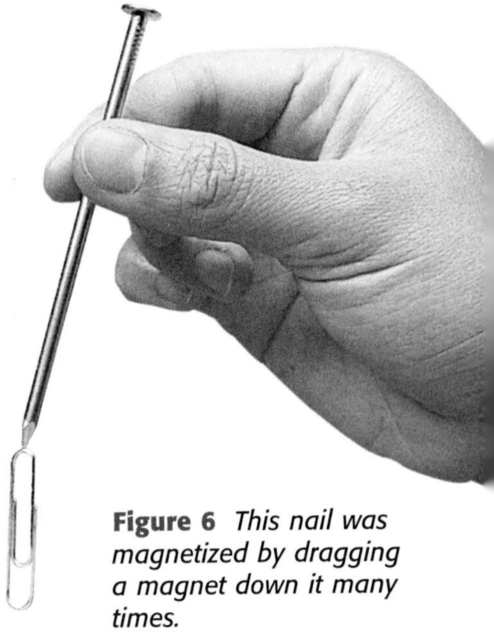

Figure 6 *This nail was magnetized by dragging a magnet down it many times.*

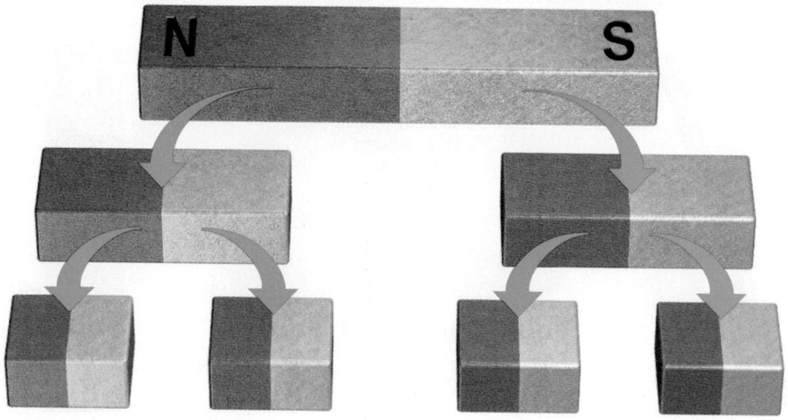

Figure 7 *If you cut a magnet in pieces, each piece will still be a magnet with two poles.*

Cutting a Magnet

What do you think would happen if you cut a magnet in half? You might think that you would end up with one north-pole piece and one south-pole piece. But that's not what happens. When you cut a magnet in half, you end up with two magnets. Each piece has its own north pole and south pole, as shown in **Figure 7.** A magnet has poles because its domains are lined up. Each domain within a magnet is like a tiny magnet with a north pole and a south pole. Even the smallest pieces of a magnet have two poles.

Figure 8 *Magnetite attracts objects containing iron and is a ferromagnet.*

Kinds of Magnets

There are different ways to describe magnets. Some magnets are made of iron, nickel, cobalt, or mixtures of those metals. Magnets made with these metals have strong magnetic properties and are called *ferromagnets*. Look at **Figure 8.** The mineral magnetite is an example of a naturally occurring ferromagnet. Another kind of magnet is the *electromagnet*. This is a magnet made by an electric current. An electromagnet usually has an iron core.

Reading Check What are ferromagnets?

Temporary and Permanent Magnets

Magnets can also be described as temporary magnets or permanent magnets. *Temporary magnets* are made from materials that are easy to magnetize. But they tend to lose their magnetization easily. Soft iron is iron that is not mixed with any other materials. It can be made into temporary magnets. *Permanent magnets* are difficult to magnetize. But they tend to keep their magnetic properties longer than temporary magnets do. Some permanent magnets are made with alnico (AL ni KOH)—an alloy of aluminum, nickel, cobalt, and iron.

Earth as a Magnet

One end of every magnet points to the north if the magnet can spin. For more than 2,000 years, travelers have used this property to find their way. In fact, you use this when you use a compass, because a compass has a freely spinning magnet.

One Giant Magnet

In 1600, an English physician named William Gilbert suggested that magnets point to the north because Earth is one giant magnet. In fact, Earth behaves as if it has a bar magnet running through its center. The poles of this imaginary magnet are located near Earth's geographic poles.

Poles of a Compass Needle

If you put a compass on a bar magnet, the marked end of the needle points to the south pole of the magnet. Does that surprise you? Opposite poles of magnets attract each other. A compass needle is a small magnet. And the tip that points to the north is the needle's north pole. Therefore, the point of a compass needle is attracted to the south pole of a magnet.

South Magnetic Pole near North Geographic Pole

Look at **Figure 9.** A compass needle points north because the magnetic pole of Earth that is closest to the geographic North Pole is a magnetic *south* pole. A compass needle points to the north because its north pole is attracted to a very large magnetic south pole.

Quick Lab

Model of Earth's Magnetic Field

1. Place a **bar magnet** on a **sheet of butcher paper.** Draw a circle on the paper with a diameter larger than the bar magnet. This represents the surface of the Earth. Label Earth's North Pole and South Pole.
2. Place the bar magnet under the butcher paper, and line up the bar magnet with the poles.
3. Sprinkle some **iron filings** lightly around the perimeter of the circle. Describe and sketch the pattern you see.

Figure 9 Earth's Geographic and Magnetic Poles

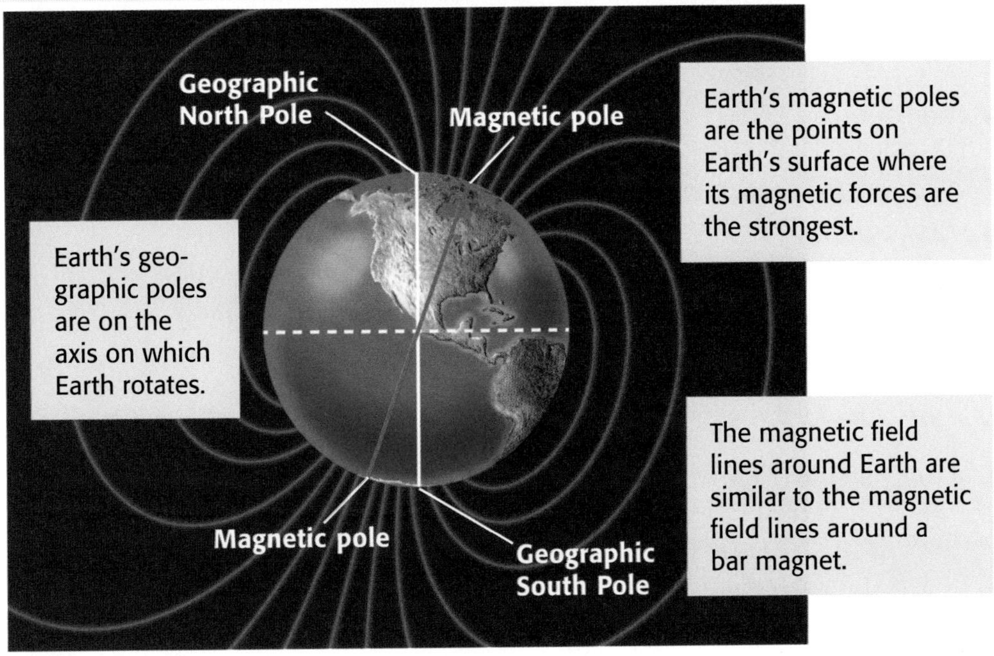

Geographic North Pole
Magnetic pole
Earth's magnetic poles are the points on Earth's surface where its magnetic forces are the strongest.
Earth's geographic poles are on the axis on which Earth rotates.
The magnetic field lines around Earth are similar to the magnetic field lines around a bar magnet.
Magnetic pole
Geographic South Pole

The Core of the Matter

Although you can think of Earth as having a giant bar magnet through its center, there isn't really a magnet there. The temperature of Earth's core (or center) is very high. The atoms in it move too violently to stay lined up in domains.

Scientists think that Earth's magnetic field is made by the movement of electric charges in the Earth's core. The Earth's core is made mostly of iron and nickel. The inner core is solid because it is under great pressure. The outer core is liquid because the pressure is not as high. As Earth rotates, the liquid in the core flows. Electric charges move, which makes a magnetic field.

Reading Check **What do scientists think causes Earth's magnetic field?**

CONNECTION TO Social Studies

History of the Compass Records from the first century BCE found in China show that people knew that the mineral lodestone (magnetite) would align to the north. But not until about 1,200 years later were floating compasses used for navigation. Research early compasses, and build a working model of one. Demonstrate to your class how it works.

ACTIVITY

A Magnetic Light Show

Look at **Figure 10.** The beautiful curtain of light is called an *aurora* (aw RAWR uh). Earth's magnetic field plays a part in making auroras. An aurora is formed when charged particles from the sun hit oxygen and nitrogen atoms in the air. The atoms become excited and then give off light of many colors.

Earth's magnetic field blocks most of the charged particles from the sun. But the field bends inward at the magnetic poles. As a result, the charged particles can crash into the atmosphere at and near the poles. Auroras seen near Earth's North Pole are called the *northern lights,* or aurora borealis (aw RAWR uh BAWR ee AL is). Auroras seen near the South Pole are called the *southern lights,* or aurora australis (aw RAWR uh aw STRAY lis).

Figure 10 *An aurora is an amazing light show in the sky.*

SECTION Review

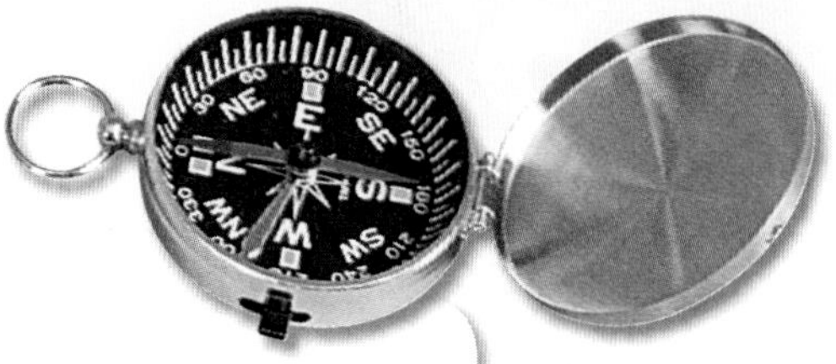

Summary

- All magnets have two poles. The north pole will always point to the north if allowed to rotate freely. The other pole is called the south pole.
- Like magnetic poles repel each other. Opposite magnetic poles attract.
- Every magnet is surrounded by a magnetic field. The shape of the field can be shown with magnetic field lines.
- A material is magnetic if its domains line up.
- Magnets can be classified as ferromagnets, electromagnets, temporary magnets, and permanent magnets.
- Earth acts as if it has a big bar magnet through its core. Compass needles and the north poles of magnets point to Earth's magnetic south pole, which is near Earth's geographic North Pole.
- Auroras are most commonly seen near Earth's magnetic poles because Earth's magnetic field bends inward at the poles.

Using Key Terms

1. Use the following terms in the same sentence: *magnet, magnetic force,* and *magnetic pole.*

Understanding Key Ideas

2. What metal is used to make ferromagnets?
   a. iron
   b. cobalt
   c. nickel
   d. All of the above
3. Name three properties of magnets.
4. Why are some iron objects magnetic and others not magnetic?
5. How are temporary magnets different from permanent magnets?

Critical Thinking

6. **Forming Hypotheses** Why are auroras more commonly seen in places such as Alaska and Australia than in places such as Florida and Mexico?
7. **Applying Concepts** Explain how you could use magnets to make a small object appear to float in air.
8. **Making Inferences** Earth's moon has no atmosphere and has a cool, solid core. Would you expect to see auroras on the moon? Explain your answer.

Interpreting Graphics

The image below shows a model of Earth as a large magnet. Use the image below to answer the questions that follow.

9. Which magnetic pole is closest to the geographic North Pole?
10. Is the magnetic field of Earth stronger near the middle of Earth (in Mexico) or at the bottom of Earth (in Antarctica)? Explain your answer.

SCILINKS. NSTA
Developed and maintained by the National Science Teachers Association

For a variety of links related to this chapter, go to www.scilinks.org

Topic: Magnetism; Types of Magnets
SciLinks code: HSM0900; HSM1566

SECTION 2

Magnetism from Electricity

What You Will Learn

- Identify the relationship between an electric current and a magnetic field.
- Compare solenoids and electromagnets.
- Describe how electromagnetism is involved in the operation of doorbells, electric motors, and galvanometers.

Vocabulary

electromagnetism
solenoid
electromagnet
electric motor

READING STRATEGY

Reading Organizer As you read this section, make a table comparing solenoids and electromagnets.

Most of the trains you see roll on wheels on top of a track. But engineers have developed trains that have no wheels. The trains actually float above the track.

They float because of magnetic forces between the track and the train cars. Such trains are called maglev trains. The name *maglev* is short for magnetic levitation. To levitate, maglev trains use a kind of magnet called an electromagnet. Electromagnets can make strong magnetic fields. In this section, you will learn how electricity and magnetism are related and how electromagnets are made.

The Discovery of Electromagnetism

Danish physicist Hans Christian Oersted (UHR STED) discovered the relationship between electricity and magnetism in 1820. During a lecture, he held a compass near a wire carrying an electric current. Oersted noticed that when the compass was close to the wire, the compass needle no longer pointed to the north. The result surprised Oersted. A compass needle is a magnet. It moves from its north-south orientation only when it is in a magnetic field different from Earth's. Oersted tried a few experiments with the compass and the wire. His results are shown in **Figure 1.**

Figure 1 **Oersted's Experiment**

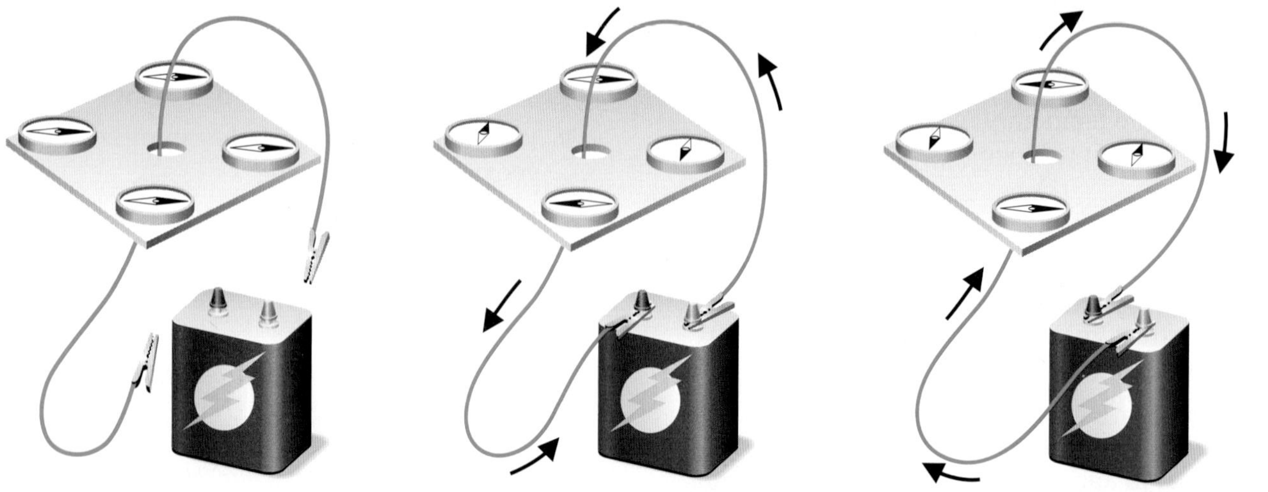

a If no electric current exists in the wire, the compass needles point in the same direction.

b Electric current in one direction in the wire causes the compass needles to deflect in a clockwise direction.

c Electric current in the opposite direction makes the compass needles deflect in a counterclockwise direction.

More Research

From his experiments, Oersted concluded that an electric current produces a magnetic field. He also found that the direction of the field depends on the direction of the current. The French scientist André-Marie Ampère heard about Oersted's findings. Ampère did more research with electricity and magnetism. Their work was the first research of electromagnetism. **Electromagnetism** is the interaction between electricity and magnetism.

Reading Check **What is electromagnetism?** (*See the Appendix for answers to Reading Checks.*)

electromagnetism the interaction between electricity and magnetism

solenoid a coil of wire with an electric current in it

Using Electromagnetism

The magnetic field generated by an electric current in a wire can move a compass needle. But the magnetic field is not strong enough to be very useful. However, two devices, the solenoid and the electromagnet, strengthen the magnetic field made by a current-carrying wire. Both devices make electromagnetism more useful.

Solenoids

A single loop of wire carrying a current does not have a very strong magnetic field. But suppose you form many loops into a coil. The magnetic fields of the individual loops will combine to make a much stronger field. A **solenoid** is a coil of wire that produces a magnetic field when carrying an electric current. In fact, the magnetic field around a solenoid is very similar to the magnetic field of a bar magnet, as shown in **Figure 2.** The strength of the magnetic field of a solenoid increases as more loops per meter are used. The magnetic field also becomes stronger as the current in the wire is increased.

INTERNET ACTIVITY

For another activity related to this chapter, go to **go.hrw.com** and type in the keyword **HP5EMGW.**

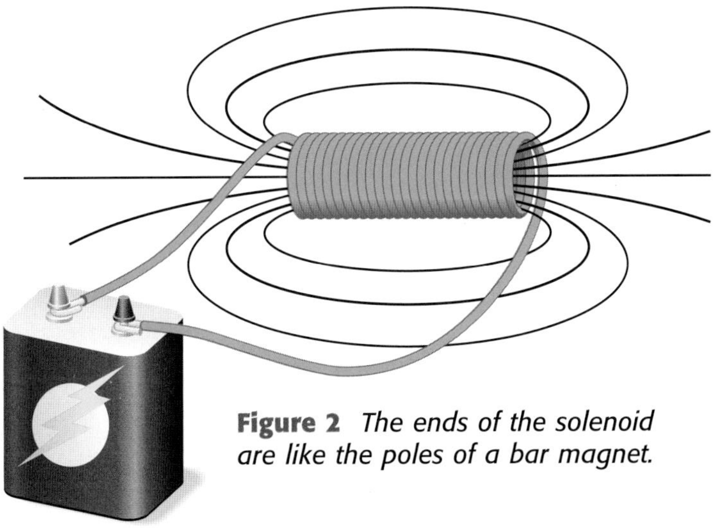

Figure 2 *The ends of the solenoid are like the poles of a bar magnet.*

Electromagnets

An **electromagnet** is made up of a solenoid wrapped around an iron core. The magnetic field of the solenoid makes the domains inside the iron core line up. The magnetic field of the electromagnet is the field of the solenoid plus the field of the magnetized core. As a result, the magnetic field of an electromagnet may be hundreds of times stronger than the magnetic field of just the solenoid.

You can make an electromagnet even stronger. You can increase the number of loops per meter in the solenoid. You can also increase the electric current in the wire. Some electromagnets are strong enough to lift a car or levitate a train! Maglev trains levitate because strong magnets on the cars are pushed away by powerful electromagnets in the rails.

Reading Check **What happens to the magnetic field of an electromagnet if you increase the current in the wire?**

Quick Lab

Electromagnets

1. Tightly wrap an **insulated copper wire** around a **large iron nail,** and leave 10 cm of wire loose at each end.
2. Use **electrical tape** to attach the bare ends of the wire against the top and bottom of a **D-cell.**
3. Hold the end of the nail near some **paper clips,** and try to lift them up.
4. While holding the clips up, remove the wires from the cell. Then, record your observations.
5. What advantage of electromagnets did you see?

Turning Electromagnets On and Off

Electromagnets are very useful because they can be turned on and off as needed. The solenoid has a field only when there is electric current in it. So, electromagnets attract things only when a current exists in the wire. When there is no current in the wire, the electromagnet is turned off. **Figure 3** shows an example of how this property can be useful.

electromagnet a coil that has a soft iron core and that acts as a magnet when an electric current is in the coil

Figure 3 *Electromagnets used in salvage yards are turned on to pick up metal objects and turned off to put them down again.*

Applications of Electromagnetism

Electromagnetism is useful in your everyday life. You already know that electromagnets can be used to lift heavy objects containing iron. But did you know that you use a solenoid whenever you ring a doorbell? Or that there are electromagnets in motors? Keep reading to learn how electromagnetism makes these things work.

Doorbells

Look at **Figure 4.** Have you ever noticed a doorbell button that has a light inside? Have you noticed that when you push the button, the light goes out? Two solenoids in the doorbell allow the doorbell to work. Pushing the button opens the circuit of the first solenoid. The current stops, causing the magnetic field to drop and the light to go out. The change in the field causes a current in the second solenoid. This current induces a magnetic field that pushes an iron rod that sounds the bell.

Figure 4 *Ringing this doorbell requires two solenoids.*

Magnetic Force and Electric Current

An electric current can cause a compass needle to move. The needle is a small magnet. The needle moves because the electric current in a wire creates a magnetic field that exerts a force on the needle. If a current-carrying wire causes a magnet to move, can a magnet cause a current-carrying wire to move? **Figure 5** shows that the answer is yes. This property is useful in electric motors.

Reading Check **Why does a current-carrying wire cause a compass needle to move?**

Figure 5 **Magnetic Force on a Current-Carrying Wire**

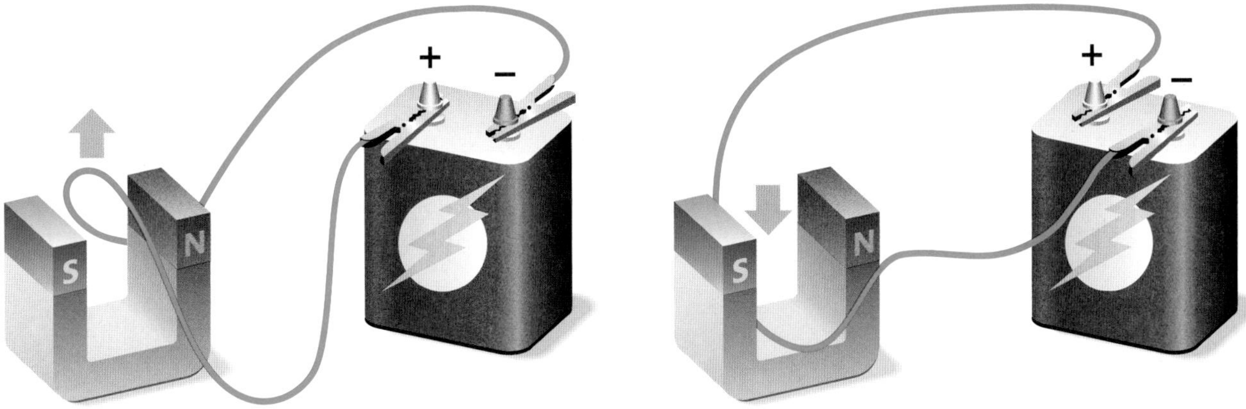

a When a current-carrying wire is placed between two poles of a magnet, the wire will jump up.

b Switching the wires at the battery reverses the direction of the current, and the wire is pushed down.

electric motor a device that converts electrical energy into mechanical energy

Electric Motors

An **electric motor** is a device that changes electrical energy into mechanical energy. All electric motors have an *armature*—a loop or coil of wire that can rotate. The armature is mounted between the poles of a permanent magnet or electromagnet.

In electric motors that use direct current, a device called a *commutator* is attached to the armature to reverse the direction of the electric current in the wire. A commutator is a ring that is split in half and connected to the ends of the armature. Electric current enters the armature through brushes that touch the commutator. Every time the armature and the commutator make a half turn, the direction of the current in the armature is reversed. **Figure 6** shows how a direct-current motor works.

Figure 6 A Direct-Current Electric Motor

Getting Started An electric current in the armature causes the magnet to exert a force on the armature. Because of the direction of the current on either side of the armature, the magnet pulls up on one side and down on the other side. This pulling makes the armature rotate.

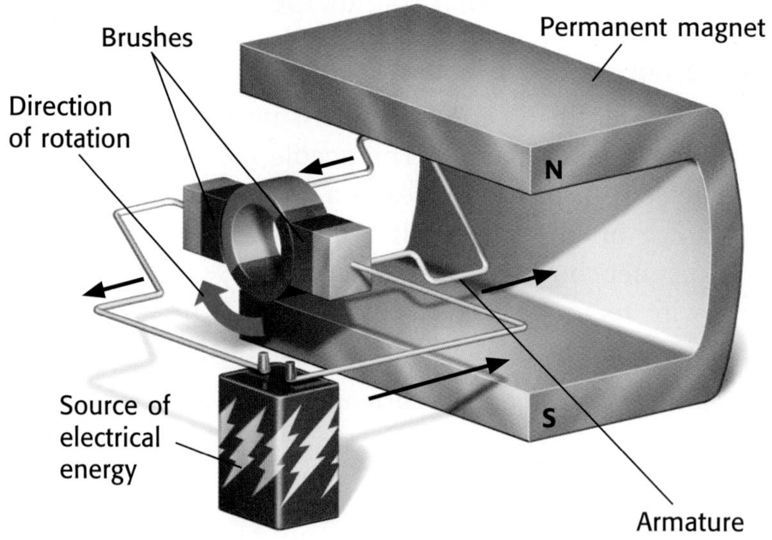

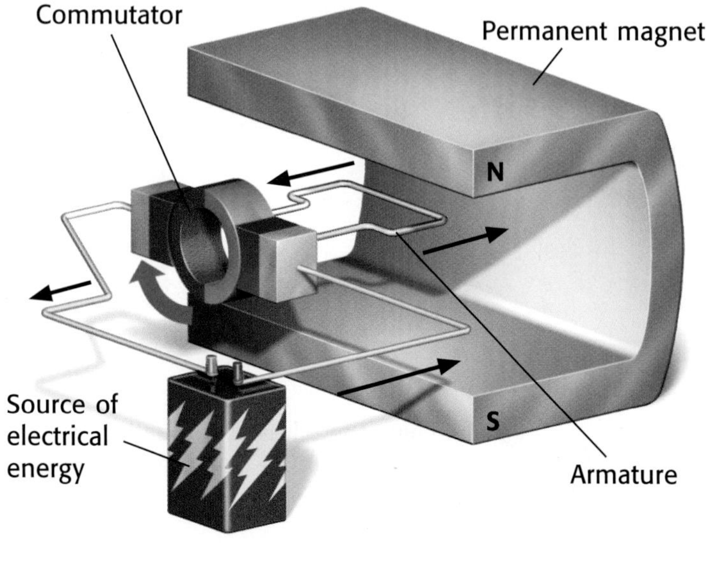

Running the Motor As the armature rotates, the commutator causes the electric current in the coil to change directions. When the electric current is reversed, the side of the coil that was pulled up is pulled down and the side that was pulled down is pulled up. This change of direction keeps the armature rotating.

Galvanometers

A galvanometer (GAL vuh NAHM uht uhr) measures current. Galvanometers are sometimes found in equipment used by electricians, such as ammeters and voltmeters, as shown in **Figure 7.** A galvanometer has an electromagnet placed between the poles of a permanent magnet. The poles of the electromagnet are pushed away by the poles of the permanent magnet. The electromagnet is free to rotate and is attached to a pointer. The pointer moves along a scale that shows the size and direction of the current.

Reading Check **What does a galvanometer measure?**

Figure 7 *This ammeter uses a galvanometer to measure electric current.*

SECTION Review

Summary

- Oersted discovered that a wire carrying a current makes a magnetic field.
- Electromagnetism is the interaction between electricity and magnetism.
- An electromagnet is a solenoid that has an iron core.
- A magnet can exert a force on a wire carrying a current.
- A doorbell, an electric motor, and a galvanometer all make use of electromagnetism.

Using Key Terms

For each pair of terms, explain how the meanings of the terms differ.

1. *electromagnet* and *solenoid*

Understanding Key Ideas

2. Which of the following actions will decrease the strength of the magnetic field of an electromagnet?
   a. using fewer loops of wire per meter in the coil
   b. decreasing the current in the wire
   c. removing the iron core
   d. All of the above
3. Describe what happens when you hold a compass close to a wire carrying a current.
4. What is the relationship between an electric current and a magnetic field?
5. What makes the armature in an electric motor rotate?

Critical Thinking

6. **Applying Concepts** What do Hans Christian Oersted's experiments have to do with a galvanometer? Explain your answer.
7. **Making Comparisons** Compare the structures and magnetic fields of solenoids with those of electromagnets.

Interpreting Graphics

8. Look at the image below. Your friend says that the image shows an electromagnet because there are loops with a core in the middle. Is your friend correct? Explain your reasoning.

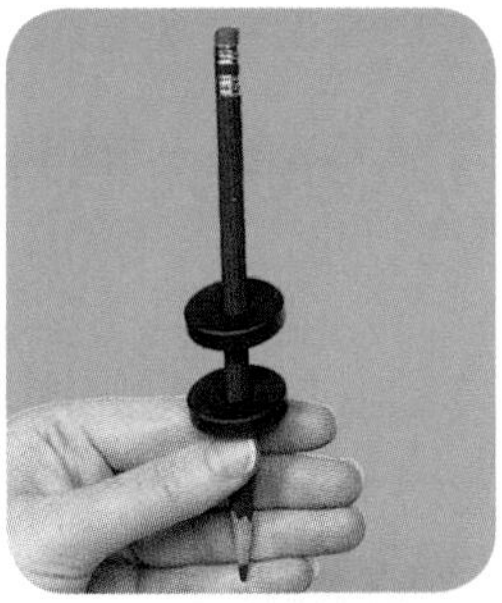

SCILINKS. NSTA Developed and maintained by the National Science Teachers Association

For a variety of links related to this chapter, go to www.scilinks.org

Topic: Electromagnetism
SciLinks code: HSM0483

SECTION 3

Electricity from Magnetism

What You Will Learn

- Explain how a magnetic field can make an electric current.
- Explain how electromagnetic induction is used in a generator.
- Compare step-up and step-down transformers.

Vocabulary

electromagnetic induction
electric generator
transformer

READING STRATEGY

Paired Summarizing Read this section silently. In pairs, take turns summarizing the material. Stop to discuss ideas that seem confusing.

When you use an electrical appliance or turn on a light in your home, you probably don't think about where the electrical energy comes from.

For most people, an electric power company supplies their home with electrical energy. In this section, you'll learn how a magnetic field can induce an electric current and how power companies use this process to supply electrical energy.

Electric Current from a Changing Magnetic Field

Hans Christian Oersted discovered that an electric current could make a magnetic field. Soon after, scientists wondered if a magnetic field could make an electric current. In 1831, two scientists each solved this problem. Joseph Henry, of the United States, made the discovery first. But Michael Faraday, from Great Britain, published his results first. Faraday also reported them in great detail, so his results are better known.

Faraday's Experiment

Faraday used a setup like the one shown in **Figure 1.** Faraday hoped that the magnetic field of the electromagnet would make—or induce—an electric current in the second wire. But no matter how strong the electromagnet was, he could not make an electric current in the second wire.

Reading Check **What was Faraday trying to do in his experiment?** (*See the Appendix for answers to Reading Checks.*)

Figure 1 **Faraday's Experiment with Magnets and Induction**

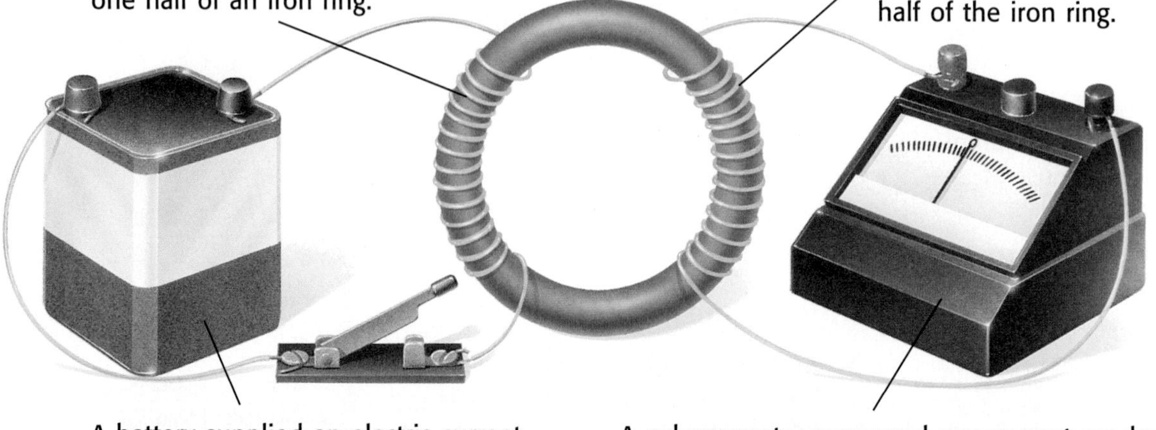

One wire was wound around one half of an iron ring.
A second wire was wound around the other half of the iron ring.
A battery supplied an electric current to the wire, making an electromagnet.
A galvanometer measured any current produced in the second wire by the magnetic field.

Figure 2 Factors that Affect an Induced Current

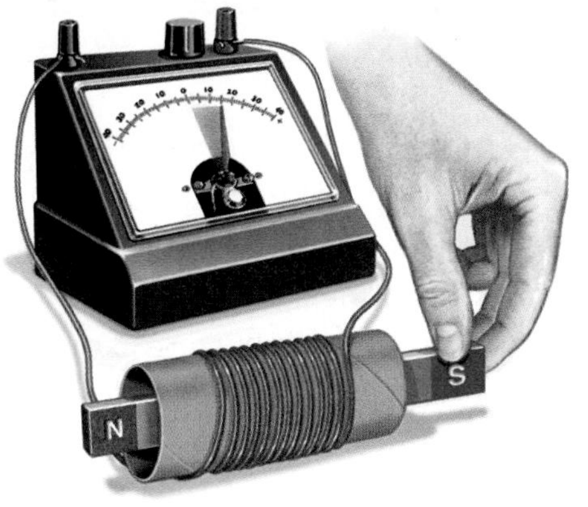

a An electric current is induced when you move a magnet through a coil of wire.

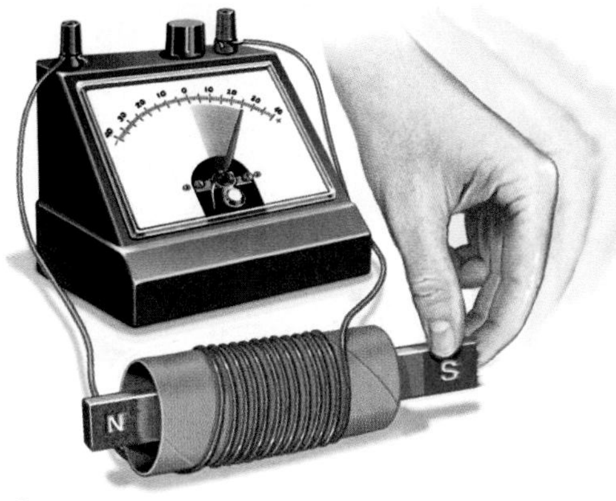

b A greater electric current is induced if you move the magnet faster through the coil because the magnetic field is changing faster.

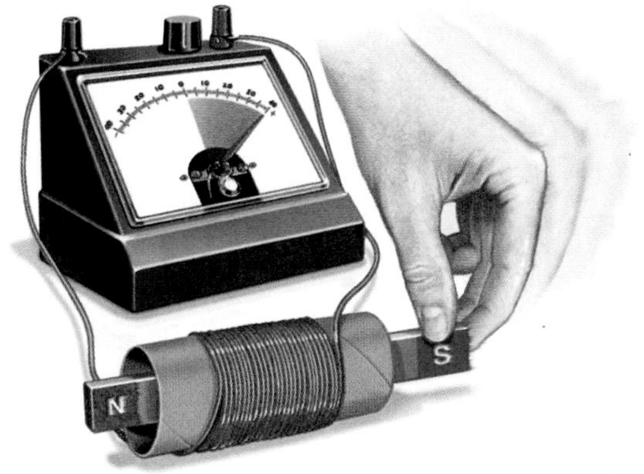

c A greater electric current is induced if you add more loops of wire. This magnet is moving at the same speed as the magnet in **b.**

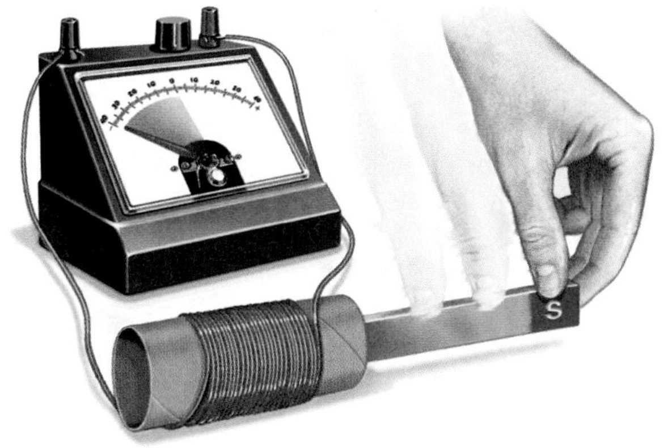

d The induced electric current reverses direction if the magnet is pulled out rather than pushed in.

Success for an Instant

As Faraday experimented with the electromagnetic ring, he noticed something interesting. At the instant he connected the wires to the battery, the galvanometer pointer moved. This movement showed that an electric current was present. The pointer moved again at the instant he disconnected the battery. But as long as the battery was fully connected, the galvanometer measured no electric current.

Faraday realized that electric current in the second wire was made only when the magnetic field was changing. The magnetic field changed as the battery was connected and disconnected. The process by which an electric current is made by changing a magnetic field is called **electromagnetic induction.** Faraday did many more experiments in this area. Some of his results are shown in **Figure 2.**

electromagnetic induction the process of creating a current in a circuit by changing a magnetic field

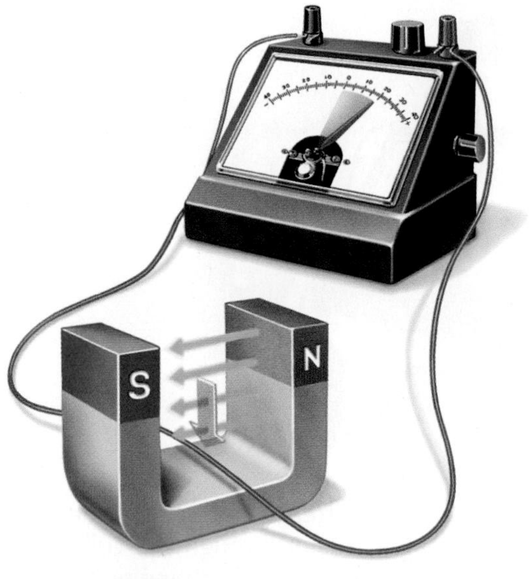

Figure 3 *As the wire moves between the poles of the magnet, it cuts through magnetic field lines, and an electric current is induced.*

electric generator a device that converts mechanical energy into electrical energy

Inducing Electric Current

Faraday's experiments also showed that moving either the magnet or the wire changes the magnetic field around the wire. So, an electric current is made when a magnet moves in a coil of wire or when a wire moves between the poles of a magnet.

Consider the magnetic field lines between the poles of the magnet. An electric current is induced only when a wire crosses the magnetic field lines, as shown in **Figure 3.** An electric current is induced because a magnetic force can cause electric charges to move. But the charges move in a wire only when the wire moves through the magnetic field.

Electric Generators

Electromagnetic induction is very important for the generation of electrical energy. An **electric generator** uses electromagnetic induction to change mechanical energy into electrical energy. **Figure 4** shows the parts of a simple generator. **Figure 5** explains how the generator works.

Reading Check **What energy change happens in an electric generator?**

Figure 4 **Parts of a Simple Generator**

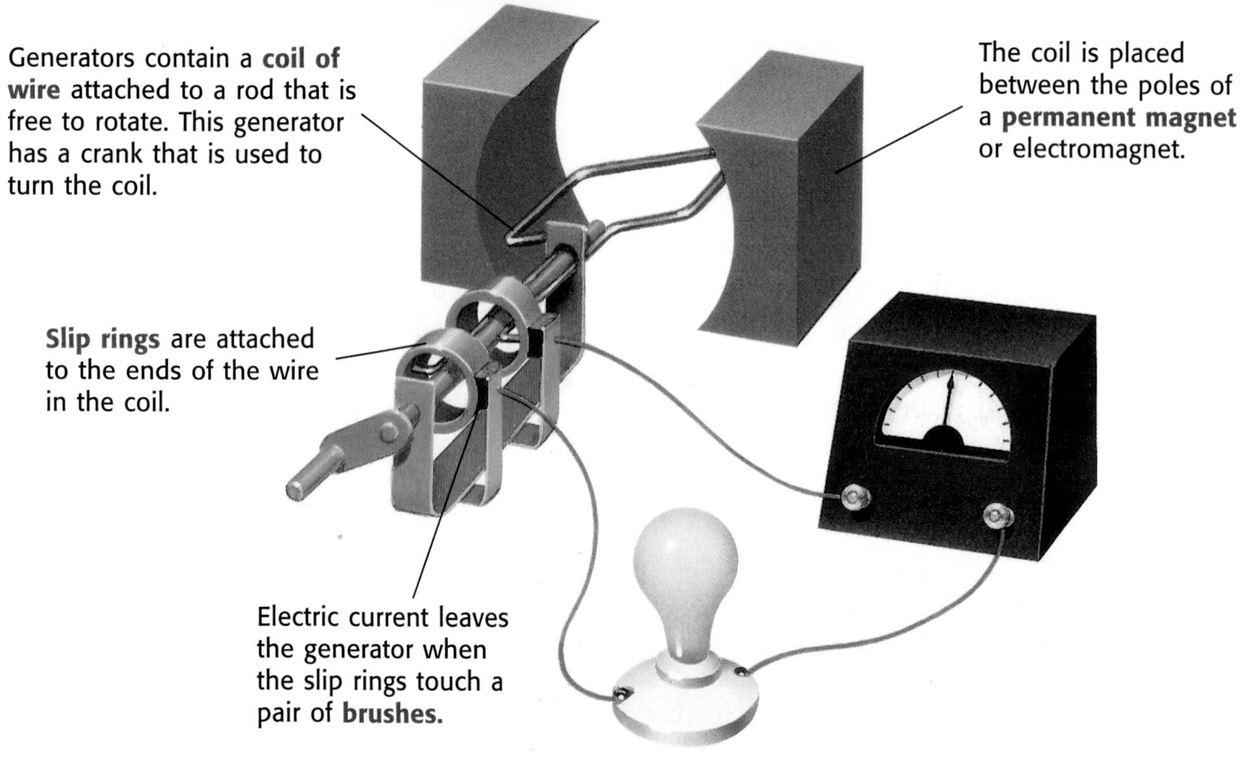

Generators contain a **coil of wire** attached to a rod that is free to rotate. This generator has a crank that is used to turn the coil.
The coil is placed between the poles of a **permanent magnet** or electromagnet.
Slip rings are attached to the ends of the wire in the coil.
Electric current leaves the generator when the slip rings touch a pair of **brushes.**

Figure 5 How a Generator Works

1. As the crank is turned, the rotating coil crosses the magnetic field lines of the magnet, and an electric current is induced in the wire.
2. When the coil is not crossing the magnetic field lines, no electric current is induced.
3. As the coil continues to rotate, the magnetic field lines are crossed in a different direction. An electric current is induced in the opposite direction.

Alternating Current

The electric current produced by the generator shown in **Figure 5** changes direction each time the coil makes a half turn. Because the electric current changes direction, it is an alternating current. Generators in power plants also make alternating current. But generators in power plants are very large. They have many coils of wire instead of just one. In most large generators, the magnet is turned instead of the coils.

Generating Electrical Energy

The energy that generators convert into electrical energy comes from different sources. The source in nuclear power plants is thermal energy from a nuclear reaction. The energy boils water into steam. The steam turns a turbine. The turbine turns the magnet of the generator, which induces an electric current and generates electrical energy. Other kinds of power plants burn fuel such as coal or gas to release thermal energy.

Energy from wind can also be used to turn turbines. **Figure 6** shows how the energy of falling water is converted into electrical energy in a hydroelectric power plant.

Reading Check **What are three sources of energy that are used to generate electrical energy?**

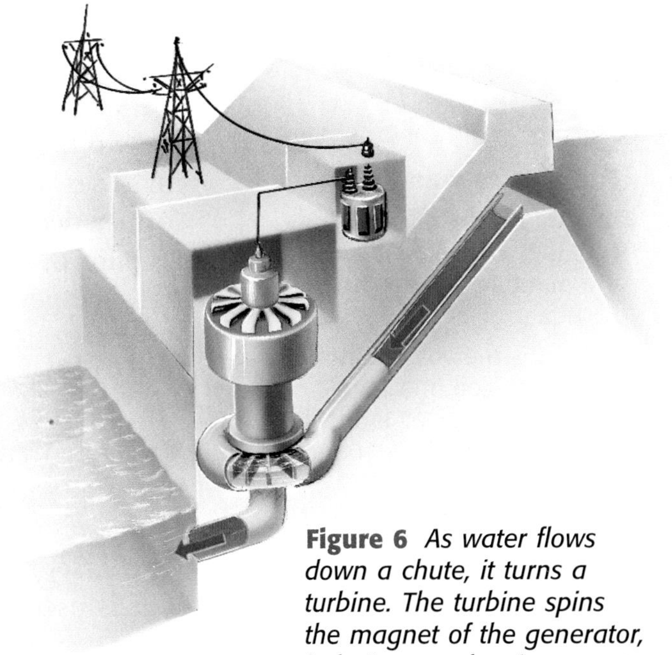

Figure 6 *As water flows down a chute, it turns a turbine. The turbine spins the magnet of the generator, inducing an electric current.*

Figure 7 **How Transformers Change Voltage**

The primary coil of a **step-up transformer** has fewer loops than the secondary coil. So, the voltage of the electric current in the secondary coil is higher than the voltage of the electric current in the primary coil. Therefore, voltage is increased.

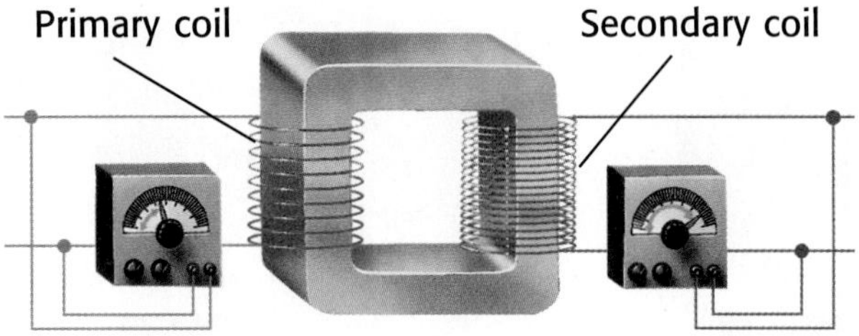

The primary coil of a **step-down transformer** has more loops than the secondary coil. So, the voltage of the electric current in the secondary coil is lower than the voltage of the electric current in the primary coil. Therefore, voltage is decreased.

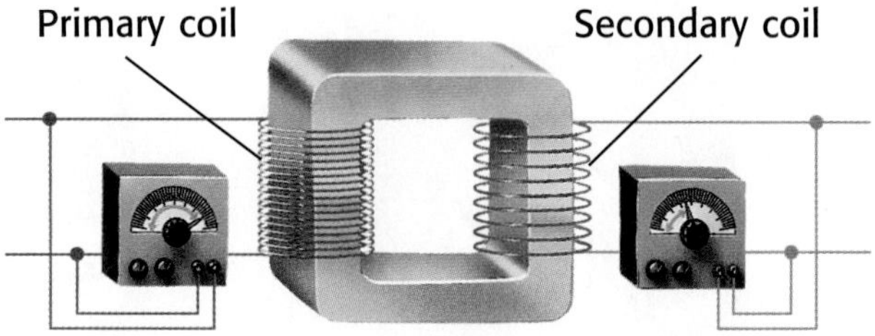

Transformers

transformer a device that increases or decreases the voltage of alternating current

Another device that relies on induction is a transformer. A **transformer** increases or decreases the voltage of alternating current. A simple transformer is made up of two coils of wire wrapped around an iron ring. The primary coil gets alternating current from an electrical energy source. The current makes the ring an electromagnet. But the current in the primary coil is alternating. The magnetic field of the electromagnet changes as the direction of the current changes. The changing magnetic field in the iron ring induces a current in the secondary coil.

✓ *Reading Check* **What does a transformer do?**

Step-Up, Step-Down

The number of loops in the primary and secondary coils of a transformer determines whether it increases or decreases the voltage, as shown in **Figure 7.** A step-up transformer increases voltage and decreases current. A step-down transformer decreases voltage and increases current. However, the amount of energy going into and out of the transformer does not change.

MATH PRACTICE

Transformers and Voltage

In a transformer, for each coil, the voltage divided by the number of loops must be equal.

What is the voltage in the secondary coil of a transformer that has 20 loops if the primary coil has 10 loops and a voltage of 1,200 V?

Electrical Energy for Your Home

The electric current that brings electrical energy to your home is usually transformed three times, as shown in **Figure 8.** At the power plants, the voltage is increased. This decreases power loss that happens as the energy is sent over long distances. Of course, the voltage must be decreased again before the current is used. Two step-down transformers are used before the electric current reaches your house.

Figure 8 **Getting Energy to Your Home**

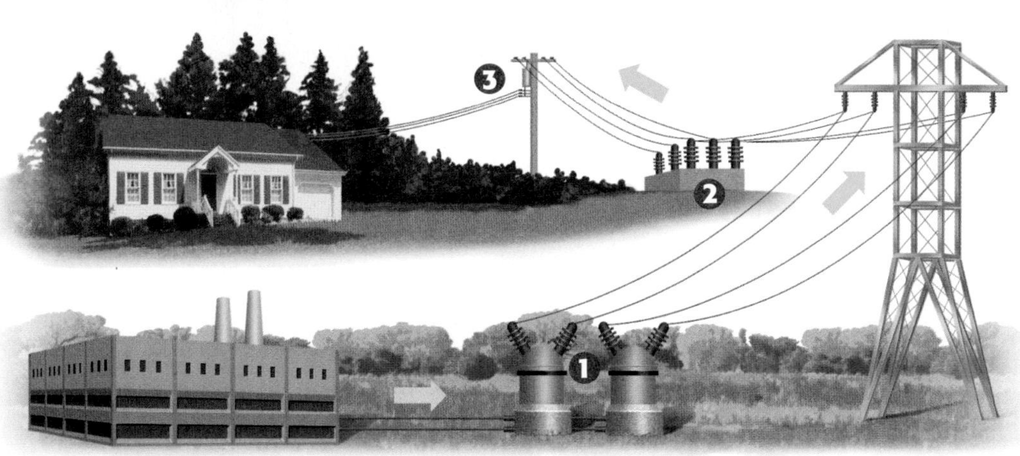

❶ The voltage is stepped up thousands of times at the power plant.

❷ The voltage is stepped down at a local power distribution center.

❸ The voltage is stepped down again at a transformer near your house.

SECTION Review

Summary

- Electromagnetic induction is the process of making an electric current by changing a magnetic field.
- An electric generator converts mechanical energy into electrical energy through electromagnetic induction.
- A step-up transformer increases the voltage of an alternating current. A step-down transformer decreases the voltage.
- The side of a transformer that has the greater number of loops has the higher voltage.

Using Key Terms

For each pair of terms, explain how the meanings of the terms differ.

1. *electric generator* and *transformer*

Understanding Key Ideas

2. Which of the following will induce an electric current in a wire?
   a. moving a magnet into a coil of wire
   b. moving a wire between the poles of a magnet
   c. turning a loop of wire between the poles of a magnet
   d. All of the above
3. How does a generator produce an electric current?
4. Compare a step-up transformer with a step-down transformer based on the number of loops in the primary and secondary coils.

Math Skills

5. A transformer has 500 loops in its primary coil and 5,000 loops in its secondary coil. What is the voltage in the primary coil if the voltage in the secondary coil is 20,000 V?
6. A transformer has 3,000 loops in its primary coil and 1,500 loops in its secondary coil. What is the voltage in the secondary coil if the voltage in the primary coil is 120 V?

Critical Thinking

7. **Analyzing Ideas** One reason that electric power plants do not send out electrical energy as direct current is that direct current cannot be transformed. Explain why not.
8. **Analyzing Processes** Explain why rotating either the coil or the magnet in a generator induces an electric current.

SCILINKS® NSTA
Developed and maintained by the National Science Teachers Association

For a variety of links related to this chapter, go to www.scilinks.org

Topic: Electromagnetic Induction
SciLinks code: HSM0481

Model-Making Lab

Build a DC Motor

Electric motors can be used for many things. Hair dryers, CD players, and even some cars and buses are powered by electric motors. In this lab, you will build a direct current electric motor—the basis for the electric motors you use every day.

OBJECTIVES

Build a model of an electric motor.

Analyze the workings of the parts of a motor.

MATERIALS

- battery, 4.5 V
- cup, plastic-foam
- magnet, disc (4)
- magnet wire, 100 cm
- marker, permanent
- paper clips, large (2)
- sandpaper
- tape
- tube, cardboard
- wire, insulated, with alligator clips, approximately 30 cm long (2)

SAFETY

Procedure

1. To make the armature for the motor, wind the wire around the cardboard tube to make a coil like the one shown below. Wind the ends of the wire around the loops on each side of the coil. Leave about 5 cm of wire free on each end.
2. Hold the coil on its edge. Sand the enamel from only the top half of each end of the wire. This acts like a commutator, except that it blocks the electric current instead of reversing it during half of each rotation.
3. Partially unfold the two paper clips from the middle. Make a hook in one end of each paper clip to hold the coil, as shown below.

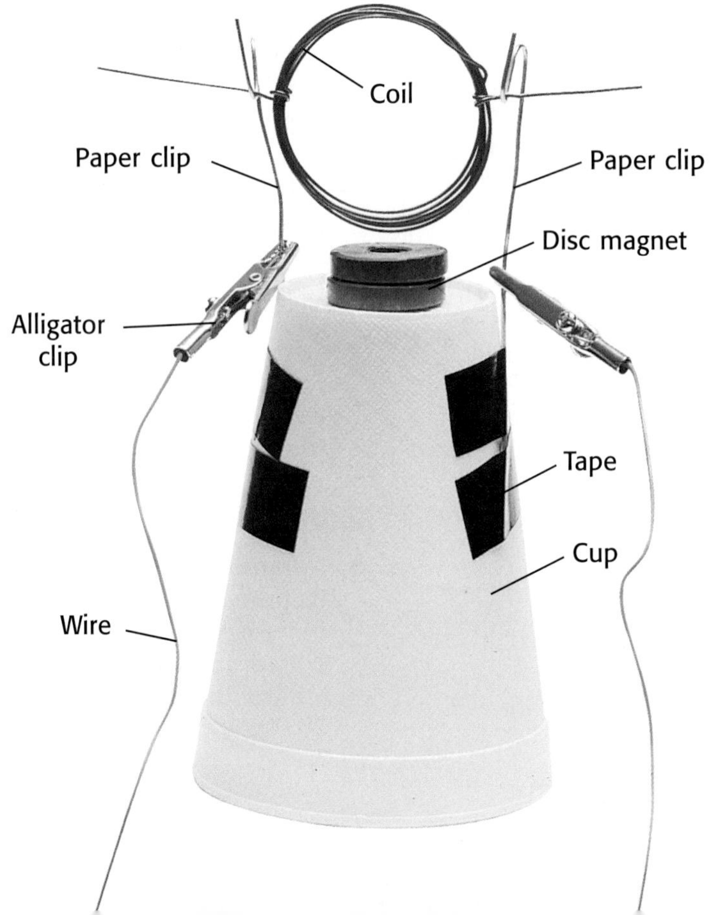

4. Place two disc magnets in the bottom of the cup, and place the other magnets on the outside of the bottom of the cup. The magnets should remain in place when the cup is turned upside down.
5. Tape the paper clips to the sides of the cup. The hooks should be at the same height, and should keep the coil from hitting the magnet.
6. Test your coil. Flick the top of the coil lightly with your finger. The coil should spin freely without wobbling or sliding to one side.
7. Make adjustments to the ends of the wire and the hooks until your coil spins freely.
8. Use the alligator clips to attach one wire to each paper clip.
9. Attach the free end of one wire to one terminal of the battery.
10. Connect the free end of the other wire to the second battery terminal, and give your coil a gentle spin. Record your observations.

11. Stop the coil, and give it a gentle spin in the opposite direction. Record your observations.
12. If the coil does not keep spinning, check the ends of the wire. Bare wire should touch the paper clips during half of the spin, and only enamel should touch the paper clips for the other half of the spin.
13. If you removed too much enamel, color half of the wire with a permanent marker.
14. Switch the connections to the battery, and repeat steps 10 and 11.

Analyze the Results

1. **Describing Events** Did your motor always spin in the direction you started it? Explain.
2. **Explaining Events** Why was the motor affected by switching the battery connections?
3. **Explaining Events** Some electric cars run on solar power. Which part of your model would be replaced by the solar panels?

Draw Conclusions

4. **Drawing Conclusions** Some people claim that electric-powered cars produce less pollution than gasoline-powered cars do. Why might this be true?
5. **Evaluating Models** List some reasons that electric cars are not ideal.
6. **Applying Conclusions** How could your model be used to help design a hair dryer?
7. **Applying Conclusions** Make a list of at least three other items that could be powered by an electric motor like the one you built.

Chapter Review

USING KEY TERMS

Complete each of the following sentences by choosing the correct term from the word bank.

electric motor, transformer, magnetic force, electric generator, magnetic pole, electromagnetism, electromagnetic induction

1. Each end of a bar magnet is a(n) ___.
2. A(n) ___ converts mechanical energy into electrical energy.
3. ___ occurs when an electric current is made by a changing magnetic field.
4. The relationship between electricity and magnetism is called ___.

UNDERSTANDING KEY IDEAS

Multiple Choice

5. In the region around a magnet in which magnetic forces act exists the
   - **a.** magnetic field.
   - **b.** domain.
   - **c.** pole.
   - **d.** solenoid.
6. An electric fan has an electric motor inside to change
   - **a.** mechanical energy into electrical energy.
   - **b.** thermal energy into electrical energy.
   - **c.** electrical energy into thermal energy.
   - **d.** electrical energy into mechanical energy.
7. The marked end of a compass needle always points directly to
   - **a.** Earth's geographic South Pole.
   - **b.** Earth's geographic North Pole.
   - **c.** a magnet's south pole.
   - **d.** a magnet's north pole.
8. A device that increases the voltage of an alternating current is called a(n)
   - **a.** electric motor.
   - **b.** galvanometer.
   - **c.** step-up transformer.
   - **d.** step-down transformer.
9. The magnetic field of a solenoid can be increased by
   - **a.** adding more loops per meter.
   - **b.** increasing the current.
   - **c.** putting an iron core inside the coil to make an electromagnet.
   - **d.** All of the above
10. What do you end up with if you cut a magnet in half?
    - **a.** one north-pole piece and one south-pole piece
    - **b.** two unmagnetized pieces
    - **c.** two pieces each with a north pole and a south pole
    - **d.** two north-pole pieces

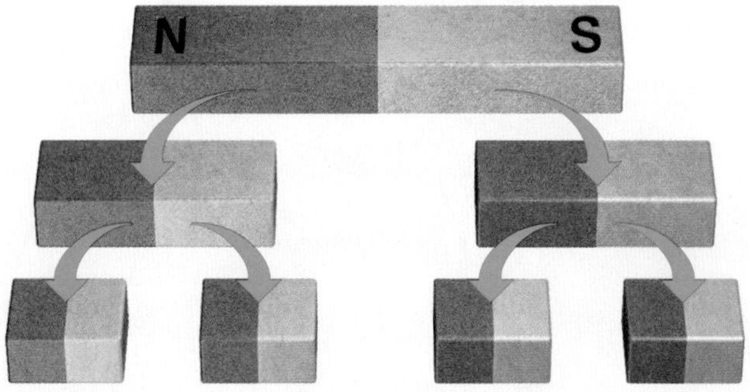

Short Answer

11. Explain why auroras are seen mostly near the North Pole and South Pole.

12. Compare the function of an electric generator with the function of an electric motor.

13. Explain why some pieces of iron are more magnetic than others are.

Math Skills

14. A step-up transformer increases voltage 20 times. If the voltage of the primary coil is 1,200 V, what is the voltage of the secondary coil?

CRITICAL THINKING

15. **Concept Mapping** Use the following terms to create a concept map: *electromagnetism, electricity, magnetism, electromagnetic induction, generators,* and *transformers.*

16. **Applying Concepts** You win a hand-powered flashlight as a prize in your school science fair. The flashlight has a clear plastic case, so you can look inside to see how it works. When you press the handle, a gray ring spins between two coils of wire. The ends of the wire are connected to the light bulb. So, when you press the handle, the light bulb glows. Explain how an electric current is produced to light the bulb. (Hint: Paper clips are attracted to the gray ring.)

17. **Identifying Relationships** Closed fire doors can slow the spread of fire between rooms. In some buildings, electromagnets controlled by the building's fire-alarm system hold the fire doors open. If a fire is detected, the doors automatically shut. Explain why electromagnets are used instead of permanent magnets.

INTERPRETING GRAPHICS

18. Look at the solenoids and electromagnets shown below. Identify which of them has the strongest magnetic field and which has the weakest magnetic field. Explain your reasoning.

a
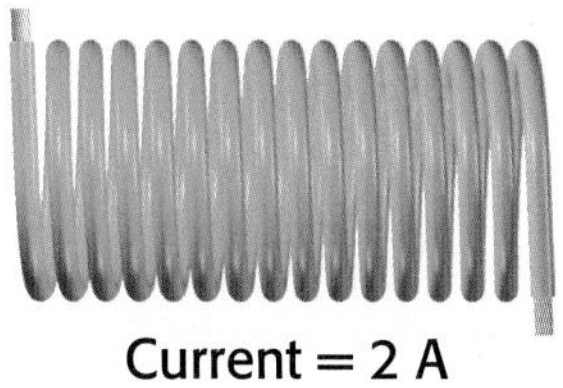
Current = 2 A

b
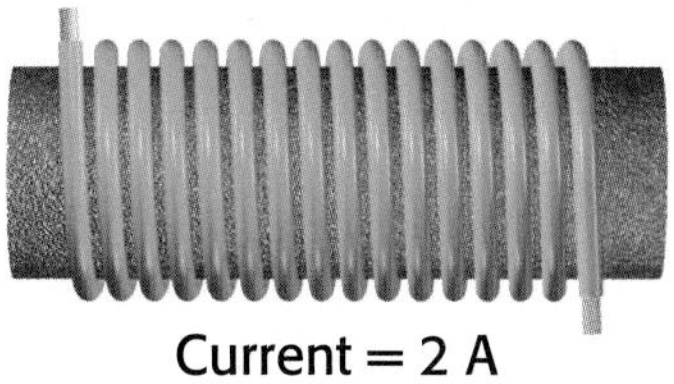
Current = 2 A

c
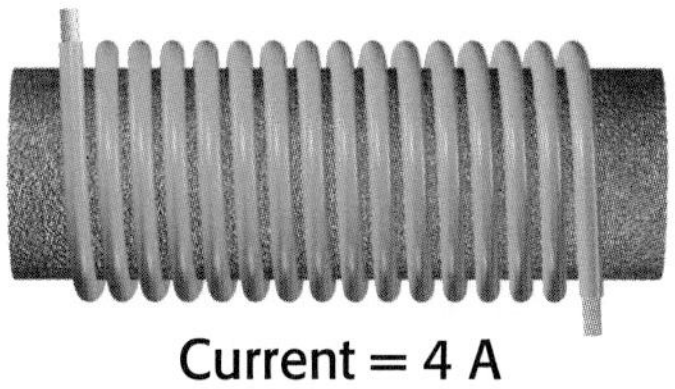
Current = 4 A

d
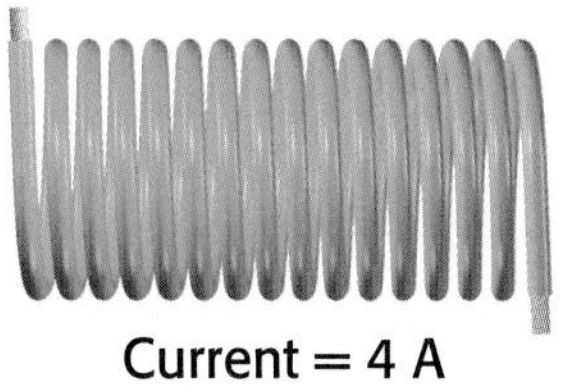
Current = 4 A

Multiple Choice

1. Putting two north poles or two south poles of two magnets together makes the magnets push each other apart. Putting a north pole with a south pole makes the magnets stick together. For which of the following could the magnets serve as a simple model?

A. parallel circuit

B. voltage

C. law of electric charges

D. potential difference

Use the diagram below to answer question 2.

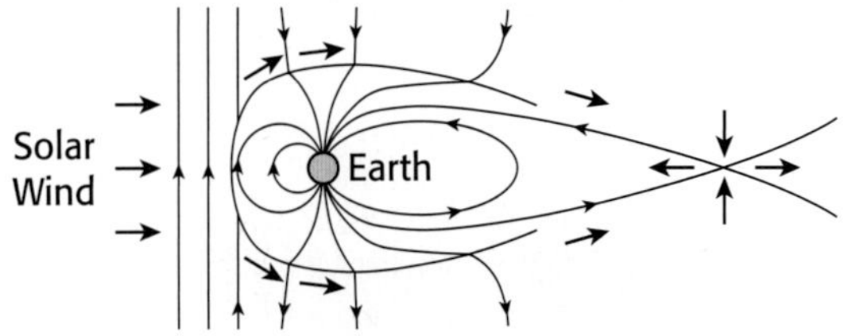

Solar Wind Around Earth

2. Charged particles in solar wind bombard Earth constantly. The image above shows how the paths of these charged particles are bent as they approach Earth. What causes the charged particles in the solar wind to change course as they approach Earth?

A. Earth's gravity

B. Earth's radiation

C. Earth's electric field

D. Earth's magnetic field

3. Which powerline would most likely have the highest voltage?

A. The one supplying a residential area.

B. The one near a power distribution center.

C. The one near a power plant.

D. The one along a highway.

4. A junkyard electromagnet is strong enough to pick up cars, but not trucks. How could it be upgraded to lift larger vehicles?

A. The electric current and the number of coils in the solenoid could be increased.

B. The electric current could be increased and the number of coils in the solenoid decreased.

C. The electric current and the number of coils in the solenoid could be decreased.

D. The electric current could be decreased and the number of coils in the solenoid increased.

5. How could engineers remodeling a hydroelectric plant increase power output from the plant without replacing its magnet?

A. increase the current flowing to the magnet and the turbine.

B. increase the height of the dam so that water will flow faster.

C. add more electrical wires coming from the generator.

D. heat the water before it enters the generator.

6. **Electric outlets in the United States provide 120 volts of alternating current, while those in England provide 230 volts. What device is needed to run an American hair dryer in a British hotel?**

   A. galvanometer

   B. step-up transformer

   C. commutator

   D. step-down transformer

Use the following description to answer questions 7–8.

John created a device to power his television made out of a stationary bike, a thick rubber band, a magnet, a coil, and wire.

7. **What kind of device did John create?**

   A. electric motor

   B. electric generator

   C. electromagnet

   D. solenoid

8. **Which form of energy was converted from electrical energy?**

   A. thermal energy

   B. mechanical energy

   C. light energy

   D. chemical energy

Use the table below to answer question 9.

Power Lines	Voltage
Line A	24,000 V
Line B	12,750 V
Line C	7,200 V
Line D	4,000 V

9. **The table shows typical voltages carried by power lines. A distribution station has a transformer that uses 3 loops of wire for every volt. The transformer's primary coil contains 38,250 loops. Its secondary coil contains 21,600 loops. Where is the station located?**

   A. between lines A and B

   B. between lines B and C

   C. between lines C and D

   D. between lines B and D

Open Response

10. **Elise tells her friends that the Earth is like a giant bar magnet. Is she right? Explain your answer.**

11. **Draw and label a simple device that could induce an electric current. Describe how your device could produce an alternating current.**

Science in Action

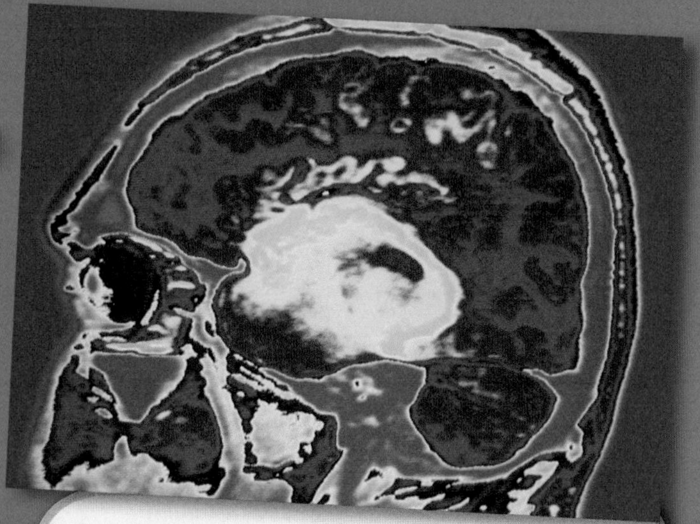

Weird Science

Geomagnetic Storms

On March 13, 1989, a geomagnetic storm hit Montreal, Quebec. It caused an electrical blackout that left about 6 million people without electricity for nine hours.

A geomagnetic storm occurs when gusts of solar wind smash into Earth's magnetic field. Powerful eruptions from the sun, called coronal mass ejections (CME), happen periodically, sending charged particles outward at high speeds. Solar winds usually travel between 300 km/s and 600 km/s. But the gusts of solar wind from a CME can travel as fast as 2,000 km/s.

Math ACTIVITY

Earth is approximately 150,000,000 km from the sun. Calculate how long it takes a solar wind that travels at 500 km/s to reach Earth from the sun.

Science, Technology, and Society

Magnets in Medicine

Like X rays, magnetic resonance imaging (MRI) creates pictures of a person's internal organs and skeleton. But MRI produces clearer pictures than X rays do, and MRI does not expose the body to the potentially harmful radiation of X rays. Instead, MRI uses powerful electromagnets and radio waves to create images. MRI allows doctors to find small tumors, see subtle changes in the brain, locate blockages in blood vessels, and observe damage to the spinal cord.

Language Arts ACTIVITY

WRITING SKILL Write a two-page story about a student who undergoes an MRI scan. In your story, include the reason he or she must have the scan, a description of the procedure, and the information the doctor can determine by looking at the scan.

People in Science

James Clerk Maxwell

Magnetic Math James Clerk Maxwell was a Scottish mathematician who lived in the 1800s. Maxwell's research led to advances in electromagnetism and in many other areas of science. He proposed that light is an electromagnetic wave—a wave that consists of electric and magnetic fields that vibrate at right angles to each other. His work on electromagnetic fields provided the foundation for Einstein's theory of relativity.

After college, Maxwell decided to study the work of Michael Faraday. Many physicists of the time thought that Faraday's work was not scientific enough. Faraday described his experiments but did not try to apply any scientific or mathematical theory to the results. Maxwell felt that this was a strength. He decided not to read any of the mathematical descriptions of electricity and magnetism until he had read all of Faraday's work. The first paper Maxwell wrote about electricity, called "On Faraday's Lines of Force," brought Faraday's experimental results together with a mathematical analysis of the magnetic field surrounding a current. This paper described a few simple mathematical equations that could be used to describe the interactions between electric and magnetic fields. Maxwell continued to work with Faraday's results and to publish papers that gave scientific explanations of some of Faraday's most exciting observations.

Social Studies ACTIVITY

Study the life of James Clerk Maxwell. Make a timeline that shows major events in his life. Include three or four historic events that happened during his lifetime.

go.hrw.com

To learn more about these Science in Action topics, visit go.hrw.com and type in the keyword HP5EMGF.

Current Science

Check out Current Science® articles related to this chapter by visiting go.hrw.com. Just type in the keyword HP5CS18.

9

Electronic Technology

The Big Idea

Electronic technology uses electrical energy to store and handle information.

SECTION

About the Photo

Can you read the expression on Kismet's face? This robot's expression can be sad, happy, angry, interested, surprised, disgusted, or just plain calm. Kismet was developed by MIT researchers to interact with humans. Electronic devices in cameras, motors, and computers allow Kismet to change its expression as it responds to its surroundings.

PRE-READING ACTIVITY

FOLDNOTES **Booklet** Before you read the chapter, create the FoldNote entitled "Booklet" described in the **Study Skills** section of the Appendix. Label each page of the booklet with a main idea from the chapter. As you read the chapter, write what you learn about each main idea on the appropriate page of the booklet.

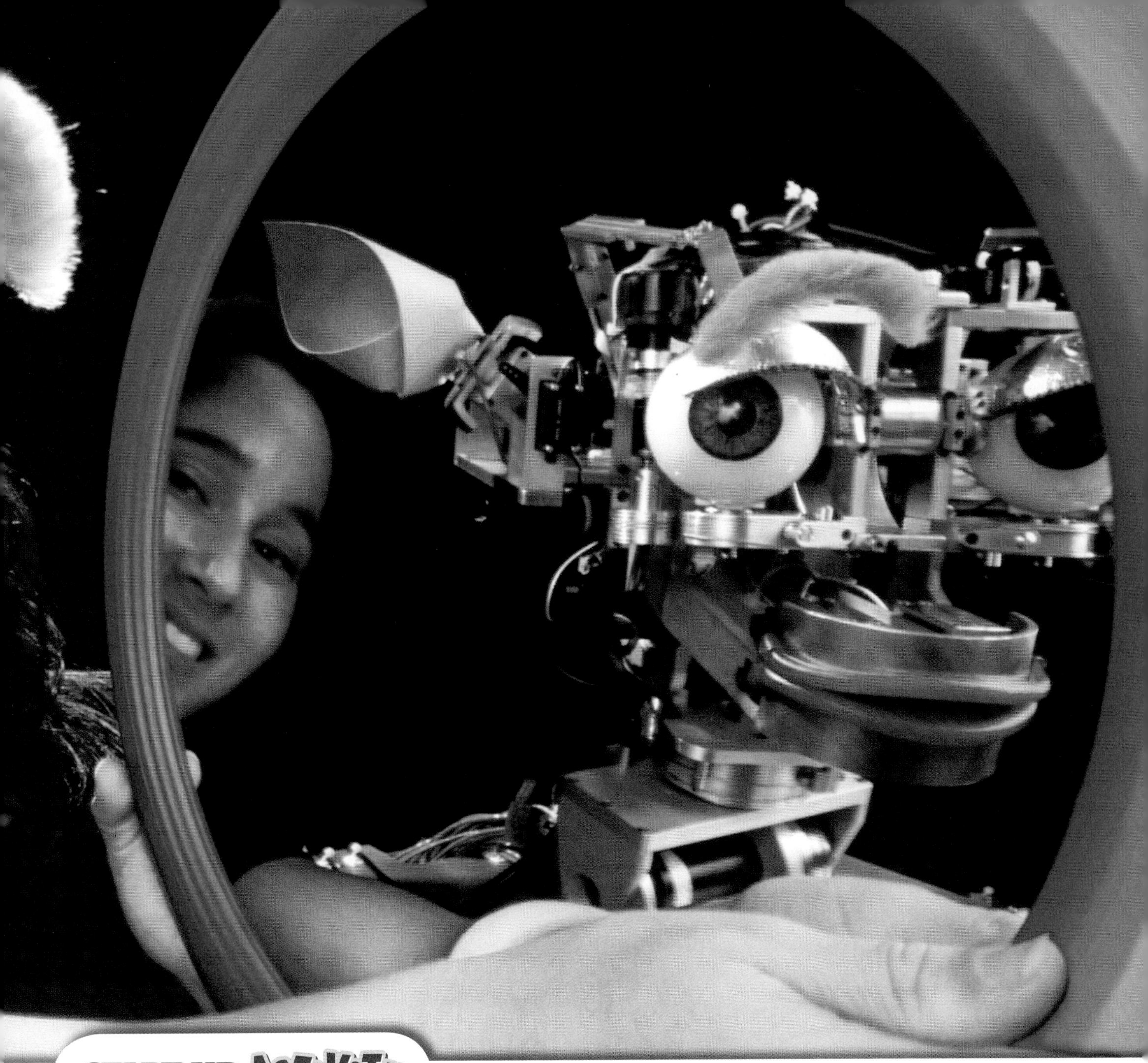

START-UP ACTIVITY

Talking Long Distance

In this activity, you'll build a model of a telephone.

Procedure

1. Thread one end of a **piece of string** through the hole in the bottom of one **empty food can.**
2. Tie a knot in the end of the string inside the can. The knot should be large enough to keep the string in place. The rest of the string should come out of the bottom of the can.
3. Repeat steps 1 and 2 with **another can** and the other end of the string.
4. Hold one can, and have a classmate hold the other. Walk away from each other until the string is fairly taut.
5. Speak into your can while your classmate holds the other can at his or her ear. Switch roles.

Analysis

1. Describe what you heard.
2. Compare your model with a real telephone.
3. How are signals sent back and forth along the string?
4. Why do you think it was important to pull the string taut?

SECTION 1

Electronic Devices

Electronic devices use electrical energy. But they do not use electrical energy in the same way that machines do.

What You Will Learn

- Identify the role of a circuit board in an electronic device.
- Describe semiconductors and how their conductivity can be changed.
- Describe diodes and how they are used in circuits.
- Describe transistors and how they are used in circuits.
- Explain how integrated circuits have influenced electronic technology.

Vocabulary

circuit board
semiconductor
doping
diode
transistor
integrated circuit

READING STRATEGY

Reading Organizer As you read this section, make a concept map by using the terms above.

Some machines can change electrical energy into other forms of energy in order to do work. Electronic devices use it to handle information.

Inside an Electronic Device

For example, a remote control sends information to a television. **Figure 1** shows the inside of a remote control. The large green board is a circuit board. A **circuit board** is a collection of many circuit parts on a sheet of insulating material. A circuit board connects the parts of the circuit to supply electric current and send signals to the parts of an electronic device.

circuit board a sheet of insulating material that carries circuit elements and that is inserted in an electronic device

Sending Information to Your Television

To change the channel or volume on the television, you push buttons on the remote control. When you push a button, you send a signal to the circuit board. The components of the circuit board process the signal to send the correct information to the television. The information is sent to the television in the form of infrared light by a tiny bulb called a *light-emitting diode* (DIE OHD), or LED. In this section, you'll learn about diodes and other components and learn about how they work.

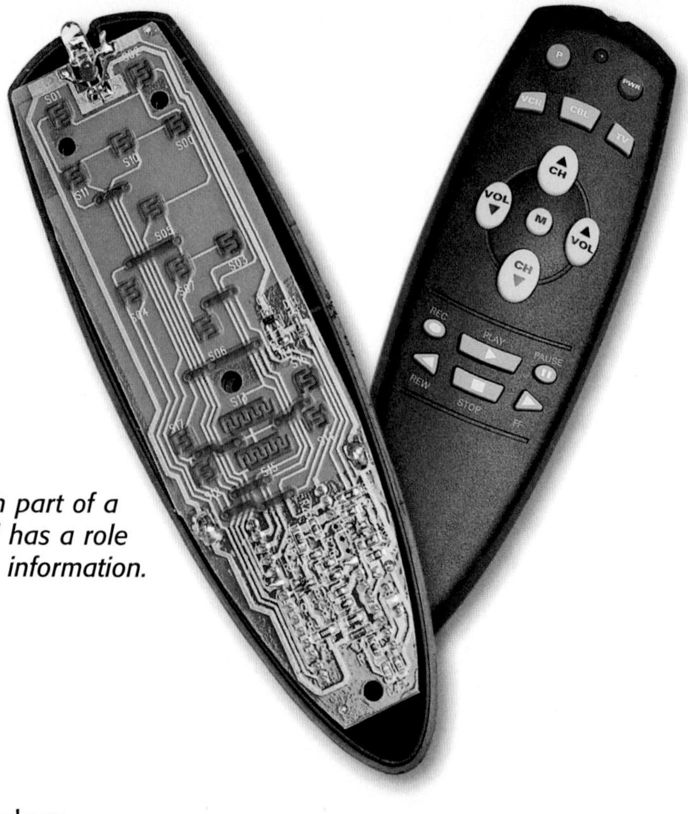

Figure 1 *Each part of a remote control has a role in transmitting information.*

Semiconductors

Semiconductors (SEM i kuhn DUHK tuhrz) are used in many electronic components. A **semiconductor** is a substance that conducts an electric current better than an insulator does but not as well as a conductor does. Semiconductors have allowed people to make incredible advances in electronic technology.

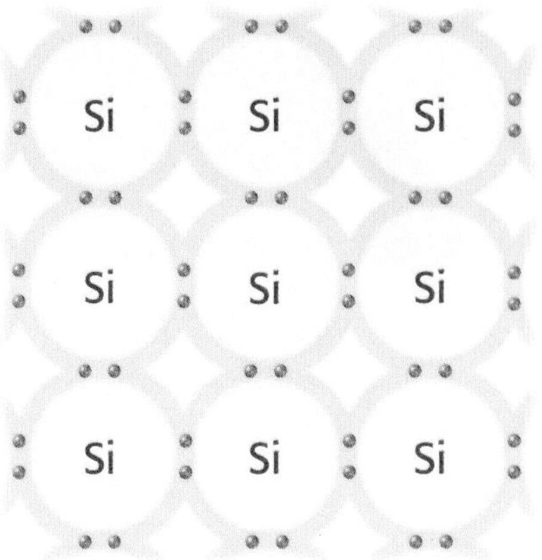

Figure 2 Each silicon atom shares its four valence electrons with other silicon atoms.

How Do Semiconductors Work?

The way a semiconductor conducts electric current is based on how its electrons are arranged. Silicon, Si, is a widely used semiconductor. As shown in **Figure 2,** when silicon atoms bond, they share all of their valence electrons. There are no electrons free to make much electric current. So, why are semiconductors such as silicon used? They are used because their conductivity can be changed.

Doping

You can change the conductivity of a semiconductor through doping (DOHP eeng). **Doping** is the addition of an impurity to a semiconductor. Adding the impurity changes the arrangement of electrons. A few atoms of the semiconductor are replaced with a few atoms of another element that has a different number of electrons, as shown in **Figure 3.**

semiconductor an element or compound that conducts electric current better than an insulator does but not as well as a conductor does

doping the addition of an impurity element to a semiconductor

Reading Check What is the result of doping a semiconductor? *(See the Appendix for answers to Reading Checks.)*

Figure 3 Types of Doped Semiconductors

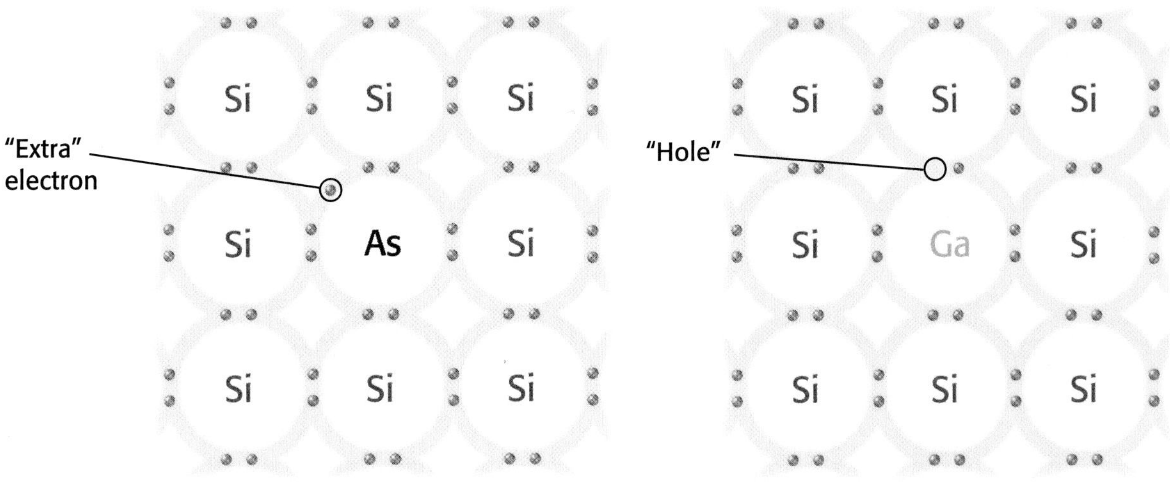

N-Type Semiconductor An atom of arsenic, As, has five electrons in its outermost energy level. Replacing a silicon atom with an arsenic atom results in an "extra" electron.

P-Type Semiconductor An atom of gallium, Ga, has three electrons in its outermost energy level. Replacing a silicon atom with a gallium atom results in a "hole" where an electron could be.

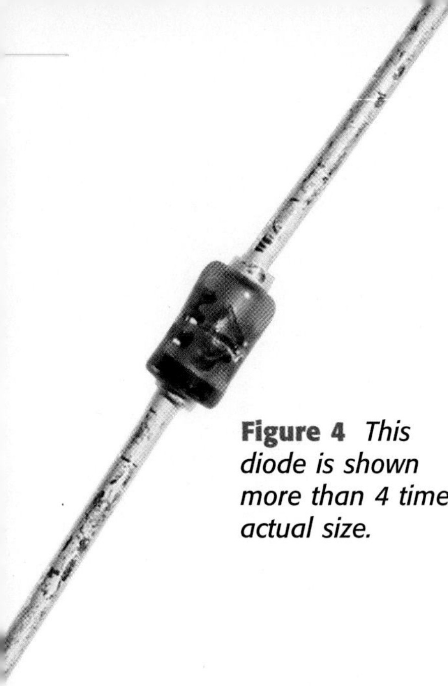

Figure 4 *This diode is shown more than 4 times actual size.*

Diodes

Layers of semiconductors can be put together like sandwiches to make electronic components. Joining an n-type semiconductor with a p-type semiconductor forms a diode. A **diode** is an electronic component that allows electric charge to move mainly in one direction. Look at **Figure 4.** Each wire joins to one of the layers in the diode.

diode an electronic device that allows electric charge to move more easily in one direction than in the other

The Flow of Electrons in Diodes

Where the two layers in a diode meet, some "extra" electrons move from the n-type layer to fill some "holes" in the p-type layer. This change gives the n-type layer a positive charge and the p-type layer a negative charge. If a diode is connected to a source of electrical energy, such as a battery, so that the positive terminal is closer to the p-type layer, a current is made. If the connections are switched so that the negative terminal is closer to the p-type layer, there is no current. **Figure 5** shows how a diode works.

Using Diodes to Change AC to DC

Power plants send electrical energy to homes by means of alternating current (AC). But many things, such as radios, use direct current (DC). Diodes can help change AC to DC. Alternating current switches direction many times each second. The diodes in an AC adapter block the current in one direction. Other components average the current in the direction that remains. As a result, AC is changed to DC.

Reading Check **Why can a diode change AC to DC?**

Figure 5 **How a Diode Works**

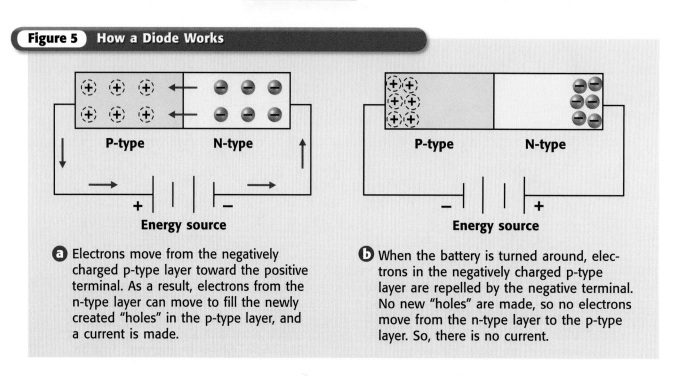

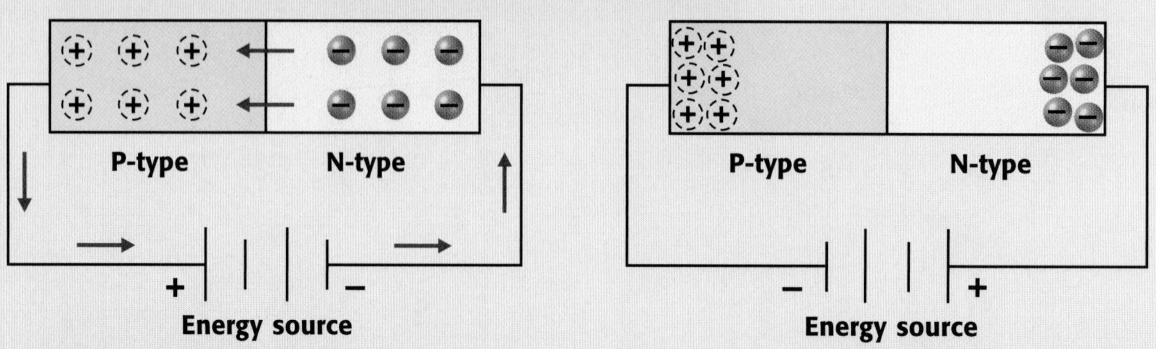

a Electrons move from the negatively charged p-type layer toward the positive terminal. As a result, electrons from the n-type layer can move to fill the newly created "holes" in the p-type layer, and a current is made.

b When the battery is turned around, electrons in the negatively charged p-type layer are repelled by the negative terminal. No new "holes" are made, so no electrons move from the n-type layer to the p-type layer. So, there is no current.

Transistors

What do you get when you sandwich three layers of semiconductors together? You get a transistor! A **transistor** is an electronic component that amplifies, or increases, current. It can be used in many circuits, including an amplifier and a switch. Transistors can be NPN or PNP transistors. An NPN transistor has a p-type layer between two n-type layers. A PNP transistor has an n-type layer between two p-type layers. Look at **Figure 6.** Each wire joins to one of the layers in the transistor.

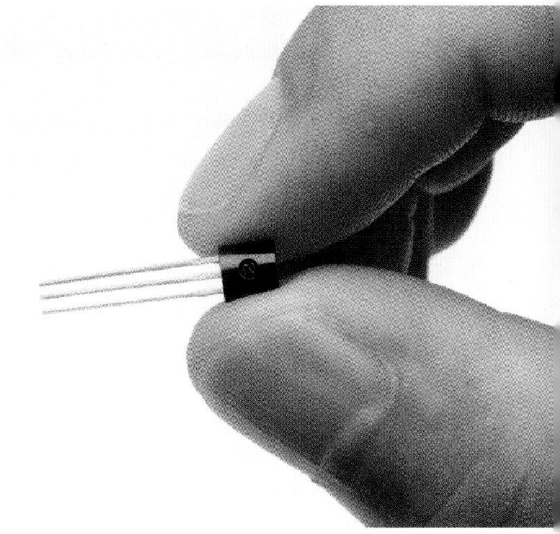

Figure 6 *This transistor is smaller than a pencil eraser!*

Reading Check **Name two kinds of transistors made from semiconductors.**

Transistors as Amplifiers

A microphone does not make a current that is large enough to run a loudspeaker. But a transistor can be used in an amplifier to make a larger current. Look at **Figure 7.** In the circuit, there is a small electric current in the microphone. This current triggers the transistor to allow a larger current in the loudspeaker. The electric current can be larger because of a large source of electrical energy in the loudspeaker side of the circuit.

transistor a semiconductor device that can amplify current and that is used in amplifiers, oscillators, and switches

Figure 7 **A Transistor as an Amplifier**

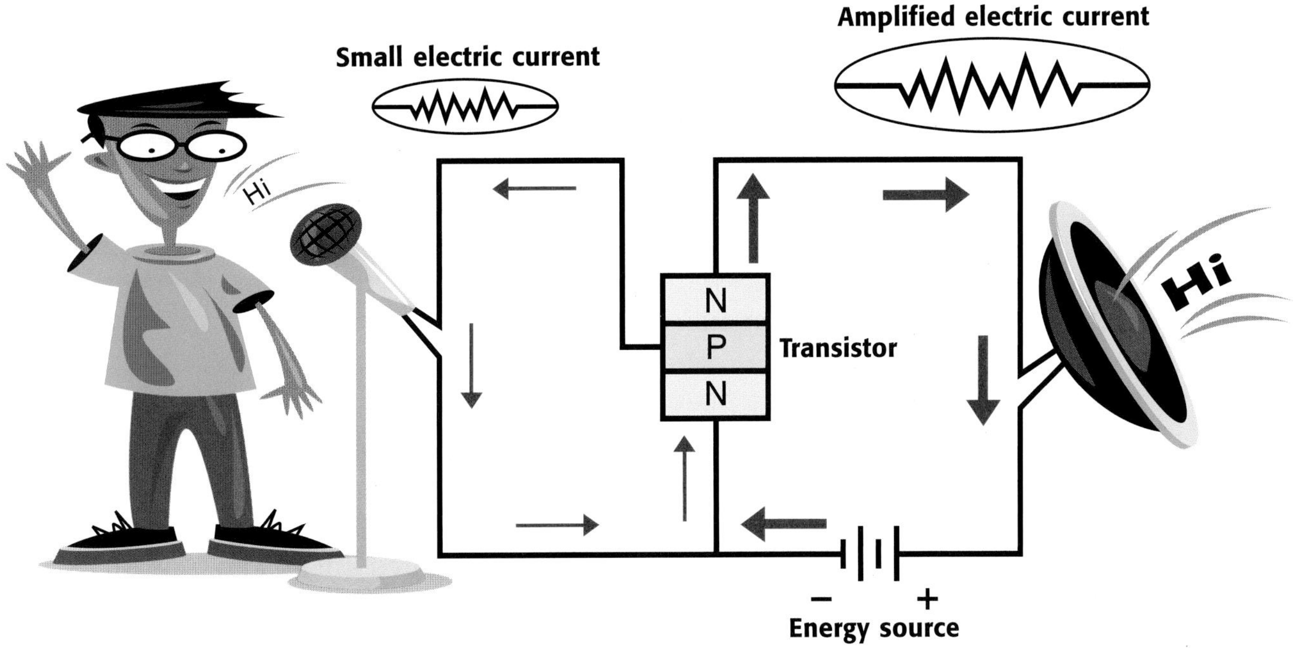

1. Sound waves from your voice enter the microphone. As a result, a small electric current is made in the microphone side of the circuit.
2. A transistor allows the small electric current to control a larger electric current that operates the loudspeaker.
3. The current in the loudspeaker is larger than the current produced by the microphone. Otherwise, the two currents are identical.

Figure 8 A Transistor as a Switch

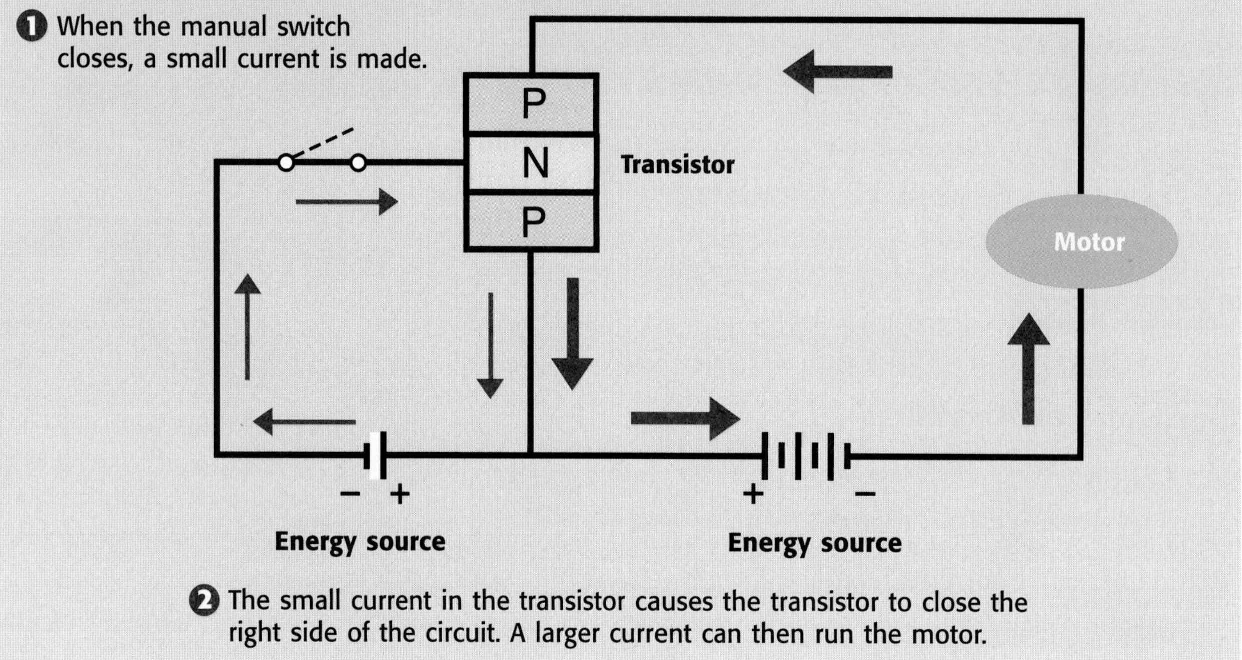

1 When the manual switch closes, a small current is made.
P
N
P
Transistor
Motor
− +
+ −
Energy source
Energy source
2 The small current in the transistor causes the transistor to close the right side of the circuit. A larger current can then run the motor.

Transistors in Switches

Remote-controlled toy cars use transistors in switches. Look at **Figure 8.** When the manual switch in the circuit is closed, a small current is made in the small loop. The small current causes the transistor to close the large loop on the right. As a result, a larger current is made in the large loop. The larger current runs the motor. You switch on a small current. The transistor switches on a larger current. If the manual switch is opened, the circuit is broken. As a result, the transistor will switch off the current that runs the motor. Computers also rely on transistors that work in switches.

integrated circuit a circuit whose components are formed on a single semiconductor

Integrated Circuits

An **integrated circuit** (IN tuh GRAYT id SUHR kit) is an entire circuit that has many components on a single semiconductor. The parts of the circuit are made by carefully doping certain spots. Look at **Figure 9.** Integrated circuits and circuit boards have helped shrink electronic devices. Many complete circuits can fit into one integrated circuit. So, complicated electronic systems can be made very small. Because the circuits are so small, the electric charges moving through them do not have to travel very far. Devices that use integrated circuits can run at very high speeds.

74HCT32N
B8809PS
Hnn9835
C

Figure 9 *This integrated circuit contains many electronic components, yet its dimensions are only about 1 cm × 3 cm!*

✓ *Reading Check* **Describe two benefits of using integrated circuits in electronic devices.**

Smaller and Smarter Devices

Before transistors and semiconductor diodes were made, vacuum tubes, like the one in **Figure 10,** were used. Vacuum tubes can amplify electric current and change AC to DC. But vacuum tubes are much larger than semiconductor components are. They also get hotter and don't last as long. Early radios had to be large. Space was needed to hold the vacuum tubes and to keep them from overheating. Modern radios are very small. They use transistors and integrated circuits. And your radio might have other features, such as a clock or a CD player. But even more importantly than waking you up to your favorite music, integrated circuits have changed the world through their use in computers.

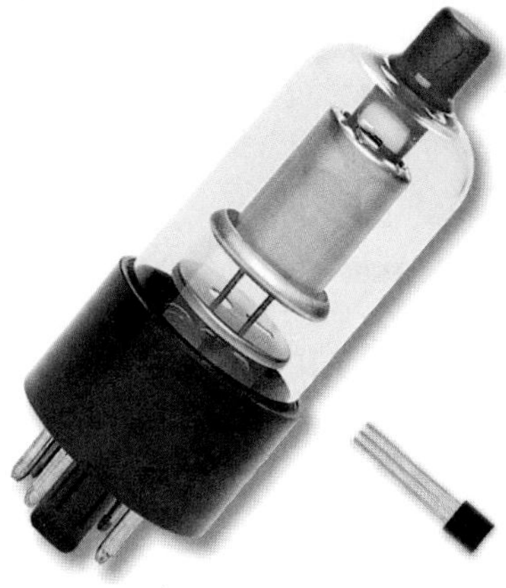

Figure 10 *Vacuum tubes are much larger than the transistors used today. So, radios that used the tubes were very large also.*

SECTION Review

Summary

- Circuit boards contain circuits that supply current to different parts of electronic devices.
- Semiconductors are often used in electronic devices because their conductivity can be changed by doping.
- Diodes allow current in one direction and can change AC to DC.
- Transistors are used in amplifiers and switches.
- Integrated circuits have made smaller, smarter electronic devices possible.

Using Key Terms

For each pair of terms, explain how the meanings of the terms differ.

1. *circuit board* and *integrated circuit*
2. *semiconductor* and *doping*
3. *diode* and *transistor*

Understanding Key Ideas

4. Which element forms the basis for semiconductors?
   a. oxygen
   b. gallium
   c. arsenic
   d. silicon
5. Describe how p-type and n-type semiconductors are made.
6. Explain how a diode changes AC to DC.
7. What are two purposes transistors serve?

Math Skills

8. An integrated circuit that was made in 1974 contained 6,000 transistors. An integrated circuit that was made in 2000 contained 42,000,000 transistors. How many times more transistors did the circuit made in 2000 have?

Critical Thinking

9. **Making Comparisons** How might an electronic system that uses vacuum tubes be different from one that uses integrated circuits?
10. **Applying Concepts** Would modern computers be possible without integrated circuits? Explain.

Interpreting Graphics

11. The graph below represents electric current in a series circuit. Does the circuit contain a diode? Explain your reasoning.

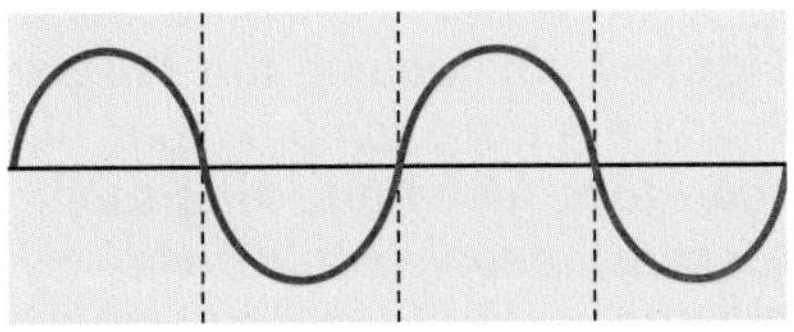

SECTION 2

Communication Technology

What electronic devices do you use to send or receive information? Your answer might include telephones, radios, or televisions.

In this section, you'll study these and other electronic devices that are used for communication. You'll also learn about two kinds of signals used to send and store information.

What You Will Learn

- Identify how signals transmit information.
- Describe analog signals and their use in telephones and records.
- Describe digital signals and their use in compact discs.
- Describe how information is transmitted and received in radios and televisions.

Vocabulary

analog signal
digital signal

READING STRATEGY

Discussion Read this section silently. Write down questions that you have about this section. Discuss your questions in a small group.

Communicating with Signals

One of the first electronic communication devices was the telegraph. It was invented in the 1830s. It used an electric current to send messages between places joined by wires. People sent messages in Morse code through the wires. **Table 1** shows the patterns of dots and dashes that stand for each letter and number in Morse code. The message was sent by tapping a telegraph key, like the one in **Figure 1.** This tapping closed a circuit, causing "clicks" at the receiving end of the telegraph.

Signals and Carriers

Electronic communication devices, including the telegraph, send information by using signals. A *signal* is anything, such as a movement, a sound, or a set of numbers and letters, that can be used to send information. Often, one signal is sent using another signal called a *carrier*. Electric current is the carrier of the signals made by tapping a telegraph key. Two kinds of signals are analog signals and digital signals.

Table 1 International Morse Code

A	•-	G	--•	Q	--•-	1	•----
B	-•••	H	••••	R	•-•	2	••---
C	-•-•	I	••	S	•••	3	•••--
D	-••	J	•---	T	-	4	••••-
E	•	K	-•-	U	••-	5	•••••
F	••-•	L	•-••	V	•••-	6	-••••
		M	--	W	•--	7	--•••
		N	-•	X	-••-	8	---••
		O	---	Y	-•--	9	----•
		P	•--•	Z	--••	0	-----

Figure 1 *By tapping this telegraph key in the right combinations of short taps (dots) and long taps (dashes), people could send messages over long distances.*

Analog Signals

An **analog signal** (AN uh LAWG SIG nuhl) is a signal whose properties change without a break or jump between values. Think of a dimmer switch on a light. You can continuously change the brightness of the light using the dimmer switch.

The changes in an analog signal are based on changes in the original information. For example, when you talk on the phone, the sound of your voice is changed into changing electric current in the form of a wave. This wave is an analog signal that is similar to the original sound wave. But remember that sound waves do not travel down your phone line!

Reading Check **What is an analog signal?** (*See the Appendix for answers to Reading Checks.*)

Talking on the Phone

Look at the telephone in **Figure 2.** You talk into the transmitter. You listen to the receiver. The transmitter changes the sound waves made when you speak into an analog signal. This signal moves through phone wires to the receiver of another phone. The receiver changes the analog signal back into the sound of your voice. Sometimes, the analog signals are changed to digital signals and back again before they reach the other person. You will learn about digital signals later in this section.

analog signal a signal whose properties can change continuously in a given range

CONNECTION TO Geology

Seismograms A *seismograph* is a device used by scientists to record waves made by earthquakes. It makes a *seismogram*—wavy lines on paper that record ground movement. Draw an example of a seismogram that shows changes in the wave, and explain why this is an example of an analog signal.

ACTIVITY

Figure 2 **How a Telephone Works**

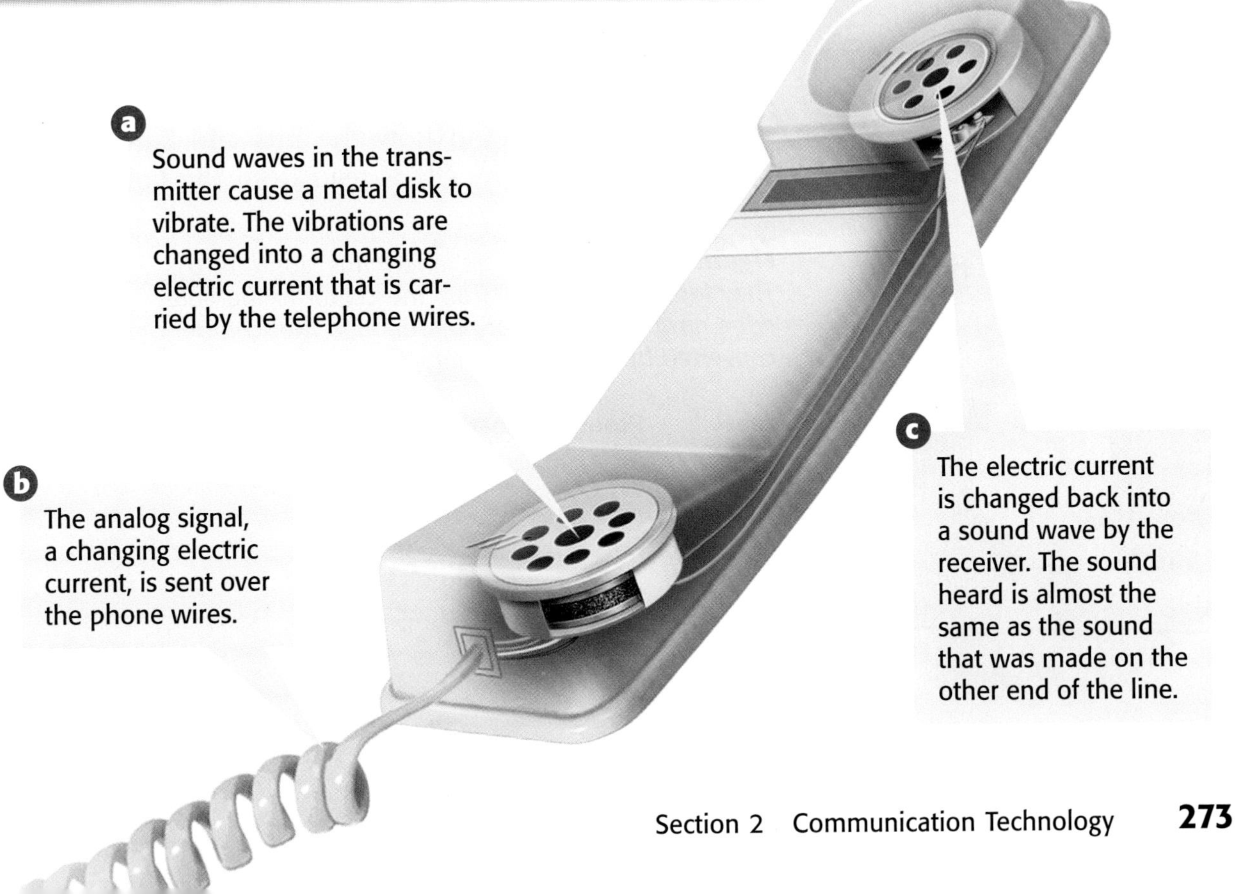

a
Sound waves in the transmitter cause a metal disk to vibrate. The vibrations are changed into a changing electric current that is carried by the telephone wires.
b
The analog signal, a changing electric current, is sent over the phone wires.
c
The electric current is changed back into a sound wave by the receiver. The sound heard is almost the same as the sound that was made on the other end of the line.

Analog Recording

If you want to save a sound, you can store an analog signal of the sound wave. In vinyl records, the signal is made into grooves on a plastic disk. The sound's properties are represented by the number and depth of the contours in the disk.

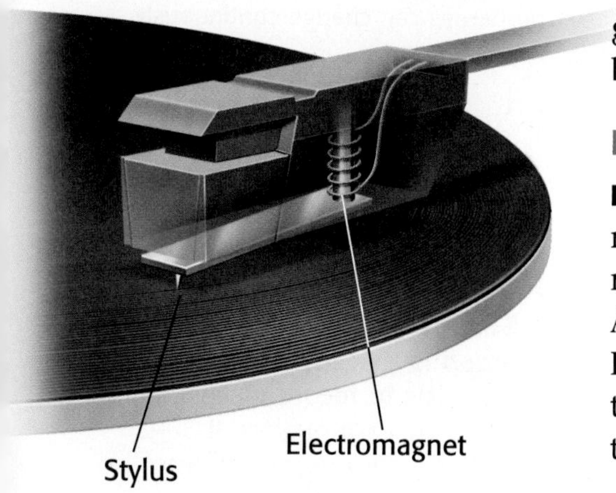

Figure 3 *As the stylus rides in the record's grooves, it causes an electromagnet to vibrate.*

Playing a Record

Figure 3 shows a record being played. The stylus (STIE luhs), or needle, makes an electromagnet vibrate. The vibrating electromagnet induces an electric current that is used to make sound. Analog recording makes sound that is very close to the original. But unwanted sounds are sometimes recorded and are not easy to remove. Also, the stylus touches the record to play it. So, the record wears out, and the sound changes over time.

Digital Signals

digital signal a signal that can be represented as a sequence of discrete values

A **digital signal** is a signal that is represented as a sequence of separate values. It does not change continuously. Think of a regular light switch. It can be either on or off. Information in a digital signal is represented as binary (BIE nuh ree) numbers. *Binary* means "two." Numbers in binary are made up of only two digits, 1 and 0. Each digit is a *bit,* which is short for *binary digit.* Computers process digital signals that are in the form of a pattern of electric pulses. Each pulse stands for a 1. Each missing pulse stands for a 0.

Digital Storage on a CD

You've probably heard digital sound from a compact disc, or CD. Sound is recorded to a CD by means of a digital signal. A CD stores the signals in a thin layer of aluminum. Look at **Figure 4.** To understand how the pits and lands are named, keep in mind that the CD is read from the bottom.

Figure 4 *Pits stand for 1s, and lands stand for 0s. They form a tight spiral from the center to the outer edge on a CD. They store information that can be converted by a CD player into sound.*

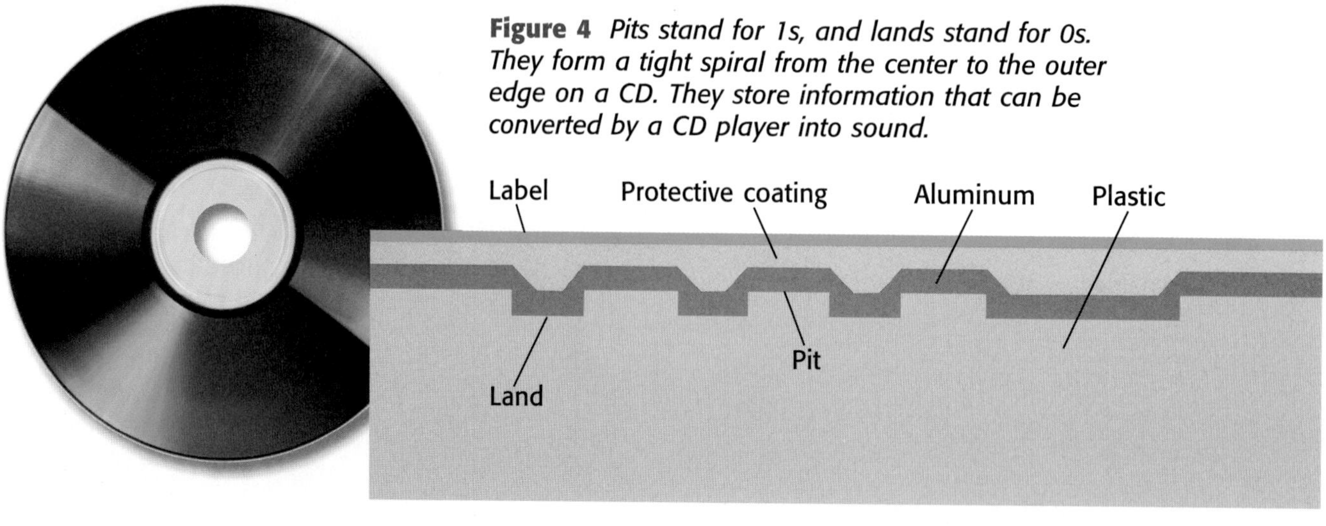

Digital Recording

In a digital recording, the sound wave is measured many times each second. **Figure 5** shows how these sample values represent the original sound. These numbers are then changed into binary values using 1s and 0s. The 1s and 0s are stored as pits and lands on a CD.

In digital recording, the sample values don't exactly match the original sound wave. So, the number of samples taken each second is important to make sure the recording sounds the way it should sound. Taking more sample values each second makes a digital sound that is closer to the original sound.

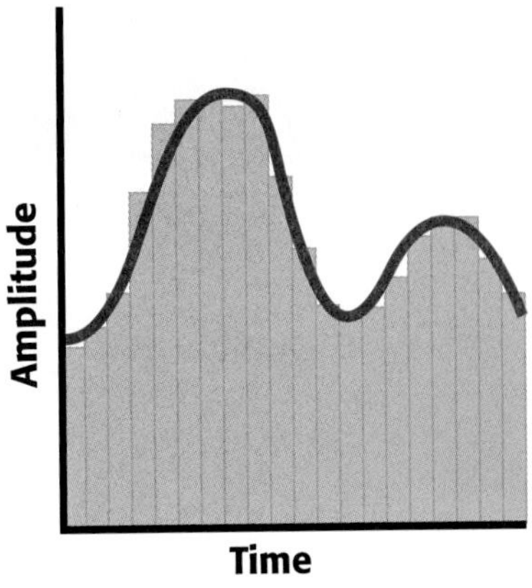

Figure 5 *Each of the bars represent a digital sample of the sound wave.*

Reading Check **How can a digital recording be made to sound more like the original sound?**

Playing a CD

In a CD player, the CD spins around while a laser shines on the CD from below. As shown in **Figure 6,** light reflected from the CD enters a detector. The detector changes the pattern of light and dark into a digital signal. The digital signal is changed into an analog signal, which is used to make a sound wave. Because only light touches the CD, the CD doesn't wear out. But errors can happen from playing a dirty or scratched CD.

Figure 6 **How a CD Player Works**

Different sequences and sizes of pits and lands will register different patterns of numbers that are converted into different sounds.

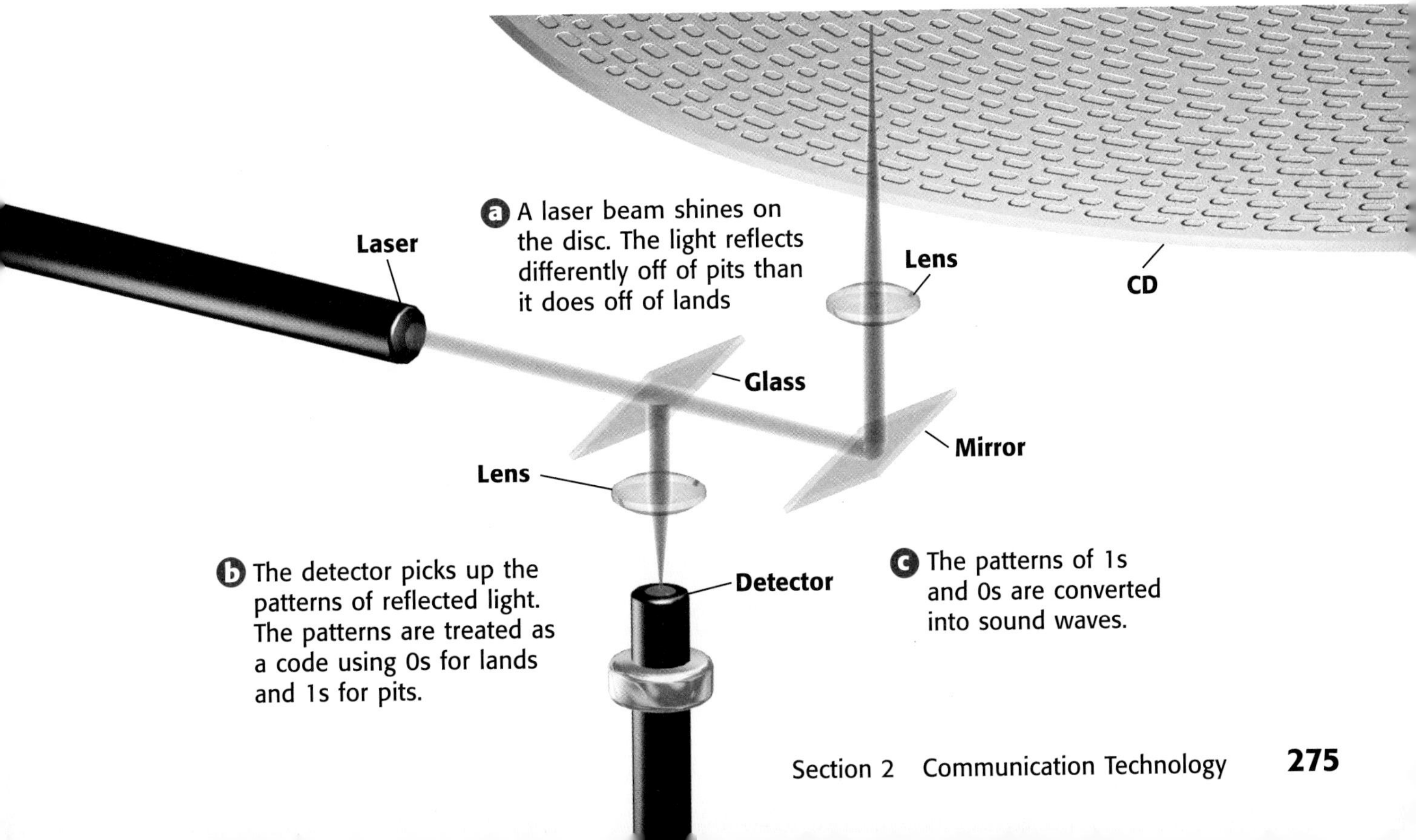

Laser
a A laser beam shines on the disc. The light reflects differently off of pits than it does off of lands
Lens
CD
Glass
Mirror
Lens
b The detector picks up the patterns of reflected light. The patterns are treated as a code using 0s for lands and 1s for pits.
Detector
c The patterns of 1s and 0s are converted into sound waves.

Radio and Television

INTERNET ACTIVITY

For another activity related to this chapter, go to **go.hrw.com** and type in the keyword **HP5ELTW.**

You hear or see shows on your radio or television that are broadcast from a station that may be many kilometers away. The radio and TV signals can be either analog or digital. An *electromagnetic* (EM) *wave* is a wave that consists of changing electric and magnetic fields. EM waves are used as carriers.

Radio

Radio waves are one kind of EM wave. Radio stations use radio waves to carry signals that represent sound. Look at **Figure 7.** Radio waves are transmitted by a radio tower. They travel through the air and are picked up by a radio antenna.

Figure 7 **How a Radio Works**

1. A microphone creates an electric current that is an analog signal of the original sound wave.
2. A modulator combines the amplified analog signal with radio waves that have a specific frequency.
3. A radio tower transmits modulated radio waves through the air.
4. The antenna in a radio "tuned in" to the correct frequency receives the modulated radio waves. The receiver separates the radio waves and the analog signal.
5. The radio's speakers convert the analog signal, the electric current, into sound.

Television

The pictures you see on your television are made by beams of electrons hitting the screen, as described in **Figure 8.** Video signals hold the information to make a picture. Audio signals hold the information to make the sound. These signals can be sent as analog or digital signals to your television. The signals can be broadcast using EM waves as carriers. The signals can be sent through cables or from satellites or broadcast towers.

More and more, television programs are going digital. This means that they are filmed using digital cameras and transmitted to homes as digital signals. You can watch digital shows on an analog TV. However, on a digital display, the images and sound of these programs are much clearer than on a television made for analog broadcasts.

Reading Check **What kinds of signals can be picked up by a color television?**

SCHOOL to HOME

TV Screen

With an adult, use a magnifying lens to look at a television screen. How are the fluorescent materials arranged? Hold the lens at various distances from the screen. What effects do you see? How does the screen's changing picture affect what you see?

ACTIVITY

Figure 8 **Images on a Color Television**

1. Video signals transmitted from a TV station are received by the antenna of a TV receiver.

2. Electronic circuits divide the video signal into separate signals for each of three electron beams. The beams, one for each primary color of light (red, green, and blue), strike the screen in varying strengths determined by the video signal.

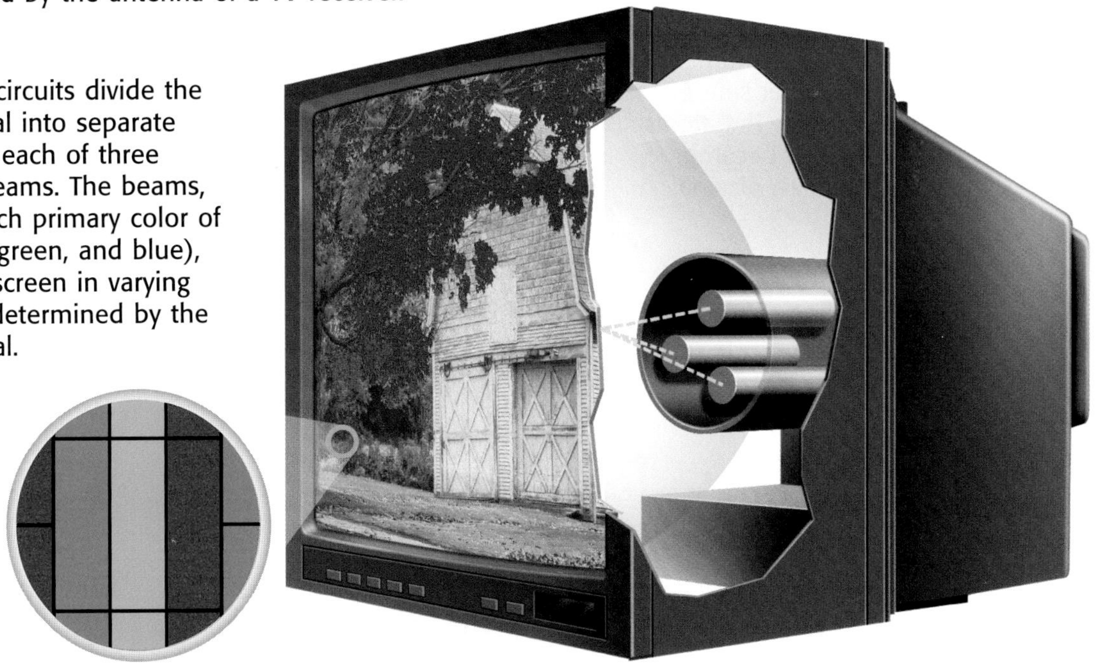

3. The screen has stripes or dots of three fluorescent (FLOO uh RES uhnt) materials. These materials glow when hit by electrons. The electron beams sweep the screen 30 times every second and activate the fluorescent materials. These materials then emit colored light that is viewed as a picture.

Plasma Display

Standard televisions must be deep enough so that the electron beams can reach all parts of the screen. So, televisions are bulky and heavy. A newer kind of screen, called a *plasma display,* is much thinner. It can be as thin as 15 cm. So, it is not much thicker than a painting on the wall!

Figure 9 shows how a plasma display works. Plasma displays do not use electron tubes. Instead, they have thousands of tiny cells with gases in them. A computer charges the cells, making a current in the gases. The current generates colored lights. Each light can be red, green, blue, or a combination. As in a regular television, these three colors are combined to make every picture on the screen.

Reading Check **Why is a plasma display thinner than a regular television?**

Figure 9 **How a Plasma Display Works**

1. Video signals transmitted from a TV station are received by a device, such as a VCR, that has a television tuner in it. The signals are then sent to the plasma display.

2. The signal includes commands to charge conductors on either side of small wells in the screen. The atoms of gas in the wells become charged and form a plasma.

3. Each well contains one of three fluorescent materials. The materials give off red, blue, or green light after absorbing energy given off by the plasma.

4. The colored light from each group of three wells blends together and makes a small dot of light in the picture on the screen.

SECTION Review

Summary

- Signals transmit information in electronic devices. Signals can be transmitted using a carrier. Signals can be analog or digital.
- Analog signals have continuous values. Telephones, record players, radios, and regular TV sets use analog signals.
- In a telephone, a transmitter changes sound waves to electric current. The current is sent across a phone line. The receiving telephone converts the signal back into a sound wave.
- Analog signals of sounds are used to make vinyl records. Changes in the groove reflect changes in the sound.
- Digital signals have discrete values, such as 0 and 1. CD players use digital signals.
- Radios and televisions use electromagnetic waves. These waves travel through the atmosphere. In a radio, the signals are converted to sound waves. In a television, electron beams convert the signals into images on the screen.

Using Key Terms

1. In your own words, write a definition for each of the following terms: *analog signal* and *digital signal.*

Understanding Key Ideas

2. Which of the following objects changes sound waves into an electric current in order to transmit information?
   a. telephone
   b. radio
   c. television
   d. telegraph
3. Why are carriers used to transmit signals?
4. What is an early example of an electrical device used for sending information over long distances? How did this device work?

Critical Thinking

5. **Applying Concepts** Is Morse code an example of an analog signal or a digital signal? Explain your reasoning.
6. **Making Comparisons** Compare how a telephone and a radio tower transmit information.
7. **Making Inferences** Does a mercury thermometer provide information in an analog or digital way? Explain your reasoning.

Interpreting Graphics

8. Look at the graphs below. They represent a sound wave that is being changed into a digital signal. Each bar represents a digital sample of the sound wave. Which graph represents the digital signal that is closer to the original sound wave? Explain your reasoning.

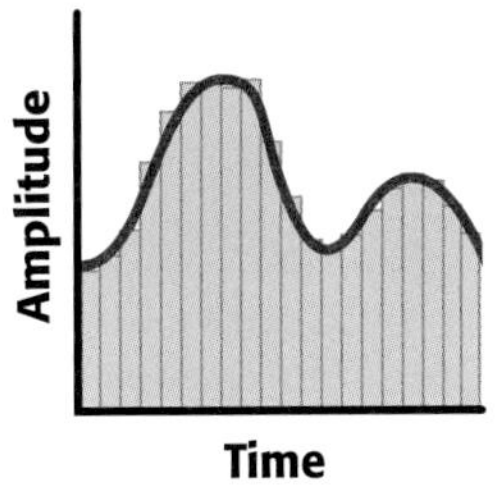

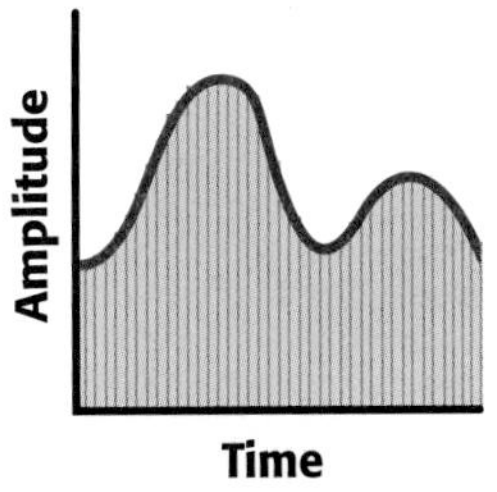

SECTION 3

Computers

Did you use a computer to wake up this morning?

What You Will Learn

- List a computer's basic functions, and describe its development.
- Identify the main components of computer hardware.
- Explain how information can be stored on CD-Rs and CD-RWs.
- Describe what computer software allows a computer to do.
- Describe computer networks.

Vocabulary

computer
microprocessor
hardware
software
Internet

READING STRATEGY

Prediction Guide Before reading this section, write the title of each heading in this section. Next, under each heading, write what you think you will learn.

You might think of a computer as something you use to send e-mail or to surf the Internet. But computers are around you all the time. Computers are in automobiles, VCRs, and telephones. Even an alarm clock is an example of a simple computer!

What Is a Computer?

A **computer** is an electronic device that performs tasks by following instructions given to it. A computer does a task when it is given a command and has the instructions necessary to carry out that command. Computers can do tasks very quickly.

Basic Functions

The basic functions of a computer are shown in **Figure 1.** The information you give to a computer is called *input.* The computer *processes* the input. Processing could mean adding a list of numbers, making a drawing, or even moving a piece of equipment. Input doesn't have to be processed right away. It can be stored until it is needed. The computer *stores* information in its memory. *Output* is the final result of the job done by the computer.

Reading Check **What are the basic functions of a computer?** *(See the Appendix for answers to Reading Checks.)*

Figure 1 **Basic Computer Functions**

The Functions of a Computer

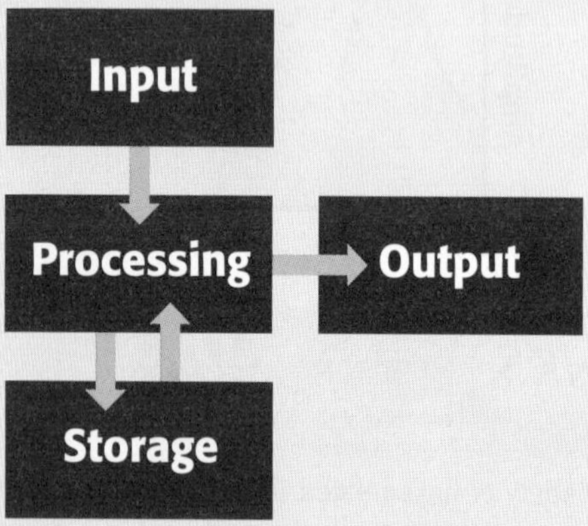

An Alarm Clock as a Computer

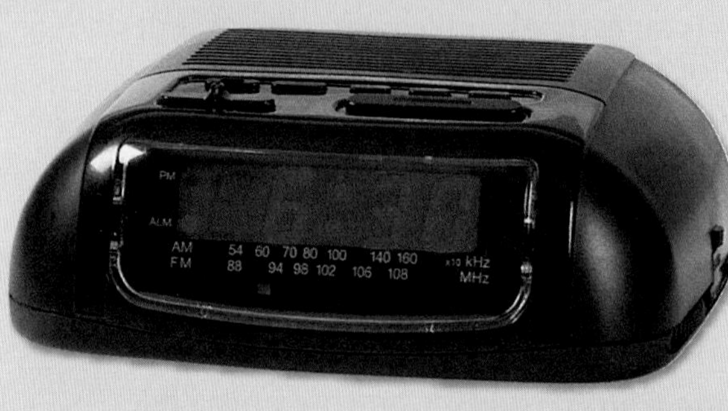

Input You set the time you need to wake up.

Processing Clock compares wake-up time to actual time.

Storage Clock remembers your wake-up time.

Output Buzzer or music sounds to wake you up.

The First Computers

Your pocket calculator is a simple computer. But computers were not always so small and easy to use. The first computers were huge! They were made up of large pieces of equipment that could fill a room. The first general-purpose computer is shown in **Figure 2.** This is the ENIAC. ENIAC stands for Electronic Numerical Integrator and Computer. It was made in 1946 by the U.S. Army. The ENIAC was made up of thousands of vacuum tubes. As a result, it had to be cooled while in use. It also cost a lot to build and to run.

Figure 2 *Fast for its time, the ENIAC could add 5,000 numbers per second.*

Modern Computers

Computers have become much smaller because of integrated circuits. Computers today use microprocessors. A **microprocessor** is a single chip that controls and carries out a computer's instructions. The first widely available microprocessor had only 4,800 transistors. But microprocessors made today may have more than 40 million transistors. Computers are now made so small that we can carry them around like a book!

computer an electronic device that can accept data and instructions, follow the instructions, and output the results

microprocessor a single semiconductor chip that controls and executes a microcomputer's instructions

Reading Check What is a microprocessor?

Quick Lab

The Speed of a Simple Computer

1. With a partner, use a **clock** to measure the time it takes each of you to solve the following items by hand.
   - a. (108 ÷ 9) + 231 − 19
   - b. 1 × 2 × 3 × 4 × 5
   - c. (4 × 6 × 8) ÷ 2
   - d. 3 × (5 + 12) − 2
2. Repeat step 1 using a **calculator.**
3. Which method was faster?
4. Which method was more accurate?
5. Will the calculator always give you the correct answer? Explain.

hardware the parts or pieces of equipment that make up a computer

CONNECTION TO Social Studies

WRITING SKILL **ENIAC** ENIAC was developed for use by the U.S. Army during World War II. Research what ENIAC was to be used for in the war and what plans were made for ENIAC after the war. Write a one-page report in your **science journal** to report your findings.

Computer Hardware

Different parts of a computer do different jobs. **Hardware** is the parts or pieces of equipment that make up a computer. As you read about each piece of hardware, look at **Figure 3** and **Figure 4** to see what the hardware looks like.

Input Devices

An *input device* gives information, or input, to the computer. You can enter information into a computer using a keyboard, a mouse, a scanner, or a digitizing pad and pen. You can even enter information using a microphone.

Central Processing Unit

A computer does tasks in the *central processing unit,* or CPU. In a personal computer, the CPU is a microprocessor. Input goes through the CPU for processing on the spot or for storage in memory. In the CPU, the computer does calculations, solves problems, and carries out instructions given to it.

Reading Check What does *CPU* stand for?

Figure 3 Computer Hardware

Memory

Information can be stored in the computer's memory until it is needed. Hard disks inside a computer and floppy disks or CDs that are put into a computer have memory to store information. Two other types of memory are *ROM* (read-only memory) and *RAM* (random-access memory).

ROM is permanent. It handles jobs such as start-up, maintenance, and hardware management. ROM normally cannot be added to or changed. It also cannot be lost when the computer is turned off. RAM is temporary. RAM stores information only while it is being used. RAM is sometimes called *working memory.* Information in RAM is lost if the power is shut off. So, it is a good habit to save your work to a hard drive or to a disk every few minutes.

Output Devices

Once a computer does a job, it shows the results on an *output device.* Monitors, printers, and speaker systems are all examples of output devices.

Modems and Interface Cards

Computers can exchange information if they are joined by modems or interface cards. Modems send information through telephone lines. Modems convert information from a digital signal to an analog signal and vice versa. Interface cards use cables or wireless connections.

MATH PRACTICE

Computer Memory

Suppose you download a document from the Internet that uses 25 kilobytes of memory. How many of those documents could you fit on a disk that has 1 gigabyte of memory? A kilobyte is 1,024 bytes, and a gigabyte is 1,073,741,824 bytes.

Figure 4 Additional Computer Hardware

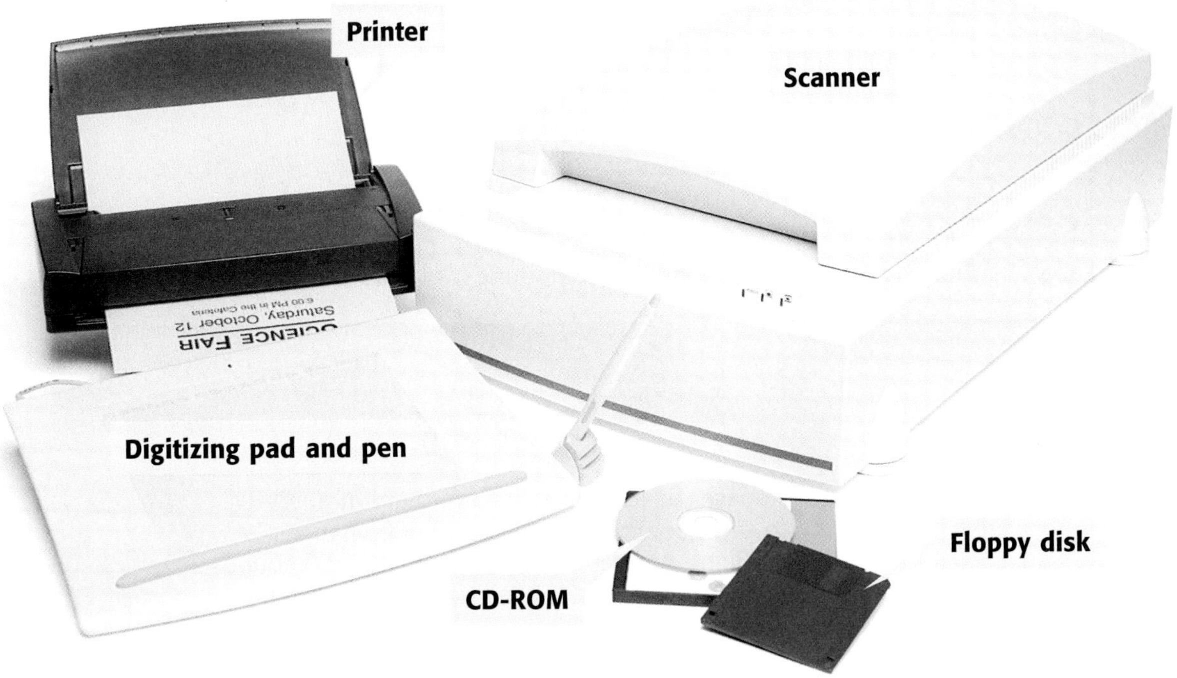

Compact Discs

Today, you can use a CD burner to make your own compact discs. A CD can hold about 500 times more information than a floppy disk. It can store digital photos, music files, and any other type of computer file.

Burning and Erasing CDs

The first kind of CD that you could put information onto, or "burn," is a CD-recordable (CD-R) disc. CD-R discs use a dye to block light. When the dye is heated, light cannot pass through to reflect off the aluminum. To burn a CD, a special laser heats some places and not others. This burning creates a pattern of "on" and "off" spots on the CD-R. These spots store information just as the pits and lands do on a regular CD. You can burn a CD-R disc only once.

A CD-rewritable (CD-RW) disc can be used more than once. CD-RW discs use a special compound that can be erased and written over again. CD-RW discs cost more than CD-R discs. But CD-RW discs cannot be read by all CD players. Look at **Figure 5** to see how CD-R and CD-RW discs work.

Figure 5 How CD-R and CD-RW Discs Work

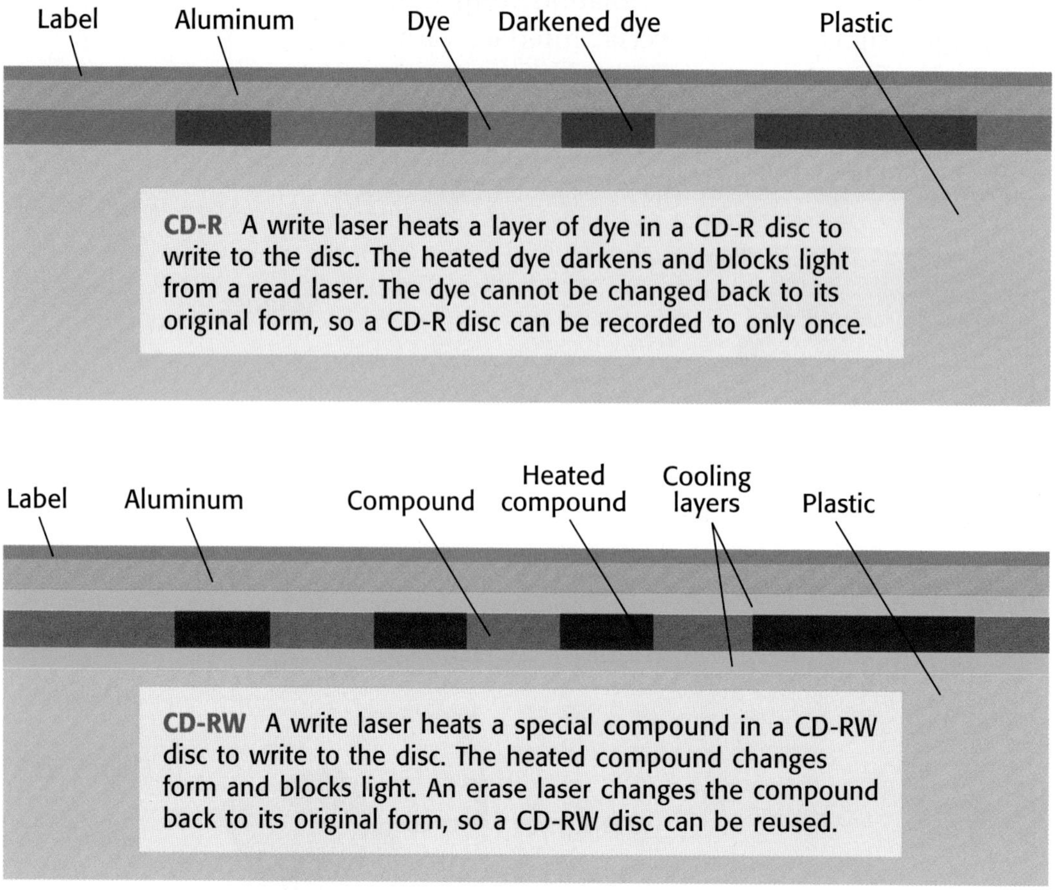

Label
Aluminum
Dye
Darkened dye
Plastic
CD-R A write laser heats a layer of dye in a CD-R disc to write to the disc. The heated dye darkens and blocks light from a read laser. The dye cannot be changed back to its original form, so a CD-R disc can be recorded to only once.
Label
Aluminum
Compound
Heated compound
Cooling layers
Plastic
CD-RW A write laser heats a special compound in a CD-RW disc to write to the disc. The heated compound changes form and blocks light. An erase laser changes the compound back to its original form, so a CD-RW disc can be reused.

Computer Software

Computers need instructions before they can do any given task. **Software** is a set of instructions or commands that tells a computer what to do. A computer program is software.

software a set of instructions or commands that tells a computer what to do; a computer program

Kinds of Software

Software can be split into two kinds: operating-system software and application software. Operating-system software handles basic operations needed by the computer. It helps the software and hardware communicate. It also handles commands from an input device. It can find programming instructions on a hard disk to be loaded into memory.

Application software tells the computer to run a utility, such as the ones shown in **Figure 6.** The pages in this book were made using many kinds of application software!

Reading Check What are the two main kinds of software?

Figure 6 **Common Types of Computer Software**

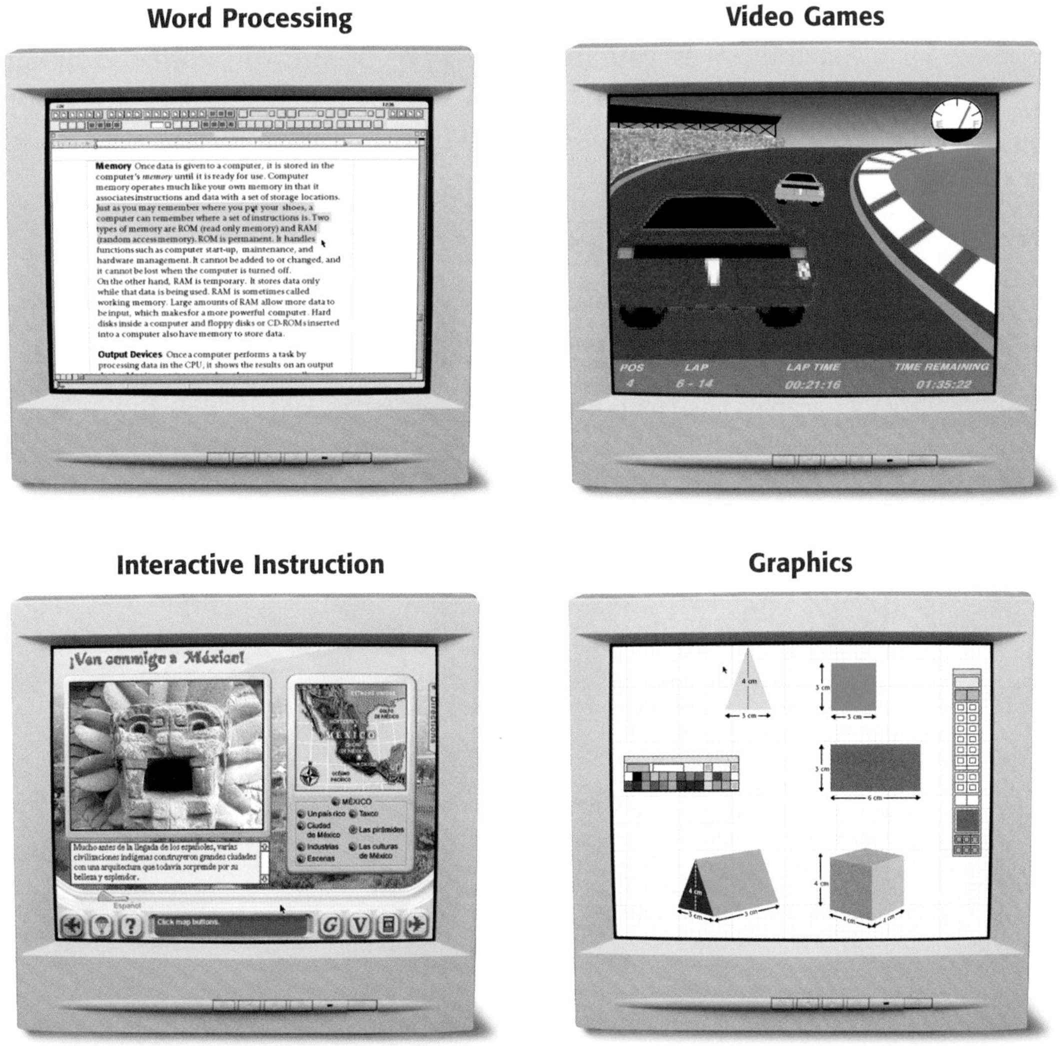

Internet a large computer network that connects many local and smaller networks all over the world

Computer Networks

By using modems and software, many computers can be connected, which allows them to communicate with one another. The **Internet** is a huge computer network made up of millions of computers that can all share information.

The Internet

Figure 7 shows some ways computers can be connected. Computers can connect on the Internet by using modems to dial into an Internet Service Provider, or ISP. A home computer often connects to an ISP over a phone or cable line. Computers in a school or business can be joined in a Local Area Network, or LAN. These computers connect to an ISP through only one line. ISPs around the world are connected by fiber optic cables.

The World Wide Web

The part of the Internet that people know best is called the *World Wide Web.* When you use a Web browser to look at pages on the Internet, you are on the World Wide Web. Web pages share a format that is simple enough that any computer can view them. They are grouped into Web sites. Clicking on a link takes you from one page or site to another. You can use a search engine to find Web pages on a topic for a report or to find out about your favorite movie!

Reading Check Describe the World Wide Web.

Figure 7 *Internet Service Providers allow computers in your home or school to connect to large routing computers that are linked around the world.*

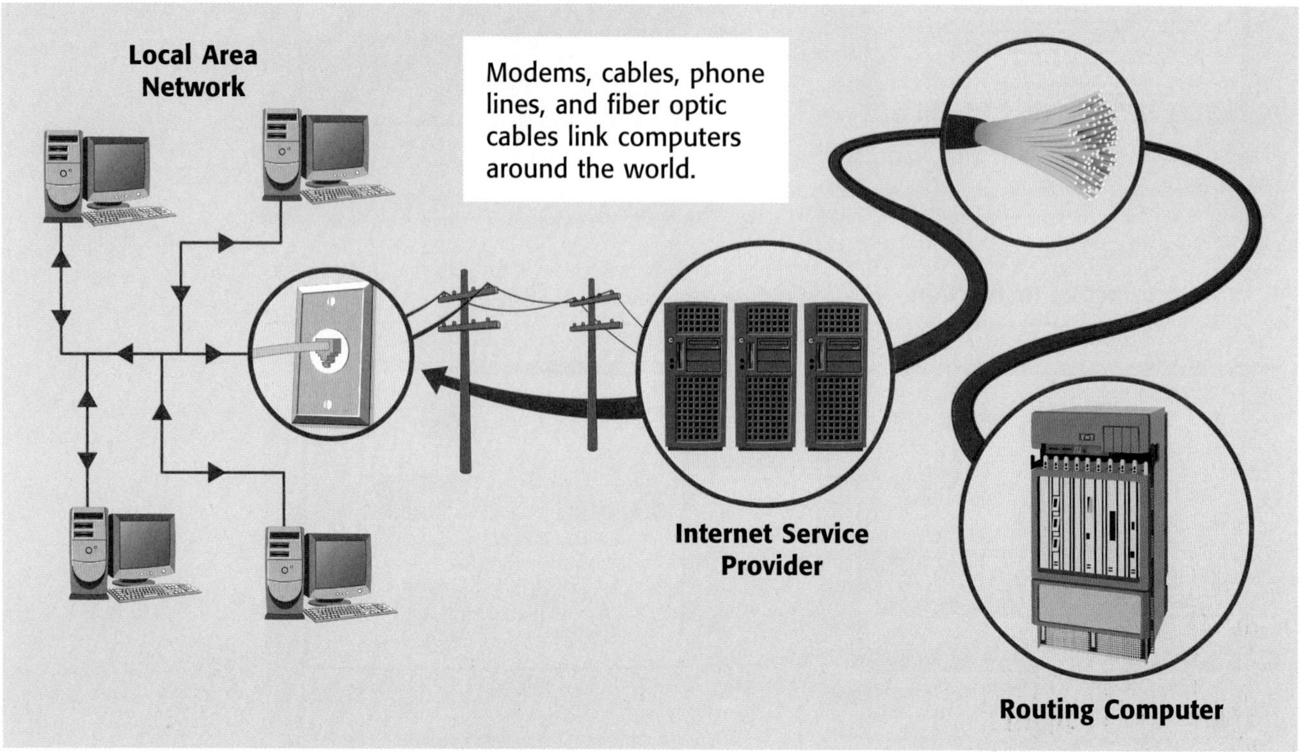
Local Area Network
Modems, cables, phone lines, and fiber optic cables link computers around the world.
Internet Service Provider
Routing Computer

SECTION Review

Summary

- All computers have four basic functions: input, processing, storage, and output.
- The first general-purpose computer, ENIAC, was made of thousands of vacuum tubes and filled an entire room. Microprocessors have made it possible to have computers the size of notebooks.
- Computer hardware includes input devices, the CPU, memory, output devices, and modems.
- CD burners can store information on recordable CDs, or CD-Rs. Rewritable CDs, or CD-RWs, can be erased and reused. Both use patterns of light and dark spots.
- Computer software is a set of instructions that tell a computer what to do. The two main types are operating systems and applications. Applications include word processors, spreadsheets, and games.
- The Internet is a huge network that allows millions of computers to share information.

Using Key Terms

The statements below are false. For each statement, replace the underlined term to make a true statement.

1. A word-processing application is an example of hardware.
2. An ISP allows you to connect to the microprocessor.

Understanding Key Ideas

3. Which of the following is an example of hardware used for input?
   a. monitor
   b. keyboard
   c. printer
   d. speaker
4. How are modern computers different from ENIAC? How are they the same?
5. What is the difference between hardware and software?
6. Explain how a CD burner works.
7. What is the Internet?

Critical Thinking

8. **Applying Concepts** Using the terms *input, output, processing,* and *store,* explain how you use a pocket calculator to add numbers.
9. **Predicting Consequences** If no phone lines were working, would there be any communication on the Internet? Explain.

Math Skills

10. How many 800 KB digital photos could you burn onto a CD-R disc that can hold 700 MB of information? (Note: 1,024 KB = 1 MB)

Interpreting Graphics

11. Look at the image of a RAM module below. Each of the black rectangles on the module is 32 MB of RAM. Each side of the module has the same number of rectangles. How much total RAM does the module have?

SCILINKS. NSTA
Developed and maintained by the National Science Teachers Association

For a variety of links related to this chapter, go to www.scilinks.org

Topic: Computer Technology; Internet
SciLinks code: HSM0334; HSM0808

Skills Practice Lab

Sending Signals

With a telegraph, you can use electric current to send signals between two telegraph keys connected by wires. In this lab, you will build a model of a telegraph that allows you to use Morse code to transmit messages to a friend.

OBJECTIVES

Build a working model of a telegraph key.

Send a message in Morse code by using your model.

Receive a message in Morse code by using your model.

MATERIALS

- battery, 6 V
- flashlight bulb with bulb holder
- paper clip (3)
- thumbtack (2)
- wire, insulated, with ends stripped, 15 cm (4)
- wood block, small

SAFETY

Procedure

1. Build a switch on the wood block, as shown below. Use a thumbtack to tack down a paper clip so that one end of the paper clip hangs over the edge of the wood block.
2. Unfold a second paper clip so that it looks like an *s*. Use the second thumbtack to tack down one end of the open paper clip on top of the remaining paper clip. The free end of the closed paper clip should hang off of the edge of the wood block opposite the first paper clip. The free end of the open paper clip should touch the thumbtack below it when pushed down.
3. Build the rest of the circuit, as shown below. Use a wire to connect one terminal of the battery to one of the paper clips that hangs over the edge of the wood block.
4. Use a second wire to connect the other paper clip that hangs over the edge of the wood block to the bulb holder.
5. Use a third wire to connect the other side of the bulb holder with the second terminal of the battery.

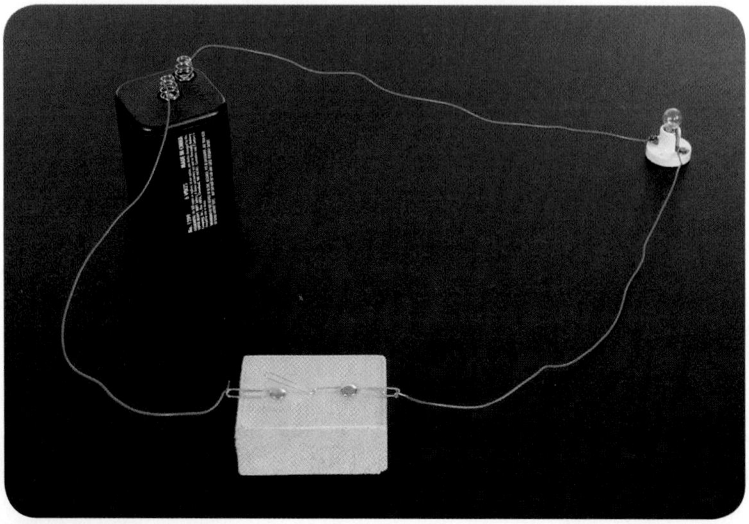

6. Test your circuit by gently pressing down on the open paper clip so that it touches the thumbtack below it. The light bulb should light. This is your model of a telegraph key.
7. Connect your model to another team's model. Use the remaining wire in each team's materials to connect the bulb holders, as shown on the next page. Test your circuit by closing each switch one at a time.

8. Write a short, four- or five-word message in Morse code. Take turns sending messages to the other team using the telegraph. To send a dot, press the paper clip down for two seconds. To send a dash, hold the clip down for four seconds. Decode the message you receive, and check to see if you got the correct message.

9. Remove one of the batteries. Test your circuit again by closing each switch one at a time.

Analyze the Results

1. **Describing Events** When both batteries are attached, what happens to the flashlight bulbs when you close your switch?

2. **Describing Events** When both batteries are attached, what happens to the flashlight bulbs when the other team closes their switch?

3. **Describing Events** How does removing one of the batteries change the way you can send or receive messages on the telegraph?

4. **Analyzing Results** Did you receive the correct message from the other team? If not, what problems did you have?

Draw Conclusions

5. **Drawing Conclusions** When the two models are connected, are the flashlight bulbs part of a series circuit or a parallel circuit?

6. **Making Predictions** How might using a telegraph to transmit messages overseas be difficult?

Table 1 **International Morse Code**

A •–	J •–––	S •••	2 ••–––
B –•••	K –•–	T –	3 •••––
C –•–•	L •–••	U ••–	4 ••••–
D –••	M ––	V •••–	5 •••••
E •	N –•	W •––	6 –••••
F ••–•	O –––	X –••–	7 ––•••
G ––•	P •––•	Y –•––	8 –––••
H ••••	Q ––•–	Z ––••	9 ––––•
I ••	R •–•	1 •––––	0 –––––

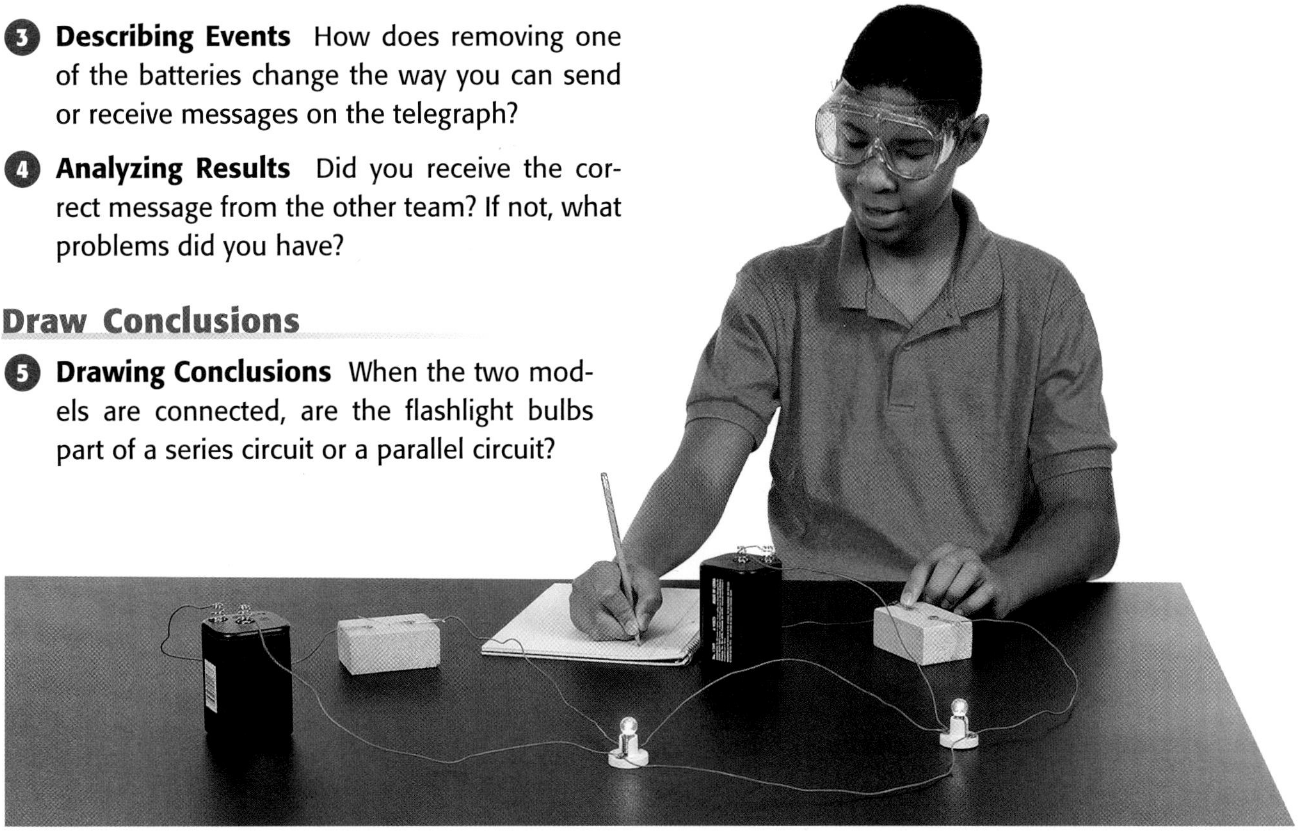

Chapter Review

USING KEY TERMS

For each pair of terms, explain how the meanings of the terms differ.

1. *semiconductor* and *integrated circuit*
2. *transistor* and *doping*
3. *analog signal* and *digital signal*
4. *computer* and *microprocessor*
5. *hardware* and *software*

UNDERSTANDING KEY IDEAS

Multiple Choice

6. All electronic devices transmit information using
   - **a.** signals.
   - **b.** electromagnetic waves.
   - **c.** radio waves.
   - **d.** modems.

7. Semiconductors are used to make
   - **a.** transistors.
   - **b.** integrated circuits.
   - **c.** diodes.
   - **d.** All of the above

8. Which of the following is an example of a telecommunication device?
   - **a.** vacuum tube
   - **b.** telephone
   - **c.** radio
   - **d.** Both (b) and (c)

9. A monitor, a printer, and a speaker are examples of
   - **a.** input devices.
   - **b.** memory.
   - **c.** computers.
   - **d.** output devices.

10. Record players play sounds that were recorded in the form of
    - **a.** digital signals.
    - **b.** electric currents.
    - **c.** analog signals.
    - **d.** radio waves.

11. Memory in a computer that is permanent and cannot be changed is called
    - **a.** RAM.
    - **b.** ROM.
    - **c.** CPU.
    - **d.** None of the above

12. Beams of electrons that shine on fluorescent materials are used in
    - **a.** telephones.
    - **b.** telegraphs.
    - **c.** televisions.
    - **d.** radios.

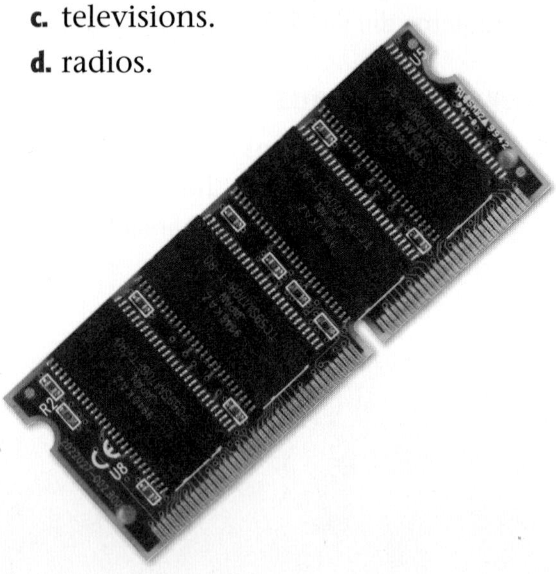

Short Answer

13 How is an electronic device different from other machines that use electrical energy?

14 In one or two sentences, describe how a television works.

15 Give three examples of how computers are used in your everyday life.

16 Explain the advantages that transistors have over vacuum tubes.

Math Skills

17 How many bits can be stored on a 20 GB hard disk? (Hint: 1 GB = 1,073,741,824 bytes; 1 byte = 8 bits.)

CRITICAL THINKING

18 **Concept Mapping** Use the following terms to create a concept map: *electronic devices, radio waves, electric current, signals,* and *information.*

19 **Applying Concepts** Your friend is preparing an oral report on the history of radio and finds the photograph shown below. He asks you why the radio is so large. Using what you know about electronic devices, how do you explain the size of this vintage radio?

20 **Making Comparisons** Using what you know about the differences between analog signals and digital signals, compare the sound from a record player to the sound from a CD player.

21 **Making Comparisons** What do Morse code and digital signals have in common?

INTERPRETING GRAPHICS

The diagram below shows a circuit that contains a transistor. Use the diagram below to answer the questions that follow.

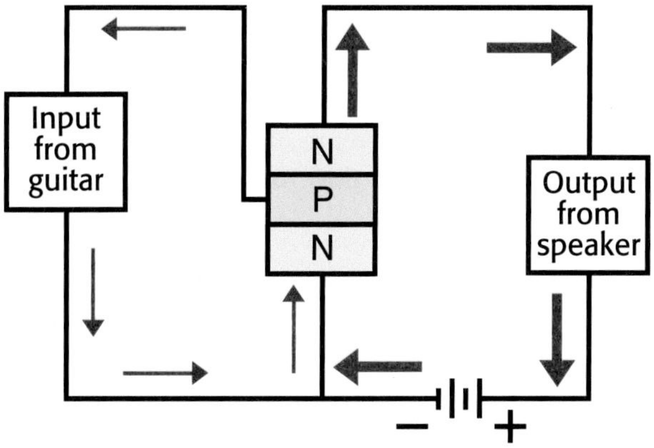

22 What purpose does the transistor serve in this diagram?

23 Compare the current in the left side of the circuit with the current in the right side of the circuit.

24 Compare the sound from the speaker with the sound from the guitar.

Multiple Choice

Use the diagram below to answer questions 1–2.

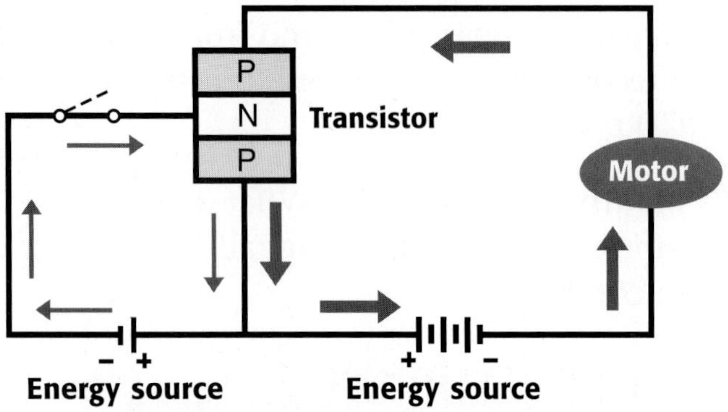

1. **In the diagram above, what happens to the current in the circuit if the manual switch is opened?**
   - A. Current stops flowing in the smaller loop but continues to flow in the larger loop.
   - B. Current stops flowing in both the smaller and larger loops.
   - C. Current stops flowing in the larger loop but continues to flow in the smaller loop.
   - D. Current continues to flow in both the smaller and larger loops.

2. **Quinn is building a remote-control car using the circuit diagram above. She switches the terminals of the energy source in the smaller loop so that the positive terminal is on the left. What else would she have to do to make the car run?**
   - A. Nothing. The position of the terminals does not affect how the energy flows within the circuit.
   - B. She would have to switch the terminals of the energy source in the larger loop.
   - C. She would have to use an NPN transistor and switch the terminals in the larger loop.
   - D. She would have to move the manual switch so that it controlled the larger loop.

3. **Which of the following most likely works in an analog way?**
   - A. remote control for a television
   - B. volume control dial on a stereo
   - C. programmable thermostat
   - D. light switch

4. **Jake hears a sound that has 3 pulses, 2 beats of silence, and 5 alternating pulses and silences. How would Jake represent the sound using digital notation?**
   - A. 0001101010
   - B. 1110101011
   - C. 0100001010
   - D. 1110010101

5. **Which of these electronic devices most likely contains a solenoid?**
   - A. record player
   - B. CD player
   - C. television set
   - D. remote control

6. Dawn wants to burn songs to a CD. Each song takes up between 3.96 and 4.54 megabytes. What is the maximum number of songs she can fit on a 700 megabyte CD?

A. 154

B. 164

C. 176

D. 189

7. Laptop computers are thin, light, and portable. How does a laptop screen produce images?

A. Electron beams sweep the screen and cause fluorescent materials to glow.

B. Laser beams shine behind the screen and create patterns of reflected light.

C. Vibrations in thousands of electron tubes transfer energy to wells of colored light.

D. Charged atoms of gas in wells on the screen transfer energy to fluorescent materials.

8. Cecily uses a remote control to turn on her DVD player. Which of the following performs a similar function as the remote control?

A. vacuum tube

B. computer mouse

C. modem

D. CD burner

Use the table below to answer question 9.

Element	Number of Electrons in Outermost Energy Level
Boron	3
Germanium	4
Phosphorus	5
Selenium	6

9. Which element in the table above could be used with silicon to make a p-type semiconductor (the type that contains a "hole")?

A. boron

B. germanium

C. phosphorus

D. selenium

Open Response

10. Would a diode containing two p-type semiconductors create a current? Explain your answer.

11. Describe how a transistor radio picks up a radio signal and converts it to sound. Then, draw and label the circuit that allows the radio to amplify sound.

Science in Action

Science, Technology, and Society

Wearable Computers

Today's thin, portable laptop computers are extremely tiny compared to the first general-purpose computer, ENIAC, which filled an entire room. But today's laptops may look bulky next to the computers of tomorrow. In the future, you might wear your computer! A wearable computer is always with you, like clothing or eyeglasses. It is easy to operate. You can even use it while moving around. You might use a wearable computer to take notes in class, look up a phone number, check e-mail, or browse the Internet. These computers are already being used today by a number of companies. As the technology evolves, wearable computers will become even easier to use and more advanced in the types of tasks they perform.

Math ACTIVITY

One wearable computer that is available today can operate from 0°C to 50°C. You can convert temperature measurements from Celsius to Fahrenheit with this equation: Fahrenheit temperature = (9/5 × Celsius temperature) + 32. What is the operating range of this computer in degrees Fahrenheit?

Science Fiction

"There Will Come Soft Rains" by Ray Bradbury

Ticktock, seven o'clock, time to get up, seven o'clock. The voice clock in the living room sent out the wake-up message, gently calling to the family to get up and begin their new day. A few minutes later, the automatic stove in the kitchen began the family breakfast. A soft rain was falling outside, so the weather box by the front door suggested that raincoats were necessary today.

But no family sounds come from the house. The house goes on talking to itself as if it were keeping itself company. Why doesn't anyone answer? Find out when you read Ray Bradbury's "There Will Come Soft Rains" in the *Holt Anthology of Science Fiction*.

Language Arts ACTIVITY

WRITING SKILL The story described above takes place in 2026. The author has imagined how the future world might be. Write a short story about how you think life will be different in the year 2050.

Careers

Agnes Riley

Computer Technician Some people take it for granted how smoothly a computer works—until it breaks down. When that happens, you may need to call in an expert, such as Agnes Riley. Agnes is a computer technician from Budapest, Hungary. When a computer isn't working properly, she will take it apart, find the problem, and fix it.

Many people go to school to learn about computer repair, but Agnes taught herself. In Hungary, the company she worked for had a set of old, run-down computers. Agnes started experimenting, trying to repair them. The more she tinkered, the more she learned.

When Agnes moved to New York City in 1999, she wanted to become a computer technician. She started out as a computer salesperson. Eventually, she got the technician training materials. Her earlier experimenting and her studying paid off. She passed the exam to become a licensed technician. Agnes enjoys solving problems and likes helping people. If you are the same type of person, you might want to become a computer technician, too!

Social Studies ACTIVITY

WRITING SKILL Agnes Riley is from Budapest, Hungary. What might you see if you visited Budapest? Do some research to find out, and then design a travel brochure to encourage tourists to visit the city. You might include information about local points of interest or Budapest's history.

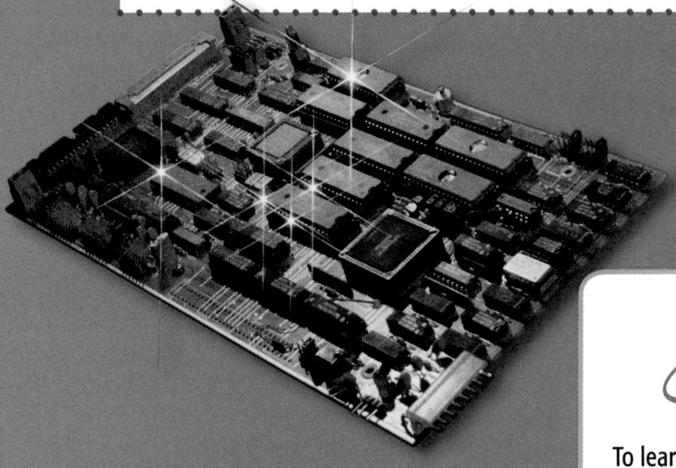

go.hrw.com

To learn more about these Science in Action topics, visit go.hrw.com and type in the keyword HP5ELTF.

Current Science

Check out Current Science® articles related to this chapter by visiting go.hrw.com. Just type in the keyword HP5CS19.

10

Energy Resources

The Big Idea

Sources of energy differ in quantity, distribution, usefulness, and the time required for formation.

SECTION

About the Photo

Would you believe that this house is made from empty soda cans and old tires? Well, it is! The Castle, named by its designer, architect Mike Reynolds, and located in Taos, New Mexico, not only uses recycled materials but also saves Earth's energy resources. All of the energy used to run this house comes directly from the sun, and the water used for household activities is rainwater.

PRE-READING ACTIVITY

Graphic Organizer

Comparison Table Before you read the chapter, create the graphic organizer entitled "Comparison Table" described in the **Study Skills** section of the Appendix. Label the columns with an energy resource from the chapter. Label the rows with "Pros" and "Cons." As you read the chapter, fill in the table with details about the pros and cons of each energy resource.

START-UP ACTIVITY

What Is the Sun's Favorite Color?

Try the following activity to see which colors are better than others at absorbing the sun's energy.

Procedure

1. Obtain **at least five balloons** that are different colors but the same size and shape. One of the balloons should be white, and one should be black. Do not inflate the balloons.
2. Place **several small ice cubes** in each balloon. Each balloon should contain the same amount of ice.
3. Line up the balloons on a flat, uniformly colored surface that receives direct sunlight. Make sure that all of the balloons receive the same amount of sunlight and that the openings in the balloons are not facing directly toward the sun.
4. Record the time that it takes the ice to melt completely in each of the balloons. You can tell how much ice has melted in each balloon by pinching the balloons open and then gently squeezing the balloon.

Analysis

1. In which balloon did the ice melt first? Why?
2. What color would you paint a device used to collect solar energy? Explain your answer.

SECTION 1

Natural Resources

What You Will Learn

- Describe how humans use natural resources.
- Compare renewable resources with nonrenewable resources.
- Explain three ways that humans can conserve natural resources.

Vocabulary

natural resource
renewable resource
nonrenewable resource
recycling

READING STRATEGY

Reading Organizer As you read this section, make a concept map by using the terms above.

What does the water you drink, the paper you write on, the gasoline used in the cars you ride in, and the air you breathe have in common?

Water, trees used to make paper, crude oil used to make gasoline, and air are just a few examples of Earth's resources. Can you think of other examples of Earth's resources?

Earth's Resources

The Earth provides almost everything needed for life. For example, the Earth's atmosphere provides the air you breathe, maintains air temperatures, and produces rain. The oceans and other waters of the Earth give you food and needed water. The solid part of the Earth gives nutrients, such as potassium, to the plants you eat. These resources that the Earth provides for you are called natural resources.

A **natural resource** is any natural material that is used by humans. Examples of natural resources are water, petroleum, minerals, forests, and animals. Most resources are changed and made into products that make people's lives more comfortable and convenient, as shown in **Figure 1.** The energy we get from many of these resources, such as gasoline and wind, ultimately comes from the sun's energy.

Figure 1 Natural Resources

This pile of lumber is made of wood, which comes from trees.
GASOLINE
The gasoline in this can is made from oil pumped from the Earth's crust.
Electrical energy generated by these wind turbines ultimately comes from the sun's energy.

Figure 2 *Trees and fresh water are just a few of the renewable resources available on Earth.*

Renewable Resources

Some natural resources can be renewed. A **renewable resource** is a natural resource that can be replaced at the same rate at which the resource is used. **Figure 2** shows two examples of renewable resources. Although many resources are renewable, they still can be used up before they can be renewed. Trees, for example, are renewable. However, some forests are being cut down faster than new forests can grow to replace them.

Reading Check **What is a renewable resource?** (*See the Appendix for answers to Reading Checks.*)

Nonrenewable Resources

Not all of Earth's natural resources are renewable. A **nonrenewable resource** is a resource that forms at a rate that is much slower than the rate at which it is consumed. Coal, shown in **Figure 3,** is an example of a nonrenewable resource. It takes millions of years for coal to form. Once coal is used up, it is no longer available. Petroleum and natural gas are other examples of nonrenewable resources. When these resources become scarce, humans will have to find other resources to replace them.

natural resource any natural material that is used by humans, such as water, petroleum, minerals, forests, and animals

renewable resource a natural resource that can be replaced at the same rate at which the resource is consumed

nonrenewable resource a resource that forms at a rate that is much slower than the rate at which it is consumed

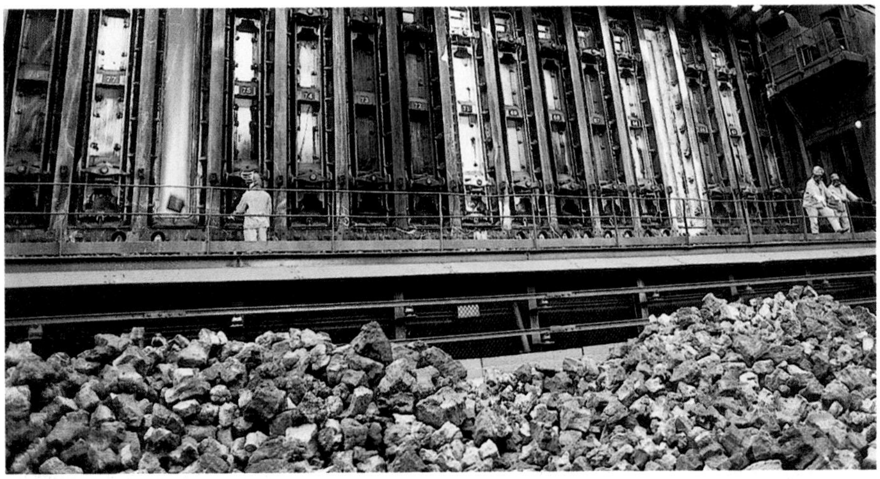

Figure 3 *The coal used in the industrial process shown here is not quickly replaced by natural processes.*

Conserving Natural Resources

Whether the natural resources you use are renewable or nonrenewable, you should be careful how you use them. To conserve natural resources, you should try to use them only when necessary. For example, leaving the faucet on while brushing your teeth wastes clean water. Turning the faucet on only to rinse your brush saves water that you may need for other uses.

Conserving resources also means taking care of the resources even when you are not using them. For example, it is important to keep lakes, rivers, and other water resources free of pollution. Polluted lakes and rivers can affect the water you drink. Also, polluted water resources can harm the plants and animals, including humans, that depend on them to survive.

SCHOOL to HOME

Renewable?

WRITING SKILL With a parent or guardian, find five products in your home that were made from natural resources. List the resource or resources from which each product was made. Label each resource as renewable or nonrenewable. What can you do to help conserve the resources you listed? In your **science journal,** describe a personal action plan to conserve some of the resources you rely on every day.

ACTIVITY

Energy Conservation

The energy we use to heat our homes, drive our cars, and run our computers comes from natural resources. The way in which we choose to use energy on a daily basis affects the availability of the natural resources. Most of the natural resources that provide us energy are nonrenewable resources. So, if we don't limit our use of energy now, the resources may not be available in the future.

As with all natural resources, conserving energy is important. You can conserve energy by being careful to use only the resources that you need. For example, turn lights off when you are not using them. And make sure the washing machine is full before you start it, as shown in **Figure 4.** You can also ride a bike, walk, or take a bus because these methods use fewer resources than a car does.

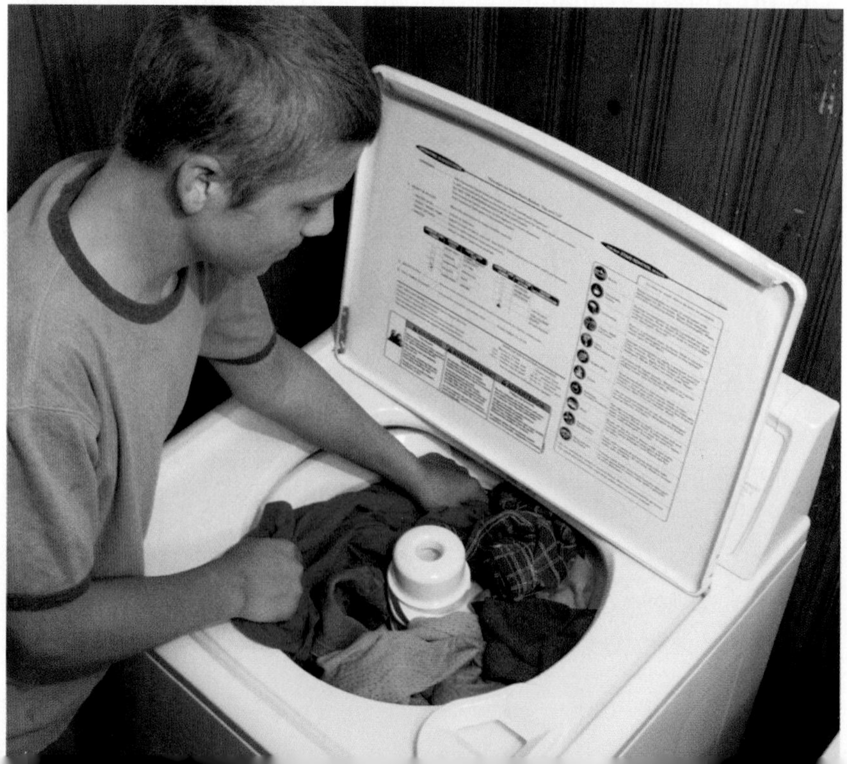

Figure 4 *Making sure the washing machine is full before running it is one way you can avoid wasting natural resources.*

Reduce, Reuse, Recycle

Another way to conserve natural resources is to recycle, as shown in **Figure 5.** **Recycling** is the process of reusing materials from waste or scrap. Recycling reduces the amount of natural resources that must be obtained from the Earth. For example, recycling paper reduces the number of trees that must be cut down to make new paper products. Recycling also conserves energy. Though energy is required to recycle materials, it takes less energy to recycle an aluminum can than it does to make a new one!

Newspaper, aluminum cans, most plastic containers, and cardboard boxes can be recycled. Most plastic containers have a number on them. This number informs you whether the item can be recycled. Plastic products with the numbers 1 and 2 can be recycled in most communities. Check with your community's recycling center to see what kinds of materials the center recycles.

Reading Check **What are some kinds of products that can be recycled?**

recycling the process of recovering valuable or useful materials from waste or scrap; the process of reusing some items

Figure 5 *You can recycle many household items to help conserve natural resources.*

SECTION Review

Summary

- We use natural resources such as water, petroleum, and lumber to make our lives more comfortable and convenient.
- Renewable resources can be replaced within a relatively short period of time, but nonrenewable resources may take thousands or even millions of years to form.
- Natural resources can be conserved by using only what is needed, taking care of resources, and recycling.

Using Key Terms

1. Use each of the following terms in a separate sentence: *natural resource, renewable resource, nonrenewable resource,* and *recycling.*

Understanding Key Ideas

2. How do humans use most natural resources?
3. Which of the following is a renewable resource?
   a. oil
   b. water
   c. coal
   d. natural gas
4. Describe three ways to conserve natural resources.

Math Skills

5. If a faucet dripped for 8.6 h and 3.3 L of water dripped out every hour, how many liters of water dripped out altogether?

Critical Thinking

6. **Making Inferences** How does human activity affect Earth's renewable and nonrenewable resources?
7. **Applying Concepts** List five products you regularly use that can be recycled.
8. **Making Inferences** Why is the availability of some renewable resources more of a concern now than it was 100 years ago?

SCILINKS® NSTA Developed and maintained by the National Science Teachers Association

For a variety of links related to this chapter, go to www.scilinks.org

Topic: Natural Resources
SciLinks code: HSM1015

SECTION

2

Fossil Fuels

How does a sunny day 200 million years ago relate to your life today?

Chances are that if you traveled to school today or used a product made of plastic, you used some of the energy from sunlight that fell on Earth several hundred million years ago. Life as you know it would be very different without the fuels or products formed from plants and animals that lived alongside the dinosaurs.

What You Will Learn

- Describe what energy resources are.
- Identify three different forms of fossil fuels.
- Explain how fossil fuels form.
- Describe how fossil fuels are found and obtained.
- Identify four problems with fossil fuels.

Vocabulary

fossil fuel
petroleum
natural gas
coal
acid precipitation
smog

READING STRATEGY

Brainstorming The key idea of this section is fossil fuels. Brainstorm words and phrases related to fossil fuels.

Energy Resources

The fuels we use to run cars, ships, planes, and factories and to generate electrical energy, shown in **Figure 1,** are energy resources. *Energy resources* are natural resources that humans use to generate energy. Most of the energy we use comes from a group of natural resources called fossil fuels. A **fossil fuel** is a nonrenewable energy resource formed from the remains of plants and animals that lived long ago. Examples of fossil fuels include petroleum, coal, and natural gas.

Energy is released from fossil fuels when they are burned. For example, the energy from burning coal in a power plant is used to produce electrical energy. However, because fossil fuels are a nonrenewable resource, once they are burned, they are gone. Therefore, like other resources, fossil fuels need to be conserved. In the 21st century, societies will continue to explore alternatives to fossil fuels. But they will also focus on developing more-efficient ways to use these fuels.

fossil fuel a nonrenewable energy resource formed from the remains of organisms that lived long ago; examples include oil, coal, and natural gas

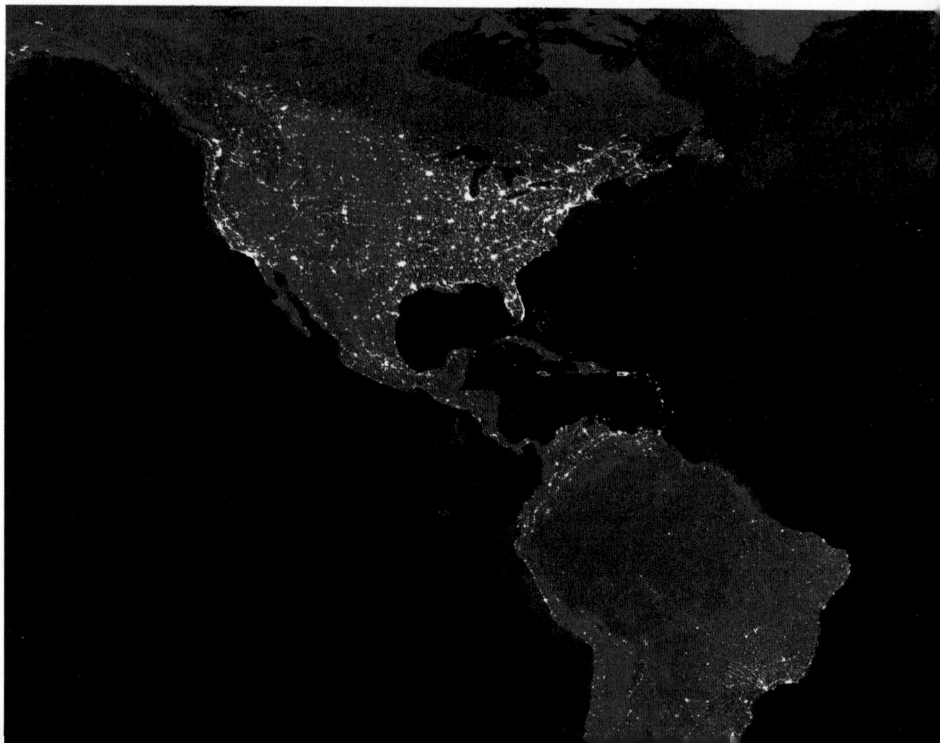

Figure 1 *Light produced from electrical energy can be seen in this satellite image taken from space.*

Figure 2 *Some refineries use a process called* distillation *to separate petroleum into various types of petroleum products.*

Types of Fossil Fuels

All living things are made up of the element carbon. Because fossil fuels are formed from the remains of plants and animals, all fossil fuels are made of carbon, too. Most of the carbon in fossil fuels exists as hydrogen-carbon compounds called *hydrocarbons*. But different fossil fuels have different forms. Fossil fuels may exist as liquids, gases, or solids.

Liquid Fossil Fuels: Petroleum

A liquid mixture of complex hydrocarbon compounds is called **petroleum.** Petroleum is also commonly known as *crude oil.* Petroleum is separated into several kinds of products in refineries, such as the one shown in **Figure 2.** Examples of fossil fuels separated from petroleum are gasoline, jet fuel, kerosene, diesel fuel, and fuel oil.

More than 40% of the world's energy comes from petroleum products. Petroleum products are the main fuel for forms of transportation, such as airplanes, trains, boats, and ships. Crude oil is so valuable that it is often called *black gold.*

petroleum a liquid mixture of complex hydrocarbon compounds; used widely as a fuel source

natural gas a mixture of gaseous hydrocarbons located under the surface of the Earth, often near petroleum deposits; used as a fuel

Gaseous Fossil Fuels: Natural Gas

A gaseous mixture of hydrocarbons is called **natural gas.** Most natural gas is used for heating, but it is also used for generating electrical energy. Your kitchen stove may be powered by natural gas. Some motor vehicles, such as the van in **Figure 3,** use natural gas as fuel. An advantage of using natural gas is that using it causes less air pollution than using oil does. However, natural gas is very flammable. Gas leaks can lead to fires or deadly explosions.

Methane, CH_4, is the main component of natural gas. But other components, such as butane and propane, can be separated from natural gas, too. Butane and propane are often used as fuel for camp stoves and outdoor grills.

Reading Check **What is natural gas most often used for?**
(See the Appendix for answers to Reading Checks.)

Figure 3 *Vehicles powered by natural gas are becoming more common.*

Figure 4 *This coal is being gathered so that it may be burned in the power plant shown in the background.*

Solid Fossil Fuels: Coal

coal a fossil fuel that forms underground from partially decomposed plant material

The solid fossil fuel that humans use most is coal. **Coal** is a fossil fuel that is formed underground from partially decomposed plant material. Coal was once the major source of energy in the United States. People burned coal in stoves to heat their homes. They also used coal in transportation. Many trains in the 1800s and early 1900s were powered by coal-burning steam locomotives.

As cleaner energy resources became available, people reduced their use of coal. People began to use coal less because burning coal produces large amounts of air pollution. Now, people use forms of transportation that use oil instead of coal as fuel. In the United States, coal is now rarely used as a fuel for heating. However, many power plants, such as the one shown in **Figure 4,** burn coal to generate electrical energy.

Reading Check **In the 1800s and early 1900s, what was coal most commonly used for?**

INTERNET ACTIVITY

For another activity related to this chapter, go to **go.hrw.com** and type in the keyword **HZ5ENRW.**

CONNECTION TO Chemistry

Hydrocarbons Both petroleum and natural gas are made of compounds called *hydrocarbons.* A hydrocarbon is an organic compound that contains only carbon and hydrogen. A molecule of propane, C_3H_8, a gaseous fossil fuel, contains three carbons and eight hydrogens. Using a molecular model set, create a model of a propane molecule. (Hint: Each carbon atom should have four bonds, and each hydrogen atom should have one bond.)

ACTIVITY

How Do Fossil Fuels Form?

All fossil fuels form from the buried remains of ancient organisms. But different kinds of fossil fuels form in different ways and from different kinds of organisms.

Petroleum and Natural Gas Formation

Petroleum and natural gas form mainly from the remains of microscopic sea organisms. When these organisms die, their remains settle on the ocean floor. There, the remains are buried in sediment. Over time, the sediment is compacted and slowly becomes rock. Through physical and chemical changes over millions of years, the remains of the organisms become petroleum and gas. Gradually, more rocks form above the rocks that contain the fossil fuels. Under the pressure of overlying rocks and sediments, the fossil fuels can move through permeable rocks. *Permeable rocks* are rocks through which fluids, such as petroleum and gas, can move. As shown in **Figure 5,** these permeable rocks become reservoirs that hold petroleum and natural gas.

The formation of petroleum and natural gas is an ongoing process. Part of the remains of today's sea life will become petroleum and natural gas millions of years from now.

Quick Lab

Rock Sponge

1. Place **samples of sandstone, limestone,** and **shale** in separate **Petri dishes.**
2. Place **five drops of light machine oil** on each rock sample.
3. Observe and record the time required for the oil to be absorbed by each of the rock samples.
4. Which rock sample absorbed the oil fastest? Why?
5. Based on your findings, describe a property that allows fossil fuels to be easily removed from reservoir rock.

Figure 5 *Petroleum and gas move through permeable rock. Eventually, these fuels are collected in reservoirs. Rocks that are folded upward are excellent fossil-fuel traps.*

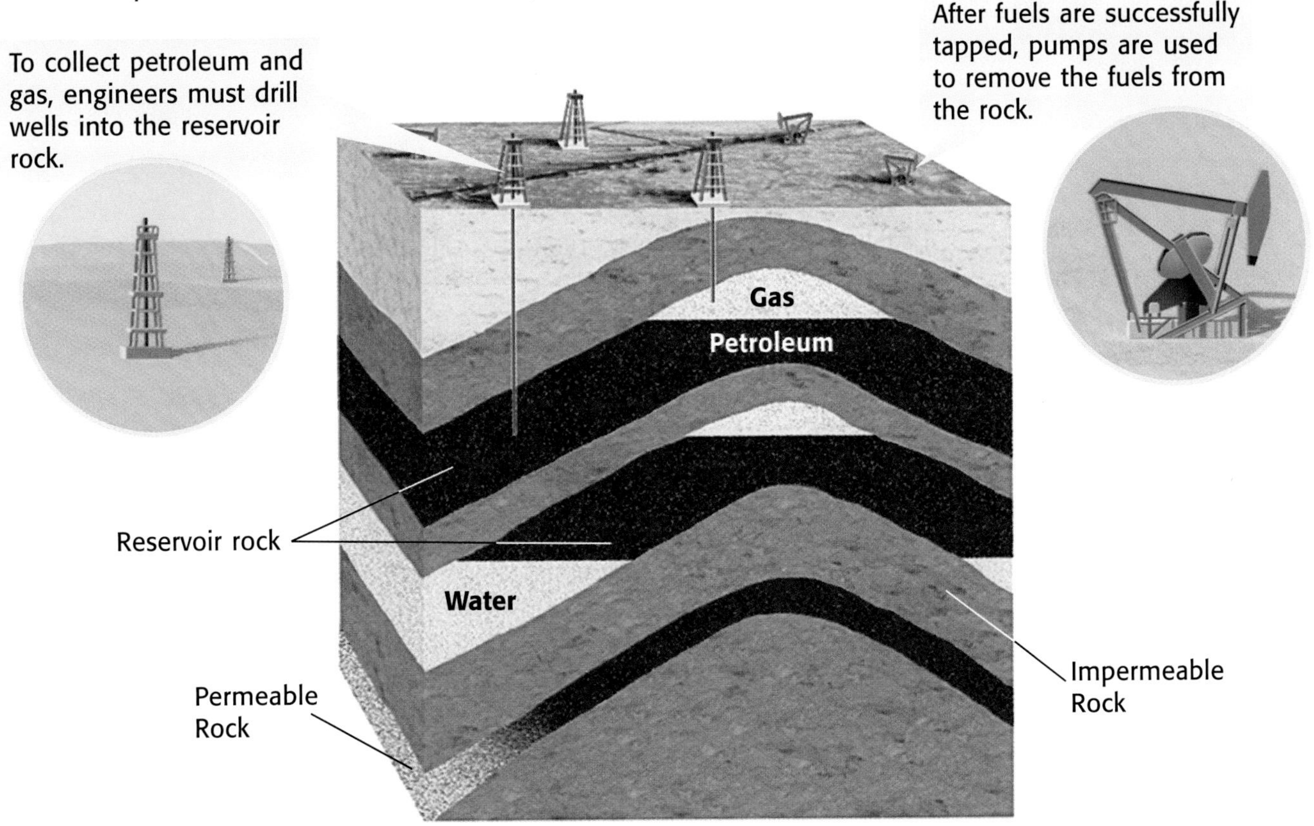

To collect petroleum and gas, engineers must drill wells into the reservoir rock.
After fuels are successfully tapped, pumps are used to remove the fuels from the rock.
Gas
Petroleum
Reservoir rock
Water
Permeable Rock
Impermeable Rock

Coal Formation

Coal forms underground over millions of years when pressure and heat cause changes in the remains of swamp plants. When these plants die, they sink to the bottom of the swamp. If they do not decay completely, coal formation may begin. The stages of coal formation are shown in **Figure 6.**

The first step of the process is the change of plant remains into peat. Peat is brown, crumbly matter made mostly of plant material and water. Peat is not coal. But, in some parts of the world, peat is dried and burned for heat or as fuel. If the peat is buried by sediment, pressure and heat are applied to the peat, and coal begins to form. The pressure and heat force water and gases out of the coal. As a result, the coal becomes harder, and its carbon content increases. The amount of heat and pressure determines the type of coal that forms. Lignite forms first, followed by bituminous coal, and, finally, anthracite. Coal formation can stop during any part of this process. Today, all three types of coal are mined throughout the world. The greater the carbon content of the coal is, the more cleanly the coal burns. But when burned, all types of coal pollute the air.

Figure 6 **Coal Formation**

Stage 1: Peat Forms
Sunken swamp plants that have not decayed completely can change into peat. About 60% of an average sample of dried peat is carbon.

Stage 2: Lignite Forms
If sediment buries the peat, pressure and temperature increase. The peat slowly changes into a type of coal called *lignite.* Lignite is harder than peat is, and about 70% of an average sample of lignite is carbon.

Stage 3: Bituminous Coal Forms
If more sediment is added, pressure and temperature force more water and gases out of the lignite. Lignite slowly changes into bituminous coal. About 80% of an average sample of bituminous coal is carbon.

Stage 4: Anthracite Forms
If more sediment accumulates, temperature and pressure continue to increase. Bituminous coal slowly changes into anthracite. Anthracite is the hardest type of coal. About 90% of an average sample of anthracite is carbon.

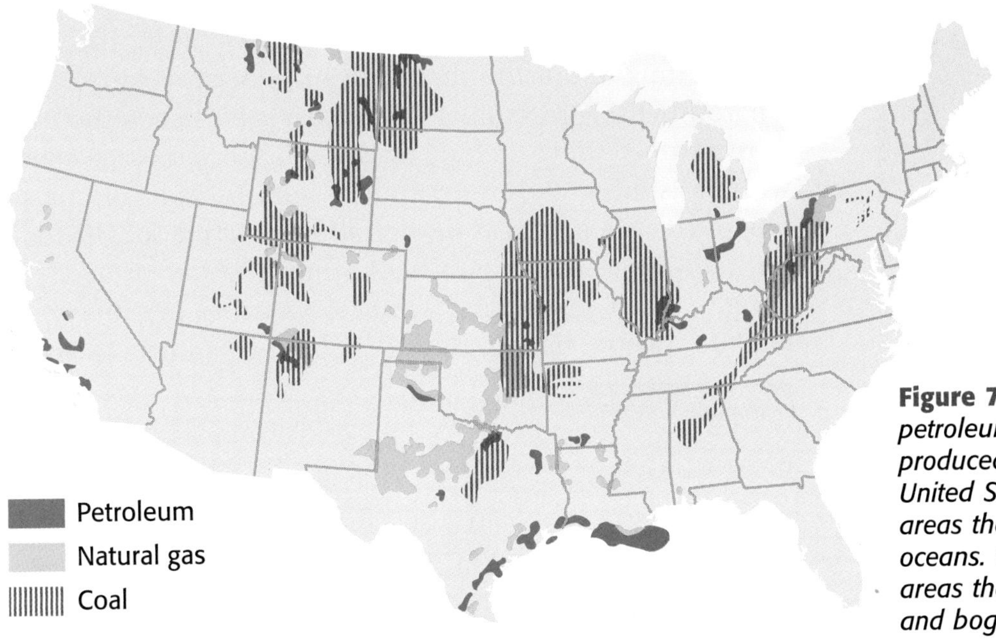

Figure 7 *Most of the petroleum and natural gas produced in the continental United States comes from areas that were prehistoric oceans. Coal comes from areas that were swamps and bogs.*

Where Are Fossil Fuels Found?

Fossil fuels are found in many parts of the world. Some fossil fuels are found on land, while other fossil fuels are found beneath the ocean. As shown in **Figure 7,** the United States has large reserves of petroleum, natural gas, and coal. Despite its large reserves of petroleum, the United States imports petroleum as well. About one-half of the petroleum used by the United States is imported from the Middle East, South America, Africa, Canada, and Mexico.

How Do We Obtain Fossil Fuels?

Humans use several methods to remove fossil fuels from the Earth's crust. The kind and location of fuel determine the method used to remove the fuel. People remove petroleum and natural gas from Earth by drilling wells into rock that contains these resources. Oil wells exist on land and in the ocean. For offshore drilling, engineers mount drills on platforms that are secured to the ocean floor or that float at the ocean's surface. **Figure 8** shows an offshore oil rig.

People obtain coal either by mining deep beneath Earth's surface or by surface mining. Surface mining, also known as *strip mining,* is the process by which soil and rock are stripped from the Earth's surface to expose the underlying coal that is to be mined.

Reading Check **How are natural gas and petroleum removed from Earth?**

Figure 8 *Large oil rigs, some of which are more than 300 m tall, operate offshore in many places, such as the Gulf of Mexico and the North Sea.*

Figure 9 *Notice how this statue looked before the effects of acid precipitation.*

Problems with Fossil Fuels

Although fossil fuels provide the energy we need, the methods of obtaining and using them can have negative effects on the environment. For example, when coal is burned without pollution controls, sulfur dioxide is released. Sulfur dioxide combines with moisture in the air to produce sulfuric acid. Sulfuric acid is one of the acids in acid precipitation. **Acid precipitation** is rain, sleet, or snow that has a high concentration of acids, often because of air pollutants. Acid precipitation negatively affects wildlife, plants, buildings, and statues, as shown in **Figure 9.**

Reading Check **How can the burning of fossil fuels affect rain?**

acid precipitation precipitation, such as rain, sleet, or snow, that contains a high concentration of acids, often because of the pollution of the atmosphere

smog photochemical haze that forms when sunlight acts on industrial pollutants and burning fuels

Coal Mining

The mining of coal can also create environmental problems. Surface mining removes soil, which some plants need for growth and some animals need for shelter. If land is not properly restored afterward, surface mining can destroy wildlife habitats. Coal mining can also lower water tables and pollute water supplies. The potential for underground mines to collapse endangers the lives of miners.

Petroleum Problems

Producing, transporting, and using petroleum can cause environmental problems and endanger wildlife. In June 2000, the carrier, *Treasure,* sank off the coast of South Africa and spilled more than 400 tons of oil. The toxic oil coated thousands of blackfooted penguins, as shown in **Figure 10.** The oil hindered the penguins from swimming and catching fish for food.

Smog

Burning petroleum products causes an environmental problem called smog. **Smog** is photochemical haze that forms when sunlight acts on industrial pollutants and burning fuels. Smog is particularly serious in cities such as Houston and Los Angeles as a result of millions of automobiles that burn gasoline. Also, mountains that surround Los Angeles prevent the wind from blowing pollutants away.

Figure 10 *The oil spilled from the carrier,* Treasure, *endangered the lives of many animals including the blackfooted penguins.*

SECTION Review

Summary

- Energy resources are resources that humans use to produce energy.
- Petroleum is a liquid fossil fuel that is made of hydrocarbon compounds.
- Natural gas is a gaseous fossil fuel that is made of hydrocarbon compounds.
- Coal is a solid fossil fuel that forms from the remains of swamp plants.
- Petroleum and natural gas form from the remains of microscopic sea life.
- Fossil fuels are found all over the world. The United States imports half of the petroleum it uses from the Middle East, South America, Africa, Mexico, and Canada.
- Fossil fuels are obtained by drilling oil wells, mining below Earth's surface, and strip mining.
- Acid precipitation, smog, water pollution, and the destruction of wildlife habitat are some of the environmental problems that are created by the use of fossil fuels.

Using Key Terms

1. Use each of the following terms in a separate sentence: *energy resource, fossil fuel, petroleum, natural gas, coal, acid precipitation,* and *smog.*

Understanding Key Ideas

2. Which of the following types of coal contains the highest carbon content?

a. lignite
b. anthracite
c. peat
d. bituminous coal

3. Name a solid fossil fuel, a liquid fossil fuel, and a gaseous fossil fuel.

4. Briefly describe how petroleum and natural gas form.

5. How do we obtain petroleum and natural gas?

6. Describe the advantages and disadvantages of fossil fuel use.

Critical Thinking

7. Making Comparisons What is the difference between the organic material from which coal forms and the organic material from which petroleum and natural gas form?

8. Making Inferences Why can't carpooling and using mass-transit systems eliminate the problems associated with fossil fuels?

Interpreting Graphics

Use the pie chart below to answer the questions that follow.

Oil Production by Region

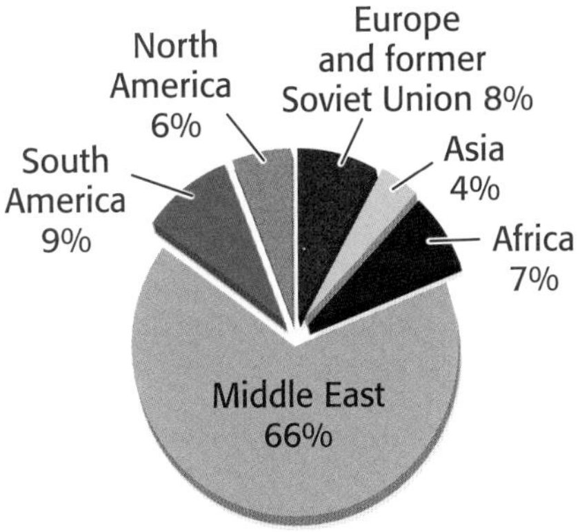

Source: International Energy Agency.

9. Which region produces the most oil?

10. If the total sales of oil in 2002 were $500 billion, what was the value of the oil produced in North America?

SECTION 3

Alternative Resources

What would your life be like if you couldn't play video games, turn on lights, microwave your dinner, take a hot shower, or take the bus to school?

What You Will Learn

- Describe alternatives to the use of fossil fuels.
- List advantages and disadvantages of using alternative energy resources.

Vocabulary

nuclear energy
chemical energy
solar energy
wind power
hydroelectric energy
biomass
gasohol
geothermal energy

READING STRATEGY

Paired Summarizing Read this section silently. In pairs, take turns summarizing the material. Stop to discuss ideas that seem confusing.

Most of your energy needs and the energy needs of others are met by the use of fossil fuels. Yet, there are two main problems with fossil fuels. First, the availability of fossil fuels is limited. Fossil fuels are nonrenewable resources. Once fossil fuels are used up, new supplies won't be available for thousands—or even millions—of years.

Second, obtaining and using fossil fuels has environmental consequences. To continue to have access to energy and to overcome pollution, we must find alternative sources of energy.

Splitting the Atom: Fission

The energy released by a fission or fusion reaction is **nuclear energy.** *Fission* is a process in which the nuclei of radioactive atoms are split into two or more smaller nuclei, as shown in **Figure 1.** When fission takes place, a large amount of energy is released. This energy can be used to generate electrical energy. The SI unit for all forms of energy is the joule. However, electrical energy and nuclear energy is often measured in megawatts (MW).

Figure 1 Fission

A neutron from a uranium-235 atom splits the nucleus into two smaller nuclei called *fission products* and two or more neutrons.

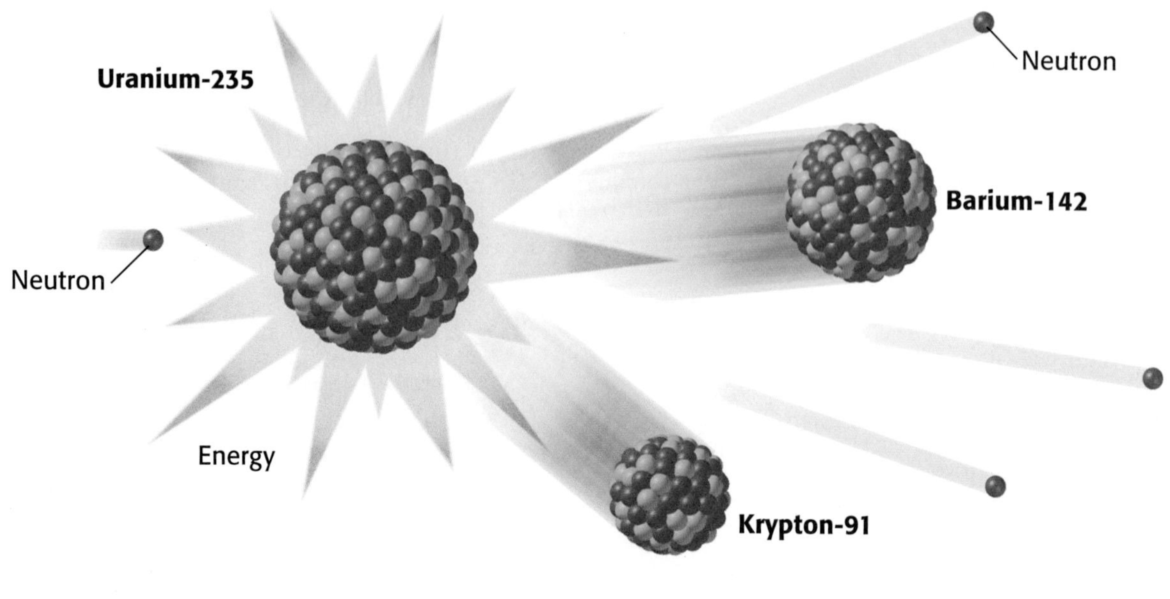

Pros and Cons of Fission

Nuclear power plants provide alternative sources of energy that do not have the problems that fossil fuels do. So, why don't we use nuclear energy more instead of using fossil fuels? Nuclear power plants produce dangerous radioactive wastes. Radioactive wastes must be removed from the plant and stored until their radioactivity decreases to a harmless level. But nuclear wastes can remain dangerously radioactive for thousands of years. These wastes must be stored in an isolated place where the radiation that they emit cannot harm anyone.

Another problem with nuclear power plants is the potential for accidental release of radiation into the environment. A release could happen if the plant overheats. If a plant's cooling system were to stop working, the plant would overheat. Then, its reactor could melt, and a large amount of radiation could escape into the environment. In addition, towers like the one shown in **Figure 2,** keep hot water from potentially disrupting the local ecosystem.

Figure 2 *Cooling towers are used to cool water leaving a nuclear power plant before the water is released into the environment.*

Combining Atoms: Fusion

Another method of getting energy from nuclei is fusion, shown in **Figure 3.** *Fusion* is the joining of two or more nuclei to form a larger nucleus. This process releases a large amount of energy and happens naturally in the sun.

nuclear energy the energy released by a fission or fusion reaction; the binding energy of the atomic nucleus

The main advantage of fusion is that it produces few dangerous wastes. The main disadvantage of fusion is that very high temperatures are required for the reaction to take place. No known material can withstand such high temperatures. Therefore, the reaction must happen within a special environment, such as a magnetic field. Controlled fusion reactions have been limited to laboratory experiments.

Reading Check **What is the advantage of producing energy through fusion?** *(See the Appendix for answers to Reading Checks.)*

Figure 3 **Fusion**

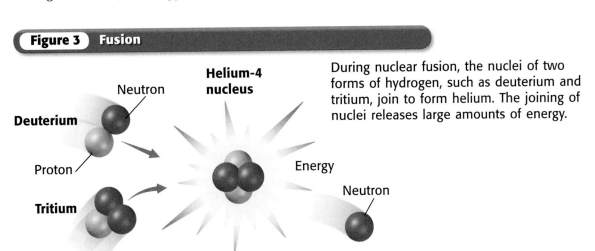

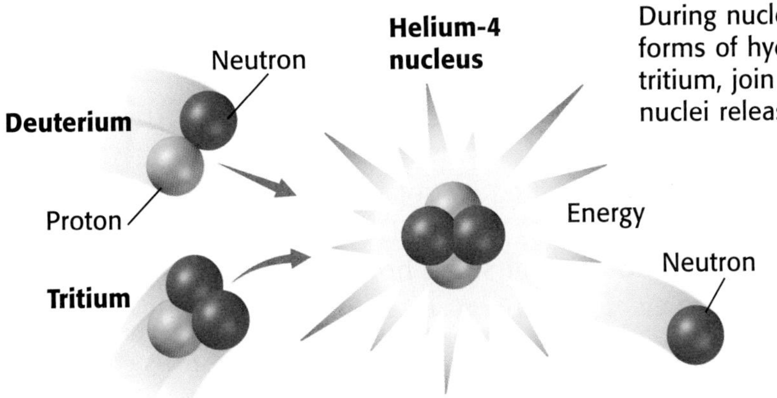

During nuclear fusion, the nuclei of two forms of hydrogen, such as deuterium and tritium, join to form helium. The joining of nuclei releases large amounts of energy.

Figure 4 *This image shows a prototype of a fuel-cell car. Power from fuel cells may be commonly used in the future.*

Chemical Energy

chemical energy the energy released when a chemical compound reacts to produce new compounds

solar energy the energy received by the Earth from the sun in the form of radiation

When you think of fuel for an automobile, you most likely think of gasoline. However, not all vehicles are fueled by gasoline. Some vehicles, such as the one shown in **Figure 4,** are powered by energy that is generated by fuel cells. Fuel cells power automobiles by converting **chemical energy** into electrical energy by reacting hydrogen and oxygen into water. One advantage of using fuel cells as energy sources is that fuel cells do not create pollution. The only byproduct of fuel cells is water. Fuel cells are also more efficient than internal combustion engines are.

The United States has been using fuel cells in space travel since the 1960s. Fuel cells have provided space crews with electrical energy and drinking water. One day, fuel-cell technology may be used to generate electrical energy in buildings, ships, and submarines, too.

Solar Energy

Almost all forms of energy, such as the energy of fossil fuels, come from the sun. The energy received by the Earth from the sun in the form of radiation is **solar energy.** The Earth receives more than enough solar energy to meet all of our energy needs. And because the Earth continuously receives solar energy, this energy is a renewable resource. Solar energy can be used directly to heat buildings and to generate electrical energy. However, we do not yet have the technology to generate the amount of electrical energy we need from solar energy.

Sunlight can be changed into electrical energy through the use of solar cells or photovoltaic cells. You may have used a calculator that is powered by solar cells. *Solar panels* are large panels made up of many solar cells wired together. Solar panels mounted on the roofs of some homes and businesses provide some of the electrical energy used in the buildings.

CONNECTION TO Language Arts

WRITING SKILL **Resources of the Future** In 100 years do you think humans will still be using fossil fuels to power their cars? Maybe humans will be using alternative energy resources. Maybe humans won't even be driving cars! Write a short, creative, science fiction story describing the energy use of humans 100 years from now.

Reading Check **Where does the energy of fossil fuels come from?**

Solar Heating

Solar energy is also used for direct heating through solar collectors. *Solar collectors* are dark-colored boxes that have glass or plastic tops. A common use of solar collectors is to heat water, as shown in **Figure 5.** More than 1 million solar water heaters have been installed in the United States. Solar water heaters are especially common in Florida and California.

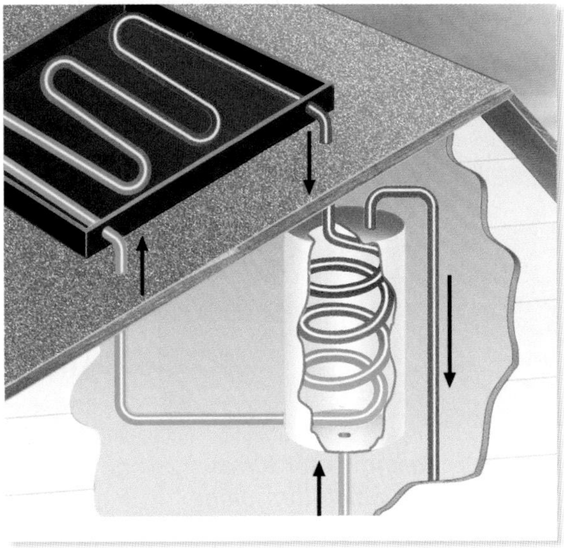

Figure 5 *The liquid in the solar collector is heated by the sun. Then, the liquid is pumped through tubes that run through a water heater, which causes the temperature of the water to increase.*

Pros and Cons of Solar Energy

One of the best things about solar energy is that it doesn't produce pollution. Also, solar energy is renewable, because it comes from the sun. However, some climates don't have enough sunny days to benefit from solar energy. Also, although solar energy is free, solar cells and solar collectors are more expensive to make than other energy systems are. The cost of installing a complete solar-power system in a house can be one-third of the total cost of the house.

Wind Power

Wind is made indirectly by solar energy through the uneven heating of air. Energy can be harnessed from wind. **Wind power** is the use of a windmill to drive an electric generator. Clusters of wind turbines, like the ones shown in **Figure 6,** can generate a significant amount of electrical energy. Wind energy is renewable, and it doesn't cause any pollution. However, in many areas, the wind isn't strong enough or frequent enough to create energy on a large scale.

wind power the use of a windmill to drive an electric generator

Figure 6 *Wind turbines take up only a small part of the ground's surface. As a result, the land on wind farms can be used for more than one purpose.*

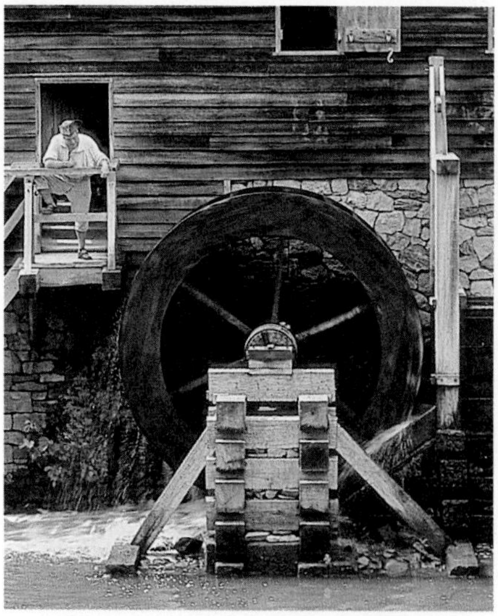

Figure 7 *Falling water turns water wheels, which turn giant millstones used to grind grain into flour.*

Hydroelectric Energy

Humans have used the energy of falling water for thousands of years. Water wheels, such as the one shown in **Figure 7,** have been around since ancient times. In the early years of the Industrial Revolution, water wheels provided energy for many factories. Today, the energy of falling water is used to generate electrical energy. Electrical energy produced by falling water is called **hydroelectric energy.**

hydroelectric energy electrical energy produced by falling water

Pros and Cons of Hydroelectric Energy

After the dam is built, hydroelectric energy is inexpensive and causes little pollution. It is renewable because water constantly cycles from water sources to the air, to the land, and back to the water source. But like wind energy, hydroelectric energy is not available everywhere. It can be produced only where large volumes of falling water can be harnessed. Huge dams, such as the one in **Figure 8,** must be built on major rivers to capture enough water to generate significant amounts of electrical energy.

Using more hydroelectric energy could reduce the demand for fossil fuels, but there are trade-offs. Building the large dams necessary for hydroelectric power plants often destroys other resources, such as forests and wildlife habitats. For example, hydroelectric dams on the lower Snake and Columbia Rivers in Washington state disrupt the migratory paths of local populations of salmon and steelhead. Large numbers of these fish die each year because their migratory path is disrupted. Dams can also decrease water quality and create erosion problems.

Reading Check **Why is hydroelectric energy renewable?**

Figure 8 *Falling water turns turbines inside hydroelectric dams and generates electrical energy for millions of people.*

Power from Plants

Plants are similar to solar collectors. Both absorb energy from the sun and store it for later use. Leaves, wood, and other parts of plants contain the stored energy. Even the dung of plant-grazing animals is high in stored energy. These sources of energy are called biomass. **Biomass** is organic matter that can be a source of energy.

biomass organic matter that can be a source of energy

gasohol a mixture of gasoline and alcohol that is used as a fuel

Burning Biomass

Biomass energy can be released in several ways. The most common way is to burn biomass. Approximately 70% of people living in developing countries, about half the world population, burn wood or charcoal to heat their homes and cook their food. In contrast, about 5% of the people in the United States heat and cook this way. Scientists estimate that the burning of wood and animal dung accounts for approximately 14% of the world's total energy use. **Figure 9** shows a woman who is preparing cow dung that will be dried and used for fuel.

Gasohol

Biomass material can also be changed into liquid fuel. Plants that contain sugar or starch can be made into alcohol. The alcohol can be burned as a fuel. Or alcohol can be mixed with gasoline to make a fuel called **gasohol.** More than 1,000 L of alcohol can be made from 1 acre of corn. But people in the United States use a large amount of fuel for their cars. And the alcohol produced from about 40% of one corn harvest in the United States would provide only 10% of the fuel used in our cars! Biomass is a renewable source of energy. However, producing biomass requires land that could be used for growing food.

MATH PRACTICE

Miles per Acre

Imagine that you own a car that runs on alcohol made from corn that you grow. You drive your car about 15,000 mi per year, and you get 240 gal of alcohol from each acre of corn that you process. If your car has a gas mileage of 25 mi/gal, how many acres of corn must you process to fuel your car for a year?

Figure 9 *In many parts of the world where firewood is scarce, people burn animal dung for energy.*

Energy from Within Earth

If you have ever seen a volcanic eruption, you know how powerful the Earth can be. The energy produced by the heat within Earth is called **geothermal energy.**

geothermal energy the energy produced by heat within the Earth

Geothermal Energy

In some areas, groundwater is heated by *magma,* or melted rock. Often, the heated groundwater becomes steam. *Geysers* are natural vents that discharge this steam or water in a column into the air. The steam and hot water can also escape through wells drilled into the rock. From these wells, geothermal power plants can harness the energy from within Earth by pumping the steam and hot water, as shown in **Figure 10.** The world's largest geothermal power plant in California, called *The Geysers,* produces electrical energy for 1.7 million households.

Geothermal energy can also be used to heat buildings. In this process, hot water and steam are used to heat a fluid. Then, this fluid is pumped through a building in order to heat the building. Buildings in Iceland are heated from the country's many geothermal sites in this way.

Reading Check How do geothermal power plants obtain geothermal energy from the Earth?

Figure 10 How a Geothermal Power Plant Works

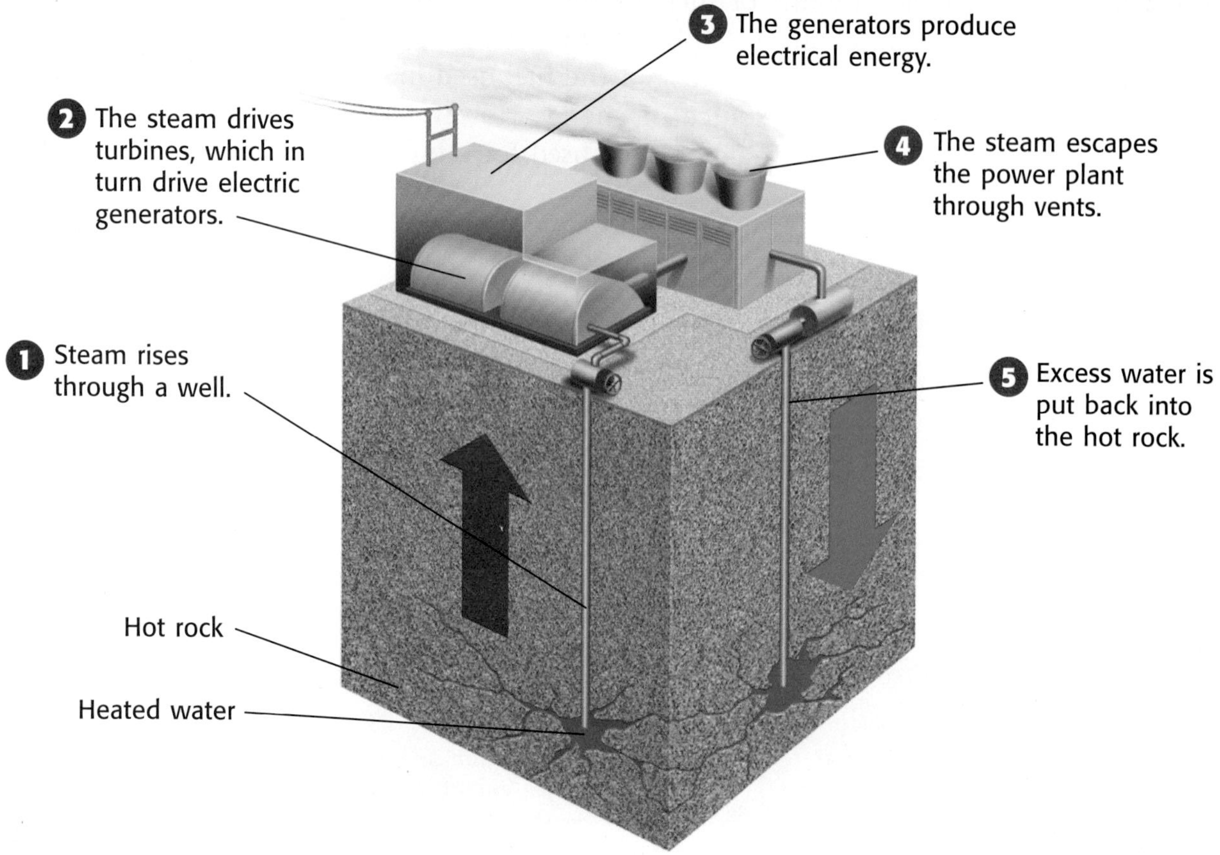

3 The generators produce electrical energy.
2 The steam drives turbines, which in turn drive electric generators.
4 The steam escapes the power plant through vents.
1 Steam rises through a well.
5 Excess water is put back into the hot rock.
Hot rock
Heated water

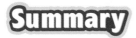

SECTION Review

Summary

- Fission and fusion are processes that release nuclear energy. The byproduct of fission is radioactive waste.
- For fusion to take place, extremely high temperatures are required.
- Fuel cells combine hydrogen and oxygen to produce electrical energy. Fuel cells release water as a byproduct.
- Solar energy is a renewable resource that doesn't emit pollution. However, solar panels and solar collectors are expensive.
- Wind power is a renewable resource that doesn't emit pollution. However, wind energy cannot be generated in all areas.
- Hydroelectric energy is a cheap, renewable resource that causes little pollution. However, it is available only in some areas.
- Burning biomass and gasohol can release energy, but not enough to meet all of our energy needs.
- Geothermal energy comes from the Earth but is available only in certain areas.

Using Key Terms

1. In your own words, write a definition for each of the following terms: *nuclear energy, solar energy, wind power, hydroelectric energy, biomass, gasohol,* and *geothermal energy.*

Understanding Key Ideas

2. Which of the following alternative resources requires hydrogen and oxygen to produce energy?

a. fuel cells
b. solar energy
c. nuclear energy
d. geothermal energy

3. Describe two ways of using solar energy.

4. Where is the production of hydroelectric energy practical?

5. Describe two ways to release biomass energy.

6. Describe two ways to use geothermal energy.

Critical Thinking

7. Analyzing Methods If you were going to build a nuclear power plant, why wouldn't you build it in the middle of a desert?

8. Predicting Consequences If an alternative resource could successfully replace crude oil, how might the use of that resource affect the environment?

Interpreting Graphics

Use the graph below to answer the questions that follow.

How Energy Is Used in the United States

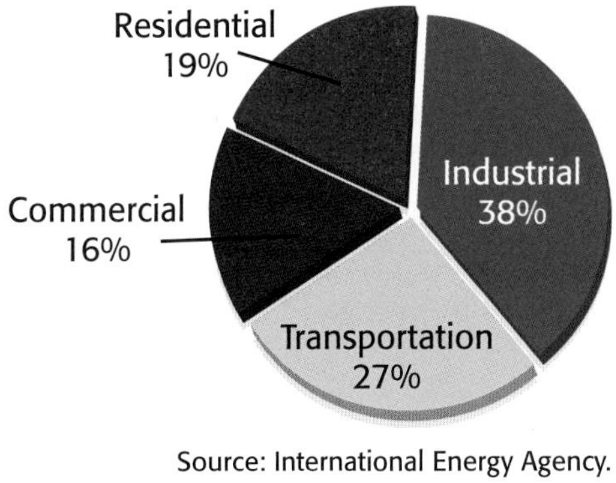

Source: International Energy Agency.

9. What is the total percentage of energy that is used for commercial and industrial purposes?

10. What is the total percentage of energy that is not used for residential purposes?

SCILINKS. NSTA Developed and maintained by the National Science Teachers Association

For a variety of links related to this chapter, go to www.scilinks.org

Topic: Renewable Resources
SciLinks code: HSM1291

Using Scientific Methods

Model-Making Lab

Make a Water Wheel

OBJECTIVES

Create a model of a water wheel.

Determine factors that influence the rate at which a water wheel lifts a weight.

MATERIALS

- bottle, soda, 2 L, filled with water
- card, index, 3 × 5 in.
- clay, modeling
- coin
- cork
- glue
- hole punch
- jug, milk, plastic
- marker, permanent, black
- meterstick
- safety razor (for teacher)
- scissors
- skewers, wooden (2)
- tape, transparent
- thread, 20 cm
- thumbtacks (5)
- watch or clock that indicates seconds

SAFETY

Lift Enterprises is planning to build a water wheel that will lift objects like a crane does. The president of the company has asked you to modify the basic water wheel design so that the water wheel will lift objects more quickly.

Ask a Question

1. What factors influence the rate at which a water wheel lifts a weight?

Form a Hypothesis

2. Change the question above into a statement to formulate a testable hypothesis.

Test the Hypothesis

3. Build a water wheel model. Measure and mark a 5 × 5 cm square on an index card. Cut the square out of the card. Fold the square in half to form a triangle.
4. Measure and mark a line 8 cm from the bottom of the plastic jug. Use scissors to cut along this line. (Your teacher may need to use a safety razor to start this cut for you.)
5. Use the paper triangle you made in step 3 as a template. Use a permanent marker to trace four triangles onto the flat parts of the top section of the plastic jug. Cut the triangles out of the plastic to form four fins.
6. Use a thumbtack to attach one corner of each plastic fin to the round edge of the cork, as shown below. Make sure the fins are equally spaced around the cork.

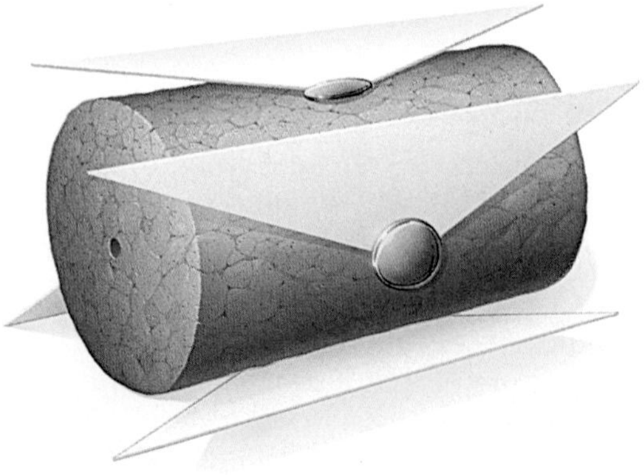

7. Press a thumbtack into one of the flat sides of the cork. Jiggle the thumbtack to widen the hole in the cork, and then remove the thumbtack. Repeat on the other side of the cork.

8. Place a drop of glue on one end of each skewer. Insert the first skewer into one of the holes in the end of the cork. Insert the second skewer into the hole in the other end of the cork.

9. Use a hole punch to carefully punch two holes in the bottom section of the plastic jug. Punch each hole 1 cm from the top edge of the jug, directly across from one another.

10. Carefully push the skewers through the holes, and suspend the cork in the center of the jug. Attach a small ball of clay to the end of each skewer. The balls should be the same size.

11. Tape one end of the thread to one skewer on the outside of the jug, next to the clay ball. Wrap the thread around the clay ball three times. (As the water wheel turns, the thread should wrap around the clay. The other ball of clay balances the weight and helps to keep the water wheel turning smoothly.)

12. Tape the free end of the thread to a coin. Wrap the thread around the coin, and tape it again.

13. Slowly pour water from the 2 L bottle onto the fins so that the water wheel spins. What happens to the coin? Record your observations.

14. Lower the coin back to the starting position. Add more clay to the skewer to increase the diameter of the wheel. Repeat step 13. Did the coin rise faster or slower this time?

15. Lower the coin back to the starting position. Modify the shape of the clay, and repeat step 13. Does the shape of the clay affect how quickly the coin rises? Explain your answer.

16. What happens if you remove two of the fins from opposite sides? What happens if you add more fins?

17. Experiment with another fin shape. How does a different fin shape affect how quickly the coin rises?

Analyze the Results

1. **Examining Data** What factors influence how quickly you can lift the coin? Explain.

Draw Conclusions

2. **Drawing Conclusions** What recommendations would you make to the president of Lift Enterprises to improve the water wheel?

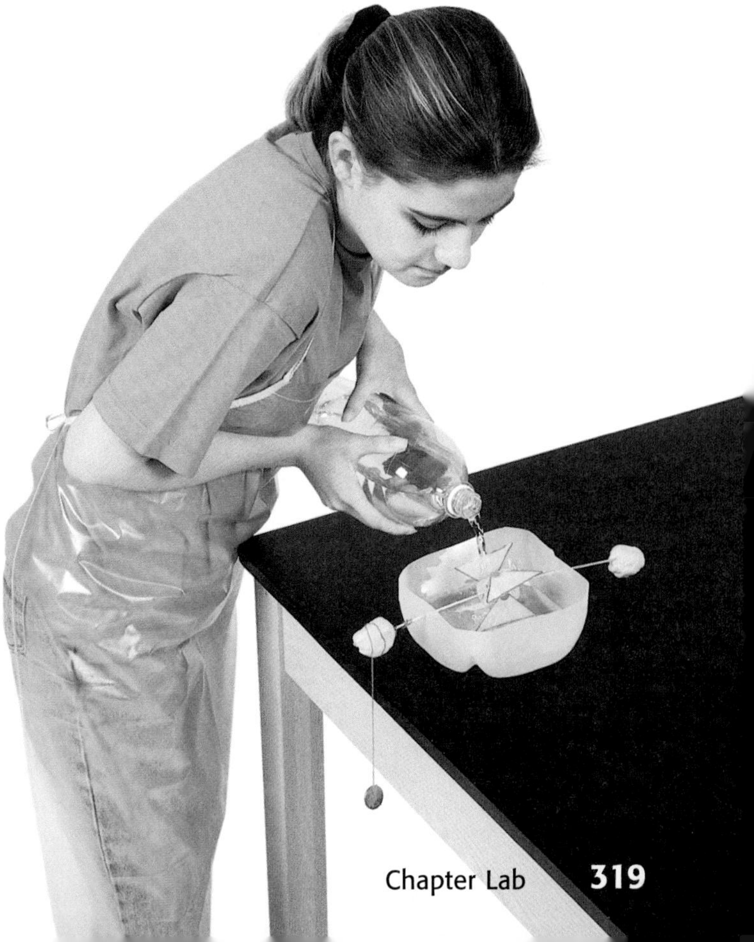

Chapter Review

USING KEY TERMS

The statements below are false. For each statement, replace the underlined term to make a true statement.

1. A liquid mixture of complex hydrocarbon compounds is called natural gas.

2. Energy that is released when a chemical compound reacts to produce a new compound is called nuclear energy.

For each pair of terms, explain how the meanings of the terms differ.

3. *solar energy* and *wind power*

4. *biomass* and *gasohol*

UNDERSTANDING KEY IDEAS

Multiple Choice

5. Which of the following resources is a renewable resource?
   a. coal
   b. trees
   c. oil
   d. natural gas

6. Which of the following fuels is NOT made from petroleum?
   a. jet fuel
   b. lignite
   c. kerosene
   d. fuel oil

7. Peat, lignite, and anthracite are all forms of
   a. petroleum.
   b. natural gas.
   c. coal.
   d. gasohol.

8. Which of the following factors contributes to smog?
   a. automobiles
   b. sunlight
   c. mountains surrounding urban areas
   d. All of the above

9. Which of the following resources is produced by fusion?
   a. solar energy
   b. natural gas
   c. nuclear energy
   d. petroleum

10. To produce energy, nuclear power plants use a process called
    a. fission.
    b. fusion.
    c. fractionation.
    d. None of the above

11. A solar-powered calculator uses
    a. solar collectors.
    b. solar panels.
    c. solar mirrors.
    d. solar cells.

Short Answer

12. How does acid precipitation form?

13. If sunlight is free, why is electrical energy from solar cells expensive?

14. Describe three ways that humans use natural resources.

15. Explain how fossil fuels are found and obtained.

CRITICAL THINKING

16 **Concept Mapping** Use the following terms to create a concept map: *fossil fuels, wind energy, energy resources, biomass, renewable resources, solar energy, nonrenewable resources, natural gas, gasohol, coal,* and *oil.*

17 **Predicting Consequences** How would your life be different if fossil fuels were less widely available?

18 **Evaluating Assumptions** Are fossil fuels nonrenewable? Explain.

19 **Evaluating Assumptions** Why do we need to conserve renewable resources even though they can be replaced?

20 **Evaluating Data** What might limit the productivity of a geothermal power plant?

21 **Identifying Relationships** Explain why the energy we get from many of our resources ultimately comes from the sun.

22 **Applying Concepts** Describe the different ways you can conserve natural resources at home.

23 **Identifying Relationships** Explain why coal usually forms in different locations from where petroleum and natural gas form.

24 **Applying Concepts** Choose an alternative energy resource that you think should be developed more. Explain the reason for your choice.

INTERPRETING GRAPHICS

Use the graph below to answer the questions that follow.

Energy Consumption and Population Growth in the United States

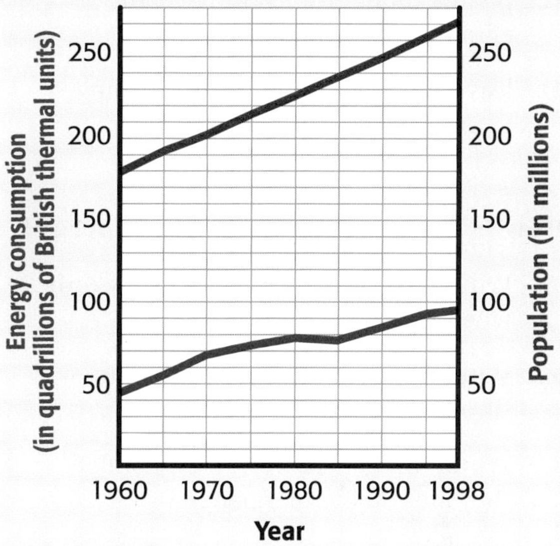

Source: U.S. Department of Energy.

25 How many British thermal units were consumed in 1970?

26 In what year was the most energy consumed?

27 Why do you think that energy consumption has not increased at the same rate as the population has increased?

Standardized Test Preparation

Multiple Choice

1. **Which of the following is one way to conserve water?**

   A. using geothermal energy

   B. using hydroelectric energy

   C. plant a drought-tolerant lawn and eliminate lawn watering

   D. leaving the faucet on while brushing your teeth

2. **How is the sun related to wind energy?**

   A. Windmills can generate electricity only when the sun is shining.

   B. Wind is made indirectly by the sun through the uneven heating of air.

   C. Windmills generate electricity only if they are run by solar panels.

   D. Wind that is heated by the sun can generate more electricity than a cold wind can.

3. **Which of the following resources is nonrenewable?**

   A. wind

   B. trees

   C. sunlight

   D. natural gas

4. **Which of the following comes from a nonrenewable natural resource?**

   A. solar energy

   B. fossil fuel energy

   C. geothermal energy

   D. hydroelectric energy

Below are pie charts that show the emissions of three pollutants from Kentucky electric power plants compared with the total emissions in the United States. Use the pie graphs to answer the question that follows.

Emissions from Electric Power Plants: Pounds per Megawatt Hour

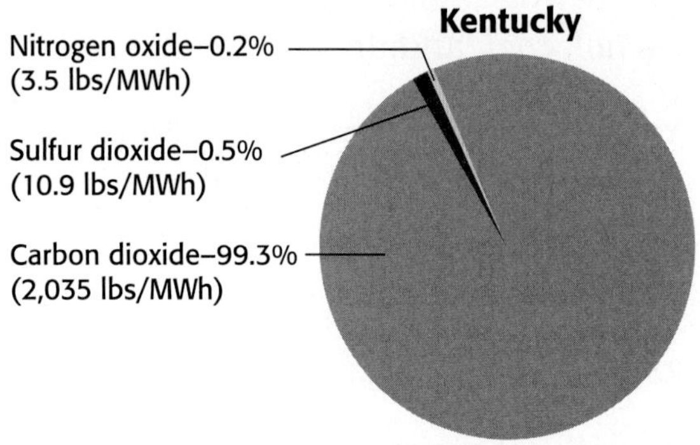

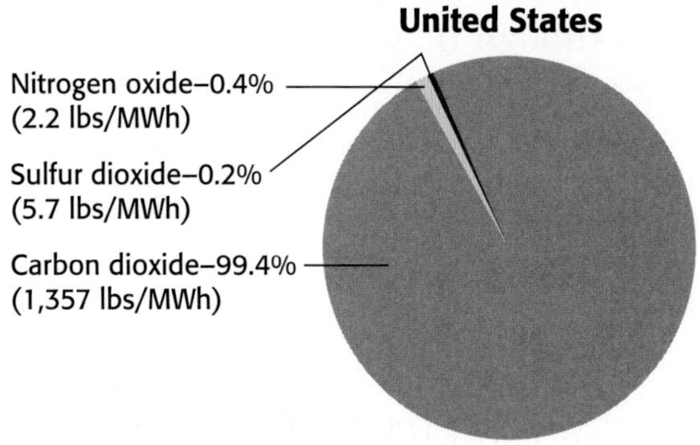

5. **In pounds per megawatt hour of greenhouse-gas emissions, how does Kentucky compare with the total for the United States?**

   A. The emissions are about the same.

   B. Kentucky's emissions are higher.

   C. Kentucky's emissions are lower.

   D. Kentucky emits about a ton of CO_2 per megawatt hour.

6. **What process releases the energy that is used in nuclear power plants to generate electrical energy?**

   A. the burning of radioactive fuel

   B. the reaction of hydrogen and oxygen to form water

   C. the splitting of nuclei into two or more smaller nuclei

   D. the joining of two or more nuclei to form a larger nucleus

7. **Which of the following is true of all fossil fuels?**

   A. Fossil fuels are liquid.

   B. Fossil fuels are found only on land.

   C. Fossil fuels move through permeable rock.

   D. Fossil fuels form from the remains of ancient organisms.

8. **Why is the energy generated at a hydroelectric dam dependent on the sun?**

   A. The sun's gravity causes water to flow.

   B. Energy from the sun powers the water cycle.

   C. Sunlight gets rid of the pollution created by hydroelectric dams.

   D. Sunlight is the source of energy in the fuels burned by hydroelectric dams.

9. **Which type of fuel forms when pressure and heat cause changes in the remains of swamp plants?**

   A. coal

   B. gasohol

   C. petroleum

   D. natural gas

10. **What is the most common way to release biomass energy?**

   A. burn it

   B. recycle it

   C. compress and heat it

   D. convert it into petroleum

Use the figure below to answer question 11.

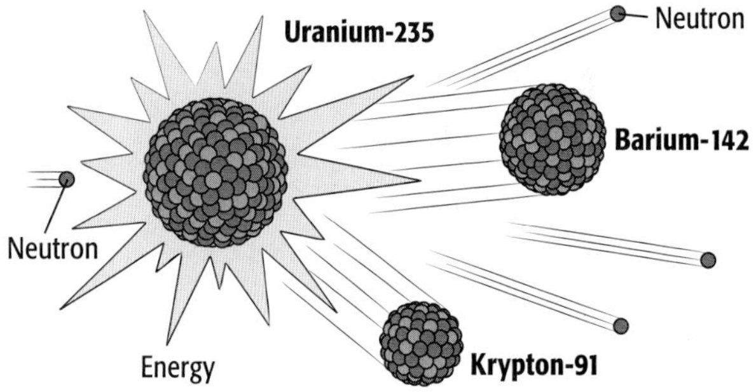

11. **What type of energy is produced from the reaction shown in the figure above?**

   A. hydroelectric energy

   B. nuclear energy

   C. solar energy

   D. chemical energy

Open Response

12. **What is the ultimate source of almost all energy in Kentucky? Explain your answer.**

13. **In what ways is the production of wind energy limited by time and place?**

Science in Action

Scientific Debate

The Three Gorges Dam

Dams provide hydroelectric energy, drinking water, and food for crops. Unfortunately, massive dam projects flood scenic landscapes and disrupt the environment around the dam. For example, the Three Gorges dam in China has displaced almost 2 million people living in the project area. Opponents of the project claim that the dam will also increase pollution levels in the Yangtze River. However, supporters of the dam say it will control flooding and provide millions of people with hydroelectric power. Engineers estimate that the dam's turbines will produce enough electrical energy to power a city 10 times the size of Los Angeles, California.

Language Arts ACTIVITY

WRITING SKILL Find out more about another dam project. Develop your own opinion on the project. What do you think the best outcome would be? Create a fictional story that expresses this outcome.

Science, Technology, and Society

Hybrid Cars

One solution to the pollution problem caused by the burning of fossil fuels for transportation purposes is to develop cars that depend less on fossil fuels. One such car is called a *hybrid*. Instead of using only gasoline for energy, a hybrid car uses gasoline and electricity. Because of its special batteries, the hybrid needs less gasoline to run than a car powered only by gasoline does. Some hybrids can have a gas mileage of as much as 45 mi/gal! Already, there are several models on the market to choose from. In the near future, you might see more hybrid cars on the roads.

Math ACTIVITY

Charlie's truck has a gas mileage of 17 mi/gal. Charlie drives his truck an average of 12,000 mi per year. Then, he sells the truck and buys a new hybrid car that has a gas mileage of 45 mi/gal. If gasoline costs $1.40 per gallon, how much money will Charlie save in a year by driving the hybrid car instead of his truck?

Careers

Fred Begay

Nuclear Physicist Generating energy by combining atoms is called *fusion*. This process is being developed by nuclear physicists, such as Dr. Fred Begay, at the Department of Energy's Los Alamos National Laboratory. Begay hopes to someday make fusion an alternative energy resource. Because fusion is the process that generates energy in the sun, Begay uses NASA satellites to study the sun. Begay explains that it is necessary to develop skills in abstract reasoning to study fusion. As a Navajo, Begay developed these skills while growing up at his Navajo home in Towaoc, Colorado, where his family taught him about nature. Today, Begay uses his skills not only to help develop a new energy resource but also to mentor Native American and minority students. In 1999, Begay won the Distinguished Scientist Award from the Society for Advancement of Chicanos and Native Americans in Science.

Social Studies ACTIVITY

Research the lifestyle of Native Americans before 1900. Then, create a poster that compares resources that Native Americans used before 1900 with resources that many people use today.

go.hrw.com

To learn more about these Science in Action topics, visit go.hrw.com and type in the keyword **HZ5ENRF.**

Current Science

Check out Current Science® articles related to this chapter by visiting go.hrw.com. Just type in the keyword HZ5CS05.

UNIT 3

TIMELINE

Oceanography

In this unit, you will learn about the Earth's oceans and the physical environments that they contain. Together, the oceans form the largest single feature on the Earth. In fact, they cover approximately 70% of the Earth's surface. The oceans not only serve as home for countless living organisms but also affect life on land. This timeline presents some milestones in the exploration of Earth's oceans. Take a deep breath, and dive in!

1851

Herman Melville's novel *Moby Dick* is published.

1938

A coelacanth is discovered in the Indian Ocean near South Africa. Called a fossil fish, the coelacanth was thought to have been extinct for 60 million years.

1978

Louise Brown, the first "test-tube baby," is born in England.

1986

Commercial whaling is temporarily stopped by the International Whaling Commission, but some whaling continues.

1872

The *HMS Challenger* begins its four-year voyage. Its discoveries lay the foundation for the science of oceanography.

1914

The Panama Canal, which links the Atlantic Ocean with the Pacific Ocean, is completed.

1927

Charles Lindbergh completes the first nonstop solo airplane flight over the Atlantic Ocean.

1943

Jacques Cousteau and Émile Gagnan invent the aqualung, a breathing device that allows divers to freely explore the silent world of the oceans.

1960

Jacques Piccard and Don Walsh dive to a record 10,916 m below sea level in their bathyscaph *Trieste*.

1977

Thermal vent communities of organisms that exist without sunlight are discovered on the ocean floor.

1994

The completion of the tunnel under the English Channel makes train and auto travel between Great Britain and France possible.

1998

Ben Lecomte of Austin, Texas, successfully swims across the Atlantic Ocean from Massachusetts to France, a distance of 5,980 km. His record-breaking feat takes 73 days.

2001

Researchers find that dolphins, like humans and the great apes, can recognize themselves in mirrors.

11

Exploring the Oceans

The Big Idea

Oceans cover 71% of Earth's surface and contain natural resources that require protection.

SECTION

About the Photo

Are two heads better than one? Although it may look like this reef lizardfish has two heads, it's actually swallowing another fish whole! Reef lizardfish are commonly found in the Western Pacific Ocean. Unlike most other types of lizardfish, the reef lizardfish prefers to rest on hard surfaces and is usually seen in pairs.

PRE-READING ACTIVITY

FOLDNOTES **Layered Book** Before you read the chapter, create the FoldNote entitled "Layered Book" described in the **Study Skills** section of the Appendix. Label the tabs of the layered book with "Characteristics of ocean water," "The ocean floor," "Ocean zones," and "Resources from the ocean." As you read the chapter, write information you learn about each category under the appropriate tab.

START-UP ACTIVITY

Exit Only?

To study what life underwater would be like, scientists sometimes live in underwater laboratories. How do these scientists enter and leave these labs? Believe it or not, the simplest way is through a hole in the lab's floor. You might think water would come in through the hole, but it doesn't. How is this possible? Do the following activity to find out.

Procedure

1. Fill a **large bowl** about two-thirds full of **water.**
2. Turn a **clear plastic cup** upside down.
3. Slowly guide the cup straight down into the water. Be careful not to guide the cup all the way to the bottom of the bowl. Also, be careful not to tip the cup.
4. Record your observations.

Analysis

1. How does the air inside the cup affect the water below the cup?
2. How do your findings relate to the hole in the bottom of an underwater research lab?

SECTION 1

Earth's Oceans

What You Will Learn

- List the major divisions of the global ocean.
- Describe the history of Earth's oceans.
- Identify the properties of ocean water.
- Describe the interactions between the ocean and the atmosphere.

Vocabulary

salinity
water cycle

READING STRATEGY

Discussion Read this section silently. Write down questions that you have about this section. Discuss your questions in a small group.

What makes Earth so different from Mars? What does Earth have that Mercury doesn't?

Earth stands out from the other planets in our solar system primarily for one reason—71% of the Earth's surface is covered with water. Most of Earth's water is found in the global ocean. The global ocean is divided by the continents into five main oceans. The divisions of the global ocean are shown in **Figure 1.** The ocean is a unique body of water that plays many parts in regulating Earth's environment.

Divisions of the Global Ocean

The largest ocean is the *Pacific Ocean.* It flows between Asia and the Americas. The volume of the *Atlantic Ocean,* the second-largest ocean, is about half the volume of the Pacific. The *Indian Ocean* is the third-largest ocean. The *Arctic Ocean* is the smallest ocean. This ocean is unique because much of its surface is covered by ice. The *Southern Ocean* extends from the coast of Antarctica to 60° south latitude.

Figure 1 *The global ocean is divided by the continents into five main oceans.*

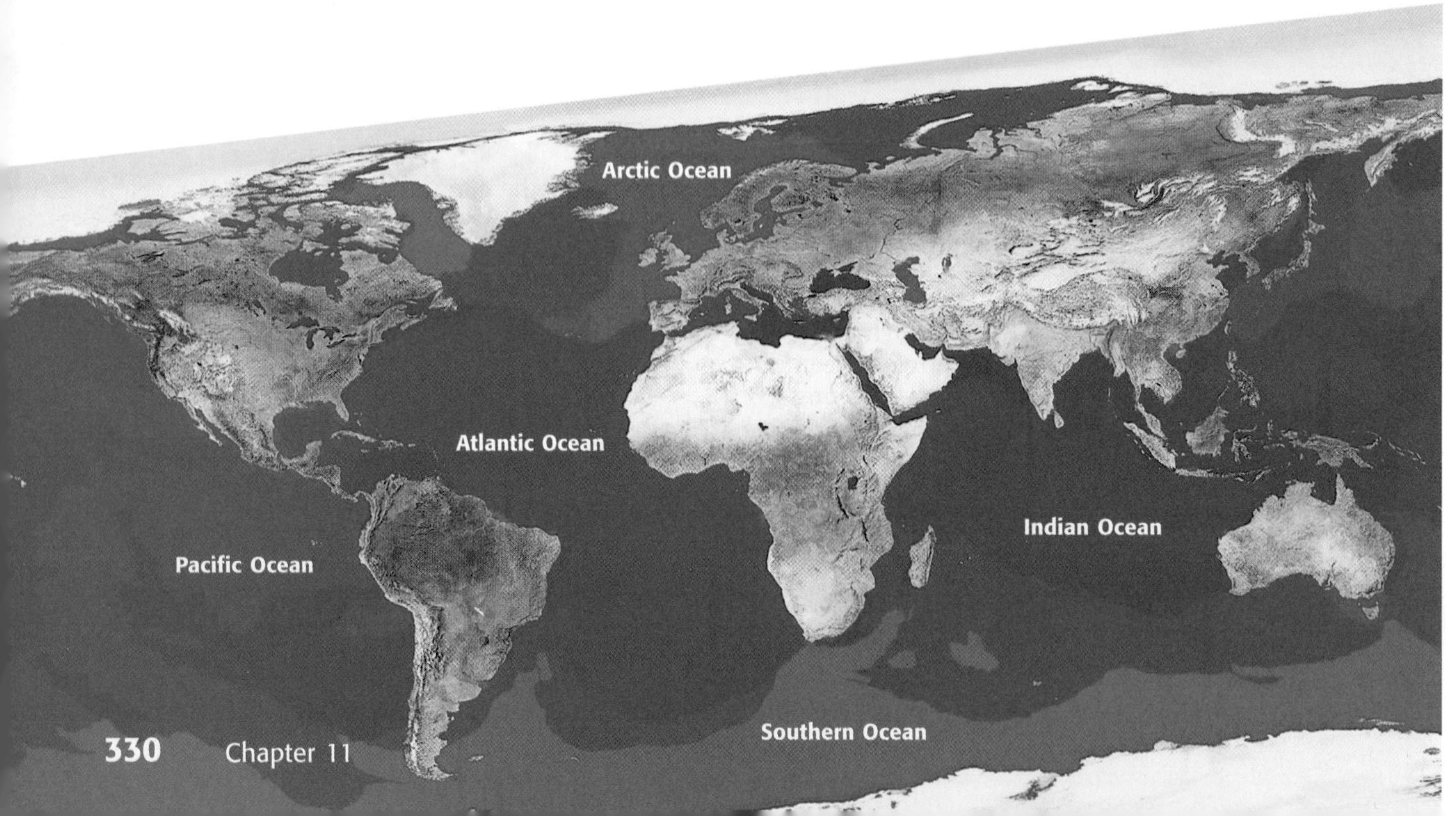

Figure 2 The History of Earth's Oceans

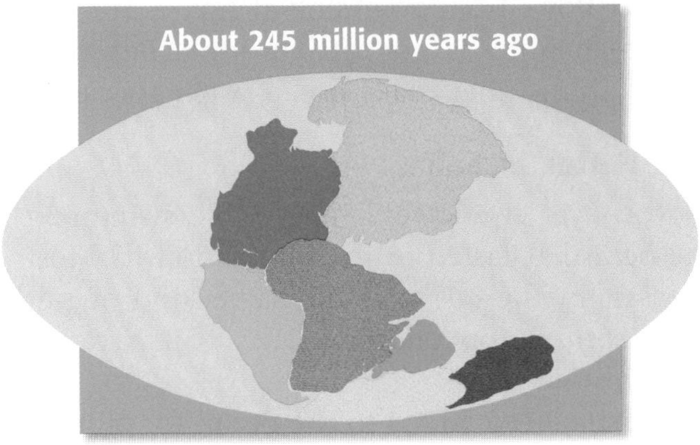

The continents were one giant landmass called Pangaea. The oceans were one giant body of water called Panthalassa.

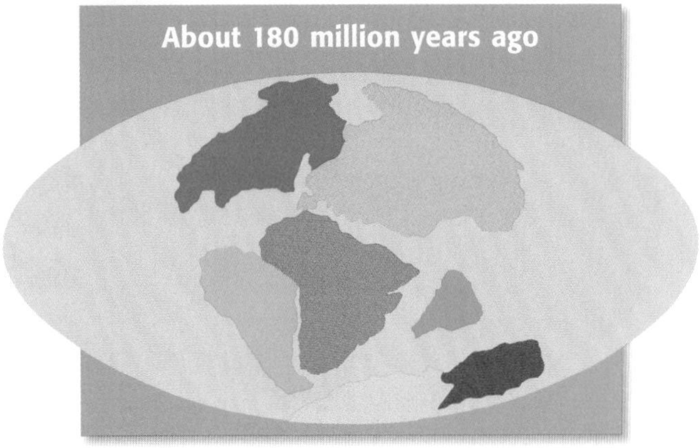

As Pangaea broke apart, the North Atlantic Ocean and the Indian Ocean began to form.

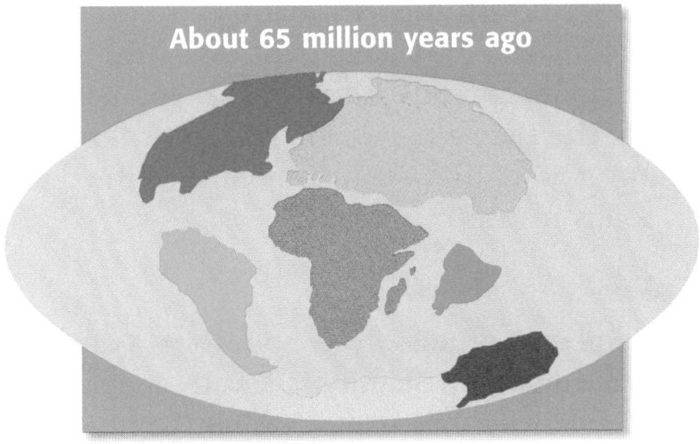

The South Atlantic Ocean was much smaller than it is today.

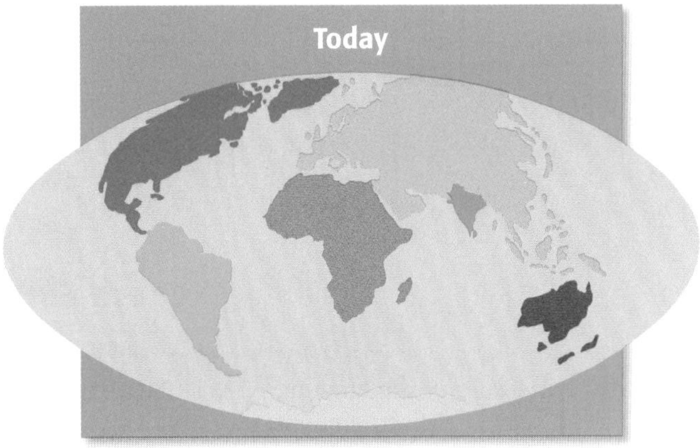

The continents continue to move at a rate of 1 to 10 cm per year. The Pacific Ocean is getting smaller. However, the other oceans are growing.

How Did the Oceans Form?

About 4.5 billion years ago, Earth was a very different place. There were no oceans. Volcanoes spewed lava, ash, and gases all over the planet. The volcanic gases began to form Earth's atmosphere. Meanwhile, Earth was cooling. Sometime before 4 billion years ago, Earth cooled enough for water vapor to condense. This water began to fall as rain. The rain filled the deeper levels of Earth's surface, and the first oceans began to form.

The shape of the Earth's oceans has changed a lot over time. Much has been learned about the oceans' history. Some of this history is shown in **Figure 2.**

Reading Check **How did the first oceans begin to form on Earth?** *(See the Appendix for answers to Reading Checks.)*

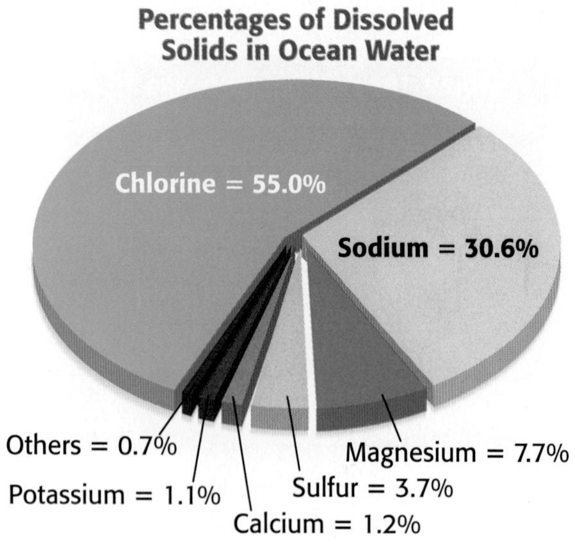

Figure 3 *This pie graph shows the relative percentages of dissolved solids (by mass) in ocean water.*

Characteristics of Ocean Water

You know that ocean water is different from the water that flows from your sink at home. For one thing, ocean water is not safe to drink. But there are other things that make ocean water special.

Ocean Water Is Salty

Have you ever swallowed water while swimming in the ocean? It tasted really salty, didn't it? Most of the salt in the ocean is the same kind of salt that we sprinkle on our food. This salt is called *sodium chloride.*

Salts have been added to the ocean for billions of years. As rivers and streams flow toward the oceans, they dissolve various minerals on land. The running water carries these dissolved minerals to the ocean. At the same time, water is *evaporating* from the ocean and is leaving the dissolved solids behind. The most abundant dissolved solid in the ocean is sodium chloride. This compound consists of the elements sodium, Na, and chlorine, Cl. **Figure 3** shows the relative amounts of the dissolved solids in ocean water.

Chock-Full of Solids

salinity a measure of the amount of dissolved salts in a given amount of liquid

A measure of the amount of dissolved solids in a given amount of liquid is called **salinity.** Salinity is usually measured as grams of dissolved solids per kilogram of water. Think of it this way: 1 kg (1,000 g) of ocean water can be evaporated to 35 g of dissolved solids, on average. Therefore, if you evaporated 1 kg of ocean water, 965 g of fresh water would be removed and 35 g of solids would remain.

Climate Affects Salinity

Some parts of the ocean are saltier than others. Coastal water in places with hotter, drier climates typically has a higher salinity. Coastal water in cooler, more humid places typically has a lower salinity. One reason for this difference is that heat increases the evaporation rate. Evaporation removes water but leaves salts and other dissolved solids behind. Salinity levels are also lower in coastal areas that have a cooler, more humid climate because more fresh water from streams and rivers runs into the ocean in these areas.

Reading Check **Why does coastal water in places with hotter, drier climates typically have a higher salinity than coastal water in places with cooler, more humid climates?**

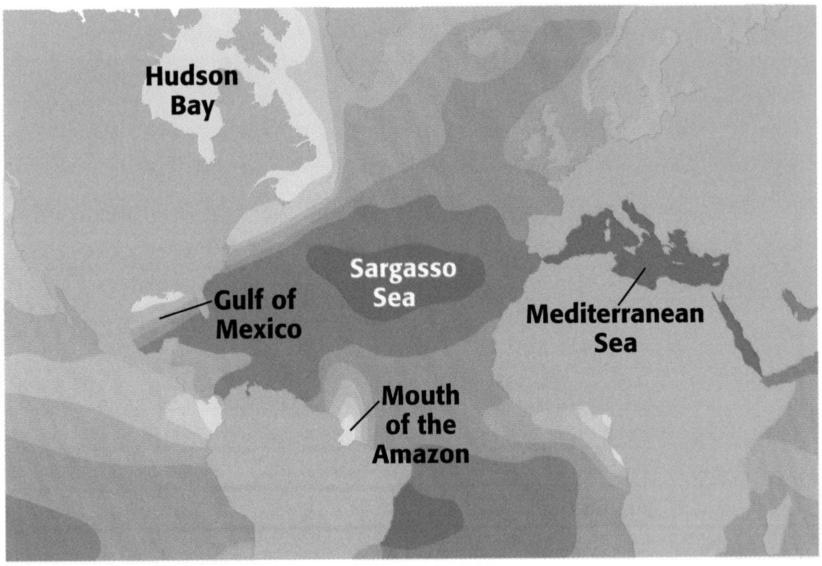

Figure 4 *Salinity varies in different parts of the ocean because of variations in evaporation, circulation, and freshwater inflow.*

Water Movement Affects Salinity

Another factor that affects ocean salinity is water movement. Some parts of the ocean, such as bays, gulfs, and seas, move less than other parts. Parts of the open ocean that do not have currents running through them can also be slow moving. Slower-moving areas of water develop higher salinity. **Figure 4** shows salinity differences in different parts of the ocean.

Temperature Zones

The temperature of ocean water decreases as depth increases. However, this temperature change does not happen gradually from the ocean's surface to its bottom. Water in the ocean can be divided into three layers by temperature. As **Figure 5** shows, the temperature at the surface is much warmer than the average temperature of ocean water.

Figure 5 **Temperature Zones in the Ocean**

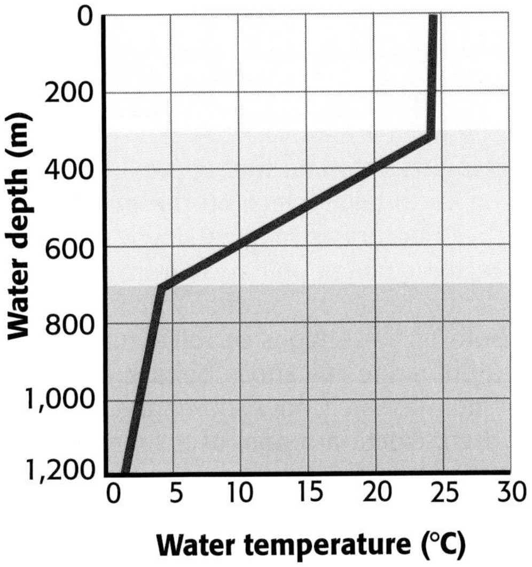

Surface zone The *surface zone* is the warm, top layer of ocean water. It can extend to 300 m below sea level. Sunlight heats the top 100 m of the surface zone. Surface currents mix the heated water with cooler water below.

Thermocline The *thermocline* is the second layer of ocean water. It can extend from 300 m below sea level to about 700 m below sea level. In the thermocline, temperature drops with increased depth faster than it does in the other two zones.

Deep zone The *deep zone* is the bottom layer that extends from the base of the thermocline to the bottom of the ocean. The temperature in this zone can range from 1°C to 3°C.

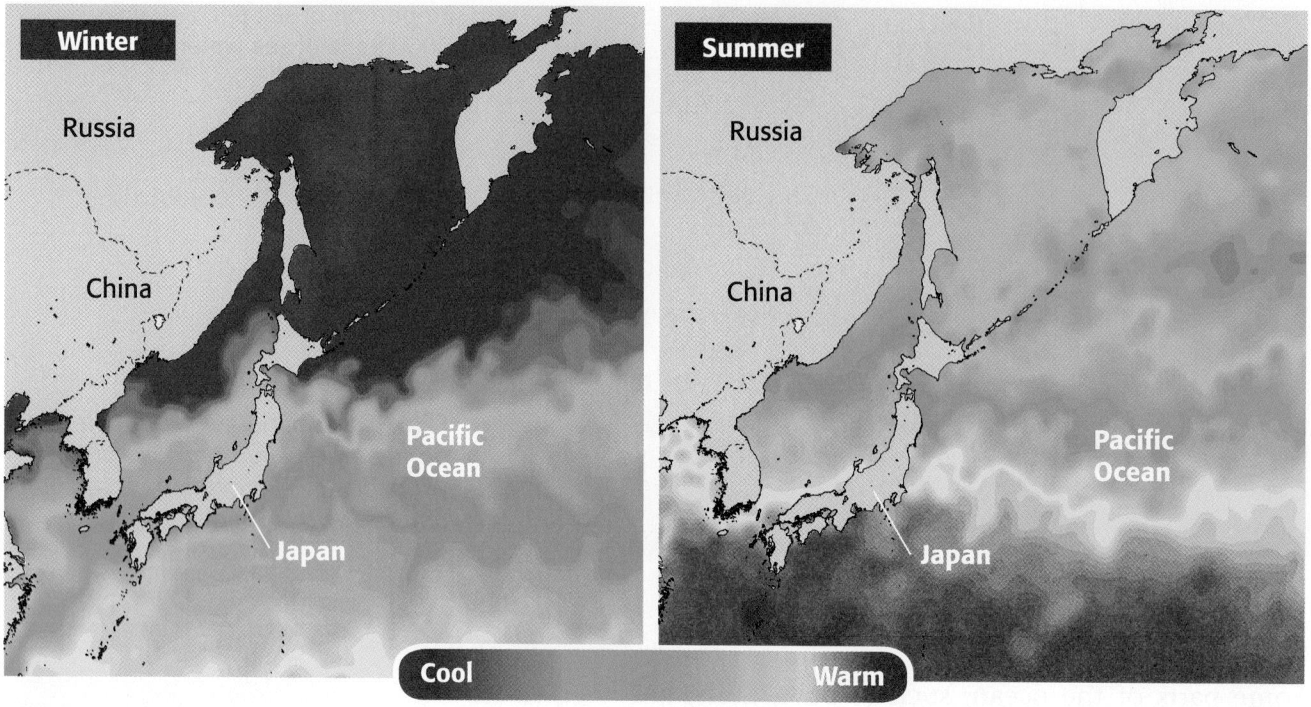

Figure 6 *These satellite images show that the surface temperatures in the northern Pacific Ocean change with the seasons.*

Surface Temperature Changes

If you live near the coast, you may know how different a swim in the ocean feels in December than it feels in July. Temperatures in the surface zone vary with latitude and the time of year. Surface temperatures range from 1°C near the poles to about 24°C near the equator. Parts of the ocean along the equator are warmer because they receive more direct sunlight per year than areas closer to the poles. However, both hemispheres receive more direct sunlight during their summer seasons. Therefore, the surface zone is heated more in the summer. **Figure 6** shows how surface-zone temperatures vary depending on the time of year.

✓ *Reading Check* **Why are parts of the ocean along the equator warmer than those closer to the poles?**

CONNECTION TO Geology

Submarine Volcanoes Geologists estimate that approximately 80% of the volcanic activity on Earth takes place on the ocean floor. Most of the volcanic activity occurs as magma slowly flows onto the ocean floor where tectonic plates pull away from each other. Other volcanic activity is the result of volcanoes that are located on the ocean floor. Both of these types of volcanoes are called *submarine volcanoes.* Submarine volcanoes behave differently than volcanoes on land do. Research how submarine volcanoes behave underwater. Then, create a model of a submarine volcano based on the information you find.

ACTIVITY

The Ocean and the Water Cycle

If you could sit on the moon and look down at Earth, what would you see? You would notice that Earth's surface is made up of three basic components—water, land, and clouds (air). All three are part of a process called the water cycle, as shown in **Figure 7.** The **water cycle** is the continuous movement of water from the ocean to the atmosphere to the land and back to the ocean. The ocean is an important part of the water cycle because nearly all of Earth's water is in the ocean.

water cycle the continuous movement of water from the ocean to the atmosphere to the land and back to the ocean

Figure 7 **The Water Cycle**

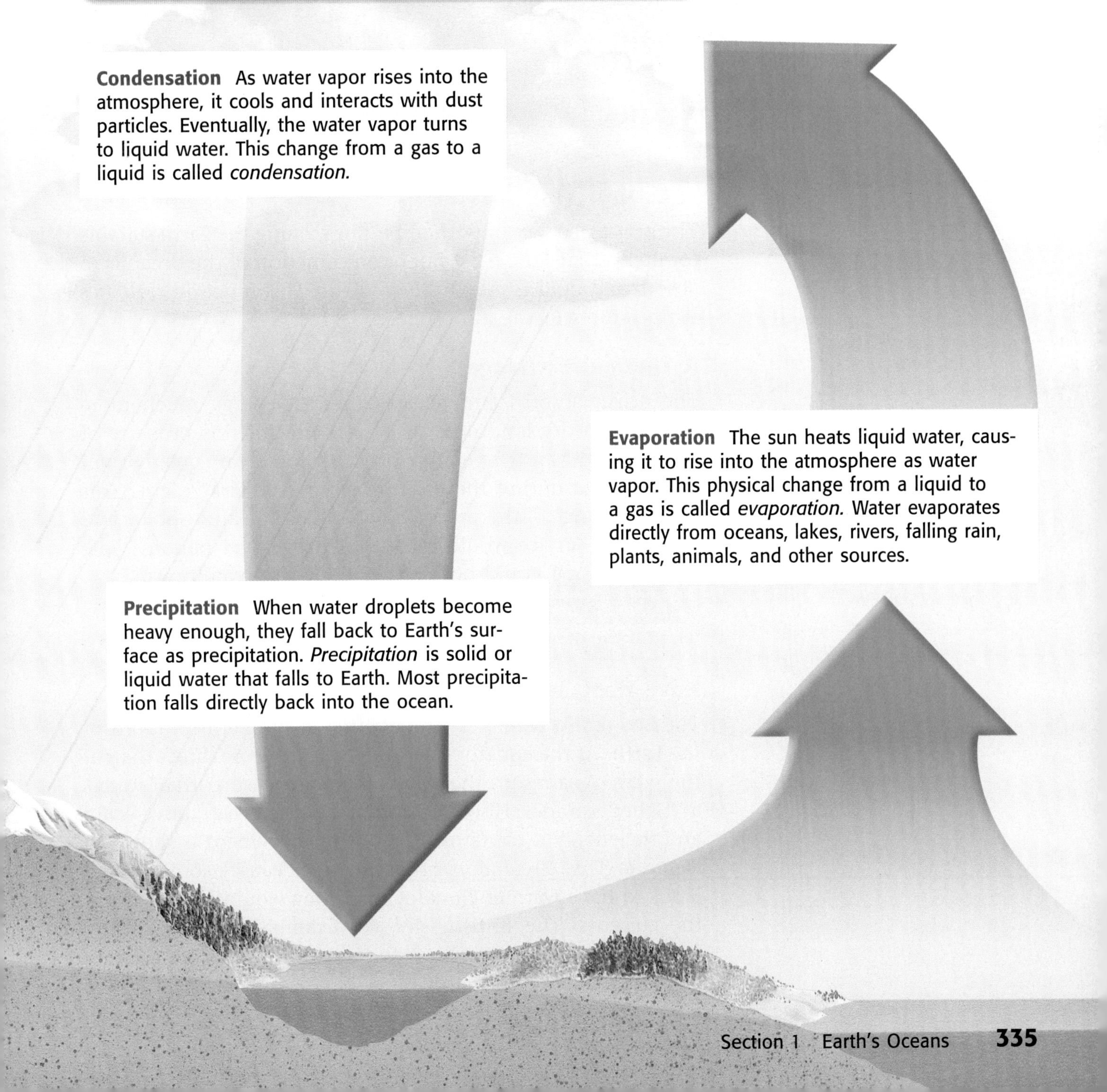

Condensation As water vapor rises into the atmosphere, it cools and interacts with dust particles. Eventually, the water vapor turns to liquid water. This change from a gas to a liquid is called *condensation.*
Evaporation The sun heats liquid water, causing it to rise into the atmosphere as water vapor. This physical change from a liquid to a gas is called *evaporation.* Water evaporates directly from oceans, lakes, rivers, falling rain, plants, animals, and other sources.
Precipitation When water droplets become heavy enough, they fall back to Earth's surface as precipitation. *Precipitation* is solid or liquid water that falls to Earth. Most precipitation falls directly back into the ocean.

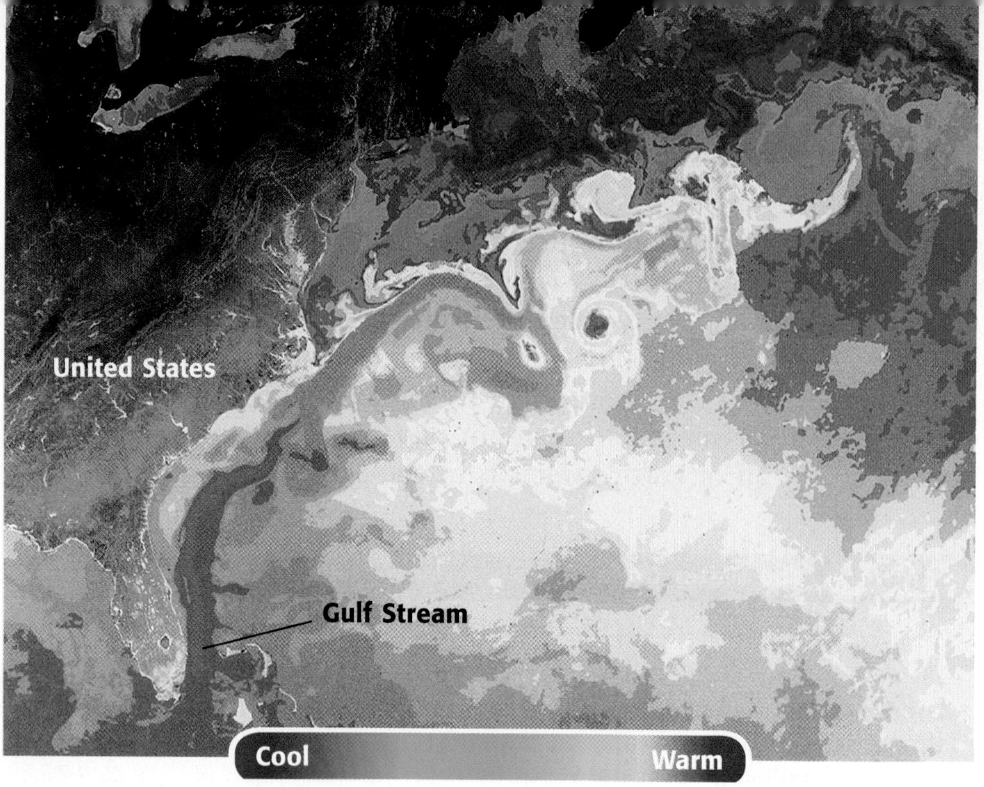

Figure 8 *This infrared satellite image shows the Gulf Stream moving warm water from lower latitudes to higher latitudes.*

A Global Thermostat

The ocean plays an important part in keeping the Earth suitable for life. Perhaps the most important function of the ocean is to absorb and hold energy from sunlight. This function regulates temperatures in the atmosphere.

A Thermal Exchange

The ocean absorbs and releases thermal energy much more slowly than dry land does. If it were not for this property of the ocean, the air temperature on Earth could vary greatly from above 100°C during the day to below –100°C at night. This rapid exchange of thermal energy between the atmosphere and the Earth's surface would cause violent weather patterns. Life as you know it could not exist under these conditions.

INTERNET ACTIVITY

For another activity related to this chapter, go to **go.hrw.com** and type in the keyword **HZ5OCEW.**

Reading Check **How would the air temperature on land be different if the ocean did not release thermal energy so slowly?**

Have Heat, Will Travel

The ocean also regulates temperatures at different locations of the Earth. At the equator, the sun's rays are more direct than at the poles. As a result, the waters there are warmer than waters at higher latitudes. However, currents in the ocean move water and the energy it contains. Part of this movement is shown in **Figure 8.** This circulation of warm water causes some coastal lands to have warmer climates than they would have without the currents. The British Isles, for example, have a warmer climate than most regions at the same latitude. This warmer climate is due to the warm water of the Gulf Stream.

SECTION Review

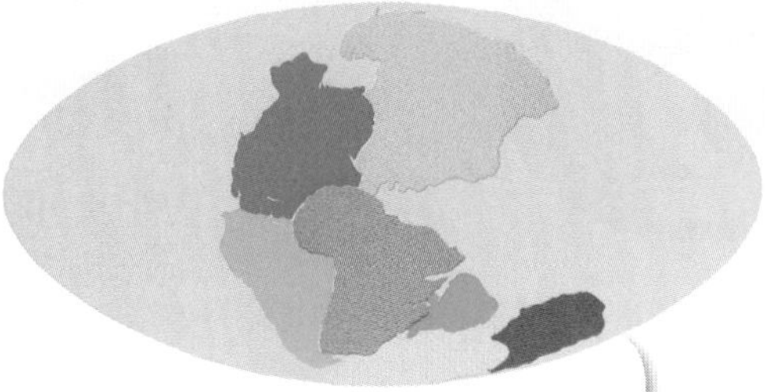

Summary

- The global ocean is divided by the continents into five main oceans: Pacific Ocean, Atlantic Ocean, Indian Ocean, Southern Ocean, and Arctic Ocean.
- The five oceans as we know them today formed within the last 300 million years.
- Salts have been added to the ocean for billions of years. Salinity is a measure of the amount of dissolved salts in a given weight or mass of liquid.
- The three temperature zones of ocean water are the surface zone, the thermocline, and the deep zone.
- The water cycle is the continuous movement of water from the ocean to the atmosphere to the land and back to the ocean. The ocean plays the largest role in the water cycle.
- The ocean stabilizes Earth's weather conditions by absorbing and holding thermal energy.

Using Key Terms

1. In your own words, write a definition for each of the following terms: *salinity* and *water cycle*.

Understanding Key Ideas

2. The top layer of ocean water that extends to 300 m below sea level is called the
   a. deep zone.
   b. surface zone.
   c. Gulf Stream.
   d. thermocline.
3. Name the major divisions of the global ocean.
4. Explain how Earth's first oceans formed.
5. Why is the ocean an important part of the water cycle?
6. Between which two steps of the water cycle does the ocean fit?

Critical Thinking

7. **Making Inferences** Describe how the ocean plays a role in stabilizing Earth's weather conditions.
8. **Identifying Relationships** List one factor that affects salinity in the ocean and one factor that affects ocean temperatures. Explain how each factor affects salinity or temperature.

Interpreting Graphics

Use the image below to answer the questions that follow.

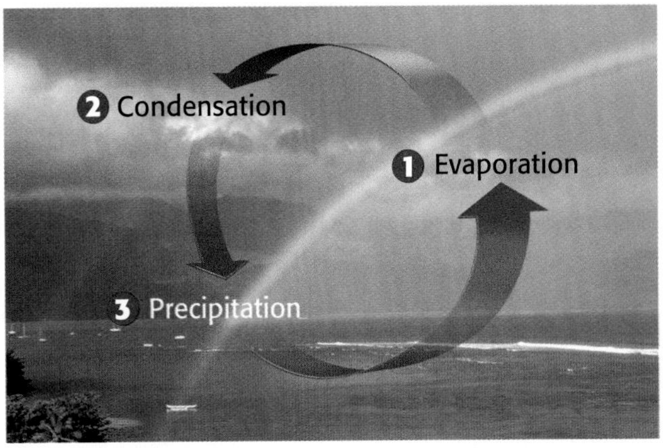

9. At which stage would solid or liquid water fall to the Earth?
10. At which stage would the sun's energy cause liquid to rise into the atmosphere as water vapor?

For a variety of links related to this chapter, go to www.scilinks.org

Topic: Exploring Earth's Oceans
SciLinks code: HSM0557

SECTION 2

The Ocean Floor

What You Will Learn

- Describe technologies for studying the ocean floor.
- Identify the two major regions of the ocean floor.
- Classify subdivisions and features of the two major regions of the ocean floor.

Vocabulary

continental shelf
continental slope
continental rise
abyssal plain
mid-ocean ridge
rift valley
seamount
ocean trench

READING STRATEGY

Reading Organizer As you read this section, create an outline of the section. Use the headings from the section in your outline.

What lies at the bottom of the ocean? How deep is the ocean?

These questions were once unanswerable. By using new technology, scientists have learned a lot about the ocean floor. Scientists have discovered landforms on the ocean floor and have measured depths for almost the entire ocean floor.

Studying the Ocean Floor

Sending people into deep water to study the ocean floor can be risky. Fortunately, there are other ways to study the deep ocean. These ways include surveying from the ocean surface and from high above in space.

Seeing by Sonar

Sonar stands for ***so****und* ***n****avigation* ***a****nd* ***r****anging*. This technology is based on the echo-ranging behavior of bats. Scientists use sonar to determine the ocean's depth by sending sound pulses from a ship down into the ocean. The sound moves through the water, bounces off the ocean floor, and returns to the ship. The deeper the water is, the longer the round trip takes. Scientists then calculate the depth by multiplying half the travel time by the speed of sound in water (about 1,500 m/s). This process is shown in **Figure 1.**

Figure 1 Ocean Floor Mapping with Sonar

3
Scientists use sonar signals to make a *bathymetric profile,* which is a map of the ocean floor that shows the ocean's depth.

Oceanography via Satellite

In the 1970s, scientists began studying Earth from satellites in orbit around the Earth. In 1978, scientists launched the satellite *Seasat.* This satellite focused on the ocean, sending images back to Earth that allowed scientists to measure the direction and speed of ocean currents.

Studying the Ocean with *Geosat*

Geosat, once a top-secret military satellite, has been used to measure slight changes in the height of the ocean's surface. Different underwater features, such as mountains and trenches, affect the height of the water above them. Scientists measure the different heights of the ocean surface and use the measurements to make detailed maps of the ocean floor. Maps made using satellite measurements, such as the map in **Figure 2,** can cover much more territory than maps made using ship-based sonar readings.

Reading Check **How do scientists use satellites to make detailed maps of the ocean floor?** (*See the Appendix for answers to Reading Checks.*)

North America
South America

Figure 2 *This map was generated by satellite measurements of different heights of the ocean surface.*

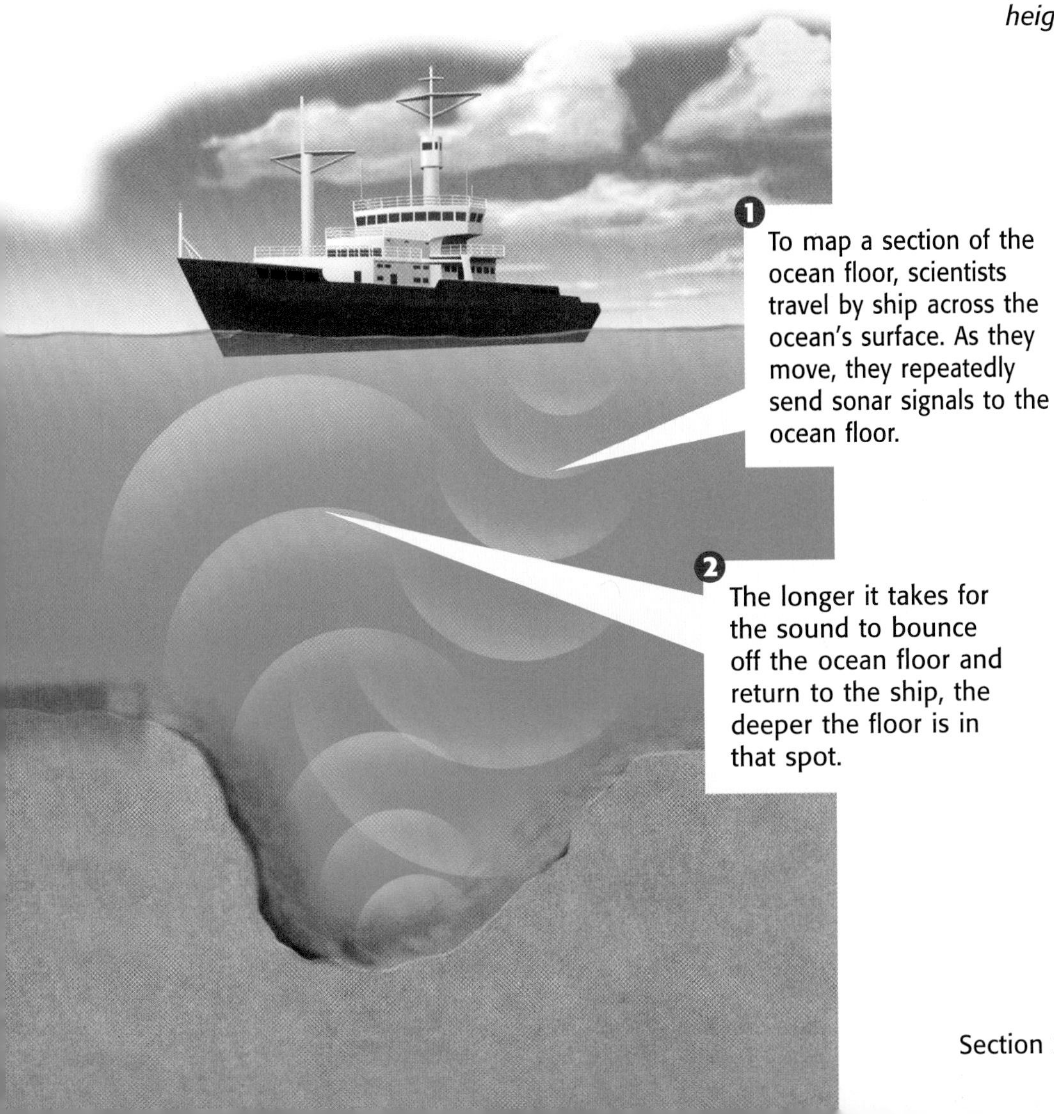
1 To map a section of the ocean floor, scientists travel by ship across the ocean's surface. As they move, they repeatedly send sonar signals to the ocean floor.
2 The longer it takes for the sound to bounce off the ocean floor and return to the ship, the deeper the floor is in that spot.

continental shelf the gently sloping section of the continental margin located between the shoreline and the continental slope

continental slope the steeply inclined section of the continental margin located between the continental rise and the continental shelf

continental rise the gently sloping section of the continental margin located between the continental slope and the abyssal plain

abyssal plain a large, flat, almost level area of the deep-ocean basin

Revealing the Ocean Floor

Can you imagine being an explorer assigned to map uncharted areas on the planet? You might think that there are not many uncharted areas left because most of the land has already been explored. But what about the bottom of the ocean?

The ocean floor is not a flat surface. If you could go to the bottom of the ocean, you would see a number of impressive features. You would see the world's longest mountain chain, which is about 64,000 km (40,000 mi) long as well as canyons deeper than the Grand Canyon. And because it is underwater and some areas are so deep, much of the ocean floor is still not completely explored.

Reading Check **How long is the longest mountain chain in the world? Where is it located?**

Figure 3 **The Ocean Floor**

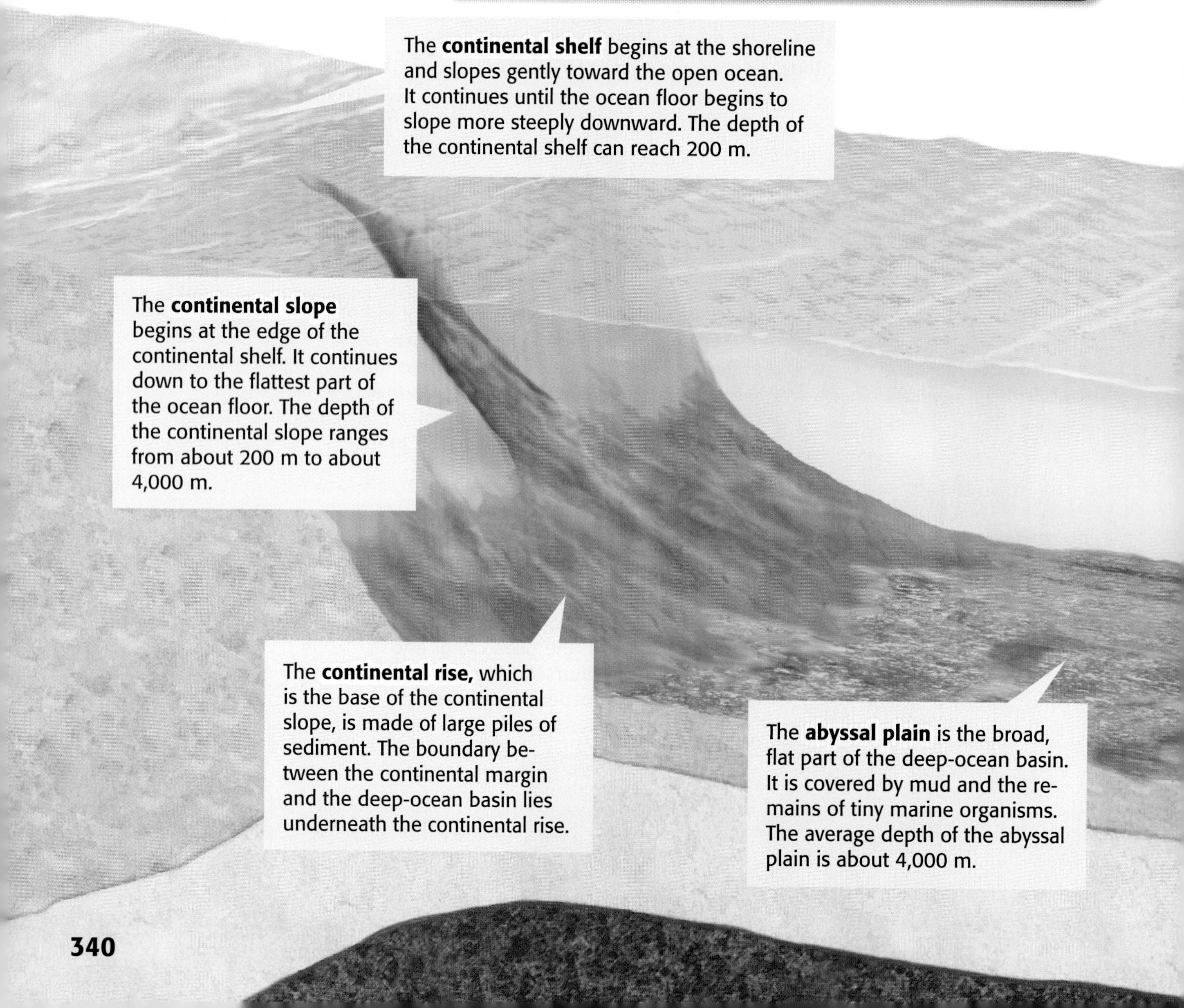

The **continental shelf** begins at the shoreline and slopes gently toward the open ocean. It continues until the ocean floor begins to slope more steeply downward. The depth of the continental shelf can reach 200 m.
The **continental slope** begins at the edge of the continental shelf. It continues down to the flattest part of the ocean floor. The depth of the continental slope ranges from about 200 m to about 4,000 m.
The **continental rise,** which is the base of the continental slope, is made of large piles of sediment. The boundary between the continental margin and the deep-ocean basin lies underneath the continental rise.
The **abyssal plain** is the broad, flat part of the deep-ocean basin. It is covered by mud and the remains of tiny marine organisms. The average depth of the abyssal plain is about 4,000 m.

Regions of the Ocean Floor

If you journeyed to the ocean floor, you would first notice two major regions. The *continental margin* is made of continental crust, and the *deep-ocean basin* is made of oceanic crust. Imagine that the ocean is a giant swimming pool. The continental margin is the shallow end of the pool, and the deep-ocean basin is the deep end of the pool. The figure below shows how these two regions are subdivided.

Underwater Real Estate

As you can see in **Figure 3** below, the continental margin is subdivided into the continental shelf, the continental slope, and the continental rise. These divisions are based on depth and changes in slope. The deep-ocean basin consists of the abyssal (uh BIS uhl) plain, mid-ocean ridges, rift valleys, and ocean trenches. All of these features form near the boundaries of Earth's *tectonic plates*. On parts of the deep-ocean basin that are not near plate boundaries, there are thousands of seamounts. Seamounts are submerged volcanic mountains on the ocean floor.

Reading Check What are the subdivisions of the continental margin?

mid-ocean ridge a long, undersea mountain chain that forms along the floor of the major oceans

rift valley a long, narrow valley that forms as tectonic plates separate

seamount a submerged mountain on the ocean floor that is at least 1,000 m high and that has a volcanic origin

ocean trench a steep, long depression in the deep-sea floor that runs parallel to a chain of volcanic islands or a continental margin

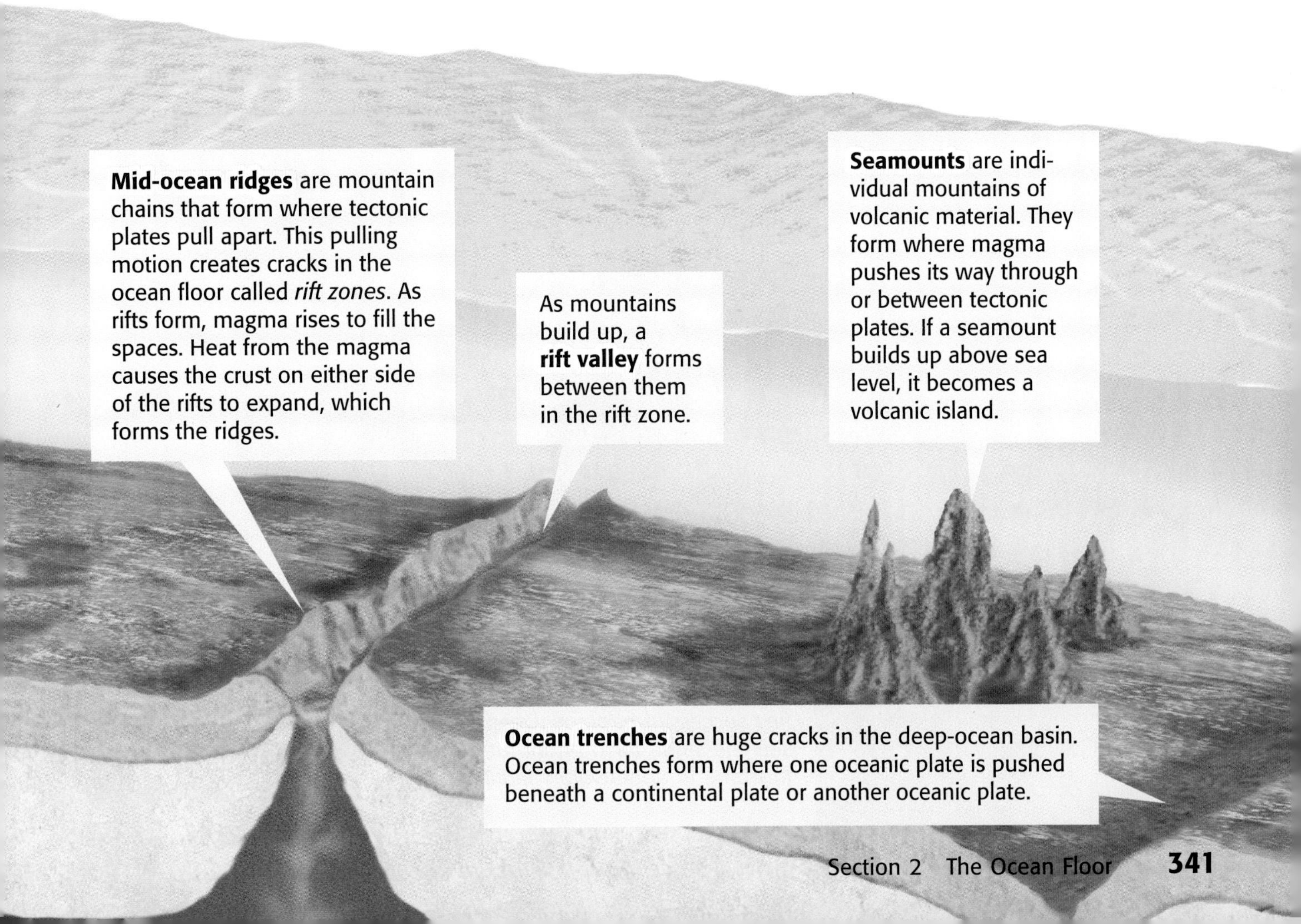

Mid-ocean ridges are mountain chains that form where tectonic plates pull apart. This pulling motion creates cracks in the ocean floor called *rift zones*. As rifts form, magma rises to fill the spaces. Heat from the magma causes the crust on either side of the rifts to expand, which forms the ridges.
As mountains build up, a **rift valley** forms between them in the rift zone.
Seamounts are individual mountains of volcanic material. They form where magma pushes its way through or between tectonic plates. If a seamount builds up above sea level, it becomes a volcanic island.
Ocean trenches are huge cracks in the deep-ocean basin. Ocean trenches form where one oceanic plate is pushed beneath a continental plate or another oceanic plate.

CONNECTION TO Social Studies

The JASON Project The JASON project, started by oceanographer Dr. Robert Ballard, allows students and teachers to take part in virtual field trips to some of the most exotic locations on Earth. Using satellite links and the Internet, students around the world have participated in scientific expeditions to places such as the Galápagos Islands, the Sea of Cortez, and deep-sea hydrothermal vents. Using the Internet, research where the JASON project is headed to next!

Exploring the Ocean with Underwater Vessels

Just as astronauts explore space with rockets, scientists explore the oceans with underwater vessels. These vessels contain the air that the explorers need to breathe and all of the scientific instruments that the explorers need to study the oceans.

Piloted Vessels: *Alvin* and *Deep Flight*

One research vessel used to travel to the deep ocean is called *Alvin*. *Alvin* is 7 m long and can reach some of the deepest parts of the ocean. Scientists have used *Alvin* for many underwater missions, including searches for sunken ships, the recovery of a lost hydrogen bomb, and explorations of the sea floor. In 1977, scientists aboard *Alvin* discovered an oasis of life around hydrothermal vents near the Galápagos Islands. Ecosystems near hydrothermal vents are unique because some organisms living around the vent do not rely on photosynthesis for energy. Instead, these organisms rely on chemicals in the water as their source of energy.

Another modern vessel that scientists use to explore the deep ocean is an underwater airplane called *Deep Flight*. This vessel, shown in **Figure 4,** moves through the water in much the same way that an airplane moves through the air. Future models of *Deep Flight* will be designed to transport pilots to the deepest parts of the ocean, which are more than 11,000 m deep.

Reading Check **Why is the ecosystem discovered by *Alvin* unique?**

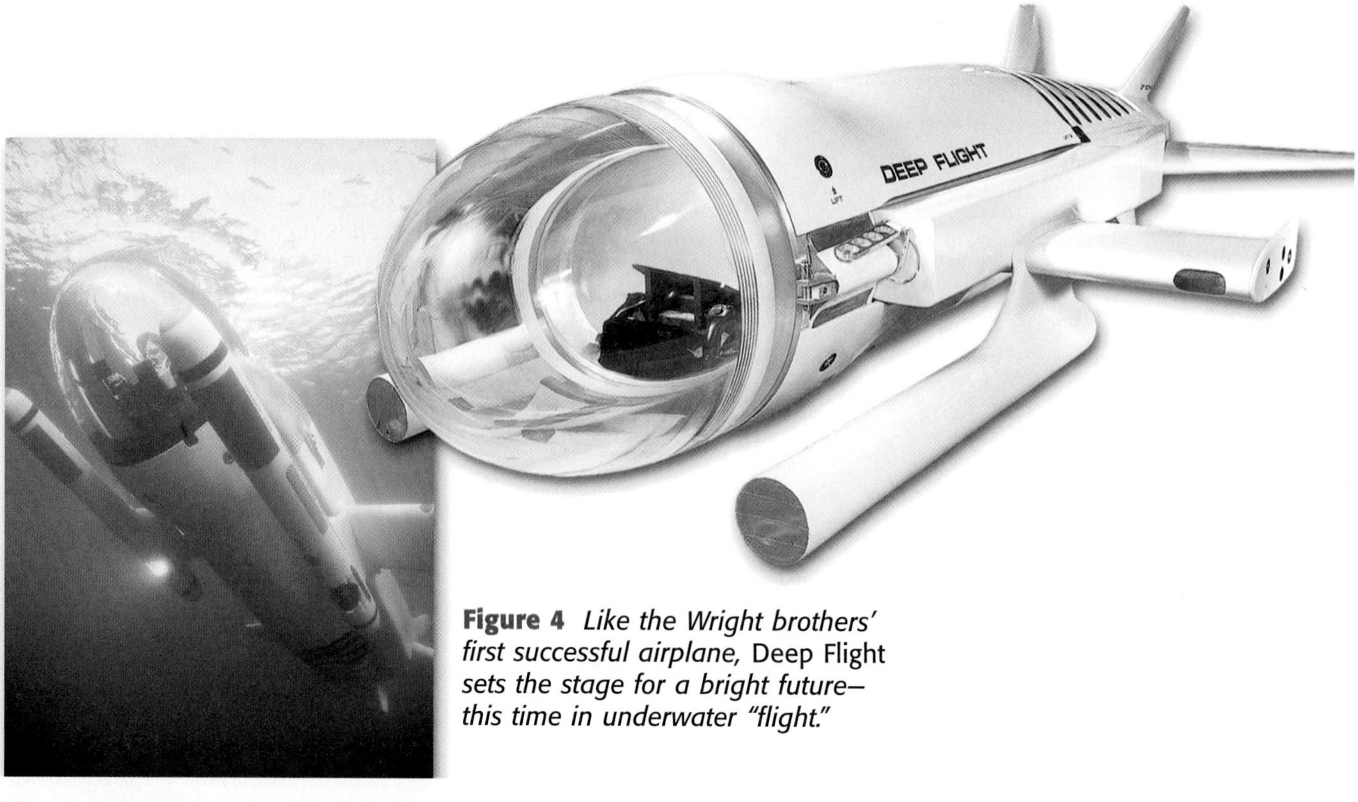

Figure 4 *Like the Wright brothers' first successful airplane,* Deep Flight *sets the stage for a bright future—this time in underwater "flight."*

Robotic Vessels: *JASON II* and *Medea*

Exploring the deep ocean by using piloted vessels is expensive and can be very dangerous. For these reasons, scientists use robotic vessels to explore the ocean. One interesting robot team consists of *JASON II* and *Medea*. These robots are designed to withstand pressures much greater than those found in the deepest parts of the ocean. *JASON II* is "flown" by a pilot at the surface and is used to explore the ocean floor. *Medea* is attached to *JASON II* with a tether and explores above the sea floor. In the future, unpiloted "drone" robots shaped like fish may be used. Another robot under development uses the ocean's thermal energy for power. These robots could explore the ocean for years and send data to scientists at the surface.

SECTION Review

Summary

- Scientists study the ocean floor from the surface using sonar and satellites.
- The ocean floor is divided into two regions—the continental margin and the deep-ocean basin.
- The continental margin consists of the continental shelf, the continental slope, and the continental rise.
- The deep-ocean basin consists of the abyssal plain, mid-ocean ridges, rift valleys, seamounts, and ocean trenches.
- Scientists explore the ocean from below the surface by using piloted vessels and robotic vessels.

Using Key Terms

For each pair of terms, explain how the meanings of the terms differ.

1. *continental shelf* and *continental slope*
2. *abyssal plain* and *ocean trench*
3. *mid-ocean ridge* and *seamount*

Understanding Key Ideas

4. Sonar is a technology based on the
   a. *Geosat* satellite.
   b. surface currents in the ocean.
   c. zones of the ocean floor.
   d. echo-ranging behavior of bats.
5. List the two major regions of the ocean floor.
6. Describe the subdivisions of the continental margin.
7. List three technologies for studying the ocean floor, and explain how they are used.
8. List three underwater missions that *Alvin* has been used for.
9. Explain how *Jason II* and *Medea* are used to explore the ocean.
10. Describe how a bathymetric profile is made.

Math Skills

11. Air pressure at sea level is 1 atmosphere (atm). Underwater, pressure increases by 1 atm every 10 m of depth. For example, at a depth of 10 m, water pressure is 2 atm. What is the pressure at 100 m?

Critical Thinking

12. **Making Comparisons** How is exploring the oceans similar to exploring space?
13. **Applying Concepts** Is the ocean floor a flat surface? Explain your answer.

SCI LINKS. NSTA Developed and maintained by the National Science Teachers Association

For a variety of links related to this chapter, go to www.scilinks.org

Topic: Ocean Floor
SciLinks code: HSM1062

SECTION 3

Life in the Ocean

In which part of the ocean does an octopus live? And where do dolphins spend most of their time?

What You Will Learn

- Identify the three groups of marine life.
- Describe the two main ocean environments.
- Identify the ecological zones of the benthic and pelagic environments.

Vocabulary

plankton
nekton
benthos
benthic environment
pelagic environment

READING STRATEGY

Mnemonics As you read this section, create a mnemonic device to help you remember the ecological zones of the ocean.

Just as armadillos and birds occupy very different places on Earth, octopuses and dolphins live in very different parts of the ocean. Trying to study life in the oceans can be a challenge for scientists. The oceans are so large that many forms of marine life have not been discovered, and there are many more organisms that scientists know little about. To make things easier, scientists classify marine organisms into three main groups.

The Three Groups of Marine Life

The three main groups of marine life, as shown in **Figure 1,** are plankton, nekton, and benthos. Marine organisms are placed into one of these three groups according to where they live and how they move.

Organisms that float or drift freely near the ocean's surface are called **plankton.** Most plankton are microscopic. Plankton are divided into two groups—those that are plant-like (*phytoplankton*) and those that are animal-like (*zooplankton*). Organisms that swim actively in the open ocean are called **nekton.** Types of nekton include mammals, such as whales, dolphins, and sea lions, as well as many varieties of fish. **Benthos** are organisms that live on or in the ocean floor. There are many types of benthos, such as crabs, starfish, worms, coral, sponges, seaweed, and clams.

Figure 1 *Plankton, nekton, and benthos are the three groups of organisms that live in the ocean.*

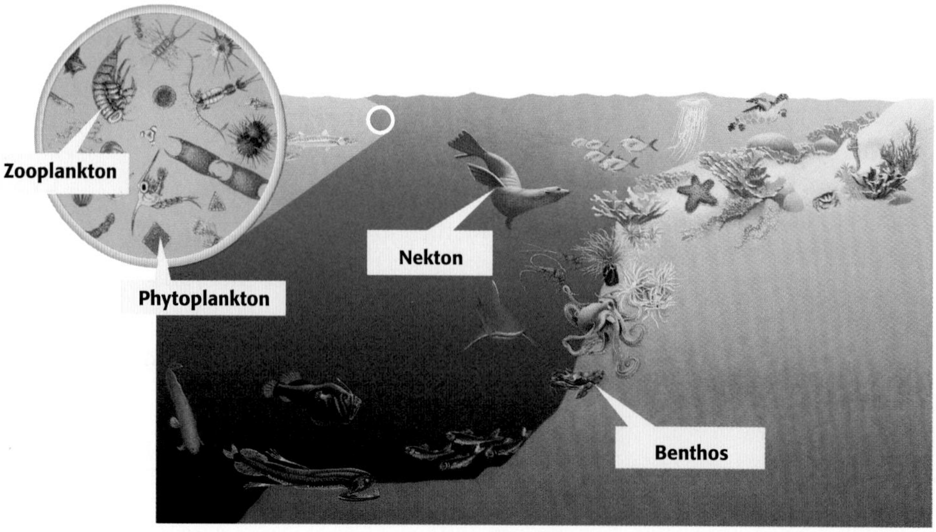

Figure 2 *Organisms such as sea anemones and starfish attach themselves to rocks and reefs. These organisms must be able to survive both wet and dry conditions.*

The Benthic Environment

In addition to being divided into zones based on depth, the ocean floor is divided into ecological zones based on where different types of benthos live. These zones are grouped into one major marine environment—the benthic environment. The **benthic environment,** or bottom environment, is the region near the ocean floor and all the organisms that live on or in it.

The Intertidal Zone

The shallowest benthic zone, called the *intertidal zone,* is located between the low-tide and high-tide limits. Twice a day, the intertidal zone changes. As the tide flows in, the zone is covered with ocean water. Then, as the tide flows out, the intertidal zone is exposed to the air and sun.

Because of the change in tides, intertidal organisms must be able to live both underwater and on exposed land. Some organisms, such as the sea anemones and starfish shown in **Figure 2,** attach themselves to rocks and reefs to avoid being washed out to sea during low tide. Other organisms, such as clams, oysters, barnacles, and crabs, have tough shells that give them protection against strong waves during high tide and against harsh sunlight during low tide. Some animals can burrow in sand or between rocks to avoid harsh conditions. Plants also protect themselves from being washed away by strong waves. Plants such as seaweed have strong *holdfasts* (rootlike structures) that allow them to grow in this zone.

Reading Check **How do clams and oysters survive in the intertidal zone during high tide and low tide?** *(See the Appendix for answers to Reading Checks.)*

plankton the mass of mostly microscopic organisms that float or drift freely in freshwater and marine environments

nekton all organisms that swim actively in open water, independent of currents

benthos the organisms that live at the bottom of the sea or ocean

benthic environment the region near the bottom of a pond, lake, or ocean

Figure 3 *Corals, like many other types of organisms, can live in both the sublittoral zone and the intertidal zone. However, they are more common in the sublittoral zone.*

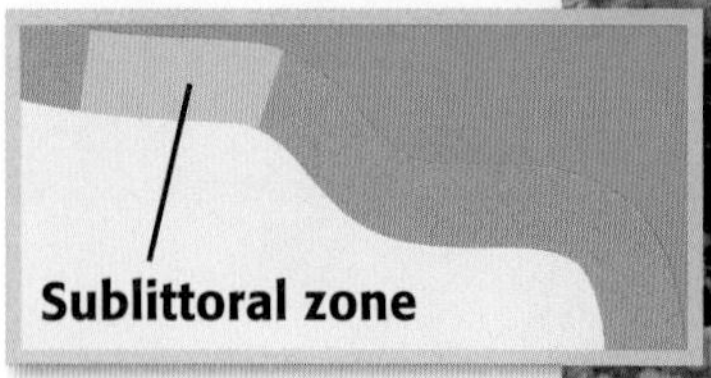

The Sublittoral Zone

The *sublittoral zone* begins where the intertidal zone ends, at the low-tide limit. The sublittoral zone ends at the edge of the continental shelf, about 200 m below sea level. The sublittoral zone is more stable than the intertidal zone. Organisms in the sublittoral zone are always covered by ocean water. The temperature, water pressure, and amount of sunlight remain fairly constant in the sublittoral zone. Sublittoral organisms, such as the corals shown in **Figure 3,** do not have to cope with as much change as intertidal organisms do. The kind of sediment on the ocean floor influences where organisms live in the sublittoral zone.

Figure 4 *Octopuses are one of the animals common to the bathyal zone.*

The Bathyal Zone

The *bathyal* (BATH ee uhl) *zone* extends from the edge of the continental shelf to the abyssal plain. The depth of this zone ranges from 200 m to 4,000 m below sea level. Because of the lack of sunlight at these depths, plant life is scarce in this part of the benthic environment. Animals in this zone include sponges, brachiopods, sea stars, echinoids, and octopuses, such as the one shown in **Figure 4.**

Figure 5 *Tube worms can tolerate higher temperatures than most other organisms can. These animals survive in water as hot as 81°C.*

The Abyssal Zone

No plants and very few animals live in the *abyssal zone,* which is on the abyssal plain. The abyssal zone is the largest ecological zone of the ocean and can reach 4,000 m in depth. Animals such as crabs, sponges, worms, and sea cucumbers live within the abyssal zone. Many of these organisms, such as the tube worms shown in **Figure 5,** live around hot-water vents called *black smokers.* Scientists know very little about this benthic environment because it is so deep and dark.

Reading Check **What types of animals live in the abyssal zone?**

The Hadal Zone

The deepest benthic zone is the *hadal* (HAYD'l) *zone.* This zone consists of the floor of the ocean trenches and any organisms found there. The hadal zone can reach from 6,000 m to 7,000 m in depth. Scientists know even less about the hadal zone than they do about the abyssal zone. So far, scientists have discovered a type of sponge, a few species of worms, and a type of clam, which is shown in **Figure 6.**

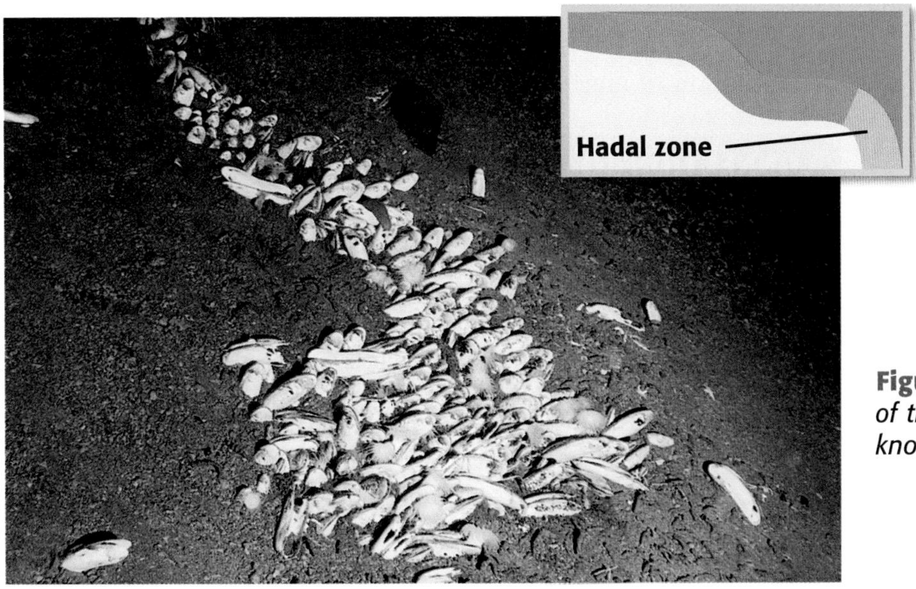

Figure 6 *These clams are one of the few types of organisms known to live in the hadal zone.*

Figure 7 *Many marine animals, such as these dolphins, live in the neritic zone.*

The Pelagic Environment

The zone near the ocean's surface and at the middle depths of the ocean is called the **pelagic environment.** It is beyond the sublittoral zone and above the abyssal zone. There are two major zones in the pelagic environment—the neritic zone and the oceanic zone.

pelagic environment in the ocean, the zone near the surface or at middle depths, beyond the sublittoral zone and above the abyssal zone

The Neritic Zone

The *neritic zone* covers the continental shelf. This warm, shallow zone contains the largest concentration of marine life. Fish, plankton, and marine mammals, such as the dolphins in **Figure 7,** are just a few of the animal groups found in this zone. The neritic zone contains diverse marine life because it receives more sunlight than the other zones in the ocean. Sunlight allows plankton, which are food for other marine organisms, to grow. The many animals in the benthic zone below the neritic zone also serve as a food supply.

Reading Check **Why does the neritic zone contain the largest concentration of marine life in the ocean?**

CONNECTION TO Language Arts

WRITING SKILL **Water, Water, Everywhere** Samuel Taylor Coleridge wrote "The Rime of the Ancient Mariner" in 1798. The following is an excerpt from the poem:

> Water, water, everywhere, / And all the boards did shrink / Water, water, everywhere, / Nor any drop to drink . . . / And every tongue through utter drought, / Was withered at the root; / We could not speak, no more than if / We had been choked with soot.

What do you think this excerpt means? Write a short essay describing the meaning of this passage.

The Oceanic Zone

The *oceanic zone* includes the volume of water that covers the entire sea floor except for the continental shelf. In the deeper parts of the oceanic zone, the water temperature is colder and the pressure is much greater than in the neritic zone. Also, organisms are more spread out in the oceanic zone than in the neritic zone. Although many of the same organisms that live in the neritic zone are found throughout the upper regions, some strange animals lurk in the darker depths, as shown in **Figure 8.** Other animals in the deeper parts of this zone include giant squids and some whale species.

Figure 8 *The angler fish is a predator that uses a wormlike lure attached to its head to attract prey.*

SECTION Review

Summary

- The three main groups of marine life are plankton, nekton, and benthos.
- The two main ocean environments are the benthic environment and the pelagic environment.
- The ecological zones of the benthic environment include the intertidal zone, sublittoral zone, bathyal zone, abyssal zone, and hadal zone.
- The ecological zones of the pelagic environment include the neritic zone and the oceanic zone.

Using Key Terms

The statements below are false. For each statement, replace the underlined term to make a true statement.

1. <u>Plankton</u> are organisms that swim actively in ocean water.
2. The intertidal zone is part of the <u>pelagic zone</u>.
3. Dolphins live in the <u>benthic environment</u>.

Understanding Key Ideas

4. The deepest benthic zone is the
   a. pelagic environment.
   b. hadal zone.
   c. oceanic zone.
   d. abyssal zone.
5. List and briefly describe the three main groups of marine organisms.
6. Name the two ocean environments. In your own words, describe where they are located in the ocean.

Critical Thinking

7. **Making Inferences** Describe why organisms in the intertidal zone must be able to live underwater and on exposed land.
8. **Applying Concepts** How would the ocean's ecological zones change if sea level dropped 300 m?

Interpreting Graphics

Use the diagram below to answer the following question.

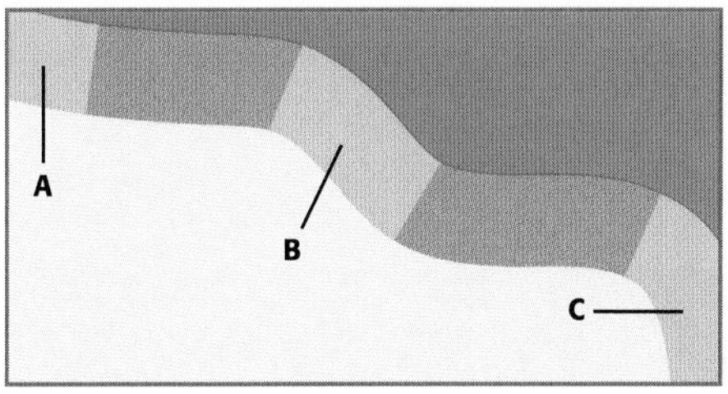

9. Identify the names of the ecological zones of the benthic environment shown above.

SCILINKS® NSTA
Developed and maintained by the National Science Teachers Association

For a variety of links related to this chapter, go to www.scilinks.org

Topic: Life in the Oceans
SciLinks code: HSM0874

SECTION 4

Resources from the Ocean

What You Will Learn

- List two ways of harvesting the ocean's living resources.
- Identify three nonliving resources in the ocean.
- Describe the ocean's energy resources.

Vocabulary

desalination

READING STRATEGY

Paired Summarizing Read this section silently. In pairs, take turns summarizing the material. Stop to discuss ideas that seem confusing.

The next time you enjoy your favorite ice cream, remember that without seaweed, it would be a runny mess!

The ocean offers a vast supply of resources. These resources are put to a number of uses. For example, a seaweed called *kelp* is used as a thickener for many food products, including ice cream. Food, raw materials, energy, and drinkable water are all harvested from the ocean. And there are probably more resources in unexplored parts of the ocean. As human populations have grown, however, the demand for these resources has increased, while the availability has decreased.

Living Resources

People have been harvesting plants and animals from the ocean for thousands of years. Many civilizations formed in coastal regions where the ocean offered plenty of food for a growing population. Today, harvesting food from the ocean is a multi-billion-dollar industry.

Fishing the Ocean

Of all the marine organisms, fish are the largest group of organisms that are taken from the ocean. Almost 75 million tons of fish are harvested each year. With improved technology, such as drift nets, fishers have become better at taking fish from the ocean. **Figure 1** shows the large number of fish that can be caught using a drift net. In recent years, many people have become concerned that we are overfishing the ocean. We are taking more fish than can be naturally replaced. Also, animals other than fish, especially dolphins and turtles, can be accidentally caught in drift nets. Today, the fishing industry is making efforts to prevent overfishing and damage to other wildlife from drift nets.

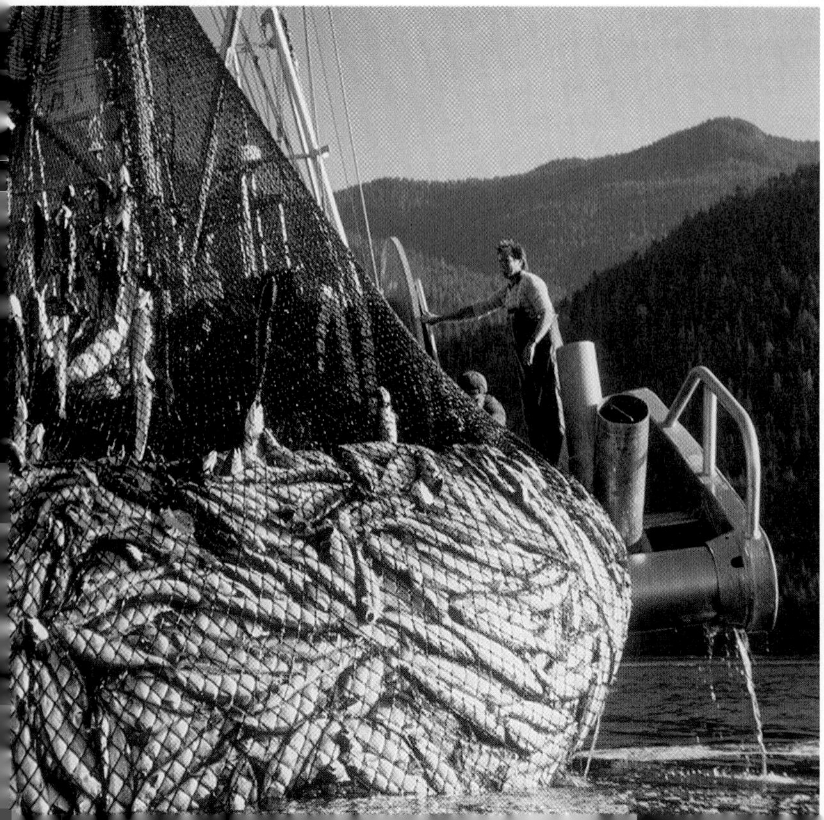

Figure 1 *Drift nets are fishing nets that cover kilometers of ocean. Whole schools of fish can be caught with a single drift net.*

Farming the Ocean

Overfishing reduces fish populations. Recently, laws regulating fishing have become stricter. As a result, it is becoming more difficult to supply our demand for fish. Many people have begun to raise ocean fish in fish farms to help meet the demand. Fish farming requires several holding ponds. Each pond contains fish at a certain level of development. **Figure 2** shows a holding pond in a fish farm. When the fish are old enough, they are harvested and packaged for shipping.

Fish are not the only seafood harvested in a farmlike setting. Shrimp, oysters, crabs, and mussels are raised in enclosed areas near the shore. Mussels and oysters are grown attached to ropes. Huge nets line the nursery area, preventing the animals from being eaten by their natural predators.

Figure 2 *Eating fish raised in a fish farm helps lower the number of fish harvested from the ocean.*

Reading Check **How can fish farms help reduce overfishing?** (*See the Appendix for answers to Reading Checks.*)

Savory Seaweed

Many types of seaweed, which are species of alga, are harvested from the ocean. For example, kelp, shown in **Figure 3,** is a seaweed that grows as much as 33 cm a day. Kelp is harvested and used as a thickener in jellies, ice cream, and similar products. Seaweed is rich in protein. In fact, several species of seaweed are staples of the Japanese diet. For example, some kinds of sushi, a Japanese dish, are wrapped in seaweed.

Figure 3 *Kelp, a type of alga, can grow up to 33 cm a day. It is harvested and used in a number of products, including ice cream.*

Nonliving Resources

Humans also harvest many nonliving resources from the ocean. These resources provide raw materials, drinkable water, and energy for our growing population. Some resources are easy to get, while others are very difficult to harvest.

Oil and Natural Gas

Modern civilization continues to be very dependent on oil and natural gas for energy. Oil and natural gas are *nonrenewable resources*. They are used up faster than they can be replenished naturally. Both oil and natural gas are found under layers of impermeable rock. Petroleum engineers must drill through this rock in order to reach these resources.

Reading Check **What are nonrenewable resources? Give an example of a nonrenewable resource.**

Searching for Oil

How do engineers know where to drill for oil and natural gas? They use seismic equipment. Special devices send powerful pulses of sound to the ocean floor. The pulses move through the water and penetrate the rocks and sediment below. The pulses are then reflected back toward the ship, where they are recorded by electronic equipment and analyzed by a computer. The computer readings indicate how rock layers are arranged below the ocean floor. Petroleum workers, such as the one in **Figure 4,** use these readings to locate a promising area to drill.

Figure 4 *Petroleum workers, such as the one below, drill for oil and gas in the ocean floor. By using seismic equipment, workers can decide which spot will be best for drilling.*

Figure 5 *The Kuwait Towers store fresh water that is produced by desalination.*

Fresh Water and Desalination

In parts of the world where fresh water is limited, people desalinate ocean water. **Desalination** (DEE SAL uh NAY shuhn) is the process of removing salt from sea water. After the salt is removed, the fresh water is then collected for human use. But desalination is not as simple as it sounds, and it is very expensive. Countries with enough annual rainfall rely on the fresh water provided by precipitation and do not need costly desalination plants. Some countries in drier parts of the world, such as Saudi Arabia and Kuwait, use desalination plants to produce fresh water. The towers shown in **Figure 5** are used to store fresh water in Kuwait.

desalination a process of removing salt from ocean water

Reading Check **Explain where desalination plants are most likely to be built.**

Quick Lab

The Desalination Plant

1. Measure **1,000 mL of warm water** in a **graduated cylinder.** Pour the water in a **large pot.**
2. Carefully, add **35 g of table salt.** Stir the water until all of the salt is dissolved.
3. Place the pot on a **hot plate,** and allow all of the water to boil away.
4. Using a **wooden spoon,** scrape the salt residue from the bottom of the pot.
5. Measure the mass of the salt that was left in the bottom of the pot. How much salt did you separate from the water?
6. How does this activity model what happens in a desalination plant? What would be done differently in a desalination plant?

Figure 6 *Manganese nodules are difficult to mine because they are located on the deep ocean floor.*

Sea-Floor Minerals

Mining companies are interested in mineral nodules that are lying on the ocean floor. These nodules are made mostly of manganese, which can be used to make certain types of steel. They also contain iron, copper, nickel, and cobalt. Other nodules are made of phosphates, which are used to make fertilizer.

Nodules are formed from dissolved substances in sea water that stick to solid objects, such as pebbles. As more substances stick to the coated pebble, a nodule begins to grow. Manganese nodules can be as small as a marble or as large as a soccer ball. The photograph in **Figure 6** shows a number of nodules on the ocean floor. Scientists estimate that 15% of the ocean floor is covered with these nodules. However, these nodules are located in the deeper parts of the ocean, and mining them is costly and difficult.

Tidal Energy

The ocean generates a great deal of energy simply because of its constant movement. The gravitational pulls of the sun and moon cause the ocean to rise and fall as tides. *Tidal energy* is energy generated from the movement of tides. Tidal energy can be an excellent source of power. If the water during high tide can be rushed through a narrow coastal passageway, the water's force can be powerful enough to generate electrical energy. **Figure 7** shows how this process works. Tidal energy is a clean, inexpensive, and renewable resource. A *renewable resource* can be replenished, in time, after being used. Unfortunately, tidal energy is practical only in a few parts of the world. These areas must have a coastline with shallow, narrow channels. For example, the coastline at Cook Inlet, in Alaska, is ideal for generating electrical energy.

Figure 7 **Using Tides to Generate Electrical Energy**

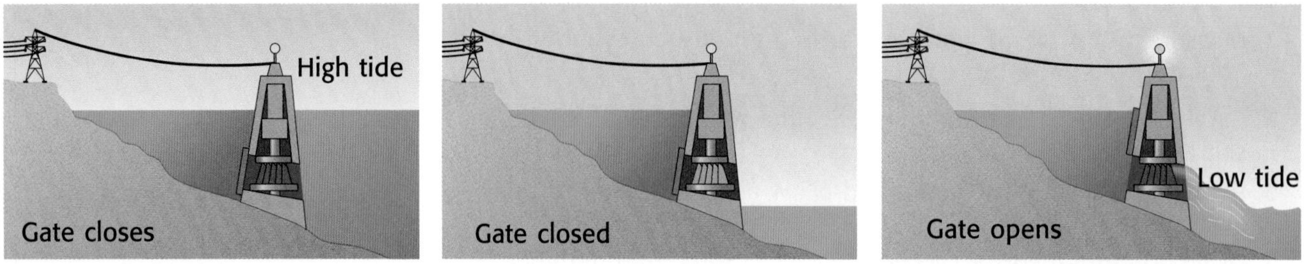

1 As the tide rises, water enters a bay behind a dam. The gate then closes at high tide.

2 The gate remains closed as the tide lowers.

3 At low tide, the gate opens, and the water rushes through the dam and moves the turbines, which, in turn, generate electrical energy.

Wave Energy

Have you ever stood on the beach and watched as waves crashed on the shore? This constant motion is an energy resource. Wave energy, like tidal energy, is a clean, renewable resource. Recently, computer programs have been developed to analyze wave energy. Researchers have found certain areas of the world where wave energy can generate enough electrical energy to make building power plants worthwhile. Wave energy in the North Sea is strong enough to produce power for parts of Scotland and England.

Reading Check **Why would wave energy be a good alternative energy resource?**

SECTION Review

Summary

- Humans depend on the ocean for living and nonliving resources.
- Fish and other marine life are being raised in ocean farms to help feed growing human populations.
- Nonliving ocean resources include oil and natural gas, water, minerals, and tidal and wave energy.

Using Key Terms

1. In your own words, write a definition for the term *desalination*.

Understanding Key Ideas

2. Mineral nodules on the ocean floor are
   a. renewable resources.
   b. easily mined.
   c. used during the process of desalination.
   d. nonliving resources.
3. List two ways of harvesting the ocean's living resources.
4. Name four nonliving resources in the ocean.
5. Explain how fish farms help meet the demand for fish.
6. Explain how engineers decide where to drill for oil and natural gas in the ocean.

Math Skills

7. A kelp plant is 5 cm tall. If it grows an average of 29 cm per day, how tall will the kelp plant be after 2 weeks?

Critical Thinking

8. **Analyzing Processes** Explain why tidal energy and wave energy are considered renewable resources.
9. **Predicting Consequences** Define the term *overfishing* in your own words. What would happen to the population of fish in the ocean if laws did not regulate overfishing? What would happen to the ocean ecosystem?
10. **Analyzing Ideas** What is one benefit and one consequence of building a desalination plant? Would a desalination plant be beneficial to your local area? Explain why or why not.

SCILINKS. NSTA Developed and maintained by the National Science Teachers Association

For a variety of links related to this chapter, go to www.scilinks.org

Topic: Ocean Resources
SciLinks code: HSM1065

SECTION 5

Ocean Pollution

What You Will Learn

- Explain the difference between point-source pollution and nonpoint-source pollution.
- Identify three different types of point-source ocean pollution.
- Describe what is being done to control ocean pollution.

Vocabulary

nonpoint-source pollution
point-source pollution

READING STRATEGY

Reading Organizer As you read this section, create an outline of the section. Use the headings from the section in your outline.

It's a hot summer day at the beach. You can hardly wait to swim in the ocean. You run to the surf only to be met by piles of trash washed up on the shore. Where did all that trash come from?

Humans have thrown their trash in the ocean for hundreds, if not thousands, of years. This trash has harmed the plants and animals that live in the oceans, as well as the people and animals that depend on them. Fortunately, we are becoming more aware of ocean pollution, and we are learning from our mistakes.

Nonpoint-Source Pollution

There are many sources of ocean pollution. Some of these sources are easily identified, but others are more difficult to pinpoint. **Nonpoint-source pollution** is pollution that comes from many sources rather than just from a single site. Some common sources of nonpoint-source pollutants are shown in **Figure 1.** Most ocean pollution is nonpoint-source pollution. Human activities on land can pollute streams and rivers, which then flow into the ocean and bring the pollutants they carry with them. Because nonpoint-source pollutants can enter bodies of water in many different ways, they are very hard to regulate and control. Nonpoint-source pollution can be reduced by using less lawn chemicals and disposing of used motor oil properly.

Figure 1 Examples of Nonpoint-Source Pollution

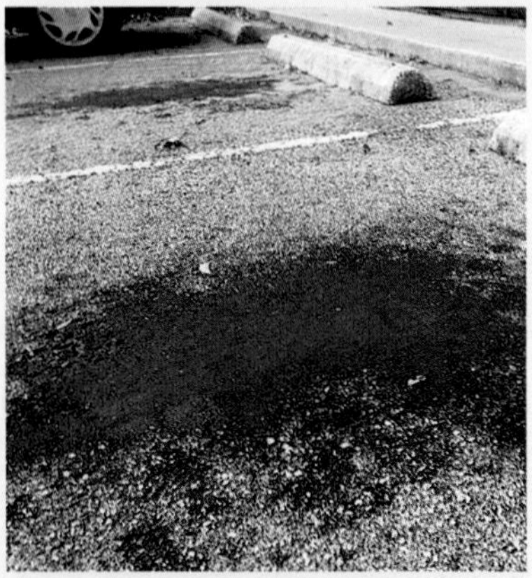

Oil and gasoline that have leaked from cars onto streets can wash into storm sewers and then drain into waterways.

Thousands of watercraft, such as boats and personal watercraft, can leak gasoline and oil directly into bodies of water.

Pesticides, herbicides, and fertilizer from residential lawns, golf courses, and farmland can wash into waterways.

Figure 2 *This barge is headed out to the open ocean, where it will dump the trash it carries.*

Point-Source Pollution

Water pollution caused by a leaking oil tanker, a factory, or a wastewater treatment plant is one type of point-source pollution. **Point-source pollution** is pollution that comes from a specific site. Even when the source of pollution is known, cleanup of the pollution is difficult.

nonpoint-source pollution pollution that comes from many sources rather than from a single, specific site

point-source pollution pollution that comes from a specific site

Trash Dumping

People dump trash in many places, including the ocean. In the 1980s, scientists became alarmed by the kinds of trash that were washing up on beaches. Bandages, vials of blood, and syringes (needles) were found among the waste. Some of the blood in the vials even contained the AIDS virus. The Environmental Protection Agency (EPA) began an investigation and discovered that hospitals in the United States produce an average of 3 million tons of medical waste each year. Because of stricter laws, much of this medical waste is now buried in sanitary landfills. However, dumping trash in the deeper part of the ocean is still a common practice in many countries. The barge in **Figure 2** will dump the trash it carries into the open ocean.

Effects of Trash Dumping

Trash thrown into the ocean can affect the organisms that live in the ocean and those organisms that depend on the ocean for food. Trash such as plastic can be particularly harmful to ocean organisms. This is because most plastic materials do not break down for thousands of years. Marine animals can mistake plastic materials for food and choke or become strangled. The sea gull in **Figure 3** is tangled up in a piece of plastic trash.

Reading Check **What is one effect of trash dumping?** (*See the Appendix for answers to Reading Checks.*)

Figure 3 *Marine animals can be strangled by plastic trash or can choke if they mistake the plastic for food.*

Figure 4 *Sludge is the solid part of waste matter and often carries bacteria. Sludge makes beaches dirty and kills marine animals.*

Sludge Dumping

By 1990, the United States alone had discharged 38 trillion liters of treated sludge into the waters along its coasts. Sludge is part of raw sewage. *Raw sewage* is all the liquid and solid wastes that are flushed down toilets and poured down drains. After collecting in sewer drains, raw sewage is sent through a treatment plant, where it undergoes a cleaning process that removes solid waste. The solid waste is called *sludge,* as shown in **Figure 4.** In many areas, people dump sludge into the ocean several kilometers offshore, intending for it to settle and stay on the ocean floor. Unfortunately, currents can stir the sludge up and move it closer to shore. This sludge can pollute beaches and kill marine life. Many countries have banned sludge dumping, but it continues to occur in many areas of the world.

Oil Spills

Because oil is in such high demand across the world, large tankers must transport billions of barrels of it across the oceans. If not handled properly, these transports can turn disastrous and cause oil spills. **Figure 5** shows some of the major oil spills that have occurred off the coast of North America.

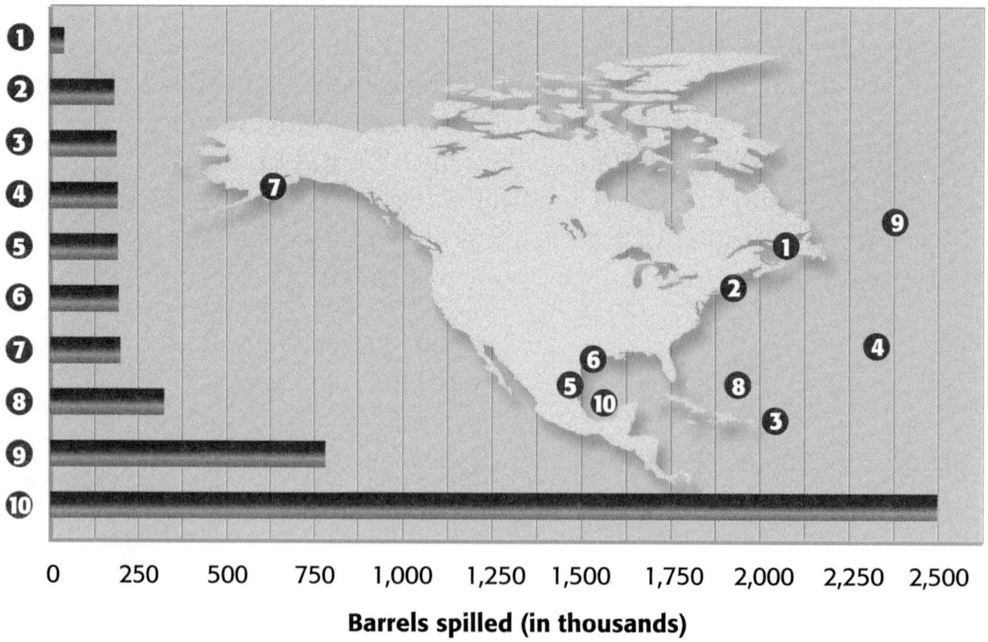

Figure 5 *This map shows some of the major oil spills that have occurred off the coast of North America in the last 30 years.*

1. *Kurdistan* Gulf of St. Lawrence, Canada, 1979
2. *Argo Merchant* Nantucket, MA, 1976
3. Storage Tank Benuelan, Puerto Rico, 1978
4. *Athenian Venture* Atlantic Ocean, 1988
5. Unnamed Tanker Tuxpan, Mexico, 1996
6. *Burmah Agate* Galveston Bay, TX, 1979
7. *Exxon Valdez* Prince William Sound, AK, 1989
8. *Epic Colocotronis* Caribbean Sea, 1975
9. *Odyssey* North Atlantic Ocean, 1988
10. Exploratory Well Bay of Campeche, 1979

Effects of Oil Spills

One of the oil spills shown on the map in **Figure 5** occurred in Prince William Sound, Alaska, in 1989. The supertanker *Exxon Valdez* struck a reef and spilled more than 260,000 barrels of crude oil along the shorelines of Alaska. The amount of spilled oil is roughly equivalent to 125 olympic-sized swimming pools.

Although some animals were saved, such as the bird in **Figure 6,** many plants and animals died as a result of the spill. Alaskans who made their living from fishing lost their businesses. The Exxon Oil Company spent $2.1 billion to try to clean up the mess. But Alaska's wildlife and economy will continue to suffer for decades.

While oil spills can harm plants, animals, and people, they are responsible for only about 5% of oil pollution in the oceans. Most of the oil that pollutes the oceans is caused by nonpoint-source pollution on land from cities and towns.

Figure 6 *Many oil-covered animals were rescued and cleaned after the* Exxon Valdez *spill.*

Preventing Oil Spills

Today, many oil companies are using new technology to safeguard against oil spills. Tankers are now being built with two hulls instead of one. The inner hull prevents oil from spilling into the ocean if the outer hull of the ship is damaged. **Figure 7** shows the design of a double-hulled tanker.

Reading Check **How can two hulls on an oil tanker help prevent an oil spill?**

Figure 7 *If the outer hull of a double-hulled tanker is punctured, the oil will still be contained within the inner hull.*

SCHOOL to HOME

Coastal Cleanup

WRITING SKILL You can be a part of a coastal cleanup. Every September, people from all over the world set aside one day to help clean up trash and debris from beaches. You can join this international effort! With a parent or guardian, write a letter to the Ocean Conservancy to see what you can do to help clean up coastal areas.

ACTIVITY

Saving Our Ocean Resources

Although humans have done much to harm the ocean's resources, we have also begun to do more to save them. From international treaties to volunteer cleanups, efforts to conserve the ocean's resources are making an impact around the world.

Nations Take Notice

When ocean pollution reached an all-time high, many countries recognized the need to work together to solve the problem. In 1989, a treaty was passed by 64 countries that prohibits the dumping of certain metals, plastics, oil, and radioactive wastes into the ocean. Even though many other international agreements and laws restricting ocean pollution have been made, waste dumping and oil spills still occur. Therefore, waste continues to wash ashore, as shown in **Figure 8.** Enforcing pollution-preventing laws at all times is often difficult.

Citizens Taking Charge

Citizens of many countries have demanded that their governments do more to solve the growing problem of ocean pollution. Because of public outcry, the United States now spends more than $130 million each year to protect the oceans and beaches. United States citizens have also begun to take the matter into their own hands. In the early 1980s, citizens began organizing beach cleanups. One of the largest cleanups is the semiannual Adopt-a-Beach program, shown in **Figure 8,** which originated with the Texas Coastal Cleanup campaign. Millions of tons of trash have been gathered from the beaches, and people are being educated about the hazards of ocean dumping.

Figure 8 *Making an effort to pick up trash on a beach can help make the beach safer for plants, animals, and people.*

Action in the United States

The United States, like many other countries, has taken additional measures to control local pollution. For example, in 1972, Congress passed the Clean Water Act, which put the Environmental Protection Agency in charge of issuing permits for any dumping of trash into the ocean. Later that year, a stricter law—the U.S. Marine Protection, Research, and Sanctuaries Act—was passed. This act prohibits the dumping of any material that would affect human health or welfare, the marine environment or ecosystems, or businesses that depend on the ocean.

Reading Check **What is the U.S. Marine Protection, Research, and Sanctuaries Act?**

SECTION Review

Summary

- The two main types of ocean pollution are nonpoint-source pollution and point-source pollution.
- Types of nonpoint-source pollution include oil and gasoline from cars, trucks, and watercraft, as well as the use of pesticides, herbicides, and fertilizers.
- Types of point-source ocean pollution include trash dumping, sludge dumping, and oil spills.
- Efforts to save ocean resources include international treaties and volunteer cleanups.

Using Key Terms

1. Use the following terms in the same sentence: *point-source pollution* and *nonpoint-source pollution.*

Understanding Key Ideas

2. Which of the following is an example of nonpoint-source pollution?
   - **a.** a leak from an oil tanker
   - **b.** a trash barge
   - **c.** an unlined landfill
   - **d.** water discharged by industries
3. List three types of ocean pollution. How can each of these types be prevented or minimized?
4. Which part of raw sewage is a type of ocean pollution?

Math Skills

5. Only 3% of Earth's water is drinkable. What portion of Earth's water is not drinkable?
6. A ship spilled 750,000 barrels of oil when it accidentally struck a reef. The oil company was able to recover 65% of the oil spilled. How many barrels of oil were not recovered?

Critical Thinking

7. **Identifying Relationships** List and describe three measures that governments have taken to control ocean pollution.
8. **Evaluating Data** What were two effects of the *Exxon Valdez* oil spill? Describe two ways in which oil spills can be prevented.
9. **Applying Concepts** List two examples of nonpoint-source pollution that occur in your area. Explain why they are nonpoint-source pollution.
10. **Predicting Consequences** How can trash dumping and sludge dumping affect food chains in the ocean?

For a variety of links related to this chapter, go to www.scilinks.org

Topic: Ocean Pollution
SciLinks code: HSM1063

Model-Making Lab

Probing the Depths

OBJECTIVES

Model a method of mapping the ocean floor.

Construct a map of an ocean-floor model.

MATERIALS

- clay, modeling (1 lb)
- pencil, unsharpened (8 of equal length)
- ruler, metric
- scissors
- shoe box with lid

SAFETY

In the 1870s, the crew of the ship the HMS *Challenger* used a wire and a weight to discover and map some of the deepest places in the world's oceans. The crew members tied a wire to a weight and dropped the weight overboard. When the weight reached the bottom of the ocean, they hauled the weight back up to the surface and measured the length of the wet wire. In this way, they were eventually able to map the ocean floor. In this activity, you will model this method of mapping by making a map of an ocean-floor model.

Procedure

1. Use the clay to make a model ocean floor in the shoe box. The model ocean floor should have some mountains and valleys.
2. Cut eight holes in a line along the center of the lid. The holes should be just big enough for a pencil to slide through. Place the lid on the box.
3. Exchange boxes with another student or group of students. Do not look into the box.
4. Copy the table shown on the facing page onto a piece of paper. Also, copy the graph shown on the facing page.
5. Measure the length of the probe (pencil) in centimeters. Record the length in your data table.
6. Gently insert the probe into the first hole position in the box until the probe touches the model ocean floor. Do not push the probe down. Pushing the probe down could affect your reading.
7. Make sure that the probe is straight up and down, and measure the length of probe showing above the lid. Record your data in the data table.
8. Use the formula below to calculate the depth in centimeters.

$$\textit{length of probe} - \textit{length of probe showing} \text{ (cm)} = \textit{depth} \text{ (cm)}$$

Ocean Depth Table				
Hole position	Length of probe	Length of probe showing (cm)	Depth (cm)	Depth (m) scale of 1cm = 200m
1				
2				
3				
4				
5				
6				
7				
8				

9. To better represent real ocean depths, use the scale 1 cm = 200 m to convert the depth in centimeters to depth in meters. Add the data to your table.
10. Plot the depth in meters for hole position 1 on your graph.
11. Repeat steps 6–10 for the other hole positions.
12. After plotting the data for the eight hole positions, connect the plotted points with a smooth curve.

Depth of Shoe Box

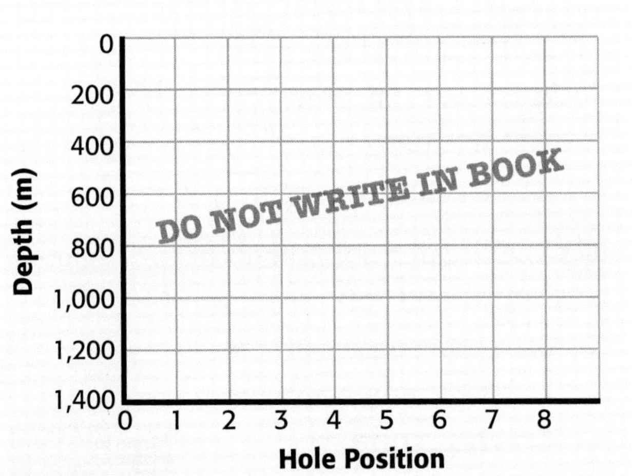

13. Put a pencil in each of the holes in the shoe box. Compare the rise and fall of the eight pencils with the shape of your graph.

Analyze the Results

1. **Describing Events** How deep was the deepest point of your ocean-floor model? How deep was the shallowest point of your ocean-floor model?
2. **Explaining Events** Did your graph resemble the ocean-floor model, as shown by the pencils in step 13? If not, why not?

Draw Conclusions

3. **Applying Conclusions** Why is measuring the real ocean floor difficult? Explain your answer.

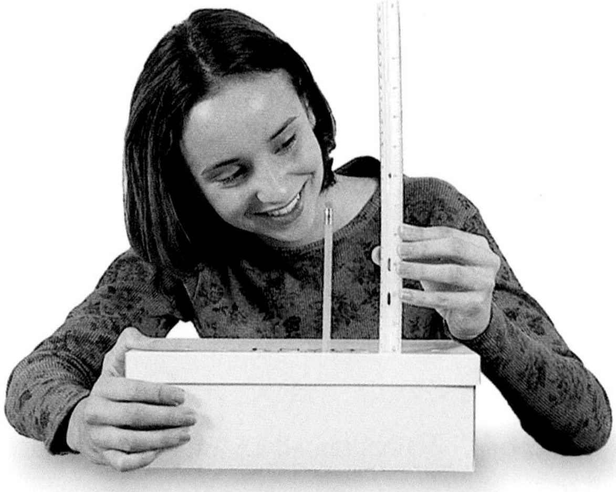

Chapter Review

USING KEY TERMS

Complete each of the following sentences by choosing the correct term from the word bank.

continental shelf
abyssal plain
salinity
nonpoint-source pollution
continental slope
desalination
benthic environment
point-source pollution

1. The region of the ocean floor that is closest to the shoreline is the ___.
2. ___ is the process of removing salt from sea water.
3. ___ is a measure of the amount of dissolved salts in a liquid.
4. The ___ is the broad, flat part of the deep-ocean basin.
5. The region near the bottom of a pond, lake, or ocean is called the ___.
6. Pollution that comes from many sources rather than a single specific source is called ___.

UNDERSTANDING KEY IDEAS

Multiple Choice

7. The largest ocean is the
   a. Indian Ocean.
   b. Pacific Ocean.
   c. Atlantic Ocean.
   d. Arctic Ocean.

8. One of the most abundant elements in the ocean is
   a. potassium.
   b. calcium.
   c. chlorine.
   d. magnesium.

9. Which of the following affects the ocean's salinity?
   a. fresh water added by rivers
   b. currents
   c. evaporation
   d. All of the above

10. Most precipitation falls
    a. on land.
    b. into lakes and rivers.
    c. into the ocean.
    d. in rain forests.

11. Which of the following is a nonrenewable resource in the ocean?
    a. fish
    b. tidal energy
    c. oil
    d. All of the above

12. Which benthic zone has a depth range between 200 m and 4,000 m?
    a. the bathyal zone
    b. the abyssal zone
    c. the hadal zone
    d. the sublittoral zone

13. The ocean floor and all of the organisms that live on or in it is the
    a. benthic environment.
    b. pelagic environment.
    c. neritic zone.
    d. oceanic zone.

Short Answer

14 Why does coastal water in areas that have hotter, drier climates typically have a higher salinity than coastal water in cooler, more humid areas does?

15 Describe two technologies used for studying the ocean floor.

16 Identify the two major regions of the ocean floor, and describe how the continental shelf, the continental slope, and the continental rise are related.

17 In your own words, write a definition for each of the following terms: *plankton, nekton,* and *benthos*. Give two examples of each.

18 List two living resources and two nonliving resources that are harvested from the ocean.

CRITICAL THINKING

19 **Concept Mapping** Use the following terms to create a concept map: *water cycle, evaporation, condensation, precipitation, atmosphere,* and *oceans*.

20 **Making Inferences** What benefit other than being able to obtain fresh water from salt water comes from desalination?

21 **Making Comparisons** Explain the difference between a bathymetric profile and a seismic reading.

22 **Analyzing Ideas** In your own words, define *nonpoint-source pollution* and *point-source pollution*. Give an example of each. What is being done to control ocean pollution?

INTERPRETING GRAPHICS

The graph below shows the ecological zones of the ocean. Use the graph below to answer the questions that follow.

Ecological Zones of the Ocean

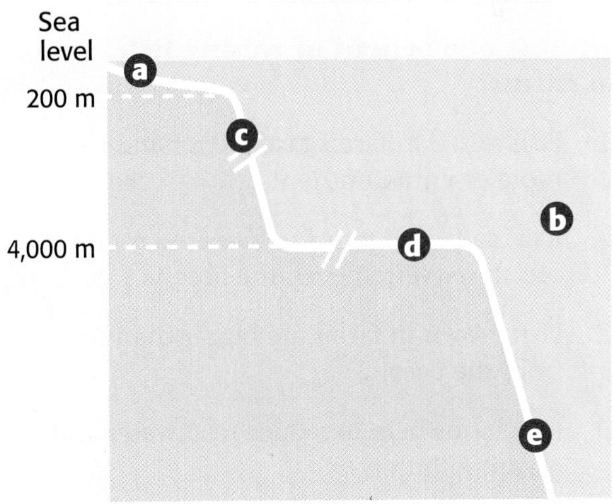

23 At which point would you most likely find an anglerfish?

24 At which point would you most likely find tube worms?

25 Which ecological zone is shown at point c? Which depth zone is shown at point c?

26 Name an organism that you might find at point e.

Standardized Test Preparation

Multiple Choice

1. **An astronaut viewed Earth from space. Which of the following did she observe?**

   A. Earth has five main oceans that are distinctly different.

   B. Earth has equal amounts of ocean and land on its surface.

   C. Ocean water covers about 71 percent of Earth's surface.

   D. Three-fourths of the water on Earth is in the Earth's oceans.

2. **What is one benefit of raising fish in farms?**

   A. Fish raised in farms taste better and have more essential nutrients.

   B. Raising fish in farms reduces the number of fish harvested from the ocean.

   C. Fish grown in farms are bigger than fish from the ocean.

   D. Fish farms help to reduce freshwater and ocean pollution.

3. **Which statement describes the main pathway of ocean water in the water cycle?**

   A. Ocean water evaporates, condenses, and precipitates back into the ocean.

   B. Ocean water flows onto shore land and into the groundwater.

   C. Ocean water evaporates, condenses, and falls onto land areas.

   D. Ocean water blows onto land and flows back into the ocean.

Use the diagram below to answer question 4.

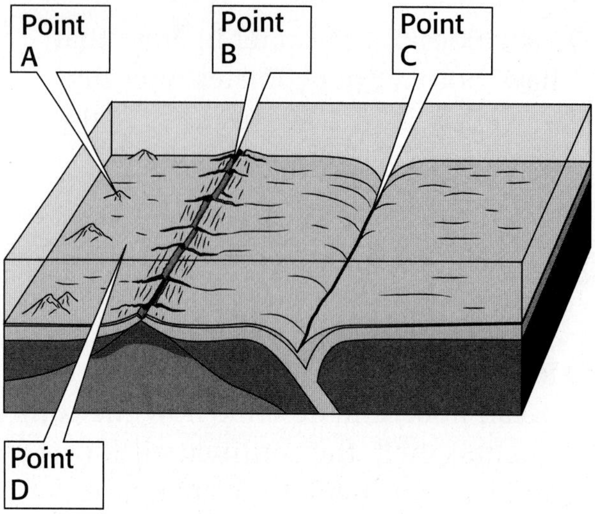

4. **Where in the diagram would hot magma most likely rise through the ocean floor and erupt underwater?**

   A. point A

   B. point B

   C. point C

   D. point D

5. **The ocean water off the coast of Maine in the United States is not as salty as the ocean water off the coast of Morocco in Africa. Which of the following factors could be responsible for this difference in salinity?**

   A. climate

   B. marine life

   C. ocean pollution

   D. deep ocean currents

Use the table below to answer question 6.

Dissolved Ions	Percentage in Ocean Water
Chlorine	55.0%
Sodium	30.6%
Magnesium	7.7%
Sulfur	3.7%
Calcium	1.2%
Potassium	1.1%
Others	0.7%

6. As part of a field investigation, Stephen analyzed a sample of ocean water. The table above summarizes the relative amounts of dissolved ions found in the sample. Based on the table, which of the following is a valid conclusion?

A. Six elements make up 99.3% of dissolved ions in Stephen's sample.

B. Chlorine only forms a compound with sodium in ocean water.

C. Magnesium is found in trace amounts in ocean water.

D. Potassium is the most abundant dissolved ion in ocean water.

7. Data show that because of tectonic plate movement the Atlantic Ocean is expanding while the Pacific Ocean is shrinking. If this pattern of tectonic plate motion continues into the future, what will probably happen to North America?

A. It will collide with Asia.

B. It will sink into the Pacific Ocean.

C. It will become part of Africa.

D. It will be covered by the Atlantic Ocean.

8. Why are mineral nodules that are found on the ocean floor considered a nonrenewable resource?

A. They are difficult and costly to locate and mine.

B. They are often composed of heavy metals.

C. They are formed from dissolved elements that cannot be recycled.

D. They cannot be created as quickly as they are mined.

9. Coral reef organisms need to be adapted to which environmental conditions?

A. strong waves and periodic exposure to air

B. warm water and plenty of light for photosynthesis

C. low light and cold water

D. hot water and no light

Open Response

10. "Marine snow" contains small pieces of dead organisms and wastes from organisms that rain down from the surface waters of the ocean to the deepest ocean zones. Sea cucumbers, worms, fish, and many other animals that live in the abyssal zone eat marine snow. Describe how energy flows from surface waters through the abyssal zone. What would happen to abyssal zone communities if marine snow stopped falling?

11. Ocean water has a high salinity because it contains high levels of sodium chloride and other dissolved mineral salts. Describe how mineral salts cycle between ocean water and land.

Science in Action

Scientific Discoveries

In Search of the Giant Squid

You might think that giant squids exist only in science fiction novels. You aren't alone, because many people have never seen a giant squid or do not know that giant squids exist. Scientists have not been able to study giant squids in the ocean. They have been able to study only dead or dying squids that have washed ashore or that have been trapped in fishing nets. As the largest of all invertebrates, giant squids range from 8 to 25 m long and have a mass of as much as 2,000 kg. Giant squids are very similar to smaller squids. But a giant squid's body parts are much larger. For example, a giant squid's eye may be as large as a volleyball! Because of the size of giant squids, you may think that they don't have any enemies in the ocean, but they do. They are usually eaten by sperm whales that can weigh 20 tons!

Math ACTIVITY

A giant squid that washed ashore has a mass of 900 kg. A deep-sea squid that washed ashore has a mass that is only 7% of the mass of the giant squid. What is the mass in kilograms of the deep-sea squid?

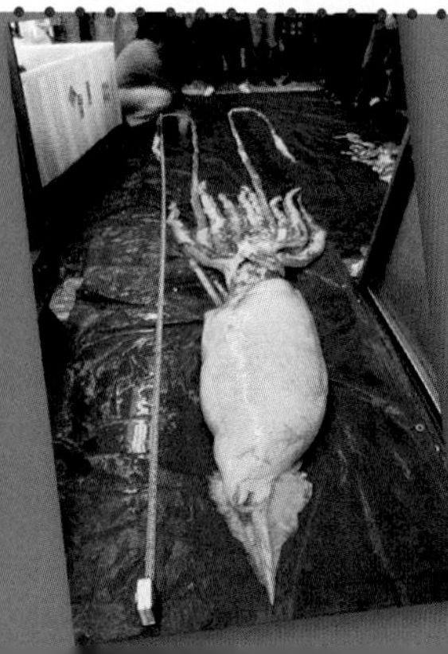

Science, Technology, and Society

Creating Artificial Reefs

If you found a sunken ship, would you look for hidden treasure? Treasure is not the only thing that sunken ships are known for. Hundreds of years ago, people found that the fishing is often good over a sunken ship. The fishing is good because many marine organisms, such as seaweed, corals, and oysters, live only where they can attach to a hard surface in clear water. They attract other organisms to the sunken ship and eventually form a reef community. Thus, in recent years, many human communities have created artificial reefs by sinking objects such as warships, barges, concrete, airplanes, and school buses in the ocean. Like natural reefs, artificial reefs provide a home for organisms and protect organisms from predators.

Social Studies ACTIVITY

WRITING SKILL Research how some artificial reefs are created off the coast of some states in the United States. Write a report that describes some of the objects used to create artificial reefs. In your report also include what countries other than the United States create artificial reefs and what are the benefits and disadvantages of creating artificial reefs.

Jacques Cousteau

Ocean Explorer Jacques Cousteau was born in France in 1910. Cousteau performed his first underwater diving mission at age 10 and became very fascinated with the possibilities of seeing and breathing underwater. As a result, in 1943, Cousteau and Emile Gagnan developed the first aqualung, a self-contained breathing system for underwater exploration. Using the aqualung and other underwater equipment that he developed, Cousteau began making underwater films. In 1950, Cousteau transformed the *Calypso*, a retired minesweeper boat, into an oceanographic vessel and laboratory. For the next 40 years, Cousteau sailed with the *Calypso* around the world to explore and film the world's oceans. Cousteau produced more than 115 films, many of which have won awards.

Jacques Cousteau opened the eyes of countless people to the sea. During his long life, Cousteau explored Earth's oceans and documented the amazing variety of life that they contain. He was an environmentalist, inventor, and teacher who inspired millions with his joy and wonder of the ocean. Cousteau was an outspoken defender of the environment. He campaigned vigorously to protect the oceans and environment. Cousteau died in 1997 at age 87. Before his death, he dedicated the *Calypso II,* a new research vessel, to the children of the world.

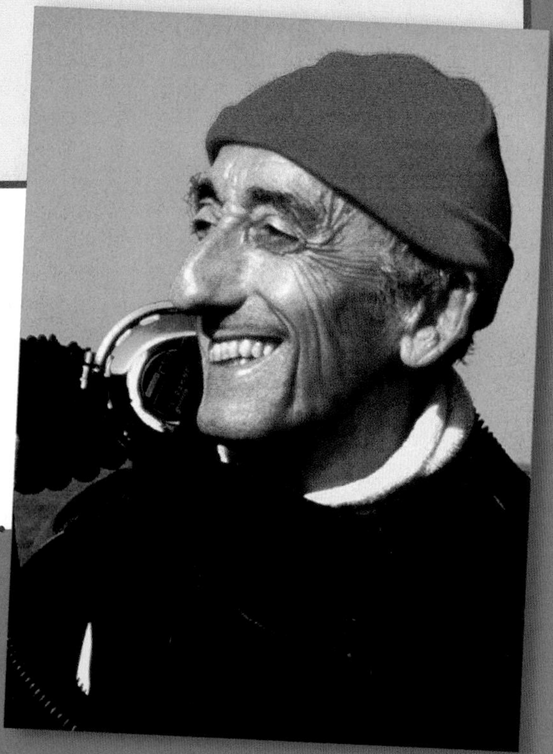

Language Arts ACTIVITY

WRITING SKILL Ocean pollution and overfishing are subjects of intense debate. Think about these issues, and discuss them with your classmates. Take notes on what you discuss with your classmates. Then, write an essay in which you try to convince readers of your point of view.

Cousteau sailed his ship, the Calypso, *around the world exploring and filming the world's oceans.*

go.hrw.com

To learn more about these Science in Action topics, visit **go.hrw.com** and type in the keyword **HZ5OCEF.**

Current Science

Check out Current Science® articles related to this chapter by visiting go.hrw.com. Just type in the keyword HZ5CS13.

12

The Movement of Ocean Water

The Big Idea

The movement of ocean water is driven by differences in density and temperature, by wind, and by the moon's gravity.

SECTION

About the Photo

No, this isn't a traffic jam or the result of careless navigation. Hurricane Hugo is to blame for this major boat pile up. When Hurricane Hugo hit South Carolina's coast in 1989, the hurricane's strong winds created large ocean waves. These ocean waves carried these boats right onto the shore.

PRE-READING ACTIVITY

Graphic Organizer

Concept Map Before you read the chapter, create the graphic organizer entitled "Concept Map" described in the **Study Skills** section of the Appendix. As you read the chapter, fill in the concept map with details about each type of ocean water movement.

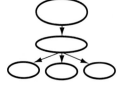

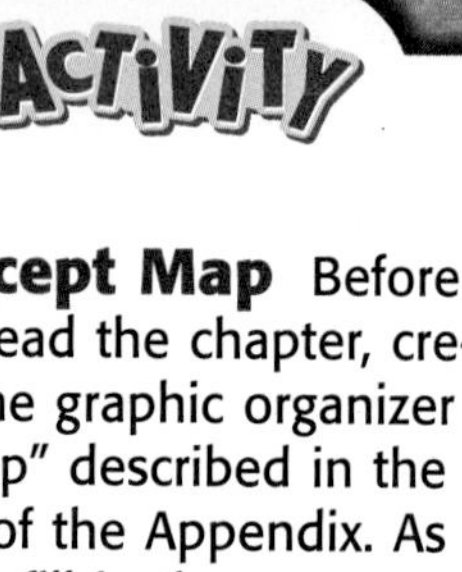

START-UP ACTIVITY

When Whirls Collide

Some ocean currents flow in a clockwise direction, while other ocean currents flow in a counterclockwise direction. Sometimes these currents collide. In this activity, you and your lab partner will demonstrate how two currents flowing in opposite directions affect one another.

Procedure

1. Fill a large **tub** with **water** 5 cm deep.
2. Add **10 drops of red food coloring** to the water at one end of the tub.
3. Add **10 drops of blue food coloring** to the water at the other end of the tub.
4. Using a **pencil,** quickly stir the water at one end of the tub in a clockwise direction while your partner stirs the water at the other end in a counterclockwise direction. Stir both ends for 5 s.
5. Draw what you see happening in the tub immediately after you stop stirring. (Both ends should be swirling.)

Analysis

1. How did the blue water and the red water interact?
2. How does this activity relate to how ocean currents interact?

SECTION 1

Currents

What You Will Learn

- Describe surface currents.
- List the three factors that control surface currents.
- Describe deep currents.
- Identify the three factors that form deep currents.

Vocabulary

ocean current
surface current
Coriolis effect
deep current

READING STRATEGY

Reading Organizer As you read this section, create an outline of the section. Use the headings from the section in your outline.

Imagine that you are stranded on a desert island. You stuff a distress message into a bottle and throw it into the ocean. Is there any way to predict where your bottle may land?

Actually, there is a way to predict where the bottle will end up. Ocean water contains streamlike movements of water called **ocean currents.** Currents are influenced by a number of factors, including weather, the Earth's rotation, and the position of the continents. With knowledge of ocean currents, people are able to predict where objects in the open ocean will be carried.

One Way to Explore Currents

In the 1940s, a Norwegian explorer named Thor Heyerdahl tried to answer questions about human migration across the ocean. Heyerdahl theorized that the inhabitants of Polynesia originally sailed from Peru on rafts powered only by the wind and ocean currents. In 1947, Heyerdahl and a crew of five people set sail from Peru on a raft, which is shown in **Figure 1.**

On the 97th day of their expedition, Heyerdahl and his crew landed on an island in Polynesia. Currents had carried the raft westward more than 6,000 km across the South Pacific. This landing supported Heyerdahl's theory that ocean currents carried the ancient Peruvians across the Pacific to Polynesia.

Reading Check **What was Heyerdahl's theory, and how did he prove it?** *(See the Appendix for answers to Reading Checks.)*

ocean current a movement of ocean water that follows a regular pattern

Figure 1 *The handcrafted Kon-Tiki was made mainly from materials that would have been available to ancient Peruvians.*

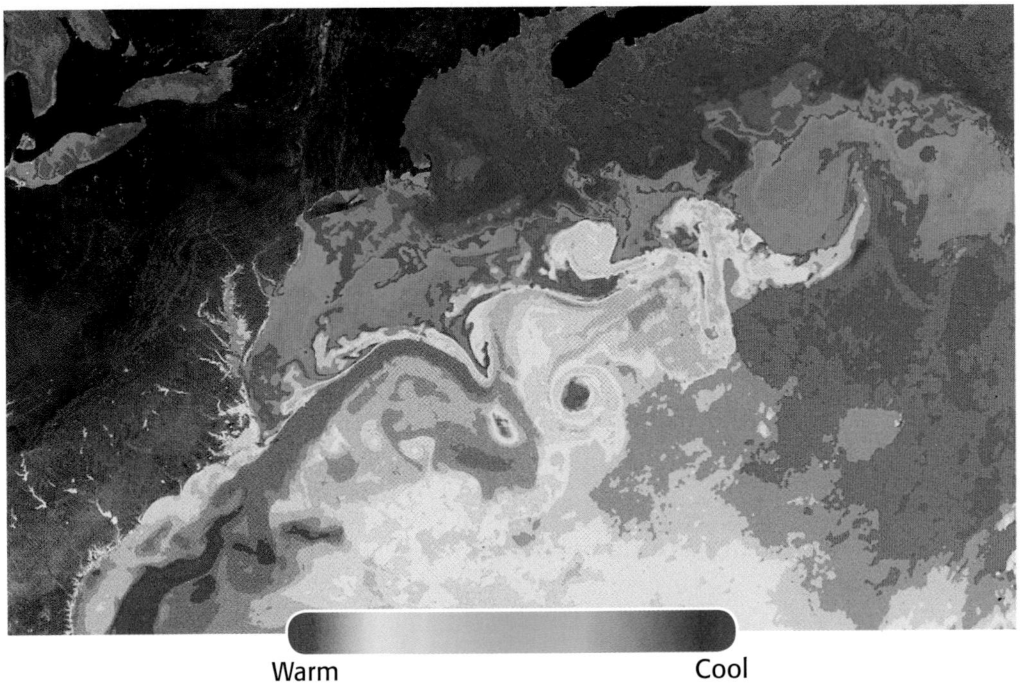

Figure 2 *This infrared satellite image shows the Gulf Stream current moving warm water from lower latitudes to higher latitudes.*

Surface Currents

Horizontal, streamlike movements of water that occur at or near the surface of the ocean are called **surface currents.** Surface currents can reach depths of several hundred meters and lengths of several thousand kilometers and can travel across oceans. The Gulf Stream, shown in **Figure 2,** is one of the longest surface currents—it transports 25 times more water than all the rivers in the world.

surface current a horizontal movement of ocean water that is caused by wind and that occurs at or near the ocean's surface

Surface currents are controlled by three factors: global winds, the Coriolis effect, and continental deflections. These three factors keep surface currents flowing in distinct patterns around the Earth.

Global Winds

Have you ever blown gently on a cup of hot chocolate? You may have noticed ripples moving across the surface, as in **Figure 3.** These ripples are caused by a tiny surface current created by your breath. In much the same way that you create ripples, winds that blow across the Earth's surface create surface currents in the ocean.

Different winds cause currents to flow in different directions. Near the equator, the winds blow ocean water east to west, but closer to the poles, ocean water is blown west to east. Merchant ships often use these currents to travel more quickly back and forth across the oceans.

Figure 3 *Winds form surface currents in the ocean, much like blowing on a cup of hot chocolate forms ripples.*

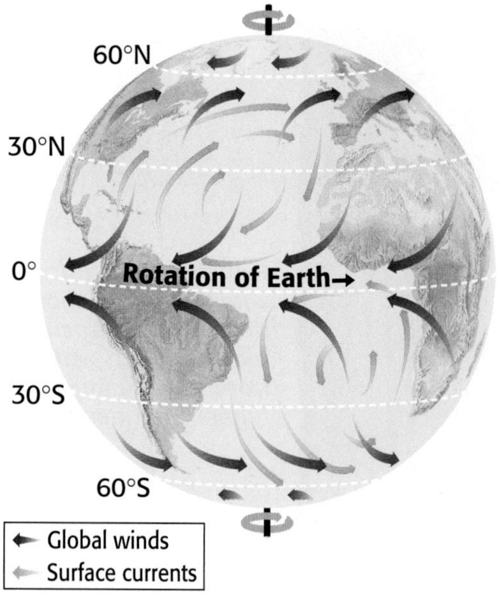

Figure 4 *The rotation of the Earth causes surface currents (yellow arrows) and global winds (purple arrows) to curve as they move across the Earth's surface.*

The Coriolis Effect

The Earth's rotation causes wind and surface currents to move in curved paths rather than in straight lines. The apparent curving of moving objects from a straight path due to the Earth's rotation is called the **Coriolis effect.** To understand the Coriolis effect, imagine trying to roll a ball straight across a turning merry-go-round. Because the merry-go-round is spinning, the path of the ball will curve before it reaches the other side. **Figure 4** shows how the Coriolis effect causes surface currents in the Northern Hemisphere to turn clockwise, and surface currents in the Southern Hemisphere to turn counterclockwise.

Reading Check **What causes currents to move in curved paths instead of straight lines?**

Coriolis effect the apparent curving of the path of a moving object from an otherwise straight path due to the Earth's rotation

Continental Deflections

If the Earth's surface were covered only with water, surface currents would travel freely across the globe in a very uniform pattern. However, you know that water does not cover the entire surface of the Earth. Continents rise above sea level over roughly one-third of the Earth's surface. When surface currents meet continents, the currents *deflect,* or change direction. Notice in **Figure 5** how the Brazil Current deflects southward as it meets the east coast of South America.

SCHOOL to HOME

Coriolis Effect in Your Sink?

WRITING SKILL Some people think the Coriolis effect can be seen in sinks. Does water draining from sinks turn clockwise in the Northern Hemisphere and counterclockwise in the Southern Hemisphere? Research this question at the library, on the Internet, and in your sink at home with an adult. Write what you learn in your **science journal.**

ACTIVITY

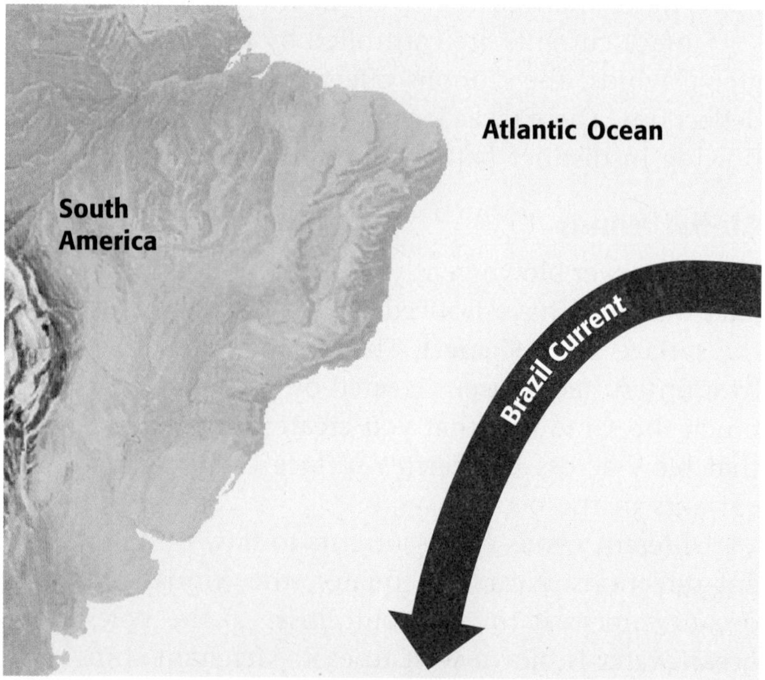

Figure 5 *If South America were not in the way, the Brazil Current would probably flow farther west.*

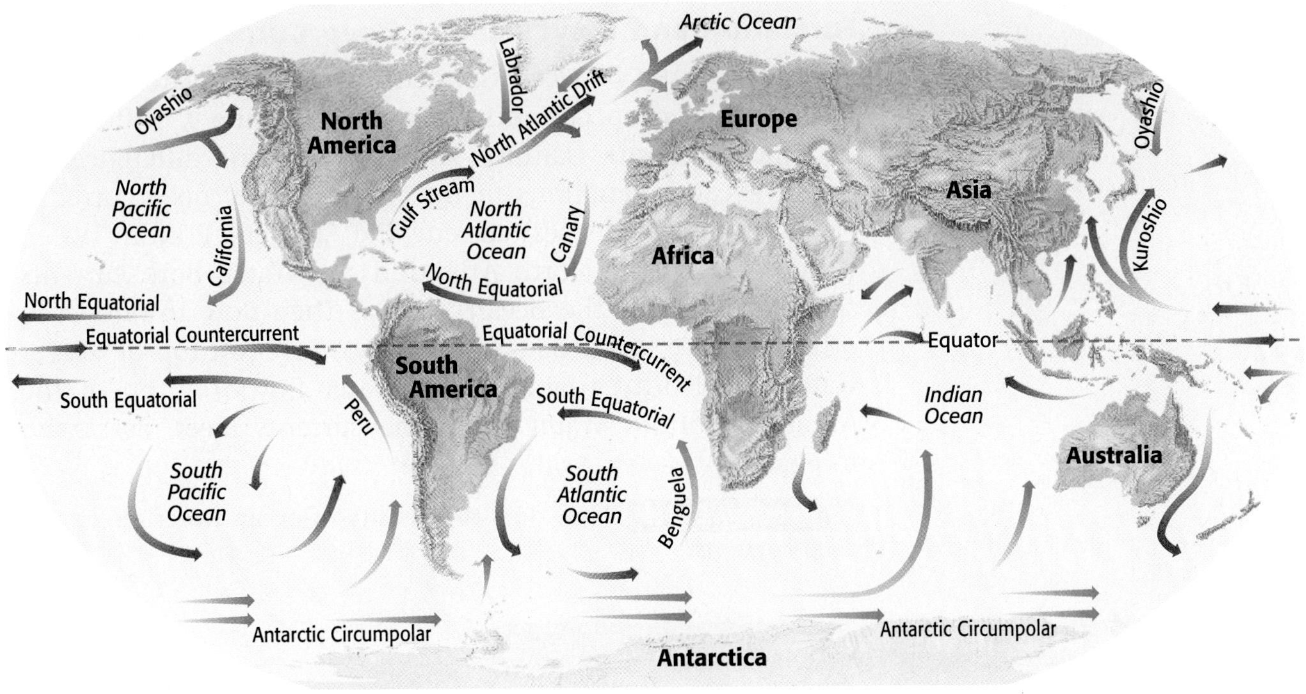

Figure 6 *This map shows Earth's surface currents. Warm-water currents are shown as red arrows, and cold-water currents are shown as blue arrows.*

Taking Temperatures

All three factors—global winds, the Coriolis effect, and continental deflections—work together to form a pattern of surface currents on Earth. But currents are also affected by the temperature of the water in which they form. Warm-water currents begin near the equator and carry warm water to other parts of the ocean. Cold-water currents begin closer to the poles and carry cool water to other parts of the ocean. As you can see on the map in **Figure 6,** all the oceans are connected and both warm-water and cold-water currents travel from one ocean to another.

Reading Check What three factors form a pattern of surface currents on Earth?

Deep Currents

Streamlike movements of ocean water located far below the surface are called **deep currents.** Unlike surface currents, deep currents are not directly controlled by wind. Instead, deep currents form in parts of the ocean where water density increases. *Density* is the amount of matter in a given space, or volume. The density of ocean water is affected by temperature and *salinity*—a measure of the amount of dissolved salts or solids in a liquid. Both decreasing the temperature of ocean water and increasing the water's salinity increase the water's density.

deep current a streamlike movement of ocean water far below the surface

CONNECTION TO Physics

Convection Currents While winds are often responsible for ocean currents, the sun is the initial energy source of the winds and currents. Because the sun heats the Earth more in some places than in others, convection currents are formed. These currents transfer thermal energy. Which ocean currents do you think carry more thermal energy, currents located near the equator or currents located near the poles?

Formation and Movement of Deep Currents

The relationship between the density of ocean water and the formation of deep currents is shown in **Figure 7.** Differences in temperature and salinity—and the resulting differences in density—cause variations in the movement of deep currents. For example, the deepest current, the Antarctic Bottom Water, is denser than the North Atlantic Deep Water. Both currents spread out across the ocean floor as they flow toward each other. Because less-dense water always flows on top of denser water, the North Atlantic Deep Water flows on top of the Antarctic Bottom Water when the currents meet, as shown in **Figure 8.**

Reading Check How does the density of ocean water affect deep currents?

Figure 7 How Deep Currents Form

Decreasing Temperature In Earth's polar regions, cold air chills the water molecules at the ocean's surface, which causes the molecules to slow down and move closer together. This reaction causes the water's volume to decrease. Thus, the water becomes denser. The dense water sinks and eventually travels toward the equator as a deep current along the ocean floor.

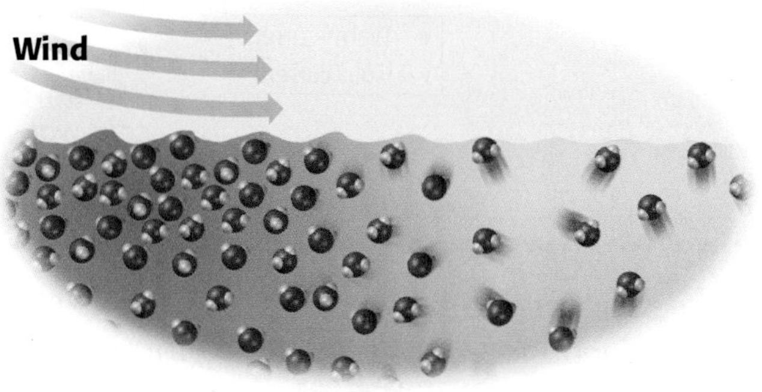

Increasing Salinity Through Freezing If the ocean water freezes at the surface, ice will float on top of the water because ice is less dense than liquid water. The dissolved solids are squeezed out of the ice and enter the liquid water below the ice. This process increases the salinity of the water. As a result of the increased salinity, the water's density increases.

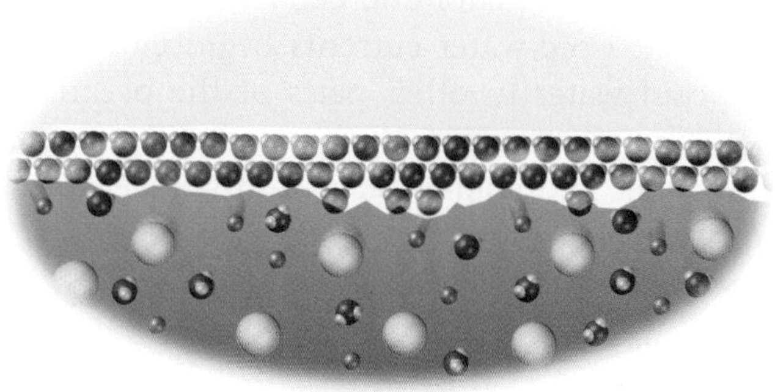

Increasing Salinity Through Evaporation Another way salinity increases is through evaporation of surface water, which removes water but leaves solids behind. This process is especially common in warm climates. Increasing salinity through freezing or evaporation causes water to become denser, to sink to the ocean floor, and to form a deep current.

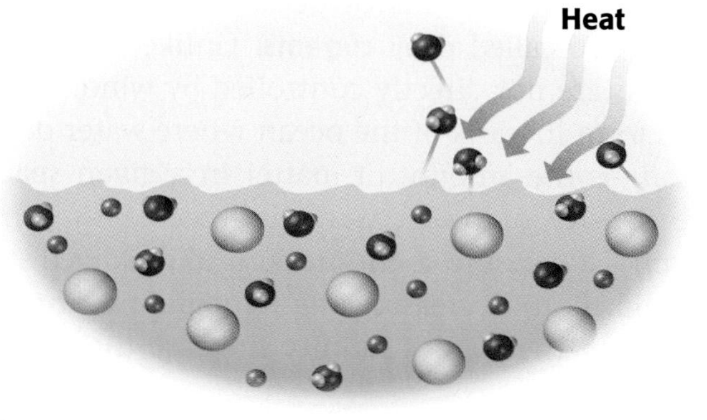

Figure 8 *The warmer, less-dense water in surface currents cools and becomes the colder, denser water in deep currents.*

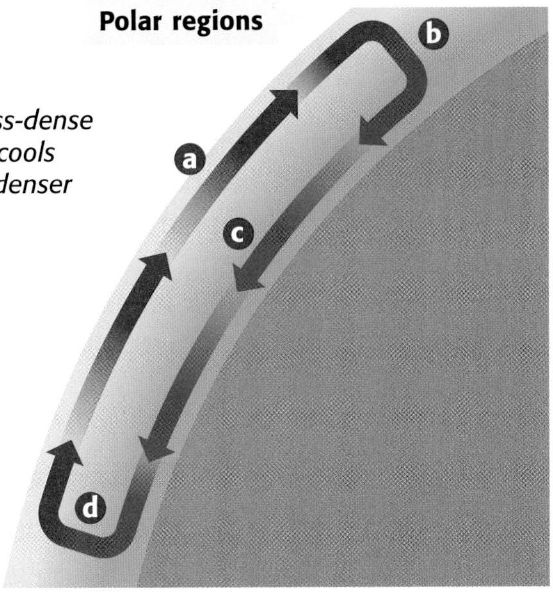

a Surface currents carry the warmer, less-dense water from other ocean regions to polar regions.

b Warm water from surface currents replaces colder, denser water that sinks to the ocean floor.

c Deep currents carry colder, denser water along the ocean floor from polar regions to other ocean regions.

d Water from deep currents rises to replace water leaving surface currents.

SECTION Review

Summary

- Surface currents are streamlike movements of water at or near the surface of the ocean.
- Surface currents are controlled by three factors: global winds, the Coriolis effect, and continental deflections.
- Deep currents are streamlike movements of ocean water located far below the surface.
- Deep currents form where the density of ocean water increases. Water density depends on temperature and salinity.

Using Key Terms

The statements below are false. For each statement, replace the underlined word to make a true statement.

1. <u>Deep currents</u> are directly controlled by wind.
2. An increase in density in parts of the ocean can cause <u>surface currents</u> to form.

Understanding Key Ideas

3. Surface currents
   a. are formed by wind.
   b. are streamlike movements of water.
   c. can travel across entire oceans.
   d. All of the above
4. List three factors that control surface currents.
5. How does a continent affect the movement of a surface current?
6. Explain how temperature and salinity affect the formation of deep currents.

Math Skills

7. The Gulf Stream flows along the North Carolina coast at 90 million cubic meters per second and at 40 million cubic meters per second when it turns eastward. How much faster is the Gulf Stream flowing along the coast than when it turns eastward?

Critical Thinking

8. **Evaluating Conclusions** If there were no land on Earth's surface, what would the pattern of surface currents look like? Explain your answer.
9. **Making Comparisons** Compare the factors that contribute to the formation of surface currents and deep currents.

SCILINKS® NSTA Developed and maintained by the National Science Teachers Association

For a variety of links related to this chapter, go to www.scilinks.org

Topic: Ocean Currents
SciLinks code: HSM1061

SECTION 2

Currents and Climate

The Scilly Isles in England are located as far north as Newfoundland in northeast Canada. But the Scilly Isles experience warm temperatures almost all year long, while Newfoundland has long winters of frost and snow. How can two places at similar latitudes have completely different climates? This difference in climate is caused by surface currents.

What You Will Learn

- Explain how currents affect climate.
- Describe the effects of El Niño.
- Explain how scientists study and predict the pattern of El Niño.

Vocabulary

upwelling
El Niño
La Niña

READING STRATEGY

Paired Summarizing Read this section silently. In pairs, take turns summarizing the material. Stop to discuss ideas that seem confusing.

Surface Currents and Climate

Surface currents greatly affect the climate in many parts of the world. Some surface currents warm or cool coastal areas year-round. Other surface currents sometimes change their circulation pattern. Changes in circulation patterns cause changes in atmosphere that affect the climate in many parts of the world.

Warm-Water Currents and Climate

Although surface currents are generally much warmer than deep currents, the temperatures of surface currents do vary. Surface currents are classified as warm-water currents or cold-water currents. Warm-water currents create warmer climates in coastal areas that would otherwise be much cooler. **Figure 1** shows how the Gulf Stream carries warm water from the Tropics to the North Atlantic Ocean. The Gulf Stream flows to the British Isles and creates a relatively mild climate for land at such high latitude. The Gulf Stream is the same current that makes the climate of the Scilly Isles very different from the climate of Newfoundland.

Figure 1 How Warm-Water Currents Affect Climate

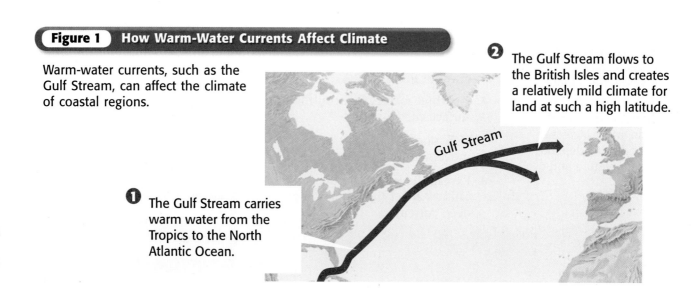

Warm-water currents, such as the Gulf Stream, can affect the climate of coastal regions.

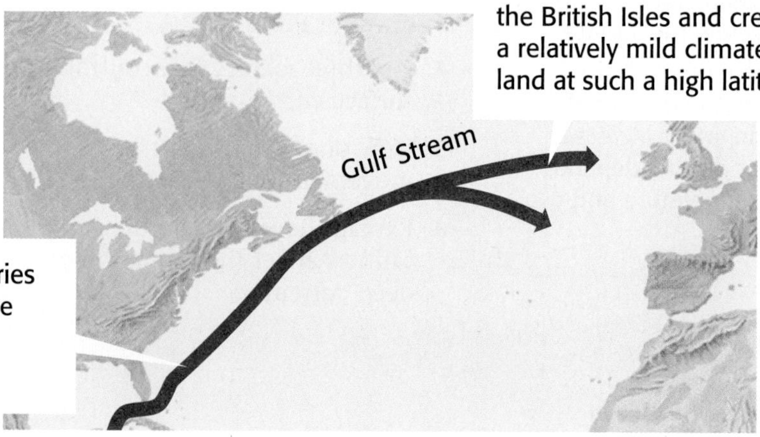

1. The Gulf Stream carries warm water from the Tropics to the North Atlantic Ocean.
2. The Gulf Stream flows to the British Isles and creates a relatively mild climate for land at such a high latitude.

Figure 2 How Cold-Water Currents Affect Climate

Cold-water currents, such as the California Current, can affect the climate of coastal regions.

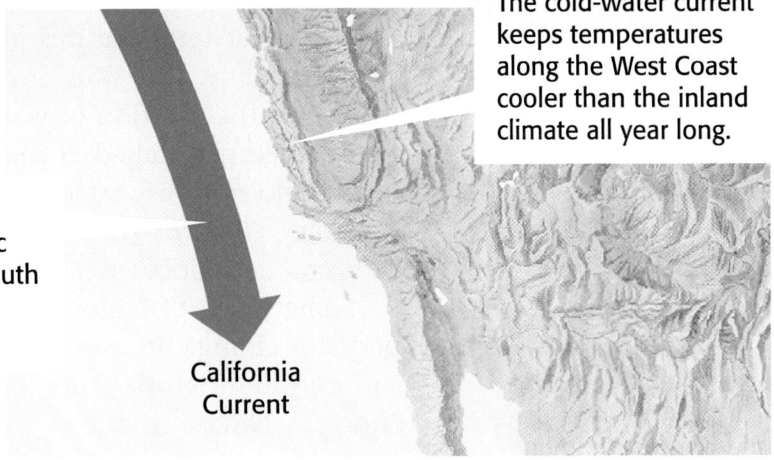

1 Cold water from the northern Pacific Ocean is carried south to Mexico by the California Current.
California Current
2 The cold-water current keeps temperatures along the West Coast cooler than the inland climate all year long.

Cold-Water Currents and Climate

Cold-water currents also affect the climate of the land near where they flow. **Figure 2** shows how the California Current carries cold water from the North Pacific Ocean southward to Mexico. The cold-water California Current keeps the climate along the West Coast cooler than the inland climate year-round.

upwelling the movement of deep, cold, and nutrient-rich water to the surface

Reading Check How do cold-water currents affect coastal regions?

Upwelling

When local wind patterns blow along the northwest coast of South America, they cause local surface currents to move away from the shore. This warm water is then replaced by deep, cold water. This movement causes upwelling to occur in the eastern Pacific. **Upwelling** is a process in which cold, nutrient-rich water from the deep ocean rises to the surface and replaces warm surface water, as shown in **Figure 3.** The nutrients from the deep ocean are made up of elements and chemicals, such as iron and nitrate. When these chemicals are brought to the sunny surface, they help tiny plants grow through the process of photosynthesis.

The process of upwelling is extremely important to organisms. The nutrients that are brought to the surface of the ocean support the growth of phytoplankton and zooplankton. These tiny plants and animals support other organisms such as fish and seabirds.

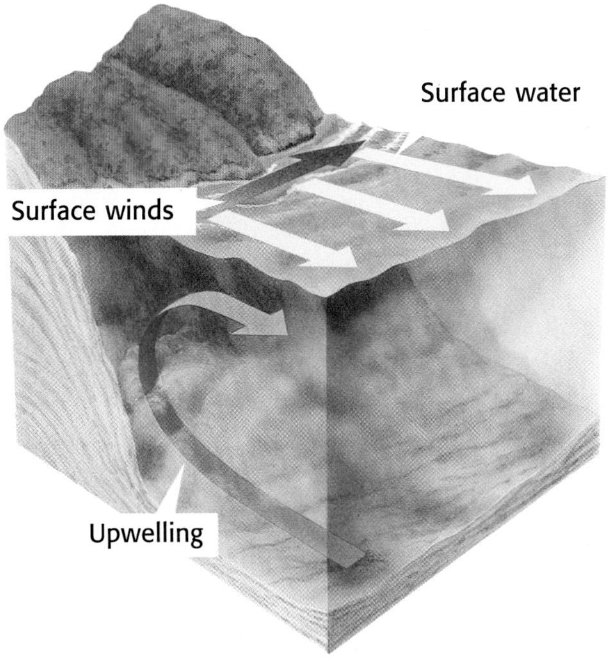

Surface water
Surface winds
Upwelling

Figure 3 *Upwelling causes cold, nutrient-rich water from the deep ocean to rise to the surface.*

El Niño

Every 2 to 12 years, the South Pacific trade winds move less warm water to the western Pacific than they usually do. Thus, surface-water temperatures along the coast of South America rise. Gradually, this warming spreads westward. This periodic change in the location of warm and cool surface waters in the Pacific Ocean is called **El Niño.** El Niño can last for a year or longer and not only affects the surface waters but also changes the interaction of the ocean and the atmosphere, which in turn changes global weather patterns.

Sometimes, El Niño is followed by La Niña. **La Niña** is a periodic change in the eastern Pacific Ocean in which the surface-water temperature becomes unusually cool. Like El Niño, La Niña also affects weather patterns.

CONNECTION TO Environmental Science

El Niño and Coral Reefs The increase of surface water temperatures during El Niño can destroy coral reefs. *Coral reefs* are fragile limestone ridges built by tiny coral animals. An increase in surface water temperature and exposure to the sun (due to a decrease in sea level) can cause corals to become bleached and die. Coral reefs support a diverse community of marine life. Create a world map that shows the locations of the coral reefs.

ACTIVITY

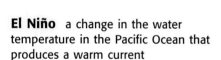

El Niño a change in the water temperature in the Pacific Ocean that produces a warm current

La Niña a change in the eastern Pacific Ocean in which the surface water temperature becomes unusually cool

Effects of El Niño

El Niño alters weather patterns enough to cause disasters. These disasters include flash floods and mudslides in areas of the world that usually receive little rain, such as the southern half of the United States and Peru. **Figure 4** shows homes in Southern California destroyed by a mudslide caused by El Niño. While some regions flood, regions that usually get a lot of rain may experience *droughts,* an unusually long period during which rainfall is below average. During El Niño, severe droughts can occur in Indonesia and Australia. Periods of severe drought can lead to crop failure.

During El Niño, the upwelling of nutrient-rich water does not occur off the coast of South America, which affects the organisms that depend on the nutrients for food.

Figure 4 *This damage in Southern California was the result of excessive rain caused by El Niño in 1997.*

Studying and Predicting El Niño

Because El Niño occurs every 2 to 12 years, studying and predicting it can be difficult. However, it is important for scientists to learn as much as possible about El Niño because of its effects on organisms and land.

One way scientists collect data to predict an El Niño is through a network of buoys operated by the National Oceanic and Atmospheric Administration (NOAA). The buoys, some of which are anchored to the ocean floor, are located along the Earth's equator. The buoys record data about surface temperature, air temperature, currents, and winds. The buoys transmit some of the data on a daily basis to NOAA through a satellite in space.

When the buoys report that the South Pacific trade winds are not as strong as they usually are or that the surface temperatures of the tropical oceans have risen, scientists can predict that an El Niño is likely to occur.

Reading Check **Why is it important to study El Niño? Describe one way scientists study El Niño.**

INTERNET ACTIVITY

For another activity related to this chapter, go to **go.hrw.com** and type in the keyword **HZ5H20W.**

SECTION Review

Summary

- Surface currents affect the climate of the land near which they flow.
- Warm-water currents bring warmer climates to coastal regions.
- Cold-water currents bring cooler climates to coastal regions.
- During El Niño, warm and cool surface waters change locations.
- El Niño can cause floods, mudslides, and drought.

Using Key Terms

1. Use each of the following terms in a separate sentence: *upwelling, El Niño,* and *La Niña.*

Understanding Key Ideas

2. The Gulf Stream carries warm water to the North Atlantic Ocean, which contributes to
   - **a.** a harsh winter in the British Isles.
   - **b.** a cold-water surface current that flows to the British Isles.
   - **c.** a mild climate for the British Isles.
   - **d.** a warm-water surface current that flows along the coast of California.
3. Why might the climate in Scotland be relatively mild even though the country is located at a high latitude?
4. Name two disasters caused by El Niño.

Math Skills

5. A fisher usually catches 540 kg of anchovies off the coast of Peru. During El Niño, the fisher caught 85% less fish. How many kilograms of fish did the fisher catch during El Niño?

Critical Thinking

6. **Applying Concepts** Many marine organisms depend on upwelling to bring nutrients to the surface. How might El Niño affect a fisher's way of life?

SCILINKS. NSTA Developed and maintained by the National Science Teachers Association

For a variety of links related to this chapter, go to www.scilinks.org

Topic: El Niño
SciLinks code: HSM0468

SECTION 3

Waves

Have you ever seen a surfer riding waves? Did you ever wonder where the waves come from? And why are some waves big, while others are small?

What You Will Learn

- Identify the parts of a wave.
- Explain how the parts of a wave relate to wave movement.
- Describe how ocean waves form and move.
- Classify types of waves.

Vocabulary

undertow
longshore current
whitecap
swell
tsunami
storm surge

READING STRATEGY

Prediction Guide Before reading this section, write the title of each heading in this section. Next, write what you think you will learn under each heading.

We all know what ocean waves look like. Even if you've never been to the seashore, you've most likely seen waves on TV. But how do waves form and move? Waves are affected by a number of different factors. They can be formed by something as simple as wind or by something as violent as an earthquake. Ocean waves can travel through water slowly or incredibly quickly. Read on to discover the many forces that affect the formation and movement of ocean waves.

Anatomy of a Wave

Waves are made up of two main parts—crests and troughs. A *crest* is the highest point of a wave. A *trough* is the lowest point of a wave. Imagine a roller coaster designed with many rises and dips. The top of a rise on a roller-coaster track is similar to the crest of a wave, and the bottom of a dip in the track resembles the trough of a wave. The distance between two adjacent wave crests or wave troughs is a *wavelength*. The vertical distance between the crest and trough of a wave is called the *wave height*. **Figure 1** shows the parts of a wave.

Reading Check **What is the lowest point of a wave called?** *(See the Appendix for answers to Reading Checks.)*

Figure 1 Parts of a Wave

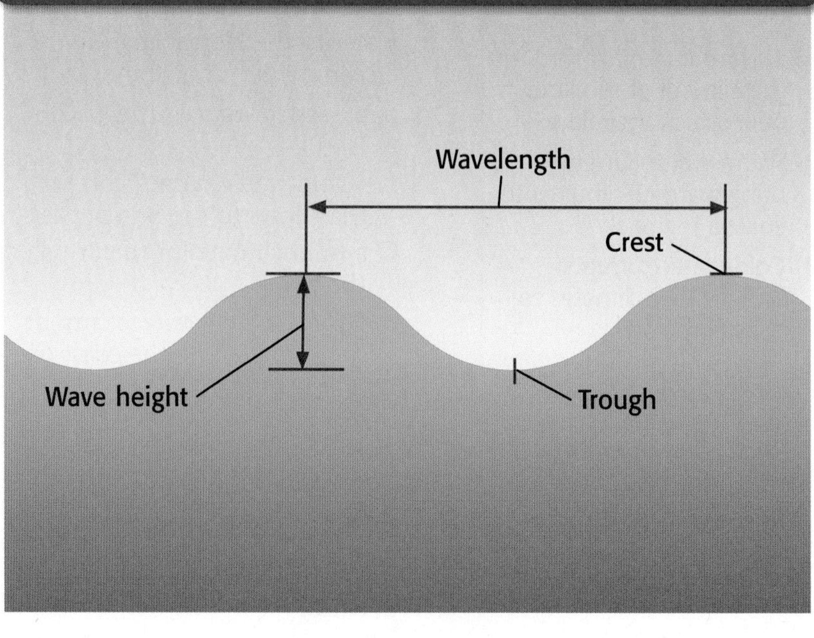

Wave Formation and Movement

If you have watched ocean waves before, you may have noticed that water appears to move across the ocean's surface. However, this movement is only an illusion. Most waves form as wind blows across the water's surface and transfers energy to the water. As the energy moves through the water, so do the waves. But the water itself stays behind, rising and falling in circular movements. Notice in **Figure 2** that the floating bottle remains in the same spot as the waves travel from left to right. This circular motion gets smaller as the water depth increases, because wave energy decreases as the water depth increases. Wave energy reaches only a certain depth. Below that depth, the water is not affected by wave energy.

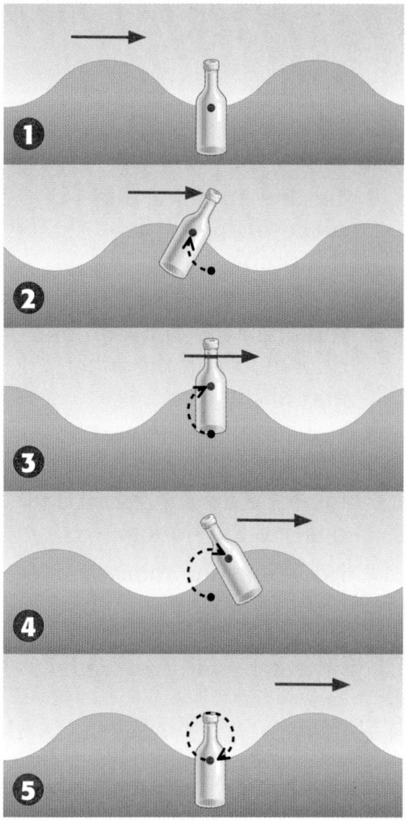

Figure 2 *Like the bottle in this figure, water remains in the same place as waves travel through it.*

Specifics of Wave Movement

Waves not only come in different sizes but also travel at different speeds. To calculate wave speed, scientists must know the wavelength and the wave period. *Wave period* is the time between the passage of two wave crests (or troughs) at a fixed point, as shown in **Figure 3.** Dividing wavelength by wave period gives you wave speed, as shown below.

$$\frac{\text{wavelength (m)}}{\text{wave period (s)}} = \text{wave speed (m/s)}$$

For any given wavelength, an increase in the wave period will decrease the wave speed and a decrease in the wave period will increase the wave speed.

Figure 3 **Determining Wave Period**

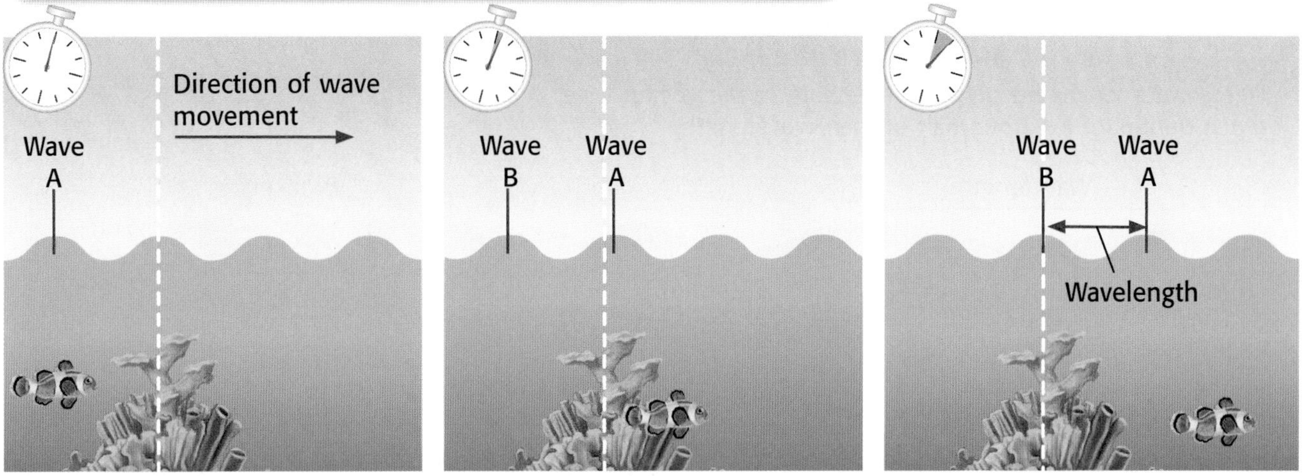

❶ Notice that the waves are moving from left to right.

❷ The clock begins running as Wave A passes the reef's peak.

❸ The clock stops as Wave B passes the reef's peak. The time shown on the clock (5 s) represents the wave period.

Types of Waves

As you learned earlier in this section, wind forms most ocean waves. Waves can also form by other mechanisms. Underwater earthquakes and landslides as well as impacts by cosmic bodies can form different types of waves. Most waves move in one way regardless of how they are formed. Depending on their size and the angle at which they hit the shore, waves can generate a variety of near-shore events, some of which can be dangerous to humans.

Deep-Water Waves and Shallow-Water Waves

Have you ever wondered why waves increase in height as they approach the shore? The answer has to do with the depth of the water. *Deep-water waves* are waves that move in water deeper than one-half their wavelength. When the waves reach water shallower than one-half their wavelength, they begin to interact with the ocean floor. These waves are called *shallow-water waves.* **Figure 4** shows how deep-water waves become shallow-water waves as they move toward the shore.

As deep-water waves become shallow-water waves, the water particles slow down and build up. This change forces more water between wave crests and increases wave height. Gravity eventually pulls the high wave crests down, which causes them to crash into the ocean floor as *breakers*. The area where waves first begin to tumble downward, or break, is called the *breaker zone*. Waves continue to break as they move from the breaker zone to the shore. The area between the breaker zone and the shore is called the *surf*.

Reading Check How do deep-water waves become shallow-water waves?

Quick Lab

Doing the Wave

1. Tie one end of a **thin piece of rope** to a **doorknob**.
2. Tie a **ribbon** around the rope halfway between the doorknob and the other end of the rope.
3. Holding the rope at the untied end, quickly move the rope up and down and observe the ribbon.
4. How does the movement of the rope and ribbon relate to the movement of water and deep-water waves?
5. Repeat step 3, but move the rope higher and lower this time.
6. How does this affect the waves in the rope?

Figure 4 Deep-Water and Shallow-Water Waves

Deep-water waves become shallow-water waves when they reach depths of less than half of their wavelength.

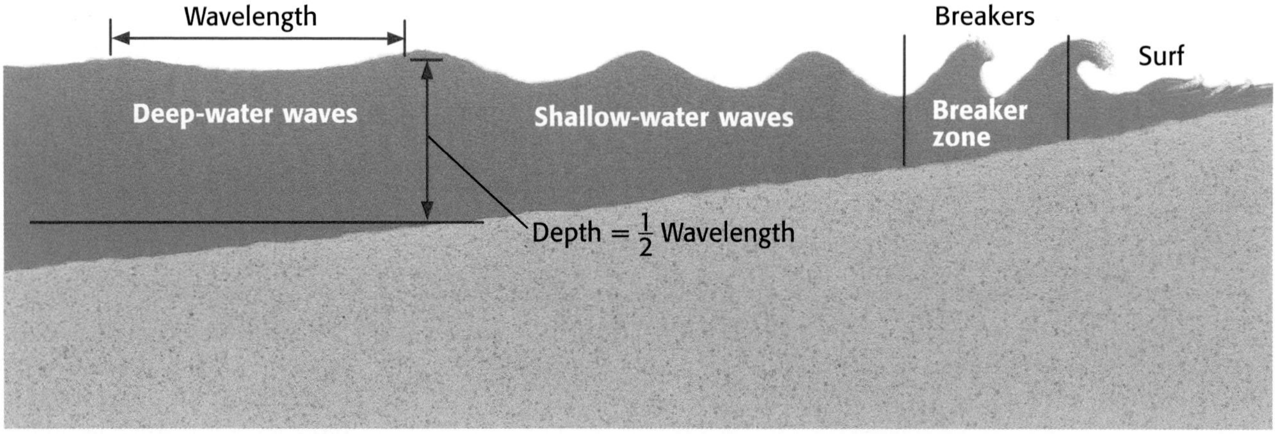

Figure 5 **Formation of an Undertow**

Head-on waves create an undertow.

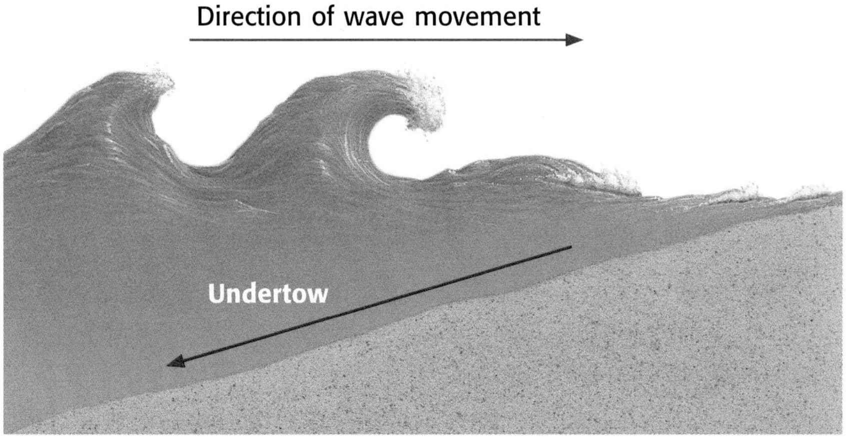

Shore Currents

When waves crash on the beach head-on, the water they moved through flows back to the ocean underneath new incoming waves. This movement of water, which carries sand, rock particles, and plankton away from the shore, is called an **undertow. Figure 5** illustrates the back-and-forth movement of water at the shore.

undertow a subsurface current that is near shore and that pulls objects out to sea

longshore current a water current that travels near and parallel to the shoreline

Longshore Currents

When waves hit the shore at an angle, they cause water to move along the shore in a current called a **longshore current,** which is shown in **Figure 6.** Longshore currents transport most of the sediment in beach environments. This movement of sand and other sediment both tears down and builds up the coastline. Unfortunately, longshore currents also carry and spread trash and other types of ocean pollution along the shore.

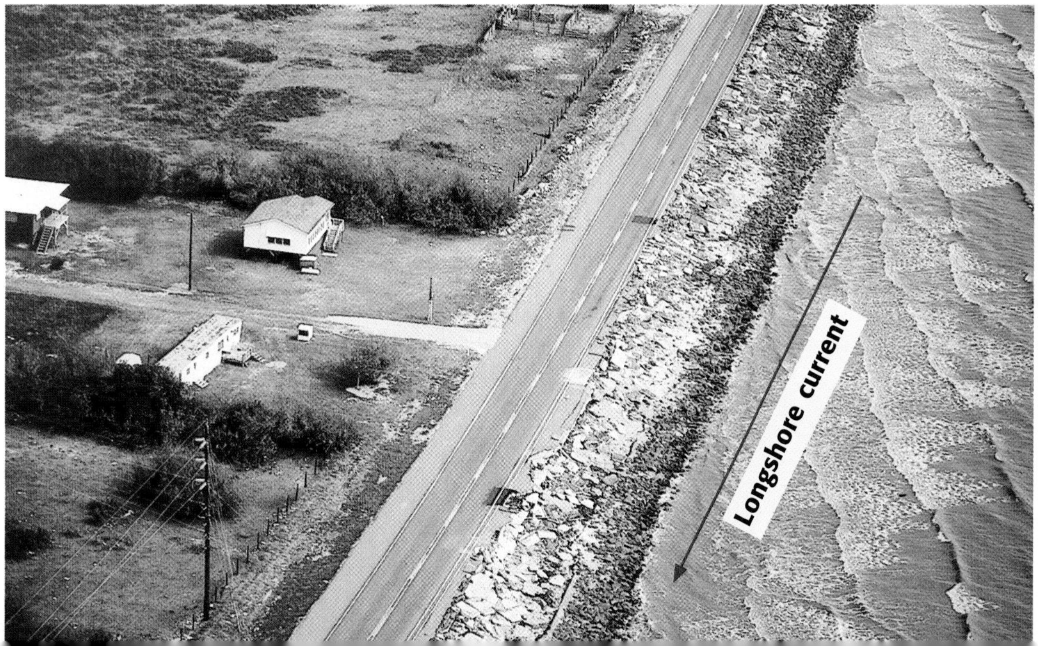

Figure 6 *Longshore currents form where waves approach beaches at an angle.*

Figure 7 *Whitecaps (left) break in the open ocean, while swells (right) roll gently in the open ocean.*

Open-Ocean Waves

Sometimes waves called *whitecaps* form in the open ocean. **Whitecaps** are white, foaming waves with very steep crests that break in the open ocean before the waves get close to the shore. These waves usually form during stormy weather, and they are usually short-lived. Winds that are far away from the shore form waves called *swells*. **Swells** are rolling waves that move steadily across the ocean. Swells have longer wavelengths than whitecaps and can travel for thousands of kilometers. **Figure 7** shows how whitecaps and swells differ.

whitecap the bubbles in the crest of a breaking wave

swell one of a group of long ocean waves that have steadily traveled a great distance from their point of generation

tsunami a giant ocean wave that forms after a volcanic eruption, submarine earthquake, or landslide

Tsunamis

Professional surfers often travel to Hawaii to catch some of the highest waves in the world. But even the best surfers would not be able to handle a tsunami. **Tsunamis** are waves that form when a large volume of ocean water is suddenly moved up or down. This movement can be caused by underwater earthquakes, volcanic eruptions, landslides, underwater explosions, or the impact of a meteorite or comet. The majority of tsunamis occur in the Pacific Ocean because of the large number of earthquakes in that region. **Figure 8** shows how an earthquake can generate a tsunami.

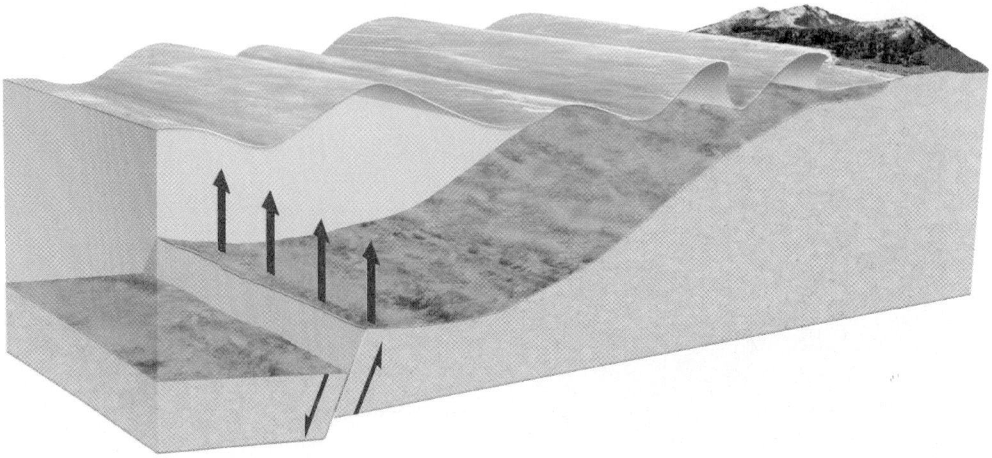

Figure 8 *An upward shift in the ocean floor creates an earthquake. The energy released by the earthquake pushes a large volume of water upward, which creates a series of tsunamis.*

Storm Surges

A local rise in sea level near the shore that is caused by strong winds from a storm, such as a hurricane, is called a **storm surge.** Winds form a storm surge by blowing water into a big pile under the storm. As the storm moves onto shore, so does the giant mass of water beneath it. Storm surges often disappear as quickly as they form, which makes them difficult to study. Storm surges contain a lot of energy and can reach about 8 m in height. Their size and power often make them the most destructive part of hurricanes.

storm surge a local rise in sea level near the shore that is caused by strong winds from a storm, such as those from a hurricane

Reading Check **What is a storm surge? Why are storm surges difficult to study?**

SECTION Review

Summary

- Waves are made up of two main parts—crests and troughs.
- Waves are usually created by the transfer of the wind's energy across the surface of the ocean.
- Waves travel through water near the water's surface, while the water itself rises and falls in circular movements.
- Wind-generated waves are classified as deep-water or shallow-water waves.
- When waves hit the shore at a certain angle, they can create either an undertow or a longshore current.
- Tsunamis are dangerous waves that can be very destructive to coastal communities.

Using Key Terms

For each pair of terms, explain how the meanings of the terms differ.

1. *whitecap* and *swell*
2. *undertow* and *longshore current*
3. *tsunami* and *storm surge*

Understanding Key Ideas

4. Longshore currents transport sediment
   a. to the open ocean.
   b. along the shore.
   c. only during low tide.
   d. only during high tide.
5. Where do deep-water waves become shallow-water waves?
6. Explain how water moves as waves travel through it.
7. Name five events that can cause a tsunami.
8. Describe the two parts of a wave.

Math Skills

9. If a barrier island that is 1 km wide and 10 km long loses 1.5 m of its width per year to erosion by a longshore current, how long will the island take to lose one-fourth of its width?

Critical Thinking

10. **Analyzing Processes** How would you explain a bottle moving across the water in the same direction that the waves are traveling? Make a drawing of the bottle's movement.
11. **Analyzing Processes** Describe the motion of a wave as it approaches the shore.
12. **Applying Concepts** Explain how energy plays a role in the creation of ocean waves.
13. **Making Comparisons** How does the formation of an undertow differ from the formation of a longshore current? How is sand on the beach affected by each?

SCILINKS. NSTA Developed and maintained by the National Science Teachers Association

For a variety of links related to this chapter, go to www.scilinks.org

Topic: Ocean Waves
SciLinks code: HSM1066

SECTION 4

Tides

What You Will Learn

- Explain tides and their relationship with the Earth, sun, and moon.
- Describe four different types of tides.
- Analyze the relationship between tides and coastal land.

Vocabulary

tide	spring tide
tidal range	neap tide

READING STRATEGY

Discussion Read this section silently. Write down questions that you have about this section. Discuss your questions in a small group.

tide the periodic rise and fall of the water level in the oceans and other large bodies of water

If you stand at some ocean shores long enough, you will see the edge of the ocean shrink away from you. Wait longer, and you will see it return to its original place on the shore. Would you believe the moon causes this movement?

You have learned how winds and earthquakes can move ocean water. But less obvious forces move ocean water in regular patterns called tides. **Tides** are daily changes in the level of ocean water. Tides are influenced by the sun and the moon, as shown in **Figure 1,** and they occur in a variety of cycles.

The Lure of the Moon

The phases of the moon and their relationship to the tides were first discovered more than 2,000 years ago by a Greek explorer named Pytheas. But Pytheas and other early investigators could not explain the relationship. A scientific explanation was not given until 1687, when Sir Isaac Newton's theories on the principle of gravitation were published.

The gravity of the moon pulls on every particle of the Earth. But the pull on liquids is much more noticeable than on solids, because liquids move more easily. Even the liquid in a carton of milk is slightly pulled by the moon's gravity.

Reading Check **How does the moon affect Earth's particles?** *(See the Appendix for answers to Reading Checks.)*

High Tide and Low Tide

How often tides occur and the difference in tidal levels depend on the position of the moon as it revolves around the Earth. The moon's pull is strongest on the part of the Earth directly facing the moon.

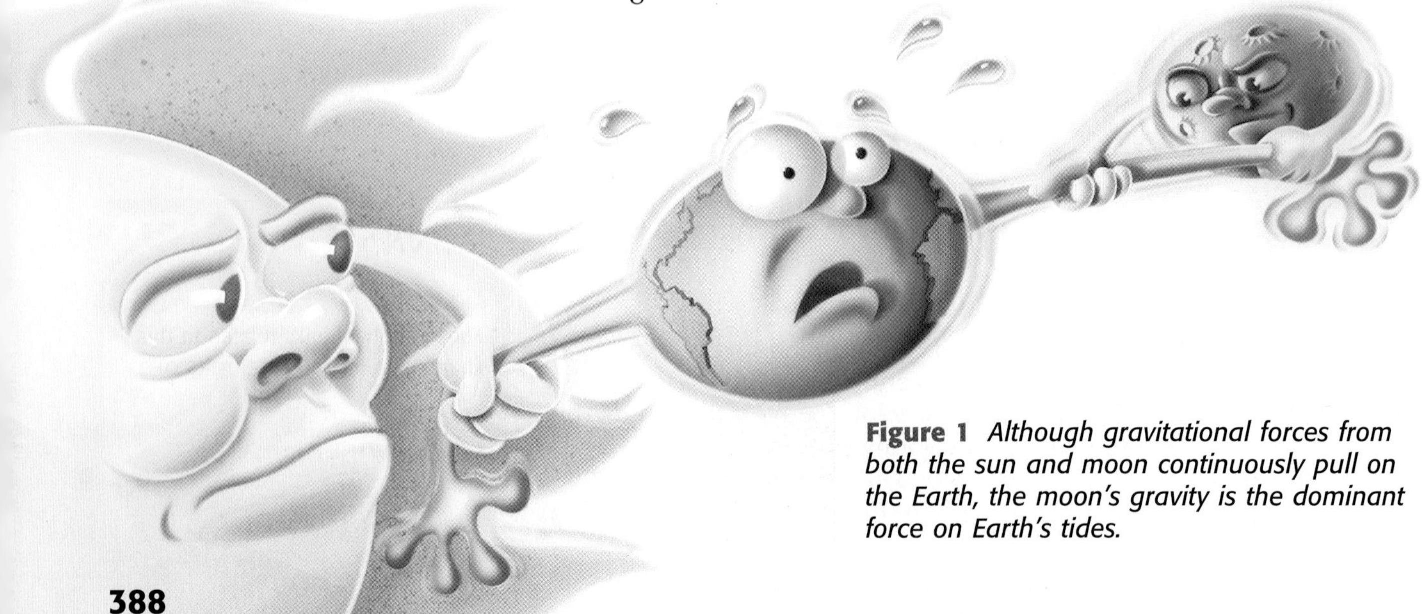

Figure 1 *Although gravitational forces from both the sun and moon continuously pull on the Earth, the moon's gravity is the dominant force on Earth's tides.*

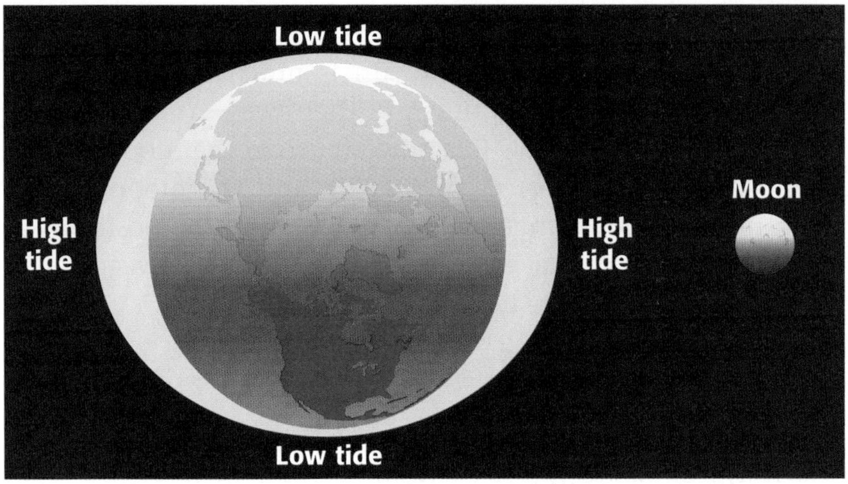

Figure 2 *High tide occurs on the part of Earth that is closest to the moon. At the same time, high tide also occurs on the opposite side of Earth.*

Battle of the Bulge

When part of the ocean is directly facing the moon, the water there bulges toward the moon. At the same time, water on the opposite side of the Earth bulges because of the rotation of the Earth and the motion of the moon around the Earth. These bulges are called *high tides.* Notice in **Figure 2** how the position of the moon causes the water to bulge. Also notice that when high tides occur, water is drawn away from the area between the high tides, which causes *low tides* to form.

Timing the Tides

The rotation of the Earth and the moon's revolution around the Earth determine when tides occur. If the Earth rotated at the same speed that the moon revolves around the Earth, the tides would not alternate between high and low. But the moon revolves around the Earth much more slowly than the Earth rotates. As **Figure 3** shows, a spot on Earth that is facing the moon takes 24 h and 50 m to rotate and face the moon again.

CONNECTION TO Language Arts

WRITING SKILL **Mont-St-Michel Is Sometimes an Island?** Mont-St-Michel is located off the coast of France. Mont-St-Michel experiences extreme tides. The tides are so extreme that during high tide, it is an island and during low tide, it is connected to the mainland. Research the history behind Mont-St-Michel and then write a short story describing what it would be like to live there for a day. Be sure to include a description of Mont-St-Michel at high tide and at low tide.

Figure 3 *Tides occur at different locations on Earth because the Earth rotates more quickly than the moon revolves around the Earth.*

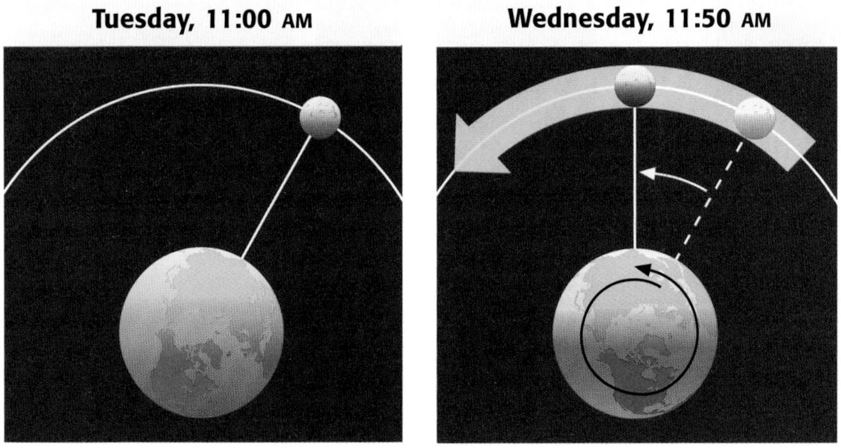

Tidal Variations

The sun also affects tides. The sun is much larger than the moon, but the sun is also much farther away. As a result, the sun's influence on tides is less powerful than the moon's influence. The combined forces of the sun and the moon on the Earth result in tidal ranges that vary based on the positions of all three bodies. A **tidal range** is the difference between levels of ocean water at high tide and low tide.

tidal range the difference in levels of ocean water at high tide and low tide

spring tide a tide of increased range that occurs two times a month, at the new and full moons

neap tide a tide of minimum range that occurs during the first and third quarters of the moon

Reading Check What is a tidal range?

Spring Tides

When the sun, Earth, and moon are aligned, spring tides occur. **Spring tides** are tides with the largest daily tidal range and occur during the new and full moons, or every 14 days. The first time spring tides occur is when the moon is between the sun and Earth. The second time spring tides occur is when the moon and the sun are on opposite sides of the Earth. **Figure 4** shows the positions of the sun, Earth, and moon during spring tides.

Neap Tides

When the sun, Earth, and moon form a 90° angle, neap tides occur. **Neap tides** are tides with the smallest daily tidal range and occur during the first and third quarters of the moon. Neap tides occur halfway between the occurrence of spring tides. When neap tides occur, the gravitational forces on the Earth by the sun and moon work against each other. **Figure 4** shows the positions of the sun, Earth, and moon during neap tides.

Figure 4 Spring Tides and Neap Tides

Spring Tides During the full moon and the new moon, the sun, Earth, and the moon are aligned. The gravitational force of the sun reinforces the high tides created by the gravitational force of the moon.

Neap Tides The sun and the moon are at right angles to each other relative to Earth. In this arrangement, the gravitational forces of the sun and moon work against each other.

Figure 5 *It's a good thing the people on this beach (left) knew when high tide occurred (right). These photos show the Bay of Fundy, in New Brunswick, Canada. The Bay of Fundy has the greatest tidal range on Earth.*

Tides and Topography

After a tidal range has been measured, the times that tides occur can be accurately predicted. This information can be useful for people who live near or visit the coast, as shown in **Figure 5.** In some coastal areas that have narrow inlets, movements of water called tidal bores occur. A *tidal bore* is a body of water that rushes up through a narrow bay, estuary, or river channel during the rise of high tide and causes a very sudden tidal rise. Tidal bores occur in coastal areas of China, the British Isles, France, and Canada.

SECTION Review

Summary

- Tides are caused by the gravitational forces of the moon and sun on the Earth.
- The moon's gravity is the main force behind the tides.
- The positions of the sun and moon relative to the position of the Earth cause tidal ranges.
- The four different types of tides are: high tides, low tides, spring tides, and neap tides.

Using Key Terms

1. In your own words, write a definition for each of the following terms: *spring tides* and *neap tides.*

Understanding Key Ideas

2. Tides are at their highest during
   a. spring tide.
   b. neap tide.
   c. a tidal bore.
   d. the daytime.
3. Which tides have minimum tidal range? Which tides have maximum tidal range?
4. What causes tidal ranges?

Math Skills

5. If it takes 24 h and 50 min for a spot on Earth that is facing the moon to rotate to face the moon again, how many minutes does it take?

Critical Thinking

6. **Applying Concepts** How many days pass between the minimum and the maximum of the tidal range in any given area? Explain your answer.
7. **Analyzing Processes** Explain how the position of the moon relates to the occurrence of high tides and low tides.

SciLinks® NSTA
Developed and maintained by the National Science Teachers Association

For a variety of links related to this chapter, go to www.scilinks.org

Topic: Tides
SciLinks code: HSM1525

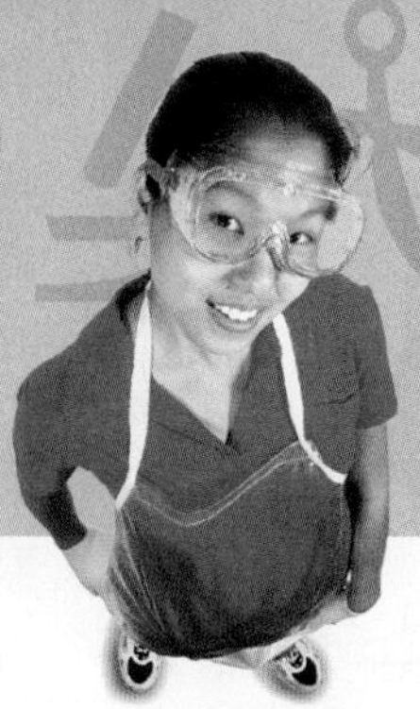

Using Scientific Methods

Skills Practice Lab

OBJECTIVES

Demonstrate the effects of temperature and salinity on the density of water.

Describe why some parts of the ocean turn over, while others do not.

MATERIALS

- beakers, 400 mL (5)
- blue and red food coloring
- bucket of ice
- gloves, heat-resistant
- hot plate
- plastic wrap, 4 pieces, approximately 30 cm × 20 cm
- salt
- spoon
- tap water
- watch or clock

SAFETY

Up from the Depths

Every year, the water in certain parts of the ocean "turns over." That is, the water at the bottom rises to the top and the water at the top falls to the bottom. This yearly change brings fresh nutrients from the bottom of the ocean to the fish living near the surface. However, the water in some parts of the ocean never turns over. By completing this activity, you will find out why not.

Keep in mind that some parts of the ocean are warmer at the bottom, and some are warmer at the top. And sometimes the saltiest water is at the bottom and sometimes not. As you complete this activity, you will investigate how these factors help determine whether the water will turn over.

Ask a Question

1. Why do some parts of the ocean turn over and not others?

Form a Hypothesis

2. Write a hypothesis that is a possible answer to the question above. Explain your reasoning.

Test the Hypothesis

3. Label the beakers 1 through 5. Fill beakers 1 through 4 with tap water.
4. Add a drop of blue food coloring to the water in beakers 1 and 2, and stir with the spoon.
5. Place beaker 1 in the bucket of ice for 10 min.
6. Add a drop of red food coloring to the water in beakers 3 and 4, and stir with the spoon.
7. Set beaker 3 on a hot plate turned to a low setting for 10 min.
8. Add one spoonful of salt to the water in beaker 4, and stir with the spoon.

9. While beaker 1 is cooling and beaker 3 is heating, copy the observations table below on a sheet of paper.

Observations Table	
Mixture of water	**Observations**
Warm water placed above cold water	
Cold water placed above warm water	DO NOT WRITE IN BOOK
Salty water placed above fresh water	
Fresh water placed above salty water	

10. Pour half of the water in beaker 1 into beaker 5. Return beaker 1 to the bucket of ice.

11. Tuck a sheet of plastic wrap into beaker 5 so that the plastic rests on the surface of the water and lines the upper half of the beaker.

12. Put on your gloves. Slowly pour half of the water in beaker 3 into the plastic-lined upper half of beaker 5 to form two layers of water. Return beaker 3 to the hot plate, and remove your gloves.

13. Very carefully, pull on one edge of the plastic wrap and remove it so that the warm, red water rests on the cold, blue water.
Caution: The plastic wrap may be warm.

14. Wait about 5 minutes, and then observe the layers in beaker 5. Did one layer remain on top of the other? Was there any mixing or turning over? Record your observations in your observations table.

15. Empty beaker 5, and rinse it with clean tap water.

16. Repeat the procedure used in steps 10–15. This time, pour warm, red water from beaker 3 on the bottom and cold, blue water from beaker 1 on top. (Use gloves when pouring warm water.)

17. Again, repeat the procedure used in steps 10–15. This time, pour blue tap water from beaker 2 on the bottom and red, salty water from beaker 4 on top.

18. Repeat the procedure used in steps 10–15 a third time. This time, pour red, salty water from beaker 4 on the bottom and blue tap water from beaker 2 on top.

Analyze the Results

1. **Analyzing Data** Compare the results of all four trials. Explain why the water turned over in some of the trials but not in all of them.

Draw Conclusions

2. **Evaluating Results** What is the effect of temperature and salinity on the density of water?

3. **Drawing Conclusions** What makes the temperature of ocean water decrease? What could make the salinity of ocean water increase?

4. **Drawing Conclusions** What reasons can you give to explain why some parts of the ocean do not turn over in the spring while some do?

Applying Your Data

Suggest a method for setting up a model that tests the combined effects of temperature and salinity on the density of water. Consider using more than two water samples and dyes.

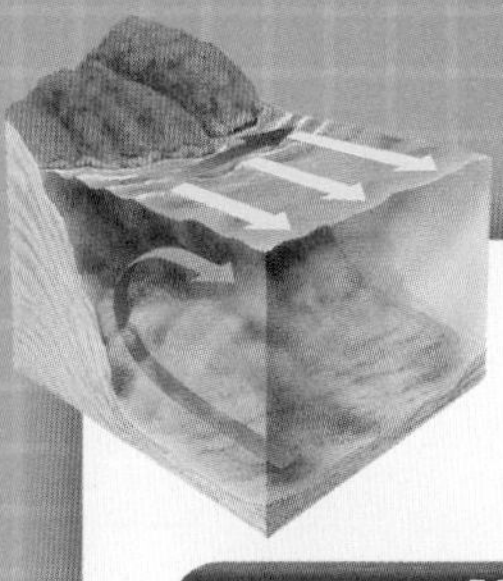

Chapter Review

USING KEY TERMS

For each pair of terms, explain how the meanings of the terms differ.

1. *surface current* and *deep current*
2. *El Niño* and *La Niña*
3. *spring tide* and *neap tide*
4. *tide* and *tidal range*

UNDERSTANDING KEY IDEAS

Multiple Choice

5. Deep currents form when
   - **a.** cold air decreases water density.
   - **b.** warm air increases water density.
   - **c.** the ocean surface freezes and solids from the water underneath are removed.
   - **d.** salinity increases.

6. When waves come near the shore,
   - **a.** they speed up.
   - **b.** they maintain their speed.
   - **c.** their wavelength increases.
   - **d.** their wave height increases.

7. Whitecaps break
   - **a.** in the surf.
   - **b.** in the breaker zone.
   - **c.** in the open ocean.
   - **d.** as their wavelength increases.

8. Tidal range is greatest during
   - **a.** spring tide.
   - **b.** neap tide.
   - **c.** a tidal bore.
   - **d.** the daytime.

9. Tides alternate between high and low because the moon revolves around the Earth
   - **a.** at the same speed the Earth rotates.
   - **b.** at a much faster speed than the Earth rotates.
   - **c.** at a much slower speed than the Earth rotates.
   - **d.** at different speeds.

10. El Niño can cause
    - **a.** droughts to occur in Indonesia and Australia.
    - **b.** upwelling to occur off the coast of South America.
    - **c.** earthquakes.
    - **d.** droughts to occur in the southern half of the United States.

Short Answer

11. Explain the relationship between upwelling and El Niño.
12. Describe the two parts of a wave. Describe how these two parts relate to wavelength and wave height.
13. Compare the relative positions of the Earth, moon, and sun during the spring and neap tides.
14. Explain the difference between the breaker zone and the surf.
15. Describe how warm-water currents affect the climate in the British Isles.
16. Describe the factors that form deep currents.

CRITICAL THINKING

17 **Concept Mapping** Use the following terms to create a concept map: *wind, deep currents, sun's gravity, types of ocean-water movement, surface currents, tides, increasing water density, waves,* and *moon's gravity.*

18 **Identifying Relationships** Why are tides more noticeable in Earth's oceans than on its land?

19 **Expressing Opinions** Explain why it's important to study El Niño and La Niña.

20 **Applying Concepts** Suppose you and a friend are planning a fishing trip to the ocean. Your friend tells you that the fish bite more in his secret fishing spot during low tide. If low tide occurred at the spot at 7 a.m. today and you are going to fish there in 1 week, at what time will low tide occur in that spot?

21 **Identifying Relationships** Describe how global winds, the Coriolis Effect, and continental deflections form a pattern of surface currents on Earth.

INTERPRETING GRAPHICS

The diagram below shows some of Earth's major surface currents that flow in the Western Hemisphere. Use the diagram to answer the questions that follow.

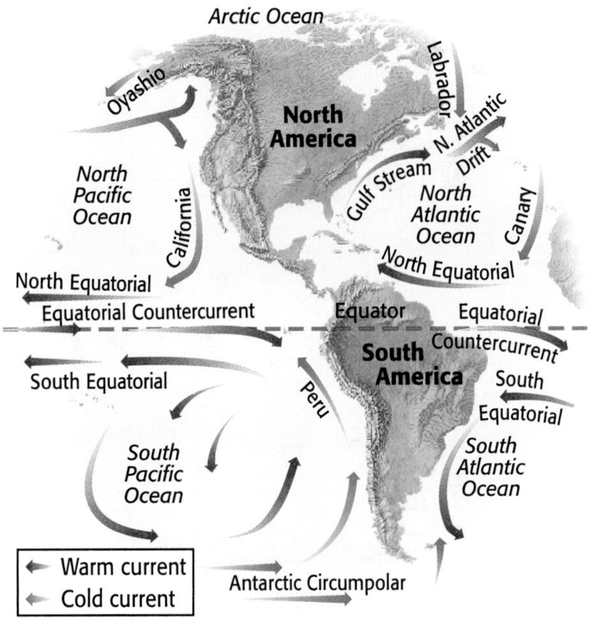

22 List two warm-water currents and two cold-water currents.

23 How do you think the Labrador Current affects the climate of Canada and Greenland?

Standardized Test Preparation

Multiple Choice

Use the diagram below to answer question 1.

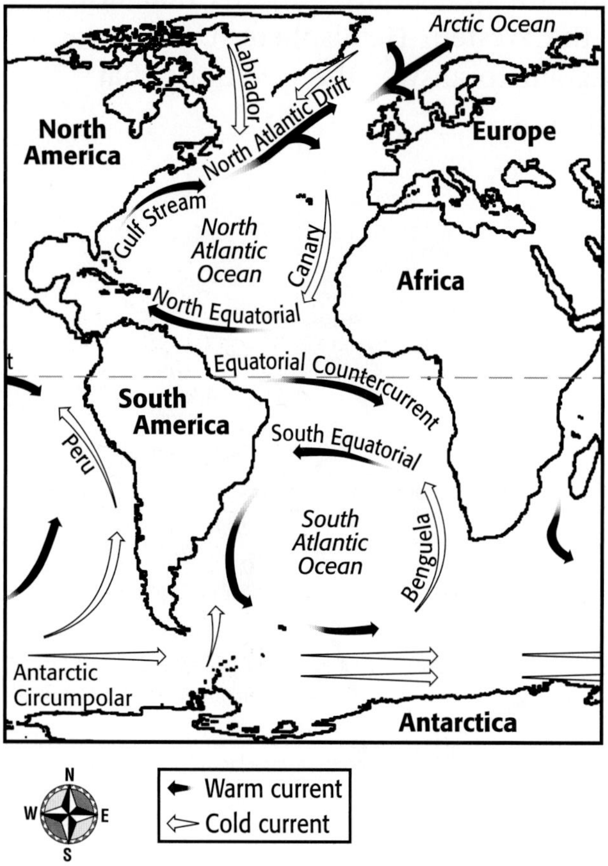

1. Which of the following most directly affects the direction of the Gulf Stream current?

A. full moon

B. continental deflection

C. upwelling

D. water density

2. Southern California has cooler temperatures than Arizona, which is at the same latitude. What causes this temperature difference?

A. a cold-water surface current off of California's coast

B. winds that form high in the California mountains

C. the shade provided by the large number of trees in California

D. the large longshore current running along California's coast

3. A longshore current moves down a sandy coastline, from north to south. Developers build a long, concrete breakwater at one point along the coast. What happens to the sandy beach to the south of that breakwater?

A. It builds up.

B. It erodes away.

C. It stays the same.

D. It accumulates trash.

4. On a clear day, a wave that looks like a wall of water suddenly hits the beach of an island in the South Pacific. What was the likely cause of the wave?

A. offshore hurricane

B. undersea earthquake

C. continental deflection

D. wind in the open ocean

5. **Karla is going to search for clams and oysters during low tide. If she knows that low tide is at 3:00 P.M. today, at what time should she plan to go searching for shellfish tomorrow?**

   A. 3:00 A.M.

   B. 2:10 P.M.

   C. 3:00 P.M.

   D. 3:50 P.M.

6. **Kelp are giant seaweeds that grow in clear, shallow coastal waters. They attach to rocks with a holdfast and grow long, leafy blades that extend to the surface. These blades create a floating kelp forest, which provides a habitat for animals such as eels, sponges, sea stars, and sea otters. Kelp require cold, nutrient-rich water and light in order to survive. Which ocean process supports the kelp forest?**

   A. cold-water surface currents

   B. warm-water surface currents

   C. upwelling

   D. deep currents

7. **Although the British Isles are at a high latitude, the climate in the isles is very mild. What is the most likely reason for this?**

   A. The British Isles receive a great deal of sunshine.

   B. The British Isles are located near a warm-water surface current.

   C. The British Isles are located near an area of upwelling.

   D. The British Isles are located near a cold-water surface current.

8. **What combination of tides is occurring at the approximate time you see the full moon directly overhead?**

   A. high tide during a neap tide

   B. low tide during a neap tide

   C. high tide during a spring tide

   D. low tide during a spring tide

Use the table below to answer question 9.

Waves	Wavelength	Wave Period
Wave A	12 meters	8 seconds
Wave B	10 meter	6 seconds
Wave C	8 meters	4 seconds
Wave D	14 meters	5 seconds

9. **If each wave hits a sandy beach head-on, which wave would cause the most erosion of sand through its undertow?**

   A. wave A

   B. wave B

   C. wave C

   D. wave D

Open Response

10. **What causes an El Niño event? List 3 effects of an El Niño.**

11. **Describe what happens to a wave's energy as it travels from deep water to the shore. How does this energy affect a sandy or rocky shoreline?**

Science in Action

Weird Science

Using Toy Ducks to Track Ocean Currents

Accidents can sometimes lead to scientific discovery. For example, on January 10, 1992, 29,000 plastic tub toys spilled overboard when a container ship traveling northwest of Hawaii ran into a storm. In November of that year, those toys began washing up on Alaskan beaches. When oceanographers heard about this, they placed advertisements in newspapers along the Alaskan coast asking people who found the toys to call them. Altogether, hundreds of toys were recovered. Using recovery dates and locations and computer models, oceanographers were able to re-create the toys' drift and figure out which currents carried the toys. As for the remaining toys, currents may carry them to a number of different destinations. Some may travel through the Arctic Ocean and eventually reach Europe!

Math ACTIVITY

Between January 10, 1992, and November 16, 1992, some of the toys were carried approximately 3,220 km from the cargo-spill site to the coast of Alaska. Calculate the average distance traveled by these toys per day. (Hint: The year 1992 was a leap year.)

Science, Technology, and Society

Red Tides

Imagine going to the beach only to find that the ocean water has turned red and that a lot of fish are floating belly up. What could cause such damage to the ocean? It may surprise you to find that the answer is single-celled algae. When certain algae grow rapidly, they clump together on the ocean's surface in what are known as algal blooms. These algal blooms have been commonly called *red tides* because the blooms often turn the water red or reddish-brown. The term scientists use for these sudden explosions in algae growth is *harmful algal blooms* (HABs). The blooms are harmful because certain species of algae produce toxins that can poison fish, shellfish, and people who eat poisoned fish or shellfish. Toxic blooms can be carried hundreds of miles on ocean currents. HABs can ride into an area on an ocean current and cause fish to die and people who eat the poisoned fish or shellfish to become ill.

Social Studies ACTIVITY

Some scientists think that factors related to human activities, such as agricultural runoff into the ocean, are causing more HABs than occurred in the past. Other scientists disagree. Find out more about this issue, and have a class debate about the roles humans play in creating HABs.

Careers

Cristina Castro

Marine Biologist Have you ever imagined watching whales for a living? Cristina Castro does. Castro works as a marine biologist with the Pacific Whale Foundation in Ecuador. She is studying the migratory patterns of a whale species known as the *humpback whale*. Each year, the humpback whale migrates from feeding grounds in the Antarctic to the warm waters off Ecuador, where the whales breed. Her studies take place largely in the Machalilla National Park. The park is a two-mile stretch of beach that is protected by the government of Ecuador.

In her research, Cristina Castro focuses on the connection between El Niño events and the number of humpback whales in the waters off Ecuador. Castro believes that during an El Niño event, the waters off Ecuador are too hot for the whales. When the whales get hot, they have a difficult time cooling off because they have a thick coat of blubber that provides insulation. So, Castro believes that the whales stay in colder waters during an El Niño event.

Language Arts ACTIVITY

WRITING SKILL Research the humpback whale's migratory route from Antarctica to Ecuador. Write a short story in which you tell of the migration from the point of view of a young whale.

go.hrw.com

To learn more about these Science in Action topics, visit go.hrw.com and type in the keyword **HZ5H2OF.**

Current Science

Check out Current Science® articles related to this chapter by visiting go.hrw.com. Just type in the keyword HZ5CS14.

13

Environmental Problems and Solutions

The Big Idea

Human activities affect the environment in positive and negative ways.

About the Photo

After an oil spill, volunteers try to capture oil-covered penguins. The oil affects the penguins' ability to float. So, oil-covered penguins often won't go into the water to get food. The penguins may also swallow oil, harming their stomach, kidneys, and lungs. Once captured, the penguins are fed activated charcoal. The charcoal helps the penguins get rid of any oil they have swallowed. Then, the birds are washed to remove oil from their feathers.

PRE-READING ACTIVITY

FOLDNOTES **Two-Panel Flip Chart** Before you read the chapter, create the FoldNote entitled "Two-Panel Flip Chart" described in the **Study Skills** section of the Appendix. Label the flaps of the two-panel flip chart with "Environmental problems" and "Environmental solutions." As you read the chapter, write information you learn about each category under the appropriate flap.

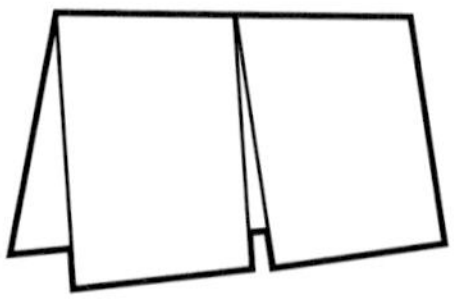

START-UP ACTIVITY

Recycling Paper

In this activity, you will be making paper without cutting down trees. You will be reusing paper that has already been made.

Procedure

1. Tear **two sheets of old newspaper** into small pieces, and put them in a **blender.** Add **1 L of water.** Cover and blend until the mixture is soupy.
2. Fill a **square pan** with **water** to a depth of 2 cm to 3 cm. Place a **wire screen** in the pan. Pour 250 mL of the paper mixture onto the screen, and spread the mixture evenly.
3. Lift the screen out of the water with the paper on it. Drain excess water into the pan.
4. Place the screen inside a **section of newspaper.** Close the newspaper, and turn it over so that the screen is on top of the paper mixture.
5. Cover the newspaper with a **flat board.** Press on the board to squeeze out excess water.
6. Open the newspaper, and let your paper mixture dry overnight. Use your recycled paper to write a note to a friend!

Analysis

1. How is your paper like regular paper? How is it different?
2. What could you do to improve your papermaking methods?

SECTION 1

Environmental Problems

What You Will Learn

- List five kinds of pollutants.
- Distinguish between renewable and nonrenewable resources.
- Describe the impact of exotic species.
- Explain why human population growth has increased.
- Describe how habitat destruction affects biodiversity.
- Give two examples of how pollution affects humans.

Vocabulary

pollution
renewable resource
nonrenewable resource
overpopulation
biodiversity

READING STRATEGY

Reading Organizer As you read this section, make a concept map by using the terms above.

Maybe you've heard warnings about dirty air, water, and soil. Or you've heard about the destruction of rain forests. Do these warnings mean our environment is in trouble?

In the late 1700s, the Industrial Revolution began. People started to rely more and more on machines. As a result, more harmful substances entered the air, water, and soil.

Pollution

Today, machines don't produce as much pollution as they once did. But there are more sources of pollution today than there once were. **Pollution** is an unwanted change in the environment caused by substances, such as wastes, or forms of energy, such as radiation. Anything that causes pollution is called a *pollutant.* Some pollutants are produced by natural events, such as volcanic eruptions. Many pollutants are human-made. Pollutants may harm plants, animals, and humans.

Garbage

The average American throws away more trash than the average person in any other nation—about 12 kg of trash a week. This trash often goes to a landfill like the one in **Figure 1.** Other landfills contain medical waste, lead paint, and other hazardous wastes. *Hazardous waste* includes wastes that can catch fire; corrode, or eat through metal; explode; or make people sick. Many industries, such as paper mills and oil refineries, produce hazardous wastes.

Reading Check What is hazardous waste? *(See the Appendix for answers to Reading Checks.)*

pollution an unwanted change in the environment caused by substances or forms of energy

Figure 1 *Every year, Americans throw away about 200 million metric tons of garbage.*

Figure 2 *Fertilizer promotes the growth of algae. As dead algae decompose, oxygen in the water is used up. So, fish die because they cannot get oxygen.*

Chemicals

People need and use many chemicals. Some chemicals are used to treat diseases. Other chemicals are used in plastics and preserved foods. Sometimes, the same chemicals that help people may harm the environment. As shown in **Figure 2,** fertilizers and pesticides may pollute soil and water.

CFCs and PCBs are two groups of harmful chemicals. Ozone protects Earth from harmful ultraviolet light. CFCs destroy ozone. CFCs were used in aerosols, refrigerators, and plastics. The second group, PCBs, was once used in appliances and paints. PCBs are poisonous and may cause cancer. Today, the use of CFCs and PCBs is banned. But CFCs are still found in the atmosphere. And PCBs are still found in even the most remote areas on Earth.

High-Powered Wastes

Nuclear power plants provide electricity to many homes and businesses. The plants also produce radioactive wastes. *Radioactive wastes* are hazardous wastes that give off radiation. Some of these wastes take thousands of years to become harmless.

Gases

Earth's atmosphere is made up of a mixture of gases, including carbon dioxide. The atmosphere acts as a protective blanket. It keeps Earth warm enough for life to exist. Since the Industrial Revolution, however, the amount of carbon dioxide in the atmosphere has increased. Carbon dioxide and other air pollutants act like a greenhouse, trapping heat around the Earth. Many scientists think the increase in carbon dioxide has increased global temperatures. If temperatures continue to rise, the polar icecaps could melt. Then, the level of the world's oceans would rise. Coastal areas could flood as a result.

CONNECTION TO Chemistry

Ozone Holes This image of two holes in the ozone layer (the purple areas over Antarctica) was taken in 2002. Ozone in the stratosphere absorbs most of the ultraviolet light that comes from the sun. Ozone is destroyed by CFCs. Research how CFCs destroy ozone. Make a model demonstrating this process. Then, identify the effects of too much ultraviolet light.

ACTIVITY

MATH PRACTICE

Water Depletion

In one day, millions of liters of water are removed from a water supply. Of this volume, 30 million liters cannot be replaced naturally. Today, the water supply has 60 billion liters of water. In years, how long would the water supply last if water continued to be removed at this rate? If water were removed at the same rate as it was replaced, how long would the water supply last?

Noise

Some pollutants affect the senses. These pollutants include loud noises. Too much noise is not just annoying. Noise pollution affects your ability to hear and think clearly. And it may damage your hearing. People who work in noisy environments, such as in construction zones, must protect their ears.

Resource Depletion

Some of Earth's resources are renewable. But other resources are nonrenewable. A **renewable resource** is one that can be replaced at the same rate at which the resource is used. Solar and wind energy are renewable resources, as are some kinds of trees. A **nonrenewable resource** is one that cannot be replaced or that can be replaced only over thousands or millions of years. Most minerals and fossil fuels, such as oil and coal, are nonrenewable resources.

Nonrenewable resources cannot last forever. These resources will become more expensive as they become harder to find. The removal of some materials from the Earth also carries a high price tag. This removal may lead to oil spills, loss of habitat, and damage from mining, as shown in **Figure 3.**

renewable resource a natural resource that can be replaced at the same rate at which the resource is consumed

nonrenewable resource a resource that forms at a rate that is much slower than the rate at which it is consumed

Renewable or Nonrenewable?

Some resources once thought to be renewable are becoming nonrenewable. For example, scientists used to think that fresh water was a renewable resource. However, in some areas, water supplies are being used faster than they are being replaced. Eventually, these areas may run out of fresh water. So, scientists are working on ways to keep these water supplies from being used up.

Figure 3 *This area has been mined for iron using a method called* strip mining.

Exotic Species

People are always on the move. Without knowing it, people carry other species with them. Plant seeds, animal eggs, and adult organisms are carried from one part of the world to another. An organism that makes a home for itself in a new place outside its native home is an *exotic species*. Exotic species often thrive in new places. One reason is that they are free from the predators found in their native homes.

Exotic species can become pests and compete with native species. In 2002, the northern snakehead fish was found in a Maryland pond. This fish, shown in **Figure 4,** is from Asia. Scientists are concerned because the northern snakehead eats other fish, amphibians, small birds, and some mammals. It can also move across land. The northern snakehead could invade more lakes and ponds.

Reading Check What are exotic species?

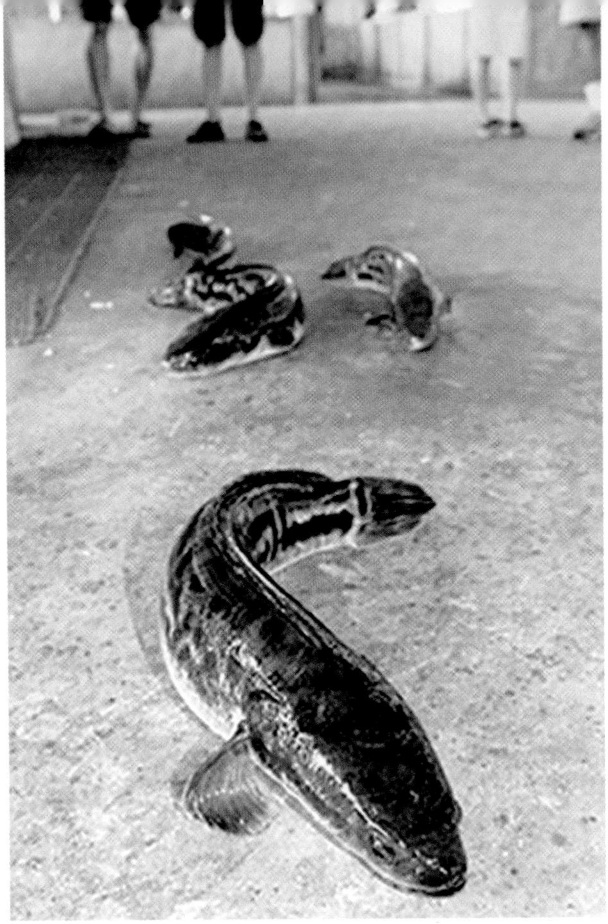

Figure 4 *Northern snakehead fish can move across land in search of water. These fish can survive out of water for up to four days!*

Human Population Growth

Look at **Figure 5.** In 1800, there were 1 billion people on Earth. By 2000, there were more than 6 billion people. Advances in medicine, such as immunizations, and advances in farming have made human population growth possible. Overall, these advances are beneficial. But some people argue that there may eventually be too many people on Earth. **Overpopulation** happens when the number of individuals becomes so large that the individuals can't get the resources they need to survive. However, many scientists think that human population growth will slow down or level off before it reaches that point.

overpopulation the presence of too many individuals in an area for the available resources

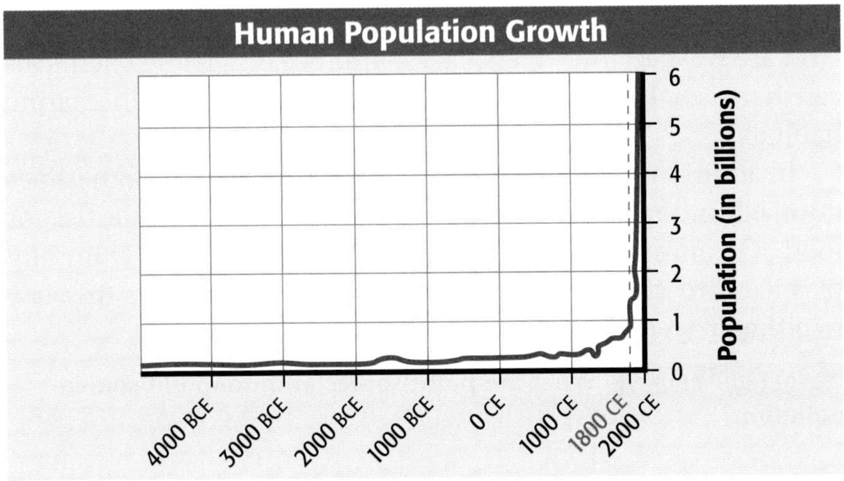

Figure 5 *Recently, the human population has been doubling every few decades.*

Figure 6 *Deforestation can leave soil exposed to erosion.*

Habitat Destruction

People need homes. People also need food and building materials. But when land is cleared for construction, crops, mines, or lumber, the topsoil may erode. Chemicals may pollute nearby streams and rivers. The organisms that were living in these areas may be left without food and shelter. These organisms may die.

An organism's *habitat* is where it lives. Every habitat has its own number and variety of organisms, or **biodiversity.** If a habitat is damaged or destroyed, biodiversity is lost.

biodiversity the number and variety of organisms in a given area during a specific period of time

Forest Habitats

Trees provide humans with oxygen, lumber, food, rubber, and paper. For some of these products, such as lumber and paper, trees must be cut down. *Deforestation* is the clearing of forest lands, as shown in **Figure 6.** At one time, many of these cleared forests were not replanted. Today, lumber companies often plant new trees to replace the trees that were cut down. However, some biodiversity is still lost.

Tropical rain forests, the most diverse habitats on Earth, are sometimes cleared for farmland, roads, and lumber. But after a tropical rain forest is cleared, the area cannot grow to be as diverse as it once was. Also, thin tropical soils are often badly damaged.

CONNECTION TO Social Studies

Wood Identify a country that is a major exporter of wood. List some of the ways this wood is used. Research the impact this exportation is having on that country's forests. Make a poster describing your findings.

ACTIVITY

Marine Habitats

Many people think of oil spills when they think of pollution in marine habitats. This is an example of *point-source pollution*, or pollution that comes from one source. Spilled oil pollutes both open waters and coastal habitats.

A second kind of water pollution is *nonpoint-source pollution*. This kind of pollution comes from many different sources. Nonpoint-source pollution often happens when chemicals on land are washed into rivers, lakes, and oceans. These chemicals can harm or kill many of the organisms that live in marine habitats.

In addition to oil and chemicals, plastics are also sometimes dumped into marine habitats. Animals may mistake plastics for food. Or animals may become tangled in plastics. Dumping plastics into the ocean is against the law. However, this law is difficult to enforce.

Reading Check What are point-source and nonpoint-source pollution?

Effects on Humans

Trees and marine life are not the only organisms affected by pollution and habitat destruction. Pollution and habitat destruction affect humans, too. Sometimes, the effect is immediate. Polluted air affects people with respiratory problems. If you drink polluted water, you may get sick. Sometimes, the damage is not apparent right away. Some chemicals cause cancers many years after a person is exposed to them. Over time, natural resources may be hard to find or used up. Your children or grandchildren may have to deal with these problems.

Anything that harms other organisms may eventually harm people, too. Caring for the environment means being aware of what is happening now and looking ahead to the future.

SECTION Review

Summary

- Pollutants include garbage, chemicals, high-energy wastes, gases, and noise.
- Renewable resources can be used over and over. Nonrenewable resources cannot be replaced or are replaced over thousands or millions of years.
- Exotic species can become pests and compete with native species.
- Overpopulation happens when a population is so large that it can't get what it needs to survive.
- Habitat destruction can lead to soil erosion, water pollution, and decreased biodiversity.
- In addition to harming the environment, pollution can harm humans.

Using Key Terms

The statements below are false. For each statement, replace the underlined term to make a true statement.

1. Coal is a <u>renewable resource</u>.
2. <u>Overpopulation</u> is the number and variety of organisms in an area.

Understanding Key Ideas

3. Which of the following can cause pollution?
   - **a.** noise
   - **b.** garbage
   - **c.** chemicals
   - **d.** All of the above
4. Pollution
   - **a.** does not affect humans.
   - **b.** can make humans sick.
   - **c.** makes humans sick only after many years.
   - **d.** None of the above
5. Compare renewable and nonrenewable resources.
6. Why has human population growth increased?
7. What is an exotic species?
8. How does habitat destruction affect biodiversity?

Math Skills

9. Jodi's family produces 48 kg of garbage each week. What is the percentage decrease if they reduce the amount of garbage to 40 kg per week?

Critical Thinking

10. **Applying Concepts** Explain how each of the following can help people but harm the environment: hospitals, old refrigerators, and road construction.
11. **Making Inferences** Explain how human population growth is related to pollution problems.
12. **Predicting Consequences** How can the pollution of marine habitats affect humans?

SCILINKS. NSTA Developed and maintained by the National Science Teachers Association

For a variety of links related to this chapter, go to www.scilinks.org

Topic: Air Pollution; Resource Depletion
SciLinks code: HSM0033; HSM1304

SECTION 2

Environmental Solutions

What You Will Learn

- Explain the importance of conservation.
- Describe the three Rs.
- Explain how biodiversity can be maintained.
- List five environmental strategies.

Vocabulary

conservation
recycling

READING STRATEGY

Discussion Read this section silently. Write down questions that you have about this section. Discuss your questions in a small group.

As the human population grows, it will need more resources. People will need food, healthcare, transportation, and waste disposal. What does this mean for the Earth?

All of these needs will have an impact on the Earth. If people don't use resources wisely, people will continue to pollute the air, soil, and water. More natural habitats could be lost. Many species could die out as a result. But there are many things people can do to protect the environment.

Conservation

One way to care for the Earth is conservation (KAHN suhr VAY shuhn). **Conservation** is the preservation and wise use of natural resources. You can ride your bike to conserve fuel. At the same time, you prevent air pollution. You can use organic compost instead of chemical fertilizer in your garden. Doing so conserves the resources needed to make the fertilizer. Also, you may reduce soil and water pollution.

Practicing conservation means using fewer natural resources. Conservation helps reduce waste and pollution. Also, conservation can help prevent habitat destruction. The three Rs are shown in **Figure 1.** They describe three ways to conserve resources: Reduce, Reuse, and Recycle.

Reading Check **What are the three Rs?** (*See the Appendix for answers to Reading Checks.*)

conservation the preservation and wise use of natural resources

Figure 1 *By reducing, reusing, and recycling, these teens are conserving resources.*

Reduce

What is the best way to conserve the Earth's natural resources? Use less of them! Doing so also helps reduce pollution.

Reducing Waste and Pollution

As much as one-third of the waste produced by some countries is packaging material. Products can be wrapped in less paper and plastic to reduce waste. For example, fast-food restaurants used to serve sandwiches in large plastic containers. Today, sandwiches are usually wrapped in thin paper instead. This paper is more biodegradable than plastic. Something that is *biodegradable* can be broken down by living organisms, such as bacteria. Scientists, such as the ones in **Figure 2,** are working to make biodegradable plastics.

Many people and companies are using less-hazardous materials in making their products. For example, some farmers don't use synthetic chemicals on their crops. Instead, they practice organic farming. They use mulch, compost, manure, and natural pest control. Agricultural specialists are also working on farming techniques that are better for the environment.

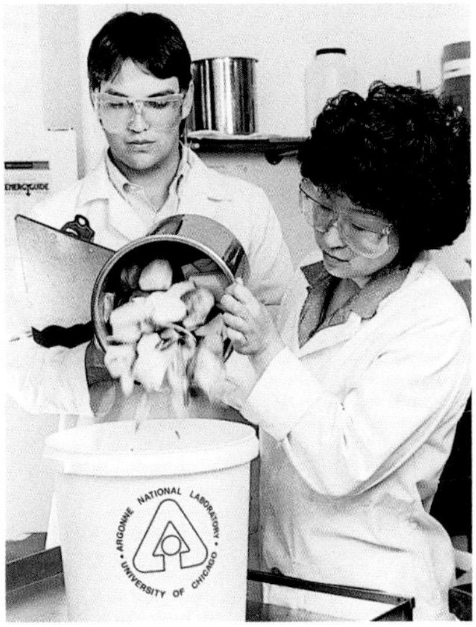

Figure 2 *These scientists are studying ways to make biodegradable plastics.*

Reducing the Use of Nonrenewable Resources

Some scientists are looking for sources of energy that can replace fossil fuels. For example, solar energy can be used to power homes, such as the home shown in **Figure 3.** Scientists are studying power sources such as wind, tides, and falling water. Car companies have developed electric and hydrogen-fueled automobiles. Driving these cars uses fewer fossil fuels and produces less pollution than driving gas-fueled cars does.

Figure 3 *The people who live in this home use solar panels to get energy from the sun.*

Figure 4 *This home was built with reused tires and aluminum cans.*

Reuse

Do you get hand-me-down clothes from an older sibling? Do you try to fix broken sports equipment instead of throwing it away? If so, you are helping conserve resources by *reusing* products.

Reusing Products

Every time you reuse a plastic bag, one bag fewer needs to be made. Reusing the plastic bag at the grocery store is just one way to reuse the bag. Reusing products is an important way to conserve resources.

You might be surprised at how many materials can be reused. For example, building materials can be reused. Wood, bricks, and tiles can be used in new structures. Old tires can be reused, too. They can be reused for playground surfaces. As shown in **Figure 4,** some tires are even reused to build new homes!

Figure 5 *This golf course is being watered with reclaimed water.*

TO CONSERVE OUR
NATURAL RESOURCES
THIS GOLF COURSE
IS IRRIGATED WITH
TREATED EFFLUENT

Reusing Water

About 100 billion liters of water are used each day in American homes. Most of this water goes down the drain. Many communities are experiencing water shortages. Some of these communities are experimenting with reusing, or reclaiming, wastewater.

One way to reclaim water is to use organisms to clean the water. These organisms include plants and filter-feeding animals, such as clams. Often, reclaimed water isn't pure enough to drink. But it can be used to water crops, lawns, and golf courses, such as the one shown in **Figure 5.** Sometimes, reclaimed water is returned to underground water supplies.

Reading Check **Describe how water is reused.**

Recycle

Another example of reuse is recycling. **Recycling** is the recovery of materials from waste. Sometimes, recyclable items, such as paper, are used to make the same kinds of products. Other recyclable items are made into different products. For example, yard clippings can be recycled into a natural fertilizer.

recycling the process of recovering valuable or useful materials from waste or scrap

Recycling Trash

Plastics, paper, aluminum, wood, glass, and cardboard are examples of materials that can be recycled. Every week, about half a million trees are used to make Sunday newspapers. Recycling newspapers could save millions of trees. Recycling aluminum saves 95% of the energy needed to change raw ore into aluminum. Glass can be recycled over and over again to make new bottles and jars.

Many communities make recycling easy. Some cities provide containers for glass, plastic, aluminum, and paper. People can leave these containers on the curb. Each week, the materials are picked up for recycling, as shown in **Figure 6.** Other cities have centers where people can take materials for recycling.

Figure 6 *In some communities, recyclable materials are picked up each week.*

Recycling Resources

Waste that can be burned can also be used to generate electricity. Electricity is generated in waste-to-energy plants, such as the one shown in **Figure 7.** Using garbage to make electricity is an example of *resource recovery.* Some companies are beginning to make electricity with their own waste. Doing so saves the companies money and conserves resources.

About 16% of the solid waste in the United States is burned in waste-to-energy plants. But some people are concerned that these plants pollute the air. Other people worry that the plants reduce recycling.

Figure 7 *A waste-to-energy plant can provide electricity to many homes and businesses.*

Figure 8 *What could happen if a fungus attacks a banana field? Biodiversity is low in fields of crops such as bananas.*

Maintaining Biodiversity

You know the three Rs. What else can you do to help the environment? You can help maintain biodiversity! So, how does biodiversity help the environment?

Imagine a forest with only one kind of tree. If a disease hit that species, the entire forest might die. Now, imagine a forest with 10 species of trees. If a disease hits one species, 9 other species will remain. Bananas, shown in **Figure 8,** are an important crop. But banana fields are not very diverse. Fungi threaten the survival of bananas. Farmers often use chemicals to control fungi. Growing other plants among the bananas, or increasing biodiversity, can also prevent the spread of fungi.

Biodiversity is also important because each species has a unique role in an ecosystem. Losing one species could disrupt an entire ecosystem. For example, if an important predator is lost, its prey will multiply. The prey might eat the plants in an area, keeping other animals from getting food. Eventually, even the prey won't have food. So, the prey will starve.

Figure 9 *Thanks to captive-breeding programs, the California condor population is increasing.*

Protecting Species

One way to maintain biodiversity is to protect individual species. In the United States, a law called the *Endangered Species Act* was designed to do just that. Endangered species are put on a special list. The law forbids activities that would harm a species on this list. The law also requires the development of recovery programs for each endangered species. Some endangered species, such as the California condor in **Figure 9,** are now increasing in number.

Anyone can ask the government to add a species to or remove a species from the endangered species list. This process can take years to complete. The government must study the species and its habitat before making a decision.

Protecting Habitats

Waiting until a species is almost extinct to begin protecting it is like waiting until your teeth are rotting to begin brushing them. Scientists want to prevent species from becoming endangered and from becoming extinct.

Plants, animals, and microorganisms depend on each other. Each organism is part of a huge, interconnected web of organisms. The entire web should be protected to protect these organisms. To protect the web, complete habitats, not just individual species, must be preserved. Nature preserves, such as the one shown in **Figure 10,** are one way to protect entire habitats.

Figure 10 *Setting aside public lands for wildlife is one way to protect habitats.*

Environmental Strategies

Laws have been passed to help protect the Earth's environment. By following those laws, people can help the environment. People can also use the following environmental strategies:

- **Reduce pollution.** Recycle as much as possible, and buy recycled products. Don't dump wastes on farmland, in forests, or into rivers, lakes, and oceans. Participate in a local cleanup project.
- **Reduce pesticide use.** Use only pesticides that are targeted specifically for harmful insects. Avoid pesticides that might harm beneficial insects, such as ladybugs or spiders. Use natural pesticides that interfere with how certain insects grow, develop, and reproduce.
- **Protect habitats.** Preserve entire habitats. Conserve wetlands. Reduce deforestation. Use resources at a rate that allows them to be replenished naturally.
- **Learn about local issues.** Attend local meetings about laws and projects that may affect your local environment. Research the impact of the project, and let people know about your concerns.
- **Develop alternative energy sources.** Increase the use of renewable energy, such as solar power and wind power.

The *Environmental Protection Agency* (EPA) is a government organization that helps protect the environment. The EPA works to help people have a clean environment in which to live, work, and play. The EPA keeps people informed about environmental issues and helps enforce environmental laws.

Reading Check What is the EPA?

INTERNET ACTIVITY

For another activity related to this chapter, go to **go.hrw.com** and type in the keyword **HL5ENVW.**

What You Can Do

Reduce, reuse, and recycle. Protect the Earth. These are jobs for everyone. Children as well as adults can help clean up the Earth. By doing so, people can improve their environment. And they can improve their quality of life.

The list in **Figure 11** offers some suggestions for how *you* can help. How many of these things do you already do? What can you add to the list?

Figure 11 **How You Can Help the Environment**

1. Volunteer at a local preserve or nature center, and help other people learn about conservation.
2. Give away your old toys.
3. Use recycled paper.
4. Fill up both sides of a sheet of paper.
5. Start an environmental awareness club at your school or in your neighborhood.
6. Recycle glass, plastics, paper, aluminum, and batteries.
7. Don't buy any products made from an endangered plant or animal.
8. Turn off electrical devices when you are not using them.
9. Wear hand-me-downs.
10. Share books with friends, or use the library.
11. Walk, ride a bicycle, or use public transportation.
12. Carry a reusable cloth shopping bag to the store.
13. Use a lunch box, or reuse your paper lunch bags.
14. Turn off the water while you brush your teeth.
15. Buy products made from biodegradable and recycled materials.
16. Use cloth napkins and kitchen towels.
17. Buy things in packages that can be recycled.
18. Use rechargeable batteries.
19. Make a compost heap.

SECTION
Review

Summary

- Conservation is the preservation and wise use of natural resources. Conservation helps reduce pollution, ensures that resources will be available in the future, and protects habitats.
- The three Rs are Reduce, Reuse, and Recycle. Reducing means using fewer resources. Reusing means using materials and products over and over. Recycling is the recovery of materials from waste.
- Biodiversity is vital for maintaining healthy ecosystems. A loss of one species can affect an entire ecosystem.
- Biodiversity can be preserved by protecting endangered species and entire habitats.
- Environmental strategies include reducing pollution, reducing pesticide use, protecting habitats, enforcing the Endangered Species Act, and developing alternative energy resources.

Using Key Terms

1. Use each of the following terms in a separate sentence: *conservation* and *recycling*.

Understanding Key Ideas

2. Which of the following is NOT a strategy to protect the environment?
   - **a.** preserving entire habitats
   - **b.** using pesticides that target all insects
   - **c.** reducing deforestation
   - **d.** increasing the use of solar power
3. Conservation
   - **a.** has little effect on the environment.
   - **b.** is the use of more natural resources.
   - **c.** involves using more fossil fuels.
   - **d.** can prevent pollution.
4. Describe the three Rs.
5. Describe why biodiversity is important. How can biodiversity be protected?

Critical Thinking

6. **Applying Concepts** Liza rode her bike to the store. She bought items that had little packaging and put her purchases into her backpack. Describe how Liza practiced conservation.
7. **Identifying Relationships** How does conservation of resources also reduce pollution and protect habitats?

Interpreting Graphics

Use the pie graph below to answer the questions that follow.

Land Use in the United States

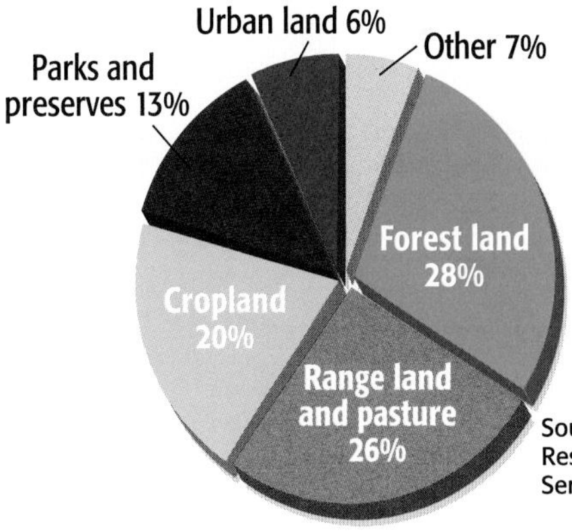

Source: Natural Resources Conservation Service.

8. If half of the forest land were made into preserves, what percentage of total land would be parks and preserves?
9. If 10% of the cropland were not planted, what percentage of land would be used for crops?

SCILINKS. NSTA Developed and maintained by the National Science Teachers Association

For a variety of links related to this chapter, go to www.scilinks.org

Topic: Recycling; Maintaining Biodiversity
SciLinks code: HSM1277; HSM0902

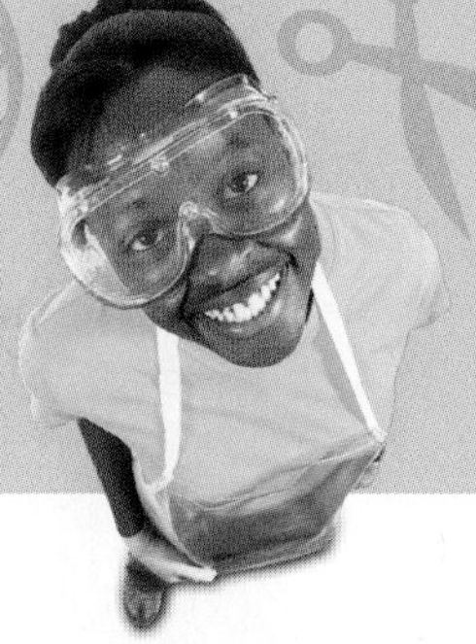

Using Scientific Methods

Inquiry Lab

Biodiversity—What a Disturbing Thought!

OBJECTIVES

Examine biodiversity in your community.

Identify which areas in your community have the greatest biodiversity.

MATERIALS

- items to be determined by the students and approved by the teacher (Possible field equipment includes a meterstick, binoculars, a magnifying lens, and forceps.)
- stakes (4)
- twine

SAFETY

Biodiversity is important for the stability of an ecosystem. Microorganisms, plants, and animals all have a role in an ecosystem. In this activity, you will investigate areas outside your school to determine which areas contain the greatest biodiversity.

Ask a Question

1. Based on your understanding of biodiversity, do you expect a forest or an area planted with crops to be more diverse?

Form a Hypothesis

2. Select an area that is highly disturbed (such as a yard) and an area that is relatively undisturbed (such as a vacant lot). Make a hypothesis about which area contains the greater biodiversity. Get your teacher's approval of your selected locations.

Test the Hypothesis

3. Design a procedure to determine which area contains the greater biodiversity. Have your plan approved by your teacher before you begin.

Prairie

Wheat Field

4. To discover smaller organisms, measure off a square meter, set stakes at the corners, and mark the area with twine. Use a magnifying lens to observe organisms. When you record your observations, refer to organisms in the following way: Ant A, Ant B, and so on. Make note of any visits by larger organisms.

5. Create any data tables that you might need for recording your data. If you observe your areas on more than one occasion, make data tables for each observation period. Organize your data into clear and understandable categories.

Analyze the Results

1. **Explaining Events** What factors did you consider before deciding which habitats were disturbed or undisturbed?

2. **Constructing Maps** Draw a map of the land around your school. Label areas of high biodiversity and those of lower biodiversity.

3. **Analyzing Data** What problems did you have while making observations and recording data for each habitat? How did you solve these problems?

Draw Conclusions

4. **Drawing Conclusions** Review your hypothesis. Did your data support your hypothesis? Explain your answer.

5. **Evaluating Methods** Describe possible errors in your investigation. What are ways you could improve your procedure to eliminate errors?

6. **Applying Conclusions** Do you think that the biodiversity around your school increased or decreased since the school was built? Explain your answer.

Applying Your Data

The photographs of the prairie and of the wheat field on this page are beautiful. One of these areas, however, is very low in biodiversity. Describe each photograph, and explain the difference in biodiversity.

Chapter Review

USING KEY TERMS

Complete each of the following sentences by choosing the correct term from the word bank.

conservation
pollution
recycling
biodiversity
overpopulation
renewable resource
nonrenewable resource

1. A(n) ___ is a resource that is replaced at a much slower rate than it is used.

2. The presence of too many individuals in a population for available resources is called ___.

3. ___ is an unwanted change in the environment caused by wastes.

4. The preservation and wise use of natural resources is called ___.

5. ___ is the number and variety of organisms in an area.

UNDERSTANDING KEY IDEAS

Multiple Choice

6. Preventing habitat destruction is important because
   - **a.** organisms do not live independently of each other.
   - **b.** protection of habitats is a way to promote biodiversity.
   - **c.** the balance of nature could be disrupted if habitats were destroyed.
   - **d.** All of the above

7. Exotic species
   - **a.** do not affect native species.
   - **b.** are species that make a home for themselves in a new place.
   - **c.** are not introduced by human activity.
   - **d.** do not take over an area.

8. A renewable resource
   - **a.** is a natural resource that can be replaced as quickly as it is used.
   - **b.** is a natural resource that takes thousands or millions of years to be replaced.
   - **c.** includes fossil fuels, such as coal or oil.
   - **d.** will eventually run out.

Short Answer

9. Describe how you can use the three Rs to conserve resources.

10. What are five kinds of pollutants?

11. Explain why human population growth has increased.

12. What are two things that can be done to maintain biodiversity?

13. List five environmental strategies.

CRITICAL THINKING

14 **Concept Mapping** Use the following terms to create a concept map: *pollution, radioactive wastes, gases, pollutants, CFCs, PCBs, hazardous wastes, chemicals, noise,* and *garbage.*

15 **Analyzing Ideas** How may deforestation have contributed to the extinction of some species?

16 **Predicting Consequences** Imagine that the supply of fossil fuels is going to run out in 50 years. What will happen if people are not prepared when the supply runs out? What might be done to prepare for such an event?

17 **Evaluating Conclusions** A scientist thinks that farms should be planted with many different kinds of crops instead of a single crop. Based on what you learned about biodiversity, evaluate the scientist's conclusion. What problems might this cause?

18 **Applying Concepts** Imagine that a new species has moved into a local habitat. The species feeds on some of the same plants that the native species do, but it has no natural predators. Describe what might happen to local habitats as a result.

19 **Making Inferences** Many scientists think that forests are nonrenewable resources. Explain why they might have this opinion.

INTERPRETING GRAPHICS

The line graph below shows the concentration of carbon dioxide in the atmosphere between 1958 and 1994. Use this graph to answer the questions that follow.

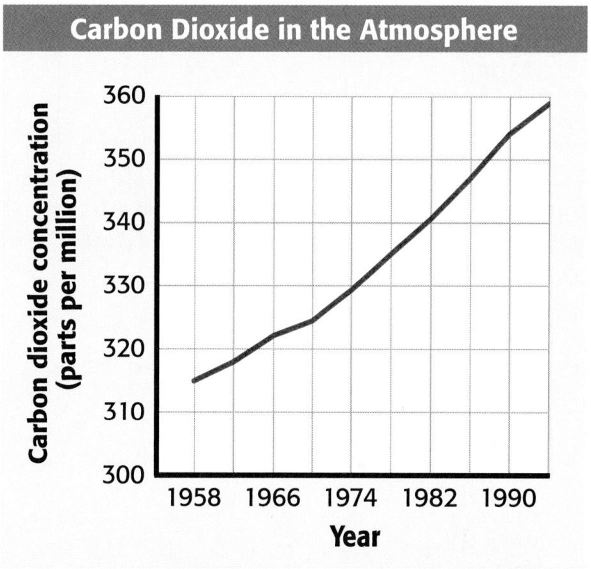

20 What was the concentration of carbon dioxide in parts per million in 1960? in 1994?

21 What is the average change in carbon dioxide concentration every 4 years?

22 If the concentration of carbon dioxide continues to change at the rate shown in the graph, what will the concentration be in 2010?

Standardized Test Preparation

Multiple Choice

Use the table below to answer question 1.

October Ozone Levels Above Halley Bay, Antarctica, in Dobson Units (DU)	
Year	**Ozone level (DU)**
1960	300
1970	280
1980	235
1990	190

1. Based on the table above, which of the following statements most likely describes the ozone layer above Antarctica in 2000?

A. The ozone layer was thinner than it was in 1990.

B. The ozone layer was thicker than it was in 1960.

C. The ozone layer was as thick as it was in 1980.

D. The ozone layer was nonexistent over Antarctica.

2. Which of the following would be the best way for students and teachers to decrease the amount of paper they use in their science class? They could

A. share handouts of class notes.

B. use both sides of each sheet of paper.

C. recycle sheets of paper when they are finished with them.

D. use blackboards and overhead projectors instead of handouts of class notes.

3. If there were a massive increase in the amount of carbon circulating in the carbon cycle, it would

A. cause no change.

B. decrease the number of plants.

C. affect photosynthesis and respiration.

D. only affect living things that have carbon in their bodies.

4. You need to choose materials for a lab investigation. Which of the following is the most environmentally friendly product to use?

A. one 1-L paper carton of water

B. two 1-L plastic bottles of water

C. four half-liter plastic bottles of water

D. two refillable 1-L glass bottles of water

5. An exotic species often thrives in its new environment because it

A. hunts prey.

B. helps native species thrive.

C. doesn't affect the existing ecosystem.

D. is free from the predators in its native habitat.

6. Habitat destruction caused by human activities can result in

A. increased rainfall.

B. an increase in the number of species.

C. a loss of biodiversity.

D. long-term loss of carbon dioxide.

Use the diagram below to answer question 7.

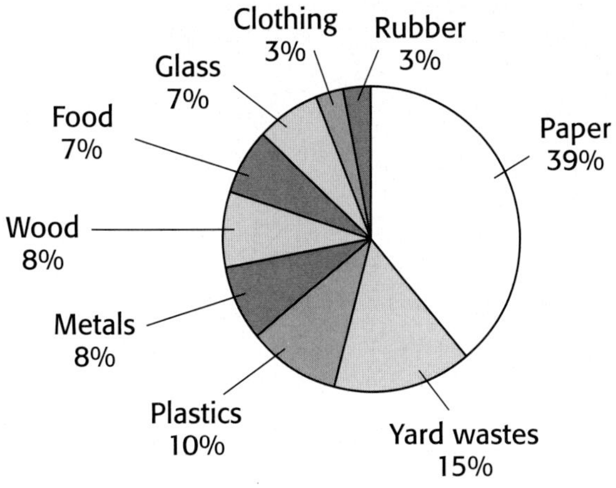

7. Ross performed a field investigation on his local landfill and created the pie chart above, which shows the types and amounts of wastes in the landfill. How much space in this landfill could be saved if people recycled all of their glass and plastic?

A. 17%

B. 25%

C. 30%

D. 59%

8. A certain object is biodegradable. How does that benefit the environment?

A. It can be recycled, reducing the use of resources.

B. It is readily broken down, so it doesn't take up space in a landfill.

C. It increases the use of renewable resources, which can be quickly replaced.

D. It releases chemicals that are less harmful than chemicals released by other items.

9. Some fertilizers are pollutants. Which of the following statements describes the effect of such fertilizers on the environment?

A. They give off radiation, which harms organisms.

B. They trap heat around Earth.

C. They destroy the ozone that protects Earth.

D. They can cause oxygen depletion in water, killing fish.

10. The loss of any habitat can affect biodiversity. The loss of which of the following habitats will have the greatest effect on biodiversity?

A. rain forest

B. wheat field

C. coniferous forest

D. banana plantation

Open Response

11. The gray bat lives in the caves of central Kentucky and is an endangered species. Discuss 2 ways the gray bat could be protected.

12. Marine habitats are affected by both point and non-point source pollution. Explain the difference between these kinds of pollution. Give an example of each point and non-point source pollution and its effect on marine habitats.

Science in Action

Scientific Debate

Where Should the Wolves Roam?

The U.S. Fish and Wildlife Service once listed the gray wolf as an endangered species and devised a plan to reintroduce the wolf to parts of the U.S. The goal was to establish a population of at least 100 wolves at each location. In April 2003, gray wolves were reclassified as a threatened species in much of the United States. Eventually, gray wolves may be removed from the endangered species list entirely. But some ranchers and hunters are uneasy about the reintroduction of gray wolves, and some environmentalists and wolf enthusiasts think the plan doesn't go far enough to protect wolves.

Math ACTIVITY

Scientists tried to establish a population of 100 wolves in Idaho. But the population grew to 285 wolves. By what percentage did the population exceed expectations?

Science, Technology, and Society

Hydrogen-Fueled Automobiles

Can you imagine a car that purrs quieter than a kitten and gives off water vapor instead of harmful pollutants? These cars may sound like science fiction. But such cars already exist! They run on one of the most common elements in the world—hydrogen. Some car companies are already speculating that one day all cars will run on hydrogen. The U.S. government has also taken notice. In 2003, President George W. Bush promised $1.2 billion to help research and develop hydrogen-fueled cars.

Language Arts ACTIVITY

WRITING SKILL Research hydrogen-fueled cars. Then, write a letter to a car company, your senator, or the President expressing your opinion about the development of hydrogen-fueled cars.

People in Science

Phil McCrory

Hairy Oil Spills Phil McCrory, a hairdresser in Huntsville, Alabama, asked a brilliant question when he saw an otter whose fur was drenched with oil from the *Exxon Valdez* oil spill. If the otter's fur soaked up all the oil, why wouldn't human hair do the same? McCrory gathered hair from the floor of his salon and took it home to perform his own experiments. He stuffed hair into a pair of his wife's pantyhose and tied the ankles together to form a bagel-shaped bundle. McCrory floated the bundle in his son's wading pool and poured used motor oil into the center of the ring. When he pulled the ring closed, not a drop of oil remained in the water!

McCrory approached the National Aeronautics and Space Administration (NASA) with his discovery. Based on tests performed by NASA, scientists estimated that 64 million kilograms of hair in reusable mesh pillows could have cleaned up all of the oil spilled by the *Exxon Valdez* within a week! Unfortunately, the $2 billion spent on the cleanup removed only about 12% of the oil.

Social Studies ACTIVITY

Make a map of an oil spill. Show the areas that were affected. Indicate some of the animal populations affected by the spill, such as penguins.

To learn more about these Science in Action topics, visit go.hrw.com and type in the keyword **HL5ENVF.**

Current Science

Check out Current Science® articles related to this chapter by visiting go.hrw.com. Just type in the keyword HL5CS21.

UNIT 4

TIMELINE

Astronomy

In this unit, you will learn about the science of astronomy. Long before science was called science, people looked up at the night sky and tried to understand the meaning of the twinkling lights above. Early astronomers charted the stars and built calendars based on the movement of the sun, moon, and planets. Today, scientists from around the world have come together to place a space station in orbit around the Earth. This timeline shows some of the events that have occurred throughout human history as scientists have come to understand more about our planet's "neighborhood" in space.

1054

Chinese and Korean astronomers record the appearance of a supernova, an exploding star. Strangely, no European observations of this event have ever been found.

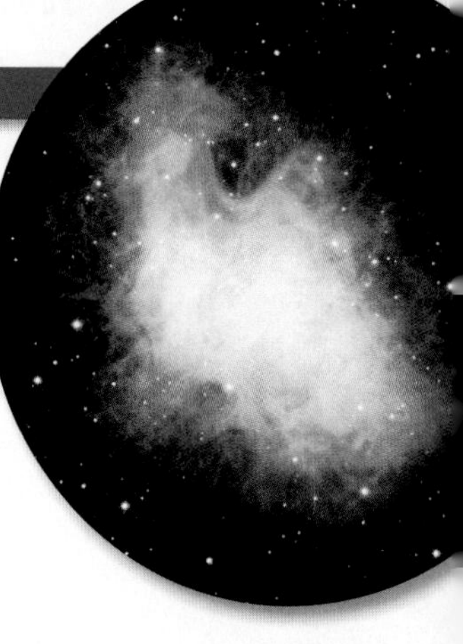

The Crab Nebula

Andromeda Nebula

1924

An astronomer named Edwin Hubble confirms the existence of other galaxies.

1983

Sally Ride becomes the first American woman to travel in space.

1582

Ten days are dropped from October as the Julian calendar is replaced by the Gregorian calendar.

1666

Using a prism, Isaac Newton discovers that white light is composed of different colors.

1898

The War of the Worlds, by H. G. Wells, is published.

1958

The National Aeronautics and Space Administration (NASA) is established to oversee the exploration of space.

1970

Apollo 13 is damaged shortly after leaving orbit. The spacecraft's three astronauts navigate around the moon to return safely to the Earth.

1977

Voyager 1 and *Voyager 2* are launched on missions to Jupiter, Saturn, and beyond. Now more than 10 billion kilometers away from the Earth, they are still sending back information about space.

Voyager 2

1992

Astronomers discover the first planet outside the solar system.

1998

John Glenn becomes the oldest human in space. His second trip into space comes 36 years after he became the first American to orbit the Earth.

2003

Astronomers discover three distant quasars that date back to a time when the universe was only 800 million years old. It takes light 13 billion years to reach Earth from the farthest of the three quasars.

14

Studying Space

The Big Idea

Studying space allows us to understand the movement of objects in space and the distances between those objects.

SECTION

About the Photo

This time-exposure photograph was taken at an observatory located high in the mountains of Chile. As the night passed, the photograph recorded the stars as they circled the southern celestial pole. Just as Earth's rotation causes the sun to appear to move across the sky during the day, Earth's rotation also causes the stars to appear to move across the night sky.

PRE-READING ACTIVITY

FOLDNOTES

Three-Panel Flip Chart

Before you read the chapter, create the FoldNote entitled "Three-Panel Flip Chart" described in the **Study Skills** section of the Appendix. Label the flaps of the three-panel flip chart with "Astronomy," "Telescopes," and "Mapping the stars." As you read the chapter, write information you learn about each category under the appropriate flap.

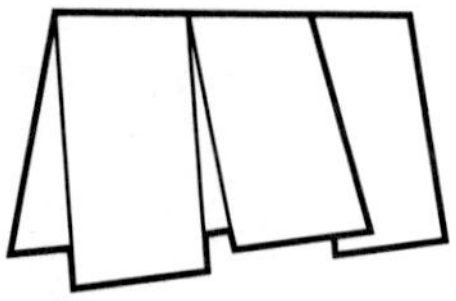

START-UP ACTIVITY

Making an Astrolabe

In this activity, you will make an astronomical device called an *astrolabe* (AS troh LAYB). Ancient astronomers used astrolabes to measure the location of stars in the sky. You will use the astrolabe to measure the angle, or altitude, of an object.

Procedure

1. Tie one end of a **piece of thread** that is 15 cm long to the center of the straight edge of a **protractor.** Attach a **paper clip** to the other end of the string.
2. Tape a **soda straw** lengthwise along the straight edge of the protractor. Your astrolabe is complete!
3. Go outside, and hold the astrolabe in front of you.
4. Look through the straw at a distant object, such as a treetop. The curve of the astrolabe should point toward the ground.
5. Hold the astrolabe still, and carefully pinch the string between your thumb and the protractor. Count the number of degrees between the string and the 90° marker on the protractor. This angle is the altitude of the object.

Analysis

1. What is the altitude of the object? How would the altitude change if you moved closer to the object?
2. Explain how you would use an astrolabe to find the altitude of a star. What are the advantages and disadvantages of this method of measurement?

SECTION 1

Astronomy: The Original Science

What You Will Learn

- Identify the units of a calendar.
- Describe two early ideas about the structure of the universe.
- Describe the contributions of Brahe, Kepler, Galileo, Newton, and Hubble to modern astronomy.

Vocabulary

astronomy
year
month
day

READING STRATEGY

Reading Organizer As you read this section, make a flowchart of the development of astronomy.

Imagine that it is 5,000 years ago. Clocks and modern calendars have not been invented. How would you tell the time or know what day it is? One way to tell the time is to study the movement of stars, planets, and the moon.

People in ancient cultures used the seasonal cycles of the stars, planets, and the moon to mark the passage of time. For example, by observing these yearly cycles, early farmers learned the best times of year to plant and harvest various crops. Studying the movement of objects in the sky was so important to ancient people that they built observatories, such as the one shown in **Figure 1.** Over time, the study of the night sky became the science of astronomy. **Astronomy** is the study of the universe. Although ancient cultures did not fully understand how the planets, moons, and stars move in relation to each other, their observations led to the first calendars.

astronomy the study of the universe

year the time required for the Earth to orbit once around the sun

Our Modern Calendar

The years, months, and days of our modern calendar are based on the observation of bodies in our solar system. A **year** is the time required for the Earth to orbit once around the sun. A **month** is roughly the amount of time required for the moon to orbit once around the Earth. (The word *month* comes from the word *moon*.) A **day** is the time required for the Earth to rotate once on its axis.

Figure 1 *This building is located at Chichén Itzá in the Yucatán, Mexico. It is thought to be an ancient Mayan observatory.*

Who's Who of Early Astronomy

Astronomical observations have given us much more than the modern calendar that we use. The careful work of early astronomers helped people understand their place in the universe. The earliest astronomers had only oral histories to learn from. Almost everything they knew about the universe came from what they could discover with their eyes and minds. Not surprisingly, most early astronomers thought that the universe consisted of the sun, the moon, and the planets. They thought that the stars were at the edge of the universe. Claudius Ptolemy (KLAW dee uhs TAHL uh mee) and Nicolaus Copernicus (NIK uh LAY uhs koh PUHR ni kuhs) were two early scientists who influenced the way that people thought about the structure of the universe.

month a division of the year that is based on the orbit of the moon around the Earth

day the time required for Earth to rotate once on its axis

Ptolemy: An Earth-Centered Universe

In 140 CE, Ptolemy, a Greek astronomer, wrote a book that combined all of the ancient knowledge of astronomy that he could find. He expanded ancient theories with careful mathematical calculations in what was called the *Ptolemaic theory.* Ptolemy thought that the Earth was at the center of the universe and that the other planets and the sun revolved around the Earth. Although the Ptolemaic theory, shown in **Figure 2,** was incorrect, it predicted the motions of the planets better than any other theory at the time did. For over 1,500 years in Europe, the Ptolemaic theory was the most popular theory for the structure of the universe.

Figure 2 *According to the Ptolemaic theory, the Earth is at the center of the universe.*

Copernicus: A Sun-Centered Universe

In 1543, a Polish astronomer named Copernicus published a new theory that would eventually revolutionize astronomy. According to his theory, which is shown in **Figure 3,** the sun is at the center of the universe, and all of the planets—including the Earth—orbit the sun. Although Copernicus correctly thought that the planets orbit the sun, his theory did not replace the Ptolemaic theory immediately. When Copernicus's theory was accepted, major changes in science and society called the *Copernican revolution* took place.

Figure 3 *According to Copernicus's theory, the sun is at the center of the universe.*

Reading Check What was Copernicus's theory? *(See the Appendix for answers to Reading Checks.)*

Figure 4 *Brahe (upper right) used a mural quadrant, which is a large quarter-circle on a wall, to measure the positions of stars and planets.*

Tycho Brahe: A Wealth of Data

In the late-1500s, Danish astronomer Tycho Brahe (TIE koh BRAW uh) used several large tools, including the one shown in **Figure 4,** to make the most detailed astronomical observations that had been recorded so far. Brahe favored a theory of an Earth-centered universe that was different from the Ptolemaic theory. Brahe thought that the sun and the moon revolved around the Earth and that the other planets revolved around the sun. While his theory was not correct, Brahe recorded very precise observations of the planets and stars that helped future astronomers.

Johannes Kepler: Laws of Planetary Motion

After Brahe died, his assistant, Johannes Kepler, continued Brahe's work. Kepler did not agree with Brahe's theory, but he recognized how valuable Brahe's data were. In 1609, after analyzing the data, Kepler announced that all of the planets revolve around the sun in elliptical orbits and that the sun is not in the exact center of the orbits. Kepler also stated three laws of planetary motion. These laws are still used today.

Galileo: Turning a Telescope to the Sky

In 1609, Galileo Galilei became one of the first people to use a telescope to observe objects in space. Galileo discovered craters and mountains on the Earth's moon, four of Jupiter's moons, sunspots on the sun, and the phases of Venus. These discoveries showed that the planets are not "wandering stars" but are physical bodies like the Earth.

Isaac Newton: The Laws of Gravity

In 1687, a scientist named Sir Isaac Newton showed that all objects in the universe attract each other through gravitational force. The force of gravity depends on the mass of the objects and the distance between them. Newton's law of gravity explained why all of the planets orbit the most massive object in the solar system—the sun. Thus, Newton helped explain the observations of the scientists who came before him.

Reading Check **How did the work of Isaac Newton help explain the observations of earlier scientists?**

Modern Astronomy

The invention of the telescope and the description of gravity were two milestones in the development of modern astronomy. In the 200 years following Newton's discoveries, scientists made many discoveries about our solar system. But they did not learn that our galaxy has cosmic neighbors until the 1920s.

Edwin Hubble: Beyond the Edge of the Milky Way

Before the 1920s, many astronomers thought that our galaxy, the Milky Way, included every object in space. In 1924, Edwin Hubble proved that other galaxies existed beyond the edge of the Milky Way. His data confirmed the beliefs of some astronomers that the universe is much larger than our galaxy. Today, larger and better telescopes on the Earth and in space, new models of the universe, and spacecraft help astronomers study space. Computers, shown in **Figure 5,** help process data and control the movement of telescopes. These tools have helped answer many questions about the universe. Yet new technology has presented questions that were unthinkable even 10 years ago.

Figure 5 *Computers are used to control telescopes and process large amounts of data.*

SECTION Review

Summary

- Astronomy, the study of the universe, is one of the oldest sciences.
- The units of the modern calendar—days, months, and years—are based on observations of objects in space.
- Ptolemaic theory states that the Earth is at the center of the universe.
- Copernican theory states that the sun is at the center of the universe.
- Modern astronomy has shown that there are billions of galaxies.

Using Key Terms

1. Use each of the following terms in a separate sentence: *year, day, month,* and *astronomy.*

Understanding Key Ideas

2. What happens in 1 year?
   a. The moon completes one orbit around the Earth.
   b. The sun travels once around the Earth.
   c. The Earth revolves once on its axis.
   d. The Earth completes one orbit around the sun.
3. What is the difference between the Ptolemaic and Copernican theories? Who was more accurate: Ptolemy or Copernicus?
4. What contributions did Brahe and Kepler make to astronomy?
5. What contributions did Galileo, Newton, and Hubble make to astronomy?

Math Skills

6. How many times did Earth orbit the sun between 140 CE, when Ptolemy introduced his theories, and 1543, when Copernicus introduced his theories?

Critical Thinking

7. **Analyzing Relationships** What advantage did Galileo have over earlier astronomers?
8. **Making Inferences** Why is astronomy such an old science?

SCiLINKS. NSTA Developed and maintained by the National Science Teachers Association

For a variety of links related to this chapter, go to www.scilinks.org

Topic: The Stars and Keeping Time; Early Theories in Astronomy

SciLinks code: HSM1449; HSM0444

SECTION 2

Telescopes

What color are Saturn's rings? What does the surface of the moon look like? To answer these questions, you could use a device called a telescope.

What You Will Learn

- Compare refracting telescopes with reflecting telescopes.
- Explain how the atmosphere limits astronomical observations, and explain how astronomers overcome these limitations.
- List the types of electromagnetic radiation that astronomers use to study objects in space.

Vocabulary

telescope
refracting telescope
reflecting telescope
electromagnetic spectrum

READING STRATEGY

Mnemonics As you read this section, create a mnemonic device to help you remember the characteristics of each type of radiation in the electromagnetic spectrum.

For professional astronomers and amateur stargazers, the telescope is the standard tool for observing the sky. A **telescope** is an instrument that gathers electromagnetic radiation from objects in space and concentrates it for better observation.

Optical Telescopes

Optical telescopes, which are the most common type of telescope, are used to study visible light from objects in the universe. Without using an optical telescope, you can see at most about 3,000 stars in the night sky. Using an optical telescope, however, you can see millions of stars and other objects.

An optical telescope collects visible light and focuses it to a focal point for closer observation. A *focal point* is the point where the rays of light that pass through a lens or that reflect from a mirror converge. The simplest optical telescope has two lenses. One lens, called the *objective lens,* collects light and forms an image at the back of the telescope. The bigger the objective lens is, the more light the telescope can gather. The second lens is located in the eyepiece of the telescope. This lens magnifies the image produced by the objective lens. **Figure 1** shows how much more of the moon you can see by using an optical telescope.

Reading Check **What are the functions of the two lenses in an optical telescope?** (*See the Appendix for answers to Reading Checks.*)

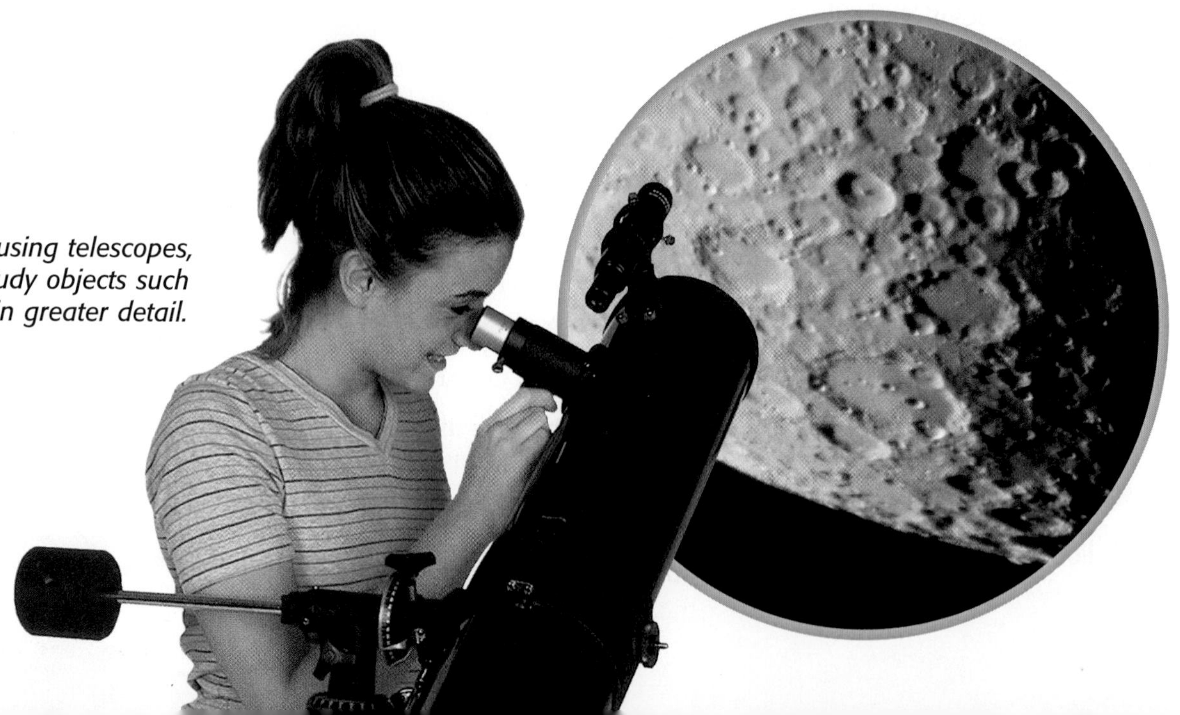

Figure 1 *By using telescopes, people can study objects such as the moon in greater detail.*

Figure 2 Refracting and Reflecting Telescopes

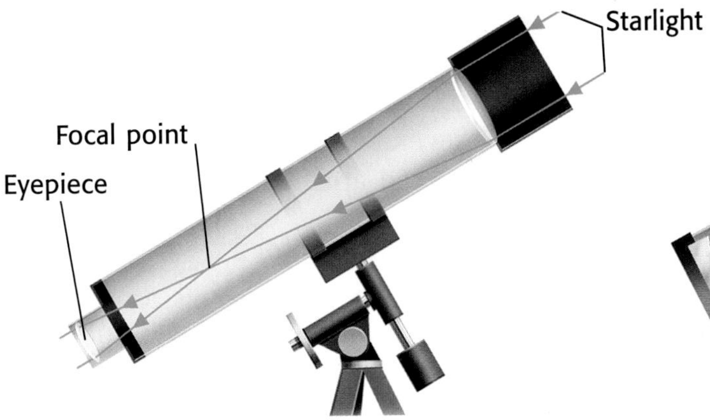

Refracting telescopes use lenses to gather and focus light.

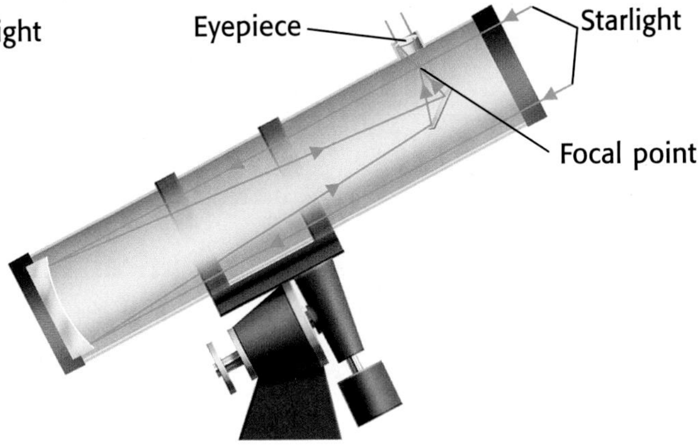

Reflecting telescopes use mirrors to gather and focus light.

Refracting Telescopes

Telescopes that use lenses to gather and focus light are called **refracting telescopes.** As shown in **Figure 2,** a refracting telescope has an objective lens that bends light that passes through it and focuses the light to be magnified by an eyepiece. Refracting telescopes have two disadvantages. First, lenses focus different colors of light at slightly different distances, so images cannot be perfectly focused. Second, the size of a refracting telescope is also limited by the size of the objective lens. If the lens is too large, the glass sags under its own weight and images are distorted. These limitations are two reasons that most professional astronomers use reflecting telescopes.

telescope an instrument that collects electromagnetic radiation from the sky and concentrates it for better observation

refracting telescope a telescope that uses a set of lenses to gather and focus light from distant objects

reflecting telescope a telescope that uses a curved mirror to gather and focus light from distant objects

Reflecting Telescopes

A telescope that uses a curved mirror to gather and focus light is called a **reflecting telescope.** Light enters the telescope and is reflected from a large, curved mirror to a flat mirror. As shown in **Figure 2,** the flat mirror focuses the image and reflects the light to be magnified by the eyepiece.

One advantage of reflecting telescopes is that the mirrors can be very large. Large mirrors allow reflecting telescopes to gather more light than refracting telescopes do. Another advantage is that curved mirrors are polished on their curved side, which prevents light from entering the glass. Thus, any flaws in the glass do not affect the light. A third advantage is that mirrors can focus all colors of light to the same focal point. Therefore, reflecting telescopes allow all colors of light from an object to be seen in focus at the same time.

Very Large Reflecting Telescopes

In some very large reflecting telescopes, several mirrors work together to collect light and focus it in the same area. The Keck Telescopes in Hawaii, shown in **Figure 3,** are twin telescopes that each have 36 hexagonal mirrors that work together. Linking several mirrors allows more light to be collected and focused in one spot.

Figure 3 *The Keck Telescopes are in Hawaii. The 36 hexagonal mirrors in each telescope (shown in the inset) combine to form a light-reflecting surface that is 10 m across.*

Optical Telescopes and the Atmosphere

The light gathered by telescopes on the Earth is affected by the atmosphere. The Earth's atmosphere causes starlight to shimmer and blur due to the motion of the air above the telescope. Also, light pollution from large cities can make the sky look bright. As a result, an observer's ability to view faint objects is limited. Astronomers often place telescopes in dry areas to avoid moisture in the air. Mountaintops are also good locations for telescopes because the air is thinner at higher elevations. In addition, mountaintops generally have less air pollution and light pollution than other areas do.

Reading Check **How does the atmosphere affect the images produced by optical telescopes?**

Optical Telescopes in Space

To avoid interference by the atmosphere, scientists have put telescopes in space. Although the mirror in the *Hubble Space Telescope,* shown in **Figure 4,** is only 2.4 m across, this optical telescope can detect very faint objects in space.

Figure 4 *The* Hubble Space Telescope *has produced very clear images of objects in deep space.*

The Electromagnetic Spectrum

For thousands of years, humans have used their eyes to observe stars and planets. But scientists eventually discovered that visible light, the light that we can see, is not the only form of radiation. In 1852, James Clerk Maxwell proved that visible light is a part of the electromagnetic spectrum. The **electromagnetic spectrum** is made up of all of the wavelengths of electromagnetic radiation.

electromagnetic spectrum all of the frequencies or wavelengths of electromagnetic radiation

Detecting Electromagnetic Radiation

Each color of light is a different wavelength of electromagnetic radiation. Humans can see radiation from red light, which has a long wavelength, to blue light, which has a shorter wavelength. But visible light is only a small part of the electromagnetic spectrum, as shown in **Figure 5.** The rest of the electromagnetic spectrum—radio waves, microwaves, infrared light, ultraviolet light, X rays, and gamma rays—is invisible. The Earth's atmosphere blocks most invisible radiation from objects in space. In this way, the atmosphere functions as a protective shield around the Earth. Radiation that can pass through the atmosphere includes some radio waves, microwaves, infrared light, visible light, and some ultraviolet light.

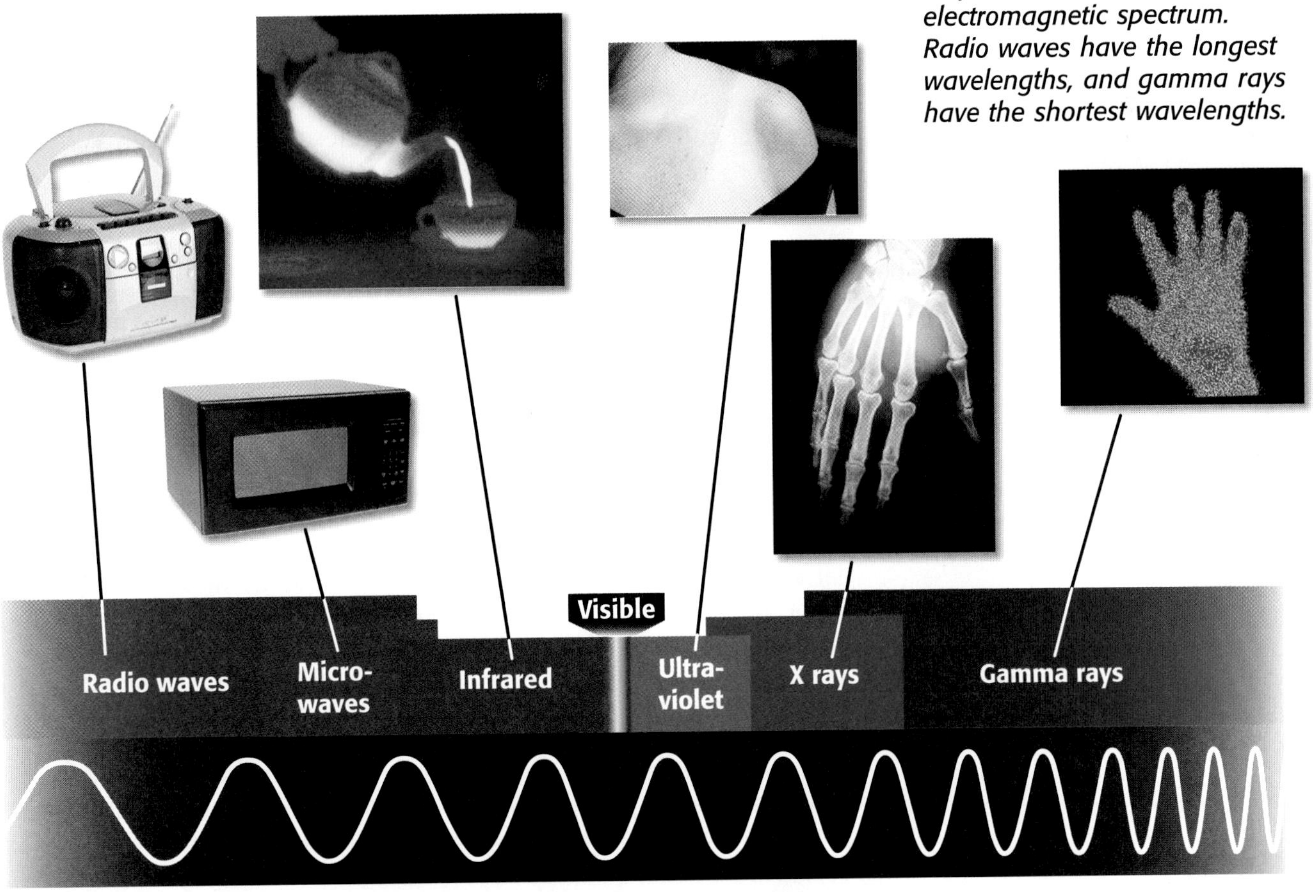

Figure 5 *Visible light is only a small band of the electromagnetic spectrum. Radio waves have the longest wavelengths, and gamma rays have the shortest wavelengths.*

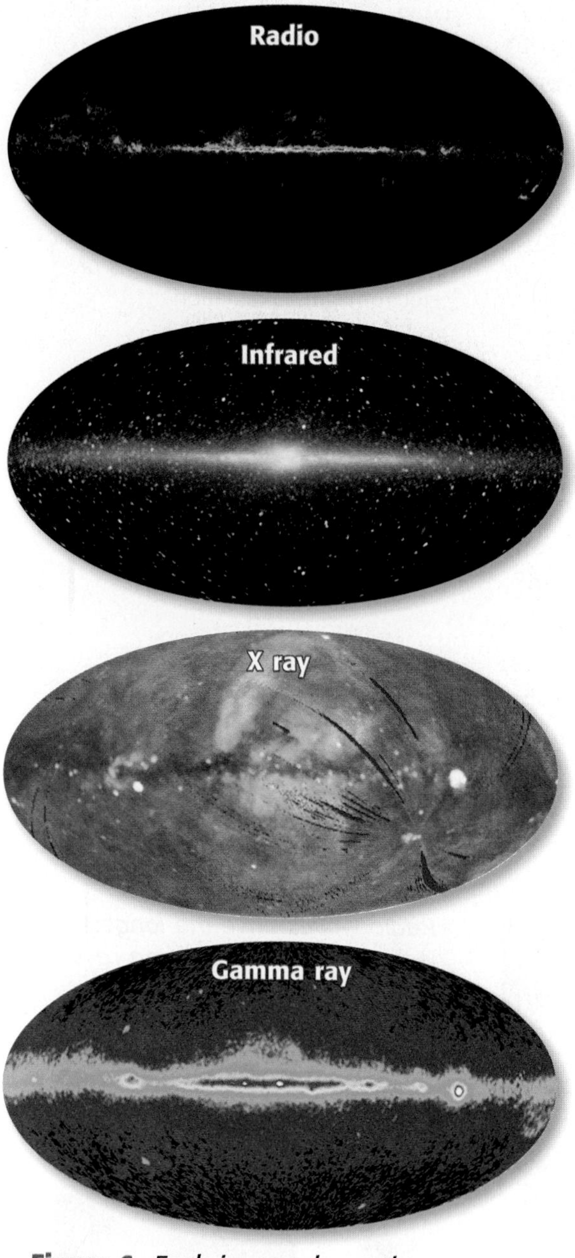

Figure 6 *Each image shows the Milky Way as it would appear if we could see other wavelengths of electromagnetic radiation.*

Nonoptical Telescopes

To study invisible radiation, scientists use nonoptical telescopes. Nonoptical telescopes detect radiation that cannot be seen by the human eye. Astronomers study the entire electromagnetic spectrum because each type of radiation reveals different clues about an object. As **Figure 6** shows, our galaxy looks very different when it is observed at various wavelengths. A different type of telescope was used to produce each image. The "cloud" that goes across the image is the Milky Way galaxy.

Radio Telescopes

Radio telescopes detect radio waves. Radio telescopes have to be much larger than optical telescopes because radio wavelengths are about 1 million times longer than optical wavelengths. Most radio radiation reaches the ground and can be detected both during the day and night. The surface of radio telescopes does not have to be as flawless as the lenses and mirrors of optical telescopes. In fact, the surface of a radio telescope does not have to be solid.

Linking Radio Telescopes

Astronomers can get more detailed images of the universe by linking radio telescopes together. When radio telescopes are linked together, they work like a single giant telescope. For example, the Very Large Array (VLA) consists of 27 radio telescopes that are spread over 30 km. Working together, the telescopes function as a single telescope that is 30 km across!

CONNECTION TO Physics

Detecting Infrared Radiation In this activity, you will replicate Sir William Herschel's discovery of invisible infrared radiation. First, paint the bulbs of three thermometers black. Place a sheet of white paper inside a tall cardboard box. Tape the thermometers parallel to each other, and place them inside the box. Cut a small notch in the top of the box, and position a small glass prism so that a spectrum is projected inside the box. Arrange the thermometers so that one is just outside the red end of the spectrum, with no direct light on it. After 10 min, record the temperatures. Which thermometer recorded the highest temperature? Explain why.

ACTIVITY

Nonoptical Telescopes in Space

Because most electromagnetic waves are blocked by the Earth's atmosphere, scientists have placed ultraviolet telescopes, infrared telescopes, gamma-ray telescopes, and X-ray telescopes in space. The *Chandra X-Ray Observatory,* a space-based telescope that detects X rays, is illustrated in **Figure 7.** X-ray telescopes in space can be much more sensitive than optical telescopes. For example, NASA has tested an X-ray telescope that can detect an object that is the size of a frisbee on the surface of the sun. If an optical telescope had a similar power, it could detect a hair on the head of an astronaut on the moon!

Reading Check Why are X-ray telescopes placed in space?

Figure 7 *The* Chandra X-Ray Observatory *can detect black holes and some of the most distant objects in the universe.*

SECTION Review

Summary

- Refracting telescopes use lenses to gather and focus light.
- Reflecting telescopes use mirrors to gather and focus light.
- Astronomers study all wavelengths of the electromagnetic spectrum, including radio waves, microwaves, infrared light, visible light, ultraviolet light, X rays, and gamma rays.
- The atmosphere blocks most forms of electromagnetic radiation from reaching the Earth. To overcome this limitation, astronomers place telescopes in space.

Using Key Terms

For each pair of terms, explain how the meanings of the terms differ.

1. *refracting telescope* and *reflecting telescope*
2. *telescope* and *electromagnetic spectrum*

Understanding Key Ideas

3. How does the atmosphere affect astronomical observations?
   - **a.** It focuses visible light.
   - **b.** It blocks most electromagnetic radiation.
   - **c.** It blocks all radio waves.
   - **d.** It does not affect astronomical observations.
4. Describe how reflecting and refracting telescopes work.
5. What limits the size of a refracting telescope? Explain.
6. What advantages do reflecting telescopes have over refracting telescopes?
7. List the types of radiation in the electromagnetic spectrum, from the longest wavelength to the shortest wavelength. Then, describe how astronomers study each type of radiation.

Math Skills

8. A telescope's light-gathering power is proportional to the area of its objective lens or mirror. If the diameter of a lens is 1 m, what is the area of the lens? (Hint: $area = 3.1416 \times radius^2$)

Critical Thinking

9. **Applying Concepts** Describe three reasons why Hawaii is a good location for a telescope.
10. **Making Inferences** Why doesn't the surface of a radio telescope have to be as flawless as the surface of a mirror in an optical telescope?
11. **Making Inferences** What limitation of a refracting telescope could be overcome by placing the telescope in space?

SCILINKS® NSTA Developed and maintained by the National Science Teachers Association

For a variety of links related to this chapter, go to www.scilinks.org

Topic: Telescopes
SciLinks code: HSM1500

SECTION 3

Mapping the Stars

Have you ever seen Orion the Hunter or the Big Dipper in the night sky? Ancient cultures linked stars together to form patterns that represented characters from myths and objects in their lives.

Today, we can see the same star patterns that people in ancient cultures saw. Modern astronomers still use many of the names given to stars centuries ago. But astronomers can now describe a star's location precisely. Advances in astronomy have led to a better understanding of how far away stars are and how big the universe is.

What You Will Learn

- Explain how constellations are used to organize the night sky.
- Describe how the altitude of a star is measured.
- Explain how the celestial sphere is used to describe the location of objects in the sky.
- Compare size and scale in the universe, and explain how red shift indicates that the universe is expanding.

Vocabulary

constellation	horizon
zenith	light-year
altitude	

READING STRATEGY

Paired Summarizing Read this section silently. In pairs, take turns summarizing the material. Stop to discuss ideas that seem confusing.

Patterns in the Sky

When people in ancient cultures connected stars in patterns, they named sections of the sky based on the patterns. These patterns are called *constellations*. **Constellations** are sections of the sky that contain recognizable star patterns. Understanding the location and movement of constellations helped people navigate and keep track of time.

Different civilizations had different names for the same constellations. For example, where the Greeks saw a hunter (Orion) in the northern sky, the Japanese saw a drum, as shown in **Figure 1.** Today, different cultures still interpret the sky in different ways, but astronomers have agreed on the names and locations of the constellations.

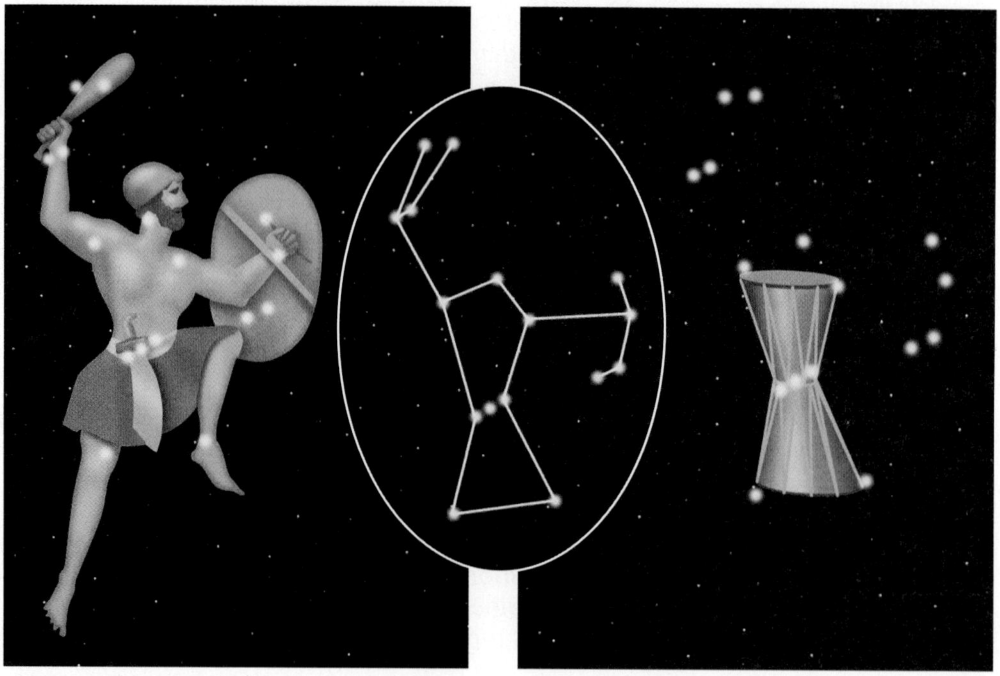

Figure 1 *The ancient Greeks saw Orion as a hunter, but the Japanese saw the same set of stars as a drum.*

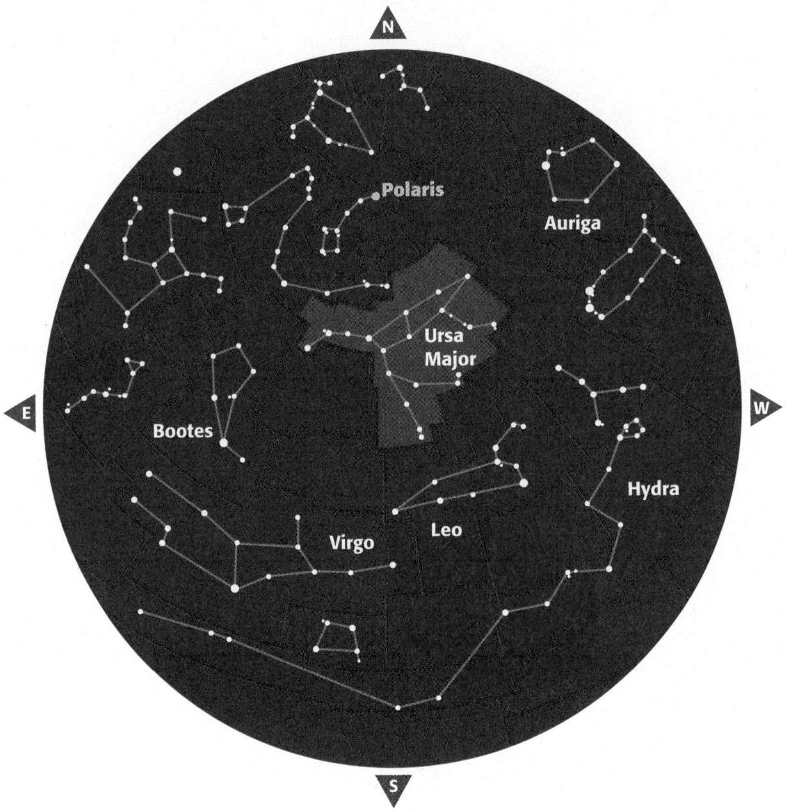

Figure 2 *This sky map shows some of the constellations in the Northern Hemisphere at midnight in the spring. Ursa Major (the Great Bear) is a region of the sky that includes all of the stars that make up that constellation.*

constellation a region of the sky that contains a recognizable star pattern and that is used to describe the location of objects in space

Constellations Help Organize the Sky

When you think of constellations, you probably think of the stick figures made by connecting bright stars with imaginary lines. To an astronomer, however, a constellation is something more. As you can see in **Figure 2,** a constellation is a region of the sky. Each constellation shares a border with neighboring constellations. For example, in the same way that the state of Texas is a region of the United States, Ursa Major is a region of the sky. Every star or galaxy is located within 1 of 88 constellations.

Seasonal Changes

The sky map in **Figure 2** shows what the midnight sky in the Northern Hemisphere looks like in the spring. But as the Earth revolves around the sun, the apparent locations of the constellations change from season to season. In addition, different constellations are visible in the Southern Hemisphere. Thus, a child in Chile can see different constellations than you can. Therefore, this map is not accurate for the other three seasons or for the Southern Hemisphere. Sky maps for summer, fall, and winter in the Northern Hemisphere appear in the Appendix of this book.

Reading Check **Why are different constellations visible in the Northern and Southern Hemispheres?** (*See the Appendix for answers to Reading Checks.*)

Quick Lab

Using a Sky Map

1. Hold your **textbook** over your head with the cover facing upward. Turn the book so that the direction at the bottom of the sky map is the same as the direction you are facing.
2. Notice the locations of the constellations in relation to each other.
3. If you look up at the sky at night in the spring, you should see the stars positioned as they are on your map.
4. Why are *E* and *W* on sky maps the reverse of how they appear on land maps?

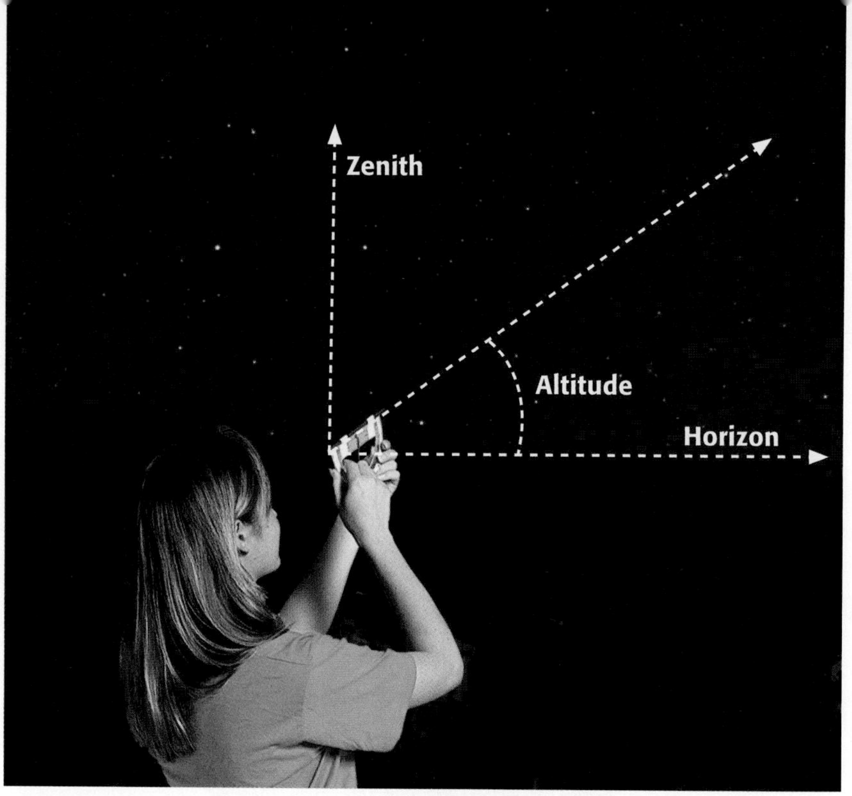
Zenith
Altitude
Horizon

Figure 3 *Using an astrolabe, you can determine the altitude of a star by measuring the angle between the horizon and a star. The altitude of any object depends on where you are and when you look.*

zenith the point in the sky directly above an observer on Earth

altitude the angle between an object in the sky and the horizon

horizon the line where the sky and the Earth appear to meet

Finding Stars in the Night Sky

Have you ever tried to show someone a star by pointing to it? Did the person miss what you were seeing? If you use an instrument called an *astrolabe,* shown in **Figure 3,** you can describe the location of a star or planet. To use an astrolabe correctly, you need to understand the three points of reference shown in **Figure 4.** This method is useful to describe the location of a star relative to where you are. But if you want to describe a star's location in relation to the Earth, you need to use the celestial sphere, shown in **Figure 5.**

Figure 4 Zenith, Altitude, and Horizon

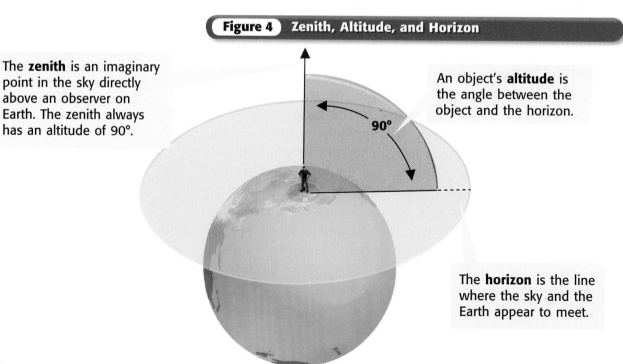

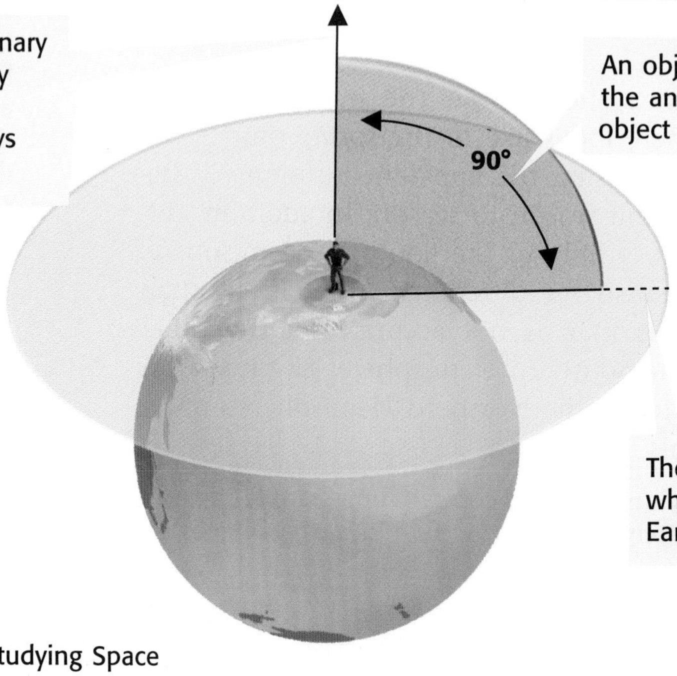
The **zenith** is an imaginary point in the sky directly above an observer on Earth. The zenith always has an altitude of 90°.
90°
An object's **altitude** is the angle between the object and the horizon.
The **horizon** is the line where the sky and the Earth appear to meet.

Figure 5 **The Celestial Sphere**

To talk to each other about the location of a star, astronomers must have a common method of describing a star's location. The method that astronomers have invented is based on a reference system known as the *celestial sphere*. The celestial sphere is an imaginary sphere that surrounds the Earth. Just as we use latitude and longitude to plot positions on Earth, astronomers use right ascension and declination to plot positions in the sky. *Right ascension* is a measure of how far east an object is from the *vernal equinox,* the location of the sun on the first day of spring. *Declination* is a measure of how far north or south an object is from the celestial equator.

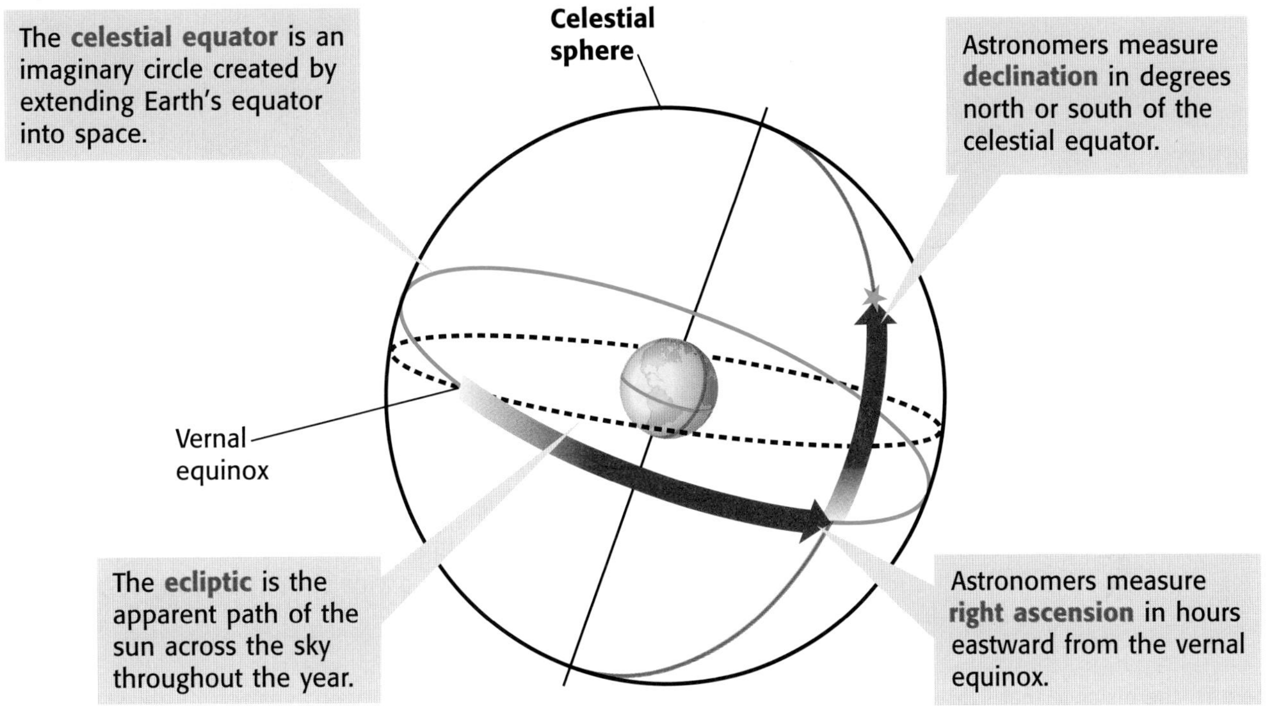

The **celestial equator** is an imaginary circle created by extending Earth's equator into space.
Celestial sphere
Astronomers measure **declination** in degrees north or south of the celestial equator.
Vernal equinox
The **ecliptic** is the apparent path of the sun across the sky throughout the year.
Astronomers measure **right ascension** in hours eastward from the vernal equinox.

The Path of Stars Across the Sky

Just as the sun appears to move across the sky during the day, most stars and planets rise and set throughout the night. This apparent motion is caused by the Earth's rotation. As the Earth spins on its axis, stars and planets appear to move. Near the poles, however, stars are circumpolar. *Circumpolar stars* are stars that can be seen at all times of year and all times of night. These stars never set, and they appear to circle the celestial poles. You also see different stars in the sky depending on the time of year. Why? The reason is that as the Earth travels around the sun, different areas of the universe are visible.

Reading Check **How is the apparent movement of the sun similar to the apparent movement of most stars during the night?**

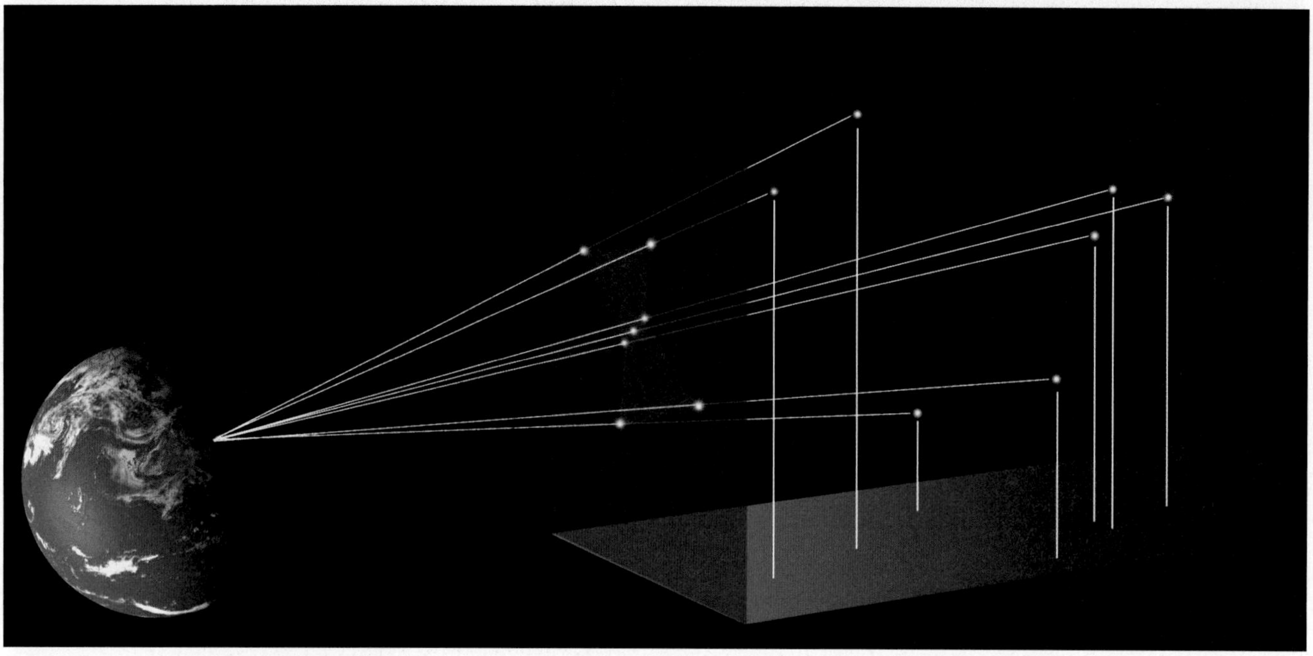

Figure 6 *While the stars in the constellation Orion may appear to be near each other when they are seen from Earth, they are actually very far apart.*

The Size and Scale of the Universe

Imagine looking out the window of a moving car. Nearby trees appear to move more quickly than farther trees do. Objects that are very far away do not appear to move at all. The same principle applies to stars and planets. In the 1500s, Nicolaus Copernicus noticed that the planets appeared to move relative to each other but that the stars did not. Thus, he thought that the stars must be much farther away than the planets.

Measuring Distance in Space

light-year the distance that light travels in one year; about 9.46 trillion kilometers

Today, we know that Copernicus was correct. The stars are much farther away than the planets are. In fact, stars are so distant that a new unit of length—the light-year—was created to measure their distance. A **light-year** is a unit of length equal to the distance that light travels in 1 year. One light-year is equal to about 9.46 trillion kilometers! The farthest objects we can observe are more than 10 billion light-years away. Although the stars may appear to be at similar distances from Earth, their distances vary greatly. For example, **Figure 6** shows how far away the stars that make up part of Orion are.

Reading Check How far does light travel in 1 year?

INTERNET ACTIVITY

For another activity related to this chapter, go to **go.hrw.com** and type in the keyword **HZ5OBSW.**

Considering Scale in the Universe

When you think about the universe and all of the objects it contains, it is important to consider scale. For example, stars appear to be very small in the night sky. But we know that most stars are a lot larger than Earth. **Figure 7** will help you understand the scale of objects in the universe.

Figure 7 From Home Plate to 10 Million Light-Years Away

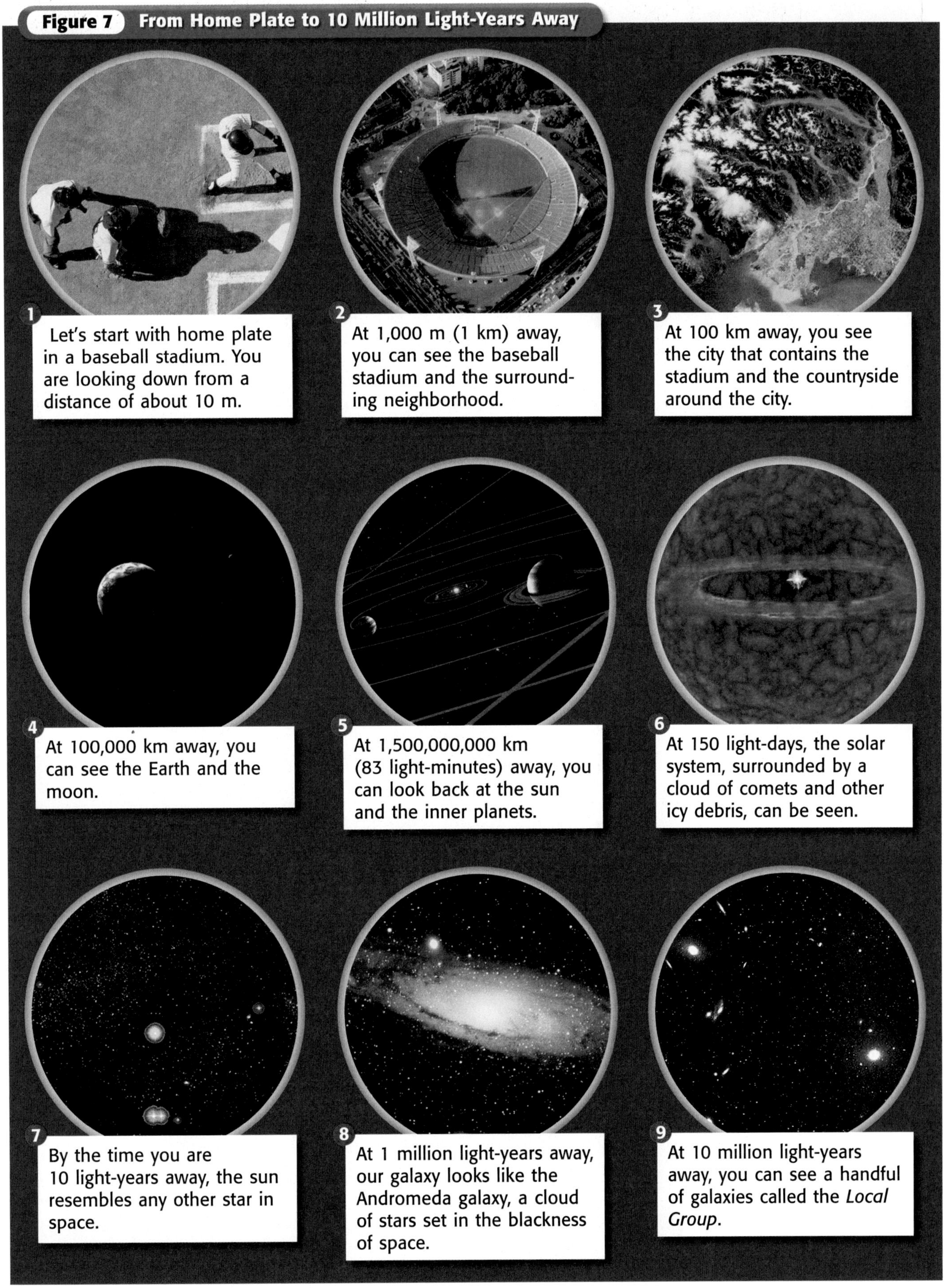

1 Let's start with home plate in a baseball stadium. You are looking down from a distance of about 10 m.

2 At 1,000 m (1 km) away, you can see the baseball stadium and the surrounding neighborhood.

3 At 100 km away, you see the city that contains the stadium and the countryside around the city.

4 At 100,000 km away, you can see the Earth and the moon.

5 At 1,500,000,000 km (83 light-minutes) away, you can look back at the sun and the inner planets.

6 At 150 light-days, the solar system, surrounded by a cloud of comets and other icy debris, can be seen.

7 By the time you are 10 light-years away, the sun resembles any other star in space.

8 At 1 million light-years away, our galaxy looks like the Andromeda galaxy, a cloud of stars set in the blackness of space.

9 At 10 million light-years away, you can see a handful of galaxies called the *Local Group*.

Figure 8 *As an object moves away from an observer at a high speed, the light from the object appears redder. As the object moves toward the observer, the light from the object appears bluer.*

The Doppler Effect

Have you ever noticed that when a driver in an approaching car blows the horn, the horn sounds higher pitched as the car approaches and lower pitched after the car passes? This effect is called the *Doppler effect.* As shown in **Figure 8,** the Doppler effect also occurs with light. If a light source, such as a star or galaxy, is moving quickly away from an observer, the light emitted looks redder than it normally does. This effect is called *redshift.* If a star or galaxy is moving quickly toward an observer, its light appears bluer than it normally does. This effect is known as *blueshift.*

An Expanding Universe

After discovering that the universe is made up of many other galaxies like our own, Edwin Hubble analyzed the light from galaxies and stars to study the general direction that objects in the universe are moving. Hubble soon made another startling discovery—the light from all galaxies except our close neighbors is affected by redshift. This means that galaxies are rapidly moving apart from each other. In other words, because all galaxies except our close neighbors are moving apart, the universe must be expanding. **Figure 9** shows evidence of redshift recorded by the *Hubble Space Telescope* in 2002.

Reading Check **What logical conclusion could be made if the light from all of the galaxies were affected by blueshift?**

Figure 9 *The galaxy that is cut off at the bottom of this image is moving away from us at a much slower speed than the other galaxies are. Distant galaxies are visible as faint disks.*

SECTION Review

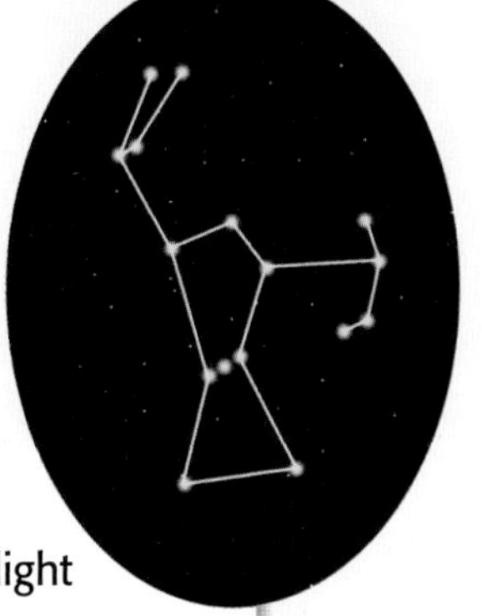

Summary

- Astronomers use constellations to organize the sky.
- Altitude, or the angle between an object and the horizon, can be used to describe the location of an object in the sky.
- The celestial sphere is an imaginary sphere that surrounds the Earth. Using the celestial sphere, astronomers can accurately describe the location of an object without reference to an observer.
- A light-year is the distance that light travels in 1 year.
- The Doppler effect causes the light emitted by objects that are moving away from an observer to appear to shift toward the red end of the spectrum. Objects moving toward an observer are shifted to the blue end of the spectrum.
- Observations of redshift and blueshift indicate that the universe is expanding.

Using Key Terms

The statements below are false. For each statement, replace the underlined term to make a true statement.

1. <u>Zenith</u> is the angle between an object and the horizon.
2. The distance that light travels in 1 year is called a <u>light-meter</u>.

Understanding Key Ideas

3. Stars appear to move across the night sky because of
   a. the rotation of Earth on its axis.
   b. the movement of the Milky Way galaxy.
   c. the movement of stars in the universe.
   d. the revolution of Earth around the sun.
4. How do astronomers use the celestial sphere to plot a star's exact position?
5. How do constellations relate to patterns of stars? How are constellations like states?
6. Why are different sky maps needed for different times of the year?
7. What are redshift and blueshift? Why are these effects useful in the study of the universe?

Critical Thinking

8. **Applying Concepts** Light from the Andromeda galaxy is affected by blueshift. What can you conclude about this galaxy?
9. **Making Comparisons** Explain how Copernicus concluded that stars were farther away than planets. Draw a diagram showing how this principle applies to another example.

Interpreting Graphics

The diagram below shows the altitude of Star A and Star B. Use the diagram below to answer the questions that follow.

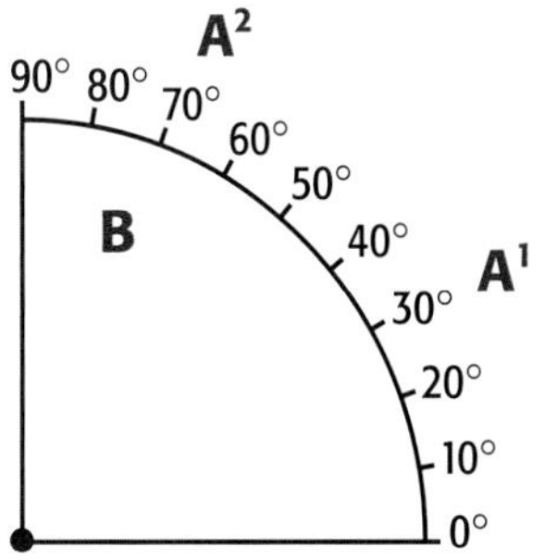

10. What is the approximate altitude of star B?
11. In 4 h, star A moved from A^1 to A^2. How many degrees did the star move each hour?

SCILINKS. NSTA Developed and maintained by the National Science Teachers Association

For a variety of links related to this chapter, go to www.scilinks.org

Topic: Constellations
SciLinks code: HSM0347

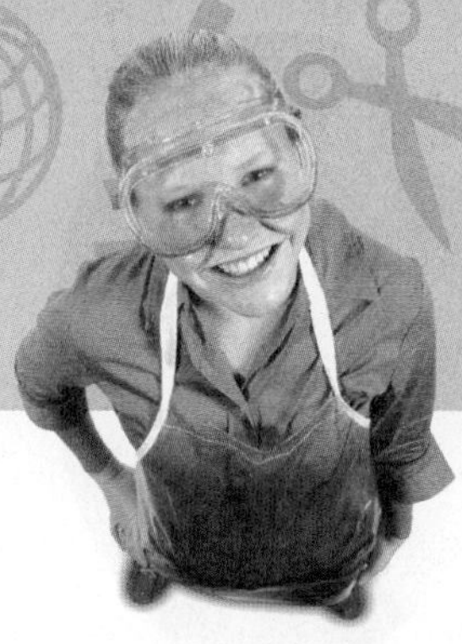

Skills Practice Lab

Through the Looking Glass

OBJECTIVES

Construct a simple model of a refracting telescope.

Observe distant objects by using your telescope.

MATERIALS

- clay, modeling (1 stick)
- convex lens, 3 cm in diameter (2 of different focal length)
- lamp, desk
- paper, white (1 sheet)
- ruler, metric
- scissors
- tape, masking (1 roll)
- toilet-paper tube, cardboard
- wrapping paper tube, cardboard

SAFETY

Have you ever looked toward the horizon or up into the sky and wished that you could see farther? Do you think that a telescope might help you see farther? Astronomers use huge telescopes to study the universe. You can build your own telescope to get a glimpse of how these enormous, technologically advanced telescopes help astronomers see distant objects.

Procedure

1. Use modeling clay to form a base that holds one of the lenses upright on your desktop. When the lights are turned off, your teacher will turn on a lamp at the front of the classroom. Rotate your lens so that the light from the lamp passes through the lens.
2. Hold the paper so that the light passing through the lens lands on the paper. To sharpen the image of the light on the paper, slowly move the paper closer to or farther from the lens. Hold the paper in the position in which the image is sharpest.
3. Using the metric ruler, measure the distance between the lens and the paper. Record this distance.

4. How far is the paper from the lens? This distance, called the *focal length,* is the distance that the paper has to be from the lens for the image to be in focus.
5. Repeat steps 1–4 using the other lens.
6. Measuring from one end of the long cardboard tube, mark the focal length of the lens that has the longer focal length. Place a mark 2 cm past this line toward the other end of the tube, and label the mark "Cut."
7. Measuring from one end of the short cardboard tube, mark the focal length of the lens that has the shorter focal length. Place a mark 2 cm past this line toward the other end of the tube, and label the mark "Cut."
8. Shorten the tubes by cutting along the marks labeled "Cut." Wear safety goggles when you make these cuts.
9. Tape the lens that has the longer focal length to one end of the longer tube. Tape the other lens to one end of the shorter tube. Slip the empty end of one tube inside the empty end of the other tube. Be sure that there is one lens at each end of this new, longer tube.
10. Congratulations! You have just constructed a telescope. To use your telescope, look through the short tube (the eyepiece) and point the long end at various objects in the room. You can focus the telescope by adjusting its length. Are the images right side up or upside down? Observe birds, insects, trees, or other outside objects. Record the images that you see. **Caution:** NEVER look directly at the sun! Looking directly at the sun could cause permanent blindness.

Analyze the Results

1. **Analyzing Results** Which type of telescope did you just construct: a refracting telescope or a reflecting telescope? What makes your telescope one type and not the other?
2. **Identifying Patterns** What factor determines the focal length of a lens?

Draw Conclusions

3. **Evaluating Results** How would you improve your telescope?

Chapter Review

USING KEY TERMS

1. Use each of the following terms in a separate sentence: *year, month, day, astronomy, electromagnetic spectrum, constellation,* and *altitude.*

For each pair of terms, explain how the meanings of the terms differ.

2. *reflecting telescope* and *refracting telescope*
3. *zenith* and *horizon*
4. *year* and *light-year*

UNDERSTANDING KEY IDEAS

Multiple Choice

5. Which of the following answer choices lists types of electromagnetic radiation from longest wavelength to shortest wavelength?
   - **a.** radio waves, ultraviolet light, infrared light
   - **b.** infrared light, microwaves, X rays
   - **c.** X rays, ultraviolet light, gamma rays
   - **d.** microwaves, infrared light, visible light

6. The length of a day is based on the amount of time that
   - **a.** Earth takes to orbit the sun one time.
   - **b.** Earth takes to rotate once on its axis.
   - **c.** the moon takes to orbit Earth one time.
   - **d.** the moon takes to rotate once on its axis.

7. Which of the following statements about X rays and radio waves from objects in space is true?
   - **a.** Both types of radiation can be observed by using the same telescope.
   - **b.** Separate telescopes are needed to observe each type of radiation, but both telescopes can be on Earth.
   - **c.** Separate telescopes are needed to observe each type of radiation, but both telescopes must be in space.
   - **d.** Separate telescopes are needed to observe each type of radiation, but only one of the telescopes must be in space.

8. According to ___, Earth is at the center of the universe.
   - **a.** the Ptolemaic theory
   - **b.** Copernicus's theory
   - **c.** Galileo's theory
   - **d.** None of the above

9. Which scientist was one of the first scientists to successfully use a telescope to observe the night sky?
   - **a.** Brahe
   - **b.** Galileo
   - **c.** Hubble
   - **d.** Kepler

10. Astronomers divide the sky into
    - **a.** galaxies.
    - **b.** constellations.
    - **c.** zeniths.
    - **d.** phases.

11. ___ determines which stars you see in the sky.
    - **a.** Your latitude
    - **b.** The time of year
    - **c.** The time of night
    - **d.** All of the above

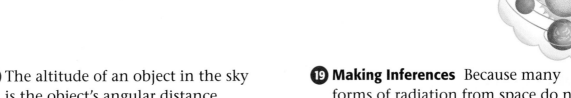

12 The altitude of an object in the sky is the object's angular distance

a. above the horizon.
b. from the north celestial pole.
c. from the zenith.
d. from the prime meridian.

13 Right ascension is a measure of how far east an object in the sky is from

a. the observer.
b. the vernal equinox.
c. the moon.
d. Venus.

14 Telescopes that work on Earth's surface include all of the following EXCEPT

a. radio telescopes.
b. refracting telescopes.
c. X-ray telescopes.
d. reflecting telescopes.

Short Answer

15 Explain how right ascension and declination are similar to latitude and longitude.

16 How does a reflecting telescope work?

CRITICAL THINKING

17 **Concept Mapping** Use the following terms to create a concept map: *right ascension, declination, celestial sphere, degrees, hours, celestial equator,* and *vernal equinox.*

18 **Making Inferences** Why was seeing objects in the sky easier for people in ancient cultures than it is for most people today? What tools help modern people study objects in space in greater detail than was possible in the past?

19 **Making Inferences** Because many forms of radiation from space do not penetrate Earth's atmosphere, astronomers' ability to detect this radiation is limited. But how does the protection of the atmosphere benefit humans?

20 **Analyzing Ideas** Explain why the Ptolemaic theory seems logical based on daily observations of the rising and setting of the sun.

INTERPRETING GRAPHICS

Use the sky map below to answer the questions that follow. (Example: The star Aldebaran is located at about 4 h, 30 min right ascension, 16° declination.)

Celestial Coordinates

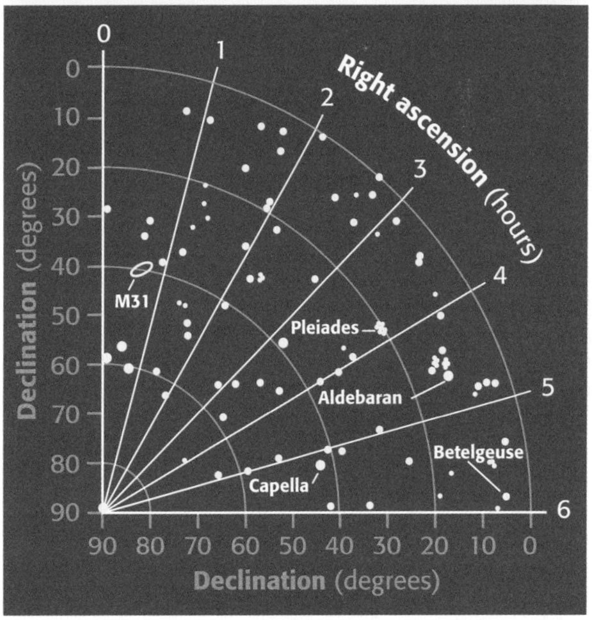

21 What object is located near 5 h, 55 min right ascension, and 7° declination?

22 What are the celestial coordinates for the Andromeda galaxy (M31)? Round off the right ascension to the nearest half-hour.

Multiple Choice

1. **Why did Copernicus think the stars are farther from the Earth than the planets are?**

   A. He believed that the Earth is the center of the universe and the other planets and the sun revolve around the Earth.

   B. He theorized that the sun is at the center of the universe and that the Earth and all of the planets orbit the sun.

   C. He noticed that the planets appear to move relative to each other and that the stars do not.

   D. He understood that all of the planets revolve around the sun in an elliptical orbit and that the sun is not in the exact center of the universe.

Use the illustration below to answer question 2.

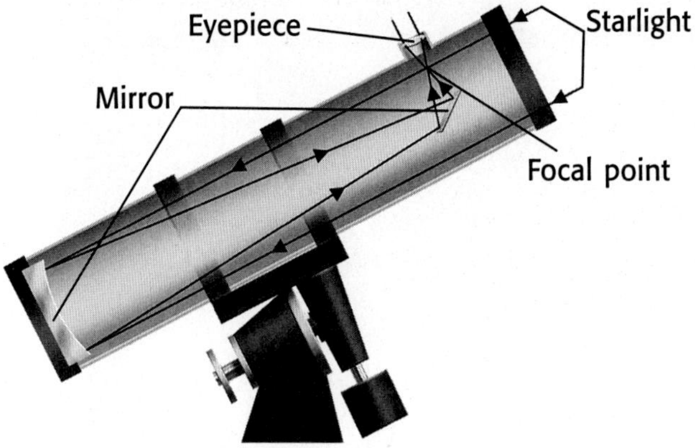

2. **The Bell Observatory near Bowling Green, Kentucky, has the same type of telescope as shown above. What type of telescope does the Bell Observatory have?**

   A. gamma ray

   B. reflecting

   C. radio

   D. refracting

3. **Dewanda has found a very bright star that is located 17 degrees less than the zenith. What is the star's altitude?**

   A. 73°

   B. 107°

   C. 163°

   D. 197°

4. **Where is an X-ray telescope most likely to be located?**

   A. in a desert

   B. on a mountaintop

   C. on an island

   D. in space

5. **What did Galileo Galilei's discovery of four of Jupiter's moons, the phases of Venus, and craters and mountains on the Earth's moon demonstrate?**

   A. The planets are physical bodies like the Earth.

   B. The planets are "wandering stars" in the solar system.

   C. The planets orbit the sun, which orbits the Earth.

   D. The planets revolve around the sun in an elliptical orbit.

6. **How does the Doppler effect demonstrate that the universe is expanding?**

   A. The light emitted from all galaxies except those closest to our galaxy looks bluer.

   B. The light emitted from all galaxies except those closest to our galaxy looks redder.

   C. The pitch from galaxies except those closest to our galaxy sounds higher.

   D. The pitch from galaxies except those closest to our galaxy sounds lower.

7. **What do astronomers use to locate a star's position in relation to the Earth?**

   A. celestial sphere

   B. handheld astrolabe

   C. mural quadrant

   D. reflecting telescope

8. **Which of the following statements best explains why astronomers study all of the wavelengths of the electromagnetic spectrum?**

   A. Each color of visible light is a different wavelength of electromagnetic radiation.

   B. Each portion of the electromagnetic spectrum gives different information about an object in space.

   C. The Earth's atmosphere blocks most invisible radiation from objects in space.

   D. Some of the different types of radiation are not visible to the human eye.

Use the table below to answer question 10.

Location	Darkness Scale	Latitude	Longitude
Area One	3.8	-85.67828°	38.20432°
Area Two	6.7	-86.48780°	37.99003°
Area Three	4.6	-85.82113°	38.02575°
Area Four	5.6	-85.86875°	37.84717°

9. **Lucas wants to set up his telescope in a place that has the least light pollution and the darkest sky. The table shows the darkness scale of four locations in Kentucky. The higher the number of the darkness scale is, the less light pollution there is and the more stars Lucas will be able to see. According to the table above, what are the latitude and longitude of the location where Lucas will see the most stars in the Kentucky night sky?**

   A. Area One

   B. Area Two

   C. Area Three

   D. Area Four

Open Response

10. **The age of the sun is estimated to be 4.6 billion years. Describe how scientists have determined the age of the sun.**

11. **Why is looking at a star through a telescope like looking back in time?**

Science in Action

Science Fiction

"Why I Left Harry's All-Night Hamburgers" by Lawrence Watt-Evans

The main character was 16, and he needed to find a job. So, he began working at Harry's All-Night Hamburgers. His shift was from midnight to 7:30 A.M. so that he could still go to school. Harry's All-Night Hamburgers was pretty quiet most nights, but once in a while some unusual characters came by. For example, one guy came in dressed for Arctic weather even though it was April. Then there were the folks who parked a very strange vehicle in the parking lot for anyone to see. The main character starts questioning the visitors, and what he learns startles and fascinates him. Soon, he's thinking about leaving Harry's. Find out why when you read "Why I Left Harry's All-Night Hamburgers," in the *Holt Anthology of Science Fiction*.

Social Studies ACTIVITY

WRITING SKILL The main character in the story learns that Earth is a pretty strange place. Find out about some of the places mentioned in the story, and create an illustrated travel guide that describes some of the foreign places that interest you.

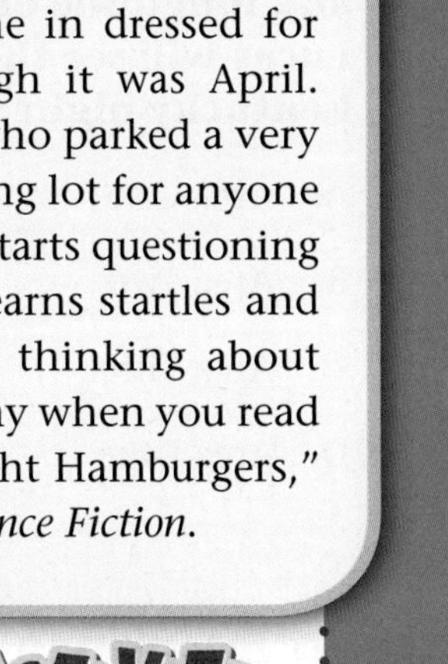

Science, Technology, and Society

Light Pollution

When your parents were your age, they could look up at the night sky and see many more stars than you can now. In a large city, seeing more than 50 stars or planets in the night sky can be difficult. Light pollution is a growing—or you could say "glowing"—problem. If you have ever seen a white glow over the horizon in the night sky, you have seen the effects of light pollution. Most light pollution comes from outdoor lights that are excessively bright or misdirected. Light pollution not only limits the number of stars that the average person can see but also limits what astronomers can detect. Light pollution affects migrating animals, too. Luckily, there are ways to reduce light pollution. The International Dark Sky Association is working to reduce light pollution around the world. Find out how you can reduce light pollution in your community or home.

Math ACTIVITY

A Virginia high school student named Jennifer Barlow started "National Dark Sky Week." If light pollution is reduced for 1 week each year, for what percentage of the year would light pollution be reduced?

People in Science

Neil deGrasse Tyson

Star Writer When Neil deGrasse Tyson was nine years old, he visited a planetarium for the first time. Tyson was so affected by the experience he decided at that moment to dedicate his life to studying the universe. Tyson began studying the stars through a telescope on the roof of his apartment building. This interest led Tyson to attend the Bronx High School of Science, where he studied astronomy and physics. Tyson's passion for astronomy continued when he was a student at Harvard. However, Tyson soon realized that he wanted to share his love of astronomy with the public. So, today Tyson is America's best-known astrophysicist. When something really exciting happens in the universe, such as the discovery of evidence of water on Mars, Tyson is often asked to explain the discovery to the public. He has been interviewed hundreds of times on TV programs and has written several books. Tyson also writes a monthly column in the magazine *Natural History*. But writing and appearing on TV isn't even his day job! Tyson is the director of the Hayden Planetarium in New York—the same planetarium that ignited his interest in astronomy when he was nine years old!

Language Arts Activity

WRITING SKILL Be a star writer! Visit a planetarium or find a Web site that offers a virtual tour of the universe. Write a magazine-style article about the experience.

go.hrw.com

To learn more about these Science in Action topics, visit **go.hrw.com** and type in the keyword **HZ5OBSF.**

Current Science

Check out Current Science® articles related to this chapter by visiting go.hrw.com. Just type in the keyword HZ5CS18.

15

Stars, Galaxies, and the Universe

The Big Idea

The structure and composition of the universe can be learned by studying stars and galaxies.

SECTION

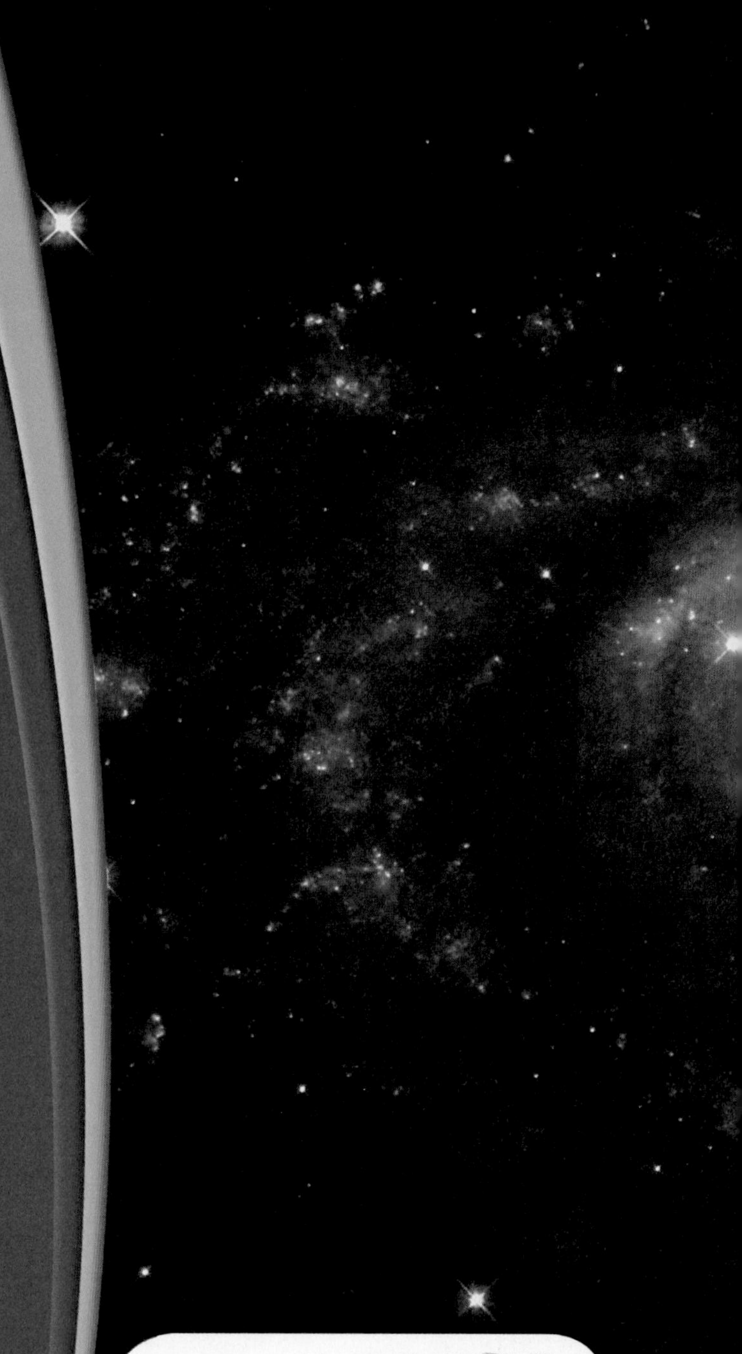

About the Photo

This image was taken by the ***Hubble Space Telescope*** and shows the IC 2163 galaxy (right) swinging past the NGC 2207 galaxy (left). Strong forces from NGC 2207 have caused stars and gas to fling out of IC 2163 into long streamers.

PRE-READING ACTIVITY

FOLDNOTES **Three-Panel Flip Chart** Before you read the chapter, create the FoldNote entitled "Three-Panel Flip Chart" described in the **Study Skills** section of the Appendix. Label the flaps of the three-panel flip chart with "Stars," "Galaxies," and "The universe." As you read the chapter, write information you learn about each category under the appropriate flap.

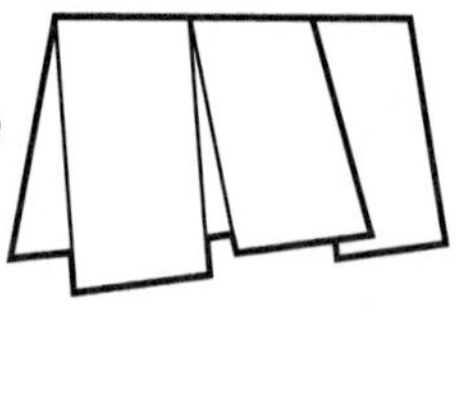

START-UP ACTIVITY

Exploring the Movement of Galaxies in the Universe

Not all galaxies are the same. Galaxies can differ by size, shape, and how they move in space. In this activity, you will explore how the galaxies in the photo move in space.

Procedure

1. Fill a **one-quart glass jar** three-fourths of the way with **water.**
2. Take a pinch of **glitter,** and sprinkle it on the surface of the water.
3. Quickly stir the water with a **wooden spoon.** Be sure to stir the water in a circular pattern.
4. After you stop stirring, look at the water from the sides of the jar and from the top of the jar.

Analysis

1. What kind of motion did the water make after you stopped stirring the water?
2. How is the motion similar to the galaxies in the photo?
3. Make up a name that describes the galaxies in the photo.

SECTION 1

Stars

What You Will Learn

- Describe how color indicates the temperature of a star.
- Explain how a scientist can identify a star's composition.
- Describe how scientists classify stars.
- Compare absolute magnitude with apparent magnitude.
- Identify how astronomers measure distances from Earth to stars.
- Describe the difference between the apparent motion and the actual motion of stars.

Vocabulary

spectrum
apparent magnitude
absolute magnitude
light-year
parallax

READING STRATEGY

Prediction Guide Before reading this section, write the title of each heading in this section. Next, under each heading, write what you think you will learn.

Do you remember the children's song "Twinkle, Twinkle Little Star"? In the song, you sing "How I wonder what you are!" Well, what are stars? And what are they made of?

Most stars look like faint dots of light in the night sky. But stars are actually huge, hot, bright balls of gas that are trillions of kilometers away from Earth. How do astronomers learn about stars when the stars are too far away to visit? Astronomers study starlight!

Color of Stars

Look at the flames on the candle and the Bunsen burner shown in **Figure 1.** Which flame is hottest? How can you tell? Although red and yellow may be thought of as "warm" colors and blue may be thought of as a "cool" color, scientists consider red and yellow to be cool colors and blue to be a warm color. For example, the blue flame of the Bunsen burner is much hotter than the yellow flame of the candle.

If you look carefully at the night sky, you might notice the different colors of some stars. Betelgeuse (BET uhl JOOZ), which is red, and Rigel (RIE juhl), which is blue, are the stars that form two corners of the constellation Orion, shown in **Figure 1.** Because these two stars are different colors, we can conclude that they have different temperatures.

Reading Check **Which star is hotter, Betelgeuse or Rigel? Explain your answer.** (*See the Appendix for answers to Reading Checks.*)

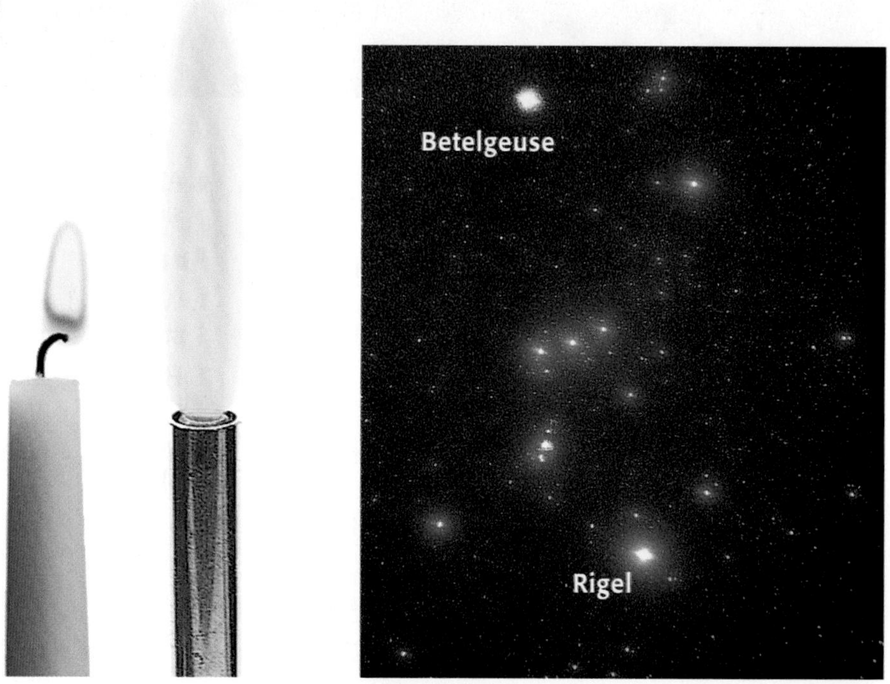

Figure 1 *In the same way that we know the blue flame of the Bunsen burner is hotter than the yellow flame of the candle, astronomers know that Rigel is hotter than Betelgeuse.*

Composition of Stars

A star is made up of different elements in the form of gases. The inner layers of a star are very dense and hot. But the outer layers of a star, or a star's atmosphere, are made up of cool gases. Elements in a star's atmosphere absorb some of the light that radiates from the star. Because different elements absorb different wavelengths of light, astronomers can tell what elements a star is made of from the light they observe from the star.

The Colors of Light

When you look at white light through a glass prism, you see a rainbow of colors called a **spectrum.** The spectrum consists of millions of colors, including red, orange, yellow, green, blue, indigo, and violet. A hot, solid object, such as the glowing wire inside a light bulb, gives off a *continuous spectrum*—a spectrum that shows all the colors. However, the spectrum of a star is different. Astronomers use an instrument called a *spectrograph* to break a star's light into a spectrum. The spectrum gives astronomers information about the composition and temperature of a star. To understand how to read a star's spectrum, think about something more familiar—a neon sign.

Making an ID

Many restaurants use neon signs to attract customers. The gas in a neon sign glows when an electric current flows through the gas. If you were to look at the sign with a spectrograph, you would not see a continuous spectrum. Instead, you would see *emission lines.* Emission lines are lines that are made when certain wavelengths of light, or colors, are given off by hot gases. When an element emits light, only some colors in the spectrum show up, while all the other colors are missing. Each element has a unique set of bright emission lines. Emission lines are like fingerprints for the elements. You can see emission lines for four elements in **Figure 2.**

CONNECTION TO Physics

WRITING SKILL **Fingerprinting Cars** Police use spectrographs to "fingerprint" cars. Car makers put trace elements in the paint of cars. Each make of car has a special paint and thus its own combination of trace elements. When a car is in a hit-and-run accident, police officers can identify the make of the car by the paint left behind. Using a spectrograph to identify a car is one of many scientific methods that police use to solve crimes. Solving crimes by using scientific equipment and methods is part of a science called *forensic science.* Research the topic of forensic science. In your **science journal,** write a short paragraph about the other scientific methods that forensic scientists use to solve crimes.

spectrum the band of color produced when white light passes through a prism

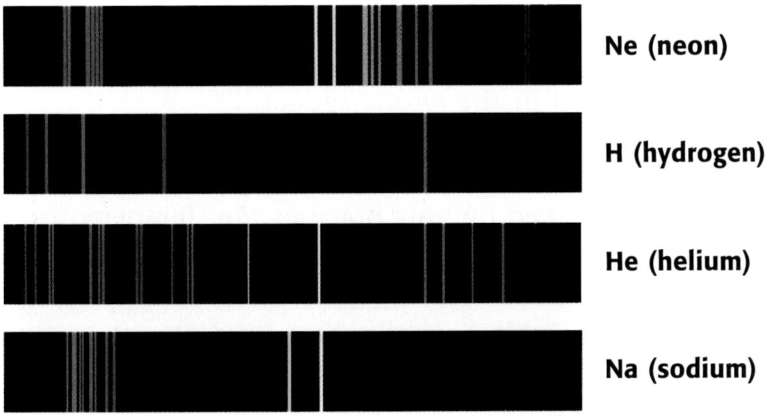

Figure 2 *Neon gas produces a unique set of emission lines, as do the elements hydrogen, helium, and sodium.*

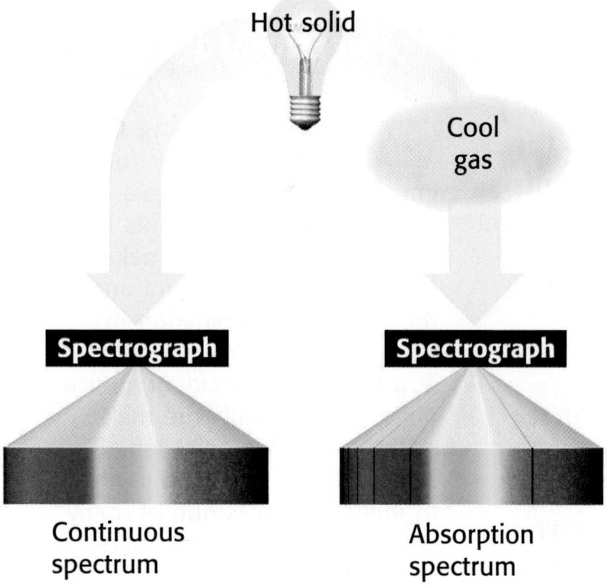

Figure 3 *A continuous spectrum (left) shows all colors while an absorption spectrum (right) absorbs some colors. Black lines appear in the spectrum where colors are absorbed.*

Trapping the Light—Cosmic Detective Work

Like an element that is charged by an electric current, a star also produces a spectrum. However, while the spectrum of an electrically charged element is made of bright emission lines, a star's spectrum is made of dark emission lines. A star's atmosphere absorbs certain colors of light in the spectrum, which causes black lines to appear.

Identifying Elements Using Dark Lines

Because a star's atmosphere absorbs colors of light instead of emitting them, the spectrum of a star is called an *absorption spectrum.* An absorption spectrum is produced when light from a hot solid or dense gas passes through a less dense, cooler gas. The cooler gas absorbs certain portions of the spectrum. Therefore, the black lines of a star's spectrum represent portions of the spectrum that are absorbed by the atmosphere. **Figure 3** compares a continuous spectrum and an absorption spectrum. How does the absorption spectrum differ from the continuous spectrum?

The pattern of lines in a star's absorption spectrum shows some of the elements that are in the star's atmosphere. If a star were made of one element, we could easily identify the element from the star's absorption spectrum. But a star is a mixture of elements and all the different sets of lines for a star's elements appear together in its spectrum. Sorting the patterns is often a puzzle.

Reading Check **What does a star's absorption spectrum show?**

CONNECTION TO Biology

Rods, Cones, and Stars

WRITING SKILL Have you ever wondered why it's hard to see the different colors of stars? Our eyes are not sensitive to colors when light levels are low. There are two types of light-sensitive cells in the eye: rods and cones. Research the functions of rods and cones. In your **science journal,** write a paragraph that explains why we can't see colors well in low light.

Classifying Stars

In the 1800s, astronomers started to collect and classify the spectra of many stars. At first, letters were assigned to each type of spectra. Stars were classified according to the elements of which they were made. Later, scientists realized that the stars were classified in the wrong order.

Differences in Temperature

Stars are now classified by how hot they are. Temperature differences between stars result in color differences that you can see. For example, the original class O stars are blue—the hottest stars. Look at **Table 1.** Notice that the stars are arranged in order from highest temperature to lowest temperature.

Table 1 Types of Stars				
Class	**Color**	**Surface temperature (°C)**	**Elements detected**	**Examples of stars**
O	blue	above 30,000	helium	10 Lacertae
B	blue-white	10,000–30,000	helium and hydrogen	Rigel, Spica
A	blue-white	7,500–10,000	hydrogen	Vega, Sirius
F	yellow-white	6,000–7,500	hydrogen and heavier elements	Canopus, Procyon
G	yellow	5,000–6,000	calcium and other metals	the sun, Capella
K	orange	3,500–5,000	calcium and molecules	Arcturus, Aldebaran
M	red	less than 3,500	molecules	Betelgeuse, Antares

Differences in Brightness

With only their eyes to aid them, early astronomers created a system to classify stars based on their brightness. They called the brightest stars in the sky *first-magnitude* stars and the dimmest stars *sixth-magnitude* stars. But when they began to use telescopes, astronomers were able to see many stars that had been too dim to see before. Rather than replace the old system of magnitudes, they added to it. Positive numbers represent dimmer stars, and negative numbers represent brighter stars. For example, by using large telescopes, astronomers can see stars as dim as 29th magnitude. And the brightest star in the night sky, Sirius, has a magnitude of -1.4. The Big Dipper, shown in **Figure 4,** contains both bright stars and dim stars.

SCHOOL to HOME

Stargazing

WRITING SKILL Someone looking at the night sky in a city would not see as many stars as someone looking at the sky in the country. With a parent or guardian, research why this is true. Try to find a place near your home that would be ideal for stargazing. If you find one, schedule a night to stargaze. Write down what you see in the night sky.

ACTIVITY

Figure 4 *The Big Dipper contains both bright stars and dim stars. What is the magnitude of the brightest star in the Big Dipper?*

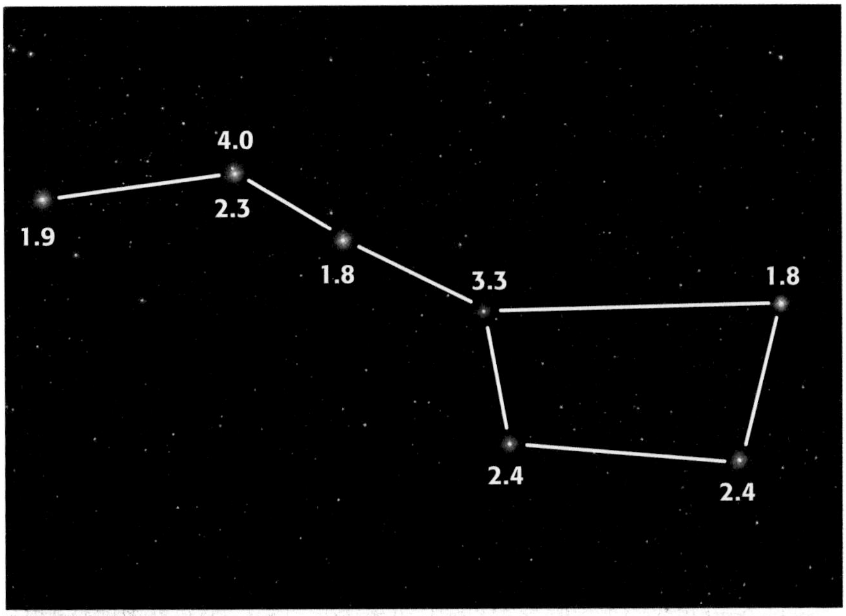

Figure 5 *You can estimate how far away each street light is by looking at its apparent brightness. Does this process work when estimating the distance of stars from Earth?*

apparent magnitude the brightness of a star as seen from the Earth

absolute magnitude the brightness that a star would have at a distance of 32.6 light-years from Earth

How Bright Is That Star?

If you look at a row of street lights, such as those shown in **Figure 5,** do they all look the same? Of course not! The nearest ones look bright, and the farthest ones look dim.

Apparent Magnitude

The brightness of a light or star is called **apparent magnitude.** If you measure the brightness of a street light with a light meter, you will find that the light's brightness depends on the square of the ratio between the light and the light meter. For example, a light that is 10 m away from you will appear 4 (2×2, or 2^2) times brighter than a light that is 20 m away from you. The same light will appear 9 (3×3, or 3^2) times brighter than a light that is 30 m away. But unlike street lights, some stars are brighter than other stars because of their size or energy output, not because of their distance from Earth. So, how can you tell how bright a star is and why?

Reading Check What is apparent magnitude?

Absolute Magnitude

Astronomers use a star's apparent magnitude and its distance from Earth to calculate its absolute magnitude. **Absolute magnitude** is the actual brightness of a star. If all stars were the same distance away, their absolute magnitudes would be the same as their apparent magnitudes. The sun, for example, has an absolute magnitude of +4.8, which is ordinary for a star. But because the sun is so close to Earth, the sun's apparent magnitude is −26.8, which makes it the brightest object in the sky.

MATH PRACTICE

Starlight, Star Bright

Magnitude is used to show how bright one object is compared with another object. Every five magnitudes is equal to a factor of 100 times in brightness. The brightest blue stars, for example, have an absolute magnitude of −10. The sun has an absolute magnitude of about +5. How much brighter is a blue star than the sun? Because each five magnitudes is a factor of 100 and the blue star is 15 magnitudes greater than the sun, the blue star must be $100 \times 100 \times 100$, or 1,000,000 (1 million), times brighter than the sun!

Figure 6 Measuring a Star's Parallax

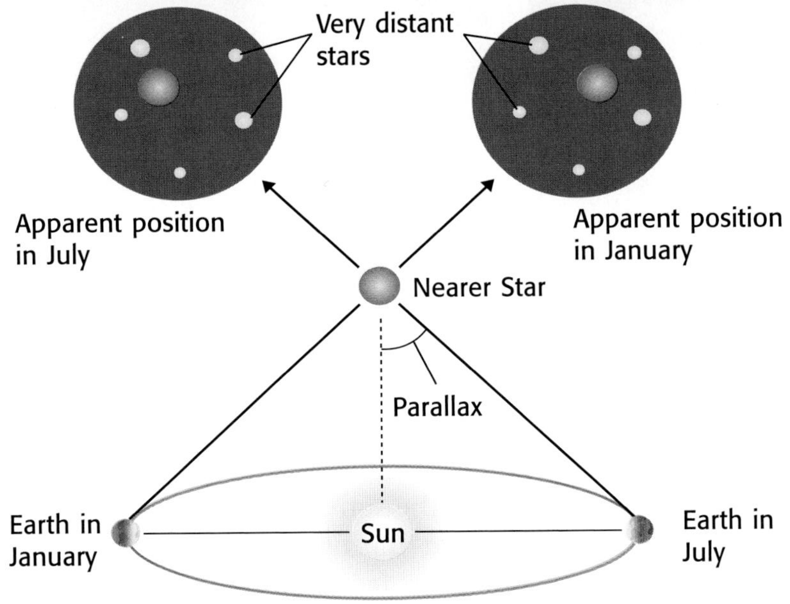

light-year the distance that light travels in one year; about 9.5 trillion kilometers

parallax an apparent shift in the position of an object when viewed from different locations

Distance to the Stars

Because stars are so far away, astronomers use light-years to measure the distances from Earth to the stars. A **light-year** is the distance that light travels in one year. Obviously, it would be easier to give the distance to the North Star as 431 light-years than as 4,080,000,000,000,000 km. But how do astronomers measure a star's distance from Earth?

Stars near the Earth seem to move, while more-distant stars seem to stay in one place as Earth revolves around the sun, as shown in **Figure 6.** A star's apparent shift in position is called **parallax.** Notice that the location of the nearer star in **Figure 6** seems to shift in relation to the pattern of more-distant stars. This shift can be seen only through telescopes. Astronomers use parallax and simple trigonometry (a type of math) to find the actual distance to stars that are close to Earth.

Reading Check What is a light-year?

Motions of Stars

As you know, daytime and nighttime are caused by the Earth's rotation. The Earth's tilt and revolution around the sun cause the seasons. During each season, the Earth faces a different part of the sky at night. Look again at **Figure 6.** In January, the Earth's night side faces a different part of the sky than it faces in July. This is why you see a different set of constellations at different times of the year.

Quick Lab

Not All Thumbs!

1. Hold your thumb in front of your face at arm's length.
2. Close one eye, and focus on an **object** some distance behind your thumb.
3. Slowly turn your head side to side a small amount. Notice how your thumb seems to be moving compared with the background you are looking at.
4. Now, move your thumb in close to your face, and move your head the same amount. Does your thumb seem to move more?

Figure 7 *As Earth rotates on its axis, the stars appear to rotate around Polaris.*

The Apparent Motion of Stars

Because of Earth's rotation, the sun appears to move across the sky. Likewise, if you look at the night sky long enough, the stars also appear to move. In fact, at night you can observe that the whole sky is rotating above us. Look at **Figure 7.** All the stars you see appear to rotate around Polaris, the North Star, which is almost directly above Earth's North Pole. Because of Earth's rotation, all of the stars in the sky appear to make one complete circle around Polaris every 24 h.

INTERNET ACTIVITY

For another activity related to this chapter, go to **go.hrw.com** and type in the keyword **HZ5UNVW.**

The Actual Motion of Stars

You now know that the apparent motion of the sun and stars in our sky is due to Earth's rotation. But each star is also moving in space. Because stars are so distant, however, their actual motion is hard to see. If you could put thousands of years into one hour, a star's movement would be obvious. **Figure 8** shows how familiar star patterns slowly change their shapes.

Reading Check **Why is the actual motion of stars hard to see?**

Figure 8 *Over time, the shapes of star patterns, such as the Big Dipper and other groups, change.*

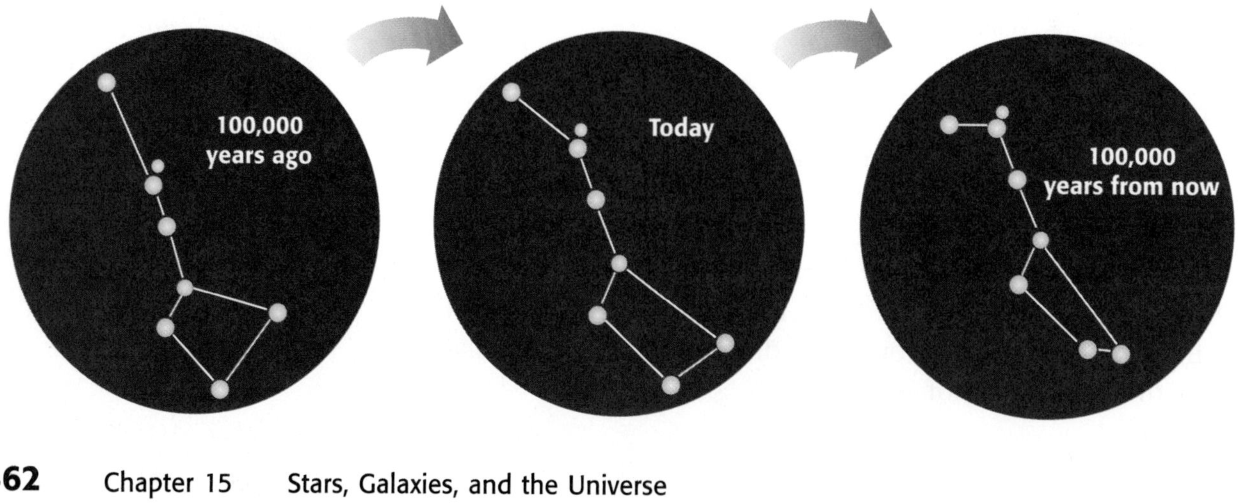

SECTION Review

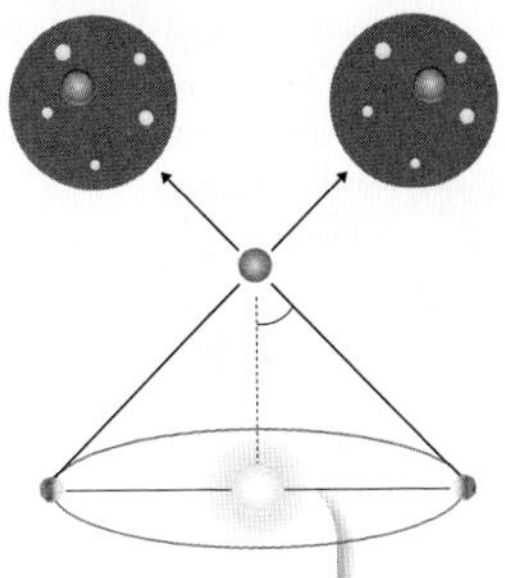

Summary

- The color of a star depends on its temperature. Hot stars are blue. Cool stars are red.
- The spectrum of a star shows the composition of a star.
- Scientists classify stars by temperature and brightness.
- Apparent magnitude is the brightness of a star as seen from Earth.
- Absolute magnitude is the measured brightness of a star at a distance of 32.6 light-years.
- Astronomers use parallax and trigonometry to measure distances from Earth to stars.
- Stars appear to move because of Earth's rotation. However, the actual motion of stars is very hard to see because stars are so distant.

Using Key Terms

1. Use the following terms in the same sentence: *apparent magnitude* and *absolute magnitude*.
2. Use each of the following terms in a separate sentence: *spectrum, light-year,* and *parallax*.

Understanding Key Ideas

3. When you look at white light through a glass prism, you see a rainbow of colors called a
   - **a.** spectograph.
   - **b.** spectrum.
   - **c.** parallax.
   - **d.** light-year.
4. Class F stars are
   - **a.** blue.
   - **b.** yellow.
   - **c.** yellow-white.
   - **d.** red.
5. Describe how scientists classify stars.
6. Explain how color indicates the temperature of a star.

Critical Thinking

7. **Applying Concepts** If a certain star displayed a large parallax, what could you say about the star's distance from Earth?
8. **Making Comparisons** Compare a continuous spectrum with an absorption spectrum. Then, explain how an absorption spectrum can identify a star's composition.
9. **Making Comparisons** Compare apparent motion with actual motion.

Interpreting Graphics

10. Look at the two figures below. How many hours passed between the first image and the second image? Explain your answer.

SECTION 2

The Life Cycle of Stars

Some stars exist for billions of years. But how are they born? And what happens when a star dies?

What You Will Learn

- Describe different types of stars.
- Describe the quantities that are plotted in the H-R diagram.
- Explain how stars at different stages in their life cycle appear on the H-R diagram.

Vocabulary

red giant
white dwarf
H-R diagram
main sequence
supernova
neutron star
pulsar
black hole

READING STRATEGY

Paired Summarizing Read this section silently. In pairs, take turns summarizing the material. Stop to discuss ideas that seem confusing.

Because stars exist for billions of years, scientists cannot observe a star throughout its entire life. Therefore, scientists have developed theories about the life cycle of stars by studying them in different stages of development.

The Beginning and End of Stars

A star enters the first stage of its life cycle as a ball of gas and dust. Gravity pulls the gas and dust together into a sphere. As the sphere becomes denser, it gets hotter and the hydrogen changes to helium in a process called *nuclear fusion.*

As stars get older, they lose some of their material. Stars usually lose material slowly, but sometimes they can lose material in a big explosion. Either way, when a star dies, much of its material returns to space. In space, some of the material combines with more gas and dust to form new stars.

Different Types of Stars

Stars can be classified by their size, mass, brightness, color, temperature, spectrum, and age. Some types of stars include *main-sequence stars*, *giants*, *supergiants*, and *white dwarf stars*. A star can be classified as one type of star early in its life cycle and then can be classified as another star when it gets older. For example, the star shown in **Figure 1** has reached the final stage in its life cycle. It has run out of fuel, which has caused the central parts of the star to collapse inward.

Figure 1 *This star (center) has entered the last stage of its life cycle.*

Main-Sequence Stars

After a star forms, it enters the second and longest stage of its life cycle known as the main sequence. During this stage, energy is generated in the core of the star as hydrogen atoms fuse into helium atoms. This process releases an enormous amount of energy. The size of a main-sequence star will change very little as long as the star has a continuous supply of hydrogen atoms to fuse into helium atoms.

Figure 2 *The red supergiant star Antares is shown above. Antares is located in the constellation of Scorpius.*

Giants and Supergiants

After the main-sequence stage, a star can enter the third stage of its life cycle. In this third stage, a star can become a red giant. A **red giant** is a star that expands and cools once it uses all of its hydrogen. Eventually, the loss of hydrogen causes the center of the star to shrink. As the center of the star shrinks, the atmosphere of the star grows very large and cools to form a red giant or a red supergiant, as shown in **Figure 2.** Red giants can be 10 or more times bigger than the sun. Supergiants are at least 100 times bigger than the sun.

Reading Check **What is the difference between a red giant star and a red supergiant star?** *(See the Appendix for answers to Reading Checks.)*

red giant a large, reddish star late in its life cycle

white dwarf a small, hot, dim star that is the leftover center of an old star

White Dwarfs

In the final stages of a star's life cycle, a star that has the same mass as the sun or smaller can be classified as a white dwarf. A **white dwarf** is a small hot star that is the leftover center of an older star. A white dwarf has no hydrogen left and can no longer generate energy by fusing hydrogen atoms into helium atoms. White dwarfs can shine for billions of years before they cool completely.

CONNECTION TO Astronomy

WRITING SKILL **Long Live the Sun** Our sun probably took about 10 million years to become a main-sequence star. It has been shining for about 5 billion years. In another 5 billion years, our sun will burn up most of its hydrogen and expand to become a red giant. When this change happens, the sun's diameter will increase. How will this change affect Earth and our solar system? Use the Internet or library resources to find out what might happen as the sun gets older and how the changes in the sun might affect our solar system. Gather your findings, and write a report on what you find out about the life cycle the sun.

A Tool for Studying Stars

In 1911, a Danish astronomer named Ejnar Hertzsprung (IE nawr HUHRTS sproong) compared the brightness and temperature of stars on a graph. Two years later, American astronomer Henry Norris Russell made some similar graphs. Although these astronomers used different data, they had similar results. The combination of their ideas is now called the Hertzsprung-Russell diagram, or H-R diagram. The **H-R diagram** is a graph that shows the relationship between a star's surface temperature and its absolute magnitude. Over the years, the H-R diagram has become a tool for studying the lives of stars. It shows not only how stars are classified by brightness and temperature but also how stars change over time.

H-R diagram Hertzsprung-Russell diagram, a graph that shows the relationship between a star's surface temperature and absolute magnitude

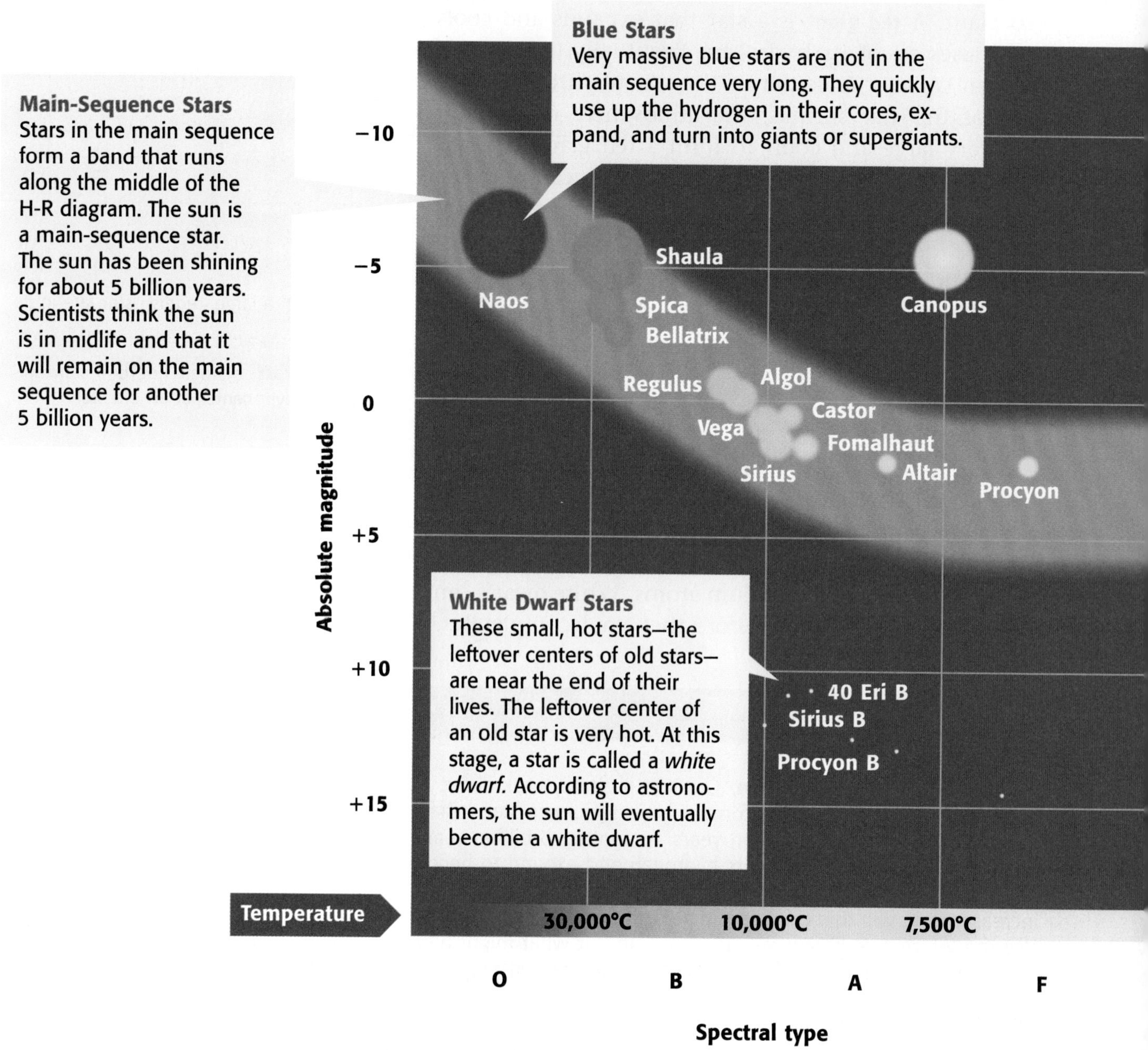
Blue Stars
Very massive blue stars are not in the main sequence very long. They quickly use up the hydrogen in their cores, expand, and turn into giants or supergiants.
Main-Sequence Stars
Stars in the main sequence form a band that runs along the middle of the H-R diagram. The sun is a main-sequence star. The sun has been shining for about 5 billion years. Scientists think the sun is in midlife and that it will remain on the main sequence for another 5 billion years.
−10
−5
0
+5
+10
+15
Absolute magnitude
Naos
Shaula
Spica
Bellatrix
Canopus
Regulus
Algol
Castor
Vega
Fomalhaut
Sirius
Altair
Procyon
White Dwarf Stars
These small, hot stars—the leftover centers of old stars—are near the end of their lives. The leftover center of an old star is very hot. At this stage, a star is called a *white dwarf.* According to astronomers, the sun will eventually become a white dwarf.
40 Eri B
Sirius B
Procyon B
Temperature
30,000°C
10,000°C
7,500°C
O
B
A
F
Spectral type

Reading the H-R Diagram

The modern H-R diagram is shown below. Temperature is given along the bottom of the diagram and absolute magnitude, or brightness, is given along the left side. Hot (blue) stars are located on the left, and cool (red) stars are on the right. Bright stars are at the top, and dim stars are at the bottom. The brightest stars are 1 million times brighter than the sun. The dimmest stars are 1/10,000 as bright as the sun. The diagonal pattern on the H-R diagram where most stars lie, is called the **main sequence.** A star spends most of its lifetime in the main sequence. As main-sequence stars age, they move up and to the right on the H-R diagram to become giants or supergiants and then down and to the left to become white dwarfs.

main sequence the location on the H-R diagram where most stars lie

Giants and Supergiants
When a star runs out of hydrogen in its core, the center of the star shrinks inward and the outer parts expand outward. For a star the size of our sun, the star's atmosphere will grow very large and become cool. When this change happens, the star becomes a *red giant.* If the star is very massive, it becomes a supergiant.

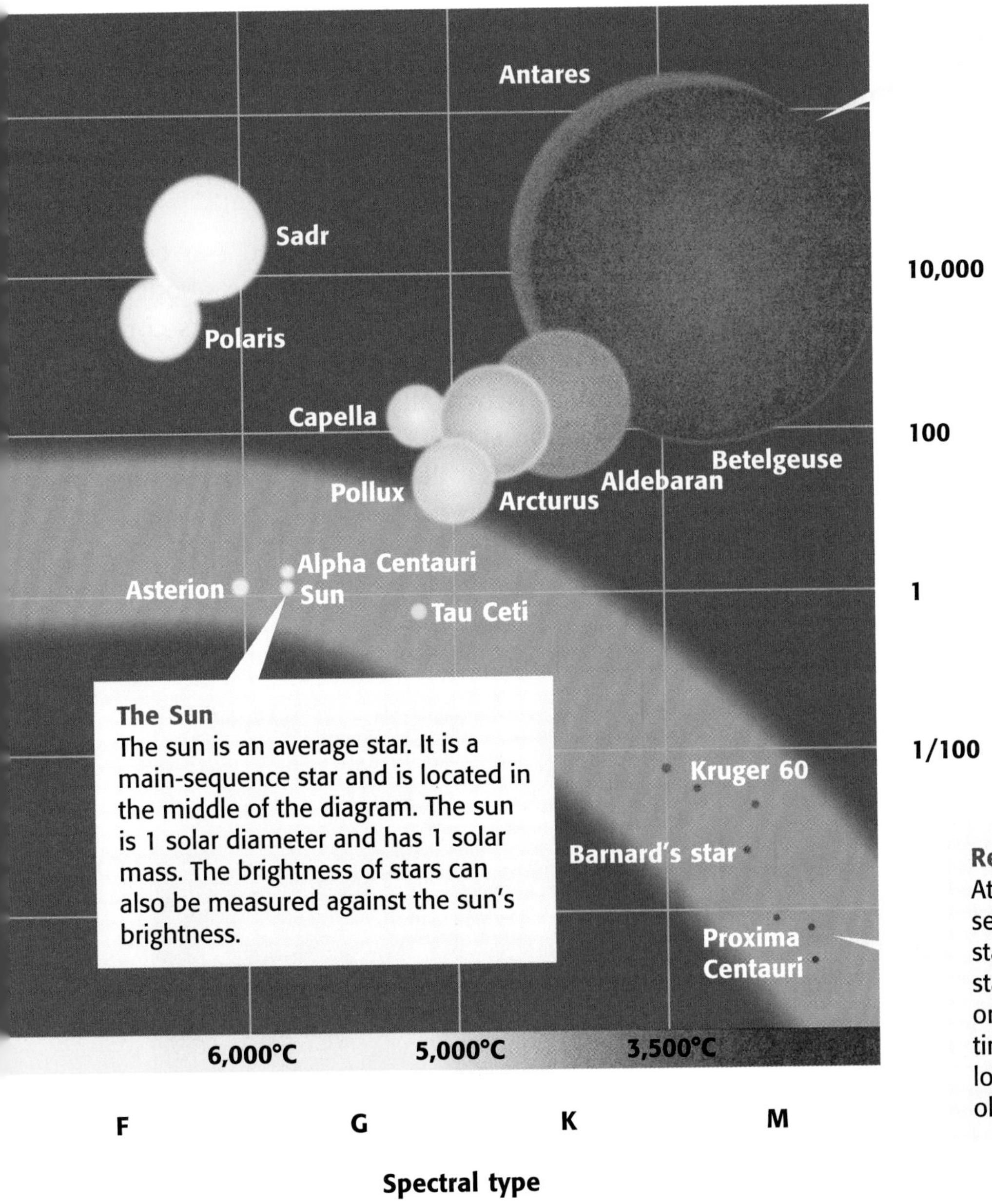

Red Dwarf Stars
At the lower end of the main sequence are the red dwarf stars, which are low-mass stars. Low-mass stars remain on the main sequence a long time. The stars that have the lowest mass are among the oldest stars in the universe.

When Stars Get Old

Although stars may stay on the main sequence for a long time, they don't stay there forever. Average stars, such as the sun, become red giants and then white dwarfs. However, stars that are more massive than the sun may explode with such intensity that they become a variety of strange objects such as supernovas, neutron stars, pulsars, and black holes.

Supernovas

Massive stars use their hydrogen much faster than stars like the sun do. As a result, massive stars generate more energy than stars like the sun do and thus are very hot! And compared with other stars, massive stars don't have long lives.

At the end of its life, a massive star may explode in a large, bright flash called a *supernova.* A **supernova** is a gigantic explosion in which a massive star collapses and throws its outer layers into space. The explosion is so powerful that it can be brighter than an entire galaxy for several days. The ringed structure shown in **Figure 3** is the result of a supernova.

supernova a gigantic explosion in which a massive star collapses and throws its outer layers into space

neutron star a star that has collapsed under gravity to the point that the electrons and protons have smashed together to form neutrons

pulsar a rapidly spinning neutron star that emits rapid pulses of radio and optical energy

Neutron Stars and Pulsars

Following a supernova, the center of the collapsed star contracts to form a new star. The mass of this new star is about 2 times the mass of the sun. The particles inside the star's core are forced together to form neutrons. A star that has collapsed under gravity to the point at which all of the star's particles are neutrons is called a **neutron star.**

If a neutron star is spinning, it is called a **pulsar.** A pulsar sends out a beam of radiation that sweeps across space. The beam is detected on Earth by radio telescopes as rapid clicks, or pulses.

Figure 3 Explosion of a Supernova

Supernova 1987A was the first supernova visible to the unaided eye in 400 years. The first image shows what the original star must have looked like only a few hours before the explosion. Today, the star's remains form a double ring of gas and dust, as shown at right.

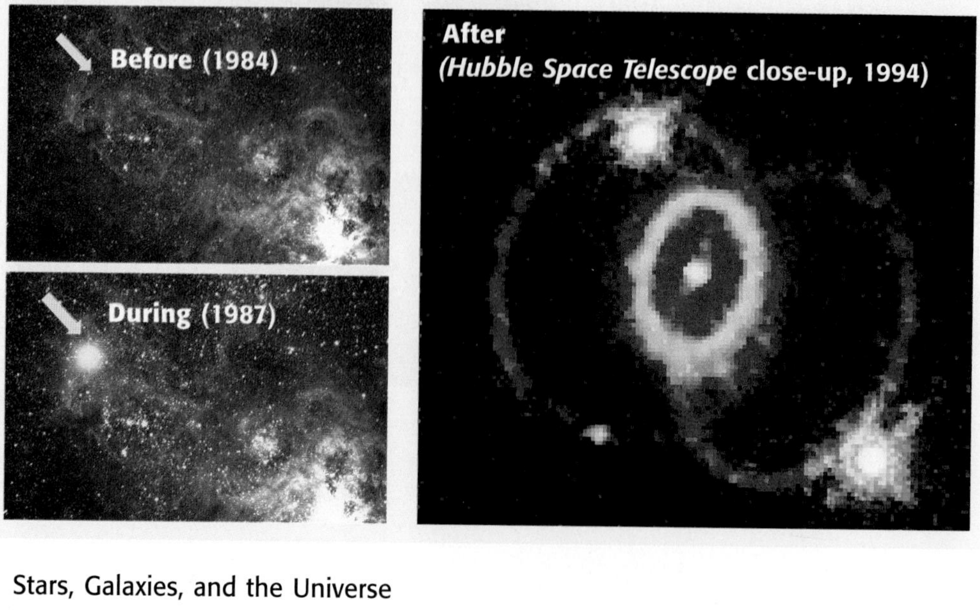

Black Holes

If the center of a collapsed star has a mass that is more than 3 times the mass of the sun, the star may contract further because of the strength of its gravity. The force of the contraction crushes the dense center of the star and leaves a black hole. A **black hole** is an object that is so massive that light cannot escape its gravity.

Because black holes do not give off light, locating them is difficult. If a star is nearby, some gas or dust from the star will spiral into the black hole and give off X rays. These X rays allow astronomers to detect the existence of black holes.

black hole an object so massive and dense that even light cannot escape its gravity

Reading Check **What is a black hole? How do astronomers detect the presence of black holes?**

SECTION Review

Summary

- New stars form from the material of old stars that have gone through their lives.
- Types of stars include main-sequence stars, giants and supergiants, and white dwarf stars.
- The H-R diagram shows the brightness of a star in relation to the temperature of a star. It also shows the life cycle of stars.
- Most stars are main-sequence stars.
- Massive stars become supernovas. Their cores can change into neutron stars or black holes.

Using Key Terms

For each pair of terms, explain how the meanings of the terms differ.

1. *white dwarf* and *red giant*
2. *supernova* and *neutron star*
3. *pulsar* and *black hole*

Understanding Key Ideas

4. The sun is a
   a. white dwarf.
   b. main-sequence star.
   c. red giant.
   d. red dwarf.
5. A star begins as a ball of gas and dust pulled together by
   a. black holes.
   b. electrons and protons.
   c. heavy metals.
   d. gravity.
6. Are blue stars young or old? How can you tell?
7. In main-sequence stars, what is the relationship between brightness and temperature?
8. Arrange the following stages in order of their appearance in the life cycle of a star: white dwarf, red giant, and main-sequence star. Explain your answer.

Math Skills

9. The sun's present radius is 700,000 km. If the sun's radius increased by 150 times, what would its radius be?

Critical Thinking

10. **Applying Concepts** Given that there are more low-mass stars than high-mass stars in the universe, do you think there are more white dwarfs or more black holes in the universe? Explain.
11. **Analyzing Processes** Describe what might happen to a star after it becomes a supernova.
12. **Evaluating Data** How does the H-R diagram explain the life cycle of a star?

SciLinks® NSTA Developed and maintained by the National Science Teachers Association

For a variety of links related to this chapter, go to www.scilinks.org

Topic: Supernova
SciLinks code: HSM1482

SECTION 3

Galaxies

What You Will Learn

- Identify three types of galaxies.
- Describe the contents and characteristics of galaxies.
- Explain why looking at distant galaxies reveals what young galaxies looked like.

Vocabulary

galaxy
nebula
globular cluster
open cluster
quasar

READING STRATEGY

Reading Organizer As you read this section, make a table comparing the different types of galaxies.

Your complete address is part of a much larger system than your street, city, state, country, and even the planet Earth. You also live in the Milky Way galaxy.

Large groups of stars, dust, and gas are called **galaxies.** Galaxies come in a variety of sizes and shapes. The largest galaxies contain more than a trillion stars. Astronomers don't count the stars, of course. They estimate how many sun-sized stars the galaxy might have by studying the size and brightness of the galaxy.

galaxy a collection of stars, dust, and gas bound together by gravity

Types of Galaxies

There are many different types of galaxies. Edwin Hubble, the astronomer for whom the *Hubble Space Telescope* is named, began to classify galaxies, mostly by their shapes, in the 1920s. Astronomers still use the galaxy classification that Hubble developed.

Spiral Galaxies

When someone says the word *galaxy,* most people probably think of a spiral galaxy. *Spiral galaxies,* such as the one shown in **Figure 1,** have a bulge at the center and spiral arms. The spiral arms are made up of gas, dust, and new stars that have formed in these denser regions of gas and dust.

Reading Check **What are two characteristics of spiral galaxies? What makes up the arms of a spiral galaxy?** (*See the Appendix for answers to Reading Checks.*)

Figure 1 **Types of Galaxies**

Spiral Galaxy
The Andromeda galaxy is a spiral galaxy that looks similar to what our galaxy, the Milky Way, is thought to look like.

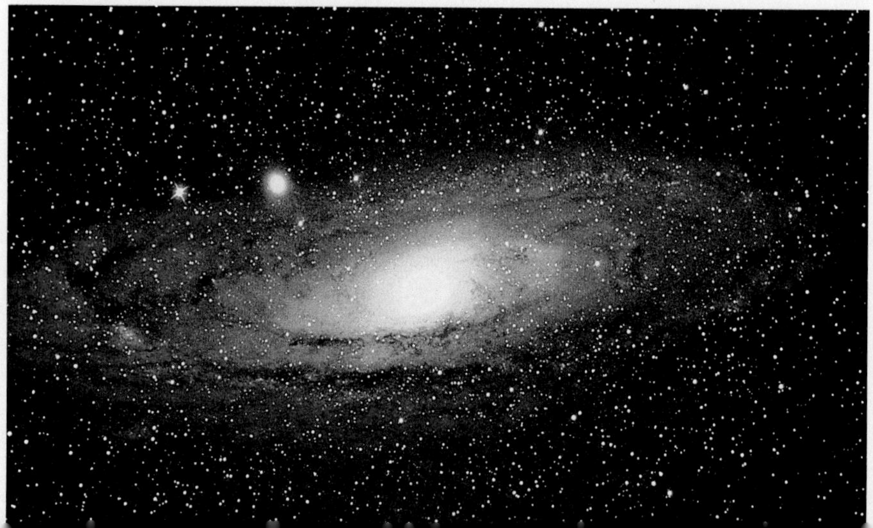

The Milky Way

It is hard to tell what type of galaxy we live in because the gas, dust, and stars keep astronomers from having a good view of our galaxy. Observing other galaxies and making measurements inside our galaxy, the Milky Way, has led astronomers to think that our solar system is in a spiral galaxy. The same elements, forces, and energy relationships that occur in the Milky Way appear to exist in other types of galaxies.

Elliptical Galaxies

About one-third of all galaxies are simply massive blobs of stars. Many look like spheres, and others are more stretched out. These galaxies are called *elliptical galaxies*. Elliptical galaxies usually have very bright centers and very little dust and gas. Elliptical galaxies contain mostly old stars. Because there is so little free-flowing gas in an elliptical galaxy, few new stars form. Some elliptical galaxies, such as M87, shown in **Figure 1,** are huge and are called *giant elliptical galaxies*. Other elliptical galaxies are much smaller and are called *dwarf elliptical galaxies*.

Irregular Galaxies

When Hubble first classified galaxies, he had a group of leftovers. He named the leftovers "irregulars." *Irregular galaxies* are galaxies that don't fit into any other class. As their name suggests, their shape is irregular. Many of these galaxies, such as the Large Magellanic Cloud, shown in **Figure 1,** are close companions of large spiral galaxies. The large spiral galaxies may be distorting the shape of these irregular galaxies.

CONNECTION TO Language Arts

WRITING SKILL **Alien Observer** As you read earlier, it's hard to tell what type of galaxy we live in because the gas, dust, and stars keep us from having a good view. But our galaxy might look different to an alien observer. Write a short story describing how our galaxy would look to an alien observer in another galaxy.

Elliptical Galaxy
Unlike the Milky Way, the galaxy known as M87 has no spiral arms.

Irregular Galaxy
The Large Magellanic Cloud, an irregular galaxy, is located within our galactic neighborhood.

Contents of Galaxies

Galaxies are composed of billions of stars and some planetary systems, too. Some of these stars form large features, such as gas clouds and star clusters, as shown in **Figure 2.**

Gas Clouds

nebula a large cloud of dust and gas in interstellar space; a region in space where stars are born or where stars explode at the end of their lives

globular cluster a tight group of stars that looks like a ball and contains up to 1 million stars

open cluster a group of stars that are close together relative to surrounding stars

The Latin word for "cloud" is *nebula*. In space, **nebulas** (or nebulae) are large clouds of gas and dust. Some types of nebulas glow, while others absorb light and hide stars. Still, other nebulas reflect starlight and produce some amazing images. Some nebulas are regions in which new stars form. **Figure 2** shows part of the Eagle nebula. Spiral galaxies usually contain nebulas, but elliptical galaxies contain very few.

Star Clusters

Globular clusters are groups of older stars. A **globular cluster** is a group of stars that looks like a ball, as shown in **Figure 2.** There may be up to one million stars in a globular cluster. Globular clusters are located in a spherical *halo* that surrounds spiral galaxies such as the Milky Way. Globular clusters are also common near giant elliptical galaxies.

Open clusters are groups of closely grouped stars that are usually located along the spiral disk of a galaxy. Newly formed open clusters have many bright blue stars, as shown in **Figure 2.** There may be a few hundred to a few thousand stars in an open cluster.

Reading Check What is the difference between a globular cluster and an open cluster?

Figure 2 Gas Clouds and Star Clusters

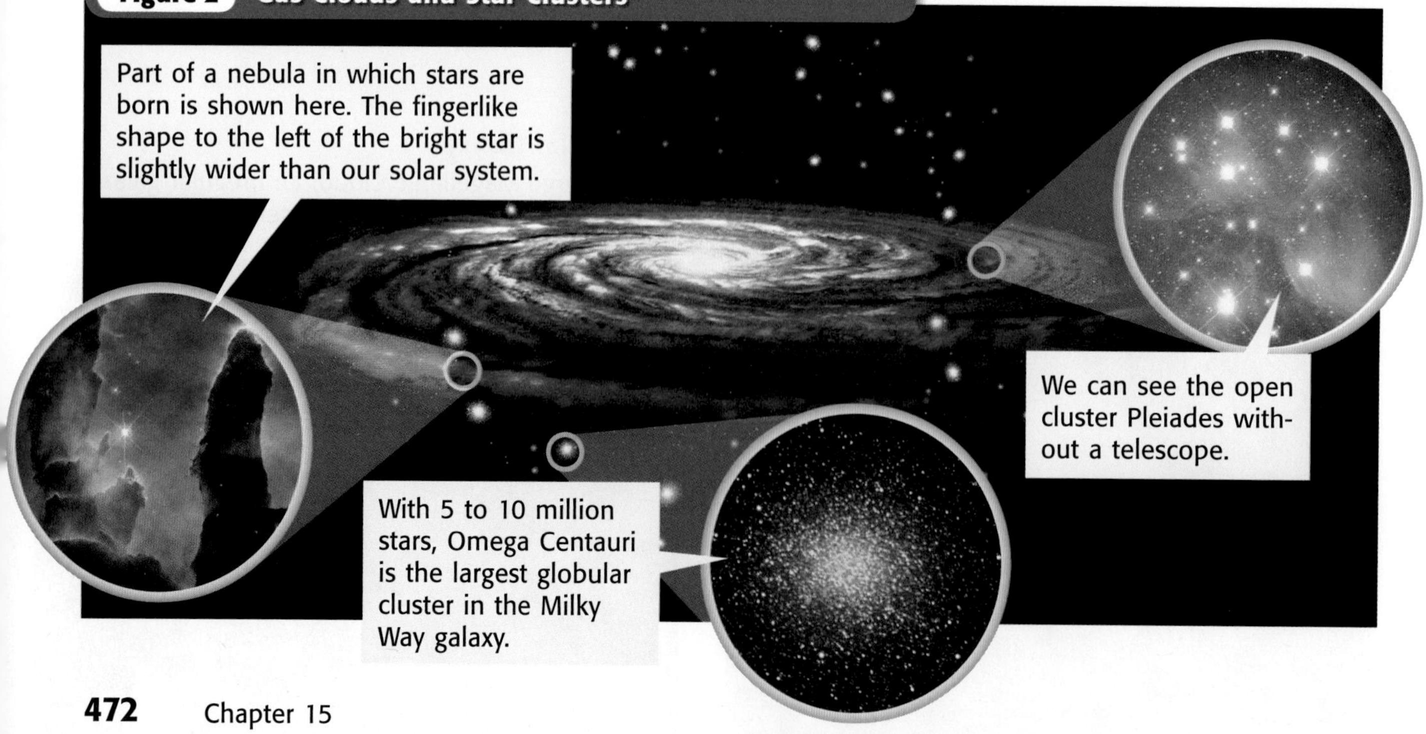

Part of a nebula in which stars are born is shown here. The fingerlike shape to the left of the bright star is slightly wider than our solar system.
We can see the open cluster Pleiades without a telescope.
With 5 to 10 million stars, Omega Centauri is the largest globular cluster in the Milky Way galaxy.

Origin of Galaxies

Scientists investigate the early universe by observing objects that are extremely far away in space. Because it takes time for light to travel through space, looking through a telescope is like looking back in time. Looking at distant galaxies reveals what early galaxies looked like. This information gives scientists an idea of how galaxies change over time and may give them insight about what caused the galaxies to form.

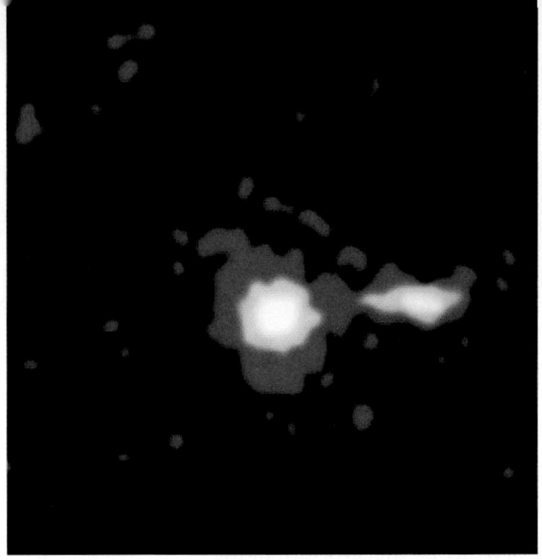

Figure 3 *The quasar known as PKS 0637-752 is as massive as 10 billion suns.*

Quasars

Among the most distant objects are quasars. **Quasars** are starlike sources of light that are extremely far away. They are among the most powerful energy sources in the universe. Some scientists think that quasars may be caused by massive black holes in the cores of some galaxies. **Figure 3** shows a quasar that is 6 billion light-years away.

quasar a very luminous, starlike object that generates energy at a high rate; quasars are thought to be the most distant objects in the universe

Reading Check **What are quasars? What do some scientists think quasars might be?**

SECTION Review

Summary

- Edwin Hubble classified galaxies according to their shape including spiral, elliptical, and irregular galaxies.
- Some galaxies consist of nebulas and star clusters.
- Nebulas are large clouds of gas and dust. Globular clusters are tightly grouped stars. Open clusters are closely grouped stars.
- Scientists look at distant galaxies to learn what early galaxies looked like.

Using Key Terms

1. Use the following terms in the same sentence: *nebula, globular cluster,* and *open cluster.*

Understanding Key Ideas

2. Arrange the following galaxies in order of decreasing size: spiral, giant elliptical, dwarf elliptical, and irregular.
3. All of the following are shapes used to classify galaxies EXCEPT
   a. elliptical.
   b. irregular.
   c. spiral.
   d. triangular.

Critical Thinking

4. **Making Comparisons** Describe the difference between an elliptical galaxy and a globular cluster.
5. **Identifying Relationships** Explain how looking through a telescope is like looking back in time.

Math Skills

6. The quasar known as PKS 0637-752 is 6 billion light-years away from Earth. The North Star is 431 light-years away from Earth. What is the ratio of the distances in kilometers these two celestial objects are from Earth? (Hint: One light-year is equal to 9.46 trillion km.)

SECTION 4

Formation of the Universe

What You Will Learn

- Describe the big bang theory.
- Explain evidence used to support the big bang theory.
- Describe the structure of the universe.
- Describe two ways scientists calculate the age of the universe.
- Explain what will happen if the universe expands forever.

Vocabulary

cosmology
big bang theory

READING STRATEGY

Prediction Guide Before reading this section, write the title of each heading in this section. Next, under each heading, write what you think you will learn.

Imagine explosions, bright lights, and intense energy. Does that scene sound like an action movie? This scene could also describe a theory about the formation of the universe.

The study of the origin, structure, and future of the universe is called **cosmology.** Like other scientific theories, theories about the beginning and end of the universe must be tested by observations or experiments.

cosmology the study of the origin, properties, processes, and evolution of the universe

Universal Expansion

To understand how the universe formed, scientists study the movement of galaxies. Careful measurements have shown that most galaxies are moving apart.

A Raisin-Bread Model

To understand how the galaxies are moving, imagine a loaf of raisin bread before it is baked. Inside the dough, each raisin is a certain distance from every other raisin. As the dough gets warm and rises, it expands and all of the raisins begin to move apart. No matter which raisin you observe, the other raisins are moving farther away from it. The universe, like the rising bread dough, is expanding. Think of the raisins as galaxies. As the universe expands, the galaxies move farther apart.

The Big Bang Theory

With the discovery that the universe is expanding, scientists began to wonder what it would be like to watch the formation of the universe in reverse. The universe would appear to be contracting, not expanding. All matter would eventually come together at a single point. Thinking about what would happen if all of the matter in the universe were squeezed into such a small space led scientists to the big bang theory.

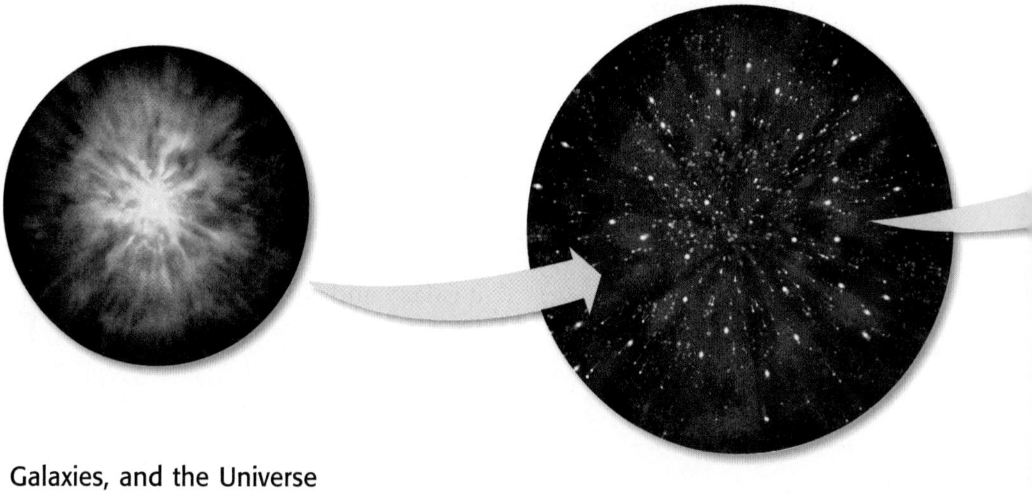

Figure 1 *Some astronomers think the big bang caused the universe to expand in all directions.*

A Tremendous Explosion

The theory that the universe began with a tremendous explosion is called the **big bang theory.** According to the theory, 13.7 billion years ago all the contents of the universe was compressed under extreme pressure, temperature, and density in a very tiny spot. Then, the universe rapidly expanded, and matter began to come together and form galaxies. **Figure 1** illustrates what the big bang might have looked like.

big bang theory the theory that states the universe began with a tremendous explosion 13.7 billion years ago

Cosmic Background Radiation

In 1964, two scientists using a huge antenna accidentally found radiation coming from all directions in space. One explanation for this radiation is that it is *cosmic background radiation* left over from the big bang. To understand the connection between the big bang theory and cosmic background radiation, think about a kitchen oven. When an oven door is left open after the oven has been used, thermal energy is transferred throughout the kitchen and the oven cools. Eventually, the room and the oven are the same temperature. According to the big bang theory, the thermal energy from the original explosion was distributed in every direction as the universe expanded. This cosmic background radiation now fills all of space.

Reading Check **Explain the relationship between cosmic background radiation and the big bang theory.** (*See the Appendix for answers to Reading Checks.*)

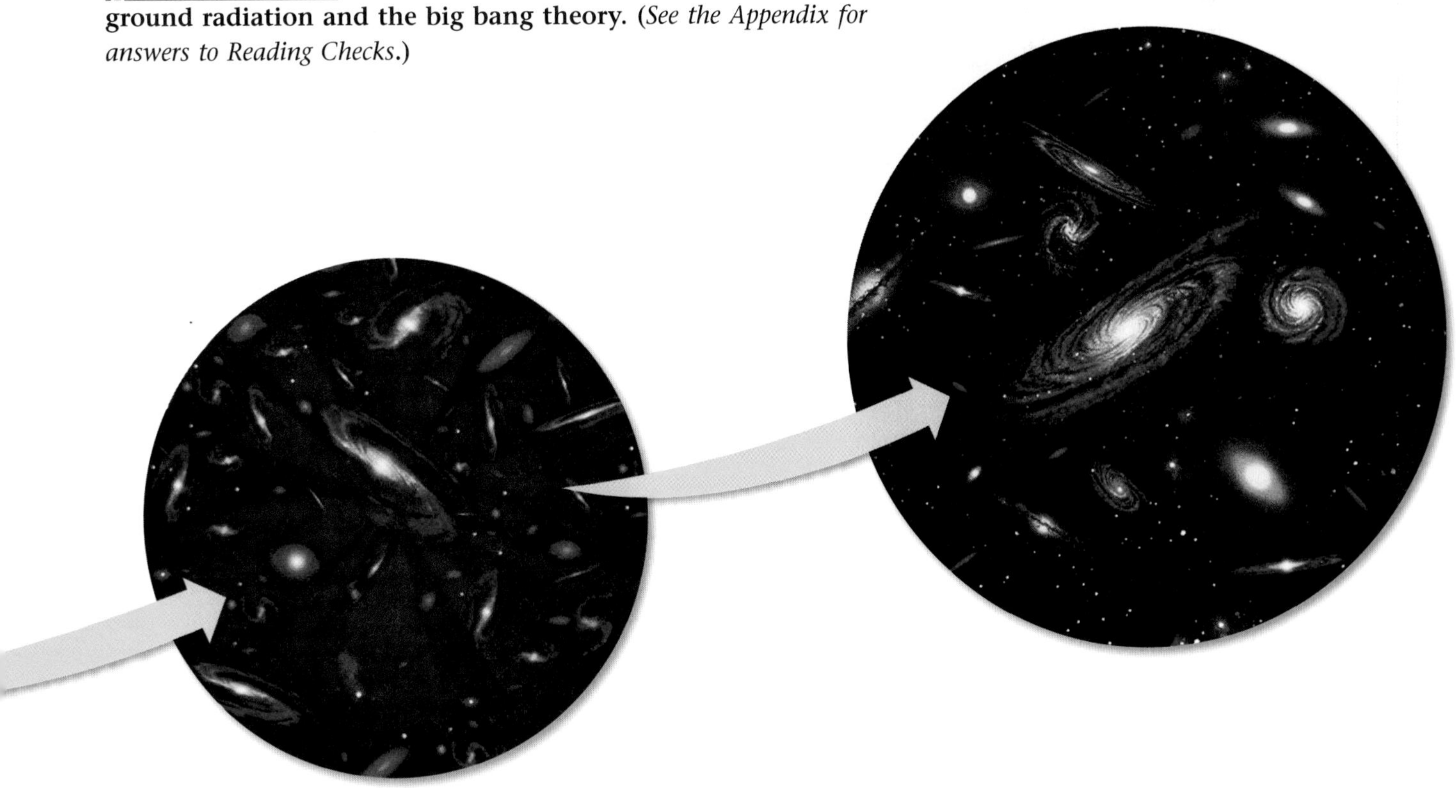

Structure of the Universe

From our home on Earth, the universe stretches out farther than astronomers can see with their most advanced instruments. The universe contains a variety of objects. But these objects in the universe are not simply scattered through the universe in a random pattern. The universe has a structure that is loosely repeated over and over again.

A Cosmic Repetition

Every object in the universe is part of a larger system. As illustrated in **Figure 2,** a cluster or group of galaxies can be made up of smaller star clusters and galaxies. Galaxies, such as the Milky Way, can include planetary systems, such as our solar system. Earth is part of our solar system. Although our solar system is the planetary system that we are most familiar with, other planets have been detected in orbit around other stars. Scientists think that planetary systems are common in the universe.

How Old Is the Universe?

One way scientists can calculate the age of the universe is to measure the distance from Earth to various galaxies. By using these distances, scientists can estimate the age of the universe and predict its rate of expansion.

Another way to estimate the age of the universe is to calculate the ages of old, nearby stars. Because the universe must be at least as old as the oldest stars it contains, the ages of the stars provide a clue to the age of the universe.

Reading Check **What is one way that scientists calculate the age of the universe?**

Figure 2 *Every object in the universe is part of a larger system. Earth is part of our solar system, which is in turn part of the Milky Way galaxy.*

A Forever Expanding Universe

What will happen to the universe? As the galaxies move farther apart, they get older and stop forming stars. The farther galaxies move apart from each other, the less visible to us they will become. The expansion of the universe depends on how much matter the universe contains. Scientists predict that if there is enough matter, gravity could eventually stop the expansion of the universe. If the universe stops expanding, it could start collapsing to its original state. This process would be a reverse of what might have happened during the big bang.

However, scientists now think that there may not be enough matter in the universe, so the universe will continue to expand forever. Therefore, stars will age and die, and the universe will probably become cold and dark after many billions of years. Even after the universe becomes cold and dark, it will continue to expand forever.

Reading Check **If the universe expanded to the point at which gravity stopped the expansion, what would happen? What will happen if the expansion of the universe continues forever?**

CONNECTION TO Physics

WRITING SKILL **Origin of the Universe** The big bang theory is one scientific theory about the origin of the universe. Use library resources to research these other scientific theories. In your **science journal,** describe in your own words the different theories of the origin of the universe. Use charts or tables to examine and evaluate these differences.

SECTION Review

Summary

- Observations show that the universe is expanding.
- The big bang theory states that the universe began with an explosion about 13.7 billion years ago.
- Cosmic background radiation helps support the big bang theory.
- Scientists use different ways to calculate the age of the universe.
- Scientists think that the universe may expand forever.

Using Key Terms

1. In your own words, write a definition for the following terms: *cosmology* and *big bang theory.*

Understanding Key Ideas

2. Describe two ways scientists calculate the age of the universe.
3. The expansion of the universe can be compared to
   a. cosmology.
   b. raisin bread baking in an oven.
   c. thermal energy leaving an oven as the oven cools.
   d. bread pudding.
4. How does cosmic background radiation support the big bang theory?
5. What do scientists think will eventually happen to the universe?

Math Skills

6. The North Star is 4.08×10^{12} km from Earth. What is this number written in its long form?

Critical Thinking

7. **Applying Concepts** Explain how every object in the universe is part of a larger system.
8. **Analyzing Ideas** Why do scientists think that the universe will expand forever?

Using Scientific Methods

Skills Practice Lab

Red Hot, or Not?

OBJECTIVES

Discover what the color of a glowing object reveals about the temperature of the object.

Describe how the color and temperature of a star are related.

MATERIALS

- battery, D cell (2)
- battery, D cell, weak
- flashlight bulb
- tape, electrical
- wire, insulated copper, with ends stripped, 20 cm long (2)

SAFETY

When you look at the night sky, some stars are brighter than others. Some are even different colors. For example, Betelgeuse, a bright star in the constellation Orion, glows red. Sirius, one of the brightest stars in the sky, glows bluish white. Astronomers use color to estimate the temperature of stars. In this activity, you will experiment with a light bulb and some batteries to discover what the color of a glowing object reveals about the temperature of the object.

Ask a Question

1. How are the color and temperature of a star related?

Form a Hypothesis

2. On a sheet of paper, change the question above into a statement that gives your best guess about the relationship between a star's color and temperature.

Test the Hypothesis

3. Tape one end of an insulated copper wire to the positive pole of the weak D cell. Tape one end of the second wire to the negative pole.

4. Touch the free end of each wire to the light bulb. Hold one of the wires against the bottom tip of the light bulb. Hold the second wire against the side of the metal portion of the bulb. The bulb should light.

5. Record the color of the filament in the light bulb. Carefully touch your hand to the bulb. Observe the temperature of the bulb. Record your observations.

6. Repeat steps 3–5 with one of the two fresh D cells.

7. Use the electrical tape to connect two fresh D cells so that the positive pole of the first cell is connected to the negative pole of the second cell.

8. Repeat steps 3–5 using the fresh D cells that are taped together.

Analyze the Results

1. **Describing Events** What was the color of the filament in each of the three trials? For each trial, compare the bulb temperature to the temperature of the bulb in the other two trials.

2. **Analyzing Results** What information does the color of a star tell you about the star?

3. **Classifying** What color are stars that have relatively high surface temperatures? What color are stars that have relatively low surface temperatures?

Draw Conclusions

4. **Applying Conclusions** Arrange the following stars in order from highest to lowest surface temperature: Sirius, which is bluish white; Aldebaran, which is orange; Procyon, which is yellow-white; Capella, which is yellow; and Betelgeuse, which is red.

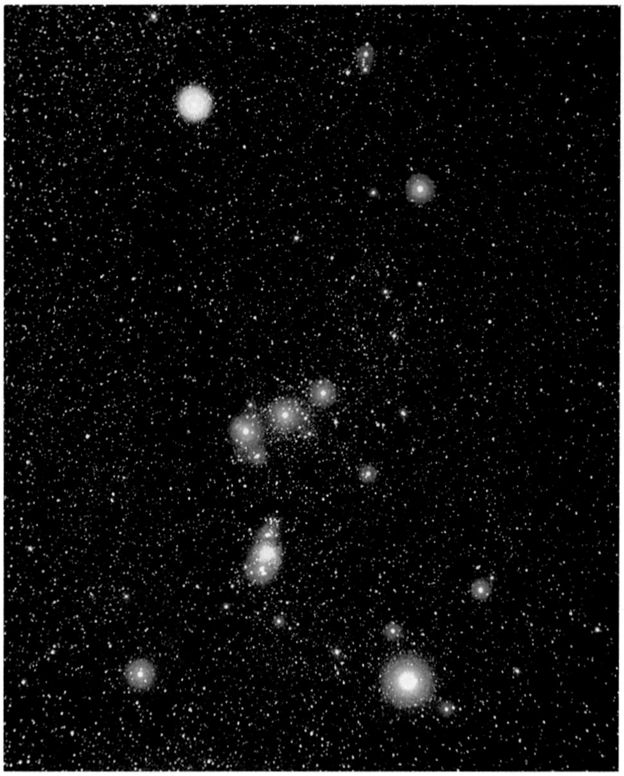

Chapter Review

USING KEY TERMS

The statements below are false. For each statement, replace the underlined term to make a true statement.

1. The distance that light travels in space in 1 year is called <u>apparent magnitude</u>.

2. <u>Globular clusters</u> are groups of stars that are usually located along the spiral disk of a galaxy.

3. Galaxies that have very bright centers and very little dust and gas are called <u>spiral galaxies</u>.

4. When you look at white light through a glass prism, you see a rainbow of colors called a <u>supernova</u>.

UNDERSTANDING KEY IDEAS

Multiple Choice

5. A scientist can identify a star's composition by looking at
   - **a.** the star's prism.
   - **b.** the star's continuous spectrum.
   - **c.** the star's absorption spectrum.
   - **d.** the star's color.

6. If the universe expands forever,
   - **a.** the universe will collapse.
   - **b.** the universe will repeat itself.
   - **c.** the universe will remain just as it is today.
   - **d.** stars will age and die and the universe will become cold and dark.

7. The majority of stars in our galaxy are
   - **a.** blue stars.
   - **b.** white dwarfs.
   - **c.** main-sequence stars.
   - **d.** red giants.

8. Which of the following is used to measure the distance between objects in space?
   - **a.** parallax
   - **b.** magnitude
   - **c.** zenith
   - **d.** altitude

9. Which of the following stars would be seen as the brightest star?
   - **a.** Alcyone, which has an apparent magnitude of 3
   - **b.** Alpheratz, which has an apparent magnitude of 2
   - **c.** Deneb, which has an apparent magnitude of 1
   - **d.** Rigel, which has an apparent magnitude of 0

Short Answer

10. Describe how scientists classify stars.

11. Describe the structure of the universe.

12. Explain how stars at different stages in their life cycle appear on the H-R diagram.

13. Explain the difference between the apparent motion and actual motion of stars.

14. Describe how color indicates the temperature of a star.

15. Describe two ways that scientists calculate the age of the universe.

CRITICAL THINKING

16 **Concept Mapping** Use the following terms to create a concept map: *main-sequence star, nebula, red giant, white dwarf, neutron star,* and *black hole.*

17 **Evaluating Conclusions** While looking through a telescope, you see a galaxy that doesn't appear to contain any blue stars. What kind of galaxy is it most likely to be? Explain your answer.

18 **Making Comparisons** Explain the differences between main-sequence stars, giant stars, supergiant stars, and white dwarfs.

19 **Evaluating Data** Why do astronomers use absolute magnitudes to plot stars? Why don't astronomers use apparent magnitudes to plot stars?

20 **Evaluating Sources** According to the big bang theory, how did the universe begin? What evidence supports this theory?

21 **Evaluating Data** If a certain star displayed a large parallax, what could you say about the star's distance from Earth?

INTERPRETING GRAPHICS

The graph below shows Hubble's law, which relates how far galaxies are from Earth and how fast they are moving away from Earth. Use the graph below to answer the questions that follow.

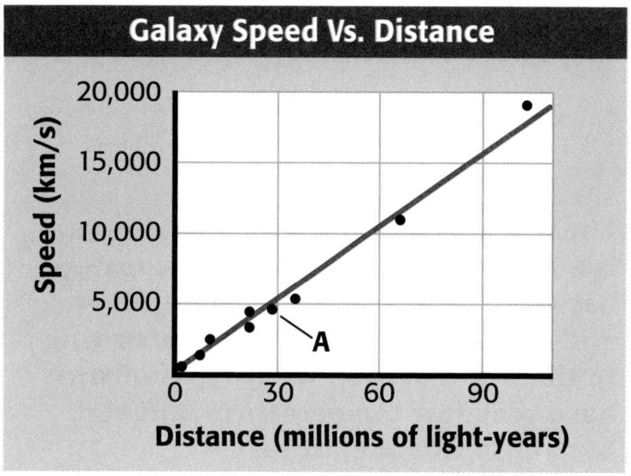

22 Look at the point that represents galaxy A in the graph. How far is galaxy A from Earth, and how fast is it moving away from Earth?

23 If a galaxy is moving away from Earth at 15,000 km/s, how far is the galaxy from Earth?

24 If a galaxy is 90,000,000 light-years from Earth, how fast is it moving away from Earth?

Standardized Test Preparation

Multiple Choice

1. The color of a star can indicate its surface temperature. Which of the following colors indicates to an astronomer that a star has a very high surface temperature?

A. blue

B. orange

C. red

D. yellow

2. The Hertzsprung-Russell (H-R) diagram is a graph that shows the relationship between a star's surface temperature and its absolute magnitude. According to the H-R diagram, what types of stars have very low temperatures and very high absolute magnitudes?

A. blue stars

B. red dwarfs

C. white dwarfs

D. giants and supergiants

3. Our solar system is located in the Milky Way. Which one of the following statements best describes the Milky Way?

A. a nebula containing about 200 billion stars

B. a spiral galaxy containing about 200 billion stars

C. an irregular galaxy containing about 200 billion stars

D. an elliptical galaxy containing about 200 billion stars

Use the images below to answer question 4.

Image I

Image II

Image III

Image IV

4. When an amateur astronomer from Kentucky discovered a nebula that is about 1,500 light-years from Earth, he saw the birth of a star that happened about 15 centuries ago. Which of the above images most closely represents a nebula?

A. Image I

B. Image II

C. Image III

D. Image IV

5. Astronomers believe that the sun has been shining for approximately 5 billion years and is in the middle of its life cycle. Astronomers estimate that in another 5 billion years, the sun will burn up most of its hydrogen fuel and will expand to become a red giant. At the very end of its life cycle, what kind of star will the sun become?

A. blue main sequence

B. red dwarf

C. supernova

D. white dwarf

Use the table below to answer question 6.

Limiting Magnitude	Actual Number of Stars Visible to the Unaided Eye	Light Pollution Level
+2.0	Less than 25	Extreme
+3.0	Less than 50	Severe
+4.0	Less than 250	Serious
+5.0	Approx. 800	Moderate
+6.0	Approx. 2,400	Some

6. Limiting magnitude is the magnitude of the dimmest star that can be seen from the Earth. The table above shows the number of stars that can be seen at night at different limiting magnitudes without using binoculars or a telescope. The limiting magnitude of the Louisville evening sky is approximately 3.8. Of the 7,000 stars that potentially can be seen, what percentage can actually be seen in Louisville at night?

A. approximately 0.07 percent

B. approximately 3.5 percent

C. approximately 11.5 percent

D. approximately 34 percent

7. Stars have different temperatures and different elemental compositions. Which one of the following properties of stars do astronomers use to determine both the temperature and composition of stars?

A. the absorption spectrum of stars

B. the absolute magnitude of stars

C. the apparent magnitude of stars

D. the apparent motion of stars

8. What happens to a star during its main-sequence stage?

A. Energy is generated in the star's core.

B. Gravity pulls gas and dust into a sphere.

C. No hydrogen is left in the star's core.

D. The center expands and then shrinks.

9. Which of the following statements best describes why a black hole is hard to locate?

A. Its absolute magnitude is a negative number.

B. Its core is filled with hydrogen and helium.

C. Its core is a cloud of gas and dust.

D. Its gravity does not allow any light to escape.

10. Why does the sun have the greatest apparent magnitude of any star?

A. It is closer to Earth than all of the other stars in the universe.

B. It is hotter than all of the other stars in the universe.

C. It is larger than all of the other stars in the universe.

D. It is older than all of the other stars in the universe.

Open Response

11. In what two ways do scientists calculate the age of the universe?

12. What do scientists predict will happen to the universe as the galaxies move farther apart?

Science in Action

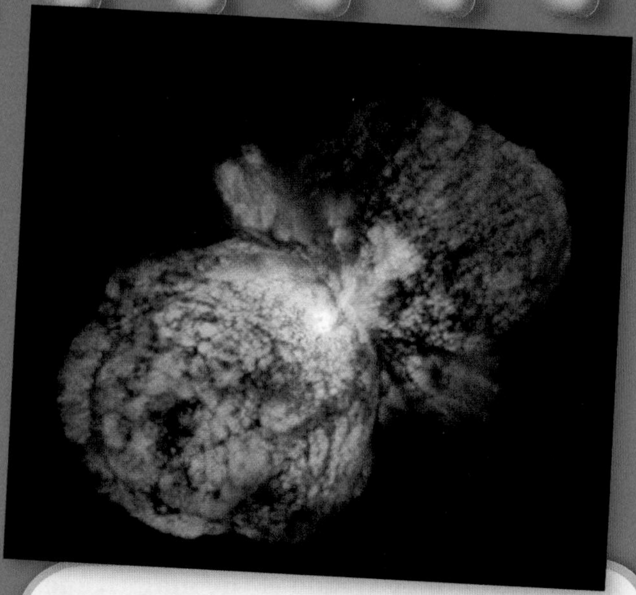

Weird Science

Holes Where Stars Once Were

An invisible phantom lurks in space, ready to swallow everything that comes near it. Once trapped in its grasp, matter is stretched, torn, and crushed into oblivion. Does this tale sound like a horror story? Guess again! Scientists call this phantom a *black hole*. As a star runs out of fuel, it cools and eventually collapses under the force of its own gravity. If the collapsing star is massive enough, it may shrink to become a black hole. The resulting gravitational attraction is so strong that even light cannot escape! Many astronomers think that black holes lie at the heart of many galaxies. Some scientists suggest that there is a giant black hole at the center of our own Milky Way.

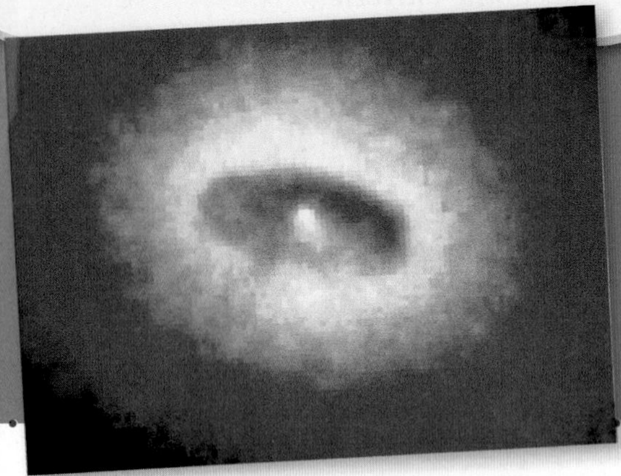

Language Arts ACTIVITY

WRITING SKILL Can you imagine traveling through a black hole? Write a short story that describes what you would see if you led a space mission to a black hole.

Scientific Discoveries

Eta Carinae: The Biggest Star Ever Discovered

In 1841, Eta Carinae was the second-brightest star in the night sky. Why is this observation a part of history? Eta Carinae's brightness is historic because before 1837, Eta Carinae wasn't even visible to the naked eye! Strangely, a few years later Eta Carinae faded again and disappeared from the night sky. Something unusual was happening to Eta Carinae, and scientists wanted to know what it was. As soon as scientists had telescopes with which they could see far into space, they took a closer look at Eta Carinae. Scientists discovered that this star is highly unstable and prone to violent outbursts. These outbursts, the last of which was seen in 1841, can be seen on Earth. Scientists also discovered that Eta Carinae is 150 times as big as our sun and about 4 million times as bright. Eta Carinae is the biggest and brightest star ever found!

Math ACTIVITY

If Eta Carinae is 8,000 light-years from our solar system, how many kilometers is Eta Carinae from our solar system? (Hint: One light-year is equal to 9.46 trillion kilometers.)

Jocelyn Bell-Burnell

Astrophysicist Imagine getting a signal from far out in space and not knowing what or whom it's coming from. That's what happened to astrophysicist Jocelyn Bell-Burnell. Bell-Burnell is known for discovering pulsars, objects in space that emit radio waves at short, regular intervals. But before she and her advisor discovered that the signals came from pulsars, they thought that the signals may have come from aliens!

Born in 1943 in Belfast, Northern Ireland, Jocelyn Bell-Burnell became interested in astronomy at an early age. At Cambridge University in 1967, Bell-Burnell, who was a graduate student, and her advisor, Anthony Hewish, completed work on a huge radio telescope designed to pick up signals from quasars. Bell-Burnell's job was to operate the telescope and analyze its chart paper recordings on a graph. Each day, the telescope recordings used 29.2 m of chart paper! After a month, Bell-Burnell noticed that the recordings showed a few "bits of scruff"—very short, pulsating radio signals—that she could not explain. Bell-Burnell and Hewish struggled to find the source of the mysterious signal. They checked the equipment and began eliminating possible sources of the signal, such as satellites, television, and radar. Shortly after finding the first signal, Bell-Burnell discovered a second. The second signal was similar to the first but came from a different position in the sky. By January 1968, Bell-Burnell had discovered two more pulsating signals. In March of 1968, her findings that the signals were from a new kind of star were published and amazed the scientific community. The scientific press named the newly discovered stars *pulsars*.

Today, Bell-Burnell is a leading expert in the field of astrophysics and the study of stars. She is currently head of the physics department at the Open University, in Milton Keynes, England.

Social Studies ACTIVITY

Use the Internet or library resources to research historical events that occurred during 1967 and 1968. Find out if the prediction that the signals from pulsars were coming from aliens affected historical events during this time.

go.hrw.com

To learn more about these Science in Action topics, visit go.hrw.com and type in the keyword HZ5UNVF.

Current Science

Check out Current Science® articles related to this chapter by visiting go.hrw.com. Just type in the keyword HZ5CS19.

16

Formation of the Solar System

The Big Idea

The way in which stars, planets, and solar systems form is controlled by gravity and pressure.

SECTION

About the Photo

The Orion Nebula, a vast cloud of dust and gas that is 35 trillion miles wide, is part of the familiar Orion constellation. Here, swirling clouds of dust and gas give birth to systems like our own solar system.

PRE-READING ACTIVITY

Graphic Organizer

Chain-of-Events Chart Before you read the chapter, create the graphic organizer entitled "Chain-of-Events Chart" described in the **Study Skills** section of the Appendix. As you read the chapter, fill in the chart with details about each step of the formation of the solar system.

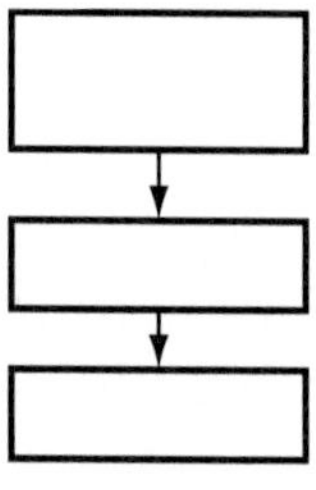

START-UP ACTIVITY

Strange Gravity

If you drop a heavy object, will it fall faster than a lighter one? According to the law of gravity, the answer is no. In 1971, *Apollo 15* astronaut David Scott stood on the moon and dropped a feather and a hammer. Television audiences were amazed to see both objects strike the moon's surface at the same time. Now, you can perform a similar experiment.

Procedure

1. Select **two pieces of identical notebook paper.** Crumple one piece of paper into a ball.
2. Place the flat piece of paper on top of a **book** and the paper ball on top of the flat piece of paper.
3. Hold the book waist high, and then drop it to the floor.

Analysis

1. Which piece of paper reached the bottom first? Did either piece of paper fall slower than the book? Explain your observations.
2. Now, hold the crumpled paper in one hand and the flat piece of paper in the other. Drop both pieces of paper at the same time. Besides gravity, what affected the speed of the falling paper? Record your observations.

SECTION 1

A Solar System Is Born

As you read this sentence, you are traveling at a speed of about 30 km/s around an incredibly hot star shining in the vastness of space!

What You Will Learn

- Explain the relationship between gravity and pressure in a nebula.
- Describe how the solar system formed.

Vocabulary

nebula
solar nebula

READING STRATEGY

Reading Organizer As you read this section, make a flowchart of the steps of the formation of a solar system.

Earth is not the only planet orbiting the sun. In fact, Earth has many fellow travelers in its cosmic neighborhood. The solar system includes a star we call the sun, the planets, and many moons and small bodies that travel around the sun. For almost 5 billion years, planets have been orbiting the sun. But how did the solar system come to be?

The Solar Nebula

All of the ingredients for building planets, moons, and stars are found in the vast, seemingly empty regions of space between the stars. Just as there are clouds in the sky, there are clouds in space. These clouds are called nebulas. **Nebulas** (or nebulae) are mixtures of gases—mainly hydrogen and helium—and dust made of elements such as carbon and iron. Although nebulas are normally dark and invisible to optical telescopes, they can be seen when nearby stars illuminate them. So, how can a cloud of gas and dust such as the Horsehead Nebula, shown in **Figure 1,** form planets and stars? To answer this question, you must explore two forces that interact in nebulas—gravity and pressure.

Gravity Pulls Matter Together

nebula a large cloud of gas and dust in interstellar space; a region in space where stars are born or where stars explode at the end of their lives

The gas and dust that make up nebulas are made of matter. The matter of a nebula is held together by the force of gravity. In most nebulas, there is a lot of space between the particles. In fact, nebulas are less dense than air! Thus, the gravitational attraction between the particles in a nebula is very weak. The force is just enough to keep the nebula from drifting apart.

Figure 1 *The Horsehead Nebula is a cold, dark cloud of gas and dust. But observations suggest that it is also a site where stars form.*

Figure 2 Gravity and Pressure in a Nebula

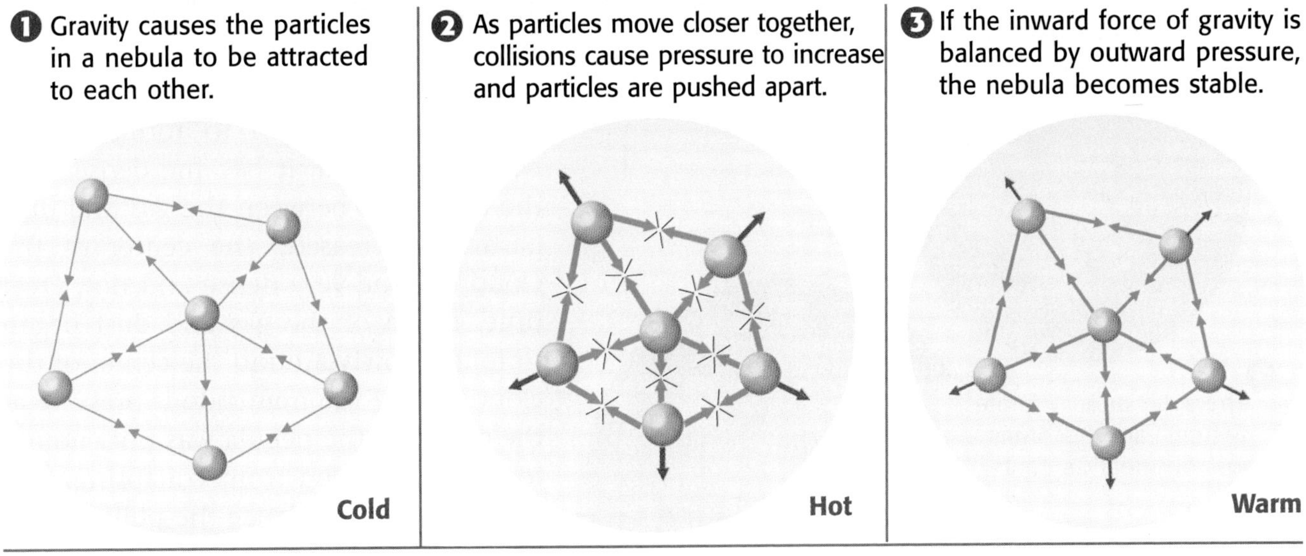

1 Gravity causes the particles in a nebula to be attracted to each other.
Cold
2 As particles move closer together, collisions cause pressure to increase and particles are pushed apart.
Hot
3 If the inward force of gravity is balanced by outward pressure, the nebula becomes stable.
Warm

Pressure Pushes Matter Apart

If gravity pulls on all of the particles in a nebula, why don't nebulas slowly collapse? The answer has to do with the relationship between temperature and pressure in a nebula. *Temperature* is a measure of the average kinetic energy, or the energy of motion, of the particles in an object. If the particles in a nebula have little kinetic energy, they move slowly and the temperature of the cloud is very low. If the particles move fast, the temperature of the cloud is high. As particles move around, they sometimes crash into each other. As shown in **Figure 2,** these collisions cause particles to push away from each other, which creates *pressure*. If you have ever blown up a balloon, you understand how pressure works—pressure keeps a balloon from collapsing. In a nebula, outward pressure balances the inward gravitational pull and keeps the cloud from collapsing.

Upsetting the Balance

The balance between gravity and pressure in a nebula can be upset if two nebulas collide or a nearby star explodes. These events compress, or push together, small regions of a nebula called *globules,* or gas clouds. Globules can become so dense that they contract under their own gravity. As the matter in a globule collapses inward, the temperature increases and the stage is set for stars to form. The **solar nebula**—the cloud of gas and dust that formed our solar system—may have formed in this way.

solar nebula the cloud of gas and dust that formed our solar system

Reading Check **What is the solar nebula?** *(See the Appendix for answers to Reading Checks.)*

Figure 3 The Formation of the Solar System

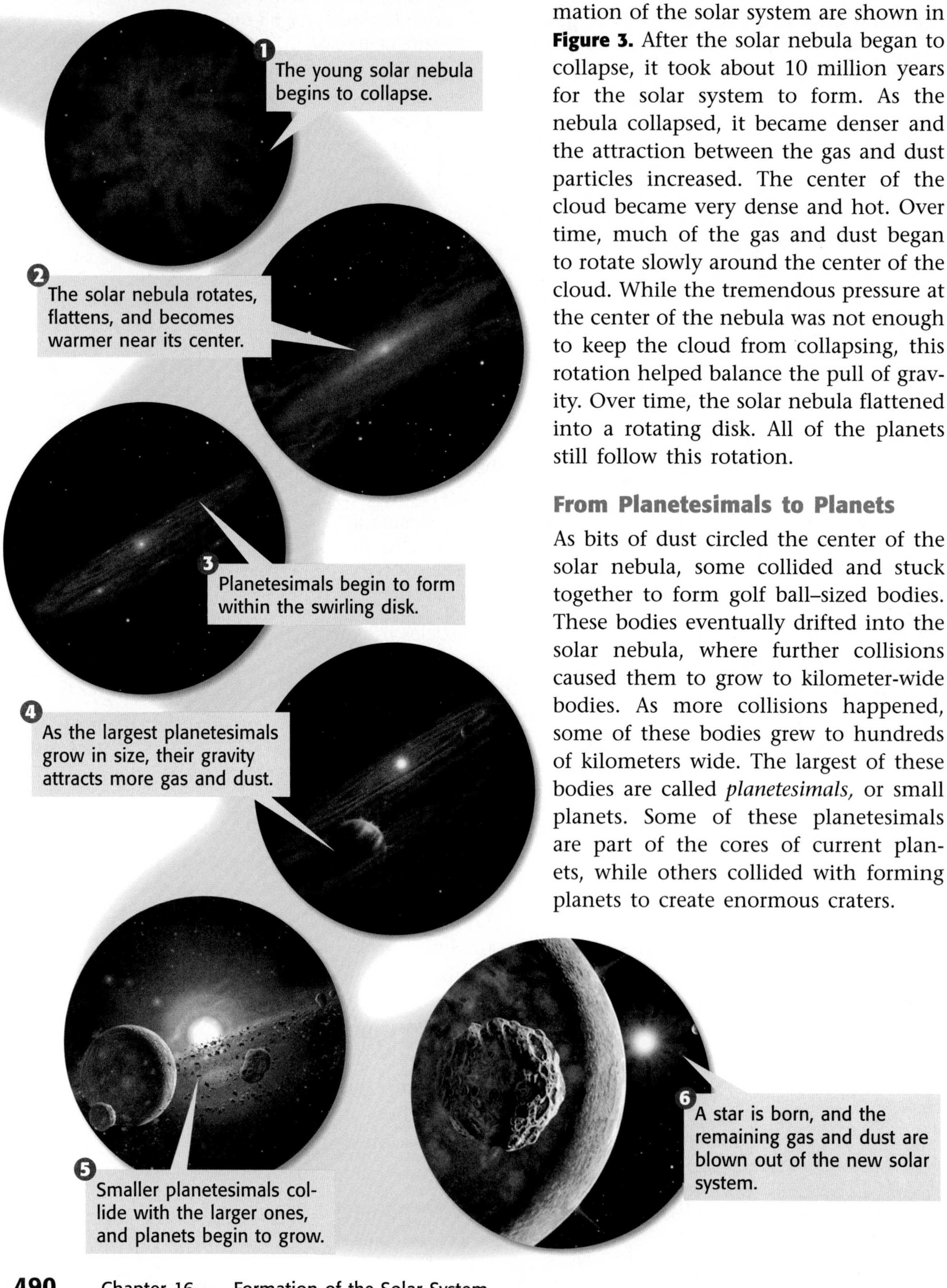

1
The young solar nebula begins to collapse.
2
The solar nebula rotates, flattens, and becomes warmer near its center.
3
Planetesimals begin to form within the swirling disk.
4
As the largest planetesimals grow in size, their gravity attracts more gas and dust.
5
Smaller planetesimals collide with the larger ones, and planets begin to grow.
6
A star is born, and the remaining gas and dust are blown out of the new solar system.

How the Solar System Formed

The events that may have led to the formation of the solar system are shown in **Figure 3.** After the solar nebula began to collapse, it took about 10 million years for the solar system to form. As the nebula collapsed, it became denser and the attraction between the gas and dust particles increased. The center of the cloud became very dense and hot. Over time, much of the gas and dust began to rotate slowly around the center of the cloud. While the tremendous pressure at the center of the nebula was not enough to keep the cloud from collapsing, this rotation helped balance the pull of gravity. Over time, the solar nebula flattened into a rotating disk. All of the planets still follow this rotation.

From Planetesimals to Planets

As bits of dust circled the center of the solar nebula, some collided and stuck together to form golf ball–sized bodies. These bodies eventually drifted into the solar nebula, where further collisions caused them to grow to kilometer-wide bodies. As more collisions happened, some of these bodies grew to hundreds of kilometers wide. The largest of these bodies are called *planetesimals,* or small planets. Some of these planetesimals are part of the cores of current planets, while others collided with forming planets to create enormous craters.

Gas Giant or Rocky Planet?

The largest planetesimals formed near the outside of the rotating solar disk, where hydrogen and helium were located. These planetesimals were far enough from the solar disk that their gravity could attract the nebula gases. These outer planets grew to huge sizes and became the gas giants—Jupiter, Saturn, Uranus, and Neptune. Closer to the center of the nebula, where Mercury, Venus, Earth, and Mars formed, temperatures were too hot for gases to remain. Therefore, the inner planets in our solar system are made mostly of rocky material.

Reading Check Which planets are gas giants?

The Birth of a Star

As the planets were forming, other matter in the solar nebula was traveling toward the center. The center became so dense and hot that hydrogen atoms began to fuse, or join, to form helium. Fusion released huge amounts of energy and created enough outward pressure to balance the inward pull of gravity. At this point, when the gas stopped collapsing, our sun was born and the new solar system was complete!

CONNECTION TO Language Arts

WRITING SKILL **Eyewitness Account** Research information on the formation of the outer planets, inner planets, and the sun. Then, imagine that you witnessed the formation of the planets and sun. Write a short story describing your experience.

SECTION Review

Summary

- The solar system formed out of a vast cloud of gas and dust called the *nebula*.
- Gravity and pressure were balanced until something upset the balance. Then, the nebula began to collapse.
- Collapse of the solar nebula caused heating at the center, while planetesimals formed in surrounding space.
- The central mass of the nebula became the sun. Planets formed from the surrounding materials.

Using Key Terms

1. In your own words, write a definition for each of the following terms: *nebula* and *solar nebula*.

Understanding Key Ideas

2. What is the relationship between gravity and pressure in a nebula?
   a. Gravity reduces pressure.
   b. Pressure balances gravity.
   c. Pressure increases gravity.
   d. None of the above
3. Describe how our solar system formed.
4. Compare the inner planets with the outer planets.

Math Skills

5. If the planets, moons, and other bodies make up 0.15% of the solar system's mass, what percentage does the sun make up?

Critical Thinking

6. **Evaluating Hypotheses** Beyond the orbit of Neptune, a field of smaller bodies orbits the sun. Some scientists think these objects are the remains of material that formed the early solar system. Use what you know about how solar systems form to evaluate this hypothesis.
7. **Making Inferences** Why do all of the planets go around the sun in the same direction, and why do the planets lie on a relatively flat plane?

SCILINKS® NSTA Developed and maintained by the National Science Teachers Association

For a variety of links related to this chapter, go to www.scilinks.org

Topic: The Planets
SciLinks code: HSM1152

SECTION 2

The Sun: Our Very Own Star

What You Will Learn

- Describe the basic structure and composition of the sun.
- Explain how the sun generates energy.
- Describe the surface activity of the sun, and identify how this activity affects Earth.

Vocabulary

nuclear fusion
sunspot

READING STRATEGY

Reading Organizer As you read this section, create an outline of the section. Use the headings from the section in your outline.

Can you imagine what life on Earth would be like if there were no sun? Without the sun, life on Earth would be impossible!

Energy from the sun lights and heats Earth's surface. Energy from the sun even drives the weather. Making up more than 99% of the solar system's mass, the sun is the dominant member of our solar system. The sun is basically a large ball of gas made mostly of hydrogen and helium held together by gravity. But what does the inside of the sun look like?

The Structure of the Sun

Although the sun may appear to have a solid surface, it does not. When you see a picture of the sun, you are really seeing through the sun's outer atmosphere. The visible surface of the sun starts at the point where the gas becomes so thick that you cannot see through it. As **Figure 1** shows, the sun is made of several layers.

Figure 1 The Structure and Atmosphere of the Sun

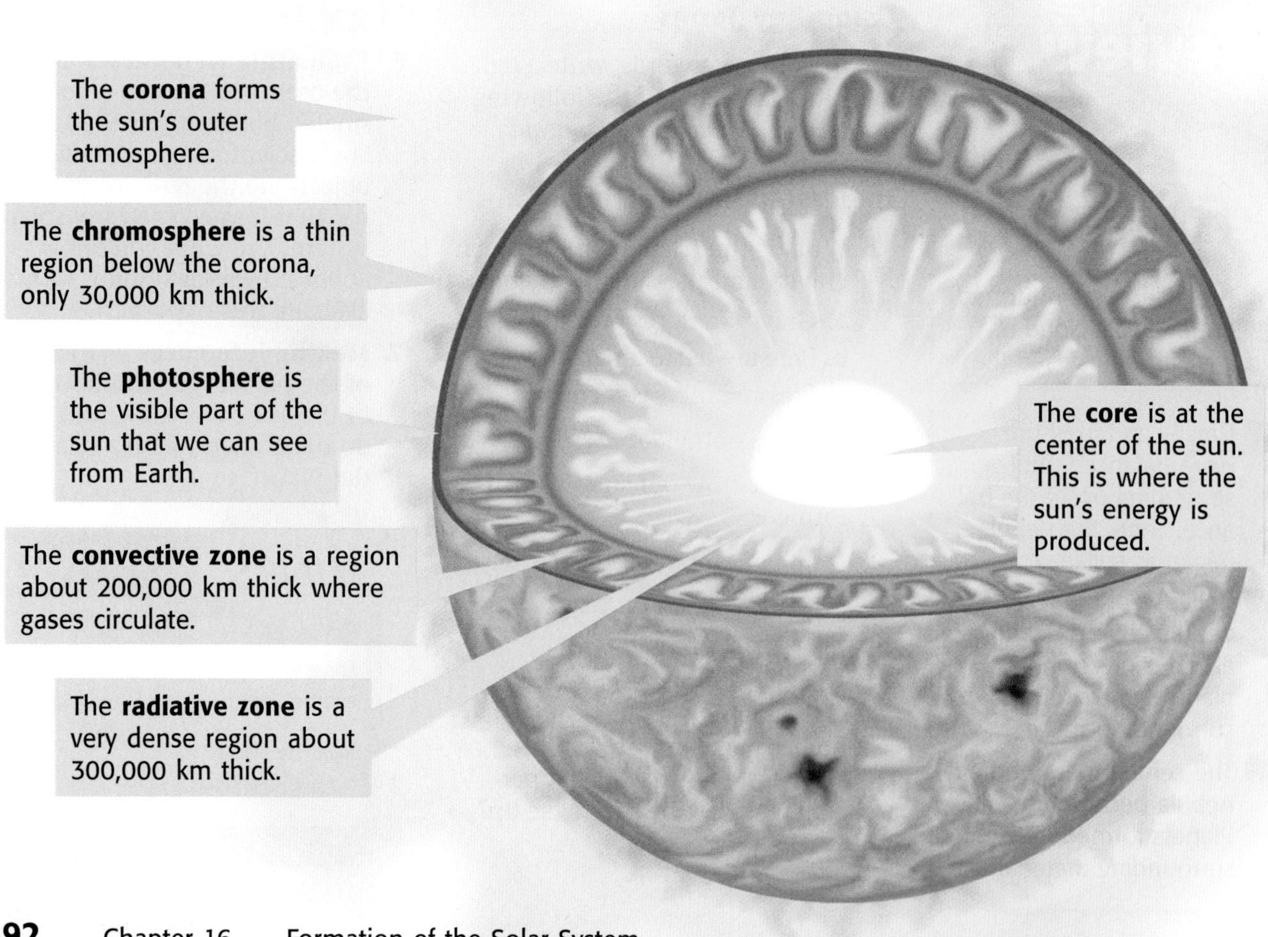

The **corona** forms the sun's outer atmosphere.
The **chromosphere** is a thin region below the corona, only 30,000 km thick.
The **photosphere** is the visible part of the sun that we can see from Earth.
The **convective zone** is a region about 200,000 km thick where gases circulate.
The **radiative zone** is a very dense region about 300,000 km thick.
The **core** is at the center of the sun. This is where the sun's energy is produced.

At first, some type of burning fuel was thought to be the source of the sun's energy.
A shrinking sun was another explanation for solar energy.

Figure 2 *Ideas about the source of the sun's energy have changed over time.*

Energy Production in the Sun

The sun has been shining on Earth for about 4.6 billion years. How can the sun stay hot for so long? And what makes it shine? **Figure 2** shows two theories that were proposed to answer these questions. Many scientists thought that the sun burned fuel to generate its energy. But the amount of energy that is released by burning would not be enough to power the sun. If the sun were simply burning, it would last for only 10,000 years.

Burning or Shrinking?

It eventually became clear to scientists that burning wouldn't last long enough to keep the sun shining. Then, scientists began to think that gravity was causing the sun to slowly shrink. They thought that perhaps gravity would release enough energy to heat the sun. While the release of gravitational energy is more powerful than burning, it is not enough to power the sun. If all of the sun's gravitational energy were released, the sun would last for only 45 million years. However, fossils that have been discovered prove that dinosaurs roamed the Earth more than 65 million years ago, so this couldn't be the case. Therefore, something even more powerful than gravity was needed.

Reading Check **Why isn't energy from gravity enough to power the sun?** (*See the Appendix for answers to Reading Checks.*)

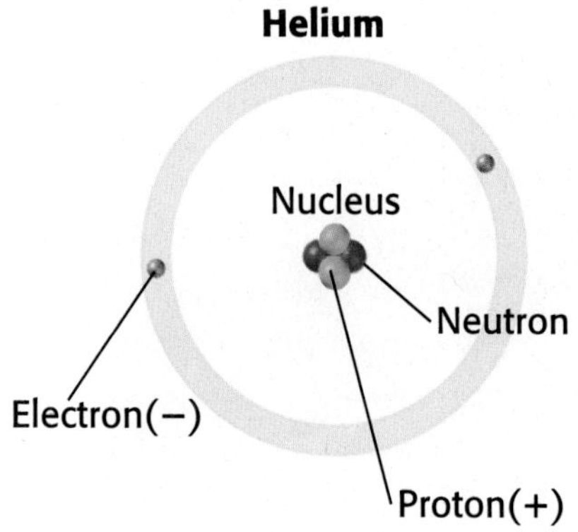

CONNECTION TO Chemistry

Atoms An atom consists of a nucleus surrounded by one or more electrons. Electrons have a negative charge. In most elements, the atom's nucleus is made up of two types of particles: *protons,* which have a positive charge, and *neutrons,* which have no charge. The protons in the nucleus are usually balanced by an equal number of electrons. The number of protons and electrons gives the atom its chemical identity. A helium atom, shown at left, has two protons, two neutrons, and two electrons. Use a Periodic Table to find the chemical identity of the following atoms: nitrogen, oxygen, and carbon.

Nuclear Fusion

At the beginning of the 20th century, Albert Einstein showed that matter and energy are interchangeable. Matter can change into energy according to his famous formula: $E = mc^2$. (E is energy, m is mass, and c is the speed of light.) Because c is such a large number, tiny amounts of matter can produce a huge amount of energy. With this idea, scientists began to understand a very powerful source of energy.

nuclear fusion the combination of the nuclei of small atoms to form a larger nucleus; releases energy

Nuclear fusion is the process by which two or more low-mass nuclei join together, or fuse, to form another nucleus. In this way, four hydrogen nuclei can fuse to form a single nucleus of helium. During the process, energy is produced. Scientists now know that the sun gets its energy from nuclear fusion. Einstein's equation, shown in **Figure 3,** changed ideas about the sun's energy source by equating mass and energy.

Figure 3 *Einstein's equation changed ideas about the sun's energy source by equating mass and energy.*

Fusion in the Sun

During fusion, under normal conditions, the nuclei of hydrogen atoms never get close enough to combine. The reason is that they are positively charged. Like charges repel each other, as shown in **Figure 4.** In the center of the sun, however, the temperature and pressure are very high. As a result, the hydrogen nuclei have enough energy to overcome the repulsive force, and hydrogen fuses into helium, as shown in **Figure 5.**

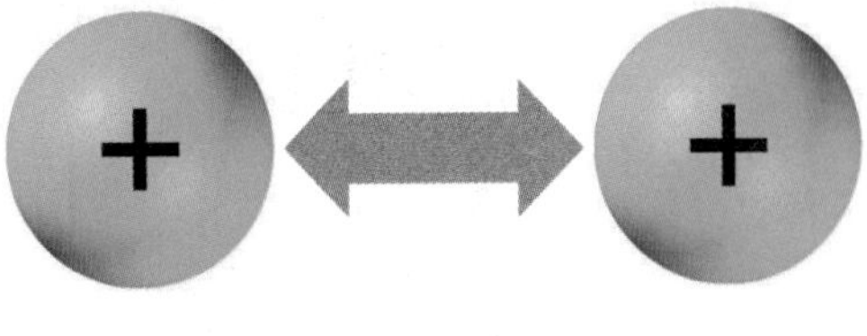

Figure 4 *Like charges repel just as similar poles on a pair of magnets do.*

The energy produced in the center, or core of the sun takes millions of years to reach the sun's surface. The energy passes from the core through a very dense region called the *radiative zone.* The matter in the radiative zone is so crowded that the light and energy are blocked and sent in different directions. Eventually, the energy reaches the *convective zone.* Gases circulate in the convective zone, which is about 200,000 km thick. Hot gases in the convective zone carry the energy up to the *photosphere,* the visible surface of the sun. From there, the energy leaves the sun as light, which takes only 8.3 min to reach Earth.

Reading Check **What causes the nuclei of hydrogen atoms to repel each other?**

Figure 5 **Fusion of Hydrogen in the Sun**

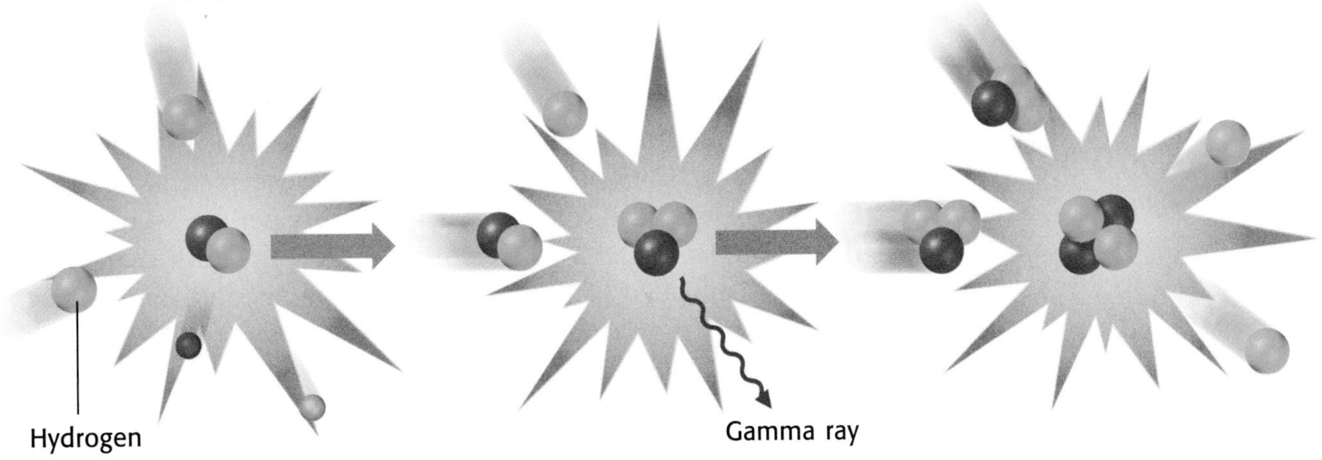

1 **Deuterium** Two hydrogen nuclei (protons) collide. One proton emits particles and energy and then becomes a neutron. The proton and neutron combine to produce a heavy form of hydrogen called *deuterium.*

2 **Helium-3** Deuterium combines with another hydrogen nucleus to form a variety of helium called *helium-3*. More energy, as well as gamma rays, is released.

3 **Helium-4** Two helium-3 atoms then combine to form ordinary helium-4, which releases more energy and a pair of hydrogen nuclei.

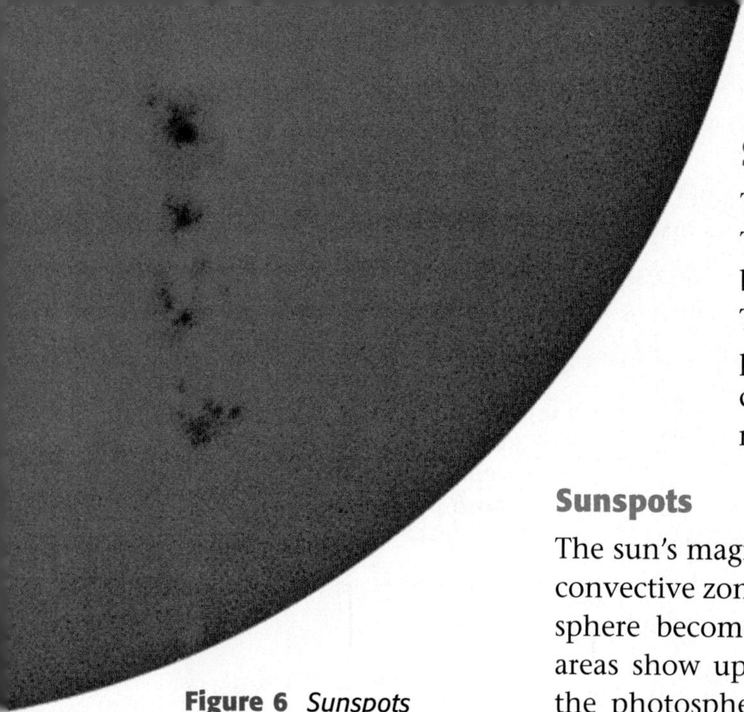

Figure 6 *Sunspots mark cooler areas on the sun's surface. They are related to changes in the magnetic properties of the sun.*

Solar Activity

The photosphere is an ever-changing place. Thermal energy moves from the sun's interior by the circulation of gases in the convective zone. This movement of energy causes the gas in the photosphere to boil and churn. This circulation, combined with the sun's rotation, creates magnetic fields that reach far out into space.

Sunspots

The sun's magnetic fields tend to slow down the activity in the convective zone. When activity slows down, areas of the photosphere become cooler than surrounding areas. These cooler areas show up as sunspots. **Sunspots** are cooler, dark spots of the photosphere of the sun, as shown in **Figure 6.** Sunspots can vary in shape and size. Some sunspots can be as large as 50,000 miles in diameter.

The numbers and locations of sunspots on the sun change in a regular cycle. Scientists have found that the sunspot cycle lasts about 11 years. Every 11 years, the amount of sunspot activity in the sun reaches a peak intensity and then decreases. **Figure 7** shows the sunspot cycle since 1610, excluding the years 1645–1715, which was a period of unusually low sunspot activity.

sunspot a dark area of the photosphere of the sun that is cooler than the surrounding areas and that has a strong magnetic field

Reading Check What are sunspots? What causes sunspots to occur?

Climate Confusion

Scientists have found that sunspot activity can affect the Earth. For example, some scientists have linked the period of low sunspot activity, 1645–1715, with the very low temperatures that Europe experienced during that time. This period is known as the "Little Ice Age." Most scientists, however, think that more research is needed to fully understand the possible connection between sunspots and Earth's climate.

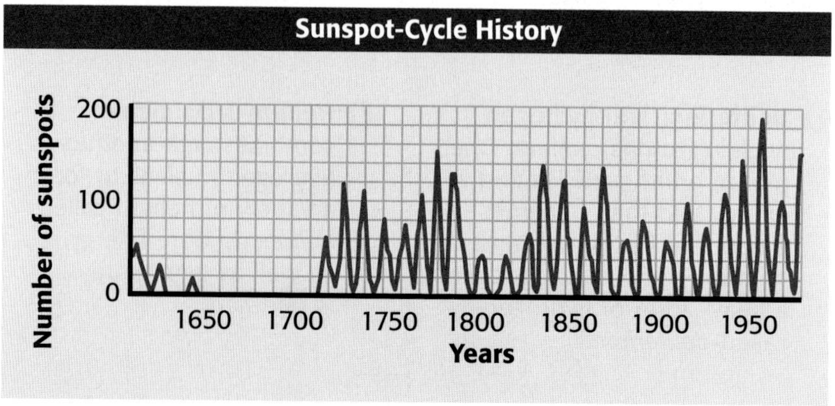

Figure 7 *This graph shows the number of sunspots that have occurred each year since Galileo's first observation in 1610.*

Solar Flares

The magnetic fields that cause sunspots also cause solar flares. *Solar flares,* as shown in **Figure 8,** are regions of extremely high temperature and brightness that develop on the sun's surface. When a solar flare erupts, it sends huge streams of electrically charged particles into the solar system. Solar flares can extend upward several thousand kilometers within minutes. Solar flares are usually associated with sunspots and can interrupt radio communications on Earth and in orbit. Scientists are trying to find ways to give advance warning of solar flares.

Figure 8 *Solar flares are giant eruptions on the sun's surface.*

SECTION Review

Summary

- The sun is a large ball of gas made mostly of hydrogen and helium. The sun consists of many layers.
- The sun's energy comes from nuclear fusion that takes place in the center of the sun.
- The visible surface of the sun, or the photosphere, is very active.
- Sunspots and solar flares are the result of the sun's magnetic fields that reach space.
- Sunspot activity may affect Earth's climate, and solar flares can interact with Earth's atmosphere.

Using Key Terms

1. In your own words, write a definition for each of the following terms: *sunspot* and *nuclear fusion.*

Understanding Key Ideas

2. Which of the following statements describes how energy is produced in the sun?
   a. The sun burns fuels to generate energy.
   b. As hydrogen changes into helium deep inside the sun, a great deal of energy is made.
   c. Energy is released as the sun shrinks because of gravity.
   d. None of the above
3. Describe the composition of the sun.
4. Name and describe the layers of the sun.
5. In which area of the sun do sunspots appear?
6. Explain how sunspots form.
7. Describe how sunspots can affect the Earth.
8. What are solar flares, and how do they form?

Math Skills

9. If the equatorial diameter of the sun is 1.39 million kilometers, how many kilometers is the sun's radius?

Critical Thinking

10. **Applying Concepts** If nuclear fusion in the sun's core suddenly stopped today, would the sky be dark in the daytime tomorrow? Explain.
11. **Making Comparisons** Compare the theories that scientists proposed about the source of the sun's energy with the process of nuclear fusion in the sun.

SCILINKS. NSTA Developed and maintained by the National Science Teachers Association

For a variety of links related to this chapter, go to www.scilinks.org

Topic: The Sun
SciLinks code: HSM1477

SECTION 3

The Earth Takes Shape

In many ways, Earth seems to be a perfect place for life.

What You Will Learn

- Describe the formation of the solid Earth.
- Describe the structure of the Earth.
- Explain the development of Earth's atmosphere and the influence of early life on the atmosphere.
- Describe how the Earth's oceans and continents formed.

Vocabulary

crust
mantle
core

READING STRATEGY

Discussion Read this section silently. Write down questions that you have about this section. Discuss your questions in a small group.

We live on the third planet from the sun. The Earth, shown in **Figure 1,** is mostly made of rock, and nearly three-fourths of its surface is covered with water. It is surrounded by a protective atmosphere of mostly nitrogen and oxygen and smaller amounts of other gases. But Earth has not always been such an oasis in the solar system.

Formation of the Solid Earth

The Earth formed as planetesimals in the solar system collided and combined. From what scientists can tell, the Earth formed within the first 10 million years of the collapse of the solar nebula!

The Effects of Gravity

When a young planet is still small, it can have an irregular shape, somewhat like a potato. But as the planet gains more matter, the force of gravity increases. When a rocky planet, such as Earth, reaches a diameter of about 350 km, the force of gravity becomes greater than the strength of the rock. As the Earth grew to this size, the rock at its center was crushed by gravity and the planet started to become round.

The Effects of Heat

As the Earth was changing shape, it was also heating up. Planetesimals continued to collide with the Earth, and the energy of their motion heated the planet. Radioactive material, which was present in the Earth as it formed, also heated the young planet. After Earth reached a certain size, the temperature rose faster than the interior could cool, and the rocky material inside began to melt. Today, the Earth is still cooling from the energy that was generated when it formed. Volcanoes, earthquakes, and hot springs are effects of this energy trapped inside the Earth. As you will learn later, the effects of heat and gravity also helped form the Earth's layers when the Earth was very young.

Reading Check **What factors heated the Earth during its early formation?** *(See the Appendix for answers to Reading Checks.)*

Figure 1 *When Earth is seen from space, one of its unique features—the presence of water—is apparent.*

How the Earth's Layers Formed

Have you ever watched the oil separate from vinegar in a bottle of salad dressing? The vinegar sinks because it is denser than oil. The Earth's layers formed in much the same way. As rocks melted, denser materials, such as nickel and iron, sank to the center of the Earth and formed the core. Less dense materials floated to the surface and became the crust. This process is shown in **Figure 2.**

The **crust** is the thin, outermost layer of the Earth. It is 5 to 100 km thick. Crustal rock is made of materials that have low densities, such as oxygen, silicon, and aluminum. The **mantle** is the layer of Earth beneath the crust. It extends 2,900 km below the surface. Mantle rock is made of materials such as magnesium and iron and is denser than crustal rock. The **core** is the central part of the Earth below the mantle. It contains the densest materials (nickel and iron) and extends to the center of the Earth—almost 6,400 km below the surface.

crust the thin and solid outermost layer of the Earth above the mantle

mantle the layer of rock between the Earth's crust and core

core the central part of the Earth below the mantle

Figure 2 **The Formation of Earth's Layers**

1. All materials in the early Earth are randomly mixed.
2. Rocks melt, and denser materials sink toward the center. Less dense elements rise and form layers.
3. According to composition, the Earth is divided into three layers: the crust, the mantle, and the core.

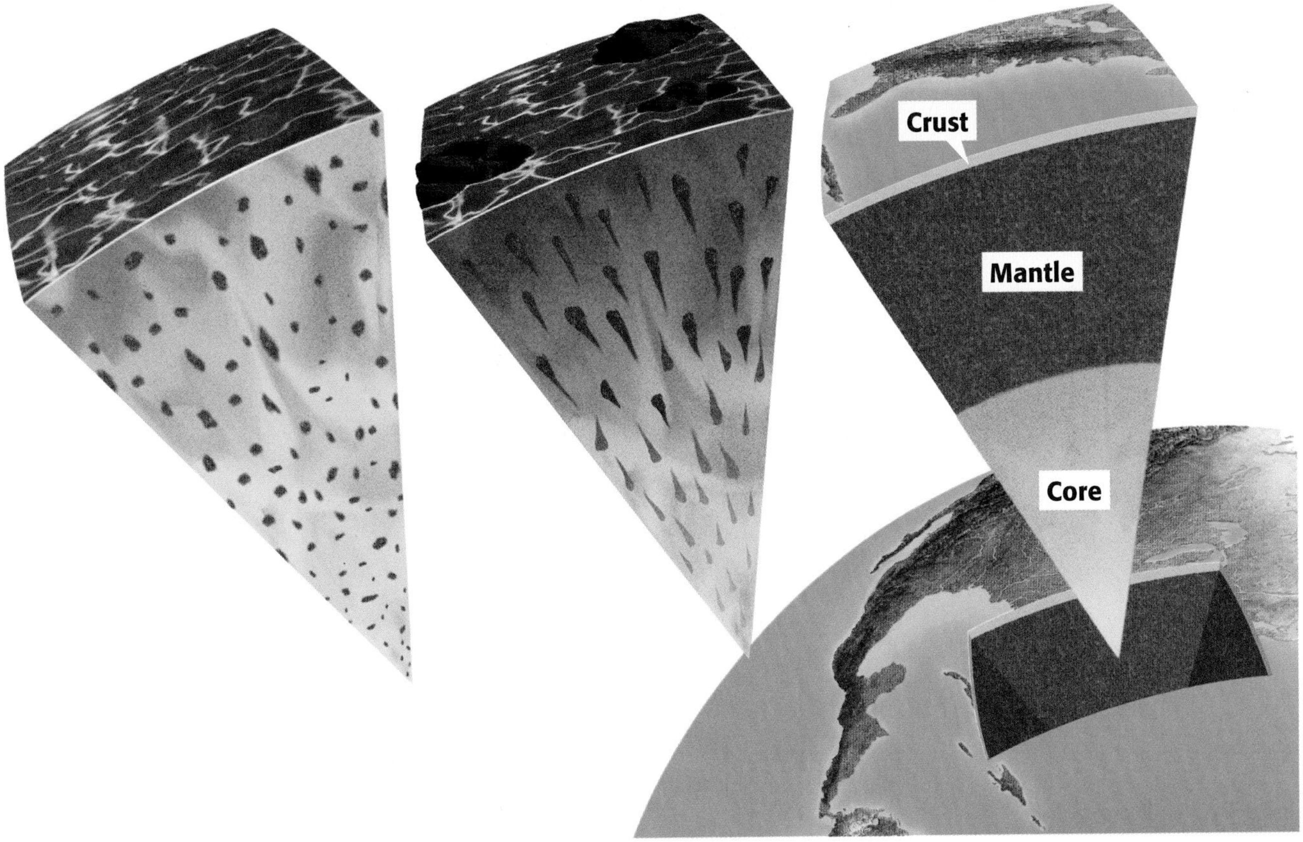

Formation of the Earth's Atmosphere

Today, Earth's atmosphere is 78% nitrogen, 21% oxygen, and about 1% argon. (There are tiny amounts of many other gases.) Did you know that the Earth's atmosphere did not always contain the oxygen that you need to live? The Earth's atmosphere is constantly changing. Scientists think that the Earth's earliest atmosphere was very different than it is today.

Earth's Early Atmosphere

Scientists think that Earth's early atmosphere was a mixture of gases that were released as Earth cooled. During the final stages of the Earth's formation, its surface was very hot—even molten in places—as shown in **Figure 3.** The molten rock released large amounts of carbon dioxide and water vapor. Therefore, scientists think that Earth's early atmosphere was a steamy mixture of carbon dioxide and water vapor.

Reading Check **Describe Earth's early atmosphere.**

CONNECTION TO Environmental Science

WRITING SKILL **The Greenhouse Effect** Carbon dioxide is a greenhouse gas. Greenhouse gases are gases that absorb thermal energy and radiate it back to Earth. This process is called the greenhouse effect because the gases function like the walls and roof of a greenhouse, which allow solar energy to enter but prevent thermal energy from escaping. Do research to find the percentage of carbon dioxide that is thought to make up Earth's early atmosphere. Write a report, and share your findings with your class.

Figure 3 *This artwork is an artist's view of what Earth's surface may have looked like shortly after the Earth formed.*

Figure 4 *As this volcano in Hawaii shows, a large amount of gas is released during an eruption.*

Earth's Changing Atmosphere

As the Earth cooled and its layers formed, the Earth's atmosphere changed again. This atmosphere probably formed from volcanic gases. Volcanoes, such as the one in **Figure 4,** released chlorine, nitrogen, and sulfur in addition to large amounts of carbon dioxide and water vapor. Some of this water vapor may have condensed to form the Earth's first oceans.

Comets, which are planetesimals made of ice, also may have contributed to this change of Earth's atmosphere. As comets crashed into the Earth, they brought in a range of elements, such as carbon, hydrogen, oxygen, and nitrogen. Comets also may have brought some of the water that helped form the oceans.

The Role of Life

How did this change of Earth's atmosphere become the air you are breathing right now? The answer is related to the appearance of life on Earth.

Ultraviolet Radiation

Scientists think that ultraviolet (UV) radiation, the same radiation that causes sunburns, helped produce the conditions necessary for life. Because UV light has a lot of energy, it can break apart molecules in your skin and in the air. Today, we are shielded from most of the sun's UV rays by Earth's protective ozone layer. But Earth's early atmosphere probably did not have ozone, so many molecules in the air and at Earth's surface were broken apart. Over time, this material collected in the Earth's waters. Water offered protection from the effects of UV radiation. In these sheltered pools of water, chemicals may have combined to form the complex molecules that made life possible. The first life-forms were very simple and did not need oxygen to live.

SCHOOL to HOME

Comets and Meteors

What is the difference between a comet and a meteor? With a parent or guardian, research the difference between comets and meteors. Then, find out if you can view meteor showers in your area!

ACTIVITY

The Source of Oxygen

Sometime before 3.4 billion years ago, organisms that produced food by photosynthesis appeared. *Photosynthesis* is the process of absorbing energy from the sun and carbon dioxide from the atmosphere to make food. During the process of making food, these organisms released oxygen—a gas that was not abundant in the atmosphere at that time. Scientists think that the descendants of these early life-forms are still around today, as shown in **Figure 5.**

Photosynthetic organisms played a major role in changing Earth's atmosphere to become the mixture of gases you breathe today. Over the next hundreds of millions of years, more and more oxygen was added to the atmosphere. At the same time, carbon dioxide was removed. As oxygen levels increased, some of the oxygen formed a layer of ozone in the upper atmosphere. This ozone blocked most of the UV radiation and made it possible for life, in the form of simple plants, to move onto land about 2.2 billion years ago.

Reading Check **How did photosynthesis contribute to Earth's current atmosphere?**

Formation of Oceans and Continents

Scientists think that the oceans probably formed during Earth's second atmosphere, when the Earth was cool enough for rain to fall and remain on the surface. After millions of years of rainfall, water began to cover the Earth. By 4 billion years ago, a global ocean covered the planet.

For the first few hundred million years of Earth's history, there may not have been any continents. Given the composition of the rocks that make up the continents, scientists know that these rocks have melted and cooled many times in the past. Each time the rocks melted, the heavier elements sank and the lighter ones rose to the surface.

Figure 5 *Stromatolites, mats of fossilized algae (left), are among the earliest evidence of life. Blue-green algae (right) living today are thought to be similar to the first life-forms on Earth.*

The Growth of Continents

After a while, some of the rocks were light enough to pile up on the surface. These rocks were the beginning of the earliest continents. The continents gradually thickened and slowly rose above the surface of the ocean. These scattered young continents did not stay in the same place, however. The slow transfer of thermal energy in the mantle pushed them around. Approximately 2.5 billion years ago, continents really started to grow. And by 1.5 billion years ago, the upper mantle had cooled and had become denser and heavier. At this time, it was easier for the cooler parts of the mantle to sink. These conditions made it easier for the continents to move in the same way that they do today.

INTERNET ACTIVITY

For another activity related to this chapter, go to **go.hrw.com** and type in the keyword **HZ5SOLW.**

SECTION Review

Summary

- The effects of gravity and heat created the shape and structure of Earth.
- The Earth is divided into three main layers based on composition: the crust, mantle, and core.
- The presence of life dramatically changed Earth's atmosphere by adding free oxygen.
- Earth's oceans formed shortly after the Earth did, when it had cooled off enough for rain to fall. Continents formed when lighter materials gathered on the surface and rose above sea level.

Using Key Terms

1. Use each of the following terms in a separate sentence: *crust, mantle,* and *core.*

Understanding Key Ideas

2. Earth's first atmosphere was mostly made of
   a. nitrogen and oxygen.
   b. chlorine, nitrogen, and sulfur.
   c. carbon dioxide and water vapor.
   d. water vapor and oxygen.

3. Describe the structure of the Earth.

4. Why did the Earth separate into distinct layers?

5. Describe the development of Earth's atmosphere. How did life affect Earth's atmosphere?

6. Explain how Earth's oceans and continents formed.

Critical Thinking

7. Applying Concepts How did the effects of gravity help shape the Earth?

8. Making Inferences How would the removal of forests affect the Earth's atmosphere?

Interpreting Graphics

Use the illustration below to answer the questions that follow.

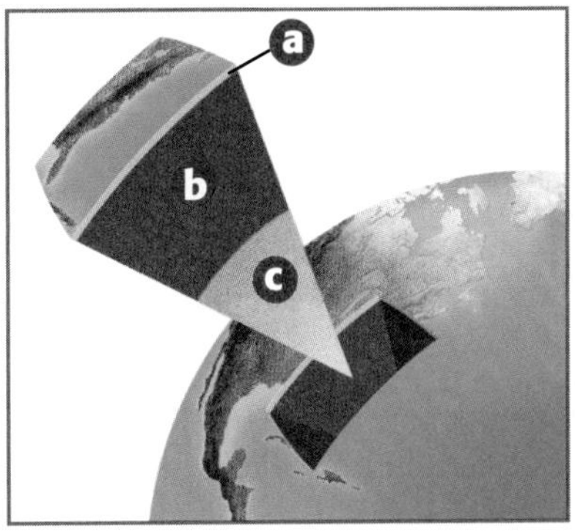

9. Which of the layers is composed mostly of the elements magnesium and iron?

10. Which of the layers is composed mostly of the elements iron and nickel?

SCILINKS. NSTA
Developed and maintained by the National Science Teachers Association

For a variety of links related to this chapter, go to www.scilinks.org

Topic: The Layers of the Earth; The Oceans
SciLinks code: HSM0862; HSM1069

SECTION 4

Planetary Motion

What You Will Learn

- Explain the difference between rotation and revolution.
- Describe three laws of planetary motion.
- Describe how distance and mass affect gravitational attraction.

Vocabulary

rotation
orbit
revolution

READING STRATEGY

Paired Summarizing Read this section silently. In pairs, take turns summarizing the material. Stop to discuss ideas that seem confusing.

Why do the planets revolve around the sun? Why don't they fly off into space? Does something hold them in their paths?

To answer these questions, you need to go back in time to look at the discoveries made by the scientists of the 1500s and 1600s. Danish astronomer Tycho Brahe (TIE koh BRAH uh) carefully observed the positions of planets for more than 25 years. When Brahe died in 1601, a German astronomer named Johannes Kepler (yoh HAHN uhs KEP luhr) continued Brahe's work. Kepler set out to understand the motions of planets and to describe the solar system.

A Revolution in Astronomy

Each planet spins on its axis. The spinning of a body, such as a planet, on its axis is called **rotation.** As the Earth rotates, only one-half of the Earth faces the sun. The half facing the sun is light (day). The half that faces away from the sun is dark (night).

The path that a body follows as it travels around another body in space is called the **orbit.** One complete trip along an orbit is called a **revolution.** The amount of time a planet takes to complete a single trip around the sun is called a *period of revolution.* Each planet takes a different amount of time to circle the sun. Earth's period of revolution is about 365.25 days (a year), but Mercury orbits the sun in only 88 days. **Figure 1** illustrates the orbit and revolution of the Earth around the sun as well as the rotation of the Earth on its axis.

rotation the spin of a body on its axis

orbit the path that a body follows as it travels around another body in space

revolution the motion of a body that travels around another body in space; one complete trip along an orbit

Figure 1 *A planet rotates on its own axis and revolves around the sun in a path called an* orbit.

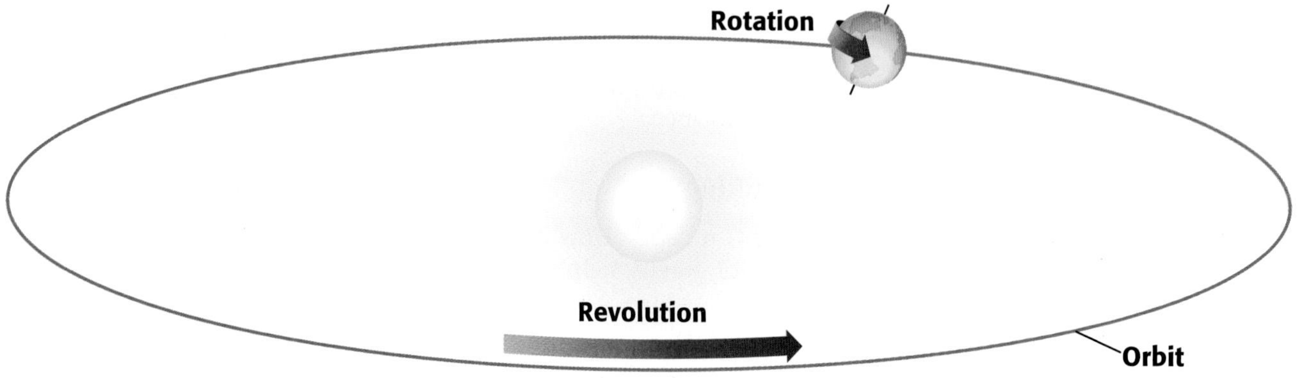

Figure 2 Parts of an Ellipse

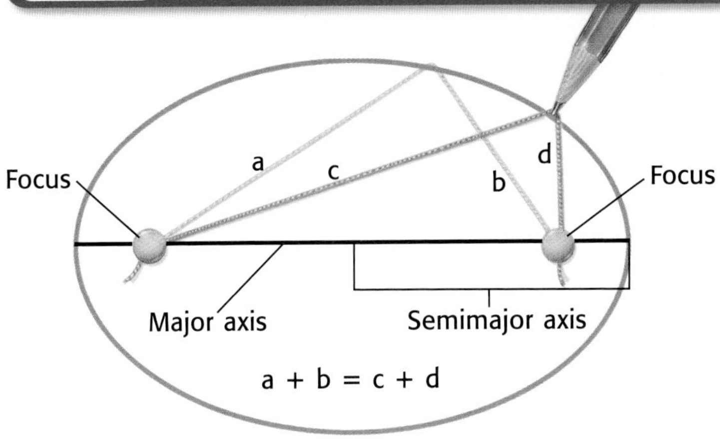

Kepler's First Law of Motion

Kepler's first discovery came from his careful study of Mars. Kepler discovered that Mars did not move in a circle around the sun but moved in an elongated circle called an *ellipse.* This finding became Kepler's first law of motion. An ellipse is a closed curve in which the sum of the distances from the edge of the curve to two points inside the ellipse is always the same, as shown in **Figure 2.** An ellipse's maximum length is called its *major axis.* Half of this distance is the *semimajor axis,* which is usually used to describe the size of an ellipse. The semimajor axis of Earth's orbit—the maximum distance between Earth and the sun—is about 150 million kilometers.

Kepler's Second Law of Motion

Kepler's second discovery, or second law of motion, was that the planets seemed to move faster when they are close to the sun and slower when they are farther away. To understand this idea, imagine that a planet is attached to the sun by a string, as modeled in **Figure 3.** When the string is shorter, the planet must move faster to cover the same area.

Kepler's Third Law of Motion

Kepler noticed that planets that are more distant from the sun, such as Saturn, take longer to orbit the sun. This finding was Kepler's third law of motion, which explains the relationship between the period of a planet's revolution and its semimajor axis. Knowing how long a planet takes to orbit the sun, Kepler was able to calculate the planet's distance from the sun.

Reading Check **Describe Kepler's third law of motion.**
(*See the Appendix for answers to Reading Checks.*)

MATH PRACTICE

Kepler's Formula

Kepler's third law can be expressed with the formula

$$P^2 = a^3$$

where P is the period of revolution and a is the semimajor axis of an orbiting body. For example, Mars's period is 1.88 years, and its semimajor axis is 1.523 AU. Thus, $1.88^2 = 1.523^3 = 3.53$. Calculate a planet's period of revolution if the semimajor axis is 5.74 AU.

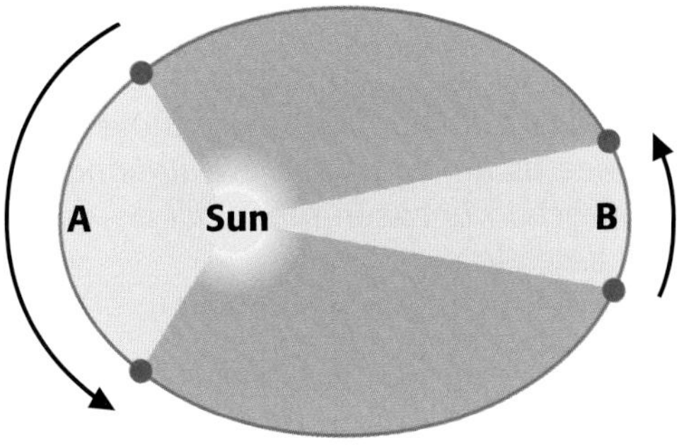

Figure 3 *According to Kepler's second law, to keep the area of* A *equal to the area of* B*, the planet must move faster in its orbit when it is closer to the sun.*

Newton to the Rescue!

Kepler wondered what caused the planets closest to the sun to move faster than the planets farther away. However, he never found an answer. Sir Isaac Newton finally put the puzzle together when he described the force of gravity. Newton didn't understand why gravity worked or what caused it. Even today, scientists do not fully understand gravity. But Newton combined the work of earlier scientists and used mathematics to explain the effects of gravity.

Quick Lab

Staying in Focus

1. Take a **short piece of string,** and pin both ends to a **piece of paper** by using **two thumbtacks.**
2. Keeping the string stretched tight at all times, use a **pencil** to trace the path of an ellipse.
3. Change the distance between the thumbtacks to change the shape of the ellipse.
4. How does the position of the thumbtacks (foci) affect the ellipse?

The Law of Universal Gravitation

Newton reasoned that an object falls toward Earth because Earth and the object are attracted to each other by gravity. He discovered that this attraction depends on the masses of the objects and the distance between the objects.

Newton's *law of universal gravitation* states that the force of gravity depends on the product of the masses of the objects divided by the square of the distance between the objects. The larger the masses of two objects and the closer together the objects are, the greater the force of gravity between the objects. For example, if two objects are moved twice as far apart, the gravitational attraction between them will decrease by 2×2 (a factor of 4), as shown in **Figure 4.** If two objects are moved 10 times as far apart, the gravitational attraction between them will decrease by 10×10 (a factor of 100).

Both Earth and the moon are attracted to each other. Although it may seem as if Earth does not orbit the moon, Earth and the moon actually orbit each other.

Reading Check **Explain Newton's law of universal gravitation.**

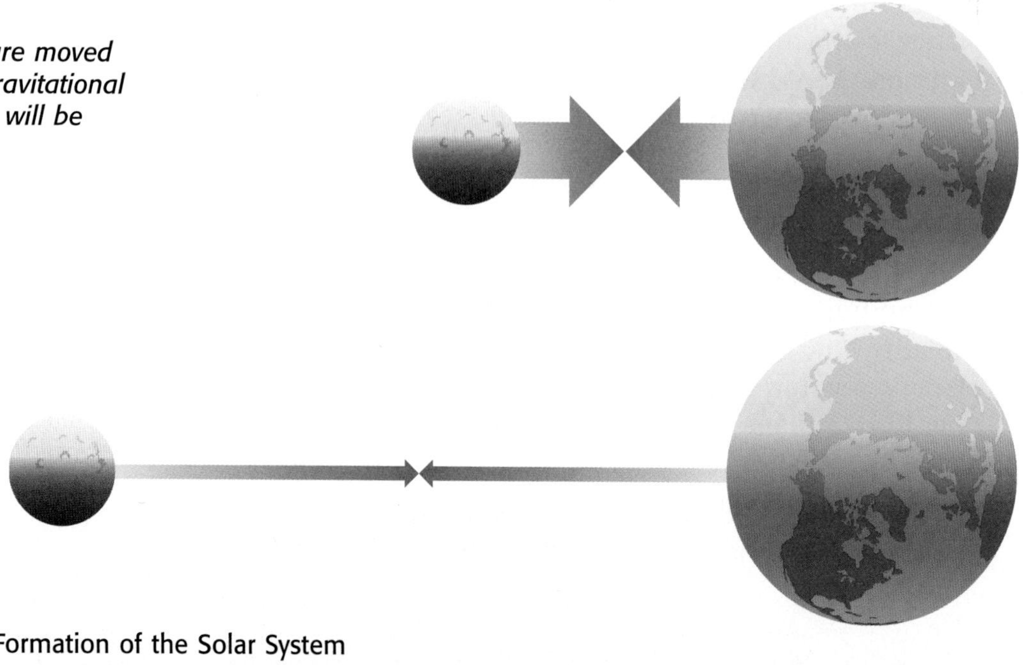

Figure 4 *If two objects are moved twice as far apart, the gravitational attraction between them will be 4 times less.*

Orbits Falling Down and Around

If you drop a rock, it falls to the ground. So, why doesn't the moon come crashing into the Earth? The answer has to do with the moon's inertia. *Inertia* is an object's resistance in speed or direction until an outside force acts on the object. In space, there isn't any air to cause resistance and slow down the moving moon. Therefore, the moon continues to move, but gravity keeps the moon in orbit, as **Figure 5** shows.

Imagine twirling a ball on the end of a string. As long as you hold the string, the ball will orbit your hand. As soon as you let go of the string, the ball will fly off in a straight path. This same principle applies to the moon. Gravity keeps the moon from flying off in a straight path. This principle holds true for all bodies in orbit, including the Earth and other planets in our solar system.

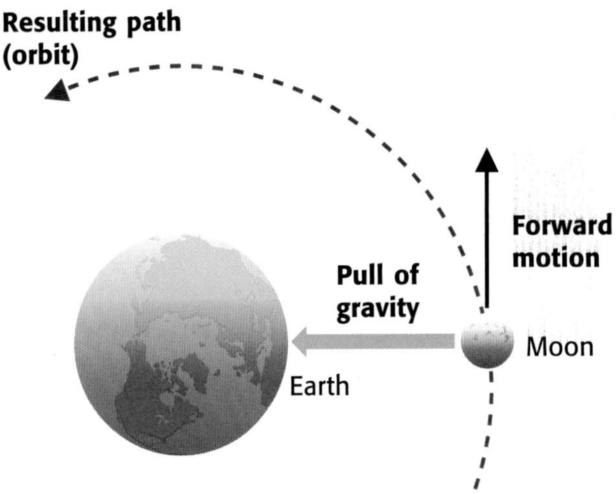

Figure 5 *Gravity causes the moon to fall toward the Earth and changes a straight-line path into a curved orbit.*

SECTION Review

Summary

- Rotation is the spinning of a planet on its axis, and revolution is one complete trip along an orbit.
- Planets move in an ellipse around the sun. The closer they are to the sun, the faster they move. The period of a planet's revolution depends on the planet's semimajor axis.
- Gravitational attraction decreases as distance increases and as mass decreases.

Using Key Terms

1. In your own words, write a definition for each of the following terms: *revolution* and *rotation.*

Understanding Key Ideas

2. Kepler discovered that planets move faster when they
   a. are farther from the sun.
   b. are closer to the sun.
   c. have more mass.
   d. rotate faster.
3. On what properties does the force of gravity between two objects depend?
4. How does gravity keep a planet moving in an orbit around the sun?

Math Skills

5. The Earth's period of revolution is 365.25 days. Convert this period of revolution into hours.

Critical Thinking

6. **Applying Concepts** If a planet had two moons and one moon was twice as far from the planet as the other, which moon would complete a revolution of the planet first? Explain your answer.
7. **Making Comparisons** Describe the three laws of planetary motion. How is each law related to the other laws?

SCILINKS. NSTA Developed and maintained by the National Science Teachers Association

For a variety of links related to this chapter, go to www.scilinks.org

Topic: Kepler's Laws
SciLinks code: HSM0827

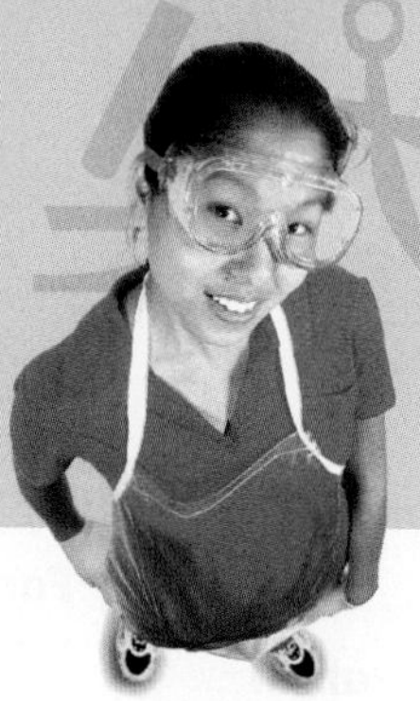

Using Scientific Methods

Skills Practice Lab

How Far Is the Sun?

It doesn't slice, it doesn't dice, but it can give you an idea of how big our universe is! You can build your very own solar-distance measuring device from household items. Amaze your friends by figuring out how many metersticks can be placed between the Earth and the sun.

OBJECTIVES

Create a solar-distance measuring device.

Calculate the Earth's distance from the sun.

MATERIALS

- aluminum foil, 5 cm × 5 cm
- card, index
- meterstick
- poster board
- ruler, metric
- scissors
- tape, masking
- thumbtack

SAFETY

Ask a Question

1. How many metersticks could I place between the Earth and the sun?

Form a Hypothesis

2. Write a hypothesis that answers the question above.

Test the Hypothesis

3. Measure and cut a 4 cm × 4 cm square from the middle of the poster board. Tape the foil square over the hole in the center of the poster board.
4. Using a thumbtack, carefully prick the foil to form a tiny hole in the center. Congratulations! You have just constructed your very own solar-distance measuring device!
5. Tape the device to a window facing the sun so that sunlight shines directly through the pinhole. **Caution:** Do not look directly into the sun.
6. Place one end of the meterstick against the window and beneath the foil square. Steady the meterstick with one hand.
7. With the other hand, hold the index card close to the pinhole. You should be able to see a circular image on the card. This image is an image of the sun.
8. Move the card back until the image is large enough to measure. Be sure to keep the image on the card sharply focused. Reposition the meterstick so that it touches the bottom of the card.

9. Ask your partner to measure the diameter of the image on the card by using the metric ruler. Record the diameter of the image in millimeters.

10. Record the distance between the window and the index card by reading the point at which the card rests on the meterstick.

11. Calculate the distance between Earth and the sun by using the following formula:

$$\textit{distance between the sun and Earth} = \textit{sun's diameter} \times \frac{\textit{distance to the image}}{\textit{image's diameter}}$$

1 cm = 10 mm
1 m = 100 cm
1 km = 1,000 m

(Hint: The sun's diameter is 1,392,000,000 m.)

Analyze the Results

1. **Analyzing Results** According to your calculations, how far from the Earth is the sun? Don't forget to convert your measurements to meters.

Draw Conclusions

2. **Evaluating Data** You could put 150 billion metersticks between the Earth and the sun. Compare this information with your result in step 11. Do you think that this activity was a good way to measure the Earth's distance from the sun? Support your answer.

Chapter Review

USING KEY TERMS

Complete each of the following sentences by choosing the correct term from the word bank.

nebula	crust
mantle	solar nebula

1. A ___ is a large cloud of gas and dust in interstellar space.

2. The ___ lies between the core and the crust of the Earth.

For each pair of terms, explain how the meanings of the terms differ.

3. *nebula* and *solar nebula*

4. *crust* and *mantle*

5. *rotation* and *revolution*

6. *nuclear fusion* and *sunspot*

UNDERSTANDING KEY IDEAS

Multiple Choice

7. To determine a planet's period of revolution, you must know its
   - **a.** size.
   - **b.** mass.
   - **c.** orbit.
   - **d.** All of the above

8. During Earth's formation, materials such as nickel and iron sank to the
   - **a.** mantle.
   - **b.** core.
   - **c.** crust.
   - **d.** All of the above

9. Planetary orbits are shaped like
   - **a.** orbits.
   - **b.** spirals.
   - **c.** ellipses.
   - **d.** periods of revolution.

10. Impacts in the early solar system
    - **a.** brought new materials to the planets.
    - **b.** released energy.
    - **c.** dug craters.
    - **d.** All of the above

11. Organisms that photosynthesize get their energy from
    - **a.** nitrogen.
    - **b.** oxygen.
    - **c.** the sun.
    - **d.** water.

12. Which of the following planets has the shortest period of revolution?
    - **a.** Mars
    - **b.** Earth
    - **c.** Mercury
    - **d.** Jupiter

13. Which gas in Earth's atmosphere suggests that there is life on Earth?
    - **a.** hydrogen
    - **b.** oxygen
    - **c.** carbon dioxide
    - **d.** nitrogen

14. Which layer of the Earth has the lowest density?
    - **a.** the core
    - **b.** the mantle
    - **c.** the crust
    - **d.** None of the above

15. What is the measure of the average kinetic energy of particles in an object?
    - **a.** temperature
    - **b.** pressure
    - **c.** gravity
    - **d.** force

Short Answer

16 Compare a sunspot with a solar flare.

17 Describe how the Earth's oceans and continents formed.

18 Explain how pressure and gravity may have become unbalanced in the solar nebula.

19 Define *nuclear fusion* in your own words. Describe how nuclear fusion generates the sun's energy.

CRITICAL THINKING

20 **Concept Mapping** Use the following terms to create a concept map: *solar nebula, solar system, planetesimals, sun, photosphere, core, nuclear fusion, planets,* and *Earth.*

21 **Making Comparisons** How did Newton's law of universal gravitation help explain the work of Johannes Kepler?

22 **Predicting Consequences** Using what you know about the relationship between living things and the development of Earth's atmosphere, explain how the formation of ozone holes in Earth's atmosphere could affect living things.

23 **Identifying Relationships** Describe Kepler's three laws of motion in your own words. Describe how each law relates to either the revolution, rotation, or orbit of a planetary body.

INTERPRETING GRAPHICS

Use the illustration below to answer the questions that follow.

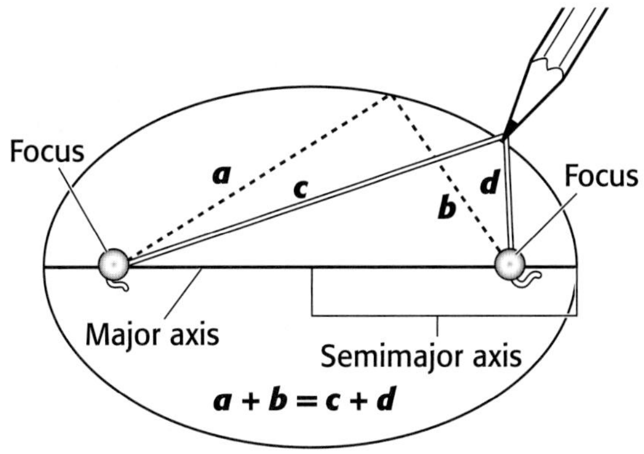

24 Which of Kepler's laws of motion does the illustration represent?

25 How does the equation shown above support the law?

26 What is an ellipse's maximum length called?

Multiple Choice

Use the table below to answer question 1.

Gravitational Force Versus Distance Data	
Distance (meters)	Force (Newtons)
1.0	4.00
2.0	1.00
4.0	0.250
8.0	0.0625

1. Which graph best fits the data provided in the table?

A. 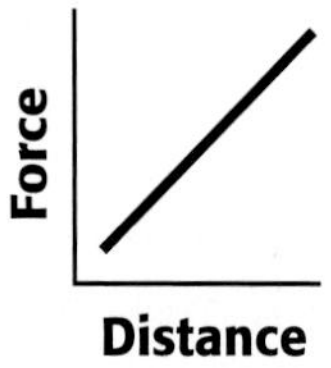

B. 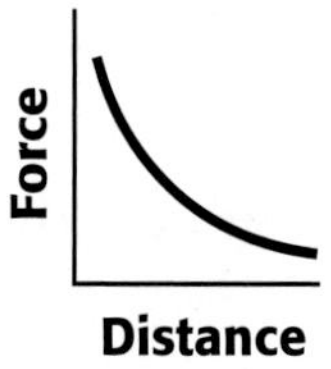

C. 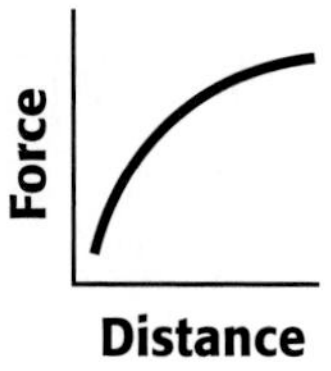

D. 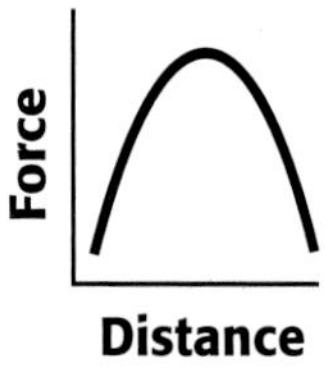

2. Which of the following planets takes the longest time to complete one revolution of the sun?

A. Earth

B. Venus

C. Mercury

D. Jupiter

3. Which of the following will most likely occur inside a cold nebula?

A. Rapid collisions will push particles far apart.

B. Particles will move closer to one another due to gravity.

C. Gravity and pressure will push particles rapidly together.

D. No forces will act on the particles, and the particles will drift apart.

4. A scientist proposes that the sun is no longer producing energy through fusion in its core. Which of the following is a reasonable response to this proposal?

A. proposing tests for the hypothesis in order for the hypothesis to be taken seriously by the scientific community

B. thinking that the proposal must be false because scientists have not detected a decrease in the amount of energy coming from the sun

C. believing that the proposal could be true because cool, dark sunspots have been appearing on the surface of the sun

D. increasing the supply of firewood and warm clothes in the family's underground bunker

5. **How has photosynthesis changed Earth's atmosphere? During photosynthesis, plants take in**

   A. carbon dioxide from the atmosphere and release oxygen.

   B. oxygen from the atmosphere and release nitrogen.

   C. nitrogen from the atmosphere and release carbon dioxide.

   D. sulfur from the atmosphere and release nitrogen.

Use the diagram below to answer questions 6–7.

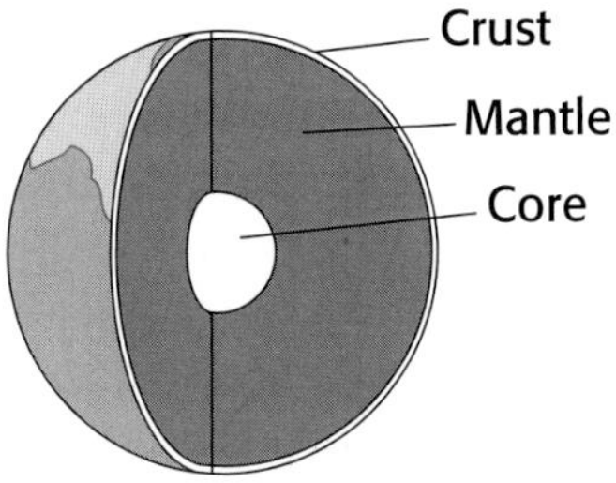

6. **Pam made the sketch of Earth's layers shown above. What is the most likely location of the densest elements?**

   A. crust

   B. mantle

   C. core

   D. all layers

7. **Pam made a second sketch of the Earth as it looked during the early period of planetary accretion. How would Pam's new sketch compare with the sketch above? The new sketch would**

   A. look about the same as the one above.

   B. have more layers than the sketch above.

   C. have only the mantle and core layers.

   D. show materials that are randomly mixed.

8. **A student swings a ball attached to a string to model the moon's orbit around the Earth. What force does the string represent?**

   A. inertia

   B. pressure

   C. gravity

   D. momentum

9. **If there were no gravitational forces acting on the moon, the moon would**

   A. quickly crash into the Earth.

   B. continue at a constant speed in a straight line through space.

   C. still orbit Earth as it does now.

   D. remain stationary, at a fixed distance from Earth.

Open Response

10. **Comets, asteroids, and meteoroids are rocky bodies in the solar system. How would the composition of these rocky bodies compare to the composition of Earth? Explain your answer.**

11. **How do Earth's crust and mantle interact to change the locations of the continents?**

Science in Action

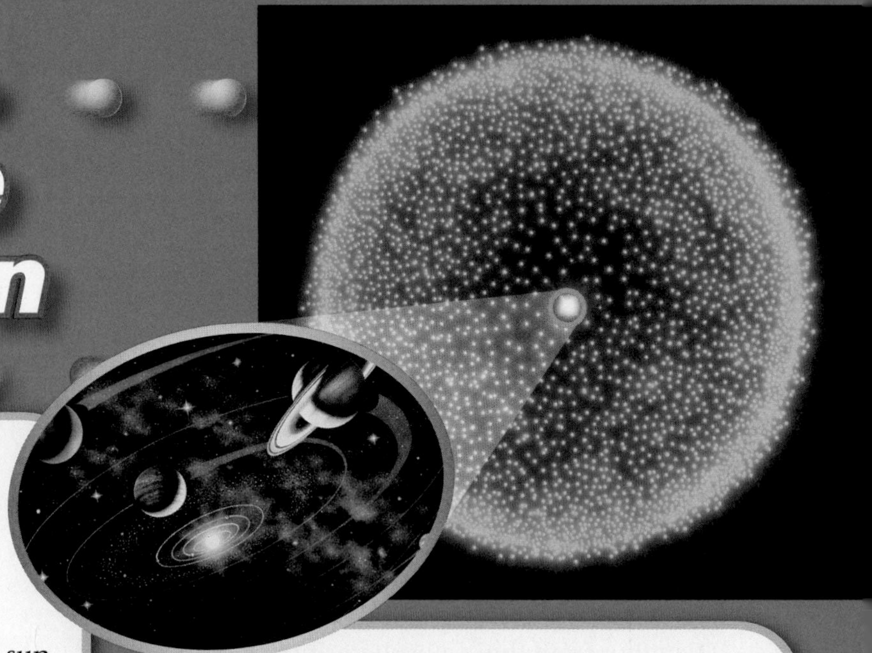

Science, Technology, and Society

Don't Look at the Sun!

How can we learn anything about the sun if we can't look at it? The answer is to use a special telescope called a *solar telescope*. The three largest solar telescopes in the world are located at Kitt Peak National Observatory near Tucson, Arizona. The largest of these telescopes, the McMath-Pierce solar telescope, creates an image of the sun that is almost 1 m wide! How is the image created? The McMath-Pierce solar telescope uses a mirror that is more than 2 m in diameter to direct the sun's rays down a diagonal shaft to another mirror, which is 152 m underground. This mirror is adjustable to focus the sunlight. The sunlight is then directed to a third mirror, which directs the light to an observing room and instrument shaft.

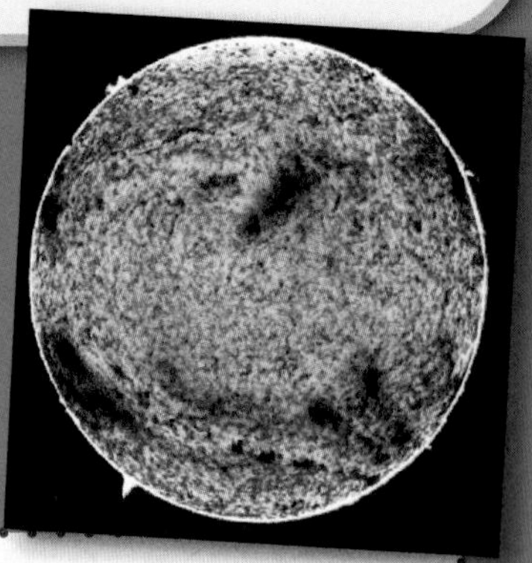

Math ACTIVITY

The outer skin of the McMath-Pierce solar telescope consists of 140 copper panels that measure 10.4 m × 2.4 m each. How many square meters of copper were used to construct the outer skin of the telescope?

Scientific Discoveries

The Oort Cloud

Have you ever wondered where comets come from? In 1950, Dutch astronomer Jan Oort decided to find out where comets originated. Oort studied 19 comets. He found that none of these comets had orbits indicating that the comets had come from outside the solar system. Oort thought that all of the comets had come from an area at the far edge of the solar system. In addition, he believed that the comets had entered the planetary system from different directions. These conclusions led Oort to theorize that the area from which comets come surrounds the solar system like a sphere and that comets can come from any point within the sphere. Today, this spherical zone at the edge of the solar system is called the *Oort Cloud*. Astronomers believe that billions or even trillions of comets may exist within the Oort Cloud.

Social Studies ACTIVITY

WRITING SKILL Before astronomers understood the nature of comets, comets were a source of much fear and misunderstanding among humans. Research some of the myths that humans have created about comets. Summarize your findings in a short essay.

People in Science

Subrahmanyan Chandrasekhar

From White Dwarfs to Black Holes You may be familiar with the *Chandra X-Ray Observatory*. Launched by NASA in July 1999 to search for x-ray sources in space, the observatory is the most powerful x-ray telescope that has ever been built. However, you may not know how the observatory got its name. The *Chandra X-Ray Observatory* was named after the Indian American astrophysicist Subrahmanyan Chandrasekhar (SOOB ruh MAHN yuhn CHUHN druh SAY kuhr).

One of the most influential astrophysicists of the 20th century, Chandrasekhar was simply known as "Chandra" by his fellow scientists. Chandrasekhar made many contributions to physics and astrophysics. The contribution for which Chandrasekhar is best known was made in 1933, when he was a 23-year-old graduate student at Cambridge University in England. At the time, astrophysicists thought that all stars eventually became planet-sized stars known as *white dwarfs*. But from his calculations, Chandrasekhar believed that not all stars ended their lives as white dwarfs. He determined that the upper limit to the mass of a white dwarf was 1.4 times the mass of the sun. Stars that were more massive would collapse and would become very dense objects. These objects are now known as *black holes*. Chandrasekhar's ideas revolutionized astrophysics. In 1983, at the age of 73, Chandrasekhar was awarded the Nobel Prize in physics for his work on the evolution of stars.

Language Arts ACTIVITY

WRITING SKILL Using the Internet or another source, research the meaning of the word *chandra*. Write a paragraph describing your findings.

To learn more about these Science in Action topics, visit go.hrw.com and type in the keyword HZ5SOLF.

Current Science

Check out Current Science® articles related to this chapter by visiting go.hrw.com. Just type in the keyword HZ5CS20.

UNIT 5

TIMELINE

Human Body Systems

Like a finely tuned machine, your body is made up of many systems that work together. Your lungs take in oxygen. Your brain reacts to things you see, hear, and smell and sends signals through your nervous system that cause you to react to those things. Your digestive system converts the food you eat into energy that the cells of your body can use. And those are just a few things that your body can do!

In this unit, you will study the systems of your body. You'll discover how the parts of your body work together.

Around 3000 BCE

Ancient Egyptian doctors are the first to study the human body scientifically.

1824

Jean Louis Prevost and Jean Batiste Dumas prove that sperm is essential for fertilization.

1766

Albrecht von Haller determines that nerves control muscle movement and that all nerves are connected to the spinal cord or to the brain.

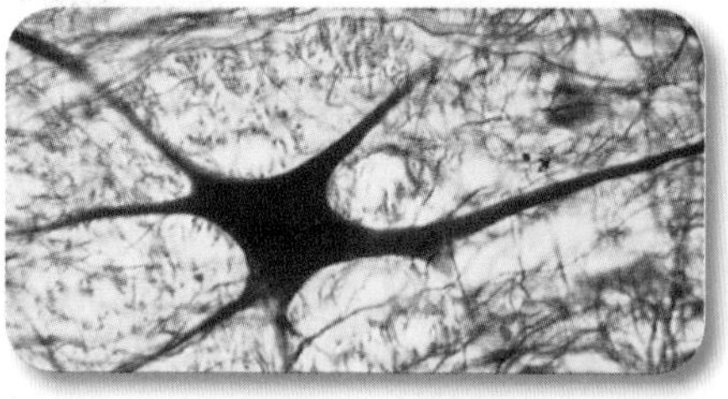

1940

During World War II in Italy, Rita Levi-Montalcini is forced to leave her work at a medical school laboratory because she is Jewish. She sets up a laboratory in her bedroom and studies the development of the nervous system.

Around
500 BCE
Indian surgeon Susrata performs operations to remove cataracts.

1492
Christopher Columbus lands in the West Indies.

1543
Andreas Vesalius publishes the first complete description of the structure of the human body.

1616
William Harvey discovers that blood circulates and that the heart acts as a pump.

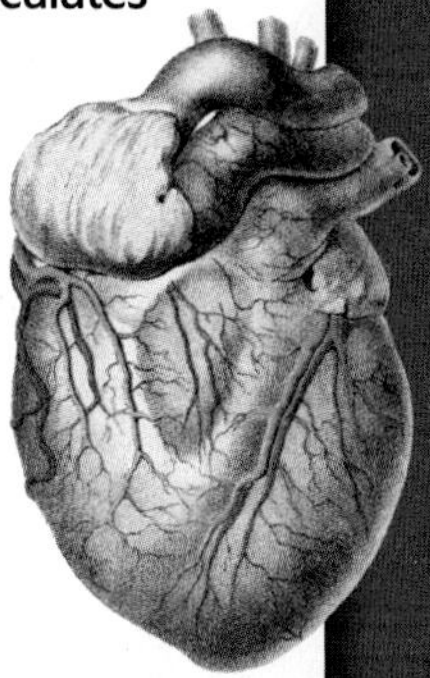

1893
Daniel Hale Williams, an African American surgeon, becomes the first person to repair a tear in the pericardium, the sac around the heart.

1922
Frederick Banting, Charles Best, and John McLeod discover insulin.

1930
Karl Landsteiner receives a Nobel Prize for his discovery of the four human blood types.

1982
Dr. William DeVries implants an artificial heart in Barney Clark.

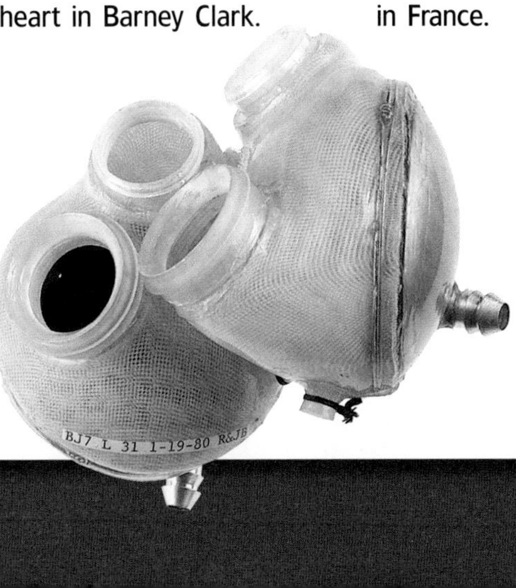

1998
The first sucessful hand transplant is performed in France.

2001
Drs. Laman A. Gray, Jr. and Robert D. Dowling at Jewish Hospital in Louisville, Kentucky, implant the first self-contained mechanical human heart.

17

Body Organization and Structure

The Big Idea

The human body is composed of major systems that have differing functions, but all of the systems work together to maintain homeostasis.

SECTION

About the Photo

Lance Armstrong has won the Tour de France several times. These victories are especially remarkable because he was diagnosed with cancer in 1996. But with medicine and hard work, he grew strong enough to win one of the toughest events in all of sports.

PRE-READING ACTIVITY

FOLDNOTES **Four-Corner Fold** Before you read the chapter, create the FoldNote entitled "Four-Corner Fold" described in the **Study Skills** section of the Appendix. Label the flaps of the four-corner fold with "The skeletal system," "The muscular system," and "The integumentary system." Write what you know about each topic under the appropriate flap. As you read the chapter, add other information that you learn.

START-UP ACTIVITY

Too Cold for Comfort

Your nervous system sends you messages about your body. For example, if someone steps on your toe, your nervous system sends you a message. The pain you feel is a message that tells you to move your toe to safety. Try this exercise to watch your nervous system in action.

Procedure

1. Hold **a few pieces of ice** in one hand. Allow the melting water to drip into a **dish.** Hold the ice until the cold is uncomfortable. Then, release the ice into the dish.
2. Compare the hand that held the ice with your other hand. Describe the changes you see.

Analysis

1. What message did you receive from your nervous system while you held the ice?
2. How quickly did the cold hand return to normal?
3. What organ systems do you think helped restore your hand to normal?
4. Think of a time when your nervous system sent you a message, such as an uncomfortable feeling of heat, cold, or pain. How did your body react?

SECTION 1

Body Organization

Imagine jumping into a lake. At first, your body feels very cold. You may even shiver. But eventually you get used to the cold water. How?

What You Will Learn

- Describe how tissues, organs, and organ systems are related.
- List 11 organ systems.
- Identify how organ systems work together to maintain homeostasis.

Vocabulary

homeostasis
organ
tissue

READING STRATEGY

Reading Organizer As you read this section, make a concept map by using the terms above.

Your body gets used to cold water because it returns to *homeostasis*. **Homeostasis** (HOH mee OH STAY sis) is the maintenance of a stable internal environment in the body. When you jump into a lake, homeostasis helps your body adapt to the cold water.

Cells, Tissues, and Organs

Maintaining homeostasis is not easy. Your internal environment is always changing. Your cells need nutrients and oxygen to survive. Your cells need wastes removed. If homeostasis is disrupted, cells may not get the materials they need. So, cells may be damaged or may die.

Cells Form Tissues

Your cells must do many jobs to maintain homeostasis. But, each of your cells does not have to do all of those jobs. Just as each person on a soccer team has a role during a game, each cell in your body has a job in maintaining homeostasis. Your cells are organized into groups. A group of similar cells working together forms a **tissue.** Your body has four main kinds of tissue. The four kinds of tissue are shown in **Figure 1.**

homeostasis the maintenance of a constant internal state in a changing environment

tissue a group of similar cells that perform a common function

Figure 1 Four Kinds of Tissue

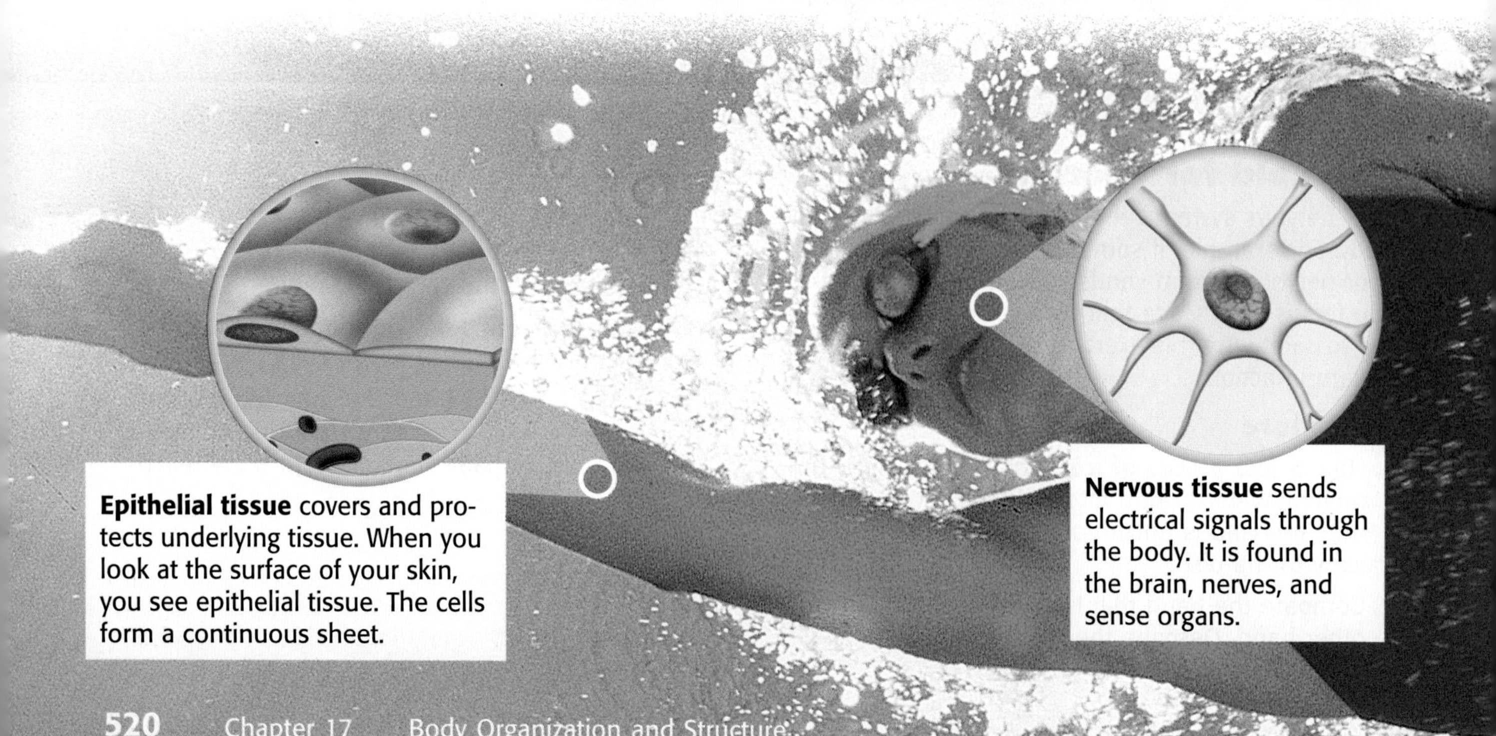

Epithelial tissue covers and protects underlying tissue. When you look at the surface of your skin, you see epithelial tissue. The cells form a continuous sheet.

Nervous tissue sends electrical signals through the body. It is found in the brain, nerves, and sense organs.

Figure 2 **Organization of the Stomach**

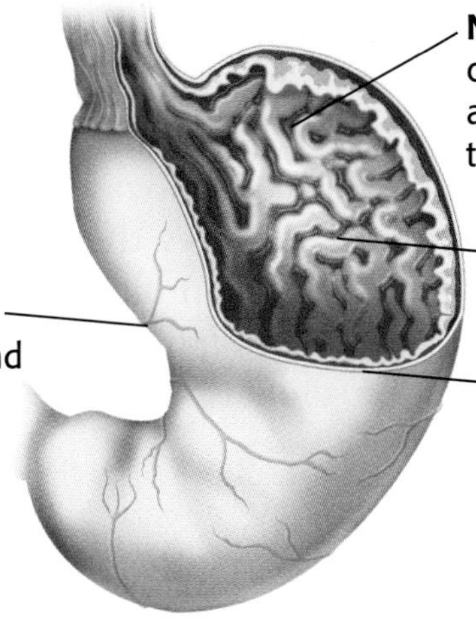

The stomach is an organ. The four kinds of tissue work together so that the stomach can carry out digestion.
Nervous tissue in the stomach partly controls the production of acids that aid in the digestion of food. Nervous tissue signals when the stomach is full.
Epithelial tissue lines the stomach.
Blood and another **connective tissue** called *collagen* are found in the wall of the stomach.
Layers of **muscle tissue** break up stomach contents.

Tissues Form Organs

One kind of tissue alone cannot do all of the things that several kinds of tissue working together can do. Two or more tissues working together form an **organ.** Your stomach, shown in **Figure 2,** uses all four kinds of tissue to carry out digestion.

organ a collection of tissues that carry out a specialized function of the body

Organs Form Systems

Your stomach does a lot to help you digest your food. But the stomach doesn't do it all. Your stomach works with other organs, such as the small and large intestines, to digest your food. Organs that work together make up an *organ system*.

Reading Check **How is the stomach part of an organ system?** *(See the Appendix for answers to Reading Checks.)*

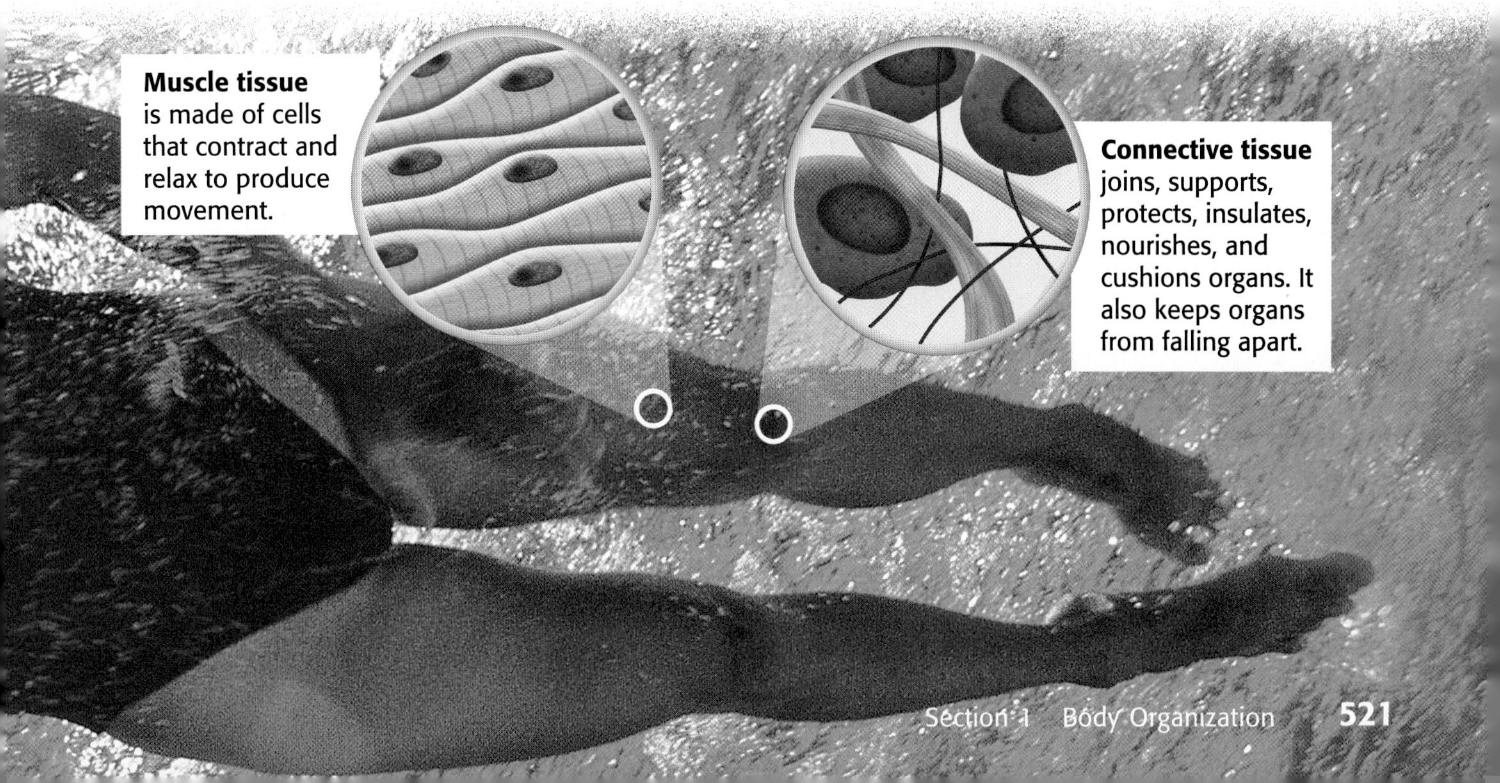

Muscle tissue is made of cells that contract and relax to produce movement.
Connective tissue joins, supports, protects, insulates, nourishes, and cushions organs. It also keeps organs from falling apart.

Working Together

Your body's 11 major organ systems, shown in **Figure 3,** work together to maintain homeostasis. For example, the cardiovascular system, which includes the heart, blood, and blood vessels, works with the respiratory system, which includes the lungs. The cardiovascular system picks up oxygen from the lungs and carries the oxygen to cells in the body. These cells produce carbon dioxide, which the cardiovascular system returns to the respiratory system. The respiratory system expels the carbon dioxide.

Reading Check **Give an example of how organ systems work together in the body.**

Figure 3 **Organ Systems**

Integumentary System Your skin, hair, and nails protect the tissue that lies beneath them.

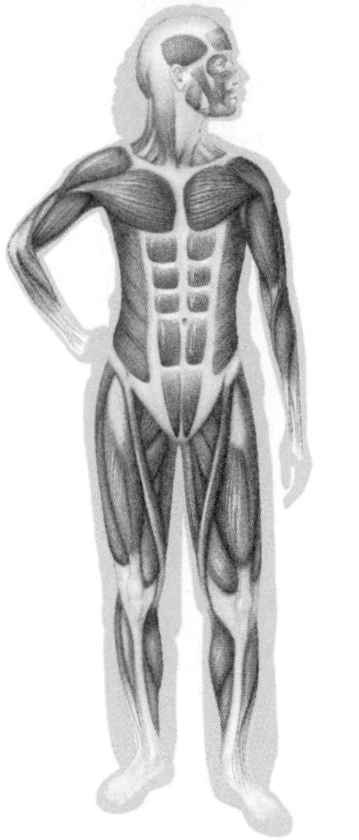

Muscular System Your muscular system works with the skeletal system to help you move.

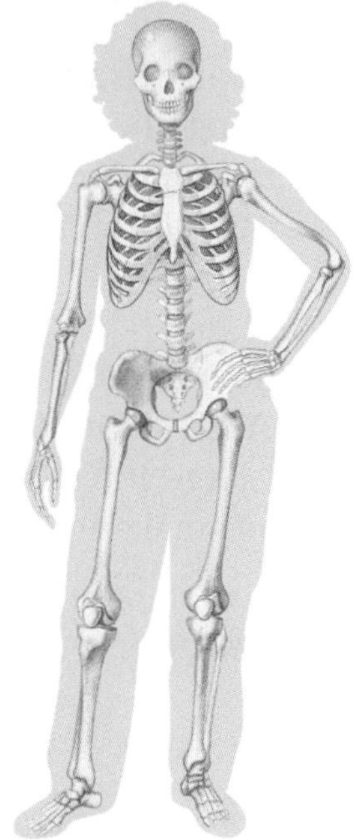

Skeletal System Your bones provide a frame to support and protect your body parts.

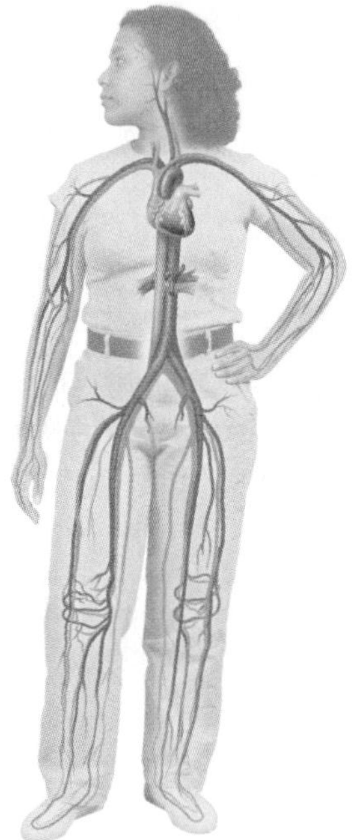

Cardiovascular System Your heart pumps blood through all of your blood vessels.

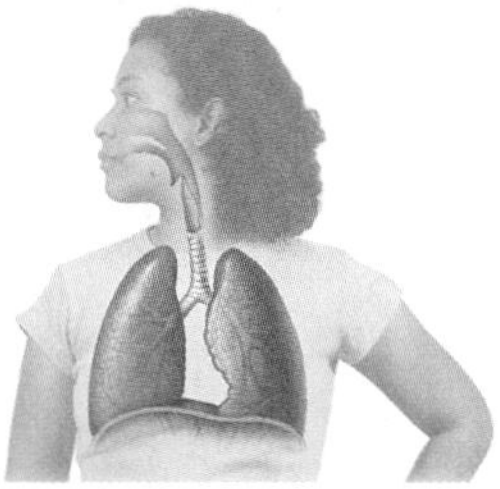

Respiratory System Your lungs absorb oxygen and release carbon dioxide.

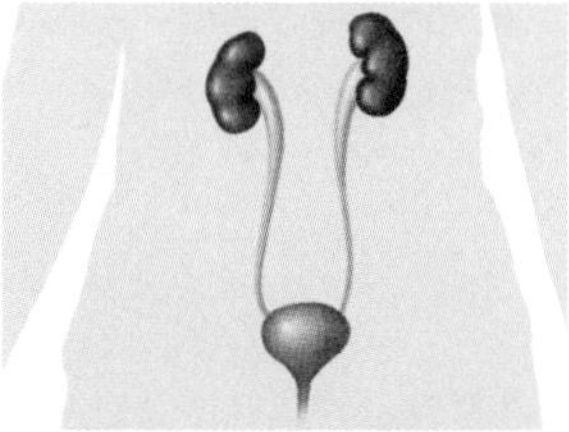

Urinary System Your urinary system removes wastes from the blood and regulates your body's fluids.

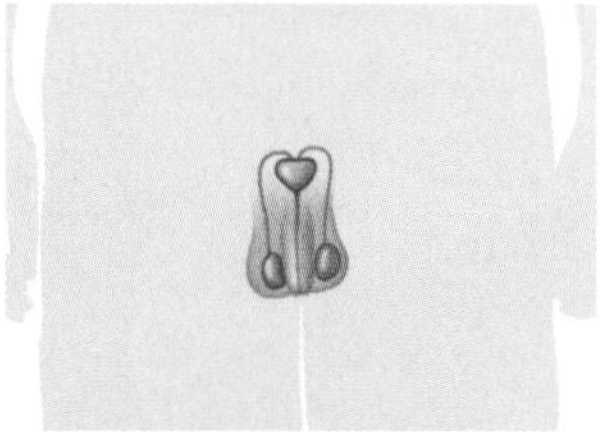

Male Reproductive System The male reproductive system produces and delivers sperm.

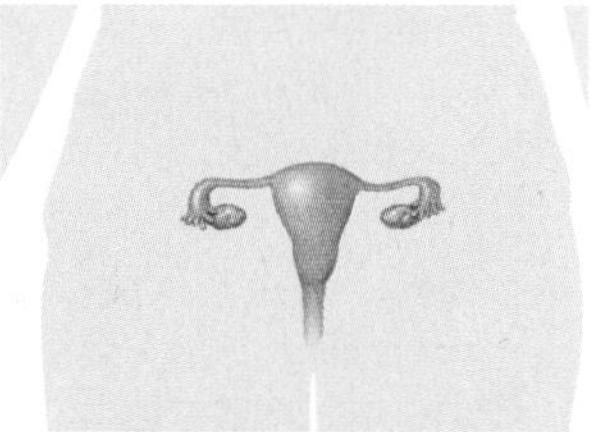

Female Reproductive System The female reproductive system produces eggs and nourishes and protects the fetus.

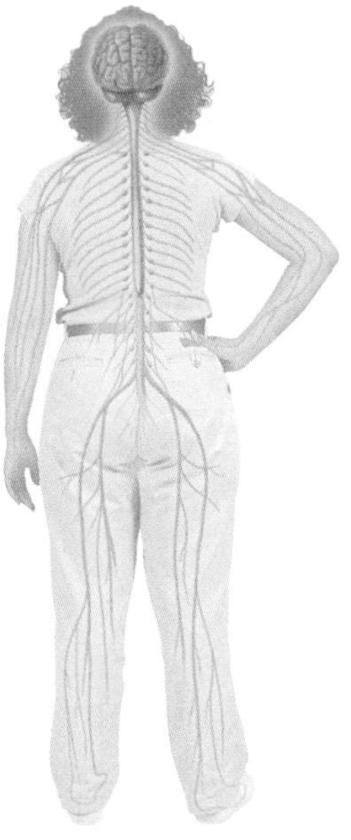

Nervous System Your nervous system receives and sends electrical messages throughout your body.

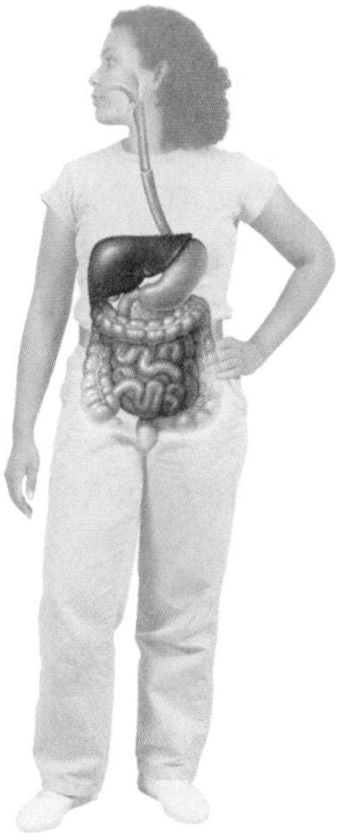

Digestive System Your digestive system breaks down the food you eat into nutrients that your body can absorb.

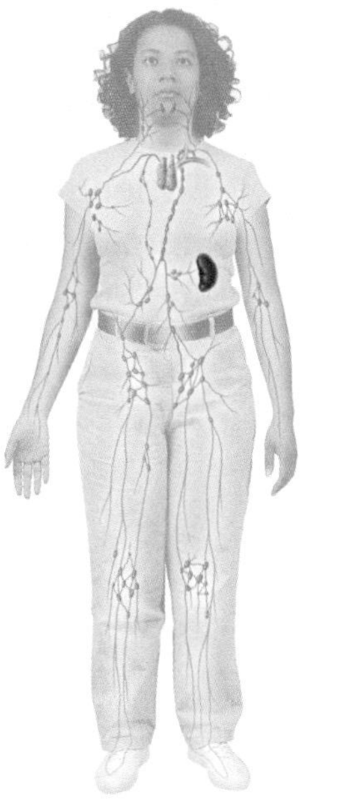

Lymphatic System The lymphatic system returns leaked fluids to blood vessels and helps get rid of bacteria and viruses.

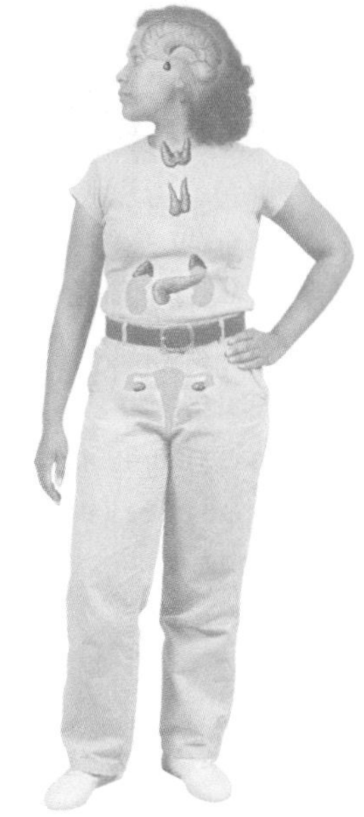

Endocrine System Your glands send out chemical messages. Ovaries and testes are part of this system.

SECTION Review

Summary

- A group of cells that work together is a tissue. Tissues form organs. Organs that work together form organ systems.
- There are four kinds of tissue in the human body.
- There are 11 major organ systems in the human body.
- Organ systems work together to help the body maintain homeostasis.

Using Key Terms

1. Use the following terms in the same sentence: *homeostasis*, *tissue*, and *organ*.

Understanding Key Ideas

2. Which of the following statements describes how tissues, organs, and organ systems are related?

a. Organs form tissues, which form organ systems.
b. Organ systems form organs, which form tissues.
c. Tissues form organs, which form organ systems.
d. None of the above

3. List the 11 organ systems.

Math Skills

4. The human skeleton has 206 bones. The human skull has 22 bones. What percentage of human bones are skull bones?

Critical Thinking

5. Applying Concepts Tanya went to a restaurant and ate a hamburger. Describe how Tanya used five organ systems to eat and digest her hamburger.

6. Predicting Consequences Predict what might happen if the human body did not have specialized cells, tissues, organs, and organ systems to maintain homeostasis.

SCILINKS. NSTA
Developed and maintained by the National Science Teachers Association

For a variety of links related to this chapter, go to www.scilinks.org

Topic: Tissues and Organs; Body Systems
SciLinks code: HSM1530; HSM0184

SECTION 2

The Skeletal System

When you hear the word *skeleton,* you may think of the remains of something that has died. But your skeleton is not dead. It is very much alive.

You may think your bones are dry and brittle. But they are alive and active. Bones, cartilage, and the connective tissue that holds bones together make up your **skeletal system.**

What You Will Learn

- Identify the major organs of the skeletal system.
- Describe four functions of bones.
- Describe three joints.
- List three injuries and two diseases that affect bones and joints.

Vocabulary

skeletal system
joint

READING STRATEGY

Reading Organizer As you read this section, create an outline of the section. Use the headings from the section in your outline.

Bones

The average adult human skeleton has 206 bones. Bones help support and protect parts of your body. They work with your muscles so you can move. Bones also help your body maintain homeostasis by storing minerals and making blood cells. **Figure 1** shows the functions of your skeleton.

skeletal system the organ system whose primary function is to support and protect the body and to allow the body to move

Figure 1 The Skeleton

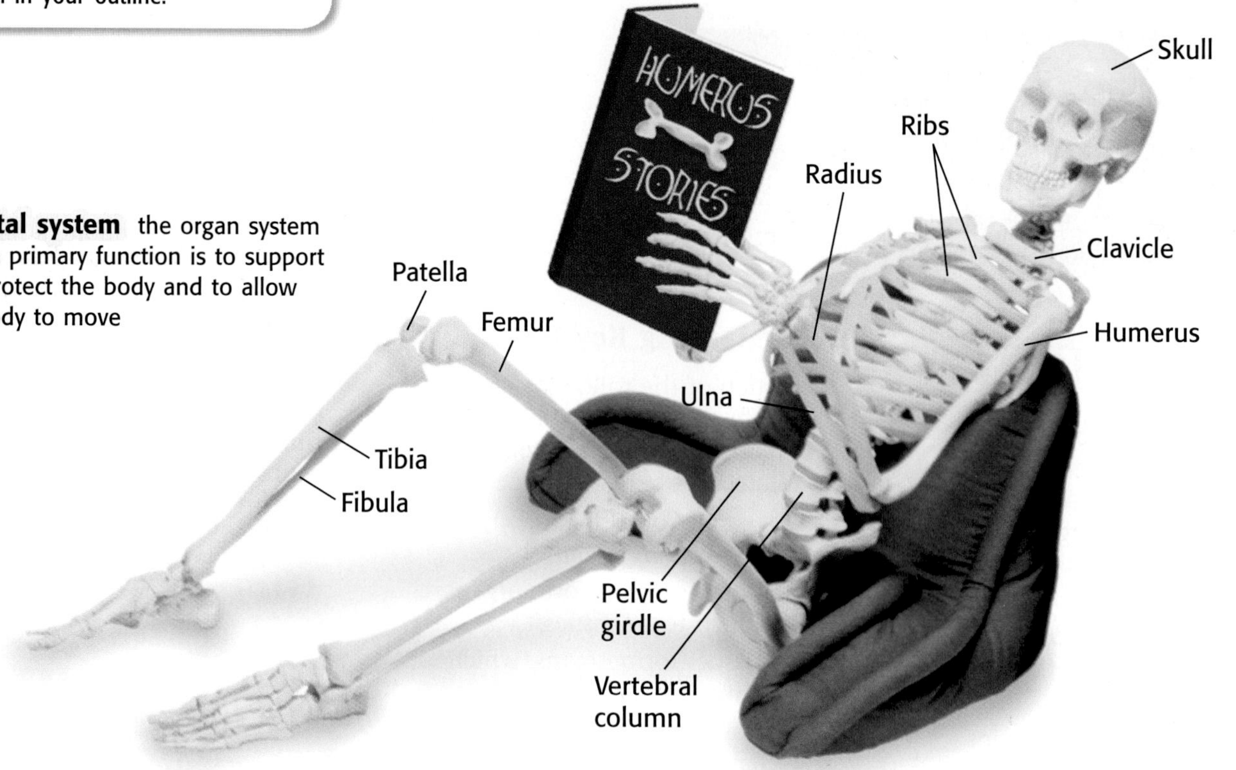

Protection Your heart and lungs are protected by ribs, your spinal cord is protected by vertebrae, and your brain is protected by the skull.

Storage Bones store minerals that help your nerves and muscles function properly. Long bones store fat that can be used for energy.

Movement Skeletal muscles pull on bones to produce movement. Without bones, you would not be able to sit, stand, walk, or run.

Blood Cell Formation Some of your bones are filled with a special material that makes blood cells. This material is called *marrow.*

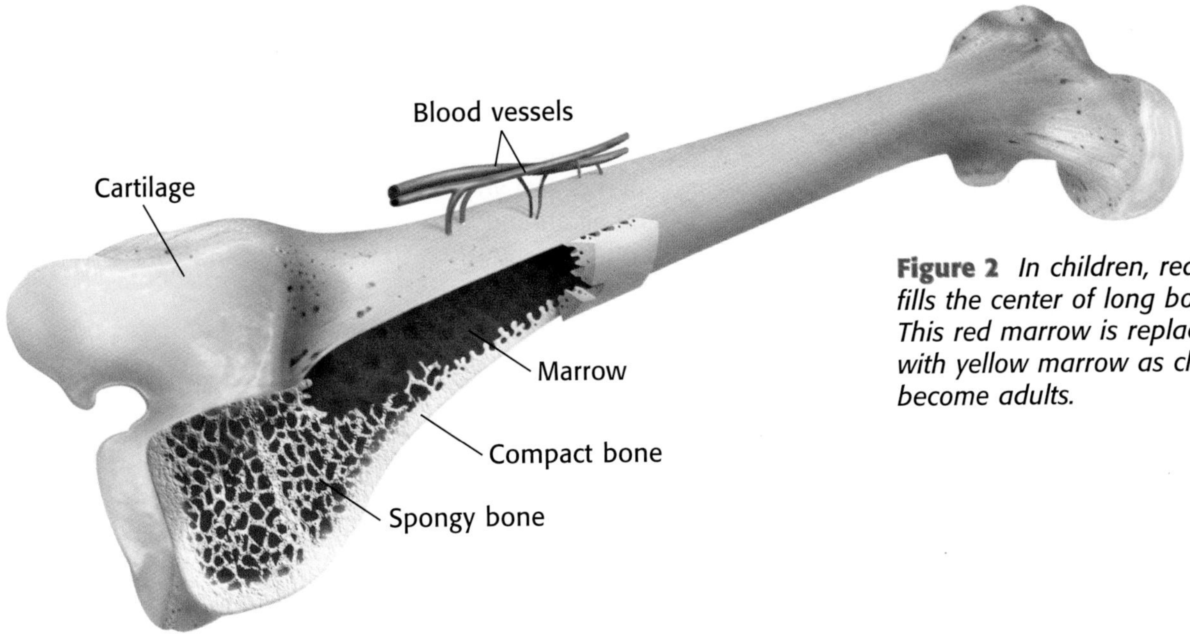

Figure 2 *In children, red marrow fills the center of long bones. This red marrow is replaced with yellow marrow as children become adults.*

Bone Structure

A bone may seem lifeless. But a bone is a living organ made of several different tissues. Bone is made of connective tissue and minerals. These minerals are deposited by living cells called *osteoblasts* (AHS tee oh BLASTS).

If you look inside a bone, you will notice two kinds of bone tissue. If the bone tissue does not have any visible open spaces, it is called *compact bone*. Compact bone is rigid and dense. Tiny canals within compact bone contain small blood vessels. Bone tissue that has many open spaces is called *spongy bone*. Spongy bone provides most of the strength and support for a bone.

Bones contain a soft tissue called *marrow*. There are two types of marrow. Red marrow produces both red and white blood cells. Yellow marrow, found in the central cavity of long bones, stores fat. **Figure 2** shows a cross section of a long bone, the femur.

Bone Growth

Did you know that most of your skeleton used to be soft and rubbery? Most bones start out as a flexible tissue called *cartilage*. When you were born, you didn't have much true bone. But as you grew, most of the cartilage was replaced by bone. During childhood, most bones still have growth plates of cartilage. These growth plates provide a place for bones to continue to grow.

Feel the end of your nose. Or bend the top of your ear. These areas are two places where cartilage is never replaced by bone. These areas stay flexible.

Reading Check **How do bones grow?** (*See the Appendix for answers to Reading Checks.*)

Quick Lab

Pickled Bones

1. Place a **clean chicken bone** in a **jar of vinegar.**
2. After 1 week, remove the bone and rinse it with **water.**
3. Describe the changes that you can see or feel.
4. How has the bone's strength changed?
5. What did the vinegar remove?

Figure 3 Three Joints

Gliding Joint
Gliding joints allow bones in the hand and wrist to glide over one another and give some flexibility to the area.

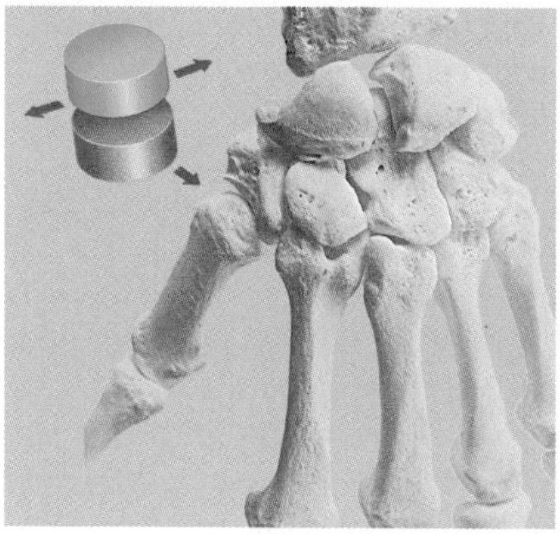

Ball-and-Socket Joint
As a video-game joystick lets you move your character all around, the shoulder lets your arm move freely in all directions.

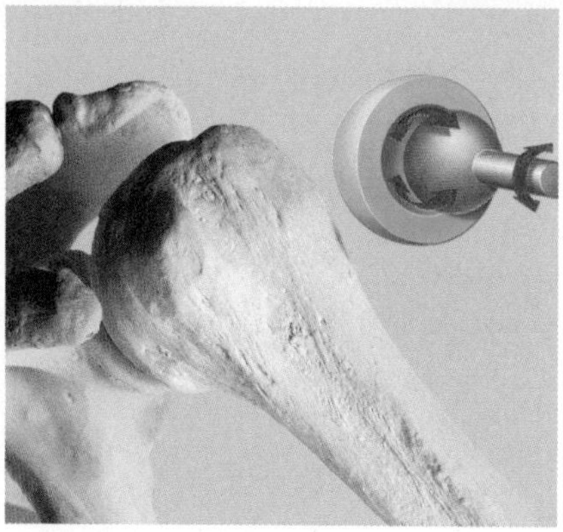

Hinge Joint
As a hinge allows a door to open and close, the knee enables you to flex and extend your lower leg.

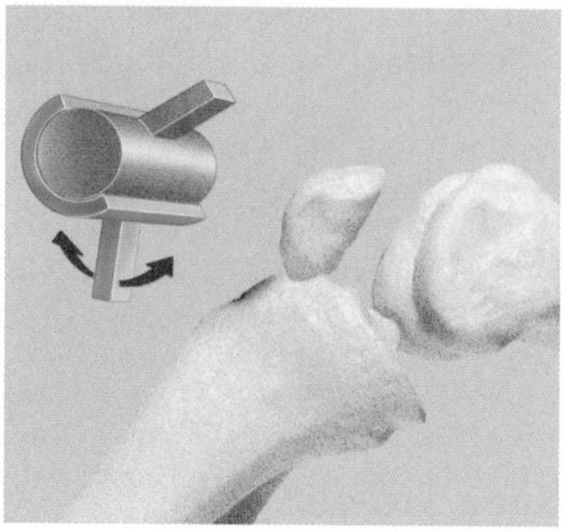

Joints

A place where two or more bones meet is called a **joint.** Your joints allow your body to move when your muscles contract. Some joints, such as fixed joints, allow little or no movement. Many of the joints in the skull are fixed joints. Other joints, such as your shoulder, allow a lot of movement. Joints can be classified based on how the bones in a joint move. For example, your shoulder is a ball-and-socket joint. Three joints are shown in **Figure 3.**

joint a place where two or more bones meet

Joints are held together by *ligaments* (LIG uh muhnts). Ligaments are strong elastic bands of connective tissue. They connect the bones in a joint. Also, cartilage covers the ends of many bones. Cartilage helps cushion the area in a joint where bones meet.

Reading Check Describe the basic structure of joints.

CONNECTION TO Environmental Science

WRITING SKILL **Bones from the Ocean** Sometimes, a bone or joint may become so damaged that it needs to be repaired or replaced with surgery. Often, replacement parts are made from a metal, such as titanium. However, some scientists have discovered that coral skeletons from coral reefs in the ocean can be used to replace human bone. Research bone surgery. Identify why doctors use metals such as titanium. Then, identify the advantages that coral may offer. Write a report discussing your findings.

Skeletal System Injuries and Diseases

Sometimes, parts of the skeletal system are injured. As shown in **Figure 4,** bones may be fractured, or broken. Joints can also be injured. A dislocated joint is a joint in which one or more bones have been moved out of place. Another joint injury, called a *sprain,* happens if a ligament is stretched too far or torn.

There are also diseases of the skeletal system. *Osteoporosis* (AHS tee OH puh ROH sis) is a disease that causes bones to become less dense. Bones become weak and break more easily. Age and poor eating habits can make it more likely for people to develop osteoporosis. Other bone diseases affect the marrow or make bones soft. A disease that affects the joints is called *arthritis* (ahr THRIET is). Arthritis is painful. Joints may swell or stiffen. As they get older, some people are more likely to have some types of arthritis.

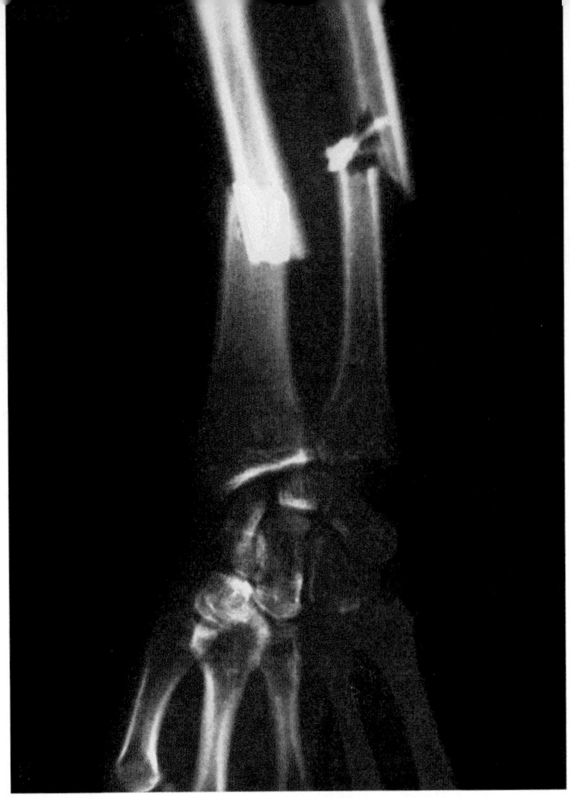

Figure 4 *This X ray shows that the two bones of the forearm have been fractured, or broken.*

SECTION Review

Summary

- The skeletal system includes bones, cartilage, and the connective tissue that connects bones.
- Bones protect the body, store minerals, allow movement, and make blood cells.
- Joints are places where two or more bones meet.
- Skeletal system injuries include fractures, dislocations, and sprains. Skeletal system diseases include osteoporosis and arthritis.

Using Key Terms

1. In your own words, write a definition for the term *skeletal system.*

Understanding Key Ideas

2. Which of the following is NOT an organ of the skeletal system?
   a. bone
   b. cartilage
   c. muscle
   d. None of the above
3. Describe four functions of bones.
4. What are three joints?
5. Describe two diseases that affect the skeletal system.

Math Skills

6. A broken bone usually heals in about six weeks. A mild sprain takes one-third as long to heal. In days, about how long does it take a mild sprain to heal?

Critical Thinking

7. **Identifying Relationships** Red bone marrow produces blood cells. Children have red bone marrow in their long bones, while adults have yellow bone marrow, which stores fat. Why might adults and children have different kinds of marrow?
8. **Predicting Consequences** What might happen if children's bones didn't have growth plates of cartilage?

SECTION 3

The Muscular System

Have you ever tried to sit still, without moving any muscles at all, for one minute? It's impossible! Somewhere in your body, muscles are always working.

What You Will Learn

- List three kinds of muscle tissue.
- Describe how skeletal muscles move bones.
- Compare aerobic exercise with resistance exercise.
- Describe two muscular system injuries.

Vocabulary

muscular system

READING STRATEGY

Discussion Read this section silently. Write down questions that you have about this section. Discuss your questions in a small group.

Your heart is a muscle. Muscles make you breathe. And muscles hold you upright. If all of your muscles rested at the same time, you would collapse. The **muscular system** is made up of the muscles that let you move.

Kinds of Muscle

Figure 1 shows the three kinds of muscle in your body. *Smooth muscle* is found in the digestive tract and in the walls of blood vessels. *Cardiac muscle* is found only in your heart. *Skeletal muscle* is attached to your bones for movement. Skeletal muscle also helps protect your inner organs.

Muscle action can be voluntary or involuntary. Muscle action that is under your control is *voluntary.* Muscle action that is not under your control is *involuntary.* Smooth muscle and cardiac muscle are involuntary muscles. Skeletal muscles can be both voluntary and involuntary muscles. For example, you can blink your eyes anytime you want to. But your eyes will also blink automatically.

Figure 1 Three Kinds of Muscle

Skeletal muscle enables bones to move.
Smooth muscle moves food through the digestive system.
Cardiac muscle pumps blood around the body.

Figure 2 A Pair of Muscles in the Arm

Skeletal muscles, such as the biceps and triceps muscles, work in pairs. When the biceps muscle contracts, the arm bends. When the triceps muscle contracts, the arm straightens.

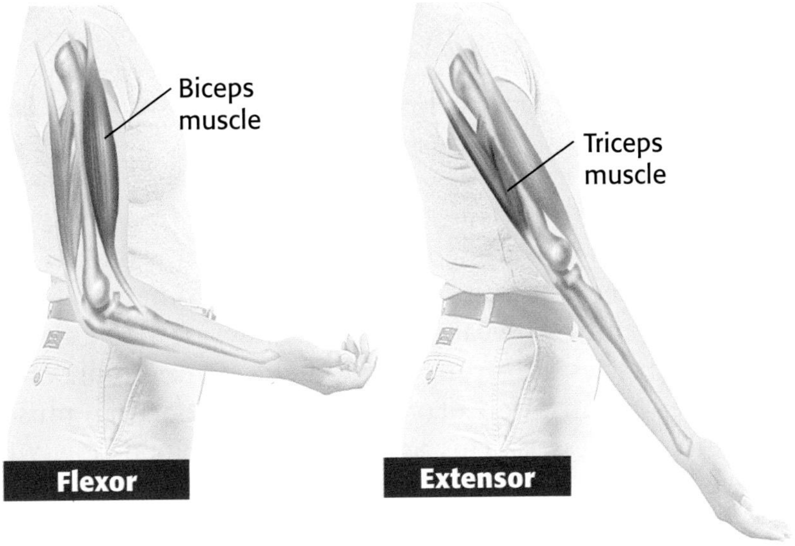

muscular system the organ system whose primary function is movement and flexibility

Movement

Skeletal muscles can make hundreds of movements. You can see many of these movements by watching a dancer, a swimmer, or even someone smiling or frowning. When you want to move, signals travel from your brain to your skeletal muscle cells. The muscle cells then contract, or get shorter.

Muscles Attach to Bones

Strands of tough connective tissue connect your skeletal muscles to your bones. These strands are called *tendons*. When a muscle that connects two bones gets shorter, the bones are pulled closer to each other. For example, tendons attach the biceps muscle to a bone in your shoulder and to a bone in your forearm. When the biceps muscle contracts, your forearm bends toward your shoulder.

Muscles Work in Pairs

Your skeletal muscles often work in pairs. Usually, one muscle in the pair bends part of the body. The other muscle straightens part of the body. A muscle that bends part of your body is called a *flexor* (FLEKS uhr). A muscle that straightens part of your body is an *extensor* (ek STEN suhr). As shown in **Figure 2,** the biceps muscle of the arm is a flexor. The triceps muscle of the arm is an extensor.

Reading Check Describe how muscles work in pairs. *(See the Appendix for answers to Reading Checks.)*

SCHOOL to HOME

Power in Pairs

Ask a parent or guardian to sit in a chair and place a hand palm up under the edge of a table. Tell your parent to apply gentle upward pressure. Feel the front and back of your parent's upper arm. Next, ask your parent to push down on top of the table. Feel your parent's arm again. What did you notice about the muscles in your parent's arm when he or she was pressing up? pushing down?

ACTIVITY

Figure 3 *This girl is strengthening her heart and improving her endurance by doing aerobic exercise. This boy is doing resistance exercise to build strong muscles.*

Use It or Lose It

What happens when someone wears a cast for a broken arm? Skeletal muscles around the broken bone become smaller and weaker. The muscles weaken because they are not exercised. Exercised muscles are stronger and larger. Strong muscles can help other organs, too. For example, contracting muscles squeeze blood vessels. This action increases blood flow without needing more work from the heart.

Certain exercises can give muscles more strength and endurance. More endurance lets muscles work longer without getting tired. Two kinds of exercise can increase muscle strength and endurance. They are resistance exercise and aerobic exercise. You can see an example of each kind in **Figure 3.**

Resistance Exercise

Resistance exercise is a great way to strengthen skeletal muscles. During resistance exercise, people work against the resistance, or weight, of an object. Some resistance exercises, such as curl-ups, use your own weight for resistance.

Aerobic Exercise

Steady, moderately intense activity is called *aerobic exercise.* Jogging, cycling, skating, swimming, and walking are aerobic exercises. This kind of exercise can increase muscle strength. However, aerobic exercise mostly strengthens the heart and increases endurance.

CONNECTION TO Chemistry

Muscle Function Body chemistry is very important for healthy muscle function. Spasms or cramps happen if too much sweating, poor diet, or illness causes a chemical imbalance in muscles. Identify three chemicals that the body needs for muscles to work properly. Make a poster explaining how people can make sure that they have enough of each chemical.

ACTIVITY

Muscle Injury

Any exercise program should be started slowly. Starting slowly means you are less likely to get hurt. You should also warm up for exercise. A *strain* is an injury in which a muscle or tendon is overstretched or torn. Strains often happen because a muscle has not been warmed up. Strains also happen when muscles are worked too hard.

People who exercise too much can hurt their tendons. The body can't repair an injured tendon before the next exercise session. So, the tendon becomes inflamed. This condition is called *tendinitis*. Often, a long rest is needed for the injured tendon to heal.

Some people try to make their muscles stronger by taking drugs. These drugs are called *anabolic steroids* (A nuh BAH lik STER OIDZ). They can cause long-term health problems. Anabolic steroids can damage the heart, liver, and kidneys. They can also cause high blood pressure. If taken before the skeleton is mature, anabolic steroids can cause bones to stop growing.

Reading Check What are the risks of using anabolic steroids?

Math Practice

Runner's Time

Jan has decided to enter a 5 km road race. She now runs 5 km in 30 min. She would like to decrease her time by 15% before the race. What will her time be when she reaches her goal?

Section Review

Summary

- The three kinds of muscle tissue are smooth muscle, cardiac muscle, and skeletal muscle.
- Skeletal muscles work in pairs. Skeletal muscles contract to move bones.
- Resistance exercise improves muscle strength. Aerobic exercise improves heart strength and muscle endurance.
- Strains are injuries that affect muscles and tendons. Tendinitis affects tendons.

Using Key Terms

1. In your own words, write a definition for the term *muscular system*.

Understanding Key Ideas

2. Muscles
   a. work in pairs.
   b. move bones by relaxing.
   c. get smaller when exercised.
   d. All of the above
3. Describe three kinds of muscle.
4. List two kinds of exercise. Give an example of each.
5. Describe two muscular system injuries.

Math Skills

6. If Trey can do one curl-up every 2.5 s, about how long will it take him to do 35 curl-ups?

Critical Thinking

7. **Applying Concepts** Describe some of the muscle action needed to pick up a book. Include flexors and extensors in your description.
8. **Predicting Consequences** If aerobic exercise improves heart strength, what likely happens to heart rate as the heart gets stronger? Explain your answer.

SCILINKS® NSTA Developed and maintained by the National Science Teachers Association

For a variety of links related to this chapter, go to www.scilinks.org

Topic: Muscular System
SciLinks code: HSM1008

SECTION 4

The Integumentary System

What part of your body has to be partly dead to keep you alive? Here are some clues: It comes in many colors, it is the largest organ in the body, and it is showing right now!

What You Will Learn

- List four functions of skin.
- Describe the two layers of skin.
- Describe the structure and function of hair and nails.
- Describe two kinds of damage that can affect skin.

Vocabulary

integumentary system
epidermis
dermis

READING STRATEGY

Paired Summarizing Read this section silently. In pairs, take turns summarizing the material. Stop to discuss ideas that seem confusing.

Did you guess your skin? If you did, you guessed correctly. Your skin, hair, and nails make up your **integumentary system** (in TEG yoo MEN tuhr ee SIS tuhm). The integumentary system covers your body and helps you maintain homeostasis.

integumentary system the organ system that forms a protective covering on the outside of the body

Functions of Skin

Why do you need skin? Here are four good reasons:

- Skin protects you by keeping water in your body and foreign particles out of your body.
- Skin keeps you in touch with the outside world. Nerve endings in your skin let you feel things around you.
- Skin helps regulate your body temperature. Small organs in the skin called *sweat glands* make sweat. Sweat is a salty liquid that flows to the surface of the skin. As sweat evaporates, the skin cools.
- Skin helps get rid of wastes. Several kinds of waste chemicals can be removed in sweat.

As shown in **Figure 1,** skin comes in many colors. Skin color is determined by a chemical called *melanin*. If a lot of melanin is present, skin is very dark. If little melanin is present, skin is very light. Melanin absorbs ultraviolet light from the sun. So, melanin reduces damage that can lead to skin cancer. However, all skin, even dark skin, is vulnerable to cancer. Skin should be protected from sunlight whenever possible.

Figure 1 *Variety in skin color is caused by the pigment melanin. The amount of melanin varies from person to person.*

Figure 2 **Structures of the Skin**

Beneath the surface, your skin is a complex organ made of blood vessels, nerves, glands, and muscles.

Blood vessels transport substances and help regulate body temperature.

Nerve fibers carry messages to and from the brain.

Hair follicles in the dermis make hair.

Muscle fibers attached to a hair follicle can contract and cause the hair to stand up.

Oil glands release oil that keeps hair flexible and waterproofs the epidermis.

Sweat glands release sweat to cool the body. Sweating is also a way to remove waste materials from the body.

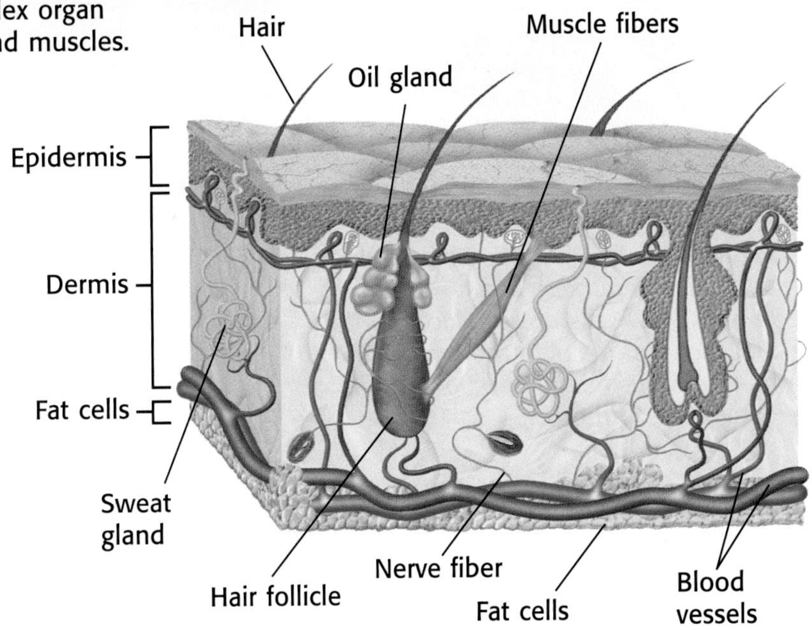

Layers of Skin

Skin is the largest organ of your body. In fact, the skin of an adult covers an area of about 2 m^2! However, there is more to skin than meets the eye. Skin has two main layers: the epidermis (EP uh DUHR mis) and the dermis. The **epidermis** is the outermost layer of skin. You see the epidermis when you look at your skin. The thicker layer of skin that lies beneath the epidermis is the **dermis.**

epidermis the surface layer of cells on a plant or animal

dermis the layer of skin below the epidermis

Epidermis

The epidermis is made of epithelial tissue. Even though the epidermis has many layers of cells, it is as thick as only two sheets of paper over most of the body. It is thicker on the palms of your hands and on the soles of your feet. Most cells in the epidermis are dead. These cells are filled with a protein called *keratin*. Keratin helps make the skin tough.

Dermis

The dermis lies beneath the epidermis. The dermis has many fibers made of a protein called *collagen*. These fibers provide strength. They also let skin bend without tearing. The dermis contains many small structures, as shown in **Figure 2.**

Reading Check **Describe the dermis. How does it differ from the epidermis?** (*See the Appendix for answers to Reading Checks.*)

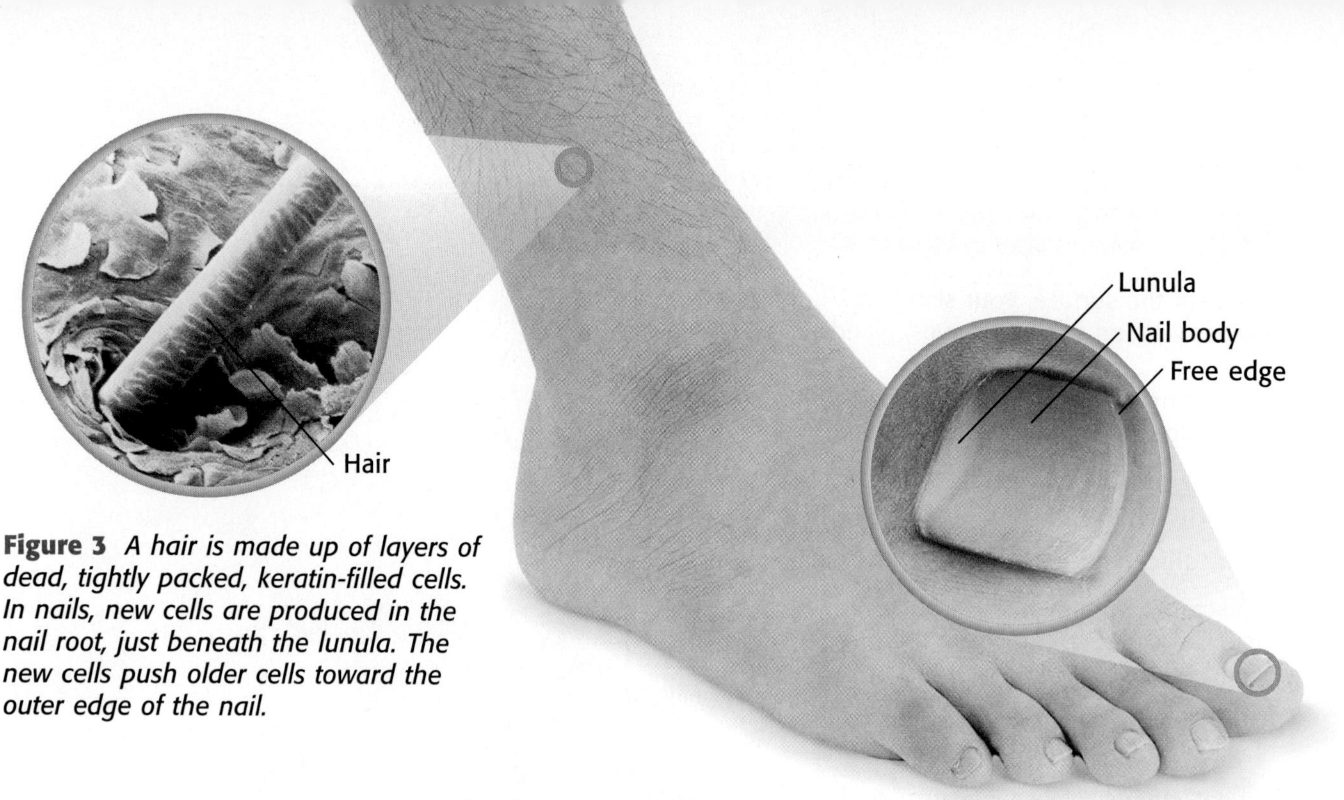

Figure 3 *A hair is made up of layers of dead, tightly packed, keratin-filled cells. In nails, new cells are produced in the nail root, just beneath the lunula. The new cells push older cells toward the outer edge of the nail.*

Hair and Nails

Hair and nails are important parts of the integumentary system. Like skin, hair and nails are made of living and dead cells. **Figure 3** shows hair and nails.

A hair forms at the bottom of a tiny sac called a *hair follicle.* The hair grows as new cells are added at the hair follicle. Older cells get pushed upward. The only living cells in a hair are in the hair follicle. Like skin, hair gets its color from melanin.

Hair helps protect skin from ultraviolet light. Hair also keeps particles, such as dust and insects, out of your eyes and nose. In most mammals, hair helps regulate body temperature. A tiny muscle attached to the hair follicle contracts. If the follicle contains a hair, the hair stands up. The lifted hairs work like a sweater. They trap warm air around the body.

A nail grows from living cells in the *nail root* at the base of the nail. As new cells form, the nail grows longer. Nails protect the tips of your fingers and toes. So, your fingers and toes can be soft and sensitive for a keen sense of touch.

Reading Check Describe how nails grow.

CONNECTION TO Social Studies

WRITING SKILL **Using Hair** Many traditional cultures use animal hair to make products, such as rugs and blankets. Identify a culture that uses animal hair. In your **science journal,** write a report describing how the culture uses animal hair.

Skin Injuries

Skin is often damaged. Fortunately, your skin can repair itself, as shown in **Figure 4.** Some damage to skin is very serious. Damage to the genetic material in skin cells can cause skin cancer. Skin may also be affected by hormones that cause oil glands in skin to make too much oil. This oil combines with dead skin cells and bacteria to clog hair follicles. The result is acne. Proper cleansing can help but often cannot prevent this problem.

Figure 4 **How Skin Heals**

❶ A blood clot forms over a cut to stop bleeding and to keep bacteria from entering the wound. Bacteria-fighting cells then come to the area to kill bacteria.

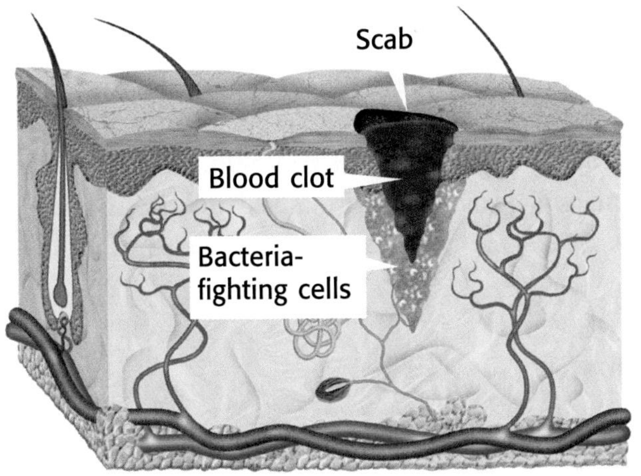

❷ Damaged cells are replaced through cell division. Eventually, all that is left on the surface is a scar.

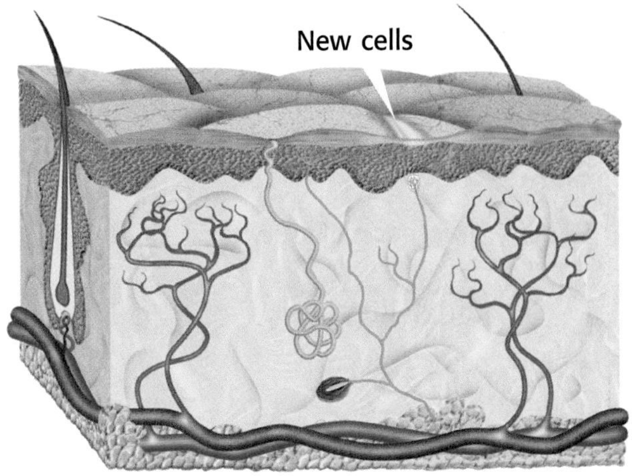

SECTION Review

Summary

- Skin keeps water in the body, keeps foreign particles out of the body, lets people feel things around them, regulates temperature, and removes wastes.
- The two layers of skin are the epidermis and the dermis.
- Hair grows from hair follicles. Nails grow from nail roots.
- Skin may develop skin cancer. Acne may develop if skin produces too much oil.

Using Key Terms

1. In your own words, write a definition for each of the following terms: *integumentary system*, *epidermis*, and *dermis*.

Understanding Key Ideas

2. Which of the following is NOT a function of skin?
   a. to regulate body temperature
   b. to keep water in the body
   c. to move your body
   d. to get rid of wastes
3. Describe the two layers of skin.
4. How do hair and nails develop?
5. Describe how a cut heals.

Math Skills

6. On average, hair grows 0.3 mm per day. How many millimeters does hair grow in 30 days? in a year?

Critical Thinking

7. **Making Inferences** Why do you feel pain when you pull on your hair or nails, but not when you cut them?
8. **Analyzing Ideas** The epidermis on the palms of your hands and on the soles of your feet is thicker than it is anywhere else on your body. Why might this skin need to be thicker?

SCILINKS® NSTA Developed and maintained by the National Science Teachers Association

For a variety of links related to this chapter, go to www.scilinks.org

Topic: Integumentary System
SciLinks code: HSM0803

Skills Practice Lab

Seeing Is Believing

OBJECTIVES

Measure nail growth over time.

Draw a graph of nail growth.

MATERIALS

- graph paper (optional)
- metric ruler
- permanent marker

SAFETY

Like your hair and skin, fingernails are part of your body's integumentary system. Nails, shown in the figure below, are a modification of the outer layer of the skin. Nails grow from the nail bed and will grow continuously throughout your life. In this activity, you will measure the rate at which fingernails grow.

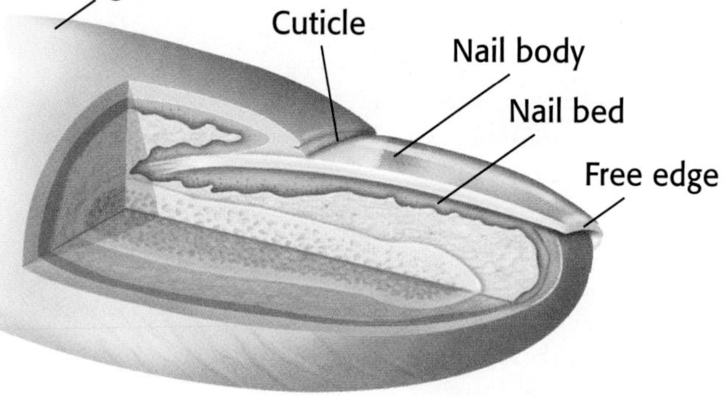

Procedure

1. Use a permanent marker to mark the center of the nail bed on your right index finger, as shown in the figure below. **Caution:** Do not get ink on your clothing.

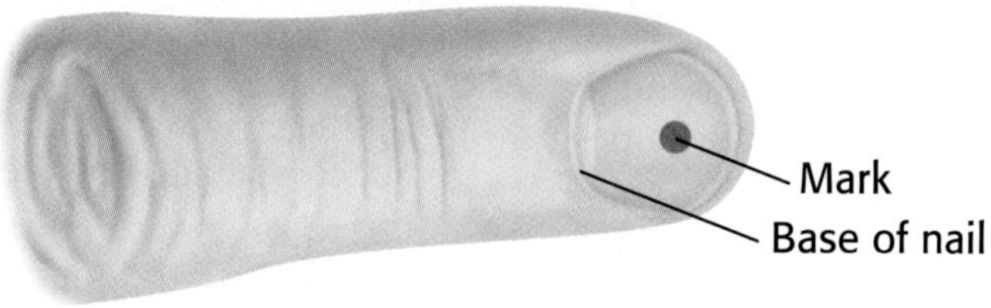

2. Measure from the mark to the base of your nail. Record the measurement, and label the measurement "Day 1."
3. Repeat steps 1 and 2 for your left index finger.
4. Let your fingernails grow for 2 days. Normal daily activity will not wash away the mark completely, but you may need to freshen the mark.
5. Measure the distance from the mark on your nail to the base of your nail. Record this distance, and label the measurement "Day 3."

6. Continue measuring and recording the growth of your nails every other day for 2 weeks. Refresh the mark as necessary. You may continue to file or trim your nails as usual throughout the course of the lab.

7. After you have completed your measurements, use them to create a graph similar to the graph below.

Fingernail Growth

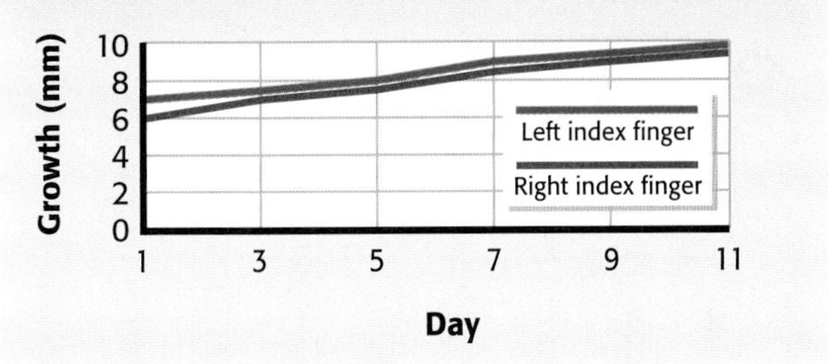

Analyze the Results

1. **Describing Events** Did the nail on one hand grow faster than the nail on the other hand?

2. **Examining Data** Did your nails grow at a constant rate, or did your nails grow more quickly at certain times?

Draw Conclusions

3. **Making Predictions** If one nail grew more quickly than the other nail, what might explain the difference in growth?

4. **Analyzing Graphs** Compare your graph with the graphs of your classmates. Do you notice any differences in the graphs based on gender or physical characteristics, such as height? If so, describe the difference.

Applying Your Data

Do additional research to find out how nails are important to you. Also, identify how nails can be used to indicate a person's health or nutrition. Based on what you learn, describe how your nail growth indicates your health or nutrition.

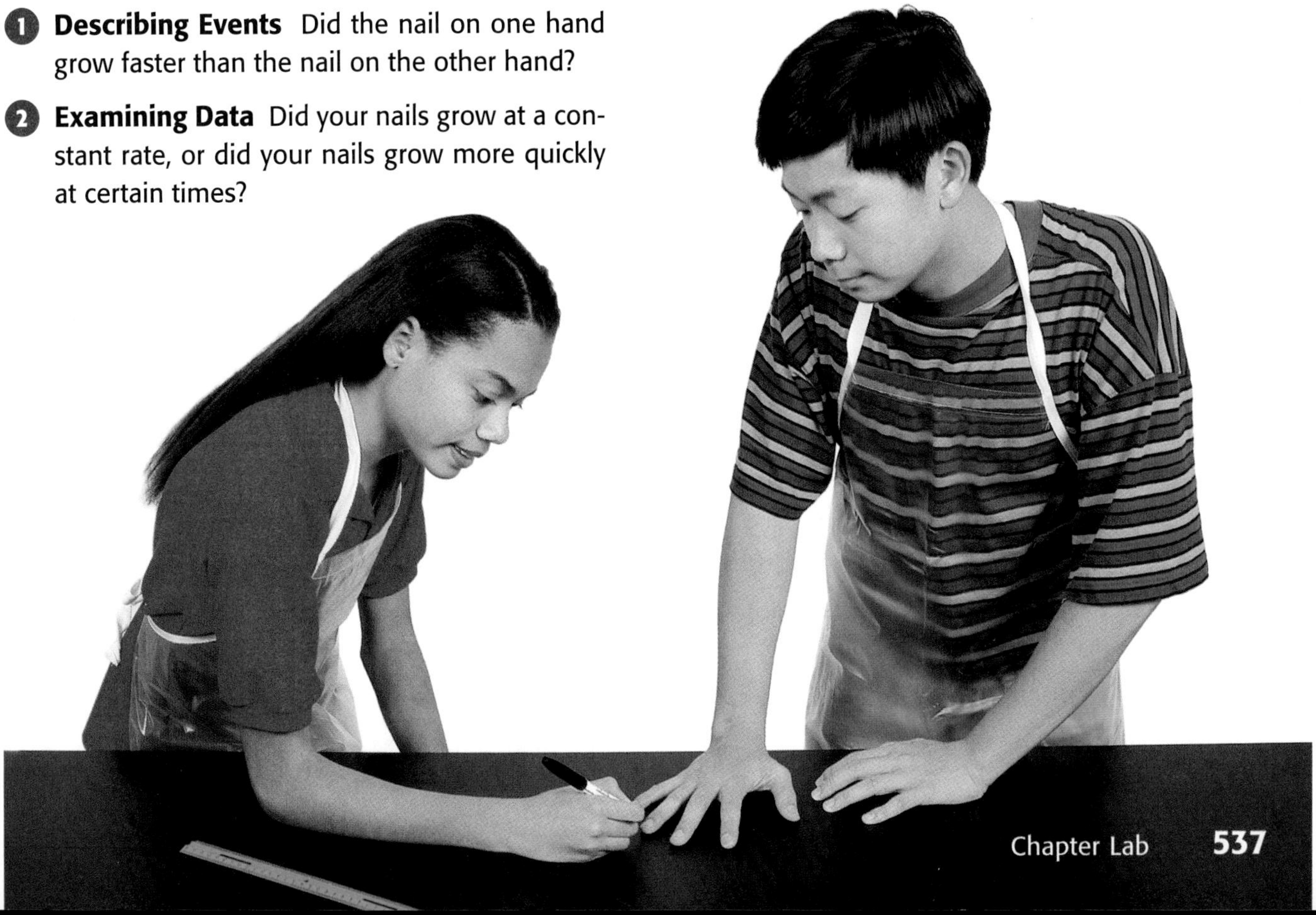

Chapter Review

USING KEY TERMS

Complete each of the following sentences by choosing the correct term from the word bank.

homeostasis	organ
joint	skeletal system
tissue	muscular system
epidermis	dermis
integumentary system	

1. A(n) ___ is a place where two or more bones meet.

2. ___ is the maintenance of a stable internal environment.

3. The outermost layer of skin is the ___.

4. The organ system that includes skin, hair, and nails is the ___.

5. A(n) ___ is made up of two or more tissues working together.

6. The ___ supports and protects the body, stores minerals, and allows movement.

UNDERSTANDING KEY IDEAS

Multiple Choice

7. Which of the following lists shows the way in which the body is organized?
   - **a.** cells, organs, organ systems, tissues
   - **b.** tissues, cells, organs, organ systems
   - **c.** cells, tissues, organs, organ systems
   - **d.** cells, tissues, organ systems, organs

8. Which muscle tissue can be both voluntary and involuntary?
   - **a.** smooth muscle
   - **b.** cardiac muscle
   - **c.** skeletal muscle
   - **d.** All of the above

9. The integumentary system
   - **a.** helps regulate body temperature.
   - **b.** helps the body move.
   - **c.** stores minerals.
   - **d.** None of the above

10. Muscles
    - **a.** work in pairs.
    - **b.** can be voluntary or involuntary.
    - **c.** become stronger if exercised.
    - **d.** All of the above

Short Answer

11. How do muscles move bones?

12. Describe the skeletal system, and list four functions of bones.

13. Give an example of how organ systems work together.

14. List three injuries and two diseases that affect the skeletal system.

15 Compare aerobic exercise and resistance exercise.

16 What are two kinds of damage that may affect skin?

CRITICAL THINKING

17 **Concept Mapping** Use the following terms to create a concept map: *tissues, muscle tissue, connective tissue, cells, organ systems, organs, epithelial tissue,* and *nervous tissue.*

18 **Making Comparisons** Compare the shapes of the bones of the human skull with the shapes of the bones of the human leg. How do the shapes differ? Why are the shapes important?

19 **Making Inferences** Compare your elbows and fingertips in terms of the texture and sensitivity of the skin on these parts of your body. Why might the skin on these body parts differ?

20 **Making Inferences** Imagine that you are building a robot. Your robot will have a skeleton similar to a human skeleton. If the robot needs to be able to move a limb in all directions, what kind of joint would be needed? Explain your answer.

21 **Analyzing Ideas** Human bones are dense and are often filled with marrow. But many bones of birds are hollow. Why might birds have hollow bones?

22 **Identifying Relationships** Why might some muscles fail to work properly if a bone is broken?

INTERPRETING GRAPHICS

Use the cross section of skin below to answer the questions that follow.

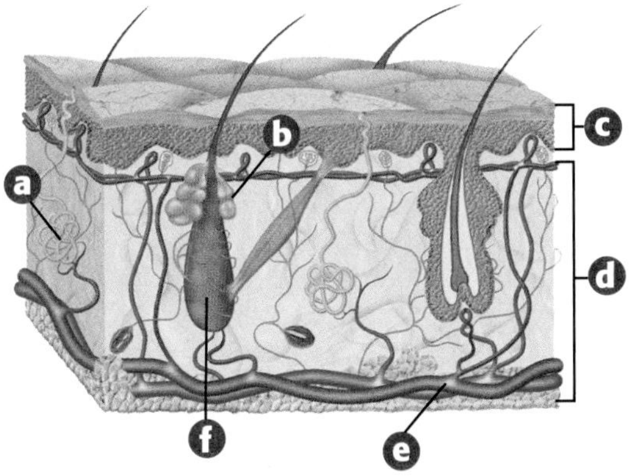

23 What is d called? What substance is most abundant in this layer?

24 What is the name and function of a?

25 What is the name and function of b?

26 Which letter corresponds to the part of the skin that is made up of epithelial tissue that contains dead cells?

27 Which letter corresponds to the part of the skin from which hair grows? What is this part called?

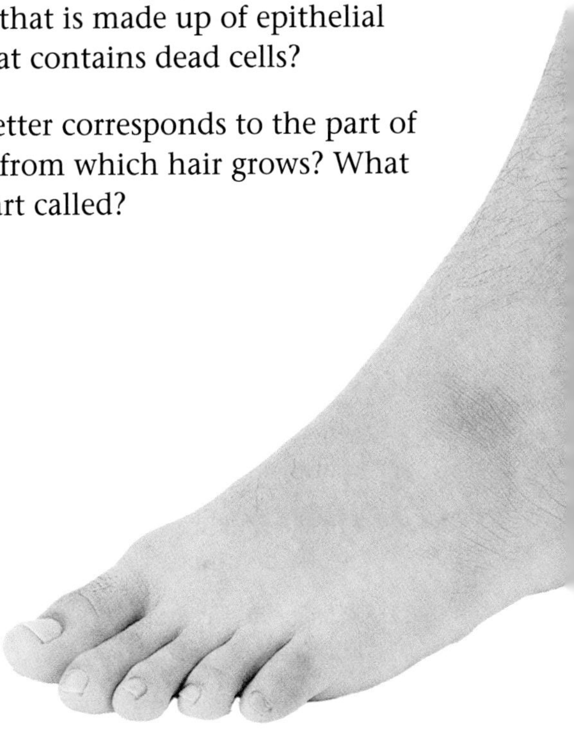

Multiple Choice

Use the figure below to answer question 1.

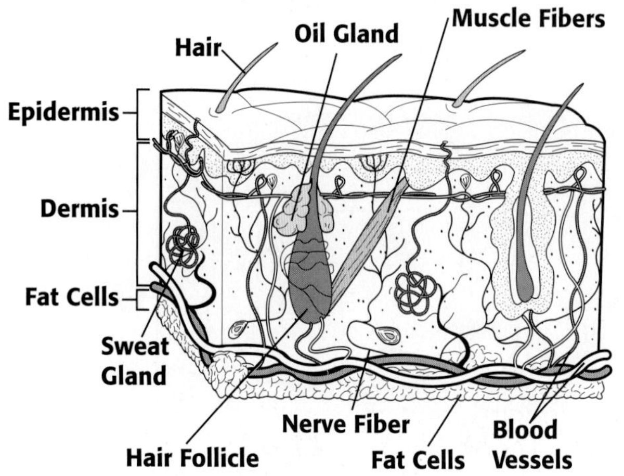

1. The body has many ways of maintaining a stable body temperature. When it is cold, hair stands up straight to help people stay warm. Based on the figure above, what happens to make the hair stand up?

A. The oil glands release oil.

B. The muscle fibers contract.

C. The blood vessels constrict.

D. The nerve fibers fire very quickly.

2. How is the structure of muscle cells different from that of other cells?

A. Muscle cells are organized into groups that work together.

B. Muscle cells contain a special pigment that picks up oxygen.

C. Muscle cells are shaped for the transfer of electrical impulses.

D. Muscle cells contain special proteins that allow them to contract.

3. Cells form tissues in the body. There are four kinds of tissues. What kind of tissue forms most of the brain?

A. muscle tissue

B. nervous tissue

C. epithelial tissue

D. connective tissue

4. Which of the following muscle contractions moves the forearm toward the shoulder?

A. The biceps muscle contracts.

B. The triceps muscle contracts.

C. The forearm muscles contract.

D. The shoulder muscle contracts.

5. Ultraviolet light can damage skin. What component of a skin cell is responsible for blocking ultraviolet rays?

A. collagen

B. dermis

C. epidermis

D. melanin

6. Donna cut her finger. A scab formed over the cut. When her scab fell off, the skin below it had healed. How did the new skin form?

A. through cell division

B. from collagen proteins

C. through keratin production

D. from bacteria-fighting cells

7. **Which of the following correctly describes a cell, tissue, organ, and organ system?**

A. osteoblasts, muscle tissue, bone, skeletal system

B. blood cells, muscle tissue, bone, muscular system

C. muscle cells, cardiac muscle tissue, esophagus, digestive system

D. fat cells, epithelial tissue, sweat gland, integumentary system

8. **Which of the following statements is about a way in which two organ systems work together?**

A. The muscles of the muscular system contract and relax.

B. The integumentary system protects the body from disease.

C. The skeletal system and muscular system make it possible to move.

D. The skeletal system and integumentary system work together to produce blood cells.

9. **Which of the following is a statement about what can happen if bone marrow is damaged?**

A. The bone may not develop normally.

B. The person might not be able to move.

C. The person might develop osteoporosis.

D. The body may not be able to develop blood cells.

Use the figure below to answer question 10.

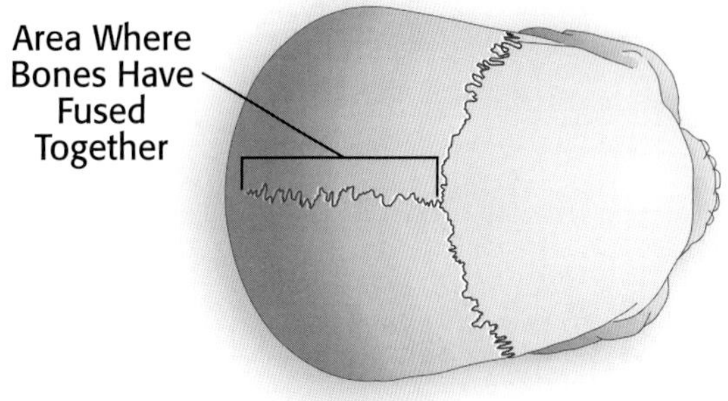

Overhead View of Human Skull

10. **This picture shows where the bones of a child's cranium have grown together. This area is called a growth plate. Earlier, this area was made up of tissues that are more flexible than bone. These tissues hold a place for bones to grow as the child matures. What changes occurred as these bones joined together?**

A. Bone cells replaced cartilage.

B. Bone cells grew in the marrow.

C. Bone cells formed a gliding joint.

D. Bone cells developed into muscle tissue.

Open Response

11. **Many hospitals perform organ transplants. One organ that they transplant is skin. Describe three functions of skin.**

12. **In single-celled organisms, all life functions are performed by one cell. Multicellular organisms have cells that perform specific functions. Describe how a multicellular organism is organized, starting with cells.**

Science in Action

Weird Science

Engineered Skin

Your skin is your first line of defense against the outside world. Your skin keeps you safe from dehydration and infection, helps regulate body temperature, and helps remove some wastes. But what happens if a large portion of skin is damaged? Skin may not be able to function properly. For someone who has a serious burn, a doctor often uses skin from an undamaged part of the person's body to repair the damaged skin. But some burn victims don't have enough undamaged skin to spare. Doctors have discovered ways to engineer skin that can be used in place of human skin.

Math ACTIVITY

A doctor repaired 0.35 m^2 of an adult patient's skin with engineered skin. If an adult has about 2 m^2 of skin, what percentage of the patient's skin was repaired?

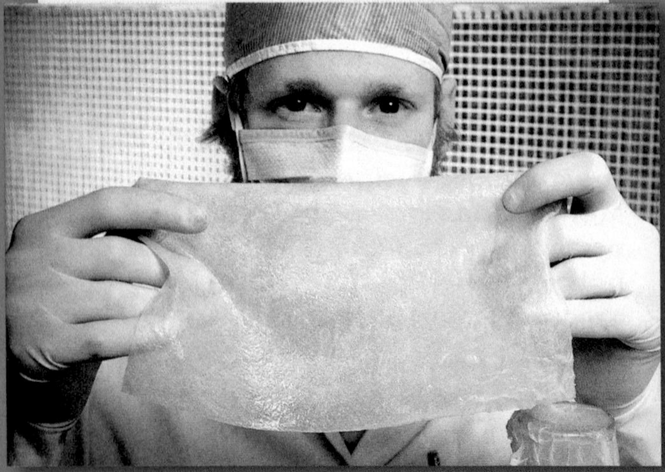

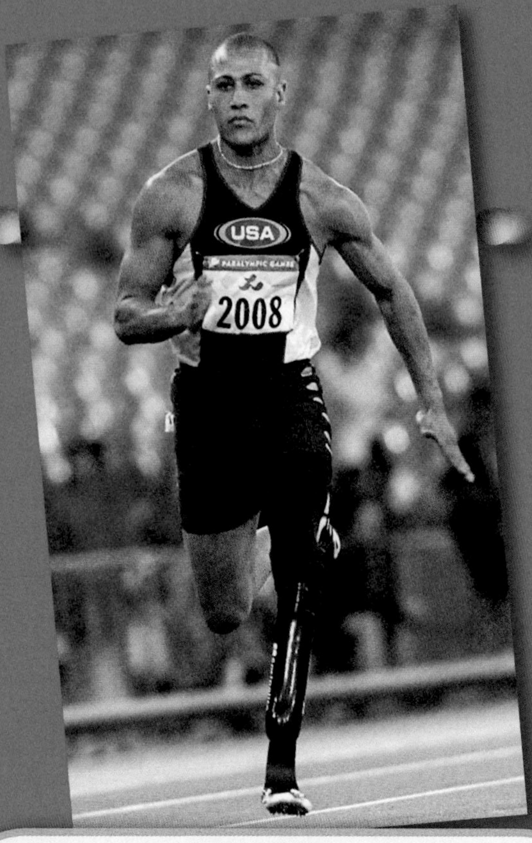

Science, Technology, and Society

Beating the Odds

Sometimes, people are born without limbs or lose limbs in accidents. Many of these people have prostheses (prahs THEE SEEZ), or human-made replacements for the body parts. Until recently, many of these prostheses made it more difficult for many people to participate in physical activities, such as sports. But new designs have led to lighter, more comfortable prostheses that move the way that a human limb does. These new designs have allowed athletes with physical disabilities to compete at higher levels.

Social Studies ACTIVITY

Research the use of prostheses throughout history. Create a timeline showing major advances in prosthesis use and design.

Careers

Zahra Beheshti

Physical Therapist A physical therapist is a licensed professional who helps people recover from injuries by using hands-on treatment instead of medicines. Dr. Zahra Beheshti is a physical therapist at the Princeton Physical Therapy Center in New Jersey. She often helps athletes who suffer from sports injuries.

After an injury, a person may go through a process called *rehabilitation* to regain the use of the injured body part. The most common mistake made by athletes is that they play sports before completely recovering from injuries. Dr. Beheshti explains, "Going back to their usual pre-injury routine could result in another injury."

Dr. Beheshti also teaches patients about preventing future sports injuries. "Most injuries happen when an individual engages in strenuous activities without a proper warm-up or cool-down period." Being a physical therapist is rewarding work. Dr. Beheshti says, "I get a lot of satisfaction when treating patients and see them regain their function and independence and return to their normal life."

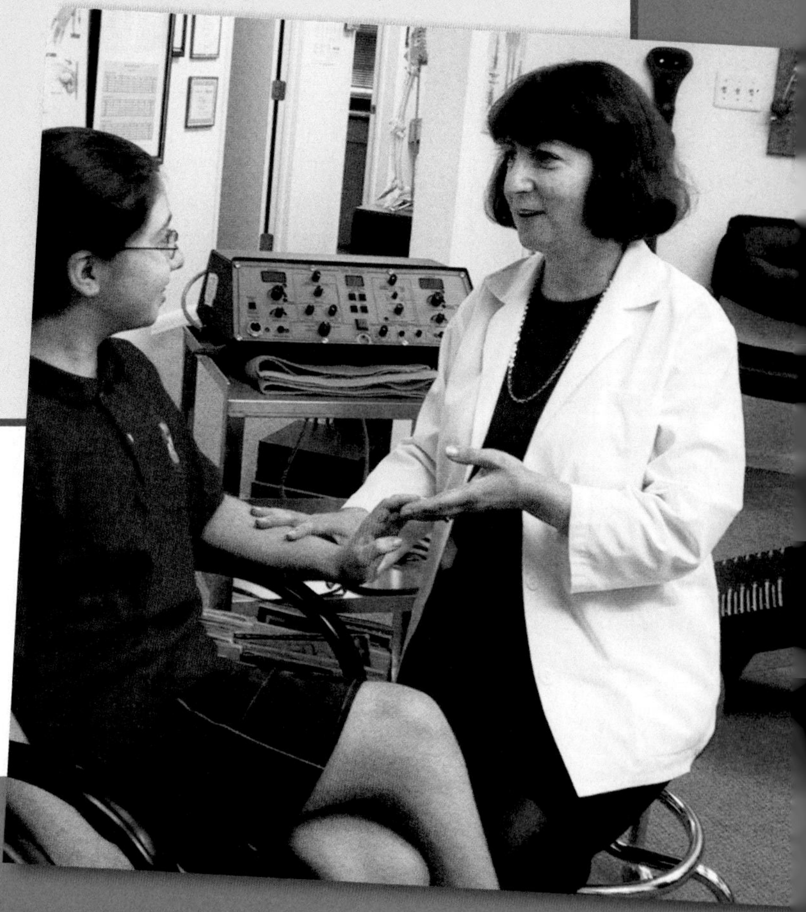

Language Arts ACTIVITY

WRITING SKILL Interview a physical therapist who works in or near your community. Write a newspaper article about your interview.

go.hrw.com

To learn more about these Science in Action topics, visit **go.hrw.com** and type in the keyword **HL5BD1F.**

Current Science

Check out Current Science® articles related to this chapter by visiting go.hrw.com. Just type in the keyword HL5CS22.

18

Circulation and Respiration

The Big Idea

The human body has systems that transport gases, nutrients, and wastes.

SECTION

About the Photo

Your cardiovascular system is made up of the heart, blood vessels, and blood. This picture is a colored scanning electron micrograph of red and white blood cells and cell fragments called ***platelets.*** Red blood cells are disk shaped, white blood cells are rounded, and platelets are the small green fragments. There are millions of blood cells in a drop of blood. Blood cells are so important that your body makes about 200 billion red blood cells every day.

PRE-READING ACTIVITY

FOLDNOTES

Four-Corner Fold

Before you read the chapter, create the FoldNote entitled "Four-Corner Fold" described in the **Study Skills** section of the Appendix. Label the flaps of the four-corner fold with the section titles "Cardiovascular system," "Blood," Lymphatic system," and "Respiratory system." Write what you know about each topic under the appropriate flap. As you read the chapter, add other information that you learn.

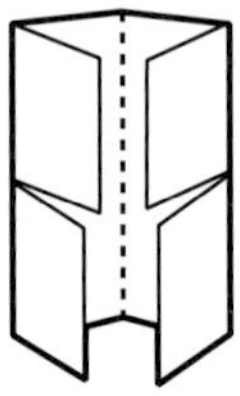

START-UP ACTIVITY

Exercise Your Heart

How does your heart respond to exercise? You can see this reaction by measuring your pulse.

Procedure

1. Take your pulse while remaining still. (Take your pulse by placing your fingers on the inside of your wrist just below your thumb.)
2. Using a **watch with a second hand,** count the number of heart beats in 15 s. Then, multiply this number by 4 to calculate the number of beats in 1 minute.
3. Do some moderate physical activity, such as jumping jacks or jogging in place, for 30 s.
4. Stop and calculate your heart rate again.

   Caution: Do not perform this exercise if you have difficulty breathing, if you have high blood pressure or asthma, or if you get dizzy easily.
5. Rest for 5 min.
6. Take your pulse again.

Analysis

1. How did exercise affect your heart rate? Why do you think this happened?
2. How does your heart rate affect the rate at which red blood cells travel throughout your body?
3. Did your heart rate return to normal (or almost normal) after you rested? Why or why not?

SECTION 1

The Cardiovascular System

What You Will Learn

- List five main parts of the cardiovascular system, and describe their functions.
- Describe the two types of circulation of blood in the body.
- List four cardiovascular problems.

Vocabulary

cardiovascular system
artery
capillary
vein
pulmonary circulation
systemic circulation

READING STRATEGY

Paired Summarizing Read this section silently. In pairs, take turns summarizing the material. Stop to discuss ideas that seem confusing.

cardiovascular system a collection of organs that transport blood throughout the body

When you hear the word **heart,** what do you think of first? Many people think of romance. Some people think of courage. But the heart is much more than a symbol of love or bravery. Your heart is an amazing pump.

The heart is an organ that is part of your cardiovascular system. The word *cardio* means "heart," and the word *vascular* means "blood vessel." The blood vessels—arteries, capillaries, and veins—carry blood pumped by the heart.

Your Cardiovascular System

Your heart, blood, and blood vessels make up your **cardiovascular system** (KAR dee OH VAS kyoo luhr SIS tuhm). Your heart creates pressure when it beats. This pressure moves blood throughout your body. **Figure 1** shows your heart, major arteries, and major veins.

The cardiovascular system helps maintain homeostasis by performing many functions. For example, this system helps maintain your body by carrying nutrients to your cells and by removing wastes from your cells. This system also helps in regulation by carrying chemical signals called *hormones* throughout the body.

Reading Check **What are the main parts of the cardiovascular system?** *(See the Appendix for answers to Reading Checks.)*

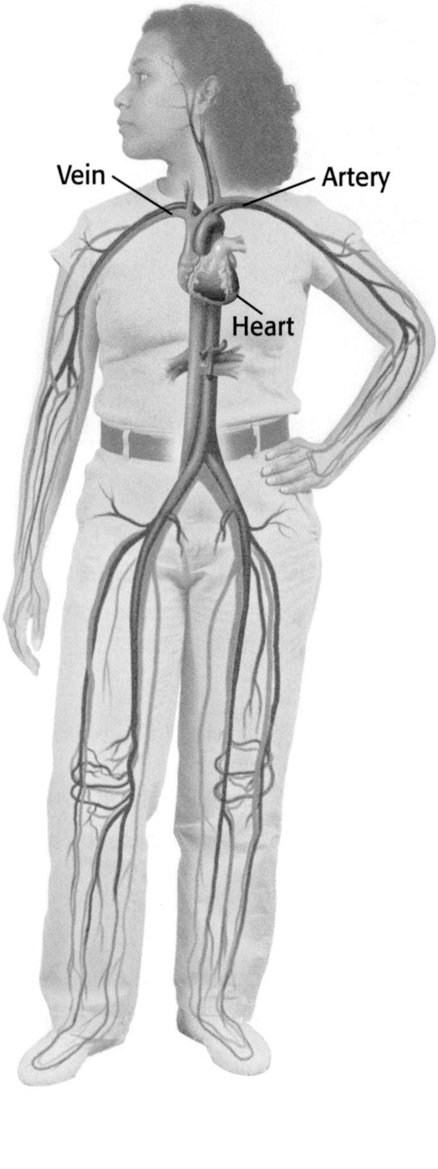

Figure 1 *The cardiovascular system carries blood to every cell in your body.*

The Heart

Your *heart* is an organ made mostly of cardiac muscle tissue. It is about the size of your fist and is almost in the center of your chest cavity. Like hearts of all mammals, your heart has a left side and a right side that are separated by a thick wall. The right side of the heart pumps oxygen-poor blood to the lungs. The left side pumps oxygen-rich blood to the body. As you can see in **Figure 2,** each side has an upper chamber and a lower chamber. Each upper chamber is called an *atrium* (plural, *atria*). Each lower chamber is called a *ventricle.*

Flaplike structures called *valves* are located between the atria and ventricles and in places where large arteries are attached to the heart. As blood moves through the heart, these valves close to prevent blood from going backward. The "lub-dub, lub-dub" sound of a beating heart is caused by the valves closing. **Figure 3** shows the flow of blood through the heart.

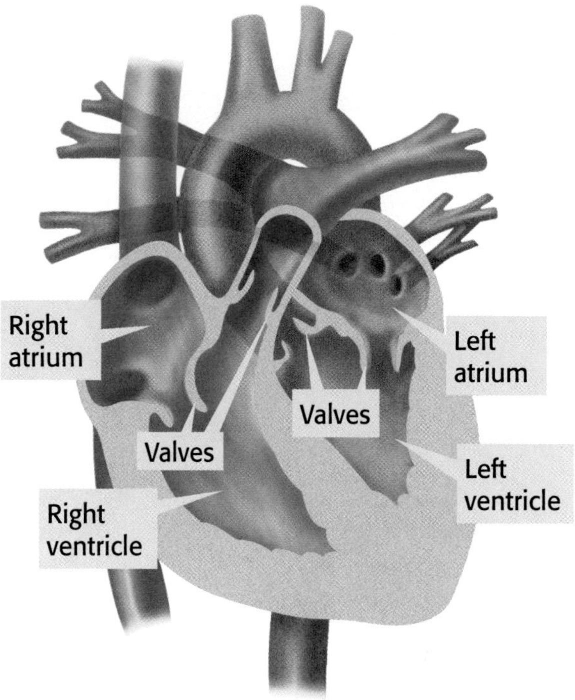

Figure 2 *The heart pumps blood through blood vessels. The vessels carrying oxygen-rich blood are shown in red. The vessels carrying oxygen-poor blood are shown in blue.*

Figure 3 The Flow of Blood Through the Heart

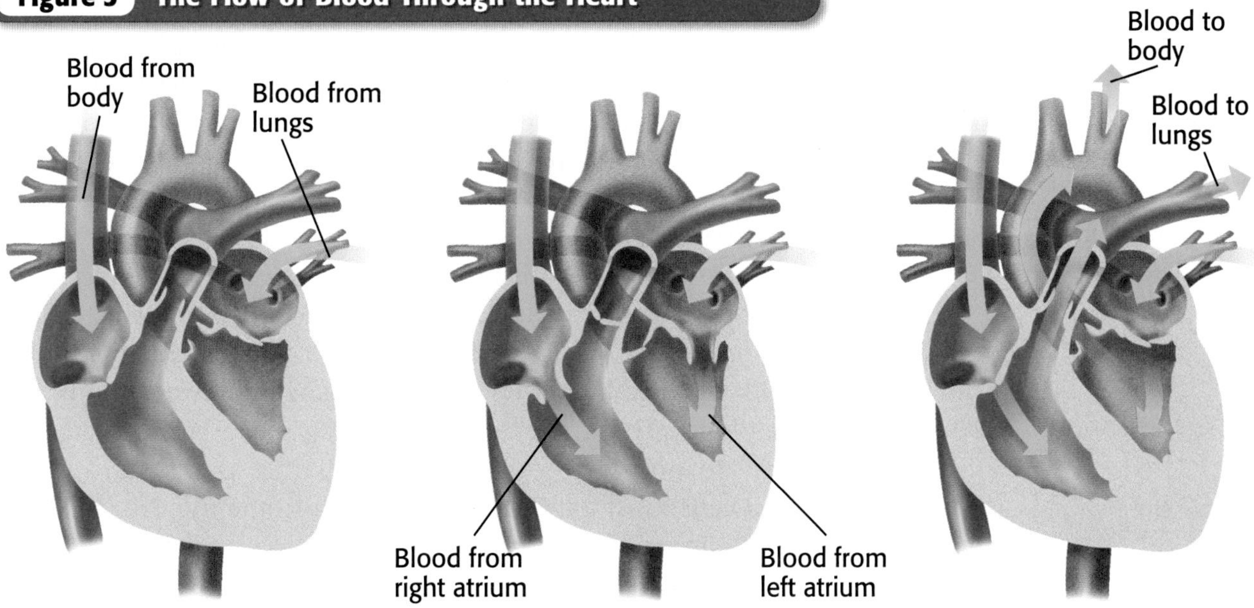

1. Blood enters the atria first. The left atrium receives oxygen-rich blood from the lungs. The right atrium receives oxygen-poor blood from the body.
2. When the atria contract, blood is squeezed into the ventricles.
3. While the atria relax, the ventricles contract and push blood out of the heart. Blood from the right ventricle goes to the lungs. Blood from the left ventricle goes to the rest of the body.

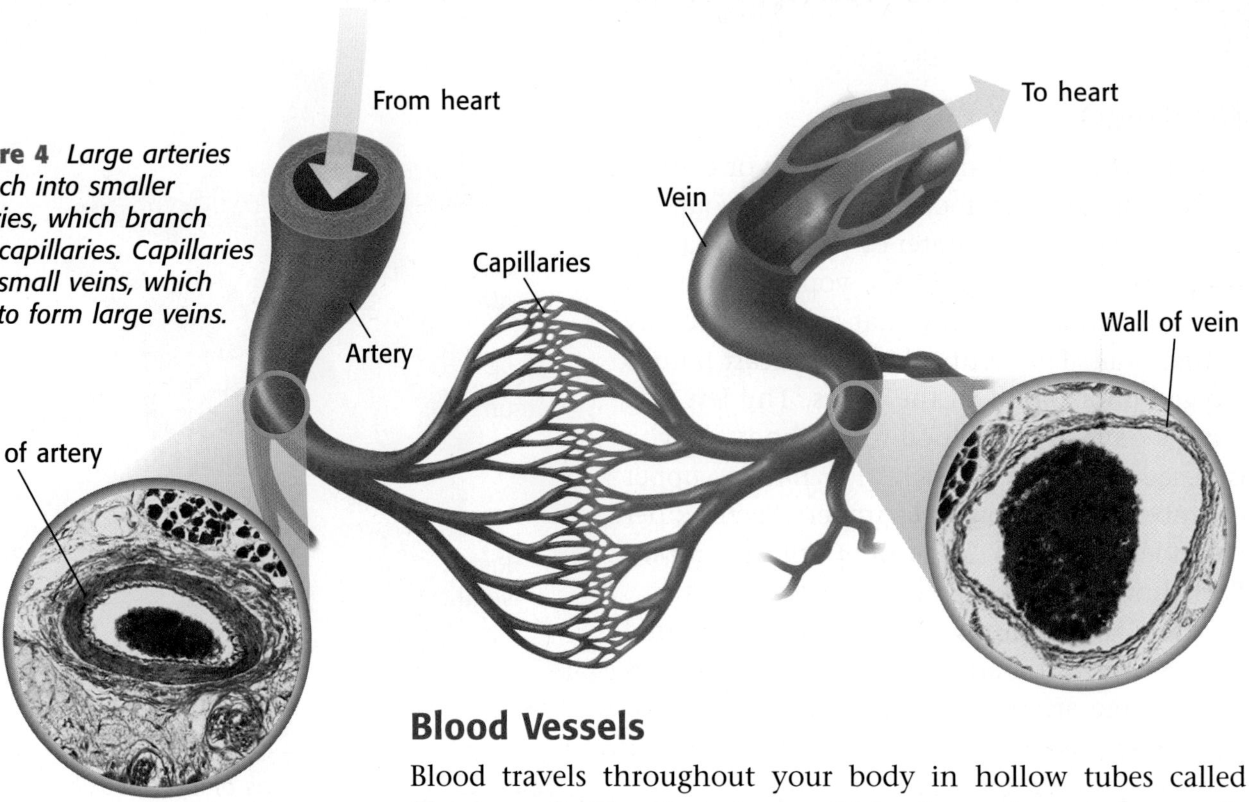

Figure 4 *Large arteries branch into smaller arteries, which branch into capillaries. Capillaries join small veins, which join to form large veins.*

Blood Vessels

Blood travels throughout your body in hollow tubes called *blood vessels.* The three types of blood vessels—arteries, capillaries, and veins—are shown in **Figure 4.**

Arteries

A blood vessel that carries blood away from the heart is an **artery.** Arteries have thick walls, which contain a layer of smooth muscle. Each heartbeat pumps blood into your arteries at high pressure. This pressure is your *blood pressure.* Artery walls stretch and are usually strong enough to stand the pressure. Your *pulse* is caused by the rhythmic change in your blood pressure.

artery a blood vessel that carries blood away from the heart to the body's organs

capillary a tiny blood vessel that allows an exchange between blood and cells in other tissue

vein in biology, a vessel that carries blood to the heart

Capillaries

Nutrients, oxygen, and other substances must leave blood and get to your body's cells. Carbon dioxide and other wastes leave body cells and are carried away by blood. A **capillary** is a tiny blood vessel that allows these exchanges between body cells and blood. These exchanges can take place because capillary walls are only one cell thick. Capillaries are so narrow that blood cells must pass through them in single file. No cell in the body is more than three or four cells away from a capillary.

Veins

After leaving capillaries, blood enters veins. A **vein** is a blood vessel that carries blood back to the heart. As blood travels through veins, valves in the veins keep the blood from flowing backward. When skeletal muscles contract, they squeeze nearby veins and help push blood toward the heart.

Reading Check **Describe the three types of blood vessels.**

Two Types of Circulation

Where does blood get the oxygen to deliver to your body? From your lungs! Your heart pumps blood to the lungs. In the lungs, carbon dioxide leaves the blood and oxygen enters the blood. The oxygen-rich blood then flows back to the heart. This circulation of blood between your heart and lungs is called **pulmonary circulation** (PUL muh NER ee SUHR kyoo LAY shuhn).

The oxygen-rich blood returning to the heart from the lungs is then pumped to the rest of the body. The circulation of blood between the heart and the rest of the body is called **systemic circulation** (sis TEM ik SUHR kyoo LAY shuhn). Both types of circulation are shown in **Figure 5.**

pulmonary circulation the flow of blood from the heart to the lungs and back to the heart through the pulmonary arteries, capillaries, and veins

systemic circulation the flow of blood from the heart to all parts of the body and back to the heart

Figure 5 The Flow of Blood Through the Body

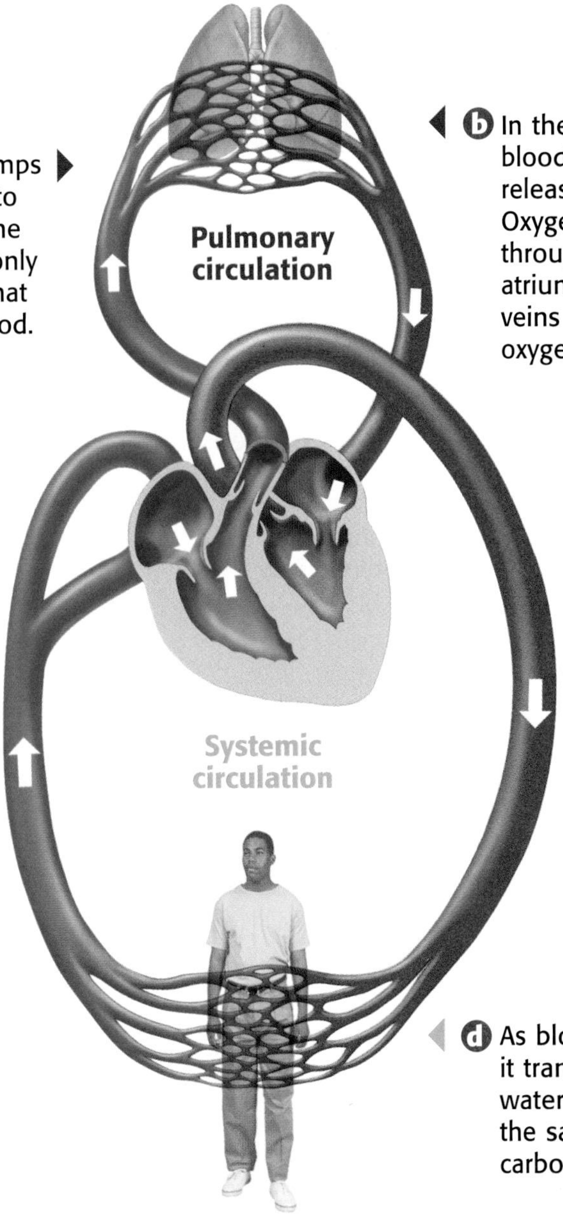

a The right ventricle pumps oxygen-poor blood into arteries that lead to the lungs. These are the only arteries in the body that carry oxygen-poor blood.
b In the capillaries of the lungs, blood takes up oxygen and releases carbon dioxide. Oxygen-rich blood travels through veins to the left atrium. These are the only veins in the body that carry oxygen-rich blood.
Pulmonary circulation
c The heart pumps oxygen-rich blood from the left ventricle into arteries and then into capillaries.
e Oxygen-poor blood travels back to the heart and is delivered into the right atrium by two large veins.
Systemic circulation
d As blood travels through capillaries, it transports oxygen, nutrients, and water to the cells of the body. At the same time, waste materials and carbon dioxide are carried away.

Cardiovascular Problems

More than just your heart and blood vessels are at risk if you have cardiovascular problems. Your whole body may be harmed. Cardiovascular problems can be caused by smoking, high levels of cholesterol in the blood, stress, physical inactivity, or heredity. Eating a healthy diet and getting plenty of exercise can reduce the risk of having cardiovascular problems.

MATH PRACTICE

The Beat Goes On

A person's heart averages about 70 beats per minute.

1. Calculate how many times a heart beats in a day.
2. If a person lives for 75 years, how many times will his or her heart beat?
3. If an athlete's heart beats 50 times a minute, how many fewer times than an average heart will his or her heart beat in 30 days?

Atherosclerosis

Heart diseases are the leading cause of death in the United States. A major cause of heart diseases is a cardiovascular disease called *atherosclerosis* (ATH uhr OH skluh ROH sis). Atherosclerosis happens when cholesterol (kuh LES tuhr AWL) builds up inside of blood vessels. This cholesterol buildup causes the blood vessels to become narrower and less elastic. **Figure 6** shows how clogged the pathway through a blood vessel can become. When an artery that supplies blood to the heart becomes blocked, the person may have a heart attack.

Reading Check **Why is atherosclerosis dangerous?**

High Blood Pressure

Atherosclerosis may be caused by hypertension. *Hypertension* is abnormally high blood pressure. The higher the blood pressure, the greater the risk of a heart attack, heart failure, kidney disease, and stroke. A *stroke* is when a blood vessel in the brain becomes clogged or ruptures. As a result, that part of the brain receives no oxygen. Without oxygen, brain cells die.

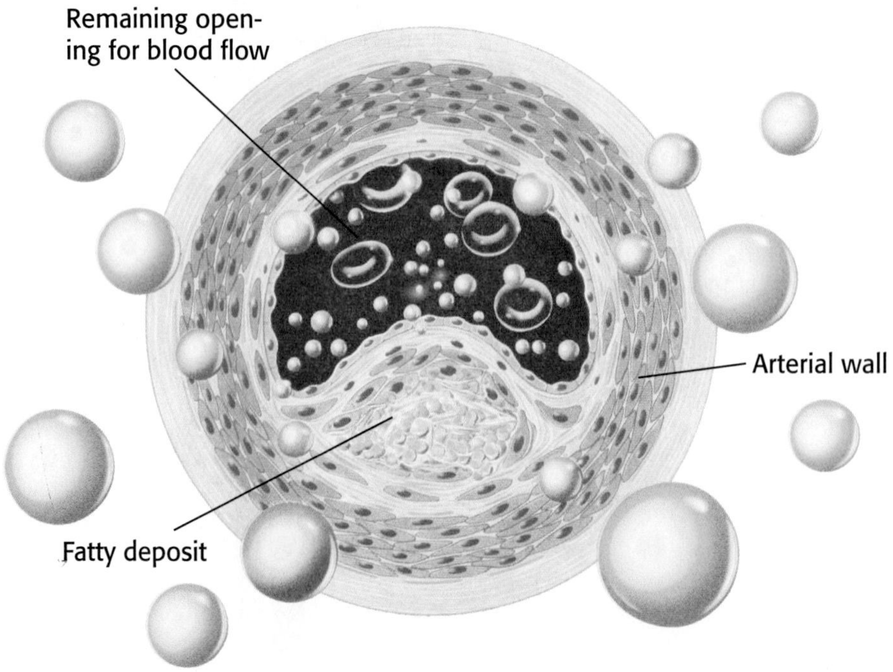

Figure 6 *This illustration shows the narrowing of an artery as the result of high levels of cholesterol in the blood. Lipid deposits (yellow) build up inside the blood vessel walls and block the flow of blood. Red blood cells and lipid particles (yellow balls) are shown escaping.*

Heart Attacks and Heart Failure

Two cardiovascular problems are heart attacks and heart failure. A *heart attack* happens when heart muscle cells die and part of the heart muscle is damaged. As shown in **Figure 7,** arteries that deliver oxygen to the heart may be blocked. Without oxygen, heart muscle cells die quickly. When enough heart muscle cells die, the heart may stop.

Heart failure is different. *Heart failure* happens when the heart cannot pump enough blood to meet the body's needs. Organs, such as the brain, lungs, and kidneys, may be damaged by lack of oxygen or nutrients, or by the buildup of fluids or wastes.

Figure 7 Heart Attack

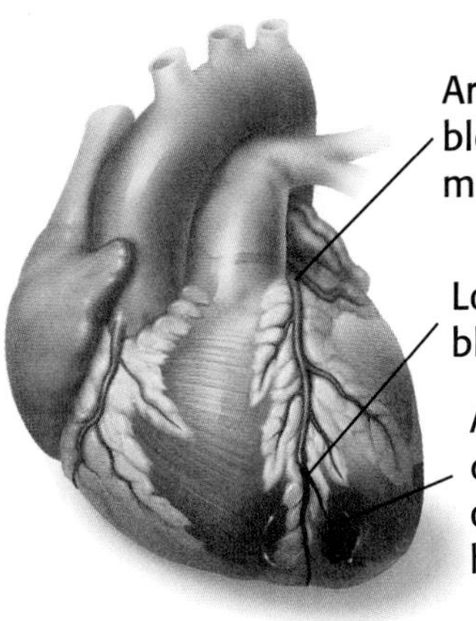

SECTION Review

Summary

- The cardiovascular system is made up of the heart, three types of blood vessels, and blood.
- The three types of blood vessels are arteries, veins, and capillaries.
- Oxygen-poor blood flows from the heart through the lungs, where it picks up oxygen.
- Oxygen-rich blood flows from the heart to the rest of the body.
- Cardiovascular problems include atherosclerosis, hypertension, heart attacks, and strokes.

Using Key Terms

For each pair of terms, explain how the meanings of the terms differ.

1. *artery* and *vein*
2. *systemic circulation* and *pulmonary circulation*

Understanding Key Ideas

3. Which of the following is true of blood in the pulmonary veins?
   a. The blood is going to the body.
   b. The blood is oxygen poor.
   c. The blood is going to the lungs.
   d. The blood is oxygen rich.
4. What are the five parts of the cardiovascular system? Describe the functions of each part.
5. What is the difference between a heart attack and heart failure?

Math Skills

6. An adult male's heart pumps about 2.8 million liters of blood a year. If his heart beats 70 times a minute, how much blood does his heart pump with each beat?

Critical Thinking

7. **Identifying Relationships** How is the structure of capillaries related to their function?
8. **Making Inferences** One of aspirin's effects is that it prevents platelets from being too "sticky." Why might doctors prescribe aspirin for patients who have had a heart attack?
9. **Analyzing Ideas** Veins and arteries are everywhere in your body. When a pulse is taken, it is usually taken at an artery in the neck or wrist. Explain why.
10. **Making Comparisons** Why is the structure of arteries different from the structure of capillaries?

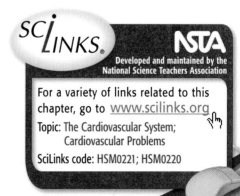

SCI LINKS. NSTA Developed and maintained by the National Science Teachers Association

For a variety of links related to this chapter, go to www.scilinks.org

Topic: The Cardiovascular System; Cardiovascular Problems

SciLinks code: HSM0221; HSM0220

SECTION 2

Blood

Blood is part of the cardiovascular system. It travels through miles and miles of blood vessels to reach every cell in your body. So, you must have a lot of blood, right?

Well, actually, an adult human body has about 5 L of blood. Your body probably has a little less than that. All the blood in your body would not fill two 3 L soda bottles.

What You Will Learn

- Identify the four main components of blood.
- Describe three functions of blood.
- Explain how blood pressure is measured.
- Explain what the ABO blood types are and why they are important.

Vocabulary

blood
blood pressure

READING STRATEGY

Reading Organizer As you read this section, create an outline of the section. Use the headings from the section in your outline.

What Is Blood?

Your cardiovascular system is made up of your heart, your blood vessels, and blood. **Blood** is a connective tissue made up of plasma, red blood cells, platelets, and white blood cells. Blood carries oxygen and nutrients to all parts of your body.

Reading Check What are the four main components of blood? *(See the Appendix for answers to Reading Checks.)*

blood the fluid that carries gases, nutrients, and wastes through the body and that is made up of plasma, red blood cells, platelets, and white blood cells

Plasma

The fluid part of the blood is called plasma (PLAZ muh). *Plasma* is a mixture of water, minerals, nutrients, sugars, proteins, and other substances. Red blood cells, white blood cells, and platelets are found in plasma.

Red Blood Cells

Most blood cells are *red blood cells,* or RBCs. RBCs, such as the ones shown in **Figure 1,** take oxygen to every cell in your body. Cells need oxygen to carry out their functions. Each RBC has hemoglobin (HEE moh GLOH bin). *Hemoglobin* is an oxygen-carrying protein. Hemoglobin clings to the oxygen you inhale. RBCs can then transport oxygen throughout the body. Hemoglobin also gives RBCs their red color.

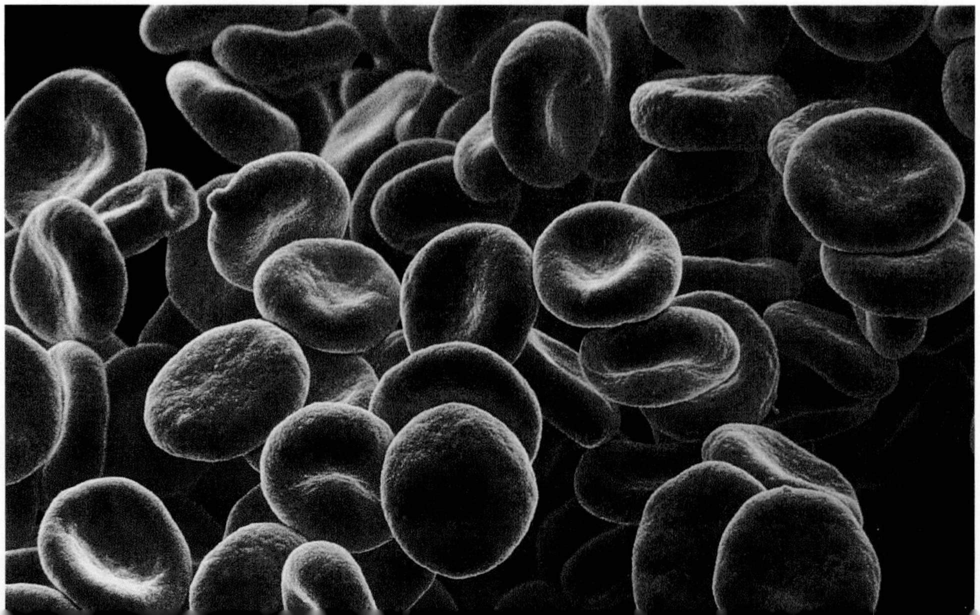

Figure 1 *Red blood cells are made in the bone marrow of certain bones. As red blood cells mature, they lose their nucleus and their DNA.*

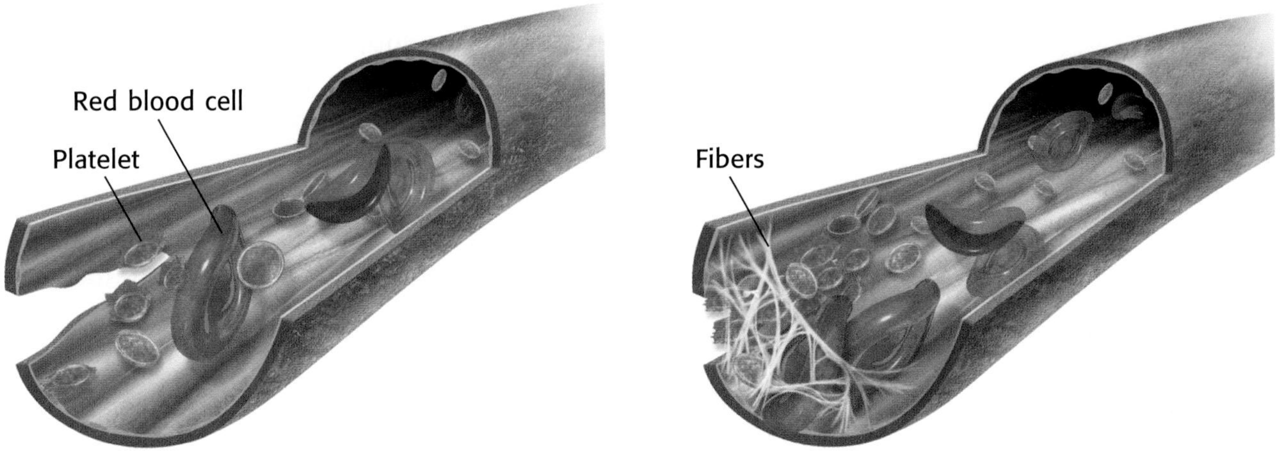

Figure 2 *Platelets release chemicals in damaged vessels and cause fibers to form. The fibers make a "net" that traps blood cells and stops bleeding.*

Platelets

Drifting among the blood cells are tiny particles called platelets. *Platelets* are pieces of larger cells found in bone marrow. These larger cells remain in the bone marrow, but fragments are pinched off and enter the bloodstream as platelets. Platelets last for only 5 to 10 days, but they are an important part of blood. When you cut or scrape your skin, you bleed because blood vessels have been opened. As soon as bleeding starts, platelets begin to clump together in the damaged area. They form a plug that helps reduce blood loss, as shown in **Figure 2.** Platelets also release chemicals that react with proteins in plasma. The reaction causes tiny fibers to form. The fibers help create a blood clot.

White Blood Cells

Sometimes *pathogens* (PATH uh juhnz)—bacteria, viruses, and other microscopic particles that can make you sick—enter your body. When they do, they often meet *white blood cells,* or WBCs. WBCs, shown in **Figure 3,** help keep you healthy by destroying pathogens. WBCs also help clean wounds.

WBCs fight pathogens in several ways. Some WBCs squeeze out of blood vessels and move around in tissues, searching for pathogens. When they find a pathogen, they destroy it. Other WBCs release antibodies. *Antibodies* are chemicals that identify or destroy pathogens. WBCs also keep you healthy by destroying body cells that have died or been damaged. Most WBCs are made in bone marrow. Some WBCs mature in the lymphatic system.

Figure 3 *White blood cells defend the body against pathogens. These white blood cells have been colored yellow to make their shape easier to see.*

Reading Check **Why are WBCs important to your health?**

Body Temperature Regulation

Your blood does more than supply your cells with oxygen and nutrients. It also helps regulate your body temperature. When your brain senses that your body temperature is rising, it signals blood vessels in your skin to enlarge. As the vessels enlarge, heat from your blood is transferred to your skin. This transfer helps lower your temperature. When your brain senses that your temperature is normal, it instructs your blood vessels to return to their normal size.

blood pressure the force that blood exerts on the walls of the arteries

Blood Pressure

Every time your heart beats, it pushes blood out of the heart and into your arteries. The force exerted by blood on the inside walls of arteries is called **blood pressure.**

Blood pressure is expressed in millimeters of mercury (mm Hg). For example, a blood pressure of 110 mm Hg means the pressure on the artery walls can push a narrow column of mercury to a height of 110 mm.

Blood pressure is usually given as two numbers, such as 110/70 mm Hg. Systolic (sis TAHL ik) pressure is the first number. *Systolic pressure* is the pressure inside large arteries when the ventricles contract. The surge of blood causes the arteries to bulge and produce a pulse. The second number, *diastolic* (DIE uh STAHL ik) *pressure,* is the pressure inside arteries when the ventricles relax. For adults, a blood pressure of 120/80 mm Hg or below is considered healthy. High blood pressure can cause heart or kidney damage.

Reading Check **What is the difference between systolic pressure and diastolic pressure?**

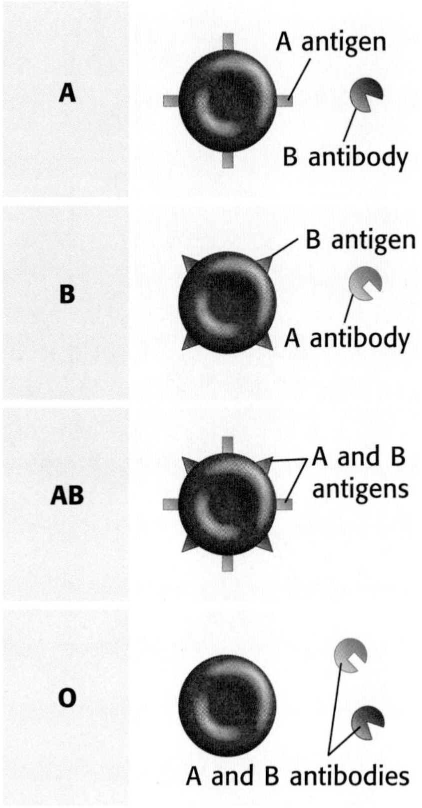

Figure 4 *This figure shows which antigens and antibodies may be present in each blood type.*

Blood Types

Every person has one of four blood types: A, B, AB, or O. Your blood type refers to the type of chemicals you have on the surface of your RBCs. These surface chemicals are called *antigens* (AN tuh juhnz). Type A blood has A antigens; type B has B antigens; and type AB has both A and B antigens. Type O blood has neither the A nor the B antigen.

The different blood types have different antigens on their RBCs. They may also have different antibodies in the plasma. These antibodies react to antigens of other blood types as if the antigens were pathogens. As shown in **Figure 4,** type A blood has antibodies that react to type B blood. If a person with type A blood receives type B blood, the type B antibodies attach themselves to the type B RBCs. These RBCs begin to clump together, and the clumps may block blood vessels. A reaction to the wrong blood type may be fatal.

Blood Types and Transfusions

Sometimes, a person must be given a blood transfusion. A *transfusion* is the injection of blood or blood components into a person to replace blood that has been lost because of surgery or an injury. **Figure 5** shows bags of blood that may be given in a transfusion. The blood type is clearly marked. Because the ABO blood types have different antigen-antibody reactions, a person receiving blood cannot receive blood from just anyone. **Table 1** shows blood transfusion possibilities.

***Table 1* Blood Transfusion Possibilities**

Type	Can receive	Can donate to
A	A, O	A, AB
B	B, O	B, AB
AB	all	AB only
O	O	all

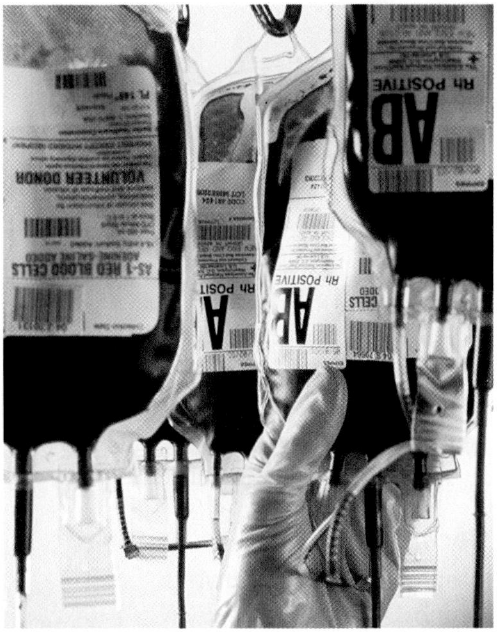

Figure 5 *The blood type must be clearly labeled on blood stored for transfusions.*

Reading Check **People with type O blood are sometimes called universal donors. Why might this be true?**

SECTION Review

Summary

- Blood's four main components are plasma, red blood cells, platelets, and white blood cells.
- Blood carries oxygen and nutrients to cells, helps protect against disease, and helps regulate body temperature.
- Blood pressure is the force blood exerts on the inside walls of arteries.
- Every person has one of four ABO blood types.
- Mixing blood types may be fatal.

Using Key Terms

1. Use each of the following terms in a separate sentence: *blood* and *blood pressure.*

Understanding Key Ideas

2. A person with type B blood can donate blood to people with which type(s) of blood?
   a. B, AB
   b. A, AB
   c. AB only
   d. All types
3. List the four main components of blood and tell what each component does.
4. Why is it important for a doctor to know a patient's blood type?

Math Skills

5. A person has a systolic pressure of 174 mm Hg. What percentage of normal (120 mm Hg) is this?

Critical Thinking

6. **Identifying Relationships** How does the body use blood and blood vessels to help maintain proper body temperature?
7. **Predicting Consequences** Some blood conditions and diseases affect the ability of red blood cells to deliver oxygen to cells of the body. Predict what might happen to a person with a disease of that type.

SciLinks® NSTA Developed and maintained by the National Science Teachers Association

For a variety of links related to this chapter, go to www.scilinks.org

Topic: Blood; Blood Donations
SciLinks code: HSM0175; HSM0178

SECTION 3

The Lymphatic System

Every time your heart pumps, a little fluid is forced out of the thin walls of the capillaries. Some of this fluid collects in the spaces around your cells. What happens to this fluid?

What You Will Learn

- Describe the relationship between the lymphatic system and the cardiovascular system.
- Identify six parts of the lymphatic system, and describe their functions.

Vocabulary

lymphatic system
lymph
lymph node
thymus
spleen
tonsils

READING STRATEGY

Prediction Guide Before reading this section, write the title of each heading in this section. Next, under each heading, write what you think you will learn.

Most of the fluid is reabsorbed through the capillaries into your blood. But some fluid is not reabsorbed. This fluid moves into your lymphatic (lim FAT ik) system.

The **lymphatic system** is the group of organs and tissues that collect the excess fluid and return it to your blood. The lymphatic system also helps your body fight pathogens.

lymphatic system a collection of organs whose primary function is to collect extracellular fluid and return it to the blood

lymph the fluid that is collected by the lymphatic vessels and nodes

Vessels of the Lymphatic System

The fluid collected by the lymphatic system is carried through vessels. The smallest vessels of the lymphatic system are *lymph capillaries*. Lymph capillaries absorb some of the fluid and particles from between the cells. These particles are too large to enter blood capillaries. Some of these particles are dead cells or pathogens. The fluid and particles absorbed into lymph capillaries are called **lymph.**

As shown in **Figure 1,** lymph capillaries carry lymph into larger vessels called *lymphatic vessels*. Skeletal muscles squeeze these vessels to force lymph through the lymphatic system. Valves inside lymphatic vessels stop backflow. Lymph drains into the large neck veins of the cardiovascular system.

Reading Check **How is the lymphatic system related to the cardiovascular system?** (*See the Appendix for answers to Reading Checks.*)

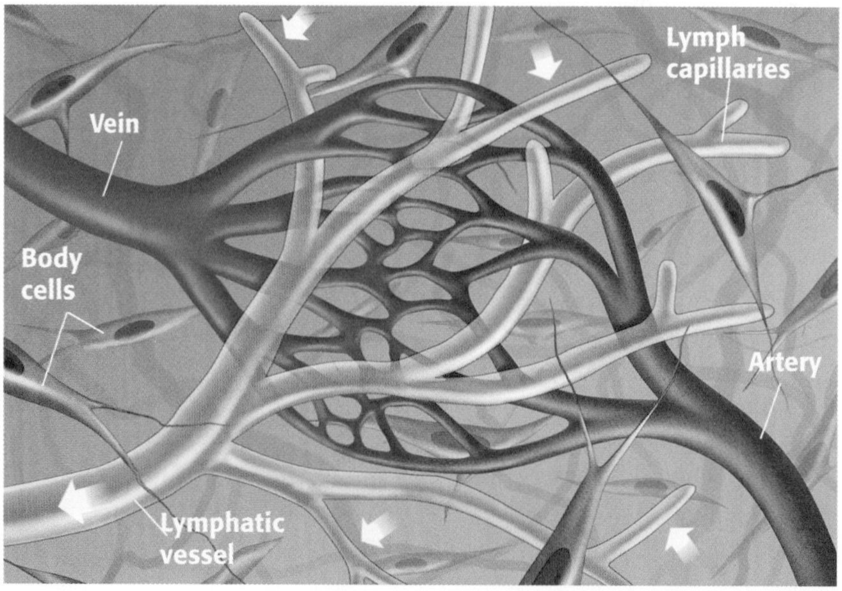

Figure 1 *The white arrows show the movement of lymph into lymph capillaries and through lymphatic vessels.*

Other Parts of the Lymphatic System

In addition to vessels and capillaries, several organs and tissues are part of the lymphatic system. These organs and tissues are shown in **Figure 2.** Bone marrow plays an important role in your lymphatic system. The other parts of the lymphatic system are the lymph nodes, the thymus gland, the spleen, and the tonsils.

lymph node an organ that filters lymph and that is found along the lymphatic vessels

thymus the main gland of the lymphatic system; it produces mature T lymphocytes

Bone Marrow

Bones—part of your skeletal system—are very important to your lymphatic system. *Bone marrow* is the soft tissue inside of bones. Bone marrow is where most red and white blood cells, including lymphocytes (LIM foh SIETS), are produced. *Lymphocytes* are a type of white blood cell that helps your body fight pathogens.

Lymph Nodes

As lymph travels through lymphatic vessels, it passes through lymph nodes. **Lymph nodes** are small, bean-shaped masses of tissue that remove pathogens and dead cells from the lymph. Lymph nodes are concentrated in the armpits, neck, and groin.

Lymph nodes contain lymphocytes. Some lymphocytes—called *killer T cells*—surround and destroy pathogens. Other lymphocytes—called *B cells*—produce antibodies that attach to pathogens. These marked pathogens clump together and are then destroyed by other cells.

When bacteria or other pathogens cause an infection, WBCs may multiply greatly. The lymph nodes fill with WBCs that are fighting the infection. As a result, some lymph nodes may become swollen and painful. Your doctor may feel these swollen lymph nodes to see if you have an infection. In fact, if your lymph nodes are swollen and sore, you or your parent can feel them, too. Swollen lymph nodes are sometimes an early clue that you have an infection.

Thymus

T cells develop from immature lymphocytes produced in the bone marrow. Before these cells are ready to fight infections, they develop further in the thymus. The **thymus** is the gland that produces T cells that are ready to fight infection. The thymus is located behind the breastbone, just above the heart. Mature lymphocytes from the thymus travel through the lymphatic system to other areas of your body.

Figure 2 **The Lymphatic System**

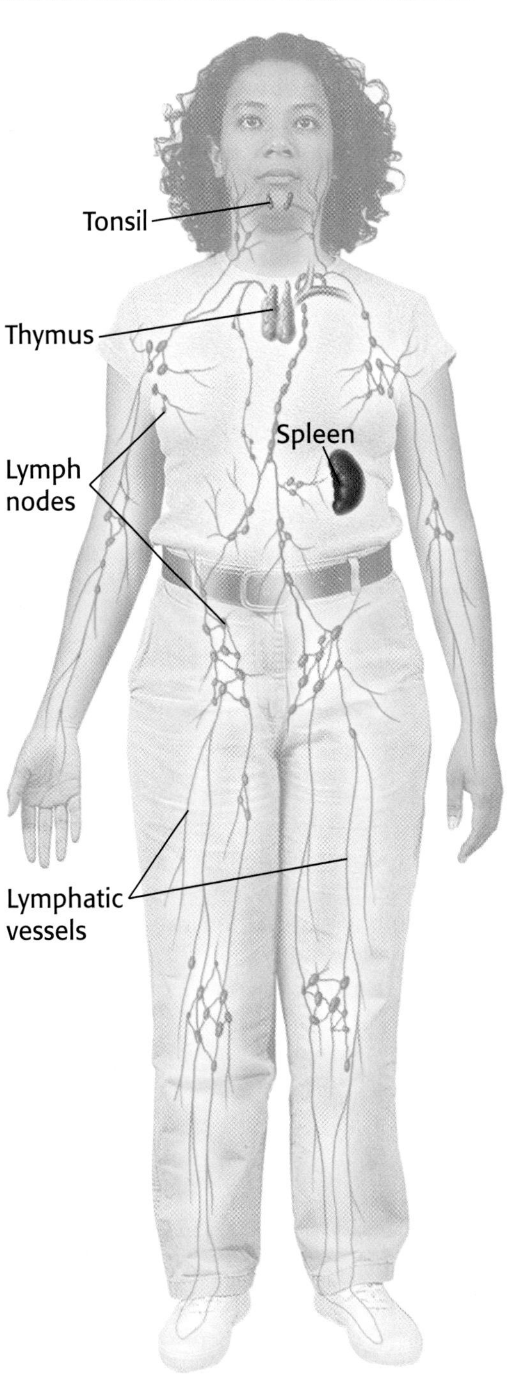

Spleen

spleen the largest lymphatic organ in the body

Your spleen is the largest lymphatic organ. The **spleen** stores and produces lymphocytes. It is a purplish organ about the size of your fist. Your spleen is soft and spongy. It is located in the upper left side of your abdomen. As blood flows through the spleen, lymphocytes attack or mark pathogens in the blood. If pathogens cause an infection, the spleen may also release lymphocytes into the bloodstream.

In addition to being part of the lymphatic system, the spleen produces, monitors, stores, and destroys blood cells. When red blood cells (RBCs) are squeezed through the spleen's capillaries, the older and more fragile cells burst. These damaged RBCs are then taken apart by some of the cells in the spleen. Some parts of these RBCs may be reused. For this reason, you can think of the spleen as the red-blood-cell recycling center.

The spleen has two important functions. The *white pulp,* shown in **Figure 3,** is part of the lymphatic system. It helps to fight infections. The *red pulp,* also shown in **Figure 3,** removes unwanted material, such as defective red blood cells, from the blood. However, it is possible to lead a healthy life without your spleen. If the spleen is damaged or removed, other organs in the body take over many of its functions.

CONNECTION TO Social Studies

WRITING SKILL **Vent Your Spleen** Why do we say that someone is "venting his spleen"? What does it mean? Conduct library or Internet research about this phrase. Write a report on what you have learned.

Reading Check **What are two important functions of the spleen?**

Figure 3 **White and Red Pulp in the Spleen**

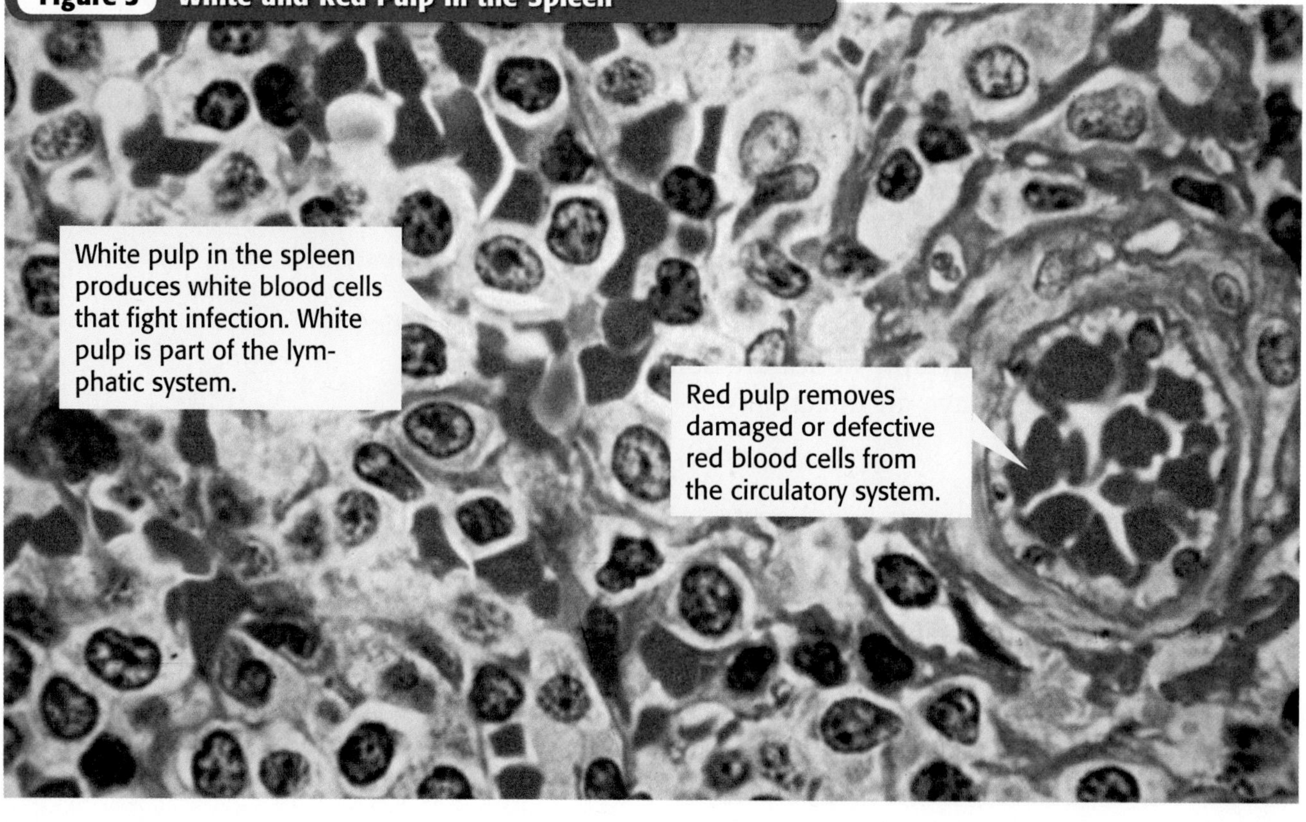
White pulp in the spleen produces white blood cells that fight infection. White pulp is part of the lymphatic system.
Red pulp removes damaged or defective red blood cells from the circulatory system.

Tonsils

The lymphatic system includes your tonsils. **Tonsils** are lymphatic tissue in the nasal cavity and at the back of the mouth on either side of the tongue. Each tonsil is about the size of a large olive.

Tonsils help defend the body against infection. Lymphocytes in the tonsils trap pathogens that enter the throat. Sometimes, tonsils become infected and are red, swollen, and very sore. Severely infected tonsils may be covered with patches of white, infected tissue. Sore, swollen tonsils, such as those in **Figure 4,** make swallowing difficult.

Sometimes, a doctor will suggest surgery to remove the tonsils. In the past, this surgery was frequently done in childhood. It is less common today. Surgery is now done only if a child has frequent, severe tonsil infections or if a child's tonsils are so enlarged that breathing is difficult.

tonsils small, rounded masses of lymphatic tissue located in the pharynx and in the passage from the mouth to the pharynx

Figure 4 *Tonsils help protect your throat and lungs from infection by trapping pathogens.*

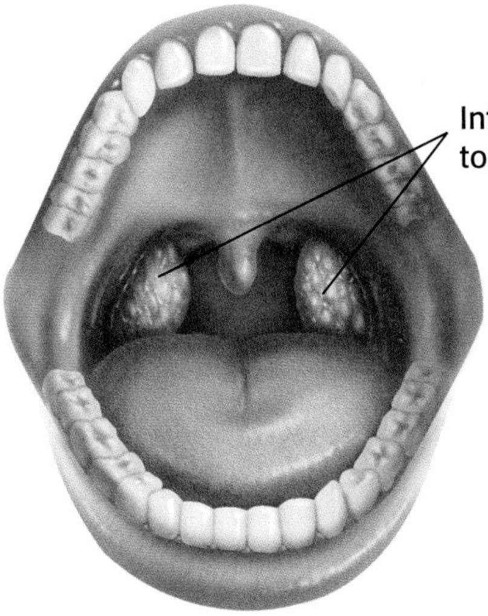

SECTION Review

Summary

- The lymphatic system collects fluid from between the cells and returns it to the blood.
- The lymphatic system contains cells that help the body fight disease.
- The lymphatic system consists of lymphatic vessels, lymph, and tissues and organs throughout the body.
- The thymus, spleen, and tonsils contain lymphocytes that help fight pathogens.

Using Key Terms

1. Use each of the following terms in a separate sentence: *lymph nodes, spleen,* and *tonsils.*

Understanding Key Ideas

2. Lymph
   a. is the same as blood.
   b. is fluid in the cells.
   c. drains into your muscles.
   d. is fluid collected by lymphatic vessels.
3. Name six parts of the lymphatic system. Tell what each part does.
4. How are your cardiovascular and lymphatic systems related?

Math Skills

5. One cubic millimeter of blood contains 5 million RBCs and 10,000 WBCs. How many times more RBCs are there than WBCs?

Critical Thinking

6. **Expressing Opinions** Some people have frequent, severe tonsil infections. These infections can be treated with medicine, and the infections usually go away after a few days. Do you think removing tonsils in such a case is a good idea? Explain.
7. **Analyzing Ideas** Why is it important that lymphatic tissue is spread throughout the body?

SECTION 4

The Respiratory System

Breathing—you do it all the time. You're doing it right now. You hardly ever think about it, though, unless you suddenly can't breathe.

Then, it becomes very clear that you have to breathe in order to live. But why is breathing important? Your body needs oxygen in order to get energy from the foods you eat. Breathing makes this process possible.

What You Will Learn

- Describe the parts of the respiratory system and their functions.
- Explain how breathing happens.
- Discuss the relationship between the respiratory system and the cardiovascular system.
- Identify two respiratory disorders.

Vocabulary

respiration
respiratory system
pharynx
larynx
trachea
bronchus
alveoli

READING STRATEGY

Reading Organizer As you read this section, make a flowchart of the steps of the process of respiration.

Respiration and the Respiratory System

The words *breathing* and *respiration* are often used to mean the same thing. However, breathing is only one part of respiration. **Respiration** is the process by which a body gets and uses oxygen and releases carbon dioxide and water. Respiration is divided into two parts. The first part is breathing, which involves inhaling and exhaling. The second part is cellular respiration, which involves chemical reactions that release energy from food.

Breathing is made possible by your respiratory system. The **respiratory system** is the group of organs that take in oxygen and get rid of carbon dioxide. The nose, throat, lungs, and passageways that lead to the lungs make up the respiratory system. **Figure 1** shows the parts of the respiratory system.

respiration the exchange of oxygen and carbon dioxide between living cells and their environment; includes breathing and cellular respiration

respiratory system a collection of organs whose primary function is to take in oxygen and expel carbon dioxide

Figure 1 *Air moves into and out of the body through the respiratory system.*

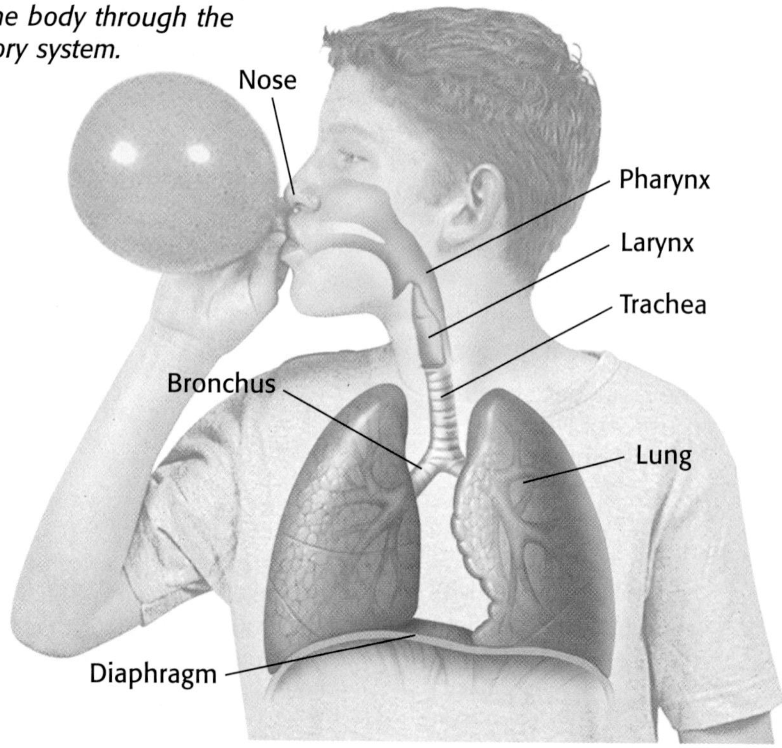

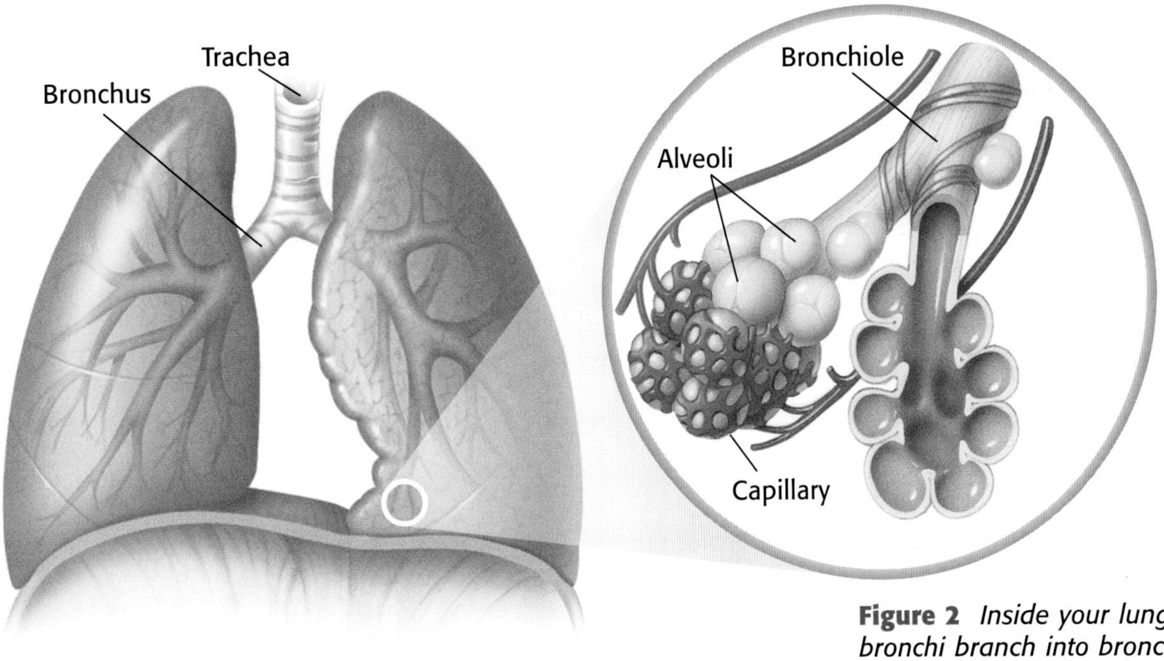

Figure 2 *Inside your lungs, the bronchi branch into bronchioles. The bronchioles lead to tiny sacs called alveoli.*

Nose, Pharynx, and Larynx

Your *nose* is the main passageway into and out of the respiratory system. Air can be breathed in through and out of the nose. Air can also enter and leave through the mouth.

From the nose, air flows into the **pharynx** (FAR ingks), or throat. Food and drink also travel through the pharynx on the way to the stomach. The pharynx branches into two tubes. One tube, the *esophagus,* leads to the stomach. The other tube is the larynx (LAR ingks). The larynx leads to the lungs.

The **larynx** is the part of the throat that contains the vocal cords. The *vocal cords* are a pair of elastic bands that stretch across the larynx. Muscles connected to the larynx control how much the vocal cords are stretched. When air flows between the vocal cords, the cords vibrate. These vibrations make sound.

pharynx the passage from the mouth to the larynx and esophagus

larynx the area of the throat that contains the vocal cords and produces vocal sounds

trachea the tube that connects the larynx to the lungs

bronchus one of the two tubes that connect the lungs with the trachea

alveoli any of the tiny air sacs of the lungs where oxygen and carbon dioxide are exchanged

Trachea

The larynx guards the entrance to a large tube called the **trachea** (TRAY kee uh), or windpipe. Your body has two large, spongelike lungs. The trachea, shown in **Figure 2,** is the passageway for air traveling from the larynx to the lungs.

Bronchi and Alveoli

The trachea splits into two branches called **bronchi** (BRAHNG KIE) (singular, *bronchus*). One bronchus connects to each lung. Each bronchus branches into smaller tubes that are called *bronchioles* (BRAHNG kee OHLZ). In the lungs, each bronchiole branches to form tiny sacs that are called **alveoli** (al VEE uh LIE) (singular, *alveolus*).

Reading Check **Describe the flow of air from your nose to your alveoli.** (*See the Appendix for answers to Reading Checks.*)

Figure 3 The Role of Blood in Respiration

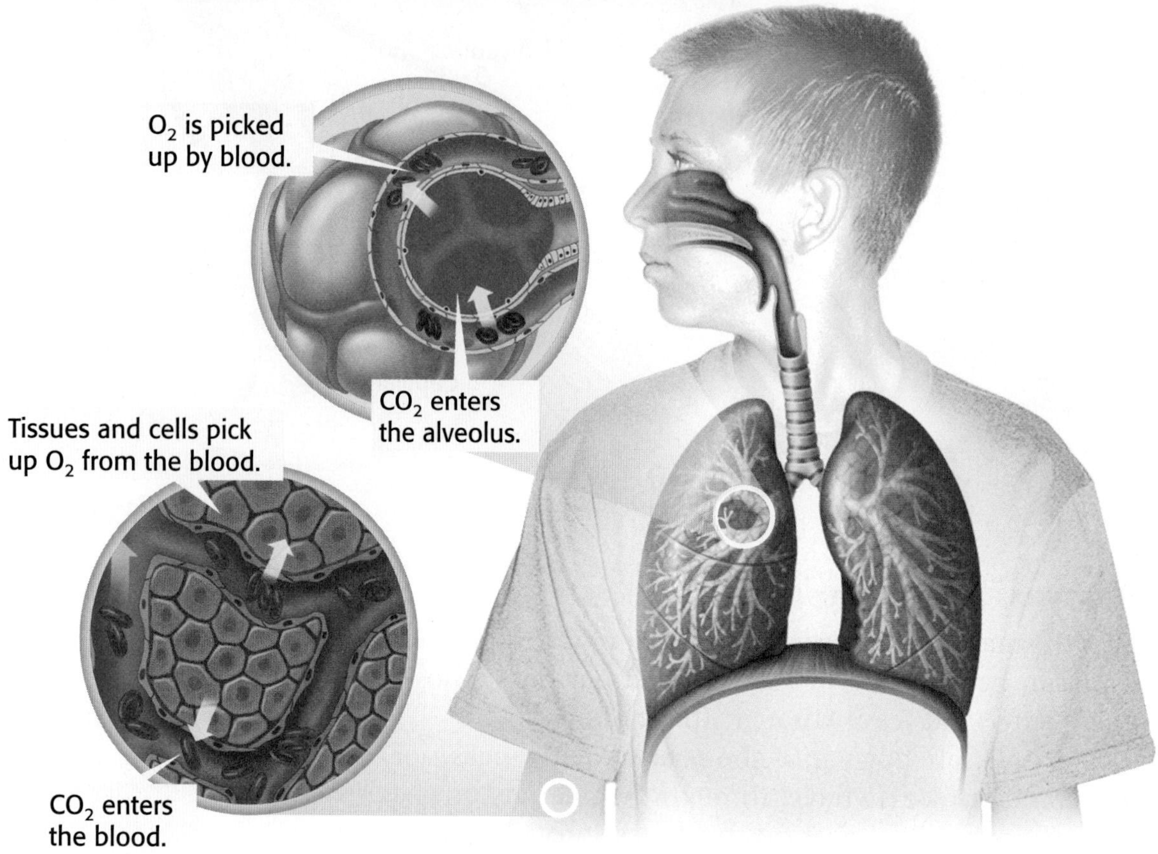
O_2 is picked up by blood.
CO_2 enters the alveolus.
Tissues and cells pick up O_2 from the blood.
CO_2 enters the blood.

Breathing

When you breathe, air is sucked into or forced out of your lungs. However, your lungs have no muscles of their own. Instead, breathing is done by the diaphragm (DIE uh FRAM) and rib muscles. The *diaphragm* is a dome-shaped muscle beneath the lungs. When you inhale, the diaphragm contracts and moves down. The chest cavity's volume increases. At the same time, some of your rib muscles contract and lift your rib cage. As a result, your chest cavity gets bigger and a vacuum is created. Air is sucked in. Exhaling is this process in reverse.

CONNECTION TO Chemistry

Oxygen and Blood When people who live at low elevations travel up into the mountains, they may find themselves breathing heavily even when they are not exerting themselves. Why might this happen?

Breathing and Cellular Respiration

In *cellular respiration,* oxygen is used by cells to release energy stored in molecules of glucose. Where does the oxygen come from? When you inhale, you take in oxygen. This oxygen diffuses into red blood cells and is carried to tissue cells. The oxygen then diffuses out of the red blood cells and into each cell. Cells use the oxygen to release chemical energy. During the process, carbon dioxide (CO_2) and water are produced. Carbon dioxide is exhaled from the lungs. **Figure 3** shows how breathing and blood circulation are related.

Reading Check What is cellular respiration?

Respiratory Disorders

Millions of people suffer from respiratory disorders. Respiratory disorders include asthma, emphysema, and severe acute respiratory syndrome (SARS). Asthma causes the bronchioles to narrow. A person who has asthma has difficulty breathing. An asthma attack may be triggered by irritants such as dust or pollen. SARS is caused by a virus. A person who has SARS may have a fever and difficulty breathing. Emphysema happens when the alveoli have been damaged. People who have emphysema have trouble getting the oxygen they need. **Figure 4** shows a lung damaged by emphysema.

Figure 4 *The photo on the left shows a healthy lung. The photo on the right shows the lung of a person who had emphysema.*

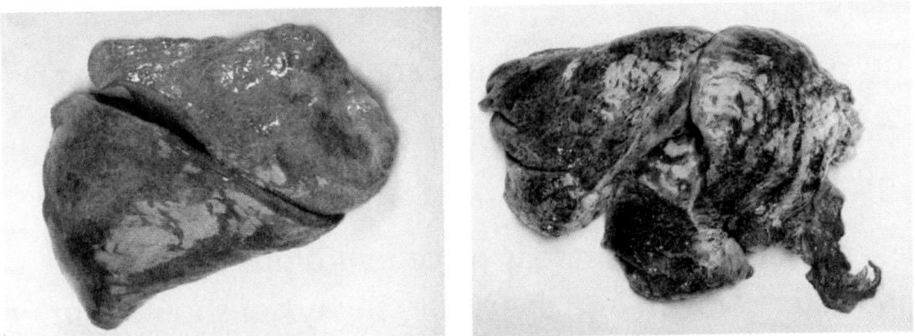

Quick Lab

Why Do People Snore?

1. Get a **15 cm^2 sheet of wax paper.**
2. Hum your favorite song.
3. Then, take the wax paper and press it against your lips. Hum the song again.
4. How was your humming different when wax paper was pressed to your mouth?
5. Use your observations to guess what might cause snoring.

SECTION Review

Summary

- Air travels to the lungs through the nose or mouth, pharynx, larynx, trachea, and bronchi.
- In the lungs, the bronchi branch into bronchioles, which branch into alveoli.
- Breathing involves lungs, muscles in the rib cage, and the diaphragm.
- Oxygen enters the blood through the alveoli in the lungs. Carbon dioxide leaves the blood and is exhaled.
- Respiratory disorders include asthma, SARS, and emphysema.

Using Key Terms

For each pair of terms, explain how the meanings of the terms differ.

1. *pharynx* and *larynx*

Understanding Key Ideas

2. Which of the following are respiratory disorders?
   a. SARS, alveoli, and asthma
   b. alveoli, emphysema, and SARS
   c. larynx, asthma, and SARS
   d. SARS, emphysema, and asthma
3. Explain how breathing happens.
4. Describe how your cardiovascular and respiratory systems work together.

Math Skills

5. Total lung capacity (TLC) is about 6 L. A person can exhale about 3.6 L. What percentage of TLC cannot be exhaled?

Critical Thinking

6. **Interpreting Statistics** About 6.3 million children in the United States have asthma. About 4 million of them had an asthma attack last year. What do these statistics tell you about the relationship between asthma and asthma attacks?
7. **Identifying Relationships** If a respiratory disorder causes lungs to fill with fluid, how might this affect a person's health?

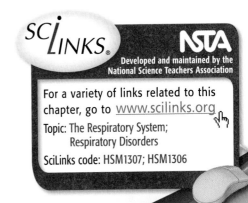

Skills Practice Lab

Carbon Dioxide Breath

OBJECTIVES

Detect the presence of carbon dioxide in your breath.

Compare the data for carbon dioxide in your breath with the data from your classmates.

MATERIALS

- calculator (optional)
- clock with a second hand, or a stopwatch
- Erlenmeyer flask, 150 mL
- eyedropper
- gloves, protective
- graduated cylinder, 150 mL
- paper towels
- phenol red indicator solution
- plastic drinking straw
- water, 100 mL

SAFETY

Carbon dioxide is important to both plants and animals. Plants take in carbon dioxide during photosynthesis and give off oxygen as a byproduct of the process. Animals—including you—take in oxygen during respiration and give off carbon dioxide as a byproduct of the process.

Procedure

1. Put on your gloves, safety goggles, and apron.
2. Use the graduated cylinder to pour 100 mL of water into a 150 mL flask.
3. Using an eyedropper, carefully place four drops of phenol red indicator solution into the water. The water should turn orange.
4. Place a plastic drinking straw into the solution of phenol red and water. Drape a paper towel over the flask to prevent splashing.
5. Carefully blow through the straw into the solution. **Caution:** Do not inhale through the straw. Do not drink the solution, and do not share a straw with anyone.

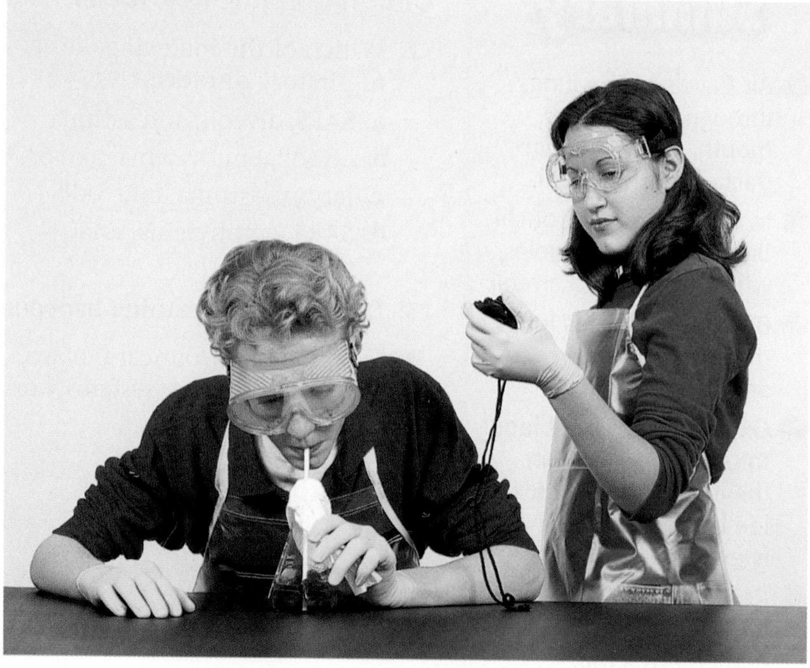

6. Your lab partner should begin keeping time as soon as you start to blow through the straw. Have your lab partner time how long the solution takes to change color. Record the time.

Analyze the Results

1. **Describing Events** Describe what happens to the indicator solution.
2. **Examining Data** Compare your data with those of your classmates. What was the longest length of time it took to see a color change? What was the shortest? How do you account for the difference?
3. **Constructing Graphs** Make a bar graph that compares your data with the data of your classmates.

Draw Conclusions

4. **Interpreting Information** Do you think that there is a relationship between the length of time the solution takes to change color and the person's physical characteristics, such as which gender the tester is or whether the tester has an athletic build? Explain your answer.
5. **Making Predictions** Predict how exercise might affect the results of your experiment. For example, would you predict that the level of carbon dioxide in the breath of someone who was exercising would be higher or lower than the carbon dioxide level in the breath of someone who was sitting quietly? Would you predict that the level of carbon dioxide in the breath would affect the timing of any color change in the phenol solution?

Applying Your Data

Do jumping jacks or sit-ups for 3 minutes, and then repeat the experiment. Did the phenol solution still change color? Did your exercising change the timing? Describe and explain any change.

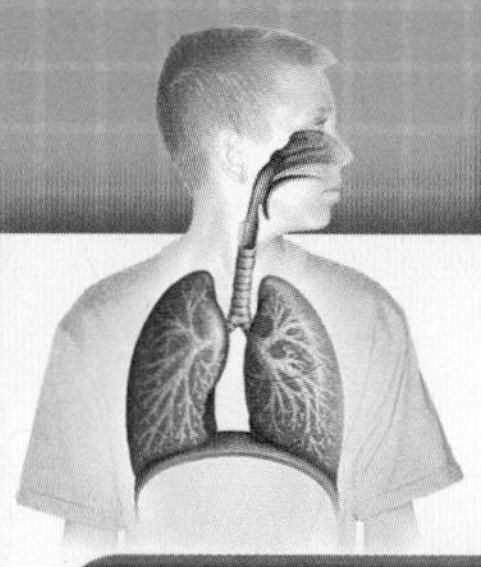

Chapter Review

USING KEY TERMS

Complete each of the following sentences by choosing the correct term from the word bank.

red blood cells	veins
white blood cells	arteries
lymphatic system	larynx
alveoli	bronchi
respiratory system	trachea

1. ___ deliver oxygen to the cells of the body.

2. ___ carry blood away from the heart.

3. The ___ helps the body fight pathogens.

4. The ___ contains the vocal cords.

5. The pathway of air through the respiratory system ends at the tiny sacs called ___.

UNDERSTANDING KEY IDEAS

Multiple Choice

6. Blood from the lungs enters the heart at the
   - **a.** left ventricle.
   - **b.** left atrium.
   - **c.** right atrium.
   - **d.** right ventricle.

7. Blood cells are made
   - **a.** in the heart.
   - **b.** from plasma.
   - **c.** from lymph.
   - **d.** in the bones.

8. Which of the following activities is a function of the lymphatic system?
   - **a.** returning excess fluid to the circulatory system
   - **b.** delivering nutrients to the cells
   - **c.** bringing oxygen to the blood
   - **d.** pumping blood to all parts of the body

9. Alveoli are surrounded by
   - **a.** veins.
   - **b.** muscles.
   - **c.** capillaries.
   - **d.** lymph nodes.

10. What prevents blood from flowing backward in veins?
    - **a.** platelets
    - **b.** valves
    - **c.** muscles
    - **d.** cartilage

11. Air moves into the lungs when the diaphragm muscle
    - **a.** contracts and moves down.
    - **b.** contracts and moves up.
    - **c.** relaxes and moves down.
    - **d.** relaxes and moves up.

Short Answer

12. What is the difference between pulmonary circulation and systemic circulation in the cardiovascular system?

13. Walton's blood pressure is 110/65. What do the two numbers mean?

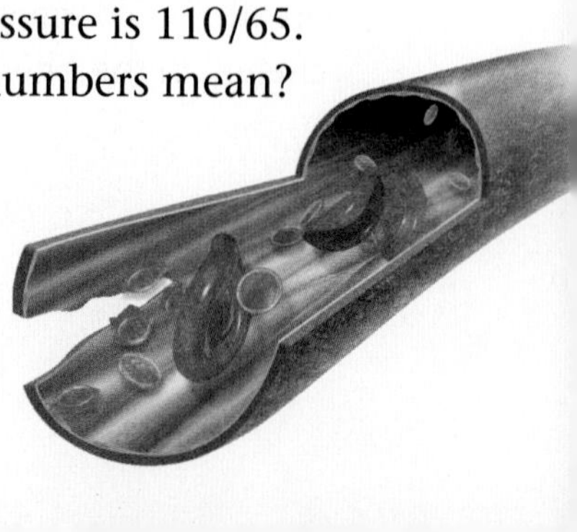

14 What body process produces the carbon dioxide you exhale?

15 Describe how the cardiovascular system and the lymphatic system work together to keep your body healthy.

16 How is the spleen important to both the lymphatic system and the cardiovascular system?

17 Briefly describe the path that oxygen follows in your respiratory system and your cardiovascular system.

CRITICAL THINKING

18 **Concept Mapping** Use the following terms to create a concept map: *blood, oxygen, alveoli, capillaries,* and *carbon dioxide.*

19 **Making Comparisons** Compare and contrast the functions of the cardiovascular system and the lymphatic system.

20 **Identifying Relationships** Why do you think there are hairs in your nose?

21 **Applying Concepts** After a person donates blood, the blood is stored in one-pint bags until it is needed for a transfusion. A healthy person has about 5 million RBCs in each cubic millimeter (1 mm^3) of blood.

a. How many RBCs are in 1 mL of blood? (One milliliter is equal to 1 cm^3 and to 1,000 mm^3.)

b. How many RBCs are there in 1 pt? (One pint is equal to 473 mL.)

22 **Predicting Consequences** What would happen if all of the red blood cells in your blood disappeared?

23 **Identifying Relationships** When a person is not feeling well, a doctor may examine samples of the person's blood to see how many white blood cells are present. Why would this information be useful?

INTERPRETING GRAPHICS

The diagram below shows how the human heart would look in cross section. Use the diagram to answer the questions that follow.

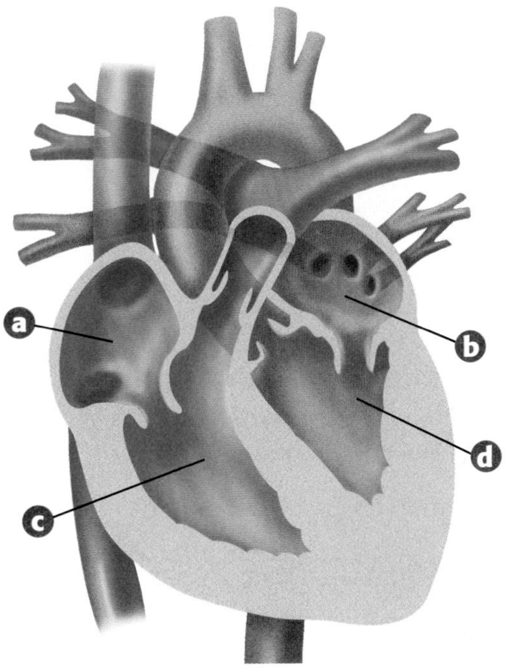

24 Which letter identifies the chamber that receives blood from systemic circulation? What is this chamber's name?

25 Which letter identifies the chamber that receives blood from the lungs? What is this chamber's name?

26 Which letter identifies the chamber that pumps blood to the lungs? What is this chamber's name?

Standardized Test Preparation

Multiple Choice

Use the figure below to answer question 1.

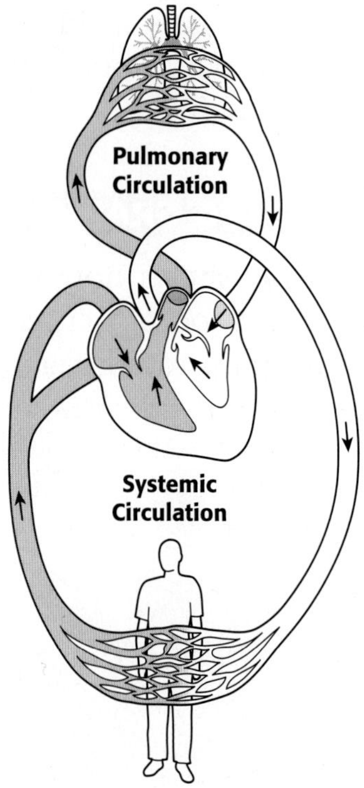

1. **Which kind of circulation provides cells with oxygen, and through which vessels does it provide it?**

   A. pulmonary circulation, arteries

   B. systemic circulation, capillaries

   C. pulmonary circulation, veins

   D. systemic circulation, arteries

2. **Which type of blood vessel allows for the exchange of gases between the blood and body cells?**

   A. arteries

   B. capillaries

   C. veins

   D. ventricles

3. **Cells form tissues, tissues form organs, organs form organ systems, and organ systems form a complete organism. Which of the following correctly follows the levels of organization from lower to higher?**

   A. spleen, lymphocytes, blood, lymph

   B. lymph, lymphocytes, blood, spleen

   C. blood, lymph, spleen, lymphocytes

   D. lymphocytes, lymph, spleen, blood

4. **If found by the doctor, which of the following signs would indicate that Angelina has an infection?**

   A. swollen lymph nodes

   B. enlarged veins and arteries

   C. more red blood cells than normal

   D. blood clots forming from platelets

5. **Which of the following is a direct cause of a stroke?**

   A. A blood vessel ruptures in the brain, cutting off oxygen flow.

   B. The heart is unable to pump enough blood to meet the body's needs.

   C. Cholesterol builds up in an artery, blocking blood flow through it.

   D. A blood vessel collapses, cutting off the flow of oxygen to the heart.

6. **White blood cells (WBCs) fight pathogens. Some WBCs engulf pathogens and break them down; others make antibodies that identify pathogens for destruction. What can you infer from this?**

A. Different kinds of WBCs have similar structures.

B. Some WBCs can become pathogens.

C. Different kinds of WBCs have different structures.

D. Some WBCs are not as effective as others.

7. **Which of the following actions pumps blood through the body?**

A. the expansion of the heart

B. the contractions of the heart

C. the expansion of blood vessels

D. the contractions of the blood vessels

8. **Which of the following are all parts of the lymphatic system?**

A. thymus, spleen, bone marrow, veins

B. capillaries, nodes, alveoli, lymphocytes

C. fluid, B cells, tonsils, valves

D. vessels, killer T cells, hormones, valves

Use the figure below to answer question 9.

Movement of Oxygen from the Atmosphere to Cells

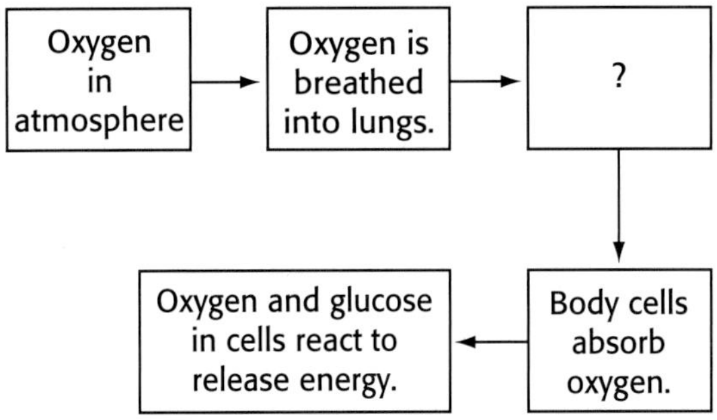

9. **Anthony made the flowchart above that shows how oxygen is taken into the body and used by cells to release energy from food. Which of the following is most likely the missing step?**

A. Oxygen is released as a waste.

B. Oxygen is exchanged for carbon dioxide.

C. Excess oxygen is carried away from body cells.

D. Oxygen enters the blood and is carried throughout the body.

Open Response

10. **List two blood types, and briefly describe how blood types affect transfusions.**

11. **Breathing is one part of respiration. The other part is cellular respiration. Describe the relationship between breathing and cellular respiration.**

Science in Action

Science, Technology, and Society

Artificial Blood

What happens when someone loses blood rapidly? Loss of blood can be fatal in a very short time, so lost blood must be replaced as quickly as possible. But what if enough blood, or blood of the right type, is not immediately available? Scientists are developing different types of artificial blood—including one based on cow hemoglobin—that may soon be used to save lives that would otherwise be lost.

Language Arts ACTIVITY

WRITING SKILL Imagine that you are a doctor and one of your patients needs surgery. Create a pamphlet or brochure that explains what artificial blood is and how it may be used in surgical procedures.

Weird Science

Circular Breathing and the Didgeridoo

Do you play a musical instrument such as a clarinet, flute, or tuba? How long can you blow into it before you have to take a breath? Can you blow into it for one minute? two minutes? And what happens when you stop to breathe? The Aboriginal people of Australia have a musical instrument called the *didgeridoo* (DIJ uh ree DOO). Didgeridoo players can play for hours without stopping to take a breath. They use a technique called *circular breathing* that lets them inhale and exhale at the same time. Circular breathing lets a musician play music without having to take breaths as often. With a little practice, maybe you can do it, too.

Social Studies ACTIVITY

WRITING SKILL Select a country from Africa or Asia. Research that country's traditional musical instruments or singing style. Write a description of how the instruments or singing style of that country differs from those of the United States. Illustrate your report.

People in Science

Anthony Roberts, Jr.

Leader in Training Anthony Roberts, Jr., has asthma. When he was in the 5th grade, his school counselor told him about a summer camp—The Boggy Creek Gang Camp—that was just being built. His counselor said that the camp was designed to serve kids who have asthma or other disabilities and diseases, such as AIDS, cancer, diabetes, epilepsy, hemophilia, heart disease, kidney disease, rheumatic diseases, and sickle cell anemia. Kids, in other words, who might otherwise never go to summer camp. Anthony jumped at the chance to go. Now, Anthony is too old to be a camper, and he is too young to be a regular counselor. But he can be a *Leader in Training* (LIT). Some camps have LIT programs that help young people make the transition from camper to counselor.

For Anthony, the chance to be an LIT fit perfectly with his love of camping and with his desire to work with kids with disabilities. Anthony remembers the fun he had and wants to help other kids have the same summer fun he did.

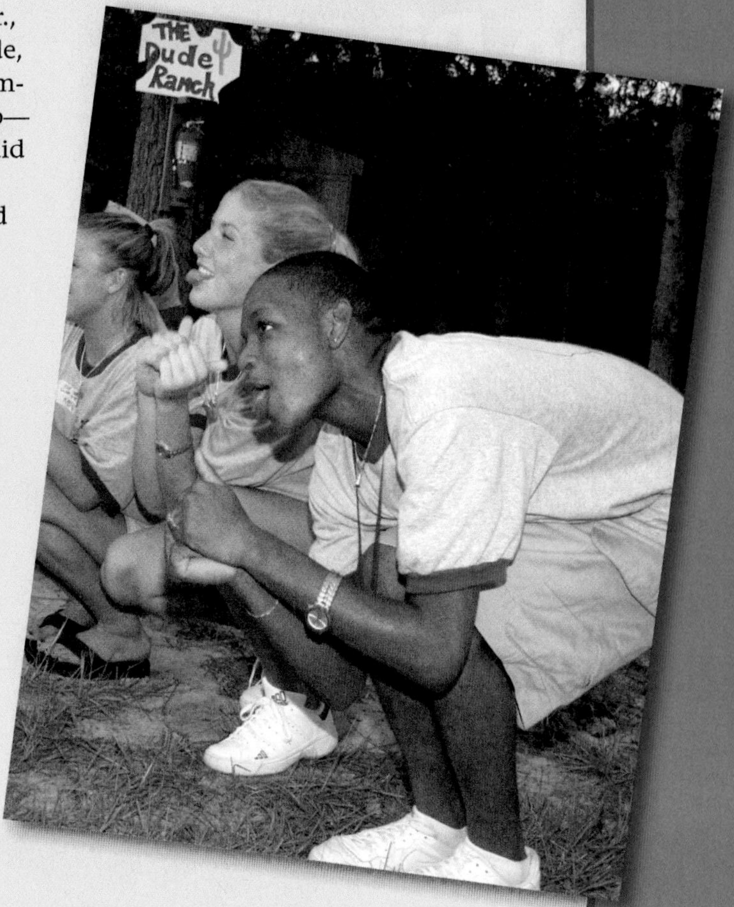

Math Activity

Research how many children under 17 years of age in the United States have asthma. Make a bar graph that shows how the number of children who have asthma has changed since 1981. What does this graph tell you about rates of asthma among children in the United States?

go.hrw.com

To learn more about these Science in Action topics, visit go.hrw.com and type in the keyword HL5BD2F.

Current Science

Check out Current Science® articles related to this chapter by visiting go.hrw.com. Just type in the keyword HL5CS23.

19

The Digestive and Urinary Systems

The Big Idea

The human body has systems that break down nutrients and remove wastes.

About the Photo

Is this a giant worm? No, it's an X ray of a healthy large intestine! Your large intestine helps your body preserve water. As mostly digested food passes through your large intestine, water is drawn out of the food. This water is returned to the bloodstream. The gray shadow behind the intestine is the spinal column. The areas that look empty are actually filled with organs. A special liquid helps this large intestine show up on the X ray.

PRE-READING ACTIVITY

Graphic Organizer

Chain-of-Events Chart Before you read the chapter, create the graphic organizer entitled "Chain-of-Events Chart" described in the **Study Skills** section of the Appendix. As you read the chapter, fill in the chart with details about each step of the processes that your body uses to digest food.

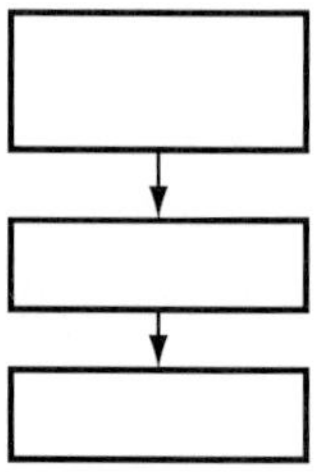

START-UP ACTIVITY

Changing Foods

The stomach breaks down food by, in part, squeezing the food. You can model the action of the stomach in the following activity.

Procedure

1. Add **200 mL of flour** and **100 mL of water** to a **resealable plastic bag.**
2. Mix **100 mL of vegetable oil** with the flour and water.
3. Seal the plastic bag.
4. Shake the bag until the flour, water, and oil are well mixed.
5. Remove as much air from the bag as you can, and reseal the bag carefully.
6. Knead the bag carefully with your hands for 5 min. Be careful to keep the bag sealed.

Analysis

1. Describe the mixture before and after you kneaded the bag.
2. How might the changes you saw in the mixture relate to how your stomach digests food?
3. Do you think this activity is a good model of how your stomach works? Explain your answer.

SECTION 1

The Digestive System

It's your last class before lunch, and you're starving! Finally, the bell rings, and you get to eat!

What You Will Learn

- Compare mechanical digestion with chemical digestion.
- Describe the parts and functions of the digestive system.

Vocabulary

digestive system
esophagus
stomach
pancreas
small intestine
liver
gallbladder
large intestine

READING STRATEGY

Prediction Guide Before reading this section, write the title of each heading in this section. Next, under each heading, write what you think you will learn.

You feel hungry because your brain receives signals that your cells need energy. But eating is only the beginning of the story. Your body must change a meal into substances that you can use. Your **digestive system,** shown in **Figure 1,** is a group of organs that work together to digest food so that it can be used by the body.

digestive system the organs that break down food so that it can be used by the body

Digestive System at a Glance

The most obvious part of your digestive system is a series of tubelike organs called the *digestive tract*. Food passes through the digestive tract. The digestive tract includes your mouth, pharynx, esophagus, stomach, small intestine, large intestine, rectum, and anus. The human digestive tract can be more than 9 m long! The liver, gallbladder, pancreas, and salivary glands are also part of the digestive system. But food does not pass through these organs.

Figure 1 The Digestive System

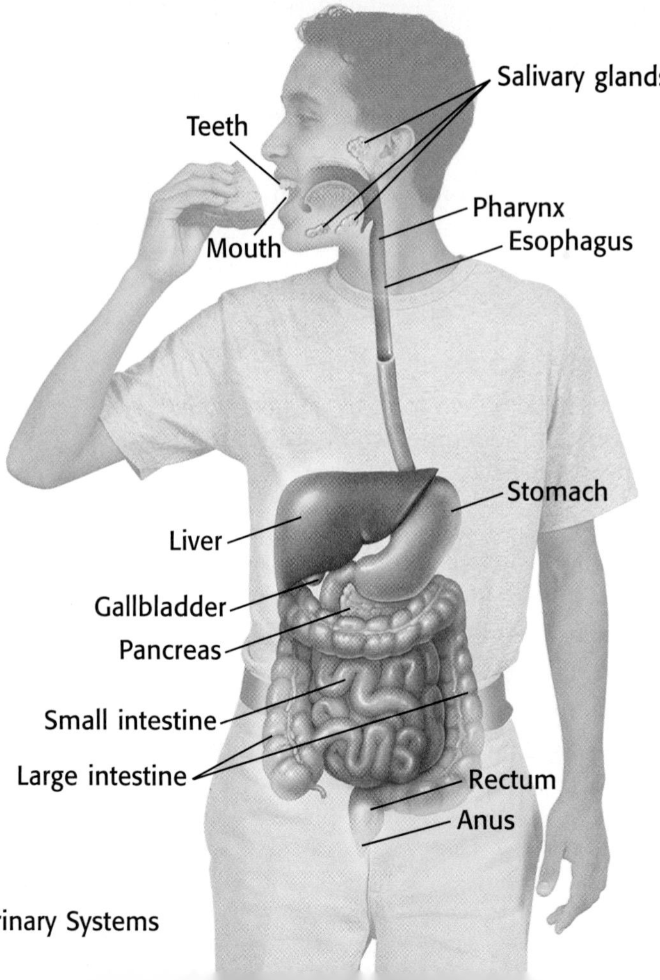

Breaking Down Food

Digestion is the process of breaking down food, such as a peanut butter and jelly sandwich, into a form that can pass from the digestive tract into the bloodstream. There are two types of digestion—mechanical and chemical. The breaking, crushing, and mashing of food is called *mechanical digestion.* In *chemical digestion,* large molecules are broken down into nutrients. Nutrients are substances in food that the body needs for normal growth, maintenance, and repair.

Three major types of nutrients—carbohydrates, proteins, and fats—make up most of the food you eat. In fact, a peanut butter and jelly sandwich contains all three of these nutrients. Substances called *enzymes* break some nutrients into smaller particles that the body can use. For example, proteins are chains of smaller molecules called *amino acids*. Proteins are too large to be absorbed into the bloodstream. So, enzymes cut up the chain of amino acids. The amino acids are small enough to pass into the bloodstream. This process is shown in **Figure 2.**

Reading Check **How do enzymes help digestion?** (*See the Appendix for answers to Reading Checks.*)

Quick Lab

Break It Up!

1. Drop **one piece of hard candy** into a **clear plastic cup of water.**
2. Wrap an **identical candy** in a **towel,** and crush the candy with a **hammer.** Drop the candy into a **second clear cup of water.**
3. The next day, examine both cups. What is different about the two candies?
4. What type of digestion is represented by breaking the hard candy?
5. How does chewing your food help the process of digestion?

Figure 2 **The Role of Enzymes in Protein Digestion**

1. Enzymes act as chemical scissors to cut the long chains of amino acids into small chains.

2. The small chains are split by other enzymes.

3. Individual amino acids are small enough to enter the bloodstream, where they can be used to make new proteins.

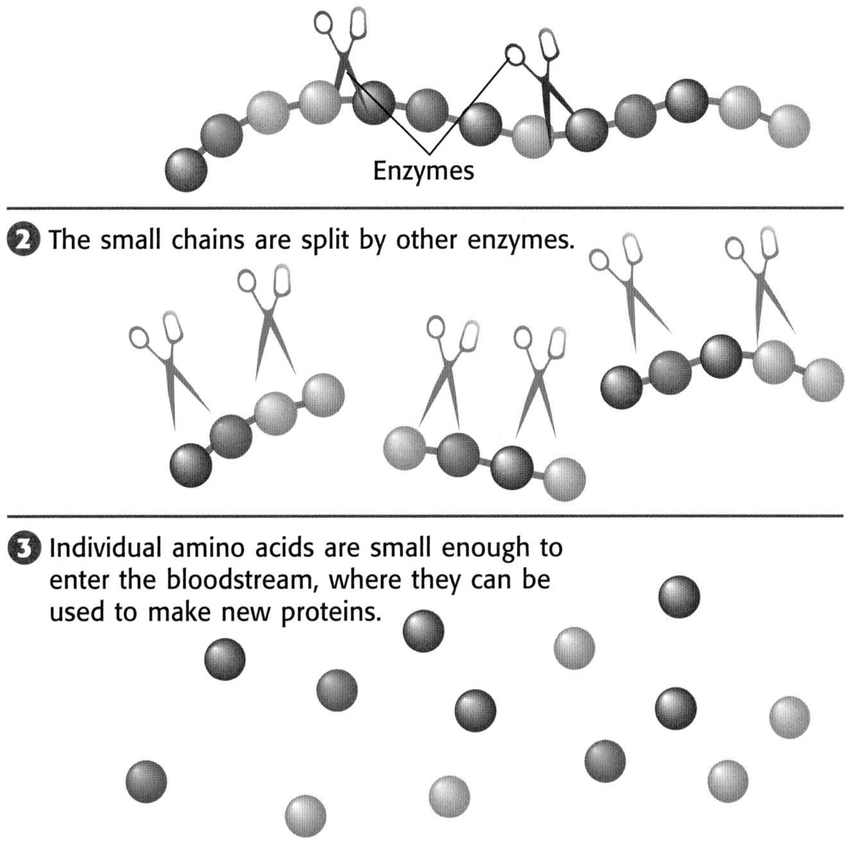

Digestion Begins in the Mouth

Chewing is important for two reasons. First, chewing creates small, slippery pieces of food that are easier to swallow than big, dry pieces are. Second, small pieces of food are easier to digest.

Teeth

Teeth are very important organs for mechanical digestion. With the help of strong jaw muscles, teeth break and grind food. The outermost layer of a tooth, the *enamel,* is the hardest material in the body. Enamel protects nerves and softer material inside the tooth. **Figure 3** shows a cross section of a tooth.

Have you ever noticed that your teeth have different shapes? Look at **Figure 4** to locate the different kinds of teeth. The molars are well suited for grinding food. The *premolars* are perfect for mashing food. The sharp teeth at the front of your mouth, the *incisors* and *canines,* are for shredding food.

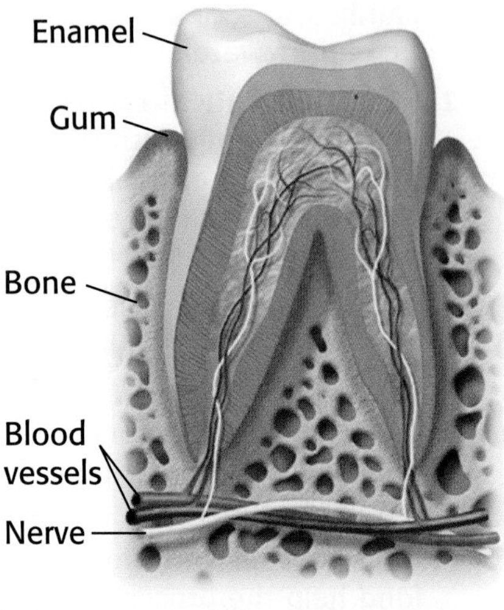

Figure 3 *A tooth, such as this molar, is made of many kinds of tissue.*

Saliva

As you chew, the food mixes with a liquid called *saliva.* Saliva is made in salivary glands located in the mouth. Saliva contains an enzyme that begins the chemical digestion of carbohydrates. Saliva changes complex carbohydrates into simple sugars.

Leaving the Mouth

Once the food has been reduced to a soft mush, the tongue pushes it into the throat, which leads to a long, straight tube called the **esophagus** (i SAHF uh guhs). The esophagus squeezes the mass of food with rhythmic muscle contractions called *peristalsis* (PER uh STAL sis). Peristalsis forces the food into the stomach.

esophagus a long, straight tube that connects the pharynx to the stomach

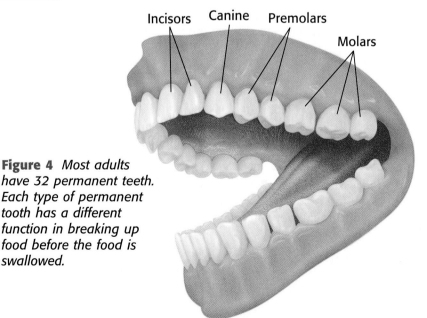

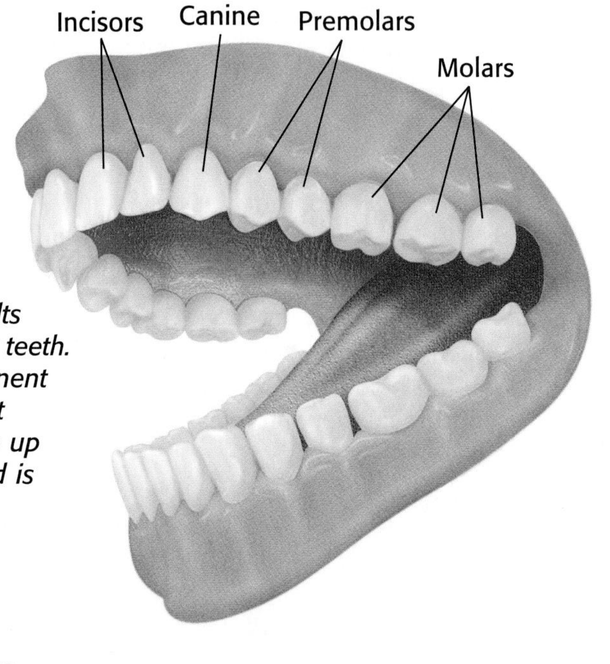

Figure 4 *Most adults have 32 permanent teeth. Each type of permanent tooth has a different function in breaking up food before the food is swallowed.*

Figure 5 **The Stomach**

The stomach squeezes and mixes food for hours before it releases the mixture into the small intestine.

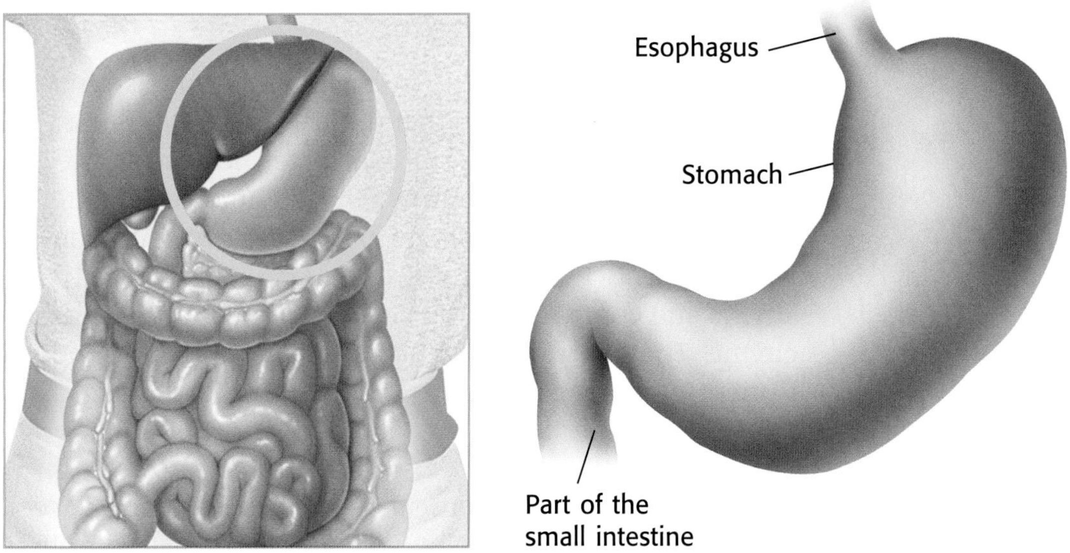

The Harsh Environment of the Stomach

The **stomach** is a muscular, saclike, digestive organ attached to the lower end of the esophagus. The stomach is shown in **Figure 5.** The stomach continues the mechanical digestion of your meal by squeezing the food with muscular contractions. While this squeezing is taking place, tiny glands in the stomach produce enzymes and acid. The enzymes and acid work together to break food into nutrients. Stomach acid also kills most bacteria that you might swallow with your food. After a few hours of combined mechanical and chemical digestion, your peanut butter and jelly sandwich has been reduced to a soupy mixture called *chyme* (KIEM).

stomach the saclike, digestive organ between the esophagus and the small intestine that breaks down food into a liquid by the action of muscles, enzymes, and acids

✓ Reading Check What is chyme?

Leaving the Stomach

The stomach slowly releases the chyme into the small intestine through a small ring of muscle that works like a valve. This valve keeps food in the stomach until the food has been thoroughly mixed with digestive fluids. Each time the valve opens and closes, it lets a small amount of chyme into the small intestine. Because the stomach releases chyme slowly, the intestine has more time to mix the chyme with fluids from the liver and pancreas. These fluids help digest food and stop the harsh acids in chyme from hurting the small intestine.

MATH PRACTICE

Tooth Truth

Young children get a first set of 20 teeth called *baby teeth*. These teeth usually fall out and are replaced by 32 permanent teeth. How many more permanent teeth than baby teeth does a person have? What is the ratio of baby teeth to permanent teeth? Be sure to express the ratio in its most reduced form.

The Pancreas and Small Intestine

Most chemical digestion takes place after food leaves the stomach. Proteins, carbohydrates, and fats in the chyme are digested by the small intestine and fluids from the pancreas.

The Pancreas

When the chyme leaves the stomach, the chyme is very acidic. The pancreas makes fluids that protect the small intestine from the acid. The **pancreas** is an oval organ located between the stomach and small intestine. The chyme never enters the pancreas. Instead, the pancreatic fluid flows into the small intestine. This fluid contains enzymes that chemically digest chyme and contains bicarbonate, which neutralizes the acid in chyme. The pancreas also functions as a part of the endocrine system by making hormones that regulate blood sugar.

pancreas the organ that lies behind the stomach and that makes digestive enzymes and hormones that regulate sugar levels

small intestine the organ between the stomach and the large intestine where most of the breakdown of food happens and most of the nutrients from food are absorbed

The Small Intestine

The **small intestine** is a muscular tube that is about 2.5 cm in diameter. Other than having a small diameter, it is really not that small. In fact, if you stretched the small intestine out, it would be longer than you are tall—about 6 m! If you flattened out the surface of the small intestine, it would be larger than a tennis court! How is this possible? The inside wall of the small intestine is covered with fingerlike projections called *villi,* shown in **Figure 6.** The surface area of the small intestine is very large because of the villi. The villi are covered with tiny, nutrient-absorbing cells. Once the nutrients are absorbed, they enter the bloodstream.

CONNECTION TO Social Studies

WRITING SKILL **Parasites** Intestinal parasites are organisms, such as roundworms and hookworms, that infect people and live in their digestive tract. Worldwide, intestinal parasites infect more than 1 billion people. Some parasites can be deadly. Research intestinal parasites in a library or on the Internet. Then, write a report on a parasite, including how it spreads, what problems it causes, how many people have it, and what can be done to stop it.

Figure 6 **The Small Intestine and Villi**

The highly folded lining of the small intestine has many fingerlike projections called *villi.*

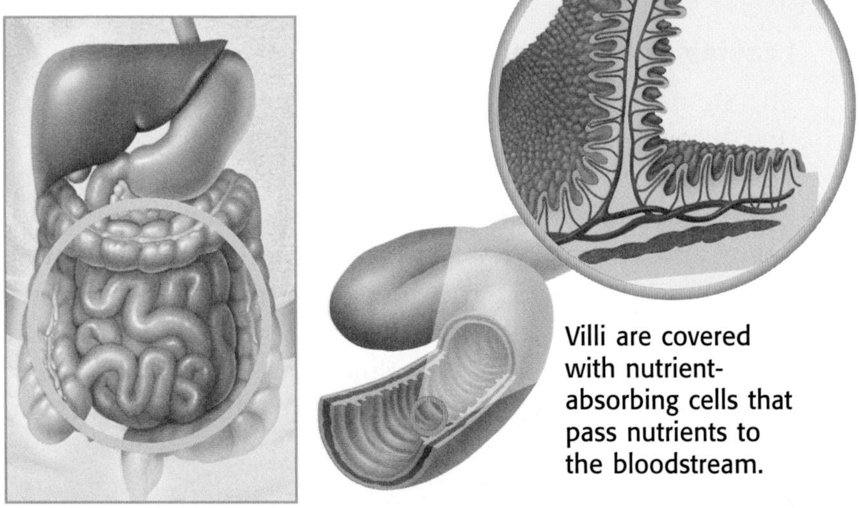

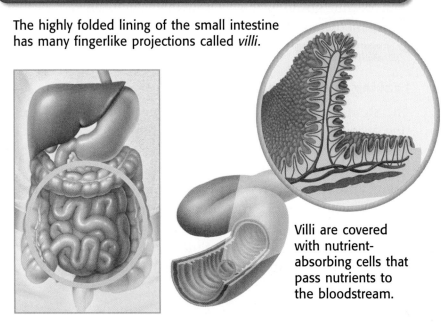

Villi are covered with nutrient-absorbing cells that pass nutrients to the bloodstream.

Figure 7 **The Liver and the Gallbladder**

Food does not move through the liver, gallbladder, and pancreas even though these organs are linked to the small intestine.

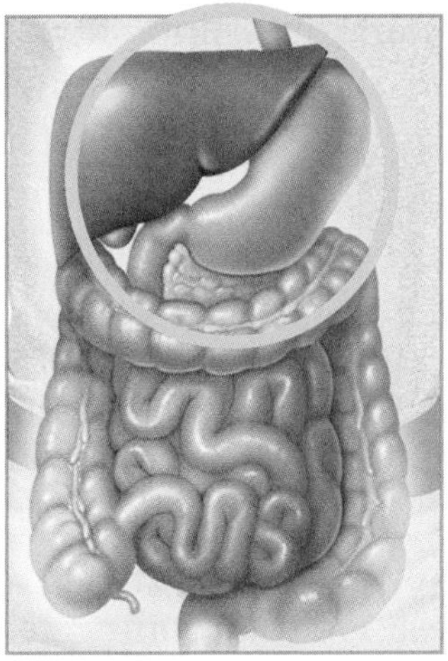

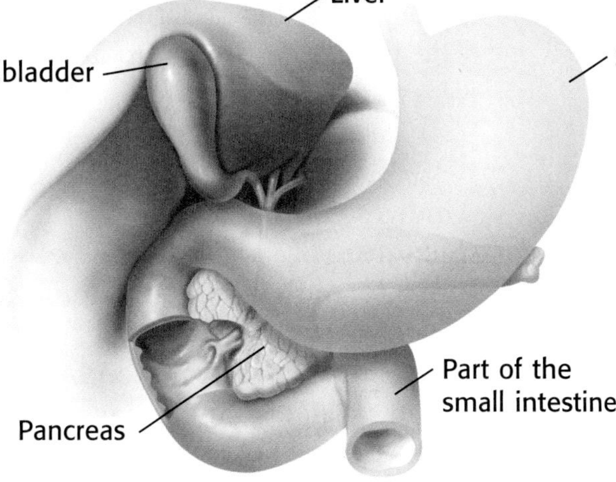

The Liver and Gallbladder

The **liver** is a large, reddish brown organ that helps with digestion. A human liver can be as large as a football. Your liver is located toward your right side, slightly higher than your stomach, as shown in **Figure 7.** The liver helps with digestion in the following ways:

- It makes bile to break up fat.
- It stores nutrients.
- It breaks down toxins.

liver the largest organ in the body; it makes bile, stores and filters blood, and stores excess sugars as glycogen

gallbladder a sac-shaped organ that stores bile produced by the liver

Breaking Up Fat

Although bile is made by the liver, bile is temporarily stored in a small, saclike organ called the **gallbladder,** shown in **Figure 7.** Bile is squeezed from the gallbladder into the small intestine, where the bile breaks large fat droplets into very small droplets. This mechanical process allows more fat molecules to be exposed to digestive enzymes.

Reading Check **How does bile help digest fat?**

Storing Nutrients and Protecting the Body

After nutrients are broken down, they are absorbed into the bloodstream and carried through the body. Nutrients that are not needed right away are stored in the liver. The liver then releases the stored nutrients into the bloodstream as needed. The liver also captures and detoxifies many chemicals in the body. For instance, the liver produces enzymes that break down alcohol and many other drugs.

SCHOOL to HOME

Bile Model

You can model the way bile breaks down fat and oil by using dish soap. At home with a parent or guardian, put a small amount of water in a small jar. Then, add a few drops of vegetable oil to the water. Notice that the two liquids separate. Draw a picture of the jar and its contents. Next, add a few drops of dishwashing soap to the water, tighten the lid securely onto the jar, and shake the jar. What happened to the three liquids in the jar? Draw another picture of the jar and its contents.

ACTIVITY

The End of the Line

large intestine the wider and shorter portion of the intestine that removes water from mostly digested food and that turns the waste into semisolid feces, or stool

Material that can't be absorbed into the blood is pushed into the large intestine. The **large intestine** is the organ of the digestive system that stores, compacts, and then eliminates indigestible material from the body. The large intestine, shown in **Figure 8,** has a larger diameter than the small intestine. The large intestine is about 1.5 m long, and has a diameter of about 7.5 cm.

In the Large Intestine

Undigested material enters the large intestine as a soupy mixture. The large intestine absorbs most of the water in the mixture and changes the liquid into semisolid waste materials called *feces,* or *stool.*

Whole grains, fruits, and vegetables contain a carbohydrate, called *cellulose,* that humans cannot digest. We commonly refer to this material as *fiber*. Fiber keeps the stool soft and keeps material moving through the large intestine.

Reading Check How does eating fiber help digestion?

Leaving the Body

The *rectum* is the last part of the large intestine. The rectum stores feces until they can be expelled. Feces pass to the outside of the body through an opening called the *anus*. It has taken your sandwich about 24 hours to make this journey through your digestive system.

CONNECTION TO Environmental Science

Waste Away Feces and other human wastes contain microorganisms and other substances that can contaminate drinking water. Every time you flush a toilet, the water and wastes go through the sewer to a wastewater treatment plant. At the wastewater treatment plant, the disease-causing microorganisms are removed, and the clean water is released back to rivers, lakes, and streams. Find out where the wastewater treatment plants are in your area. Report to your class where their wastewater goes.

ACTIVITY

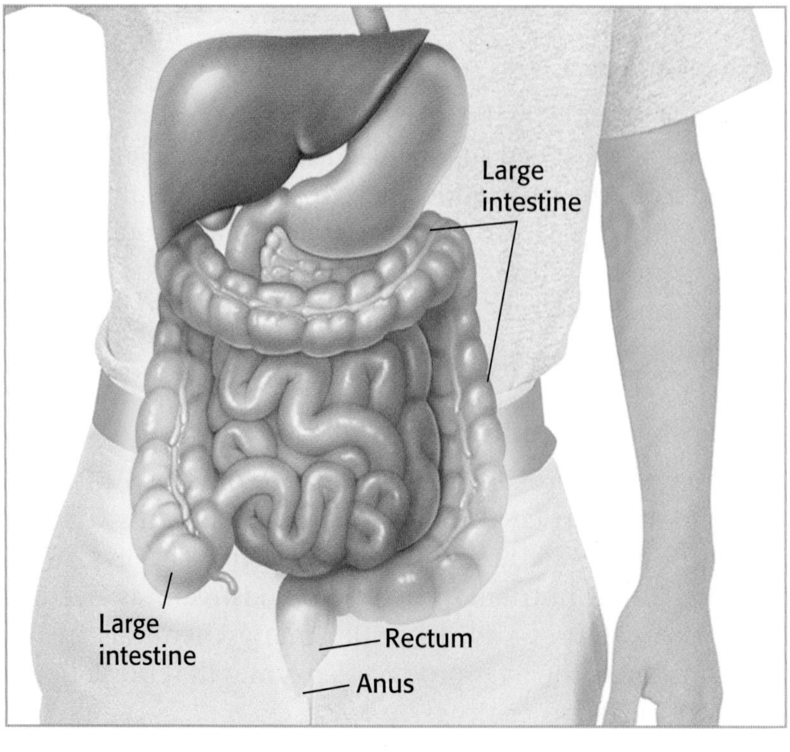

Figure 8 *The large intestine is the final organ of digestion.*

SECTION
Review

Summary

- Your digestive system is a group of organs that work together to digest food so that the nutrients from food can be used by the body.
- The breaking and mashing of food is called *mechanical digestion*. Chemical digestion is the process that breaks large food molecules into simpler molecules.
- The stomach mixes food with acid and enzymes that break down nutrients. The mixture is called *chyme.*
- In the small intestine, pancreatic fluid and bile are mixed with chyme.
- From the small intestine, nutrients enter the bloodstream and are circulated to the body's cells.
- The liver makes bile, stores nutrients, and breaks down toxins.
- The large intestine absorbs water, changing liquid waste into semisolid stool, or feces.

Using Key Terms

1. Use each of the following terms in a separate sentence: *digestive system, large intestine,* and *small intestine.*

Understanding Key Ideas

2. Which of the following is NOT a function of the liver?
   - **a.** to secrete bile
   - **b.** to store nutrients
   - **c.** to detoxify chemicals
   - **d.** to compact wastes
3. What is the difference between mechanical digestion and chemical digestion?
4. What happens to the food that you eat when it gets to your stomach?
5. Describe the role of the liver, gallbladder, and pancreas in digestion.
6. Put the following steps of digestion in order.
   - **a.** Food is chewed by the teeth in the mouth.
   - **b.** Water is absorbed by the large intestine.
   - **c.** Food is reduced to chyme in the stomach.
   - **d.** Food moves down the esophagus.
   - **e.** Nutrients are absorbed by the small intestine.
   - **f.** The pancreas releases enzymes.

Critical Thinking

7. **Evaluating Conclusions** Explain the following statement: "Digestion begins in the mouth."
8. **Identifying Relationships** How would the inability to make saliva affect digestion?

Interpreting Graphics

9. Label and describe the function of each of the organs in the diagram below.

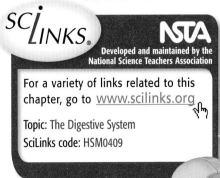

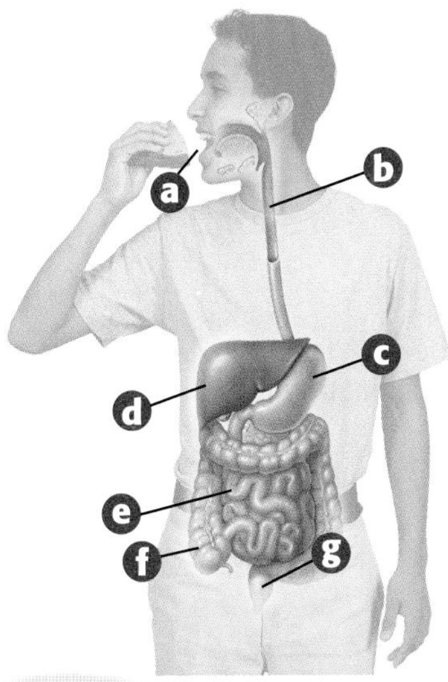

SECTION 2

The Urinary System

What You Will Learn

- Describe the parts and functions of the urinary system.
- Explain how the kidneys filter blood.
- Describe three disorders of the urinary system.

Vocabulary

urinary system
kidney
nephron

READING STRATEGY

Reading Organizer As you read this section, create an outline of the section. Use the headings from the section in your outline.

As blood travels through the tissues, it picks up waste produced by the body's cells. Your blood is like a train that comes to town to drop off supplies and take away garbage. If the waste is not removed, your body can actually be poisoned.

Excretion is the process of removing waste products from the body. Three of your body systems have a role in excretion. Your integumentary system releases waste products and water when you sweat. Your respiratory system releases carbon dioxide and water when you exhale. Finally, the **urinary system** contains the organs that remove waste products from your blood.

Cleaning the Blood

As your body performs the chemical activities that keep you alive, waste products, such as carbon dioxide and ammonia, are made. Your body has to get rid of these waste products to stay healthy. The urinary system, shown in **Figure 1,** removes these waste products from the blood.

urinary system the organs that produce, store, and eliminate urine

Figure 1 Urinary System

The Kidneys as Filters

The **kidneys** are a pair of organs that constantly clean the blood. Your kidneys filter about 2,000 L of blood each day. Your body holds only 5.6 L of blood, so your blood cycles through your kidneys about 350 times per day!

Inside each kidney, shown in **Figure 2,** are more than 1 million nephrons. **Nephrons** are microscopic filters in the kidney that remove wastes from the blood. Nephrons remove many harmful substances. One of the most important substances removed by nephrons is urea (yoo REE uh), which contains nitrogen and is formed when cells use protein for energy.

kidney one of the pair of organs that filter water and wastes from the blood and that excrete products as urine

nephron the unit in the kidney that filters blood

Reading Check **How are nephrons related to kidneys?** (*See the Appendix for answers to Reading Checks.*)

Figure 2 **How the Kidneys Filter Blood**

1. A large artery brings blood into each kidney.
2. Tiny blood vessels branch off the main artery and pass through part of each nephron.
3. Water and other small substances, such as glucose, salts, amino acids, and urea, are forced out of the blood vessels and into the nephrons.
4. As these substances flow through the nephrons, most of the water and some nutrients are moved back into blood vessels that wrap around the nephrons. A concentrated mixture of waste materials is left behind in the nephrons.
5. The cleaned blood, which has slightly less water and much less waste material, leaves each kidney in a large vein to recirculate in the body.
6. The yellow fluid that remains in the nephrons is called *urine.* Urine leaves each kidney through a slender tube called the *ureter* and flows into the *urinary bladder,* where urine is stored.
7. Urine leaves the body through another tube called the *urethra*. *Urination* is the process of expelling urine from the body.

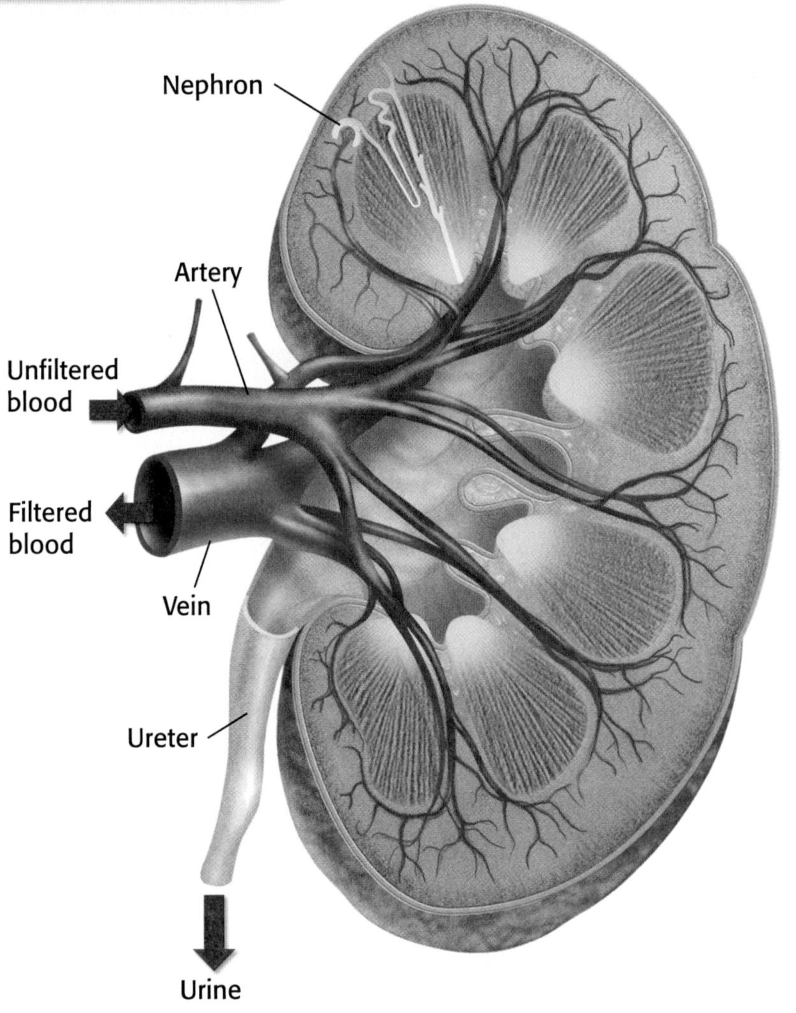

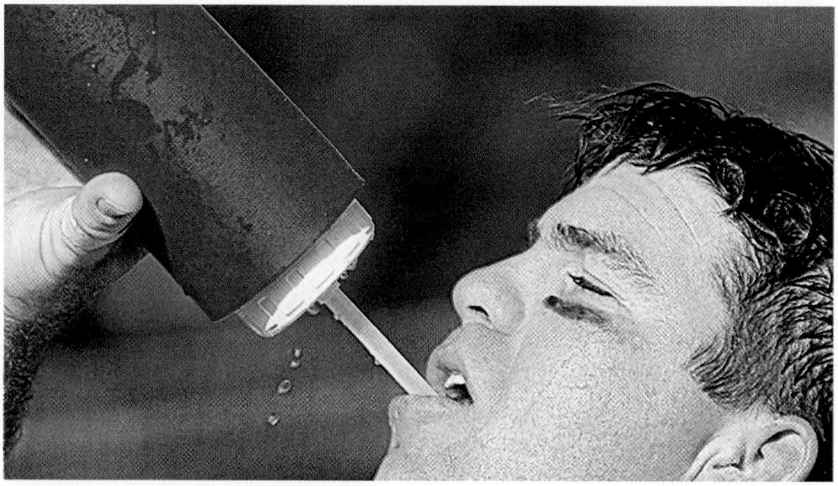

Figure 3 *Drinking water when you exercise helps replace the water you lose when you sweat.*

Water In, Water Out

You drink water every day. You lose water every day in sweat and urine. You need to get rid of as much water as you drink. If you don't, your body will swell up. So, how does your body keep the water levels in balance? The balance of fluids is controlled by chemical messengers in the body called *hormones.*

Sweat and Thirst

When you are too warm, as the boy in **Figure 3** is, you lose a lot of water in the form of sweat. The evaporation of water from your skin cools you down. As the water content of the blood drops, the salivary glands produce less saliva. This is one of the reasons you feel thirsty.

Antidiuretic Hormone

When you get thirsty, other parts of your body react to the water shortage, too. A hormone called *antidiuretic hormone* (AN tee DIE yoo RET ik HAWR MOHN), or ADH, is released. ADH signals the kidneys to take water from the nephrons. The nephrons return the water to the bloodstream. Thus, the kidneys make less urine. When your blood has too much water, small amounts of ADH are released. The kidneys react by allowing more water to stay in the nephrons and leave the body as urine.

Diuretics

Some beverages contain caffeine, which is a *diuretic* (DIE yoo RET ik). Diuretics cause the kidneys to make more urine, which decreases the amount of water in the blood. When you drink a beverage that contains water and caffeine, the caffeine increases fluid loss. So, your body gets to use less of the water from the caffeinated beverage than from a glass of water.

Reading Check **What are diuretics?**

CONNECTION TO Language Arts

WRITING SKILL **Beverage Ban** During football season, a football coach insists that all members of the team avoid caffeinated beverages. Many of the players are upset by the news. Pretend that you are the coach. Write a letter to the members of the team explaining why it is better for them to drink water than to drink beverages that contain caffeine. Read the letter aloud to members of your family. Ask them how you could make your letter more convincing.

Urinary System Problems

The urinary system regulates body fluids and removes wastes from the blood. Any problems with water regulation can become dangerous for your body. Some common urinary system problems are described below.

- **Bacterial Infections** Bacteria can get into the bladder and ureters through the urethra and cause painful infections. Infections should be treated early, before they spread to the kidneys. Infections in the kidneys can permanently damage the nephrons.
- **Kidney Stones** Sometimes, salts and other wastes collect inside the kidneys and form kidney stones like the one in **Figure 4.** Some kidney stones interfere with urine flow and cause pain. Most kidney stones pass naturally from the body, but sometimes they must be removed by a doctor.
- **Kidney Disease** Damage to nephrons can prevent normal kidney functioning and can lead to kidney disease. If a person's kidneys do not function properly, a kidney machine can be used to filter waste from the blood.

Figure 4 *This kidney stone had to be removed from a patient's urinary system.*

SECTION Review

Summary

- The urinary system removes liquid waste as urine. The filtering structures in the kidney are called *nephrons.*
- Most of the water in the blood is returned to the bloodstream. Urine passes through the ureter, into the bladder, and out of the body through the urethra.
- Disorders of the urinary system include infections, kidney stones, and kidney disease.

Using Key Terms

1. In your own words, write a definition for the term *urinary system.*

Understanding Key Ideas

2. Which event happens first?
   a. Water is absorbed into blood.
   b. A large artery brings blood into the kidney.
   c. Water enters the nephrons.
   d. The nephron separates water from wastes.
3. How do kidneys filter blood?
4. Describe three disorders of the urinary system.

Math Skills

5. A study has shown that 75% of teenage boys drink 34 oz of soda per day. How many 12 oz cans of soda would a boy drink in a week if he drank 34 oz per day?

Critical Thinking

6. **Applying Concepts** Which of the following contains more water: the blood going into the kidney or the blood leaving it?
7. **Predicting Consequences** When people have one kidney removed, their other kidney can often keep their blood clean. But the remaining kidney often changes. Predict how the remaining kidney may change to do the work of two kidneys.

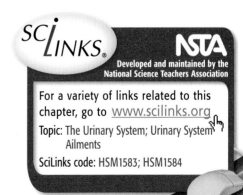

SciLinks. NSTA Developed and maintained by the National Science Teachers Association

For a variety of links related to this chapter, go to www.scilinks.org

Topic: The Urinary System; Urinary System Ailments

SciLinks code: HSM1583; HSM1584

Using Scientific Methods

Skills Practice Lab

As the Stomach Churns

The stomach, as you know, performs not only mechanical digestion but also chemical digestion. As the stomach churns, which moves the food particles around, the digestive fluids—acid and enzymes—are added to begin protein digestion.

Commercially prepared meat tenderizers contain enzymes from plants that break down, or digest, proteins. Two types of meat tenderizer are commonly available at grocery stores. One type of tenderizer contains an enzyme called *papain,* from papaya. Another type of tenderizer contains an enzyme called *bromelain,* from pineapple. In this lab, you will test the effects of these two types of meat tenderizers on beef stew meat.

OBJECTIVES

Demonstrate chemical digestion in the stomach.

Investigate three forms of chemical digestion.

MATERIALS

- beef stew meat, 1 cm cubes (3)
- eyedropper
- gloves, protective
- graduated cylinder, 25 mL
- hydrochloric acid, very dilute, 0.1 M
- measuring spoon, 1/4 tsp
- meat tenderizer, commercially prepared, containing bromelain
- meat tenderizer, commercially prepared, containing papain
- tape, masking
- test tubes (4)
- test-tube marker
- test-tube rack
- water

SAFETY

Ask a Question

1. Determine which question you will answer through your experiment. That question may be one of the following: Which meat tenderizer will work faster? Which one will make the meat more tender? Will the meat tenderizers change the color of the meat or water? What might these color changes, if any, indicate?

Form a Hypothesis

2. Form a hypothesis from the question you formed in step 1. **Caution:** Do not taste any of the materials in this activity.

Test the Hypothesis

3. Identify all variables and controls present in your experiment. In your notebook, make a data table that includes these variables and controls. Use this data table to record your observations and results.

4. Label one test tube with the name of one tenderizer, and label the other test tube with the name of the other tenderizer. Label the third test tube "Control." What will the test tube labeled "Control" contain?

5. Pour 20 mL of water into each test tube.
6. Use the eyedropper to add four drops of very dilute hydrochloric acid to each test tube. **Caution:** Hydrochloric acid can burn your skin. If any acid touches your skin, rinse the area with running water and tell your teacher immediately.
7. Use the measuring spoon to add 1/4 tsp of each meat tenderizer to its corresponding test tube.
8. Add one cube of beef to each test tube.
9. Record your observations for each test tube immediately, after 5 min, after 15 min, after 30 min, and after 24 h.

Analyze the Results

1. **Describing Events** Did you immediately notice any differences in the beef in the three test tubes? At what time interval did you notice a significant difference in the appearance of the beef in the test tubes? Explain the differences.
2. **Examining Data** Did one meat tenderizer perform better than the other? Explain how you determined which performed better.

Draw Conclusions

3. **Evaluating Results** Was your hypothesis supported? Explain your answer.
4. **Applying Conclusions** Many animals that sting have venom composed of proteins. Explain how applying meat tenderizer to the wound helps relieve the pain of such a sting.

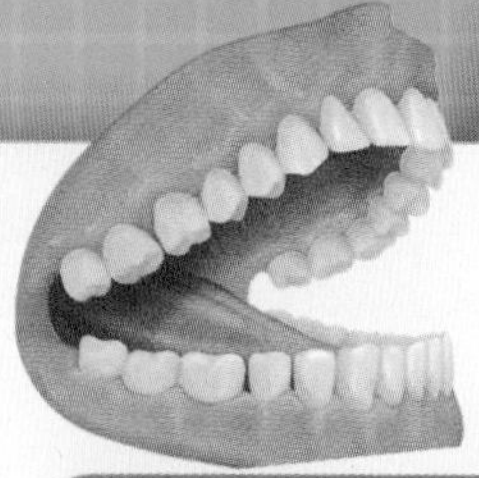

Chapter Review

USING KEY TERMS

Complete each of the following sentences by choosing the correct term from the word bank.

pancreas	digestive system
large intestine	stomach
kidney	small intestine
nephron	urinary system

1. The ____ secretes juices into the small intestine.

2. The saclike organ at the end of the esophagus is called the ____.

3. The ___ is an organ that contains millions of nephrons.

4. A group of organs that removes waste from the blood and excretes it from the body is called the ____.

5. The ____ is a group of organs that work together to break down food.

6. Indigestible material is formed into feces in the ____.

UNDERSTANDING KEY IDEAS

Multiple Choice

7. The hormone that signals the kidneys to make less urine is
   a. urea.
   b. caffeine.
   c. ADH.
   d. ATP.

8. Which of the following organs aids digestion by producing bile?
   a. stomach
   b. pancreas
   c. small intestine
   d. liver

9. The part of the kidney that filters the blood is the
   a. artery.
   b. ureter.
   c. nephron.
   d. urethra.

10. The fingerlike projections that line the small intestine are called
    a. emulsifiers.
    b. fats.
    c. amino acids.
    d. villi.

11. Which of the following is NOT part of the digestive tract?
    a. mouth
    b. kidney
    c. stomach
    d. rectum

12. The soupy mixture of food, enzymes, and acids in the stomach is called
    a. chyme.
    b. villi.
    c. urea.
    d. vitamins.

13. The stomach helps with
    a. storing food.
    b. chemical digestion.
    c. physical digestion.
    d. All of the above

14. The gall bladder stores
    a. food.
    b. urine.
    c. bile.
    d. villi.

15. The esophagus connects the
    a. pharynx to the stomach.
    b. stomach to the small intestine.
    c. kidneys to the nephrons.
    d. stomach to the large intestine.

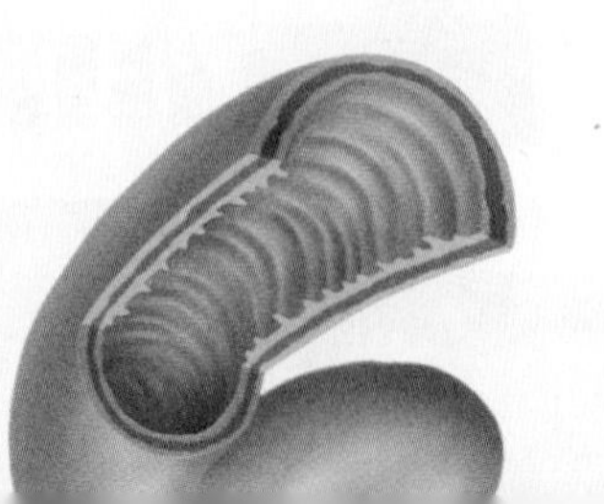

Short Answer

16 Why is it important for the pancreas to release bicarbonate into the small intestine?

17 How does the structure of the small intestine help the small intestine absorb nutrients?

18 What is a kidney stone?

CRITICAL THINKING

19 **Concept Mapping** Use the following terms to create a concept map: *teeth, stomach, digestion, bile, saliva, mechanical digestion, gallbladder,* and *chemical digestion.*

20 **Predicting Consequences** How would digestion be affected if the liver were damaged?

21 **Analyzing Processes** When you put a piece of carbohydrate-rich food, such as bread, a potato, or a cracker, into your mouth, the food tastes bland. But if this food sits on your tongue for a while, the food will begin to taste sweet. What digestive process causes this change in taste?

22 **Making Comparisons** The recycling process for one kind of plastic begins with breaking the plastic into small pieces. Next, chemicals are used to break the small pieces of plastic down to its building blocks. Then, those building blocks are used to make new plastic. How is this process both like and unlike human digestion?

INTERPRETING GRAPHICS

The bar graph below shows how long the average meal spends in each portion of your digestive tract. Use the graph below to answer the questions that follow.

Length of Time in Digestive Organs

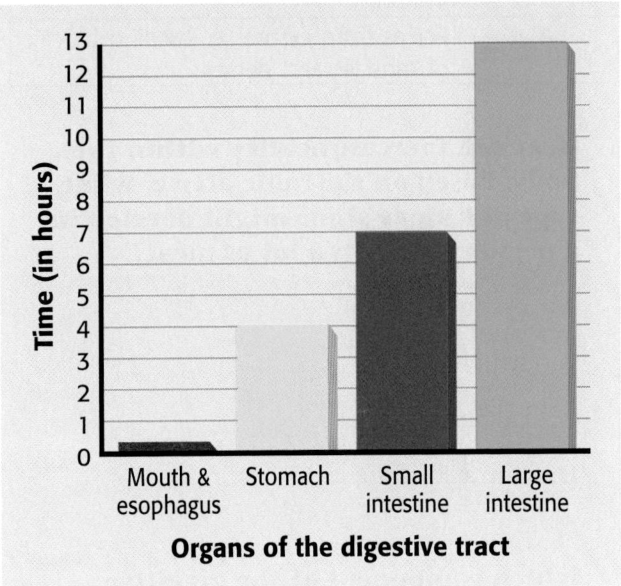

23 In which part of your digestive tract does the food spend the longest amount of time?

24 On average, how much longer does food stay in the small intestine than in the stomach?

25 Which organ mixes food with special substances to make chyme? Approximately how long does food remain in this organ?

26 Bile breaks large fat droplets into very small droplets. How long is the food in your body before it comes into contact with bile?

Standardized Test Preparation

Multiple Choice

Use the table below to answer question 1.

Types of Kidney Stones	
Type	**Description**
Calcium stone	Made up of calcium that is not removed by kidneys
Struvite stone	Made up of magnesium and ammonia
Uric acid stone	Forms when there is too much acid in urine
Cystine stone	Forms from cystine, a building block of muscles and nerves

1. Meat can increase acidity within the body. Based on the table above, what type of kidney stone might develop in a person who eats a lot of meat?

A. cystine stone

B. struvite stone

C. calcium stone

D. uric acid stone

2. Which component of the digestive tract includes the enzymes that begin digestion of carbohydrates?

A. bile

B. chyme

C. saliva

D. urea

3. Which organ of the digestive system absorbs water from waste materials?

A. liver

B. gallbladder

C. large intestine

D. small intestine

4. The digestive system breaks down various substances into smaller molecules, which the cells of the body can use for their life processes. How are molecules, such as proteins, broken down into amino acids, the components used by cells?

A. mechanical digestion in the mouth

B. chemical digestion in the esophagus

C. chemical digestion involving enzymes

D. mechanical digestion involving stomach acids

5. The integumentary system and respiratory system help remove wastes from the body, as does the urinary system. Which organ of the urinary system functions as an exit for wastes from the body?

A. bladder

B. kidney

C. ureter

D. urethra

6. Which of the following describes how blood is filtered in the kidneys?

A. Wastes and other substances are forced into the nephrons, from which water and useful substances are moved back into blood.

B. Water and useful substances are retained by blood while wastes are forced into the nephrons.

C. Blood flows into the nephrons, where it is cleaned, and it is forced back into blood vessels.

D. Water and useful substances are filtered from the nephrons into blood, then wastes are removed.

Use the figure below to answer question 7.

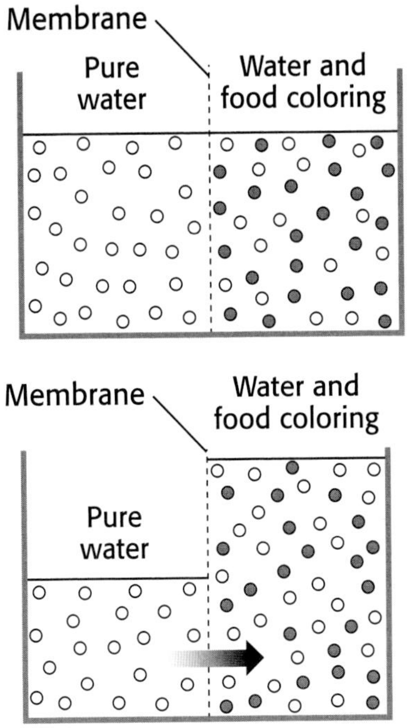

7. The figure above shows a membrane, and the food coloring represents wastes. How is the membrane similar to a nephron?

A. The membrane filters the water.

B. The membrane slows water to pass through.

C. The membrane allows wastes to pass through.

D. The membrane keeps the wastes and water separate.

8. Teeth are part of the skeletal system, but they are also part of the digestive system. Why are they part of the digestive system?

A. They start mechanical digestion.

B. They release enzymes in the saliva.

C. They play a role in chemical digestion.

D. They begin the breakdown of carbohydrates into simple sugars.

9. How does the body respond to thirst?

A. by sweating

B. by producing diuretics

C. by producing more urine

D. by releasing antidiuretic hormone

10. Which of the following harmful substances is removed from the blood by the kidneys?

A. carbon dioxide

B. bile

C. urea

D. urine

11. Which organ of the digestive system makes bicarbonate, which neutralizes stomach acid?

A. liver

B. pancreas

C. gallbladder

D. small intestine

Open Response

12. Describe the movement of food through the organs of the digestive tract, from mouth to rectum.

13. Urinary system problems can affect the entire body, causing problems with water regulation or waste removal. Describe three disorders of the urinary system.

Science in Action

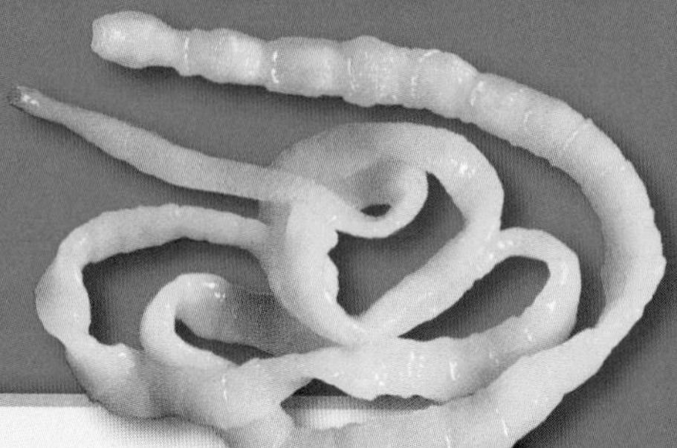

Weird Science

Tapeworms

What if you found out that you had a constant mealtime companion who didn't want just a bite but wanted it all? And what if that companion never asked for your permission? This mealtime companion might be a tapeworm. Tapeworms are invertebrate flatworms. These flatworms are parasites. A parasite is an organism that obtains its food by living in or on another organism. A tapeworm doesn't have a digestive tract of its own. Instead, a tapeworm absorbs the nutrients digested by the host. Some tape worms can grow to be over 10 m long. Cooking beef, pork, and fish properly can help prevent people from getting tapeworms. People or animals who get tapeworms can be treated with medicines.

Social Studies ACTIVITY

WRITING SKILL The World Health Organization and the Pan American Health Organization have made fighting intestinal parasites in children a high priority. Conduct library or Internet research on Worm Busters, which is a program for fighting parasites. Write a brief report of your findings.

Science, Technology, and Society

Pill Cameras

Open wide and say "Ahhhh." When you have a problem with your mouth or teeth, doctors can examine you pretty easily. But when people have problems that are further down their digestive tract, examination becomes more difficult. So, some doctors have recently created a tiny, disposable camera that patients can swallow. As the camera travels down the digestive tract, the camera takes pictures and sends them to a tiny recorder that patients wear on their belt. The camera takes about 57,000 images during its trip. Later, doctors can review the pictures and see the pictures of the patient's entire digestive tract.

Math ACTIVITY

If a pill camera takes 57,000 images while it travels through the digestive system and takes about two pictures per second, how many hours is the camera in the body?

Careers

Christy Krames

Medical Illustrator Christy Krames is a medical illustrator. For 19 years, she has created detailed illustrations of the inner workings of the human body. Medical illustrations allow doctors and surgeons to share concepts, theories, and techniques with colleagues and allow students to learn about the human body.

Medical illustrators often draw tiny structures or body processes that would be difficult or impossible to photograph. For example, a photograph of a small intestine can show the entire organ. But a medical illustrator can add to the photograph an enlarged drawing of the tiny villi inside the intestine. Adding details helps to better explain how small parts of organs work together so that the organs can function.

Medical illustration requires knowledge of both art and science. So, Christy Krames studied both art and medicine in college. Often, Krames must do research before she draws a subject. Her research may include reading books, observing surgical procedures, or even dissecting a pig's heart. This research results in accurate and educational drawings of the inner body.

Language Arts ACTIVITY

WRITING SKILL Pretend you are going to publish an atlas of the human body. Write a classified advertisement to hire medical illustrators. Describe the job, and describe the qualities that the best candidates will have. As you write the ad, remember you are trying to persuade the best illustrators to contact you.

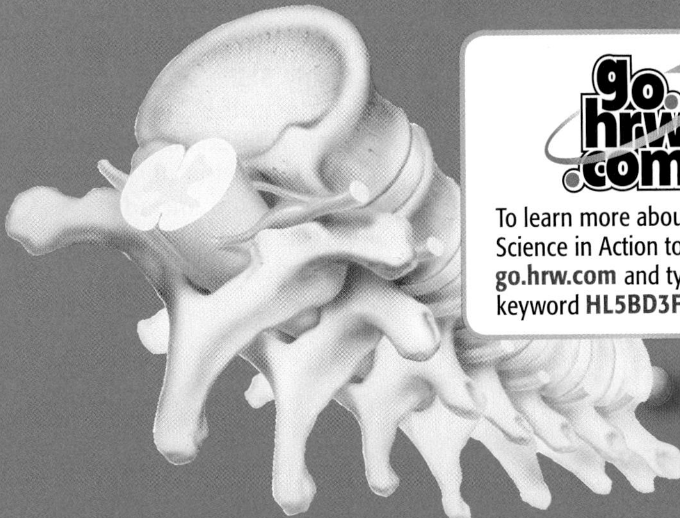

go.hrw.com

To learn more about these Science in Action topics, visit go.hrw.com and type in the keyword **HL5BD3F.**

Current Science

Check out Current Science® articles related to this chapter by visiting go.hrw.com. Just type in the keyword HL5CS24.

20

Communication and Control

The Big Idea The human body has systems that respond to its internal and external environments.

SECTION

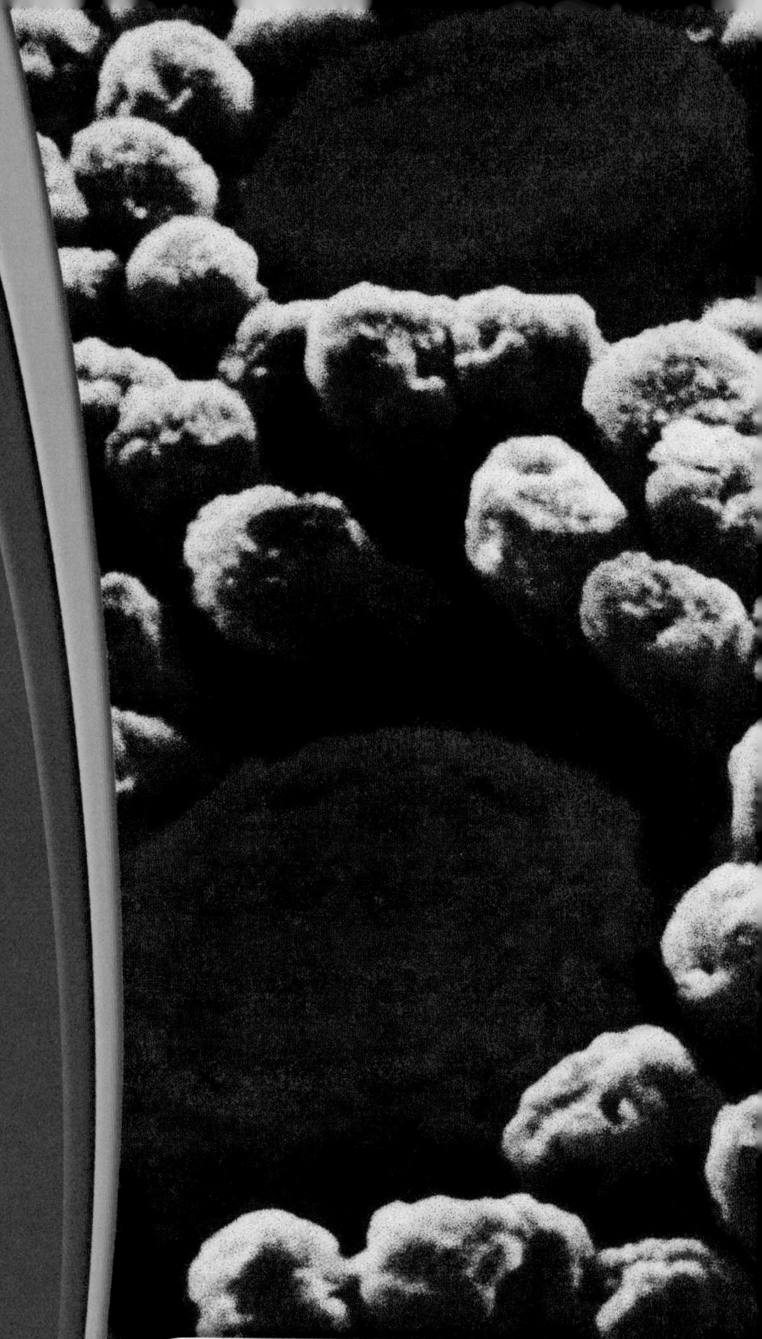

About the Photo

This picture may look like it shows a flower garden or a coral reef. But it really shows something much closer to home. It shows the human tongue (magnified thousands of times, of course). Those round bumps are taste buds. You use taste and other senses to gather information about your surroundings.

PRE-READING ACTIVITY

Graphic Organizer

Concept Map Before you read the chapter, create the graphic organizer entitled "Concept Map" described in the **Study Skills** section of the Appendix. As you read the chapter, fill in the concept map with details about each part or division of the nervous system. Include details about what each part or division does.

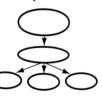

START-UP ACTIVITY

Act Fast!

If you want to catch an object, your brain sends a message to the muscles in your arm. In this exercise, you will see how long sending that message takes.

Procedure

1. Sit in a **chair** with one arm in a "handshake" position. Your partner should stand facing you, holding a **meterstick** vertically. The stick should be positioned so that it will fall between your thumb and fingers.
2. Tell your partner to let go of the meterstick without warning you. Catch the stick between your thumb and fingers. Your partner should catch the meterstick if it tips over.
3. Record the number of centimeters that the stick dropped before you caught it. That distance represents your reaction time.
4. Repeat steps 1–3 three times. Calculate the average distance.
5. Repeat steps 1–4 with your other hand.
6. Trade places with your partner, and repeat steps 1–5.

Analysis

1. Compare the reaction times of your own hands. Why might one hand react more quickly than the other?
2. Compare your results with your partner's. Why might one person react more quickly than another?

SECTION 1

The Nervous System

What You Will Learn

- Describe the relationship between the central nervous system and the peripheral nervous system.
- Compare the somatic nervous system with the autonomic nervous system.
- List one function of each part of the brain.

Vocabulary

central nervous system
peripheral nervous system
neuron
nerve
brain

READING STRATEGY

Discussion Read this section silently. Write down questions that you have about this section. Discuss your questions in a small group.

Which of the following activities do NOT involve your nervous system: eating, playing a musical instrument, reading a book, running, or sleeping?

This is a trick question. All of these activities involve your nervous system. In fact, your nervous system controls almost everything you do.

Two Systems Within a System

The nervous system acts as the body's central command post. It has two basic functions. First, it gathers and interprets information. This information comes from inside your body and from the world outside your body. Then, the nervous system responds to that information as needed.

The nervous system has two parts: the central nervous system and the peripheral (puh RIF uhr uhl) nervous system. The **central nervous system** (CNS) is your brain and spinal cord. The CNS processes and responds to all messages coming from the peripheral nervous system. The **peripheral nervous system** (PNS) is all of the parts of the nervous system except for the brain and the spinal cord. The PNS connects all parts of the body to the CNS. The PNS uses specialized structures, called *nerves*, to carry information between your body and your CNS. **Figure 1** shows the major divisions of the nervous system.

✓ *Reading Check* **Explain the difference between the CNS and the PNS.** (*See the Appendix for answers to Reading Checks.*)

central nervous system (CNS) the brain and the spinal cord

peripheral nervous system (PNS) all of the parts of the nervous system except for the brain and the spinal cord

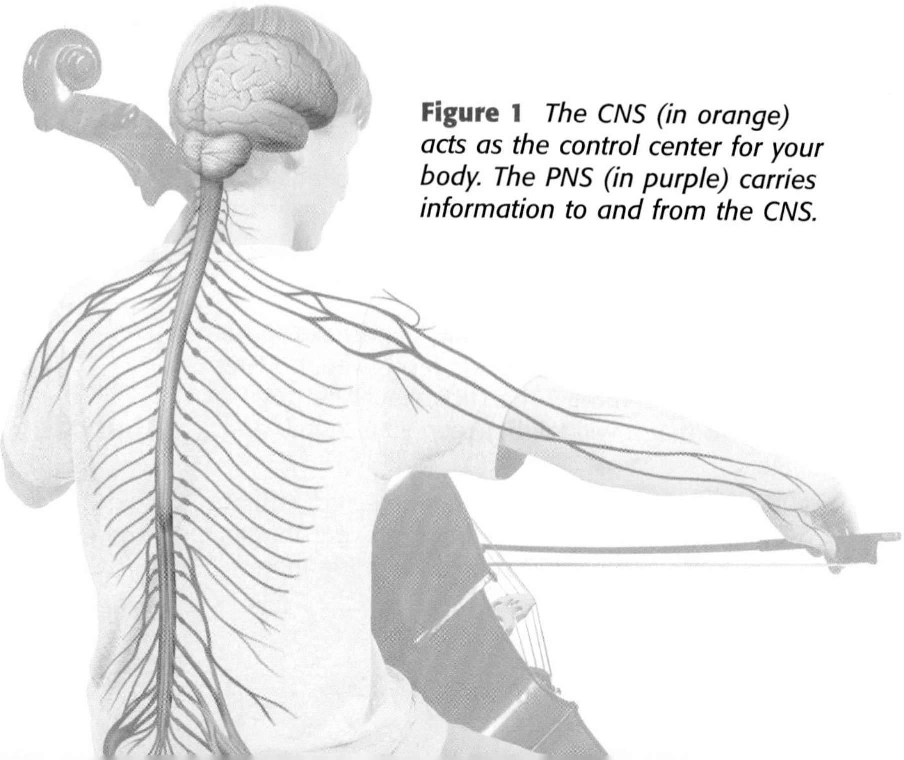

Figure 1 *The CNS (in orange) acts as the control center for your body. The PNS (in purple) carries information to and from the CNS.*

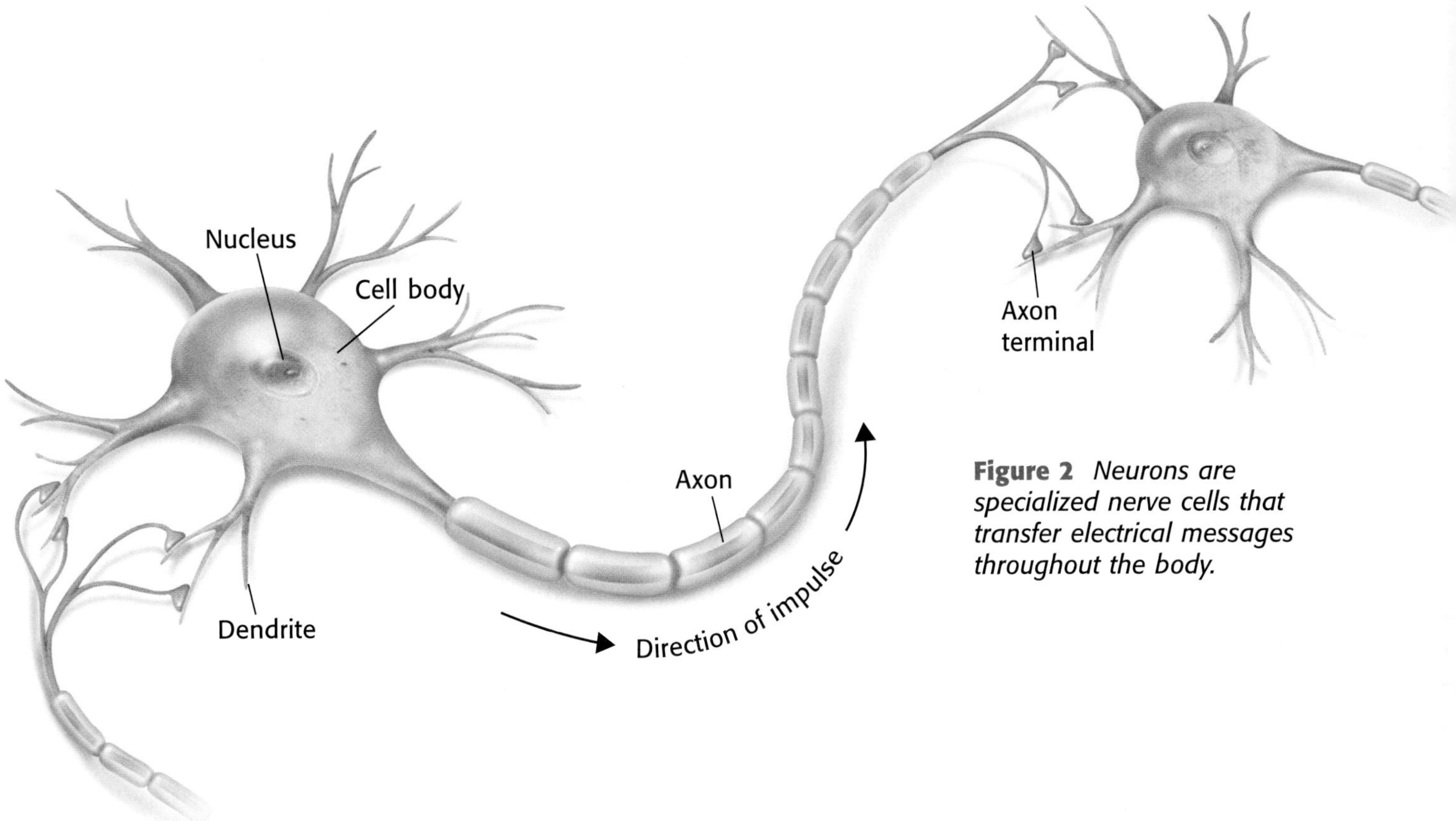

Figure 2 *Neurons are specialized nerve cells that transfer electrical messages throughout the body.*

The Peripheral Nervous System

Messages about your environment travel through the nervous system along neurons. A **neuron** (NOO RAHN) is a nerve cell that is specialized to transfer messages in the form of fast-moving electrical energy. These electrical messages are called *impulses.* Impulses may travel as fast as 150 m/s or as slow as 0.2 m/s. **Figure 2** shows a typical neuron transferring an impulse.

neuron a nerve cell that is specialized to receive and conduct electrical impulses

Neuron Structure

In many ways, a neuron is similar to other cells. A neuron has a large region in its center called the *cell body.* The cell body has a nucleus and cell organelles. But neurons also have special structures called dendrites and axons. *Dendrites* are usually short, branched extensions of the cell. Neurons receive information from other cells through their dendrites. A neuron may have many dendrites, which allows it to receive impulses from thousands of other cells.

Impulses are carried away from the cell body by axons. *Axons* are elongated extensions of a neuron. They can be very short or quite long. Some long axons extend almost 1 m from your lower back to your toes. The end of an axon often has branches that allow information to pass to other cells. The tip of each branch is called an *axon terminal.*

Reading Check **In your own words, describe a neuron.**

MATH PRACTICE

Time to Travel

To calculate how long an impulse takes to travel a certain distance, you can use the following equation:

$$time = \frac{distance}{speed}$$

If an impulse travels 100 m/s, about how long would it take an impulse to travel 10 m?

Information Collection

Remember that neurons are a type of nerve cell that carries impulses. Some neurons are *sensory neurons.* These neurons gather information about what is happening in and around your body. They have specialized nerve endings called *receptors.* Receptors detect changes inside and outside the body. For example, receptors in your eyes detect light. Sensory neurons then send this information to the CNS for processing.

nerve a collection of nerve fibers (axons) through which impulses travel between the central nervous system and other parts of the body

Delivering Orders

Neurons that send impulses from the brain and spinal cord to other systems are called *motor neurons.* When muscles get impulses from motor neurons, they respond by contracting. For example, motor neurons cause muscles around your eyes to contract when you are in bright light. These muscles make you squint. Squinting lets less light enter the eyes. Motor neurons also send messages to your glands, such as sweat glands. These messages tell sweat glands to start or stop making sweat.

Nerves

The central nervous system is connected to the rest of your body by nerves. A **nerve** is a collection of axons bundled together with blood vessels and connective tissue. Nerves are everywhere in your body. Most nerves have axons of both sensory neurons and motor neurons. Axons are parts of nerves, but nerves are more than just axons. **Figure 3** shows the structure of a nerve. The axon in this nerve transmits information from the spinal cord to muscle fibers.

Reading Check What is a nerve?

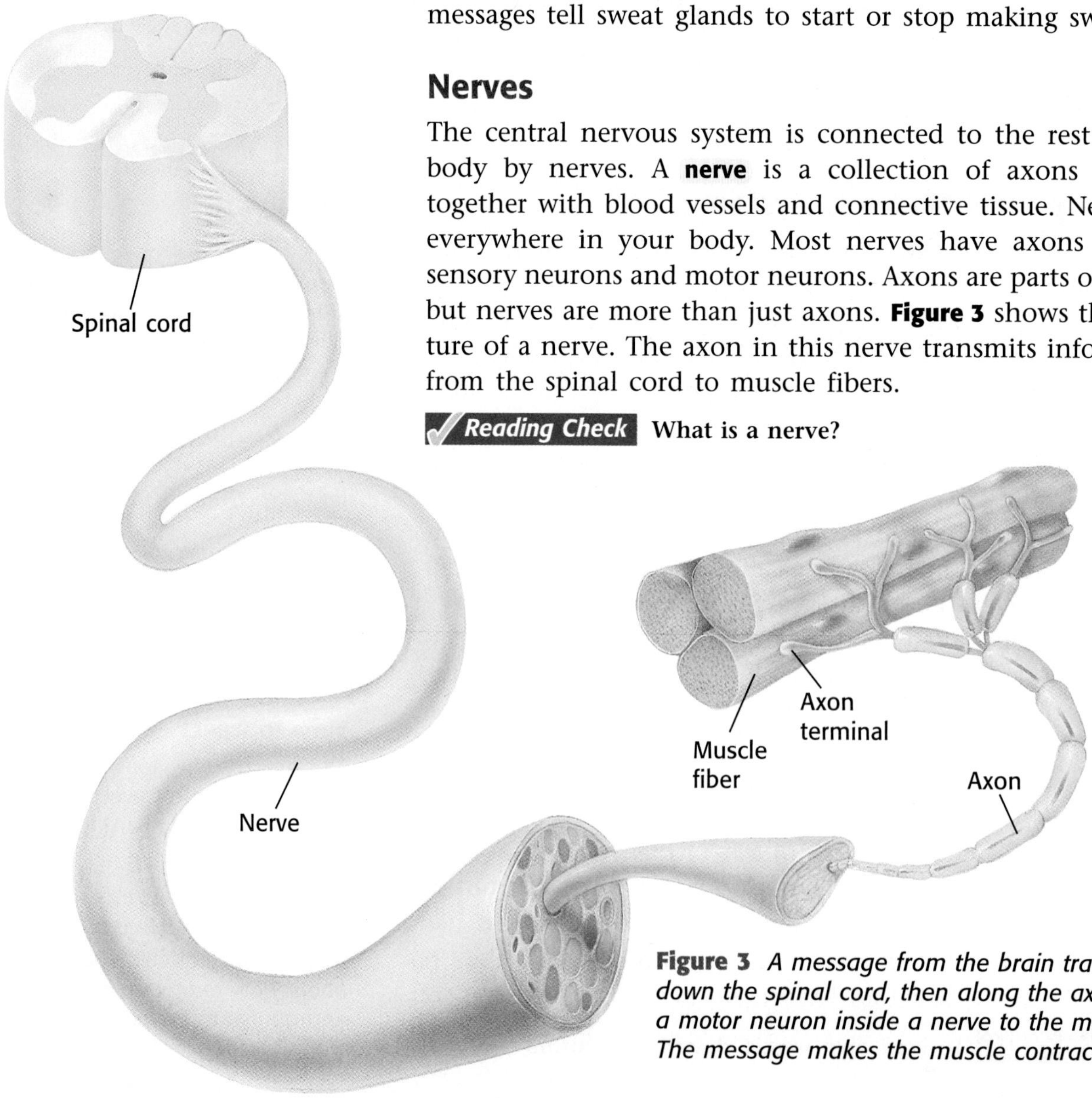

Figure 3 *A message from the brain travels down the spinal cord, then along the axon of a motor neuron inside a nerve to the muscle. The message makes the muscle contract.*

Somatic and Autonomic Nervous Systems

Remember, the PNS connects your CNS to the rest of your body. And the PNS has two main parts—the sensory part (sensory neurons) and the motor part (motor neurons). You know that sensory nerves collect information from your senses and send that information to the CNS. You also know that motor nerves carry out the CNS's responses to that sensory information. To carry those responses, the motor part of the PNS has two kinds of nerves: somatic nerves and autonomic nerves.

Somatic Nervous System

Most of the neurons that are part of the *somatic nervous system* are under your conscious control. These are the neurons that stimulate skeletal muscles. They control voluntary movements, such as writing, talking, smiling, or jumping.

Autonomic Nervous System

Autonomic nerves do not need your conscious control. These neurons are part of the autonomic nervous system. The *autonomic nervous system* controls body functions that you don't think about, such as digestion and heart rate (the number of times your heart beats per minute).

The main job of the autonomic nervous system is to keep all the body's functions in balance. Depending on the situation, the autonomic nervous system can speed up or slow down these functions. The autonomic nervous system has two divisions: the *sympathetic nervous system* and the *parasympathetic nervous system.* These two divisions work together to keep your internal environment stable. This is called *homeostasis.* Some of these functions are shown in **Table 1.**

Reading Check Describe three functions of the PNS.

CONNECTION TO Chemistry

Keeping Your Balance The autonomic nervous system has two parts—the sympathetic division and the parasympathetic division. These parts of your nervous system help keep all of your body systems in balance. Research these two parts of the nervous system, and make a poster showing how they keep your body healthy.

ACTIVITY

Table 1 Effects of the Autonomic Nervous System on the Body

Organ	Effect of sympathetic division	Effect of parasympathetic division
Eyes	pupils dilate (grow larger; makes it easier to see objects)	pupils constrict (vision normal)
Heart	heart rate increases (increases blood flow)	heart rate slows (blood flow slows)
Lungs	bronchioles dilate (grow larger; increases oxygen in blood)	bronchioles constrict
Blood vessels	blood vessels dilate (increases blood flow except to digestion)	little or no effect
Intestines	digestion slows (reduces blood flow to stomach and intestines)	digestion returns to normal

The Central Nervous System

The central nervous system receives information from the sensory neurons. Then it responds by sending messages to the body through motor neurons in the PNS.

The Control Center

brain the mass of nerve tissue that is the main control center of the nervous system

The largest organ in the nervous system is the brain. The **brain** is the main control center of the nervous system. Many processes that the brain controls happen automatically. These processes are called *involuntary.* For example, you couldn't stop digesting food even if you tried. On the other hand, some actions controlled by your brain are *voluntary.* When you want to move your arm, your brain sends signals along motor neurons to muscles in your arm. Then, the muscles contract, and your arm moves. The brain has three main parts—the cerebrum (suh REE bruhm), the cerebellum (SER uh BEL uhm), and the medulla (mi DUHL uh). Each part has its own job.

Reading Check **What is the difference between a voluntary action and an involuntary action?**

The Cerebrum

The largest part of your brain is called the *cerebrum.* It looks like a mushroom cap. This dome-shaped area is where you think and where most memories are stored. It controls voluntary movements and allows you to sense touch, light, sound, odors, taste, pain, heat, and cold.

The cerebrum has two halves, called *hemispheres.* The left hemisphere directs the right side of the body, and the right hemisphere directs the left side of the body. **Figure 4** shows some of the activities that each hemisphere controls. However, most brain activities use both hemispheres.

Figure 4 **The Cerebral Hemispheres**

The **left hemisphere** primarily controls activities such as speaking, reading, writing, and solving problems.

The **right hemisphere** primarily controls activities such as spatial thinking, processing music, and interpreting emotions.

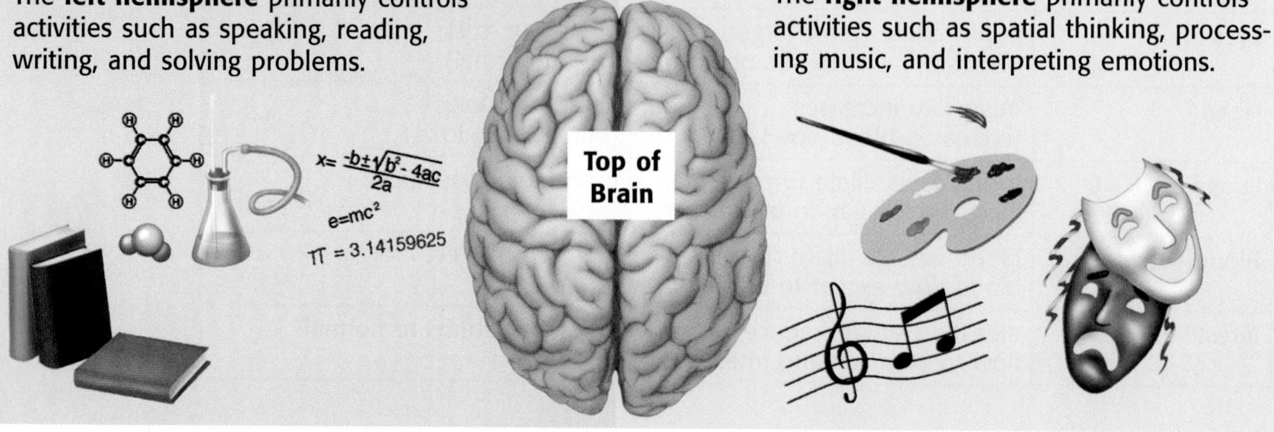

$x = \frac{-b \pm \sqrt{b^2 - 4ac}}{2a}$
$e = mc^2$
$\pi = 3.14159625$
Top of Brain

The Cerebellum

The second-largest part of your brain is the *cerebellum.* It lies beneath the back of the cerebrum. The cerebellum processes sensory information from your body, such as from skeletal muscles and joints. This allows the brain to keep track of your body's position. If you begin to lose your balance, the cerebellum sends impulses telling different skeletal muscles to contract. Those muscles shift a person's weight and keep a person, such as the girl in **Figure 5,** from losing her balance.

Figure 5 *Your cerebellum causes skeletal muscles to make adjustments so that you will stay upright.*

The Medulla

The *medulla* is the part of your brain that connects to your spinal cord. The medulla is about 3 cm long, and you can't live without it. The medulla controls involuntary processes, such as blood pressure, body temperature, heart rate, and involuntary breathing.

Your medulla constantly receives sensory impulses from receptors in your blood vessels. It uses this information to regulate your blood pressure. If your blood pressure gets too low, the medulla sends out impulses that tell blood vessels to tighten up. As a result, blood pressure rises. The medulla also sends impulses to the heart to make the heart beat faster or slower. **Figure 6** shows the location of the parts of the brain and some of the functions of each part.

Reading Check Explain why the medulla is important.

Figure 6 Areas of the Brain at Work

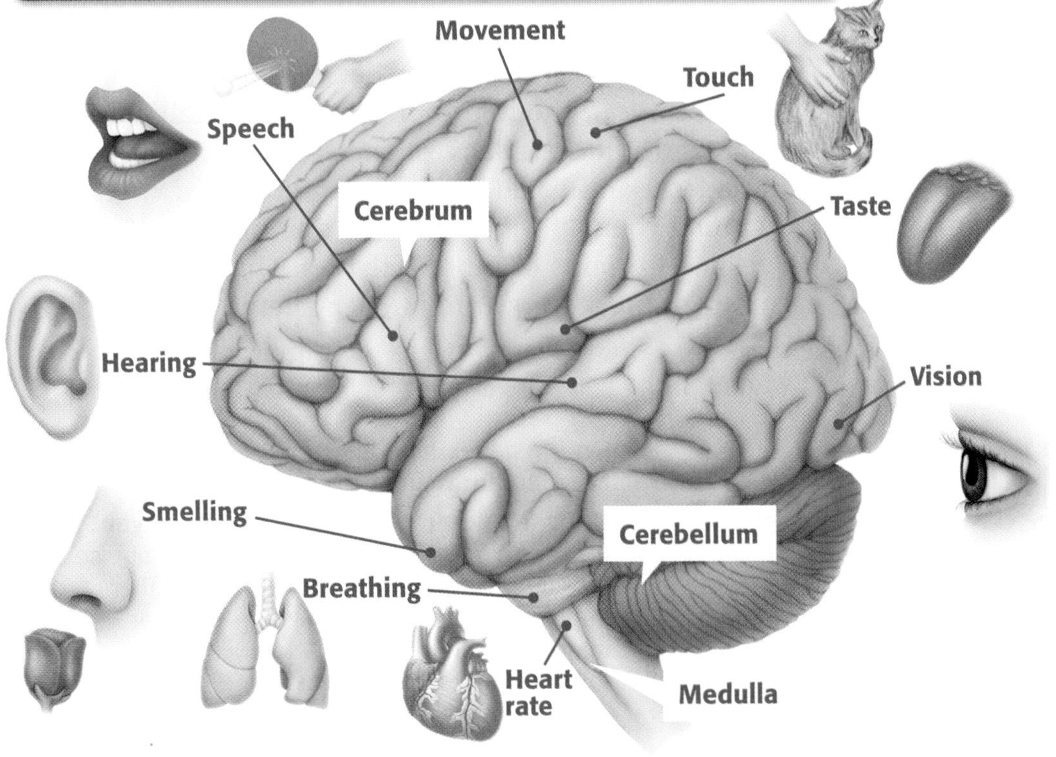

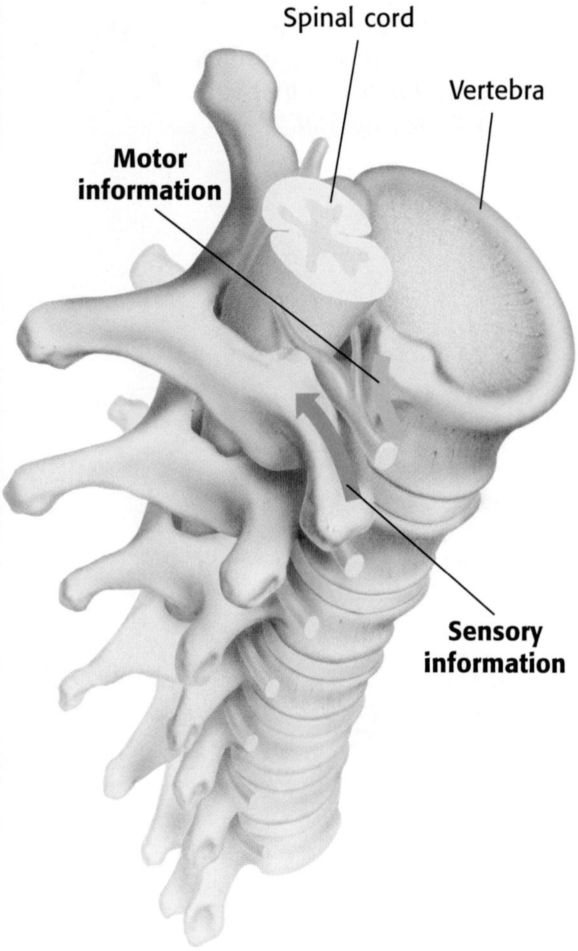

Figure 7 *The spinal cord carries information to and from the brain. Vertebrae protect the spinal cord.*

The Spinal Cord

Your spinal cord, which is part of your central nervous system, is about as big around as your thumb. The spinal cord is made of neurons and bundles of axons that pass impulses to and from the brain. As shown in **Figure 7,** the spinal cord is surrounded by protective bones called *vertebrae* (VUHR tuh BRAY).

The nerve fibers in your spinal cord allow your brain to communicate with your peripheral nervous system. Sensory neurons in your skin and muscles send impulses along their axons to your spinal cord. The spinal cord carries impulses to your brain. The brain interprets these impulses as pain, temperature, or other sensations. The brain then responds to the situation. Impulses moving from the brain down the spinal cord are relayed to motor neurons. Motor neurons carry the impulses along their axons to muscles and glands all over your body.

Reading Check **Describe the path of an impulse from the skin to the brain and the path of the response.**

Spinal Cord Injury

A spinal cord injury may block all information to and from the brain. Sensory information coming from below the injury may not get to the brain. For example, a spinal cord injury may block all sensory impulses from the feet and legs. People with such an injury would not be able to sense pain, touch, or temperature with their feet. And motor commands from the brain to the injured area may not reach the peripheral nerves. So, the person would not be able to move his or her legs.

Each year, thousands of people are paralyzed by spinal cord injuries. Many of these injuries happen in car accidents and could be avoided by wearing a seat belt. Among young people, spinal cord injuries are sometimes related to sports or other activities. These injuries might be prevented by wearing proper safety equipment.

Quick Lab

Building a Neuron

1. Your teacher will provide at least four different colors of **modeling clay.** Build a model of a neuron by using different-colored clay for the various parts of the neuron.
2. Use **tape** to attach your model neuron to a **piece of plain white paper.**
3. On the paper, label each part of the neuron. Draw an arrow from the label to the part.
4. Using a **colored pencil, marker,** or **crayon,** draw arrows showing the path of an impulse traveling in your neuron. Tell whether the impulse is a sensory impulse or a motor impulse. Then, describe what will happen when the impulse reaches its destination.

SECTION
Review

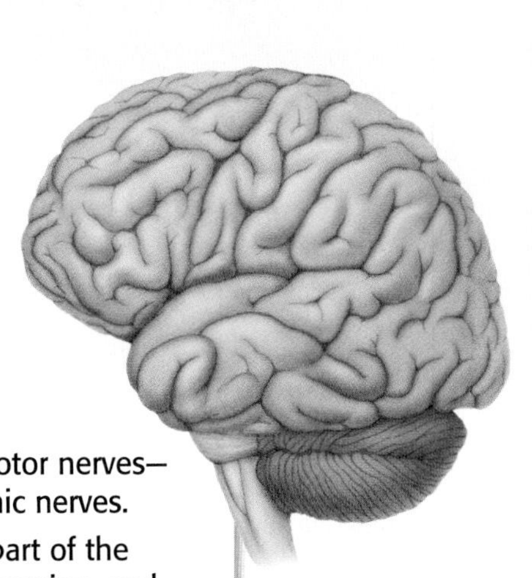

Summary

- The central nervous system (CNS) includes the brain and the spinal cord.
- The peripheral nervous system (PNS) is all the parts of the nervous system except the brain and spinal cord.
- The peripheral nervous system has nerves made up of axons of neurons.
- Sensory neurons have receptors that detect information about the body and its environment. Motor neurons carry messages from the brain and spinal cord to other parts of the body.
- The PNS has two types of motor nerves—somatic nerves and autonomic nerves.
- The cerebrum is the largest part of the brain and controls thinking, sensing, and voluntary movement.
- The cerebellum is the part of the brain that keeps track of the body's position and helps maintain balance.
- The medulla controls involuntary processes, such as heart rate, blood pressure, body temperature, and breathing.

Using Key Terms

1. In your own words, write a definition for each of the following terms: *neuron* and *nerve*.
2. Use the following terms in the same sentence: *brain* and *peripheral nervous system*.

Understanding Key Ideas

3. Someone touches your shoulder and you turn around. Which sequence do your impulses follow?
   - **a.** motor neuron, sensory neuron, CNS response
   - **b.** motor neuron, CNS response, sensory neuron
   - **c.** sensory neuron, motor neuron, CNS response
   - **d.** sensory neuron, CNS response, motor neuron
4. Describe one function of each part of the brain.
5. Compare the somatic nervous system with the autonomic nervous system.
6. Explain how a severe injury to the spinal cord can affect other parts of the body.

Critical Thinking

7. **Applying Concepts** Some medications slow a person's nervous system. These drugs are often labeled "May cause drowsiness." Explain why a person needs to know about this side effect.
8. **Predicting Consequences** Explain how your life would change if your autonomic nervous system suddenly stopped working.

Interpreting Graphics

Use the figure below to answer the questions that follow.

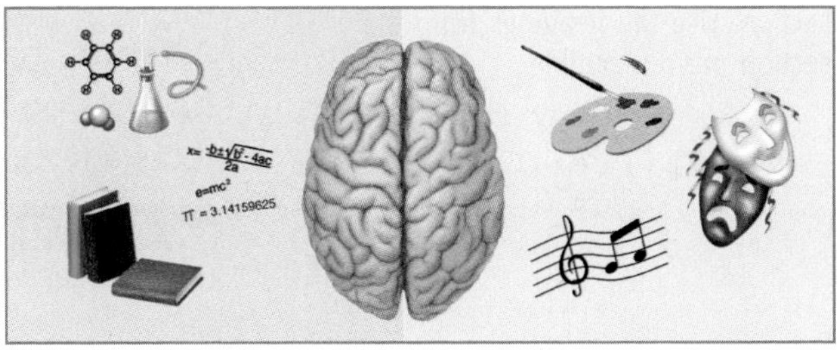

9. Which hemisphere of the brain recognizes and processes words, numbers, and letters? faces, places, and objects?
10. For a person whose left hemisphere is primarily in control, would it be easier to learn to play a new computer game by reading the rules and following instructions or by watching a friend play and imitating his actions?

SciLINKS® NSTA
Developed and maintained by the National Science Teachers Association

For a variety of links related to this chapter, go to www.scilinks.org

Topic: Nervous System
SciLinks code: HSM1023

SECTION 2

Responding to the Environment

What You Will Learn

- List four sensations that are detected by receptors in the skin.
- Describe how a feedback mechanism works.
- Describe how light relates to sight.
- Describe how the senses of hearing, taste, and smell work.

Vocabulary

integumentary system
reflex
feedback mechanism
retina
cochlea

READING STRATEGY

Reading Organizer As you read this section, create an outline of the section. Use the headings from the section in your outline.

You feel a tap on your shoulder. Who tapped you? You turn to look, hoping to see a friend. Your senses are on the job!

The tap produces impulses in sensory receptors on your shoulder. These impulses travel to your brain. Once the impulses reach your brain, they create an awareness called a *sensation*. In this case, the sensation is of your shoulder being touched. But you still do not know who tapped you. So, you turn around. The sensory receptors in your eyes send impulses to your brain. Now, your brain recognizes your best friend.

Sense of Touch

Touch is what you feel when sensory receptors in the skin are stimulated. It is the sensation you feel when you shake hands or feel a breeze. As shown in **Figure 1,** skin has different kinds of receptors. Each kind of receptor responds mainly to one kind of stimulus. For example, *thermoreceptors* respond to temperature change. Each kind of receptor produces a specific sensation of touch, such as pressure, temperature, pain, or vibration. Skin is part of the integumentary (in TEG yoo MEN tuhr ee) system. The **integumentary system** protects the body from damage. It includes hair, skin, and nails.

Reading Check List four sensations that your skin can detect. (*See the Appendix for answers to Reading Checks.*)

integumentary system the organ system that forms a protective covering on the outside of the body

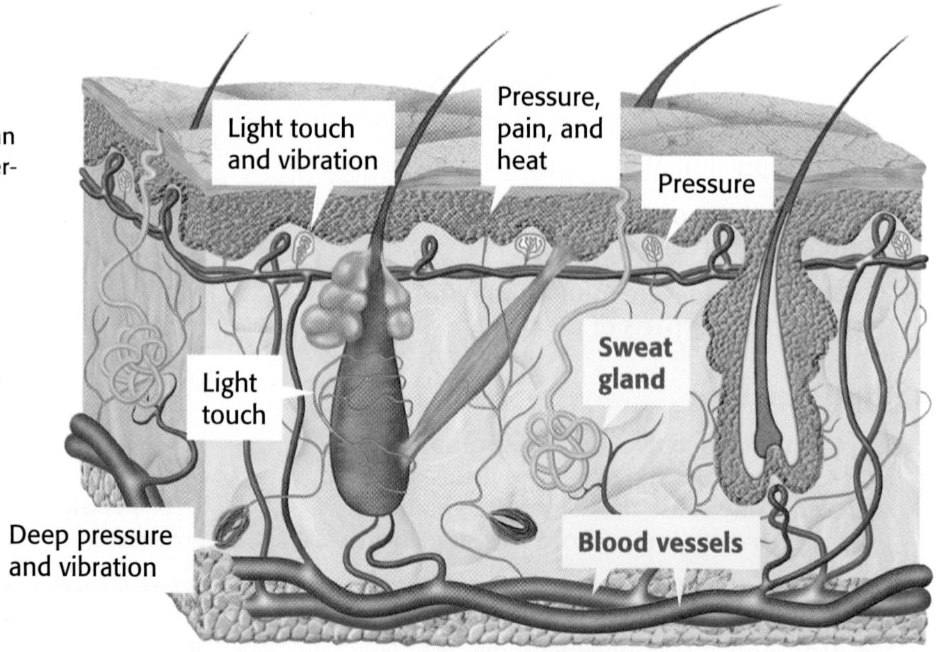

Figure 1 *Each type of receptor in your skin has its own structure and function.*

Responding to Sensory Messages

When you step on something sharp, as the man in **Figure 2** did, pain receptors in your foot or toe send impulses to your spinal cord. Almost immediately, a message to move your foot travels back to the muscles in your leg and foot. Without thinking, you quickly lift your foot. This immediate, involuntary action is called a **reflex.** Your brain isn't telling your leg to move. In fact, by the time the message reaches your brain, your leg and foot have already moved. If you had to wait for your brain to act, you toes might be seriously hurt!

reflex an involuntary and almost immediate movement in response to a stimulus

feedback mechanism a cycle of events in which information from one step controls or affects a previous step

Reading Check **Why are reflexes important?**

Feedback Mechanisms

Most of the time, the brain processes information from skin receptors. For example, on a hot day, heat receptors in your skin detect an increase in your temperature. The receptors send impulses to the brain. Your brain responds by sending messages to your sweat glands to make sweat. As sweat evaporates, it cools your body. Your brain also tells the blood vessels in your skin to dilate (open wider). Blood flow increases. Thermal energy from the blood in your skin moves to your surroundings. This also cools your body. As your body cools, it sends messages to your brain. The brain responds by sending messages to sweat glands and blood vessels to reduce their activity.

This cooling process is one of your body's feedback mechanisms. A **feedback mechanism** is a cycle of events in which information from one step controls or affects a previous step. The temperature-regulating feedback mechanism helps keep your body temperature within safe limits. This cooling mechanism works like a thermostat on an air conditioner. Once a room reaches the right temperature, the thermostat sends a message to the air conditioner to stop blowing cold air.

Figure 2 *A reflex, such as lifting your foot when you step on something sharp, is one way your nervous system responds to your environment.*

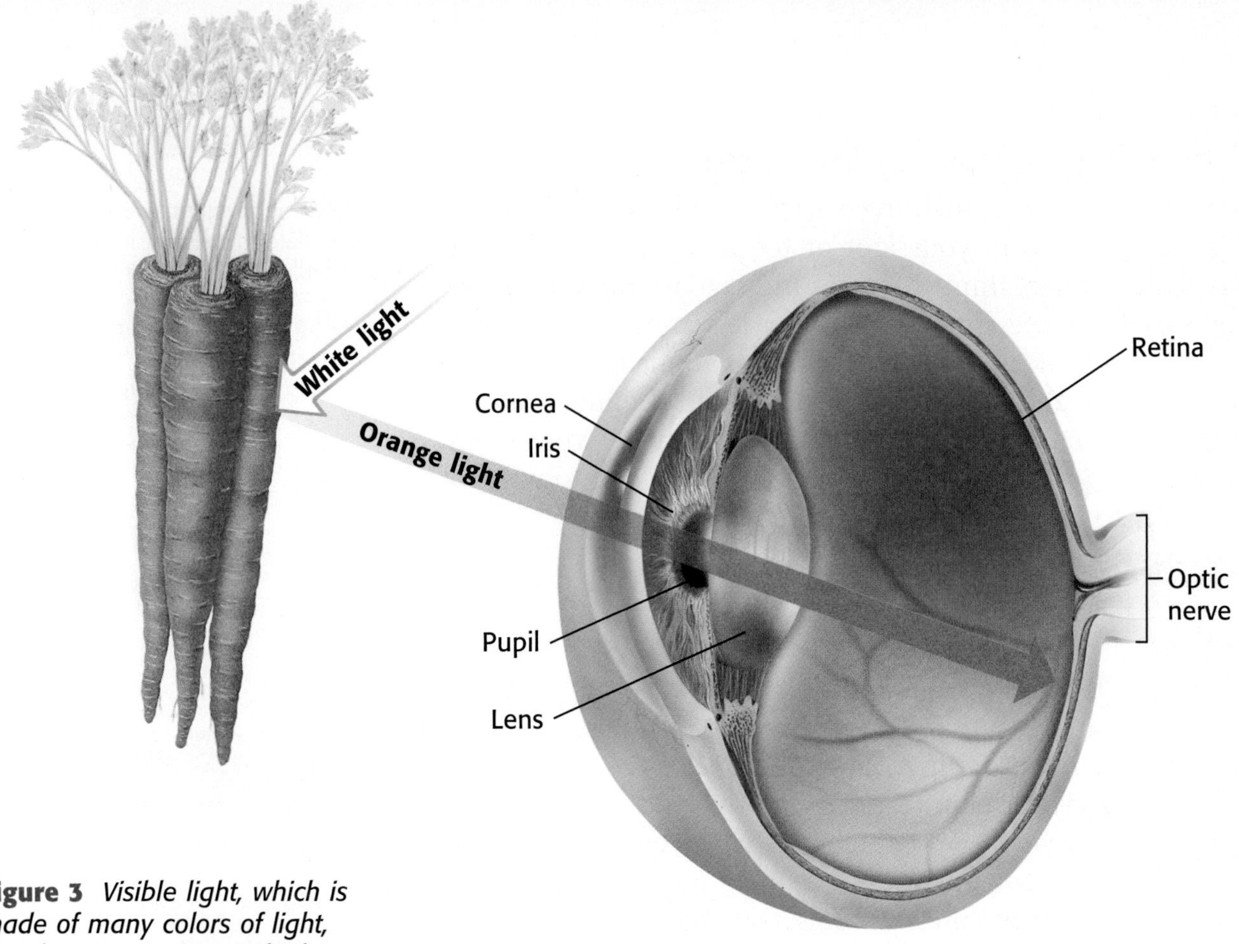

Figure 3 *Visible light, which is made of many colors of light, hits the carrots. Carrots look orange because they reflect orange light to your eyes.*

retina the light-sensitive inner layer of the eye; it receives images formed by the lens and transmits them through the optic nerve to the brain

INTERNET ACTIVITY

For another activity related to this chapter, go to **go.hrw.com** and type in the keyword **HL5BD4W.**

Sense of Sight

Sight is the sense that allows you to see the size, shape, motion, and color of objects around you. You see an object when it sends or reflects visible light toward your eyes. Your eyes detect this light, which enables your brain to form visual images.

Your eyes are complex sensory organs, as you can see in **Figure 3.** The front of the eye is covered by a clear membrane called the *cornea.* The cornea protects the eye but allows light to enter. Light from an object enters the front of your eye through an opening called the *pupil.* The light then travels through the lens to the back of the eye. There, the light strikes the **retina,** a layer of light-sensitive cells.

The retina is packed with photoreceptors. A *photoreceptor* is a special neuron that changes light into electrical impulses. The retina has two kinds of photoreceptors: rods and cones. Rods are very sensitive to dim light. They are important for night vision. Impulses from rods are interpreted as black-and-white images. Cones are very sensitive to bright light. Impulses from cones allow you to see fine details and colors.

Impulses from the rods and cones travel along axons. The impulses leave the back of each eye through an optic nerve. The optic nerve carries the impulses to your brain, where the impulses are interpreted as the images that you see.

Reading Check **Describe how light and sight are related.**

Reacting to Light

Your pupil looks like a black dot in the center of your eye. In fact, it is an opening that lets light enter the eye. The pupil is surrounded by the *iris,* a ring of muscle. The iris controls the amount of light that enters the eye and gives the eye its color. In bright light, the iris contracts, which makes the pupil smaller. A smaller pupil reduces the amount of light entering the eye and passing onto the retina. In dim light, the iris opens the pupil and lets in more light.

Reading Check **How does your iris react to bright light?**

Focusing the Light

Light travels in straight lines until it passes through the cornea and the lens. The *lens* is an oval-shaped piece of clear, curved material behind the iris. Muscles in the eye change the shape of the lens in order to focus light onto the retina. When you look at objects close to the eye, the lens becomes more curved. When you look at objects far away, the lens gets flatter.

Figure 4 shows some common vision problems. In some eyes, the lens focuses the light in front of the retina, which results in nearsightedness. If the lens focuses the light just behind the retina, the result is farsightedness. Glasses, contact lenses, or surgery can usually correct these vision problems.

Quick Lab

Where's the Dot?

1. Hold your **book** at arm's length, and close your right eye. Focus your left eye on the black dot below.

2. Slowly move the book toward your face until the white dot disappears. You may need to try a few times to get this result. The white dot doesn't always disappear for every person.
3. Describe your observations.
4. Use the library or the Internet to research the optic nerve and to find out why the white dot disappears.

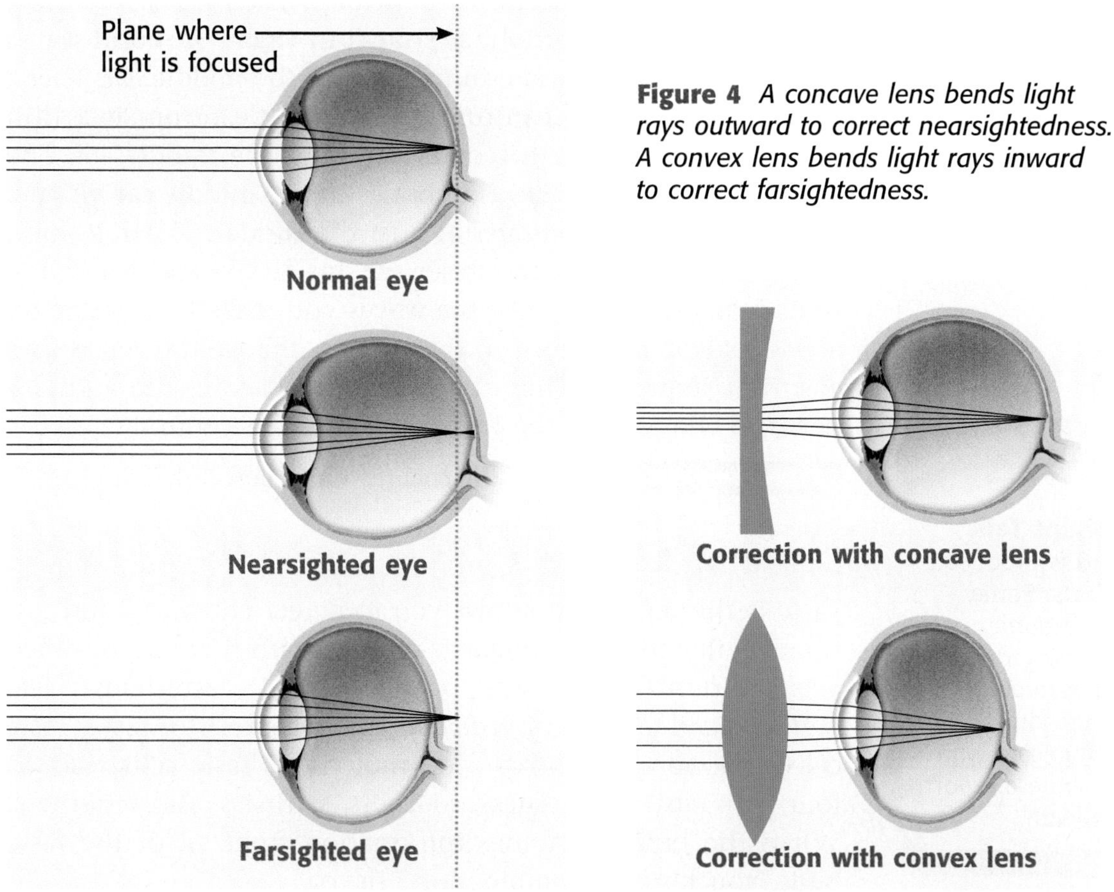

Figure 4 *A concave lens bends light rays outward to correct nearsightedness. A convex lens bends light rays inward to correct farsightedness.*

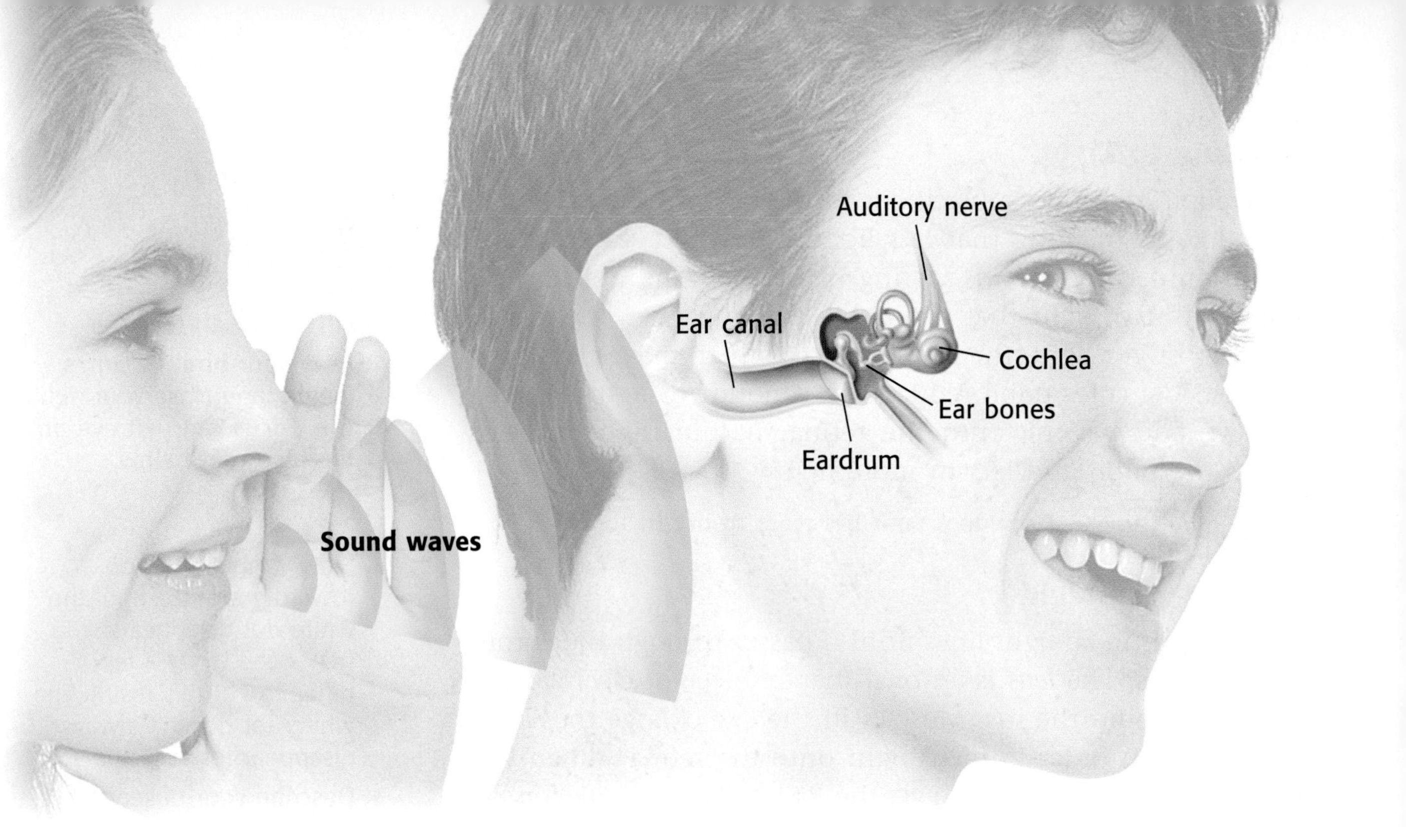

Figure 5 *A sound wave travels into the outer ear. It is converted into bone vibrations in the middle ear, then into liquid vibrations in the inner ear, and finally, into nerve impulses that travel to the brain.*

Sense of Hearing

Sound is produced when something, such as a drum, vibrates. Vibrations push on nearby air particles, which push on other air particles. The vibrations create waves of sound energy. Hearing is the sense that allows you to experience sound energy.

Ears are organs specialized for hearing. Each ear has an outer, middle, and inner portion, as shown in **Figure 5.** Sound waves reaching the outer ear are funneled into the middle ear. There, the waves make the eardrum vibrate. The eardrum is a thin membrane separating the outer ear from the middle ear. The vibrating eardrum makes tiny bones in the middle ear vibrate. One of these bones vibrates against the **cochlea** (KAHK lee uh), a fluid-filled organ of the inner ear. Inside the cochlea, vibrations make waves just like the waves you make by tapping on a glass of water. Neurons in the cochlea change the waves into electrical impulses. These impulses travel along the auditory nerve to the area of the brain that interprets sound.

cochlea a coiled tube that is found in the inner ear and that is essential to hearing

Reading Check **Why is the cochlea important to hearing?**

CONNECTION TO Physics

WRITING SKILL **Elephant Talk** Sound is produced by vibrating objects. Some sounds, called *infrasonic sounds*, are too low for human ears to detect. Research how elephants use infrasonic sounds to communicate with each other, and write a report about what you learn.

Sense of Taste

Taste is the sense that allows you to detect chemicals and distinguish flavors. Your tongue is covered with tiny bumps called *papillae* (puh PIL ee). Most papillae contain taste buds. Taste buds contain clusters of *taste cells,* the receptors for taste. Taste cells respond to dissolved food molecules. Taste cells react to four basic tastes: sweetness, sourness, saltiness, and bitterness. When the brain combines information from all of the taste buds, you taste a “combination” flavor.

Sense of Smell

As you can see in **Figure 6,** receptors for smell are located on *olfactory cells* in the upper part of your nasal cavity. An olfactory cell is a nerve cell that responds to chemical molecules in the air. You smell something when the receptors react to molecules that have been inhaled. The molecules dissolve in the moist lining of the nasal cavity and trigger an impulse. Olfactory cells send those impulses to the brain, which interprets the impulses as odors.

Taste buds and olfactory cells both detect dissolved molecules. Your brain combines information from both senses to give you sensations of flavor.

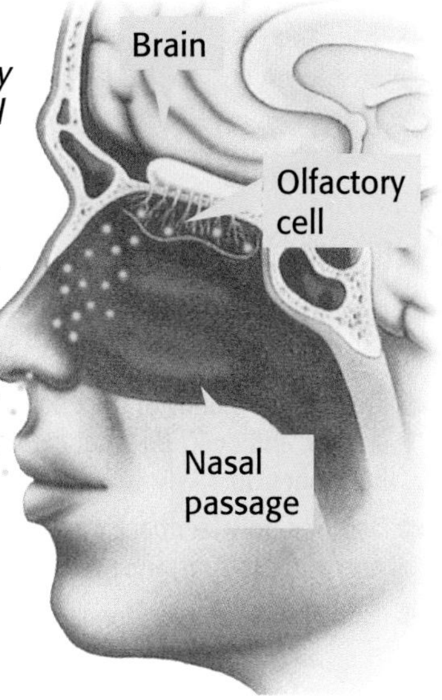

Figure 6 *Olfactory cells line the nasal cavity. These cells are sensory receptors that react to chemicals in the air.*

SECTION Review

Summary

- Touch allows you to respond to temperature, pressure, pain, and vibration on the skin.
- Reflexes and feedback mechanisms help you respond to your environment.
- Sight allows you to respond to light energy.
- Hearing allows you to respond to sound energy.
- Taste allows you to distinguish flavors.
- Smell allows you to perceive different odors.

Using Key Terms

1. In your own words, write a definition for each of the following terms: *reflex* and *feedback mechanism.*
2. Use each of the following terms in a separate sentence: *retina* and *cochlea.*

Understanding Key Ideas

3. Three sensations that receptors in the skin detect are
   - **a.** light, smell, and sound.
   - **b.** touch, pain, and odors.
   - **c.** temperature, pressure, and pain.
   - **d.** pressure, sound, and touch.
4. Explain how light and sight are related.
5. Describe how your senses of hearing, taste, and smell work.
6. Explain why you might have trouble seeing bright colors at a candlelit dinner.
7. How is your sense of taste similar to your sense of smell, and how do these senses work together?
8. Describe how the feedback mechanism that regulates body temperature works.

Math Skills

9. Suppose a nerve impulse must travel 0.90 m from your toe to your central nervous system. If the impulse travels at 150 m/s, calculate how long it will take the impulse to arrive. If the impulse travels at 0.2 m/s, how long will it take the impulse to arrive?

Critical Thinking

10. **Making Inferences** Why is it important for the human body to have reflexes?
11. **Applying Concepts** Rods help you detect objects and shapes in dim light. Explain why it is important for human eyes to have both rods and cones.

SECTION 3

The Endocrine System

What You Will Learn

- Explain why the endocrine system is important to the body.
- Identify five glands of the endocrine system, and describe what their hormones do.
- Describe how feedback mechanisms stop and start hormone release.
- Name two hormone imbalances.

Vocabulary

endocrine system
gland
hormone

READING STRATEGY

Discussion Read this section silently. Write down questions that you have about this section. Discuss your questions in a small group.

Have you ever heard of an epinephrine (EP uh NEPH rin) rush? You might have had one without realizing it. Exciting situations, such as riding a roller coaster or watching a scary movie, can cause your body to release epinephrine.

Epinephrine is one of the body's chemical messengers made by the endocrine system. Your endocrine system regulates body processes, such as fluid balance, growth, and development.

Hormones as Chemical Messengers

The **endocrine system** controls body functions by using chemicals that are made by the endocrine glands. A **gland** is a group of cells that make special chemicals for your body. Chemical messengers made by the endocrine glands are called hormones. A **hormone** is a chemical messenger made in one cell or tissue that causes a change in another cell or tissue in another part of the body. Hormones flow through the bloodstream to all parts of the body. Thus, an endocrine gland near your brain can control an organ that is somewhere else in your body.

Endocrine glands may affect many organs at one time. For example, in the situation shown in **Figure 1,** the adrenal glands release the hormone *epinephrine,* which is sometimes called *adrenaline.* Epinephrine increases your heartbeat and breathing rate. This response is called the "fight-or-flight" response. When you are frightened, angry, or excited, the "fight-or-flight" response prepares you to fight the danger or to run from it.

endocrine system a collection of glands and groups of cells that secrete hormones that regulate growth, development, and homeostasis

gland a group of cells that make special chemicals for the body

Figure 1 *When you have to move quickly to avoid danger, your adrenal glands make more blood glucose available for energy.*

More Endocrine Glands

Your body has several other endocrine glands. Some of these glands have many functions. For example, your pituitary gland stimulates skeletal growth and helps the thyroid gland work properly. It also regulates the amount of water in the blood. And the pituitary gland stimulates the birth process in women.

Your thyroid gland is very important during infancy and childhood. Thyroid hormones control the secretion of growth hormones for normal body growth. Thyroid hormones also control the development of the central nervous system. And they control your metabolism. *Metabolism* is the sum of all the chemical processes that take place in an organism.

Your thymus gland is important to your immune system. Cells called *killer T cells* grow and mature in the thymus gland. These T cells help destroy or neutralize cells or substances that invade your body. The names and some of the functions of endocrine glands are shown in **Figure 2.**

Reading Check **Name two endocrine glands, and explain why they are important to your body.** *(See the Appendix for answers to Reading Checks.)*

hormone a substance that is made in one cell or tissue and that causes a change in another cell or tissue in a different part of the body

CONNECTION TO Language Arts

WRITING SKILL **Fight or Flight?** Write a paragraph describing a time when you had a fight-or-flight experience. Include in your description the following terms: *hormones, fight-or-flight,* and *epinephrine.* If you cannot think of a personal experience, write a short story describing someone else's fight-or-flight experience.

Figure 2 **Endocrine Glands and Their Functions**

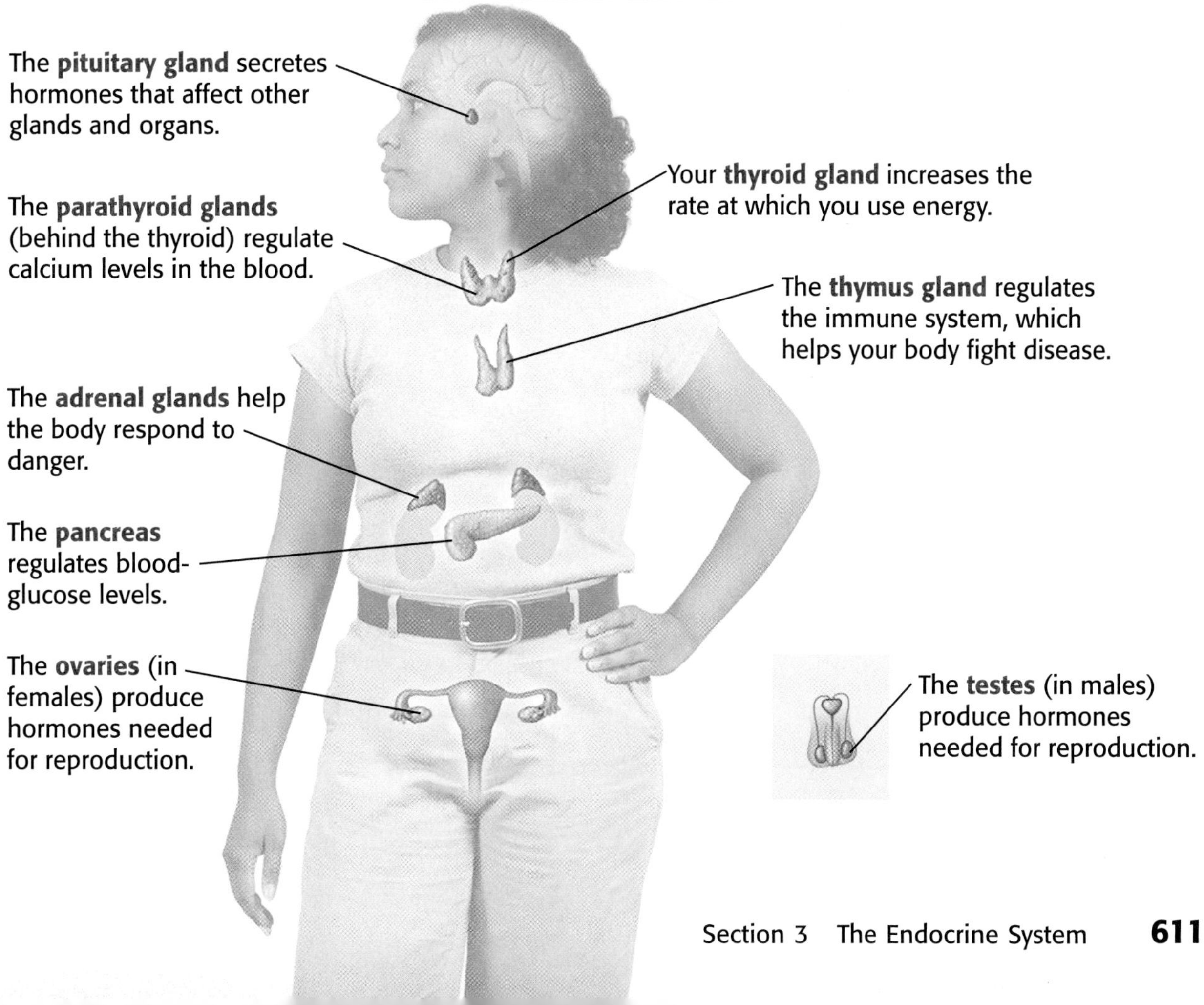

The **pituitary gland** secretes hormones that affect other glands and organs.
Your **thyroid gland** increases the rate at which you use energy.
The **parathyroid glands** (behind the thyroid) regulate calcium levels in the blood.
The **thymus gland** regulates the immune system, which helps your body fight disease.
The **adrenal glands** help the body respond to danger.
The **pancreas** regulates blood-glucose levels.
The **ovaries** (in females) produce hormones needed for reproduction.
The **testes** (in males) produce hormones needed for reproduction.

Controlling the Endocrine Glands

Do you remember the feedback mechanisms at work in the nervous system? Endocrine glands control similar feedback mechanisms. For example, the pancreas has specialized cells that make two different hormones, *insulin* and *glucagon*. As shown in **Figure 3,** these two hormones control the level of glucose in the blood. Insulin lowers blood-glucose levels by telling the liver to convert glucose into glycogen and to store glycogen for future use. Glucagon has the opposite effect. It tells the liver to convert glycogen into glucose and to release the glucose into the blood.

Reading Check **What does insulin do?**

Figure 3 **Blood-Glucose Feedback Control**

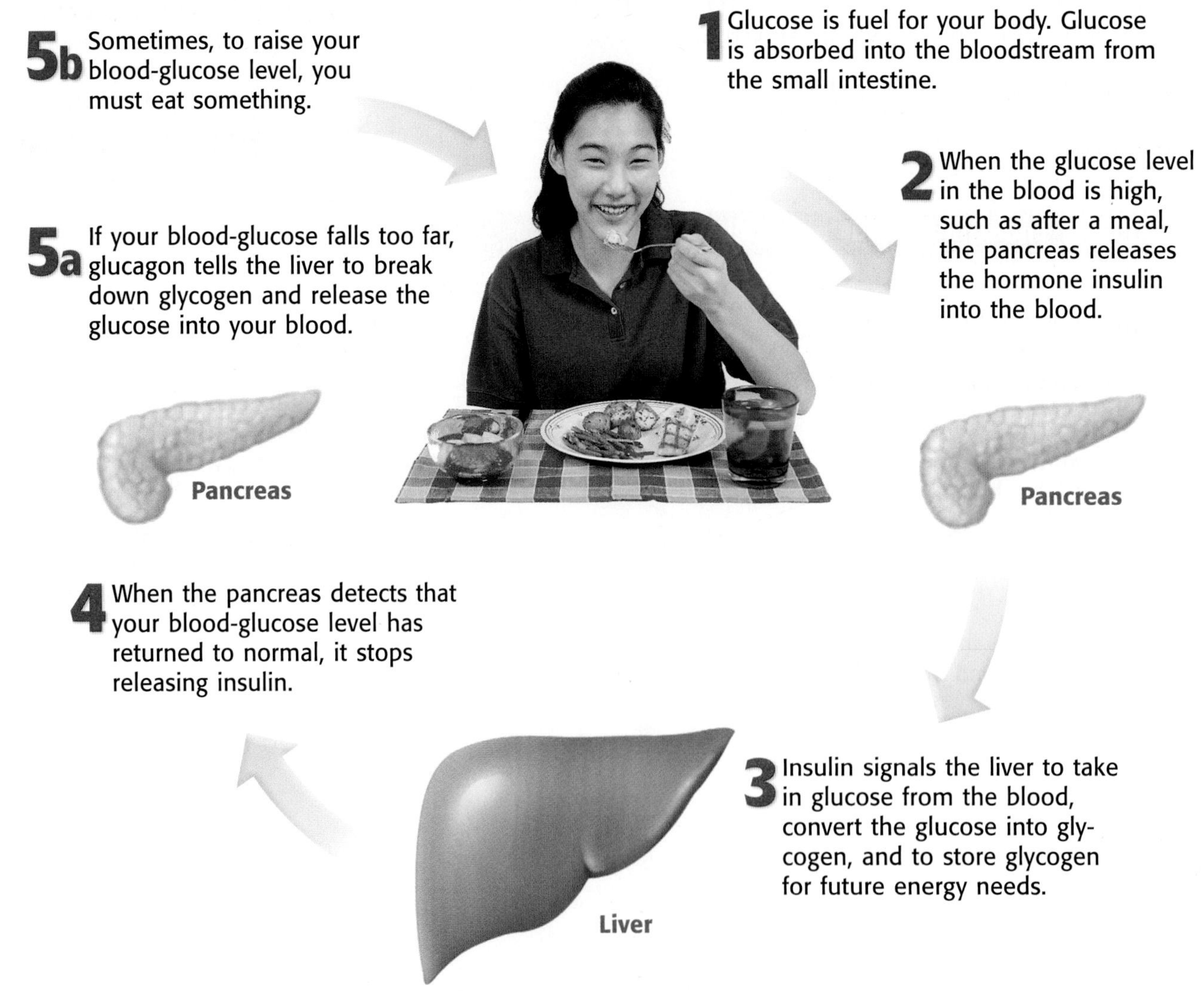

1 Glucose is fuel for your body. Glucose is absorbed into the bloodstream from the small intestine.
2 When the glucose level in the blood is high, such as after a meal, the pancreas releases the hormone insulin into the blood.
Pancreas
3 Insulin signals the liver to take in glucose from the blood, convert the glucose into glycogen, and to store glycogen for future energy needs.
Liver
4 When the pancreas detects that your blood-glucose level has returned to normal, it stops releasing insulin.
Pancreas
5a If your blood-glucose falls too far, glucagon tells the liver to break down glycogen and release the glucose into your blood.
5b Sometimes, to raise your blood-glucose level, you must eat something.

Hormone Imbalances

Occasionally, an endocrine gland makes too much or not enough of a hormone. For example, when a person's blood-glucose level rises, the pancreas secretes insulin. Insulin sends a message to the liver to convert glucose into glycogen. The liver stores glycogen for future use. But a person whose body does not use insulin properly or whose pancreas does not make enough insulin has a condition called *diabetes mellitus* (DIE uh BEET EEZ muh LIET uhs). A person who has diabetes may need daily injections of insulin to keep his or her blood-glucose levels within safe limits. Some patients, such as the woman in **Figure 4,** receive their insulin automatically from a small machine worn next to the body.

Another hormone imbalance is when a child's pituitary gland doesn't make enough growth hormone. As a result, the child's growth is stunted. Fortunately, if the problem is detected early, a doctor can prescribe growth hormone and monitor the child's growth. If the pituitary makes too much growth hormone, a child may grow taller than expected.

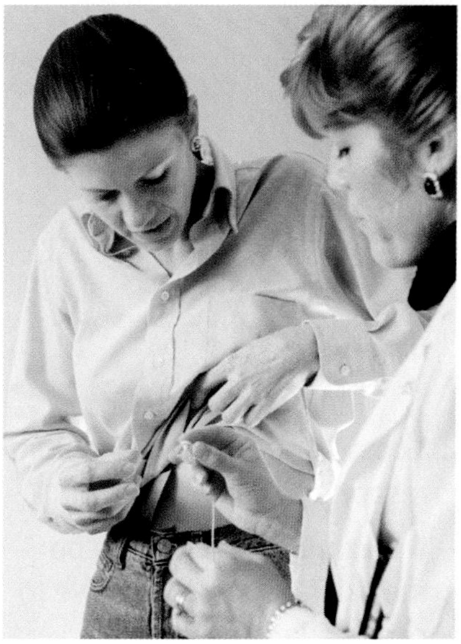

Figure 4 *This woman has diabetes and receives insulin from a device that monitors her blood-glucose level.*

SECTION Review

Summary

- Glands in the endocrine system use chemical messengers called *hormones*.
- Hormones regulate body functions by causing changes in cells or tissues.
- Feedback mechanisms tell endocrine glands when to turn hormones on and off.
- A hormone imbalance is when a gland releases too much or too little of a hormone.

Using Key Terms

1. Use the following terms in the same sentence: *endocrine system, glands,* and *hormone.*

Understanding Key Ideas

2. Identify five endocrine glands, and explain why their hormones are important to your body.
3. Hormone imbalances may cause
   - **a.** feedback and insulin.
   - **b.** diabetes and stunted growth.
   - **c.** thyroid and pituitary.
   - **d.** glucose and glycogen.
4. How do feedback mechanisms control hormone production?

Math Skills

5. One's bedtime blood-glucose level is normally 140 mg/dL. Ty's blood-glucose level is 189 mg/dL at bedtime. What percentage above 140 mg/dL is Ty's level?

Critical Thinking

6. **Making Inferences** Glucose is a source of energy. Epinephrine quickly increases the blood-glucose level. Why is epinephrine important in times of stress?
7. **Applying Concepts** The hormone glucagon is released when glucose levels fall below normal. Explain how the hormones glucagon and insulin work together to control blood-glucose levels.

SCILINKS® NSTA
Developed and maintained by the National Science Teachers Association

For a variety of links related to this chapter, go to www.scilinks.org

Topic: Hormones
SciLinks code: HSM0758

Skills Practice Lab

You've Gotta Lotta Nerve

OBJECTIVES

Locate areas on the skin that respond to certain stimuli.

Determine which areas on the skin are more sensitive to certain kinds of stimuli.

MATERIALS

- dissecting pin with a small piece of cork or a small rubber stopper covering the sharp end
- eyedropper, plastic
- paper, graphing
- pens or markers, washable, fine point
- ruler, metric
- tap water, hot
- water, very cold

SAFETY

Your skin has thousands of nerve receptors that detect sensations, such as temperature, pain, and pressure. Your brain is designed to filter out or ignore most of the input it receives from these skin receptors. If the brain did not filter input, simply wearing clothes would trigger so many responses that you couldn't function.

Some areas of the skin, such as the back of your hand, are more sensitive than others. In this activity, you will map the skin receptors for heat, cold, and pressure on the back of your hand.

Procedure

1. Form a group of three. One of you will volunteer the back of your hand for testing, one will do the testing, and the third will record the results.
2. Use a fine-point, washable marker or pen and a metric ruler to mark a 3 cm × 3 cm square on the back of one person's hand. Draw a grid within the area. Space the lines approximately 0.5 cm apart. You will have 36 squares in the grid when you are finished, as shown in the photograph below.
3. Mark off three 3 cm × 3 cm areas on a piece of graph paper. Make a grid in each area exactly as you did on the back of your partner's hand. Label one grid "Cold," another grid "Hot," and the third grid "Pressure."

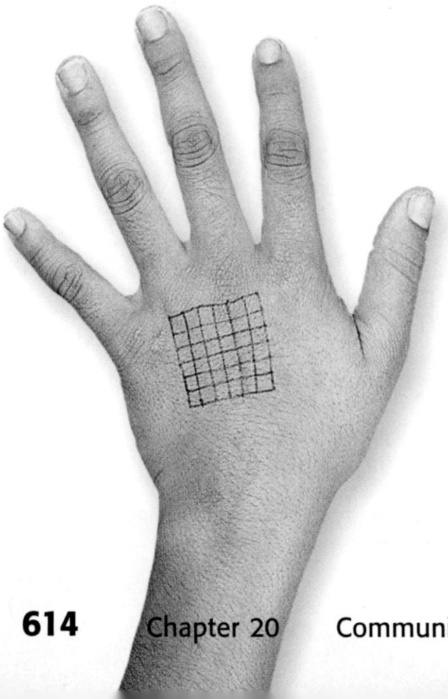

4. Use the eyedropper to apply one small droplet of cold water on each square in the grid on your partner's hand. Your partner should turn away while being tested. On your graph paper, mark an X on the "Cold" grid to show where your partner felt the cold droplet. Carefully blot the water off your partner's hand after several drops.

5. Repeat the test using hot-water droplets. The hot water should not be hot enough to hurt your partner. Mark an X on the "Hot" grid to indicate where your partner felt the hot droplet.

6. Repeat the test by using the head (not the point!) of the pin. Touch the skin to detect pressure receptors. Use a very light touch. On the graph paper, mark an X on the "Pressure" grid to indicate where your partner felt the pressure.

Analyze the Results

1. **Organizing Data** Count the number of Xs in each grid. How many heat receptor responses are there per 3 cm^2? How many cold receptor responses are there? How many pressure receptor responses are there?

2. **Explaining Events** Do you have areas on the back of your hand where the receptors overlap? Explain your answer.

3. **Recognizing Patterns** How do you think the results of this experiment would be similar or different if you mapped an area of your forearm? of the back of your neck? of the palm of your hand?

Draw Conclusions

4. **Interpreting Information** Prepare a written report that includes a description of your investigation and a discussion of your answers to items 1–3. What conclusions can you draw from your results?

Applying Your Data

Use the library or the Internet to research what happens if a receptor is continuously stimulated. Does the kind of receptor make a difference? Does the intensity or strength of the stimulus make a difference? Explain your answers.

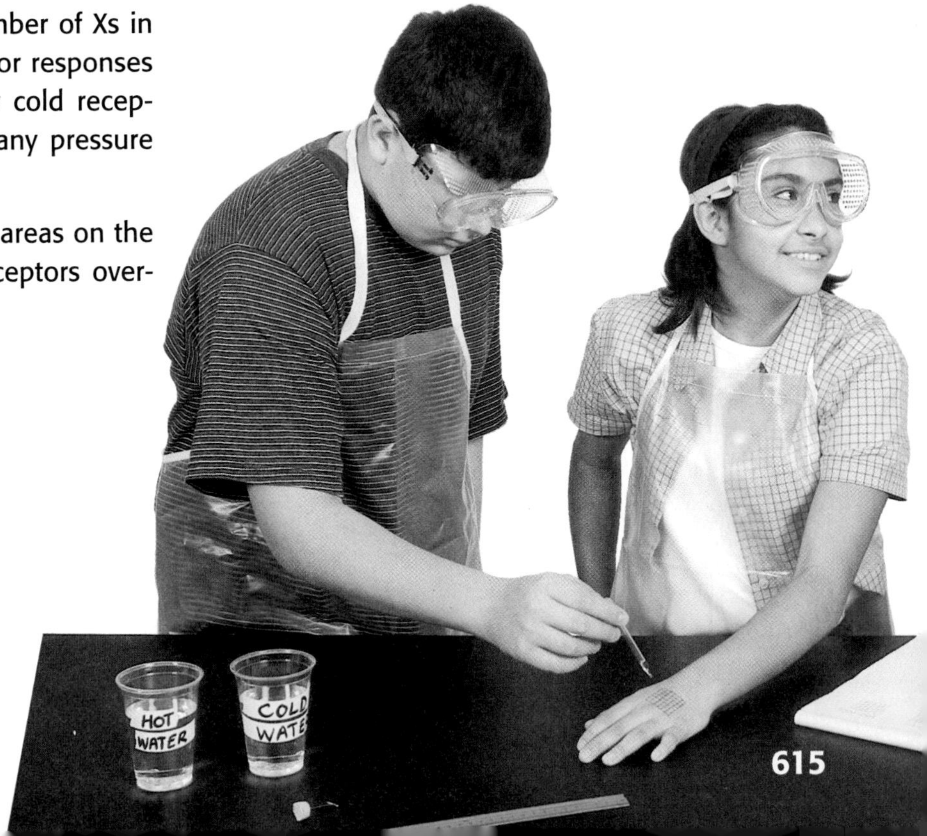

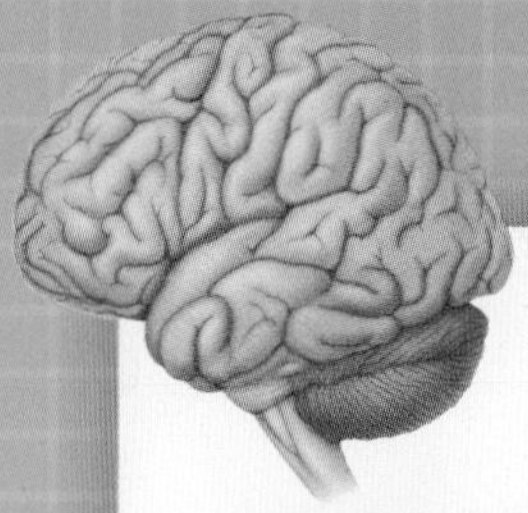

Chapter Review

USING KEY TERMS

Complete each of the following sentences by choosing the correct term from the word bank.

insulin	axon
hormone	nerve
retina	central nervous system
neuron	
reflex	

1. The two parts of your _____ are your brain and spinal cord.

2. Sensory receptors in the _____ detect light.

3. Epinephrine is a(n) _____ that triggers the fight-or-flight response.

4. A(n) _____ is an involuntary and almost immediate movement in response to a stimulus.

5. One hormone that helps to regulate blood-glucose levels is _____ .

6. A(n) _____ is a specialized cell that receives and conducts electrical impulses.

UNDERSTANDING KEY IDEAS

Multiple Choice

7. Which of the following has receptors for smelling?
   - **a.** cochlea cells
   - **b.** thermoreceptors
   - **c.** olfactory cells
   - **d.** optic nerve

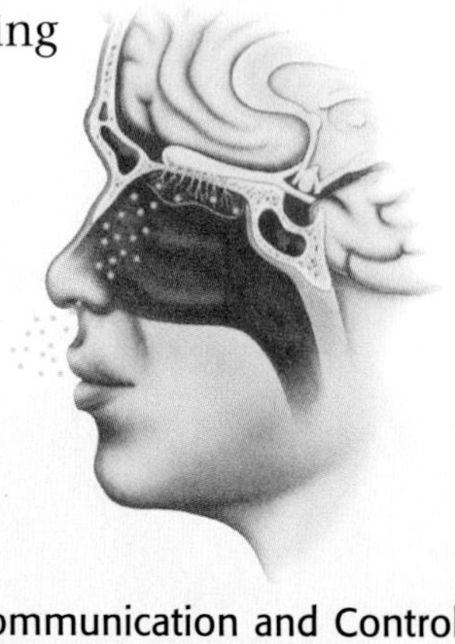

8. Which of the following allow you to see the world in color?
   - **a.** cones
   - **b.** rods
   - **c.** lenses
   - **d.** retinas

9. Which of the following glands makes insulin?
   - **a.** adrenal gland
   - **b.** pituitary gland
   - **c.** thyroid gland
   - **d.** pancreas

10. The peripheral nervous system does NOT include
    - **a.** the spinal cord.
    - **b.** axons.
    - **c.** sensory receptors.
    - **d.** motor neurons.

11. Which part of the brain regulates blood pressure?
    - **a.** right cerebral hemisphere
    - **b.** left cerebral hemisphere
    - **c.** cerebellum
    - **d.** medulla

12. The process in which the endocrine system, the digestive system, and the circulatory system control the level of blood glucose is an example of
    - **a.** a reflex.
    - **b.** an endocrine gland.
    - **c.** the fight-or-flight response.
    - **d.** a feedback mechanism.

Short Answer

13 What is the difference between the somatic nervous system and the autonomic nervous system? Why are both systems important to the body?

14 Why is the endocrine system important to your body?

15 What is the relationship between the CNS and the PNS?

16 What is the function of the bones in the middle ear?

17 Describe two interactions between the endocrine system and the body that happen when a person is frightened.

CRITICAL THINKING

18 **Concept Mapping** Use the following terms to create a concept map: *nervous system, spinal cord, medulla, peripheral nervous system, brain, cerebrum, central nervous system,* and *cerebellum.*

19 **Making Comparisons** Compare a feedback mechanism with a reflex.

20 **Analyzing Ideas** Why is it important to have a lens that can change shape inside the eye?

21 **Applying Concepts** Why it is important that reflexes happen without thinking about them?

22 **Predicting Consequences** What would happen if your autonomic nervous system stopped working?

23 **Making Comparisons** How are the nervous system and the endocrine system similar? How are they different?

INTERPRETING GRAPHICS

Use the diagram below to answer the questions that follow.

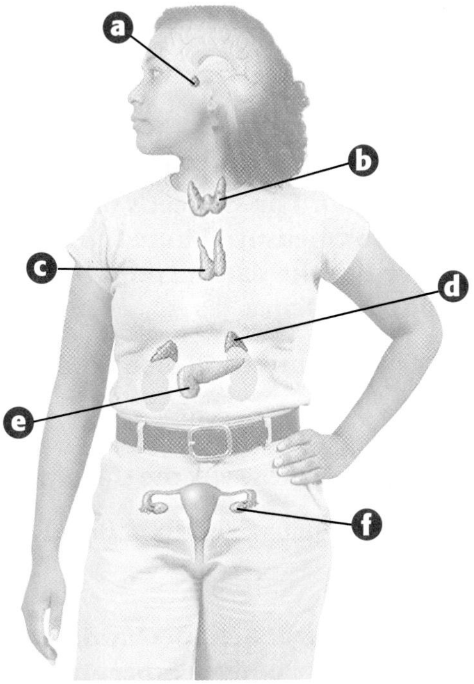

24 Which letter identifies the gland that regulates blood-glucose level?

25 Which letter identifies the gland that releases a hormone that stimulates the birth process?

26 Which letter identifies the gland that helps the body fight disease?

Multiple Choice

Use the table below to answer question 1.

Blood Glucose	
Time tested	Blood glucose level (mg/1000 mL)
1:00 P.M.	150
2:00 P.M.	110
3:00 P.M.	100
4:00 P.M.	89

1. The table above shows a person's blood glucose tests. The subject ate a regular meal at 12:00. The subject's blood glucose was measured hourly after that. Predict the data's trend based on the above evidence.

A. The blood glucose will drop slowly.

B. The blood glucose will rise slowly.

C. The blood glucose will rise sharply.

D. The blood glucose will drop sharply.

2. Identify the feedback mechanism that maintains your body temperature when your surroundings are very hot.

A. The brain sends a message to the skin. The muscles in the skin contract, or shiver, cooling the body.

B. The muscles in the skin contract, which sends a message to the brain that you feel hot. The brain sends a message to the skin's heat receptors.

C. Heat receptors in skin send a message to the brain. The brain sends a response to start sweating, which cools the body.

D. The skin starts sweating. The sweat sends a message to the brain, which sends a response to stop sweating.

3. Sensory neurons gather information from the environment. A neuron is a cell that has specialized structures to carry out its function. One part of the cell gathers information and another part of the cell carries information to other parts of the body. Which part of the neuron gathers information from other cells?

A. axon

B. nucleus

C. dendrite

D. cell body

4. It is 10 P.M., and Paul is getting very sleepy. Paul's parasympathetic nervous system sends signals to different parts of his body to prepare it for sleep. What would you expect to find occurring inside his body as he turns out the light and gets into bed?

A. His bronchioles are getting larger to allow more oxygen into his blood.

B. His heart rate is decreasing so that blood flows more slowly through the body.

C. His pupils are getting bigger so that it becomes easier to see objects in the dark.

D. His digestion is slowing down so that his muscles can use the food they already have.

5. What two organs make up the central nervous system?

A. skin and vertebrae

B. cerebrum and eyes

C. neurons and receptors

D. brain and the spinal cord

Use the figure below to answer question 6.

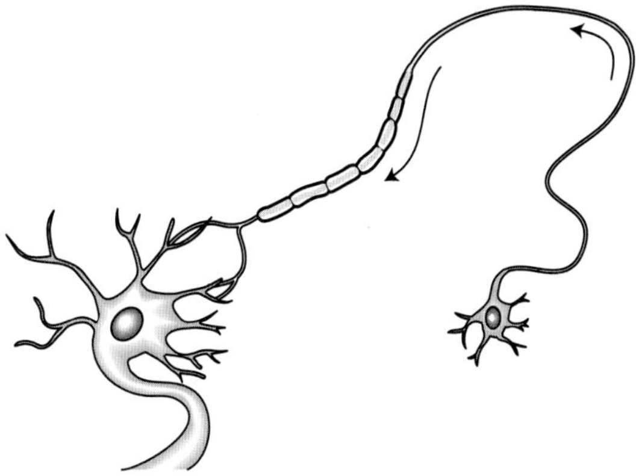

6. **The figure above shows two nerve cells. What do the arrows in the figure represent?**

   A. A signal is being sent to the brain.

   B. A stimulus is detected by a nerve cell.

   C. A signal is being passed from the axon of one cell to the dendrites of another cell.

   D. A signal is being passed from the cell body of one cell to the axon of another cell.

7. **The ear is designed to sense sound and includes various parts that play a role in sensing sound. What role does the cochlea play in hearing?**

   A. It changes sound waves into electric impulses.

   B. It catches and funnels sound into the middle ear.

   C. It causes the stirrup, a bone in the ear, to vibrate.

   D. It makes the tympanic membrane, or eardrum, vibrate.

8. **What role does the peripheral nervous system play in the body?**

   A. It connects all parts of the body to the central nervous system.

   B. It sends messages along the spinal cord to muscles and glands.

   C. It controls activities such as speaking, reading, and writing.

   D. It interprets electric impulses from the nerves as sensations.

9. **When you are startled, your heart rate increases, your pupils dilate, and your digestion slows. Which part of the nervous system controls this response?**

   A. central nervous system

   B. somatic nervous system

   C. sympathetic nervous system

   D. parasympathetic nervous system

Open Response

10. **Your brain interprets information from the taste buds in your tongue and the olfactory cells in your nose to give you sensations of flavor. Jose doesn't like broccoli so he always holds his nose closed when he has to eat it. Describe why Jose finds it easier to eat broccoli when he holds his nose closed.**

11. **Gayle was skateboarding and had to make a sudden turn to avoid a rock. Describe how Gayle's nervous system allowed her to avoid an accident. Be sure to mention which parts of her brain were involved during the response.**

Science in Action

Scientific Discoveries

The Placebo Effect

A placebo (pluh SEE boh) is an inactive substance, such as a sugar pill, used in experimental drug trials. Some of the people who are test subjects are given a placebo as if it were the drug being tested. Usually, neither the doctor conducting the trial nor the test subjects know whether a person is taking a placebo or the test drug. In theory, any change in a subject's condition should be the result of the test drug. But for many years, scientists have known about the *placebo effect,* the effect of feeling better after taking the placebo pill. What makes someone who takes the placebo feel better? By studying brain activity, scientists are beginning to understand the placebo effect.

Social Studies ACTIVITY

Research the differences and similarities between ancient Chinese medical practices and traditional Western medical treatment. Both types of treatment rely in part on a patient's mental and emotional response to treatment. How might the placebo effect be part of both medical traditions? Create a poster showing the results of your research.

Science, Technology, and Society

Robotic Limbs

Cyborgs, or people that are part human and part robot, have been part of science fiction for many years and usually have super-human strength and X-ray vision. Meanwhile there are ordinary people on Earth who have lost the use of their arms and legs and could use some robot power. However, until recently, they have had to settle for clumsy mechanical limbs that were not a very good substitute for a real arm or hand. Today, thanks to advances in technology, scientists are developing artificial limbs—and eyes and ears—that can be wired directly into the nervous system and can be controlled by the brain. In the near future, artificial limbs and some artificial organs will be much more like the real thing.

Language Arts ACTIVITY

WRITING SKILL At the library or on the Internet, find examples of optical or visual illusions. Research how the brain processes visual information and how the brain "sees" and interprets these illusions. Write a report about why the brain seems to be fooled by visual tricks. How can understanding the brain's response to illusions help scientists create artificial vision?

People in Science

Bertha Madras

Studying Brain Activity The brain is an amazing organ. Sometimes, though, drugs or disease keep the brain from working properly. Bertha Madras is a biochemist who studies drug addiction. Dr. Madras studies brain activity to see how substances, such as cocaine, target cells or areas in the brain. Using a variety of brain scanning techniques, Dr. Madras can observe a brain on drugs. She can see how a drug affects the normal activity of the brain. During her research, Dr. Madras realized that some of her results could be applied to Parkinson's disease and to attention deficit hyperactivity disorder (ADHD) in adults. Her research has led to new treatments for both problems.

Math Activity

Using a search engine on a computer connected to the Internet, search the Internet for "reaction time experiment." Go to one of the Web sites and take the response-time experiment. Record the time that it took you to respond. Repeat the test nine more times, and record your response time for each trial. Then, make a line graph or a bar graph of your response times. Did your response times change? In what way did they change?

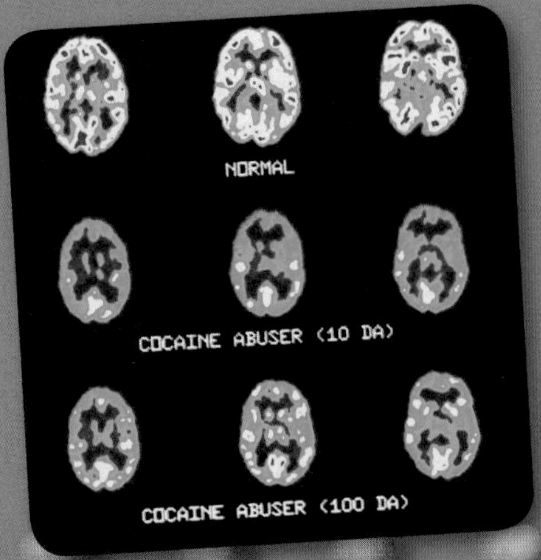

go.hrw.com

To learn more about these Science in Action topics, visit go.hrw.com and type in the keyword **HL5BD4F.**

Current Science

Check out Current Science® articles related to this chapter by visiting go.hrw.com. Just type in the keyword HL5CS25.

21

Reproduction and Development

The Big Idea

The human body has systems that function in reproduction and growth.

SECTION

About the Photo

If someone had taken your picture when your mother was about 13 weeks pregnant with you, that picture would have looked much like this photograph. You have changed a lot since then, haven't you? You started out as a single cell, and you became a complete person. And you haven't stopped growing and changing yet. In fact, you will continue to change for the rest of your life.

PRE-READING ACTIVITY

Graphic Organizer

Spider Map Before you read the chapter, create the graphic organizer entitled "Spider Map" described in the **Study Skills** section of the Appendix. Label the circle "Reproduction and Development." Create a leg for each section title. As you read the chapter, fill in the map with details about reproduction and development from each section.

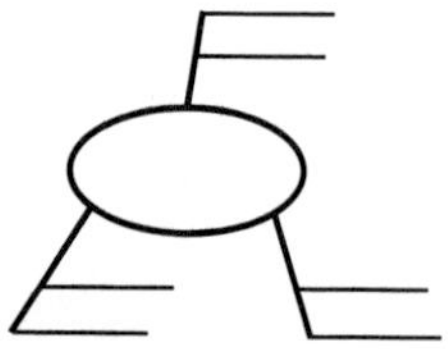

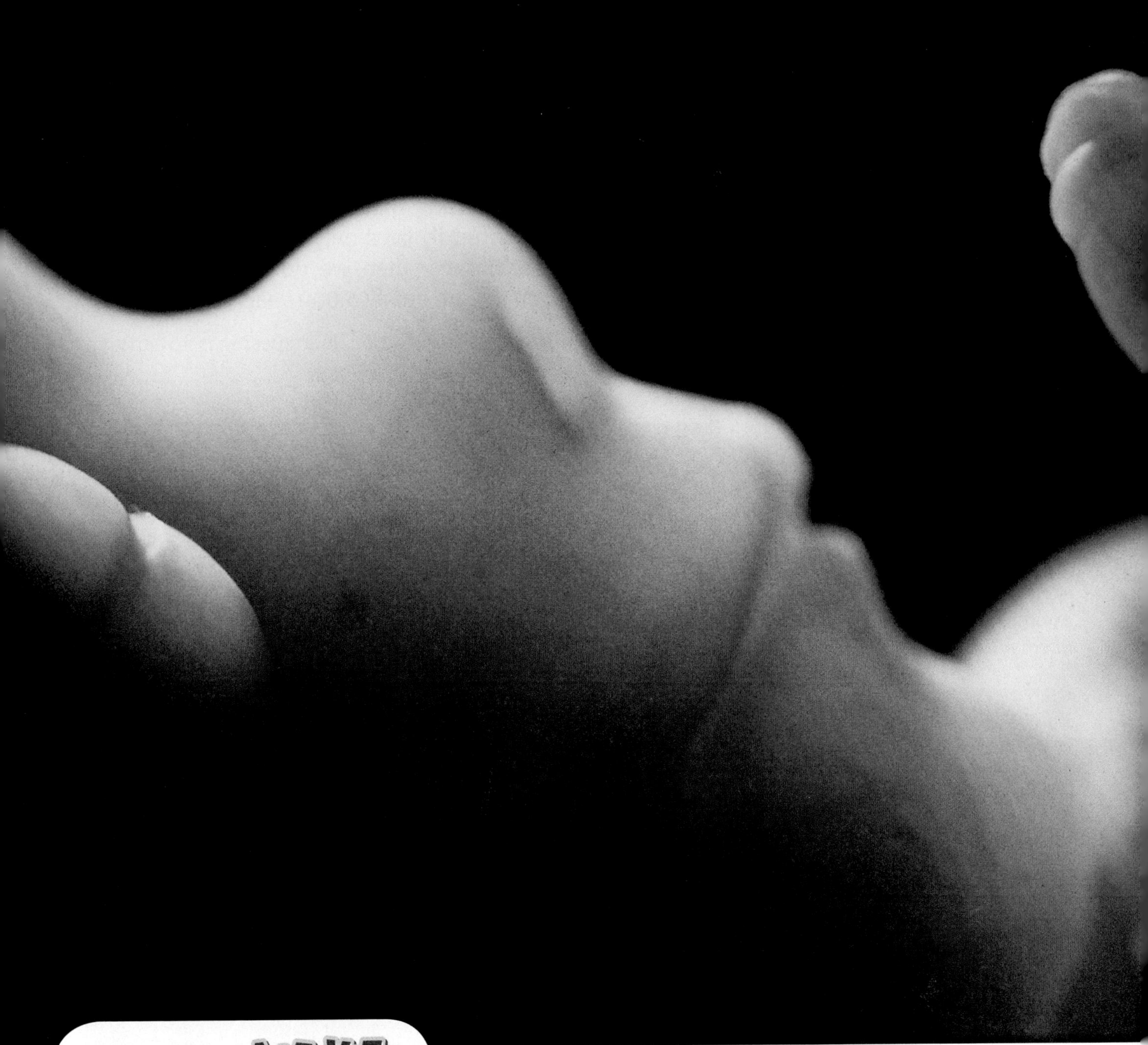

START-UP ACTIVITY

How Grows It?

As you read this paragraph, you are slowly aging. Your body is growing into the body of an adult. But does your body have the same proportions that an adult's body has? Complete this activity to find out.

Procedure

1. Have a classmate use a **tape measure** and **meterstick** to measure your total height, head height, and leg length. Your teacher will tell you how to take these measurements.
2. Use the following equations to calculate your head height–to–total body height proportion and your leg length–to–total body height proportion.

$$\text{head proportion} = \frac{\text{head height}}{\text{body height}} \times 100$$

$$\text{leg proportion} = \frac{\text{leg length}}{\text{body height}} \times 100$$

3. Your teacher will give you the head, body, and leg measurements of three adults. Calculate the head-body and leg-body proportions of each of the three adults. Record all of the measurements and calculations.

Analysis

1. Compare your proportions with the proportions of the three adults.

SECTION 1

Animal Reproduction

What You Will Learn

- Distinguish between asexual and sexual reproduction.
- Explain the difference between external and internal fertilization.
- Identify the three different types of mammalian reproduction.

Vocabulary

asexual reproduction
sexual reproduction
egg
sperm
external fertilization
internal fertilization

READING STRATEGY

Prediction Guide Before reading this section, write the title of each heading in this section. Next, under each heading, write what you think you will learn.

The life span of some living things is short compared with ours. For example, a fruit fly lives only about 40 days. Other organisms live much longer than we do. Some bristlecone pine trees, for example, are nearly 5,000 years old.

But all living things eventually die. If a species is to survive, its members must reproduce.

Asexual Reproduction

Some animals, particularly simpler ones, reproduce asexually. In **asexual reproduction,** a single parent has offspring that are genetically identical to the parent.

One kind of asexual reproduction is called budding. *Budding* happens when a part of the parent organism pinches off and forms a new organism. The new organism separates from the parent and lives independently. The hydra, shown in **Figure 1,** reproduces by budding. The new hydra is genetically identical to its parent.

Fragmentation is a second kind of asexual reproduction. In *fragmentation,* parts of an organism break off and then develop into a new individual that is identical to the original one. Certain organisms, such as flatworms called *planaria,* reproduce by fragmentation. A third type of asexual reproduction, similar to fragmentation, is *regeneration.* When an organism capable of regeneration, such as the sea star in **Figure 2,** loses a body part, that part may develop into an entirely new organism.

asexual reproduction reproduction that does not involve the union of sex cells and in which a single parent produces offspring that are genetically identical to the parent

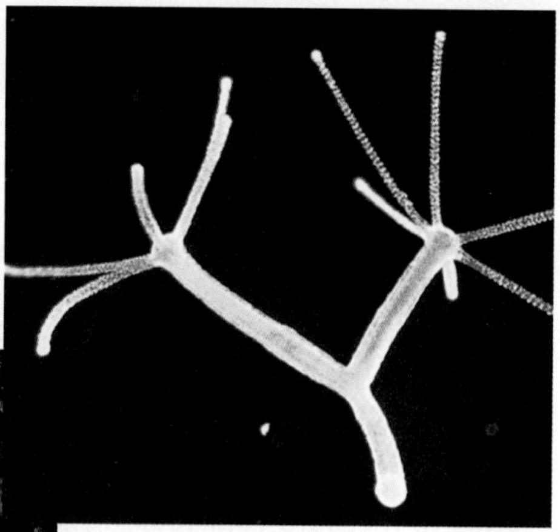

Figure 1 *The hydra bud will separate from its parent. Buds from other organisms, such as certain corals, remain attached to the parent.*

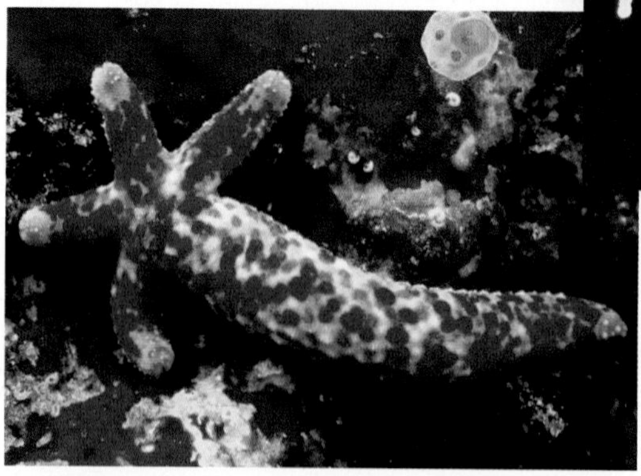

Figure 2 *The largest arm on this sea star was a fragment, from which a new sea star will regenerate. In time, all of the sea star's arms will grow to the same size.*

Sexual Reproduction

Most animals reproduce sexually. In **sexual reproduction,** offspring are formed when genetic information from more than one parent combines. Sexual reproduction in animals usually requires two parents—a male and a female. The female parent produces sex cells called **eggs.** The male parent produces sex cells called **sperm.** When an egg's nucleus and a sperm's nucleus join, a fertilized egg, called a *zygote* (ZIE GOHT), is created. This joining of an egg and sperm is known as *fertilization.*

Human cells—except eggs and sperm and mature red blood cells—contain 46 chromosomes. Eggs and sperm are formed by a process called *meiosis.* In humans, meiosis is the division of one cell that has 46 chromosomes into four cells that have 23 chromosomes each. When an egg and a sperm join to form a zygote, the original number of 46 chromosomes is restored.

Genetic information is found in *genes.* Genes are located on *chromosomes* (KROH muh SOHMZ) made of the cell's DNA. During fertilization, the egg and sperm each contribute chromosomes to the zygote. The combination of genes from the two parents results in a zygote that grows into a unique individual. **Figure 3** shows how genes mix through three generations.

Reading Check **What is sexual reproduction?** (*See the Appendix for answers to Reading Checks.*)

sexual reproduction reproduction in which sex cells from two parents unite to produce offspring that share traits from both parents

egg a sex cell produced by a female

sperm the male sex cell

Figure 3 Inheriting Genes

Eggs and sperm contain chromosomes. You inherit chromosomes—and the genes on them—from both of your parents. Your parents each inherited chromosomes from their parents.

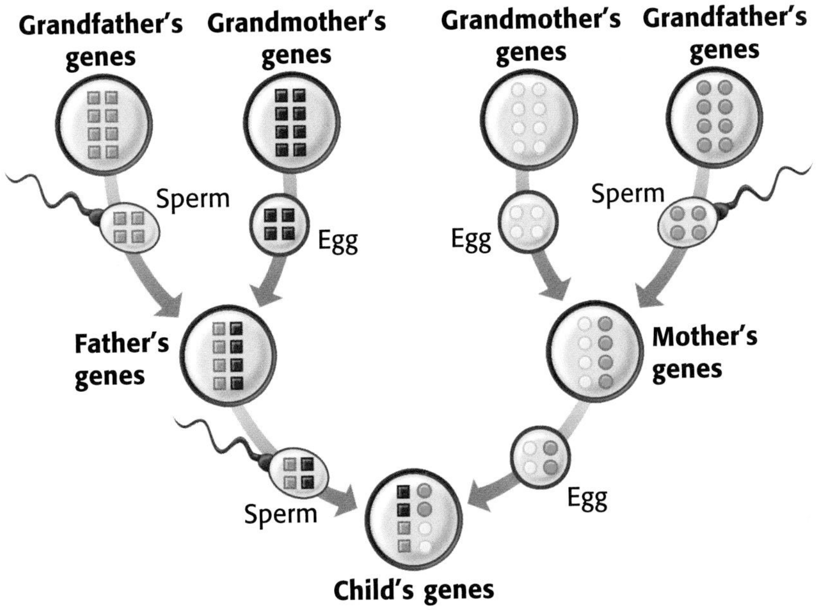

CONNECTION TO Language Arts

WRITING SKILL **Nature or Nurture?** Scientists debate whether genetics or upbringing is more important in shaping people. Use the Internet or library to research the issue of "nature versus nurture." Find information about identical twins who were raised apart. When you finish your research, write a persuasive essay supporting one side of the debate. Include evidence to support your argument.

Figure 4 *Some fish, such as these clownfish, fertilize their eggs externally. The eggs are the orange mass on the rock.*

Internal and External Fertilization

Fertilization can happen either outside or inside the female's body. When the sperm fertilizes the eggs outside the female's body, the process is called **external fertilization.** External fertilization must take place in a moist environment so that the delicate zygotes won't dry out. Some fishes, such as those in **Figure 4,** reproduce by external fertilization.

Many amphibians, such as frogs, use external fertilization. For example, the female frog releases her eggs. At the same time, the male frog releases his sperm over the eggs to fertilize them. Frogs usually leave the zygotes to develop on their own. In about two weeks, the fertilized eggs hatch into tadpoles.

Internal Fertilization

When the egg and sperm join inside the female's body, the process is called **internal fertilization**. Internal fertilization allows the female animal to protect the developing egg inside her body. Reptiles, birds, mammals, and some fishes reproduce by internal fertilization. Many animals that use internal fertilization can lay fertilized eggs. Female chickens, for example, usually lay one or two eggs after internal fertilization has taken place.

In most mammals, one or more fertilized eggs develop inside the mother's body. Many mammals give birth to young that are well developed. Young zebras, such as the one in **Figure 5,** can stand up and nurse almost immediately after birth.

external fertilization the union of sex cells outside the bodies of the parents

internal fertilization fertilization of an egg by sperm that occurs inside the body of a female

Reading Check **What is the difference between external and internal fertilization?**

Figure 5 *This zebra has just been born, but he is already able to stand. Within an hour, he will be able to run.*

Mammals

All mammals reproduce sexually. All mammals nurture their young with milk. And all mammals reproduce in one of the following three ways:

- **Monotreme** *Monotremes* (MAHN oh TREEMZ) are mammals that lay eggs. After the eggs are incubated and hatch, the young are nourished by milk that oozes from pores on the mother's belly. Echidnas and platypuses are monotremes.
- **Marsupial** Mammals that give birth to partially developed live young, such as the kangaroo in **Figure 6,** are *marsupials* (mahr SOO pee uhlz). Most marsupials have pouches where their young continue to develop after birth. Opossums, koalas, wombats, and Tasmanian devils are marsupials.
- **Placental Mammal** There are more than 4,000 species of placental mammals, including armadillos, humans, and bats. Placental mammals are nourished inside their mother's body before birth. Newborn placental mammals are more developed than newborn monotremes or marsupials are.

Figure 6 *The red kangaroo is a marsupial. A young kangaroo, such as this one in its mother's pouch, is called a* joey.

Reading Check Name two ways that all mammals are alike.

SECTION Review

Summary

- In asexual reproduction, a single parent produces offspring that are genetically identical to the parent.
- In sexual reproduction, an egg from one parent combines with a sperm from the other parent.
- Fertilization can be external or internal.
- All mammals reproduce sexually and nurture their young with milk.

Using Key Terms

For each pair of terms, explain how the meanings of the terms differ.

1. *internal fertilization* and *external fertilization*
2. *asexual reproduction* and *sexual reproduction*

Understanding Key Ideas

3. In humans, each egg and each sperm contain
   a. 23 chromosomes.
   b. 46 chromosomes.
   c. 69 chromosomes.
   d. 529 chromosomes.
4. List three types of asexual reproduction.
5. How do monotremes differ from marsupials?
6. Describe the process of meiosis.
7. Are humans placental mammals, monotremes, or marsupials? Explain.

Math Skills

8. Some bristlecone pine needles last 40 years. If a tree lives for 3,920 years, how many sets of needles might it grow?

Critical Thinking

9. **Making Inferences** Why is reproduction as important to a bristlecone pine as it is to a fruit fly?
10. **Applying Concepts** Describe one advantage of internal fertilization over external fertilization.

SECTION 2

Human Reproduction

About nine months after a human sperm and egg combine, a mother gives birth to her baby. But how do humans make eggs and sperm?

What You Will Learn

- Identify the structures and functions of the male and female reproductive systems.
- Describe two reproductive system problems.

Vocabulary

testes, uterus, penis, vagina, ovary

READING STRATEGY

Reading Organizer As you read this section, create an outline of the section. Use the headings from the section in your outline.

The Male Reproductive System

The male reproductive system, shown in **Figure 1,** produces sperm and delivers it to the female reproductive system. The **testes** (singular, *testis*) are a pair of organs that make sperm and testosterone (tes TAHS tuhr OHN). Testosterone is the main male sex hormone. It helps regulate the production of sperm and the development of male characteristics.

As sperm leave a testis, they are stored in a tube called an *epididymis* (EP uh DID i mis). Sperm mature in the epididymis. Another tube, called a *vas deferens* (vas DEF uh RENZ), passes from the epididymis into the body and through the *prostate gland.* The prostate gland surrounds the neck of the bladder. As sperm move through the vas deferens, they mix with fluids from several glands, including the prostate gland. This mixture of sperm and fluids is called *semen.*

To leave the body, semen passes through the vas deferens into the *urethra* (yoo REE thruh). The urethra is the tube that runs through the penis. The **penis** is the external organ that transfers semen into the female's body.

Reading Check **Describe the path that sperm take from the testes to the penis.** (*See the Appendix for answers to Reading Checks.*)

testes the primary male reproductive organs, which produce sperm and testosterone (singular, *testis*)

penis the male organ that transfers sperm to a female and that carries urine out of the body

Figure 1 **The Male Reproductive System**

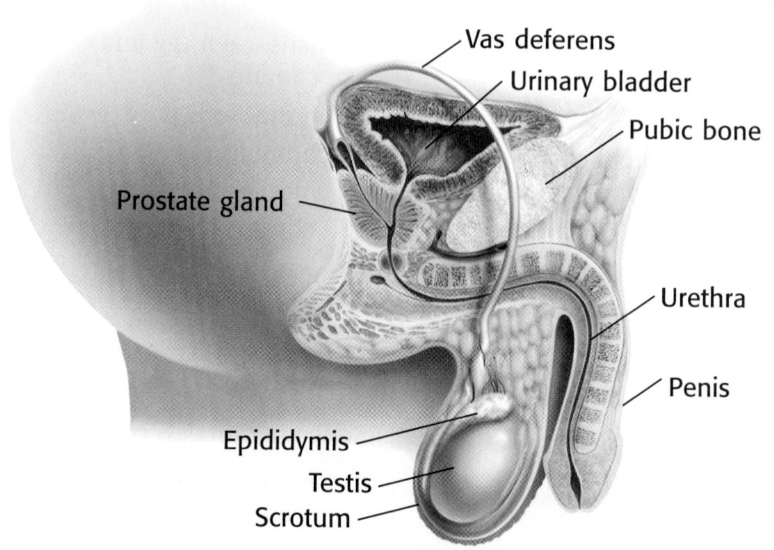

Figure 2 The Female Reproductive System

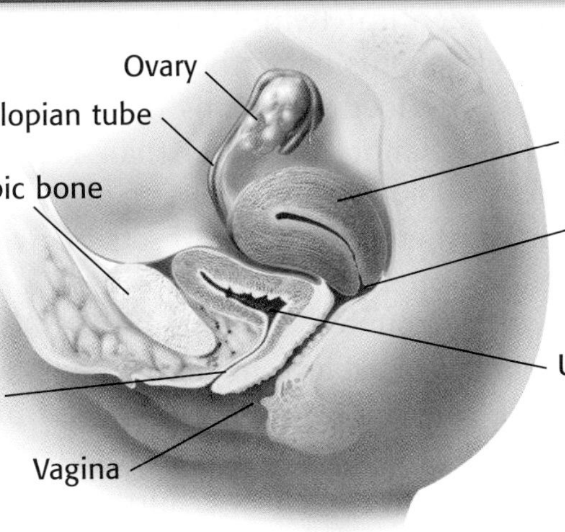

The Female Reproductive System

The female reproductive system, shown in **Figure 2,** produces eggs, nurtures developing individuals, and gives birth. The two **ovaries** are the organs that make eggs. Ovaries also release estrogen (ES truh juhn) and progesterone (proh JES tuhr OHN), the main female sex hormones. These hormones regulate the release of eggs and development of female characteristics.

ovary in the female reproductive system of animals, an organ that produces eggs

uterus in female placental mammals, the hollow, muscular organ in which an embryo embeds itself and develops into a fetus

vagina the female reproductive organ that connects the outside of the body to the uterus

The Egg's Journey

During *ovulation* (AHV yoo LAY shuhn), an egg is released from an ovary and passes into a *fallopian* (fuh LOH pee uhn) *tube.* A fallopian tube leads from each ovary to the uterus. The egg passes through the fallopian tube into the uterus. Fertilization usually happens in the fallopian tube. If the egg is fertilized, the resulting embryo enters the uterus. The embryo may become embedded in the thickened lining of the uterus. The **uterus** is the organ in which an embryo develops into a fetus.

When a baby is born, he or she passes from the uterus through the vagina and emerges outside the body. The **vagina** is the canal between the outside of the body and the uterus.

Menstrual Cycle

From puberty through her late 40s or early 50s, a woman's reproductive system goes through monthly changes. These changes prepare the body for pregnancy and are called the *menstrual cycle* (MEN struhl SIE kuhl). The first day of *menstruation* (MEN STRAY shuhn), the monthly discharge of blood and tissue from the uterus, is counted as the first day of the cycle. Menstruation lasts about 5 days. When menstruation ends, the lining of the uterus thickens. Ovulation occurs on about the 14th day of the cycle. If the egg is not fertilized within a few days, menstruation begins and flushes the egg away. The cycle—which usually takes about 28 days—starts again.

MATH PRACTICE

Counting Eggs

1. The average woman ovulates each month from about age 12 to about age 50. How many mature eggs could she produce from age 18 to age 50?
2. A female's ovaries typically contain 2 million immature eggs. If she ovulates regularly from age 12 to age 50, what percentage of her eggs will mature?

Figure 3 *Identical twins have genes that are exactly the same. Many identical twins who are raised apart have similar personalities and interests.*

Multiple Births

Have you ever seen identical twins? Sometimes, they are so similar that even their parents have trouble telling them apart. The boys in **Figure 3** are identical twins. Fraternal twins, the other type of twins, are more common than identical twins are. Fraternal twins can look very different from each other. In every 1,000 births, there are about 30 sets of twins. About one-third of all twin births are identical twins.

Twins are the most common multiple births. But humans sometimes have triplets (3 babies). In the United States, there are about two sets of triplets in every 1,000 births. Humans also have quadruplets (4 babies), quintuplets (5 babies), and more. These types of multiple births are rare. Births of quintuplets or more happen only once in about 53,000 births.

Reading Check **What is the frequency of twin births?**

Reproductive System Problems

In most cases, the reproductive system functions flawlessly. But like any body system, the reproductive system sometimes has problems. These problems include disease and infertility.

STDs

Chlamydia, herpes, and hepatitis B are common sexually transmitted diseases. A *sexually transmitted disease,* or STD, is a disease that can pass from a person who is infected with the STD to an uninfected person during sexual contact. STDs are also called *sexually transmitted infections,* or STIs. These diseases affect many people each year, as shown in **Table 1.**

An STD you may have heard of is *acquired immune deficiency syndrome* (AIDS). AIDS is caused by *human immunodeficiency virus* (HIV). But you may not have heard of the STD *hepatitis B,* a liver disease also caused by a virus. This virus is spread in several ways, including sexual contact. In the United States, about 140,000 new cases of hepatitis B happen each year.

Table 1 **The Spread of STDs in the United States**

STD	Approximate number of new cases each year
Chlamydia	3 to 10 million
Genital HPV (human papillomavirus)	5.5 million
Genital herpes	1 million
Gonorrhea	650,000
Syphilis	70,000
HIV/AIDS	40,000 to 50,000

SCHOOL to HOME

Twins and More

With a parent, discuss some challenges that are created by the birth of twins, triplets, quadruplets, or other multiples. Include financial, mental, emotional, and physical challenges.

Create a poster that shows these challenges and ways to meet them.

If twins or other multiples are in your family, discuss how the individuals differ and how they are alike.

ACTIVITY

Cancer

Sometimes, cancer happens in reproductive organs. *Cancer* is a disease in which cells grow at an uncontrolled rate. Cancer cells start out as normal cells. Then, something triggers uncontrolled cell growth. Different kinds of cancer have different triggers.

In men, the two most common reproductive system cancers are cancer of the testes and cancer of the prostate gland. In women, the two most common reproductive system cancers are breast cancer and cancer of the cervix. The *cervix* is the lower part, or neck, of the uterus. The cervix opens to the vagina.

Infertility

In the United States, about 15% of married couples have difficulty producing offspring. Many of these couples are *infertile,* or unable to have children. Men may be infertile if they do not produce enough healthy sperm. Women may be infertile if they do not ovulate normally.

Sexually transmitted diseases, such as gonorrhea and chlamydia, can lead to infertility in women. STD-related infertility occurs in men, but not as commonly as it does in women.

CONNECTION TO Social Studies

Understanding STDs Select one of the STDs in **Table 1.** Make a poster or brochure that identifies the cause of the disease, describes its symptoms, explains how it affects the body, and tells how it can be treated. Include a bar graph that shows the number of cases in different age groups.

ACTIVITY

SECTION Review

Summary

- The male reproductive system produces sperm and delivers it to the female reproductive system.
- The female reproductive system produces eggs, nurtures developing individuals, and gives birth.
- Humans usually have one child per birth, but multiple births, such as those of twins or triplets, are possible.
- Human reproduction can be affected by cancer, infertility, and disease.

Using Key Terms

1. Use the following terms in the same sentence: *uterus* and *vagina.*

Understanding Key Ideas

2. Describe two problems of the reproductive system.
3. Identify the structures and functions of the male and female reproductive systems.
4. Identical twins happen once in 250 births. How many pairs of these twins might be at a school with 2,750 students?
   a. 1
   b. 11
   c. 22
   d. 250

Math Skills

5. In one country, 7 out of 1,000 infants die before their first birthday. Convert this figure to a percentage. Is your answer greater than or less than 1%?

Critical Thinking

6. **Making Inferences** What is the purpose of the menstrual cycle?
7. **Applying Concepts** Twins can happen when an embryo splits in two or when two eggs are fertilized. How can these two ways of twin formation explain how identical twins differ from fraternal twins?
8. **Predicting Consequences** How might cancer of the testes affect a man's ability to make sperm?

SECTION 3

Growth and Development

Every one of us started out as a single cell. How did that cell become a person made of trillions of cells?

What You Will Learn

- Summarize the processes of fertilization and implantation.
- Describe the development of the embryo and the fetus.
- Identify the stages of human development from birth to death.

Vocabulary

embryo
placenta
umbilical cord
fetus

READING STRATEGY

Discussion Read this section silently. Write down questions that you have about this section. Discuss your questions in a small group.

A single cell divides many times and develops into a baby. But the development of a baby from a single cell is only the first stage of human development. Think about how you will change between now and when you become a grandparent!

From Fertilization to Embryo

Ordinarily, the process of human development starts when a man deposits millions of sperm into a woman's vagina. A few hundred sperm make it through the uterus into a fallopian tube. There, a few sperm cover the egg. Usually, only one sperm gets through the outer coating of the egg. When this happens, it triggers a response—a membrane forms around the egg to keep other sperm from entering. When the sperm's nucleus joins with the nucleus of the egg, the egg becomes fertilized.

The fertilized egg (zygote) becomes an **embryo** once the first cell division occurs. The embryo travels down the fallopian tube to the uterus over five to six days. During the trip, the embryo undergoes many cell divisions, becoming a tiny ball of cells. Eleven to 12 days after fertilization, implantation occurs. *Implantation* is the embedding of the embryo in the thick, nutrient-rich lining of the uterus. **Figure 1** shows fertilization and implantation.

Reading Check **Describe the process of fertilization and implantation.** (*See the Appendix for answers to Reading Checks.*)

embryo in humans, a developing individual from first division after fertilization through the 10th week of pregnancy

placenta the partly fetal and partly maternal organ by which materials are exchanged between a fetus and the mother

Figure 1 **Fertilization and Implantation**

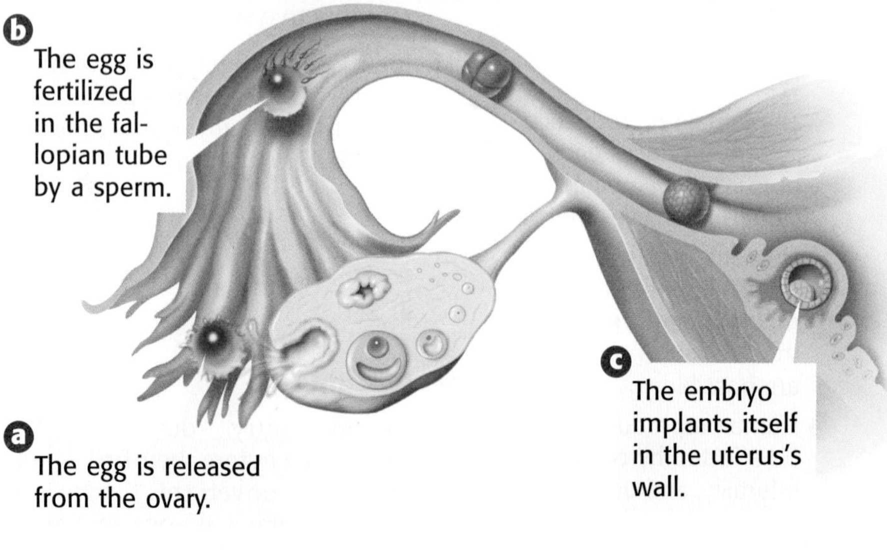
b
The egg is fertilized in the fal-lopian tube by a sperm.
a
The egg is released from the ovary.
c
The embryo implants itself in the uterus's wall.

From Embryo to Fetus

After implantation, the placenta (pluh SEN tuh) begins to grow. The **placenta** is a special two-way exchange organ. It has a network of blood vessels that provides the embryo with oxygen and nutrients from the mother's blood. Wastes produced by the embryo are removed in the placenta. They are carried by the mother's blood so that her body can excrete them. The embryo's blood and the mother's blood flow very near each other in the placenta, but they normally do not mix.

Reading Check Why is the placenta important?

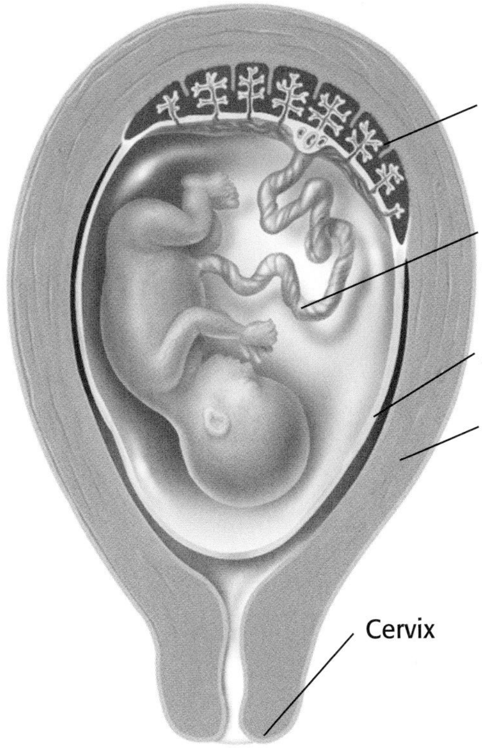

Figure 2 *The placenta, amnion, and umbilical cord are the life support system for the fetus. This fetus is about 20 to 22 weeks old.*

Weeks 1 and 2

Doctors commonly count the time of a woman's pregnancy as starting from the first day of her last menstrual period. Even though fertilization has not yet taken place, that day is a convenient date from which to start counting. A normal pregnancy lasts about 280 days, or 40 weeks, from that day.

Weeks 3 and 4

Fertilization takes place at about the end of week 2. In week 3, after fertilization, the zygote becomes an *embryo* as it moves to the uterus. As the embryo travels, it divides many times. It becomes a ball of cells that implants itself in the wall of the uterus. At the end of week 4, implantation is complete and the woman is pregnant. The embryo's blood cells begin to form. At this point, the embryo is about 0.2 mm long.

umbilical cord the ropelike structure through which blood vessels pass and by which a developing mammal is connected to the placenta

Weeks 5 to 8

Weeks 5 to 8 of pregnancy are weeks 3 to 6 of embryonic development. In this stage, the embryo becomes surrounded by a thin membrane called the *amnion* (AM nee AHN). The amnion is filled with amniotic fluid and protects the growing embryo from bumps and injury. During week 5, the umbilical cord forms. The **umbilical cord** (uhm BIL i kuhl KAWRD) is a cord that connects the embryo to the placenta. **Figure 2** shows the umbilical cord, amnion, and placenta.

In this stage, the heart, brain, other organs, and blood vessels start to form. They grow quickly. In weeks 5 and 6, eyes and ears take shape. The spinal cord begins to develop. In week 6, tiny limb buds appear. These buds will become arms and legs. In week 8, muscles start developing. Nerves grow into the shoulders and upper arms. Fingers and toes start to form. The embryo, now about 16 mm long, can swallow and blink.

SCHOOL to HOME

Growing Up

With a parent, discuss the physical and mental changes that you went through between your birth and your first day of school. Make a poster illustrating those changes.

ACTIVITY

fetus a developing human from the 10th week of pregnancy until birth

Weeks 9 to 16

At week 9, the embryo may begin to make tiny movements. After week 10, the embryo is called a **fetus** (FEET uhs). In about week 13, the fetus's face begins to look more human. During this stage, fetal muscles grow stronger. As a result, the fetus can make a fist and begins to move. The fetus grows rapidly during this stage. It doubles, and then triples, its size within a month. For example, in week 10, the fetus is about 36 mm long. A little later, at week 16, the fetus is about 108 mm to 116 mm long. Use **Figure 3** to follow some of the changes that take place in the fetus as it develops.

Reading Check **Describe three changes the fetus undergoes during weeks 9 to 16.**

Weeks 17 to 24

By week 17, the fetus can make faces. Usually, in week 18, the fetus starts to make movements that the mother can feel. By week 18, the fetus can hear sounds through the mother's uterus. It may even jump at loud noises. By week 23, the fetus's movements may be quite vigorous! If the fetus were born after week 24, it might survive. But babies born at 24 weeks require a lot of help. In weeks 17 to 24, the fetus grows to between 25 cm and 30 cm in length.

CONNECTION TO Physics

Using Ultrasound Doctors often use ultrasound to view a fetus in the uterus. Research how an ultrasound machine works, and make a poster explaining how sound waves can show what is happening inside a human body.

ACTIVITY

Weeks 25 to 36

At about 25 or 26 weeks, the fetus's lungs are well developed but not fully mature. The fetus still gets oxygen from its mother through the placenta. The fetus will not take its first breath of air until it is born. By the 32nd week, the fetus's eyes can open and close. Studies of fetal heart rate and brain activity show that fetuses respond to light. Some scientists have observed brain activity and eye movements in sleeping fetuses that resemble those activities in sleeping children or adults. These scientists think that a sleeping fetus may dream. After 36 weeks, the fetus is almost ready to be born.

Birth

At 37 to 38 weeks, the fetus is fully developed. A full-term pregnancy usually lasts about 40 weeks. Typically, as birth begins, the mother's uterus begins a series of muscular contractions called *labor.* Usually, these contractions push the fetus through the mother's vagina, and the baby is born. The newborn is still connected to the placenta by its umbilical cord, which is tied and cut. All that will remain of the point where the umbilical cord was attached is the baby's navel. Soon, the mother expels the placenta, and labor is complete.

Figure 3 **Pregnancy Timeline**

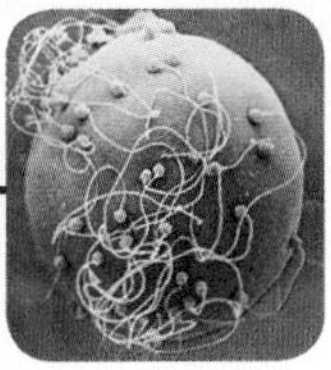

Fertilization takes place.

The fertilized egg becomes hundreds of cells.

Implantation is complete.

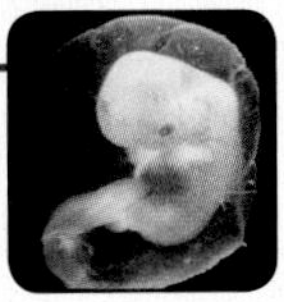

The spinal cord and brain begin to form.

Well-defined tiny fingers and toes become apparent.

The embryo may make tiny movements that may be detected by ultrasound.

The embryo is now called a fetus.

Bones and bone marrow continue to form.

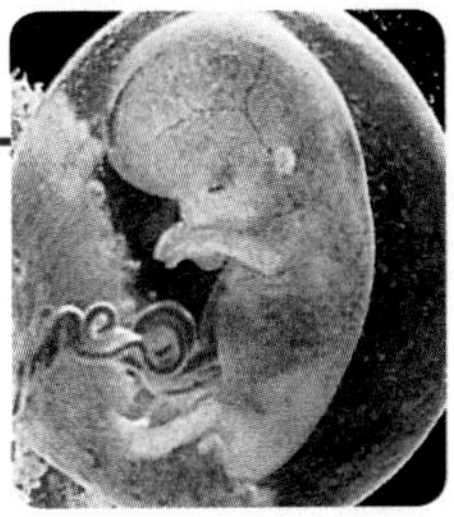

A layer of fat begins to form under the skin.

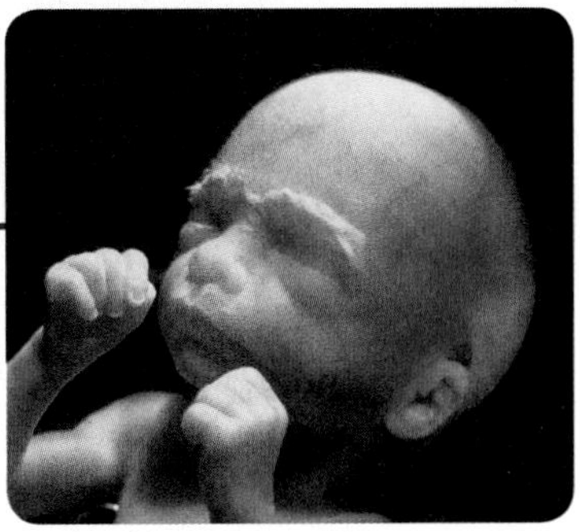

The fetus is developing taste buds and its brain is growing rapidly.

The fetus's lungs are almost ready to breathe air.

The fetus practice breathes and has brain wave activity.

The fetus's eyes are open and it may turn toward a bright light.

The fetus's skin turns from red to pink.

The fetus's skull has hardened.

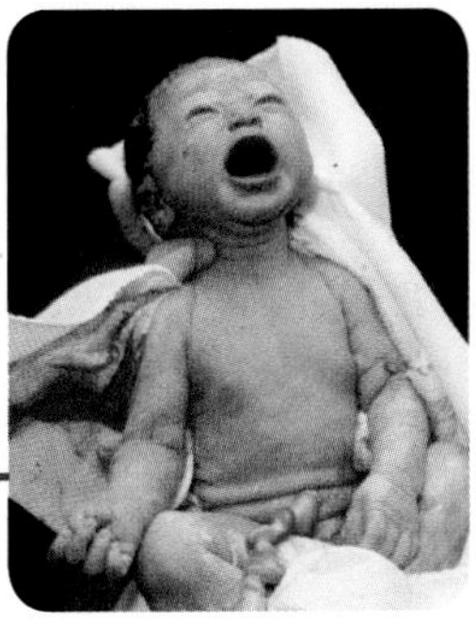

The baby is born.

Figure 4 Stages of Human Development

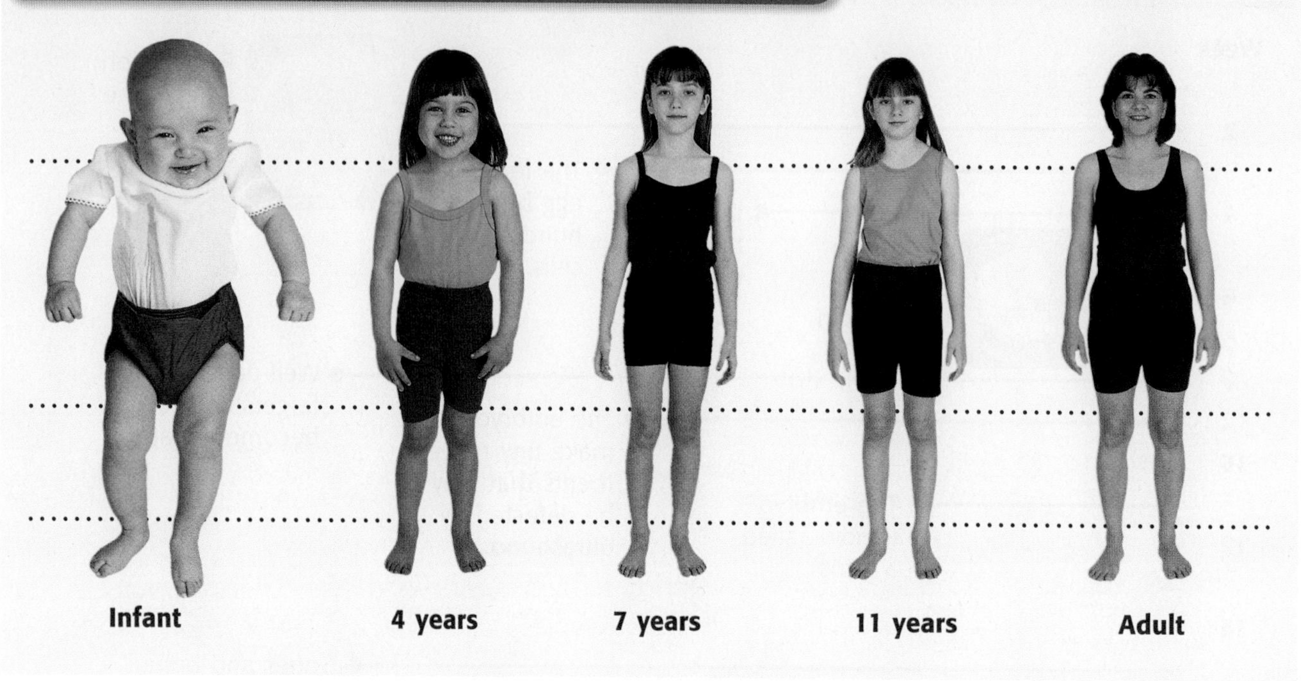

From Birth to Death

After birth, the human body goes through several stages of development. Some of those stages are shown in **Figure 4.**

Infancy and Childhood

Generally, infancy is the stage from birth to age 2. During infancy, you grew quickly and your baby teeth appeared. As your nervous system developed, you became more coordinated and started to walk.

Childhood—another period of fast growth—lasts from age 2 to puberty. Your baby teeth were replaced by permanent teeth. And your muscles became more coordinated, which allowed you to ride a bicycle, jump rope, and do other activities.

Adolescence

The stage from puberty to adulthood is adolescence. During puberty, a person's reproductive system becomes mature. In most boys, puberty takes place between the ages of 11 and 16. During this time, the young male's body becomes more muscular, his voice becomes deeper, and body and facial hair appear. In most girls, puberty takes place between the ages of 9 and 14. During puberty in females, the amount of fat in the hips and thighs increases, the breasts enlarge, body hair appears, and menstruation begins.

Reading Check **Name an important change that takes place during adolescence.**

Quick Lab

Life Grows On

Use **Figure 4** to complete this activity.

1. Use a **ruler** to measure the infant's head height. Then, measure the infant's entire height, including the head.
2. Calculate the ratio of the infant's head height to the infant's total height.
3. Repeat these measurements and calculations for the other stages.
4. Does a baby's head grow faster or slower than the rest of the body? Why do you think this is so?

Adulthood

From about age 20 to age 40, you will be a young adult. You will be at the peak of your physical development. Beginning around age 30, changes associated with aging begin. These changes are gradual and different for everyone. Some early signs of aging include loss of flexibility in muscles, deterioration of eyesight, increase in body fat, and some loss of hair.

The aging process continues in middle age (between 40 and 65 years old). During this time, hair may turn gray, athletic abilities will decline, and skin may wrinkle. A person who is more than 65 years old is considered an older adult. Although the aging process continues, many older adults lead very active lives, as is shown in **Figure 5.**

Figure 5 *Older adults can still enjoy activities that they enjoyed when they were younger.*

SECTION Review

Summary

- Fertilization occurs when a sperm from the male joins with an egg from the female and their nuclei fuse.
- The embryo and fetus undergo many changes between implantation and birth.
- The first stage of human development lasts from fertilization to birth.
- After birth, a human goes through four more stages of growth and development.

Using Key Terms

1. In your own words, write a definition for the term *umbilical cord.*
2. Use the following terms in the same sentence: *embryo* and *fetus.*

Understanding Key Ideas

3. After birth, the two periods of most rapid growth are
   a. infancy and adolescence.
   b. childhood and adulthood.
   c. infancy and childhood.
   d. adolescence and adulthood.
4. After birth, which stage of human development is the longest?
   a. infancy
   b. childhood
   c. adolescence
   d. adulthood
5. Describe the development of the embryo and the fetus.
6. What is the function of the placenta?
7. Summarize the processes of fertilization and implantation.
8. What are five stages of human development?

Math Skills

9. Suppose a person is 80 years old and that puberty took place when he or she was 12 years old.
   a. Calculate the percentage of the person's life that he or she spent in each of the four stages of development that follow birth.
   b. Make a bar graph showing the percentage for each stage.

Critical Thinking

10. **Applying Concepts** Why does the egg's covering change after a sperm has entered the egg?
11. **Analyzing Ideas** Do you think any one stage of development is more important than other stages? Explain your answer.

SciLinks® NSTA
Developed and maintained by the National Science Teachers Association

For a variety of links related to this chapter, go to www.scilinks.org

Topic: Before Birth; Growth and Development

SciLinks code: HSM0140; HSM0700

Using Scientific Methods

Skills Practice Lab

It's a Comfy, Safe World!

OBJECTIVES

Construct a model of a human uterus protecting a fetus.

Compare the protection that a bird's egg gives a developing baby bird with the protection that a human uterus gives a fetus.

MATERIALS

- computer (optional)
- cotton, soft fabric, or other soft materials
- eggs, soft-boiled and in the shell (2 to 4)
- eggs, soft-boiled and peeled (3 or 4)
- gloves, protective
- mineral oil, cooking oil, syrup, or other thick liquid
- plastic bags, sealable
- water

SAFETY

Before birth, baby birds live inside a hard, protective shell until the baby has used up all the food supply. Most mammal babies develop within their mother's uterus, in which they are surrounded by fluid and connected to a placenta, before they are born. Before human babies are born, they lead a comfy life. By the seventh month, they lie around sucking their thumb, blinking their eyes, and perhaps even dreaming.

Ask a Question

1. Inside which structure is a developing organism better protected from bumps and blows: the uterus of a placental mammal or the egg of a bird?

Form a Hypothesis

2. A placental mammal's uterus protects a developing organism from bumps and blows better than a bird's egg does.

Test the Hypothesis

3. Brainstorm several ideas about how you will construct and test your model of a mammalian uterus. Then, use the materials provided by your teacher to build your model. A peeled, soft-boiled egg will represent the fetus inside your model uterus.

4. Make a data table similar to **Table 1** below. Test your model, examine the egg for damage, and record your results.

***Table 1* First Model Test**

Original model	Modified model
DO NOT	WRITE
IN B	OOK

5. Modify your model as necessary; test this modified model using another peeled, soft-boiled egg; and record your results.

6. When you are satisfied with the design of your model, obtain another peeled, soft-boiled egg and an egg in the shell. The egg in the shell represents the baby bird inside the egg.

7. Make a data table similar to **Table 2** below. Test your new eggs, examine them for damage, and record your results in your data table.

Table 2 Final Model Test

	Test Results
Model	DO NOT WRITE
Egg in shell	IN BOOK

Analyze the Results

1. **Explaining Events** Explain any differences in the test results for the model and the egg in a shell.

2. **Analyzing Results** What modification to your model was the most effective in protecting the fetus?

Draw Conclusions

3. **Evaluating Data** Review your hypothesis. Did your data support your hypothesis? Why or why not?

4. **Evaluating Models** What modifications to your model might make it more like a uterus?

Applying Your Data

Use the Internet or the library to find information about the development of monotremes, such as the echidna or the platypus, and marsupials, such as the koala or the kangaroo. Then, using what you have learned in this lab, compare the development of placental mammals with that of marsupials and monotremes.

Chapter Review

USING KEY TERMS

For each pair of terms, explain how the meanings of the terms differ.

1 *internal fertilization* and *external fertilization*

2 *testes* and *ovaries*

3 *asexual reproduction* and *sexual reproduction*

4 *fertilization* and *implantation*

5 *umbilical cord* and *placenta*

UNDERSTANDING KEY IDEAS

Multiple Choice

6 The sea star reproduces asexually by

- **a.** fragmentation.
- **b.** budding.
- **c.** external fertilization.
- **d.** internal fertilization.

7 Which list shows in order sperm's path through the male reproductive system?

- **a.** testes, epididymis, urethra, vas deferens
- **b.** epididymis, urethra, testes, vas deferens
- **c.** testes, vas deferens, epididymis, urethra
- **d.** testes, epididymis, vas deferens, urethra

8 Identical twins are the result of

- **a.** an embryo splitting in two.
- **b.** two separate eggs being fertilized.
- **c.** budding in the uterus.
- **d.** external fertilization.

9 If the onset of menstruation is counted as the first day of the menstrual cycle, on what day of the cycle does ovulation typically occur?

- **a.** 2nd day
- **b.** 5th day
- **c.** 14th day
- **d.** 28th day

10 How do monotremes differ from placental mammals?

- **a.** Monotremes are not mammals.
- **b.** Monotremes have hair.
- **c.** Monotremes nurture their young with milk.
- **d.** Monotremes lay eggs.

11 All of the following are sexually transmitted diseases EXCEPT

- **a.** chlamydia.
- **b.** AIDS.
- **c.** infertility.
- **d.** genital herpes.

12 Where do fertilization and implantation, respectively, take place?

- **a.** uterus, fallopian tube
- **b.** fallopian tube, vagina
- **c.** uterus, vagina
- **d.** fallopian tube, uterus

Short Answer

13 Which human reproductive organs produce sperm? produce eggs?

14 Explain how the fetus gets oxygen and nutrients and how it gets rid of waste.

15 What are four stages of human life following birth?

16 Name three problems that can affect the human reproductive system, and explain why each is a problem.

17 Draw a diagram showing the structures of the male and female reproductive systems. Label each structure, and explain how each structure contributes to fertilization and implantation.

CRITICAL THINKING

18 **Concept Mapping** Use the following terms to create a concept map: *asexual reproduction, budding, external fertilization, fragmentation, reproduction, internal fertilization,* and *sexual reproduction.*

19 **Identifying Relationships** The environment in which organisms live may change over time. For example, a wet, swampy area may gradually become a grassy area with a small pond. Explain how sexual reproduction may give species that live in a changing environment a survival advantage.

20 **Applying Concepts** What is the function of the uterus? How is this function related to the menstrual cycle?

21 **Making Inferences** In most human body cells, the 46 chromosomes are duplicated during cell division so that each new cell receives 46 chromosomes. Cells that make eggs and sperm also split and duplicate their 46 chromosomes. But then, in the process of meiosis, the two cells split again to form four cells (egg or sperm) that each have 23 chromosomes. Why is meiosis important to human reproduction and to the human species?

INTERPRETING GRAPHICS

The following graph illustrates the cycles of the female hormone estrogen and the male hormone testosterone. The blue line shows the estrogen level in a female over 28 days. The red line shows the testosterone level in a male over the same amount of time. Use the graph below to answer the questions that follow.

Hormone Cycles

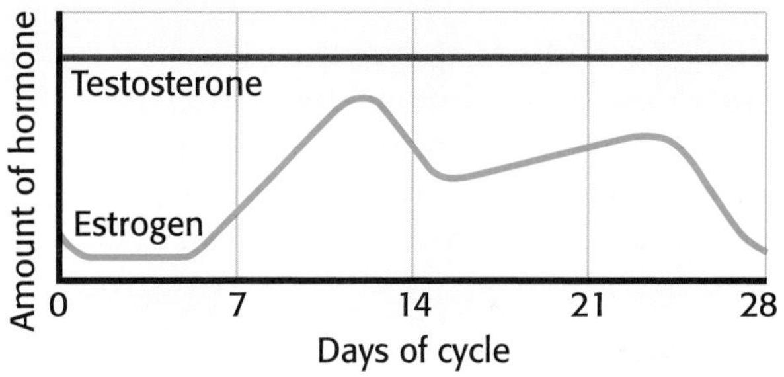

22 What is the major difference between the levels of the two hormones over the 28 days?

23 What cycle do you think estrogen affects?

24 Why might the level of testosterone stay the same?

25 Do you think that the above estrogen cycle would change in a pregnant woman? Explain your answer.

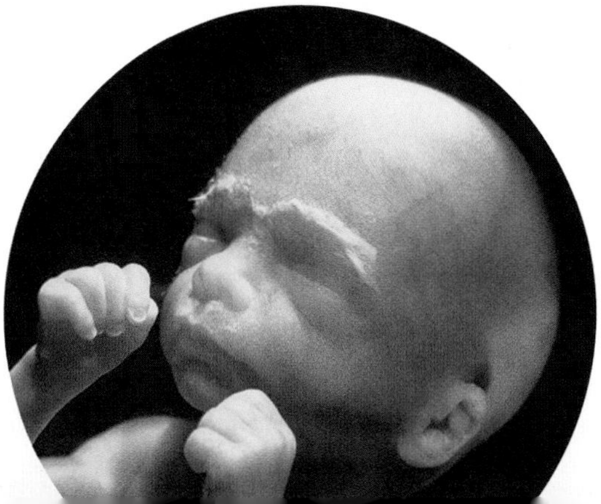

Multiple Choice

Use the figure below to answer question 1.

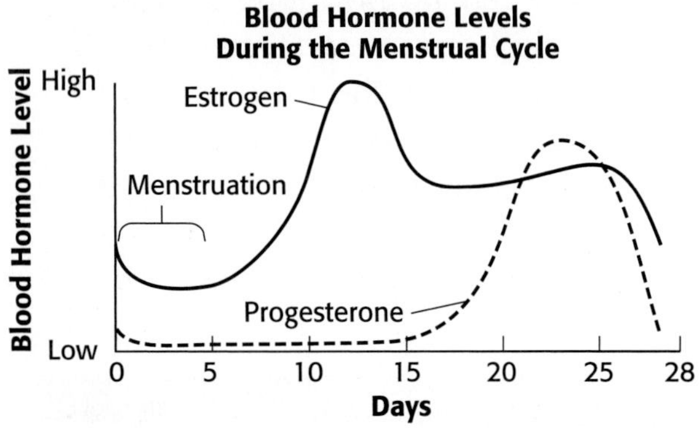

1. The graph above shows the blood hormone levels during the menstrual cycle. Ovulation occurs around the 14th day of the cycle. According to the graph, what happens to the levels of estrogen and progesterone right after ovulation?

A. The levels stay the same.

B. Both estrogen and progesterone decrease.

C. Progesterone decreases and estrogen increases.

D. Estrogen decreases and progesterone increases.

2. The pituitary gland regulates the release of sex hormones. Which of the following reproductive structures interacts with this gland?

A. testes

B. scrotum

C. vas deferens

D. fallopian tubes

3. A fetus develops in a woman's reproductive system, but the fetus is nourished by the woman's

A. lymphatic system.

B. circulatory system.

C. immune system.

D. endocrine system.

4. Which of the following is a valid conclusion that can be drawn about the development of a human fetus?

A. The fetus develops from only the mother's sex cells.

B. The fetus develops from a zygote made from the joining of two sex cells.

C. The fetus receives its 46 chromosomes in its fourth month of development.

D. At fertilization, a zygote is formed from 46 of the father's chromosomes.

5. As a fetus develops, it is dependent on the placenta to help it obtain nutrition and get rid of wastes. Which of the following statements about the placenta's function is true?

A. The placenta allows the exchange of materials between the fetus and the mother.

B. The placenta allows nutrients to move into the fetus and breaks down wastes from the fetus.

C. The placenta allows the mother's blood to mix with the blood of the fetus for the exchange of materials.

D. The placenta makes nutrients for the fetus and allows wastes from the fetus to move into the mother's blood so that her body can excrete them.

6. **A baby girl already has all of the organs that she needs to have babies of her own when she is old enough. Many of these organs must undergo hormonal changes before she can reproduce. During what phase of human development does the reproductive system fully mature?**

   A. adolescence

   B. adulthood

   C. childhood

   D. infancy

7. **A human develops from a single cell. Many tissues and organs are growing as the fetus develops in the uterus. Which of the following statements describes what cells undergo to allow the fetus to develop?**

   A. Cells are becoming larger.

   B. Cells are becoming smaller.

   C. Cells are growing and dividing.

   D. Cells are dying and breaking down.

8. **Why does a child usually have physical characteristics from both parents?**

   A. The child inherits genes from each parent.

   B. The child's cells differentiate during development.

   C. The child's genes are mixed while the child is in the uterus.

   D. The environment of the child is the same as that of the parents.

Use the chart below to answer question 9.

Age group in years	Average height in centimeters	
	Female	Male
At birth	50	51
2	87	88
4	103	104
6	117	118
8	128	128
10	139	139
12	152	149
14	160	162
16	163	172
18	163	174

9. **Svetlana is going to perform a laboratory experiment about height. She receives the chart above from her teacher. According to the chart, at what age are females taller than males?**

   A. 2 years old

   B. 6 years old

   C. 10 years old

   D. 12 years old

Open Response

10. **Both males and females have the hormones testosterone, estrogen, and progesterone. Which hormone is responsible for male characteristics? Describe two characteristics that are a result of this hormone in males.**

11. **Asexual reproduction is one way by which organisms reproduce. Other organisms, including humans, reproduce sexually. Briefly compare asexual reproduction and sexual reproduction.**

Science in Action

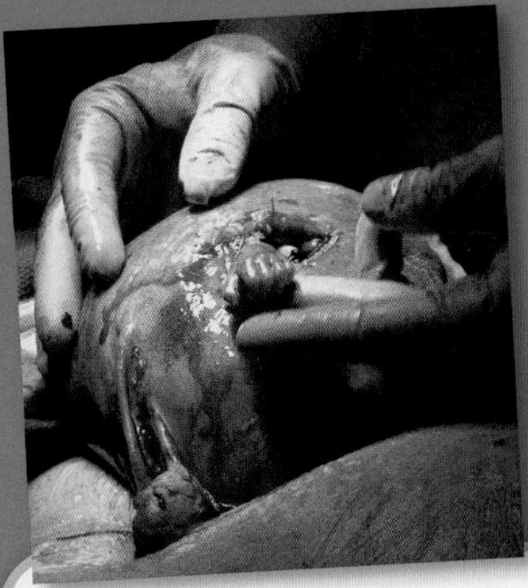

Doctors operated on a fetus, whose hand is visible in this photo, to correct spina bifida.

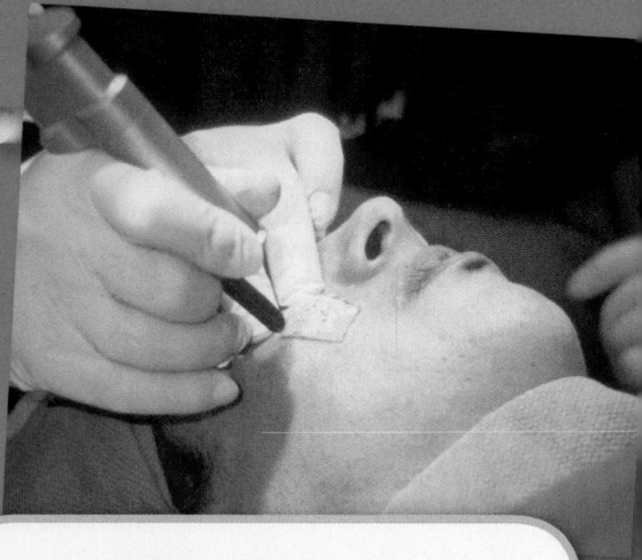

Science, Technology, and Society

Fetal Surgery

Sometimes, a developing fetus has a serious medical problem. In many cases, surgery after birth can correct the problem. But some problems can be treated while the fetus is still in the uterus. For example, fetal surgery may be used to correct spina bifida (part of the spinal cord is exposed because the backbone doesn't form properly). Doctors now can fix several types of problems before a baby is born.

Social Studies ACTIVITY

WRITING SKILL Research the causes of spina bifida. Write a brochure telling expectant mothers what precautions they can take to prevent spina bifida.

Scientific Discoveries

Lasers and Acne

Many people think that acne affects only teenagers, but acne can strike at any age. Some acne is mild, but some is severe. Now, for some severe cases of acne, lasers may provide relief. That's right—lasers can be used to treat acne! Surgeons who specialize in the health and diseases of the skin use laser light to treat the skin disease known as *acne*.

In addition, laser treatments may stimulate the skin cells that produce collagen. Collagen is a protein found in connective tissue. Increased production of collagen in the skin improves the skin's texture and helps smooth out acne scars.

Language Arts ACTIVITY

WRITING SKILL Write a story about how severe acne affects a teen's life. Tell what happens when a doctor refers the teen to a specialist for laser treatment and how the successful treatment changes the teen's life.

Careers

Reva Curry

Diagnostic Medical Sonographer Sounds are everywhere in our world. But only some of those sounds—such as your favorite music playing on the stereo or the dog barking next door—are sounds that we can hear. There are sound waves whose frequency is too high for us to hear. These high-pitched sounds are called *ultrasound*. Some animals, such as bats, use ultrasound to hunt and to avoid midair collisions.

Humans use ultrasound, too. Ultrasound machines can peer inside the human body to look at hearts, blood vessels, and fetuses. Diagnostic medical sonographers are people who use sonography equipment to diagnose medical problems and to follow the growth and development of a fetus before it is born. One of the leading professionals in the field of diagnostic medical sonography is Dr. Reva Curry. Dr. Curry spent many years as a sonographer. Her primary job was to use high-tech instruments to create ultrasound images of parts of the body and interpret the results for other medical professionals. Today, Dr. Curry works with students as the dean of a community college.

Math Activity

At 20°C, the speed of sound in water is 1,482 m/s and in steel is 5,200 m/s. How long would it take a sound to travel 815.1 m in water? In that same length of time, how far would a sound travel in a steel beam?

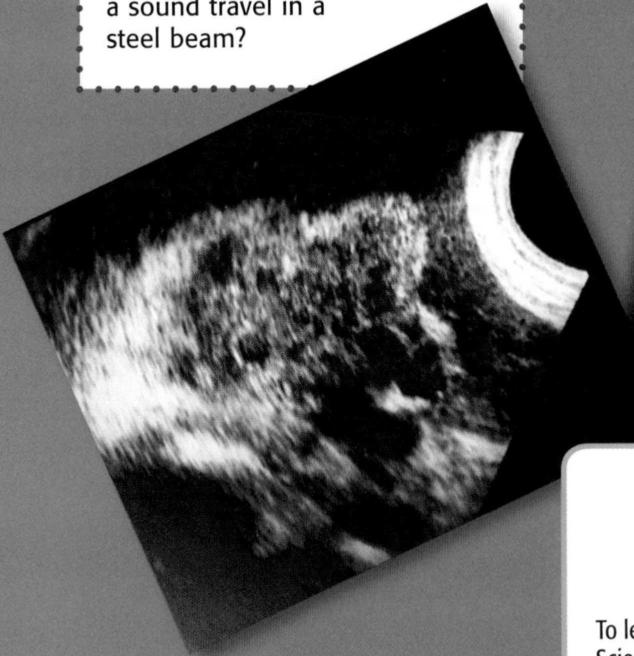

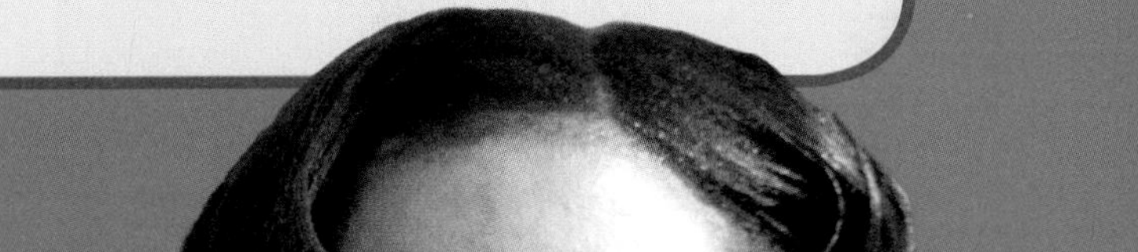

To learn more about these Science in Action topics, visit go.hrw.com and type in the keyword **HL5BD5F.**

Current Science

Check out Current Science® articles related to this chapter by visiting go.hrw.com. Just type in the keyword HL5CS26.

UNIT 6

TIMELINE

Human Health

In many ways, living in the 21st century is good for your health. Many deadly diseases that plagued our ancestors now have cures. Some diseases, such as smallpox, have been wiped out entirely. And others can be prevented by vaccines and other methods. Many researchers, including the people on this timeline, have worked to understand diseases and to find cures.

But people still get sick, and many diseases have no cure. In this unit, you will learn how your body protects itself and fights illness. You will also learn about ways to keep yourself healthy so that your body can operate in top form.

1403

The first quarantine is imposed in Venice, Italy, to stop the spread of the plague, or Black Death.

1717

Lady Mary Wortley Montague introduces a smallpox vaccine in England.

1854

Nurse Florence Nightingale introduces hygienic standards into military hospitals during the Crimean War.

1895

X rays are discovered by Wilhelm Roentgen.

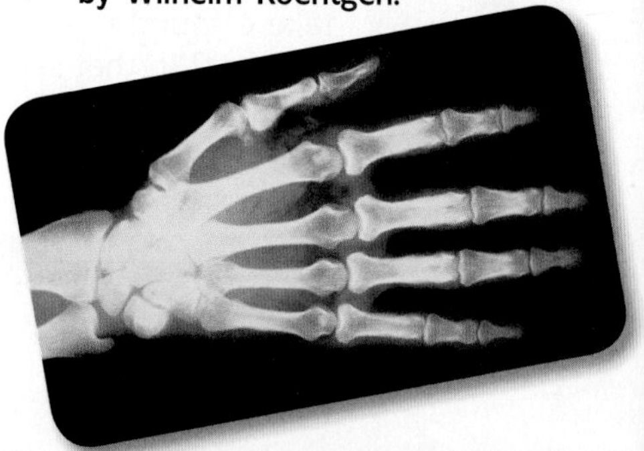

1953

Cigarette smoking is linked to lung cancer.

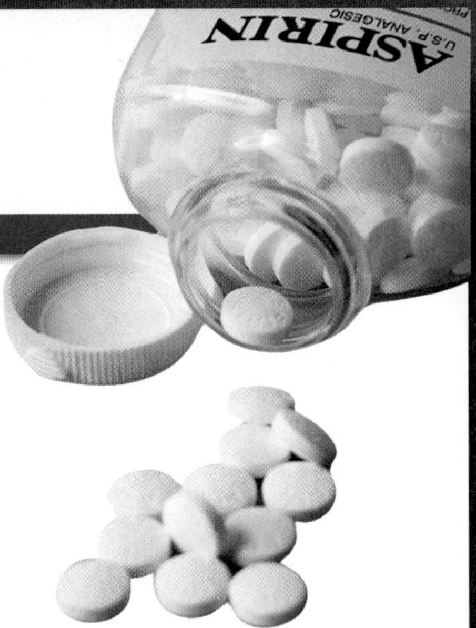

1816

R. T. Laënnec invents the stethoscope.

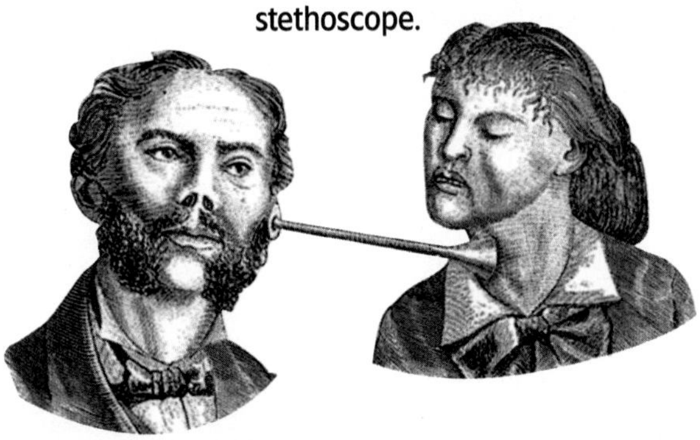

1853

Charles Gerhardt synthesizes aspirin for the first time.

1900

Walter Reed discovers that yellow fever is carried by mosquitoes.

1906

Upton Sinclair writes *The Jungle*, which describes unsanitary conditions in the Chicago stockyards and leads to the creation of the Pure Food and Drug Act.

1921

A tuberculosis vaccine is produced.

1979

Smallpox is eradicated.

1997

Researchers discover that high doses of alcohol in early pregnancy switch off a gene that controls brain, heart, limb, and skull development in the fetus.

2003

More than 8,000 people are infected with severe acute respiratory syndrome (SARS), which is caused by a newly discovered virus.

22

Body Defenses and Disease

The Big Idea

The human body has systems that protect the body from disease.

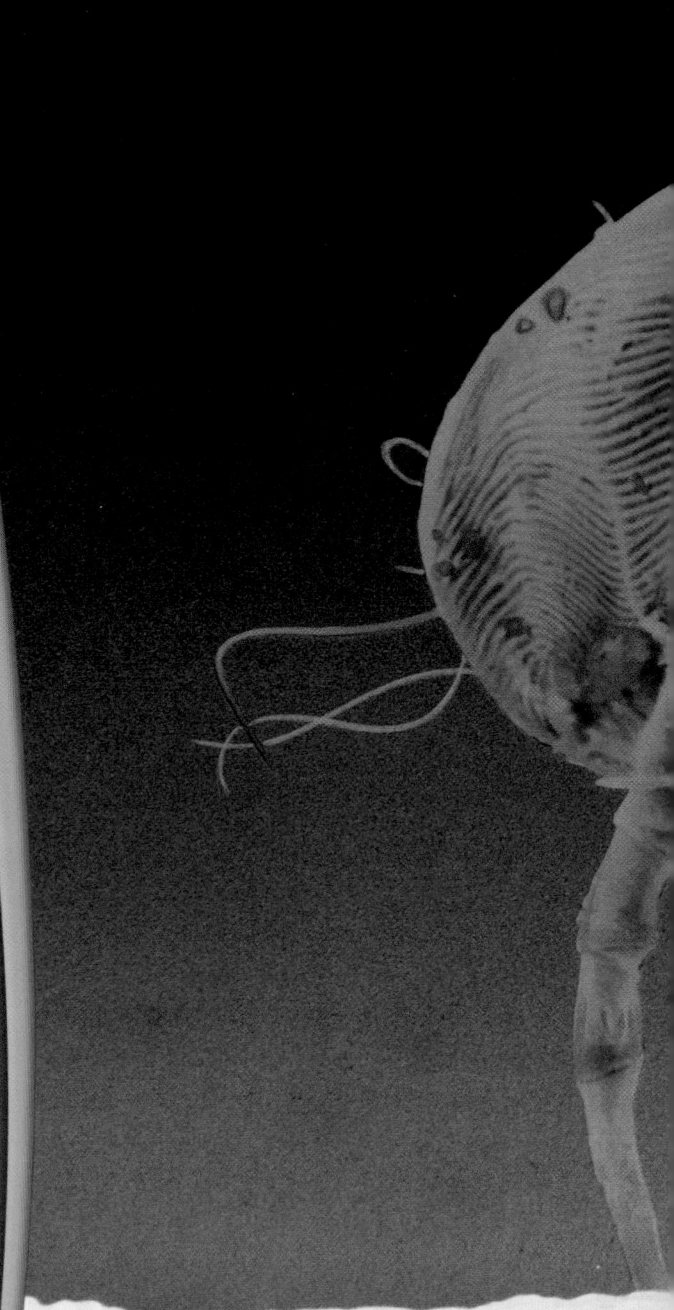

SECTION

About the Photo

No, this photo is not from a sci-fi movie. It is not an alien insect soldier. This is, in fact, a greatly enlarged image of a house dust mite that is tinier than the dot of an ***i.*** Huge numbers of these creatures live in carpets, beds, and sofas in every home. Dust mites often cause problems for people who have asthma or allergies. The body's immune system fights diseases and alien factors, such as dust mites, that cause allergies.

PRE-READING ACTIVITY

FOLDNOTES **Tri-Fold** Before you read the chapter, create the FoldNote entitled "Tri-Fold" described in the **Study Skills** section of the Appendix. Write what you know about the body's defenses in the column labeled "Know." Then, write what you want to know in the column labeled "Want." As you read the chapter, write what you learn about the body's defenses in the column labeled "Learn."

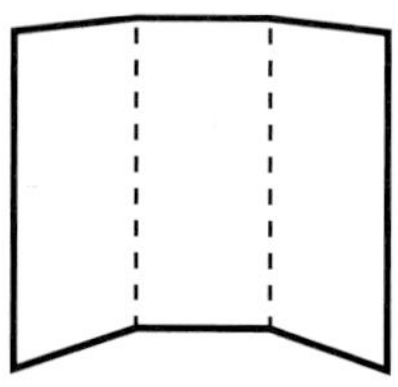

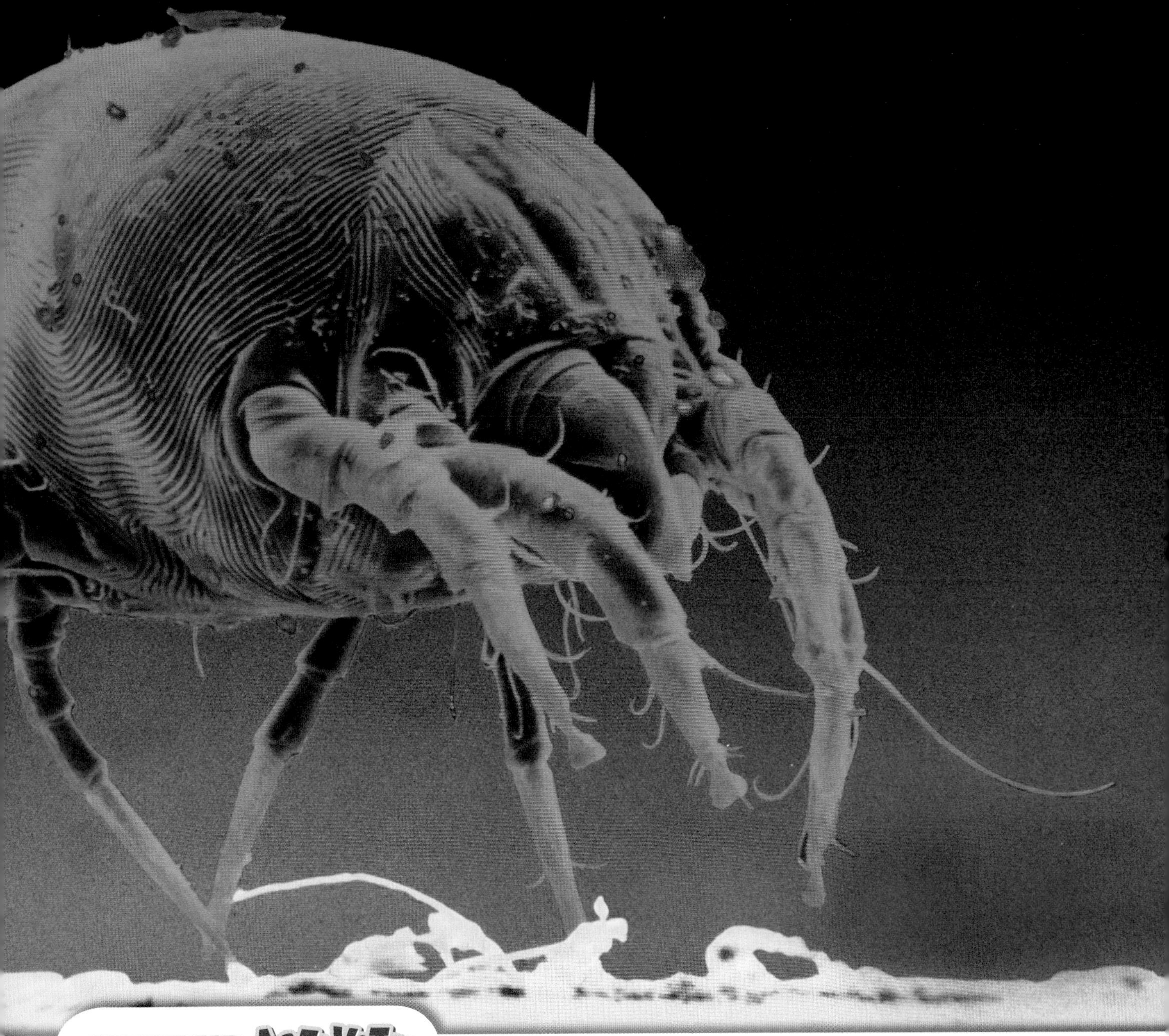

START-UP ACTIVITY

Invisible Invaders

In this activity, you will see tiny organisms grow.

Procedure

1. Obtain **two Petri dishes containing nutrient agar.** Label them "Washed" and "Unwashed."
2. Rub **two marbles** between the palms of your hands. Observe the appearance of the marbles.
3. Roll one marble in the Petri dish labeled "Unwashed."
4. Put on a pair of **disposable gloves.** Wash the other marble with **soap** and **warm water** for 4 min.
5. Roll the washed marble in the Petri dish labeled "Washed."
6. Secure the lids of the Petri dishes with **transparent tape.** Place the dishes in a warm, dark place. Do not open the Petri dishes after they are sealed.
7. Record changes in the Petri dishes for 1 week.

Analysis

1. How did the washed and unwashed marbles compare? How did the Petri dishes differ after several days?
2. Why is it important to wash your hands before eating?

SECTION 1

Disease

You've probably heard it before: "Cover your mouth when you sneeze!" "Wash your hands!" "Don't put that in your mouth!"

What is all the fuss about? When people say these things to you, they are concerned about the spread of disease.

What You Will Learn

- Explain the difference between infectious diseases and noninfectious diseases.
- Identify five ways that you might come into contact with a pathogen.
- Discuss four methods that have helped reduce the spread of disease.

Vocabulary

noninfectious disease
infectious disease
pathogen
immunity

READING STRATEGY

Paired Summarizing Read this section silently. In pairs, take turns summarizing the material. Stop to discuss ideas that seem confusing.

Causes of Disease

When you have a *disease,* your normal body functions are disrupted. Some diseases, such as most cancers and heart disease, are not spread from one person to another. They are called **noninfectious diseases.**

Noninfectious diseases can be caused by a variety of factors. For example, a genetic disorder causes the disease hemophilia (HEE moh FIL ee uh), in which a person's blood does not clot properly. Smoking, lack of physical activity, and a high-fat diet can greatly increase a person's chances of getting certain noninfectious diseases. Avoiding harmful habits may help you avoid noninfectious diseases.

A disease that can be passed from one living thing to another is an **infectious disease.** Infectious diseases are caused by agents called **pathogens,** such as a virus. Viruses are tiny, noncellular particles that depend on living things to reproduce. Some bacteria, fungi, protists, worms, and proteins also may cause diseases. **Figure 1** shows some enlarged images of common pathogens.

noninfectious disease a disease that cannot spread from one individual to another

infectious disease a disease that is caused by a pathogen and that can be spread from one individual to another

pathogen a microorganism, another organism, a virus, or a protein that causes disease

Figure 1 Pathogens

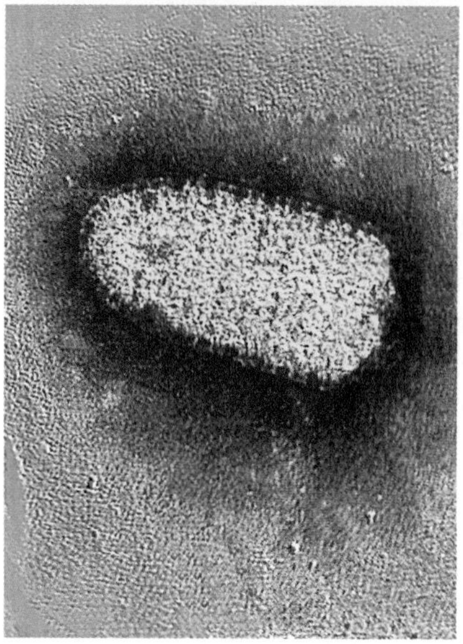

▲ This virus causes rabies.

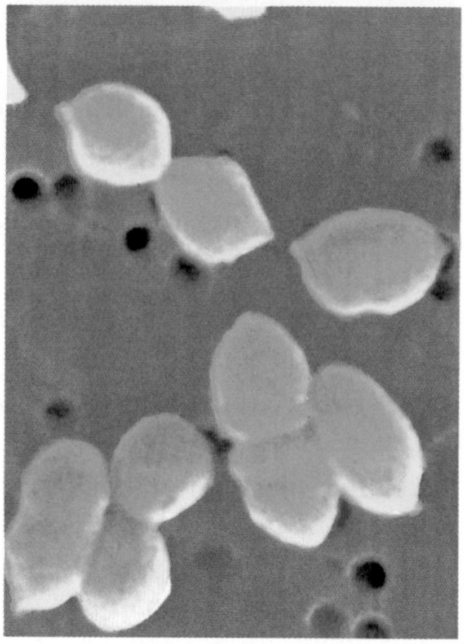

▲ *Streptococcus* bacteria can cause strep throat.

Pathways to Pathogens

There are many ways pathogens can be passed from one person to another. Being aware of them can help you stay healthy.

Air

Some pathogens travel through the air. For example, a single sneeze, such as the one shown in **Figure 2,** releases thousands of tiny droplets of moisture that can carry pathogens.

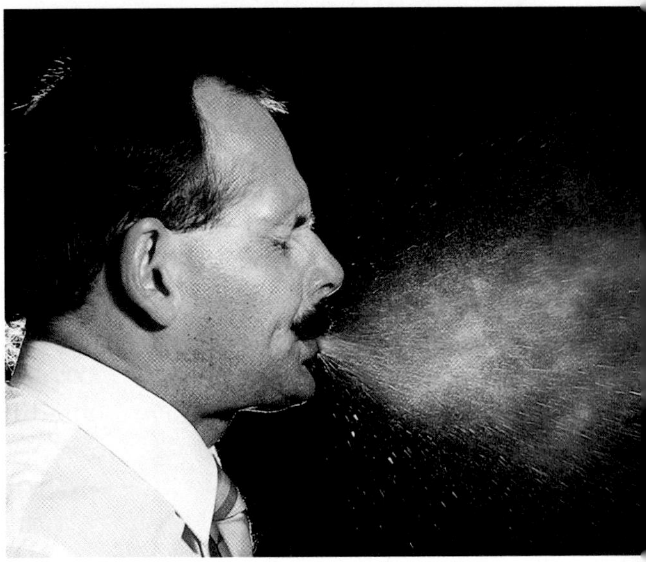

Figure 2 *A sneeze can force thousands of pathogen-carrying droplets out of your body at up to 160 km/h.*

Contaminated Objects

You may already know that if you drink from a glass that an infected person has just used, you could become infected with a pathogen. A person who is sick may leave bacteria or viruses on many other objects, too. For example, contaminated doorknobs, keyboards, combs, and towels can pass pathogens.

Person to Person

Some pathogens are spread by direct person-to-person contact. You can become infected with some illnesses by kissing, shaking hands, or touching the sores of an infected person.

Animals

Some pathogens are carried by animals. For example, humans can get a fungus called *ringworm* from handling an infected dog or cat. Also, ticks may carry bacteria that cause Lyme disease or Rocky Mountain spotted fever.

Food and Water

Drinking water in the United States is generally safe. But water lines can break, or treatment plants can become flooded. These problems may allow microorganisms to enter the public water supply. Bacteria growing in foods and beverages can cause illness, too. For example, meat, fish, and eggs that are not cooked enough can still contain dangerous bacteria or parasites. Even leaving food out at room temperature can give bacteria such as salmonella the chance to grow and produce toxins in the food. Refrigerating foods can slow the growth of many of these pathogens. Because bacteria grow in food, washing all used cooking surfaces and tools is also important.

✓ Reading Check **Why must you cook meat and eggs thoroughly?** (*See the Appendix for answers to Reading Checks.*)

CONNECTION TO Social Studies

Disease and History Many diseases have shaped history. For example, yellow fever, which is caused by a virus that is spread by mosquitoes, was one of the obstacles in building the Panama Canal. Only after people learned how to prevent the spread of the yellow fever virus could the canal be completed.

Use information from Internet and library research to create a poster describing how one infectious disease affected history.

ACTIVITY

SCHOOL to HOME

Label Check

At home or in a local store, find a product that has been pasteurized. In your **science journal,** write down other safety information you find on the label, including the product's refrigeration needs. Why do you think most products that require pasteurization also require refrigeration?

ACTIVITY

immunity the ability to resist or to recover from an infectious disease

Putting Pathogens in Their Place

Until the twentieth century, surgery patients often died of bacterial infections. But doctors learned that simple cleanliness could help prevent the spread of some diseases. Today, hospitals and clinics use a variety of technologies to prevent the spread of pathogens. For example, ultraviolet radiation, boiling water, and chemicals are used to kill pathogens in health facilities.

Pasteurization

During the mid-1800s, Louis Pasteur, a French scientist, discovered that microorganisms caused wine to spoil. The uninvited microorganisms were bacteria. Pasteur devised a method of using heat to kill most of the bacteria in the wine. This method is called *pasteurization* (PAS tuhr i ZAY shuhn), and it is still used today. The milk that the girl in **Figure 3** is drinking has been pasteurized.

Vaccines and Immunity

In the late 1700s, no one knew what a pathogen was. During this time, Edward Jenner studied a disease called *smallpox*. He observed that people who had been infected with cowpox seemed to have protection against smallpox. These people had a resistance to the disease. The ability to resist or recover from an infectious disease is called **immunity.** Jenner's work led to the first modern vaccine. A *vaccine* is a substance that helps your body develop immunity to a disease.

Today, vaccines are used all over the world to prevent many serious diseases. Modern vaccines contain pathogens that are killed or specially treated so that they can't make you very sick. The vaccine is enough like the pathogen to allow your body to develop a defense against the disease.

Figure 3 *Today, pasteurization is used to kill pathogens in many different types of food, including dairy products, shellfish, and juices.*

Antibiotics

Have you ever had strep throat? If so, you have had a bacterial infection. Bacterial infections can be a serious threat to your health. Fortunately, doctors can usually treat these kinds of infections with antibiotics. An *antibiotic* is a substance that can kill bacteria or slow the growth of bacteria. Antibiotics may also be used to treat infections caused by other microorganisms, such as fungi. You may take an antibiotic when you are sick. Always take antibiotics according to your doctor's instructions to ensure that all the pathogens are killed.

Viruses, such as those that cause colds, are not affected by antibiotics. Antibiotics can kill only living things. Viruses are not considered to be alive because they cannot reproduce on their own. Therefore, to reproduce, viruses are dependent on organisms. In the past, the only way to destroy viruses in the body was to locate and kill the cells that the viruses had invaded. Today, although there are only a few, an increasing number of antiviral medicines are being developed.

Reading Check **Explain whether antibiotics useful in treating colds?**

MATH PRACTICE

Epidemic!

You catch a cold and return to your school while sick. Your friends don't have immunity to your cold. On the first day, you expose five friends to your cold. The next day, each of those friends passes the virus to five more people. If this pattern continues for 5 more days, how many people will be exposed to the virus?

SECTION Review

Summary

- Noninfectious diseases cannot be spread from one person to another.
- Infectious diseases are caused by pathogens that are spread from one organism to another.
- Pathogens are spread by contact with infected organisms and through contaminated objects, food, water, or air.
- Cleanliness, antibiotics, pasteurization, vaccines, and antiviral medicines help control diseases.

Using Key Terms

1. In your own words, write a definition for each of the following terms: *infectious disease, noninfectious disease,* and *immunity.*

Understanding Key Ideas

2. Vaccines contain
   a. treated pathogens.
   b. heat.
   c. antibiotics.
   d. pasteurization.
3. List five ways that you might come into contact with a pathogen.
4. Name five ways to avoid and/or fight pathogens.

Math Skills

5. If 10 people with the virus each expose 25 more people to the virus, how many people will be exposed to the virus?

Critical Thinking

6. **Identifying Relationships** Why might the risk of infectious disease be high in a community that has no water treatment facility?
7. **Analyzing Methods** Explain what might happen if a doctor did not wear gloves when treating patients.
8. **Applying Concepts** Why do vaccines for diseases in animals help prevent some illnesses in people?

SCILINKS. NSTA Developed and maintained by the National Science Teachers Association

For a variety of links related to this chapter, go to www.scilinks.org

Topic: Pathogens; What Causes Diseases?
SciLinks code: HSM1118; HSM1653

SECTION 2

Your Body's Defenses

Bacteria and viruses can be in the air, in the water, and on all the surfaces around you.

What You Will Learn

- Describe how your body keeps out pathogens.
- Explain how the immune system fights infections.
- Describe four challenges to the immune system.

Vocabulary

immune system
macrophage
T cell
B cell
antibody
memory B cell
allergy
autoimmune disease
cancer

READING STRATEGY

Reading Organizer As you read this section, make a flowchart of the steps of how your body responds to a virus.

Your body must constantly protect itself against pathogens that are trying to invade it. But how does your body do that? Luckily, your body has its own built-in defense system.

First Lines of Defense

For a pathogen to harm you, it must attack a part of your body. Usually, though, very few of the pathogens around you make it past your first lines of defense.

Many organisms that try to enter your eyes or mouth are destroyed by special enzymes. Pathogens that enter your nose are washed down the back of your throat by mucus. The mucus carries the pathogens to your stomach, where most are quickly digested.

Your skin is made of many layers of flat cells. The outermost layers are dead. As a result, many pathogens that land on your skin have difficulty finding a live cell to infect. As **Figure 1** shows, the dead skin cells are constantly dropping off your body as new skin cells grow from beneath. As the dead skin cells flake off, they carry away viruses, bacteria, and other microorganisms. In addition, glands secrete oil onto your skin's surface. The oil contains chemicals that kill many pathogens.

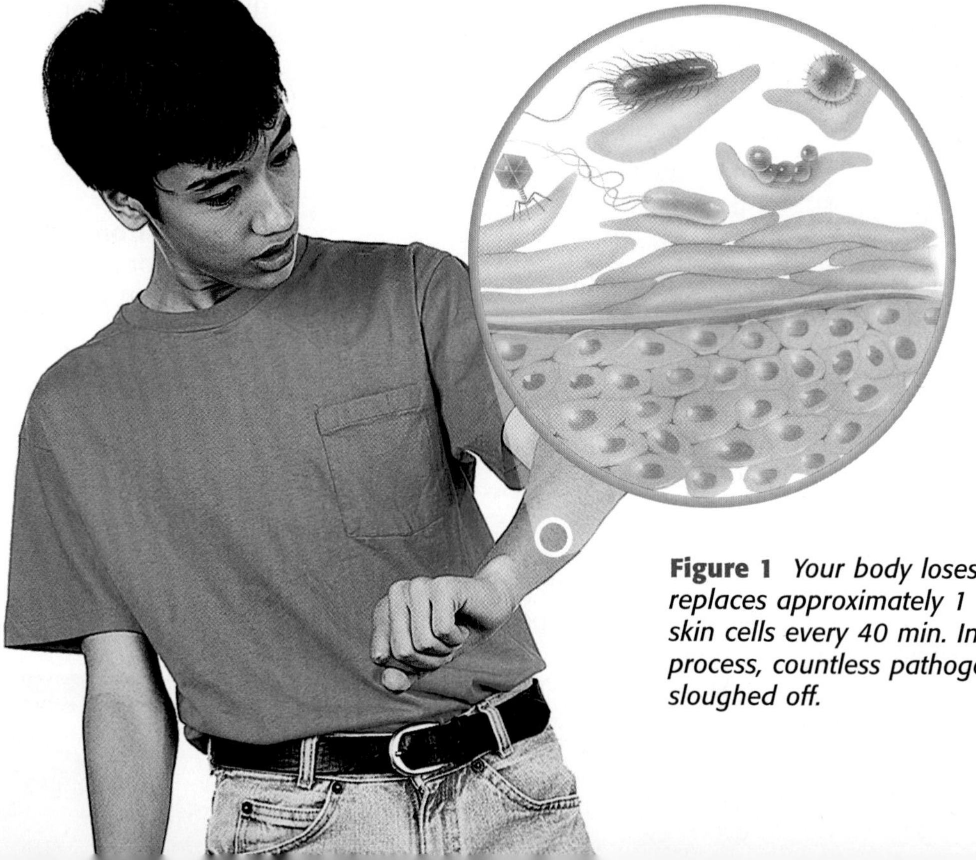

Figure 1 *Your body loses and replaces approximately 1 million skin cells every 40 min. In the process, countless pathogens are sloughed off.*

Failure of First Lines

Sometimes, skin is cut or punctured and pathogens can enter the body. The body acts quickly to keep out as many pathogens as possible. Blood flow to the injured area increases. Cell parts in the blood called *platelets* help seal the open wound so that no more pathogens can enter.

The increased blood flow also brings cells that belong to the **immune system,** the body system that fights pathogens. The immune system is not localized in any one place in your body. It is not controlled by any one organ, such as the brain. Instead, it is a team of individual cells, tissues, and organs that work together to keep you safe from invading pathogens.

immune system the cells and tissues that recognize and attack foreign substances in the body

macrophage an immune system cell that engulfs pathogens and other materials

T cell an immune system cell that coordinates the immune system and attacks many infected cells

B cell a white blood cell that makes antibodies

antibody a protein made by B cells that binds to a specific antigen

Cells of the Immune System

The immune system consists mainly of three kinds of cells. One kind is the macrophage (MAK roh FAYJ). **Macrophages** engulf and digest many microorganisms or viruses that enter your body. If only a few microorganisms or viruses have entered a wound, the macrophages can easily stop them.

The other two main kinds of immune-system cells are T cells and B cells. **T cells** coordinate the immune system and attack many infected cells. **B cells** are immune-system cells that make antibodies. **Antibodies** are proteins that attach to specific antigens. *Antigens* are substances that stimulate an immune response. Your body is capable of making billions of different antibodies. Each antibody usually attaches to only one kind of antigen, as illustrated in **Figure 2.**

Reading Check **How do macrophages help fight disease?** *(See the Appendix for answers to Reading Checks.)*

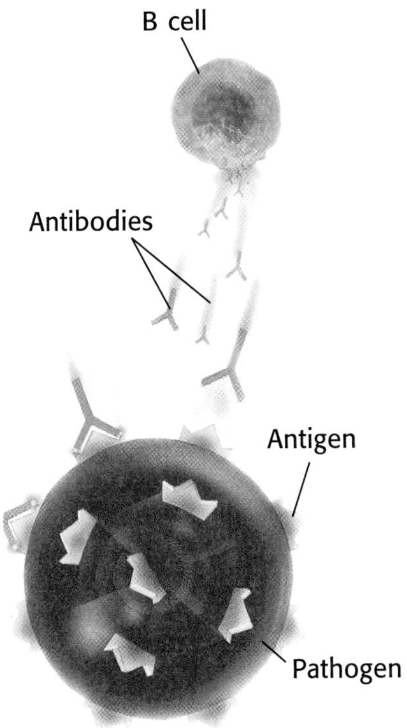

Figure 2 *An antibody's shape is very specialized. It matches an antigen like a key fits a lock.*

Quick Lab

Only Skin Deep

1. Cut an **apple** in half.
2. Place **plastic wrap** over each half. The plastic wrap will act as skin.
3. Use **scissors** to cut the plastic wrap on one of the apple halves, and then use an **eyedropper** to drip **food coloring** on each apple half. The food coloring represents pathogens coming into contact with your body.
4. What happened to each apple half?
5. How is the plastic wrap similar to skin?
6. How is the plastic wrap different from skin?

INTERNET ACTIVITY

For another activity related to this chapter, go to **go.hrw.com** and type in the keyword **HL5BD6W.**

Responding to a Virus

If virus particles enter your body, some of the particles may pass into body cells and begin to replicate. Other virus particles will be engulfed and broken up by macrophages. This is just the beginning of the immune response. The process your immune system uses to fight an invading virus is summarized in the figure below.

Reading Check **What are two things that can happen to virus particles when they enter the body?**

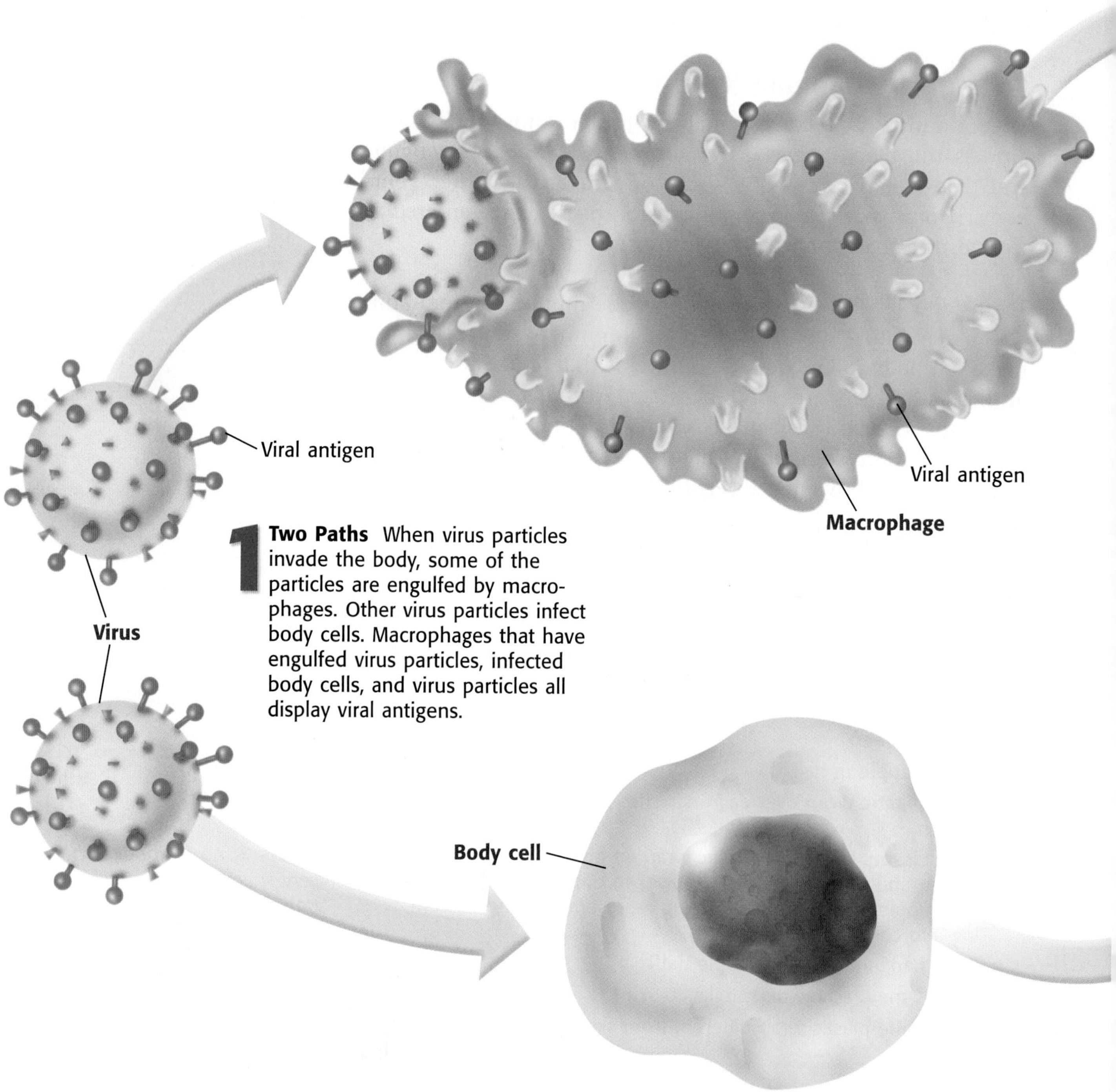

1 Two Paths When virus particles invade the body, some of the particles are engulfed by macrophages. Other virus particles infect body cells. Macrophages that have engulfed virus particles, infected body cells, and virus particles all display viral antigens.

2 Two Responses Helper T cells have receptor proteins that recognize the shape of the viral antigen on the macrophages. These helper T cells begin two responses: a T cell response and a B cell response.

3 T Cell Response Helper T cells activate killer T cells.

4 Destroying Infected Cells Killer T cells recognize the viral antigen on infected cells. The killer T cells destroy the infected cells so that the virus particles inside the cell cannot replicate.

5 B Cell Response Meanwhile, helper T cells also activate B cells. Activated B cells divide to make cells that can make antibodies. The antibodies recognize the shape of the viral antigen.

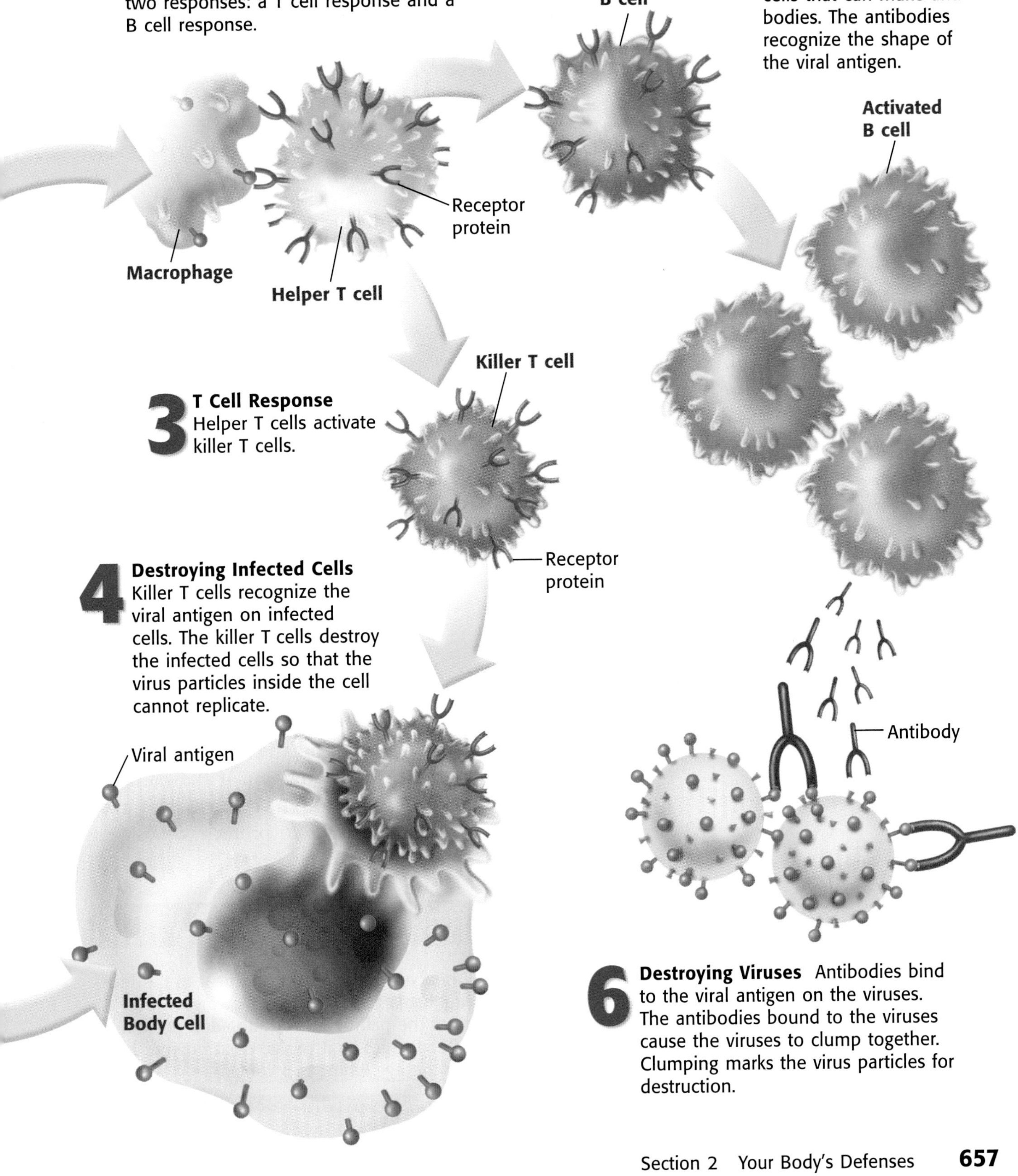

6 Destroying Viruses Antibodies bind to the viral antigen on the viruses. The antibodies bound to the viruses cause the viruses to clump together. Clumping marks the virus particles for destruction.

Figure 3 *You may not feel well when you have a fever. But a fever is one way that your body fights infections.*

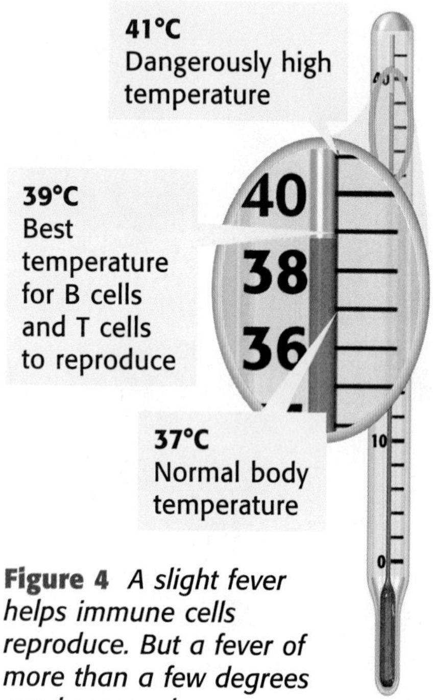

Figure 4 *A slight fever helps immune cells reproduce. But a fever of more than a few degrees can become dangerous.*

Fevers

The man in **Figure 3** is sick and has a fever. What is a fever? When macrophages activate the helper T cells, they send a chemical signal that tells your brain to turn up the thermostat. In a few minutes, your body's temperature can rise several degrees. A moderate fever of one or two degrees actually helps you get well faster because it slows the growth of some pathogens. As shown in **Figure 4,** a fever also helps B cells and T cells multiply faster.

Memory Cells

Your immune system can respond to a second encounter faster than it can respond the first time. B cells must have had previous contact with a pathogen before they can make the correct antibodies. During the first encounter with a new pathogen, specialized B cells make antibodies that are effective against that particular invader. This process takes about 2 weeks, which is far too long to prevent an infection. Therefore, the first time you are infected, you usually get sick.

A few of the B cells become memory B cells. **Memory B cells** are cells in your immune system that "remember" how to make an antibody for a particular pathogen. If the pathogen shows up again, the memory B cells produce B cells that make enough antibodies in just 3 or 4 days to protect you.

memory B cell a B cell that responds to an antigen more strongly when the body is reinfected with an antigen than it does during its first encounter with the antigen

CONNECTION TO Chemistry

Bent out of Shape When you have a fever, the heat of the fever changes the shape of viral or bacterial proteins, slowing or preventing the reproduction of the pathogen. With an adult present, observe how an egg white changes as it cooks. What do you think happens to the protein in the egg white as it cooks?

ACTIVITY

Challenges to the Immune System

The immune system is a very effective body-defense system, but it is not perfect. The immune system is unable to deal with some diseases. There are also conditions in which the immune system does not work properly.

allergy a reaction to a harmless or common substance by the body's immune system

autoimmune disease a disease in which the immune system attacks the organism's own cells

Allergies

Sometimes, the immune system overreacts to antigens that are not dangerous to the body. This inappropriate reaction is called an **allergy.** Allergies may be caused by many things, including certain foods and medicines. Many people have allergic reactions to pollen, shown in **Figure 5.** Symptoms of allergic reactions range from a runny nose and itchy eyes to more serious conditions, such as asthma.

Doctors are not sure why the immune system overreacts in some people. Scientists think allergies might be useful because the mucus draining from your nose carries away pollen, dust, and microorganisms.

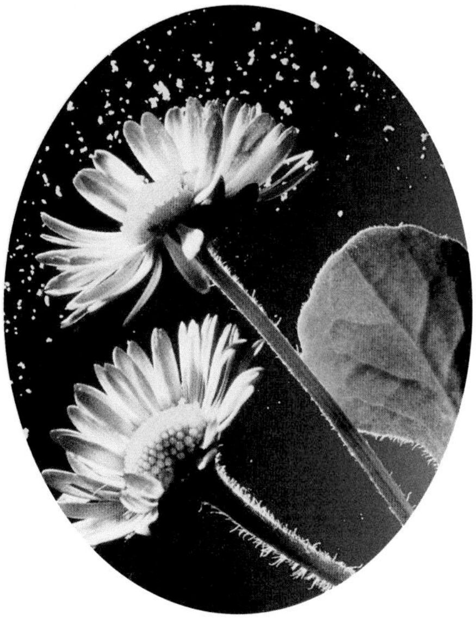

Figure 5 *Pollen is one substance that can cause allergic reactions.*

Autoimmune Diseases

A disease in which the immune system attacks the body's own cells is called an **autoimmune disease.** In an autoimmune disease, immune-system cells mistake body cells for pathogens. One autoimmune disease is rheumatoid arthritis (ROO muh TOYD ahr THRIET IS), in which the immune system attacks the joints. A common location for rheumatoid arthritis is the joints of the hands, as shown in **Figure 6.** Other autoimmune diseases include type 1 diabetes, multiple sclerosis, and lupus.

Reading Check Name four autoimmune diseases.

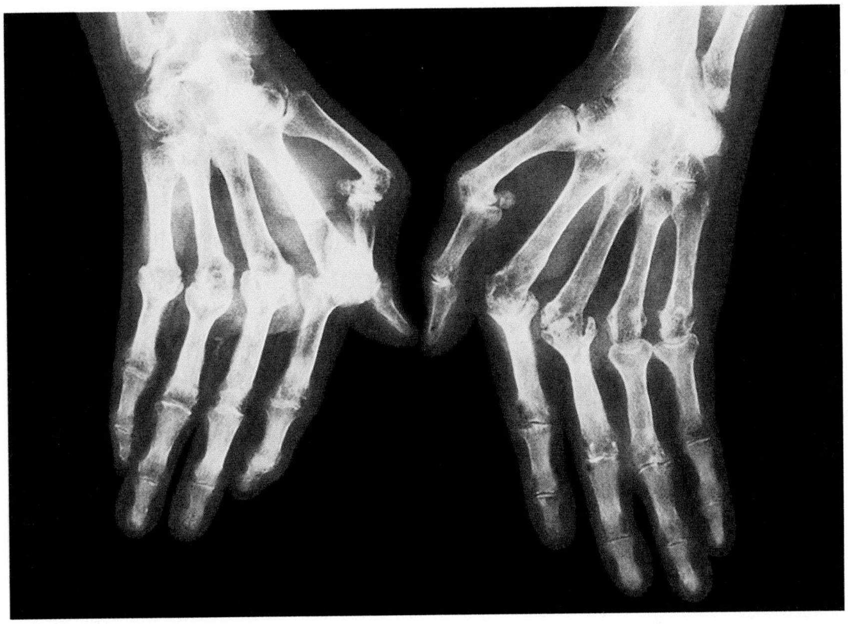

Figure 6 *In rheumatoid arthritis, immune-system cells cause joint-tissue swelling, which can lead to joint deformities.*

Figure 7 **Immune Cells Fighting Cancer**

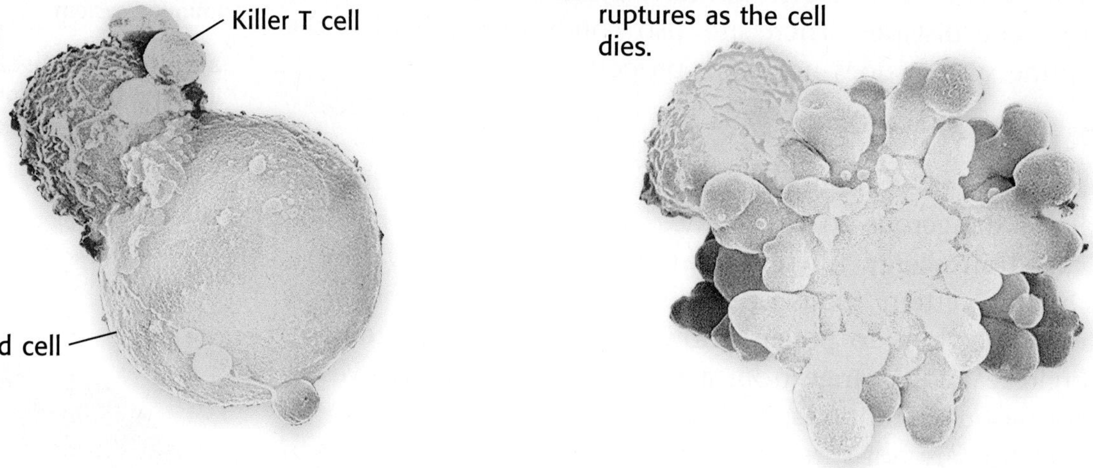

1 A killer T cell attacks an unregulated cell.
Killer T cell
Unregulated cell
2 The cell's membrane ruptures as the cell dies.

Cancer

cancer a disease in which the cells begin dividing at an uncontrolled rate and become invasive

Healthy cells divide at a carefully regulated rate. Occasionally, a cell doesn't respond to the body's regulation and begins dividing at an uncontrolled rate. As can be seen in **Figure 7,** killer T cells destroy this type of cell. Sometimes, the immune system cannot control the division of these cells. **Cancer** is the condition in which cells divide at an uncontrolled rate.

Many cancers will invade nearby tissues. They can also enter the cardiovascular system or lymphatic system. Cancers can then be transported to other places in the body. Cancers disrupt the normal activities of the organs they have invaded, sometimes leading to death. Today, though, there are many treatments for cancer. Surgery, radiation, and certain drugs can be used to remove or kill cancer cells or slow their division.

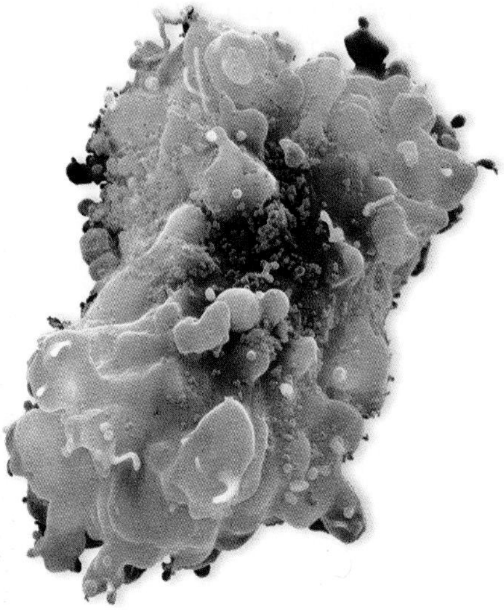

Figure 8 *The blue particles on this helper T cell are human immunodeficiency viruses. They replicated inside the T cell.*

AIDS

The human immunodeficiency virus (HIV) causes acquired immune deficiency syndrome (AIDS). Most viruses infect cells in the nose, mouth, lungs, or intestines, but HIV is different. HIV infects the immune system itself, using helper T cells as factories to produce more viruses. You can see HIV particles in **Figure 8.** The helper T cells are destroyed in the process. Remember that the helper T cells put the B cells and killer T cells to work.

People with AIDS have very few helper T cells, so nothing activates the B cells and killer T cells. Therefore, the immune system cannot attack HIV or any other pathogen. People with AIDS don't usually die of AIDS itself. They die of other diseases that they are unable to fight off.

Reading Check What virus causes AIDS?

SECTION Review

Summary

- Macrophages engulf pathogens, display antigens on their surface, and activate helper T cells. The helper T cells put the killer T cells and B cells to work.
- Killer T cells kill infected cells. B cells make antibodies.
- Fever helps speed immune-cell growth and slow pathogen growth.
- Memory B cells remember how to make an antibody for a pathogen that the body has previously fought.
- An allergy is the overreaction of the immune system to a harmless antigen.
- Autoimmune diseases are responses in which the immune system attacks healthy tissue.
- Cancer cells are cells that undergo uncontrolled division.
- AIDS is a disease that results when the human immunodeficiency virus kills helper T cells.

Using Key Terms

For each pair of terms, explain how the meanings of the terms differ.

1. *B cell* and *T cell*
2. *autoimmune disease* and *allergy*

Understanding Key Ideas

3. Your body's first line of defense against pathogens includes
   a. skin.
   b. macrophages.
   c. T cells.
   d. B cells.
4. List three ways your body defends itself against pathogens.
5. Name three different cells in the immune system, and describe how they respond to pathogens.
6. Describe four challenges to the immune system.
7. What characterizes a cancer cell?

Critical Thinking

8. **Identifying Relationships** Can your body make antibodies for pathogens that you have never been in contact with? Why or why not?
9. **Applying Concepts** If you had chickenpox at age 7, what might prevent you from getting chickenpox again at age 8?

Interpreting Graphics

10. Look at the graph below. Over time, people with AIDS become very sick and are unable to fight off infection. Use the information in the graph below to explain why this occurs.

T Cell Count of a Person with AIDS

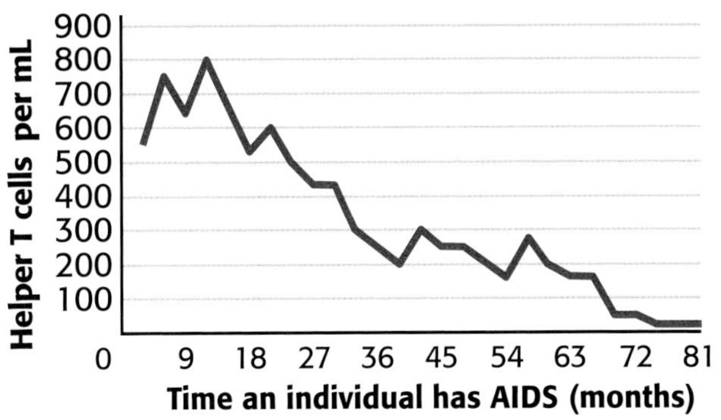

SCILINKS. NSTA Developed and maintained by the National Science Teachers Association

For a variety of links related to this chapter, go to www.scilinks.org

Topic: Body Defenses; Allergies
SciLinks code: HSM0181; HSM0048

Using Scientific Methods

Skills Practice Lab

Passing the Cold

OBJECTIVES

Investigate how diseases spread.

Analyze data about how diseases spread.

MATERIALS

- beaker or a cup, 200 mL
- eyedropper
- gloves, protective
- solution, unknown, 50 mL

SAFETY

There are more than 100 viruses that cause the symptoms of the common cold. Any of the viruses can be passed from person to person—through the air or through direct contact. In this activity, you will track the progress of an outbreak in your class.

Ask a Question

1. With other members of your group, form a question about the spread of disease. For example "How are cold viruses passed from person to person?" or "How can the progress of an outbreak be modeled?"

Form a Hypothesis

2. Form a hypothesis based on the question you asked.

Test the Hypothesis

3. Obtain an empty cup or beaker, an eyedropper, and 50 mL of one of the solutions from your teacher. Only one student will have the "cold virus" solution. You will see a change in your solution when you have become "infected."
4. Your teacher will divide the class into two equal groups. If there is an extra student, that person will record data on the board. Otherwise, the teacher will act as the recorder.
5. The two groups should form straight lines, facing each other.
6. Each time your teacher says the word *mix,* fill your eyedropper with your solution, and place 10 drops of your solution in the beaker of the person in the line opposite you without touching your eyedropper to the other liquid.
7. Gently stir the liquid in your cup with your eyedropper. Do not put your eyedropper in anyone else's solution.
8. If your solution changes color, raise your hand so that the recorder can record the number of students who have been "infected."
9. Your teacher will instruct one line to move one person to the right. Then, the person at the end of the line without a partner should go to the other end of the line.

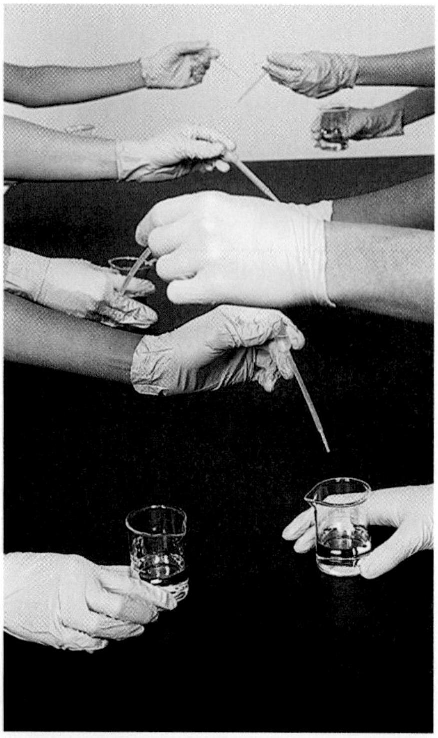

Results of Experiment			
Trial	Number of infected people	Total number of people	Percentage of infected people
1			
2			
3			
4			
5			
6			
7			
8			
9			
10			

10. Repeat steps 5–9 nine more times for a total of 10 trials.

11. Return to your desk, and create a data table in your notebook similar to the table above. The column with the title "Total number of people" will remain the same in every row. Enter the data from the board into your data table.

12. Find the percentage of infected people for the last column by dividing the number of infected people by the total number of people and multiplying by 100 in each line.

Analyze the Results

1. **Describing Events** Did you become infected? If so, during which trial did you become infected?

2. **Examining Data** Did everyone eventually become infected? If so, how many trials were necessary to infect everyone?

Draw Conclusions

3. **Interpreting Information** Explain at least one reason why this simulation may underestimate the number of people who might have been infected in real life.

4. **Applying Conclusions** Use your results to make a line graph showing the change in the infection percentage per trial.

Applying Your Data

Do research in the library or on the Internet to find out some of the factors that contribute to the spread of a cold virus. What is the best and easiest way to reduce your chances of catching a cold? Explain your answer.

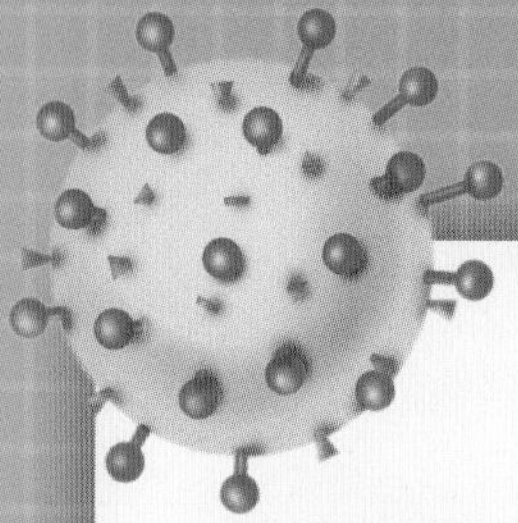

Chapter Review

USING KEY TERMS

Complete each of the following sentences by choosing the correct term from the word bank.

antibody	cancer
infectious disease	B cell
noninfectious disease	T cell
pathogen	allergy

1. A(n) ____ is caused by a pathogen.

2. Antibiotics can be used to kill a(n) ____.

3. Macrophages attract helper ____.

4. A(n) ____ binds to an antigen.

5. An immune-system overreaction to a harmless substance is a(n) ____.

6. ____ is the unregulated growth of cells.

UNDERSTANDING KEY IDEAS

Multiple Choice

7. Pathogens are
   - **a.** all viruses and microorganisms.
   - **b.** viruses and microorganisms that cause disease.
   - **c.** noninfectious organisms.
   - **d.** all bacteria that live in water.

8. Which of the following is an infectious disease?
   - **a.** allergies
   - **b.** rheumatoid arthritis
   - **c.** asthma
   - **d.** a common cold

9. The skin keeps pathogens out by
   - **a.** staying warm enough to kill pathogens.
   - **b.** releasing killer T cells onto the surface.
   - **c.** shedding dead cells and secreting oils.
   - **d.** All of the above

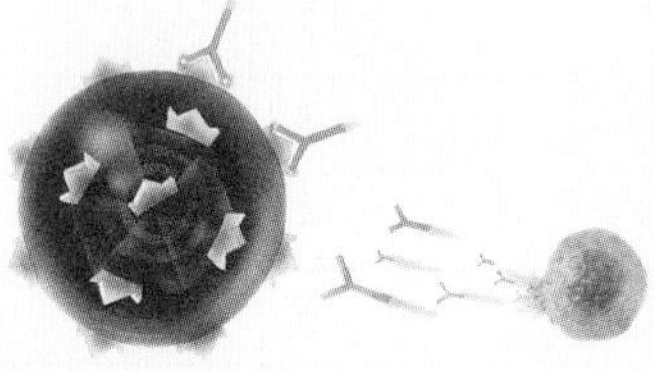

10. Memory B cells
    - **a.** kill pathogens.
    - **b.** activate killer T cells.
    - **c.** activate killer B cells.
    - **d.** produce B cells that make antibodies.

11. A fever
    - **a.** slows pathogen growth.
    - **b.** helps B cells multiply faster.
    - **c.** helps T cells multiply faster.
    - **d.** All of the above

12. Macrophages
    - **a.** make antibodies.
    - **b.** release helper T cells.
    - **c.** live in the gut.
    - **d.** engulf pathogens.

Short Answer

13. Explain how macrophages start an immune response.

14. Describe the role of helper T cells in responding to an infection.

15. Name two ways that you come into contact with pathogens.

CRITICAL THINKING

16 **Concept Mapping** Use the following terms to create a concept map: *macrophages, helper T cells, B cells, antibodies, antigens, killer T cells,* and *memory B cells.*

17 **Identifying Relationships** Why does the disappearance of helper T cells in AIDS patients damage the immune system?

18 **Predicting Consequences** Many people take fever-reducing drugs as soon as their temperature exceeds 37°C. Why might it not be a good idea to reduce a fever immediately with drugs?

19 **Evaluating Data** The risk of dying from a whooping cough vaccine is about one in 1 million. In contrast, the risk of dying from whooping cough is about one in 500. Discuss the pros and cons of this vaccination.

INTERPRETING GRAPHICS

The graph below compares the concentration of antibodies in the blood the first time you are exposed to a pathogen with the concentration of antibodies the next time you are exposed to the pathogen. Use the graph below to answer the questions that follow.

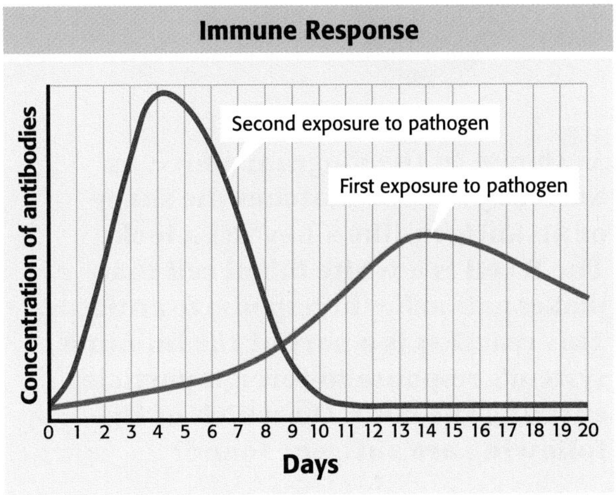

20 Are there more antibodies present during the first week of the first exposure or the first week of the second exposure? Why do you think this is so?

21 What is the difference in recovery time between the first exposure and second exposure? Why?

Standardized Test Preparation

Multiple Choice

Use the diagram below to answer question 1.

1. As shown in the diagram above, an antibody's shape matches the shape of an antigen like a key fits a lock. The B cell is a white blood cell that makes antibodies in response to antigens. This reaction is a part of the immune system's response to foreign particles entering the body. On which of the following are antigens found?

A. antibiotics

B. pathogens

C. plasma

D. platelets

2. Antibiotics are substances that kill or slow the growth of bacteria. They can also be used to treat some infections caused by fungi and other microorganisms. Why are antibiotics unable to cure diseases caused by viruses?

A. because viruses cannot reproduce on their own

B. because virus infection spreads in the body too quickly

C. because viruses are too infectious to be treated by antibiotics

D. because viruses are not alive and antibiotics only kill living things

3. During the late 1700s, a scientist named Edward Jenner observed that people who had been infected by cowpox seemed to have resistance to smallpox. This ability to resist a disease is called immunity. Jenner's work led to the creation of substances that help people develop immunity to diseases. What are these substances called?

A. T cells

B. vaccines

C. antibiotics

D. antibodies

4. Which of the following is a pathway for infectious diseases?

A. exposure to rain

B. exposure to other people

C. exposure to cold weather

D. exposure to cigarette smoke

Use the diagram below to answer question 5.

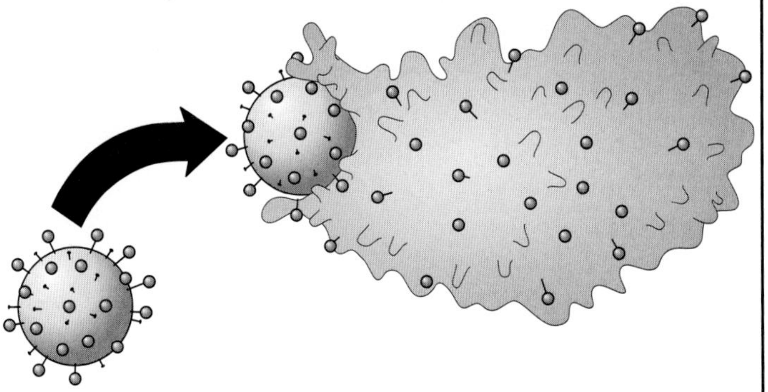

5. The illustration above shows one way the body's immune system can respond to a virus. The sphere on the left represents a virus. What is happening to the right of the arrow?

A. A virus is infecting a T cell.

B. A virus is infecting a B cell.

C. A macrophage is engulfing a virus.

D. A platelet is absorbing a virus.

6. A scientist at the Centers for Disease Control and Prevention in Atlanta collects experimental data on bacteria that live inside a freezer. Knowing that the freezer's temperature is -5°C, what can be inferred about the bacteria?

A. The bacteria entered the freezer through the water line in the icemaker.

B. The bacteria would multiply quickly if they were moved to a hot environment.

C. Some bacteria can live at temperatures below the freezing point of water.

D. Frozen foods contained in the freezer are not exposed to bacteria.

7. Viruses need the cells of living organisms to thrive and replicate. When viruses infect cells in a human body, the immune system responds by destroying the infected cells. Which of the following describes the sequence of events that leads to the destruction of infected cells?

A. Killer B cells kill infected T cells; helper T cells activate B cells, which divide and produce antibodies that bind viruses.

B. Killer T cells kill infected cells; helper T cells activate B cells, which divide and produce antibodies that bind viruses.

C. Helper T cells kill infected cells; killer T cells activate B cells, which divide and produce antibiotics that bind viruses.

D. Helper B cells kill infected T cells; killer T cells activate B cells, which divide and produce antibiotics that bind viruses.

Open Response

8. Living things are made up of one or more cells, have DNA, reproduce themselves, grow and develop, can sense and respond to stimuli, and use energy. Should a virus be considered a living thing or not? Explain your answer.

9. Describe the systems that form the body's first line of defense against pathogens.

Science in Action

Weird Science

Frogs in the Medicine Cabinet?

Frog skin, mouse intestines, cow lungs, and shark stomachs are all being tested to make more effective medicines to combat harmful bacteria. In 1896, a biologist named Michael Zasloff was studying African clawed frogs. He noticed that cuts in the frogs' skin healed quickly and never became infected. Zasloff decided to investigate further. He found that when a frog was cut, its skin released a liquid antibiotic that killed invading bacteria. Furthermore, sand sharks, moths, pigs, mice, and cows also contain chemicals that kill bacteria and other microorganisms. These useful antibiotics are even found in the small intestines of humans!

Social Studies ACTIVITY

Many medicines were discovered in plants or animals by people living near those plants or animals. Research the origin of one or two common medicines discovered this way. Make a poster showing a world map and the location of the medicines that you researched.

Scientific Discoveries

Medicine for Peanut Allergies

Scientists estimate that 1.5 million people in the United States suffer from peanut allergies. Every year 50 to 100 people in the United States die from an allergic reaction to peanuts. Peanuts and peanut oil are used to make many foods. People who have a peanut allergy sometimes mistakenly eat these foods and suffer severe reactions. A new drug has been discovered to help people control severe reactions. The drug is called TNX-901. The drug is actually an antibody that binds to the antibodies that the body makes during the allergic reaction to the peanuts. By binding these antibodies, the drug controls the allergic response.

Math ACTIVITY

During the testing of the new drug, 84 people were given four injections over the course of 4 months. One-fourth of the people participating received injections of a control that had no medicine in it. The rest of the people participating received different doses of the drug. How many people received the control? How many people received medicine? How many shots containing medicine were administered during the 4-month test?

Careers

Terrel Shepherd III

Nurse Terrel Shepherd III is a registered nurse (RN) at Texas Children's Hospital in Houston, Texas. RNs have many responsibilities. These responsibilities include giving patients their medications, assessing patients' health, and establishing intravenous access. Nurses also serve as a go-between for the patient and the doctor. Although most nurses work in hospitals or clinics, some nurses work for corporations. Pediatric nurses such as Shepherd work specifically with infants, children, and adolescents. The field of nursing offers a wide variety of job opportunities including home-care nurses, traveling nurses, and flight nurses. The hospital alone has many areas of expertise for nurses, including geriatrics (working with the elderly), intensive care, administration, and surgery. Traditionally, nursing has been considered to be a woman's career. However, since nursing began as a profession, men and women have practiced nursing. A career in nursing is possible for anyone who does well in science, enjoys people, and wants to make a difference in people's lives.

Language Arts Activity

WRITING SKILL Create a brochure that persuades people to consider a career in nursing. Describe nursing as a career, the benefits of becoming a nurse, and the education needed to be a nurse. Illustrate the brochure with pictures of nurses from the Internet or from magazines.

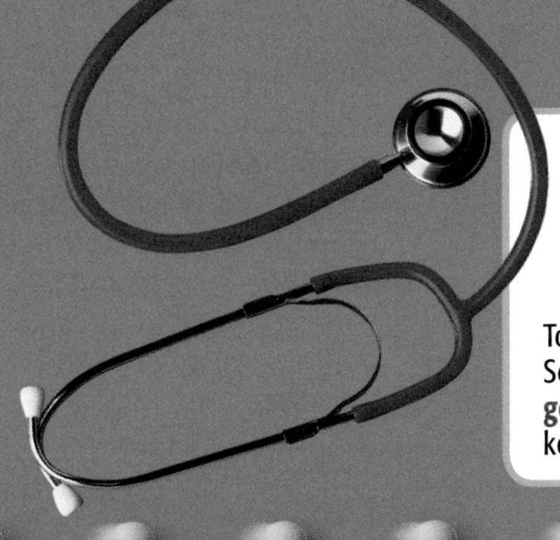

go.hrw.com

To learn more about these Science in Action topics, visit **go.hrw.com** and type in the keyword **HL5BD6F.**

Current Science

Check out Current Science® articles related to this chapter by visiting go.hrw.com. Just type in the keyword HL5CS27.

23

Staying Healthy

The Big Idea

A balanced and nutritious diet, exercise, and good habits are important parts of living a healthy life.

SECTION

About the Photo

What do you see in this photo? Sure, you can see five students facing the camera, but what else does the picture tell you? The bright eyes, happy smiles, and shiny hair show radiant health. Having a clear mind and a long, active life depend on having a healthy body. Keeping your body healthy depends on eating well; avoiding drugs, cigarettes, and alcohol; and staying safe.

PRE-READING ACTIVITY

FOLDNOTES **Booklet** Before you read the chapter, create the FoldNote entitled "Booklet" described in the **Study Skills** section of the Appendix. Label each page of the booklet with a main idea from the chapter. As you read the chapter, write what you learn about each main idea on the appropriate page of the booklet.

START-UP ACTIVITY

Conduct a Survey

How healthy are the habits of your classmates? Find out for yourself.

Procedure

1. Copy and answer yes or no to each of the five questions at right. Do not put your name on the survey.

Analysis

1. As a class, record the data from the completed surveys in a chart. For each question, calculate the percentage of your class that answered yes.
2. What good and bad habits do your classmates have?

1. Do you exercise at least three times a week?
2. Do you wear a seat belt every time you ride in a car?
3. Do you eat five or more servings of fruits and vegetables every day?
4. Do you use sunscreen to protect your skin when you are outdoors?
5. Do you eat a lot of high-fat foods?

Nutrition Facts

Serving Size 1/2 cup (120 ml)
Servings per Container 2.5

Amount per Serving	**Prepared**
Calories	70
Calories from Fat	25
	% Daily Value
Total Fat 2.5 g	4%
Saturated Fat 1 g	5%
Trans Fat 0 g	
Cholesterol 15 mg	5%
Sodium 960 mg	40%
Total Carbohydrate 8 g	3%
Dietary Fiber less than 1 g	4%
Sugars 1 g	
Protein 3 g	
Vitamin A	15%
Vitamin C	0%
Calcium	0%
Iron	4%

*Percent Daily Values are based on a 2,000 Calorie diet. Your daily values may be higher or lower depending on your Calorie needs:

	Calories	2,000	2,500
Total Fat	Less than	65g	80g
Sat Fat	Less than	20g	25g
Cholesterol	Less than	300mg	300mg
Sodium	Less than	2,400mg	2,400mg
Total Carbohydrate		300g	375g
Dietary Fiber		25g	30g
Protein		50g	60g

Figure 5 *Nutrition Facts labels provide a lot of information.*

Reading Food Labels

Packaged foods must have Nutrition Facts labels. **Figure 5** shows a Nutrition Facts label for chicken noodle soup. Nutrition Facts labels show what amount of each nutrient is in one serving of the food. You can tell whether a food is high or low in a nutrient by looking at its daily value. Reading food labels can help you make healthy eating choices. The percentage of daily values shown is based on a diet that consists of 2,000 Cal per day. Most teenagers need more than 2,000 Cal per day. The number of Calories needed depends on factors such as height, weight, age, and level of activity. Playing sports and exercising use up Calories that need to be replaced for you to grow.

Reading Check **For what nutrients does chicken noodle soup provide more than 10% of the daily value?**

Nutritional Disorders

Unhealthy eating habits can cause nutritional disorders. **Malnutrition** occurs when someone does not eat enough of the nutrients needed by the body. Malnutrition can result from eating too few or too many Calories or not taking in enough of the right nutrients. Malnutrition affects how one looks and how quickly one's body can repair damage and fight illness.

malnutrition a disorder of nutrition that results when a person does not consume enough of each of the nutrients that are needed by the human body

Anorexia Nervosa and Bulimia Nervosa

Anorexia nervosa (AN uh REKS ee uh nuhr VOH suh) is an eating disorder characterized by self-starvation and an intense fear of gaining weight. Anorexia nervosa can lead to severe malnutrition.

Bulimia nervosa (boo LEE mee uh nuhr VOH suh) is a disorder characterized by binge eating followed by induced vomiting. Sometimes, people suffering from bulimia nervosa use laxatives or diuretics to rid their bodies of food and water. Bulimia nervosa can damage teeth and the digestive system and can lead to kidney and heart failure.

Both anorexia and bulimia can cause weak bones, low blood pressure, and heart problems. These eating disorders can be fatal if not treated. If you are worried that you or someone you know may have an eating disorder, talk to an adult.

Math Practice

What Percentage?

Use the Nutrition Facts label above to answer the following question. The recommended daily value of fat is 72 g for teenage girls and 90 g for teenage boys. What percentage of the daily recommended fat value is provided in one cup of soup?

Obesity

Eating too much food that is high in fat and low in other nutrients, such as junk food and fast food, can lead to malnutrition. *Obesity* (oh BEE suh tee) is having an extremely high percentage of body fat. People suffering from obesity may not be eating a variety of foods that provide them with the correct balance of essential nutrients. Having an inactive lifestyle can also contribute to obesity.

Obesity increases the risk of high blood pressure, heart disease, and diabetes. Eating a more balanced diet and exercising regularly can help reduce obesity. Obesity may also be caused by other factors. Scientists are studying the links between obesity and heredity.

SECTION Review

Summary

- A healthy diet has a balance of carbohydrates, proteins, fats, water, vitamins, and minerals.
- MyPyramid is a good guide for healthy eating.
- Nutrition Facts labels provide information needed to plan a healthy diet.
- Anorexia nervosa and bulimia nervosa cause malnutrition and damage to many body systems.
- Obesity can lead to heart disease and diabetes.

Using Key Terms

1. In your own words, write a definition for each of the following terms: *nutrient, mineral,* and *vitamin.*

Understanding Key Ideas

2. Malnutrition can be caused by
   a. obesity.
   b. bulimia nervosa.
   c. anorexia nervosa.
   d. All of the above
3. What information is found on a Nutrition Facts label?
4. Give an example of a carbohydrate, a protein, and a fat.
5. If vitamins and minerals do not supply energy, why are they important to a healthy diet?
6. How do anorexia nervosa and bulimia nervosa differ?
7. How can someone who is obese suffer from malnutrition?

Math Skills

8. If you eat 2,500 Cal per day and 20% are from fat, 30% are from protein, and 50% are from carbohydrates, how many Calories of each nutrient do you eat?

Critical Thinking

9. **Applying Concepts** Name some of the nutrients that can be found in a glass of milk.
10. **Identifying Relationships** Explain how eating a variety of foods can help ensure good nutrition.
11. **Predicting Consequences** How would your growth be affected if your diet consistently lacked important nutrients?
12. **Applying Concepts** Explain how you can use the Nutrition Facts label to choose food that is high in calcium.

SCILINKS. NSTA Developed and maintained by the National Science Teachers Association

For a variety of links related to this chapter, go to www.scilinks.org

Topic: Food Pyramids; Nutritional Disorders
SciLinks code: HSM0598; HSM1057

SECTION 2

Risks of Alcohol and Other Drugs

What You Will Learn

- Describe the difference between psychological and physical dependence.
- Explain the hazards of tobacco, alcohol, and illegal drugs.
- Distinguish between the positive and negative uses of drugs.

Vocabulary

drug
addiction
nicotine
alcoholism
narcotic

READING STRATEGY

Reading Organizer As you read this section, make a table comparing the positive and negative uses of drugs.

You see them in movies and on television and read about them in magazines. But what are drugs?

You are exposed to information, and misinformation, about drugs every day. So, how can you make the best decisions?

What Is a Drug?

Any chemical substance that causes a physical or psychological change is called a **drug.** Drugs come in many forms, as shown in **Figure 1.** Some drugs enter the body through the skin. Other drugs are swallowed, inhaled, or injected. Drugs are classified by their effects. *Analgesics* (AN'l JEE ziks) relieve pain. *Antibiotics* (AN tie bie AHT iks) fight bacterial infections, and *antihistamines* (AN tie HIS tuh MEENZ) control cold and allergy symptoms. *Stimulants* speed up the central nervous system, and *depressants* slow it down. When used correctly, legal drugs can help your body heal. When used illegally or improperly, however, drugs can do great harm.

Dependence and Addiction

The body can develop *tolerance* to a drug. Tolerance means that larger and larger doses of the drug are needed to get the same effect. The body can also form a *physical dependence* or need for a drug. If the body doesn't receive a drug that it is physically dependent on, withdrawal symptoms occur. Withdrawal symptoms include nausea, vomiting, pain, and tremors.

Addiction is the loss of control of drug-taking behavior. Once addicted, a person finds it very hard to stop taking a drug. Sometimes, the need for a drug is not due only to physical dependence. Some people also form *psychological dependence* on a drug, which means that they feel powerful cravings for the drug.

Figure 1 *All of these products contain drugs.*

Types of Drugs

There are many kinds of drugs. Some drugs are made from plants, and some are made in a lab. You can buy some drugs at the grocery store, while others can be prescribed only by a doctor. Some drugs are illegal to buy, sell, or possess.

drug any substance that causes a change in a person's physical or psychological state

addiction a dependence on a substance, such as alcohol or another drug

Herbal Medicines

Information about herbal medicines has been handed down for centuries, and some herbs contain chemicals with important healing properties. The tea in **Figure 2** contains chamomile and is made from a plant. Chamomile has chemicals in it that can help you sleep. However, herbs are drugs and should be used carefully. The Federal Drug Administration does not regulate herbal medicines or teas and cannot guarantee their safety.

Figure 2 *Some herbs can be purchased in health-food stores. Medicinal herbs should always be used with care.*

Over-the-Counter and Prescription Drugs

Over-the-counter drugs can be bought without a prescription. A prescription is written by a doctor and describes the drug, directions for use, and the amount of the drug to be taken.

Many over-the-counter and prescription drugs are powerful healing agents. However, some drugs also produce unwanted side effects. *Side effects* are uncomfortable symptoms, such as nausea, headaches, drowsiness, or more serious problems.

Whether purchased with or without a prescription, all drugs must be used with care. Information on proper use can be found on the label. **Figure 3** shows some general drug safety tips.

Reading Check **What is the difference between an over-the-counter drug and a prescription drug?** (*See the Appendix for answers to Reading Checks.*)

Figure 3 **Drug Safety Tips**

- Never take another person's prescription medicine.
- Read the label before each use. Always follow the instructions on the label and those provided by your doctor or pharmacist.
- Do not take more or less medication than prescribed.
- Consult a doctor if you have any side effects.
- Throw away leftover and out-of-date medicines.

Figure 4 **Effects of Smoking**

▼ Healthy lung tissue of a nonsmoker

▼ Damaged lung tissue of a smoker

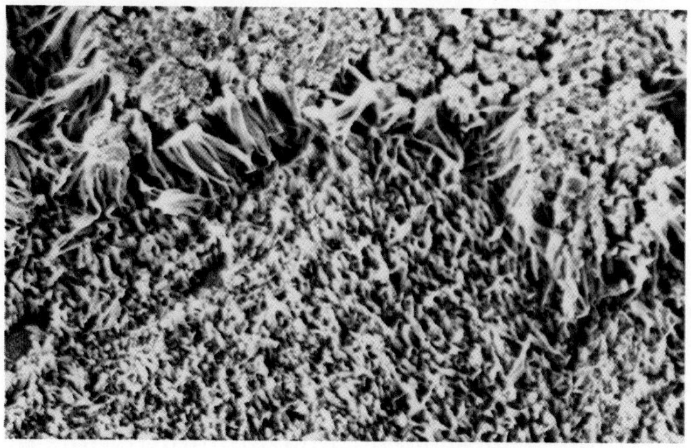

nicotine a toxic, addictive chemical that is found in tobacco and that is one of the major contributors to the harmful effects of smoking

alcoholism a disorder in which a person repeatedly drinks alcoholic beverages in an amount that interferes with the person's health and activities

Tobacco

Cigarettes are addictive, and smoking has serious health effects. **Nicotine** (NIK uh TEEN) is a chemical in tobacco that increases heart rate and blood pressure and is extremely addictive. Smokers experience a decrease in physical endurance. **Figure 4** shows the effects of smoking on the cilia of your lungs. Cilia clean the air you breathe and prevent debris from entering your lungs. Smoking increases the chances of lung cancer, and it has been linked to other cancers, emphysema, chronic bronchitis, and heart disease. Experts estimate that there are more than 430,000 deaths related to smoking each year in the United States. Secondhand smoke also poses significant health risks.

Like cigarettes, smokeless, or chewing, tobacco is addictive and can cause health problems. Nicotine is absorbed through the lining of the mouth. Smokeless tobacco increases the risk of several cancers, including mouth and throat cancer. It also causes gum disease and yellowing of the teeth.

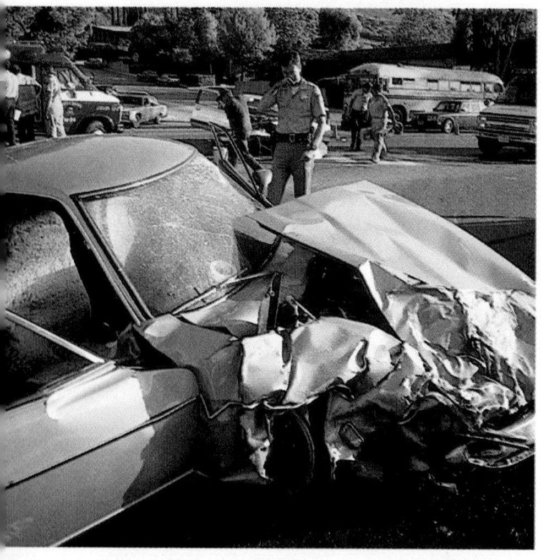

Figure 5 *This car was in an accident involving a drunk driver.*

Alcohol

It is illegal in most of the United States for people under the age of 21 to use alcohol. Alcohol slows down the central nervous system and can cause memory loss. Excessive use of alcohol can damage the liver, pancreas, brain, nerves, and cardiovascular system. In very large quantities, alcohol can cause death. Alcohol is a factor in more than half of all suicides, murders, and accidental deaths. **Figure 5** shows the results of one alcohol-related accident. Alcohol also affects decision making and can lead you to take unhealthy risks.

People can suffer from **alcoholism,** which means that they are physically and psychologically dependent on alcohol. Alcoholism is considered a disease, and genetic factors are thought to influence the development of alcoholism in some people.

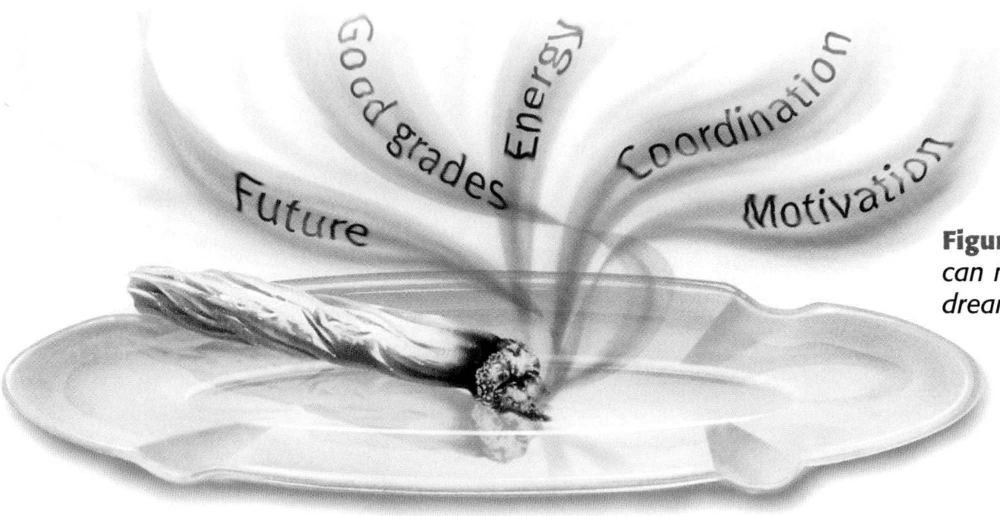

Figure 6 *Smoking marijuana can make your health and dreams go up in smoke.*

Marijuana

Marijuana is an illegal drug that comes from the Indian hemp plant. Marijuana affects different people in different ways. It may increase anxiety or cause feelings of paranoia. Marijuana slows reaction time, impairs thinking, and causes a loss of coordination. Regular use of marijuana can affect many areas of your life, as described in **Figure 6.**

narcotic a drug that is derived from opium and that relieves pain and induces sleep

Cocaine

Cocaine and its more purified form, crack, are made from the coca plant. Both drugs are illegal and highly addictive. Users can become addicted to them in a very short time. Cocaine can produce feelings of intense excitement followed by anxiety and depression. Both drugs increase heart rate and blood pressure and can cause heart attacks, even among first-time users.

Reading Check What are two dangers to users of cocaine?

Narcotics and Designer Drugs

Drugs made from the opium plant are called **narcotics.** Some narcotics are used to treat severe pain. Narcotics are illegal unless prescribed by a doctor. Some narcotics are never legal. For example, heroin is one of the most addictive narcotics and is always illegal. Heroin is usually injected, and users often share needles. Therefore, heroin users have a high risk of becoming infected with diseases such as hepatitis and AIDS. Heroin users can also die of an overdose of the drug.

Other illegal drugs include inhalants, barbiturates (bahr BICH uhr itz), amphetamines (am FET uh MEENZ), and *designer drugs*. Designer drugs are made by making small changes to existing drugs. Ecstasy, or "X," is a designer drug that causes feelings of well-being. Over time, the drug causes lesions (LEE zhuhnz), or holes, in a user's brain, as shown in **Figure 7.** Ecstasy users are also more likely to develop depression.

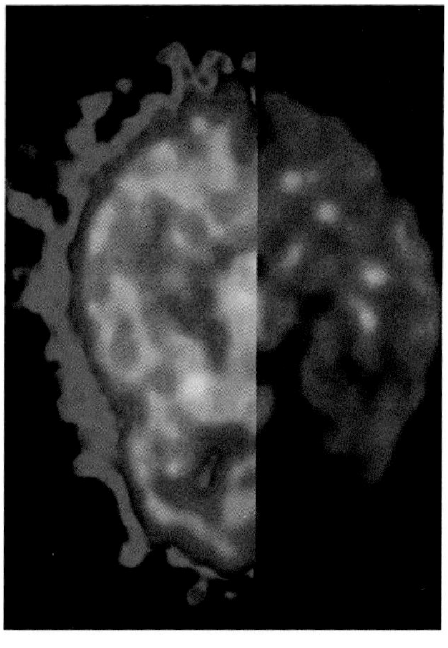

Figure 7 *The brain scan on the left shows a healthy brain. The scan on the right is from a teenager who has regularly used Ecstasy.*

Figure 8 *Drug abuse can leave you depressed and feeling alone.*

Hallucinogens

Hallucinogens (huh LOO si nuh juhnz) distort the senses and cause mood changes. Users have hallucinations, which means that they see and hear things that are not real. LSD and PCP are powerful, illegal hallucinogens. Sniffing glue or solvents can also cause hallucinations and serious brain damage.

Drug Abuse

A drug user takes a drug to prevent or improve a medical condition. The drug user obtains the drug legally and uses the drug properly. A drug abuser does not take a drug to relieve a medical condition. An abuser may take drugs for the temporary good feelings they produce, to escape from problems, or to belong to a group. The drug is often obtained illegally, and it is often taken without knowledge of the drug's dangers.

Reading Check **What is the difference between drug use and drug abuse?**

How Drug Abuse Starts

Nicotine, alcohol, and marijuana are sometimes called *gateway drugs* because they are often the first drugs a person abuses. The abuse of other, more dangerous drugs may follow the abuse of gateway drugs. Peer pressure is often the reason that young people begin to use drugs. Teenagers may drink, smoke, or try marijuana to make friends or avoid being teased. Because drug abusers often stand out, it can sometimes be hard to see that many teenagers do not abuse drugs.

Many teenagers begin using illegal drugs to feel part of a group, but drug abuse has many serious consequences. Drug abuse can lead to problems with friends, family, school, and handling money. These problems often lead to depression and social isolation, as shown in **Figure 8.**

Many people who start using drugs do not recognize the dangers. Misinformation about drugs is everywhere. Several common drug myths are discussed in **Figure 9.**

Figure 9 Drug Myths

Myth ***"It's only alcohol, not drugs."***

Reality Alcohol is a mood-altering and mind-altering drug. It affects the central nervous system and is addictive.

Myth ***"I won't get hooked on one or two cigarettes a day."***

Reality Addiction is not related to the amount of a drug used. Some people become addicted after using a drug once or twice.

Myth ***"I can quit any time I want."***

Reality Addicts may quit and return to drug usage many times. Their inability to stay drug-free shows how powerful the addiction is.

SCHOOL to HOME

Good Reasons

WRITING SKILL Discuss with your parent the possible effects of drug abuse on your family. Then, write yourself a letter giving reasons why you should stay drug-free. Put your letter in a safe place. If you ever find yourself thinking about using drugs, take out your letter and read it.

ACTIVITY

Getting Off Drugs

People who abuse drugs undergo emotional and physical changes. Teenagers who had few problems often begin to have problems with school, family, and money when they start to use drugs.

The first step to quitting drugs is to admit to abusing drugs and to decide to stop. It is important for the addicted person to get the proper medical treatment. There are drug treatment centers, like the one shown in **Figure 10,** available to help. Getting off drugs can be extremely difficult. Withdrawal symptoms are often painful, and powerful cravings for a drug can continue long after a person quits. But people who stop abusing drugs lead happier and healthier lives.

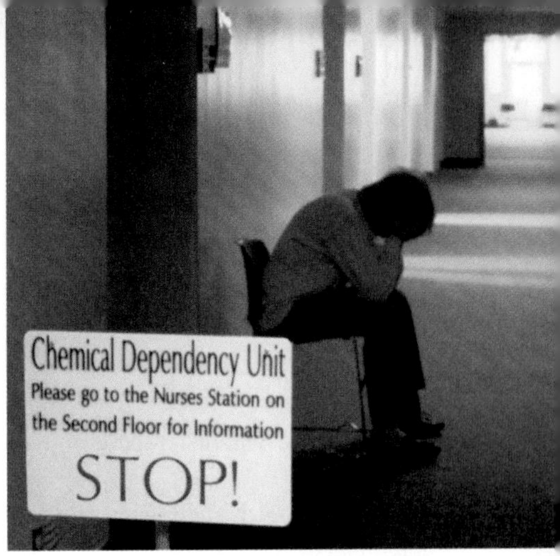

Figure 10 *Drug treatment centers help people get off drugs and back on track to healthier, happier lives.*

SECTION Review

Summary

- Physical dependence causes withdrawal symptoms when a person stops using a drug. Psychological dependence causes powerful cravings.
- There are many types of drugs, including over-the-counter, prescription, and herbal medicines.
- Tobacco contains the highly addictive chemical nicotine.
- Abuse of alcohol can lead to alcoholism.
- Illegal drugs include marijuana, cocaine, hallucinogens, designer drugs, and many narcotics.
- Getting off drugs requires proper medical treatment.

Using Key Terms

1. In your own words, write a definition for the terms *drug, addiction,* and *narcotic.*

Understanding Key Ideas

2. Which of the following products does NOT contain a drug?
   - **a.** cola
   - **b.** fruit juice
   - **c.** herbal tea
   - **d.** cough syrup
3. Describe the difference between physical and psychological dependence.
4. What is the difference between drug use and drug abuse?
5. How does addiction occur, and what are two consequences of drug addiction?
6. Name two different kinds of illegal drugs, and give examples of each.

Math Skills

7. If 2,200 people between the ages of 16 and 20 die every year in alcohol-related car crashes, how many die every day?

Critical Thinking

8. **Analyzing Relationships** How are nicotine, alcohol, heroin, and cocaine similar? How are they different?
9. **Analyzing Ideas** What are two ways that a person who abuses drugs can get in trouble with the law?
10. **Predicting Consequences** How can drug abuse damage family relationships?
11. **Making Inferences** Driving a car while under the influence of drugs can put others in danger. Describe another situation in which one person's drug abuse could put other people in danger.

SCI LINKS. NSTA
Developed and maintained by the National Science Teachers Association

For a variety of links related to this chapter, go to www.scilinks.org

Topic: Drug and Alcohol Abuse
SciLinks code: HSM0428

SECTION 3

Healthy Habits

Do you like playing sports or acting in plays? How does your health affect your favorite activities?

Whatever you do, the better your health is, the better you can perform. Keeping yourself healthy is a daily responsibility.

What You Will Learn

- Describe three important aspects of good hygiene.
- Explain why exercise and sleep are important to good health.
- Describe methods of handling stress.
- List three ways to stay safe at home, on the road, and outdoors.
- Plan what you would do in the case of an accident.

Vocabulary

hygiene
aerobic exercise
stress

READING STRATEGY

Prediction Guide Before reading this section, write the title of each heading in this section. Next, under each heading, write what you think you will learn.

Taking Care of Your Body

The science of preserving and protecting your health is known as **hygiene.** It sounds simple, but washing your hands is the best way to prevent the spread of disease and infection. You should always wash your hands after using the bathroom and before and after handling food. Taking care of your skin, hair, and teeth is important for good hygiene. Good hygiene includes regularly using sunscreen, shampooing your hair, and brushing and flossing your teeth daily.

hygiene the science of health and ways to preserve health

Good Posture

Posture is also important to health. Good posture helps you look and feel your best. Bad posture strains your muscles and ligaments and makes breathing difficult. To have good posture, imagine a vertical line passing through your ear, shoulder, hip, knee, and ankle when you stand, as shown in **Figure 1.** When working at a desk, you should maintain good posture by pulling your chair forward and planting your feet firmly on the floor.

When you have good posture, your ear, shoulder, hip, knee, and ankle are in a straight line.

Bad posture strains your muscles and ligaments and can make breathing difficult.

Figure 1 *A slumped posture strains your lower back.*

Exercise

Aerobic exercise at least three times a week is essential to good health. **Aerobic exercise** is vigorous, constant exercise of the whole body for 20 minutes or more. Walking, running, swimming, and biking are all examples of aerobic exercise. **Figure 2** shows another popular aerobic exercise—basketball.

Aerobic exercise increases the heart rate. As a result, more oxygen is taken in and distributed throughout the body. Over time, aerobic exercise strengthens the heart, lungs, and bones. It burns Calories, helps your body conserve some nutrients, and aids digestion. It also gives you more energy and stamina. Aerobic exercise protects your physical and mental health.

Figure 2 *Aerobic exercise can be fun if you choose an activity you enjoy.*

Reading Check **What are two benefits of regular exercise?** *(See the Appendix for answers to Reading Checks.)*

Sleep

Believe it or not, teenagers actually need more sleep than younger children. Do you ever fall asleep in class, like the girl in **Figure 3,** or feel tired in the middle of the afternoon? If so, you may not be getting enough sleep. Scientists say that teenagers need about 9.5 hours of sleep each night.

At night, the body goes through several cycles of progressively deeper sleep, with periods of lighter sleep in between. If you do not sleep long enough, you will not enter the deepest, most restful period of sleep.

aerobic exercise physical exercise intended to increase the activity of the heart and lungs to promote the body's use of oxygen

Figure 3 *If you fall asleep easily during the day, you are probably not getting enough sleep.*

CONNECTION TO Language Arts

Dreamy Poetry

You are not wrong, who deem
That my days have been a dream;
Yet if hope has flown away
In a night, or in a day,
In a vision, or in none,
Is it therefore the less gone?
All that we see or seem
Is but a dream within a dream.

(Edgar Allan Poe,
"A Dream Within a Dream")

What do you think Poe means by "a dream within a dream?" Why do you think there are many poems written about dreams or sleep?

Coping with Stress

Figure 4 *Can you identify all of the things in this picture that could cause stress?*

You have a big soccer game tomorrow. Are you excited and ready for action? You got a low grade on your English paper. Are you upset or angry? The game and the test are causing you stress. **Stress** is the physical and mental response to pressure.

Some stress is a normal part of life. Stress stimulates your body to prepare for difficult or dangerous situations. However, sometimes you may have no outlet for the stress, and it builds up. Many things are causing stress for the girl shown in **Figure 4.** Excess stress is harmful to your health and can decrease your ability to carry out your daily activities.

You may not even realize you are stressed until your body reacts. Perhaps you get a headache, have an upset stomach, or lie awake at night. You might feel tired all the time or begin an old nervous habit, such as nail-biting. You may become irritable or resentful. All of these things can be signs of too much stress.

Dealing with Stress

stress a physical or mental response to pressure

Different people are stressed by different things. Once you identify the source of the stress, you can find ways to deal with it. If you cannot remove the cause of stress, here are some ideas for handling stress.

- Share your problems. Talk things over with someone you trust, such as a parent, friend, teacher, or school counselor.
- Make a list of all the things you would like to get done, and rank the things in order of importance. Do the most important things first.
- Exercise regularly, and get enough sleep.
- Pet a friendly animal.
- Spend some quiet time alone, or practice deep breathing or other relaxation techniques.

INTERNET ACTIVITY

For another activity related to this chapter, go to **go.hrw.com** and type in the keyword **HL5BD7W.**

Injury Prevention

Have you ever fallen off your bike or sprained your ankle? Accidents happen, and they can cause injury and even death. It is impossible to prevent all accidents, but you can decrease your risk by using your common sense and following basic safety rules.

Safety Outdoors

Always dress appropriately for the weather and for the activity. Never hike or camp alone. Tell someone where you are going and when you expect to return. If you do not bring water from home, be sure to purify any water you drink in the wilderness.

Learn how to swim. It could save your life! Never swim alone, and do not dive into shallow water or water of unknown depth. When in a boat, wear a life jacket. If a storm threatens, get out of the water and seek shelter.

Reading Check Name three safety tips for the outdoors.

Safety at Home

Many accidents can be avoided. **Figure 5** shows tips for safety around the house.

Figure 5 Home Safety Tips

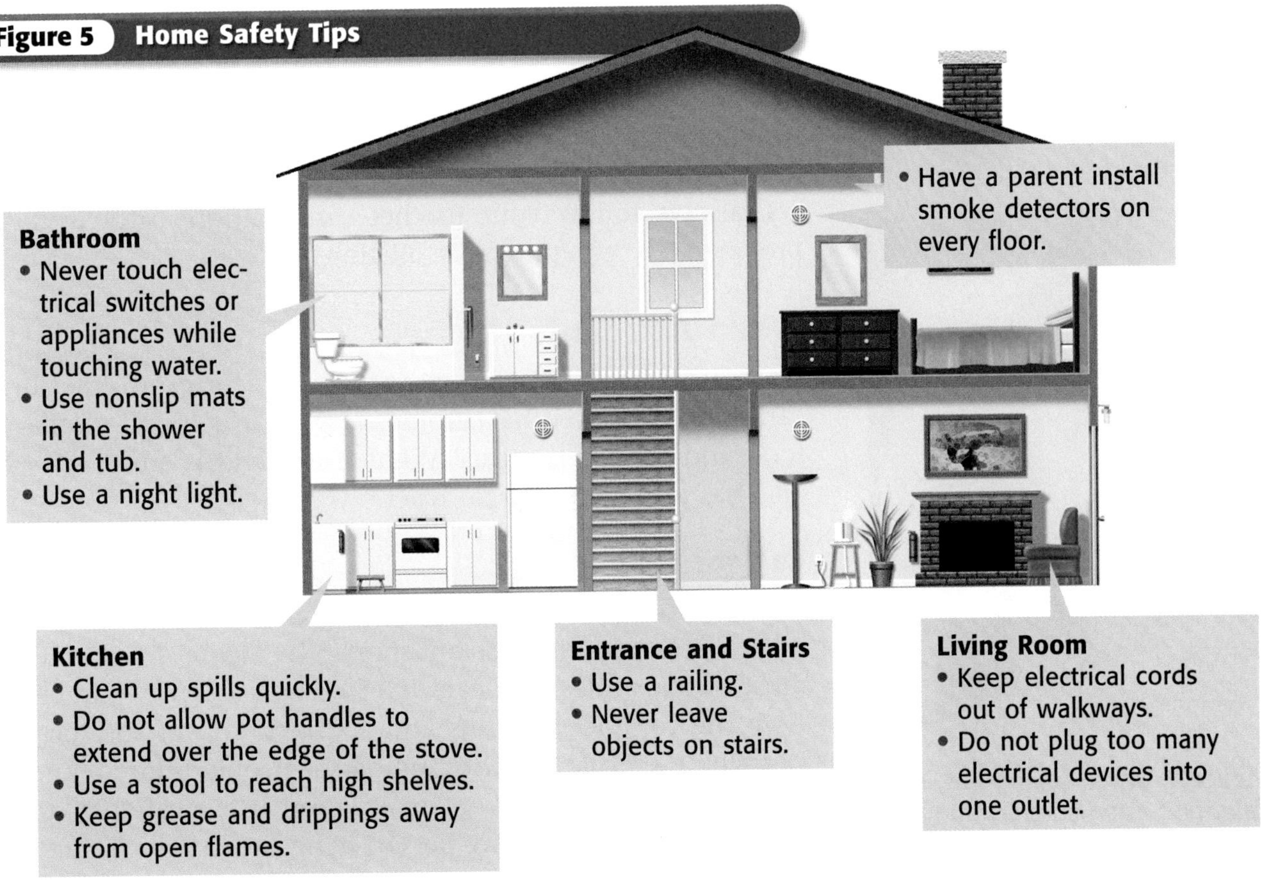

• Have a parent install smoke detectors on every floor.
Bathroom
• Never touch electrical switches or appliances while touching water.
• Use nonslip mats in the shower and tub.
• Use a night light.
Kitchen
• Clean up spills quickly.
• Do not allow pot handles to extend over the edge of the stove.
• Use a stool to reach high shelves.
• Keep grease and drippings away from open flames.
Entrance and Stairs
• Use a railing.
• Never leave objects on stairs.
Living Room
• Keep electrical cords out of walkways.
• Do not plug too many electrical devices into one outlet.

Figure 6 *It is always important to use the appropriate safety equipment.*

Safety on the Road

In the car, always wear a seat belt, even if you are traveling only a short distance. Never ride in a car with someone who has been drinking. Safety equipment and common sense are your best defense against injury. When riding a bicycle, always wear a helmet like those shown in **Figure 6.** Ride with traffic, and obey all traffic rules. Be sure to signal when stopping or turning.

Safety in Class

Accidents can happen in school, especially in a lab class or during woodworking class. To avoid hurting yourself and others, always follow your teacher's instructions, and wear the proper safety equipment at all times.

Figure 7 *When calling 911, stay calm and listen carefully to what the dispatcher tells you.*

When Accidents Happen

No matter how well you practice safety measures, accidents can still happen. What should you do if a friend chokes on food and cannot breathe? What if a friend is stung by a bee and has a violent allergic reaction?

Call for Help

Once you've checked for other dangers, call for medical help immediately, as the person shown in **Figure 7** is doing. In most communities, you can dial 911. Speak slowly and clearly. Give the complete address and a description of the location. Describe the accident, the number of people injured, and the types of injuries. Ask what to do, and listen carefully to the instructions. Let the other person hang up first to be sure there are no more questions or instructions for you.

Learn First Aid

If you want to learn more about what to do in an emergency, you can take a first-aid or CPR course, such as the one shown in **Figure 8.** *CPR* can revive a person who is not breathing and has no heartbeat. If you are over 12 years old, you can become certified in both CPR and first aid. Some baby-sitting classes also provide information on first aid. The American Red Cross, community organizations, and local hospitals offer these classes. However, you should not attempt any lifesaving procedure unless you have been trained.

✓ Reading Check **What is CPR, and how can you learn it?**

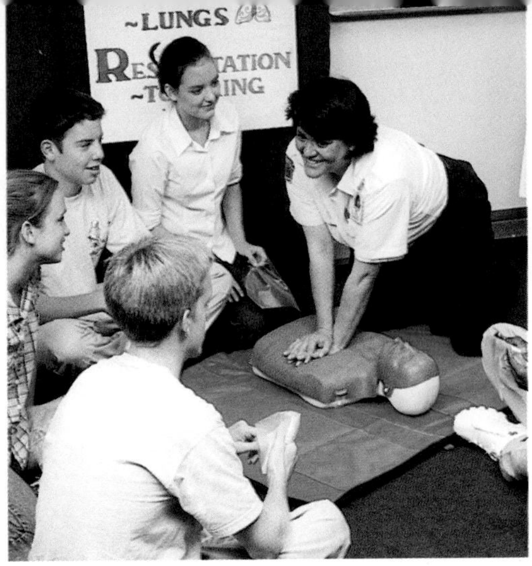

Figure 8 *These teenagers are taking a CPR course to prepare themselves for emergency situations.*

SECTION Review

Summary

- Good hygiene includes taking care of your skin, hair, and teeth.
- Good posture is important to health.
- Exercise keeps your heart, lungs, and bones healthy.
- Teenagers need more than 9 hours of sleep to stay rested and healthy.
- Coping with stress is an important part of staying physically and emotionally healthy.
- It is important to be aware of the possible hazards around your home, outdoors, and at school. Using the appropriate safety equipment can also help keep you safe.

Using Key Terms

Complete each of the following sentences by choosing the correct term from the word bank.

hygiene	aerobic exercise
sleep	stress

1. The science of protecting your health is called ___.
2. ___ strengthens your heart, lungs, and bones.
3. ___ is the physical and mental response to pressure.

Understanding Key Ideas

4. Which of the following is important for good health?
   a. irregular exercise
   b. getting your hair cut
   c. taking care of your teeth
   d. getting plenty of sun
5. List two things you should do when calling for help in a medical emergency.
6. List three ways to stay safe when you are outside, and three ways to stay safe at home.
7. How do seat belts and safety equipment protect you?

Math Skills

8. It is estimated that only 65% of adults wear their seat belts. If there are 10,000 people driving in your area right now, how many of them are wearing their seat belts?

Critical Thinking

9. **Applying Concepts** What situations cause you stress? What can you do to help relieve the stress you are feeling?
10. **Making Inferences** According to the newspaper, the temperature outside is 61°F right now. Later, it will be 90°F outside. If you and your friends want to play soccer in the park, what should you wear? What should you bring with you?

SCILINKS® NSTA
Developed and maintained by the National Science Teachers Association

For a variety of links related to this chapter, go to www.scilinks.org

Topic: Safety
SciLinks code: HSM1339

Skills Practice Lab

Keep It Clean

OBJECTIVES

Investigate how well antibacterial soap works.

Practice counting bacterial colonies.

MATERIALS

- incubator
- pencil, wax
- Petri dishes, nutrient agar–filled, sterile (3)
- scrub brush, new
- soap, liquid antibacterial
- stopwatch
- tape, transparent

SAFETY

One of the best ways to prevent the spread of bacterial and viral infections is to frequently wash your hands with soap and water. Many companies advertise that their soap ingredients can destroy bacteria normally found on the body. In this activity, you will investigate how effective antibacterial soaps are at killing bacteria.

Procedure

1. Keeping the agar plates closed at all times, use the wax pencil to label the bottoms of three agar plates. Label one plate "Control," one plate "No soap," and one plate "Soap."
2. Without washing your hands, carefully press several surfaces of your hands on the agar plate marked "Control." Have your partner immediately put the cover back on the plate. After you touch the agar, do not touch anything with either hand.
3. Hold your right hand under running water for 2 min. Ask your partner to scrub all surfaces of your right hand with the scrub brush throughout these 2 min. Be sure that he or she scrubs under your fingernails. After scrubbing, your partner should turn off the water and open the plate marked "No soap." Touching only the agar, carefully press on the "No soap" plate with the same surfaces of your right hand that you used to press on the "Control" plate.

4. Repeat step 3, but use your left hand instead of your right. This time, ask your partner to scrub your left hand with liquid antibacterial soap and the scrub brush. Use the plate marked "Soap" instead of the plate marked "No soap."

5. Secure the lid of each plate to its bottom half with transparent tape. Place the plates upside down in the incubator. Incubate all three plates overnight at 37°C.

6. Remove the plates from the incubator, and turn them right side up. Check each plate for the presence of bacterial colonies, and count the number of colonies present on each plate. Record this information. **Caution:** Do not remove the lids on any of the plates.

Analyze the Results

1. **Examining Data** Compare the bacterial growth on the plates. Which plate contained the most growth? Which contained the least?

Draw Conclusions

2. **Drawing Conclusions** Does water alone effectively kill bacteria? Explain.

Applying Your Data

Repeat this experiment, but scrub with regular, not antibacterial, liquid soap. Describe how the results of the two experiments differ.

Chapter Review

USING KEY TERMS

Complete each of the following sentences by choosing the correct term from the word bank.

nutrients	MyPyramid
addiction	drug
malnutrition	

1. Carbohydrates, proteins, fats, vitamins, minerals, and water are the six categories of ___.
2. The ___ divides foods into six groups and gives a recommended number of servings for each group.
3. Both bulimia nervosa and anorexia nervosa cause ___.
4. A physical or psychological dependence on a drug can lead to ___.
5. A(n) ___ is any substance that causes a change in a person's physical or psychological state.

UNDERSTANDING KEY IDEAS

Multiple Choice

6. Which of the following statements about drugs is true?
   a. A child cannot become addicted to drugs.
   b. Smoking just one or two cigarettes is safe for anyone.
   c. Alcohol is not a drug.
   d. Withdrawal symptoms may be painful.
7. What does alcohol do to the central nervous system (CNS)?
   a. It speeds the CNS up.
   b. It slows the CNS down.
   c. It keeps the CNS regulated.
   d. It has no effect on the CNS.
8. To keep your teeth healthy,
   a. brush your teeth as hard as you can.
   b. use a toothbrush until it is worn out.
   c. brush at least twice a day.
   d. floss at least once a week.
9. According to MyPyramid, what foods should you eat most?
   a. meats
   b. milk, yogurt, and cheese
   c. fruits and vegetables
   d. bread, cereal, rice, and pasta
10. Which of the following can help you deal with stress?
    a. ignoring your homework
    b. drinking a caffeinated drink
    c. talking to a friend
    d. watching television
11. Tobacco use increases the risk of
    a. lung cancer.
    b. car accidents.
    c. liver damage.
    d. depression.

Short Answer

12 Are all narcotics illegal? Explain.

13 What are three dangers of tobacco and alcohol use?

14 What are the three types of nutrients that provide energy in Calories, and what is the main function of each type in the body?

15 Name two conditions that can lead to malnutrition.

16 Explain why you should always wear safety equipment when you ride your bicycle.

CRITICAL THINKING

17 **Concept Mapping** Use the following terms to create a concept map: *carbohydrates, water, proteins, nutrients, fats, vitamins, minerals, saturated fats,* and *unsaturated fats.*

18 **Applying Concepts** You have recently become a vegetarian, and you worry that you are not getting enough protein. Name two foods that you could eat to get more protein.

19 **Analyzing Ideas** Your two-year-old cousin will be staying with your family. Name three things that you can do to make sure that the house is safe for a young child.

INTERPRETING GRAPHICS

Look at the photos below. The people in the photos are not practicing safe habits. List the unsafe habits shown in these photos. For each unsafe habit, tell what the corresponding safe habit is.

20

21

Multiple Choice

Use the chart below to answer questions 1–2.

Nutrition Facts

Serving Size 3 ounces
Servings per package: 1

Amount per serving	
Calories 154	Calories from Fat 18
	% Daily Value
Total Fat 2g	3%
Saturated Fat 0.5%	2.5%
Cholesterol 0mg	0%
Sodium 95mg	4%
Total Carbohydrates 30g	10%
Dietary Fiber 5g	20%
Sugars 0g	
Protein 3g	
Vitamin A 2% •	Vitamin C 10%
Calcium 0% •	Iron 2%

*Percent Daily Values are based on a 2,000 calorie diet. Your daily values may be higher or lower depending on your calorie needs.

	Calories	2,000	3,000
Total Fat	Less than	65g	80g
Sat Fat	Less than	20g	25g
Cholesterol	Less than	300mg	300mg
SodiumTotal	Less than	2,400mg	2,400mg
Carbohydrates		300g	375g
Dietary Fiber		25g	30g

Calories per gram:
Fat 9 Carbohydrates 4 Protein 4

1. **Daneeka is using the chart to perform a laboratory experiment about nutrition. According to the chart, how much fat would Daneeka take in if she were to eat this entire package of food?**

   A. 0 g

   B. 2 g

   C. 6 g

   D. 30 g

2. **Look at the chart. Which of these nutrients has the lowest Percent Daily Value?**

   A. calcium

   B. vitamin A

   C. vitamin C

   D. iron

3. **Which nutrient is your main source of energy?**

   A. carbohydrates

   B. minerals

   C. proteins

   D. water

4. **According to the Centers for Disease Control and Prevention in Atlanta, about 16 million Americans between ages 6 and 19 are overweight. Which of these problems are associated with obesity?**

   A. headaches and dizzy spells

   B. tooth decay and gum disease

   C. heart disease and diabetes

   D. colds and flu

Use the line graph below to answer question 5.

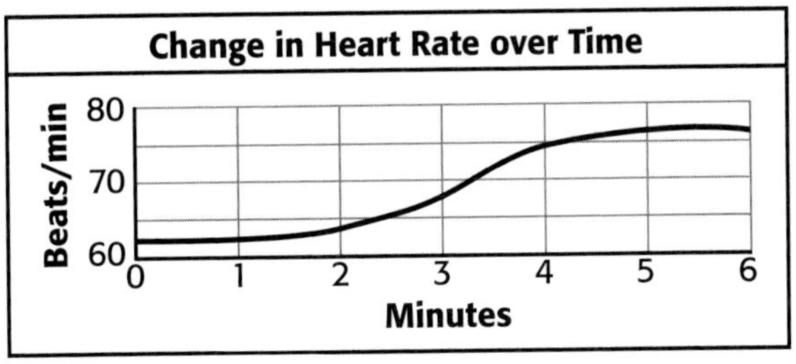

5. Look at the line graph above. What is the most likely explanation for the change seen after the two-minute mark?

A. The person started exercising.

B. The person fell asleep.

C. The person inhaled.

D. The person sat down.

6. Which of the following is addictive?

A. vitamin A

B. calcium

C. antibiotics

D. nicotine

7. Which of the following is a benefit of good posture?

A. clearer skin

B. high intelligence

C. muscle relief

D. fewer allergies

8. To maintain good health, 20 minutes of aerobic exercise should be done

A. once a week.

B. at least twice a week.

C. at least three times a week.

D. no more than three times a week.

9. Proteins play a role in most cell processes. From what substances do cells make proteins?

A. amino acids

B. lipids

C. nucleic acids

D. carbohydrates

10. Why is washing your hands an important part of good hygiene?

A. It keeps your hands smelling fresh.

B. It keeps your fingers soft and sensitive.

C. It makes other people trust you.

D. It prevents the spread of diseases and infection.

Open Response

11. What are three ways of dealing with stress?

12. Distinguish the six food groups and describe how they relate to MyPyramid.

Science in Action

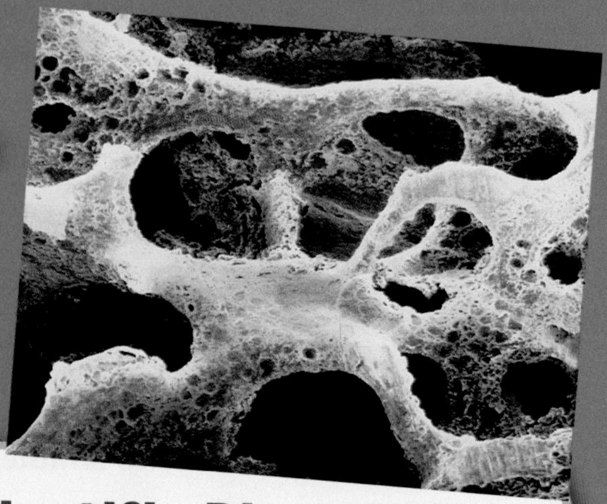

Bones can become severely weakened by the female athlete triad.

Science, Technology, and Society

Meatless Munching

Recent studies suggest that a vegetarian diet may reduce the risk of heart disease, adult-onset diabetes, and some forms of cancer. However, a vegetarian diet takes careful planning. Vegetarians must ensure that they get the proper balance of protein and vitamins in their diet. New foods that can help vegetarians remain healthy are being developed constantly. Meat substitutes are now made from soybeans, textured vegetable protein, and tofu. One new food, which is shown above, is made of a fungus that is a relative of mushrooms and truffles.

Social Studies ACTIVITY

WRITING SKILL Research a culture that has a mostly vegetarian diet, such as Hindu or Buddhist. What kinds of food do the people eat? Why don't they eat animals? Write a short report on your findings.

Scientific Discoveries

Female Athlete Triad

Getting enough exercise is an important part of staying healthy. But in 1992, doctors learned that too much exercise can be harmful for women. When a girl or woman exercises too much, three things can happen. She may lose too much weight. She may stop having her period. And her bones may become very weak. These three symptoms form the female athlete triad. To prevent this condition, female athletes need to take in enough Calories. Women who exercise heavily and try to lose weight may have a reduction in estrogen. Estrogen is the hormone that helps regulate the menstrual cycle. Low levels of estrogen and inadequate nutrition can cause bones to become weak and brittle. The photo above shows bone that has been weakened greatly.

Math ACTIVITY

Some scientists recommend that teenagers get 1,200 to 1,500 mg of calcium every day. A cup of milk has 300 mg of calcium, and a serving of yogurt has 400 mg of calcium. Calculate two combinations of milk and yogurt that would give you the recommended 1,500 mg of calcium.

Careers

Russell Selger

Guidance Counselor Guidance counselors help students think about their future by helping them discover their interests. After focusing their interests, a guidance counselor helps students plan a good academic schedule. A guidance counselor might talk to you about taking an art or computer science class that may help you discover a hidden talent. Many skills are vital to being a good guidance counselor. The job requires empathy, which is the ability to understand and sympathize with another person's feelings. Counselors also need patience, good listening skills, and a love of helping young people. Russell Selger, a guidance counselor at Timberlane Middle School, has a great respect for middle school students. "The kids are just alive. They want to learn. There's something about the spark that they have, and it's so much fun to guide them through all of this stuff," he explains.

Language Arts ACTIVITY

WRITING SKILL Visit the guidance counselor's office at your school. What services does your guidance counselor offer? Conduct an interview with a guidance counselor. Ask why he or she became a counselor. Write an article for the school paper about your findings.

go.hrw.com

To learn more about these Science in Action topics, visit go.hrw.com and type in the keyword **HL5BD7F.**

Current Science

Check out Current Science® articles related to this chapter by visiting go.hrw.com. Just type in the keyword HL5CS28.

LabBook

Contents

Using Scientific Methods

Skills Practice Lab

Layering Liquids

You have learned that liquids form layers according to the densities of the liquids. In this lab, you'll discover whether it matters in which order you add the liquids.

- beaker (or other small, clear container)
- funnel (3)
- graduated cylinder, 10 mL (3)
- liquid A
- liquid B
- liquid C

SAFETY

Ask a Question

1. Does the order in which you add liquids of different densities to a container affect the order of the layers formed by those liquids?

Form a Hypothesis

2. Write a possible answer to the question above.

Test the Hypothesis

3. Using the graduated cylinders, add 10 mL of each liquid to the clear container. Remember to read the volume at the bottom of the meniscus, as shown below. Record the order in which you added the liquids.
4. Observe the liquids in the container. Sketch what you see. Be sure to label the layers and the colors.
5. Add 10 mL more of liquid C. Observe what happens, and record your observations.
6. Add 20 mL more of liquid A. Observe what happens, and record your observations.

Analyze the Results

1. Which of the liquids has the greatest density? Which has the least density? How can you tell?
2. Did the layers change position when you added more of liquid C? Explain your answer.
3. Did the layers change position when you added more of liquid A? Explain your answer.
4. Find out in what order your classmates added the liquids to the container. Compare your results with those of a classmate who added the liquids in a different order. Were your results different? Explain why or why not.

Draw Conclusions

5. Based on your results, evaluate your hypothesis from step 2.

Skills Practice Lab

Wave Speed, Frequency, and Wavelength

Wave speed, frequency, and wavelength are three related properties of waves. In this lab, you will make observations and collect data to determine the relationship among these properties.

MATERIALS

- meterstick
- stopwatch
- toy, coiled spring

SAFETY

Part A: Wave Speed

Procedure

1. Copy Table 1.

Table 1 Wave Speed Data

Trial	Length of spring (m)	Time for wave (s)	Speed of wave (m/s)
1			
2			
3			
Average			

2. Two students should stretch the spring to a length of 2 m to 4 m on the floor or on a table. A third student should measure the length of the spring. Record the length in Table 1.

3. One student should pull part of the spring sideways with one hand, as shown at right, and release the pulled-back portion. This action will cause a wave to travel down the spring.

4. Using a stopwatch, the third student should measure how long it takes for the wave to travel down the length of the spring and back. Record this time in Table 1.

5. Repeat steps 3 and 4 two more times.

Part B: Wavelength and Frequency

Procedure

1. Keep the spring the same length that you used in Part A.
2. Copy Table 2.

***Table 2* Wavelength and Frequency Data**

Trial	Length of spring (m)	Time for 10 cycles (s)	Wave frequency (Hz)	Wavelength (m)
1				
2				
3				
Average				

DO NOT WRITE IN BOOK

3. One of the two students holding the spring should start shaking the spring from side to side until a wave pattern appears that resembles one of those shown.
4. Using the stopwatch, the third student should measure and record how long it takes for 10 cycles of the wave pattern to occur. (One back-and-forth shake is 1 cycle.) Keep the pattern going so that measurements for three trials can be made.

Analyze the Results

Part A

1. Calculate and record the wave speed for each trial. (Speed equals distance divided by time; distance is twice the spring length.)
2. Calculate and record the average time and the average wave speed.

Part B

3. Calculate the frequency for each trial by dividing the number of cycles (10) by the time. Record the answers in Table 2.
4. Determine the wavelength using the equation at right that matches your wave pattern. Record your answer in Table 2.
5. Calculate and record the average time and frequency.

Wave Patterns

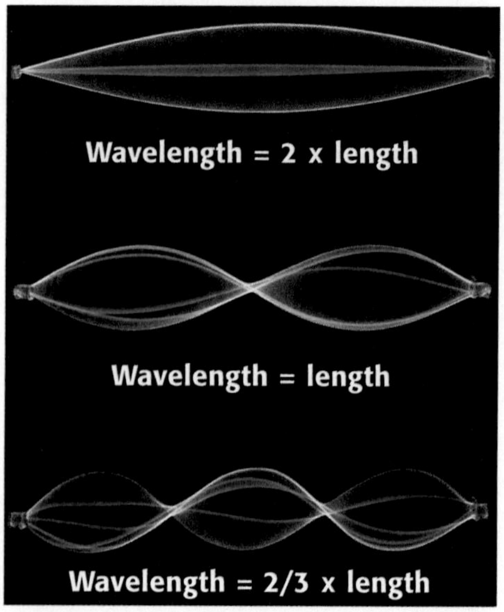

Draw Conclusions: Parts A and B

6. Analyze the relationship among speed, wavelength, and frequency. Multiply or divide any two of them to see if the result equals the third. (Use the averages from your data tables.) Write the equation that shows the relationship.

Inquiry Lab

The Speed of Sound

In the chapter entitled "The Nature of Sound," you learned that the speed of sound in air is 343 m/s at 20°C (approximately room temperature). In this lab, you'll design an experiment to measure the speed of sound yourself—and you'll determine if you're "up to speed"!

MATERIALS

- items to be determined by the students and approved by the teacher

Procedure

1. Brainstorm with your teammates to come up with a way to measure the speed of sound. Consider the following as you design your experiment:

   a. You must have a method of making a sound. Some simple examples include speaking, clapping your hands, and hitting two boards together.

   b. Remember that speed is equal to distance divided by time. You must devise methods to measure the distance that a sound travels and to measure the amount of time it takes for that sound to travel that distance.

   c. Sound travels very rapidly. A sound from across the room will reach your ears almost before you can start recording the time! You may wish to have the sound travel a long distance.

   d. Remember that sound travels in waves. Think about the interactions of sound waves. You might be able to include these interactions in your design.

2. Discuss your experimental design with your teacher, including any equipment you need. Your teacher may have questions that will help you improve your design.

3. Once your design is approved, carry out your experiment. Be sure to perform several trials. Record your results.

Analyze the Results

1. Was your result close to the value given in the introduction to this lab? If not, what factors may have caused you to get such a different value?

2. Why was it important for you to perform several trials in your experiment?

Draw Conclusions

3. Compare your results with those of your classmates. Determine which experimental design provided the best results. Explain why you think this design was so successful.

Skills Practice Lab

Tuneful Tube

If you have seen a singer shatter a crystal glass simply by singing a note, you have seen an example of resonance. For the glass to shatter, the note has to match the resonant frequency of the glass. A column of air within a cylinder can also resonate if the air column is the proper length for the frequency of the note. In this lab, you will investigate the relationship between the length of an air column, the frequency, and the wavelength during resonance.

MATERIALS

- eraser, pink, rubber
- graduated cylinder, 100 mL
- paper, graph
- plastic tube, supplied by your teacher
- ruler, metric
- tuning forks, different frequencies (4)
- water

SAFETY

Procedure

1. Copy the data table below.

Data Collection Table				
Frequency (Hz)				
Length (cm)	DO NOT WRITE IN BOOK			

2. Fill the graduated cylinder with water.
3. Hold a plastic tube in the water so that about 3 cm is above the water.
4. Record the frequency of the first tuning fork. Gently strike the tuning fork with the eraser, and hold the tuning fork so that the prongs are just above the tube, as shown at right. Slowly move the tube and fork up and down until you hear the loudest sound.
5. Measure the distance from the top of the tube to the water. Record this length in your data table.
6. Repeat steps 3–5 using the other three tuning forks.

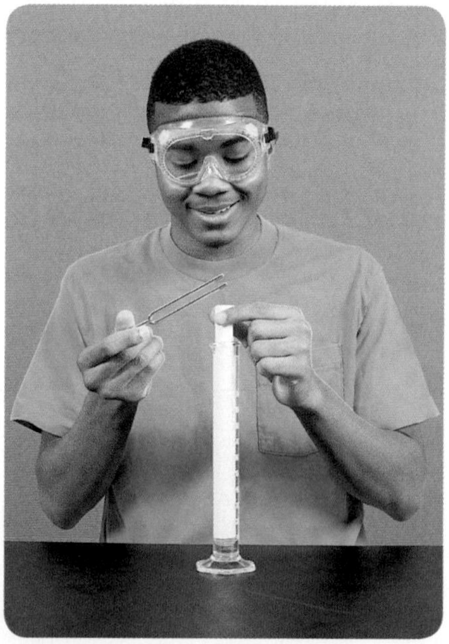

Analyze the Results

1. Calculate the wavelength (in centimeters) of each sound wave by dividing the speed of sound in air (343 m/s at 20°C) by the frequency and multiplying by 100.
2. Make the following graphs: air column length versus frequency and wavelength versus frequency. On both graphs, plot the frequency on the *x*-axis.
3. Describe the trend between the length of the air column and the frequency of the tuning fork.
4. How are the pitches you heard related to the wavelengths of the sounds?

Skills Practice Lab

The Energy of Sound

In the chapter entitled "The Nature of Sound," you learned about various properties and interactions of sound. In this lab, you will perform several activities that will demonstrate that the properties and interactions of sound all depend on one thing—the energy carried by sound waves.

MATERIALS

- cup, plastic, small, filled with water
- eraser, pink, rubber
- rubber band
- string, 50 cm
- tuning forks, same frequency (2), different frequency (1)

SAFETY

Part A: Sound Vibrations

Procedure

1. Lightly strike a tuning fork with the eraser. Slowly place the prongs of the tuning fork in the plastic cup of water. Record your observations.

Part B: Resonance

Procedure

1. Strike a tuning fork with the eraser. Quickly pick up a second tuning fork in your other hand, and hold it about 30 cm from the first tuning fork.
2. Place the first tuning fork against your leg to stop the tuning fork's vibration. Listen closely to the second tuning fork. Record your observations, including the frequencies of the two tuning forks.
3. Repeat steps 1 and 2, using the remaining tuning fork as the second tuning fork.

Part C: Interference

Procedure

1. Use the two tuning forks that have the same frequency, and place a rubber band tightly over the prongs near the base of one tuning fork, as shown at right. Strike both tuning forks against the eraser. Hold the stems of the tuning forks against a table, 3 cm to 5 cm apart. If you cannot hear any differences, move the rubber band up or down the prongs. Strike again. Record your observations.

Part D: The Doppler Effect

Procedure

1. Your teacher will tie the piece of string securely to the base of one tuning fork. Your teacher will then strike the tuning fork and carefully swing the tuning fork in a circle overhead. Record your observations.

Analyze the Results

1. How do your observations demonstrate that sound waves are carried through vibrations?
2. Explain why you can hear a sound from the second tuning fork when the frequencies of the tuning forks used are the same.
3. When using tuning forks of different frequencies, would you expect to hear a sound from the second tuning fork if you strike the first tuning fork harder? Explain your reasoning.
4. Did you notice the sound changing back and forth between loud and soft? A steady pattern like this one is called a *beat frequency.* Explain this changing pattern of loudness and softness in terms of interference (both constructive and destructive).
5. Did the tuning fork make a different sound when your teacher was swinging it than when he or she was holding it? If yes, explain why.
6. Is the actual pitch of the tuning fork changing when it is swinging? Explain.

Draw Conclusions

7. Explain how your observations from each part of this lab verify that sound waves carry energy from one point to another through a vibrating medium.
8. Particularly loud thunder can cause the windows of your room to rattle. How is this evidence that sound waves carry energy?

Using Scientific Methods

Skills Practice Lab

What Color of Light Is Best for Green Plants?

Plants grow well outdoors under natural sunlight. However, some plants are grown indoors under artificial light. A variety of colored lights are available for helping plants grow indoors. In this experiment, you'll test several colors of light to discover which color best meets the energy needs of green plants.

MATERIALS

- bean seedlings
- colored lights, supplied by your teacher
- marker, felt-tip
- paper towels
- Petri dishes with covers
- tape, masking
- water

SAFETY

Ask a Question

1. Which color of light is best for growing green plants?

Form a Hypothesis

2. Write a hypothesis that answers the question above. Explain your reasoning.

Test the Hypothesis

3. Use the masking tape and marker to label the side of each Petri dish with your name and the type of light under which you will place the dish.
4. Place a moist paper towel in each Petri dish. Place 5 seedlings on top of the paper towel. Cover each dish.
5. Record your observations of the seedlings, such as length, color, and number of leaves.
6. Place each dish under the appropriate light.
7. Observe the Petri dishes every day for at least 5 days. Record your observations.

Analyze the Results

1. Based on your results, which color of light is best for growing green plants? Which color of light is worst?

Draw Conclusions

2. Remember that the color of an opaque object (such as a plant) is determined by the colors the object reflects. Use this information to explain your answer to question 1 above.
3. Would a purple light be good for growing purple plants? Explain.

Skills Practice Lab

Which Color Is Hottest?

Will a navy blue hat or a white hat keep your head warmer in cool weather? Colored objects absorb energy, which can make the objects warmer. How much energy is absorbed depends on the object's color. In this experiment, you will test several colors under a bright light to determine which colors absorb the most energy.

MATERIALS

- light source
- paper, colored, squares
- paper, graph
- paper towels
- pencils or pens, colored
- tape, transparent
- thermometer
- water, room-temperature

SAFETY

Procedure

1. Copy the table below. Be sure to have one column for each color of paper you use and enough rows to end at 3 min.

Data Collection Table

Time (s)	White	Red	Blue	Black
0				
15				
30				
45				
etc.				

2. Tape a piece of colored paper around the bottom of a thermometer, and hold it under the light source. Record the temperature every 15 s for 3 min.
3. Cool the thermometer by removing the piece of paper and placing the thermometer in the cup of room-temperature water. After 1 min, remove the thermometer, and dry it with a paper towel.
4. Repeat steps 2 and 3 with each color, making sure to hold the thermometer at the same distance from the light source.

Analyze the Results

1. Prepare a graph of temperature (y-axis) versus time (x-axis). Using a different colored pencil or pen for each set of data, plot all data on one graph.
2. Rank the colors you used in order from hottest to coolest.

Draw Conclusions

3. Compare the colors, based on the amount of energy each absorbs.
4. In this experiment, a white light was used. How would your results be different if you used a red light? Explain.
5. Use the relationship between color and energy absorbed to explain why different colors of clothing are used for different seasons.

Using Scientific Methods

Skills Practice Lab

Stop the Static Electricity!

Imagine this scenario: Some of your clothes cling together when they come out of the dryer. This annoying problem is caused by static electricity—the buildup of electric charges on an object. In this lab, you'll discover how this buildup occurs.

MATERIALS

- cloth, silk
- cloth, woolen
- packing peanut, plastic-foam
- rod, glass
- rod, rubber
- tape
- thread, 30 cm

SAFETY

Ask a Question

1. How do electric charges build up on clothes in a dryer?

Form a Hypothesis

2. Write a statement that answers the question above. Explain your reasoning.

Test the Hypothesis

3. Tie a piece of thread approximately 30 cm in length to a packing peanut. Hang the peanut by the thread from the edge of a table. Tape the thread to the table.
4. Rub the rubber rod with the wool cloth for 10 to 15 s. Bring the rod near, but do not touch, the peanut. Observe the peanut, and record your observations. If nothing happens, repeat this step.
5. Touch the peanut with the rubber rod. Pull the rod away from the peanut, and then bring it near again. Record your observations.
6. Repeat steps 4 and 5 with the glass rod and silk cloth.
7. Now, rub the rubber rod with the wool cloth, and bring the rod near the peanut again. Record your observations.

Analyze the Results

1. What caused the peanut to act differently in steps 4 and 5?
2. Did the glass rod have the same effect on the peanut as the rubber rod did? Explain how the peanut reacted in each case.
3. Was the reaction of the peanut the same in steps 5 and 7? Explain.

Draw Conclusions

4. Based on your results, was your hypothesis correct? Explain your answer, and write a new statement if necessary.

Applying Your Data

Do some research to find out how a dryer sheet helps stop the buildup of electric charges in the dryer.

Model-Making Lab

Potato Power

Have you ever wanted to look inside a D cell from a flashlight or an AA cell from a portable radio? All cells include the same basic components, as shown below. There is a metal "bucket," some electrolyte (a paste), and a rod of some other metal (or solid) in the middle. Even though cell construction is simple, companies that manufacture cells are always trying to make a product with the highest voltage possible from the least expensive materials. Sometimes, companies try different pastes, and sometimes they try different combinations of metals. In this lab, you will make your own cell. Using inexpensive materials, you will try to produce the highest voltage you can.

MATERIALS

- metal strips, labeled
- potato
- ruler, metric
- voltmeter

SAFETY

Procedure

1. Choose two metal strips. Carefully push one of the strips into the potato at least 2 cm deep. Insert the second strip the same way, and measure how far apart the two strips are. (If one of your metal strips is too soft to push into the potato, push a harder strip in first, remove it, and then push the soft strip into the slit.) Record the two metals you have used and the distance between the strips. **Caution:** The strips of metal may have sharp edges.
2. Connect the voltmeter to the two strips, and record the voltage.
3. Move one of the strips closer to or farther from the other. Measure the new distance and voltage. Record your results.
4. Repeat steps 1 through 3, using different combinations of metal strips and distances until you find the combination that produces the highest voltage.

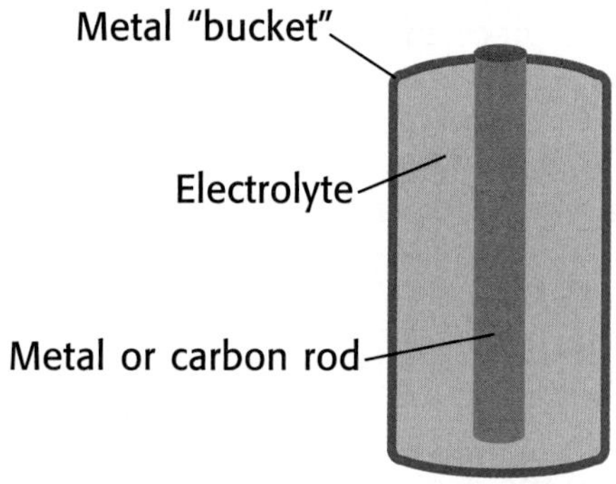

D cell

Analyze the Results

1. What combination of metals and distance produced the highest voltage?
2. If you change only the distance but use the same metal strips, what is the effect on the voltage?
3. One of the metal strips tends to lose electrons, and the other tends to gain electrons. What do you think would happen if you used two strips of the same metal?

Using Scientific Methods

Skills Practice Lab

Magnetic Mystery

Every magnet is surrounded by a magnetic field. Magnetic field lines show the shape of the magnetic field. These lines can be modeled by using iron filings. The iron filings are affected by the magnetic field, and they fall into lines showing the field. In this lab, you will first learn about magnetic fields, and then you will use this knowledge to identify a mystery magnet's shape and orientation based on observations of the field lines.

MATERIALS

- acetate, clear (1 sheet)
- iron filings
- magnets, different shapes (2)
- shoe box
- tape, masking

SAFETY

Ask a Question

1. Can a magnet's shape and orientation be determined without seeing the magnet?

Form a Hypothesis

2. Write a possible answer to the question above. Explain your reasoning.

Test the Hypothesis

3. Lay one of the magnets flat on a table.
4. Place a sheet of clear acetate over the magnet. Sprinkle some iron filings on the acetate to see the magnetic field lines.
5. Draw the magnet and the magnetic field lines.
6. Remove the acetate, and return the filings to the container.
7. Place your magnet so that one end is pointing up. Repeat steps 4 through 6.
8. Place your magnet on its side. Repeat steps 4 through 6.
9. Repeat steps 3 through 8 with the other magnet.
10. Remove the lid from a shoe box, and tape a magnet underneath the lid. Once the magnet is secure, place the lid on the box.
11. Exchange boxes with another team.
12. Without opening the box, use the sheet of acetate and the iron filings to determine the shape of the magnetic field.
13. Draw the magnetic field lines.

Analyze the Results

1. Use your drawings from steps 3 through 9 to find the shape and orientation of the magnet in your box. Draw a picture of your conclusion.

Applying Your Data

Examine your drawings. Can you identify the north and south poles of a magnet from the shape of the magnetic field lines? Design a procedure that would allow you to determine the poles of a magnet.

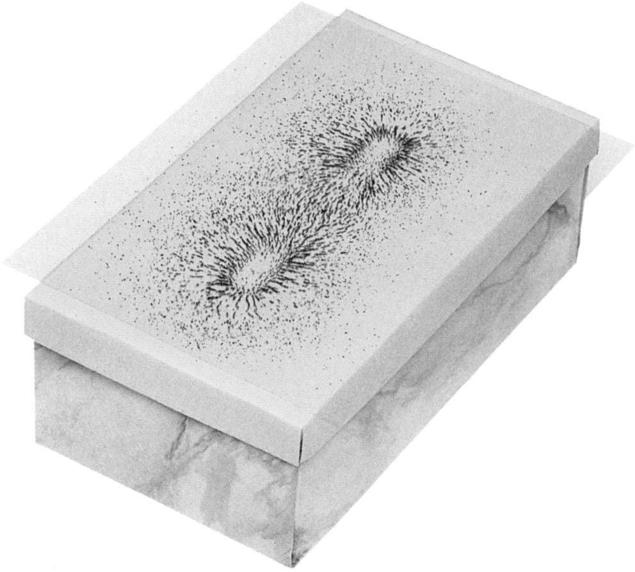

Using Scientific Methods

Model-Making Lab

Tune In!

You probably have listened to radios many times in your life. Modern radios are complicated electronic devices. However, radios do not have to be so complicated. The basic parts of all radios include a diode, an inductor, a capacitor, an antenna, a ground wire, and an earphone (or a speaker and amplifier on a large radio). In this activity, you will examine each of these components one at a time as you build a working model of a radio-wave receiver.

MATERIALS

- aluminum foil
- antenna
- cardboard, 20 cm × 30 cm
- cardboard tubes (2)
- connecting wires, 30 cm each (7)
- diode
- earphone
- ground wire
- paper (1 sheet)
- paper clips (3)
- scissors
- tape
- wire, insulated, 2 m

SAFETY

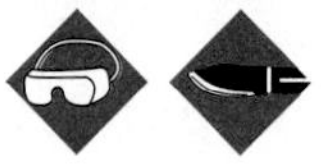

Ask a Question

1. Write a question you can test using the procedure in this lab.

Form a Hypothesis

2. Write a possible answer to the question you wrote in the step above. Explain your reasoning.

Test the Hypothesis

3. Examine the diode. Describe it on another sheet of paper.
4. A diode carries current in only one direction. Draw the inside of a diode, and illustrate how the diode might allow current in only one direction.
5. An inductor controls the amount of electric current because of the resistance of the wire. Make an inductor by winding the insulated wire around a cardboard tube approximately 100 times. Wind the wire so that all the turns of the coil are neat and in an orderly row, as shown below. Leave about 25 cm of wire on each end of the coil. The coil of wire may be held on the tube using tape.

6. Now, you will construct the variable capacitor. A capacitor stores electrical energy when an electric current is applied. A variable capacitor is a capacitor in which the amount of energy stored can be changed. Cut a piece of aluminum foil to go around the tube but only half the length of the tube, as shown at right. Keep the foil as wrinkle-free as possible as you wrap it around the tube, and tape the foil to itself. Now, tape the foil to the tube.
7. Use the sheet of paper and tape to make a sliding cover on the tube. The paper should completely cover the foil on the tube with about 1 cm extra.
8. Cut another sheet of aluminum foil to wrap completely around the paper. Leave approximately 1 cm of paper showing at each end of the foil. Tape this foil sheet to the paper sleeve. If you have done this correctly, you have a paper/foil sheet that will slide up and down the tube over the stationary foil. The two pieces of foil should not touch.
9. Stand your variable capacitor on its end so that the stationary foil is at the bottom. The amount of stored energy is greater when the sleeve is down than when the sleeve is up.
10. Use tape to attach one connecting wire to the stationary foil at the end of the tube. Use tape to attach another connecting wire to the sliding foil sleeve. Be sure that the metal part of the wire touches the foil.

Capacitor

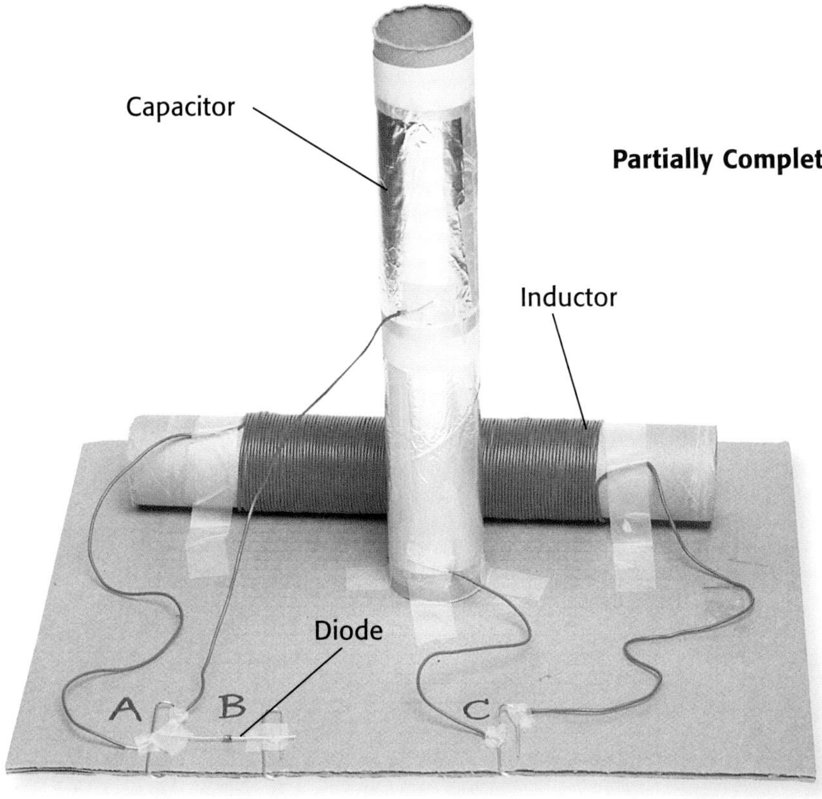

Partially Completed Model Receiver

11. Hook three paper clips on one edge of the cardboard, as shown below. Label one paper clip "A," the second one "B," and the third one "C."
12. Lay the inductor on the piece of cardboard, and tape it to the cardboard.
13. Stand the capacitor next to the inductor, and tape the tube to the cardboard. Be sure not to tape the sleeve—it must be free to slide.
14. Use tape to connect the diode to paper clips A and B. The cathode should be closest to paper clip B. (The cathode end of the diode is the one with the dark band.) Make sure that all connections have good metal-to-metal contact.
15. Connect one end of the inductor to paper clip A and the other end to paper clip C. Use tape to hold the wires in place.
16. Connect the wire from the sliding part of the capacitor to paper clip A. Connect the other wire (from the stationary foil) to paper clip C.
17. The antenna receives radio waves transmitted by a radio station. Tape a connecting wire to your antenna. Then, connect this wire to paper clip A.

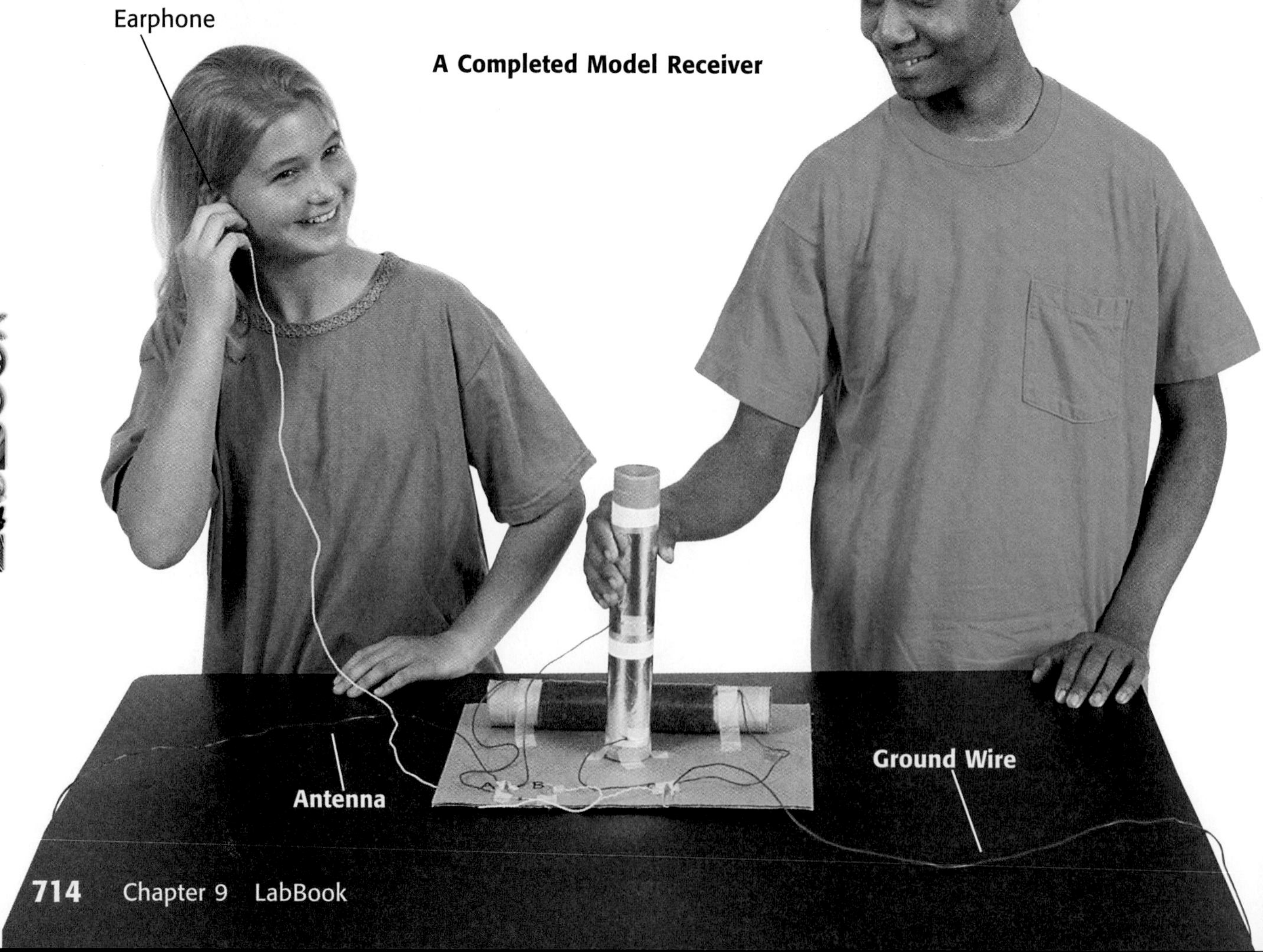

A Completed Model Receiver

18 Use tape to connect one end of the ground wire to paper clip C. The other end of the ground wire should be connected to an object specified by your teacher.

19 The earphone will allow you to detect the radio waves you receive. Connect one wire from the earphone to paper clip B and the other wire to paper clip C.

20 You are now ready to begin listening. With everything connected and the earphone in your ear, slowly slide the paper/foil sheet of the capacitor up and down. Listen for a very faint sound. You may have to troubleshoot many of the parts to get your receiver to work. As you troubleshoot, check to be sure there is good contact between all the connections.

Analyze the Results

1. Describe the process of operating your receiver.
2. Considering what you have learned about a diode, why is it important to have the diode connected the correct way?
3. A function of the inductor on a radio is to "slow the current down." Why does the inductor you made slow the current down more than does a straight wire the length of your coil?
4. A capacitor consists of any two conductors separated by an insulator. For your capacitor, list the two conductors and the insulator.

Draw Conclusions

5. Explain why the amount of stored energy is increased down when you slide the foil sleeve and decreased when you slide the foil sleeve up.
6. Make a list of ways that your receiver is similar to a modern radio. Make a second list of ways that your receiver is different from a modern radio.

Skills Practice Lab

Power of the Sun

The sun radiates energy in every direction. Like the sun, the energy radiated by a light bulb spreads out in all directions. But how much energy an object receives depends on how close that object is to the source. As you move farther from the source, the amount of energy you receive decreases. For example, if you measure the amount of energy that reaches you from a light and then move three times farther away, you will discover that nine times less energy will reach you at your second position. Energy from the sun travels as light energy. When light energy is absorbed by an object it is converted into thermal energy. Power is the rate at which one form of energy is converted to another, and it is measured in watts. Because power is related to distance, nearby objects can be used to measure the power of far-away objects. In this lab you will calculate the power of the sun using an ordinary 100-watt light bulb.

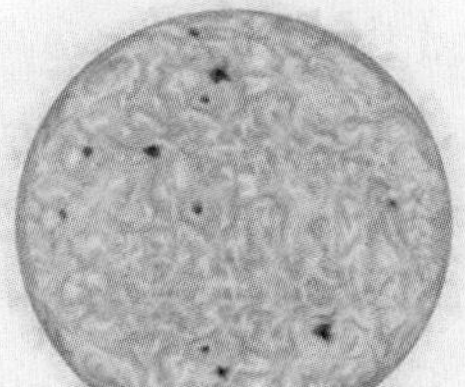

MATERIALS

- aluminum strip, 2 × 8 cm
- calculator, scientific
- clay, modeling
- desk lamp with a 100 W bulb and removable shade
- gloves, protective
- marker, black permanent
- mason jar, cap, and lid with hole in center
- pencil
- ruler, metric
- thermometer, Celsius
- watch (or clock) that indicates seconds

SAFETY

Procedure

1. Gently shape the piece of aluminum around a pencil so that it holds on in the middle and has two wings, one on either side of the pencil.
2. Bend the wings outward so that they can catch as much sunlight as possible.
3. Use the marker to color both wings on one side of the aluminum strip black.
4. Remove the pencil and place the aluminum snugly around the thermometer near the bulb. **Caution:** Do not press too hard—you do not want to break the thermometer! Wear protective gloves when working with the thermometer and the aluminum.
5. Carefully slide the top of the thermometer through the hole in the lid. Place the lid on the jar so that the thermometer bulb is inside the jar, and screw down the cap.
6. Secure the thermometer to the jar lid by molding clay around the thermometer on the outside of the lid. The aluminum wings should be in the center of the jar.
7. Read the temperature on the thermometer. Record this as room temperature.
8. Place the jar on a windowsill in the sunlight. Turn the jar so that the black wings are angled toward the sun.
9. Watch the thermometer until the temperature reading stops rising. Record the temperature.
10. Remove the jar from direct sunlight, and allow it to return to room temperature.
11. Remove any shade or reflector from the lamp. Place the lamp at one end of a table.
12. Place the jar about 30 cm from the lamp. Turn the jar so that the wings are angled toward the lamp.

13. Turn on the lamp, and wait about 1 minute.
14. Move the jar a few centimeters toward the lamp until the temperature reading starts to rise. When the temperature stops rising, compare it with the reading you took in step 9.
15. Repeat step 14 until the temperature matches the temperature you recorded in step 9.
16. If the temperature reading rises too high, move the jar away from the lamp and allow it to cool. Once the reading has dropped to at least 5°C below the temperature you recorded in step 9, you may begin again at step 12.
17. When the temperature in the jar matches the temperature you recorded in step 9, record the distance between the center of the light bulb and the thermometer bulb.

Analyze the Results

1. The thermometer measured the same amount of energy absorbed by the jar at the distance you measured to the lamp. In other words, your jar absorbed as much energy from the sun at a distance of 150 million kilometers as it did from the 100 W light bulb at the distance you recorded in step 17.
2. Use the following formula to calculate the power of the sun (be sure to show your work):

$$\frac{\text{power of the sun}}{(\text{distance to the sun})^2} = \frac{\text{power of the lamp}}{(\text{distance to the lamp})^2}$$

Hint: $(\text{distance})^2$ means that you multiply the distance by itself. If you found that the lamp was 5 cm away from the jar, for example, the $(\text{distance})^2$ would be 25.

Hint: Convert 150,000,000 km to 15,000,000,000,000 cm.

3. Review the discussion of scientific notation in the Math Refresher found in the Appendix at the back of this book. You will need to understand this technique for writing large numbers in order to compare your calculation with the actual figure. For practice, convert the distance to the sun given above in step 2 of Analyze the Results to scientific notation.

15,000,000,000,000 cm = $1.5 \times 10^{?}$ cm

Draw Conclusions

4. The sun emits 3.7×10^{26} W of power. Compare your answer in step 2 with this value. Was this a good way to calculate the power of the sun? Explain.

Using Scientific Methods

Skills Practice Lab

Investigating an Oil Spill

Have you ever wondered why it is important to recycle motor oil rather than pour it down the drain or sewer? Or have you ever wondered why a seemingly small oil spill can cause so much damage? The reason is that a little oil goes a long way.

MATERIALS

- calculator (optional)
- gloves, protective
- goggles
- graduated cylinder
- oil, light machine, 15 mL
- pan, large, at least 22 cm in diameter
- pipet
- ruler, metric
- water

SAFETY

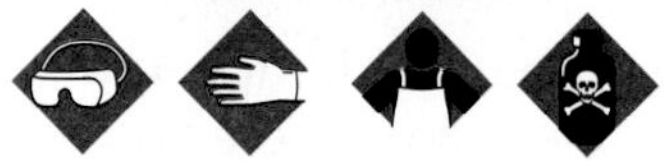

Observing Oil and Water

Maybe you've heard the phrase "Oil and water don't mix." Oil dropped in water will spread out thinly over the surface of the water. In this activity, you'll learn how far a drop of oil can spread.

Ask a Question

1. How far will one drop of oil spread in a pan of water?

Form a Hypothesis

2. Write a hypothesis that could answer the question above.

Test the Hypothesis

3. Use a pipet to place one drop of oil into the middle of a pan of water. **Caution:** Machine oil is poisonous. Wear goggles and gloves. Keep materials that have contacted oil out of your mouth and eyes.
4. Observe what happens to the drop of oil for the next few seconds. Record your observations.
5. Using a metric ruler, measure the diameter of the oil slick to the nearest centimeter.
6. Determine the area of the oil slick in square centimeters. Use the formula below to find the area of a circle ($A = \pi r^2$). The radius (r) is equal to the diameter you measured in step 5 divided by 2. Multiply the radius by itself to get the square of the radius (r^2). Pi (π) is equal to 3.14. Record your answer.

Example

If your diameter is 10 cm,

$r = 5$ cm, $r^2 = 25$ cm^2, $\pi = 3.14$

$$A = \pi r^2$$

$$A = 3.14 \times 25 \text{ cm}^2$$

$$A = 78.5 \text{ cm}^2$$

Analyze the Results

1. What happened to the drop of oil when it came in contact with the water?
2. What total surface area was covered by the oil slick? (Show your calculations.)

Draw Conclusions

3. What can you conclude about the density of oil compared with the density of water?

Finding the Number of Drops in a Liter

"It's only a few drops," you may think as you spill something toxic on the ground. But those drops eventually add up. Just how many drops does it take to make a difference? In this activity, you'll learn just what an impact a few drops can have.

Procedure

1. Using a clean pipet, count the number of water drops it takes to fill the graduated cylinder to 10 mL. Be sure to add the drops slowly so you get an accurate count.
2. Since there are 1,000 mL in a liter, multiply the number of drops in 10 mL by 100. The result is the number of drops in a liter.

Analyze the Results

1. How many drops of water from your pipet did it take to fill a 1 L container?
2. What would happen if someone spilled 4 L of oil into a lake?

Applying Your Data

Can you devise a way to clean the oil from the water? Get permission from your teacher before testing your cleaning method.

Do you think oil behaves the same way in ocean water? Devise an experiment to test your hypothesis.

Model-Making Lab

Turning the Tides

Daily tides are caused by two "bulges" on the ocean's surface—one on the side of the Earth facing the moon and the other on the opposite side of the Earth. The bulge on the side facing the moon is caused by the moon's gravitational pull on the water. But the bulge on the opposite side of the Earth is slightly more difficult to explain. Whereas the moon pulls the water on one side of the Earth, the combined rotation of the Earth and the moon "pushes" the water on the opposite side of the Earth. In this activity, you will model the motion of the Earth and the moon to investigate the tidal bulge on the side of Earth facing away from the moon.

MATERIALS

- cardboard, 1 cm × 1 cm piece
- corrugated cardboard, one large and one small, with centers marked (2 disks)
- dowel, $\frac{1}{4}$ in. in diameter and 36 cm long
- glue, white
- pencil, sharp
- stapler with staples
- string, 5 cm length

SAFETY

Procedure

1. Draw a line from the center of each disk along the folds in the cardboard to the edge of the disk. This line is the radius.
2. Place a drop of white glue on one end of the dowel. Lay the larger disk flat, and align the dowel with the line for the radius you drew in step 1. Insert about 2.5 cm of the dowel into the edge of the disk.
3. Add a drop of glue to the other end of the dowel, and push that end into the smaller disk, again along its radius. The setup should look like a large, two-headed lollipop, as shown below. This setup is a model of the Earth-moon system.
4. Staple the string to the edge of the large disk on the side opposite the dowel. Staple the cardboard square to the other end of the string. This smaller piece of cardboard represents the Earth's oceans that face away from the moon.

5. Place the tip of the pencil at the center of the large disk, as shown in the figure on the next page, and spin the model. You may poke a small hole in the bottom of the disk with your pencil, but DO NOT poke all the way through the cardboard. Record your observations. **Caution:** Be sure you are at a safe distance from other people before spinning your model.

6. Now, find your model's center of mass. The center of mass is the point at which the model can be balanced on the end of the pencil. (Hint: It might be easier to find the center of mass by using the eraser end. Then, use the sharpened end of the pencil to balance the model.) This balance point should be just inside the edge of the larger disk.
7. Place the pencil at the center of mass, and spin the model around the pencil. Again, you may wish to poke a small hole in the disk. Record your observations.

Analyze the Results

1. What happened when you tried to spin the model around the center of the large disk? This model, called the Earth-centered model, represents the incorrect view that the moon orbits the center of the Earth.
2. What happened when you tried to spin the model around its center of mass? This point, called the *barycenter,* is the point around which both the Earth and the moon rotate.
3. In each case, what happened to the string and cardboard square when the model was spun?

Draw Conclusions

4. Which model—the Earth-centered model or the barycentric model—explains why the Earth has a tidal bulge on the side opposite the moon? Explain.

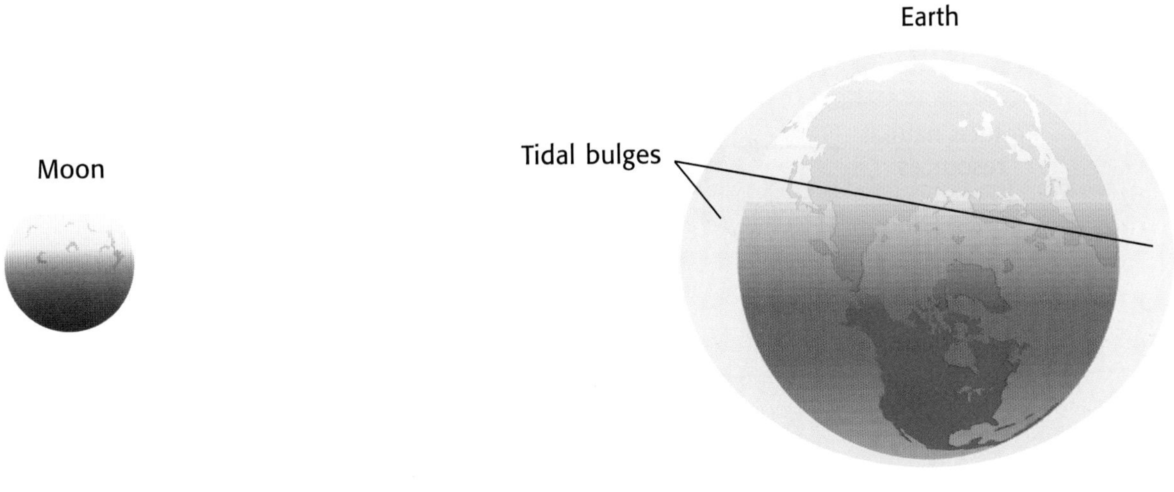

Skills Practice Lab

Deciding About Environmental Issues

You make hundreds of decisions every day. Some of them are complicated, but many of them are very simple, such as what to wear or what to eat for lunch. Deciding what to do about an environmental issue can be very difficult. There are many different factors that must be considered. How will a certain solution affect people's lives? How much will it cost? Is it ethically right?

In this activity, you will analyze an issue in four steps to help you make a decision about it. Find out about environmental issues that are being discussed in your area. Examine newspapers, magazines, and other publications to find out what the issues are. Choose one local issue to evaluate. For example, you could evaluate whether the city should spend the money to provide recycling bins and special trucks for picking up recyclable trash.

MATERIALS

- newspapers, magazines, and other publications containing information about environmental issues

A Four-Step Decision-Making Model

Gather Information
↓
Consider Values
↓
Explore Consequences
↓
Make a Decision

Procedure

1. Write a statement about an environmental issue.
2. Read about your issue in several publications. On a separate sheet of paper, summarize important facts.
3. The values of an issue are the things that you consider important. Examine the diagram below. Several values are given. Which values do you think apply most to the environmental issue you are considering? Are there other values that you believe will help you make a decision about the issue? Consider at least four values in making your decision.

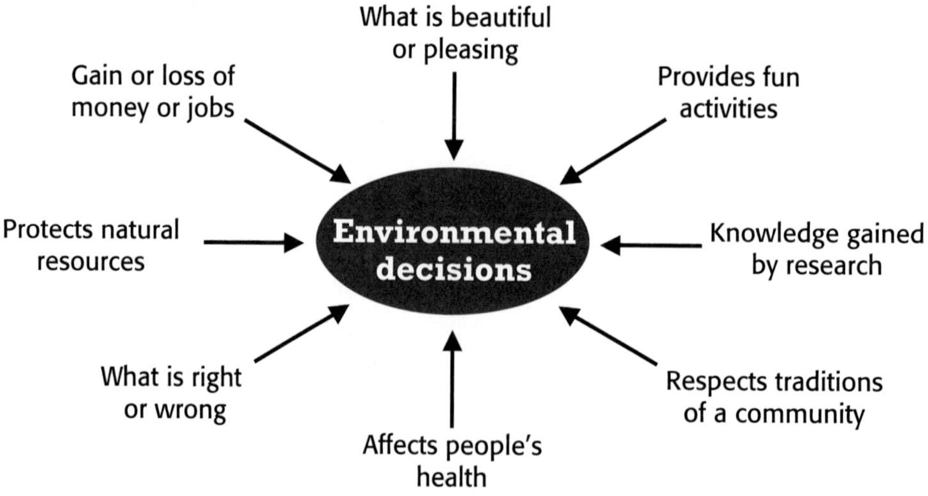

4. Consequences are the things that result from a certain course of action. Create a table similar to the one below. Use your table to organize your thoughts about consequences related to your environmental issue. List your values at the top. Fill in each space with the consequences for each value.

Consequences Table				
	Values			
Consequences				
Positive short-term consequences				
Negative short-term consequences		DO NOT WRITE IN BOOK		
Positive long-term consequences				
Negative long-term consequences				

5. Thoroughly consider all of the consequences you have recorded in your table. Evaluate how important each consequence is. Make a decision about what course of action you would choose on the issue.

Analyze the Results

1. In your evaluation, did you consider short-term consequences or long-term consequences to be more important? Why?

2. Which value or values had the greatest influence on your final decision? Explain your reasoning.

Communicating Your Data

Compare your table with your classmates' tables. Did you all make the same decision about a similar issue? If not, form teams, and organize a formal classroom debate of a specific environmental issue.

Using Scientific Methods

Skills Practice Lab

The Sun's Yearly Trip Through the Zodiac

During the course of a year, the sun appears to move through a circle of 12 constellations in the sky. The 12 constellations make up a "belt" in the sky called the *zodiac.* Each month, the sun appears to be in a different constellation. The ancient Babylonians developed a 12-month calendar based on the idea that the sun moved through this circle of constellations as it revolved around the Earth. They believed that the constellations of stars were fixed in position and that the sun and planets moved past the stars. Later, Copernicus developed a model of the solar system in which the Earth and the planets revolve around the sun. But how can Copernicus's model of the solar system be correct when the sun appears to move through the zodiac?

MATERIALS

- ball, inflated
- box, cardboard, large
- cards, index (12)
- chairs (12)
- tape, masking (1 roll)

Ask a Question

1. If the sun is at the center of the solar system, why does it appear to move with respect to the stars in the sky?

Form a Hypothesis

2. Write a possible answer to the question above. Explain your reasoning.

Test the Hypothesis

3. Set the chairs in a large circle so that the backs of the chairs all face the center of the circle. Make sure that the chairs are equally spaced, like the numbers on the face of a clock.
4. Write the name of each constellation in the zodiac on the index cards. You should have one card for each constellation.
5. Stand inside the circle with the masking tape and the index cards. Moving counterclockwise, attach the cards to the backs of the chairs in the following order: Aries, Taurus, Gemini, Cancer, Leo, Virgo, Libra, Scorpio, Sagittarius, Capricorn, Aquarius, and Pisces.

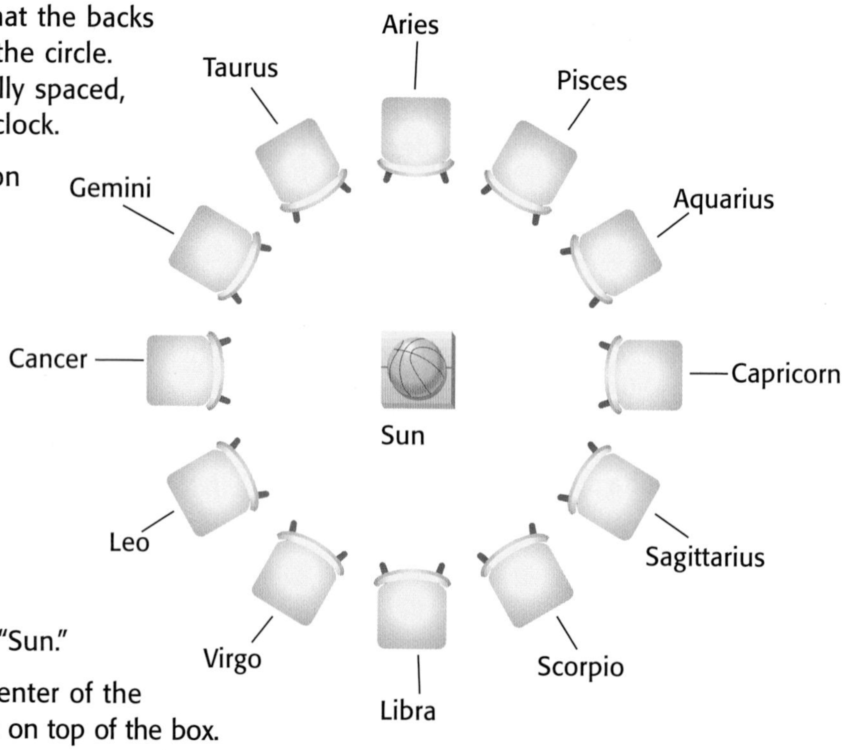

6. Use masking tape to label the ball "Sun."
7. Place the large, closed box in the center of the circle. Set the roll of masking tape flat on top of the box.

8 Place the ball on top of the roll of masking tape so that the ball stays in place.

9 Stand inside the circle of chairs. You will represent the Earth. As you move around the ball, you will model the Earth's orbit around the sun. Notice that even though only the "Earth" is moving, as seen from the Earth, the sun appears to move through the entire zodiac!

10 Stand in front of the chair labeled "Aries." Look at the ball representing the sun. Then, look past the ball to the chair at the opposite side of the circle. Where in the zodiac does the sun appear to be?

11 Move to the next chair on your right (counterclockwise). Where does the sun appear to be? Is it in the same constellation? Explain your answer.

12 Repeat step 10 until you have observed the position of the sun from each chair in the circle.

Analyze the Results

1 Did the sun appear to move through the 12 constellations, even though the Earth was orbiting around the sun? How can you explain this apparent movement?

Draw Conclusions

2 How does Copernicus's model of the solar system explain the apparent movement of the sun through the constellations of the zodiac?

Using Scientific Methods

Skills Practice Lab

I See the Light!

How do you find the distance to an object you can't reach? You can do it by measuring something you can reach, finding a few angles, and using mathematics. In this activity, you'll practice measuring the distances of objects here on Earth. When you get used to it, you can take your skills to the stars!

MATERIALS

- calculator, scientific
- meterstick
- pencil, sharp
- poster board, 16 × 16 cm
- protractor
- ruler, metric
- scissors
- string, 30 cm
- tape measure, metric
- tape, transparent

SAFETY

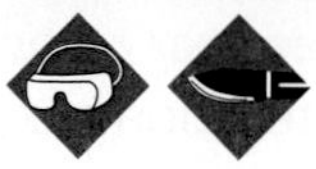

Ask a Question

1. How can you measure the distance to a star?

Form a Hypothesis

2. Write a hypothesis that might answer this question. Explain your reasoning.

Test the Hypothesis

3. Draw a line 4 cm away from the edge of one side of the piece of poster board. Fold the poster board along this line.
4. Tape the protractor to the poster board with its flat edge against the fold, as shown in the photo below.

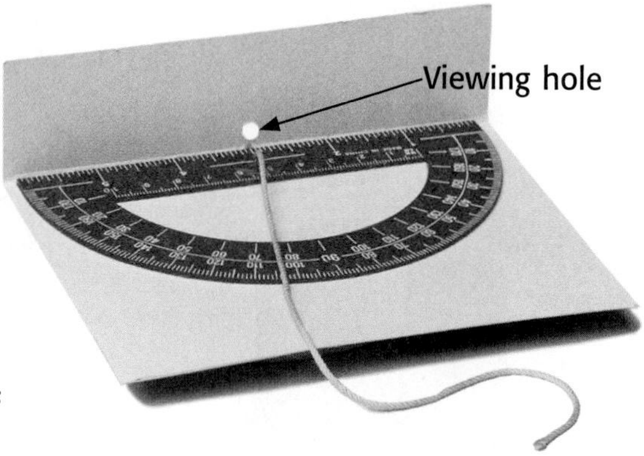

5. Use a pencil to carefully punch a hole through the poster board along its folded edge at the center of the protractor.
6. Thread the string through the hole, and tape one end to the underside of the poster board. The other end should be long enough to hang off the far end of the poster board.
7. Carefully punch a second hole in the smaller area of the poster board halfway between its short sides. The hole should be directly above the first hole and should be large enough for the pencil to fit through. This hole is the viewing hole of your new parallax device. This device will allow you to measure the distance of faraway objects.
8. Find a location that is at least 50 steps away from a tall, narrow object, such as the school's flagpole or a tall tree. (This object will represent background stars.) Set the meterstick on the ground with one of its long edges facing the flagpole.
9. Ask your partner, who represents a nearby star, to take 10 steps toward the flagpole, starting at the left end of the meterstick. You will be the observer. When you stand at the left end of the meterstick, which represents the location of the sun, your partner's nose should be lined up with the flagpole.

10. Move to the other end of the meterstick, which represents the location of Earth. Does your partner appear to the left or right of the flagpole? Record your observations.

11. Hold the string so that it runs straight from the viewing hole to the 90° mark on the protractor. Using one eye, look through the viewing hole along the string, and point the device at your partner's nose.

12. Holding the device still, slowly move your head until you can see the flagpole through the viewing hole. Move the string so that it lines up between your eye and the flagpole. Make sure the string is taut, and hold it tightly against the protractor.

13. Read and record the angle made by the string and the string's original position at 90° (count the number of degrees between 90° and the string's new position).

14. Use the measuring tape to find and record the distance from the left end of the meterstick to your partner's nose.

15. Now, find a place outside that is at least 100 steps away from the flagpole. Set the meterstick on the ground as before, and repeat steps 9–14.

Analyze the Results

1. The angle you recorded in step 13 is called the *parallax angle.* The distance from one end of the meterstick to the other is called the *baseline.* With this angle and the length of your baseline, you can calculate the distance to your partner.

2. To calculate the distance (d) to your partner, use the following equation:

$$d = b/\tan A$$

In this equation, A is the parallax angle, and b is the length of the baseline (1 m). (Tan A means the tangent of angle A, which you will learn more about in math classes.)

3. To find d, enter 1 (the length of your baseline in meters) into the calculator, press the division key, enter the value of A (the parallax angle you recorded), then press the tan key. Finally, press the equals key.

4. Record this result. It is the distance in meters between the left end of the meterstick and your partner. You may want to use a table like the one below.

5. How close is this calculated distance to the distance you measured?

6. Repeat steps 1–3 under Analyze the Results using the angle you found when the flagpole was 100 steps away.

Draw Conclusions

7. At which position, 50 steps or 100 steps from the flagpole, did your calculated distance better match the actual distance as measured?

8. What do you think would happen if you were even farther from the flagpole?

9. When astronomers use parallax, their "flagpoles" are distant stars. Might this affect the accuracy of their parallax readings?

Distance by Parallax Versus Measuring Tape

	At 50 steps	At 100 steps
Parallax		
angle		
Distance (calculated)		
Distance (measured)		

Using Scientific Methods

Inquiry Lab

Muscles at Work

Have you ever exercised outside on a cold fall day wearing only a thin warm-up suit or shorts? How did you stay warm? The answer is that your muscle cells contracted, and when contraction takes place, some energy is used to do work, and the rest is converted to thermal energy. This process helps your body maintain a constant temperature in cold conditions. In this activity, you will learn how the release of energy can cause a change in your body temperature.

MATERIALS

- clock (or watch) with a second hand
- thermometer, small, hand held
- other materials as approved by your teacher

Ask a Question

1. Write a question that you can test about how activity affects body temperature.

Form a Hypothesis

2. Form a group of four students. In your group, discuss several exercises that can produce a change in body temperature. Write a hypothesis that could answer the question you asked.

Test the Hypothesis

3. Develop an experimental procedure that includes the steps necessary to test your hypothesis. Be sure to get your teacher's approval before you begin.
4. Assign tasks to individuals in the group, such as note taking, data recording, and timing. What observations and data will you be recording? Design your data tables accordingly.
5. Perform your experiment as planned by your group. Be sure to record all observations in your data tables.

Analyze the Results

1. How did you determine if muscle contractions cause the release of thermal energy? Was your hypothesis supported by your data? Explain your results in a written report. Describe how you could improve your experimental method.

Applying Your Data

Why do humans shiver in the cold? Do all animals shiver? Find out why shivering is one of the first signs that your body is becoming too cold.

Model-Making Lab

Build a Lung

When you breathe, you actually pull air into your lungs because your diaphragm muscle causes your chest to expand. You can see this is true by placing your hands on your ribs and inhaling slowly. Did you feel your chest expand?

In this activity, you will build a model of a lung by using some common materials. You will see how the diaphragm muscle works to inflate your lungs. Refer to the diagrams at right as you construct your model.

MATERIALS

- bag, trash, small plastic
- balloon, small
- bottle, top half, 2 L
- clay, golf-ball-sized piece
- rubber bands (2)
- ruler, metric
- straw, plastic
- tape, transparent

Procedure

1. Attach the balloon to the end of the straw with a rubber band. Make a hole through the clay, and insert the other end of the straw through the hole. Be sure at least 8 cm of the straw extends beyond the clay. Squeeze the ball of clay gently to seal the clay around the straw.
2. Insert the balloon end of the straw into the neck of the bottle. Use the ball of clay to seal the straw and balloon into the bottle.
3. Turn the bottle gently on its side. Place the trash bag over the cut end of the bottle. Expand a rubber band around the bottom of the bottle to secure the bag. You may wish to reinforce the seal with tape. Before the plastic is completely sealed, gather the excess material of the bag into your hand, and press toward the inside of the bottle slightly. (You may need to tie a knot about halfway up from the bottom of the bag to take up excess material.) Use tape to finish sealing the bag to the bottle with the bag in this position. The excess air will be pushed out of the bottle.

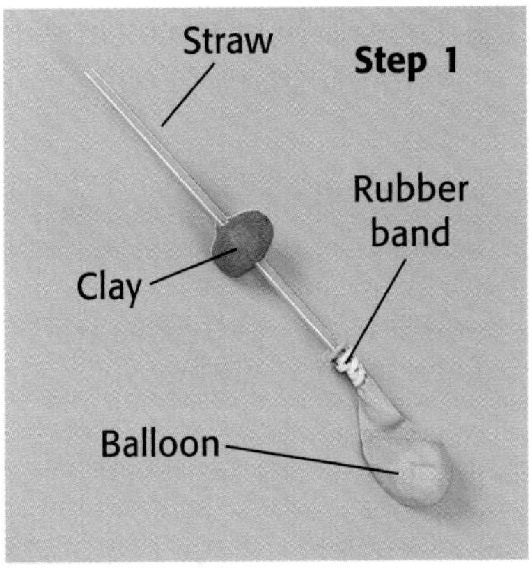

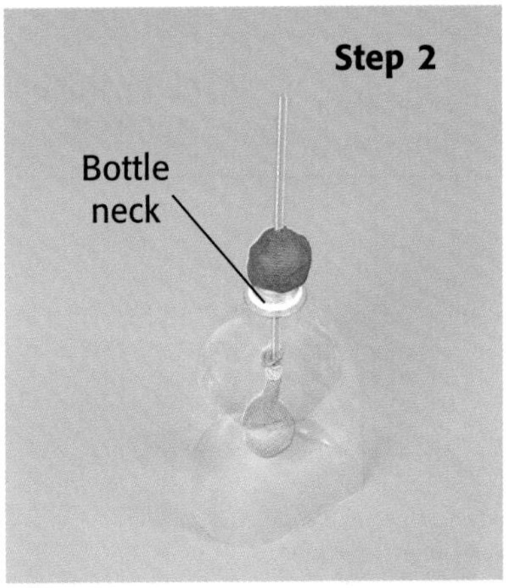

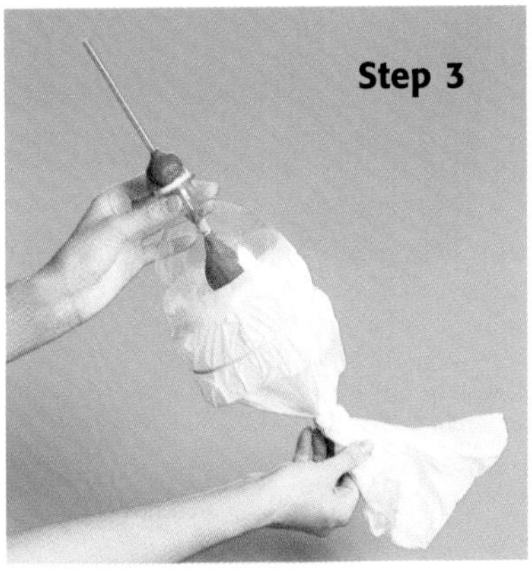

Analyze the Results

1. What can you do with your model to make the "lung" inflate?
2. What do the balloon, the plastic wrap, and the straw represent in your model?
3. Using your model, demonstrate to the class how air enters the lung and how air exits the lung.

Applying Your Data

Do some research to find out what an "iron lung" is and why it was used in the past. Research and write a report about what is used today to help people who have difficulty breathing.

LabBook

Skills Practice Lab

Enzymes in Action

You know how important enzymes are in the process of digestion. This lab will help you see enzymes at work. Hydrogen peroxide is continuously produced by your cells. If it is not quickly broken down, hydrogen peroxide will kill your cells. Luckily, your cells contain an enzyme that converts hydrogen peroxide into two nonpoisonous substances. This enzyme is also present in the cells of beef liver. In this lab, you will observe the action of this enzyme on hydrogen peroxide.

MATERIALS

- beef liver, 1 cm cubes (3)
- gloves, protective
- graduated cylinder, 10 mL
- hydrogen peroxide, fresh (4 mL)
- mortar and pestle (or fork and watch glass)
- plate, small
- spatula
- test tube (3)
- test-tube rack
- tweezers
- water

SAFETY

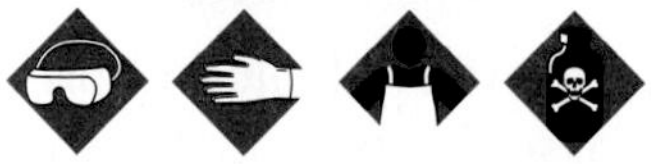

Procedure

1. Draw a data table similar to the one below. Be sure to leave enough space to write your observations.

Data Table

Size and condition of liver	Experimental liquid	Observations
1 cm cube beef liver	2 mL water	
1 cm cube beef liver	2 mL hydrogen peroxide	DO NOT WRITE IN BOOK
1 cm cube beef liver (mashed)	2 mL hydrogen peroxide	

2. Get three equal-sized pieces of beef liver from your teacher, and use your forceps to place them on your plate.
3. Pour 2 mL of water into a test tube labeled "Water and liver."
4. Using the tweezers, carefully place one piece of liver in the test tube. Record your observations in your data table.
5. Pour 2 mL of hydrogen peroxide into a second test tube labeled "Liver and hydrogen peroxide."
   Caution: Do not splash hydrogen peroxide on your skin. If you do get hydrogen peroxide on your skin, rinse the affected area with running water immediately, and tell your teacher.
6. Using the tweezers, carefully place one piece of liver in the test tube. Record your observations of the second test tube in your data table.
7. Pour another 2 mL of hydrogen peroxide into a third test tube labeled "Ground liver and hydrogen peroxide."
8. Using a mortar and pestle (or fork and watch glass), carefully grind the third piece of liver.
9. Using the spatula, scrape the ground liver into the third test tube. Record your observations of the third test tube in your data table.

Analyze the Results

1. What was the purpose of putting the first piece of liver in water? Why was this a necessary step?
2. Describe the difference you observed between the liver and the ground liver when each was placed in the hydrogen peroxide. How can you account for this difference?

Applying Your Data

Do plant cells contain enzymes that break down hydrogen peroxide? Try this experiment using potato cubes instead of liver to find out.

Skills Practice Lab

My, How You've Grown!

In humans, the process of development that takes place between fertilization and birth lasts about 266 days. In 4 weeks, the new individual grows from a single fertilized cell to an embryo whose heart is beating and pumping blood. All of the organ systems and body parts are completely formed by the end of the seventh month. During the last 2 months before birth, the baby grows, and its organ systems mature. At birth, the average mass of a baby is about 33,000 times as much as that of an embryo at 2 weeks of development! In this activity, you will discover just how fast a fetus grows.

MATERIALS

- paper, graph
- pencils, colored

Procedure

1. Using graph paper, make two graphs—one entitled "Length" and one entitled "Mass." On the length graph, use intervals of 25 mm on the *y*-axis. Extend the *y*-axis to 500 mm. On the mass graph, use intervals of 100 g on the *y*-axis. Extend this *y*-axis to 3,300 g. Use 2-week intervals for time on the *x*-axes for both graphs. Both *x*-axes should extend to 40 weeks.
2. Examine the data table at right. Plot the data in the table on your graphs. Use a colored pencil to draw the curved line that joins the points on each graph.

Increase of Mass and Length of Average Human Fetus

Time (weeks)	Mass (g)	Length (mm)
2	0.1	1.5
3	0.3	2.3
4	0.5	5.0
5	0.6	10.0
6	0.8	15.0
8	1.0	30.0
13	15.0	90.0
17	115.0	140.0
21	300.0	250.0
26	950.0	320.0
30	1,500.0	400.0
35	2,300.0	450.0
40	3,300.0	500.0

Analyze the Results

1. Describe the change in mass of a developing fetus. How can you explain this change?
2. Describe the change in length of a developing fetus. How does the change in mass compare to the change in length?

Applying Your Data

Using the information in your graphs, estimate how tall a child would be at age 3 if he or she continued to grow at the same average rate that a fetus grows.

Model-Making Lab

Antibodies to the Rescue

Some cells of the immune system, called *B cells,* make antibodies that attack and kill invading viruses and microorganisms. These antibodies help make you immune to disease. Have you ever had chickenpox? If you have, your body has built up antibodies that can recognize that particular virus. Antibodies will attach themselves to the virus, tagging it for destruction. If you are exposed to the same disease again, the antibodies remember that virus. They will attack the virus even quicker and in greater number than they did the first time. This is the reason that you will probably never have chickenpox more than once.

In this activity, you will construct simple models of viruses and their antibodies. You will see how antibodies are specific for a particular virus.

MATERIALS

- craft materials, such as buttons, fabric scraps, pipe cleaners, and recycled materials
- paper, colored
- scissors
- tape (or glue)

Procedure

1. Draw the virus patterns shown on this page on a separate piece of paper, or design your own virus models from the craft supplies. Remember to design different receptors on each of your virus models.
2. Write a few sentences describing how your viruses are different.
3. Cut out the viruses, and attach them to a piece of colored paper with tape or glue.

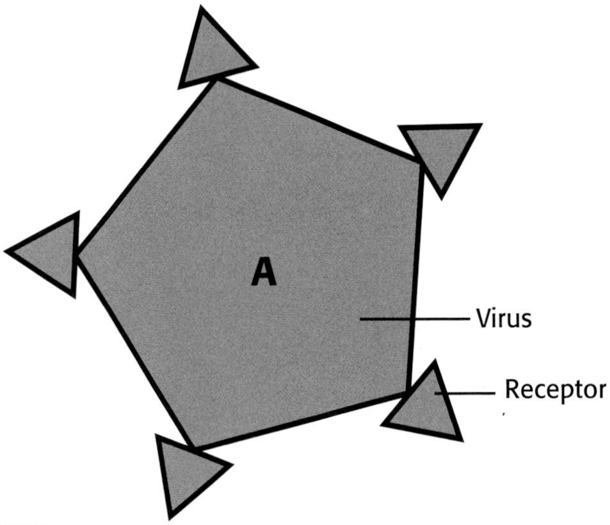

Viruses

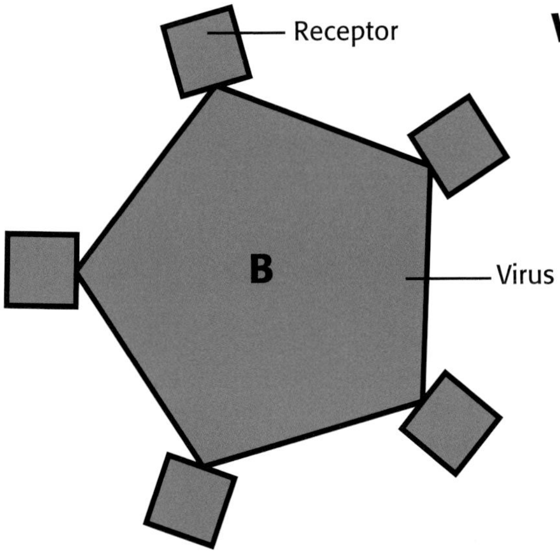

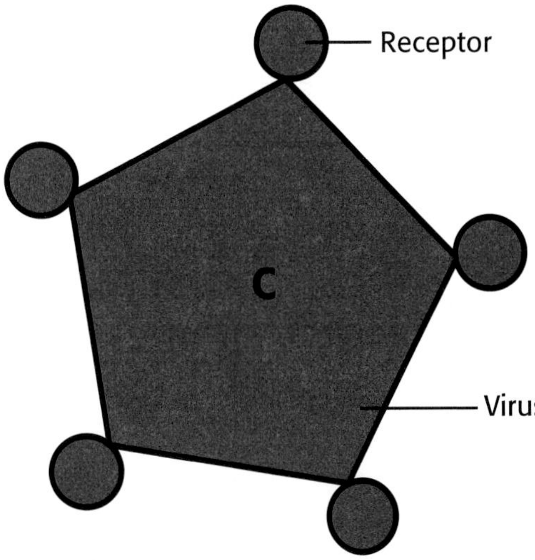

4. Select the antibodies drawn below, or design your own antibodies that will exactly fit on the receptors on your virus models. Draw or create each antibody enough times to attach one to each receptor site on the virus.

Antibodies

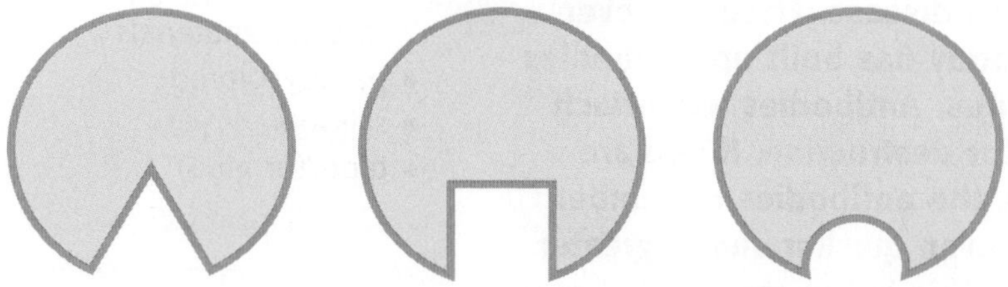

5. Cut out the antibodies you have drawn. Arrange the antibodies so that they bind to the virus at the appropriate receptor. Attach them to the virus with tape or glue.

Analyze the Results

1. Explain how an antibody "recognizes" a particular virus.
2. After the attachment of antibodies to the receptors, what would be the next step in the immune response?
3. Many vaccines use weakened copies of the virus to protect the body. Use the model of a virus and its specific antibody to explain how vaccines work.

Draw Conclusions

4. Use your model of a virus to demonstrate to the class how a receptor might change or mutate so that a vaccine would no longer be effective.

Applying Your Data

Research in the library or on the Internet to find information about the discovery of the Salk vaccine for polio. Include information on how polio affects people today.

Research in the library or on the Internet to find information and write a report about filoviruses. What do they look like? What diseases do they cause? Why are they especially dangerous? Is there an effective vaccine against any filovirus? Explain.

Skills Practice Lab

To Diet or Not to Diet

There are six main classes of foods that we need in order to keep our bodies functioning properly: water, vitamins, minerals, carbohydrates, fats, and proteins. In this activity you will investigate the importance of a well-balanced diet in maintaining a healthy body. Then you will create a poster or picture that illustrates the importance of one of the three energy-producing nutrients—carbohydrates, fats, and proteins.

MATERIALS

- crayons (or markers), assorted colors
- diet books
- menus, fast-food (optional)
- nutrition reference books
- paper, white unlined

Procedure

1. Draw a table like the one below. Research in the library, on nutrition labels, in nutrition or diet books, or on the Internet to find the information you need to fill out the chart.

Nutrition Data Table

	Fats	Carbohydrates	Proteins
Found in which foods			
Functions in the body		DO NOT WRITE IN BOOK	
Consequences of deficiency			

2. Choose one of the foods you have learned about in your research, and create a poster or picture that describes its importance in a well-balanced diet.

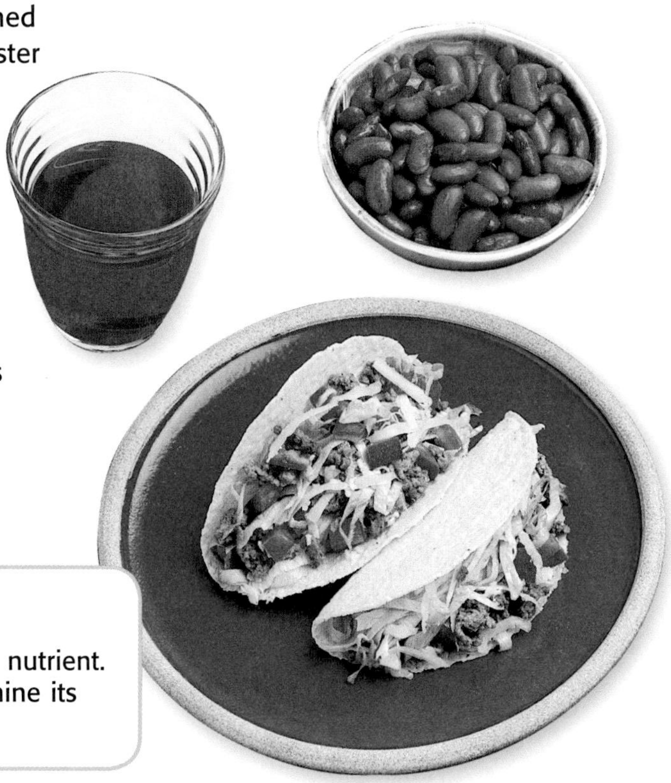

Analyze the Results

1. Based on what you have learned in this lab, how might you change your eating habits to have a well-balanced diet? Does the nutritional value of foods concern you? Why or why not? Write down your answers, and explain your reasoning.

Communicating Your Data

Write a paragraph explaining why water is a nutrient. Analyze a typical fast-food meal, and determine its overall nutritional value.

Contents

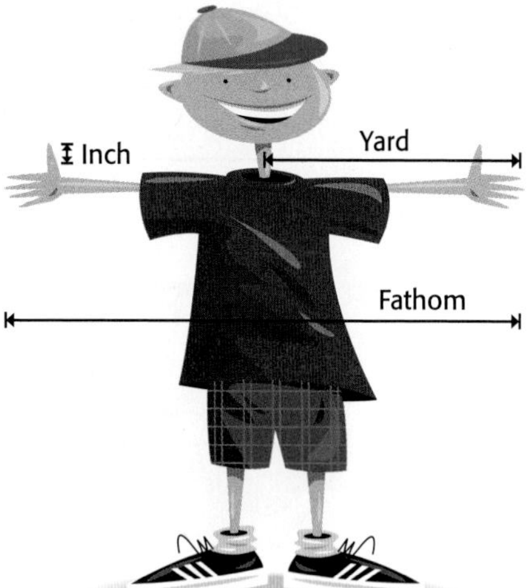

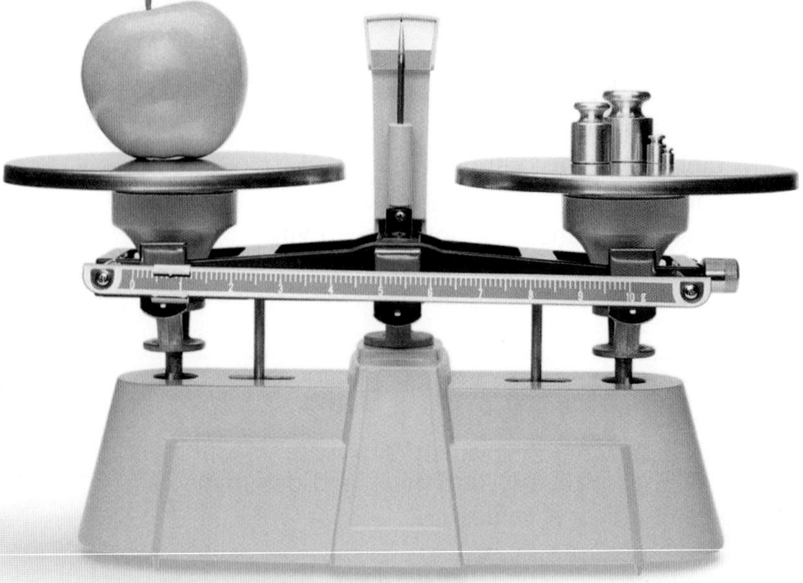

✓Reading Check Answers

Chapter 1 Science in Our World

Section 1

Page 5: If your materials are hard to find, you can do more research and look for new ideas or resources from the results of someone else's experiment.

Page 7: A meteorologist is a scientist who studies Earth's atmosphere.

Page 9: A science illustrator uses art and science skills to draw scientific diagrams.

Section 2

Page 13: A prediction is a statement that describes what a scientist thinks will happen during the test of a hypothesis.

Page 15: Once you have your data, you must analyze them.

Section 3

Page 19: A conceptual model is a system of ideas or a model based on making comparisons with familiar things to explain an idea.

Page 20: A theory is a unifying explanation for a broad range of hypotheses and observations that have been supported by testing.

Section 4

Page 23: Stopwatches, metersticks, and balances are some of the tools that you can use to make measurements.

Page 26: The kelvin is the SI basic unit for temperature.

Chapter 2 Introduction To Matter

Section 1

Page 40: All matter has mass and volume.

Page 41: Weight is a measure of gravitational force acting on an object, but mass is a measure of the amount of matter in an object.

Page 43: Sample answer: If two substances have the same volume, you can tell the difference between them by finding the mass of each substance. Because most substances have different densities, the masses of the two substances with the same volume will probably be different.

Section 2

Page 45: An atom is made up of protons, neutrons, and electrons.

Page 46: The charge of a nucleus is important because opposite charges attract. Because the nucleus contains positive protons, negatively charged electrons are attracted to it.

Page 49: Atoms gain, lose, or share electrons with other atoms to form different substances.

Section 3

Page 50: The three states of matter are solid, liquid, and gas. Atoms or molecules in a solid of a substance have fixed positions and move more slowly than atoms or molecules in a liquid or gas of the substance do. Atoms or molecules in liquids and gases do not have fixed positions.

Page 51: The particles in a crystalline solid are arranged in a repeating pattern of rows that forms an orderly, three-dimensional arrangement.

Page 52: Viscosity is a liquid's resistance to flow.

Page 53: Compared with atoms of molecules in a liquid, atoms or molecules in a gas move more freely and are arranged in a less orderly fashion.

Page 54: Water drops forming on the outside of a cold glass are an example of condensation.

Section 4

Page 56: Physical properties are characteristics that can be observed without changing the identity of the material. Chemical properties are characteristics that describe how a substance is able to change into other substances.

Page 59: Flammability and reactivity are two chemical properties that can be used to identify substances.

Page 60: Substances have unique combinations of physical and chemical properties. When several properties are used, it is possible to quickly identify an unknown substance.

Section 5

Page 62: In a physical change, no new substance is formed. In a chemical change, one or more new substances are formed.

Page 64: A chemical change results in the formation of one or more new substances. A physical change does not result in the formation of a new substance.

Chapter 3 The Energy of Waves

Section 1

Page 76: All waves are disturbances that transmit energy.

Page 78: Electromagnetic waves do not require a medium.

Page 80: A sound wave is a longitudinal wave.

Section 2

Page 83: Shaking the rope faster makes the wavelength shorter; shaking the rope more slowly makes the wavelength longer.

Page 84: 3 Hz

Section 3

Page 87: It refracts.

Page 89: Constructive interference occurs when the crests of one wave overlap the crests of another wave.

Page 90: A standing wave results from a wave that is reflected between two fixed points. Interference from the wave and reflected waves causes certain points to remain at rest and certain points to remain at a large amplitude.

Chapter 4 The Nature of Sound

Section 1

Page 103: Sound waves consist of longitudinal waves carried through a medium.

Page 104: Sound needs a medium in order to travel.

Page 106: Tinnitus is caused by long-term exposure to loud sounds.

Section 2

Page 109: Frequency is the number of crests or troughs made in a given time.

Page 111: The amplitude of a sound increases as the energy of the vibrations that caused the sound increases.

Page 112: An oscilloscope turns sounds into electrical signals and graphs the signals.

Section 3

Page 115: Echolocation helps some animals find food.

Page 116: Sound wave interference can be either constructive or destructive.

Page 118: A standing wave is a pattern of vibration that looks like a wave that is standing still.

Section 4

Page 121: Musical instruments differ in the part of the instrument that vibrates and in the way that the vibrations are made.

Page 123: Music consists of sound waves that have regular patterns, and noise consists of a random mix of frequencies.

Chapter 5 The Nature of Light

Section 1

Page 135: Electric fields can be found around every charged object.

Page 136: The speed of light is about 880,000 times faster than the speed of sound.

Section 2

Page 138: The speed of a wave is determined by multiplying the wavelength and frequency of the wave.

Page 140: Radio waves carry TV signals.

Page 142: White light is the combination of visible light of all wavelengths.

Page 143: Ultraviolet light waves have shorter wavelengths and higher frequencies than visible light waves do.

Page 144: Patients are protected from X rays by special lead-lined aprons.

Section 3

Page 146: The law of reflection states that the angle of incidence equals the angle of reflection.

Page 147: Sample answer: Four light sources are a television screen, a fluorescent light in the classroom, a light bulb, and the tail of a firefly.

Page 148: You can see things outside of a beam of light because light is scattered outside of the beam.

Page 151: The amount that a wave diffracts depends on the wavelength of the wave and the size of the barrier or opening.

Page 152: Constructive interference is interference in which the resulting wave has a greater amplitude than the original waves had.

Section 4

Page 155: Sample answer: Two translucent objects are a frosted window and wax paper.

Page 156: When white light shines on a colored opaque object, some of the colors of light are absorbed and some are reflected.

Page 158: A pigment is a material that gives color to a substance by absorbing some colors of light and reflecting others.

Chapter 6 Light and Our World

Section 1

Page 171: A virtual image is an image through which light does not travel.

Page 172: A concave mirror can be used to make a powerful beam of light by putting a light source at the focal point of the mirror.

Page 174: A convex lens in thicker in the middle than it is at the edges.

Section 2

Page 177: Nearsightedness happens when a person's eye is too long. Farsightedness happens when a person's eye is too short.

Page 178: The three kinds of cones are red, blue, and green.

Section 3

Page 181: When light is coherent, light waves move together as they travel away from their source. Individual waves behave as one wave.

Page 183: Holograms are like photographs because both are images recorded on film.

Page 185: A cordless telephone sends signals by using radio waves.

Page 186: Sample answer: GPS can be used by hikers and campers to find their way in the wilderness. GPS can also be used for treasure hunt games.

Chapter 7 Introduction to Electricity

Section 1

Page 200: protons and electrons

Page 202: friction, conduction, and induction

Page 203: You can use an electroscope to detect whether an object is charged.

Page 205: Electric discharge is the release of electricity stored in a source.

Page 206: Sample answer: A person in an open area might be the tallest object and might provide a path for lightning.

Section 2

Page 208: amperes (A)

Page 209: alternating current (AC) and direct current (DC)

Page 210: volts (V)

Page 213: wet cells and dry cells

Page 214: a photocell

Section 3

Page 217: watt (W) and kilowatt (kW)

Page 218: kilowatt-hour (kWh)

Section 4

Page 220: an energy source, wires, and a load

Page 221: series circuits and parallel circuits

Page 222: Loads are connected in a single loop in a series circuit.

Page 223: Loads are connected side by side in branches in a parallel circuit.

Page 224: fuses and circuit breakers

Chapter 8 Electromagnetism

Section 1

Page 236: A magnet is any material that attracts iron or things made of iron.

Page 237: The poles of the magnets are identical.

Page 238: The magnetic fields of the individual atoms cancel each other out.

Page 239: A magnet can lose its magnetic properties if it is dropped, hit, placed in a strong magnetic field that is opposite to its own, or heated.

Page 240: Ferromagnets are magnets made of iron, nickel, cobalt, or mixtures of these metals.

Page 242: Scientists think that the Earth's magnetic field is caused by the movement of electric charges in the Earth's liquid outer core.

Section 2

Page 245: the interaction between electricity and magnetism

Page 246: The magnetic field gets stronger.

Page 247: The electric current creates a magnetic field that exerts a force on the compass needle and causes the compass needle to move.

Page 249: electric current

Section 3

Page 250: Faraday was trying to induce a current in a wire by using the magnetic field of an electromagnet.

Page 252: Mechanical energy is converted into electrical energy in an electric generator.

Page 253: A nuclear reaction, fossil fuels, and wind are sources of energy that are used to generate electrical energy.

Page 254: A transformer increases or decreases the voltage of alternating current.

Chapter 9 Electronic Technology

Section 1

Page 267: The conductivity of the semiconductor is changed by doping.

Page 268: A diode allows current in only one direction, so it blocks current that is in the other direction.

Page 269: NPN and PNP

Page 270: Devices can be made smaller and can run faster by using integrated circuits.

Section 2

Page 273: An analog signal is a signal whose properties can change continuously in a given range.

Page 275: A digital recording can be made to sound more like the original sound by taking more samples each second.

Page 277: analog signals and digital signals

Page 278: A plasma display does not use electron beams to activate the fluorescent materials. Instead, each tiny cell is activated individually.

Section 3

Page 280: input, processing, storage, and output

Page 281: A microprocessor is a single semiconductor chip that controls and executes a microcomputer's instructions.

Page 282: central processing unit

Page 285: operating-system software and application software

Page 286: Sample answer: The World Wide Web is a collection of pages that share a format that can be viewed on any computer.

Chapter 10 Energy Resources

Section 1

Page 299: A renewable resource is a natural resource that can be replaced at the same rate at which the resource is used.

Page 301: Answers may vary. Sample answer: newspapers, plastic containers, and cardboard boxes.

Section 2

Page 303: Natural gas is most often used for heating and for generating electrical energy.

Page 304: Coal was most commonly used to power trains.

Page 307: Natural gas and petroleum are removed from the Earth by drilling wells into rock that contains petroleum and natural gas.

Page 308: The sulfur dioxide released from the burning coal combines with moisture in the air to produce acid rain.

Section 3

Page 311: Fusion produces few dangerous wastes.

Page 312: The energy of fossil fuels comes from the sun.

Page 314: Hydroelectric energy is renewable because water is constantly recycled.

Page 316: Geothermal power plants obtain energy from the Earth by pumping steam and hot water from wells drilled into the rock.

Chapter 11 Exploring the Oceans

Section 1

Page 331: The first oceans began to form sometime before 4 billion years ago as the Earth cooled enough for water vapor to condense and fall as rain.

Page 332: Coastal water in places with hotter, drier climates has a higher salinity because less fresh water runs into the ocean in drier areas and because heat increases the evaporation rate.

Page 334: Parts of the ocean along the equator are warmer because they receive more sunlight per year.

Page 336: If the ocean did not release thermal energy so slowly, the air temperature on land would vary greatly from above 100°C during the day to below 100°C at night.

Section 2

Page 339: Satellite photos from *Seasat* send images of the ocean back to Earth. These images allow scientists to measure the direction and speed of ocean currents. Satellite photos and information from *Geosat* have been used to measure slight changes in the height of the ocean's surface.

Page 340: 64,000 km; on the ocean floor

Page 341: continental shelf, continental slope, and continental rise

Page 342: It is unique because some organisms living around the vent do not rely on photosynthesis for energy.

Section 3

Page 345: The tough shells of clams and oysters protect the organisms against strong waves and harsh sunlight.

Page 347: crabs, sponges, worms, and sea cucumbers

Page 348: The neritic zone contains the largest concentration of marine life in the ocean because it receives more sunlight than the other zones in the ocean.

Section 4

Page 351: Fish farms can help reduce overfishing because the fish are raised instead of fished directly out of the ocean.

Page 352: Nonrenewable resources are resources that cannot be replenished. Oil and natural gas are nonrenewable resources.

Page 353: Desalination plants are most likely to be built in drier parts of the world, and where governments can afford to buy expensive equipment. Most desalination plants are in the Middle East, where the fuel needed to run the plants is relatively inexpensive.

Page 355: Wave energy would be a good alternative energy resource because it is a clean and renewable resource.

Section 5

Page 357: One effect of trash dumping is that plastic materials may harm and kill marine animals because these animals may mistake the trash for food.

Page 359: An oil tanker that has two hulls can prevent an oil spill, because if the outer hull is damaged, the inner hull will prevent oil from spilling into the ocean.

Page 361: The U.S. Marine Protection, Research, and Sanctuaries Act prohibits the dumping of any material that would affect human health or welfare, the marine environment or ecosystems, or businesses that depend on the ocean.

Chapter 12 The Movement of Ocean Water

Section 1

Page 372: Heyerdahl theorized that the inhabitants of Polynesia originally sailed from Peru on rafts powered only by the wind and ocean currents. Heyerdahl proved his theory by sailing from Peru to Polynesia on a raft powered only by wind and ocean currents.

Page 374: The Earth's rotation causes surface currents to move in curved paths rather than in straight lines.

Page 375: The three factors that form a pattern of surface currents on Earth are global winds, the Coriolis effect, and continental deflections.

Page 376: Density causes variations in the movement of deep currents.

Section 2

Page 379: Cold-water currents keep coastal climates cooler than inland climates all year long.

Page 381: Answers may vary. Sample answer: It is important to study El Niño because El Niño can greatly affect organisms and land. One way that scientists study El Niño is through a network of buoys located along the equator. These buoys record information that helps scientists predict when an El Niño is likely to occur.

Section 3

Page 382: The lowest point of a wave is called a *trough*.

Page 384: Deep-water waves become shallow-water waves as they move toward the shore and reach water that is shallower than one-half their wavelength.

Page 387: A storm surge is a local rise in sea level near the shore and is caused by strong winds from a storm, such as a hurricane. Storm surges are difficult to study because they disappear as quickly as they form.

Section 4

Page 388: The gravity of the moon pulls on every particle of the Earth.

Page 390: A tidal range is the difference between levels of ocean water at high tide and low tide.

Chapter 13 Environmental Problems and Solutions

Section 1

Page 402: Sample answer: Hazardous waste is waste that can catch fire, wear through metal, explode, or make people sick.

Page 405: Sample answer: Exotic species are organisms that make a home for themselves in a new place.

Page 406: Point-source pollution is pollution that comes from one place. Nonpoint-source pollution is pollution that comes from many places.

Section 2

Page 408: reduce, reuse, and recycle

Page 410: Sample answer: Water is reclaimed with plants or filter-feeding animals. Then, it can be used to water crops, parks, lawns, and golf courses.

Page 413: Sample answer: The EPA is a government organization that helps protect the environment.

Chapter 14 Studying Space

Section 1

Page 429: Copernicus believed in a sun-centered universe.

Page 430: Newton's law of gravity helped explain why the planets orbit the sun and moons orbit planets.

Section 2

Page 432: The objective lens collects light and forms an image at the back of the telescope. The eyepiece magnifies the image produced by the objective lens.

Page 434: The motion of air, air pollution, water vapor, and light pollution distort the images produced by optical telescopes.

Page 437: because the atmosphere blocks most X-ray radiation from space

Section 3

Page 439: Different constellations are visible in the Northern and Southern Hemispheres because different portions of the sky are visible from the Northern and Southern hemispheres.

Page 441: The apparent movement of the sun and stars is caused by the Earth's rotation on its axis.

Page 442: 9.46 trillion kilometers

Page 444: One might conclude that all of the galaxies are traveling toward the Earth and that the universe is contracting.

Chapter 15 Stars, Galaxies, and the Universe

Section 1

Page 456: Rigel is hotter than Betelgeuse because blue stars are hotter than red stars.

Page 458: A star's absorption spectrum indicates some of the elements that are in the star's atmosphere.

Page 460: Apparent magnitude is the brightness of a light or star.

Page 461: A light-year is the distance that light travels in 1 year.

Page 462: The actual motion of stars is hard to see because the stars are so distant.

Section 2

Page 465: A red giant star is a star that expands and cools once it uses all of its hydrogen. As the center of a star continues to shrink a red giant star can become a red supergiant star.

Page 469: A black hole is an object that is so massive that even light cannot escape its gravity. A black hole can be detected when it gives off X-rays.

Section 3

Page 470: Spiral galaxies have a bulge at the center and spiral arms. The arms of spiral galaxies are made up of gas, dust, and new stars.

Page 472: A globular cluster is a tight group of up to 1 million stars that looks like a ball. An open cluster is a group of closely grouped stars that are usually located along the spiral disk of a galaxy.

Page 473: Quasars are starlike sources of light that are extremely far away. Some scientists think that quasars may be the core of young galaxies that are in the process of forming.

Section 4

Page 475: Cosmic background radiation is radiation that is left over from the big bang. After the big bang, cosmic background radiation was distributed everywhere and filled all of space.

Page 476: One way to calculate the age of the universe is to measure the distance from Earth to various galaxies.

Page 477: If gravity stops the expansion of the universe, the universe might collapse. If the expansion of the universe continues forever, stars will age and die. The universe will eventually become cold and dark.

Chapter 16 Formation of the Solar System

Section 1

Page 489: The solar nebula is the cloud of gas and dust that formed our solar system.

Page 491: Jupiter, Saturn, Uranus, and Neptune

Section 2

Page 493: Energy from gravity is not enough to power the sun, because if all of the sun's gravitational energy were released, the sun would last for only 45 million years.

Page 495: The nuclei of hydrogen atoms repel each other because they are positively charged and like charges repel each other.

Page 496: Sunspots are cooler, dark spots on the sun. They occur because when activity slows down in the convective zone, areas of the photosphere become cooler.

Section 3

Page 498: During Earth's early formation, planetesimals collided with the Earth. The energy of their motion heated the planet.

Page 500: Scientists think that the Earth's first atmosphere was a mixture of CO_2 and water vapor.

Page 502: When photosynthetic organisms appeared on Earth, they released oxygen into the Earth's atmosphere. Over several million years, more and more oxygen was added to the atmosphere, which helped form Earth's current atmosphere.

Section 4

Page 505: Kepler's third law of motion states that planets that are farther away from the sun take longer to orbit the sun.

Page 506: Newton's law of universal gravitation states that the force of gravity depends on the product of the masses of the objects divided by the square of the distance between the objects.

Chapter 17 Body Organization and Structure

Section 1

Page 521: The stomach works with other organs, such as the small and large intestines, to digest food.

Page 522: the cardiovascular and respiratory systems; The respiratory system draws in oxygen which the cardiovascular system transports to every cell in the body. The cardiovascular system also carries the carbon dioxide (which cells produce) to the respiratory system. The respiratory system then expels the carbon dioxide from the body.

Section 2

Page 525: Sample answer: As people grow, most of the cartilage that they start out with is replaced with bone.

Page 526: Sample answer: Joints are held together by ligaments. Cartilage cushions the area in a joint where bones meet.

Section 3

Page 529: Sample answer: One muscle, the flexor, bends part of the body. Another muscle, the extensor, straightens part of the body.

Page 531: Sample answer: Anabolic steroids can damage the heart, liver, and kidneys. They can also cause high blood pressure. Anabolic steroids can cause bones to stop growing.

Section 4

Page 533: The dermis is the layer of skin that lies beneath the epidermis. The dermis is composed of a protein called *collagen,* while the epidermis contains keratin.

Page 534: Sample answer: A nail grows from living cells in the nail root at the base of the nail. As new cells form, the nail grows longer.

Chapter 18 Circulation and Respiration

Section 1

Page 546: The five main parts of the cardiovascular system are the heart, arteries, capillaries, veins, and blood.

Page 548: Arteries have thick, stretchy walls and carry blood away from the heart. Capillaries are tiny blood vessels that allow the exchange of oxygen, carbon dioxide, and nutrients between cells and blood. Veins are blood vessels that carry blood back to the heart.

Page 550: Atherosclerosis is dangerous because it is the build-up of material inside an artery. When the artery becomes blocked, blood can't flow and can't reach the cells. In some cases, a person can have a heart attack from a blocked artery.

Section 2

Page 552: plasma, red blood cells, white blood cells, and platelets

Page 553: White blood cells identify and attack pathogens that may make you sick.

Page 554: Systolic pressure is the pressure inside arteries when the ventricles contract. Diastolic pressure is the pressure inside the arteries when the ventricles are relaxed.

Page 555: The red blood cells of a person who has type O blood have no A or B antigens. The A or B antibodies in another person's blood will not react to the type O cells. It is safe for anyone to receive type O blood.

Section 3

Page 556: The lymphatic system is a group of organs and tissues that collect excess fluid and return the fluid to the cardiovascular system.

Page 558: The white pulp of the spleen is part of the lymphatic system. It helps fight infections by storing and producing lymphocytes. The red pulp of the spleen removes unwanted material, such as defective red blood cells, from the circulatory system.

Section 4

Page 561: nose, pharynx, larynx, trachea, bronchi, bronchioles, alveoli

Page 562: Cellular respiration is the process inside a cell in which oxygen is used to release energy stored in molecules of glucose. During the process, carbon dioxide (CO_2) and water are released.

Chapter 19 The Digestive and Urinary Systems

Section 1

Page 575: Enzymes cut proteins into amino acids that the body can use.

Page 577: Chyme is a soupy mixture of partially digested food in the stomach.

Page 579: Bile breaks large fat droplets into very small droplets. This process allows more fat molecules to be exposed to digestive enzymes.

Page 580: Fiber keeps the stool soft and keeps material moving through the large intestine.

Section 2

Page 583: Nephrons are microscopic filters inside the kidneys.

Page 584: Diuretics are chemicals that cause the kidneys to make more urine.

Chapter 20 Communication and Control

Section 1

Page 596: The CNS is the brain and the spinal cord. The PNS is all of the parts of the nervous system except the brain and the spinal cord.

Page 597: A neuron is a cell that has a cell body and a nucleus. A neuron also has dendrites that receive signals from other neurons and axons that send signals to other neurons.

Page 598: A nerve is a collection of nerve fibers, or axons, bundled together with blood vessels through which impulses travel between the central nervous system and other parts of the body.

Page 599: The PNS connects your CNS to the rest of your body, controls voluntary movements, and keeps your body's functions in balance.

Page 600: A voluntary action is an action over which you have conscious control. Voluntary activities include throwing a ball, playing a video game, talking to your friends, taking a bite of food, and raising your hand to answer a question in class. An involuntary action is an action that happens automatically. It is an action or process over which you do not have conscious control.

Page 601: The medulla is important because it controls your heart rate, blood pressure, and ordinary breathing.

Page 602: When someone touches your skin, an impulse that travels along a sensory neuron to your spinal cord and then to your brain is created. The response travels back from your brain to your spinal cord and then along a motor neuron to a muscle.

Section 2

Page 604: Skin can detect pressure, temperature, pain, and vibration.

Page 605: Reflexes are important because they can protect you from injury.

Page 606: Light strikes cells on the retina and triggers impulses in those cells. The impulses are carried to the brain, which interprets the impulses as images that you "see."

Page 607: In bright light, your iris contracts and reduces the amount of light entering the eye.

Page 608: Neurons in the cochlea convert waves into electrical impulses that the brain interprets as sound.

Section 3

Page 611: Sample answer: The thyroid gland increases the rate at which the body uses energy. The thymus gland regulates the immune system, which helps your body fight disease.

Page 612: Insulin helps regulate the amount of glucose in the blood.

Chapter 21 Reproduction and Development

Section 1

Page 625: Sexual reproduction is reproduction in which the sex cells (egg and sperm) of two parents unite to form a new individual.

Page 626: External fertilization happens when the sex cells unite outside of the female's body. Internal fertilization happens when the sex cells unite inside the female's body.

Page 627: All mammals reproduce sexually and nurture their young with milk.

Section 2

Page 628: testes, epididymis, vas deferens, urethra, penis

Page 630: Twin births occur about 30 times in every 1,000 births.

Section 3

Page 632: Fertilization happens when the nucleus of a sperm unites with the nucleus of an egg, forming a zygote. A zygote becomes an embryo after first cell division. Implantation happens after the embryo travels down the fallopian tube to the uterus and embeds itself in the wall of the uterus.

Page 633: The placenta is important because it provides the embryo with oxygen and nutrients from the mother's blood. Wastes from the embryo also travel to the placenta, where they are carried to the mother so that she can excrete them.

Page 634: The embryo is now called a *fetus.* The fetus's face begins to look more human, and the fetus can swallow, grows rapidly (triples in size), and begins to make movements that the mother can feel.

Page 636: A person's reproductive system becomes mature.

Chapter 22 Body Defenses and Disease

Section 1

Page 651: Cooking kills dangerous bacteria or parasites living in meat, fish, and eggs.

Page 653: Antibiotics can kill only living things. Therefore, antibiotics are not useful in treating colds, because colds are caused by viruses, which are not considered to be alive.

Section 2

Page 655: Macrophages engulf, or eat, any microorganisms or viruses that enter your body.

Page 656: If a virus particle enters the body, the virus may pass into body cells and begin to replicate. Or it may be engulfed and broken up by macrophages.

Page 659: rheumatoid arthritis, diabetes, multiple sclerosis, and lupus

Page 660: HIV causes AIDS.

Chapter 23 Staying Healthy

Section 1

Page 673: An incomplete protein does not contain all of the essential amino acids.

Page 675: Sample answer: a peanut butter sandwich, a glass of milk, and fresh fruit and vegetable slices

Page 676: One serving of chicken noodle soup provides more than 10% of the daily recommended allowance of vitamin A and sodium.

Section 2

Page 679: Over-the-counter drugs can be bought without a prescription. Prescription drugs can be bought only with a prescription from a doctor or other medical professional.

Page 681: First-time use of cocaine can cause a heart attack or can cause a person to become addicted.

Page 682: Drug use is the proper use of a legal drug. Drug abuse is either the use of an illegal drug or the improper use of a legal drug.

Section 3

Page 685: Aerobic exercise strengthens the heart, lungs, and bones and reduces stress. Regular exercise also burns Calories and can give you more energy.

Page 687: Sample answers: Never hike or camp alone, dress for the weather, learn how to swim, wear a life jacket, and never drink unpurified water.

Page 689: CPR is a way to revive someone whose heart has stopped beating. CPR classes are available in many places in the community.

Study Skills

FoldNote Instructions

Have you ever tried to study for a test or quiz but didn't know where to start? Or have you read a chapter and found that you can remember only a few ideas? Well, FoldNotes are a fun and exciting way to help you learn and remember the ideas you encounter as you learn science!

FoldNotes are tools that you can use to organize concepts. By focusing on a few main concepts, FoldNotes help you learn and remember how the concepts fit together. They can help you see the "big picture." Below you will find instructions for building 10 different FoldNotes.

Pyramid

1. Place a sheet of paper in front of you. Fold the lower left-hand corner of the paper diagonally to the opposite edge of the paper.
2. Cut off the tab of paper created by the fold (at the top).
3. Open the paper so that it is a square. Fold the lower right-hand corner of the paper diagonally to the opposite corner to form a triangle.
4. Open the paper. The creases of the two folds will have created an X.
5. Using scissors, cut along one of the creases. Start from any corner, and stop at the center point to create two flaps. Use tape or glue to attach one of the flaps on top of the other flap.

Double Door

1. Fold a sheet of paper in half from the top to the bottom. Then, unfold the paper.
2. Fold the top and bottom edges of the paper to the crease.

Booklet

1. Fold a sheet of paper in half from left to right. Then, unfold the paper.
2. Fold the sheet of paper in half again from the top to the bottom. Then, unfold the paper.
3. Refold the sheet of paper in half from left to right.
4. Fold the top and bottom edges to the center crease.
5. Completely unfold the paper.
6. Refold the paper from top to bottom.
7. Using scissors, cut a slit along the center crease of the sheet from the folded edge to the creases made in step 4. Do not cut the entire sheet in half.
8. Fold the sheet of paper in half from left to right. While holding the bottom and top edges of the paper, push the bottom and top edges together so that the center collapses at the center slit. Fold the four flaps to form a four-page book.

Layered Book

1. Lay one sheet of paper on top of another sheet. Slide the top sheet up so that 2 cm of the bottom sheet is showing.
2. Hold the two sheets together, fold down the top of the two sheets so that you see four 2 cm tabs along the bottom.
3. Using a stapler, staple the top of the FoldNote.

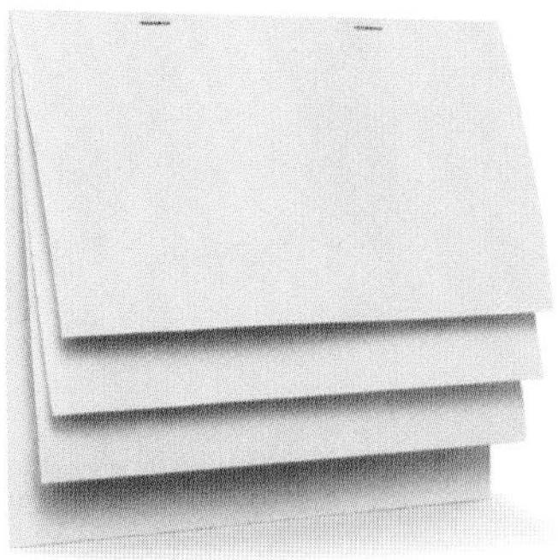

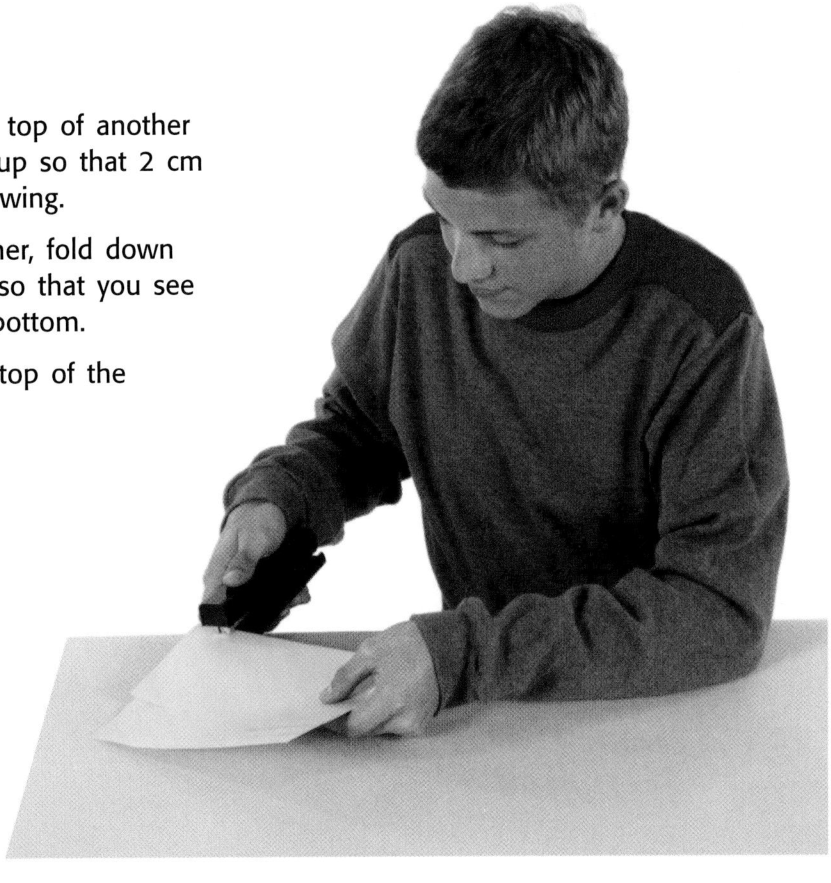

Key-Term Fold

1. Fold a sheet of lined notebook paper in half from left to right.
2. Using scissors, cut along every third line from the right edge of the paper to the center fold to make tabs.

Four-Corner Fold

1. Fold a sheet of paper in half from left to right. Then, unfold the paper.
2. Fold each side of the paper to the crease in the center of the paper.
3. Fold the paper in half from the top to the bottom. Then, unfold the paper.
4. Using scissors, cut the top flap creases made in step 3 to form four flaps.

Three-Panel Flip Chart

1. Fold a piece of paper in half from the top to the bottom.
2. Fold the paper in thirds from side to side. Then, unfold the paper so that you can see the three sections.
3. From the top of the paper, cut along each of the vertical fold lines to the fold in the middle of the paper. You will now have three flaps.

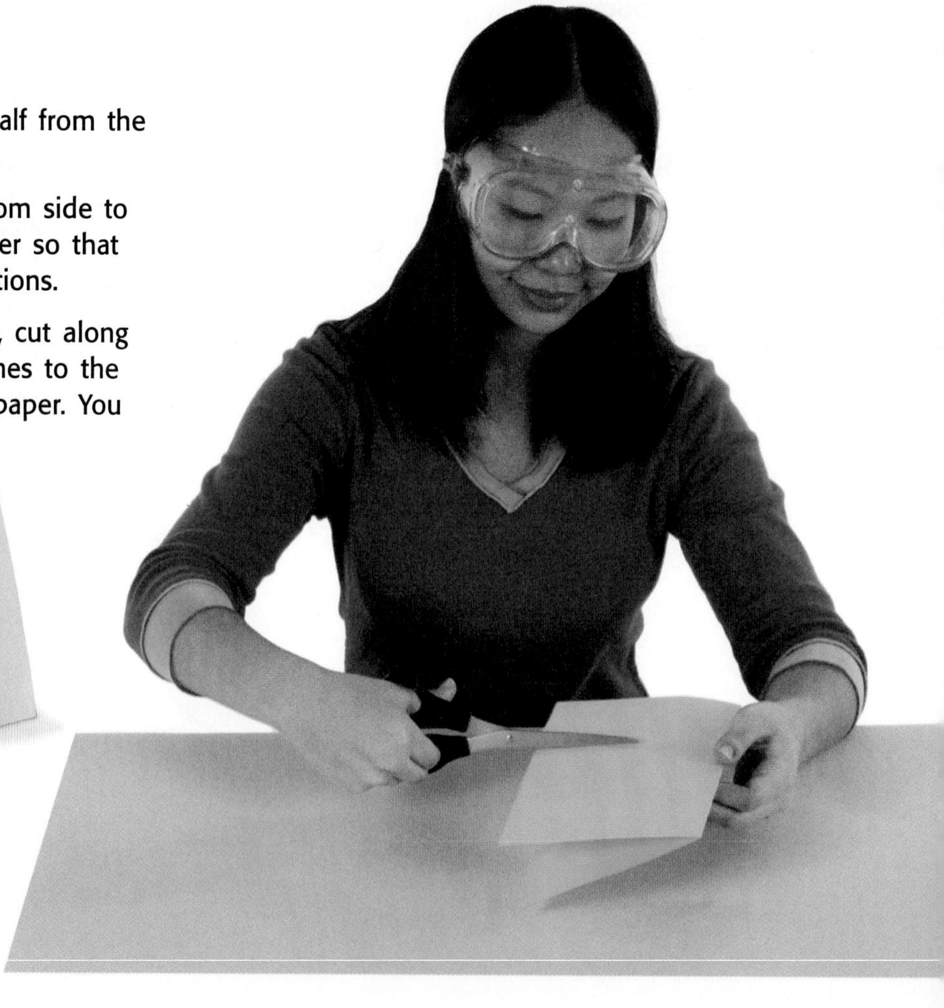

Table Fold

1. Fold a piece of paper in half from the top to the bottom. Then, fold the paper in half again.
2. Fold the paper in thirds from side to side.
3. Unfold the paper completely. Carefully trace the fold lines by using a pen or pencil.

Two-Panel Flip Chart

1. Fold a piece of paper in half from the top to the bottom.
2. Fold the paper in half from side to side. Then, unfold the paper so that you can see the two sections.
3. From the top of the paper, cut along the vertical fold line to the fold in the middle of the paper. You will now have two flaps.

Tri-Fold

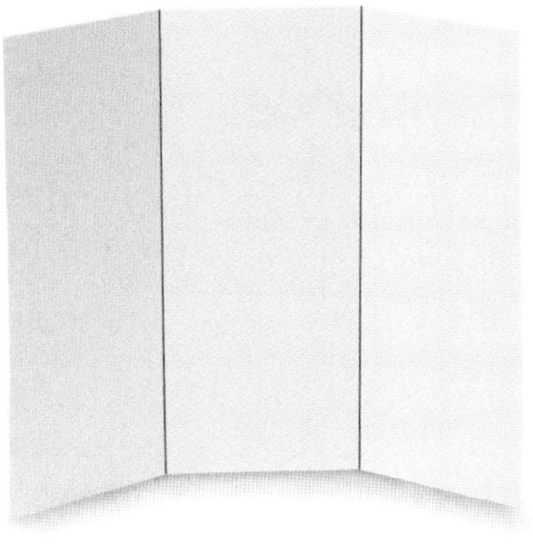

1. Fold a piece a paper in thirds from the top to the bottom.
2. Unfold the paper so that you can see the three sections. Then, turn the paper sideways so that the three sections form vertical columns.
3. Trace the fold lines by using a pen or pencil. Label the columns "Know," "Want," and "Learn."

Graphic Organizer Instructions

Have you ever wished that you could "draw out" the many concepts you learn in your science class? Sometimes, being able to *see* how concepts are related really helps you remember what you've learned. Graphic Organizers do just that! They give you a way to draw or map out concepts.

All you need to make a Graphic Organizer is a piece of paper and a pencil. Below you will find instructions for four different Graphic Organizers designed to help you organize the concepts you'll learn in this book.

Spider Map

1. Draw a diagram like the one shown. In the circle, write the main topic.
2. From the circle, draw legs to represent different categories of the main topic. You can have as many categories as you want.
3. From the category legs, draw horizontal lines. As you read the chapter, write details about each category on the horizontal lines.

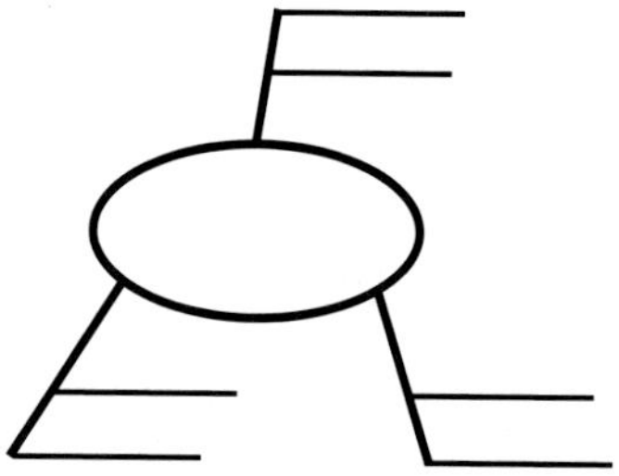

Comparison Table

1. Draw a chart like the one shown. Your chart can have as many columns and rows as you want.
2. In the top row, write the topics that you want to compare.
3. In the left column, write characteristics of the topics that you want to compare. As you read the chapter, fill in the characteristics for each topic in the appropriate boxes.

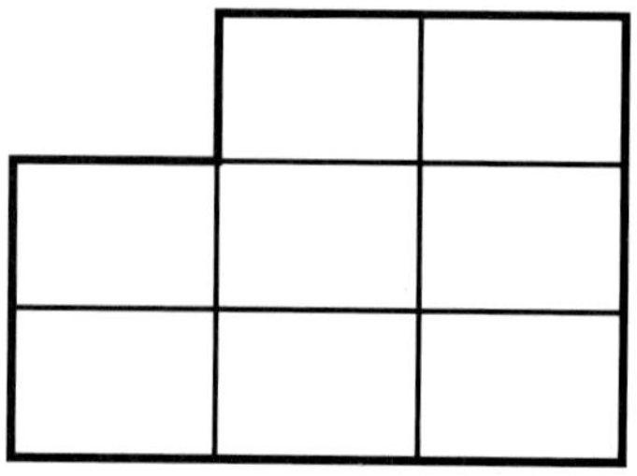

Chain-of-Events-Chart

1. Draw a box. In the box, write the first step of a process or the first event of a timeline.
2. Under the box, draw another box, and use an arrow to connect the two boxes. In the second box, write the next step of the process or the next event in the timeline.
3. Continue adding boxes until the process or timeline is finished.

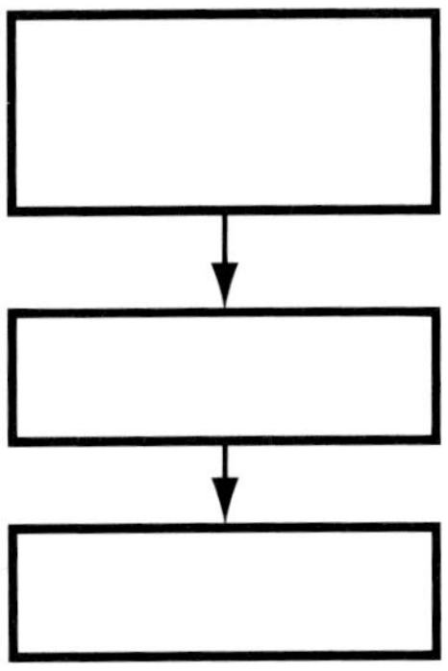

Concept Map

1. Draw a circle in the center of a piece of paper. Write the main idea of the chapter in the center of the circle.
2. From the circle, draw other circles. In those circles, write characteristics of the main idea. Draw arrows from the center circle to the circles that contain the characteristics.
3. From each circle that contains a characteristic, draw other circles. In those circles, write specific details about the characteristic. Draw arrows from each circle that contains a characteristic to the circles that contain specific details. You may draw as many circles as you want.

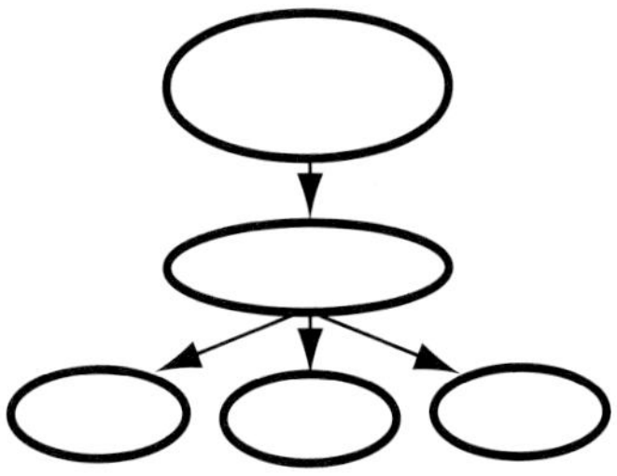

Appendix

Physical Science Laws and Principles

Law of Conservation of Mass

Mass cannot be created or destroyed during ordinary chemical or physical changes.

The total mass in a closed system is always the same no matter how many physical changes or chemical reactions occur.

Law of Conservation of Energy

Energy can be neither created nor destroyed.

The total amount of energy in a closed system is always the same. Energy can be changed from one form to another, but all of the different forms of energy in a system always add up to the same total amount of energy no matter how many energy conversions occur.

Law of Universal Gravitation

All objects in the universe attract each other by a force called *gravity.* The size of the force depends on the masses of the objects and the distance between the objects.

The first part of the law explains why lifting a bowling ball is much harder than lifting a marble. Because the bowling ball has a much larger mass than the marble does, the amount of gravity between the Earth and the bowling ball is greater than the amount of gravity between the Earth and the marble.

The second part of the law explains why a satellite can remain in orbit around the Earth. The satellite is carefully placed at a distance great enough to prevent the Earth's gravity from immediately pulling the satellite down but small enough to prevent the satellite from completely escaping the Earth's gravity and wandering off into space.

Newton's Laws of Motion

Newton's first law of motion states that an object at rest remains at rest and an object in motion remains in motion at constant speed and in a straight line unless acted on by an unbalanced force.

The first part of the law explains why a football will remain on a tee until it is kicked off or until a gust of wind blows it off.

The second part of the law explains why a bike rider will continue moving forward after the bike comes to an abrupt stop. Gravity and the friction of the sidewalk will eventually stop the rider.

Newton's second law of motion states that the acceleration of an object depends on the mass of the object and the amount of force applied.

The first part of the law explains why the acceleration of a 4 kg bowling ball will be greater than the acceleration of a 6 kg bowling ball if the same force is applied to both balls.

The second part of the law explains why the acceleration of a bowling ball will be larger if a larger force is applied to the bowling ball.

The relationship of acceleration (*a*) to mass (*m*) and force (*F*) can be expressed mathematically by the following equation:

$$acceleration = \frac{force}{mass}, \text{ or } a = \frac{F}{m}$$

This equation is often rearranged to the form

$$force = mass \times acceleration, \text{ or } F = m \times a$$

Newton's third law of motion states that whenever one object exerts a force on a second object, the second object exerts an equal and opposite force on the first.

This law explains that a runner is able to move forward because of the equal and opposite force that the ground exerts on the runner's foot after each step.

Law of Reflection

The law of reflection states that the angle of incidence is equal to the angle of reflection. This law explains why light reflects off a surface at the same angle that the light strikes the surface.

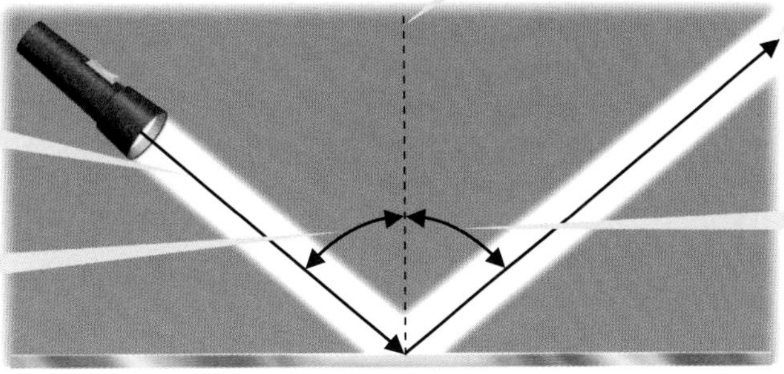

A line perpendicular to the mirror's surface is called the *normal.*
The beam of light reflected off the mirror is called the *reflected beam.*
The beam of light traveling toward the mirror is called the *incident beam.*
The angle between the incident beam and the normal is called the *angle of incidence.*
The angle between the reflected beam and the normal is called the *angle of reflection.*

Charles's Law

Charles's law states that for a fixed amount of gas at a constant pressure, the volume of the gas increases as the temperature of the gas increases. Likewise, the volume of the gas decreases as the temperature of the gas decreases.

If a basketball that was inflated indoors is left outside on a cold winter day, the air particles inside the ball will move more slowly. They will hit the sides of the basketball less often and with less force. The ball will get smaller as the volume of the air decreases.

Boyle's Law

Boyle's law states that for a fixed amount of gas at a constant temperature, the volume of a gas increases as the pressure of the gas decreases. Likewise, the volume of a gas decreases as its pressure increases.

If an inflated balloon is pulled down to the bottom of a swimming pool, the pressure of the water on the balloon increases. The pressure of the air particles inside the balloon must increase to match that of the water outside, so the volume of the air inside the balloon decreases.

Pascal's Principle

Pascal's principle states that a change in pressure at any point in an enclosed fluid will be transmitted equally to all parts of that fluid.

When a mechanic uses a hydraulic jack to raise an automobile off the ground, he or she increases the pressure on the fluid in the jack by pushing on the jack handle. The pressure is transmitted equally to all parts of the fluid-filled jacking system. As fluid presses the jack plate against the frame of the car, the car is lifed off the ground.

Archimedes' Principle

Archimedes' principle states that the buoyant force on an object in a fluid is equal to the weight of the volume of fluid that the object displaces.

A person floating in a swimming pool displaces 20 L of water. The weight of that volume of water is about 200 N. Therefore, the buoyant force on the person is 200 N.

Appendix

Bernoulli's Principle

Bernoulli's principle states that as the speed of a moving fluid increases, the fluid's pressure decreases.

The lift on an airplane wing or on a Frisbee® can be explained in part by using Bernoulli's principle. Because of the shape of the Frisbee, the air moving over the top of the Frisbee must travel farther than the air below the Frisbee in the same amount of time. In other words, the air above the Frisbee is moving faster than the air below it. This faster-moving air above the Frisbee exerts less pressure than the slower-moving air below it does. The resulting increased pressure below exerts an upward force and pushes the Frisbee up.

Useful Equations

Average speed

$$\textit{average speed} = \frac{\textit{total distance}}{\textit{total time}}$$

Example: A bicycle messenger traveled a distance of 136 km in 8 h. What was the messenger's average speed?

$$\frac{136\text{ km}}{8\text{ h}} = 17\text{ km/h}$$

The messenger's average speed was **17 km/h.**

Average acceleration

$$\textit{average acceleration} = \frac{\textit{final velocity} - \textit{starting velocity}}{\textit{time it takes to change velocity}}$$

Example: Calculate the average acceleration of an Olympic 100 m dash sprinter who reaches a velocity of 20 m/s south at the finish line. The race was in a straight line and lasted 10 s.

$$\frac{20\text{ m/s} - 0\text{ m/s}}{10\text{s}} = 2\text{ m/s/s}$$

The sprinter's average acceleration is **2 m/s/s south.**

Net force

Forces in the Same Direction

When forces are in the same direction, add the forces together to determine the net force.

Example: Calculate the net force on a stalled car that is being pushed by two people. One person is pushing with a force of 13 N northwest, and the other person is pushing with a force of 8 N in the same direction.

$$13\text{ N} + 8\text{ N} = 21\text{ N}$$

The net force is **21 N northwest.**

Forces in Opposite Directions

When forces are in opposite directions, subtract the smaller force from the larger force to determine the net force. The net force will be in the direction of the larger force.

Example: Calculate the net force on a rope that is being pulled on each end. One person is pulling on one end of the rope with a force of 12 N south. Another person is pulling on the opposite end of the rope with a force of 7 N north.

$$12\text{ N} - 7\text{ N} = 5\text{ N}$$

The net force is **5 N south.**

Appendix

Work

Work is done by exerting a force through a distance. Work has units of joules (J), which are equivalent to Newton-meters.

$$Work = F \times d$$

Example: Calculate the amount of work done by a man who lifts a 100 N toddler 1.5 m off the floor.

Work = 100 N × 1.5 m = 150 N•m = 150 J

The man did **150 J** of work.

Power

Power is the rate at which work is done. Power is measured in watts (W), which are equivalent to joules per second.

$$P = \frac{Work}{t}$$

Example: Calculate the power of a weightlifter who raises a 300 N barbell 2.1 m off the floor in 1.25 s.

Work = 300 N × 2.1 m = 630 N•m = 630 J

$$P = \frac{630 \text{ J}}{1.25 \text{ s}} = \frac{504 \text{ J}}{\text{s}} = 504 \text{ W}$$

The weightlifter has **504 W** of power.

Pressure

Pressure is the force exerted over a given area. The SI unit for pressure is the pascal (Pa).

$$pressure = \frac{force}{area}$$

Example: Calculate the pressure of the air in a soccer ball if the air exerts a force of 25,000 N over an area of 0.15 m^2.

$$pressure = \frac{25{,}000 \text{ N}}{0.15 \text{ m}^2} = \frac{167{,}000 \text{ N}}{\text{m}^2} = 167{,}000 \text{ Pa}$$

The pressure of the air inside the soccer ball is **167,000 Pa.**

Density

$$density = \frac{mass}{volume}$$

Example: Calculate the density of a sponge that has a mass of 10 g and a volume of 40 cm^3.

$$\frac{10 \text{ g}}{40 \text{ cm}^3} = \frac{0.25 \text{ g}}{\text{cm}^3}$$

The density of the sponge is $\mathbf{\frac{0.25 \text{ g}}{\text{cm}^3}}$.

Concentration

$$concentration = \frac{mass\ of\ solute}{volume\ of\ solvent}$$

Example: Calculate the concentration of a solution in which 10 g of sugar is dissolved in 125 mL of water.

$$\frac{10 \text{ g of sugar}}{125 \text{ mL of water}} = \frac{0.08 \text{ g}}{\text{mL}}$$

The concentration of this solution is $\mathbf{\frac{0.08 \text{ g}}{\text{mL}}}$.

Appendix

Math Refresher

Science requires an understanding of many math concepts. The following pages will help you review some important math skills.

Averages

An **average,** or **mean,** simplifies a set of numbers into a single number that *approximates* the value of the set.

Example: Find the average of the following set of numbers: 5, 4, 7, and 8.

Step 1: Find the sum.

$$5 + 4 + 7 + 8 = 24$$

Step 2: Divide the sum by the number of numbers in your set. Because there are four numbers in this example, divide the sum by 4.

$$\frac{24}{4} = 6$$

The average, or mean, is **6.**

Ratios

A **ratio** is a comparison between numbers, and it is usually written as a fraction.

Example: Find the ratio of thermometers to students if you have 36 thermometers and 48 students in your class.

Step 1: Make the ratio.

$$\frac{\text{36 thermometers}}{\text{48 students}}$$

Step 2: Reduce the fraction to its simplest form.

$$\frac{36}{48} = \frac{36 \div 12}{48 \div 12} = \frac{3}{4}$$

The ratio of thermometers to students is **3 to 4,** or $\frac{3}{4}$. The ratio may also be written in the form 3:4.

Proportions

A **proportion** is an equation that states that two ratios are equal.

$$\frac{3}{1} = \frac{12}{4}$$

To solve a proportion, first multiply across the equal sign. This is called *cross-multiplication*. If you know three of the quantities in a proportion, you can use cross-multiplication to find the fourth.

Example: Imagine that you are making a scale model of the solar system for your science project. The diameter of Jupiter is 11.2 times the diameter of the Earth. If you are using a plastic-foam ball that has a diameter of 2 cm to represent the Earth, what must the diameter of the ball representing Jupiter be?

$$\frac{11.2}{1} = \frac{x}{2 \text{ cm}}$$

Step 1: Cross-multiply.

$$\frac{11.2}{1} \times \frac{x}{2}$$

$$11.2 \times 2 = x \times 1$$

Step 2: Multiply.

$$22.4 = x \times 1$$

Step 3: Isolate the variable by dividing both sides by 1.

$$x = \frac{22.4}{1}$$

$$x = 22.4 \text{ cm}$$

You will need to use a ball that has a diameter of **22.4** cm to represent Jupiter.

Percentages

A **percentage** is a ratio of a given number to 100.

Example: What is 85% of 40?

Step 1: Rewrite the percentage by moving the decimal point two places to the left.

0.85

Step 2: Multiply the decimal by the number that you are calculating the percentage of.

$0.85 \times 40 = 34$

85% of 40 is **34.**

Decimals

To **add** or **subtract decimals,** line up the digits vertically so that the decimal points line up. Then, add or subtract the columns from right to left. Carry or borrow numbers as necessary.

Example: Add the following numbers: 3.1415 and 2.96.

Step 1: Line up the digits vertically so that the decimal points line up.

$$\begin{array}{r} 3.1415 \\ +\ 2.96 \\ \hline \end{array}$$

Step 2: Add the columns from right to left, and carry when necessary.

$$\begin{array}{r} {\scriptstyle 1\ 1} \\ 3.1415 \\ +\ 2.96 \\ \hline 6.1015 \end{array}$$

The sum is **6.1015.**

Fractions

Numbers tell you how many; **fractions** tell you *how much of a whole.*

Example: Your class has 24 plants. Your teacher instructs you to put 5 plants in a shady spot. What fraction of the plants in your class will you put in a shady spot?

Step 1: In the denominator, write the total number of parts in the whole.

$$\frac{?}{24}$$

Step 2: In the numerator, write the number of parts of the whole that are being considered.

$$\frac{5}{24}$$

So, $\mathbf{\frac{5}{24}}$ of the plants will be in the shade.

Reducing Fractions

It is usually best to express a fraction in its simplest form. Expressing a fraction in its simplest form is called *reducing* a fraction.

Example: Reduce the fraction $\frac{30}{45}$ to its simplest form.

Step 1: Find the largest whole number that will divide evenly into both the numerator and denominator. This number is called the *greatest common factor* (GCF).

Factors of the numerator 30:

1, 2, 3, 5, 6, 10, **15,** 30

Factors of the denominator 45:

1, 3, 5, 9, **15,** 45

Step 2: Divide both the numerator and the denominator by the GCF, which in this case is 15.

$$\frac{30}{45} = \frac{30 \div 15}{45 \div 15} = \frac{2}{3}$$

Thus, $\frac{30}{45}$ reduced to its simplest form is $\mathbf{\frac{2}{3}}$.

Appendix

Adding and Subtracting Fractions

To **add** or **subtract fractions** that have the **same denominator,** simply add or subtract the numerators.

Examples:

$$\frac{3}{5} + \frac{1}{5} = ? \text{ and } \frac{3}{4} - \frac{1}{4} = ?$$

Step 1: Add or subtract the numerators.

$$\frac{3}{5} + \frac{1}{5} = \frac{4}{\ } \text{ and } \frac{3}{4} - \frac{1}{4} = \frac{2}{\ }$$

Step 2: Write the sum or difference over the denominator.

$$\frac{3}{5} + \frac{1}{5} = \frac{4}{5} \text{ and } \frac{3}{4} - \frac{1}{4} = \frac{2}{4}$$

Step 3: If necessary, reduce the fraction to its simplest form.

$\mathbf{\frac{4}{5}}$ cannot be reduced, and $\frac{2}{4} = \mathbf{\frac{1}{2}}$.

To **add** or **subtract fractions** that have **different denominators,** first find the least common denominator (LCD).

Examples:

$$\frac{1}{2} + \frac{1}{6} = ? \text{ and } \frac{3}{4} - \frac{2}{3} = ?$$

Step 1: Write the equivalent fractions that have a common denominator.

$$\frac{3}{6} + \frac{1}{6} = ? \text{ and } \frac{9}{12} - \frac{8}{12} = ?$$

Step 2: Add or subtract the fractions.

$$\frac{3}{6} + \frac{1}{6} = \frac{4}{6} \text{ and } \frac{9}{12} - \frac{8}{12} = \frac{1}{12}$$

Step 3: If necessary, reduce the fraction to its simplest form.

The fraction $\frac{4}{6} = \mathbf{\frac{2}{3}}$, and $\mathbf{\frac{1}{12}}$ cannot be reduced.

Multiplying Fractions

To **multiply fractions,** multiply the numerators and the denominators together, and then reduce the fraction to its simplest form.

Example:

$$\frac{5}{9} \times \frac{7}{10} = ?$$

Step 1: Multiply the numerators and denominators.

$$\frac{5}{9} \times \frac{7}{10} = \frac{5 \times 7}{9 \times 10} = \frac{35}{90}$$

Step 2: Reduce the fraction.

$$\frac{35}{90} = \frac{35 \div 5}{90 \div 5} = \mathbf{\frac{7}{18}}$$

Dividing Fractions

To **divide fractions,** first rewrite the divisor (the number you divide by) upside down. This number is called the *reciprocal* of the divisor. Then multiply and reduce if necessary.

Example:

$$\frac{5}{8} \div \frac{3}{2} = ?$$

Step 1: Rewrite the divisor as its reciprocal.

$$\frac{3}{2} \rightarrow \frac{2}{3}$$

Step 2: Multiply the fractions.

$$\frac{5}{8} \times \frac{2}{3} = \frac{5 \times 2}{8 \times 3} = \frac{10}{24}$$

Step 3: Reduce the fraction.

$$\frac{10}{24} = \frac{10 \div 2}{24 \div 2} = \mathbf{\frac{5}{12}}$$

Appendix

Scientific Notation

Scientific notation is a short way of representing very large and very small numbers without writing all of the place-holding zeros.

Example: Write 653,000,000 in scientific notation.

Step 1: Write the number without the place-holding zeros.

653

Step 2: Place the decimal point after the first digit.

6.53

Step 3: Find the exponent by counting the number of places that you moved the decimal point.

6.53000000

The decimal point was moved eight places to the left. Therefore, the exponent of 10 is positive 8. If you had moved the decimal point to the right, the exponent would be negative.

Step 4: Write the number in scientific notation.

$\mathbf{6.53 \times 10^8}$

Area

Area is the number of square units needed to cover the surface of an object.

Formulas:

area of a square = side × side

area of a rectangle = length × width

area of a triangle = $\frac{1}{2}$ *× base × height*

Examples: Find the areas.

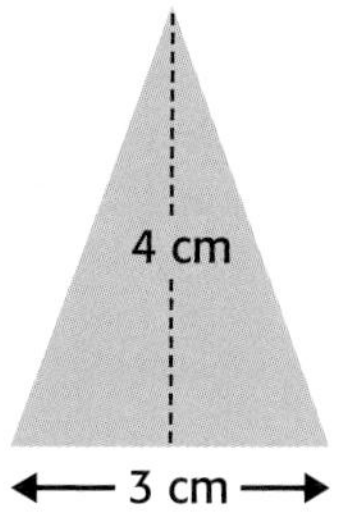

Triangle

area = $\frac{1}{2}$ × *base* × *height*

area = $\frac{1}{2}$ × 3 cm × 4 cm

area = **6 cm²**

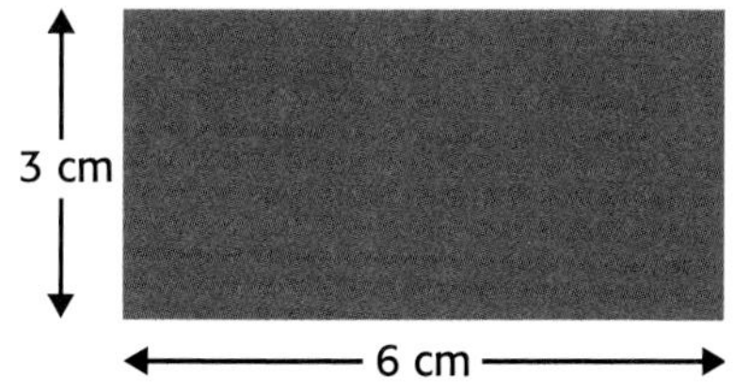

Rectangle

area = length × width

area = 6 cm × 3 cm

area = $\mathbf{18\ cm^2}$

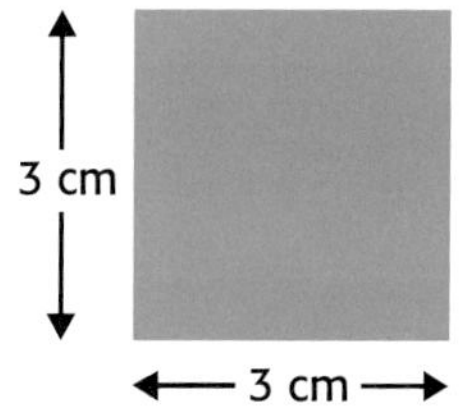

Square

area = side × side

area = 3 cm × 3 cm

area = $\mathbf{9\ cm^2}$

Volume

Volume is the amount of space that something occupies.

Formulas:

volume of a cube = side × side × side

volume of a prism = area of base × height

Examples:

Find the volume of the solids.

Cube

volume = side × side × side

volume = 4 cm × 4 cm × 4 cm

volume = $\mathbf{64\ cm^3}$

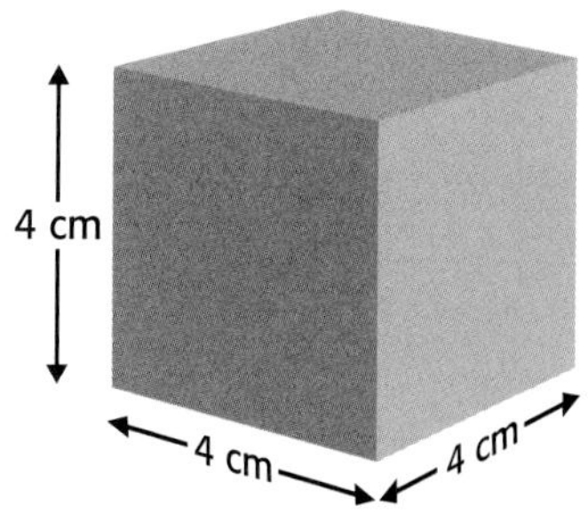

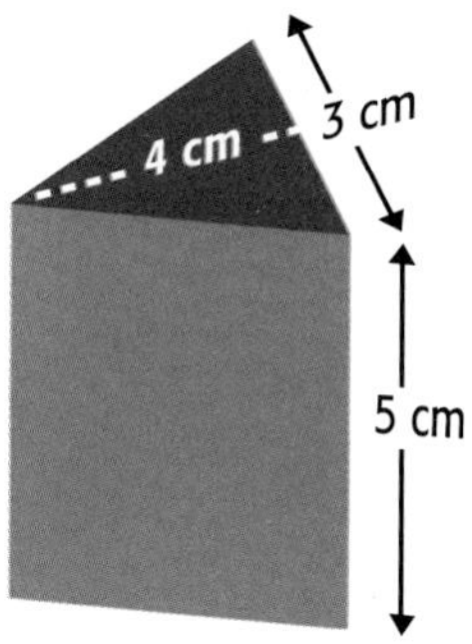

Prism

volume = area of base × height

volume = (area of triangle) × height

volume = ($\frac{1}{2}$ × 3 cm × 4 cm) × 5 cm

volume = 6 cm² × 5 cm

volume = $\mathbf{30\ cm^3}$

Making Charts and Graphs

Pie Charts

A pie chart shows how each group of data relates to all of the data. Each part of the circle forming the chart represents a category of the data. The entire circle represents all of the data. For example, a biologist studying a hardwood forest in Wisconsin found that there were five different types of trees. The data table at right summarizes the biologist's findings.

Wisconsin Hardwood Trees

Type of tree	Number found
Oak	600
Maple	750
Beech	300
Birch	1,200
Hickory	150
Total	3,000

How to Make a Pie Chart

1. To make a pie chart of these data, first find the percentage of each type of tree. Divide the number of trees of each type by the total number of trees, and multiply by 100.

$$\frac{600 \text{ oak}}{3{,}000 \text{ trees}} \times 100 = 20\%$$

$$\frac{750 \text{ maple}}{3{,}000 \text{ trees}} \times 100 = 25\%$$

$$\frac{300 \text{ beech}}{3{,}000 \text{ trees}} \times 100 = 10\%$$

$$\frac{1{,}200 \text{ birch}}{3{,}000 \text{ trees}} \times 100 = 40\%$$

$$\frac{150 \text{ hickory}}{3{,}000 \text{ trees}} \times 100 = 5\%$$

2. Now, determine the size of the wedges that make up the pie chart. Multiply each percentage by 360°. Remember that a circle contains 360°.

$20\% \times 360° = 72°$ $25\% \times 360° = 90°$

$10\% \times 360° = 36°$ $40\% \times 360° = 144°$

$5\% \times 360° = 18°$

3. Check that the sum of the percentages is 100 and the sum of the degrees is 360.

$20\% + 25\% + 10\% + 40\% + 5\% = 100\%$

$72° + 90° + 36° + 144° + 18° = 360°$

4. Use a compass to draw a circle and mark the center of the circle.
5. Then, use a protractor to draw angles of 72°, 90°, 36°, 144°, and 18° in the circle.
6. Finally, label each part of the chart, and choose an appropriate title.

A Community of Wisconsin Hardwood Trees

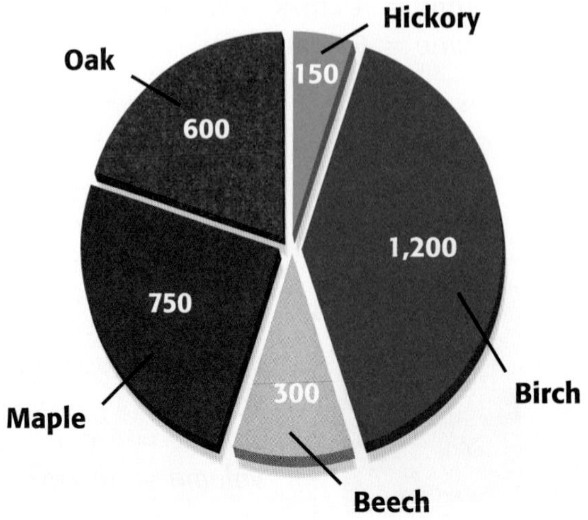

Appendix

Line Graphs

Line graphs are most often used to demonstrate continuous change. For example, Mr. Smith's students analyzed the population records for their hometown, Appleton, between 1900 and 2000. Examine the data at right.

Because the year and the population change, they are the *variables.* The population is determined by, or dependent on, the year. Therefore, the population is called the **dependent variable,** and the year is called the **independent variable.** Each set of data is called a **data pair.** To prepare a line graph, you must first organize data pairs into a table like the one at right.

Population of Appleton, 1900–2000

Year	Population
1900	1,800
1920	2,500
1940	3,200
1960	3,900
1980	4,600
2000	5,300

How to Make a Line Graph

1. Place the independent variable along the horizontal (x) axis. Place the dependent variable along the vertical (y) axis.
2. Label the x-axis "Year" and the y-axis "Population." Look at your largest and smallest values for the population. For the y-axis, determine a scale that will provide enough space to show these values. You must use the same scale for the entire length of the axis. Next, find an appropriate scale for the x-axis.
3. Choose reasonable starting points for each axis.
4. Plot the data pairs as accurately as possible.
5. Choose a title that accurately represents the data.

Population of Appleton, 1900–2000

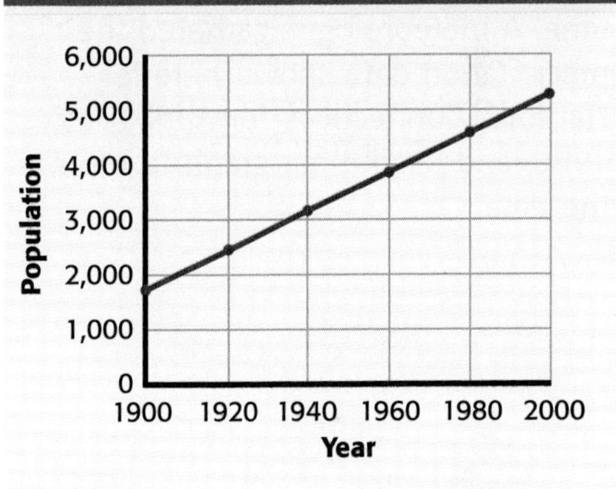

How to Determine Slope

Slope is the ratio of the change in the y-value to the change in the x-value, or "rise over run."

1. Choose two points on the line graph. For example, the population of Appleton in 2000 was 5,300 people. Therefore, you can define point a as (2000, 5,300). In 1900, the population was 1,800 people. You can define point b as (1900, 1,800).
2. Find the change in the y-value. (y at point a) − (y at point b) = 5,300 people − 1,800 people = 3,500 people
3. Find the change in the x-value. (x at point a) − (x at point b) = 2000 − 1900 = 100 years
4. Calculate the slope of the graph by dividing the change in y by the change in x.

$$slope = \frac{change\ in\ y}{change\ in\ x}$$

$$slope = \frac{3{,}500 \text{ people}}{100 \text{ years}}$$

$$slope = 35 \text{ people per year}$$

In this example, the population in Appleton increased by a fixed amount each year. The graph of these data is a straight line. Therefore, the relationship is **linear.** When the graph of a set of data is not a straight line, the relationship is **nonlinear.**

Using Algebra to Determine Slope

The equation in step 4 may also be arranged to be

$$y = kx$$

where y represents the change in the y-value, k represents the slope, and x represents the change in the x-value.

$$slope = \frac{change\ in\ y}{change\ in\ x}$$

$$k = \frac{y}{x}$$

$$k \times x = \frac{y \times x}{x}$$

$$kx = y$$

Bar Graphs

Bar graphs are used to demonstrate change that is not continuous. These graphs can be used to indicate trends when the data cover a long period of time. A meteorologist gathered the precipitation data shown here for Hartford, Connecticut, for April 1–15, 1996, and used a bar graph to represent the data.

Precipitation in Hartford, Connecticut April 1–15, 1996

Date	Precipitation (cm)	Date	Precipitation (cm)
April 1	0.5	April 9	0.25
April 2	1.25	April 10	0.0
April 3	0.0	April 11	1.0
April 4	0.0	April 12	0.0
April 5	0.0	April 13	0.25
April 6	0.0	April 14	0.0
April 7	0.0	April 15	6.50
April 8	1.75		

How to Make a Bar Graph

1. Use an appropriate scale and a reasonable starting point for each axis.
2. Label the axes, and plot the data.
3. Choose a title that accurately represents the data.

Precipitation in Hartford, Connecticut, April 1–15, 1996

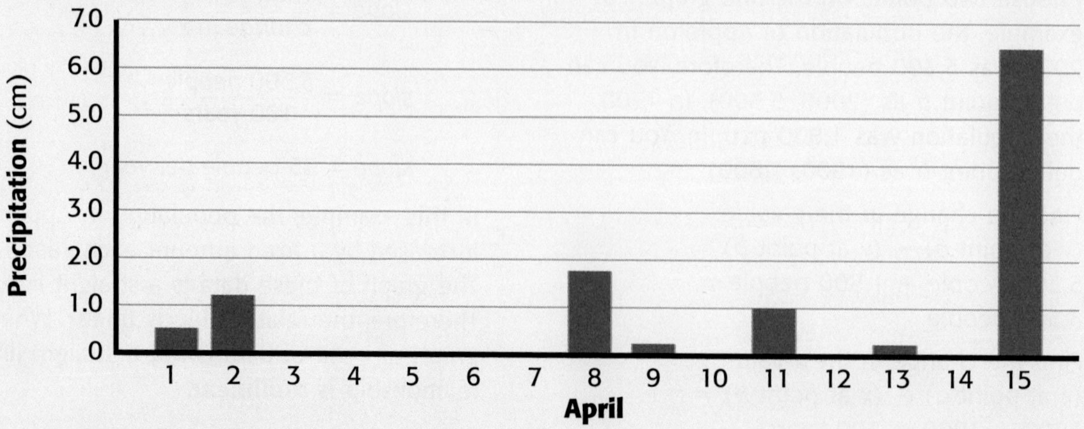

Measuring Skills

Using a Graduated Cylinder

When using a graduated cylinder to measure volume, keep the following procedures in mind:

1. Place the cylinder on a flat, level surface before measuring liquid.
2. Move your head so that your eye is level with the surface of the liquid.
3. Read the mark closest to the liquid level. On glass graduated cylinders, read the mark closest to the center of the curve in the liquid's surface.

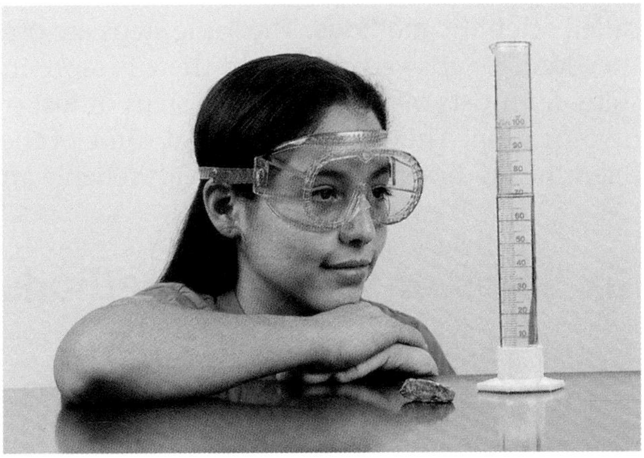

Using a Meterstick or Metric Ruler

When using a meterstick or metric ruler to measure length, keep the following procedures in mind:

1. Place the ruler firmly against the object that you are measuring.
2. Align one edge of the object exactly with the 0 end of the ruler.
3. Look at the other edge of the object to see which of the marks on the ruler is closest to that edge. (Note: Each small slash between the centimeters represents a millimeter, which is one-tenth of a centimeter.)

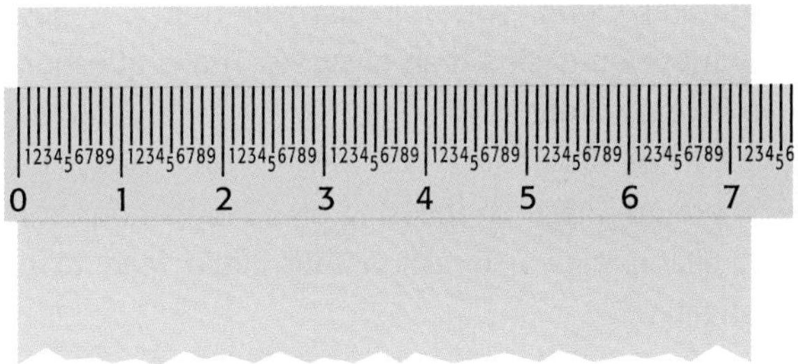

Using a Triple-Beam Balance

When using a triple-beam balance to measure mass, keep the following procedures in mind:

1. Make sure the balance is on a level surface.
2. Place all of the countermasses at 0. Adjust the balancing knob until the pointer rests at 0.
3. Place the object you wish to measure on the pan. **Caution:** Do not place hot objects or chemicals directly on the balance pan.
4. Move the largest countermass along the beam to the right until it is at the last notch that does not tip the balance. Follow the same procedure with the next-largest countermass. Then, move the smallest countermass until the pointer rests at 0.
5. Add the readings from the three beams together to determine the mass of the object.
6. When determining the mass of crystals or powders, first find the mass of a piece of filter paper. Then, add the crystals or powder to the paper, and remeasure. The actual mass of the crystals or powder is the total mass minus the mass of the paper. When finding the mass of liquids, first find the mass of the empty container. Then, find the combined mass of the liquid and container. The mass of the liquid is the total mass minus the mass of the container.

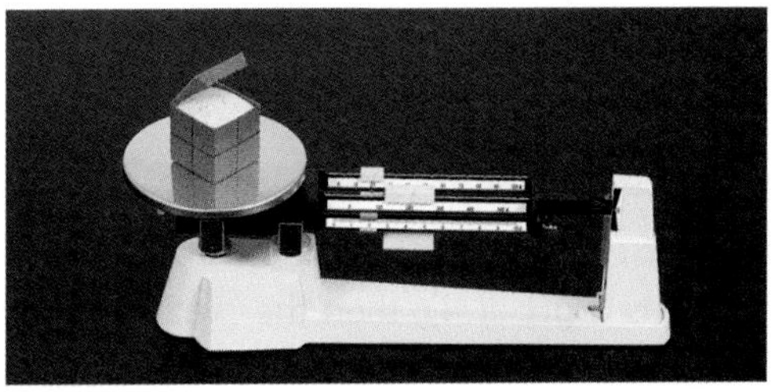

Scientific Methods

The ways in which scientists answer questions and solve problems are called **scientific methods.** The same steps are often used by scientists as they look for answers. However, there is more than one way to use these steps. Scientists may use all of the steps or just some of the steps during an investigation. They may even repeat some of the steps. The goal of using scientific methods is to come up with reliable answers and solutions.

Six Steps of Scientific Methods

1 Ask a Question

Good questions come from careful **observations.** You make observations by using your senses to gather information. Sometimes, you may use instruments, such as microscopes and telescopes, to extend the range of your senses. As you observe the natural world, you will discover that you have many more questions than answers. These questions drive investigations.

Questions beginning with *what, why, how,* and *when* are important in focusing an investigation. Here is an example of a question that could lead to an investigation.

Question: How does acid rain affect plant growth?

2 Form a Hypothesis

After you ask a question, you need to form a **hypothesis.** A hypothesis is a clear statement of what you expect the answer to your question to be. Your hypothesis will represent your best "educated guess" based on what you have observed and what you already know. A good hypothesis is testable. Otherwise, the investigation can go no further. Here is a hypothesis based on the question, "How does acid rain affect plant growth?"

Hypothesis: Acid rain slows plant growth.

The hypothesis can lead to predictions. A prediction is what you think the outcome of your experiment or data collection will be. Predictions are usually stated in an if-then format. Here is a sample prediction for the hypothesis that acid rain slows plant growth.

Prediction: If a plant is watered with only acid rain (which has a pH of 4), then the plant will grow at half its normal rate.

3 Test the Hypothesis

After you have formed a hypothesis and made a prediction, your hypothesis should be tested. One way to test a hypothesis is with a controlled experiment. A **controlled experiment** tests only one factor at a time. In an experiment to test the effect of acid rain on plant growth, the **control group** would be watered with normal rain water. The **experimental group** would be watered with acid rain. All of the plants should receive the same amount of sunlight and water each day. The air temperature should be the same for all groups. However, the acidity of the water will be a variable. In fact, any factor that is different from one group to another is a **variable.** If your hypothesis is correct, then the acidity of the water and plant growth are *dependant variables.* The amount a plant grows is dependent on the acidity of the water. However, the amount of water each plant receives and the amount of sunlight each plant receives are *independent variables.* Either of these factors could change without affecting the other factor.

Sometimes, the nature of an investigation makes a controlled experiment impossible. For example, the Earth's core is surrounded by thousands of meters of rock. Under such circumstances, a hypothesis may be tested by making detailed observations.

4 Analyze the Results

After you have completed your experiments, made your observations, and collected your data, you must analyze all the information you have gathered. Tables and graphs are often used in this step to organize the data.

5 Draw Conclusions

After analyzing your data, you can determine if your results support your hypothesis. If your hypothesis is supported, you (or others) might want to repeat the observations or experiments to verify your results. If your hypothesis is not supported by the data, you may have to check your procedure for errors. You may even have to reject your hypothesis and make a new one. If you cannot draw a conclusion from your results, you may have to try the investigation again or carry out further observations or experiments.

6 Communicate Results

After any scientific investigation, you should report your results. By preparing a written or oral report, you let others know what you have learned. They may repeat your investigation to see if they get the same results. Your report may even lead to another question and then to another investigation.

Scientific Methods in Action

Scientific methods contain loops in which several steps may be repeated over and over again. In some cases, certain steps are unnecessary. Thus, there is not a "straight line" of steps. For example, sometimes scientists find that testing one hypothesis raises new questions and new hypotheses to be tested. And sometimes, testing the hypothesis leads directly to a conclusion. Furthermore, the steps in scientific methods are not always used in the same order. Follow the steps in the diagram, and see how many different directions scientific methods can take you.

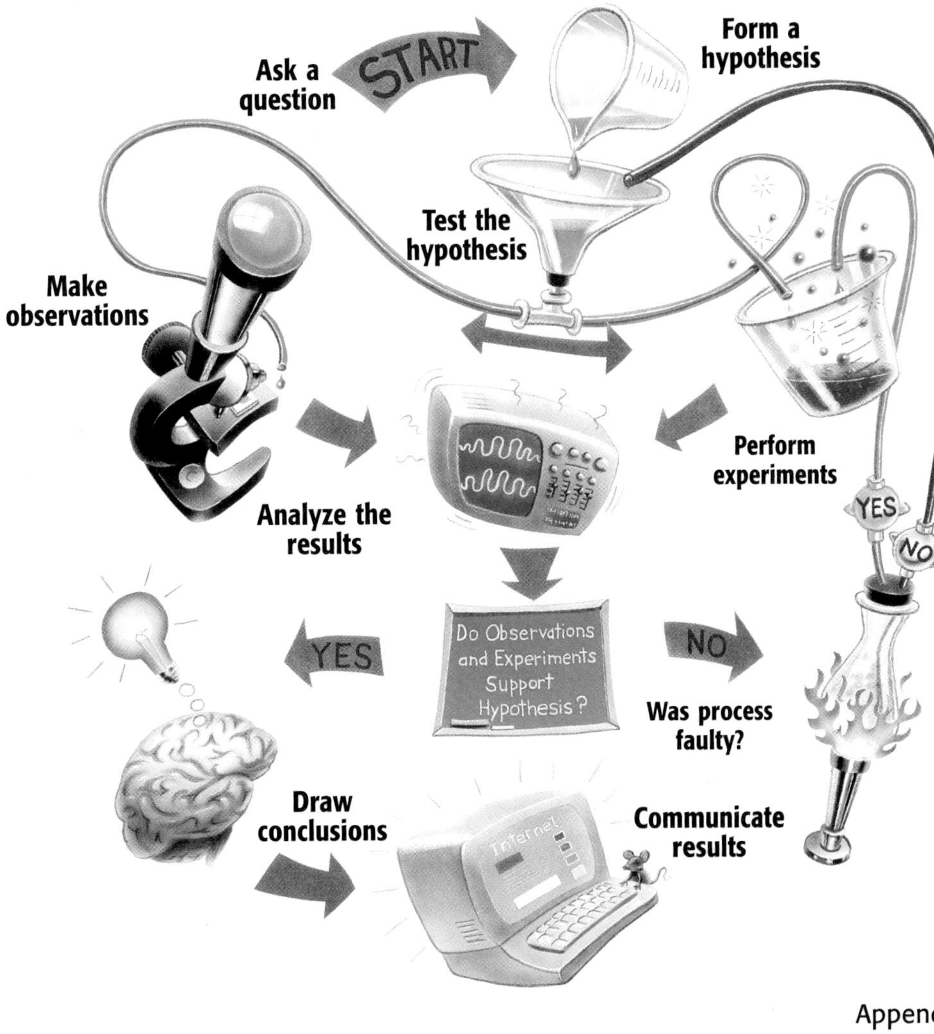

Using the Microscope

Parts of the Compound Light Microscope

- The **ocular lens** magnifies the image 10×.
- The **low-power objective** magnifies the image 10×.
- The **high-power objective** magnifies the image either 40× or 43×.
- The **revolving nosepiece** holds the objectives and can be turned to change from one magnification to the other.
- The **body tube** maintains the correct distance between the ocular lens and objectives.
- The **coarse-adjustment knob** moves the body tube up and down to allow focusing of the image.
- The **fine-adjustment knob** moves the body tube slightly to bring the image into sharper focus. It is usually located in the center of the coarse-adjustment knob.
- The **stage** supports a slide.
- **Stage clips** hold the slide in place for viewing.
- The **diaphragm** controls the amount of light coming through the stage.
- The light source provides a **light** for viewing the slide.
- The **arm** supports the body tube.
- The **base** supports the microscope.

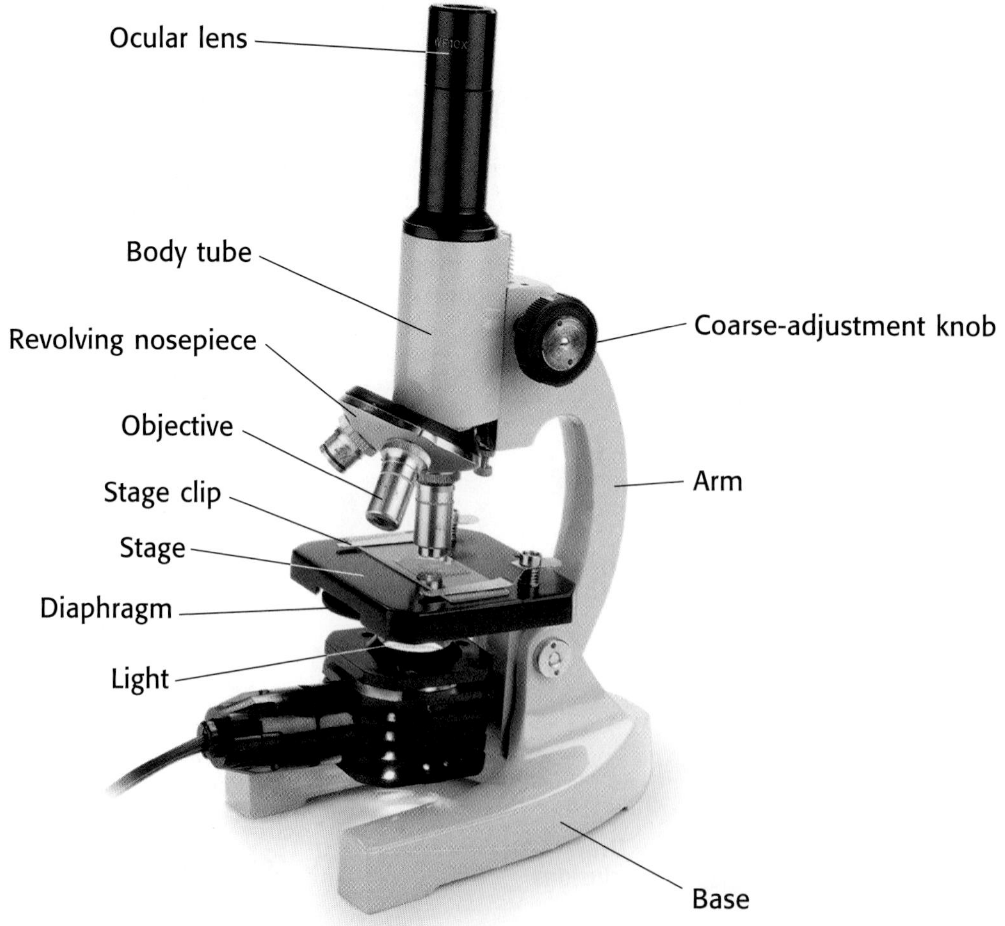

Proper Use of the Compound Light Microscope

1. Use both hands to carry the microscope to your lab table. Place one hand beneath the base, and use the other hand to hold the arm of the microscope. Hold the microscope close to your body while carrying it to your lab table.
2. Place the microscope on the lab table at least 5 cm from the edge of the table.
3. Check to see what type of light source is used by your microscope. If the microscope has a lamp, plug it in and make sure that the cord is out of the way. If the microscope has a mirror, adjust the mirror to reflect light through the hole in the stage. **Caution:** If your microscope has a mirror, do not use direct sunlight as a light source. Direct sunlight can damage your eyes.
4. Always begin work with the low-power objective in line with the body tube. Adjust the revolving nosepiece.
5. Place a prepared slide over the hole in the stage. Secure the slide with the stage clips.
6. Look through the ocular lens. Move the diaphragm to adjust the amount of light coming through the stage.
7. Look at the stage from eye level. Slowly turn the coarse adjustment to lower the objective until the objective almost touches the slide. Do not allow the objective to touch the slide.
8. Look through the ocular lens. Turn the coarse adjustment to raise the low-power objective until the image is in focus. Always focus by raising the objective away from the slide. Never focus the objective downward. Use the fine adjustment to sharpen the focus. Keep both eyes open while viewing a slide.
9. Make sure that the image is exactly in the center of your field of vision. Then, switch to the high-power objective. Focus the image by using only the fine adjustment. Never use the coarse adjustment at high power.
10. When you are finished using the microscope, remove the slide. Clean the ocular lens and objectives with lens paper. Return the microscope to its storage area. Remember to use both hands when carrying the microscope.

Making a Wet Mount

1. Use lens paper to clean a glass slide and a coverslip.
2. Place the specimen that you wish to observe in the center of the slide.
3. Using a medicine dropper, place one drop of water on the specimen.
4. Hold the coverslip at the edge of the water and at a 45° angle to the slide. Make sure that the water runs along the edge of the coverslip.
5. Lower the coverslip slowly to avoid trapping air bubbles.
6. Water might evaporate from the slide as you work. Add more water to keep the specimen fresh. Place the tip of the medicine dropper next to the edge of the coverslip. Add a drop of water. (You can also use this method to add stain or solutions to a wet mount.) Remove excess water from the slide by using the corner of a paper towel as a blotter. Do not lift the coverslip to add or remove water.

SI Measurement

The International System of Units, or SI, is the standard system of measurement used by many scientists. Using the same standards of measurement makes it easier for scientists to communicate with one another.

SI works by combining prefixes and base units. Each base unit can be used with different prefixes to define smaller and larger quantities. The table below lists common SI prefixes.

SI Prefixes

Prefix	Symbol	Factor	Example
kilo-	k	1,000	kilogram, 1 kg = 1,000 g
hecto-	h	100	hectoliter, 1 hL = 100 L
deka-	da	10	dekameter, 1 dam = 10 m
		1	meter, liter, gram
deci-	d	0.1	decigram, 1 dg = 0.1 g
centi-	c	0.01	centimeter, 1 cm = 0.01 m
milli-	m	0.001	milliliter, 1 mL = 0.001 L
micro-	μ	0.000 001	micrometer, 1 μm = 0.000 001 m

SI Conversion Table

SI units	From SI to English	From English to SI
Length		
kilometer (km) = 1,000 m	1 km = 0.621 mi	1 mi = 1.609 km
meter (m) = 100 cm	1 m = 3.281 ft	1 ft = 0.305 m
centimeter (cm) = 0.01 m	1 cm = 0.394 in.	1 in. = 2.540 cm
millimeter (mm) = 0.001 m	1 mm = 0.039 in.	
micrometer (μm) = 0.000 001 m		
nanometer (nm) = 0.000 000 001 m		
Area		
square kilometer (km^2) = 100 hectares	1 km^2 = 0.386 mi^2	1 mi^2 = 2.590 km^2
hectare (ha) = 10,000 m^2	1 ha = 2.471 acres	1 acre = 0.405 ha
square meter (m^2) = 10,000 cm^2	1 m^2 = 10.764 ft^2	1 ft^2 = 0.093 m^2
square centimeter (cm^2) = 100 mm^2	1 cm^2 = 0.155 $in.^2$	1 $in.^2$ = 6.452 cm^2
Volume		
liter (L) = 1,000 mL = 1 dm^3	1 L = 1.057 fl qt	1 fl qt = 0.946 L
milliliter (mL) = 0.001 L = 1 cm^3	1 mL = 0.034 fl oz	1 fl oz = 29.574 mL
microliter (μL) = 0.000 001 L		
Mass		*Equivalent weight at Earth's surface
kilogram (kg) = 1,000 g	1 kg = 2.205 lb*	1 lb* = 0.454 kg
gram (g) = 1,000 mg	1 g = 0.035 oz*	1 oz* = 28.350 g
milligram (mg) = 0.001 g		
microgram (μg) = 0.000 001 g		

Temperature Scales

Temperature can be expressed by using three different scales: Fahrenheit, Celsius, and Kelvin. The SI unit for temperature is the kelvin (K).

Although 0 K is much colder than 0°C, a change of 1 K is equal to a change of 1°C.

Three Temperature Scales

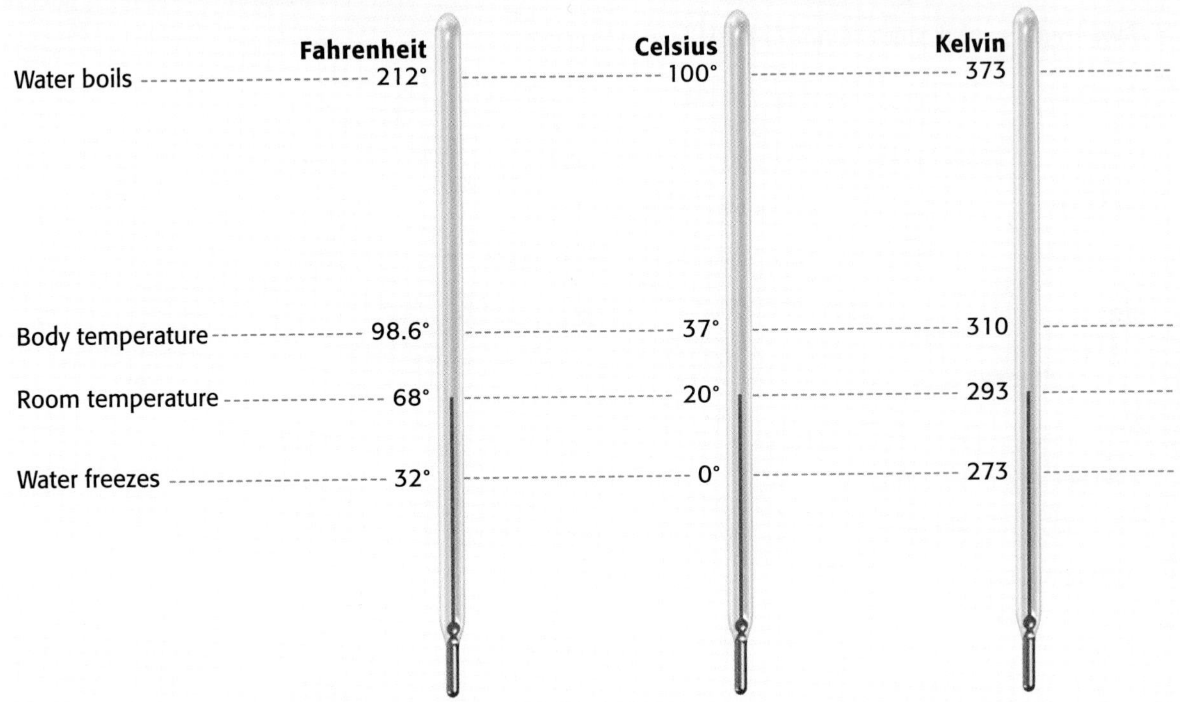

Temperature Conversions Table

To convert	Use this equation:	Example
Celsius to Fahrenheit °C → °F	$°F = \left(\frac{9}{5} \times °C\right) + 32$	Convert 45°C to °F. $°F = \left(\frac{9}{5} \times 45°C\right) + 32 = 113°F$
Fahrenheit to Celsius °F → °C	$°C = \frac{5}{9} \times (°F - 32)$	Convert 68°F to °C. $°C = \frac{5}{9} \times (68°F - 32) = 20°C$
Celsius to Kelvin °C → K	$K = °C + 273$	Convert 45°C to K. $K = 45°C + 273 = 318\ K$
Kelvin to Celsius K → °C	$°C = K - 273$	Convert 32 K to °C. $°C = 32K - 273 = -241°C$

Properties of Common Minerals

	Mineral	Color	Luster	Streak	Hardness
Silicate Minerals	**Beryl**	deep green, pink, white, bluish green, or yellow	vitreous	white	7.5–8
	Chlorite	green	vitreous to pearly	pale green	2–2.5
	Garnet	green, red, brown, black	vitreous	white	6.5–7.5
	Hornblende	dark green, brown, or black	vitreous	none	5–6
	Muscovite	colorless, silvery white, or brown	vitreous or pearly	white	2–2.5
	Olivine	olive green, yellow	vitreous	white or none	6.5–7
	Orthoclase	colorless, white, pink, or other colors	vitreous	white or none	6
	Plagioclase	colorless, white, yellow, pink, green	vitreous	white	6
	Quartz	colorless or white; any color when not pure	vitreous or waxy	white or none	7
Nonsilicate Minerals	**Native Elements**				
	Copper	copper-red	metallic	copper-red	2.5–3
	Diamond	pale yellow or colorless	adamantine	none	10
	Graphite	black to gray	submetallic	black	1–2
	Carbonates				
	Aragonite	colorless, white, or pale yellow	vitreous	white	3.5–4
	Calcite	colorless or white to tan	vitreous	white	3
	Halides				
	Fluorite	light green, yellow, purple, bluish green, or other colors	vitreous	none	4
	Halite	white	vitreous	white	2.0–2.5
	Oxides				
	Hematite	reddish brown to black	metallic to earthy	dark red to red-brown	5.6–6.5
	Magnetite	iron-black	metallic	black	5.5–6.5
	Sulfates				
	Anhydrite	colorless, bluish, or violet	vitreous to pearly	white	3–3.5
	Gypsum	white, pink, gray, or colorless	vitreous, pearly, or silky	white	2.0
	Sulfides				
	Galena	lead-gray	metallic	lead-gray to black	2.5–2.8
	Pyrite	brassy yellow	metallic	greenish, brownish, or black	6–6.5

Density (g/cm^3)	Cleavage, Fracture, Special Properties	Common Uses
2.6–2.8	1 cleavage direction; irregular fracture; some varieties fluoresce in ultraviolet light	gemstones, ore of the metal beryllium
2.6–3.3	1 cleavage direction; irregular fracture	
4.2	no cleavage; conchoidal to splintery fracture	gemstones, abrasives
3.0–3.4	2 cleavage directions; hackly to splintery fracture	
2.7–3	1 cleavage direction; irregular fracture	electrical insulation, wallpaper, fireproofing material, lubricant
3.2–3.3	no cleavage; conchoidal fracture	gemstones, casting
2.6	2 cleavage directions; irregular fracture	porcelain
2.6–2.7	2 cleavage directions; irregular fracture	ceramics
2.6	no cleavage; conchoidal fracture	gemstones, concrete, glass, porcelain, sandpaper, lenses
8.9	no cleavage; hackly fracture	wiring, brass, bronze, coins
3.5	4 cleavage directions; irregular to conchoidal fracture	gemstones, drilling
2.3	1 cleavage direction; irregular fracture	pencils, paints, lubricants, batteries
2.95	2 cleavage directions; irregular fracture; reacts with hydrochloric acid	no important industrial uses
2.7	3 cleavage directions; irregular fracture; reacts with weak acid; double refraction	cements, soil conditioner, whitewash, construction materials
3.0–3.3	4 cleavage directions; irregular fracture; some varieties fluoresce	hydrofluoric acid, steel, glass, fiberglass, pottery, enamel
2.1–2.2	3 cleavage directions; splintery to conchoidal fracture; salty taste	tanning hides, salting icy roads, food preservation
5.2–5.3	no cleavage; splintery fracture; magnetic when heated	iron ore for steel, pigments
5.2	no cleavage; splintery fracture; magnetic	iron ore
3.0	3 cleavage directions; conchoidal to splintery fracture	soil conditioner, sulfuric acid
2.3	3 cleavage directions; conchoidal to splintery fracture	plaster of Paris, wallboard, soil conditioner
7.4–7.6	3 cleavage directions; irregular fracture	batteries, paints
5	no cleavage; conchoidal to splintery fracture	sulfuric acid

Sky Maps

Spring

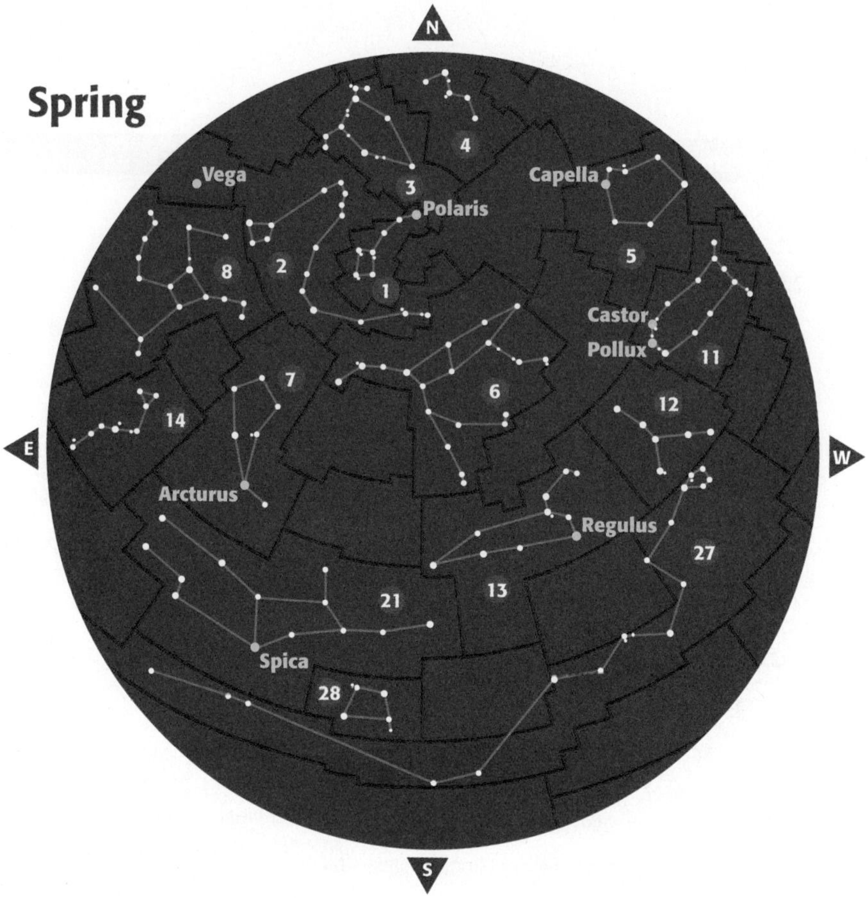

Summer

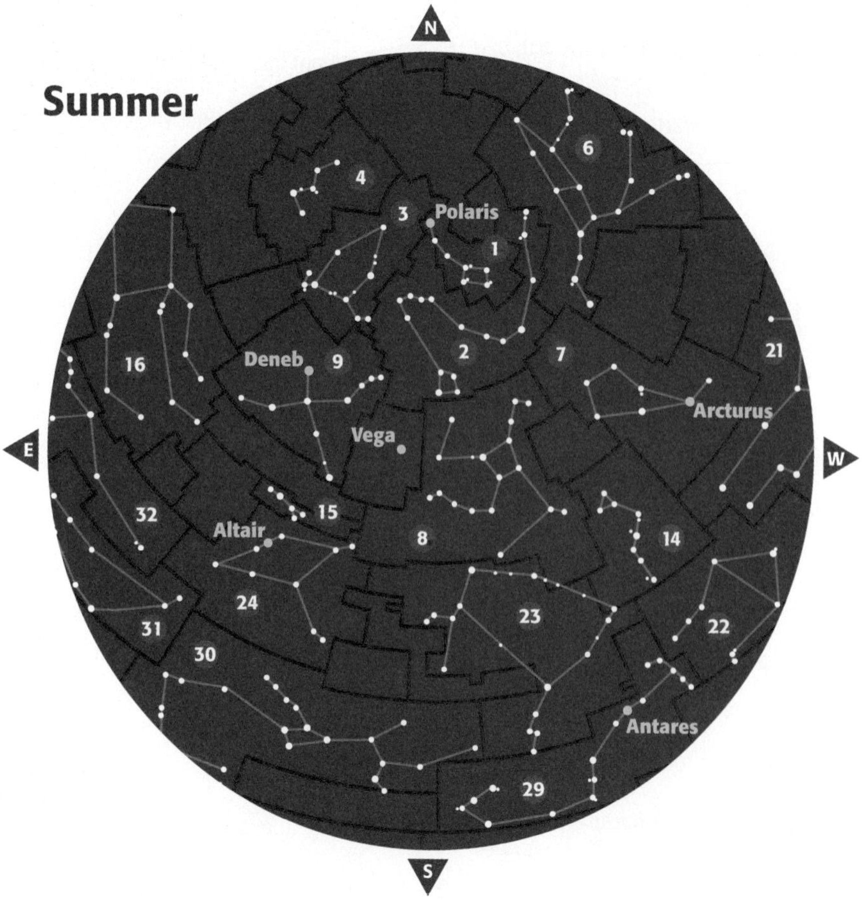

Constellations

1 Ursa Minor
2 Draco
3 Cepheus
4 Cassiopeia
5 Auriga
6 Ursa Major
7 Bootes
8 Hercules
9 Cygnus
10 Perseus
11 Gemini
12 Cancer
13 Leo
14 Serpens
15 Sagitta
16 Pegasus
17 Pisces

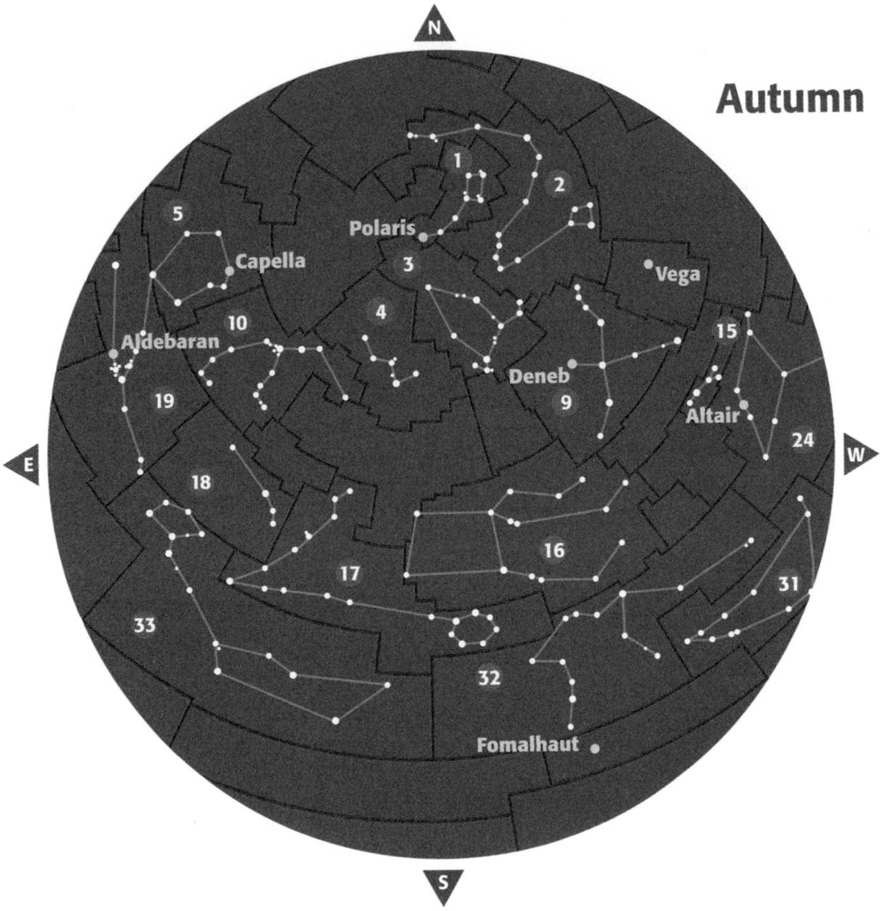

Constellations

18 Aries
19 Taurus
20 Orion
21 Virgo
22 Libra
23 Ophiuchus
24 Aquila
25 Lepus
26 Canis Major
27 Hydra
28 Corvus
29 Scorpius
30 Sagittarius
31 Capricornus
32 Aquarius
33 Cetus
34 Columba

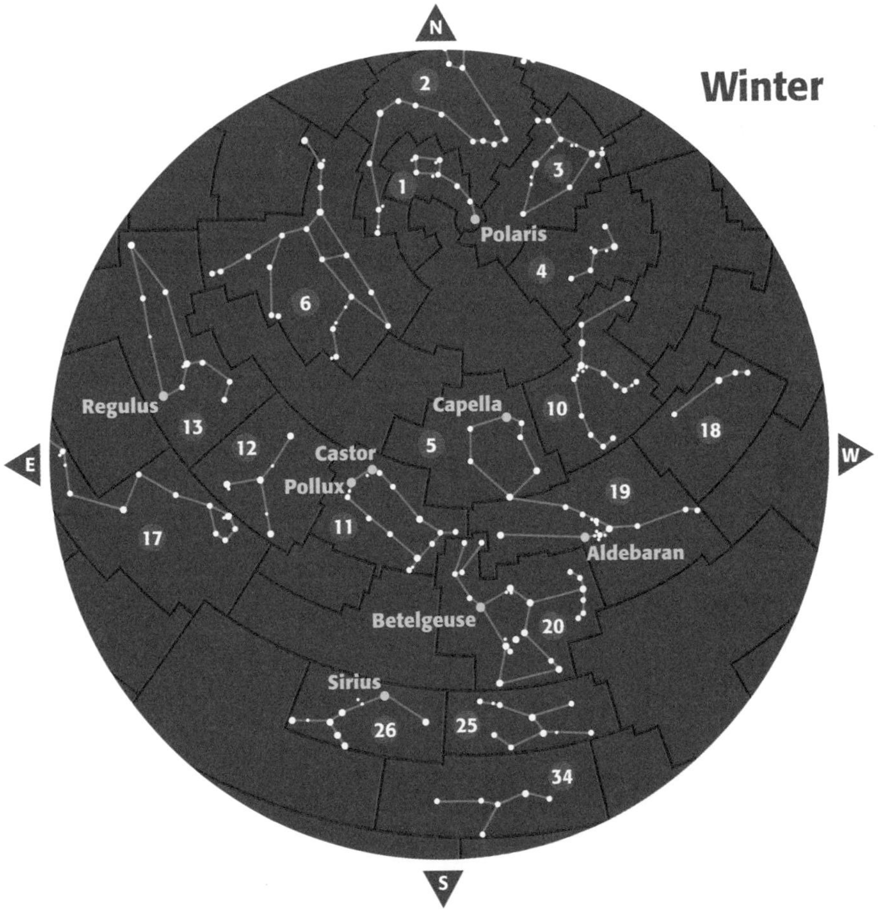

Appendix

Glossary

A

absolute magnitude the brightness that a star would have at a distance of 32.6 light-years from Earth (460)

absorption in optics, the transfer of light energy to particles of matter (148)

abyssal plain a large, flat, almost level area of the deep-ocean basin (340)

acid precipitation rain, sleet, or snow that contains a high concentration of acids (308)

addiction a dependence on a substance, such as alcohol or drugs (679)

aerobic exercise physical exercise intended to increase the activity of the heart and lungs to promote the body's use of oxygen (685)

alcoholism a disorder in which a person repeatedly drinks alcoholic beverages in an amount that interferes with the person's health and activities (680)

allergy a reaction to a harmless or common substance by the body's immune system (659)

altitude the angle between an object in the sky and the horizon (440)

alveoli (al VEE uh LIE) any of the tiny air sacs of the lungs where oxygen and carbon dioxide are exchanged (561)

amplitude the maximum distance that the particles of a wave's medium vibrate from their rest position (82)

analog signal (AN uh LAWG SIG nuhl) a signal whose properties can change continuously in a given range (273)

antibody a protein made by B cells that binds to a specific antigen (655)

apparent magnitude the brightness of a star as seen from the Earth (460)

area a measure of the size of a surface or a region (24)

artery a blood vessel that carries blood away from the heart to the body's organs (548)

asexual reproduction reproduction that does not involve the union of sex cells and in which one parent produces offspring that are genetically identical to the parent (624)

astronomy the study of the universe (429)

atom the smallest unit of an element that maintains the properties of that element (44)

autoimmune disease a disease in which the immune system attacks the organism's own cells (659)

B

B cell a white blood cell that makes antibodies (655)

benthic environment the region near the bottom of a pond, lake, or ocean (345)

benthos the organisms that live at the bottom of the sea or ocean (345)

big bang theory the theory that states that the universe began with a tremendous explosion about 13.7 billion years ago (475)

biodiversity the number and variety of organisms in a given area during a specific period of time (406)

biomass organic matter that can be a source of energy; the total mass of the organisms in a given area (315)

black hole an object so massive and dense that even light cannot escape its gravity (469)

blood the fluid that carries gases, nutrients, and wastes through the body and that is made up of platelets, white blood cells, red blood cells, and plasma (552)

blood pressure the force that blood exerts on the walls of the arteries (554)

brain the mass of nerve tissue that is the main control center of the nervous system (600)

bronchus (BRAHNG kuhs) one of the two tubes that connect the lungs with the trachea (561)

C

cancer a tumor in which the cells begin dividing at an uncontrolled rate and become invasive (660)

capillary a tiny blood vessel that allows an exchange between blood and cells in tissue (548)

carbohydrate a class of energy-giving nutrients that includes sugars, starches, and fiber; contains carbon, hydrogen, and oxygen (672)

cardiovascular system a collection of organs that transport blood throughout the body (546)

cell in electricity, a device that produces an electric current by converting chemical or radiant energy into electrical energy (213)

central nervous system the brain and the spinal cord; its main function is to control the flow of information in the body (596)

change of state the change of a substance from one physical state to another (52)

chemical change a change that occurs when one or more substances change into entirely new substances with different properties (63)

chemical energy the energy released when a chemical compound reacts to produce new compounds (312)

chemical property a property of matter that describes a substance's ability to participate in chemical reactions (56)

circuit board a sheet of insulating material that carries circuit elements and that is inserted in an electronic device (266)

coal a fossil fuel that forms underground from partially decomposed plant material (304)

cochlea (KAHK lee uh) a coiled tube that is found in the inner ear and that is essential to hearing (608)

computer an electronic device that can accept data and instructions, follow the instructions, and output the results (281)

concave lens a lens that is thinner in the middle than at the edges (174)

concave mirror a mirror that is curved inward like the inside of a spoon (172)

conservation (KAHN suhr VAY shuhn) the preservation and wise use of natural resources (408)

constellation a region of the sky that contains a recognizable star pattern and that is used to describe the location of objects in space (439)

continental rise the gently sloping section of the continental margin located between the continental slope and the abyssal plain (340)

continental shelf the gently sloping section of the continental margin located between the shoreline and the continental slope (340)

continental slope the steeply inclined section of the continental margin located between the continental rise and the continental shelf (340)

convex lens a lens that is thicker in the middle than at the edges (174)

convex mirror a mirror that is curved outward like the back of a spoon (172)

core the central part of the Earth below the mantle (499)

Coriolis effect the apparent curving of the path of a moving object from an otherwise straight path due to the Earth's rotation (374)

cosmology the study of the origin, properties, processes, and evolution of the universe (474)

crust the thin and solid outermost layer of the Earth above the mantle (499)

D

data any pieces of information acquired through observation or experimentation (15)

day the time required for Earth to rotate once on its axis (429)

decibel the most common unit used to measure loudness (symbol, dB) (112)

deep current a streamlike movement of ocean water far below the surface (375)

density the ratio of the mass of a substance to the volume of the substance (25, 43)

dermis the layer of skin below the epidermis (533)

desalination (DEE SAL uh NAY shuhn) a process of removing salt from ocean water (353)

diffraction a change in the direction of a wave when the wave finds an obstacle or an edge, such as an opening (88, 151)

digestive system the organs that break down food so that it can be used by the body (574)

digital signal a signal that can be represented as a sequence of discrete values (274)

diode an electronic device that allows electric charge to move more easily in one direction than in the other (268)

doping (DOHP eeng) the addition of an impurity element to a semiconductor (267)

Doppler effect an observed change in the frequency of a wave when the source or observer is moving (110)

drug any substance that causes a change in a person's physical or psychological state (679)

E

echo a reflected sound wave (114)

echolocation the process of using reflected sound waves to find objects; used by animals such as bats (115)

egg a sex cell produced by a female (625)

El Niño a change in the surface water temperature in the Pacific Ocean that produces a warm current (380)

electric current the rate at which charges pass through a given point; measured in amperes (209)

electric discharge the release of electricity stored in a source (205)

electric field the space around a charged object in which another charged object experiences an electric force (201)

electric force the force of attraction or repulsion on a charged particle that is due to an electric field (201)

electric generator a device that converts mechanical energy into electrical energy (252)

electric motor a device that converts electrical energy into mechanical energy (240)

electric power the rate at which electrical energy is converted into other forms of energy (217)

electrical conductor a material in which charges can move freely (204)

electrical insulator a material in which charges cannot move freely (204)

electromagnet a coil that has a soft iron core and that acts as a magnet when an electric current is in the coil (246)

electromagnetic induction the process of creating a current in a circuit by changing a magnetic field (251)

electromagnetic spectrum all of the frequencies or wavelengths of electromagnetic radiation (139, 435)

electromagnetic wave a wave that consists of electric and magnetic fields that vibrate at right angles to each other (134)

electromagnetism the interaction between electricity and magnetism (245)

electron a subatomic particle that has a negative charge (45)

element a substance that cannot be separated or broken down into simpler substances by chemical means (44)

embryo (EM bree OH) in humans, a developing individual from first division after fertilization through the 10th week of pregnancy (632)

endocrine system a collection of glands and groups of cells that secrete hormones that regulate growth, development, and homeostasis; includes the pituitary, thyroid, parathyroid, and adrenal glands, the hypothalamus, the pineal body, and the gonads (610)

epidermis (EP uh DUHR mis) the surface layer of cells on a plant or animal (533)

esophagus (i SAHF uh guhs) a long, straight tube that connects the pharynx to the stomach (576)

external fertilization the union of sex cells outside the bodies of the parents (626)

F

farsightedness a condition in which the lens of the eye focuses distant objects behind rather than on the retina (177)

fat an energy-storage nutrient that helps the body store some vitamins (673)

feedback mechanism a cycle of events in which information from one step controls or affects a previous step (605)

fetus (FEET uhs) a developing human from the 10th week of pregnancy until birth (634)

fossil fuel a nonrenewable energy resource formed from the remains of organisms that lived long ago (302)

frequency the number of waves produced in a given amount of time (85)

G

galaxy a collection of stars, dust, and gas bound together by gravity (470)

gallbladder a sac-shaped organ that stores bile produced by the liver (579)

gas a form of matter that does not have a definite volume or shape (52)

gasohol a mixture of gasoline and alcohol that is used as a fuel (315)

geothermal energy the energy produced by heat within the Earth (316)

gland a group of cells that make special chemicals for the body (610)

globular cluster a tight group of stars that looks like a ball and contains up to 1 million stars (472)

H

hardware the parts or pieces of equipment that make up a computer (282)

hologram a piece of film that produces a three-dimensional image of an object; made by using laser light (183)

homeostasis (HOH mee OH STAY sis) the maintenance of a constant internal state in a changing environment (520)

horizon the line where the sky and the Earth appear to meet (440)

hormone a substance that is made in one cell or tissue and that causes a change in another cell or tissue in a different part of the body (611)

H-R diagram Hertzsprung-Russell diagram, a graph that shows the relationship between a star's surface temperature and absolute magnitude (466)

hydroelectric energy electrical energy produced by falling water (314)

hygiene the science of health and ways to preserve health (684)

hypothesis (hie PAHTH uh sis) an explanation that is based on prior scientific research or observations and that can be tested (13)

I

immune system the cells and tissues that recognize and attack foreign substances in the body (655)

immunity the ability to resist or recover from an infectious disease (652)

infectious disease a disease that is caused by a pathogen and that can be spread from one individual to another (650)

integrated circuit (IN tuh GRAYT id SUHR kit) a circuit whose components are formed on a single semiconductor (270)

integumentary system (in TEG yoo MEN tuhr ee SIS tuhm) the organ system that forms a protective covering on the outside of the body (532, 604)

interference the combination of two or more waves that results in a single wave (89, 116, 152)

internal fertilization fertilization of an egg by sperm that occurs inside the body of a female (626)

Internet a large computer network that connects many local and smaller networks all over the world (286)

ion a charged particle that forms when an atom or group of atoms gains or loses one or more electrons (48)

J

joint a place where two or more bones meet (526)

K

kidney one of the pair of organs that filter water and wastes from the blood and that excrete products as urine (583)

L

La Niña a change in the eastern Pacific Ocean in which the surface water temperature becomes unusually cool (380)

large intestine the wider and shorter portion of the intestine that removes water from mostly digested food and that turns the waste into semisolid feces, or stool (580)

larynx (LAR ingks) the area of the throat that contains the vocal cords and produces vocal sounds (561)

laser a device that produces intense light of only one wavelength and color (181)

law a summary of many experimental results and observations; a law tells how things work (20)

law of electric charges the law that states that like charges repel and opposite charges attract (201)

lens a transparent object that refracts light waves such that they converge or diverge to create an image (174)

light-year the distance that light travels in one year; about 9.46 trillion kilometers (442, 461)

liquid the state of matter that has a definite volume but not a definite shape (52)

liver the largest organ in the body; it makes bile, stores and filters blood, and stores excess sugars as glycogen (579)

longitudinal wave a wave in which the particles of the medium vibrate parallel to the direction of wave motion (80)

longshore current a water current that travels near and parallel to the shoreline (385)

loudness the extent to which a sound can be heard (111)

lymph the fluid that is collected by the lymphatic vessels and nodes (556)

lymph node an organ that filters lymph and that is found along the lymphatic vessels (557)

lymphatic system (lim FAT ik SIS tuhm) a collection of organs whose primary function is to collect extracellular fluid and return it to the blood; the organs in this system include the lymph nodes and the lymphatic vessels (556)

M

macrophage (MAK roh FAYJ) an immune system cell that engulfs pathogens and other materials (655)

magnet any material that attracts iron or materials containing iron (236)

magnetic force the force of attraction or repulsion generated by moving or spinning electric charges (237)

magnetic pole one of two points, such as the ends of a magnet, that have opposing magnetic qualities (236)

main sequence the location on the H-R diagram where most stars lie; it has a diagonal pattern from the lower right (low temperature and luminosity) to the upper left (high temperature and luminosity) (466)

malnutrition a disorder of nutrition that results when a person does not consume enough of each of the nutrients that are needed by the human body (676)

mantle the layer of rock between the Earth's crust and core (499)

mass a measure of the amount of matter in an object (24, 40)

memory B cell a B cell that responds to an antigen more strongly when the body is reinfected with an antigen than it does during its first encounter with the antigen (658)

meter the basic unit of length in the SI (symbol, m) (24)

microprocessor a single semiconductor chip that controls and executes a microcomputer's instructions (281)

mid-ocean ridge a long, undersea mountain chain that forms along the floor of the major oceans (341)

mineral a class of nutrients that are chemical elements that are needed for certain body processes (674)

model a pattern, plan, representation, or description designed to show the structure or workings of an object, system, or concept (18)

month a division of the year that is based on the orbit of the moon around the Earth (429)

muscular system the organ system whose primary function is movement and flexibility (529)

N

narcotic a drug that is derived from opium and that relieves pain and induces sleep; examples include heroine, morphine, and codeine (681)

natural gas a mixture of gaseous hydrocarbons located under the surface of the Earth, often near petroleum deposits; used as a fuel (303)

natural resource any natural material that is used by humans, such as water, petroleum, minerals, forests, and animals (299)

neap tide a tide of minimum range that occurs during the first and third quarters of the moon (390)

nearsightedness a condition in which the lens of the eye focuses distant objects in front of rather than on the retina (177)

nebula a large cloud of gas and dust in interstellar space; a region in space where stars are born or where stars explode at the end of their lives (472, 488)

nekton all organisms that swim actively in open water, independent of currents (345)

nephron the unit in the kidney that filters blood (583)

nerve a collection of nerve fibers through which impulses travel between the central nervous system and other parts of the body (598)

neuron (NOO RAHN) a nerve cell that is specialized to receive and conduct electrical impulses (597)

neutron a subatomic particle that has no charge and that is found in the nucleus of an atom (45, 468)

nicotine (NIK uh TEEN) a toxic, addictive chemical that is found in tobacco and that is one of the major contributors to the harmful effects of smoking (680)

noise a sound that consists of a random mix of frequencies (123)

noninfectious disease a disease that cannot spread from one individual to another (650)

nonpoint-source pollution pollution that comes from many sources rather than from a single, specific site (357)

nonrenewable resource a resource that forms at a rate that is much slower than the rate at which it is consumed (299, 404)

nuclear energy the energy released by a fission or fusion reaction; the binding energy of the atomic nucleus (311)

nuclear fusion the combination of the nuclei of small atoms to form a larger nucleus; releases energy (494)

nucleus in a eukaryotic cell, a membrane-bound organelle that contains the cell's DNA and that has a role in processes such as growth, metabolism, and reproduction (46)

nutrient a substance in food that provides energy or helps form body tissues and that is necessary for life and growth (672)

O

observation the process of obtaining information by using the senses (11)

ocean current a movement of ocean water that follows a regular pattern (372)

ocean trench a steep and long depression in the deep-sea floor that runs parallel to a chain of volcanic islands or a continental margin (341)

opaque (oh PAYK) describes an object that is not transparent or translucent (155)

open cluster a group of stars that are close together relative to surrounding stars (472)

orbit the path that a body follows as it travels around another body in space (504)

organ a collection of tissues that carry out a specialized function of the body (521)

ovary in flowering plants, the lower part of a pistil that produces eggs in ovules; in the female reproductive system of animals, an organ that produces eggs (629)

overpopulation the presence of too many individuals in an area for the available resources (405)

P

pancreas the organ that lies behind the stomach and that makes digestive enzymes and hormones that regulate sugar levels (578)

parallax an apparent shift in the position of an object when viewed from different locations (461)

parallel circuit a circuit in which the parts are joined in branches such that the potential difference across each part is the same (223)

pathogen a microorganism, another organism, a virus, or a protein that causes disease (650)

pelagic environment in the ocean, the zone near the surface or at middle depths, beyond the sublittoral zone and above the abyssal zone (348)

penis the male organ that transfers sperm to a female and that carries urine out of the body (628)

peripheral nervous system (puh RIF uhr uhl NUHR vuhs SIS tuhm) all of the parts of the nervous system except for the brain and the spinal cord (596)

petroleum a liquid mixture of complex hydrocarbon compounds; used widely as a fuel source (303)

pharynx (FAR ingks) in flatworms, the muscular tube that leads from the mouth to the gastrovascular cavity; in animals with a digestive tract, the passage from the mouth to the larynx and esophagus (561)

photocell a device that converts light energy into electrical energy (214)

physical change a change of matter from one form to another without a change in chemical properties (63)

physical property a characteristic of a substance that does not involve a chemical change, such as density, color, or hardness (56)

pigment a substance that gives another substance or a mixture its color (158)

pitch a measure of how high or low a sound is perceived to be, depending on the frequency of the sound wave (109)

placenta (pluh SEN tuh) the partly fetal and partly maternal organ by which materials are exchanged between a fetus and the mother (632)

plane mirror a mirror that has a flat surface (171)

plankton the mass of mostly microscopic organisms that float or drift freely in freshwater and marine environments (345)

point-source pollution pollution that comes from a specific site (357)

pollution an unwanted change in the environment caused by substances or forms of energy (402)

protein a molecule that is made up of amino acids and that is needed to build and repair body structures and to regulate processes in the body (673)

proton a subatomic particle that has a positive charge and that is found in the nucleus of an atom (45)

pulmonary circulation (PUL muh NER ee SUHR kyoo LAY shuhn) the flow of blood from the heart to the lungs and back to the heart through the pulmonary arteries, capillaries, and veins (549)

pulsar a rapidly spinning neutron star that emits rapid pulses of radio and optical energy (468)

Q

quasar a very luminous, starlike object that generates energy at a high rate; quasars are thought to be the most distant objects in the universe (473)

R

radiation the transfer of energy as electromagnetic waves (135)

recycling the process of recovering valuable or useful materials from waste or scrap (301, 411)

red giant a large, reddish star late in its life cycle (465)

reflecting telescope a telescope that uses a curved mirror to gather and focus light from distant objects (433)

reflection the bouncing back of a ray of light, sound, or heat when the ray hits a surface that it does not go through (86, 147)

reflex an involuntary and almost immediate movement in response to a stimulus (605)

refracting telescope a telescope that uses a set of lenses to gather and focus light from distant objects (433)

refraction the bending of a wave as the wave passes between two substances in which the speed of the wave differs (87, 149)

renewable resource a natural resource that can be replaced at the same rate at which the resource is consumed (299, 404)

resistance in physical science, the opposition presented to the current by a material or device (211)

resonance a phenomenon that occurs when two objects naturally vibrate at the same frequency; the sound produced by one object causes the other object to vibrate (91, 118)

respiration in biology, the exchange of oxygen and carbon dioxide between living cells and their environment; includes breathing and cellular respiration (560)

respiratory system a collection of organs whose primary function is to take in oxygen and expel carbon dioxide; the organs of this system include the lungs, the throat, and the passageways that lead to the lungs (560)

retina the light-sensitive inner layer of the eye, which receives images formed by the lens and transmits them through the optic nerve to the brain (606)

revolution the motion of a body that travels around another body in space; one complete trip along an orbit (504)

rift valley a long, narrow valley that forms as tectonic plates separate (341)

rotation the spin of a body on its axis (504)

S

salinity a measure of the amount of dissolved salts in a given amount of liquid (332)

scattering an interaction of light with matter that causes light to change its energy, direction of motion, or both (148)

science the knowledge obtained by observing natural events and conditions in order to discover facts and formulate laws or principles that can be verified or tested (4)

scientific methods a series of steps followed to solve problems (11)

seamount a submerged mountain on the ocean floor that is at least 1,000 m high and that has a volcanic origin (341)

semiconductor (SEM i kuhn DUHK tuhr) an element or compound that conducts electric current better than an insulator does but not as well as a conductor does (267)

series circuit a circuit in which the parts are joined one after another such that the current in each part is the same (222)

sexual reproduction reproduction in which the sex cells from two parents unite to produce offspring that share traits from both parents (625)

skeletal system the organ system whose primary function is to support and protect the body and to allow the body to move (524)

small intestine the organ between the stomach and the large intestine where most of the breakdown of food happens and most of the nutrients from food are absorbed (578)

smog photochemical haze that forms when sunlight acts on industrial pollutants and burning fuels (308)

software a set of instructions or commands that tells a computer what to do; a computer program (285)

solar energy the energy received by the Earth from the sun in the form of radiation (312)

solar nebula the cloud of gas and dust that formed our solar system (489)

solenoid a coil of wire with an electric current in it (245)

solid the state of matter in which the volume and shape of a substance are fixed (51)

sonic boom the explosive sound heard when a shock wave from an object traveling faster than the speed of sound reaches a person's ears (116)

sound quality the result of the blending of several pitches through interference (121)

sound wave a longitudinal wave that is caused by vibrations and that travels through a material medium (103)

spectrum the band of colors produced when white light passes through a prism (457)

sperm the male sex cell (625)

spleen the largest lymphatic organ in the body; serves as a blood reservoir, disintegrates old red blood cells, and produces lymphocytes and plasmids (558)

spring tide a tide of increased range that occurs two times a month, at the new and full moons (390)

standing wave a pattern of vibration that simulates a wave that is standing still (91, 118)

states of matter the physical forms of matter, which include solid, liquid, and gas (51)

static electricity electric charge at rest; generally produced by friction or induction (204)

stomach the saclike, digestive organ between the esophagus and the small intestine that breaks down food by the action of muscles, enzymes, and acids (577)

storm surge a local rise in sea level near the shore that is caused by strong winds from a storm, such as those from a hurricane (387)

stress a physical or mental response to pressure (686)

sunspot a dark area of the photosphere of the sun that is cooler than the surrounding areas and that has a strong magnetic field (496)

supernova a gigantic explosion in which a massive star collapses and throws its outer layers into space (468)

surface current a horizontal movement of ocean water that is caused by wind and that occurs at or near the ocean's surface (373)

swell one of a group of long ocean waves that have steadily traveled a great distance from their point of generation (386)

systemic circulation (sis TEM ik SUHR kyoo LAY shuhn) the flow of blood from the heart to all parts of the body and back to the heart (549)

T

T cell an immune system cell that coordinates the immune system and attacks many infected cells (655)

technology the application of science for practical purposes; the use of tools, machines, materials, and processes to meet human needs (11)

telescope an instrument that collects electromagnetic radiation from the sky and concentrates it for better observation (433)

temperature a measure of how hot (or cold) something is; specifically, a measure of the average kinetic energy of the particles in an object (26)

testes the primary male reproductive organs, which produce sperm cells and testosterone (singular, *testis*) (628)

theory an explanation that ties together many hypotheses and observations (20)

thermocouple a device that converts thermal energy into electrical energy (214)

thymus the main gland of the lymphatic system; it releases mature T lymphocytes (557)

tidal range the difference in levels of ocean water at high tide and low tide (390)

tide the periodic rise and fall of the water level in the oceans and other large bodies of water (388)

tissue a group of similar cells that perform a common function (520)

tonsils small, rounded masses of lymphatic tissue located in the pharynx and in the passage from the mouth to the pharynx (559)

trachea (TRAY kee uh) in insects, myriapods, and spiders, one of a network of air tubes; in vertebrates, the tube that connects the larynx to the lungs (561)

transformer a device that increases or decreases the voltage of alternating current (254)

transistor a semiconductor device that can amplify current and that is used in amplifiers, oscillators, and switches (269)

translucent (trans LOO suhnt) describes matter that transmits light but that does not transmit an image (155)

transmission the passing of light or other form of energy through matter (154)

transparent describes matter that allows light to pass through with little interference (155)

transverse wave a wave in which the particles of the medium move perpendicularly to the direction the wave is traveling (79)

tsunami a giant ocean wave that forms after a volcanic eruption, submarine earthquake, or landslide (386)

U

umbilical cord (uhm BIL i kuhl KAWRD) the rope-like structure through which blood vessels pass and by which a developing mammal is connected to the placenta (633)

undertow a subsurface current that is near shore and that pulls objects out to sea (385)

upwelling the movement of deep, cold, and nutrient-rich water to the surface (379)

urinary system the organs that make, store, and eliminate urine (582)

uterus in female placental mammals, the hollow muscular organ in which an embryo embeds itself and develops into a fetus (629)

V

vagina the female reproductive organ that connects the outside of the body to the uterus (629)

vein in biology, a vessel that carries blood to the heart (548)

vitamin a class of nutrients that contain carbon and that are needed in small amounts to maintain health and allow growth (674)

voltage the potential difference between two points; measured in volts (210)

volume a measure of the size of a body or region in three-dimensional space (25, 40)

W

water cycle the continuous movement of water from the ocean to the atmosphere to the land and back to the ocean (335)

wave a periodic disturbance in a solid, liquid, or gas as energy is transmitted through a medium (76)

wave speed the speed at which a wave travels through a medium (85)

wavelength the distance from any point on a wave to an identical point on the next wave (83)

weight a measure of the gravitational force exerted on an object; its value can change with the location of the object in the universe (41)

white dwarf a small, hot, dim star that is the leftover center of an old star (465)

whitecap the bubbles in the crest of a breaking wave (386)

wind power the use of a windmill to drive an electric generator (313)

Y

year the time required for the Earth to orbit once around the sun (428)

Z

zenith the point in the sky directly above an observer on Earth (440)

Spanish Glossary

A

absolute magnitude/magnitud absoluta el brillo que una estrella tendría a una distancia de 32.6 años luz de la Tierra (460)

absorption/absorción en la óptica, la transferencia de energía luminosa a las partículas de materia (148)

abyssal plain/llanura abisal un área amplia, llana y casi plana de la cuenca oceánica profunda (340)

acid precipitation/precipitación ácida lluvia, aguanieve o nieve que contiene una alta concentración de ácidos (308)

addiction/adicción dependencia de substancia, tal como el alcohol u otra droga (679)

aerobic exercise/ejercicio aeróbico ejercicio físico cuyo objetivo es aumentar la actividad del corazón y los pulmones para hacer que el cuerpo use más oxígeno (685)

alcoholism/alcoholismo un trastorno en el cual una persona consume bebidas alcohólicas repetidamente en una cantidad tal que interfiere con su salud y sus actividades (680)

allergy/alergia una reacción del sistema inmunológico del cuerpo a una substancia inofensiva o común (659)

altitude/altitud el ángulo que se forma entre un objeto en el cielo y el horizonte (440)

alveoli/alveolo cualquiera de las diminutas bolsas de aire de los pulmones, en donde ocurre el intercambio de oxígeno y dióxido de carbono (561)

amplitude/amplitud la distancia máxima a la que vibran las partículas del medio de una onda a partir de su posición de reposo (82)

analog signal/señal análoga una señal cuyas propiedades cambian continuamente en un rango determinado (273)

antibody/anticuerpo una proteína producida por las células B que se une a un antígeno específico (655)

apparent magnitude/magnitud aparente el brillo de una estrella como se percibe desde la Tierra (460)

area/área una medida del tamaño de una superficie o región (24)

artery/arteria un vaso sanguíneo que transporta sangre del corazón a los órganos del cuerpo (548)

asexual reproduction/reproducción asexual reproducción que no involucra la unión de células sexuales, en la que un solo progenitor produce descendencia que es genéticamente igual al progenitor (624)

astronomy/astronomía el estudio del universo (429)

atom/átomo la unidad más pequeña de un elemento que conserva las propiedades de ese elemento (44)

autoimmune disease/enfermedad autoinmune una enfermedad en la que el sistema inmunológico ataca las células del propio organismo (659)

B

B cell/célula B un glóbulo blanco de la sangre que fabrica anticuerpos (655)

benthic environment/ambiente béntico la región que se encuentra cerca del fondo de una laguna, lago u océano (345)

benthos/benthos los organismos que viven en el fondo del mar o del océano (345)

big bang theory/teoría del Big Bang la teoría que establece que el universo comenzó con una tremenda explosión hace aproximadamente 13.7 mil millones de años (475)

biodiversity/biodiversidad el número y la variedad de organismos que se encuentran en un área determinada durante un período específico de tiempo (406)

biomass/biomasa materia orgánica que puede ser una fuente de energía; la masa total de los organismos en un área determinada (315)

black hole/hoyo negro un objeto tan masivo y denso que ni siquiera la luz puede salir de su campo gravitacional (469)

blood/sangre el líquido que lleva gases, nutrientes y desechos por el cuerpo y que está formado por plaquetas, glóbulos blancos, glóbulos rojos y plasma (552)

blood pressure/presión sanguínea la fuerza que la sangre ejerce en las paredes de las arterias (554)

brain/encéfalo la masa de tejido nervioso que es el centro principal de control del sistema nervioso (600)

bronchus/bronquio uno de los dos tubos que conectan los pulmones con la tráquea (561)

C

cancer/cáncer un tumor en el cual las células comienzan a dividirse a una tasa incontrolable y se vuelven invasivas (660)

capillary/capilar diminuto vaso sanguíneo que permite el intercambio entre la sangre y las células de los tejidos (548)

carbohydrate/carbohidrato una clase de nutrientes que proporcionan energía; incluye los azúcares, los almidones y las fibras; contiene carbono, hidrógeno y oxígeno (672)

cardiovascular system/aparato cardiovascular un conjunto de órganos que transportan la sangre a través del cuerpo (546)

cell/célula en electricidad, un aparto que produce una corriente eléctricia transformando la energía química o radiante en energía eléctrica (213)

central nervous system/sistema nervioso central el cerebro y la médula espinal; su principal función es controlar el flujo de información en el cuerpo (596)

change of state/cambio de estado el cambio de una substancia de un estado físico a otro (52)

chemical change/cambio químico un cambio que ocurre cuando una o más substancias se transforman en substancias totalmente nuevas con propiedades diferentes (63)

chemical energy/energía química la energía que se libera cuando un compuesto químico reacciona para producir nuevos compuestos (312)

chemical property/propiedad química una propiedad de la materia que describe la capacidad de una substancia de participar en reacciones químicas (56)

circuit board/cuadro del circuito una lámina de material aislante que lleva elementos del circuito y que es insertado en un aparato electrónico (266)

coal/carbón un combustible fósil que se forma en el subsuelo a partir de materiales vegetales parcialmente descompuestos (304)

cochlea/cóclea un tubo enrollado que se encuentra en el oído interno y es esencial para poder oír (608)

Computer/computadora un aparato electrónico que acepta información e instrucciones, sigue instrucciones y produce una salida para los resultados (281)

concave lens/lente cóncava una lente que es más delgada en la parte media que en los bordes (174)

concave mirror/espejo cóncavo un espejo que está curvado hacia adentro como la parte interior de una cuchara (172)

conservation/conservación la preservación y el uso inteligente de los recursos naturales (409)

constellation/constelación una región del cielo que contiene un patrón reconocible de estrellas y que se utiliza para describir la ubicación de los objetos en el espacio (439)

continental rise/elevación continental la sección del margen continental que tiene un ligero declive, ubicada entre el talud continental y la llanura abisal (340)

continental shelf/plataforma continental la sección del margen continental que tiene un ligero declive, ubicada entre la costa y el talud continental (340)

continental slope/talud continental la sección del margen continental que tiene una gran inclinación, ubicada entre la elevación continental y la plataforma continental (340)

convex lens/lente convexa una lente que es más gruesa en la parte media que en los bordes (174)

convex mirror/espejo convexo un espejo que está curvado hacia fuera como la parte de atrás de una cuchara (172)

core/núcleo la parte central de la Tierra, debajo del manto (499)

Coriolis effect/efecto de Coriolis la desviación aparente de la trayectoria recta que experimentan los objetos en movimiento debido a la rotación de la Tierra (374)

cosmology/cosmología el estudio del origen, propiedades, procesos y evolución del universo (474)

crust/corteza la capa externa, delgada y sólida de la Tierra, que se encuentra sobre el manto (499)

D

data/datos cualquier parte de la información que se adquiere por medio de la observación o experimentación (15)

day/día el tiempo que se requiere para que la Tierra rote una vez sobre su eje (429)

decibel/decibel la unidad más común que se usa para medir el volumen del sonido (símbolo: dB) (112)

deep current/corriente profunda un movimiento del agua del océano que es similar a una corriente y ocurre debajo de la superficie (375)

density/densidad la relación entre la masa de una substancia y su volumen (25, 43)

dermis/dermis la capa de piel que está debajo de la epidermis (533)

desalination/desalación (o desalinización) un proceso de remoción de sal del agua del océano (353)

diffraction/difracción un cambio en la dirección de una onda cuando ésta se encuentra con un obstáculo o un borde, tal como una abertura (88, 151)

digestive system/aparato digestivo los órganos que descomponen la comida de modo que el cuerpo la pueda usar (574)

digital signal/señal digital una señal que se puede representar como una secuencia de valores discretos (274)

diode/diodo un aparato electrónico que permite que la corriente eléctrica pase más fácilmente en una dirección que en otra (268)

doping/adulteración la adición de un elemento impuro a un semiconductor (267)

Doppler effect/efecto Doppler un cambio que se observa en la frecuencia de una onda cuando la fuente o el observador está en movimiento (110)

drug/droga cualquier substancia que produce un cambio en el estado físico o psicológico de una persona (679)

E

echo/eco una onda de sonido reflejada (114)

echolocation/ecolocación el proceso de usar ondas de sonido reflejadas para buscar objetos; utilizado por animales tales como los murciélagos (115)

egg/óvulo una célula sexual producida por una hembra (625)

El Niño/El Niño un cambio en la temperatura del agua superficial del océano Pacífico que produce una corriente caliente (380)

electric current/corriente eléctrica la tasa a la que las cargas pasan por un punto determinado; se mide en amperes (209)

electric discharge/descarga eléctrica la liberación de electricidad almacenada en una fuente (205)

electric field/campo eléctrico el espacio que se encuentra alrededor de un objeto con carga y en el que otro objecto con carga experimenta una fuerza eléctrica (201)

electric force/fuerza eléctrica la fuerza de atracción o repulsión en una partícula con carga debido a un campo eléctrico (201)

electric generator/generador eléctrico un aparato que transforma la energía mecánica en energía eléctrica (252)

electric motor/motor eléctrico un aparato que transforma la energía eléctrica en energía mecánica (240)

electric power/potencia eléctrica la tasa a la que la energía eléctrica se transforma en otras formas de energía (217)

electrical conductor/conductor eléctrico un material en el que las cargas se mueven libremente (204)

electrical insulator/aislante eléctrico un material en el que las cargas no pueden moverse libremente (204)

electromagnet/electroimán una bobina que tiene un centro de hierro suave y que funciona como un imán cuando hay una corriente eléctrica en la bobina (246)

electromagnetic induction/inducción electromagnética el proceso de crear una corriente en un circuito por medio de un cambio en el campo magnético (251)

electromagnetic spectrum/espectro electromagnético todas las frecuencias o longitudes de onda de la radiación electromagnética (139, 435)

electromagnetic wave/onda electromagnética una onda que está formada por campos eléctricos y magnéticos que vibran formando un ángulo recto unos con otros (134)

electromagnetism/electromagnetismo la interacción entre la electricidad y el magnetismo (245)

electron/electrón una partícula subatómica que tiene carga negativa (45)

element/elemento una substancia que no se puede separar o descomponer en substancias más simples por medio de métodos químicos (44)

embryo/embrión una planta o un animal en una de las primeras etapas de su desarrollo; en los seres humanos, un individuo en desarrollo desde la primera división después de la fecundación hasta el final de la décima semana del embarazo (632)

endocrine system/sistema endocrino un conjunto de glándulas y grupos de células que secretan hormonas que regulan el crecimiento, el desarrollo y la homeostasis; incluye las glándulas pituitaria, tiroides, paratiroides y suprarrenal, el hipotálamo, el cuerpo pineal y las gónadas (610)

epidermis/epidermis la superficie externa de las células de una planta o animal (533)

esophagus/esófago un conducto largo y recto que conecta la faringe con el estómago (576)

external fertilization/fecundación externa la unión de células sexuales fuera del cuerpo de los progenitores (626)

F

farsightedness/hipermetropía condición en la que el cristalino del ojo enfoca los objetos lejanos detrás de la retina en lugar de en ella (177)

fat/grasa un nutriente que almacena energía y ayuda al cuerpo a almacenar algunas vitaminas (673)

feedback mechanism/mecanismo de retroalimentación un ciclo de sucesos en el que la información de una etapa controla o afecta a una etapa anterior (605)

fetus/feto un ser humano en desarrollo desde el final de la décima semana del embarazo hasta el nacimiento (634)

fossil fuel/combustible fósil un recurso energético no renovable formado a partir de los restos de organismos que vivieron hace mucho tiempo (302)

frequency/frecuencia el número de ondas producidas en una cantidad de tiempo determinada (85)

G

galaxy/galaxia un conjunto de estrellas, polvo y gas unidos por la gravedad (470)

gallbladder/vesícula biliar un órgano que tiene la forma de una bolsa y que almacena la bilis producida por el hígado (579)

gas/gas un estado de la materia que no tiene volumen ni forma definidos (52)

gasohol/gasohol una mezcla de gasolina y alcohol que se usa como combustible (315)

geothermal energy/energía geotérmica la energía producida por el calor del interior de la Tierra (316)

gland/glándula un grupo de células que elaboran ciertas substancias químicas para el cuerpo (610)

globular cluster/cúmulo globular un grupo compacto de estrellas que parece una bola y contiene hasta un millón de estrellas (472)

H

hardware/hardware las partes o piezas de equipo que forman una computadora (282)

hologram/holograma una porción de película que produce una imagen tridimensional de un objeto mediante luz láser (183)

homeostasis/homeostasis la capacidad de mantener un estado interno constante en un ambiente en cambio (520)

horizon/horizonte la línea donde parece que el cielo y la Tierra se unen (440)

hormone/hormona una substancia que es producida en una célula o tejido, la cual causa un cambio en otra célula o tejido ubicado en una parte diferente del cuerpo (611)

H-R diagram/diagrama H-R diagrama de Hertzsprung-Russell; una gráfica que muestra la relación entre la temperatura de la superficie de una estrella y su magnitud absoluta (466)

hydroelectric energy/energía hidroeléctrica energía eléctrica producida por agua en caída (314)

hygiene/higiene la ciencia de la salud y las formas de preservar la salud (684)

hypothesis/hipótesis una explicación que se basa en observaciones o investigaciones científicas previas y que se puede probar (13)

I

immune system/sistema inmunológico las células y tejidos que reconocen y atacan substancias extrañas en el cuerpo (655)

immunity/inmunidad la capacidad de resistir una enfermedad infecciosa o recuperarse de ella (652)

infectious disease/enfermedad infecciosa una enfermedad que es causada por un patógeno y que puede transmitirse de un individuo a otro (650)

integrated circuit/circuito integrado un circuito cuyos componentes están formados en un solo semiconductor (270)

integumentary system/sistema integumentario el sistema de órganos que forma una cubierta de protección en la parte exterior del cuerpo (532, 604)

interference/interferencia la combinación de dos o más ondas que resulta en una sola onda (89, 116, 152)

internal fertilization/fecundación interna fecundación de un óvulo por un espermatozoide, la cual ocurre dentro del cuerpo de la hembra (626)

Internet/Internet una amplia red de computadoras que conecta muchas redes locales y redes más pequeñas por todo el mundo (286)

ion/ion una partícula cargada que se forma cuando un átomo o grupo de átomos gana o pierde uno o más electrones (48)

J

joint/articulación un lugar donde se unen dos o más huesos (526)

K

kidney/riñón uno de los dos órganos que filtran el agua y los desechos de la sangre y excretan productos en forma de orina (583)

L

La Niña/La Niña un cambio en el océano Pacífico oriental por el cual el agua superficial se vuelve más fría que de costumbre (380)

large intestine/intestino grueso la porción más ancha y más corta del intestino, que elimina el agua de los alimentos casi totalmente digeridos y convierte los desechos en heces semisólidas o excremento (580)

larynx/laringe el área de la garganta que contiene las cuerdas vocales y que produce sonidos vocales (561)

laser/láser un aparato que produce una luz intensa de únicamente una longitud de onda y color (181)

law/ley un resumen de muchos resultados y observaciones experimentales; una ley dice cómo funcionan las cosas (20)

law of electric charges/ley de las cargas eléctricas la ley que establece que las cargas iguales se repelen y las cargas opuestas se atraen (201)

lens/lente un objeto transparente que refracta las ondas de luz de modo que converjan o diverjan para crear una imagen (174)

light-year/año luz la distancia que viaja la luz en un año; aproximadamente 9.46 trillones de kilómetros (442, 461)

liquid/líquido el estado de la materia que tiene un volumen definido, pero no una forma definida (52)

liver/hígado el órgano más grande del cuerpo; produce bilis, almacena y filtra la sangre, y almacena el exceso de azúcares en forma de glucógeno (579)

longitudinal wave/onda longitudinal una onda en la que las partículas del medio vibran paralelamente a la dirección del movimiento de la onda (80)

longshore current/corriente de ribera una corriente de agua que se desplaza cerca de la costa y paralela a ella (385)

loudness/volumen el grado al que se escucha un sonido (111)

lymph/linfa el fluido que es recolectado por los vasos y nodos linfáticos (556)

lymph node/nodo linfático un órgano que filtra la linfa y que se encuentra a lo largo de los vasos linfáticos (557)

lymphatic system/sistema linfático un conjunto de órganos cuya función principal es recolectar el fluido extracelular y regresarlo a la sangre; los órganos de este sistema incluyen los nodos linfáticos y los vasos linfáticos (556)

M

macrophage/macrófago una célula del sistema inmunológico que envuelve a los patógenos y otros materiales (655)

magnet/imán cualquier material que atrae hierro o materiales que contienen hierro (236)

magnetic force/fuerza magnética la fuerza de atracción o repulsión generadas por cargas eléctricas en movimiento o que giran (237)

magnetic pole/polo magnético uno de dos puntos, tales como los extremos de un imán, que tienen cualidades magnéticas opuestas (236)

main sequence/secuencia principal la ubicación en el diagrama H-R donde se encuentran la mayoría de las estrellas; tiene un patrón diagonal de la parte inferior derecha (baja temperatura y luminosidad) a la parte superior izquierda (alta temperatura y luminosidad) (407)

malnutrition/desnutrición un trastorno de nutrición que resulta cuando una persona no consume una cantidad suficiente de cada nutriente que el cuerpo humano necesita (676)

mantle/manto la capa de roca que se encuentra entre la corteza terrestre y el núcleo (499)

mass/masa una medida de la cantidad de materia que tiene un objeto (24, 40)

memory B cell/célula B de memoria una célula B que responde con mayor eficacia a un antígeno cuando el cuerpo vuelve a infectarse con él que cuando lo encuentra por primera vez (658)

meter/metro la unidad fundamental de longitud en el sistema internacional de unidades (símbolo: m) (24)

microprocessor/microprocesador un chip único de un semiconductor, el cual controla y ejecuta las instrucciones de una microcomputadora (281)

mid-ocean ridge/dorsal oceánica una larga cadena submarina de montañas que se forma en el suelo de los principales océanos (341)

mineral/mineral una clase de nutrientes que son elementos quínicos necesarios para ciertos procesos del cuerpo (674)

model/modelo un diseño, plan, representación o descripción cuyo objetivo es mostrar la estructura o funcionamiento de un objeto, sistema o concepto (18)

month/mes una división del año que se basa en la órbita de la Luna alrededor de la Tierra (429)

muscular system/sistema muscular el sistema de órganos cuya función principal es permitir el movimiento y la flexibilidad (529)

N

narcotic/narcótico una droga que proviene del opio, la cual alivia el dolor e induce el sueño; entre los ejemplos se encuentran la heroína, morfina y codeína (681)

natural gas/gas natural una mezcla de hidrocarburos gaseosos que se encuentran debajo de la superficie de la Tierra, normalmente cerca de los depósitos de petróleo, y los cuales se usan como combustible (303)

natural resource/recurso natural cualquier material natural que es utilizado por los seres humanos, como agua, petróleo, minerales, bosques y animales (299)

neap tide/marea muerta una marea que tiene un rango mínimo, la cual ocurre durante el primer y el tercer cuartos de la Luna (390)

nearsightedness/miopía condición en la que el cristalino del ojo enfoca los objetos lejanos delante de la retina en lugar de en ella (177)

nebula/nebulosa una nube grande de gas y polvo en el espacio interestelar; una región en el espacio donde las estrellas nacen o donde explotan al final de su vida (472, 488)

nekton/necton todos los organismos que nadan activamente en las aguas abiertas, de manera independiente de las corrientes (345)

nephron/nefrona la unidad del riñón que filtra la sangre (583)

nerve/nervio un conjunto de fibras nerviosas a través de las cuales se desplazan los impulsos entre el sistema nervioso central y otras partes del cuerpo (598)

neuron/neurona una célula nerviosa que está especializada en recibir y transmitir impulsos eléctricos (597)

neutron/neutrón una partícula subatómica que no tiene carga y que se encuentra en el núcleo de un átomo (45, 468)

nicotine/nicotina una substancia química tóxica y adictiva que se encuentra en el tabaco y que es una de las principales causas de los efectos dañinos de fumar (680)

noise/ruido un sonido que está constituido por una mezcla aleatoria de frecuencias (123)

noninfectious disease/enfermedad no infecciosa una enfermedad que no se contagia de una persona a otra (650)

nonpoint-source pollution/contaminación no puntual contaminación que proviene de muchas fuentes, en lugar de provenir de un solo sitio específico (357)

nonrenewable resource/recurso no renovable un recurso que se forma a una tasa que es mucho más lenta que la tasa a la que se consume (299, 404)

nuclear energy/energía nuclear la energía liberada por una reacción de fisión o fusión; la energía de enlace del núcleo atómico (311)

nuclear fusion/fusión nuclear combinación de los núcleos de átomos pequeños para formar un núcleo más grande; libera energía (494)

nucleus/núcleo en ciencias físicas, la región central de un átomo, la cual está constituida por protones y neutrones (46)

nutrient/nutriente una substancia de los alimentos que proporciona energía o ayuda a formar tejidos corporales y que es necesaria para la vida y el crecimiento (672)

O

observation/observación el proceso de obtener información por medio de los sentidos (11)

ocean current/corriente oceánica un movimiento del agua del océano que sigue un patrón regular (372)

ocean trench/fosa oceánica una depresión empinada y larga del suelo marino profundo, paralela a una cadena de islas volcánicas o al margen continental (341)

opaque/opaco término que describe un objeto que no es transparente ni translúcido (155)

open cluster/conglomerado abierto un grupo de estrellas que se encuentran juntas respecto a las estrellas que las rodean (472)

orbit/órbita la trayectoria que sigue un cuerpo al desplazarse alrededor de otro cuerpo en el espacio (504)

organ/órgano un conjunto de tejidos que desempeñan una función especializada en el cuerpo (521)

ovary/ovario en las plantas con flores, la parte inferior del pistilo que produce óvulos; en el aparato reproductor femenino de los animales, un órgano que produce óvulos (629)

overpopulation/sobrepoblación la presencia de demasiados individuos en un área para los recursos disponibles (405)

P

pancreas/páncreas el órgano que se encuentra detrás del estómago y que produce las enzimas digestivas y las hormonas que regulan los niveles de azúcar (578)

parallax/paralaje un cambio aparente en la posición de un objeto cuando se ve desde lugares distintos (461)

parallel circuit/circuito paralelo un circuito en el que las partes están unidas en ramas de manera tal que la diferencia de potencial entre cada parte es la misma (223)

pathogen/patógeno un microorganismo, otro organismo, un virus o una proteína que causa enfermedades (650)

pelagic environment/ambiente pelágico en el océano, la zona ubicada cerca de la superficie o en profundidades medias, más allá de la zona sublitoral y por encima de la zona abisal (348)

penis/pene el órgano masculino que transfiere espermatozoides a una hembra y que lleva la orina hacia el exterior del cuerpo (628)

peripheral nervous system/sistema nervioso periférico todas las partes del sistema nervioso, excepto el encéfalo y la médula espinal (596)

petroleum/petróleo una mezcla líquida de compuestos hidrocarburos complejos; se usa ampliamente como una fuente de combustible (303)

pharynx/faringe en los gusanos planos, el tubo muscular que va de la boca a la cavidad gastrovascular; en los animales que tienen tracto digestivo, el conducto que va de la boca a la laringe y al esófago (561)

photocell/fotocelda un aparato que transforma la energía luminosa en energía eléctrica (214)

physical change/cambio físico un cambio de materia de una forma a otra sin que ocurra un cambio en sus propiedades químicas (63)

physical property/propiedad física una característica de una substancia que no implica un cambio químico, tal como la densidad, el color o la dureza (56)

pigment/pigmento una substancia que le da color a otra substancia o mezcla (158)

pitch/altura tonal una medida de qué tan agudo o grave se percibe un sonido, dependiendo de la frecuencia de la onda sonora (109)

placenta/placenta el órgano parcialmente fetal y parcialmente materno por medio del cual se intercambian materiales entre el feto y la madre (632)

plane mirror/espejo plano un espejo que tiene una superficie plana (171)

plankton/plancton la masa de organismos en su mayoría microscópicos que flotan o se encuentran a la deriva en ambientes de agua dulce o marina (345)

point-source pollution/contaminación puntual contaminación que proviene de un lugar específico (357)

pollution/contaminación un cambio indeseable en el ambiente producido por substancias o formas de energía (402)

protein/proteína una molécula formada por aminoácidos que es necesaria para construir y reparar estructuras corporales y para regular procesos del cuerpo (673)

proton/protón una partícula subatómica que tiene una carga positiva y que se encuentra en el núcleo de un átomo (45)

pulmonary circulation/circulación pulmonar el flujo de sangre del corazón a los pulmones y de vuelta al corazón a través de las arterias, los capilares y las venas pulmonares (549)

pulsar/pulsar una estrella de neutrones que gira rápidamente y emite pulsaciones rápidas de energía radioeléctrica y óptica (468)

Q

quasar/cuasar un objeto muy luminoso, parecido a una estrella, que genera energía a una gran velocidad; se piensa que los cuásares son los objetos más distantes del universo (473)

R

radiation/radiación la transferencia de energía en forma de ondas electromagnéticas (135)

recycling/reciclar el proceso de recuperar materiales valiosos o útiles de los desechos o de la basura; el proceso de reutilizar algunas cosas (301, 411)

red giant/gigante roja una estrella grande de color rojizo que se encuentra en una etapa avanzada de su vida (465)

reflecting telescope/telescopio reflector un telescopio que utiliza un espejo curvo para captar y enfocar la luz de objetos lejanos (433)

reflection/reflexión el rebote de un rayo de luz, sonido o calor cuando el rayo golpea una superficie pero no la atraviesa (86, 147)

reflex/reflejo un movimiento involuntario y prácticamente inmediato en respuesta a un estímulo (605)

refracting telescope/telescopio refractante un telescopio que utiliza un conjunto de lentes para captar y enfocar la luz de objetos lejanos (433)

refraction/refracción el curvamiento de una onda cuando ésta pasa entre dos substancias en las que su velocidad difiere (87, 149)

renewable resource/recurso renovable un recurso natural que puede reemplazarse a la misma tasa a la que se consume (299, 404)

resistance/resistencia en ciencias físicas, la oposición que un material o aparato presenta a la corriente (211)

resonance/resonancia un fenómeno que ocurre cuando dos objetos vibran naturalmente a la misma frecuencia; el sonido producido por un objeto hace que el otro objeto vibre (91, 118)

respiration/respiración en biología, el intercambio de oxígeno y dióxido de carbono entre células vivas y su ambiente; incluye la respiración y la respiración celular (560)

respiratory system/aparato respiratorio un conjunto de órganos cuya función principal es tomar oxígeno y expulsar dióxido de carbono; los órganos de este aparato incluyen a los pulmones, la garganta y las vías que llevan a los pulmones (560)

retina/retina la capa interna del ojo, sensible a la luz, que recibe imágenes formadas por el lente ocular y las transmite al cerebro por medio del nervio óptico (606)

revolution/revolución el movimiento de un cuerpo que viaja alrededor de otro cuerpo en el espacio; un viaje completo a lo largo de una órbita (504)

rift valley/fosa tectónica un valle largo y estrecho que se forma cuando se separan las placas tectónicas (341)

rotation/rotación el giro de un cuerpo alrededor de su eje (504)

S

salinity/salinidad una medida de la cantidad de sales disueltas en una cantidad determinada de líquido (332)

scattering/dispersión una interacción de la luz con la materia que hace que la luz cambie su energía, la dirección del movimiento o ambas (148)

science/ciencia el conocimiento que se obtiene por medio de la observación natural de acontecimientos y condiciones con el fin de descubrir hechos y formular leyes o principios que puedan ser verificados o probados (4)

scientific methods/métodos científicos una serie de pasos que se siguen para solucionar problemas (11)

seamount/montaña submarina una montaña sumergida que se encuentra en el fondo del océano, la cual tiene por lo menos 1,000 m de altura y cuyo origen es volcánico (341)

semiconductor/semiconductor un elemento o compuesto que conduce la corriente eléctrica mejor que un aislante, pero no tan bien como un conductor (267)

series circuit/circuito en serie un circuito en el que las partes están unidas una después de la otra de manera tal que la corriente en cada parte es la misma (222)

sexual reproduction/reproducción sexual reproducción en la que se unen las células sexuales de los dos progenitores para producir descendencia que comparte caracteres de ambos progenitores (625)

skeletal system/sistema esquelético el sistema de órganos cuya función principal es sostener y proteger el cuerpo y permitir que se mueva (524)

small intestine/intestino delgado el órgano que se encuentra entre el estómago y el intestino grueso en el cual se produce la mayor parte de la descomposición de los alimentos y se absorben la mayoría de los nutrientes (578)

smog/esmog bruma fotoquímica que se forma cuando la luz solar actúa sobre contaminantes industriales y combustibles (308)

software/software un conjunto de instrucciones o comandos que le dicen qué hacer a una computadora; un programa de computadora (285)

solar energy/energía solar la energía que la Tierra recibe del Sol en forma de radiación (312)

solar nebula/nebulosa solar la nube de gas y polvo que formó nuestro Sistema Solar (489)

solenoid/solenoide una bobina de alambre que tiene una corriente eléctrica (245)

solid/sólido el estado de la materia en el cual el volumen y la forma de una sustancia están fijos (51)

sonic boom/estampido sónico el sonido explosivo que se escucha cuando la onda de choque de un objeto que se desplaza a una velocidad superior a la de lo sonido llega a los oídos de una persona (116)

sound quality/calidad del sonido el resultado de la combinación de varios tonos por medio de la interferencia (121)

sound wave/onda de sonido una onda longitudinal que se origina debido a vibraciones y que se desplaza a través de un medio material (103)

spectrum/espectro la banda de colores que se produce cuando la luz blanca pasa a través de un prisma (457)

sperm/espermatozoide la célula sexual masculina (625)

spleen/bazo el órgano linfático más grande del cuerpo; funciona como depósito para la sangre, desintegra los glóbulos rojos viejos y produce linfocitos y plásmidos (558)

spring tide/marea muerta una marea de mayor rango que ocurre dos veces al mes, durante la luna nueva y la luna llena (390)

standing wave/onda estacionaria un patrón de vibración que simula una onda que está parada (91, 118)

states of matter/estados de la material las formas físicas de la materia, que son sólida, líquida y gaseosa (51)

static electricity/electricidad estática carga eléctrica en reposo; por lo general se produce por fricción o inducción (204)

stomach/estómago el órgano digestivo con forma de bolsa ubicado entre el esófago y el intestino delgado, que descompone los alimentos por la acción de músculos, enzimas y ácidos (577)

storm surge/marea de tempestad un levantamiento local del nivel del mar cerca de la costa, el cual es resultado de los fuertes vientos de una tormenta, como por ejemplo, los vientos de un huracán (387)

stress/estrés una respuesta física o mental a la presión (686)

sunspot/mancha solar un área oscura en la fotosfera del Sol que es más fría que las áreas que la rodean y que tiene un campo magnético fuerte (496)

supernova/supernova una explosión gigantesca en la que una estrella masiva se colapsa y lanza sus capas externas hacia el espacio (468)

surface current/corriente superficial un movimiento horizontal del agua del océano que es producido por el viento y que ocurre en la superficie del océano o cerca de ella (373)

swell/mar de leva un grupo de olas oceánicas grandes que se han desplazado una gran distancia desde el punto en el que se originaron (386)

systemic circulation/circulación sistémica el flujo de sangre del corazón a todas las partes del cuerpo y de vuelta al corazón (549)

T

T cell/célula T una célula del sistema inmunológico que coordina el sistema inmunológico y ataca a muchas células infectadas (655)

technology/tecnología la aplicación de la ciencia con fines prácticos; el uso de herramientas, máquinas, materiales y procesos para satisfacer las necesidades de los seres humanos (11)

telescope/telescopio un instrumento que capta la radiación electromagnética del cielo y la concentra para mejorar la observación (433)

temperature/temperatura una medida de qué tan caliente (o frío) está algo; específicamente, una medida de la energía cinética promedio de las partículas de un objeto (26)

testes/testículos los principales órganos reproductores masculinos, los cuales producen espermatozoides y testosterona (628)

theory/teoría una explicación que relaciona muchas hipótesis y observaciones (20)

thermocouple/termopar un aparato que transforma la energía térmica en energía eléctrica (214)

thymus/timo la glándula principal del sistema linfático; libera linfocitos T maduros (557)

tidal range/rango de marea la diferencia en los niveles del agua del océano entre la marea alta y la marea baja (390)

tide/marea el ascenso y descenso periódico del nivel del agua en los océanos y otras masas grandes de agua (388)

tissue/tejido un grupo de células similares que llevan a cabo una función común (520)

tonsils/amígdalas masas pequeñas y redondas de tejido linfático, ubicadas en la faringe y en el paso de la boca a la faringe (559)

trachea/tráquea en los insectos, miriápodos y arañas, uno de los conductos de una red de conductos de aire; en los vertebrados, el conducto que une la laringe con los pulmones (561)

transformer/transformador un aparato que aumenta o disminuye el voltaje de la corriente alterna (254)

transistor/transistor un aparato semiconductor que puede amplificar la corriente y se usa en los amplificadores, osciladores e interruptores (269)

translucent/traslúcido término que describe la materia que transmite luz, pero que no transmite una imagen (155)

transmission/transmisión el paso de la luz u otra forma de energía a través de la materia (154)

transparent/transparente término que describe materia que permite el paso de la luz con poca interferencia (155)

transverse wave/onda transversal una onda en la que las partículas del medio se mueven perpendicularmente respecto a la dirección en la que se desplaza la onda (79)

tsunami/tsunami una ola gigante del océano que se forma después de una erupción volcánica, terremoto submarino o desprendimiento de tierras (386)

U

umbilical cord/cordón umbilical la estructura con forma de cuerda a través de la cual pasan vasos sanguíneos y por medio de la cual un mamífero en desarrollo está unido a la placenta (633)

undertow/resaca un corriente subsuperficial que está cerca de la orilla y que arrastra los objetos hacia el mar (385)

upwelling/surgencia el movimiento de las aguas profundas, frías y ricas en nutrientes hacia la superficie (379)

urinary system/sistema urinario los órganos que producen, almacenan y eliminan la orina (582)

uterus/útero en los mamíferos placentarios hembras, el órgano hueco y muscular en el que el embrión se incrusta y se desarrolla hasta convertirse en feto (629)

V

vagina/vagina el órgano reproductivo femenino que conecta la parte exterior del cuerpo con el útero (629)

vein/vena en biología, un vaso que lleva sangre al corazón (548)

vitamin/vitamina una clase de nutrientes que contiene carbono y que es necesaria en pequeñas cantidades para mantener la salud y permitir el crecimiento (674)

voltage/voltaje la diferencia de potencial entre dos puntos, medida en voltios (210)

volume/volumen una medida del tamaño de un cuerpo o región en un espacio de tres dimensiones (25, 40)

W

water cycle/ciclo del agua el movimiento continuo del agua: del océano a la atmósfera, de la atmósfera a la tierra y de la tierra al océano (335)

wave/onda una perturbación periódica en un sólido, líquido o gas que se transmite a través de un medio en forma de energía (76)

wave speed/rapidez de onda la rapidez a la cual viaja una onda a través de un medio (85)

wavelength/longitud de onda la distancia entre cualquier punto de una onda y un punto idéntico en la onda siguiente (83)

weight/peso una medida de la fuerza gravitacional ejercida sobre un objeto; su valor puede cambiar en función de la ubicación del objeto en el universo (41)

white dwarf/enana blanca una estrella pequeña, caliente y tenue que es el centro sobrante de una estrella vieja (465)

whitecap/cabrillas las burbujas de la cresta de una ola rompiente (386)

wind power/potencia eólica el uso de un molino de viento para hacer funcionar un generador eléctrico (313)

Y

year/año el tiempo que se requiere para que la Tierra le dé la vuelta al Sol una vez (428)

Z

zenith/cenit el punto del cielo situado directamente sobre un observador en la Tierra (440)

Index

Boldface page numbers refer to illustrative materials, such as figures, tables, margin elements, photographs, and illustrations

A

B

Index

Index

D

E

F

G

H

M

N

O

P

S

T

U

V

Index

Index

Acknowledgments

continued from page ii

Howard L. Brooks, Ph.D.
Professor of Physics & Astronomy
Department of Physics & Astronomy
DePauw University
Greencastle, Indiana

Dan Bruton, Ph.D.
Associate Professor
Department of Physics and Astronomy
Stephen F. Austin State University
Nacogdoches, Texas

Wesley N. Colley, Ph.D.
Lecturer
Department of Astronomy
University of Virginia
Charlottesville, Virginia

William E. Dunscombe
Associate Professor and Chairman
Biology Department
Union County College
Cranford, New Jersey

Simonetta Frittelli, Ph.D.
Associate Professor
Department of Physics
Duquesne University
Pittsburgh, Pennsylvania

William Grisham, Ph.D.
Lecturer
Psychology Department
University of California, Los Angeles
Los Angeles, California

P. Shiv Halasyamani, Ph.D.
Associate Professor of Chemistry
Department of Chemistry
University of Houston
Houston, Texas

David S. Hall, Ph.D.
Assistant Professor of Physics
Department of Physics
Amherst College
Amherst, Massachusetts

William H. Ingham, Ph.D.
Professor of Physics
James Madison University
Harrisonburg, Virginia

Ping H. Johnson, M.D., Ph.D., C.H.E.S.
Assistant Professor of Health Education
Department of Health, Physical Education and Sport Science
Kennesaw State University
Kennesaw, Georgia

Linda Jones
Program Manager
Texas Department of Public Health
Austin, Texas

David Lamp, Ph.D.
Associate Professor of Physics
Physics Department
Texas Tech University
Lubbock, Texas

Joel S. Leventhal, Ph.D.
Emeritus Scientist, Geochemistry
U.S. Geological Survey
Denver, Colorado

Mark Mattson, Ph.D.
Director, College of Science and Mathematics Learning Center
James Madison University
Harrisonburg, Virginia

Richard F. Niedziela, Ph.D.
Assistant Professor of Chemistry
Department of Chemistry
DePaul University
Chicago, Illinois

Eva Oberdoerster, Ph.D.
Lecturer
Department of Biology
Southern Methodist University
Dallas, Texas

Sten Odenwald, Ph.D.
Astronomer
NASA Goddard Space Flight Center and Raytheon ITSS
Greenbelt, Maryland

Kenneth H. Rubin, Ph.D.
Associate Professor
Department of Geology & Geophysics
University of Hawaii at Manoa
Honolulu, Hawaii

Laurie Santos, Ph.D.
Assistant Professor
Department of Psychology
Yale University
New Haven, Connecticut

H. Michael Sommermann, Ph.D.
Professor of Physics
Physics Department
Westmont College
Santa Barbara, California

Teacher Reviewers

Laura Buchanan
Science Teacher and Department Chair
Corkran Middle School
Glen Burnie, Maryland

Randy Dye, M.S.
Science Department Head
Wood Middle School
Fort Leonard Wood, Missouri

Trisha Elliott
Science and Mathematics Teacher
Chain of Lakes Middle School
Orlando, Florida

Liza M. Guasp
Science Teacher
Celebration K–8 School
Celebration, Florida

Ronald W. Hudson
Science Teacher
Batchelor Middle School
Bloomington, Indiana

Denise Hulette
Science Teacher
Conway Middle School
Orlando, Florida

Laura Kitselman
Science Teacher and Coordinator
Loudoun Country Day School
Leesburg, Virginia

Debra S. Kogelman, MAed.
Science Teacher
University of Chicago Laboratory Schools
Chicago, Illinois

Deborah L. Kronsteiner
Science Teacher
Spring Grove Area Middle School
Spring Grove, Pennsylvania

Jennifer L. Lamkie
Science Teacher
Thomas Jefferson Middle School
Edison, New Jersey

Rebecca Larsen
Science Teacher
Fernandina Beach Middle School
Fernandina Beach, Florida

Sally M. Lesley
ESL Science Teacher
Burnet Middle School
Austin, Texas

Stacy Loeak
Science Teacher and Department Chair
Baker Middle School
Columbus, Georgia

Augie Maldonado
Science Teacher
Grisham Middle School
Round Rock, Texas

Bill Martin
Science Teacher
Southeast Middle School
Kernersville, North Carolina

Maureen Martin
Green Team Science Teacher
Jackson Creek Middle School
Bloomington, Indiana

Jean Pletchette
Health Educator
Winterset Community Schools
Winterset, Iowa

Thomas Lee Reed
Science Teacher
Rising Starr Middle School
Fayetteville, Georgia

Shannon Ripple
Science Teacher
Canyon Vista Middle School
Round Rock, Texas

Elizabeth J. Rustad
Science Department Chair
Coronado Elementary
Gilbert, Arizona

Helen P. Schiller
Instructional Coach
The School District of Greenville County
Greenville, South Carolina

Mark Schnably
Science Instructor
Thomas Jefferson Middle School
Winston-Salem, North Carolina

Marci L. Stadiem
Science Department Head
Cascade Middle School
Seattle, Washington

Martha Tedrow
Science Teacher
Thomas Jefferson Middle School
Winston-Salem, North Carolina

Martha B. Trisler
Science Teacher
Rising Starr Middle School
Fayetteville, Georgia

Sherrye Valenti
Curriculum Leader
Science Department
Wildwood Middle School
Wildwood, Missouri

Florence Vaughan
Science Teacher
University of Chicago Laboratory Schools
Chicago, Illinois

Roberta Young
Science Teacher
Gunn Junior High School
Arlington, Texas

Lab Testing

Barry L. Bishop
Science Teacher
San Rafael Junior High
Ferron, Utah

Paul Boyle
Science Teacher
Perry Heights Middle School
Evansville, Indiana

Yvonne Brannum
Science Teacher
Hine Junior High School
Washington, D.C.

Daniel Bugenhagen
Science Teacher
Yutan Junior-Senior High School
Yutan, Nebraska

Randy Christian
Science Teacher
Stovall Junior HS
Houston, Texas

James Chin
Science Teacher
Frank A. Day Middle School
Newtonville, Massachusetts

Laura Fleet
Science Teacher
Alice B. Landrum Middle School
Ponte Vedra Beach, Florida

Jennifer Ford
Science Teacher
North Ridge Middle School
North Richland Hills, Texas

Susan Gorman
Science Teacher
North Ridge Middle School
North Ridge, Texas

Norman Holcomb
Science Teacher
Marion Elementary School
Maria Stein, Ohio

Tracy Jahn
Science Teacher
Berkshire Junior-Sr. HS
Canaan, New York

Martha Kisiah
Science Teacher
Fairview Middle School
Tallahassee, Florida

Michael E. Krai
Science Teacher
West Hardin Middle School
Cecilia, Kentucky

Kathy Laroe
Science Teacher
East Valley Middle School
East Helena, Montana

Edith McAlanis
Science Teacher
Socorro Middle School
El Paso, Texas

Kevin McCurdy
Science Teacher
Elmwood Junior High
Rogers, Arkansas

Kathy McKee
Science Teacher
Hoyt Middle School
Des Moines, Iowa

Alyson Mike
Science Teacher
Radley Middle School
East Helena, Montana

Joseph W. Price
Science Teacher
H.M. Browne Junior High
Washington, D.C.

Terry Rakes
Science Teacher
Elmwood Junior HS
Rogers, Arkansas

Elizabeth Rustad
Science Teacher
Crane Junior HS
Yuma, Arizona

Debra Sampson
Science Teacher
Booker T. Washington Middle School
Elgin, Texas

Rodney A. Sandefur
Science Teacher
Naturita Middle School
Naturita, Colorado

Patricia McFarlane Soto
Science Teacher
George Washington Carver Middle School
Miami, Florida

David Sparks
Science Teacher
Redwater Junior HS
Redwater, Texas

Ivora Washington
Science Teacher
Hyattsville Middle School
Hyattsville, Maryland

Christopher Woods
Science Teacher
Western Rockingham Middle School
Madison, North Carolina

Gordon Zibelman
Science Teacher
Drexel Hill Middle School
Drexel Hill, Pennsylvania

Answer Checking

Hatim Belyamani
Austin, Texas

John A. Benner
Austin, Texas

Catherine Podeszwa
Duluth, Minnesota

Credits

PHOTOGRAPHY

Abbreviations used: (t) top, (c) center, (b) bottom, (l) left, (r) right, (bkgd) background

Front Cover (tl) James L. Amos/Photo Researchers, Inc.; (bl) Robert Essel/Corbis; (r) Daryl Benson/Masterfile; (earth) NASA Goddard Space Flight Center

Skills Practice Lab Teens Sam Dudgeon/HRW

Connection to Astronomy Corbis Images; **Connection to Biology** David M. Phillips/Visuals Unlimited; **Connection to Chemistry** Digital Image copyright © 2005 PhotoDisc; **Connection to Environment** Digital Image copyright © 2005 PhotoDisc; **Connection to Geology** Letraset Phototone; **Connection to Language Arts** Digital Image copyright © 2005 PhotoDisc; **Connection to Meteorology** Digital Image copyright © 2005 PhotoDisc; **Connection to Oceanography** © ICONOTEC; **Connection to Physics** Digital Image copyright © 2005 PhotoDisc

Table of Contents iii (tr), Sam Dudgeon/HRW; iii (b), NASA; iv (tl), Howard B. Bluestein; iv (bl), age fotostock/Fabio Cardoso; v (tl), Pete Saloutos/The Stock Market; v (bl), Sam Dudgeon/HRW; vi (tl), © Cameron Davidson; vi (b), © Digital Vision Ltd.; vii (tl), John Langford/HRW; vii (bl), Victoria Smith/HRW; viii (tl), © Reuters NewMedia Inc./CORBIS; viii (b), Laurent Gillieron/Keystone/AP/Wide World Photos; ix (tl), Stuart Westmorland/CORBIS; ix (tl) © Sindre Ellingsen/Alamy Photos; ix (bl), Peter Van Steen/HRW; xi (tl), Bill & Sally Fletcher/Tom Stack & Associates; xi (b), NASA/TSADO/Tom Stack & Associates; xii (tl), Sam Dudgeon/HRW; xii (bl), © Nih/Science Source/Photo Researchers, Inc.; xiii (all), Sam Dudgeon/HRW; xiv (tl), Photo Lennart Nilsson/Albert Bonniers Forlag AB, A Child Is Born, Dell Publishing Company; xv (tl), © Rob Van Petten/Getty Images/The Image Bank; xvi (br), Sam Dudgeon/HRW; xix (tc), Victoria Smith/HRW; xx (tr), Victoria Smith/HRW; xxi (tr), Victoria Smith/HRW; xxii (bl), Victoria Smith/HRW

Safety First! xxvi, Sam Dudgeon/HRW; xxvii(t), John Langford/HRW; xxvii(bc), xxviii(br) & xxviii(tl), Sam Dudgeon/HRW xxviii(bl), Stephanie Morris/HRW; xxix(tl), Sam Dudgeon/HRW xxix(tr), Jana Birchum/HRW; xxix(b), Sam Dudgeon/HRW

Chapter One 2-3 (all), © Kevin Schafer/Getty Images; 4 bl Peter Van Steen/HRW Photo; 5 (tr) Peter Van Steen/HRW Photo; 5 (br) Peter Van Steen/HRW Photo; 6 (tl) Regis Bossu/Sygma; 6 (bl) Richard R. Hansen/Photo Researchers, Inc.; 7 (br) Howard B. Bluestein; 8 (tl) Andy Christiansen/HRW Photo; 8 (bl) © G. Brad Lewis/Getty Images/Stone; 9 (tr) Andy Christiansen/HRW Photo; 11 (r) HRW photo by Stephen Malcone; 11 (l) Barry Chin/Boston Globe; 14 Donna Coveney/MIT News; 18 (l) Peter Van Steen/HRW Photo; 18 (l) Peter Van Steen/HRW Photo; 19 (b) Chris Butler/Science Photo Library/Photo Researchers, Inc.; 19 (t) John Langford/HRW photo; 20 (tl) Sam Dudgeon/HRW Photo; 21 Victoria Smith/HRW Photo; 21 (c) Victoria Smith/HRW Photo; 24 (t) Otis Imboden/National Geographic Image Collection; 25 (tr) Andy Christiansen/HRW Photo; 25 (bl) Peter Van Steen/HRW Photo; 25 (br) Peter Van Steen/HRW Photo; 26 (tl) Tony Freeman/PhotoEdit; 26 (bl) Corbis Images; 26 (tr) Victoria Smith/HRW; 27 (b), Sam Dudgeon/HRW; 28 (bl), Digital Image copyright © 2005 PhotoDisc; 30 Sam Dudgeon/HRW photo; 31 (cl) John Langford/HRW photo; 31 (cr) HRW photo by Victoria Smith; 34 (tr), © Layne Kennedy/CORBIS; 35 (all), Louis Fronkier/Art Louis Photographics/HRW

Unit One 36 (c), Photofest; 36 (br), Sam Dudgeon/HRW; 36 (tr), © Archivo Iconografico, S.A./CORBIS; 37 (tl), David Parker/Science Photo Library/Photo Researchers, Inc.; 37 (tr), Dr. E.R. Degginger; 37 (cr), Fotos International/Hulton Archive/Getty Images; 37 (bl), Victoria Smith/HRW; 37 (br), Kieran Doherty/REUTERS/NewsCom

Chapter Two 38-39, © Tina Buckman/Index Stock Imagery, Inc.; 40 (l), Victoria Smith/HRW; 40 (r), Victoria Smith/HRW; 41, NASA Marshall Space Flight Center (NASA-MSFC); 42, Victoria Smith/HRW; 43 (l), © William Gottlieb/CORBIS; 43 (r), PhotoDisc/gettyimages; 44 (l), © Imagestate 2003 all rights reserved; 51 (l), PhotoDisc/gettyimages; 51 (r), Susumu Nishinaga/SPL/Photo Researchers, Inc.; 52 (t), Victoria Smith/HRW; 52 (b), © Dr. Jeremy Burgess/Photo Researchers, Inc.; 53 (r), Scott Van Osdol/HRW; 54 (bl), © Layne Kennedy/CORBIS; 54 (br), © John Warden/Index Stock Imagery, Inc.; 54 (bc), © Dennis Galante/Envision - All rights reserved.; 55, © Matt Meadows/SPL/Photo Researchers, Inc.; 56 (b), Peter Van Steen/HRW; 56 r-(inset), Peter Van Steen/HRW; 56 l-(inset), Peter Van Steen/HRW; 57, © SHEILA TERRY/SCIENCE PHOTO LIBRARY/Photo Researchers, Inc.; 58 (bl), Sergio Purtell/Foca/HRW; 58 (br), Sergio Purtell/Foca/HRW; 58 (bc), © Astrid & Hanns-Frieder Michler/SPL/Photo Researchers, Inc.; 59 (bc), Sergio Purtell/Foca/HRW; 59 (bl), © Royalty Free/CORBIS; 59 (br), © Jose Luis Pelaez, Inc./CORBIS; 60, Victoria Smith/HRW; 61, © Jose Luis Pelaez, Inc./CORBIS; 62, © Fukuhara, Inc./CORBIS; 63, Copley News Service Photo by Russell Johnson/NewsCom; 64 (l), Joan Iaconetti/Bruce Coleman, Inc.; 64 (r), Norman Owne Tomalin/Bruce Coleman, Inc.; 65 l-(inset), Sam Dudgeon/HRW; 65 (t), Sam Dudgeon/HRW; 65 r-(inset), Sam Dudgeon/HRW; 66 (t), Sam Dudgeon/HRW; 66 (b), Sam Dudgeon/HRW; 67 (t), John Langford/HRW; 67 (b), NASA; 68, © SHEILA TERRY/SCIENCE PHOTO LIBRARY/Photo Researchers, Inc.; 69 (tl), Victoria Smith/HRW; 69 (tr), Victoria Smith/HRW; 69 (b), © Imagestate 2003 all rights reserved; 72 (tr), Glenn Anderson/Jacksonville Museum of Science and History; 73 (t), Courtesy of Aundra Nix; 73 (b), Astrid & Hans-Frieder Michler/SPL/Photo Researchers, Inc.

Chapter Three 74-75 (all), © Jason Childs/Getty Images; 77 (tr), Robert Mathena/Fundamental Photographs, New York; 77 (bl), © Albert Copley/Visuals Unlimited; 78 (t), NASA; 85 (tr), © Steve Kaufman/CORBIS; 86 (br), Erich Schrempp/Photo Researchers, Inc.; 87 (tl), Richard Megna/Fundamental Photographs; 88 (tc), Educational Development Center; 90 (tl), Richard Megna/Fundamental Photographs; 90 (bl), John Langford/HRW; 92 (br), James H. Karales/Peter Arnold, Inc.; 93 (b), Sam Dudgeon/HRW; 94 (bl), Richard Megna/Fundamental Photographs; 95 (bl), Martin Bough/Fundamental Photographs; 98 (tl), Pete Saloutos/The Stock Market; 98 (tr), The Granger Collection, New York; 99 (all), Peter Van Steen/HRW

Chapter Four 100-101 (all), © Flip Nicklin/Minden Pictures; 103 (tl), John Langford/HRW; 104 (tr), Sam Dudgeon/HRW; 106 (tr), Sam Dudgeon/HRW; 107 (tr), Mary Kate Denny/PhotoEdit; 108 (all), Archive Photos; 110 (t), John Langford/HRW; 111 (bl), John Langford/HRW; 113 (tr), Charles D. Winters; 115 (t), © Stephen Dalton/Photo Researchers, Inc.; 116 (tl), Matt Meadows/Photo Researchers, Inc.; 118 (all), Richard Megna/Fundamental Photographs; 119 (tr), Sam Dudgeon/HRW; 120 (bc), Sam Dudgeon/HRW; 121 (bl), Digital Image copyright © 2005 EyeWire; 121 (br), John Langford/HRW; 122 (tr, tl), Digital Image copyright © 2005 EyeWire; 122 (bc), Bob Daemmrich/HRW; 124 (bl), Richard Megna/Fundamental Photographs; 125 (br), Sam Dudgeon/HRW; 126 (tl), © Flip Nicklin/Minden Pictures; 126 (bc), Sam Dudgeon/HRW; 127 (tc), © Ross Harrison Koty/Getty Images; 127 (cl), Dick Luria/Photo Researchers, Inc.; 127 (br), John Langford/HRW; 131 (all), Victoria Smith/HRW

Chapter Five 132-133 (all), Matt Meadows/Peter Arnold, Inc.; 135 (tl), Charlie Winters/Photo Researchers, Inc.; 135 (tr), Richard Megna/Fundamental Photographs; 136 (t), © A.T. Willett/Getty Images; 137 (tr), © Detlev Van Ravenswaay/Photo Researchers, Inc.; 138 (bc), Sam Dudgeon/HRW; 138 (br, bl), John Langford/HRW; 139 (bcr), Hugh Turvey/Science Photo Library/Photo Researchers, Inc.; 139 (br), Blair Seitz/Photo Researchers, Inc.; 139 (bcl), Leonide Principe/Photo Researchers, Inc.; 139 (tc, tr), Sam Dudgeon/HRW; 141 (br), © Tony Mcconnell/Photo Researchers, Inc.; 141 (tl), © Najlah Feanny/CORBIS SABA; 142 (t), © Cameron Davidson; 143 (cr), © Sinclair Stammers/SPL/Photo Researchers, Inc.; 144 (br), © Michael English/Custom Medical Stock Photo; 145 (tr), Hugh Turvey/Science Photo Library/Photo Researchers, Inc.; 147 (br), © Darwin Dale/Photo Researchers, Inc.; 148 (bl), Sovfoto/Eastfoto; 149 (bl), Richard Megna/Fundamental Photographs; 151 (br), Ken Kay/Fundamental Photographs; 153 (cr), Ken Kay/Fundamental Photographs; 154 (br), Stephanie Morris/HRW; 155 (all), John Langford/HRW; 156 (tl), Image copyright ©1998 PhotoDisc, Inc.; 156 (tr), Renee Lynn/Davis/Lynn Images; 156 (bl), Robert Wolf/HRW; 157 (tl), Leonard Lessin/Peter Arnold, Inc.; 158 (br), Sam Dudgeon/HRW; 159 (t), Index Stock Photography, Inc.; 159 (cr), Peter Van Steen/HRW; 161 (tr), Sam Dudgeon/HRW; 162 (br), Matt Meadows/Peter Arnold, Inc.; 162 (tl), Image copyright © 2005 PhotoDisc, Inc.; 163 (cr), Charles D. Winters/Photo Researchers, Inc.; 163 (bcr), © Mark E. Gibson; 163 (br), Richard Megna/Fundamental Photographs; 166 (tl), Dr. E. R. Degginger; 166 (tr), courtesy of the Raytheon Company; 167 (cr), © Underwood & Underwood/CORBIS

Chapter Six 168-169 (all), Data courtesy Marc Imhoff of NASA GSFC and Christopher Elvidge of NOAA NGDC. Image by Craig Mayhew and Robert Simmon, NASA GSFC.; 170 (b), Yoav Levy/Phototake; 171 (tr), Stephanie Morris/HRW; 171 (bl, br), John Langford/HRW; 172 (tl), John Langford/HRW; 172 (tr), Richard Megna/Fundamental Photographs; 174 (tl, tr), Fundamental Photographs, New York; 178 (tl), © Digital Vision Ltd.; 178 (tr), Courtesy www.vischeck.com (program)/©Digital Vision Ltd. (frogs); 179 (tr), © Yoav Levy/Phototake; 183 (tr), Sam Dudgeon/HRW; 183 (bl), Don Mason/The Stock Market; 184 (all), Victoria Smith/HRW; 185 (cr), © Steve Dunwell/Getty Images; 189 (br), Sam Dudgeon/HRW; 190 (tl), Yoav Levy/Phototake; 190 (br), © Digital Vision Ltd.; 194 (tr), Digital Image copyright © 2005; 194 (tl), M. Spencer Green/AP/Wide World Photos; 195 (bc), Photo courtesy R.R. Jones, Hubble Deep field team, NASA; 195 (cr), NASA

Unit Two 196 (t), AKG Photo, London; 196 (c), Getty Images; 196 (bl), Enrico Tedeschi; 197 (tr), Property of AT&T Archives. Printed with permission of AT&T.; 197 (c), Peter Southwick/AP/Wide World Photos; 197 (bl), Enrico Tedeschi; 197 (bc), Ilkka Uimonen/Sygma

Chapter Seven 198-199 (all), Courtesy Sandia National Laboratories; 202 (bc), John Langford/HRW; 202 (bl), Sam Dudgeon/HRW; 203 (tr), John Langford/HRW; 204 (tl), © COMSTOCK, Inc.; 206 (br), Paul Katz/Index Stock Imagery/PictureQuest; 207 (cr), Michelle Bridwell/HRW; 207 (tr), Sam Dudgeon/HRW; 210 (br), Sam Dudgeon/HRW; 211 (tl), © National Geographic Image Collection/Richard T. Nowitz; 212 (br), Takeshi Takahara/Photo Researchers, Inc.; 213 (br), John Langford/HRW; 215 (tr), John Langford/HRW; 217 (br), Sam Dudgeon/HRW; 218 (tl, tc), Sam Dudgeon/HRW; 219 (cl), Digital Image copyright © 2005 PhotoDisc; 219 (c), © Brand X Pictures; 220 (bl), Richard T. Nowitz/Photo Researchers, Inc.; 220 (bc, br, inset), Sam Dudgeon/HRW; 221 (all), John Langford/HRW; 222 (b), John Langford/HRW; 223 (b), Sam Dudgeon/HRW; 224 (tl), Paul Silverman/Fundamental Photographs; 224 (bc), Sam Dudgeon/HRW; 225 (all), Sam Dudgeon/HRW; 226 (bl), John Langford/HRW; 227 (b), Victoria Smith/HRW; 228 (br), Sam Dudgeon/HRW; 229 (br), John Langford/HRW; 229 (tl), © COMSTOCK, Inc.; 232 (tr), Daniel L. Osborne, University of Alaska/Detlev Van Ravenswaay/Science Photo Library/Photo Researchers, Inc.; 232 (tl), Sonia S. Wasco/Grant Heilman Photography, Inc.; 232 (cr), STARLab, Stanford University; 233 (cr), Sam Dudgeon/HRW

Chapter Eight 234-235 (all), © NASA/Photo Researchers, Inc.; 236 (bc), Sam Dudgeon/HRW; 237 (tr, bc, br), Richard Megna/Fundamental Photographs; 237 (cr), Sam Dudgeon/HRW; 238 (tr), Richard Megna/Fundamental Photographs; 239 (br), Sam Dudgeon/HRW; 240 (cl), Sam Dudgeon/HRW; 242 (br), Pekka Parviainen/Science Photo Library/Photo Researchers, Inc.; 243 (tr), Sam Dudgeon/HRW; 246 (br), © Tom Tracy/The Stock Shop; 247 (tr), Victoria Smith/HRW; 249 (cr), Victoria Smith/HRW; 249 (tr), Sam Dudgeon/HRW; 256 (cr), Sam Dudgeon/HRW; 257 (bl), David Young Wolf/PhotoEdit; 258 (tl), Sam Dudgeon/HRW; 262 (cl), © Getty Images; 262 (tr), Howard Sochurek; 263 (tr), © Baldwin Ward/CORBIS

Chapter Nine 264-265 (all), © Peter Menzel Photography; 266 (all), Sam Dudgeon/HRW; 268 (tl), Sam Dudgeon/HRW; 269 (tr), Sam Dudgeon/HRW; 270 (bl), Sam Dudgeon/HRW; 271 (all), Sam Dudgeon/HRW; 272 (bl), Digital Image copyright © 2005 PhotoDisc; 274 (bl), Digital Image copyright © 2005 PhotoDisc; 277 (inset), Corbis Images; 278 (inset), Corbis Images; 280 (br), Sam Dudgeon/HRW; 281 (tr), Corbis-Bettmann; 282 (b), Sam Dudgeon/HRW; 283 (b), Sam Dudgeon/HRW; 287 (all), Sam Dudgeon/HRW; 288 (bl), Sam Dudgeon/HRW; 289 (b), Sam Dudgeon/HRW; 290 (br), Sam Dudgeon/HRW; 291 (bl), Sam Dudgeon/HRW; 294 (tl), © Reuters NewMedia Inc./CORBIS; 295 (cr), Courtesy Agnes Riley; 295 (bl), Digital Image copyright © 2005 PhotoDisc

Chapter Ten 296-297 (inset), Novovitch/Liaison/Getty Images; 296 (t), Roger Ressmeyer/CORBIS; 298 (tc), Andy Christiansen/HRW; 298 (tl), © Russell Illiq/Photodisc/gettyimages; 298 (tr), Mark Lewis/Getty Images/Stone; 299 (tl), James Randklev/Getty Images/Stone; 299 (b), Ed Malles; 299 (tr), Myrleen Furgusson Cate/PhotoEdit; 300, Victoria Smith/HRW; 302, Data courtesy Marc Imhoff of NASA/GSFC and Christopher Elvidge of NOAA/NGDC. Image by Craig Mayhew and Robert Simmon, NASA/GSFC.; 303 (b), John Zoiner; 303 (t), Mark Green/Getty Images/Taxi; 304, John Zoiner; 306, 2, Paolo Koch/Photo Researchers, Inc.; 306, 1, Horst Schafer/Peter Arnold, Inc.; 306, 3, Brian Parker/Tom Stack & Associates; 306, 4, C. Kuhn/Getty Images/The Image Bank; 307 (br), Alberto Incrocci/Getty Images/The Image Bank; 308 (inset), ©1994 NYC Parks Photo Archive/Fundamental Photographs; 308 (tl), © 1994 Kristen Brochmann/Fundamental Photographs; 308, Martin Harvey; 311 (tr), Tom Myers/Photo Researchers, Inc; 312 (t), Laurent Gillieron/Keystone/AP/Wide World Photos; 313 (b), Terry W. Eggers/CORBIS; 314 (t), Craig Sands/National Geographic Image Collection/Getty Images; 314 (b), Caio Coronel/Reuters/NewsCom; 315, G.R. Roberts Photo Library; 317, Laurent Gillieron/Keystone/AP/Wide World Photos; 319, Sam Dudgeon/HRW; 320, HRW; 321; Martin Harvey; 324 (t), Junko Kimura/Getty Images; 324 (b), STR/AP/Wide World Photos; 325 (t), Courtesy of Los Alamos National Laboratories; 325 (b), Corbis Images

Unit Three 326 (tl), Herman Melville: Classics Illustrated/Kenneth Spencer Research Library; 326 (c), Peter Scoones/Woodfin Camp & Associates; 326 (bl), Mark Votier/Sygma/CORBIS; 326 (br), D. DeMillo ©Wildlife Conservation Society, New York Aquarium; 327 (tr), National Air and Space Museum/Smithsonian; 327 (cl), Photo HO by The Cousteau Society REUTERS/NewsCom; 327 (cr), Hulton-Deutsch Collection/Corbis; 327 (bl), Jeremy Horner/CORBIS

Chapter Eleven 328-329, Henry Wolcott/Getty Images/National Geographic; 330, Tom Van Sant, Geosphere Project/Planetary Visions/Science Photo Library; 334 (l), U.S. Navy; 334 (r), U.S. Navy; 336, Rosenstiel School of Marine and Atmospheric Science, University of Miami; 337, Pam Ostrow/Index Stock Imagery, Inc.; 338 (l), W. Haxby, Lamont-Doherty Earth Observatory/Science Photo Library/Photo Researchers, Inc.; 339 (t), NOAA/NSDS; 342 (r), James Wilson/Woodfin Camp & Associates; 342 (l), Norbert Wu; 345, Stuart Westmoreland/CORBIS; 345, Stuart Westmoreland/CORBIS; 346 (t), Mike Bacon/Tom Stack & Associates; 346 (b), James B. Wood; 347 (t), Al GIddings/Al Giddings Images; 347 (b), JAMESTEC; 348, Mike Hill/Getty Images/Photographer's Choice; 349, ©2005 Norbert Wu/www.norbertwu.com; 350, Joel W. Rogers; 351 (t), Breg Vaughn/Tom Stack & Associates; 351 (b), Gregory Ochocki/Photo Researchers, Inc.; 352, Terry Vine/Getty Images/Stone; 353, Steve Raymer/National Geographic Society Image Collection; 354 (tl), Institute of Oceanographic Sciences/NERC/Science Photo Library/Photo Researchers, Inc.; 354 (inset), Charles D. Winters/Photo Researchers, Inc.; 355, Gregory Ochocki/Photo Researchers, Inc.; 356 (r), Tony Freeman/Photo Edit; 356 (l), Andy Christiansen/HRW; 356 (c), Richard Hamilton Smith/CORBIS; 357 (t), E. R. Degginger/Color-Pic, Inc.; 357 (b), Fred Bavendam/Peter Arnold, Inc.; 358, Greenpeace International; 359 (t), Ben Osborne/Getty Images/Stone; 359 (b), Courtesy Mobil; 360 (l), Courtesy Texas General Land Office Adopt-A-Beach Program; 360 (r), © Tony Amos/The University of Texas Marine Science Institute; 361, Ben Osborne/Getty Images/Stone; 363, Sam Dudgeon/HRW; 364, ©2005 Norbert Wu/www.norbertwu.com; 368 (b), © Reuters NewMedia Inc./CORBIS; 368 (tr), ©Patricia Jordan/Peter Arnold, Inc.; 368 (tl), ©Aldo Brando/Peter Arnold, Inc.; 369 (r), HO/The Cousteau Society/Reuters Photo Archive/NewsCom; 369 (l), Parrot Pascal/Corbis Sygma

Chapter Twelve 370-371, Tom Salyer/Reuters NewMedia Inc./CORBIS; 372, Hulton Archive/Getty Images; 373 (r), Sam Dudgeon/HRW; 373 (t), Rosenstiel School of Marine and Atmospheric Science, University of Miami; 380, Lacy Atkins/San Francisco Examiner/AP/Wide World Photos; 385 (b), CC Lockwood/Bruce Coleman, Inc.; 386 (tl), Darrell Wong/Getty Images/Stone; 386 (tr), Jack Fields/CORBIS; 391 (tl), VOSCAR/The Maine Photographer; 391 (tr), VOSCAR/The Maine Photographer; 392, Andy Christiansen/HRW; 398 (t), J.A.L. Cooke/Oxford Scientific Films/Animals Animals/Earth Scenes; 399 (t), Pacific Whale Foundation; 399 (b), Flip Nicklin/Minden Pictures

Chapter Thirteen 400-401 Martin Harvey/NHPA; 402 Larry Lefever/Grant Heilman Photography; 403 (t), J. Roche/Peter Arnold, Inc.; 403 (b), NASA; 404 (b), © Jacques Jangoux/Getty Images/Stone; 405 REUTERS/Jonathan Searle/NewsCom; 406 © Rex Ziak/Getty Images/Stone; 407 REUTERS/Jonathan Searle/NewsCom; 408 (l), Peter Van Steen/HRW; 408 (c), Peter Van Steen/HRW; 408 (r), Peter Van Steen/HRW; 409 (t), Argonne National Laboratory, University of Chicago/U.S. Department of Energy; 409 (b), Digital Image copyright © 2005 PhotoDisc; 410 (b), PhotoEdit; 410 (t), Kay Park-Rec Corp.; 411 (t), Peter Van Steen/HRW; 411 (b), Martin Bond/Science Photo Library/Photo Researchers; 412 (b), K. W. Fink/Bruce Coleman; 412 (t), © Sindre Ellingsen/Alamy Photos; 413 Stephen J. Krasemann/DRK Photo; 414 (bl), Sam Dudgeon/HRW; 414 (t), © Will & Deni McIntyre/Getty Images/Stone; 414 (br), Stephen J. Krasemann/DRK Photo; 415 (t), K. W. Fink/Bruce Coleman; 416 Peter Van Steen/HRW; 417 (tl), Tom Bean/DRK Photo; 417 (tr), Darrell Gulin/DRK Photo; 418 (l), Peter Van Steen/HRW; 418 (r), Peter Van Steen/HRW; 419 Larry Lefever/Grant Heilman Photography; 422 (l), Art Wolfe; 422 (r), © Toru Yamanaka/AFP/CORBIS; 423 (b), John S. Lough/Visuals Unlimited; 423 (t), Huntsville Times

Unit Four 424 (t), Astronomical Society of Pacific/Peter Arnold, Inc; 424 (c), Warren Faidley/NASA/Image State; 424 (bl), NASA/JPL; 425 (tl), Alfred Pasieka/Peter Arnold, Inc.; 425 (tr), Hulton Archive/Getty Images; 425 (cl, bc), NASA; 425 (cr), NASA/JPL; 425 (paper), Hulton Archive/Getty Images

Tuesday, November 26th, 2013

Chapter Fourteen 426-427, Roger Ressmeyer/CORBIS; 428, David L. Brown/Tom Stack & Associates; 430, The Bridgeman Art Library; 431, Roger Ressmeyer/Corbis; 432 (bl), Peter Van Steen/HRW; 432 (r), Fred Espenek; 434 (tl), Simon Fraser/Science Photo Library/Photo Researchers, Inc.; 434 (b), NASA; 434 (inset), Roger Ressmeyer/Corbis; 435 (radio), Sam Dudgeon/HRW; 435 (microwave) Sam Dudgeon/HRW; 435 (keyboard), Chuck O'Rear/Woodfin Camp & Associates, Inc.; 435 (sunburn), HRW; 435 (x-ray), David M. Dennis/Tom Stack & Associates; 435 (gamma) Alfred Pasieka/Photo Researchers, Inc.; 435 (tea), Tony McConnell/SPL/Photo Researchers, Inc.; 436 (gamma), NASA; 436 (radio), NASA; 436 (x-ray), NASA; 436 (infrared), NASA; 437, MSFC/NASA; 440, Peter Van Steen/HRW; 440 (bkgd), Frank Zullo/Photo Researchers, Inc.; 443 (tl), Jim Cummings/Getty Images/Taxi; 443 (tc), Mike Yamashita/Woodfin Camp/Picture Quest; 443 (tr), NASA; 443 (cr), Nozomi MSI Team/ISAS; 443 (bc), Jerry Lodriguss/Photo Researchers, Inc.; 443 (br), Tony & Daphne Hallas/Science Photo Library/Photo Researchers, Inc.; 444 (b), Jane C. Charlton, Penn State/HST/ESA/NASA; 444 (tc), NCAR/Tom Stack & Associates; 446, Peter Van Steen/HRW; 447, Peter Van Steen/HRW; 448 (t), MSFC/NASA; 448 (tea), Tony McConnell/SPL/Photo Researchers, Inc.; 452 (t), Craig Matthew and Robert Simmon/NASA/GSFC/DMSP; 453 (t), American Museum of Natural History; 453 (bl), Richard Berenholtz/CORBIS

Chapter Fifteen 454-455, NASA; 456 (bl), Phil Degginger/Color-Pic, Inc.; 456 (br), John Sanford/Astrostock; 457, Sam Dudgeon/HRW; 459, Roger Ressmeyer/CORBIS; 460, Andre Gallant/Getty Images/The Image Bank; 464, V. Bujarrabal (OAN, Spain), WFPC2, HST, ESA/NASA; 465, Royal Observatory, Edinburgh/SPL/Photo Researchers, Inc.; 468 (br), Dr. Christopher Burrows, ESA/STScI/NASA; 468, (blt), Anglo-Australian Telescope Board; 468 (bl), Anglo-Australian Telescope Board; 469, V. Bujarrabal (OAN, Spain), WFPC2, HST, ESA/NASA; 470, Bill & Sally Fletcher/Tom Stack & Associates; 471 (br), Dennis Di Cicco/Peter Arnold, Inc.; 471 (bl), David Malin/Anglo-Australian Observatory; 472 (bl), NASA Headquarters - GReatest Images of NASA (NASA-HQ-GRIN); 472 (br), Bill & Sally Fletcher/Tom Stack & Associates; 472 (bc), Jerry Lodriguss/Photo Researchers, Inc; 473, NASA/CXC/Smithsonian Astrophysical Observatory; 478, Sam Dudgeon/HRW; 479, John Sanford/Photo Researchers, Inc.; 484 (bl), NASA; 484 (tr), Jon Morse (University of Colorado)/NASA; 485 (r), The Open University; 485 (bkgd), Detlev Van Ravenswaay/SPL/Photo Researchers, Inc.

Chapter Sixteen 486-487, Anglo-Australian Observatory/Royal Obs. Edinburgh; 488, David Malin/Anglo-Australian Observatory/Royal Observatory, Edinburgh; 496, NASA/Mark Marten/Photo Researchers, Inc.; 497, NASA/TSADO/Tom Stack & Associates; 498, Earth Imaging/Getty Images/Stone; 501, SuperStock; 502 (l), Breck P. Kent/Animals Animals/Earth Scenes; 502 (r), John Reader/Science Photo Library/Photo Researchers, Inc; 504 (bc), Scott Van Osdol/HRW; 508, Sam Dudgeon/HRW; 510, Earth Imaging/Getty Images/Stone; 514 (b), NSO/NASA; 514 (tr), Jon Lomberg/Science Photo Library/Photo Researchers, Inc.; 514 (inset), David A. Hardy/Science Photo Library/Photo Researchers, Inc.; 515 (r), AIP/Photo Researchers, Inc.; 515 (l), Corbis Sygma

Unit Five 516 (t), Geoffrey Clifford/Woodfin Camp; 516 (c), J & L Weber/Peter Arnold; 516 (b), AP/Wide World Photos; 517 (cl), Brown Brothers; 517 (cr), SuperStock; 517 (tl), © Reuters/CORBIS; 517 (bl), Enrico Ferorelli; 517 (tr), Sheila Terry/Science Photo Library/Photo Researchers, Inc.; 517 (br), © CORBIS

Chapter Seventeen 518-519 AFP/CORBIS; 520-521 (b-bkgd), © David Madison/Getty Images/Stone; 522 Sam Dudgeon/HRW; 524 Sam Dudgeon/HRW; 526 (c), HRW Photo by Sergio Purtell/FOCA; 526 (r), HRW Photo by Sergio Purtell/FOCA; 526 (l), SP/FOCA/HRW Photo; 527 Scott Camazine/Photo Researchers, Inc.; 528 (bkgd), © Bob Torrez/Getty Images/Stone; 528 (bl-inset), Dr. E.R. Degginger; 528 (r-inset), Manfred Kage/Peter Arnold, Inc.; 528 (tl-inset), Gladden Willis, M.D./Visuals Unlimited; 530 (r), Sam Dudgeon/HRW; 530 (l), Chris Hamilton; 532 Sam Dudgeon/HRW; 534 (bkgd), Peter Van Steen/HRW; 534 (l), Dr. Robert Becker/Custom Medical Stock Photo; 534 (r), Peter Van Steen/HRW; 537 Sam Dudgeon/HRW; 538 Sam Dudgeon/HRW; 539 (t), Sam Dudgeon/HRW; 539 (b), Peter Van Steen/HRW; 542 (l), © Dan McCoy/Rainbow; 542 (r), Reuters/David Gray/NewsCom; 543 (t), Photo courtesy of Dr. Zahra Beheshti; 543 (b), Creatas/PictureQuest

Chapter Eighteen 544-545 © Nih/Science Source/Photo Researchers, Inc.; 548 (l), O. Meckes/Nicole Ottawa/Photo Researchers; 548 (r), O. Meckes/Nicole Ottawa/Photo Researchers; 550 © John Bavosi/Photo Researchers, Inc.; 552 Susumu Nishinaga/Science Photo Library/Photo Researchers, Inc.; 553 (b), Don Fawcett/Photo Researchers; 555 © Getty Images/The Image Bank; 558 © Collection CNRI/Phototake Inc./Alamy Photos; 563 (l), Matt Meadows/Peter Arnold, Inc.; 563 (r), Matt Meadows/Peter Arnold, Inc.; 564 (b), Sam Dudgeon/HRW; 570 (l), Richard T. Nowitz/Phototake; 570 (r), © Paul A. Souders/CORBIS; 571 Courtesy of Camp Boggy Creek

Chapter Nineteen 572-573 © ISM/Phototake; 581 (t), Victoria Smith/HRW; 584 Getty Images/The Image Bank; 585 Stephen J. Krasemann/DRK Photo; 586 (b), Sam Dudgeon/HRW; 592 (l), J.H. Robinson/Photo Researchers; 592 (r), REUTERS/David Gray/NewsCom; 593 (t), Peter Van Steen/HRW

Chapter Twenty 594-595 Omikron/Photo Researchers, Inc.; 601 (t), Sam Dudgeon/HRW; 605 Sam Dudgeon/HRW; 612 (c), Sam Dudgeon/HRW; 613 Will & Deni McIntyre/Photo Researchers; 614 (r), Sam Dudgeon/HRW; 614 (l), Sam Dudgeon/HRW; 615 Sam Dudgeon/HRW; 617 (t), Sam Dudgeon/HRW; 620 (l), Victoria Smith/HRW; 620 (r), Mike Derer/AP/Wide World Photos; 621 (t), Photo courtesy of Dr. Bertha Madras; 621 (b), SPL/Photo Researchers, Inc.

Chapter Twenty One 622-623 Photo Lennart Nilsson/Albert Bonniers Forlag AB, A Child Is Born, Dell Publishing Company; 624 (r), Visuals Unlimited/Cabisco; 624 (l), Innerspace Visions; 626 (b), Photo Researchers; 626 (t), Digital Image copyright © 2005 PhotoDisc Green; 627 © Charles Phillip/CORBIS; 630 Chip Henderson; 635 (tl), Petit Format/Nestle/Science Source/Photo Researchers, Inc.; 635 (cl), Photo Lennart Nilsson/Albert Bonniers Forlag AB, A Child Is Born, Dell Publishing Company; 635 (cr), Photo Lennart Nilsson/Albert Bonniers Forlag AB, A Child Is Born, Dell Publishing Company; 635 (br), Keith/Custom Medical Stock Photo; 635 (tr), David M. Phillips/Photo Researchers, Inc.; 636 (l), Peter Van Steen/HRW; 636 (cl), Peter Van Steen/HRW; 636 (c), Peter Van Steen/HRW; 636 (cr), Peter Van Steen/HRW; 636 (r), Peter Van Steen/HRW; 637 © Mark Harmel/Getty Images/FPG International; 639 Digital Image copyright © 2005 PhotoDisc; 640 Peter Van Steen/HRW; 641 Photo Lennart Nilsson/Albert Bonniers Forlag AB, A Child Is Born, Dell Publishing Company; 644 (r), Jim Tunell/Zuma Press/NewsCom; 644 (l), © Michael Clancy; 645 (l), ZEPHYR/Science Photo Library/Photo Researchers, Inc.; 645 (r), Salem Community College

Unit Six 646 (c), Erich Schrempp/Photo Researchers, Inc.; 646 (t), Gervase Spencer/E.T. Archive; 647 (tl), Mary Evans Picture Library; 647 (tr), Wayne Floyd/Unicorn Stock Photos; 647 (cl), © LSHTM/Getty Images/Stone; 647 (cr), UPI/Corbis-Bettmann; 647 (b), Wang Haiyan/China Features/CORBIS

Chapter Twenty Two 648-649 (t), © K. Kjeldsen/Photo Researchers, Inc.; 650 (br), CNRI/Science Photo Library/Photo Researchers; 650 (bl), Tektoff-RM/CNRI/Science Photo Library/Photo Researchers; 651 (t), Kent Wood/Photo Researchers; 652 (b), Peter Van Steen/HRW; 654 (b), Peter Van Steen/HRW; 658 (t), John Langford/HRW Photo; 659 (b), Clinical Radiology Dept., Salisbury District Hospital/Science Photo Library/Photo Researchers; 659 (t), SuperStock; 660 (b), Photo Lennart Nilsson/Albert Bonniers Forlag AB; 660 (tl), Dr. A. Liepins/Science Photo Library/Photo Researchers; 660 (tr), Dr. A. Liepins/Science Photo Library/Photo Researchers; 662 Sam Dudgeon/HRW; 665 (t), Peter Van Steen/HRW; 668 (l), E. R. Degginger/Bruce Coleman; 668 (r), Chris Rogers/Index Stock Imagery, Inc.; 669 (t), Peter Van Steen/HRW; 669 (b), Corbis

Chapter Twenty Three 670-671 © Arthur Tilley/Getty Images/Taxi; 672 Peter Van Steen/HRW; 673 (b), Peter Van Steen/HRW; 673 (t), Sam Dudgeon/HRW; 674 (c), Image Copyright ©2004 PhotoDisc, Inc./HRW; 674 (t), Image Copyright ©2004 PhotoDisc, Inc./HRW; 674 (bl), CORBIS Images/HRW; 674 (br), CORBIS Images/HRW; 675 U. S. Department of Agriculture; 676 John Burwell/FoodPix; 677 Peter Van Steen/HRW; 678 Peter Van Steen/HRW; 679 (b), Peter Van Steen/HRW; 679 (t), © Wally Eberhart/Botonica/Getty Images; 680 (t), E. Dirksen/Photo Researchers; 680 (b), Spencer Grant/Photo Researchers, Inc.; 680 (tr), Dr. Andrew P. Evans/Indiana University; 682 Jeff Greenberg/PhotoEdit; 683 Mike Siluk/The Image Works; 684 Sam Dudgeon/HRW; 685 (t), © Rob Van Petten/Getty Images/The Image Bank; 685 (b), Peter Van Steen/HRW; 686 Sam Dudgeon/HRW; 688 (b), Peter Van Steen/HRW; 688 (t), © Mug Shots/CORBIS; 689 Peter Van Steen/HRW; 690 Digital Image copyright © 2005 PhotoDisc; 692 (t), © John Kelly/Getty Images/Stone; 692 (b), Peter Van Steen/HRW; 693 (t), Peter Van Steen/HRW; 693 (b), Peter Van Steen/HRW; 696 (l), Brian Hagiwara/FoodPix; 697 (r), Courtesy Russell Selger; 697 (l), © Eyebyte/Alamy Photos

STAFF CREDITS

The people who contributed to *Holt Science & Technology* are listed below. They represent editorial, design, production, eMedia, permissions, and marketing.

Chris Allison, Melanie Baccus, Wesley M. Bain, Juan Baquera, Angela Beckmann, Ed Blake, Sara Buller, Marc Burgamy, Rebecca Calhoun, Kimberly Cammerata, Soojinn Choi, Eddie Dawson, Julie Dervin, Michelle Dike, Lydia Doty, Jen Driscoll, Leigh Ann García, Catherine Gnader, Diana Goetting, Tim Hovde, Wilonda Ieans, Jevara Jackson, Simon Key, Jane A. Kirschman, Cathy Kuhles, Laura Likon, Denise Mahoney, Michael Mazza, Kristen McCardel, Richard Metzger, Micah Newman, Janice Noske, Joeleen Ornt, Cathy Paré, Jenny Patton, Laura Prescott, Bill Rader, Peter D. Reid, Curtis Riker, Michael Rinella, Jeff Robinson, Audrey Rozsypal, Beth Sample, Margaret Sanchez, Kay Selke, Elizabeth Simmons, Chris Smith, Dawn Marie Spinozza, Sherry Sprague, Jeff Streber, JoAnn Stringer, Roshan Strong, Jeannie Taylor, Bob Tucek, Tam Voynick, Clay Walton, Kira J. Watkins, Ken Whiteside, Holly Whittaker, David Wisnieski, Monica Yudron, Patty Zepeda